SACRED CODES

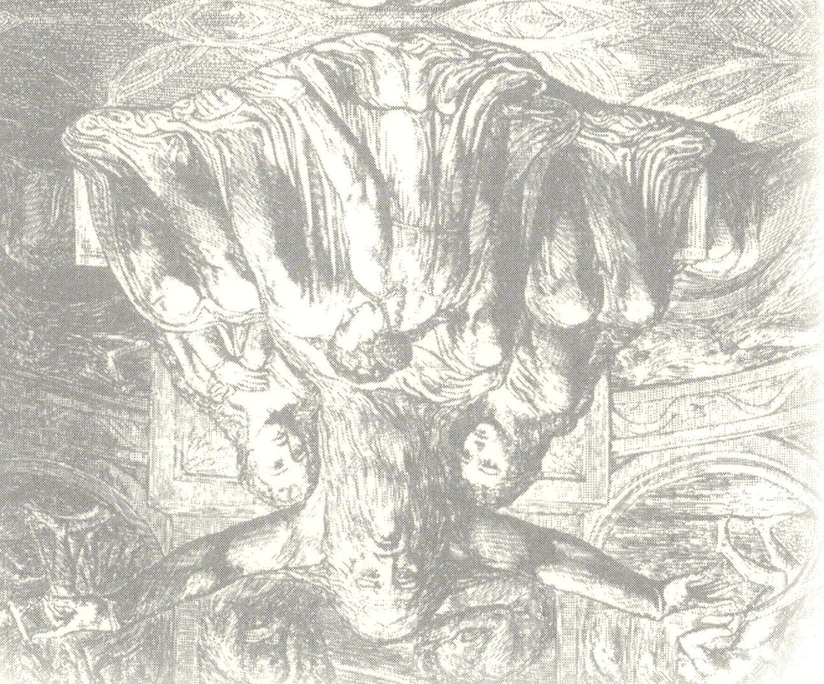

SACRED CODES – VOLUME I

Published by Recluse Publishing
First paperback edition – 2017

Library of Congress cataloguing-in-publication data
Caruana, Laurence, 1962 -
Sacred Codes:
The Forgotten Principles of Painting Revived by Visionary Art
Volume I
1st edition – Recluse Publishing
ISBN: 978-0-9782637-6-8
1. Fine Arts - Painting - General
2. Visual Arts - Theory. Philosophy. Aesthestics of the visual arts

SACRED CODES

THE FORGOTTEN PRINCIPLES OF PAINTING
REVIVED BY VISIONARY ART

VOLUME 1
THE DRAWING STAGE

He who has only experience
knows that a thing is so, but not why it is so,
whereas the artist knows the why and the wherefore.
This is why a master craftsman in any trade
is more highly esteemed, is considered to know more,
and therefore to be wiser than an artisan,
because he understands the reason for what is done.
Aristotle, *Metaphysics*[1]

L. CARUANA
AD SACRUM – TOWARD THE SACRED

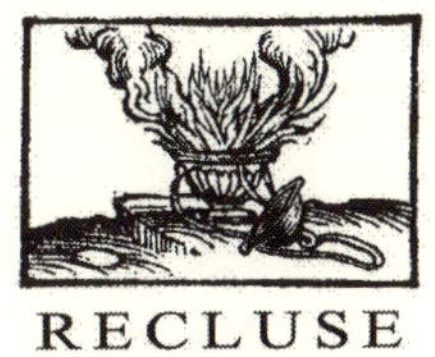

RECLUSE
2017

ABOUT THE AUTHOR:

Artist, author and lecturer, Laurence Caruana's multifaceted works explore the interplay of myth, visions and dreams while integrating views from different sacred traditions. Born in Toronto Canada of Maltese descent, he is a graduate of *The University of Toronto* (B.A. Hons. Philosophy) and also studied painting at *die Akademie der bildenden Künste* in Vienna before assisting Prof. Ernst Fuchs in his studios in Monaco and Castillon, where he learned classical techniques of painting in the traditional manner of master to apprentice.

For years, the artist led an itinerant existence, living variously in Malta, Vienna, Munich and Monaco while travelling extensively through Asia, Europe and Central America to explore sacred sites, study art techniques and enrich his passion for different cultural iconographies. With his French wife he settled in Paris, alternating between a studio in the Bastille quarter and a farmhouse in the Bourgogne region of France. In 2012, he co-founded the Vienna Academy of Visionary Art, where he serves as director.

BY THE SAME AUTHOR:

The First Manifesto of Visionary Art (2000)
The Hidden Passion: A Novel of the Gnostic Christ Based on the Nag Hammadi Texts (2007)
Enter Through the Image: The Ancient Image Language of Myth, Art & Dreams (2009)

CONTENTS

TO

PROF. ERNST FUCHS

My Father in Art, Eternal

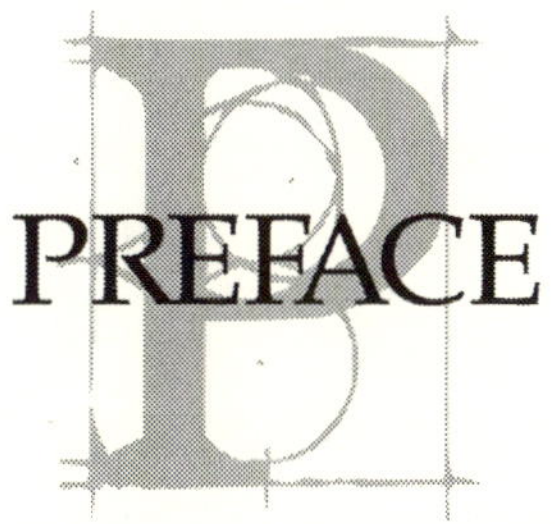

PREFACE

To be sure, the artist who does not learn early on
the principles and the style that he intends to adopt
and who does not gradually solve the problems of his art by practice,
striving to learn and master every aspect of it,
will rarely become perfect.
Vasari, Lives of the Artists[2]

The Art of Painting has slowly become lost over the last century, falling into a period which we call 'Modernist', but which other centuries will call by a very different name. How we are judged by the coming ages will depend on the choices we make now, the paths we choose to follow in our culture. Like an underground current, Visionary Art has traversed all ages, continents and cultures, encapsulated in the works of anonymous craftsmen and a few recognized masters. Though caught up in the currents of their own times, these artists have produced images that transcend their epoch – passing on secrets, as in the days of old, from gifted master to watchful apprentice.

This book recounts how I learned to paint while apprenticing myself to a 20th century master, whose name is Ernst Fuchs. Like any true master, he had opened his eyes and absorbed the teachings of other great practitioners of our art – a lineage which extends back, beyond the 20th century, to Visionaries like Gustave Moreau, William Blake and Michelangelo Buonarroti. By painting side-by-side with Ernst Fuchs for many hours and days, my mentor opened my eyes to *new ways of seeing* – indeed, to forms of perception which I would never have dreamt of or imagined were possible. That process is ongoing even today, as he, the eternal artist, continues to watch over the history of art through my eyes.

I also learned from him a venerable technique of painting, called the *Mischtechnik*, which attempts to revive two great lineages of the craft: tempera and oils. But, equally important to me were the forgotten principles of painting, and the extraordinary forms of perception which can arise, if only one is fully immersed in the act of painting. Such alternative ways of seeing, which I will describe here as 'Visionary', require new ways of experiencing our sight – such as the active immersion of our awareness into the watery depths of perception.

Over the last twenty years I have practiced Visionary Seeing in a variety of forms, some learned from my master, others acquired through diligent practice. More recently, a variety of young and inquisitive artists have approached me, asking me to teach them these techniques. So, I have been placed in a position where it is now my duty to transmit these unusual ways of seeing to others. Mostly, I have done this one-on-one with artists who come to me seeking a deeper understanding of art and the immersion into hidden worlds made possible through Visionary painting.

...A need to clarify my vision, to educate and advance it, arose in my forty-ninth year. I took a hiatus from painting, barely touching a brush for five years – because a great task awaited me, requiring new eyes and a new worldview. I felt I could no longer paint until my vision had been sufficiently cleansed and renewed.

Thus began the writing of this book, in anticipation of a project far larger than any I had undertaken in my life thus far. Having first met my master in a chapel, working with him in his *Apocalypse Chapel* in southern Austria, I undertook the sacred task of creating my own *Apocryphon Chapel.* This life-task, which arose shortly after the birth of my son, will require years of sustained effort. So I made a vow – a wish, a heart-felt prayer to God, to dedicate myself to one unique form of worship: sitting before the easel, contemplating the Sacred, and rendering its great mystery into form.

Knowing I had a long journey ahead of me, I began to prepare myself by reflecting deeply on the nature of art. I needed to peer down the corridors of time and visit other cultures, studying their traditions as passed on from master to apprentice. I needed to reach beyond my own century, as an artist, and experience *other* worldviews – indeed, a variety of distant and ancient cultures, immersing myself into their spiritual practices, to experience *from whence* their art had emerged. I began this process while living in my farmhouse in Bourgogne France, for a period of about three years.

As the research and writing of this book progressed, their momentum propelled me into a much different sphere: that of full-time teacher and administrator. I became the director of The Vienna Academy of Visionary Art. And so, most of the writing and research for this book transpired in Vienna – as if my master had called me back to that strange city during (what turned out to be) the last years of his prolific life. Under his supervision, and with the help of my students and colleagues, this treatise has slowly been hammered into form.

I would like to thank here my Academy colleagues for their inspiration and many amiable conversations – especially Kuba Ambrose, Daniel Mirante, Kevin Campeau and Daniel Kage. Indeed, *all* the teachers and students have made some valuable contribution to this work – alas, their names are too numerous to mention here. Since I spend many hours writing in cafés, I must thank *Le Voltigeur* in Paris and the *Strozzi Café* in Vienna for their warmth and hospitality, as well as the beautiful village of Torri Superiore in Italy, where several chapters were written during my stay there each summer. I also wish to acknowledge Andrew Stewart and Alexandra Oberrauch for help in preparing the images for print. Last of all, I have to express love and gratitude to my wife and son for their continued patience and good humour, as they urged me to 'finish the damn book!' Their loving presence has sustained me.

I must stress at the outset that this is a treatise on *Visionary* Painting. Countless texts have been written declaiming the rules of the painter's craft. But this work is concerned with one genre of painting which I have described in previous books, articles and manifestoes[3] as 'Visionary Art.' Such an art seeks to manifest those spiritual realms which remain otherwise unseen by the unilluminated eye. By this same token, the methods and techniques of the Visionary artist are not, at first glance, easily detectable.

Nevertheless, master craftsmen from the East and the West have left behind signs of their methods which – though in plain sight – remain hidden to the untrained eye. They pass unnoticed because they are inserted, quite often, *in the details* (where no one but the most committed of craftsmen would bother to search for them...). Other times, they require a much different manner of *viewing* the work to actually be seen and understood.

Over time, I have come to read these hidden marks and signs as codes – as a series of Sacred Codes which have been transmitted in an unbroken chain from time immemorial. The aim of this work is to present a series of these Sacred Codes, which structure and support each of the various stages of Visionary Painting.

Since this first volume is dedicated to The Drawing Stage, I have sought out 'lines' above all. And most of these, as it turns out, *are invisible.* Such unseen lines are still passed on, nowadays, in the various demonstrations and constructions of Linear Perspective. But a rich variety of other such lines have been taught to young painters, beginning with Proportion – a huge field actually, especially when approached from different cultural perspectives.

Less known, but equally important, are the many invisible lines that traverse the Pose. The most obvious is the plumb line, descending from the eye or the pit of the neck down to the weight-bearing foot, and offering an axis for various *contrapposto* twists and turns. The variety of bends (one, two or three) and the types of forces at work in the figure (will, repose) constitute an arcane knowledge almost entirely lost to time. I have laboured hard to revive these forgotten principles.

Composition is taught in schools, but only in the most rudimentary of fashions. We have forgotten the laws of Harmony (the *diapason*, *diapente* and *diatessaron*), and why *concordia* was once so important. The art of Armature – with its rich matrix of invisible lines, thus generating new forms and figures – has also fallen into dis-use. Understanding the complex relationship of Composition to Figuration, and again of Composition to Perspective, constitute other important areas of knowledge, well-known to artists of the Renaissance, but shared by only a handful of practitioners today.

The science of line known as Geometry, when thoroughly studied and understood, becomes an art in itself. This lost art was pursued, most clearly and expressively, in Ornament. I make no apologies for investigating Geometry and Ornament *in depth* – an aspect of sacred creation far too neglected in our modern times. As we shall see, the rules of Composition can only be fully understood and appreciated, once their history in Ornament is recognized.

Last of all I shall investigate that aspect of line which remains the most elusive and evasive of all: its Style. Each culture and, indeed, each individual artist, has the ability to render a pose or expression in a manner that is entirely unique. How artists like Leonardo or Michelangelo arrived at their characteristic styles remains something of a mystery. Yet, no serious investigation into the Drawing Stage can ignore these vital questions.

One evening in 2003, while sitting alone in my studio in Paris, I saw all the works from a variety of cultural traditions as divided into two distinct types. It did not matter if the painting came from the Occident or the Orient, whether the work was Egyptian or Mayan, Buddhist or Byzantine – all were executed in either the Humanist or Hieratic Style (Hieratic, in this case, meaning 'sacred' – the tradition of art dedicated to the creation of 'holy images').

Such a way of seeing, once acquired, could not easily be abandoned or forgotten. For we are living in a time of *the Hieratic Revival*, while still fully immersed in *our Humanist Inheritance*. The distinction between Humanist and Hieratic Styles will become fundamental to all that follows, since it allows us to transcend and unite cultural differences, in a variety of works from different epochs and locales.

My fascination for Visionary Seeing, combined with my travels through Egypt, India and Tibet, compelled me to investigate the forgotten act of *consecration*. In the Occident, this took the form of Theurgy – a spiritual practice emerging in 2nd century Alexandria, based on older Egyptian rituals, which sought to consecrate, and hence, *activate* a divine statue – opening a visionary portal into the higher realms, where souls journeyed after death, and where we ourselves could journey – in this life – in a visionary state.

Similar practices, I discovered, exist in India and Tibet, where thangkas, mandalas and sacred statues are activated through meditation and ritual – granting access to higher dimensions, in order to map the soul's journey through the afterlife realms. My investigations into Visionary Seeing, Theurgy and Mandala Meditation have been gathered together at the end of this volume, so the reader may discover how works of art were *spiritually activated* in distant and ancient cultures. By performing similar such meditations *on their own works*, contemporary Visionary artists may experience their creations as portals to the higher spheres.

I will not hesitate to record here all the things I learned while working with Ernst Fuchs in his studios in Monaco and Castillon. And I dare say now, after ten years of reflection, that he did not take me on as his assistant due to my refined technique. Rather, I came to him with the unusual desire to 'see perfection.' And it was this, the capacity for Visionary Seeing, which he honed and refined as we spent countless hours together painting, painting, painting.

To see perfection is to see unity in a work of art. For a Visionary artist to portray the higher realm, he or she must first have had a *direct experience* of the Sacred. Such an experience, as Wisdom Traditions from around the world have taught, involves a sudden, overwhelming experience *of unity*. In a rare moment of epiphany, the One at the centre of all creation reveals itself, as our singular Source and Inspiration. Mystical texts from all traditions have expressed this truth poetically in words. And Visionary artists have sought nothing less than to express that same eternal truth – in images.

For a Visionary work of art to be genuinely *visionary*, it must not only depict the Sacred, but manifest its sacred oneness. In the parts, in the composition, in the colours and the forms – at all times a balance and harmony emerges, to hold the pieces together and integrate them into a holistic vision of divine beauty and mystery. In this way, the sacred oneness is not only symbolized, but *shown to us* directly; it permeates and activates the artist's work.

There are many paths, in my experience, to seeing unity, and I intend to convey all the ones I have experienced directly. Some involve sacred plants; others require a prolonged meditation and contemplation on the work at hand.

How the artist may come *to see* the Sacred is indeed a great mystery. For years I have made notes in my Museum Journals, Painter's Notebooks, Entheogen Journals and Travel Diaries, pondering and approaching this question from many different angles. In preparation for this treatise, the most relevant sections have been reviewed and transcribed. Chapters have been written and discarded. The first two chapters of the book, including this preface, disappeared when my computer was stolen late one night in Paris, on the terrace of *Café Select* (I was too deeply engaged in conversation to notice that the wandering flower seller, who held the roses under my face, had an accomplice...). I wracked my memory in an attempt to re-transcribe my own words and phrasings. Despite these hardships, the book has reached its conclusion, and I now look forward to returning to painting with renewed vigour.

In the first three chapters of this volume, I will introduce the reader to Envisioning the Work. To begin, we must learn how *to see* the Sacred Codes, *to see* the Humanist and Hieratic Styles, and *to see unity* in a work of art. Through extended contemplation, we will learn how to 'enter through the image' so the higher world, beyond the picture's surface, will become manifest in all its divine beauty and perfection.

After this introduction (which is absolutely vital and necessary for all that follows) we will pursue the task of painting in earnest, following the three main stages of Ernst Fuchs' *Mischtechnik.*

The Sacred Codes series is conceived as a trilogy, which I hope will advance from *The Drawing Stage* in Volume I, to *The Monochrome Underpainting* in Volume II, to the *Complete Colour Painting* in Volume III. The first two volumes treat questions of figure and composition, of light and shadow, of line, volume and style – and so are printed in black and white. The third volume, translating dark and light values into chroma and hue, will be printed in colour so that visionary colour harmonies may be experienced in the full spectrum of their glory.

With alchemy, as with painting, the aim is not only to produce a work of perfection, but to transfigure, in the process, the very soul of the artist-alchemist engaged in the experiment. With the help of my colleagues and students, I hope to see these volumes expand in future editions to become a rich compendium of knowledge for the Visionary Art of Painting.

To be an artist requires a certain mastery of technique. To be a Visionary artist, we must not only master technique, but apply that mastery to the betterment of ourselves, the work, and the world. Through the acquisition of the Divine Eye, we immerse ourselves fully in the act of creation, feeling a sacred oneness at the very heart of our being. At that moment, the divine sees us, and we see the divine, with one sight for all eternity.

L. Caruana

16th of February 2012 – Montenoison France
Amended: 8th of November 2016 – Vienna Austria

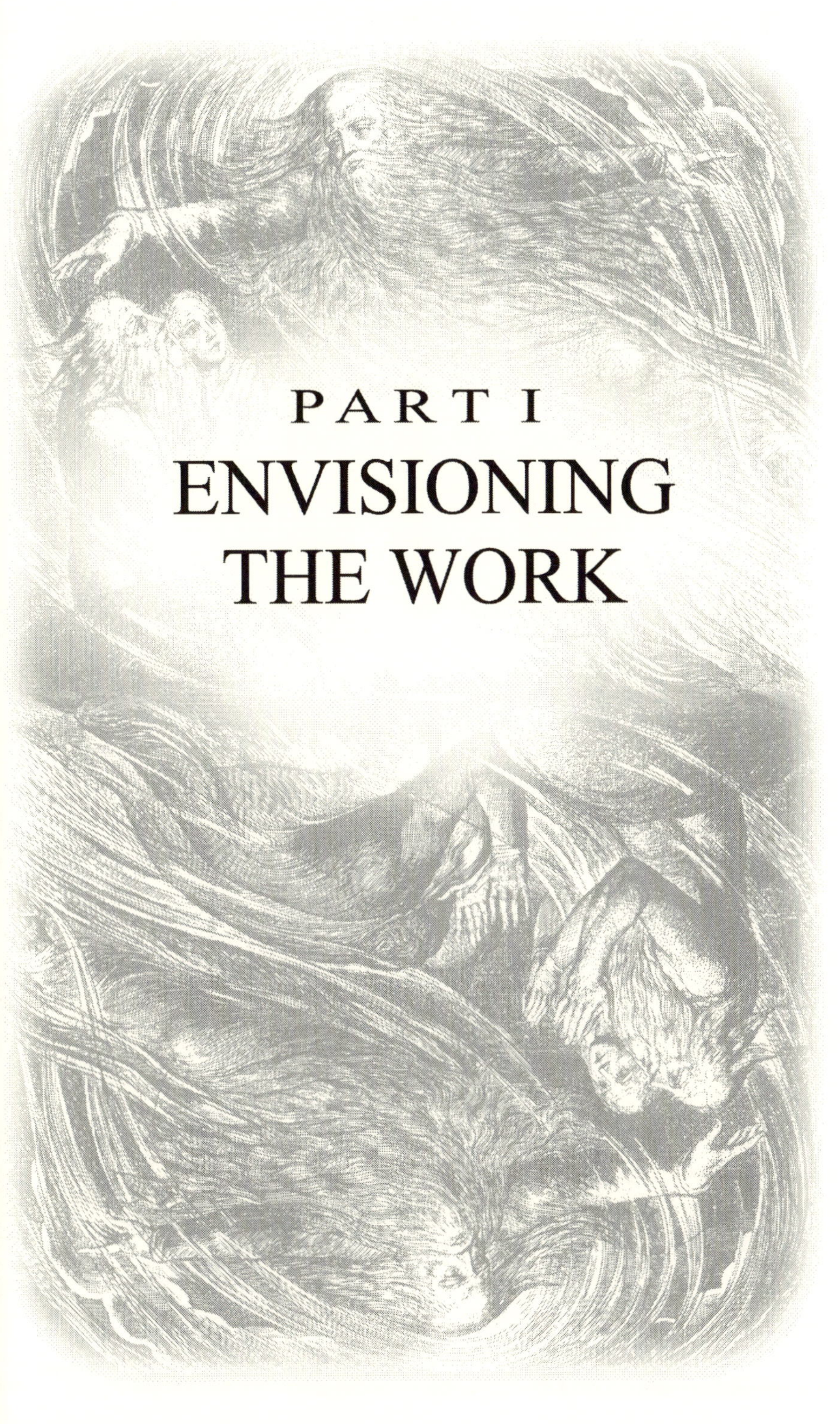

PART I

ENVISIONING THE WORK

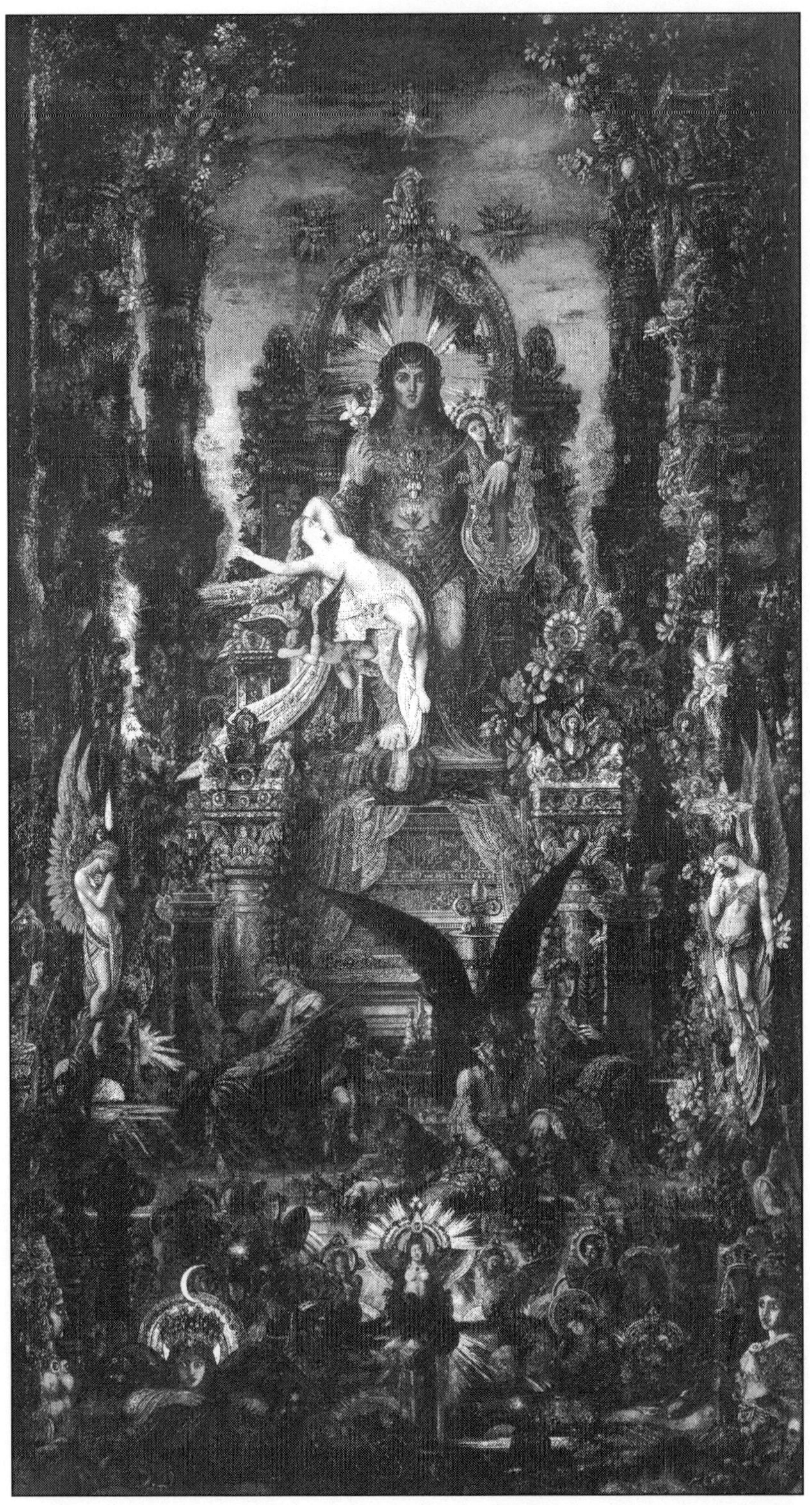

JUPITER AND SEMELE
Text by Gustave Moreau[1]

A towering, colossal architecture rises up with neither foundation nor summit, its sacred flora quivering and alive against the sombre blue solitude of the sky. Here, the oft-invoked God appears in his still-veiled splendour.

Semele – thunderstruck – dies and yet regenerates; purged in the holy fire and purified by the sacred overflowing – and with her, a cloven-hoofed angel, the Spirit of Earthly Love.

Through this holy exorcism and enchantment, all are transformed into a higher and purer ideal. The eternally Sacred expands into the all; and the all, though not yet fully-formed, give praise to the one true Light.

Denizens of the water and woods, dryads, satyrs and fauns – all are overcome by ecstasy, love and joy. Leaving behind their earthen beds, they rise up and assume new shapes as sacred beings in the celestial hierarchy.

Two hierophants, flanking the throne with outspread wings, bow their heads with hallowed reverence before the god.

Meanwhile, at the dais below, Death and Suffering form the tragic foundation to our human existence. Enshadowed by Jupiter's eagle, the great god Pan, symbol of our earthly predicament, lowers his brow in sad remembrance of our enslaved and exiled state. In the darkness below, beings of mystery and shade mingle in the depths. These indecipherable enigmas, children of Erebus and Night, are those unformed entities who still await their life in the light.

Sleeping in the lowest depths of the abyss are the creatures of darkness – hydras, lemurs, griffons – hybrid in form, ill-fated spirits ruled over by the silent Moon, and Hecate of the oblique gaze.

Finally, two great sphinxes, one facing the past and the other the future, stand as guardians to this herd and their heavenly ascent – and contemplate each other with a smiling and hieratic stillness.

Fig. 1.1 Left - Gustave Moreau: *Jupiter and Semele* 1895

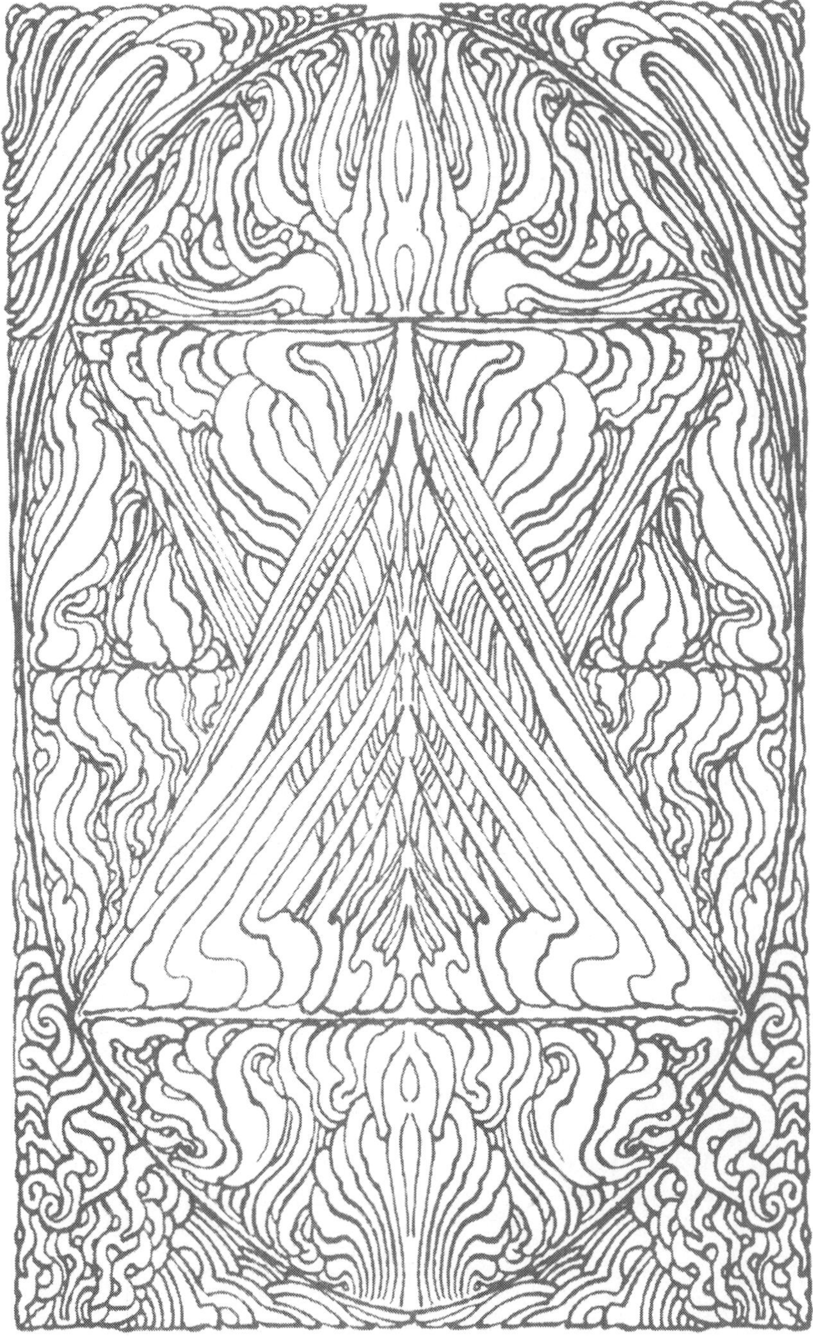

Fig. 1.2 - Ernst Fuchs: Ornamental Design from *Symbolik des Traumes* 1968

CHAPTER I
SEEING UNITY

I. Vision & Annihilation

After forty years of wandering in the wilderness, Moses led his people to Mount Sinai. And there, in the mountain's shadow, he withdrew for a while and addressed his God with the words, *"Show me your glory, I pray."* (Exodus 33:18)[2] The Lord's response to Moses was firm and canonical: *"You cannot see my face; for no one can see me, and live."* (Exodus 33:20)

In the myths and legends of many cultures, this same mysterious injunction appears: No One May Gaze upon the Face of God – and Survive. For, to gaze upon the divine countenance – particularly if the initiate is not prepared – is to risk blindness, madness or, even worse, utter annihilation.

In the Greek and Roman tradition, this same tale is told through the tragedy of Jupiter and Semele. The fair nymph Semele, daughter of king Cadmus, was visited one night by the god of thunder in human guise. Her womb soon swelling with child, Semele was determined to discover the true face of her night visitor. The next time he appeared, she bade him grant her one request and the god swore to comply. Her voice rising, Semele commanded, *"Show yourself to me!"* And though Jupiter *"...tried to stop her lips as she spoke,"* even he, the father of all the gods, was bound by his oath. In a blinding epiphany, Jupiter revealed himself in the full power and glory of his effulgence. *"Semele's mortal frame could not endure the exaltation and,"* as Ovid recounts, *"she was burned to ashes."*[3]

This image of vision and annihilation so fascinated the French Symbolist Gustave Moreau that he dedicated the last years of his life to painting its epiphany. From the first sketches made in 1889 to the final finished canvas in 1895, Moreau worked obsessively on (what was destined to be) his last finished work – sketching out the colour schemes, photographing models, refining the figures and adding an infinity of details up to the very corners of his composition. Moving beyond the Greek and Roman sources, he researched Egyptian, Hindu and Babylonian myths, incorporating their symbols in his rich tapestry: a Shiva lingam here, an Egyptian scarab there. Moreau even dismantled the painting and re-stretched the canvas, so its larger dimensions could encompass the ever-growing panoply of angels, satyrs and demons.

All the while, he also wrote obsessively about his intentions: scribbling notes on the back of drawings, reworking the phrasings, and completing no less than three alternative texts. The final version appears in a letter addressed to Léopold Goldschmidt, the purchaser of the painting – a letter which Moreau, overcome by doubt, *never sent.* In the opening passage, Moreau questions the necessity of articulating his intentions: *"All that I'm writing here need be neither expressed nor explained through words."*[4]

I have taken the time to research his writings and translate his text (Fig. 1.1) because Gustave Moreau has become, in my eyes, one of the four great masters of Visionary Art as practiced in the Western tradition. While working with Ernst Fuchs, I soon learned that my master had his masters. And so, my inquisitive gaze compelled me to seek out and understand the unbroken chain that descended from Michelangelo to Blake to Moreau to Fuchs. Each of these four masters displayed an intimate knowledge of the same Sacred Codes, which re-appear inexorably – altered, yet the same – in so many of their works.

As a young artist struggling in Paris, Fuchs often visited the *Musée Gustave Moreau*. At that time, in the early sixties, it was a sad and neglected place. Fuchs recounted to me fondly how he would ring the bell and wait until the guardian obligingly unlocked the door and turned on the lights to accommodate him, the young acolyte, as the *only* visitor to the museum that afternoon. While living in Paris, I too became a *habitué* of the museum, as the mysterious French Symbolist imparted to me aspects of his vision.

II. Jupiter & Semele: The Eternally Sacred Expands into the All

Despite Moreau's misgivings, his text of the painting's *histoire* (narrative) reveals much to us about the artist's hidden higher ideals. His intention was nothing short of visionary: to behold the face of God and render that epiphany in paint. In Moreau's splendrous image, the Sacred reveals itself to us in a blinding revelation. In a flash of red and yellow light, *"the oft-invoked God appears in his still-veiled splendor."* Though the god reveals himself in a blinding effulgence of light, he also appears 'still veiled' in his human form: enthroned, bejewelled, upholding a sacred flower while gesturing to us majestically. The god gazes upon us *directly*, his hieratic features frozen *in a timeless stare* of infinite knowledge and awareness.

Hence, above and beyond this human appearance, Moreau sought to evoke the Sacred as the hidden, unified source of all creation. Following the Wisdom Traditions of the Orphics, Gnostics and Neo-Platonists, Moreau describes this divinity as the source of all life and light, which seeks its own reflection in the infinite variety of images manifest in creation. In the artist's own words: *"The eternally Sacred expands into the all; and the all, though not yet fully-formed, give praise to the one true Light."* This well-spring of existence is also described as a sacred fountain or flame in which we eternally die and are reborn: *"Semele – thunderstruck – dies and yet regenerates; purged in the holy fire and purified by the sacred overflowing."*

His painting depicts nothing less than the unfolding of the Sacred into ever-lower hypostases of its own infinite being. At the summit is the unified source of creation. Meanwhile, all the figures below are arranged like so many mirrors, descending row on row, into ever-lower forms in the celestial hierarchy. In Moreau's vision, the divine throne forms a 'towering colossal architecture' in which all of creation descends, step by step, into darkness and unknowing. Yet, each form bears the mark of its maker, and reflects the divine radiance in descending shades of darkness and light.

The question, for the Visionary artist, is how to see and behold this overwhelming vision, and how to ultimately depict it in a work of art.

Moreau gives us several important clues in the construction of his image. As we gaze upon this crowded composition, our eye naturally wanders away from the central figure, and begins to examine the infinity of fine details below. Because we, like the figures below, are fallen creatures. *"Death and Suffering form the tragic foundation to our human existence,"* Moreau writes. We are no longer angelic beings, deathless and free, gazing without cease upon the divine countenance and singing its endless praise. Due to our incarnation in the flesh, we have become the children of Pan (archaic Greek for, literally, "the All"). This god, *"the symbol of our earthly predicament, lowers his brow in sad remembrance of our enslaved and exiled state."* Like satyrs and fauns, we are now enslaved by our own fleshly yearnings, and exiled from our higher spiritual state within the celestial order.

Hence, *"sleeping in the lowest depths of the abyss,"* we are like *"creatures of darkness."* Our gaze, errant and wandering, absorbs a thousand different forms moving in and out of shadowy manifestation. If only we could remember to look up and focus our gaze on the light, we would begin to *"rise up and assume new shapes as sacred beings in the celestial hierarchy."* Like the *"two hierophants, flanking the throne with outspread wings,"* we too could remember *"with hallowed reverence"* our origin in the Divine. Although we are beings *"not yet fully-formed,"* through prayer, concentration and meditation we may yet be *"transformed into a higher and purer ideal."*

And so our wandering eye, rising ever higher, finally comes to rest upon Semele's graceful form. Her curving figure, with its *contrapposto* movement, focusses all the energy of her body *into her gaze* – a direct line of sight into the hieratic features of the divine countenance. Thus we stare fixedly, for a few precious moments, into Jupiter's eyes. If we, like Semele, are not yet prepared to accept the god's infinite gaze, then we shall die, thunderstruck, by its overpowering glory and transcendence. Glancing downward, we avert our eyes, and our lids slowly descend in death.

Through the eternal cycle of death and rebirth, we return once more to the depths. Like the winged satyr just below Semele, we fall blinded from the sight of the god. As our gaze follows the gesture of Semele's extended arm, we may suddenly become aware of the falling stars, which take on new forms and incarnations, descending as jewels, vegetation, heraldic animals and human allegorical figures, all integrated into the celestial architecture, all expressing forgetfulness, sleep and fallenness.

We become again those *"beings of mystery and shade* [who] *mingle in the depths. These indecipherable enigmas, children of Erebus* [the Underworld] *and Night, are those unformed entities who still await their life in the light."* What is worse, we may become *"ill-fated spirits ruled over by the silent Moon, and Hecate of the oblique gaze."*

The Moon, by its very nature, is inconstant and ever-changing. So too does our wandering gaze drift once more in the darkness, seeking some momentary diversion to fix and attract its attention. Unmindful, distracted, we are indeed ruled over by *"Hecate of the oblique gaze"* – she whose line of sight is never direct, but askew and askance, continually diverging from the straight path...

Meanwhile, at the very base of the composition stand two great sphinxes 'one facing the past and the other the future.' If we wish to escape this endless cycle of death and rebirth, then we must make our way past these two enigmatic figures, who *"...stand as guardians to this herd and their heavenly ascent."* We must, in essence, solve the riddle of the sphinx. These two mysterious beings *"...contemplate each other with a smiling and hieratic stillness."*

Herein lies the greatest clue left to us by Gustave Moreau for the decipherment of his final masterpiece. Though a good number of Sacred Codes are woven into the details of this painting, this is without doubt the most important sign. Stepping back from the painting, we can see that he has mastered the seven steps of painting: the figure, composition, lines, light and shadow, volume, colour and style. All of these work together harmoniously to redirect our gaze to one fixed point. That point is most obviously indicated by the composition: a hierarchal and symmetrical rectangle wherein an immense triangle is inscribed, with a perfect circle at its summit. And there – where the contrast of colour, light and darkness are most pronounced – appears the face of God.

If we wish to solve the riddle of the sphinx and transcend our human condition, then we must gaze directly and without cease into the hieratic features of that great god, who gazes directly upon us – 'frozen in a timeless stare of infinite knowledge and awareness.' As beings mortal and immortal, we must *"...contemplate each other with a smiling and hieratic stillness."*

Sitting in quiet solitude and repose, with a relaxed and steadfast gaze, we may stare for minutes if not hours (for time has no meaning now) until the silent truth reveals itself: God and I are one. The human form before me, delineated with such mastery and grace, reflects my higher, sacred aspect. I am, in origin, divine. The flesh – adorned with a beautifully-jewelled scarab and lily – may die and be reborn, may rise up and ultimately be transfigured into a flashing effulgence of glory. I am the light, eternal, flawless and crystalline. At that moment, our Divine Eye opens, and the painting dissolves into a pure and perfect vision of our sacred oneness.

III. *I Give You my Divine Eye – Behold!*

The highest task of the artist is to render our eternal aspect – the soul in its perennial quest for union with the Sacred. To open our eyes in that holy Presence, and actually *see* what lies before us, we must acquire new eyes and a new outlook. We must sacrifice our human sight, with its endless need for distraction, and open our vision to Divine Sight. How is this possible?

To answer this question, we must first join with Arjuna, the prince of Pandava, as he awaits a great battle in the *Bhagavad Gita*.[5] His charioteer, who is none other than the great god Krishna, appears to the prince *in human form*. As Arjuna surveys the armies aligned for battle, his heart sinks in his chest and he loses his resolve, because he sees in the opposing ranks only his companions and kinsmen. The prince questions Krishna on the purpose of doing one's duty, and thus begins one of the greatest Sanskrit epics in the Hindu Wisdom Tradition.

Although Krishna appears to Arjuna in human form, he also possesses a higher, transcendent aspect. Indeed, he is nothing less than the unified source of all creation. *"All this visible universe,"* Krishna reveals to Arjuna, *"comes from my invisible Being."* (9:4) *"I am the source of all beings,"* (9:5) he re-asserts. *"Thus through my nature I bring forth all creation, and this rolls round in the circles of time."* (9:8)

Hence *The Bhagavad Gita* expresses once more, in the Eastern tradition, the same eternal truth as revealed in the West through the Orphic, Gnostic and Neo-Platonic texts. Like Moreau's painting, *The Bhagavad Gita* addresses the same burning question confronting the Visionary artist: how may we see and behold such an overwhelming vision of divine unity, and depict its majestic splendour in paint?

As Krishna explains to Arjuna, all mortals are blind beings caught in the 'circles of time' because *"...the mind has become bound to the passion of the wandering senses."* (2:67) Indeed, our *"soul is darkened by delusion* [...and] *vision is veiled by the cloud of appearance."* (7:15) Hence, our wandering eye and restless mind, continually distracted, seek ever-new divertissements within the shadowy realm of appearance.

To combat this *"confusion of mind"* (2:63), the East developed the spiritual practice of yoga. In the West, yoga is generally understood as a series of postures, meditations and breathings to calm the body and focus the mind. But there is also a yoga of vision. *"To those who are ever in harmony, and who worship me with their love,"* Krishna says, *"I give the yoga of vision, and with this they come to me."* (10:10)

In other, more mystical passages from the Gita, Krishna describes in detail those adepts who practice the yoga of vision: *"The greatest of these is the man of vision, who is ever one, who loves the One. For I love the man of vision, and the man of vision loves me..."* (7:17) *"The man of vision and I are one. His whole soul is one in me, and I am his path supreme."* (7:18) *"At the end of many lives, the man of vision comes to me. 'God is all' this great man says."* (7:19)

In these passages, we learn that the yoga of vision not only requires a mindful gaze, steadfast and unwavering, but also a higher awareness of the fundamental unity between the seer and the seen. Essentially, the seer must recognize the higher source of all that he sees – and that, indeed, his own vision and awareness come to him from above. The moment the seer discovers the source of his vision, the Sacred reveals itself in their fundamental unity.

At a turning point in the epic, Arjuna beseeches Krishna with the words: *"If thou thinkest, O my Lord, that it can be seen by me, show me, O God of Yoga, the glory of thine own Supreme Being."* (11:4) In the classic Arnold translation, Prince Arjuna's plea is even more dramatic: *"If I may bear the sight, make Thyself visible, Lord of all prayers! Show me Thy very self, the Eternal God!"*

Krishna's response to Arjuna is not unlike the Lord's response to Moses: *"Thou never canst see me with these thy mortal eyes,"* (11:8) he declares. As with Moses, so here – the divine visage remains inscrutable...

But then, Krishna bestows upon humanity a great gift, which allows us to see beyond the fleshly veil, to behold God 'face to face' in the full glory of his heavenly splendour. Although Krishna warns, *"Thou never canst see me with these thy mortal eyes,"* the great Boon-bestower also adjoins, *"I will give thee divine sight. Behold my wonder and glory!"* (11:8) The Sanskrit phrase *divyaṃ dadāmi te cakṣuḥ* may be translated literally as: I Give You My Divine Eye – Behold!

It is this, the gift of the Divine Eye, which allows the yogi of vision – and the Visionary artist in particular – to transcend the limits of human sight and gaze unimpeded into the higher world.

As the narrator of *The Bhagavad Gita* relates:

"When Krishna, the God of Yoga, had thus spoken... he appeared then to Arjuna in his supreme divine form. And Arjuna saw in that form countless visions of wonder: eyes from innumerable faces, numerous celestial ornaments... The Infinite Divinity was facing all sides, all marvels in him containing. If the light of a thousand suns suddenly arose in the sky, that splendour might be compared to the radiance of the Supreme Spirit. And Arjuna saw in that radiance the whole universe in its variety, standing in a vast unity in the body of the God of gods. Trembling with awe and wonder, Arjuna bowed his head, and joining his hands in adoration he thus spoke to his God... 'How difficult thou art to see! But I see thee...'" (11:9-17)

IV. Seeing Unity

While working with Ernst Fuchs, one of the greatest challenges I had was *to see* a painting the way he saw it. I soon learned that I had to forget my usual ways of looking at art and radically alter my gaze. This new way of seeing was acquired in three distinct ways.

First of all, there was the direct transmission of Visionary Seeing, which happened by painting for hours and days on his works. To paint in the way he demanded of me, I *had to see the painting* 'through his eyes', and render the forms in accord with his more expanded vision.

Secondly, he dropped many hints and key phrases during our conversations, which helped me to articulate and understand these new ways of seeing. Some of these remarks, like "colour is space," made no sense at all until years afterward. Others, like "see the general forms before you render the particulars," made sense to me immediately. Each phrase, though deceptively simple, encapsulated years of experience.

Thirdly, he came to me repeatedly in dreams. This happened *before* we ever met, in a series of inter-related dreams over a period of years, where I gradually came to meet and work with him in his studio. Though I never expected this to *actually occur*, once it did transpire, I finally understood many strange and unexplained omens from my dreams. Shortly after I finished working with him, I had an important dream where he and I were working together on a large 'Vision Tree' with an 'eye in the triangle' embedded in its crown. This collaboration in the dream-sphere moved our relationship onto a different level, into a more timeless and trans-personal sphere, where I continue to dream of him to this day.

Our conversations roved near and far over the history of art and poetry and philosophy, but always came back to one central theme – the Sacred. Fuchs knew the Bible inside and out, and could – much to my surprise – quote long passages of the King James version *in English*. His knowledge also extended into many arcane domains, and he had a fairly intimate knowledge of the Orphic, Gnostic and Neo-Platonic philosophies.

Brasserie Quai des Artistes, that excellent restaurant just below Fuchs' studio in Monaco, became the backdrop to many a conversation between he and I. During one long discussion, he described the Sacred to me as *"...a single light at the centre of the many."* And he went on to say that our aim in this existence was *"...to remember our origin in the Divine."*

These discussions sent me back to Plato, as well as the Gnostic and Neo-Platonic texts, studying their writings with a new eye. In particular, I realized that the Gnostic myth of creation, as portrayed in *The Apocryphon of John*,[6] was not a contrived and constructed story, but described in detail their authentic visionary experience of the cosmos' creation.

More than that, this myth offered a new way of seeing and beholding the creation. It was founded upon Aristotle's insight that God is the unity of *noesis noeseos noesis*, that is, 'the thinking a thought of itself thinking' (often translated less literally as 'thought thinking itself'). In other words, the creation begins when God becomes *conscious*, and so begins 'thinking a thought' (*noesis noeseos*). This is portrayed mythically in *The Apocryphon* as the divine Oneness (or Monad) dividing into the dyad of the Father (*the thinking*) and the Mother (*the thought*). Hence, God *is* consciousness, and the dyad reflects this, making it visible through images.

In the next step of creation, the divine Father and Mother turn to each other and beget a third: the Child, who is also an image and reflection of the divine Oneness. The Child completes the trinity, as the third part of the triad, the concluding *noeseos*. And so, God is not just the two-in-one of 'thinking a thought' (*noesis noeseos*) – but the three-in-one of 'thinking a thought *of itself thinking*' (*noesis noeseos noesis*). God becomes *self*-consciousness.

After this, the cosmos continues to expand outward in a unified hierarchy of heavenly beings (tetrad, pentad... dodecad), all of whom are images and reflections of the divine Oneness. Each possesses a particle of the Divine Light – which is nothing less than a particle of divine consciousness and self-consciousness. Through Adam and Eve at the Tree of Knowledge (*gnosis*), Humanity also acquires the divine spark – which is manifest in our own God-like consciousness and self-consciousness. Through it, we may recognize our origin in the Divine, and so return to it – through the mystical union of 'higher consciousness.'

The divine Oneness, in *The Apocryphon,* is not only the source of all creation – it is an immense Self-Consciousness that sees itself reflected in all the luminous images surrounding it. Every aspect of the creation that possesses consciousness, possesses a luminous spark that 'lights up' its image, making it visible to the creator, as a mirror of its own awareness. The One sees the all – as itself; it knows and is consciously aware of the all – as itself. The entire cosmos is a mirrored array of its own self-awareness.

Throughout *The Apocryphon of John* an extended metaphor is used to describe this mirrored array. It is called the Watery Light of the Aeons – the 'aeons' being nothing less than the emanations of the One's own unified being, the ever-descending hierarchy of its own manifest forms in creation. And so, all of creation surrounds the One like 'images in its watery light' – liquid reflections of the divine source, which are 'luminous' due to their share of its light, their particle of divine self-awareness.

This Gnostic text is of great importance because it offers us a radically new way of seeing. It offers us the chance to 'see unity' – to behold the creation as a unified whole. This is, by no means, an easy task. But, the Gnostic worldview constructs the cosmos in such a way that we, in a higher state of self-awareness, are able to *see as God sees* – to activate the divine spark in us and behold the cosmos *as unified and one*.

For the Visionary artist, the task is to depict the Sacred in such a way that this self-same experience of 'seeing unity' may be achieved while gazing at a work of art. The work itself must possess enough of the Sacred Codes so as to induce this 'higher seeing' in the viewer.

V. *"...In the Contemplation of Beauty Absolute."*

In my case, while working with Fuchs, I learned to stop looking at the painting and start *seeing the vision.* At first, I was a bit startled, as I never expected the painting to come alive in this way. But, by fixing my gaze on one point, I began to see how the paint would slowly give way to the higher hidden shapes. At first, the image became extremely clear and precise. As the circle of my focus widened, the perspective deepened, so that architecture appeared (as Moreau said) 'with neither foundation nor summit.' All the objects became surprisingly voluminous, and the colours began to harmonize and fuse. Everything had a luminous quality, as if glowing from within.

As my sight adjusted to this new way of seeing, the colours started glowing with an eerie liquid depth, and I became wholly submersed in their watery splendour (which the Gnostics had described as 'the realm of watery light'). None of this happened immediately, but it did happen naturally over the course of many months. Typically, we spent eight to ten hours a day painting, for weeks at a stretch. These marathon painting sessions encouraged, what Fuchs called, *"concentration on the fixation of the picture surface."*[7] It was his way of naturally entering into the same visionary state which had previously been revealed to him *"through drugs."*[8] Following Fuchs, I entered the visionary sphere – through concentration and contemplation.

Later, with sacred plants, I learned to re-enter this realm. And the plants gave me the strange ability to understand and articulate to myself the way the vision worked. In contrast to some of my colleagues, I rarely paint under the effects of entheogens. But I do journey through paintings (my own and others) as well as the art and sculpture of other epochs, to see and understand their Sacred Codes.

To transcend the picture plane and 'enter through the image,' we must allow the Sacred Codes, imbedded in the art, to work their magic. We must, for example, allow our wandering gaze to rest and become focussed on one point. That is why symmetry and a central point are so often imbedded in a sacred work of art – they draw our eye inexorably to that spot, to the face of the deity whose Divine Eye, once it is engaged, activates our higher seeing.

We know the Divine Eye in us has opened wide because we, like the Divine Source, see everything *as unified.* Such an experience lies beyond words, but the greatest mystics of our culture have endeavoured hard to bear witness to it in writing, and render an authentic, personal account. My experiences with Fuchs sent me back to Plato, Plotinus and the Gnostics, because their words suddenly found a rich new resonance in me.

In his text 'On Beauty'[9] Plotinus describes his experience while gazing upon a work of art. Unlike many of his contemporaries, he saw beauty as *"...something detected at a first glance, something that the soul – remembering – names, recognizes, gives welcome to and, in a way, fuses with."* (I.6.2)

But, what is it that the soul recognizes in beauty, and fuses with? Plotinus goes on: *"At a stroke, one grasps the scattered multiplicity, gathers it together, and draws it within one's self to present it there, to one's interior and indivisible oneness, as concordant, congenial, and friend."* (I.6.3) In other words, through beauty, the picture becomes a unity. What is more, it awakens us to the source of unity in ourselves, the divine Unity which he calls 'the One'. Thus, Plotinus concludes: *"In what is compacted to unity, there beauty resides – present to the parts and to the whole."* (I.6.2)

Much of this text is inspired by Plato's *Symposium*,[10] where he attempts to articulate the transcendent experience of beauty. Through the voice of a goddess addressing Socrates, Plato writes, "*These are the lesser mysteries of love, into which even you, Socrates, may enter; to the greater and more hidden ones which are the crown of these, and to which, if you pursue them in a right spirit, they will lead, I know not whether you will be able to attain. But I will do my utmost to inform you...*" (209e)

She proceeds to lay out the stages of contemplation necessary to pass from personal and fleeting images of beauty to those forms that are universal and timeless. For, *"the quest for the universal beauty must find him ever mounting the heavenly ladder, stepping from rung to rung... until at last he comes to know what beauty is..."* (211c)

She then describes 'the final revelation' as an experience like *"...drawing towards and contemplating the vast sea of beauty."* (210d)

"And now," she says, *"there bursts upon him that wondrous vision which is the very soul of the beauty he has toiled so long for. It is an everlasting loveliness which neither comes nor goes, which neither flowers nor fades... but subsisting of itself and by itself in an eternal oneness, while every lovely thing partakes of it in such sort that, however much the parts may wax and wane, it will be neither more nor less, but still the same inviolable whole."* (211b)

Having gained that experience, the visionary seer becomes one *"...whose eyes had been opened to the vision, and who had gazed upon it in true contemplation until it had become his own forever."* (211e)

"This, my dear Socrates," she concludes, *"is that life above all others which man should live, in the contemplation of beauty absolute."* (211d)

These words explain, as much as any text can, the experience I have while gazing upon a work of art. 'At a stroke,' I come to see the unity manifest in diversity: how the forms, the lines, the colours – all – acquire a certain harmony and, transcending that, a total relationship to each other as a unified whole. Beauty comes from harmony, and harmony from unity. And so, while gazing at a work of art, the beauty and harmony of the forms suddenly remind us of our origins 'in the One.'

My aim, throughout this treatise, will be to examine the seven steps of painting – the figure, composition, lines, light and shadow, volume, colour and style – and to explain how ancient craftsmen have used Sacred Codes throughout time to *unify* each aspect of the work, to open the Divine Eye in us so we can actually *see unity*.

VI. The Hidden Sign of the Hieratic

One evening in the studio at Castel Caramel, Fuchs stared at me over his glasses while reciting from memory a long fragment by Anaxagoras: *"All things will be in everything; nor is it possible for them to be apart, but all things have a portion of everything. Since they cannot be separated, or be by themselves; they must be now, just as they were in the beginning, all-together, always."* I was floored. Somehow, he had transmitted to me a vision of universal cohesion, beyond all thought or understanding.

Several months later, I came across a text[11] he had written to describe 'the eye in the egg' motif (Fig. 1.3) which appears at the centre of his *Battle of the Transformed Gods* painting (Fig. 1.11). This motif always struck a deep chord in me, because I had dreamt of something similar, and rendered it as 'the child in the chalice' (Fig. 1.4) in my *Christ Alchemist* painting (Fig. 2.1). I had no words to describe the original appearance of this figure to me (in a

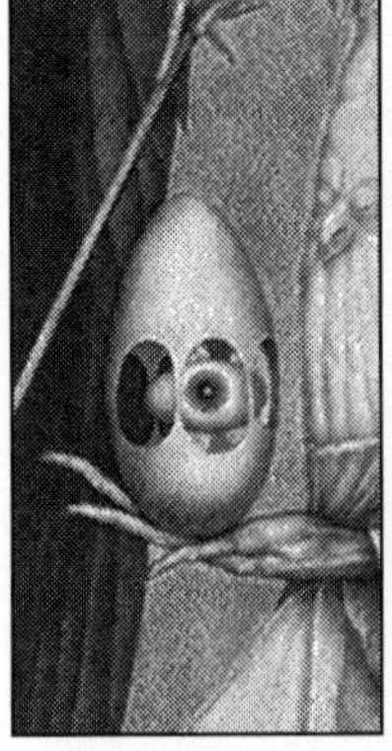

Fig. 1.3 - Fuchs: *Vessel of the Universe*

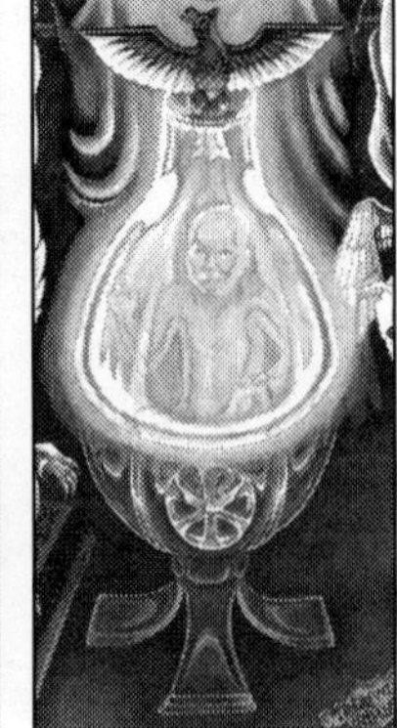

Fig. 1.4 - Caruana: *Child in the Chalice*

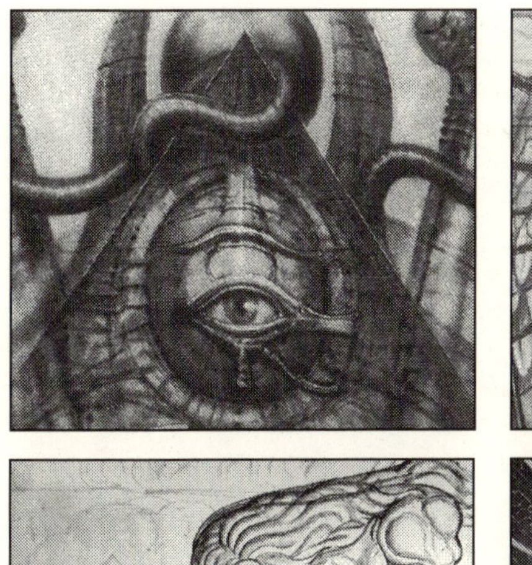

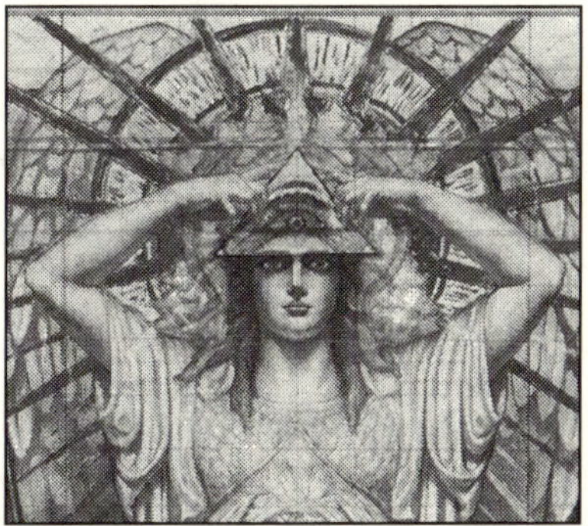

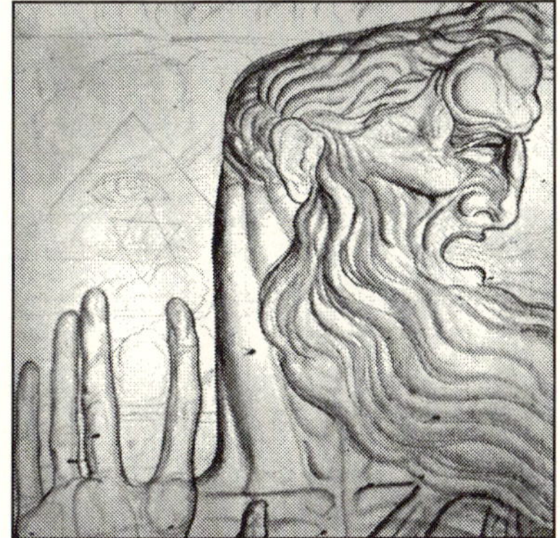

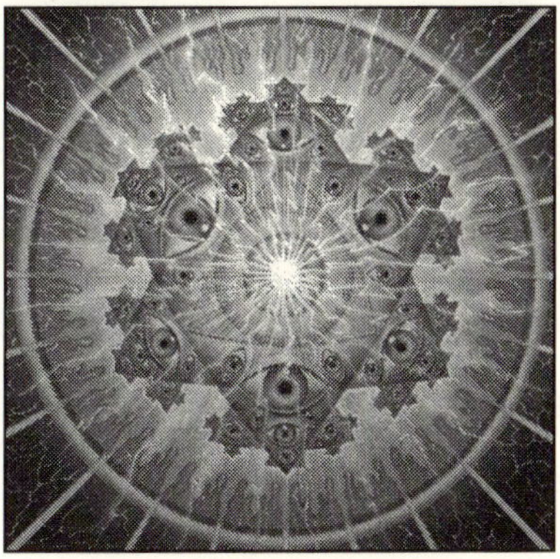

Fig. 1.5 Top - H. R. Giger: *Illuminatis I* 1978 (detail)

Fig. 1.6 Bottom - Ernst Fuchs: *Moses* 1945

Fig. 1.7 Top - Jean Delville: *Ideal Justice* 1914 (detail)

Fig. 1.8 Bottom - Aex Grey: *Vision Crystal* 1997

dream), but when I read Fuchs' writing, the moment returned to me with all its earth-shaking power.

He called that central motif, the *"Behälter des Weltalls"* – the Vessel of the Universe – and it evoked in me a sudden flashback, like remembering a long-submerged memory, of *'everything that is, was and will-be'* brought together, *now*, in one moment of seeing and being. (The German word *Behälter,* meaning *a vessel*, also evokes the English word *beholder* – to see and contain all things in a single moment or glance).

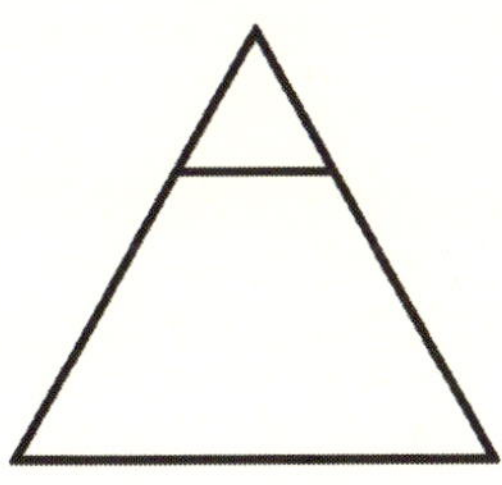

Fig. 1.9 - The Hidden Sign of the Hieratic

As an important sign or sigil of this experience, some of the greatest artists of our times have not hesitated to include examples of the Divine Eye in their works. This ranges from Jean Delville and Ernst Fuchs to H. R. Giger and Alex Grey (Figs. 1.5 - 8). In this way, each of them has recognized and acknowledged the gift of divine sight.

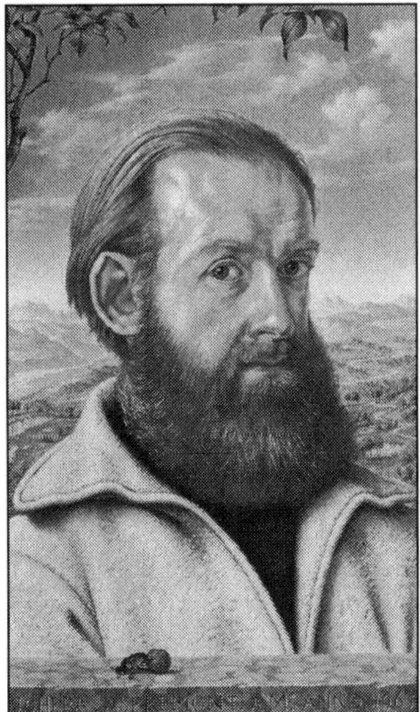

Fig. 1.10 - Johfra
Self-Portrait 1965

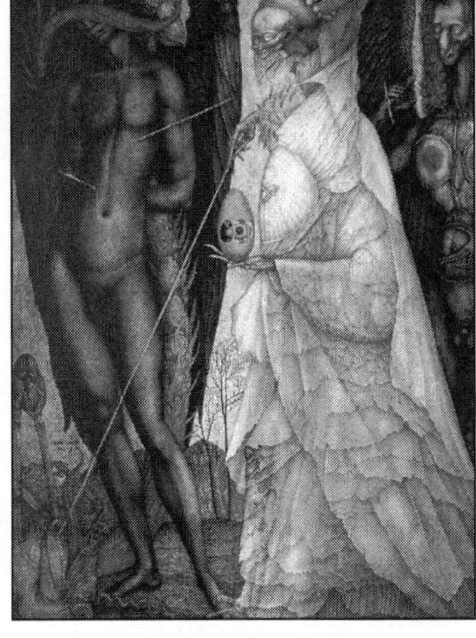

Fig. 1.11 - Ernst Fuchs
Battle of the Transformed Gods 1952

If we take the time to look a bit deeper, we discover that many great artists have left behind hidden signs and traces of this design in their works. Turning to examples by Johfra and Fuchs (Figs. 1.10 - 11), I invite the reader to gaze upon their compositions and seek out traces of this ancient motif. In Figs. 1.13 - 14 (two pages over), we see how the triangle underlies their design, such that, the eye always appears at the apex of the triangle. I call this ever-recurring motif 'The Hidden Sign of the Hieratic' (Fig. 1.9).

The eye at the apex of the triangle appears often in Hieratic art, as a sign of the Sacred. Alas, it has also been misread as a malevolent sign, since its use in Freemasonry led to an association with Illuminati conspiracies. But, the eye in the triangle *has always existed* in art, in the East and the West. In Christian iconography, it is quite a traditional and orthodox sign of the three-in-one God. But, since the Renaissance, it has submerged, and is more often inserted into the armature of the artist's work. We can see traces of it, for example, in Duccio, Raphael, Rembrandt and Blake (Fig. 1.12). Rather than appearing fully formed, it becomes *a hidden sign* of the ancient Hieratic tradition...

The word *Hieratic* simply means 'sacred' (from the Greek word *hieros* for 'holy'), and I will use that word throughout this treatise to denote those works of art wherein the Sacred *becomes manifest* – not just symbolized, but evoked and made present through the artwork's inner constructs, calling upon balance, harmony and unity. 'Religious art,' even 'Sacred art,' are terms which nowadays denote any work of art that is religious in its intentions or theme. 'Hieratic art' moves beyond that, and is sacred in its very structure, not just its content.

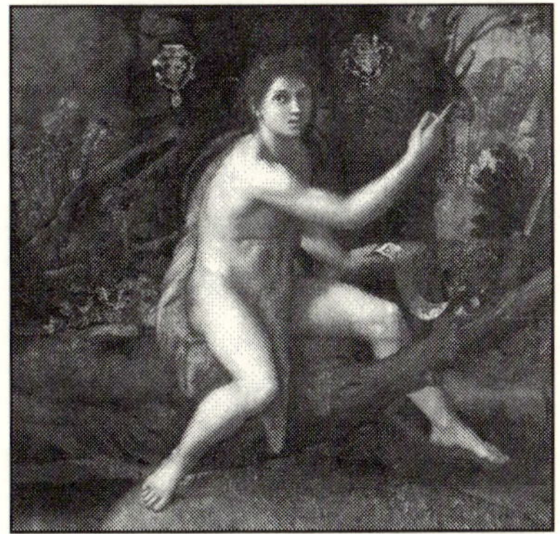

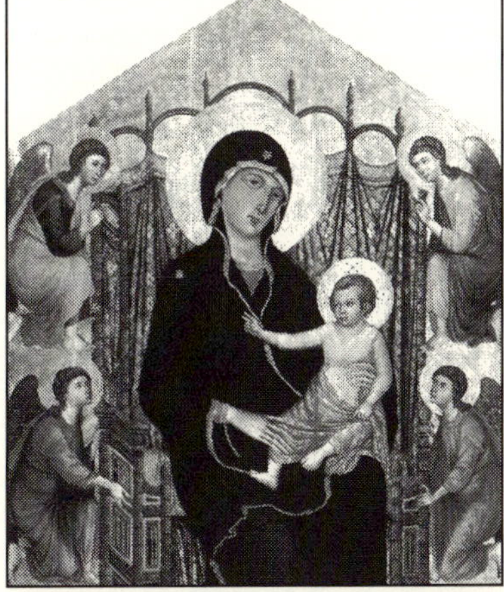

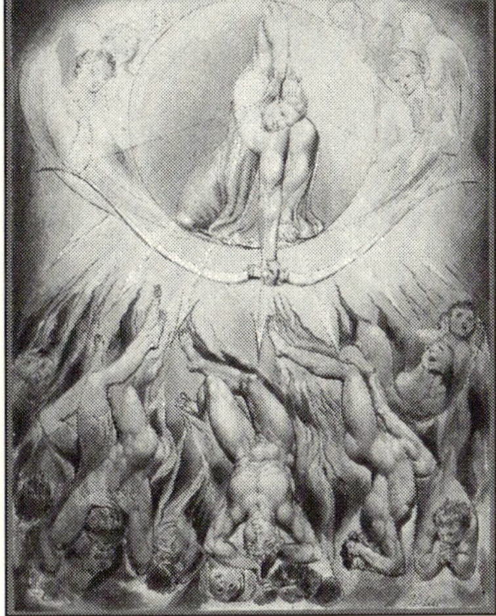

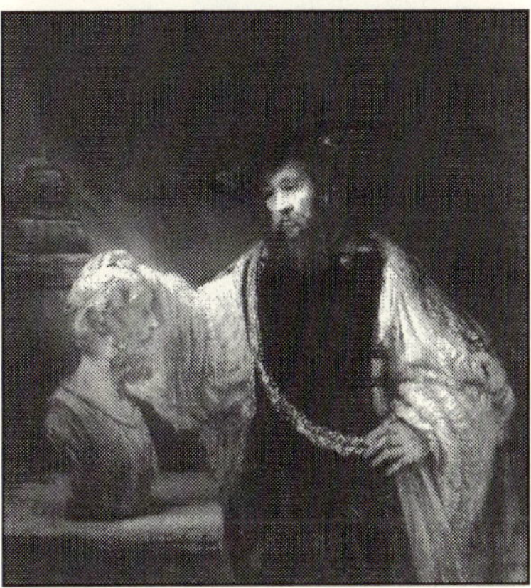

Fig. 1.12 - The Hidden Sign of the Hieratic
Top: Raphael, Duccio; Bottom: Blake, Rembrandt

Visionary art, when executed with an awareness of these perennial structures or codes, is a Hieratic art. But, examples of the Hieratic Style have occurred throughout history, and reached their apogees in the art of the Egyptians and Babylonians, the Hindus and Buddhists, the Mayans and Aztecs. In the West, it arose primarily during the Byzantine and Gothic periods, though Netherlandish art also evinces these qualities. The art of all these epochs manifest a distinctive cultural style that is hieratic in purpose.

As a Sacred Code, the Hidden Sign of the Hieratic is one of the many codes that have descended through time – concealed yet manifest in the works of those timeless craftsmen who have sought and actually seen the Divine. But, it would be wrong to think that this sign was somehow hidden to make it 'esoteric' – as a knowledge only for the initiated. Rather, it is a specific instrument or device with the express function of unconcealing the Sacred.

Its purpose is not only to indicate the Divine Eye, hidden in the eye of the beholder, but *to awaken and activate it.* Occurring always at the centre of the composition, its purpose is to attract and fix our regard, to draw it

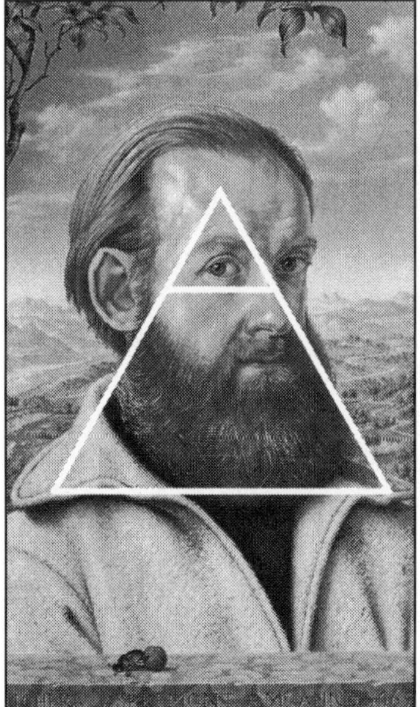

Fig. 1.13 - Johfra:
Self-Portrait 1965

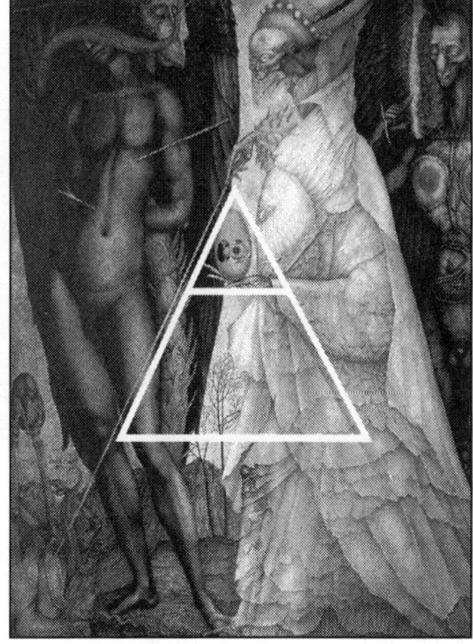

Fig. 1.14 - Ernst Fuchs:
Battle of the Transformed Gods 1952

inexorably to one point of focus. Like the gaze of god in Moreau's altarpiece, it demands a prolonged meditation and contemplation, until the true source of our vision is suddenly awakened. Once the Divine Eye *in us* has opened wide, then we begin *to see* the Sacred – not only in the point at the centre of the painting, but in the composition *as a whole*. Our vision expands, and the unified source of creation becomes manifest in each aspect and detail.

VII. The Hieratic and Humanist Traditions

We in the West, particularly those artists practicing the craft of painting, have inherited a way of seeing which can best be described as 'Humanist.' We have come to focus on ourselves, on Humanity as a whole, with its Human, all-too-Humanist triumphs and tragedies. This began in the Renaissance and has continued onward to this very day. It is a slow transition in which the Sacred has slowly disappeared from Western art.

Meanwhile, with Visionary Art, we are slowly turning our gaze once more 'toward the Sacred' (*Ad Sacrum*). We are rediscovering, in the Sacred Art of the past, long-forgotten wonders. In my mind, the greatest achievement of Visionary art today is that it seeks its inspiration *in both* the Humanist and Hieratic traditions. What is more, Visionary artists seek to *revive* the Hieratic style, so as to *re-unite* it with our Humanist inheritance. In the art of my masters and colleagues, I have seen this tendency, and I wish to share its beauty and mystery here.

What is Hieratic art? And what is our Humanist inheritance? As I mentioned above, the Hieratic Style reached its apogee in ancient cultures like Egypt, Mesopotamia, Crete and Archaic Greece. Towards the East, it could be found in Hindu and Buddhist art from India, Nepal and Tibet all the way to China, Thailand and Japan. During the Middle Ages, Persian miniatures and Islamic art evolved side-by-side with Byzantine icons and Gothic sculpture. In the new world, it arose among the Olmecs, Mayans and Aztecs. Other cultural examples come to mind, such as 'Primitive' art, Inca, Nordic and Celtic art. Netherlandish painting is a special case in point, since it shows a gradual transition from the Hieratic to the Humanist style.

I must add here that I have made Netherlandish art one of my personal life-long obsessions, but have not included it in this volume (with a few exceptions) to maintain a certain focus. I intend to remedy that in the next volume, where Netherlandish art will emerge as an important area for the development of painting methods and materials.

What I will call the Humanist Style began in the Classical age of Ancient Greece and progressed through Hellenistic art up to the Roman period. This style was re-discovered during the Renaissance in Italy and parts of Northern Europe. It is not only a style, but a world outlook and philosophy which places Man and Rationality at the centre of our vision. For the last five hundred years, its secular worldview has increasingly dominated painting, up to Modernist and Contemporary art.

Over the course of this treatise, we will witness the interplay of these two distinctive styles, as their differing forms converge and unite during each of the seven steps of painting. It is particularly in the works of my four recognized masters – Michelangelo, Blake, Moreau and Fuchs – that the Humanist and Hieratic Styles *wondrously unite*. But other great Visionaries – some from the past, others still painting today – have also achieved this magnificent fusion of styles.

To better understand the Hieratic and Humanist traditions, let us begin with a few key examples...

• The Figure:

The Hieratic figure is *symmetrically balanced*, emphasizing stillness and repose. The countenance is calm, perhaps adorned with an archaic smile. The gestures are symbolic, as with mudras, or upholding symbolic attributes. Examples include free-standing statues of Osiris or Ptah, or seated statues of Sekhmet the leonine goddess, the Buddha in the *padmasana* position or Medieval depictions of Christ in glory surrounded by the tetramorph. Standing and seated figures in profile, especially from Mesopotamia (steles of Marduk, Hammurabi), also fall into this category. All these figures inspire a calm meditation and contemplation.

The Humanist figure is *dynamically balanced*, with an arcing *contrapposto* movement. The face is filled with human emotion and the gestures convey inner states of passion, joy or suffering. The figure may recline in languid repose but more often struggles against adverse forces. Through the *contrapposto* movement, a burst of energy traverses the body, exploding in a glance or hand-gesture. Examples include the Laocoön sculpture in the Vatican, Bernini's *Ecstasy of St. Theresa* and Munch's *The Scream*. Their dramatic movements express vivid *human* emotions like terror, ecstasy or angst.

• The Face:

In Hieratic art, there is a preference for *profiles or the full frontal position*. Often, the god gazes at us directly, his eyes opened wide. Or, in the case of the Buddha, through eyes half-closed in contemplation. The 'eyeless stare' of ancient and mediaeval statuary is common here. Meanwhile, the profile gives the face a hieroglyphic quality: a simplified and stylized delineation of its silhouette. We gaze upon this epic being with fear and reverence.

In Humanist art, there is a preference for *the three-quarter angle*. In this way, the figure offers us a side-glance, and the greatest play of light and shadow falls upon the corner of the mouth and eye, amplifying their expression. The spark of light in the pupil expresses the soul of the sitter. Portraiture emerges, emphasizing the human over the hieratic. We feel an intimate relationship with the person depicted.

• Composition:

In a Hieratic work of art, the overall composition is *symmetrical*. Often an equilateral or isosceles triangle underlies the composition. Examples that come to mind include Christian altarpieces (triptychs), Buddhist thangkas, Babylonian reliefs of the Tree of Life flanked by winged genies, the Djed pillar of Osiris flanked by Isis and Nephthys, the Mayan Tree of Life, etc. The aim of these symmetrical compositions is to organize space around a central axis, and focus the eye on its mid-point.

In a Humanist work of art, the overall composition is *dynamic*. Often a mixture of scalene triangles underlie the composition. Examples from Classical Greece include panels from the frieze of the Parthenon, and the Gigantomachia Frieze on the Pergamon Altar in Berlin. During the Renaissance and afterward, consider Botticelli's *Primavera*, Gericault's *Raft of the Medusa*, and Picasso's *Guernica*. These dynamic compositions excite the eye and encourage it to move around the image.

• Perspective:

In a Hieratic composition, perspective is *determined by the divine figure within the painting*, which creates and organizes the space around it. Typically, this is a form of Axonometric perspective, where parallel lines do not converge but remain orthogonal, or at best, oblique diagonals. A geometric organization of space leads to flat but complex divisions in the form of tessellations and tilings. For example, Chinese, Persian and Islamic art, where space is treated as a regular whole. In Buddhist mandalas, all the flattened architectural shapes offer entrance to the titular deity at the centre. Byzantine art uses so-called 'inverse' perspective to create diagonal lines in the corners, while moving inward to the central figure. The deity gazes outward from sacred space, and we enter into its presence, in order *to be seen*.

In a Humanist composition, perspective is *determined by the humanist viewer outside the painting*. Using Linear Perspective, the Renaissance artist measures out the orthogonals and transversals of space by deciding on a distance point on the horizon line – a distance point which 'folds out' to where the viewer is standing. The sight lines of the viewer define the pictorial space, and their eye is invited to wander and explore a multiplicity of figures moving within this space. In this more mundane space, the sacred or mythological figures *are seen by* the viewer.

• Time:

In a Hieratic work, the image portrays *a timeless moment in the eternal mythic time.* The features of the god appear frozen for all time. His symbolic gestures of protection or blessing occur in a timeless moment. Standing upright and immobile, the figure balances on a fixed point. Meanwhile, a deity performing a mythic action is 'playing' at expressing an emotion, ritually re-enacting an event from the mythic time, in a purely dance-like and symbolic way. Through stylization and grace, the action has a higher meaning, and seems to take place *outside* our mundane and linear passage of time. Our eye is invited to linger on these ancient beings, who exist for all eternity.

In a Humanist work, the image portrays *a historical moment in linear time.* The features and gestures express a human emotion that occurred once in the past, and move us to feel that same emotion *now.* The action occurs historically, at some moment in the past, but along *the same* segment of linear time which we experience now. We *share the same time line.* The figure is poised to act, in a pregnant moment where the significant action has either just happened or is about to happen. This dynamic action seems to be caught in mid-motion (as if Western painting had invented the photograph, before the construction of the camera). Our eye quickly reacts to the spectacle with fear, pleasure or joy.

These five examples offer a brief introduction to the Humanist and Hieratic Styles. If we return to Moreau's *Jupiter and Semele* (Fig. 1.1), we find a fine example of how this Visionary master has managed to combine such different, even conflicting qualities in one work.

In this painting, the composition is hierarchal and symmetrical, but a variety of allegorical figures invite our eye to explore the space and construct a narrative. The event in the painting, drawn from Ovid's *Metamorphoses*, expresses a definite story or *histoire*, but also expands into a more timeless and spiritual allegory. Jupiter's pose is still and hieratic, but Semele twists and turns to express her humanist suffering. A surprisingly large number of the faces are delineated in frontal or profile, while others prefer the Renaissance three-quarter view. The square caps of the columns measure out space according to humanist perspective, but this is inconsistent, and the architecture plays a more symbolic role as the hierarchal Throne where 'all of creation descends, step by step, into darkness and unknowing.'

In this way, Moreau revives aspects of the Hieratic Style while continuing to work in the Humanist tradition. We have already seen how our gaze is invited to roam and scan the dark figures at the bottom of his composition. *Through the Humanist Style*, we experience to the full the terrible truth of our tragic, fallen condition. Meanwhile, our eye is also invited to rise up and rest upon Jupiter's godly gaze. *Through the Hieratic Style*, we may also transcend our fallen state and experience a momentary oneness with the Divine. The Humanist and Hieratic Styles *combine* to render this unique vision of death and transcendence.

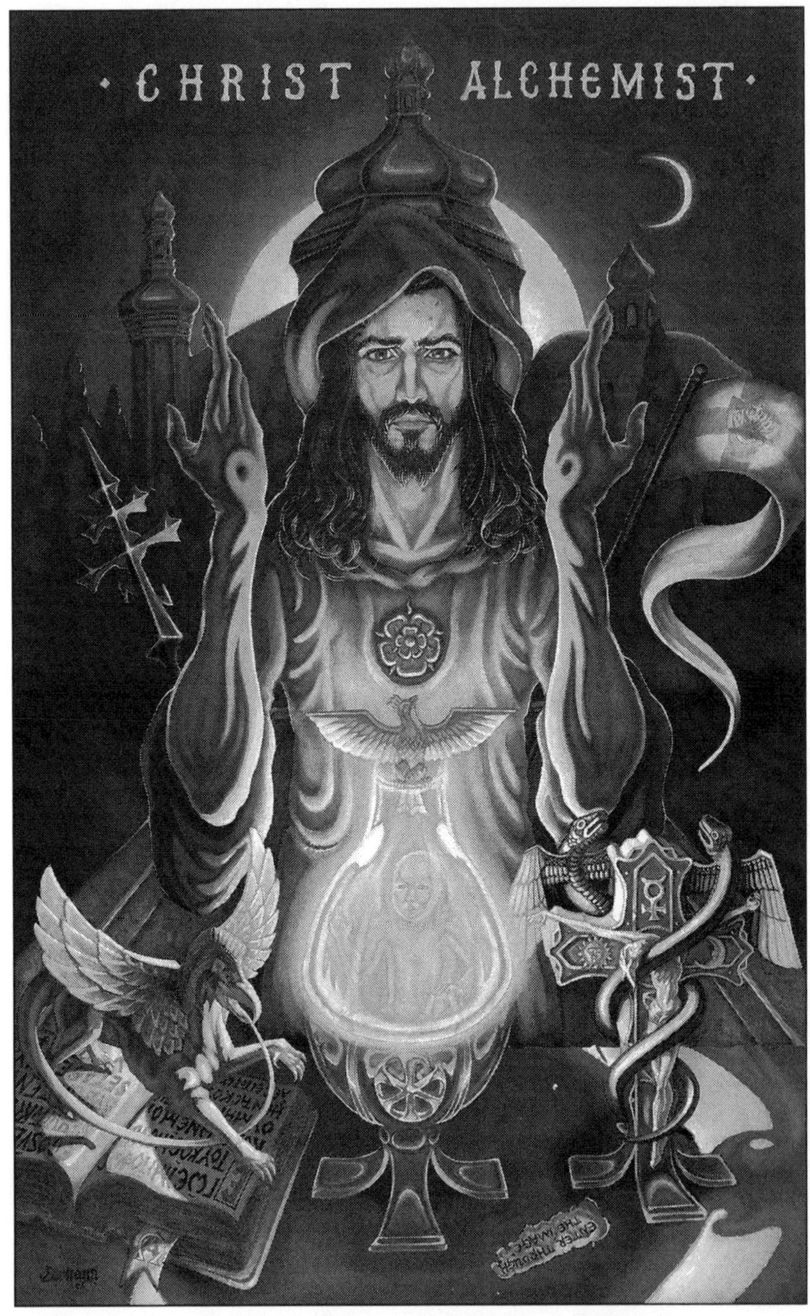

Fig. 2.1 - L. Caruana: *Christ Alchemist* 1997

CHAPTER II
ENTER THROUGH THE IMAGE

"The painter must always take care however,
that everything is in relation to the work as a whole;
so that when the picture is looked at, one can recognize in it
a harmonious unity."
Giorgio Vasari[1]

I. A New Way of Seeing

On May 13th, 1995 I made a discovery that would forever alter the course of my life. I was thirty-three years of age at the time, and living in Munich. Over the course of that night, while gazing upon my painting of Christ Alchemist, I *entered through the image* for the first time. The experience was like none other I had encountered before, and to this day it lies beyond the power of my abilities to describe the overwhelming sense of wonder and awe.

The object of my meditation – the image portrayed in my painting – had been given to me five years before... in a dream. During my travels from Toronto to Vienna and then from Malta to Munich, I had managed to paint and destroy one version of *Christ Alchemist*, then begin again and complete a monochrome underpainting in burnt umber. The experience that evening shook me so deeply that, the next day, I painted the words *"Enter through the image"* on a fragment of text at the bottom – to never forget that profound experience...

Over the next five years, as I *entered through* images time and again, I taught myself the techniques necessary for meditating on images, and even described them in a book, which was naturally entitled *Enter Through the Image*. In the summer of 2000, I had my painting of *Christ Alchemist* with me when I met Ernst Fuchs in the Apocalypse Chapel in Klagenfurt. He took one look at the finished painting and declared that I should work with him.

Over the course of that year in Monaco and Castillon, my perception of painting began to alter radically. This occurred quite naturally, while working on paintings with him. But, for years afterward, I also meditated on images with the aid of sacred plants and noted in detail the many possible modalities of perception. I came to see the underlying shapes and hidden signs which I eventually called Sacred Codes. Gathering these diverse texts together, I began to write a book (the book in your hands) under the working title of Seeing Unity. The emphasis, I had clearly decided, must be upon 'seeing'.

Because, while working with Fuchs, I came to realize that my way of 'entering through the image' had significantly altered. Previously, as I describe in my book *Enter Through the Image*, my meditation involved a psychological journey through personal and cultural memory-images, which ended with a rare experience of oneness at their core. I also described the different ways we can 'think through' images, and how different cultural symbols may be combined in myth, art and dreams. The journey involved meditation, thinking, knowledge and *gnosis* – and indeed, I still pursue the 'Gnostic path' to this day.

But, with Fuchs, I did not just come to 'know' the experience of unity – I came to *see* it. This was the great revelation; the 'new way of seeing' that he revealed to me. Still, it would be misleading to think that Fuchs pointed out these things directly. Rather, he required that I mix colours and apply them in a way that *demanded* these ways of seeing.

Since then, I have been teaching artists how to 'enter through the image', both in groups and one-on-one, with or without sacred plants, in Europe and the U.S.A. The results, to say the least, have been surprising, rewarding and (at times) even miraculous. As I travel round the globe, I am pleased to find that many people have already discovered these techniques for themselves, and are happy to share the experience. It is amazing how this new way of seeing extends beyond the individual, so that visionary experience may be shared.

As an artist engaged in teaching Visionary art, I consider this form of meditation to be absolutely essential. It has shown me how to 'see unity' at each of the painting's different stages of development, such as composition and the figure, as well as the stylistic and practical concerns like line, volume, light, shadow and colour. Having learned many of their Sacred Codes through image-meditation, I implement them while painting.

Indeed, if there is one thing I learned from Fuchs – painting *is* seeing, a continual process of watching the image come to life while rendering. In this way, the on-going contemplation inspires my work, it shows me where I should go with a work in progress, and a final meditation upon the finished work is like its ritual activation or consecration: I become fully aware of the deity who has continually inspired the painting's creation.

To this day, I continue my own practice of 'entering through the image' and always in a sacramental way. Despite the hours and days of preparation before a single séance, I am not always successful. Often, I have the feeling of standing at the threshold, and peering in, but not entirely stepping across. Meanwhile, during those moments when I have been successful, there is no fragment of doubt left in my mind: I am entirely there.

The experience is so overwhelming that it often brings me to tears, and I feel such intense gratitude for this moment of divine grace, that I am left in a state of awe for hours and days afterward. During those timeless moments, I have entirely forgotten that I am sitting in a room and staring at a painting. Rather, I am so fully immersed in the vision that I no longer know where it begins and I end. I am fully immersed in a state of seeing – seeing with the Divine Eye – simultaneously seeing and being seen, in the oneness of divine perception.

II. Sacred Plants & Visionary Art

In the not-too-distant future I hope to write a book on the subject of sacred plants and Visionary Art, where I can discuss the subject at length. For now, I would be negligent if I did not mention the topic, but I also approach it with the greatest of misgivings. There is just so much misinformation with regard to 'drugs' in our culture, that whatever I write here will surely be misinterpreted due to pre-conceived notions.

Nevertheless, I am not alone among those Visionary artists who have chosen to speak openly about sacred plants, their role in traditional cultures, and the possibility that they could serve a similar role in our own. As cultural attitudes cycle through freedom and repression, artists often stand at the vanguard of change.

Without a doubt, psychedelics reveal contents of the psyche otherwise inaccessible most of the time. Although the veracity of those contents remains open to debate, their phenomenology includes, not only images, sounds and narratives, but also states of mind, feelings and attitudes. Some are extremely dark and negative – causing inexperienced initiates to draw the conclusion that they are so for everyone, all the time. Other experiences are full of light and positive. In the proper context and setting, preferably with a guide, all these experiences have the potential of initiating a profound and positive transformation in the initiate – a unique experience of awakening and healing.

Having experienced a range of effects, both positive and negative, I tend to refer to these substances as sacred plants, entheogens, medicine, and even sacraments. I have also used them in conjunction with image contemplation, and found different results with different types of plant (as well as their quality, quantity and familiarity). Ideally, the entheogen should not be so powerful as to entirely dominate the experience with full-blown open-eye visions that are in a continual state of transformation. While these may be valued by some, my own aims have always been directed towards stasis and stillness, through contemplation of the image at hand.

Nevertheless, for hours and days after an intense experience of full-blown open-eye visuals with, say, ayahuasca, mushrooms or LSD, the lingering after-effects are indeed suitable for image contemplation. Otherwise, I have come to respect less intense entheogens, such as cannabis, for its unique ability to bridge the inner and outer worlds, leaving a continuous link or 'open door' between the two. In the form of marijuana and hashish, both inhaled and ingested, cannabis was the plant teacher of my master, and has since become my teacher as well.

Fuchs has written at length about his experiences with hashish (and peyote) in his essay 'The Hidden Prime of Styles'[2] and I also published the essay 'A Mirror Delirious'[3] which describes some of my own experiences with hashish (and absinthe). As narratives, both Fuchs' writing and my own describe a willing descent, even a plunge, into momentary darkness before re-emerging into a world full of light, feeling a certain lingering ambivalence towards the plants by the end.

During my apprenticeship with Fuchs, this ambivalence was maintained. Although we discussed our experiences, and may even have used sacred plants in private, in the studio a professional atmosphere reigned. The most important aspect of our studio practice was to maintain eight to ten hours of concentrated painting per day (often ten to twelve hours, and always for two to three weeks in a row). This discipline in regard to painting was absolute.

Thanks to the continual practice, I entered into visionary states naturally, and continue to do so to this day. Nevertheless, I practice image contemplation with entheogens in a sacramental way. By this, I mean that, even for a journey with cannabis (which others may smoke daily), I prepare three to four days in advance, then journey for one to two days, while leaving at least a week in between sessions. I do not impose my own practice on anyone, but I do vocalize my dissatisfaction when sacred plants are not treated with due respect.

III. To Enter Through the Image: The First Steps

The impetus to begin a journey will be a certain conjunction of time, place and the sacred image itself. While I often journey through my own images, I also learn much from the works of artists I admire, such as the Old Masters, but also my own colleagues and students. All sources are valid – images from different cultures and epochs, culled from books, posters, giclées or – most preferably – with the originals themselves. Journeying in museums may be difficult, but rewarding. Journeying in temples and sacred spaces has been, for me, the most profound of all experiences.

If a certain image has come my way, beseeching further contemplation, I set aside a time – preferably in alignment with the sun, moon and stars (though religious feasts may also be observed). For several days before, I moderate my diet (no meat, fats or alcohol) and avoid all extremes (no emotional conflicts, fatigue or illness). I cultivate good thoughts and positive intentions, particularly in the moments before sleep and after waking.

On the day of my journey I prepare both myself and the space – arranging all lighting, music and the images themselves well beforehand. All distractions, I know, must be kept to a minimum – a dark room, the image perfectly arranged in terms of its level and height, well-lit by spot lights, with music on the headphones or speakers nearby. As I lock the door of my studio, all electronic connections to the outside world are severed. I always do yoga just beforehand, to prepare my breathing and posture, then clearly express my intentions with the sacrament before an altar.

As part of my preparation, several images are at hand, and a very flexible order for viewing is decided. More often than not, the images themselves tell me where to go next, so I accept the new order as the journey naturally unfolds, moving from one image to the next. In all, I may meditate on three, perhaps four images over the course of a 3-hour session. Another session is scheduled for the next day, to go a bit further and possibly resolve questions from the day before.

Once the spirit of the plant is accepted (with gratitude) into my body, I place myself before the painting, sitting with an upright posture and maintaining a natural rhythm of deep breathing. My posture and breathing allow me to maintain a certain mental 'stance' during the journey. When I fall too far into the visionary trance-state, my posture relaxes and breathing becomes shallow (like falling into a dream). By consciously correcting my posture and breathing, I maintain my 'stance' of wakefulness within the dream.

At first, I allow my eyes and thoughts to wander over the image, absorbing minor details along the periphery. In a gentle state of revery, insights come naturally, and I follow the trains and digressions of thought, no matter how bizarre they may seem. Time naturally loses its constant measure, and I accept these alterations without fear.

My heart may beat faster, thoughts accelerate and body temperature elevate. Tingling in the fingers, nausea, sweating – all of these are accepted without panic. If my body tenses, I shake away the tension and relax, focussing on my posture and breathing. Morbid thoughts, inner voices, vicious circles – everyone has experienced these; they are the first steps of a labyrinthine journey.

By focussing on something of interest in the image, these distractions may soon be forgotten. Typically, something appears in the field of vision which seems unusual. Even by moving the eyes away and returning them – the unusual element remains. This means that the doorway to the visionary realm is now slightly ajar.

With more fascination than fear, my eye focusses upon some detail, which gains a greater clarity from my attention. Aspects of the painting which were formerly two-dimensional gain a greater depth. Indeed, as this new mode of seeing is accepted, the entire painting ceases to be a flat surface and becomes a window onto another world. The doorway to the visionary realm is opening wide.

If I still feel stuck at the threshold, I have certain techniques which I have taught to myself and my students. Many of these concern the different types of *gaze* that are possible. The most immediate and effective is the 'one-eyed gaze' where I simply close my right eye (always my *right* eye, directing all vision through my left eye, and hence, all mentation through my right brain). Although I can effortlessly sustain a closed right eye for hours, I have learned that a raised right hand or even an eye patch (I have indeed provided eye patches for my students...) will allow for continuous one-eyed meditation with ease.

I resort to the one-eyed gaze near the beginning of a journey, to initiate myself deeper into the experience. Despite the fact that only one eye is open, the painting acquires all the depth and perspective usually associated with two eyes. What is more, the colours may acquire greater luminosity and depth, leading the viewer to understand how, indeed, *"colour is space."* I have often performed an entire meditation with only one eye open.

Another technique is to squint with both eyes. While trying out these different eye postures, my thoughts are still wandering, making new connections. Often I am struck by a profound insight, but I resist the temptation to write it down. I trust that whatever is important will remain in my memory. Later, as more insights emerge, I do at times begin writing or drawing, but these inevitably interrupt the natural flow of my meditation.

The initial stages of 'entering through the image' take fifteen to thirty minutes, though I know that time has lost its usual measure, so this may feel like an hour. Over the course of a 3 hour journey, the greatest insights and moments of revelation come around the second hour – so I have plenty of time to gradually initiate myself deeper into new ways of seeing.

Each of these *ways of seeing* relates to a section or chapter of this book, and may be described as a different Sacred Code. What I have learned over time is that the Deity, gently evoked through the image, is calling to me. The Deity is calling to be seen, gradually, in a step by step initiation into wonder. Each element of the painting, carefully constructed, is so conceived as to reveal a new aspect of the Deity, a new way of seeing.

Each of these ways of seeing, I have learned over time, is based on unity. But it is the Divine in us, once we become aware of it, which awakens this sense of unity. Indeed, unified thinking and perceiving constitute the very essence of Divinity, as I described earlier with the Gnostic worldview. We know we are entering into the presence of the Sacred when our thinking and seeing alter so as to manifest unity – we begin to 'see unity'.

Over the course of two to three hours, these different ways of 'seeing unity' emerge, as ways of seeing that are completely different and unfamiliar to 'everyday sight'. An experienced Visionary artist will learn, gradually, to initiate him or herself into many of these different modes. Through study into the works of past masters, we can also learn the underlying structures, or codes, which support them and allow them to work their magic.

IV. To Enter Through the Image: Steps to Seeing Unity

Returning to the contemplation of the painting, the first sign of 'seeing unity' is that *the painting acquires greater depth.* It is no longer a flat surface, but like a world onto itself. In our expanded state of consciousness, the underlying lines of perspective are now joining up and finding their central, unifying point. What source, we may ask, grants such all-encompassing unity to these lines of perspective, so that the painting now appears *like a window into another world?* Is it my ego? Or are we suddenly becoming aware of a far greater source, which grants its more expansive unity to all our thoughts and perceptions?

As the image acquires greater depth, another momentary realization occurs: *the extent of our focus has widened.* Where once, we only saw a small circle with clarity, now all the elements along the periphery of our vision have become perfectly clear. Indeed, this often produces a natural reaction of fear, as we suddenly shift our glance away from the centre and onto some new object calling to us from the corner of our eye. But after a while we learn to accept this new state of 'expanded vision'.

Not only has the circle of our sight expanded, but everything in the painting has acquired *a sharper focus, a greater degree of clarity.* We begin to marvel at *the beauty of details*, and wonder why these details escaped our vision before. It seems like we could sit here pleasantly for hours and marvel at all the information encoded in those details. And indeed, many a craftsman has left behind important signs in these smaller designs – 'hidden in plain sight'.

If a recurring pattern, such as seen on Persian rugs, Amazonian *kene* weavings, or textiles from Indigenous peoples, covers most of the visual field, then our seeing may so expand as to behold *the entire pattern* rather than its individual motifs. To our wonderment, the pattern stretches across our entire spatial field, as a unified whole. At times, it may even glow with neon-like brilliance.

As our fascination increases, our eye remains open for longer periods of time. Gradually, *a white haze settles over our vision*, unifying all things in our visual field into a more cohesive, collective display. Words like *maya* (the ocean of appearances) or *chitta* (the mind's endless stream of thoughts and impressions) describe the initial impression left by this white haze, since we often begin to question the disturbing beauty and perfection that has settled over our sight.

Once again, fear may emerge, as we begin to doubt our sanity. How can the vision presented by the painting acquire, not just greater depth, clarity and precision than everyday reality, *but also greater meaning, presence and veracity?* As the fear of 'losing touch with reality' arises, we feel we can no longer distinguish 'appearance' (the images in a painting) from so-called 'reality' (the objects in the room).

At this point, we are certainly 'hallucinating'. But this beauteous apparition before us – is it merely a drug-inspired delusion or an unobstructed glimpse into the higher and unseen realm? Our rational mind finds this perfected state of vision to be impossible, indeed, insane, and momentarily fears it will be trapped forever in this new way of seeing. (For example, some of my students feared they would become trapped forever in the painting).

I have often wondered if the white haze were not indeed a kind of screen upon which our mind is able to project its inner archetypes. The images arising before our eyes acquire a distinct familiarity, as if we were remembering and 'recollecting' (in the Platonic sense of *anamnesis*) what was once known to us in our eternal soul. Everything may momentarily appear *huge, epic and monumental,* as if it has *existed since greatest antiquity*. And, ascending to a higher realm, the vision may appear timeless, perfect and true.

Over the course of the first hour, our state of fascination may become so intense that our eye will remain open and *focussed on a single point* for longer and longer periods. Shifting our sight from point to point is no longer as interesting as remaining focused on a single point near the centre of the painting – marveling at how everything comes together and coheres into a singularly overwhelming vision of sacred Oneness.

During my meditations, I may remain focussed on one point for twenty minutes or more – though the measure of time (as I have said) is irrelevant. At this point, the 'see-er' has truly entered into a state of contemplation (*theoria*), seeing the Divine (*darśan*), with the eye and mind fixed 'on a single point' (*ekāgratā*). All these ancient traditions, from a variety of different cultures, begin to make sense – as sacred practices leading to actual experience. They are not just the stuff of esoteric lore... (We shall elaborate upon *theoria, darśan* and *ekāgratā* in Ch. 26 on Visionary Seeing).

Eventually the mind becomes so focussed (and totally undisturbed by distractions), that an inner sense of *stillness* arises. We feel 'at rest', and can hear – above and beyond whatever music may be playing – a more comforting and all-encompassing *silence*. We enter the spaces in between, the places where the otherworldly light shines through all forms. We have entered into the presence of the Sacred.

If grace is with me, I may experience at this moment *a shift of focus*. Suddenly, I seem to remember that a different way of focussing my eyes exists. In the span of a heartbeat, *I re-focus my eyes*, and all appears flawless, resplendent and overwhelmingly divine. I am now fully immersed in the Sacred.

It is difficult not to shed tears of sadness, wonder and joy at this moment – sadness, because this more-perfect world lay beyond our reach most of the time; wonder, because we find it hard to believe that such a world has always existed, just beyond the reach of our sight; and joy, because we are now immersed, for an unmeasured moment, in the Source from whence we came, and to which we will eventually return – the timeless and eternal One.

V. Varieties of Seeing Unity

Once the state of 'unified vision' has been fully achieved, we may be further amazed to discover that we can now shift our gaze to anywhere else within the painting, *and the perfect state of vision persists*. We may open both eyes, stretch our body and casually glance at another painting in the room – only to discover that it too is beckoning to us like a doorway into another realm.

After placing another painting on the well-lit easel or support, and perhaps changing the music, we prepare ourselves for another plunge into the visionary realm – this time freed of our initial fears, and more at ease with the wondrous state of vision that may occur.

I find that, as an artist, I may become more acutely aware of the methods and techniques that have induced such an amazing experience in me. I now become more aware how each aspect of the painting – the composition, colour, etc – is a different way of 'seeing unity'. More precisely, it is my present state of unified awareness which allows me to fully experience these aspects of the painting.

For example, the colours which I first saw with my 'everyday sight' as dull, lifeless and flat (I may return to seeing them this way, simply by changing my focus) have instead transformed into something far more phenomenal. In the visionary state, *the colours have acquired an extreme richness and depth*, like the blues seen by a swimmer underwater when transpierced by sunlight from above. All the colours in the painting now *glow from within*, or *shine with an ethereal light*, and have a brightness and intensity far above normal. We are reminded of Mediaeval stained-glass, of the scintillating reflections of silver and gold, or the deep translucent hues of rubies, sapphires and beryls.

Due to this higher vibration, the neighbouring colours (which would otherwise appear *separate* in 'everyday sight') are now able *to mix and blend in the eye of the beholder*. For the Visionary artist, this new awareness of how colours may combine in our vision constitutes a rare and important discovery. New harmonies and colour combinations await, as yet untried, which produce hues otherwise unseen to normal sight. We have now gained a direct view onto 'the higher colours', as if we have poked our heads above the dark grey atmosphere of the sublunar realm, and suddenly seen the sun-drenched colours – pure, original and true – of the higher spheres.

In certain rare and wondrous moments, I have witnessed a whole spectrum of colours combine and unify into a single blinding white light. Which gave me pause to think: from whence comes the unity that combines colours in our vision? Has not the Deity, as the higher source of unity in me, granted its all-encompassing oneness onto the colours, so that they may combine harmoniously in my vision? And so, in this way, I have come to 'see unity' in the colours...

With this new-found awareness, I begin to marvel at the many other 'ways of seeing' – and of 'seeing unity' – granted to me in this elevated state. In the *composition* of the painting, I come to recognize how my *expanded vision* – seeing everything with a wider circle of focus – is indeed due to the One working through me. I am seeing all with Divine Sight, and this allows me to see 'the many' as unified into one.

Hence, the composition becomes a series of embedded polygons, expanding outward from a common centre – like Islamic *girih* designs, where a single shape at the centre expands geometrically into increasingly complex but unified patterns as it reaches the periphery of our vision. The composition of the painting before me now possesses this quality – the disposition of figures above and below, and from side to side, are reaching out to each other in new and varied arrangements, forming previously-unseen relationships, even up to the corners and the bounding shape of the canvas. The figures at the periphery relate to each other and to the centre, all in one massive harmonious configuration of the interior cosmos, like a painted *microcosm* expanding outward to the bounding limits of its outermost shape.

This new way of 'seeing unity' in the composition allows me, as an artist, to re-think the design of my works in important new ways. Suddenly, traditional rules of harmonic composition and sacred geometry combine in my mind, exploring new possibilities – and this extends to the sacred proportions of the figure as viewed in many different cultures. From Islamic tilings to Gothic architecture and Hindu sculpture – all these different measures are connected, as Sacred Codes, for the harmonious arrangement of figures in space.

When I focus my vision onto *the figure*, it too appears in an entirely new light. *Sacred proportion*, I realize, is nothing less than the attempt, in Hieratic art, to 'see unity' in the human figure – to see the relationship of the parts to the whole as a single harmoniously unified totality. All avatars of the Sacred, from Buddha to Krishna to Quetzalcoatl to Christ, are perfected images of humanity – they are the divine One manifest in the flesh, and flesh transfigured into the supremely measured and geometrically disposed, perfectly conceived and described human shape.

This elevated manner of viewing the figure also extends to its other dimensions within the painting. While proportion attempts to geometrically define its horizontal and vertical measure, *the volume* of the figure – as defined through *light and shadow* – suggests new dimensions. But this volume is not just the illusion of three-dimensional shapes on a 2D plane.

Rather, it is the attempt to convey the huge, epic and monumental quality of timeless mythic figures. As we see in the art of Michelangelo, Blake, Moreau and Fuchs, but also in the winged *Lamassu* guardians of Babylon, the huge heads of the Olmecs, or the leonine *'Shi'* guardians of Asian art – these epic figures seem to be carved from another dimension. Arising from the timeless realm of myth, they stand eternally stilled in their colossal beauty.

For the artist to convey this other-worldly light, shadow and volume, he or she must be fully immersed in the visionary realm. More than that, to build up the volumes in the *Mischtechnik* (painting white over dark in layer after layer), the artist must have an extraordinary sensitivity to the way light and shadow *combine* in our vision to render volume.

In essence, the artist must be able to 'see unity' in light and shadow – see how these two play over the surface of any figure, and ultimately merge and fuse. It is only in a state of 'higher seeing', when all appears unified, that the single outermost highlight may be touched with the tip of the brush, and then dispersed and blended into ever more transparent shadows, as the rest of the figure recedes into darkness and the lower volumes. That highlight at the centre grants unity to the ever descending shadows that constitute the volume of the whole. Such sensitivity to volume and form has only been achieved by the greatest sculptors and craftsmen of antiquity, and has endlessly been sought-after ever-since by painters and draughtsmen in their works of fresco and oil extending across the centuries.

In conjunction with volume is the figure's bounding line, its silhouette, which extends beyond geometric shapes and proportion to become *the cultural style*. Somehow, each of the greatest cultures in history – from Antiquity to the Levant; from the Occident to the Orient – have succeeded in rendering the Sacred in a *hieratically-perfected* human form. Each cultural style, we may say, is 'flawless and timeless'. All are different, yet eternally true.

One has the impression that the divine unity, by transcending time, is able to achieve a mirrored reflection of itself, not only spatially through different geographical locations around the globe, but also temporally through different historical epochs unfolding over time. Each cultural style is a temporal reflection of the eternal One underlying all of history. This is what Fuchs meant by his on-going quest for 'the Hidden Prime of Styles'.

In an elevated state, the Visionary artist *is able to experience time differently*. The visionary artist is able to perceive linear time *as a construct* (what Robert Anton Wilson calls a 'reality tunnel' or 'consensus reality') and so is able to rise above it. When the measures of time are rescinded, one may experience the eternal now. For a moment, history is transcended and all the epochs of art history, with their accompanying cultural styles, appear equal and comparable. We may literally rise above time and *combine cultural styles*, just as we would combine colours or compositional shapes in our vision. We combine cultural styles in order to perceive the time-transcending unity beyond its present appearance.

This temporally-expanded style of rendering does not only apply to the human figure, but *all figures, whether animal, plant or mineral*. In paradise, and in the visionary realm, time has no measure. As we seek to delineate animals, plants or minerals within this abode, we naturally seek a more timeless, perfect and true rendering of the transcendental and ideal. Heaven is not a blue sky with soft fluffy clouds, but the earth transfigured, a garden regained, and a whole tapestry populated by timeless archetypes. It is the realm of angels, elves and unicorns, but also every species of flora and fauna known to humanity now transfigured into its eternal state of being.

While in this elevated state, we also take great delight in *observing every detail* because time has lost its finitude, its pressing sense of urgency. We are no longer being pulled along a single thread of time (or lifeline) that ends with our pre-destined death. Instead – sensing our true eternal nature – *time feels abundant*, and we take advantage of this prosperity and profusion to dwell upon every minute wonder in creation. Thus, the details of a painting – *the ornaments and arabesques* – take on a new meaning, as essential to the whole. Each seemingly insignificant figure, as a member of the multitude, contains a germ of the whole and equally reflects the Divine.

If there are random swirls or gestures in the paint, the Visionary artist *begins to perceive faces and figures in the random forms* (*pareidolia*). In the ornaments and peripheral figures of Gothic and Hindu stone carving, we find many historical examples of this unique way of seeing, though lately, Visionary artists have begun many a painting in this manner. Ernst Fuchs, for example, would often 'see' and suddenly delineate a figure hiding in a section of the painting.

Let us not under-estimate what is happening here. In more ancient times, prophets and seers would listen to rushing water or gaze into a flashing fire and hear voices or see visions. The words and images arising from these random elements were accepted as Divine in origin. They were oracles, signs and even full-blown manifestations of the Sacred. The Visionary artist treats the figures arising from the painting's *'matière'* as spirits – whether plant, animal or angelic – calling to become manifest in this realm.

In the end, the disturbing beauty and perfection that settles over our visionary seeing is nothing less than the emergence of 'the Ideal'. What 20th century art has lost (and which we hope to regain in the art of the 21st century) is the quest for Beauty. To depict it, the artist must first *see* it – in a higher state of being. Beauty is not just the refinement of forms, but the echo of divine perfection. It is the momentary transfiguration of the mundane into a higher, stilled and timeless image of divine movement and grace in eternity.

VI. The Narrative Journey

Meanwhile, I have not as yet mentioned one of the most important aspects of image meditation. And that is *the narrative journey* which transpires, due to the momentary meeting and conjunction of the images with their beholder.

I will never forget (nor will I cease to repeat in my writings) something that Ernst Fuchs said to me, which clarifies the deep inner connection between life, art and myth-making: *"Myth,"* he said, *"is the eternal prefiguration of a human life."* While meditating on a painting – if its subject matter is indeed mythic, sacred or visionary – we bring our life *to* the images, and the images *transform our life thereby* – granting us a more timeless and eternal view onto our present life-unfolding.

No one, I believe, can meditate on an image without bringing themselves into the picture. By meditating on a sacred image, we bring our own life, as lived now, to the image and witness its transfiguration.

Every mythic being and event depicted in art is like a step by step unfolding of life's gradual evolution from the darkest suffering to the dance of joy in the light. Our heroic life-journey requires the crossing of numerous life-thresholds, such as marriage, finding a vocation, building a home, the death of a beloved, or confronting one's own mortality. Great works of art address these themes and offer us images of healing and transcendence, to overcome life's greatest traumas and triumphs.

When I meditate on an image, I know that any thought or feeling entering into my meditative state (especially at the beginning, when making an intention and accepting the sacrament) will come back repeatedly over the course of the session. This need not be one thought, but may be several seemingly-disconnected thoughts or feelings. Nevertheless, over the course of two to three hours, my heart and mind will slowly construct a narrative, integrating some if not all of these concerns into my vision-journey through the painting.

The narrative arises through the seemingly 'chance encounter' of my roving eye with the images in the painting. As my gaze shifts from one image to the next, new thoughts arise in my mind, observing and connecting my own unique interest in the painting with the artist's rendition of a higher theme. The narrative emerges as image after image are encountered, considered and newly understood.

In a moment of revelation, I understand how the higher theme finds its unique echo and example in me and the greater striving for life now moving through me, body and soul.

During such moments, I find myself viewing my life from a higher perspective, that is mythic and eternal (*sub specie aeternitatis* – 'under the aspect of eternity'). We witness ourselves, not just as mundane human beings crossing over life's many thresholds, but as immortal, spiritual beings momentarily incarnated here to gain some insight or revelation into our true nature, though these teaching experiences.

Rising ever higher, I eventually become aware of my true relationship to the god, goddess or angelic being in the painting: the Sacred finds its momentary reflection in me, and I – at that rare moment – see myself in the Sacred. I can completely identify myself with the Sacred figure – seeing the painting, in Alex Grey words, as a 'sacred mirror' and experiencing the state of oneness between the image and its beholder.

What is more, if we meditate on a painting that we ourselves have created, then the higher self in us – the Over Self – may reveal its hidden workings. Suddenly, an image or symbol which we painted from a vision or a dream reveals its higher hidden intent. New levels of meaning emerge, and unexpected associations arise, revealing aspects of our own life previously unconsidered. We feel like Oedipus who, trapped by the deathly gaze of the Sphinx, suddenly divines the mysterious answer to her riddle – an answer which only a life fully lived and experienced may reveal.

The artist, like the eternal hero, is that unique individual who knows how to read the signs and omens arising enigmatically in art, legends and dreams – and lives their life according to these deeper portents. They have the courage to follow their dreams – not the ego-based dream of success and financial reward – but the deeper dream-stuff, of confronting fears and embracing the unknown. By rendering their dreams and visions in paint, artists have the unique opportunity of re-encountering those symbols, meditating upon them, and integrating their higher truths into their lives.

VII. *The ego is a continuous forgetting...*

Almost twenty years have transpired from my first experience of 'entering through the image'. Following my ritual observance of this practice, I have 'pierced the veil' perhaps two hundred times in my life – recording each unique experience in my notebooks and journals.

Looking back over those experiences, I can see that, almost every time, I succeeded in 'seeing' another world and 'thinking' in a different way – as the awareness of unity granted me a new perspective and outlook onto the world. And yet, *the direct experience of Oneness,* as a complete immersion into mystical experience, has only happened a handful of times.

If there were a single, simple direct path to that experience, I would surely describe it here, for the benefit of myself and others. But the most I can offer is practice – spiritual practice, of breathing, posture, and concentration, combined with meditation upon a sacred image. And yet, that practice will only meet its highest intention through the blessings of Divine grace.

During those moments, I *know* (in the deepest sense of *gnosis*) that the ego is a continuous *forgetting* of our true nature, as we become blinded by wants, needs and desires. Suddenly, I *remember* that I am part of something much greater: an all-encompassing light and awareness, of which 'I' am but the tiniest reflection.

Perhaps I am a particle of divinity, a spark of light descended into darkness and matter, so this 'world of becoming' is all an illusion. Perhaps I am a breath of life, a vital spirit passing through this vast network of beautiful earthen shapes, generated by Nature, our mother. We make images of gods and goddesses to direct our focus towards these experiences – but the images only serve their higher purpose once they are completely 'entered through' – activated, consecrated, and transcended.

During my meditation on an image, there may arrive a rare moment of divine dispensation, where I 'know' and 'remember' that all these different ways of seeing and thinking have led me *here*, to *this* place. It is a state of being with neither beginning nor end; complete in itself; total, perfect, one and true. My eyes are still open and I am still gazing at the image – but my perspective has utterly transformed.

My only desire, at that moment, is to remain in this state for all of eternity. And so, tirelessly, effortlessly, I remain focussed on the image, on a single point, feeling with each intake of breath a greater immersion into spirit and plenitude. The image itself – a face, figure or sacred symbol – is now fully alive in my vision, a living memory and clear reflection of its true Source. Time has lost all measure, so I sit there staring – with tears in my eyes – immersed in the watery light, awash with gratitude and awareness of that greater Consciousness that grants us greater vision and knowing.

The Wisdom traditions from East to West have described these rare moments of total immersion into wonder – as *the direct experience of Oneness*. Such experiences have taught me that the greatest form of image-contemplation consists of stillness, focus and concentration. During the first parts of the vision journey, our eyes wander over the image, seeking out narrative and allegory, combining symbols, learning the language of the image. We construct narratives for ourselves, and see the synchronicities, as our own life questions find their answers in the mythic unfolding of figures in the painting – their 'eternal pre-figuration of a human life.'

But eventually, if we are able to exhaust this ego-striving for experience and self-understanding, we may immerse ourselves in a different way of seeing. With our mind wide open, we witness the One's circular self-knowing in a limitless ocean of pure awareness. And with our *eyes* wide open, we witness the One's circular *self-seeing* in a boundless ocean of *pure sight* – the images aglow in a sphere of clear watery light.

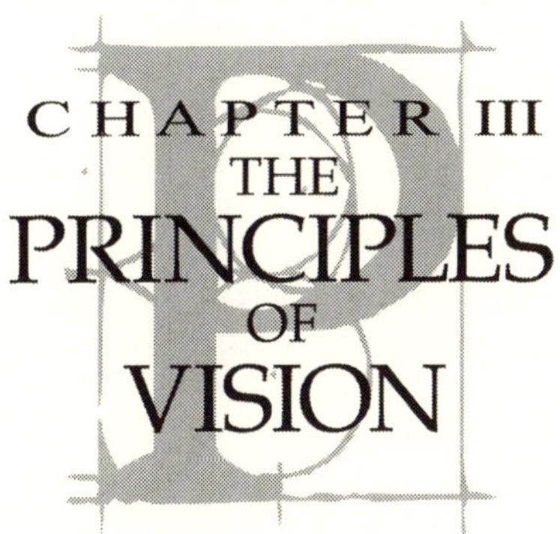

CHAPTER III THE PRINCIPLES OF VISION

The light of the body is the eye:
if therefore thine eye be single,
thy whole body shall be full of light.
Mt 6:22, King James version

I. The Outpouring of Vision

Since the time of the Renaissance, we have developed a scientific and Humanist explanation of sight based on the empirical method and its 'corroboration of the senses'. According to this "intromission" theory of vision, rays of light from the sun bounce off the object and enter the eye. In this sense, *the object* is primary, sending out images of itself to the receptive eye, which records it. In contrast, the "extramission" theory of vision, which is more ancient and Hieratic, perceives *the eye* as primary, *projecting rays of light* onto objects in order to seize their shape and form.

Perhaps the first and greatest exponent of the Humanist "intromission" theory was Leonardo da Vinci, who wrote of the visual object:

"Just as a stone flung into the water becomes the centre and cause of many circles, and as sound diffuses itself in circles in the air: so any object placed in the luminous atmosphere diffuses itself in circles, and fills the surrounding air with infinite images of itself."[1]

Here, in stark contrast to the Divine Eye of the Gnostics, which 'fills the surrounding watery aeons with luminous images of itself', it is *the object* which 'fills the surrounding air with infinite images of itself.' The object, and not the eye, is the primary source of all perception.

For Leonardo, the discovery of Renaissance perspective was nothing less than the confirmation of this new way of seeing – a passive reception of the object's manifold images projected into space. Again, the artist wrote:

"Perspective is a rational demonstration by which experience confirms that every object sends its images to the eye."[2]

We have become the unquestioning heirs to this Humanist model of perception, developed during the Renaissance and reaching its apex with Kepler's *Ad Vitellionem paralipomena, quibus astronimiae pars optica traditur* (Optics: A Supplement to Witelo and the Optical Part of Astronomy - 1604) and, a century later, Newton's *Opticks* (1704). But, prior to that time, a more ancient and "Hieratic" model of vision governed over perception, from the time of the Classical Greeks all the way through to the Mediaeval period of Gothic, Byzantine and Netherlandish art.

In the Gnostic way of seeing described above, the One at the centre of all things "pours out" its luminous vision into the watery aeons, thus *actively creating* all the objects within its field of vision, as mirror reflections of its own all-inclusive seeing. This unified model of Divine Vision, written around the 1st century, had in fact existed since the earliest expositions of Greek thinking.

In the 5th century BCE, the Pre-Socratic philosopher Empedocles was the first to give voice to the more Hieratic, extramission model of vision, by attributing sight to the Greek Goddess of Love: *"Divine Aphrodite,"* he wrote, *"fashioned the unwearying eyes."*[3] In a longer passage, he described how she fashioned the eye so that the luminous fire of vision could *pass outward* from it, while watery membranes held the pupil (or lens) in place:

"As when a man, thinking to travel through the stormy night, gets ready a lamp, a flame of blazing fire, and puts round it a lantern to keep out all manner of winds so that the light may shine outward and across the threshold with unfailing beams; even so did she [Aphrodite, create the eye so as to] *entrap primaeval fire within the round pupil, whose gentle membranes and delicate garments are pierced through with wondrous passages. These keep out the water that surrounds the pupil, but let the fire pass through."*[4]

A century later, Plato expounded a similar view in his *Timaeus*, describing the primaeval intra-ocular fire as *"...such a fire as has the property, not of burning, but of yielding a gentle light."*[5] He goes on to say that, *"The pure fire within us is akin to this, and they* [the gods] *caused it to flow through the eyes."*[6] When the intra-ocular fire reaches the light of day, Plato says, it fuses with it to become a transparent medium for the transmission of vision: *"Accordingly, whenever there is daylight round about, the visual current issues forth* [from the eye], *like to like, and coalesces with it, to form a single homogeneous body in a direct line with the eyes."*[7]

Plato's emphasis on 'the direct line' between the eye and its object was taken up by Euclid in his *Optica*. Here, the Alexandrian logician provided the first *geometrical* definition of extramission vision, where 'rectilinear' (i.e. straight) rays of light proceed from the eye *in conical form* to describe the object. In the *Optica*, the first of the seven postulates begins: *"Let it be assumed: 1. That the rectilinear rays proceeding from the eye diverge indefinitely."*[8]

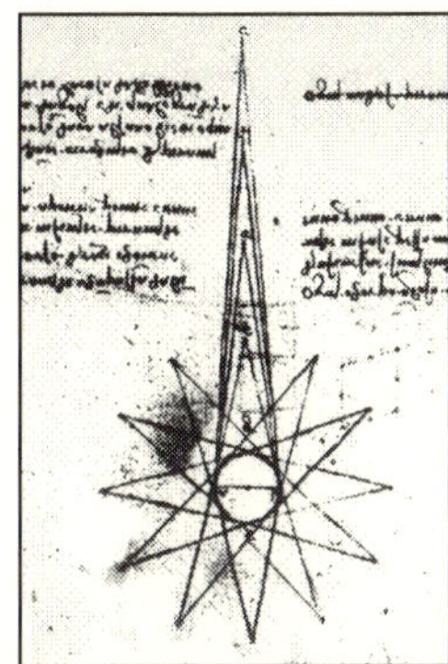

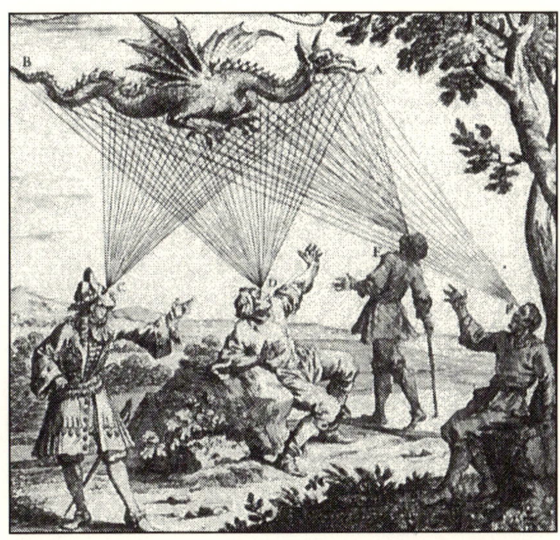

Fig. 3.1 Above - Leonardo da Vinci: *"The object ...fills the air with infinite images of itself."*
Fig. 3.2 Right - The Extra-mission Theory of Vision

Euclid's eighth theorem offered the first definition of perspective for artists. Interestingly, he did not establish the distance between objects by comparing their difference in size (object is primary), but rather, by comparing their differing angles of conical vision as emitted from the eye (the eye is primary). This view onto perspective – of the eye's active creation of its spatial field – would influence artists in their construction of spatial perspective from Classical Greek to Mediaeval times (a view to which we will return in our exposition on Perspective).

But, more than that, the Hieratic model of vision granted artists the power to see their creations as sacred unfoldings of Divine Vision. Rather than being bound to the veridical recording of Nature, artists opened themselves up to the higher outpourings of the heavenly realm, with its graceful lines and divine shapes manifesting the more archetypal beauty of 'the ideal' world.

If we truly wish to become Visionary artists – seeing the Sacred as the ancient craftsmen did – then we must acquire the Divine Eye. In the deepest sense, this means that we must radically alter our model of vision so as to understand 'seeing' as *an active creation of the world*, rather than a passive reception of it through the senses.

The Divine Eye created the cosmos by 'seeing' it in the watery light, actively forming and manifesting it. Visionary Seeing requires that we, similarly, open our eyes to the possibility that vision is *the active transmission* of Divine Sight, rather than the passive reception of worldly objects. The Sacred *sees the world through us*, and manifests its higher world, in particular, *through Visionary artists*, whose hands delineate with perfection the graceful lines and harmonious shapes of the archetypal realm. Such artists become the *artifex* – the divine craftsman – and the *pantocrator* – the ruler of all creation.

Ultimately, Visionary Art seeks a synthesis of the Humanist and Hieratic traditions, of Nature and the Ideal. But modern Western art has gone so far down the secular Humanist path that we are now in dire need of Sacred art as a panacea and healing herb to the injurious malady of Contemporary Art. Throughout this treatise, I will emphasize the more active Hieratic manner of seeing which, according to William Blake, is the only true form of vision:

This life's dim windows of the soul
Distorts the heavens from pole to pole
And leads you to believe a lie
When you see with, not through, the eye.[9]

II. The Hieratic Style in India

In the spring of 2003, I spent several months in India, Nepal and Tibet, opening my eyes to the art of the East. One experience that marked me profoundly occurred during the Hindu festival of Holi. Having smoked some of the local *bhang*, I entered the temples of Khajuraho, those glorious stone cathedrals built by the Chandella rulers in the 10th to 12th centuries. My sense of time altered, becoming distinctly cyclic, and the temple itself, dedicated to the goddess Devi, became a House of the Holy.

After circumnavigating the Devi Jagadambi temple, I reverently removed my sandals and ascended the steps. Passing under the porch and entering the vestibule, I really felt myself in the presence of the Holy. The stones themselves seemed to reverberate with ancient time. The deity of this place emanated her presence across the land and over the centuries, drawing people from far and near to her sanctuary.

When a Hindu family came in to worship, I respectfully stood to the side. Standing 'outside' history I watched the timeless, ever-repeated acts of *pūjā, sparśa* and *nyāsa.*[10] Greeting the statue with a namaste gesture, the devotee laid her flowers at the Goddess's feet, touched the statue with her hand then moved her hand to her heart, forehead and lips. Through these simple, timeless gestures, the statue was ritually activated, and the ever-present deity became manifest, for a few brief moments, through her earthly receptacle.

For me, at that moment, the bounds of linear time dissolved, and I saw the thousands upon thousands who had come to this place, prayed and worshipped here. Holiness was emanating from every block and stone, but especially from the stone statue of the Goddess enshrined within.

After making my own offering to Devi, she granted me several hours of illuminated exploration among the various temples (with insights and revelations far too numerous to recount here). Toward dusk, I watched spellbound as the light of the setting sun entered the neighbouring Chitragupta temple and fused with the statue inside, a majestic sculpture of the sun god Surya. While admiring the statues flanking the entrance to this sanctuary, I was inexorably drawn towards two figures on the right, of a male *gandharva* and female *apsara*.

For an uninterrupted moment I gazed at these carvings and 'saw' the unique Hindu style for delineating the human figure. This 'seeing' was like an initiation into a new way of perceiving the human form – how its graceful lines 'carved out' their surrounding space. But, more than just space, they were

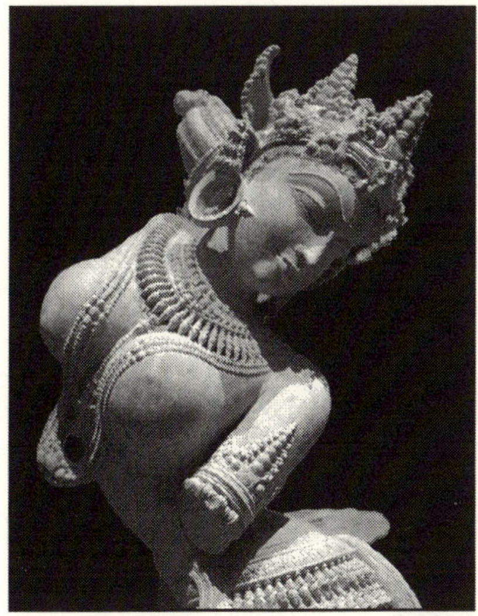
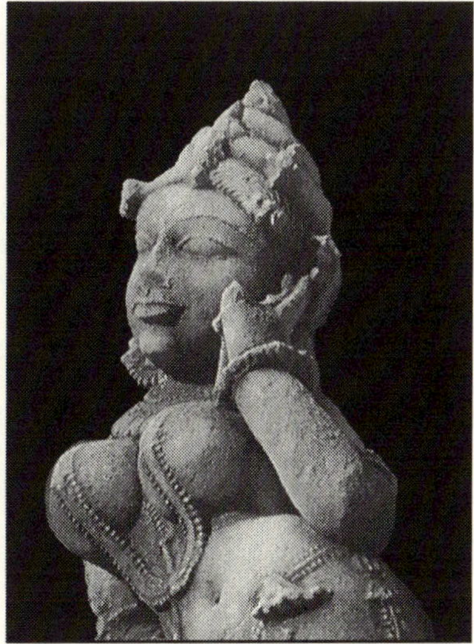

Fig. 3.3 - Khajuraho Statues, 10th century, Chandella Dynasty

reshaping the watery expanse of perception before me. I felt such an intimate oneness with the figures before me that the 'space' which was 'separating' us was more like a liquid pool of vision which, while momentarily uniting us, was also capable of metamorphosing into ten thousand things.

Everything in my visual field was sculpted from the waters of creation, and these particular statues were reshaping that liquid expanse in the most beautiful and harmonious of ways. Gazing at their faces, I saw how all this came together in *the style* – what we call the recognizable 'Chandella' style of Khajuraho sculpture. All the artists of that epoch were familiar with the same Sacred Codes, and so could execute a work in that style – not just by copying the superficial outlines, but by working within the set principles of proportion, balance and pose which undergird the figure, giving it energy and life from within.

What struck me even more strongly about the flanking statues is that I could 'see' how they were rendered *by different hands*, each of which followed the codes of *a different family lineage*. Although both statues shared the Chandella style, each family of craftsmen – each master in the *guild* – had subtly altered and played within the rules of that style, leaving their own unique mark. (Indeed, I even found evidence of these mason's marks on the stones, and copied them into my notebook).

These family lineages of sculptors from India found their equivalent in the workshops of Master artists from Mediaeval Europe. After all, the building of the Khajuraho temples in the 10th to 12th centuries paralleled the building of the first French cathedrals in Paris and Chartres.

Since I was living in Paris at that time, I was already piercing the veil – slowly but surely – of Mediaeval French sculpture, learning to distinguish its uniquely Gothic codes that united craftsmen into recognizable family-lineages, workshops and guilds.

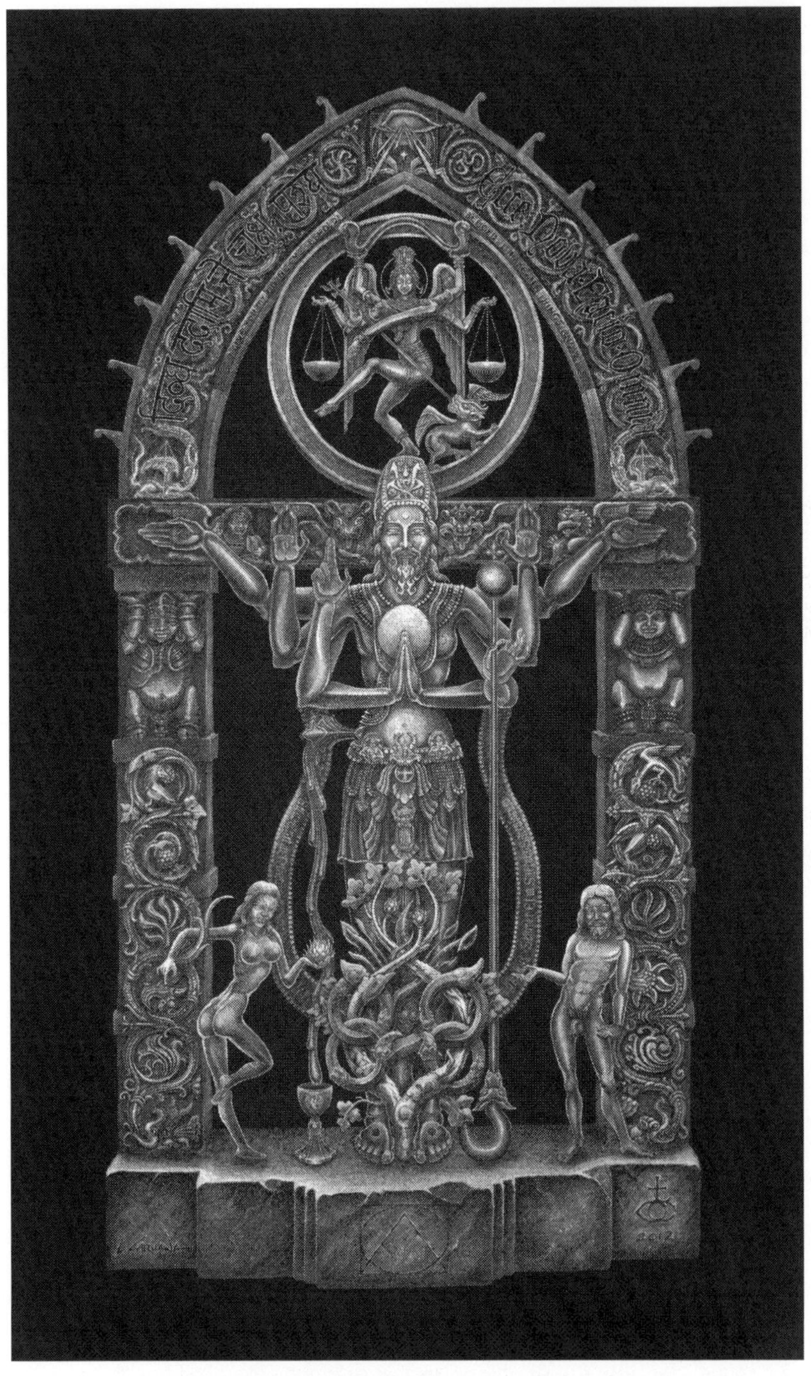

Fig. 3.4 - L. Caruana: *Vishnu-Christ Avatar* 2012

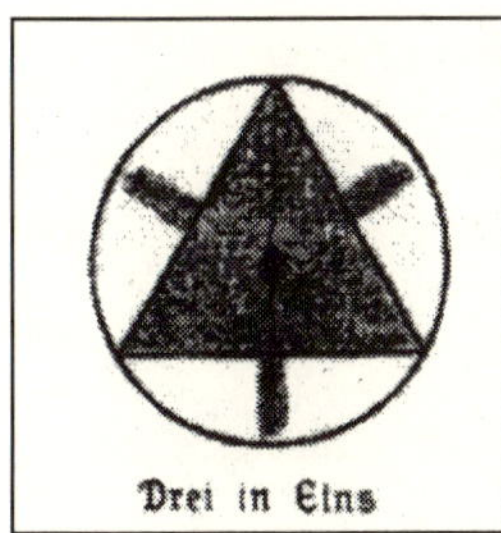

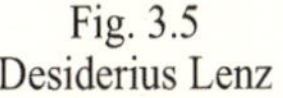

Fig. 3.5
Desiderius Lenz

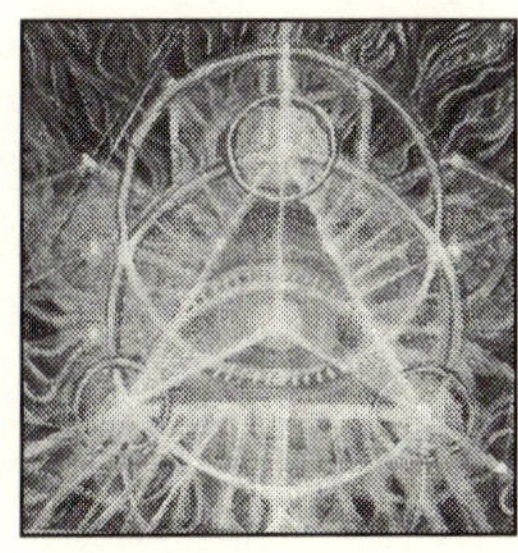

Fig. 3.6
Kuba Ambrose

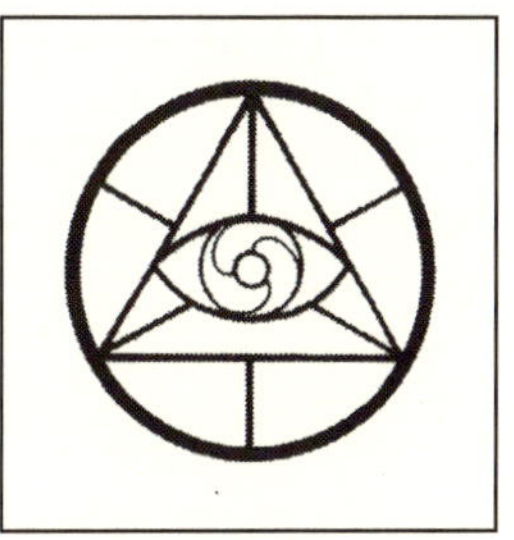

Fig. 3.7
Alex Grey

Through my painting *Vishnu-Christ Avatar*, (Fig. 3.4), I even attempted to fuse the Gothic style of Chartres and Notre Dame with the 'Chandella' style of Khajuraho. To accomplish this, I repeatedly entered into visionary states over the course of its execution, *to see* the invisible lines of balance, proportion and pose which constituted so many Sacred Codes for the creation of a consecrated statue.

III. The Archetype of the Divine Eye

To render a face or figure in the Hieratic style, I realized, you must begin by visualizing the simple perfect shapes which are associated with it. These shapes, such as a circle, square and triangle, are called 'simple' because they emanate oneness. From a single invisible point at their centre, they expand outward in space, reshaping it in a unified and harmonic way. We could say that each of these shapes echoes outward through space, like circles rippling outward in larger circles, squares expanding outward into ever greater squares, and triangles producing an infinity of triangles.

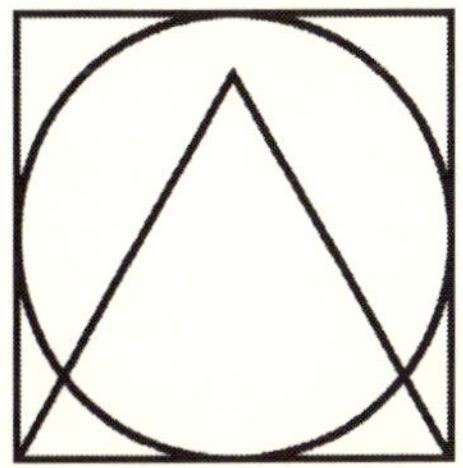

Fig. 3.8 - Trimorphic Matrix Subocularis

It was only after I had drawn the entire lower half of *Vishnu-Christ Avatar* that I recognized the same basic shape which lay behind every composition on every block. This was an inlaid arrangement of a circle, square and triangle which I then traced out and drew at the base of the statue, calling it (rather poetically) my Trimorphic Matrix Subocularis (Fig. 3.8).

I do not, for a moment, believe that this particular arrangement is the *only* possible one, the only armature that combines a circle, square and triangle. Each guild, even each artist, will discover their own signature shape over time. For example, while I inscribe the base of the triangle *in the square*, Alex Grey inscribes his triangle *in the circle* – a method which Desiderius Lenz used before, and which Kuba Ambrose has used afterward (Figs. 3.5 - 7). The purpose of these armatures is to harmonize and 'hieraticize' the liquid expanse of our vision.

By the time I reached the top of *Vishnu-Christ Avatar* (which had taken me seven years to complete), I was able to render the Divine Eye as the ultimate exemplar and apotheosis of this recurring geometric shape. And so I named this design on the capstone 'the Archetype of the Divine Eye' (Fig. 3.9).

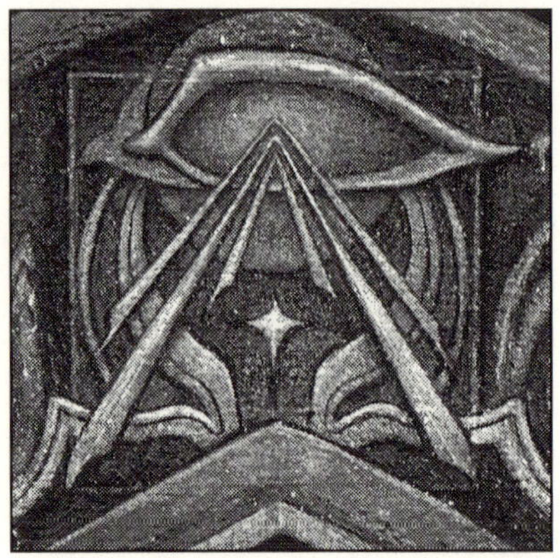
Fig. 3.9 - The Archetype of the Divine Eye

To the left, in Sanskrit, I had inscribed the words *Divyaṃ Dadāmi Te Cakṣuḥ* – Vishnu's stirring declaration, uttered as Krishna in the *Baghavad Gita*: *"I Give You My Divine Eye – Behold!"* And, on the right, in Gothic script, came the Latin phrase from the *Book of Revelation*: *Ecce Nova Facio Omnium* – which Christ utters at the end of time as *"Behold – I Make All Things Anew!"* These two phrases, uttered by Vishnu and Christ, summarized *the new way of seeing* which I had acquired ...through the opening of the Divine Eye.

After repeated meditations on this image, I had learned that – through contemplation – the image may become activated once the seer and the seen unite as one, in a state which the Hindu tradition calls *samadhi*. Once our gaze has become fixed, elevated and mirrored by the Divine Gaze, then the contemplator *sees* the Sacred and, indeed, the Sacred sees the contemplator.

Gazing at The Archetype of the Divine Eye, I could not help but recognize that the eye itself was conscious, aware, and gazing directly at me (as a momentary reflection of its divine seeing). More than that, vision was flowing *outward* from the eye, like the stream of watery light in the Gnostic tradition, or the 'extramission' theory of the ancient Greeks. Through its active sacred seeing, the Divine Eye was creating circles upon circles of forms, which were flowing outward and returning to it, in a grand, mirrored reflection of its all-creative vision.

To express this outpouring of vision, I had drawn two basic forms: the rays of light that flow along the diagonals of the triangle (the 'Alpha' of creation), and the undulating forms that follow the curves of the circle (the 'Omega' of forms that flow outward and eventually return to their source as reflective images). Both of these are bounded by a space that is basically square. As the years progressed and I researched the Sacred Codes contained in this book, I was surprised to discover that all works of art follow these three basic principles of vision:

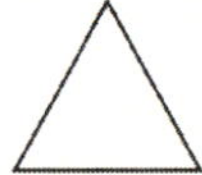

• From the triangle, the straight diagonal lines give us the creative flow of vision moving outward from the eye. These diagonals govern the creation of armature and perspective in painting.

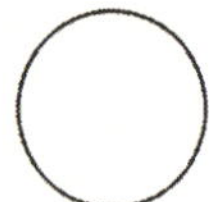

• From the circle, the curving lines give us the stylized forms that flow into creation. Hence, curves govern the creation of all forms and their stylistic rendering.

• From the square, we develop the spatial field of the painting. The orthogonals measure out the basic harmonies of architectural space and human proportion.

All of these – the diagonals, curves and orthogonals – dynamically work together to create a Visionary work of art. However, none of these lines appear directly in a painting, *but remain invisible,* as so many secret tracings or Sacred Codes passed on through the generations, from master to apprentice. In the Middle Ages, both in the East and the West, they were transmitted through family lineages, workshops and guilds. Then, with the rise of the Renaissance in the West, royal patrons eventually established Academies of Art, where the rules of design (*disegno*) were taught from the 1600's up until the early 20th century.

It is my personal belief that Gustave Moreau was *the last* Visionary artist to receive the transmission of these principles *through the academy*, and his works bear evidence of this claim. By the end of this treatise, I will show how these three basic shapes structure the flow of vision in major works by Michelangelo, Blake, Moreau and Fuchs – and how Moreau's *Jupiter and Semele* in particular manifests the active implementation and harmonious integration of these three basic principles of vision.

Like the musical score underlying the production of a symphony, the invisible lines of a painting need not be seen directly for the work of art to accomplish its true purpose – but their underlying presence is absolutely vital and necessary for the work to achieve its narrative cohesion and harmonic unity. While researching this treatise I have brought to light as many different types of invisible line as I could possibly find – yet their number remains undetermined and infinite.

Nevertheless, the moment vision becomes active, all the differing configurations become the linear descendants of these three basic shapes: the diagonals from the triangle, the curves from the circle, and the orthogonals from the square. When brought together, they create a flow of energy which directs the movement of our eye through the painting, thus creating an allegorical narrative which reaches its climax with the stilled and timeless gaze of the central sacred figure, as the transcendent source of all these images.

IV. The Three Basic Principles of Visions

• The Circle – Curving Lines

Over the course of this treatise we shall explore two basic types of curving lines – those that create the figure's *form*, and those that give the figure a certain *style*. We shall explore style in depth by the end of this chapter. For now, let us focus on form. During the drawing stage, the artist often renders the figure's form in pencil, thus delineating its basic silhouette in dark lines. The curves thus created may mislead the artist in believing that they have rendered the most important lines of the figure. Nothing could be further from the truth...

Through a deeper understanding of 'The Pose', the artist learns that two basic forces are always at work in the figure, which may be described variously as will and repose, energy and gravity, or more poetically as soul and body, spirit and flesh. In those places where the figure is relaxed, we see the force of the body, as gravity and repose, moving *downward* through the torso and limbs. Meanwhile, in those places where the figure is tensed or moving, we see the force of the soul, as will and energy, moving *upward* through the torso and limbs.

The soul's energetic movement begins at the bottom, *on the weight-bearing foot*, and moves upward through the figure to finally be released in a gesture or glance. Meanwhile, the body's repose begins *at the pit of the neck* and moves downward through the figure, along the relaxed limbs. In Humanist works of art, from Classical times to the Renaissance, artists 'saw' the figure in this way, and clearly delineated these two movements around the vertical plumb line (another 'invisible line'). At times, the movements crossed ('chiasmus') creating an 'X' shape ('chia' in Greek), giving rise to 'Chiastic Ponderation', called the *Contrapposto* during the Renaissance. We shall examine this dynamic interplay of will and repose in the chapters on the Pose.

The figure's *form* becomes the visible expression of these forces, and yet, the invisible lines describing those forces are never drawn directly. At times, the drapery may suggest them, as do the highlights on the flesh. Which brings us back to the drawing of a dark silhouette in pencil. One of the main properties of the *Mischtechnik*, which we shall explore in depth in these volumes, is the *rendering with whites* (usually in egg tempera or casein). Rendering with whites teaches us *a whole new way of seeing*, since we are obliged to render *the innermost forms and highlights*, rather than the dark shadows and silhouettes. In this way, we learn to *see the volume* of the figure, and how the serpentine highlight does, in fact, express the subtle interplay of will and repose.

Once the movement of energy escapes the body, it travels along invisible lines connected to *the gesture or glance*. At this point, the invisible lines, in fact, become straight rather than curved, since they are carried by the armature and composition. These, as we shall see, are primarily diagonal, the linear descendants of the triangle.

• The Triangle – Diagonal Lines

The straight lines in a painting are basically of two types: diagonal or orthogonal. Both types work together and are not easily separated.

However, if we focus on the diagonals, as the descendants of the triangle, we find that they too are basically of two types. This may be illustrated by drawing my Trimorphic Matrix Subocularis over the figure of Vishnu-Christ (Fig. 3.10), so that the two squares form a 1:2 rectangle: the upper square with an upright triangle and the lower square with an inverted triangle. As a result, a ◇ diamond is created within the 1:2 rectangle, with its uppermost tip at the third eye and its lowermost tip near the pierced feet.

As well, we shall draw an X within the double square, which basically crosses the figure at the pubis. The purpose of these drawings is to reveal the two basic shapes that result from all diagonals: the ◇ diamond (as the upright and inverted triangles base to base), and the X (as the upright and inverted triangles tip to tip).

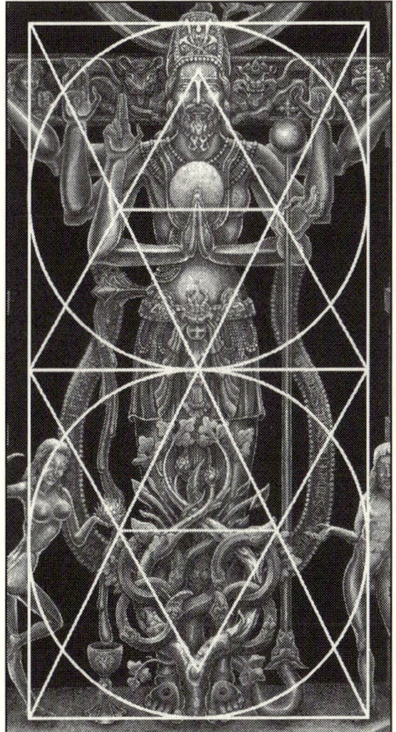

Fig. 3.10 - Trimorphic Matrix Subocularis over *Vishnu-Christ Avatar*

If we meditate on these two shapes for some time, we come to realize another basic principle of vision: that the ◇ diamond relates more to form, and hence, the circle (or oval), since it acts as a vehicle or container for the curving volume; meanwhile the X relates more to perspectival space, and hence, the square, since it reaches out to the corners of the square (or rectangle). It is a curious constant of human vision that we tend to visualize forms through the enclosed ◇ diamond, and space through the open-ended X.

This principle may be seen particularly in the case of armatures in composition. When artists divide up groupings of figures, they draw diagonals in the form of triangles or diamonds, since these shapes unify the groupings into recognizable masses.

Meanwhile, those same figures exist in a perspectival space that is basically determined by an X drawn to the corners of the frame. The X suggests space rather than form.

As we shall see in the chapters on Composition, armatures use diagonal lines to determine the harmonious points in a painting. But, since the frame is usually orthogonal, the most harmonious points vibrate or resonate within a squared space. The eye moves from figure to figure along the diagonals, but it comes to rest upon a figure that sounds its harmonic note within that squared space. As the eye moves to another figure, a new note is sounded, which resonates harmoniously within the whole.

Hence, once the flow of energy escapes a single figure, it tends to move around the painting *on diagonal lines*, since these create a more dynamic movement through the painting. From the gesture or glance of the principle figure, the flow of energy moves around to the second and third most important figures (or objects), which are placed in diagonally-related points determined by the armature. These lesser points sound their own harmonious notes within the squared space as a whole.

The lines of armature and perspective may become incredibly intricate and involved – yet the vast majority of these lines are never seen in the final painting. They remain invisible, as so many Sacred Codes supporting the structure of the composition.

• The Square – Orthogonal Lines

In any pictorial space, the artist cannot easily escape two major orthogonals – the vertical line of gravity and the horizontal line of the horizon.

The vertical line of gravity has been closely examined by craftsmen throughout the centuries as the *plumb line* (French *ligne de plomb*, Sanskrit *Brahmasutra*) which traverses the figure and determines its balance. The form of a static figure moves *along* the plumb line, and evokes thereby a Hieratic calm, which expresses higher states of mind such as wisdom, understanding and compassion. The form of a dynamic figure moves *around* the plumb line and evokes thereby a more Humanist attitude, expressing passions of the soul like longing, anger or regret.

The main horizontal line of a painting has also been closely examined by craftsmen across time, as the *horizon line* which gives the space its basic orientation. From here, all manner of architecture may be developed, to measure out the space in a visible, harmonious manner.

But, from the time of the Egyptians up until the French academies, artists have also measured out the basic proportions of the human figure. Dividing the vertical plumb line into constant measures, all manner of proportions have been developed in the East and West, as we shall see in our chapters on Proportion.

One proportion which has gained prevalence in the West, used by Jean Cousins, Leonardo da Vinci and Desiderius Lenz, is the 8-head measure. The advantage of this proportion is that it simplifies the body into eight distinct parts, dividing the figure in two at the pubis, with the upper body divided in two once more at the nipple line, and the lower body again in two, just below the knees. This can be seen in the diagram of *Vishnu-Christ Avatar* (Fig. 3.10), where the figure also stands eight heads tall.

The main role of the horizon line is to determine the painting's perspective. As with armature, the diagonals (called 'transversals') play an important role by determining the distance and placement of the orthogonal lines in perspective. Different systems of perspective may shift the vanishing points, but the space remains fundamentally square, related to the bounding frame. And so the square grids anchor the painting, as *the space* in which the curvilinear forms and diagonal sight-lines interact.

To extend the musical analogy, the orthogonals are like the timing in a symphony, the curving figures are much like the notes, and their movement along the diagonals are like the developing themes or melodies. This movement may also take on a narrative quality, as the painting develops a specific allegory (which Alberti called the *historia*). Ultimately, all three basic principles must be combined in service to the painting's theme – the higher world which the Visionary artist hopes to convey.

Keeping all these principles in mind, we may visualize the process of drawing a face or figure.

V. Drawing in the Hieratic & Humanist Styles

To render a face or figure in the Hieratic style, the artist must first draw the 'invisible' lines which grant the human form its divine harmony and unity. Over time and with practice, one should learn to visualize the shapes without actually drawing them. But first, the artist must change their usual way of seeing – by focusing only on one point at the centre, and expanding their vision until it encompasses the face as a whole. The centering point for the Hieratic visage, as sacred traditions from East to West have shown, is the 'third eye' – the Divine Eye located just above the brow.

While drawing a Hieratic visage, such as the face of Vishnu-Christ, I first visualize my basic armature (Fig. 3.11). So, I focus on the apex of the triangle as the centre of vision, located at the third eye. From this point, everything flows outward in a play of straight and curving lines.

In this case, the straight lines are the diagonals, beginning at the third eye and tracing the flow of Divine Vision outward through the two corporeal eyes. The square provides the space and outermost limit for this visual expansion. And the circle provides the graceful curving lines of the face with their harmony and unity. These move like waves in the watery expanse, infinitely shifting, seeking a more simplified line that gives contour and shape to every volume in the Divine Face. The volume, light and shadow must come together as a whole, while each facet of the face is finely chiselled into its most simple and essential shape, creating a curvilinear style that we recognize as 'Hieratic'.

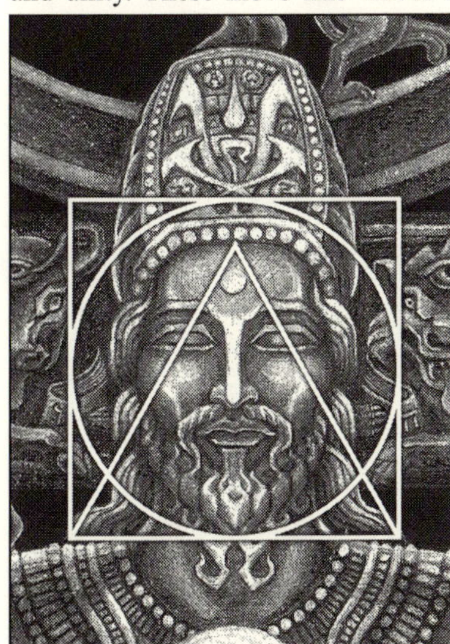

Fig. 3.11 - Trimorphic Matrix Subocularis over *Vishnu-Christ Avatar*

In this way, the divine visage takes form in front of me – if I am able 'to see' it. Since I am gazing through the Divine Eye, it would be wiser to say that the Divine in me sees *its own face* taking form in the drawing. This face, to be a true reflection, must possess harmony, grace and beauty. That harmony is achieved, in part, through the underlying triangle, circle and square of the armature, which guide the graceful movement of the artist's hand.

To draw the whole figure in the Hieratic Style, we simply extend this principle. As we saw in Fig. 3.10, the basic armature is enlarged so that the square reaches from the top of the head to the pubis, and another armature is drawn, inversed, from the pubis down to the feet. The two triangles create a diamond in which the divine figure seeks to manifest itself in human form (like Christ in a vesica-shaped mandorla). To establish symmetry, a vertical plumb line may also be drawn through the apices of the two triangles.

With this addition, the plumb line also becomes a 'line of Divine Sight' which actively 'sees' and creates the emergent figure, as a harmonious 'form' flowing into creative manifestation. That form is symmetrical: the body 'standing at rest' along the plumb line in perfect equipoise. The gesture, the glance – they all aim, in Hieratic art, towards an effect of inner calm, tranquility and stillness. In my rendering of Vishnu-Christ, the hieratic stare and symbolic gestures all strive towards the effect of timelessness.

In the case of the Humanist face, the principles remain the same. Though symmetry may be forsaken, a certain balance and equilibrium is maintained. Now, the soul of the sitter comes to the fore, as the sparkle in the eye reveals their deep inner life, and the slightest variance in the lids or lips alters their expression.

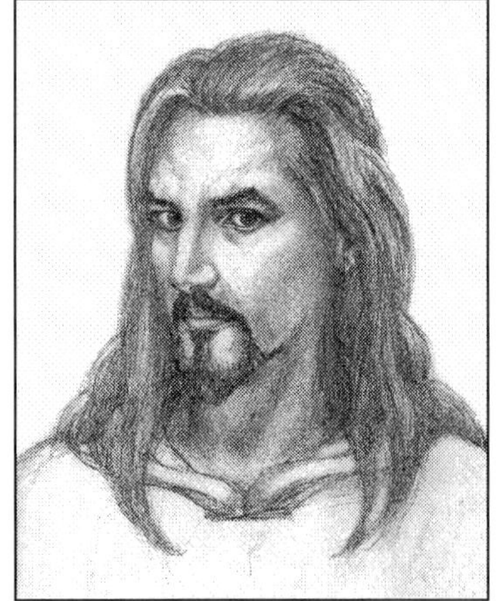

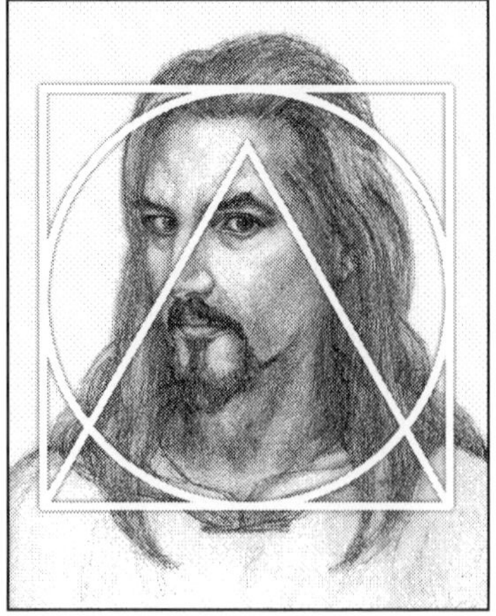

Fig. 3.12 - L. Caruana: *Self-Portrait* 2012

During the Renaissance, the three-quarter angle gained greater preference over the simple symmetry of the frontal view. A close examination of portraiture reveals that, in its more Classical examples, the underlying armature was nevertheless maintained. We may see this in Johfra's *Self-Portrait* (Fig. 1.9) or in the example of my own self-portrait (Fig. 3.12), where one eye appears at the apex of the triangle – to which we may add a circle and square to complete the armature.

Now, divine vision no longer flows from the third eye on the brow (frontal view, Hieratic visage), but from one eye at the centre of the three-quarter angle – an eye which looks directly at us. As we focus our gaze on that eye, the face gradually takes form within the encompassing circle and square. Many artists, from Byzantine to Renaissance times, drew the halo round the head such that, the centre of the circle lay exactly at the eye. The more the human features reflect the hidden perfect shapes, the more harmonious and graceful its unique features appear. Even a half-turned face in the Humanist Style should maintain balance, proportion and stylistic grace.

To draw the whole figure in the Humanist Style, we resort once more to the enlarged armature with its basic

◇ diamond and X shapes, but this time we add the plumb line. Now we must focus on two distinct movements, one of *will* and the other of *repose*, which revolve around the central plumb line.

However, we would be sorely mistaken if we thought that Greek and Renaissance artists sought out 'movement' as their highest form of expression. True, many Humanist figures did express dynamic movement through figures that were distinctly 'off balance'. Indeed, as Humanism progressed, figures became increasingly unbalanced through the ever-more dynamic expressions of passion. But the Classical Ideal, established by Polykleitus in his statue of the Doryphorus (Fig. 3.13), strove instead to *unite will and repose into a perfectly balanced figure* which manifest 'potential movement' (to be addressed later in the chapters on The Pose).

In the Classical contrapposto, *the forces of will and repose balance one another*, to establish a point of equilibrium which, in the French tradition, was called 'aplomb'. According to this principle, the figure establishes a point of balance *in direct relationship to the plumb line* ('aplomb' means 'on the plumb line') from which he or she may potentially move in any direction. This 'potential movement' (the pose) manifests a distinct *grace and poise*, a harmony of the limbs and torso, which we sense as 'Classically Beautiful'. Although the *lack of* movement may strike us as unnatural, the figure is striving to express a higher state of being, a timeless expression of feeling or emotion, which is 'ideal' rather than actual.

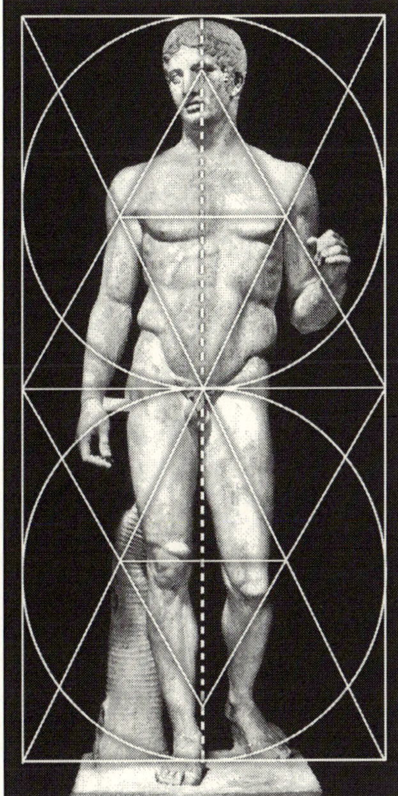

Fig. 3.13
Polykleitus: *Doryphorus*

And so, the whole figure now twists and turns in a graceful movement *around the plumb line* – the will moving up from the weight-bearing foot; the repose moving down from the pit of the neck – to create a balanced harmony and fusion of these two contrary forces – one arising from the torpor of the body; the other, from the passions of the soul.

VI. Style: The Dance of the Serpentine Line

The first volume of this trilogy is dedicated to the Drawing Stage, where questions of the Figure, Composition and Ornament will naturally come to the fore. But, the initial drawing, as such, must be motivated by two major impulses: *the original idea* which moves through the painting, and *the style* which ultimately expresses it. All the foundational principles laid out in this treatise – on the figure's proportion and pose, on the underlying armature and composition – have but *one* purpose: to structure and support the emerging artist's *style of expression...*

Beginning with a series of quick sketches, the artist may wish to capture that first idea (*"la première idée"* Moreau called it) – roughing out compositional strategies and multiple figures that captivate the eye and move the soul. Next, the artist may seek out a canvas of some definite shape and proportion, to begin visualizing the full composition and roughing in the figures. With the *istoria* or 'narrative idea' firmly in mind, the design of the figures in their compositional space should strive towards a higher sense of beauty, harmony and unity.

It is at this stage that the experienced craftsman will call upon certain basic practices, to assure that the disposition of figures possesses a good degree of harmony. For example, a simple X drawn from corner to corner reveals the centre point of all pictorial space. This initial 'drawing of the X' is recorded in painting manuals from both Byzantine and Buddhist traditions, and reveals thereby their conscious creation of a Sacred Centre for the exfoliation of divine vision.

Moving outward from that centre, the harmonic division of space may continue along orthogonals and diagonals, harmoniously dividing space into measures of armature and perspective. And, within this greater expanse, each figure may receive some finer measure of balance and proportion through the pose around a plumb line notched into its respective harmonious parts.

Alas, the inexperienced craftsman will soon become enmired in a dense mesh of criss-crossing lines, imprisoning their vision behind so many black iron bars. We recall Rilke's panther, pacing back and forth in its small cell in the fauverie du Jardin des Plantes: *"His gaze against the sweeping of the bars has grown so weary, it can hold no more. To him there seems to be a thousand bars, and back behind those thousand bars, no world."*[11]

But the experienced craftsman, through practice and apprenticeship, will have memorized those invisible lines and learned their harmonizing principles. Hence, the visible movement of their stylus traces out flowing lines which *move in accord* with these principles, dancing round their hidden shapes and over their balancing forms.

Indeed, his pencil or brush performs *"the dance of a curving line around a straight line, which remains invisible."* That is the way I remember hearing it from Ernst Fuchs when we discussed these things. Looking back through his book *Architectura Caelestis*, I find that he describes it thus:

"At the time [of drawing Job and the Judgement of Paris, The Anti-Laocoön, and The Triumph of Christ], *I had drawn soft architecture which was dominated by a* [curving] *line which searched flexibly, in a wave-like dance, for the straight line... I recognized the 'play-around' of the straight line was the musical, the vibrating principle of 'the hidden prime of styles'. The pictures which I had drawn show quite clearly the movement of all lines and one straight line which, however, never appears directly... the horizontal and the vertical are related to each other (never at a right angle) in a swaying rhythm, playing around an undrawn vertical and horizontal line."*[12]

While drawing *Vishnu-Christ Avatar*, I began to understand what Fuchs had in mind. I recognized that the *invisible* lines, in this case, were my armature, with its geometric shapes offering simple orthogonals and diagonals (my Trimorphic Matrix Subocularis). Meanwhile the *visible* lines, which were the actual lines I drew, created a liquid flow of forms between the straight diagonals and the outer limits of the squared circle. The moment those curving lines manifest ease and grace, my drawing hand had moved with a certain 'style'.

Fuchs referred to 'the play-around of the straight line' as the musical, vibrating principle of the Hidden Prime of Styles. We shall explore this theme in depth later on, where Fuchs' Hidden Prime may be viewed, ultimately, as the fusion of the Humanist and Hieratic Styles. Whether we speak of the artist's *individual* style or the greater *cultural* style, whether we speak of a Humanist, Hieratic or Hidden Prime of Styles, that ever-elusive, free-flowing line which visibly weaves around the unseen straight lines characterizes the artist's chief means of *stylistic expression* while drawing.

The aim of this treatise is to investigate those unseen lines which underlie the painting's geometry, its armature and proportion. Yet, all these marks and measures must ultimately be memorized, erased and transcended. Their segments must dissolve into so many faint points, guiding the graceful movement of artist's eye and hand. And now, rather than a black panther behind bars, the artist's original idea will shine like Blake's tyger, prompting the draughtsman to ask of his invention: *"What immortal hand or eye could frame thy fearful symmetry?"*[13]

VII. The Principle of Style

In 1875, the French restorer of Gothic monuments, Eugène Viollet-le-Duc, published his Magnum Opus, *Dictionnaire raisoné de l'architecture française du XIe au XVIe siècle (Dictionary of French Architecture from 11th to 16th Century)*. In the eighth volume, he offered a definition of style which strikes me as perhaps the best and most precise characterization of this elusive concept.

"Le style," he wrote, *"est la manifestation d'un idéal établi sur un principe"* – which is to say: *"Style is the manifestation of an ideal founded upon a principle.* [We could also say that...] *style is the natural consequence of a principle followed methodically. Hence, only one kind of form may emerge naturally, without force. If it is forced, it becomes a mannerism. Mannerism grows old, the style – never."*[14]

Later in this treatise we will see examples where the climbing vines and spiralling tendrils so characteristic of the Gothic style had, indeed, wrapped themselves round invisible lines of armature traced out in *ad triangulum* grids ('from the triangle'). These geometric shapes undergird the Gothic style, making it 'the natural consequence of a principle followed methodically.'

Indeed, as we trace Ornament from the Gothic period to its roots in Islamic art, we learn that 'geometry generates form'. This fundamental principle, which first emerges in Ornament, ultimately evolves into the dynamic relationship of Figuration and Composition in large-scale easel paintings. The armatures of all figure paintings, both in the East and the West, have their roots in Sacred Geometry, which manifest itself most clearly in Islamic art, but also emerged through history as Ornament. In the long-lost art of Ornamental design (a skill which Fuchs possessed in abundance), the figure and composition are subordinated to a greater impetus for stylistic design ('following a principle'), which makes each culture's 'ornamental style' so instantly recognizable.

Every artist has their own individual style, a particular way of rendering hands and faces that is uniquely all their own. If this is true, then why bother with so many measures and lines, which might possibly inhibit their expression? The artist who depends solely upon their signature style will soon become a Mannerist, as Viollet-le-Duc says. Toward the end of the Renaissance, the Italian word *'maniere'* described those artists whose works demonstrated great individual flair, but lacked a Classical foundation in harmonizing principles – those eternal principles which grant unity and timelessness to any work of art, allowing it to transcend its own time and become a part of the immortal Canon.

Those principles are not arbitrary or contrived, but the manifestation of a divine vision in man. ...The circle, the square and the triangle – these perfect shapes manifest order, beauty and harmony on every level. Though proportions may differ from culture to culture, the eternal striving for order remains the same. The beautiful and the ideal find their origin, ultimately, in a higher sphere of archetypes, where tranquil forms and timeless gestures express divinity's eternal reflection upon itself through moving images in time.

VIII. The Hieratic Style in Egypt

In 2003, I made the pilgrimage of a lifetime, and immersed myself fully in the sacred art and temples of three great traditions: ancient Egypt, India and Tibet.

Beginning my journey in Egypt, I visited each temple and tomb with a passionate longing to rediscover the Visionary sources of their art. From my base in Thebes at the mud-walled Marsam Hotel, I could easily access the temples west of the Nile – Merneptah, Tuthmosis and Medinet Habu – or hike across the desert hills to the tombs below in the Valley of the Kings. But, a recent terrorist attack at Hatshepsut's temple made the more outlying sites difficult to access.

Nevertheless, in Qena I bribed a taxi driver to transport me to the Hathor Temple at Dendera and the Osireion in Abydos. At the third roadblock, our pick-up truck was halted by the police, and we could only continue under military escort (two jeeps, with a nervous soldier – machine gun at the ready – standing in the back of our pick-up). In this way, we passed through the market town of Nag Hammadi (...where the Gnostic texts were discovered in the outlying hills – how I wish we could have stopped there!) and on to Abydos. At the Osireion and its nearby Temple of Seti, I had the singular pleasure of visiting these sites all by myself – except for the escort of four soldiers surrounding me, automatic weapons pointed skyward...

In Hathor's Temple at Dendera, I was left to myself and able to immerse myself fully into the atmosphere of that sacred precinct. The astronomical observations of the Ptolemaic priesthood (inscribed on the famous Dendera ceiling) and their complex lunar rituals celebrating Osiris' death and rebirth engraved themselves permanently in my memory. For a few rare moments, I joined the Egyptian priesthood and participated in their ancient rites.

Meanwhile, in the Valley of the Kings, I spent many an afternoon sepulchered in the Pharaoh's tombs, reading the images incised on the walls. Aided by the detailed diagrams in Erik Hornung's *Ancient Egyptian Books of the Afterlife,* I traversed the gates and caverns of the *Am Duat*, gaining new insight into the theurgic practices of the Egyptian priesthood. Accompanying Re on his solar barque, I overcame the serpent Apophis, stood in Osiris' hall of judgement, and rose with the scarab Khepri to a new morning of existence.

I had already spent the better part of a week scrutinizing friezes of the pharaohs, carved in *bas relief,* on Karnak's inner walls. But when my eyes fell upon the statue of King Thutmosis III (in the Luxor Museum on the Nile's East bank), I suddenly 'saw' those hidden shapes that give Egyptian art its unique style and power. My eyes opened wide, for the first time, to *the Hieratic style of all cultures*.

...Let us begin with Egyptian *bas relief,* since these stone friezes hinted at notions of the Hieratic Style, which Thutmosis' statue then revealed to me in their full glory.

When gazing at a *bas relief* (Fig. 3.14), we should not forget that the Egyptian eye was accustomed to hieroglyphs, which delineate natural forms like a falcon, feather, or human head *in their simplest, most basic and essential shapes*. Thus, each natural form takes on the quality of a 'holy letter' or hiero-glyph. So the human face, for example, achieves its most archetypal form *in profile*, which is why profiles appears so often in Hieratic art – not just in ancient art, but also the works of those timeless Visionaries like Michelangelo, Blake, Moreau and Fuchs, who continually call upon this Sacred Code.

As a hieroglyph, the face in profile becomes a kind of sacred sigil, where the divine features may be recognized immediately. This archetypal shape, through its harmony and unity, *manifests* the Sacred. It is not just a sign that signifies; it is a theurgic instrument for activating the sacred experience. It is in this sense that the Egyptian priests viewed their hieroglyphs – as 'magical' tokens which actively manifest the invisible, underlying holiness of the One behind the all.

If we now cast our gaze upon an Egyptian *bas relief,* we may notice how the bounding silhouette of the headdress and features seems to glide gently from one transition to the next. Meanwhile, the natural human face, lest we forget, is filled with imperfections. The lines of the brow, nose and lips will fall, dip and curve, almost randomly and unpredictably. In its natural or 'realistic' state, the human profile is an amorphous, unharmonious meander of straight and curving lines.

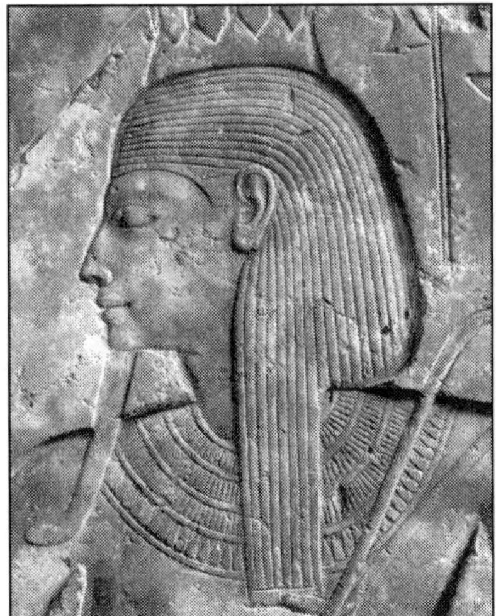
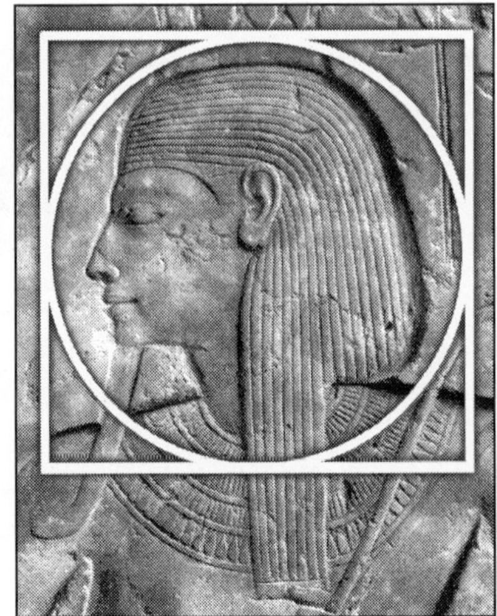

Fig. 3.14 - Egyptian Bas Relief

However, the moment we envision an invisible square and circle around the head, these bounding shapes structure, harmonize and unify the surrounding space. The square and circle are manifestly perfect in 2D space. Through stylistic rendering, the amorphous profile begins to *absorb* parts of the perfect whole. When enough of the square or circle is absorbed into the meandering lines of the head, it becomes harmonious with the surrounding perfect shapes. There is a kind of 'echo' or 'resonance' – a uniting of the two – which we may describe as 'harmonious'. Through *the style* – its distinctly Hieratic Style – the amorphous shape is harmoniously linked to the perfect and, dare I say, *divine* shapes of the circle and square, which grant it simplicity, grace, and divine unity.

The Egyptians had, in fact, two types of relief – raised and sunk. The *sunk* relief, which cut the face *into* the smooth surface, was mostly used on the outside of buildings, to catch the sun's strong rays with sharply cut shadows. The *raised* relief, which cut *away* the smooth surface around the embossed face, was mostly used inside buildings, to allow for the play of atmospheric light or torchlight over the gently molded forms. It is here that we see the first signs of 'form' emerging, and their play of light and shadow.

In *sunk* relief, a dark line traces out each shape with consistent linear precision. But, with *raised* relief, that line begins to expand in width and dissolve in shadow. While the deeply incised lines remain sharp, the shallow lines begin to soften and dissolve. That which we call 'volume' appears, as the play of light and shadow over the rounded surface. This third dimension – *volume* – becomes the new place of expression for the Hieratic Style. It is the place where light and darkness – the curved surface and the bounding line – meet in new, harmonic relationships.

Turning now to the statue of King Thutmosis III from Karnak (Fig. 3.15), we may begin to see how geometrical shapes harmonize its surrounding space *in three dimensions*. The sharply chiseled lines, with linear consistency, are

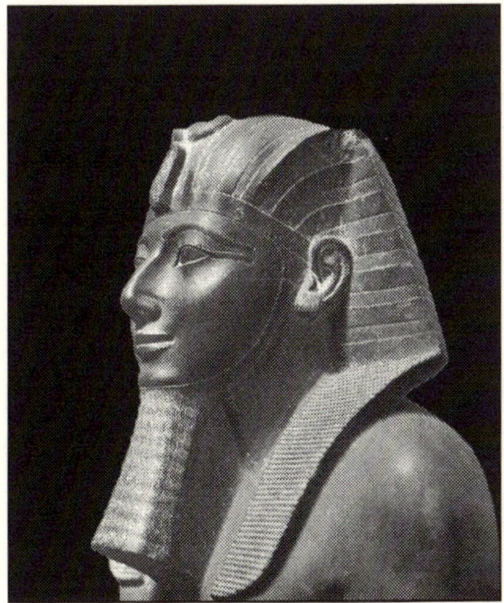
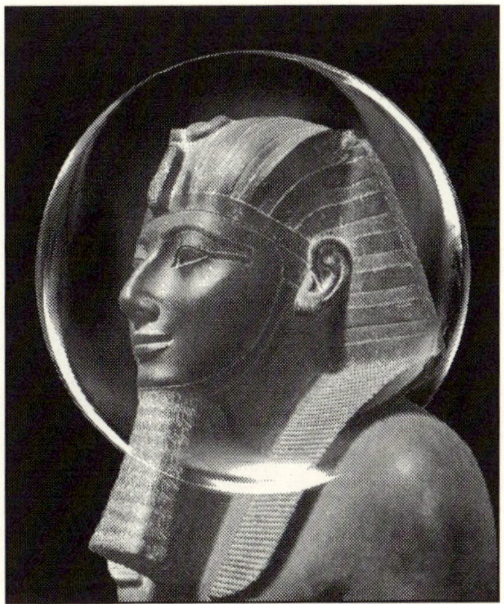

Fig. 3.15 - Egyptian Statue of King Thutmosis III, Karnak c. 1479 - 1425 BCE

still present. However, if we follow the line delineating the outermost edge of the volume, something new appears. At the very top of the headdress, there is a sharp line that descends, like the foremost edge of a pyramid, with light to its left and shadow to its right. But, as it approaches the brow, this line begins to dissolve in the soft merging of light and shadow. Continuing downward, its gentle transition still defines the temple and cheekbone, even the nostril and corner of the mouth, by blending light and darkness, keeping them separate yet unite.

This play of light and shadow over the volume is the distinguishing feature of sculpture in the round. It is here that we must transfer our gaze if we wish to distinguish the Sacred Codes that constitute the Hieratic Style of Egyptian sculpture.

If we now envision a sphere around the face, we begin to see how the stylizing lines of the face harmonize with this perfect shape. The contour lines (which were stylistically perfected in the time of *bas relief* as 'the profile') continue to show a strong relationship to the bounding sphere. But, as we move our gaze inward to admire the eyes, nose and lips, we see how these too have been simplified: their amorphous shapes have been softened and smoothened to resonate with the curves of the outer sphere. This is most strongly evident in the jaw, which has been altered from a corner to a curve.

Returning to the line delineating the outermost edge of the volume, we can now see that the sharp line at the very top of the headdress curves in accord with the upper left of the sphere. But as it descends, it shifts in the shadows, meandering in a serpentine motion. At the cheekbone the curve reverses, and resonates instead with the jaw and the lower right of the sphere. And so on, past the corner of the mouth and on to the chin.

This line, this barely visible meandering line, *is the most important line in the face* when viewed three-dimensionally from the three-quarter angle. Passing, as it does, the corner of the eyes and the corner of the mouth while grazing the lids, nostrils and lips – it is charged with feeling and expression.

...The slightest alteration of its course, the slightest movement toward the light or shadow, and the expression in the face is totally altered.

It is no wonder then that Egyptian sculptors went to such pains to measure each proportion of the face, define its every line, and set each volume in its single perfect place. Later in this treatise we will return to volumes, and learn how to render them, using the egg tempera whites of the *Mischtechnik.* For now, let us stop and admire how gracefully the whites fall over the surface of this sculpture, the way the light plays over the forms, creating their volumes. Each of the lines we described surrounds the volume in some way, defining its shape. The sculptor has reduced each part to its ideal shape, and proportioned the parts to the whole. Everything is simplified, but really, it is manifesting the *essential* qualities of a face, seeking its sacred unity.

What does this sculpture say? It says – This is thc King, the highest of men, the Perfect Man. This is man elevated to the deity – and this is the Divine manifest in man. The Egyptian sculpture of a king both 'says' this through its iconography and 'shows' it through the perfection of its forms, the hieratic stylization, harmonizing the human shape with a perfect bounding sphere of light, like a brightly shining, luminescent halo. The Pharaoh in ancient times was, what Christ is for Christian art: the union of God and Man; the divine made incarnate, and humanity transfigured.

As the twentieth century draws to a close and a new century (indeed, a new millennium) struggles into existence, I believe that the ill-shaped monsters and abominations of Contemporary Art will gradually cede their place to a new Spiritual Renaissance in Art. Craftsmen like Michelangelo, Blake, Moreau and Fuchs have shown us the way. The Western Humanist tradition will fuse with the Hieratic traditions of other cultures, so that Visionary Art may emerge as the *Ars Sacrum* of our times. But it is up to each individual artist, practising their art today, to reveal the soulful dimension and healing power of this otherwise neglected art form.

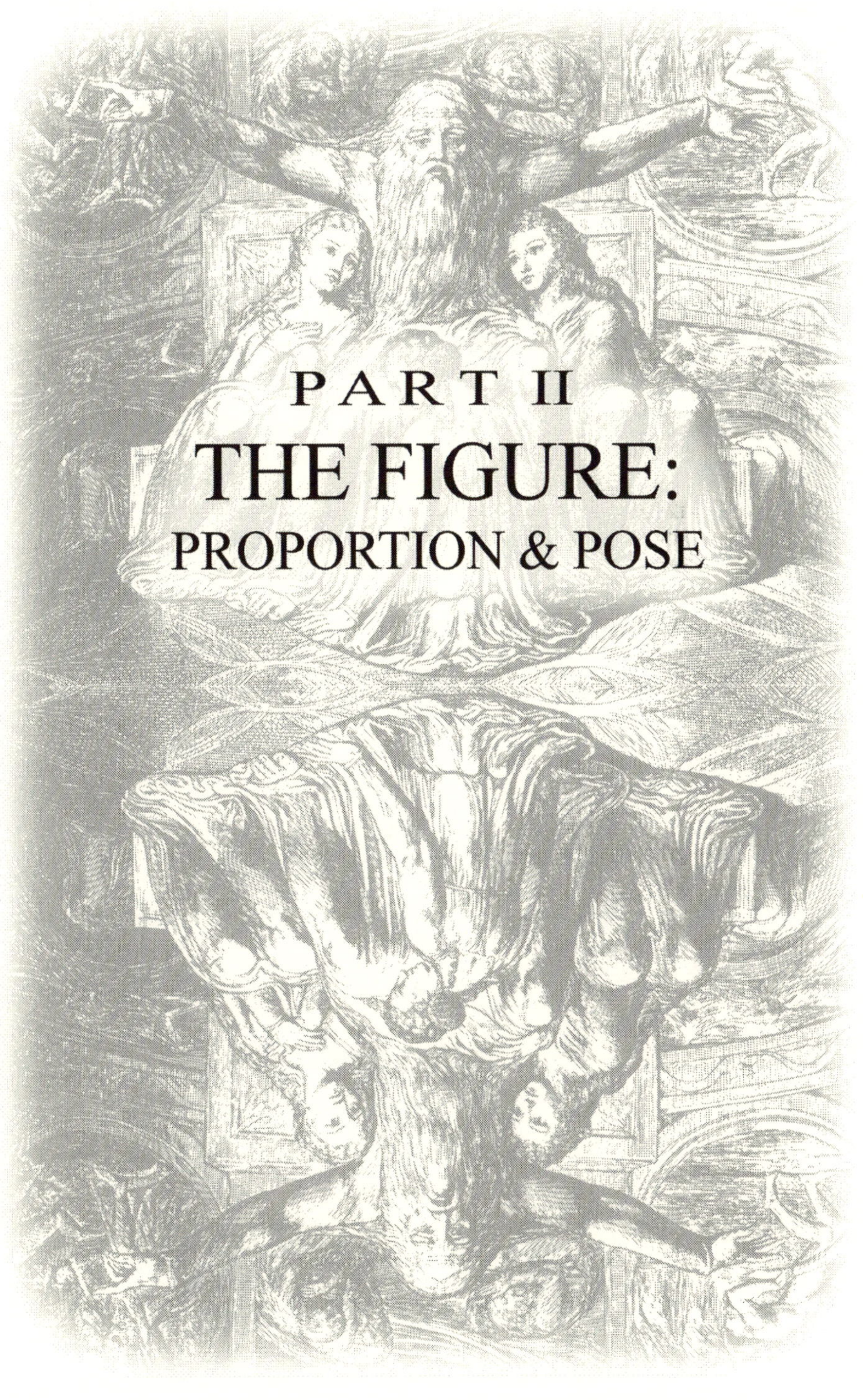

PART II
THE FIGURE:
PROPORTION & POSE

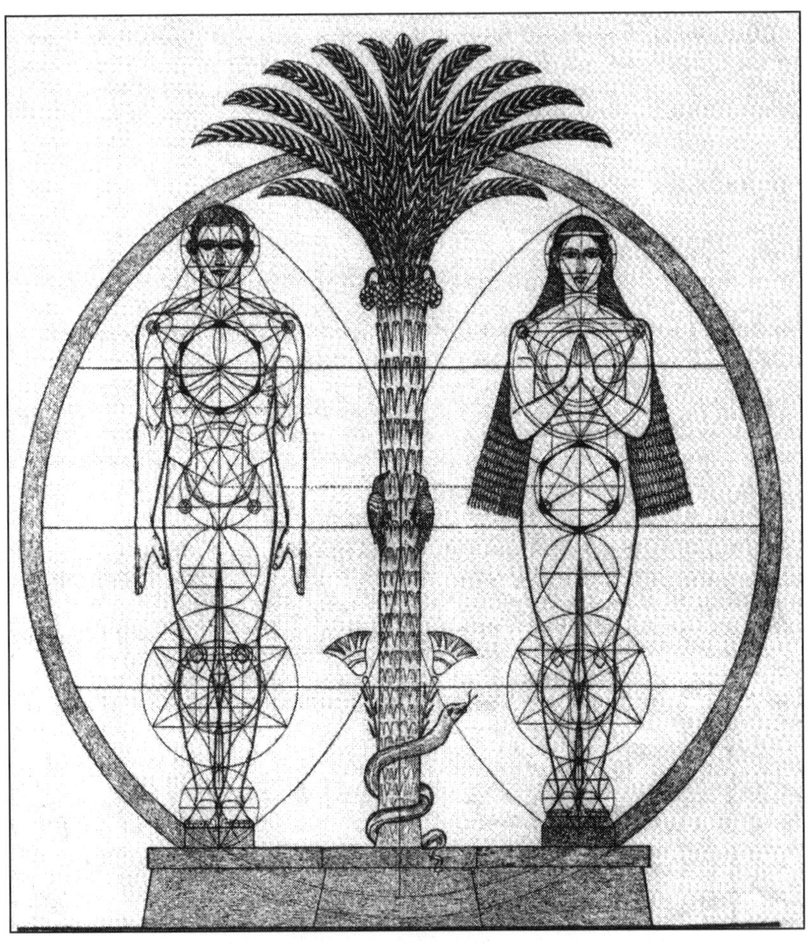

Fig. 4.1 - Desiderius Lenz:
The Canon of the Normative Human Pair in Two Sexes

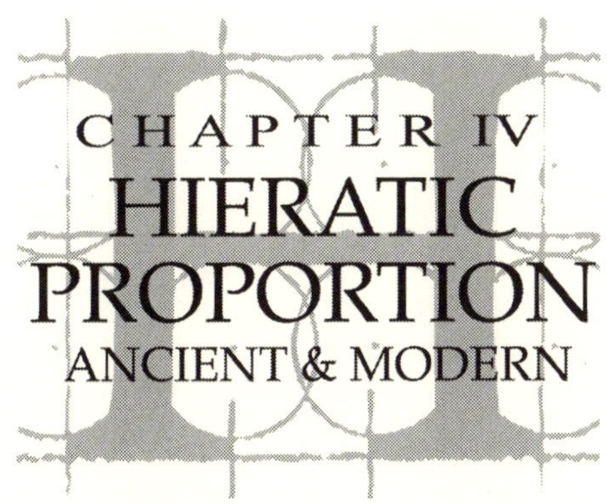

I. Seeing Sacred Codes

When we survey some of the magnificent sculptures hewn in the Hieratic style, we must ask ourselves why their ancient craftsmen delineated the gods in this manner. Why was the sacred countenance stylized into gently-curving surfaces and lines? Why do these epic beings sit or stand with such majestic stillness? What blessed proportions, beyond their human likeness, move us to regard them as Holy and sacrosanct?

All these qualities invite profound reverence and veneration. Anointed and adored within their hallowed shrines, these stone statues invite us still to contemplate their deeper mysteries. Though they stood high up, above altars where flowers, incense and animals were once sacrificed, now they appear isolated, in museums or photographs, awaiting a more mundane gaze. Only we, through our higher seeing, can restore a more sacred regard to these decayed and fragmented gods.

Within their ruined faces, ravaged by impiety and time, there remain still the traces of Sacred Codes, inviting us to view them with eyes opened wide with wonder. All that is required of us is that we take the time to view them fixedly, with an unbroken regard, for extended periods of time. As spiritual practitioners, we may do this through contemplation, worship and prayer. But as artists, we do this rather through observation, initiation and imitation. Through each work of art, we see, understand and transmit those codes, in praise of the divine creator.

By studying the texts of these cultures, what measures and proportions can we uncover, passed on from master to apprentice? And by staring at these statues, what Sacred Codes can we see, to awaken the divinity within the stone?

II. Desiderius Lenz

One evening during dinner with Alex and Allyson Grey, the subject turned to proportion and Alex mentioned the works of Father Desiderius. I had never heard the name before and Alex assured me that I was in for a pleasant surprise. Back home in France, I managed to procure a copy of *The Aesthetics of Beuron*, (*Zur Ästhetik der Beuroner Schule,* first published in Vienna in 1898) and was soon spiralling down through the vortex of his writings and personality.

Father Desiderius (Fig. 4.2) was born Peter Lenz in 1832, the son of a sculptor and cabinet maker who made Neo-Gothic furnishings for the church. In 1852 he was accepted into the Academy in Munich, where he studied sculpture. During that time he discovered the frescoes by Peter Cornelius decorating the Glyptothek, and was drawn to the spirit of these works.

Eventually, Lenz met Cornelius, who was a member of the monastic brotherhood of painters known as the Nazarenes. The movement had originated in Vienna, when a group of students at the Academy had formed a medieval type of guild to promote the practice of Sacred Art over the prevailing Neo-Classicism.

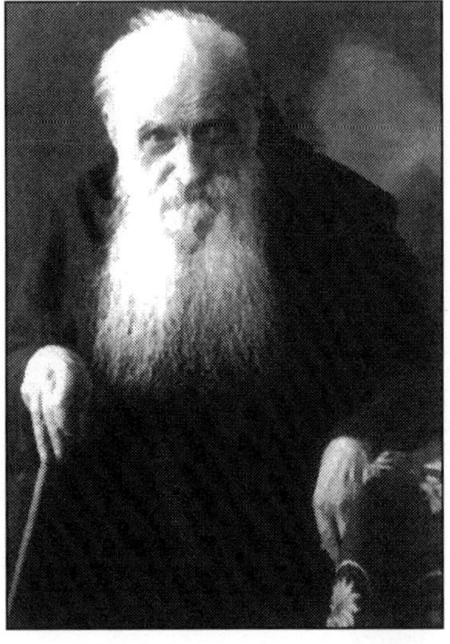

Fig. 4.2 - Father Desiderius c. 1920

Inspired by this call towards renewed spirituality in the arts, Lenz organized a similar brotherhood at the Benedictine Monastery of Beuron, where he eventually took orders as Father Desiderius. From 1872 until his death in 1928, Desiderius and his brothers created an entirely new style of art, making murals, furniture and liturgicals for the Beuron Archabbey near Stuttgart, the Convent of St. Gabriel in Prague, and the Torretta of Monte Cassino near Rome (destroyed in WWII).

Although his name is little remembered today, the ideas of Desiderius Lenz had significant impact on the art of the 20th century.

This was certainly the case with the group of French painters called *Les Nabis* (*The Prophets*), which included Maurice Denis, Pierre Bonnard, Edouard Vuillard, Paul Sérusier and Jan Verkade – artists who are remembered primarily as Post-Impressionists that opened the door to Abstract art.

Sérusier, Denis and Verkade had all visited Desiderius at different times in Beuron. Sérusier translated *The Aesthetic of Beuron* from German to French in 1905, and published it with a preface by Denis. Sérusier also summarized the monk's ideas in his *ABC de la Peinture* (1921) where Desiderius' geometrical constructions underlie much of Sérusier's theory on harmonic composition.

But the strongest link came about through Jan Verkade. Although he was a part of the *Nabis* circle in 1891, he fell so deeply under Desiderius' spell that he became a monk at Beuron three years later, and subsequently collaborated with Desiderius at the Convent of St. Gabriel in Prague. It was Verkade who organized, illustrated and published Desiderius' writings ten year's after the Benedictine's death in 1928.

More interesting still is the effect of Desiderius on Gustav Klimt. In 1905, an exhibition on Sacred Art was held at the golden domed Secession building, with one room entirely dedicated to the Beuron School. Over 10,000 people attended the exhibition, which then travelled to Aachen in 1907, Düsseldorf in 1909, and Regensburg in 1910 before becoming part of a much larger exhibition in Brussels in 1912.

Several theorists have commented upon the change in Klimt's work after 1905, when the Viennese artist began to situate his figures within large abstract shapes while incorporating Egyptian elements in his design. According to M. E. Warlick, *"Both* [Desiderius and Klimt] *shared the feeling that truly modern art should be based on ancient principles, as well as the observation of nature interpreted as a geometric language of form."*[1]

III. A Sacred Spark of Primordial Wisdom

While researching Greek and Roman statuary at the archaeological library in 1864, Desiderius came across Lepsius' twelve volume opus, *Denkmäler aus Aegypten und Aethiopien* (Egyptian and Ethiopian Monuments - 1849 - 1856) and was immediately overwhelmed by the austerity and purity of the Egyptian style. But, as a devout Catholic, he was also overcome by fear:

"I felt as one does when in a quiet moment a sacred spark of primordial wisdom falls into one's consciousness, and one follows its career into the infinite; this feeling alternated with dread and terror on the other hand, when I saw those shapes of idols, the work of Hell. I asked myself: Am I allowed to get involved with these things, is it not grievous sin?"[2]

Mastering his fears, Desiderius returned to the library the next day and began copying these 'pagan' models of the human form. As he delved deeper into the wisdom of the ancients, two monumental discoveries emerged: the Ancients – Greek and Egyptian alike – held *"the magic key"* to sacred style and sacred proportion.

Desiderius began executing Christian works in a style that was entirely Egyptian – going so far as to call a sculpture of The Virgin and Child 'The Isis Madonna' (1872). In his writings, he castigated the art of his times for its glorification of the 'natural' human figure (i.e. Humanism) at the cost of a more sacred or 'monumental' style, which he referred to elsewhere as *"the hieratic style."*[3] Gazing back over the history of art, Desiderius lamented the triumph of the Humanist style over the Hieratic:

"What was lacking [in contemporary art] *was the monumental, the static, which is denied to nature because she is of the moment, but which monumental art, especially religious art, must possess... We find it at the beginning of all art, in Egypt. It forms the basis of classical art; we find it among the Byzantines (the Greeks become Christians) and especially in their old mosaics... We find it too in the Gothic, the heir of the Romanesque. It is only in the late Renaissance that it is entirely lost."*[4]

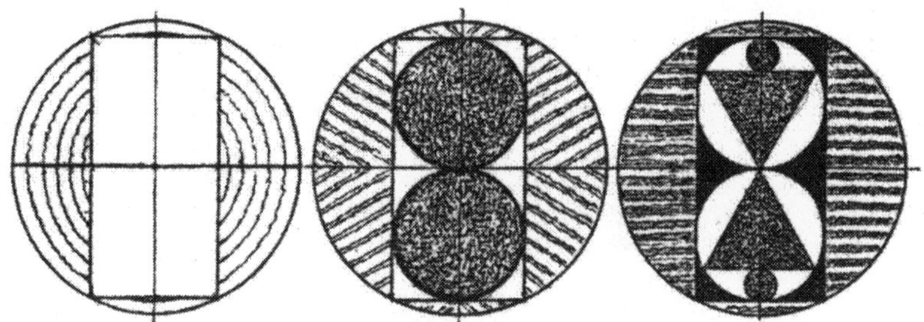

Die Fundamente des Kanon

Fig. 4.3 - Desiderius: The Fundamentals of the Canon

What makes the art of the Ancients so unique is that they were closer to 'the source': *"The nearer to the origin, the source, unity – the better, the holier, the more able to express the sacred."*[5]

For Desidierius, the human figure was a manifestation of God's mindful design. To fashion the cosmos, the divine creator had first taken up his compass and drawn a circle. Likewise, Man was created in accord with this order – the human figure was geometrically constructed *from within*: *ad triangulum* and *ad quadratum*. And indeed, such was the case with art from Egypt all the way to the Gothics.

But, during the Renaissance, artists turned to nature and the live model, to reference the human figure 'from without': *"...Prematurely plucking the forbidden fruit by the use of live models, in violation of the Holy Commandment,"* Desiderius wrote, *"this was done in the Renaissance which, far from achieving this high ambition by such means, on the contrary suffered a moral collapse and turned putrid."*[6]

The chief instigator of this moral collapse, according to the Benedictine, was Michelangelo: *"But I, for my part, must recognize this truth: Michelangelo in his own time was a hero of art, but for us he is the element we must avoid like the plague; because that uncontrolled caprice and tribulation was inflicted on almost three centuries, and still we can feel its deathly weariness in our bones."*[7]

With 'the Beuron Style' Father Desiderius called for the elimination of all traces of Humanism, and a return to the purity and simplicity of the Hieratic style. Meanwhile, with sacred proportion, Desiderius had found *"God's miracles of measure"*[8] in the sculpture of the Ancients, first and foremost. For him, the Egyptians *"...preserved, as implicit in the very notion of religious art, a measuring, an apportioning, a division in space."*[9]

IV. To Draw the Human Figure We Must Begin with a Circle...

Reading Desiderius' prose is a delight, even if his thoughts turn round in circles and never seem to reach their desired conclusion. Indeed, his texts begin to resemble Gnostic or Alchemical treatises, loaded with allusions, allegories and diagrams, but no clear method ever emerging. Although the monastery at Beuron has preserved hundreds of pages in manuscript form, the majority of these remain unpublished. Those few texts that have been

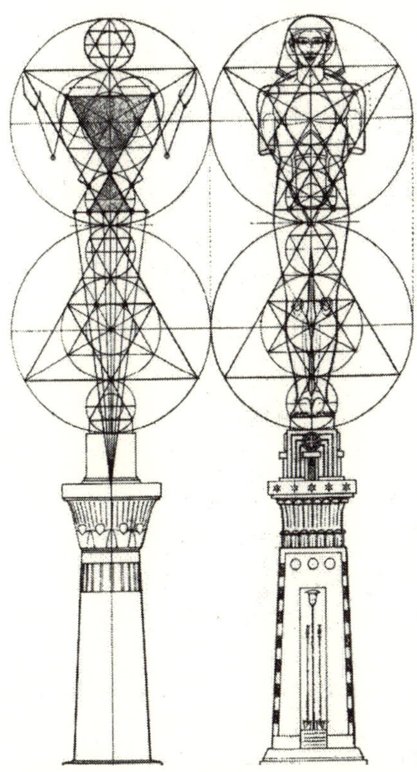
Fig. 4.4 - Desiderius: The Normative Human Image Constructed from the Square, Circle and Triangle

translated and published offer only a partial glimpse into his seemingly endless geometrical investigations.

The starting point for his sacred geometry were the true proportions of the male and female figure. Like God with compass and straight rule in hand, we must begin their construction through the circle, square and triangle:

"This art, in brief, springs from the understanding of those biblical words 'God created everything according to measure, weight and number' (Wisdom 11:20), whose highest fulfillment and most spiritual manifestation has been in the normative image of man in both sexes – in the knowledge that the three symbolic figures are symbols of the all-holy Trinity: the cube corresponding to the Father, the tetrahedron to the Son, and the sphere to the Holy Spirit; and that these three primordial figures (square, triangle, circle) alone are all that is needed to enable us to measure, to form and to construct the normative human image."[10]

Hence, to draw the human figure we must begin with a circle, the most perfect and divine of shapes. As we see in the first step of Fig. 4.3, we begin by inscribing a cross, the four-fold division of the circle into its respective quadrants. Then, a double square is inscribed within the limits of the circle.

In the second step, smaller circles are inscribed in each of the smaller squares. In the third step, we proceed *ad triangulum* – inscribing inverted triangles in each of the circles. In the top and bottom spaces, we add another smaller circle. As we can see in Fig. 4.4, this geometrical configuration offers *"the fundamentals of the Canon,"*[11] since its primordial circle, square and triangle determine all the measures of the human form. The human being as a whole stands within the double square, and his figure is divided perfectly in half at the pubis.

To determine the smaller proportions, we must construct the hexagrams, which Desiderius calls *"the Seal of Solomon."*[12] Beginning with the first circle in Fig. 4.5 (over), we note that the inverted triangle corresponds to the upper inverted triangle of 'the normative human image' in Fig. 4.4. As such, it measures the length of the torso, from below the chin to the pubis.

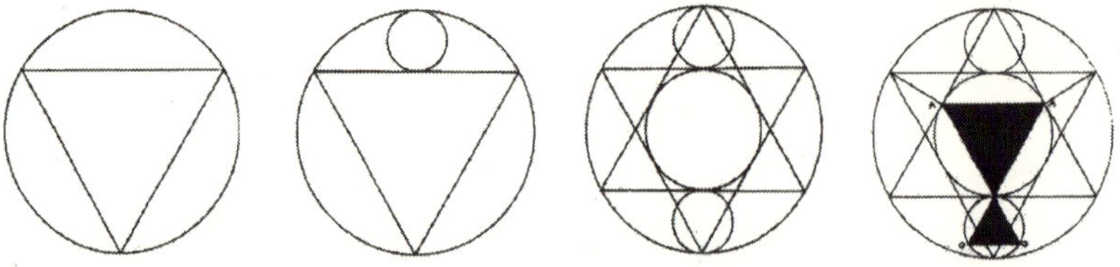

Fig. 4.5 - Desiderius: The Seal of Solomon and the Polyclitean Double Triangle

In the next step, the smaller circle above the inverted triangle, corresponds to the head, from the top of the head to the chin. In the third step, we add an upward-pointing triangle and a smaller circle below, so the hexagram is now inscribed in the larger circle. This 'Seal of Solomon' will give birth to many important measurements.

The first of these is the *"Polyclitean double triangle"*[13] which can be seen in the fourth step. It consists of the dark inverted triangle which is now inscribed in the innermost circle, and the dark upright triangle below inscribed in the small circle. This hour-glass design is the 'Polyclitean double triangle'. As we can see in Fig. 4.7, the horizontal of the dark inverted triangle corresponds to the shoulder joints, while, the horizontal of the dark upright triangle corresponds to the hip joints. Thus, the 'Polyclitean double triangle' gives us the four major point of articulation for the limbs.

If we focus on the lower half of the body in Fig. 4.7, we notice that the hexagram inscribed in the circle offers two points where the upright and inverted triangles meet. These two points mark the location of the joints in the legs i.e. the knees.

In order to differentiate between the male and female figures, Desiderius makes one more geometrical construction, which he calls *"the Five-fold Key."*[14] (Fig. 4.6) Beginning with the hexagram, we focus on the smaller hexagon within it and inscribe two circles: one *inner* circle whose circumference touches the mid-point of each of the six sides of the hexagon, and one *outer* circle whose circumference touches each of the six outermost points of the hexagon.

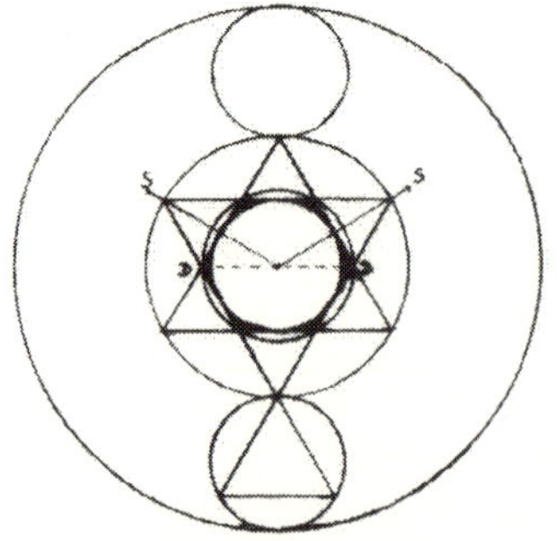

Fig. 4.6 - Desiderius: The Five-fold Key

As we can see in 'The Canon of the Normative Human Pair in Two Sexes' (Fig. 4.1 at the head of the chapter), these inner and outer circles vary between man and woman, even if their centres remain the same. In man, the outer circle measures the breast, while in woman it measures the abdomen – *"the man having its centre in the heart, the woman in her womb."*[15]

This exquisite drawing from the hand of Desiderius showing a man and woman beneath a palm tree (Fig. 4.1) is not just a proportional diagram of the normative human pair, but also of *the divine pair*. The diagram shows *"...the normative human pair as it emerged from the mind of God: in Adam and Eve, of whom it is said: 'God created man in His image and likeness.' This is the likeness which appeared on earth in Christ and the Blessed Virgin as its prototypes."*[16]

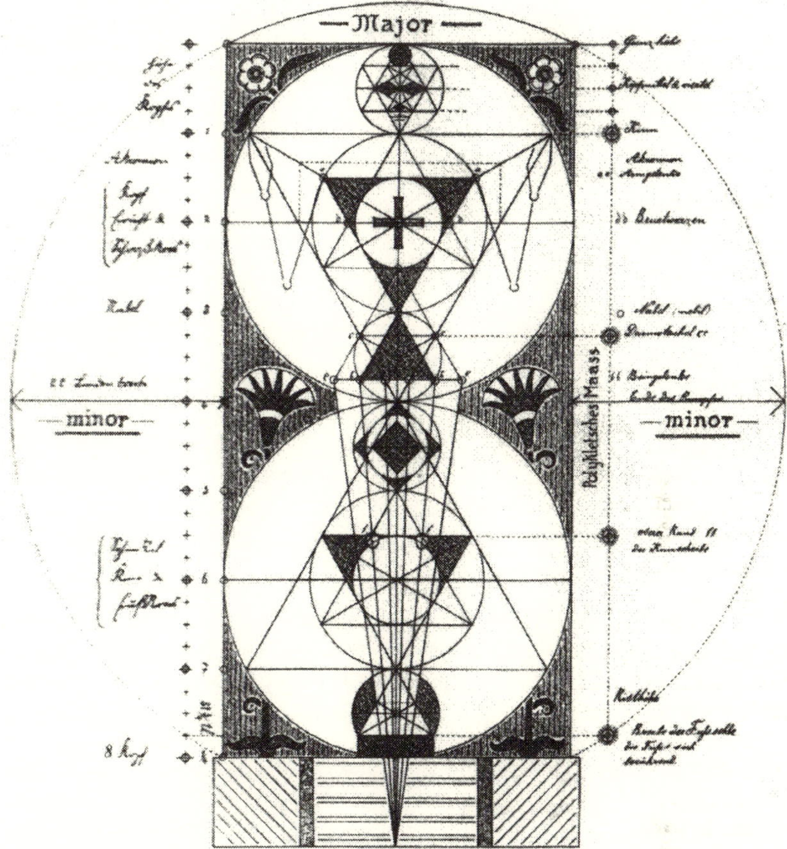

Fig. 4.7 - Desidierius: The Human Figure with the Polyclitean Double Triangle

In another treatise called 'The Canon' (1921), the 90-year-old monk elaborated upon his idea, which he called 'the Canon of the Normative Human Form in Two Sexes':

"Our manhood was, in Christ, in its normative form, just as the norm of all women appeared in His most holy mother, the Virgin... Adam and Eve alone had these normative numbers and measures, as prototypes of the original images in the Heart of God. But, with the fall into sin, they came to be lost; and the human race that followed them, in its numberless variations, disfigured by sin, can no longer show us these original – norm – measures...

"We know, however, that the ancient Egyptian art, and the art (which we term classical) of the Greeks as the heirs of the Egyptians, demonstrably knew this canonical norm of man and woman. They realized it in their works and from it they created the images of the art which we call the classical ideal... as something divine, not human."[17]

It follows from this theologic, that no male or female figure drawn from the live nude model – no matter how beautiful the figure or how accurate the drawing – will ever approach the norm, the canon, the ideal, which is founded upon geometric perfection.

Just as the primordial shapes of the circle, square and triangle underlie the construction of the human figure, so do they give God's order and design to the human face (Fig. 4.8). Once again, the Seal of Solomon or hexagram appears, to measure out the placement of the main features. Desiderius divides the face, from the top of the head to the chin, into 4 equal parts, each of the horizontals determined by the hexagram.

In this way, the eyes lie vertically half-way up the face. Meanwhile, their horizontal placement is determined by two verticals which are drawn from the points where the interpenetrating triangles cross. The outer circle, let us not forget, is the same circle that appears at the top of Fig. 4.7, making it one small part of the figure as a whole.

In fact, the circle of the head is exactly ¼ of the vertical diameter of the upper circle (see again Fig. 4.7). That being the case, the figure as a whole would be exactly 8 heads high, were it not for the fact that he is standing on a small pedestal that occupies ¼ of the small circle at the bottom. Nevertheless, Desiderius seems to be aware of this. In Fig 4.7, he clearly marks out a kind of Egyptian grid system on the left, numbering each head-length (*Kopf*) from 1 – 8, including the pedestal at the bottom. Each head-length is subdivided into 4, making 32 measures in all. He writes at the bottom left that the figure stands 31¾ *tl* (*Teile* or parts) high.

V. The Hieratic Revival

In the conclusion to *The Aesthetic of Beuron*, Father Desiderius writes, *"These theories may seem all too bold, perhaps arrogant and presumptuous; but my thoughts have come from contemplating the art of all ages which surrounds me; and He Who gave me eyes to see and the grace to seek the truth, He too is the same Who changes outer vision into inner. Let it be His will alone that moves me!"*[18]

With the Canon of Desiderius Lenz, the figure takes on a more spiritual and visionary quality. Through the greater outlying geometries of the circle, square and triangle, a certain harmony and perfection permeates the human form. Desiderius went so far as to discover the internal design, *ad quadratum* and *ad triangulum*, by which God measured out and constructed Man's figure in accord with these primordial shapes.

And yet, when I gaze upon the art of the Beuron School, I am often left cold. While his writings are full of passion and fury, Desiderius' figures remain stiff and lifeless. It was only when I saw Desiderius' work in person – visiting the Convent of St. Gabriel in Prague just a short time before this volume was published – that the inner spirit and piety of the figures came through. As his tirade against Michelangelo makes clear, the Benedictine preferred a rigid and precise Hieraticism, with no room for Humanist expression.

Although I have lamented that Western art, for the last 500 years, has been dominated by a Humanist style in decline, I do not suggest – as Desiderius certainly did – that Humanism should be eliminated completely, or replaced entirely by a Hieratic revival. Rather, in the works of the greatest Visionaries – Fuchs, Moreau, Blake (and yes) Michelangelo – the Humanist and Hieratic styles combine to seek a perfect balance.

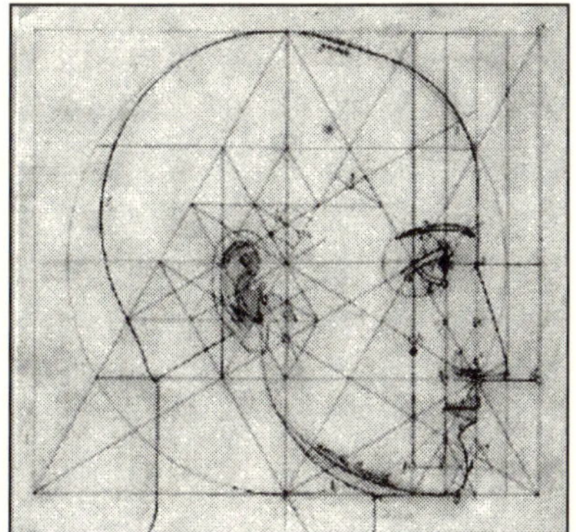
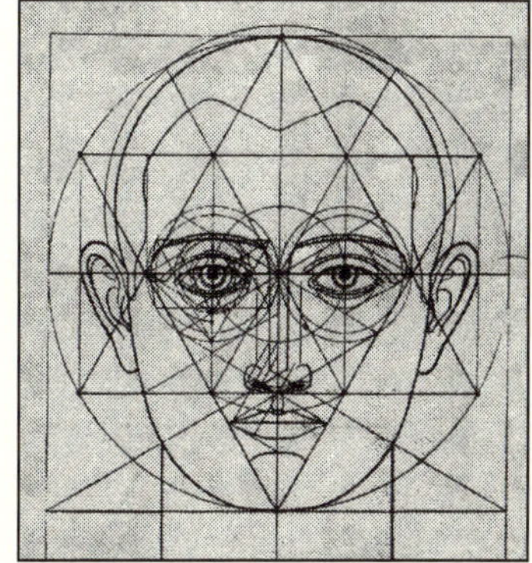

Fig. 4.8 - Desiderius: The Human Face, Profile and Frontal View
Divided by the Seal of Solomon into Four Equal Parts

As Visionary artists, it is our historical task to revive the Hieratic Style, marry it with the Humanist, and so, express the Sacred in an entirely new form of art, in time with the new millennium. With these thoughts in mind, we may approach Humanist and Hieratic figures, their respective poses and proportions, with a new spirit.

VI. Stylizing the Face – the Craftsmen of Ancient Egypt

We are fortunate that teaching pieces of the Egyptian craftsmen have come down to us through time. These so-called 'sculptors' models' (Fig. 4.8) are busts of kings and queens that show the various stages of carving, with their grid lines left in tact. Most were pedagogic pieces made by the masters, or trial pieces left by their apprentices. But some have been found in tombs, perhaps as offerings made by the apprentices to their departed masters.

In *Sculptors' Models of the Late and Ptolemaic Periods,* Nadja Tomoum studied numerous examples in order to reconstruct the artists' working methods. Beginning with a perfectly smoothened block, the sculptor first drew the guidelines on all sides to measure out the proportions. With red or black paint, he drew the face on each side of the block, in frontal view, back view and the left and right profiles.

Using a variety of tools,* he cut the basic profile into the block, then the outer sides of the face, so that the three major facets of the front and sides became clearly visible. The back was left untouched to preserve the grid lines as a reference. After re-drawing the features in accord with the grid lines (extending them from the back), he began again, removing a very shallow layer from each of the three sides before re-drawing and re-commencing. This gradual shaving away from different angles, called the 'facet technique', was repeated up to a hundred times.

---

*Sculptors' toolboxes have been found, and the Papyrus Feisner II gives a list of implements. The most important tools were the wooden mallet, flat or pointed chisel, and the adze. They also used the set-square, plumb line, knotted cord, saws, drills and polishing stones.[19]

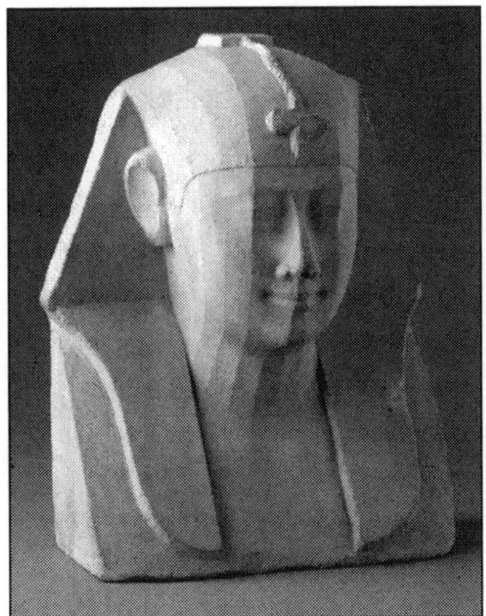

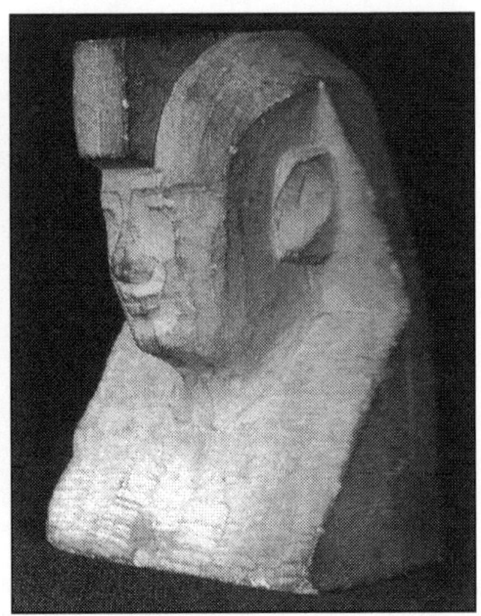

Fig. 4.9 - Egyptian Sculptors' Models

By the end, the sculptor was left with a bust that preserved up to nine vertical 'ridges' dividing up the face: *"The division into ridges enables the eye of the apprentice – when looking at the mass – not to get lost in the flowing curves, the anatomical structure and difficult balance... the system of ridges allows one to analyze the mass."*[20]

It was only in the very last stages of the work that these vertical ridges were sanded away and polished. In this way, the curves of the 'barely visible meandering line' which passed along the corners of the eyes and mouth could be carefully determined in relation to the verticals. Indeed, it became *"the dance of a curving line around a straight line, which remains invisible,"* (as Fuchs expressed it). Once the vertical ridges were removed, only the softly meandering contour lines of the face remained.

The guidelines that were cut or painted onto the block were of two distinct types (Fig. 4.10). First came the 'main' verticals and horizontals, which formed a basic grid on all sides of the block. Between these, the shorter 'secondary' lines were drawn on each side to mark the placement of specific details. It is the 'main' orthogonals of the basic grid that gives us the Egyptian system of proportions for the face.

Concentrating on the face alone, from the frontal view (leaving aside the shoulders and headdress), we note in Fig. 4.10 that the grid was 2 squares wide and 2 squares tall. The main vertical divided the face symmetrically in half, so that the face itself was 2 squares wide. The main horizontal divided the face vertically *at the tip of the nose*, so the top half of the face ended *at the hairline* and the bottom half ended just below the chin.

As we shall see, these two reference points measured out the module for many systems of proportion, Egyptian and beyond.

VII. Proportions of the Face in Ancient Egypt

C. C. Edgar was the first Egyptologist to study the facial proportions offered by these grid lines. In his 1905 article 'Remarks on Egyptian Sculptors' models' he wrote: *"The size of the square, or the length of the unit* [i.e. module] *stands in a fixed ratio to the proportions of the head. Thus in the matter of height we invariably find that the unit is equal to the distance from the lower end of the nose... to a point on the forehead a little above the eyebrows."*[21] This module, called *the nose-length*, will re-appear in Byzantine and even Indian systems of proportion.

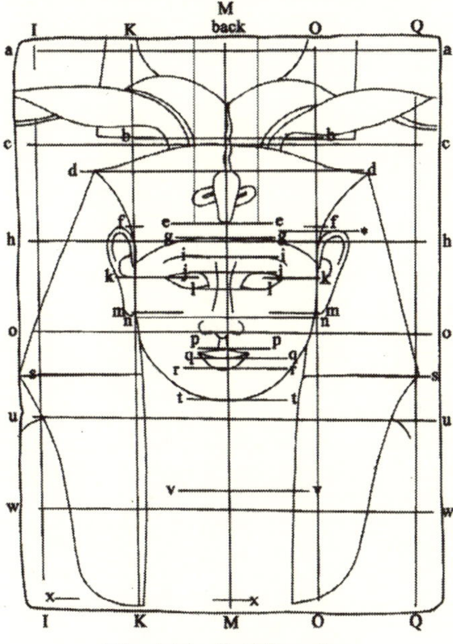

Fig. 4.10 - Grid lines from Bust CG 33337 in the Cairo Museum

If we now concentrate on the remainder of the grid for the frontal view (Fig. 4.10), we note that most of the busts were 4 squares wide and 5 – 6 squares high. On the sides, the extra 2 squares measure the outer limits of the *klaft* or headdress. Below the face, 2 squares measure the bottom limit of the headdress, and above the hairline, 1 square measures the top of the headdress, while another square is added for the decorative ears and horns.

Regarding the secondary lines, they were undoubtedly placed to mark out the eye, ears, lips and other fine features but, as C. C. Edgar noted, *"There was no fixed system for the employment of the secondary lines."*[22] Rather, with the basic facial proportions of the hairline and tip of the nose, the remaining features were drawn in accord with the artist's skill.

Through the 2 by 2 square grid lines, and the 9 vertical ridges, the Egyptian craftsmen measured out each facet of the hieratic face. With consummate skill, he then delineated the curves of the eyes, nose and mouth, each feature cut in the distinctive Egyptian Style. *"Style,"* Eugène Viollet-le-Duc reminds us, *"is the natural consequence of a principle followed methodically."*[23] The lines of proportion furnished the Egyptian craftsman with the foundation for his stylistic rendering.

Once the curves and volumes of the face had been carved, their original guidelines could be removed, thus becoming 'invisible'. Nevertheless the sense of order and perfection which those measure imparted to the face, remain – granting the divine visage its profound harmony and unity.

VIII. Hieratic Proportions of the Figure in Ancient Egypt

There is an oft-cited story from Diodorus Siculus, dating back to the first century BCE, about the statue of Pythian Apollo in Samos made by the two sons of Rhoecus, a famed sculptor in ancient Greece. The sons, named Telecles and Theodoros, made their statue of Apollo *"in conformity with the ingenious method of the Egyptians."* And, as Diodorus recounts:

"One half of the statue was worked by Telecles in Samos, and the other half was finished by his brother Theodorus at Ephesus; and when the two parts were brought together they fitted so perfectly that the whole work had the appearance of having been done by one man."

Marveling at the Egyptians' ingenuity, Diodorus goes on to explain:

"This method of working is practised nowhere among the Greeks, but is followed generally among the Egyptians. For with them the symmetrical proportions of the statues are not fixed in accordance with the appearance they present to the artist's eye, as is done among the Greeks. [...Rather,] *they take the proportions, from the smallest parts to the largest; for, dividing the structure of the entire body into twenty-one parts and one-fourth in addition, they express in this way the complete figure in its symmetrical proportions".*[24]

Over the last two hundred years, Egyptian archaeologists have in fact discovered numerous *bas reliefs* which confirm this measure of 21 parts for the proportion of the Egyptian figure. Unfinished *bas reliefs* within temples and tombs still show how the craftsmen used square grids to measure out the figures (Fig. 4.11). These grids were created by dipping string in red paint and snapping it onto the flat surface of the stone. Skilled draftsmen then drew the stylistic outline of the figures in red, using the grid as a guide for the proportions. Later, their outlines were corrected by the master draftsman, who drew over the figure in black before the stone cutting commenced.[26]

The relationship of these grids to the Egyptian system of proportion has occupied Egyptologists for centuries, and no single formula is easily discernible. But, in 1879, the French Egyptologist Achille Prisse d'Avennes (1807 – 1879) published the second volume of his *L'histoire de l'art égyptien* where he correctly observed that, in fact, *two different grid systems were used.*

Prisse identified an 'Early Grid' of 19 squares and a 'Later Grid' of 23 squares. However, he measured the figure from the soles to the top of the head. As later research showed, the Egyptians measured the figure *to the top of the eyelids or the hairline*, since the crowns and headdresses obscured the top of the head. Hence, the 'Later' grid of 23 squares identified by Prisse was actually 21¼ when measured up to the top of the eyelids – the exact measure given by Diodorus Siculus twenty centuries before...

The slight discrepancy caused by the distance between the hairline and the top of the head threw many researchers off track. Copying a gridded figure from the temple of Karnak in 1869, Charles Blanc was disappointed to report in his *Voyage de la Haute-Égypte* (1876) that the total height was 22¼ squares. Later, he revised this total to 19 squares, after a close reading of Lepsius.[25]

In 1849, Karl Richard Lepsius published the first book of his twelve volume opus, *Denkmäler aus Aegypten und Aethiopien* (Egyptian and Ethiopian Monuments - 1849 - 1856). This work, as we saw, had a profound effect upon Desiderius Lenz. Lepsius was the first to measure the Egyptian figure up to the hairline. But, his early researches postulated the division of the Egyptian figure into 18 parts up to the hairline which, in 1884, he derived from a 6 part proportional system used in the Old Kingdom.

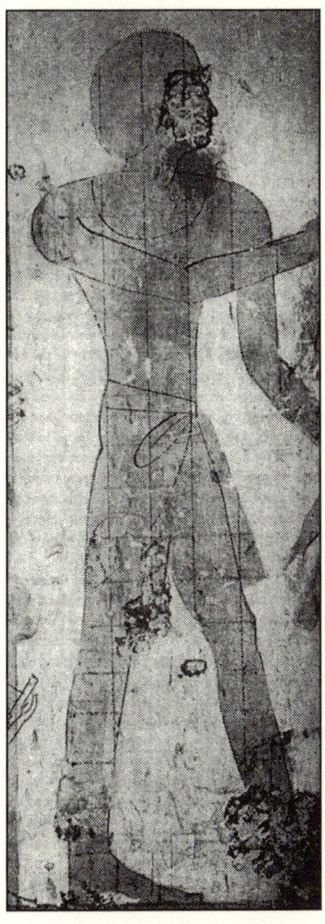

Fig. 4.11 - Figure with Grid Lines

In the last year of his life, Lepsius published his research into the module used by the Egyptians to develop their grids and proportions, offering the foot (c. 30 cm) as two thirds of a cubit (c. 45 cm). Although feet appear on Egyptian figures, and could be measured as such, the Egyptians themselves used the cubit (a measure from the elbow to the fingertips) as the basic module of measure, which was divided into 6 palms, each palm subdivided into 4 fingers. The quest for the Egyptian module was taken up by Erik Iversen, who developed an elaborate theoretical system to explain that one clenched 'fist' equalled one square of the grid, and that this equalled 5⅓ fingers in the Egyptian system of measurement.

More recently, Gay Robins did extensive fieldwork on grids which she published in 1994 as *Proportion and Style in Ancient Egyptian Art.* After examining numerous examples of grid systems throughout Egyptian history, her researches basically confirmed Prisse's discovery of two grid systems, of 19 and 23 squares respectively. While Robins showed that changes in the grid caused changes in style, she left the question of modules and proportion unanswered. Nevertheless, from her work we can make some important deductions concerning proportion.

The first grid system in use (Fig. 4.12, over), dating from the 12th dynasty (1938 BCE), may now be called more accurately the 'Middle Kingdom Grid' (Prisse's Early Grid). It consists of 19 squares, measuring the standing figure from the soles of the feet to the hairline. Although evidence of the grid dates back to the 12th dynasty, the actual proportions of the figures date back as far as the 5th dynasty (middle of the Old Kingdom, 2520 BCE). The figures bearing these proportions were executed in 'the Classical Style'.

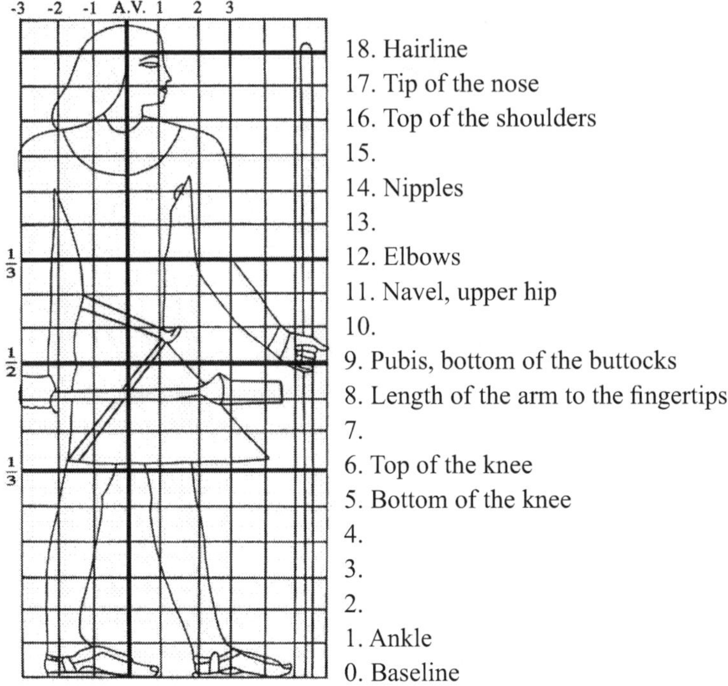

Fig. 4.12 - The 19 Square Middle Kingdom Grid

In the 26th dynasty (664 BCE), a second grid system (Fig. 4.13, on the following page) was introduced, which may be called the 'Late Period Grid' (Prisse's Later Grid). It consists of 21 squares, measuring the standing figure from the soles of the feet to the upper eyelids. This new grid led to a change in the proportions of the figure. But, rather than 'modernizing' its shape through the development of new proportions, the 21 square grid was, in fact, an attempt to 'archaize' the Egyptian figure.

The step pyramid of Djoser, which dates from the third dynasty (2705 BCE) of the Old Kingdom, offered up a fascinating discovery. In room III, grid traces were found on two stele of the king. However, the grids were not put there by the original craftsmen, since the lines run *on top of* the reliefs. Rather, these grids of 21 squares were traced *over the figures* centuries later by craftsmen of the Late Period, who were trying to *rediscover* the 'Archaic proportions' of the Old Kingdom. When the 21 square grid was introduced in the 26th dynasty, it was actually an attempt to antiquate the figure by reverting back to the 'Archaic style'[27]

It should be mentioned that a third grid was briefly used during the Amarna period, when Akhenaten radically altered, not only the sacred cults of ancient Egypt, but also its sacred style. The 20 square Amarna grid measured the figure from the soles of the feet to the hairline. Its use only lasted through the seventeen years of Akhenaten's reign (1353 – 1336 BCE) in the latter half of the 18th dynasty (although some relics in the tomb of Tutankhamun, his son, also bear traces of the Amarna style).

IX. Egyptian Proportion: the Middle Kingdom Grid

A closer analysis of the Middle Kingdom Grid (Fig. 4.12) shows how the figure's proportions were determined by the 19 square measures. Numbering each line from the base to the hairline, certain proportional constants appear from figure to figure, as follows:

Regarding the vertical lines of measure, the most important line was the Axial Vertical (A.V.) which descended through the ear, cutting the figure laterally in two. Moving outward from this line, the following constants appear:

1. Profile of the face
2. The armpits
3. Outer limits of the shoulders

It is rare for the top of the head to actually touch the 19th horizontal, usually remaining below it. Hence, the figure is usually measured as 18 squares tall (to the hairline) and 6 squares wide.

Through the 18 measures of the 19 square grid, the figure could be quickly divided into halves (9 squares), thirds (6 squares), and sixths (3 squares). The most important horizontal lines, relating the parts proportionally to the whole, were the half, third and two thirds:

- Upper third – line 12 – Elbows
- Half – line 9 – Pubis
- Lower third – line 6 – Top of the knee

As we shall see, the pubis (the point where the male sex attaches to the body) becomes an important indicator in proportions, marking the half-way point in height (rather than the navel, which appears in some systems). The Egyptian craftsmen indicated this halfway point through the clear indent of the lower buttock.

By measuring 3 squares up or down from here, they knew where to bend the elbows and knees, since these points marked the thirds – the knees at the lower third and the elbows at the upper.

The shoulders could be quickly determined by measuring 2 squares down from the hairline (or 7 squares up from the lower buttock). Other parts of the body usually fell within certain measures:

- The cubit (elbow to fingertips) – 5 squares
- The foot – 3 squares
- The width of the fist – 1 square

Surprisingly, the head – which is such an important module in later canons of proportion – does not fall within clear guidelines in the Egyptian grid. Rather, the hairline and the tip of the nose become the two main reference points for the face. Using the Axial Vertical, these two points could be quickly situated in the profile, on the first vertical line that measures 1 square over.

X. Egyptian Proportion: the Late Period Grid

To return to the more Archaic Style of the early dynasties, Egyptian craftsmen from the 26th dynasty onward used the 21 square grid of the Late Period. Instead of the hairline, *the top of the eyelids* now formed the uppermost horizontal, at line 21. The pubis remained the halfway point of the figure, between lines 10 and 11. But the other proportional constants shifted.

Regarding the vertical lines of measure, the Axial Vertical remained the most important, descending through the ear and cutting the figure laterally in two. Moving outward from this line, the figure appeared broader:

1 - 2. Profile of the face
2. The armpits
3 - 4. Outer limits of the shoulders

In the Late Period Grid, the pubis at line 10.5 remained the simplest coordinate, marking the halfway point through the indent of the lower buttock. From here, the craftsman could measure 3.5 squares up to obtain the bend in the elbow, and 3.5 squares down to the bend in the knee. The shoulders could still be quickly determined by counting 2 squares down from the top of the eyelids.

Meanwhile, the resulting measures of the limbs may strike us, initially, as rather strange. The forearm, which was 5 squares long in the Classical Style now extends to 6 squares. The legs below the knee also grow noticeably longer (from 5 to 6 squares), as do the feet (from 3 to 4 squares). Laterally, the figure gets noticeably wider (from 6 to 7 squares).

Egyptologists did not fail to notice the shift in certain key body parts which had also been used as modules in Egyptian measure. Most important was the forearm, which shifted from 6 palms in length (a 'cubit') to 7 palms in length (a 'royal cubit'). The 'royal cubit' dates back to the time of King Djoser, and its measure permeates his step pyramid – that same step pyramid where Late Period craftsmen traced their 21 square grid over the *bas relief* figures to determine their Archaic proportions...

When we step back and consider Egyptian representation as a whole, we must remember that they often presented objects in a purely schematic way, laying each hieroglyphic hand, arm or head next to each other in the grid. The most obvious example is their turning of the upper body to the frontal position, while the rest of the body remains in profile. This depicts the figure in axonometric perspective – a subject which we will return to in our chapters on Hieratic Perspective..

This same tendency appears with the Archaic Style, which gave the human figure a forearm 6 squares long to show, in a schematic way, the royal cubit (7 palms in length) rather than the standard cubit (6 palms in length).

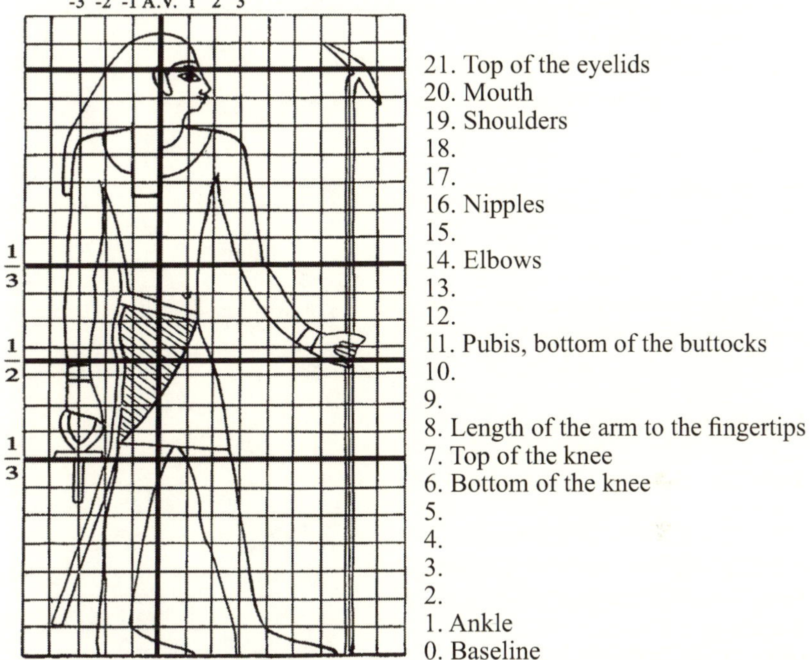

Fig. 4.13 - The 21 Square New Kingdom Grid

Meanwhile the same was true, as Lepsius argued, of the foot, which increased from 3 squares to 4 to show its new measure as three quarters of the royal cubit (rather than the shorter standard cubit).

Hence, it would be wrong for us to compare the human figure in the Archaic Style with a natural human being – that was never the Egyptians' intent. On the other hand, the Archaic Style gave the human figure a unique set of proportions which may indeed be termed 'Hieratic'. Elongating the forearms and feet accentuate their importance, thus increasing their symbolic expression. Extending the lower legs increases the effect of stature, while broadening of the figure made it seem more powerful and monumental.

This movement in the 26th dynasty (664 BCE) toward a more Hieratic style may be compared to Akhenaten's earlier and more radical stylization of the figure in the 18th dynasty (1353 BCE). Although some Egyptologists argue that Akhenaten was 'naturalizing' the body (to reflect, as they claim, his genetic disorder), I would argue, on the contrary, that he was hieratically 'idealizing' the figure in his own unique manner.

By comparison, the figures rendered in the Classical Style, using the 19 square grid of the Middle Kingdom, seem 'well-proportioned' to us. They reflect our preference for a canon that delivers a more natural representation of the human body – a 'naturalism' which we might better refer to as Humanist in proportion.

Whether the Egyptian style be Archaic, Classical or Amarna, one constant remains: the grids which the craftsmen used to determine their human proportions. These demonstrate without a doubt that so many straight but 'invisible' lines were used to determine the 'visible' curves and contours that make up the Egyptian figure. The Hieratic Style thrives within these lines, meandering around them and eventually matching their course, to give the figure a certain divine harmony and grace.

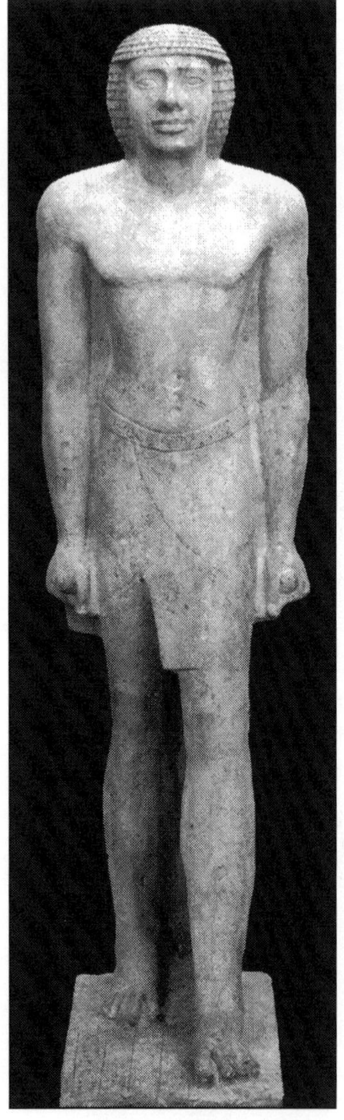

Fig. 4.14 -Statue of Tjayasetimu, 26th dynasty

XI. Archaic Greek Proportion

When Diodorus Siculus wrote that a statue of Pythian Apollo was carved *'in conformity with the ingenious method of the Egyptians,'* many scholars became intrigued by the possibility that Archaic Greek statuary may have shared the same proportional schema as Egyptian carvings. Like the Egyptian statues of the standing Horus (who was identified with the sun), the Archaic Greek *'Kouroi'* depicted a free-standing youth (identified as Apollo – the sun god) with his arms pressed to his sides and his left foot advancing.

In the late 1970's, Eleanor Guralnick[28] measured twenty-four of these *Kouroi* statues and determined that at least *two-thirds* were carved in accord with the Egyptian Late Period Grid of 21 squares. Thus, the Archaic statuary of 6th century BCE Greece shared the same proportional system as 26th dynasty Egypt (664 BCE).

What I find intriguing about this fact is that the statuary of two different cultures *could share the same proportions, but not the same style.* Granted, the similarity of pose and proportion give both Greek and Egyptian statuary a certain 'Hieratic' quality, of majestic stillness and calm. Yet, how different is the delineation of the human form..!

Following the same grids and measures, the craftsmen of both cultures simplified the volumes and stylized the outlines, yet each in a different manner. Each has *idealized* the human form, granting it divine harmony and grace, yet – expressed that transcendent aspect in a style that was unique to their own time and place (Figs. 4.14 - 4.15).

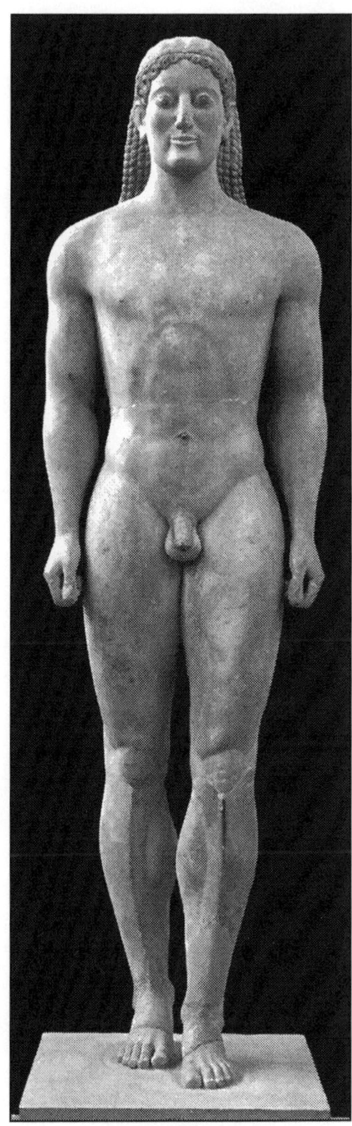

Fig. 4.15 - Archaic Greek Kouros, 6th c. BCE

Despite these differences, the same underlying principles – the same Sacred Codes – grant permanence and transcendence to their Hieratic art. They reach beyond their own times, to our own. As Hieratic artists, we too may recognize and revive these divinely-inspired proportions in our art. As Visionary artists, we should not neglect Kenneth Clark's stern warning that *"styles, like civilizations, collapse from within... whenever the discipline of an ideal scheme is relaxed."*[29] Does the art of our century follow 'the discipline of an ideal scheme?' Artists today owe it to themselves – and to their culture – to strive towards art's highest ideals, through the well-defined schemata of proportion and style.

The Egyptian method of block carving gives rise to another interesting and distinctive quality: the *quadrata* or 'squareness' of the Hieratic Style. In his essay *'The History of the Theory of Human Proportions as a Reflection of the History of Styles'* Erwin Panofsky mentions a papyrus in Berlin (Fig. 4.16) which preserves the sculptural blueprint of a sphinx. Although only fragments of the papyrus remain (it was found among mummy wrappings), its pieces clearly delineate a sphinx *from the front, top and side,* with each section divided by grid lines along their axis of symmetry.[30]

The fact that the Egyptian artisan began carving his sphinx from a block, with a square grid laid out on three of its faces, naturally led to the 'squarish' proportions of his final handiwork. Granted, the Great Sphinx at Giza has charmed pilgrims for generations, but her sinuous lines and graceful curves are best approached *from the front or side* – for it is only then that their underlying proportions work their mystery and magic.

And so it is that Hieratic works of art often manifest both symmetry and squarish proportions, while displaying the human aspect *from either the frontal or profile view.* This gives the Hieratic Style its *quadrata* quality of *squarishness*, arising from the 'block-like statures' (*quadratas staturas*) of ancient sculpture.

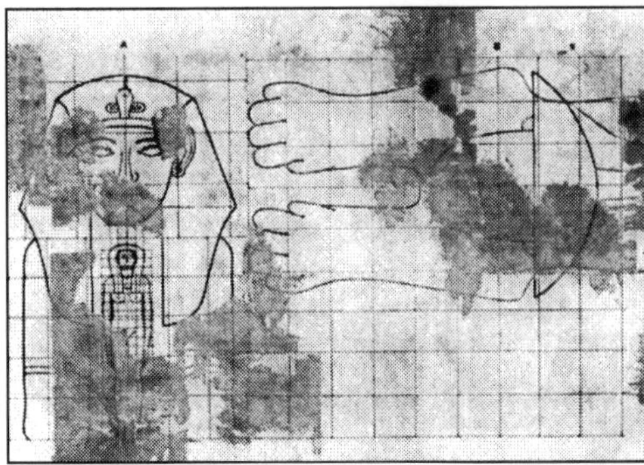

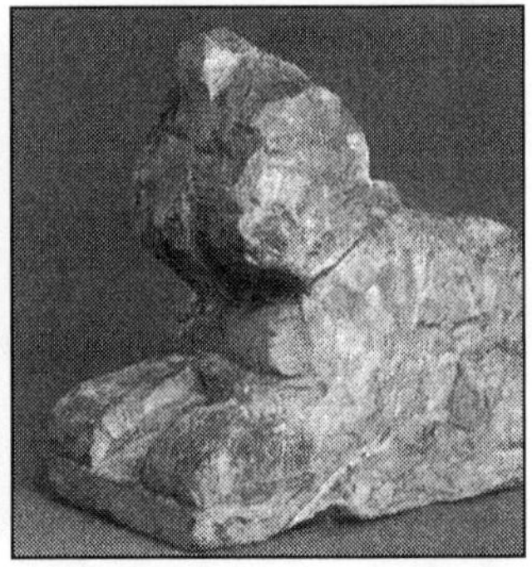

Fig. 4.16 - Papyrus of Squared Sphinx Front and Top View - Berliner Museum P11775

Fig. 4.17 - Blocked in Sphinx, Late Period, Cairo Museum JE 87825

This *ad quadratum* division of space extends from Egyptian times all the way through Hindu and Gothic architecture to Neo-Classical painting. In each case, the *'quadierung'* (German) or *'mise au carreau'* (French) leads to an arrangement of figures that harmonizes with the cubed or squared space surrounding them (temples, cathedrals, rectangular compositions). Although the square – oriented to the four cardinal directions on the horizon – measures space from a human and terrestrial point of view, the figures in its confines may rise up to higher and more divine spheres when designed with curving lines and angled shapes that resonate, as well, with the divine circle and triangle. Through the inspiration and combination of all these shapes, art achieves its highest purpose.

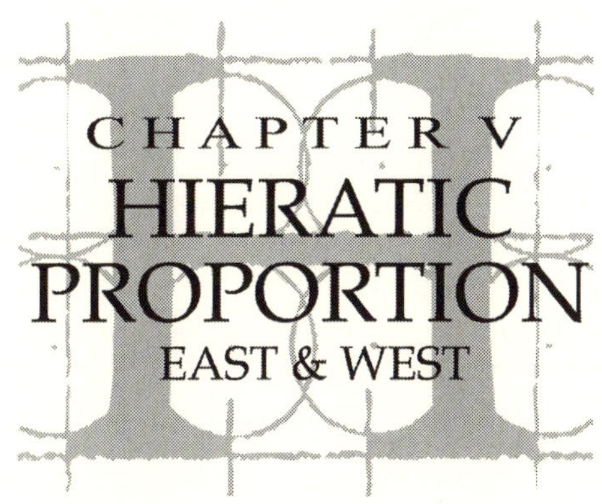

CHAPTER V
HIERATIC PROPORTION
EAST & WEST

I. The Lineage of Craftsmanship

"Works of art by man," says the *Aitareya Brāmaṇa, "are an imitation of divine forms."*[1] Hence, the Hindu craftsman follows, as a matter of course and without question, the stylistic measures and proportions learned during his apprenticeship. According to Heinrich Zimmer in his massive two-volume work, *The Art of Indian Asia*:

"In India, one is not free to choose to become an artist. The vocation is supposed to have been inherited from primordial times, from divine ancestral master craftsmen, and to be confined to certain families... Moreover, the craftsman has to be trained from childhood. Commencing as his father's apprentice, he follows unquestioningly, and as a matter of course, the ancestral calling."[2]

However, as Stella Kramrisch notes in *'The Traditions of the Indian Craftsman'*, young apprentices were also 'adopted' into families, not just born into them: *"The crafts were hereditary, or the succession was by apprenticeship and adoption. ...The craftsman was trained from childhood in the workshop of the master, whose son, or younger brother, or apprentice he was... He learned the trade secrets. With devoted receptiveness, he prepared colours and tools and learned the form and theory of his branch of the Tradition. He was initiated into his craft."*[3]

Although certain cities and towns had their local workshops, craftsmen also banded together into entire villages of a thousand sculptors or more. Guilds guaranteed the quality of materials and design. *"Membership of a guild was also hereditary,"* Kramrisch writes. *"When the son had mastered his father's craft, he took his place in the guild."*[4]

But what of women? As one master craftsman explained in a contemporary interview: *"...woman are specifically excluded from learning the tradition of sculpture because* [under the caste system] *they must marry outside the family into families that practice the same occupation as their own. Thus, teaching the women of the family the trade secrets of a family's livelihood was forbidden."*[5]

Since trade secrets were transmitted along different family lineages, *"each craft,"* Kramrisch reports, *"had an initiation imparted through the idiom of that craft. For the painter, the free hand drawing of certain abstract curves and curvilineal configurations served this purpose."*[6]

II. Hindu Proportions of the Figure

The third part of the *Vishnudharmattara* is a 7th century manual for painters. After elaborating a complex system of proportion, it warns the artist to be accurate, citing theurgic grounds for this precision:

"Even when duly invoked by the best of Brahmins, the gods never enter images short of measurements and devoid of the marks (lakshanas) of divine form. But demons, ghosts and hobgoblins always enter them, and so a great care should be taken to avoid shortness of measurements."[7]

The basic modules used in measuring Hindu statues (iconometry) are the *tāla* and *aṅgula. Tāla* means literally a 'palm' and is the distance between the tips of an outstretched thumb and middle finger. This corresponds exactly to the length of the face (hairline to chin) and so it may be understood as one 'face-length'. *Aṅgula* means 'digit' or 'finger' and corresponds to the middle segment of the middle finger.[8] There are 12 *aṅgulas* in 1 *tāla.*

Different types of divine figures have different heights. The four major types are the *daśatāla* (10 faces), *návatāla* (9 faces), *aṣtátāla* (8 faces), and *saptátāla* (7 faces), though these can go lower for dwarfs and animals. The purest proportion, used for Deities, is the *návatāla* or *nine face-lengths.* From this standard, the other proportions are developed, such as the *daśatāla* (10 faces) used expressly for Brahma, Vishnu and Shiva, and the *aṣtátāla* (8 faces) reserved for goddesses.[9] Since deities wear a variety of specific crowns and headdresses, their height is measured *"up to the root of the hair on the forehead,"* the *Śukranitisāra* (IV. 4) says.[10]

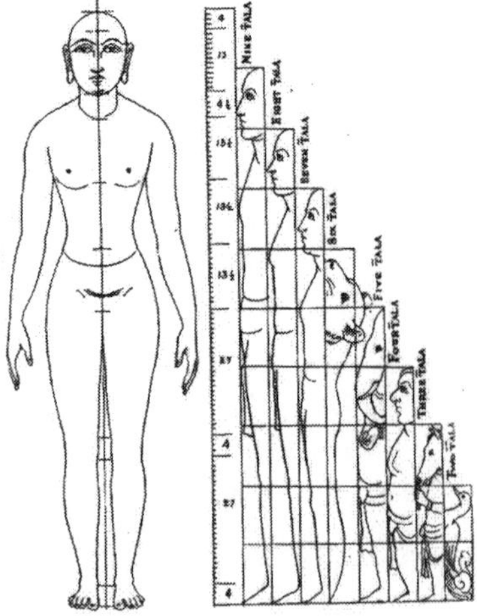

Fig. 5.1 - From 10 to 2 Face Measures

Concentrating on the *návatāla* figure of nine face-lengths, the statue's proportions are measured as follows:

For a figure 9 *tālas* tall:

- The face is 1 *tāla* (12 *aṅgulas*)
- The neck is ⅓ *tāla* (4 *aṅgulas*)
- The trunk is divided into 3 equal parts, each 1 *tāla* in length:
- From the pit of the neck to the nipple line is 1 *tāla* (12 *aṅgulas*)
- From the nipple line to the navel is 1 *tāla* (12 *aṅgulas*)
- From the navel to the pubis is 1 *tāla* (12 *aṅgulas*)
- The upper leg is 2 *tālas* (2 x 12 *aṅgulas*)
- The knee is ⅓ *tāla* (4 *aṅgulas*)
- The lower leg is 2 *tālas* (2 x 12 *aṅgulas*)
- The foot is ⅓ *tāla* (4 *aṅgulas*)

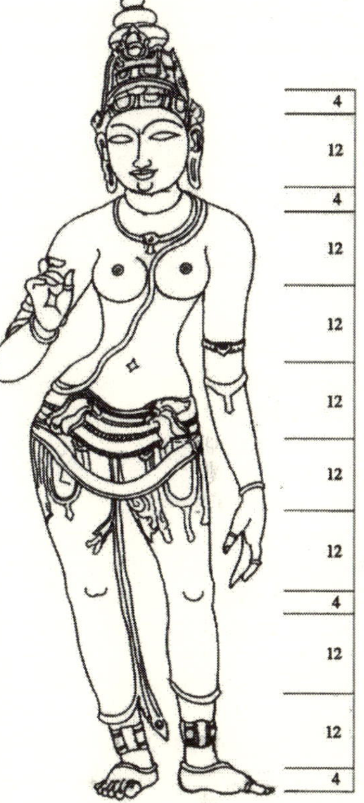

Fig. 5.2 - The *Návatāla* or 9 Face Measure

To summarize: the face is 1 *tāla*, the torso is 3, the upper and lower legs are 2 each, while the neck, knee and foot each make ⅓ of the final *tāla*, for a total of 9. Since there are 12 *aṅgulas* in each *tāla*, the figure as a whole stands 108 *aṅgulas* tall when we measure up to the hairline. The number 108 has an auspicious meaning in India where the *japa mala* or rosary has 108 beads for the recitation of the 108 names of Surya, Shiva or Devi. There are also 108 Upanishads.

As we can see in Figure 5.2, an extra ⅓ *tāla* (4 *aṅgulas*) has been added above the hairline to give the figure's full height to the top of the head (112 *aṅgulas*). In this case, the pubis now appears *exactly at the half-way point*, measuring 56 *aṅgulas* up and down from the top of the head to the soles of the feet.

Later in this treatise, we shall see that the *návatāla* figure corresponds to the basic proportions used in the West by the Roman architect Vitruvius (see Ch. VI. Section VII), as well as those appearing later in the writings of the Byzantine icon painter, Dionysius of Fournos (see Ch. V. Section V).

The face, according to the *Vishnudharmattara*[11] (Part III, Ch. 36) also follows a three-part division below the hairline:

- The forehead is 4 *aṅgulas*
- The nose is 4 *aṅgulas*
- Each lip is 1 *aṅgula* high and the chin is 2 *aṅgulas,* making 4 *aṅgulas*

Craftsmen have developed various systems for transferring these proportions to the stones for carving. According to the *Shilpa Śāstras,* five to seven vertical axes (*sutras,* literally 'threads') descend the figure, marking out the lateral proportions.

The first is the central vertical (*madhyasutra*) which descends through the middle, dividing the figure laterally in two. Flanking the sides of the face are two more lines (*parsvasutra*) which vertically descend through the middle of the knees and ankles. Further out, another two verticals (*kaksasutra*) descend from the armpits, marking the outer limit of the hips (in males). And last are the two framing verticals (*bahusutra*) marking the outer limits of the shoulders.[12]

The *brahmasutra* is a vertical line, similar to the central vertical (*madhyasutra*), but it indicates the pull of gravity. Like the western 'plumb line', it is the axial vertical of the statue, at the centre of all four directions.

When Indologists like Gopinatha Rao and Ananda Coomaraswamy visited sculptors' workshops in the early 1900's, they remarked upon the use of a *lambaphalakā* or wooden frame, from which the various plumb lines were hung around the stone block.[13]

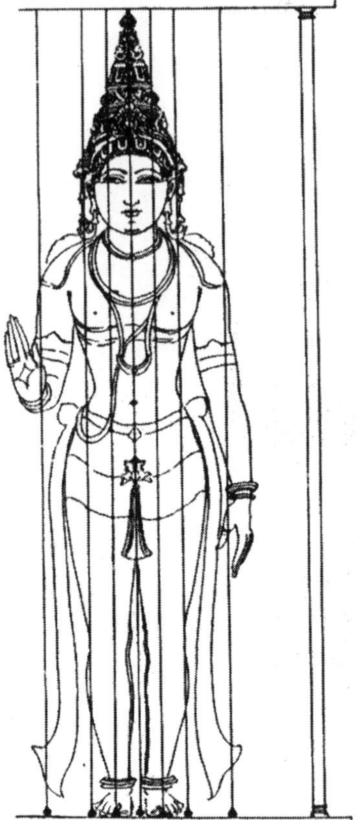

Fig. 5.3 - The *lambaphalakā* with seven plumb lines

In the 1980's, scholars such as John F. Moesteller investigated the working methods of more modern craftsmen in Kerala, finding that they followed the same basic proportions as laid out in the *Shilpa Śāstras*. However, they simplified the 5 – 7 verticals of the *śāstras* down to the 1 central *brahmasutra* or plumb line.

Using the face-length as the module, the central vertical (*brahmasutra*) was cut by a series of horizontal lines, marking out the basic vertical proportions. The most important of these are listed in the *Vishnudharmattara*: the hairline (*mastaka*), face (*vadana*), neck (*kaṇṭha*), heart (*hṛdaya*), navel (*nābhi*), genitals (*meḍra*), upper leg (*ūrū*), knee (*jānu*), lower leg (*jaṅghā*) and foot (*pāda*), all dividing the figure into the proportions given for a figure of the *návatāla* type. The face could be further subdivided into the three basic parts, the forehead (*lalāṭa*), nose (*nāsā*) and mouth/chin (*mukha*).[14]

When altering the proportions of a *návatāla* (9 face-lengths) figure to make a statue of the *aṣṭátāla* (8 face-lengths) or *daśatāla* (10 face-lengths) type, the 3 *tāla* of the trunk remained constant, while *aṅgulas* were variously

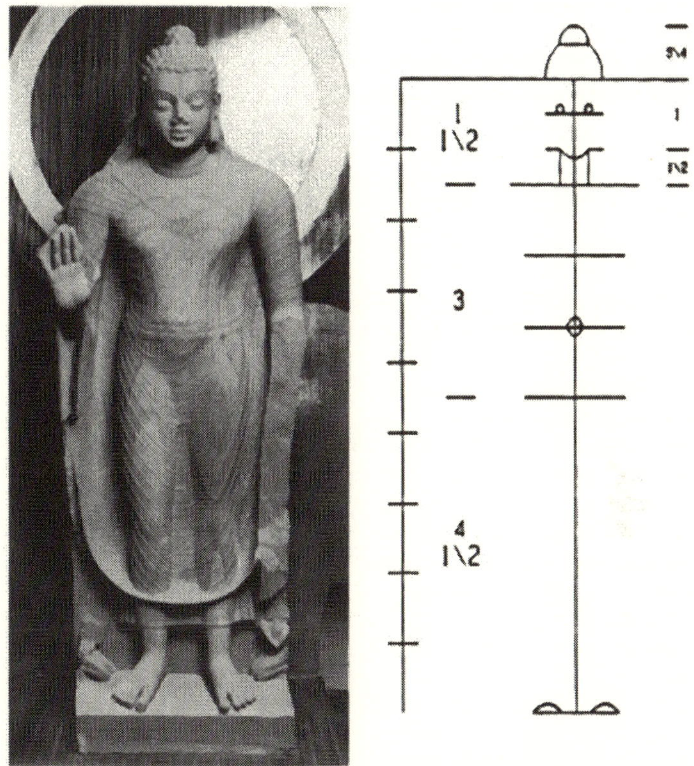

Fig. 5.4 - A Standing Buddha in the Gupta Style, accompanied by the brahmasutra cut in seven parts

added and subtracted to the other parts. This is why, for example, the standing Buddhas in the Gupta style have unusually long legs compared to their torsos (See Fig. 5.4, above).[15]

III. Buddhist Proportions of the Figure

After the Dalai Lama's departure into self-exile and the brutal suppression of the Tibetan people's uprising in March of 1959, increasing numbers of monks, scholars and artists fled to India, Nepal and the West. As a result, our knowledge of Tibetan thangka painting has dramatically increased in the last fifty years.

In 1983, Gega Lama published his two-volume *Principles of Tibetan Art*, a detailed manual transmitting the Lama's knowledge of painting from the Karma Gandri tradition. One year later, David and Janice Jackson published their seminal book, *Tibetan Thangka Painting* (illustrated by Robert Beer), giving a practical and detailed summary of what they had learned by studying with three Tibetan masters in India during the early seventies. Since then, a variety of other important historical texts on the principles of Tibetan painting have been published.

All these books offer proportional grids with iconometric measures and, as can be expected, these differ in parts. According to Gega Lama, such difference, duly acknowledged, allow for a degree of freedom in creation:

"Since there are many points in the tantras which are unclear, there exist minor differences (as well as many similarities) between the traditions known as the Indian, Nepalese, and Tibetan styles.... So one should consider all these traditions to be authentic and compatible, without holding one's own school to be the only correct interpretation and the others to be in error. Traditionally it is said that standardized proportions exist to avoid degeneration in the arts, and were set forth by accomplished artists: they are not rigidly fixed... One who is qualified is free to improvise and to introduce his own innovations wherever the standards are incomplete or there is something not clearly delineated by tradition."[16]

Despite this apparent freedom, the canons of Buddhist proportion are very rigorous, and this also extends to the poses, gestures, ornaments and detailed iconography – all of which are learned at an early age during the artist's apprenticeship. Gega Lama recounts that he entered the Chökor Namgyal Ling monastery in 1942, at the age of eleven, and began his first serious study of painting at the age of sixteen. To do this, he actively sought out his master, the greatly respected artist Tangla Tsewang. *"Studying design and proportion and absorbing his personal instructions, I became an artist in my own right by the age of twenty-two."*[17] In 1959, like so many other Tibetans, he escaped to India.

"Regarding an artist's worthy qualities," Gega Lama writes, *"these are to be skilled in drawing; to be well-versed in correct proportion; to maintain properly the lineage of artistic transmission and technique... and to portray faithfully the elements of composition – ornaments, gestures, and so forth – just as they are set forth in the appropriate canonical descriptions."*[18]

David and Janice Jackson also noted the apprentice's disciplined acquisition of proportion, pose and iconography. At least four of the six main scales of iconometry had to be memorized, while also drawing heads, hands and feet, before the first figure could even be attempted:

"The neophyte usually spent years familiarizing himself with the main proportional classes and with the frequently recurring designs and motifs, meanwhile mastering the basic techniques of paint application and shading."[19]

Once he was sufficiently prepared, the apprentice was invited to draw the full figure:

"When the student attempted to draw a complete figure for the first time, he had to begin by establishing a grid of correctly spaced lines [thig khang or thig chen] *within which he could construct the figure itself... As always, the vertical axis was the starting point and main reference... When the student had completed the grid he next drew the main outlines of the naked figure. He worked with an example by his teacher before him, constantly referring back*

to it to check the accuracy of his copy. Finally, after the completion of the figure in an unclothed state, he drew in whatever robes and ornaments were required."[20]

In their book, David and Janice Jackson provide many examples of iconometric grids, but do not illustrate the three-stage process. Gega Lama's book, which is much more pedagogic, consistently gives us the grid, the simple figure within the grid, and the final figure (without grid) draped with all its detailed ornaments and attributes. Considering the complexity of detail in the ornament, it is no wonder that the artist began with the simple figure, striving to match the canons of proportion.

Once that artist had reached a higher level of competence, he could dispense with most of the grid lines and work from an abbreviated version of it (*sdom tshad*). He could also dispense with the second stage, the simple figure, and draw the clothed figure immediately, with all its ornaments.

Although this highly-structured and stylized manner of drawing may strike the Western artist as constricting, we should not forget the definition of style given earlier. Style, according to Viollet-le-Duc, is the natural consequence of a principle, followed methodically. *Without* the principle, style cannot emerge. For it is the free-play, the delicate movement, the 'serpentine line', as Ernst Fuchs says, around the invisible straight line which gives birth to style. For Tibetan artists, iconometric grids, in all their complexity, provide the matrix within which distinctive styles and entire schools have demonstratively emerged.

IV. The Thangka Painter

Thangka painting is a Hieratic art. The artist, if he is to faithfully fashion a vessel for the Sacred, must himself practice a degree of piety, humility and austerity.

"At the start of a project," Gega Lama writes, the artist, *"...should perform a ceremony to eliminate all potential obstacles: meditating himself in the form of the appropriate protective divinity, the artist purifies the canvas; next, visualizing himself in the forms of the buddhas of the five families, or of Vairocana (the buddha of the central buddha family), he consecrates the pigments and brushes in a particular ceremony. Then he must be able to paint in gold, at the centre of the canvas, the seed-syllable of the divinity in question, surrounded by the mantra, as explained in the appropriate tantra. Until the project is completed, he must be able to devote unceasingly energy to it, without procrastination: and when it has been completed, he should know how to explain its qualities in order to gladden the patron, and to dedicate the virtue of the endeavour for the welfare of others in a spirit of celebration."*[21]

The Lama adds a long list of qualities, both positive and negative, worthy of the diligent artist. On the positive side, he should be patient, compassionate, and generally of a restrained disposition, slow to anger, lacking in vanity, with little concern for wealth and substance. He should also 'bathe regularly'. On the negative side, he should avoid being oversensitive and taciturn, quick to anger, greedy, coveting others' wealth, overtalkative and profane. *"An artist who has such flaws,"* he remarks, *"cannot develop his creative talent."*[22]

Certainly, in comparison to the Western concept of the tormented artist and genius, this strikes us as strange. Here, we tolerate and even celebrate the Bohemian artist, romanticizing their quirks and obsessions, ignoring their immense vanity while forgiving them their childish weakness and deceit, as if the artist were somehow above morality.

David and Janice Jackson write of another interesting contrast encountered in the Tibetan Painters they met: those who were willing to share their methods and those who guarded them as secret. In most cases, they were greeted by artists 'who took pleasure in imparting their knowledge,' understanding the importance of transmission, to assure that such a precious knowledge and practice would not be lost. On the other hand, they also encountered *"...a small number of brilliantly talented artists who were very reticent about their work... One such artist whom we met in India was sometimes even said to be a 'divinely emanated fashioner of images' (sprul pa'i lha bzo). Such artists had a reputation of taking no students, and often they would die without passing on their knowledge."*[23]

With these thoughts in mind, we turn to the stunningly complex art of Tibetan proportion and iconometry. Following David and Janice Jackson, we shall use as our classical source the *'Sku gzugs kyi cha tshad kyi rab tu byed pa yid bzhin nor bu'* by Smanthang-pa Sman-bla-don-grub (15th century), which is cited by Zhu-chen Tshul-khrims-rin-chen in the 18th century. These iconometric measures appear in a recently-discovered manuscript from the late 17th century called 'Illustrations of Measurements: A Refresher for the Cognoscenti' (*Cha tshad kyi dpe ris Dpyod ldan yid gsos*) produced by Sangs rgyas rgya mtsho (1653 – 1705), regent of the 5th Dalai Lama, and published in 2012 under the title *Handbook of Tibetan Iconography: A guide to the Arts of the 17th Century*.

The system for measuring out figures is derived, fundamentally, from the Indian system given above, where one *tāla* or face equals twelve *aṅgulas* or fingers. In Tibet, the face is one *zhal* which equals twelve *sors* or fingers. As the 'larger unit' (*cha chen*), the *zhal* may also be measured out as 'the distance from extended thumb to the tip of the middle finger' (a span or *mtho*), or as 'the palm plus the fingers' (a palm or *thal mo*). The overall height of a figure is typically given in the 'smaller unit' (*cha chung*) of *sors* or fingers.

David and Janice Jackson give grids and measures for Six Major Proportional Classes, according to the system of Smanthang-pa:

1. Buddhas: 125 *sor* (10 *zhal* or faces, but of 12½ *sors*)
2. Peaceful Bodhisattvas: 120 *sor* (10 *zhal* or faces)
3. Goddesses: 108 *sor* (9 *zhal* or faces)
4. Tall Wrathful figures: 96 *sor* (8 *zhal* or faces)
5. Short Wrathful figures: 72 *sor* (6 *zhal* or faces, sometimes 5)
6. Humans: 96 *sor* (8 *zhal* or faces)

The first thing we notice is the strong similarity between Tibetan proportion and the system of Hindu proportion just given above, where divine figures measure out as *daśatāla* (10 faces), *návatāla* (9 faces), *aṣṭátāla* (8 faces) and so on. To make a finer comparison, we will examine the Peaceful Bodhisattva first, since it stands at exactly 10 faces and is not encumbered by the extra ½ *sor* that makes the Buddha's measure so unique.

Concentrating on the Peaceful Bodhisattvas of 10 faces, the figure's proportions are measured as follows:

Standing Bodhisattva
where 1 *zhal* is *12 sors*

- The head protuberance (*uṣṇīṣa*) is ⅓ *zhal* (4 *sors*)
- The hair is ⅓ *zhal* (4 *sors*)
- The face is 1 *zhal* (12 *sors*)
- The neck is ⅓ *zhal* (4 *sors*)
- The trunk is divided into 3 equal parts, each 1 *zhal* in length:
- From the pit of the neck to the nipple line is 1 *zhal* (12 *sors*)
- From the nipple line to the navel is 1 *zhal* (12 *sors*)
- From the navel to the pubis is 1 *zhal* (12 *sors*)
- Below the pubis is 1 *zhal* (12 *sors*)
- The upper leg is 2 *zhal* (24 *sors*)
- The knee is ⅓ *zhal* (4 *sors*)
- The lower leg is 2 *zhal* (24 *sors*)
- The foot is ⅓ *zhal* (4 *sors*)

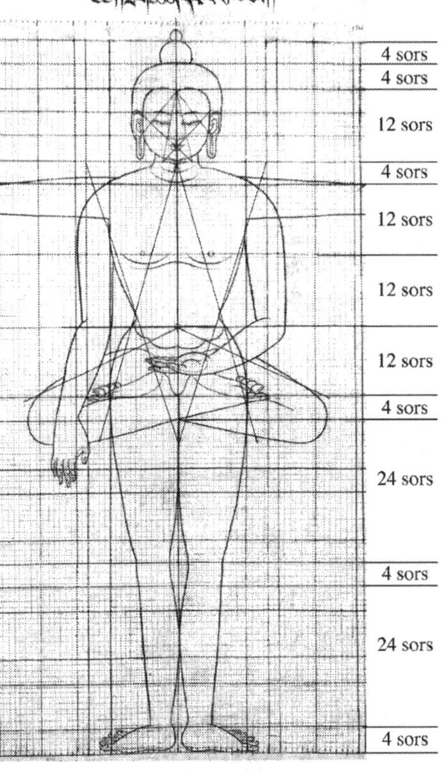

Fig. 5.5 - Peaceful Boddhisattva:
10 *zhal* of 12 *sors* each

From this, we can see that the Tibetan 10 *zhal* (10 face) system is based, fundamentally, on the Hindu *návatāla* (9 face) system of proportion. The chief difference is that the Tibetan system *includes the measures above the hairline* (⅔ *zhal*) and adds an additional ⅓ *zhal* below the pubis to gain the extra *zhal* or face measure. If we leave aside those parts and measure the figure in the Hindu fashion, up to the hairline, then all the parts of the Peaceful Bodhisattva in Buddhism correspond to those of a Deity in Hinduism (not including Brahma, Vishnu and Shiva, who are 10 *tālas* tall): the head is 1 *zhal*, the torso is 3, the upper and lower legs are 2 each, while the neck, knee and foot each make ⅓ of the final *zhal*, for a total of 9.

When we turn to the Seated Bodhisattva (Fig. 5.6), we begin to understand where the additional ⅓ *zhal* below the pubis comes from. In the grid for the Seated Bodhisattva, the proportions above the pubis correspond, part by part, to the Standing Bodhisattva and its homologue, the Hindu *návatāla* figure. Below the pubis, 2 x ⅓ *zhal* have been added for the crossed legs.

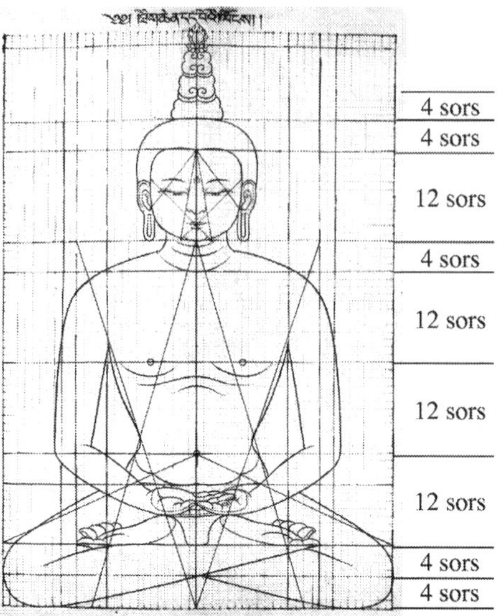

Fig. 5.6 - Seated Boddhisattva: 10 *zhal* of 12 *sors* each

This may seem arbitrary, but when we take the time to measure the entire height of a Seated Bodhisattva, from the top of the head (not including the head protuberance or *uṣṇīṣa*) to the bottom of the folded legs, we arrive at 64 *sor*. This means that the exact halfway point lies at 32 *sor*, which we locate at the nipple line but, symbolically, is the place of the Bodhisattva's heart. In a Seated Bodhisattva, the exact centre of the figure lies at the heart.

From this centre point, the artist extends his compass to draw the aura of compassion around the upper body, just as the aura of enlightenment is drawn from the point atop the hairline to encircle the head. In the composition as a whole, the heart of the Seated Bodhisattva becomes the centre point (meditation point) of the thangka. The number 32, of course, has great symbolic meaning in Buddhism, since the Buddha possessed the 32 'marks of a great man' (*mahāpuruṣa lakṣaṇa*), including slender fingers, arched insteps, long earlobes, a mysterious protuberance on the crown of his head (*uṣṇīṣa*) and a hair whorl or circle on the brow, emitting a ray of light (*ūrṇā*).

When we now turn to the Standing Buddha (Fig. 5.7), we must take into account that he too stands 10 faces tall, but each *zhal* measures 12½ *sors*.

- The head protuberance (*uṣṇīṣa*) is ⅓ *zhal* (4 *sors*)
- The hair is ⅓ *zhal* plus a ½ *sor* (4½ *sors*)
- The face is 1 *zhal* plus a ½ *sor* (12½ *sors*)
- The neck is ⅓ *zhal* (4 *sors*)
- The trunk is divided into 3 equal parts, each 1 *zhal* in length:
- From the pit of the neck to the nipple line is 1 *zhal* plus a ½ *sor* (12½ *sors*)
- From the nipple line to the navel is 1 *zhal* plus a ½ *sor* (12½ *sors*)
- From the navel to the genitals is 1 *zhal* plus a ½ *sor* (12½ *sors*)
- The upper leg is 2 *zhal* plus a 2 x ½ *sor* (25 *sors*)
- The knee is ⅓ *zhal* (4 *sors*)
- The lower leg is 2 *zhal* plus a 2 x ½ *sor* (25 *sors*)
- The foot is ⅓ *zhal* plus a ½ *sor* (4½ *sors*)

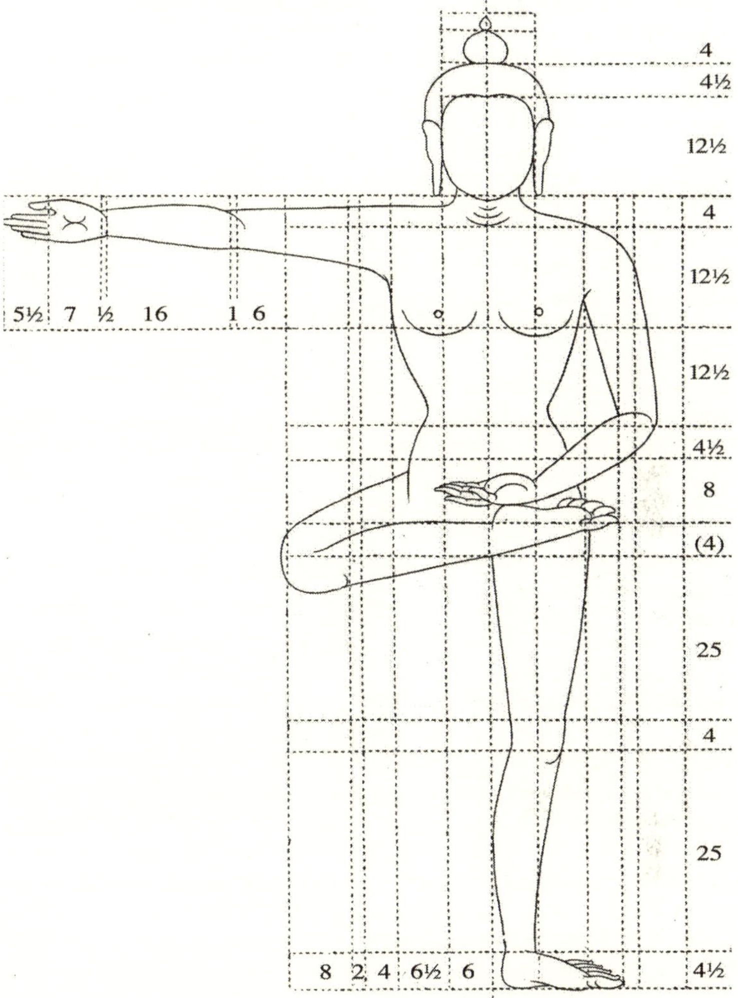

Fig. 5.7 - Standing Buddha:
10 *zhal* of 12½ *sors* each

In essence, not much has changed. Like the Bodhisattva, the Buddha includes two parts above the hairline (4 + 4½ sors) and adds an additional 4 *sors* below the pubis to gain the extra *zhal* or face measure of 12½ *sors*, giving the 10-head measure. If we leave aside those parts and measure the figure up to the hairline, then the Buddha also follows the *návatāla* (9 face) system of proportion for Hindu deities. But, in the standing Buddha, an extra ½ *sor* is added to the head, torso (3x), upper leg (2x), lower leg (2x) and foot, increasing the overall height to 125 *sors*.

The Buddha's face is basically divided into three, using the nose-length as the module of 4 *sors*. So the brow, from the tip of the hairline to the hair whorl (*ūrṇā*) is 4 *sors*, the nose from the hair whorl (*ūrṇā*) to the tip is another 4 *sors*, and the mouth from the tip of the nose to the chin is also 4 *sors*. This three-part division of the face is known to craftsmen from both the East and the West.

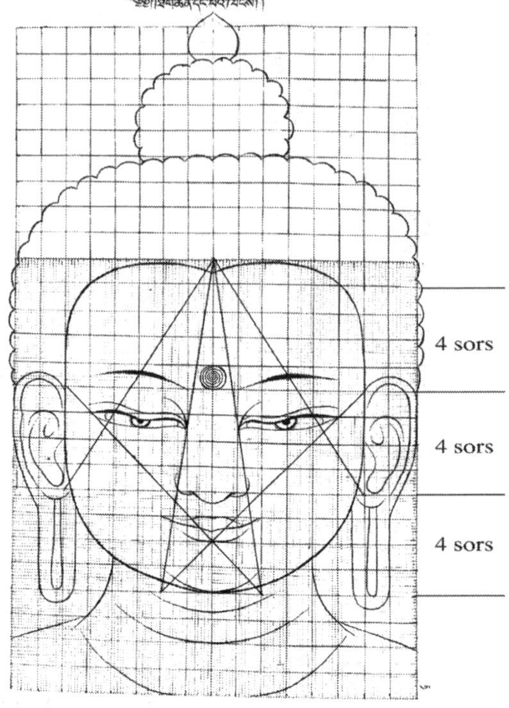

Fig. 5.8 - Face Proportions of the Buddha

The gaze in the eyes expresses 'the fourth level of *dhyana* or meditative stability'. The lower eyelid lies above the line which cuts the face in half. Hence, the eyes are almost exactly halfway up the face. The hair, from the hairline to the top of the head, adds 4½ *sors* above the hairline (just as the neck adds 4½ *sors* below the chin). This means that, from the top of the head (not including the cranial protuberance or hair knot) to the bottom of the chin, the hair whorl (*ūrṇā*) appears at the exact centre of the head, both horizontally and vertically. If the *ūrṇā* is interpreted as the place of the third eye, then this point becomes the main focal point for meditation upon the face.

In sculpture, the *ūrṇā* also often becomes the centre point for the halo, though in thangkas, it is the indented tip of the hair that becomes, instead, the compass point for drawing the *prabhà* or halo. This point is also used to draw a series of diagonals that aid determine the outer limits of the eyes and nose.

V. Byzantine Proportions

In the West, the Hieratic Style has manifest itself most clearly in Byzantine icons and Gothic sculpture. In the case of Byzantine icons, our main source for their Sacred Codes is the *Hermeneia* or *Painter's Manual* of Dionysius of Fournos. Dionysius was an 18th century icon painter trained at Mount Athos who compiled much of his knowledge into one treatise, citing previous painters like Panselinos, while offering traditional recipes, painters' methods and – of greater interest here – a system of proportion.

He begins his treatise with advice to the novice on finding a master, and the spiritual practices which a good icon painter should carry out devotedly. To the novice, he writes:

"Know therefore, diligent student, that when you wish to undertake this science, you must look for and find a learned master, whom you will soon wish to surpass in some respects if he teaches you clearly... If you only find one who is unlearned and unskilful, do as we did and see if you can find some original works by Manuel Panselinos and copy them at any opportunity, drawing them... until you master the forms and proportions of the original. Then go into the churches that he has painted and make copies... Only do not just carry out the work haphazardly, but with the fear of God and with the veneration due to a sacred task."[24]

In another passage, Dionysius describes the novice's initiation into the painterly brotherhood, addressing his readers as 'my friends and fellow-artists in Christ':

"He who wishes to learn the science of painting, let him first be brought to it by carrying out preliminary training for a set period only, just drawing without proportions, so that he may show his worth. Then let there be a prayer on his behalf to the Lord Jesus Christ, and supplication before the icon of the Mother of God Hodegetria. When the priest gives the blessing... he should mark his head and say aloud:

"...Lord Jesus Christ our God, uncircumscribed in your divine nature, having become inexpressibly incarnate for the salvation of man... who, having imprinted the sacred character of thy immaculate face on the holy veil... [may you] *enlighten and bring wisdom to the soul and heart and mind of thy servant, and direct these hands for the irreproachable and excellent depiction of the form of thy person.*

"...After the prayer he should lay in the proportions and characteristics of the figures exactly, and draw them thenceforth in such a manner, copying them often with any calculations that are necessary; with the help of God, if he wishes to he will learn very well."[25]

Since walls were painted in fresco, artists had to work fast and make measures in the most expedient way. The principle tool for measuring was the compass:

How to draw when you are working on a wall:

When you want to draw on a wall, first level the surface and then attach pieces of wood to the legs of a pair of metal compasses, to make them as long as you want, and tie a brush to one end so that you can mark with colour the proportions of the figure and describe their haloes. When you have marked the proportions of the figure, take some ochre and draw first with a watery solution.[26]

As Dionysius notes, the compass was used to *"mark with colour the proportions of the figure and describe their haloes."* The halo, as we shall see, was an important module for measuring out large surfaces, while the length of the nose, as described in the passage below, was the typical unit of measure for small surfaces.

It is likely that the measures described here were made with a compass. Dionysius writes:

Explanation of the proportions of the human figure:

[Proportion of the whole figure:] *Learn, O pupil, that in the whole figure of a man there are nine faces, that is to say nine measures, from the forehead to the soles of the feet.*

[Proportion of the face:] *First make the first face, which you divide into three, making the first division the forehead, the second the nose and the third the beard. Draw the hair above the face to the height of one nose-length; again measure into thirds the distance between the beard and the nose; the chin takes up two of the divisions and the mouth one, while the throat is one nose-length.*

[Measuring the length of the figure:] *Next divide from the chin to the middle of the body into three* [face] *measures, and from there to the knees two more* [face-measures]*; for each knee you take one nose-length. Take again two more* [face] *measures to the ankle bones, and from them to the soles of the feet one more nose-length, and from there to the toe nails one more measure.*

[Measuring the width of the figure:] *From the pit of the throat to the shoulder is one measure, and likewise to the other shoulder. For the thickness of the upper arm, take one nose-length and measure to the elbow from above one measure, and again one more to the base of the hand; from there to the fingertips is one more measure.*

[Measuring the facial features:] *Both the eyes are equal and the distance separating them is equal to one eye. When the head is in profile the nose and the ear are the length of two eyes apart, and when it is full face you put them one eye's length apart; the ear should be equal to the nose.*

[Measuring the width of the figure:] *When a man is naked his waist should be four nose-lengths across, and when he is clothed, one and a half faces.*[27]

By comparing this text to Fig. 5.9, we may gain a fairly clear vision of Byzantine proportion. Basically, the nose-measure is one third of the face-measure. In total, the figure is nine faces tall (from the forehead to the feet):

- (The head above the hairline is 1 extra nose-length)
- The face is 1 face-measure (divided in 3 nose-lengths)
- The neck is ⅓ of a face-measure (= 1 nose-length)
- The torso is 3 face-measures
- The upper leg is 2 face-measures
- The knee is ⅓ of a face-measure (= 1 nose-length)
- The lower leg is 2 face-measures
- The foot is ⅓ of a face-measure (= 1 nose-length)
- (The toes are 1 extra nose-length)

To summarize: the face is 1 face-measure, the torso is 3, the upper and lower legs are 2 each, while the neck, knee and foot each make ⅓ of the final face-measure for a total of 9.

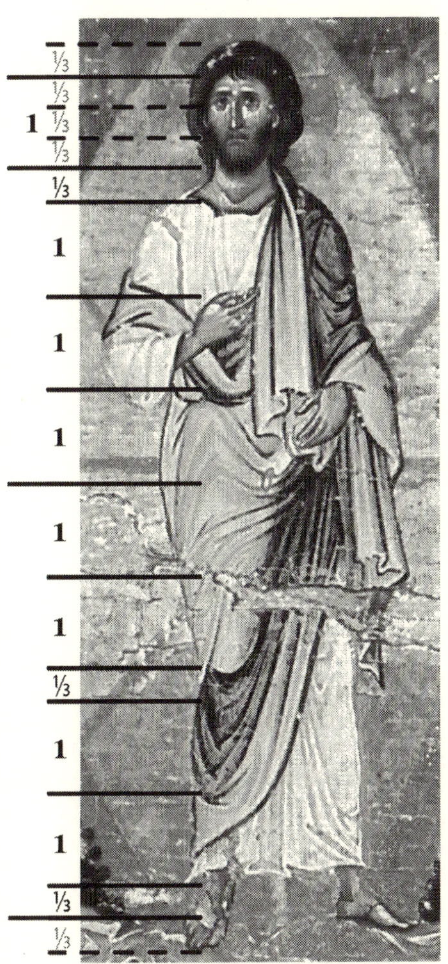

Fig. 5.9 - Byzantine 9-Face Proportion

Note that the Byzantines, like the Egyptians and Hindus, measured the figure *to the forehead.* It is the face, and not the head, which offers the 9:1 ratio. As well, the Byzantines used the nose-length, in the same manner of the Egyptians (and Hindus), as the module for the face in its 3:1 ratio.

It is quite stunning to realize that the 9-face Byzantine proportion is basically identical to the Hindu *návatāla* system, which itself lies at the root of the Tibetan proportional classes for Buddhas and Bodhisattvas (when these are measured from the hairline down).

The numbers underlying the Byzantine proportional system are also highly symbolic. In his 4th century treatise *On the Celestial Hierarchies*, Dionysius the Areopagite wrote that nine orders of angels surround the Godhead. These nine types of angels (seraphim, cherubim, etc) are divided into three categories (contemplative, potential and active), each category containing three kinds of angel.

In this way, the Trinity of the Godhead (three-in-one) expands into nine (a trinity of trinities) with no loss of unity. Similarly, the numbers three and nine underlie the proportions of Christ, to show that the parts, both in the face and figure, form a trinity of trinities, and hence, a harmonious and unified whole.

Many Byzantine figures are indeed nine faces in height. But, to reflect their transcendent aspect, other figures were stylistically elongated to ten or even twelve faces. This is the case with Christ in Theophanes the Greek's *Transfiguration*, whose elongated figure appears twelve faces tall.

VI. Byzantine Proportions of the Face

Dionysius of Fournos clearly divided the face into three, using the nose-length as his module. The most expedient way for an artist to measure out the nose-length and transfer it, was to use a compass. Placing his compass at the centre of the face, the artist drew, not one, but three concentric circles.

In *l'Icône: image de l'invisible,* Egon Sendler explains this 'system of the three circles':

"For the proportions of the face and its details, the Byzantine iconographer used a module which always corresponded to the length of the nose. Thus, the head was inscribed in two circles, with the halo often determined by a third. The centre of these circles was situated at the root of the nose, between the eyes. Most likely, this explains why that particular part of the nose was modelled so uniquely in Byzantine art."[28]

A close look at Byzantine art does indeed show a small semi-circular dip between the eyebrows, marking a ridge near the top of the nose. Taking the *Christos Acheiropooietos* ('The Image Not Made By Human Hands' - Fig. 5.10) as our example, we can see that the point of the compass was placed between the eyebrows to draw a circle from the tip of the nose, around to the hairline, then back down.

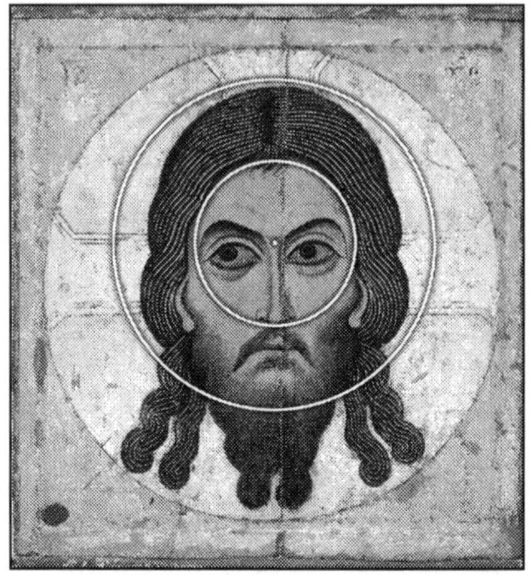

Fig. 5.10 - *The Christos Acheiropoietos*
Novgorod Icon, 12th century

Next, moving the sharp point of the compass to the tip of the nose, the icon-painter drew a short arc at the chin, thus marking the next circle. Expanding his compass and returning the sharp point to the centre of the eyebrows, he drew the second, larger circle, from the chin round to the top of the head and back again, encompassing the hair in its circumference. This explains why so many Byzantine figures have rounded coiffures or, in the case of the Virgin, a rounded hood.

Following Dionysius' rule of proportion, the face was *three nose-lengths in height*. Each radius of the inner circle marked out the first 2 measures, from the top of the nose to its tip (1 measure), and from the top of the nose to the hairline (1 measure). Then, with the outer circle, the third measure was added, from the tip of the nose to the chin.

To mark the halo, a third, larger circle was drawn, using the nose-length as the module. In the icon of St. Florian of Lorch from the Convent of Nonnberg (Austria, 12th century - Fig. 5.11), the centre was drawn lower down, but the three circles can still be clearly seen. Sometimes, as much as two or three nose-lengths were used to mark out the placement of the halo. This halo, as we shall see,

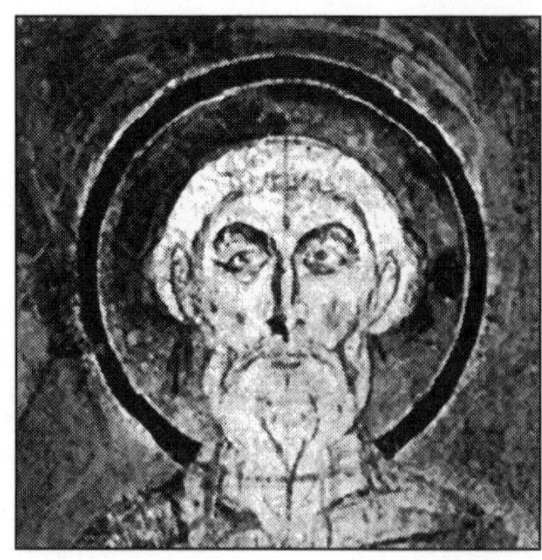

Fig. 5.11 - *St. Florian of Lorch* - 12th c.

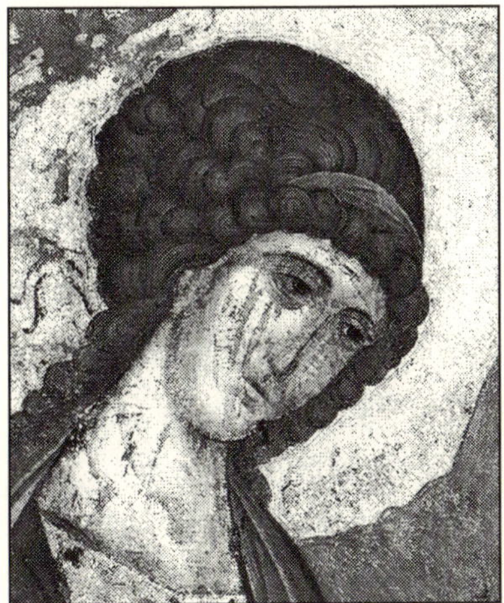

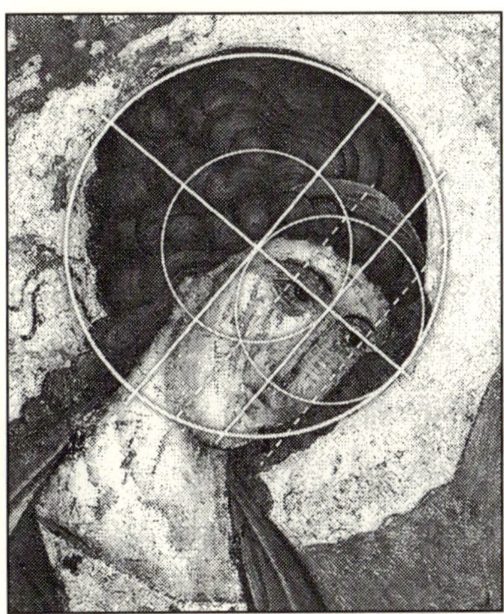

Fig. 5.12 - Andrei Rublev: *The Archangel Michael*, c. 1407

became a new module for measuring out the length of the figure, as well as determining the placement of figures in a composition.

The harmonic armature of three concentric circles worked well when the face was depicted in the full frontal position. But related systems had to be developed when dealing with the face in profile and a three-quarter angle. *"The profile,"* Sendler tells us, *"is rare and awkwardly drawn. It signifies that the figure is of lesser importance, if not downright evil. In icons of The Last Supper, the representation of the figure in profile is striking... Only Judas is represented in profile, since the profile violates the circle, destroying its perfection."*[29] Contrast this to Egyptian and Babylonian art, where the profile was a mark of holiness and the Hieratic Style...

For the face at a three-quarter angle, Byzantine artists developed many fascinating methods for its representation. As with perspective, it was never in their interest to develop a schema that accurately reflected the natural world in three dimensions. Instead, they came up with various planimetric constructions for displacing the circles.

For his explanation, Sendler found examples in two of the finest Byzantine icons. The first is *The Archangel Michael* by Andrei Rublev, painted around 1407. The other is *Our Lady of the Don* painted by Theophanes the Greek at the end of the 14th century. In both cases, we can see that the three-quarter angle is obtained by a variation on the three circle process.

As per tradition, the first circle was drawn by placing the sharp end of the compass between the eyebrows, thus drawing a circle from the tip of the nose up and around to the hairline then back down (an arc marked in Rublev's Archangel by the hairband).

After drawing a descending diagonal, another circle of the same dimensions was drawn, using the circumference of the first as the centre of the second (the *vesica piscis*). This displaced second circle became the new centre for the head, now viewed at the three-quarter angle.

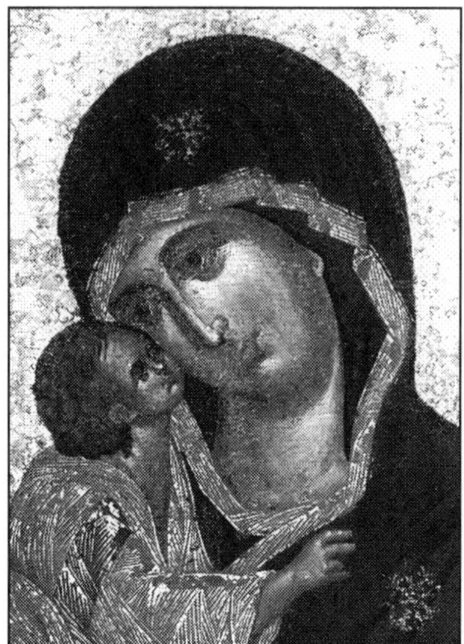

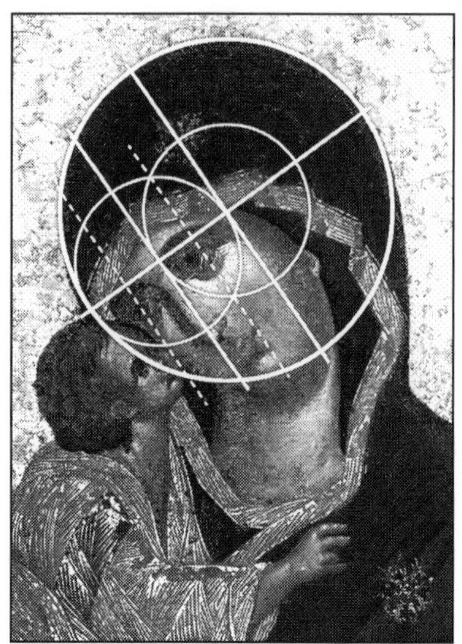

Fig. 5.13 - Theophanes the Greek: *Our Lady of the Don*, late 14th century

After this intermediary step, the artist returned to his usual procedure. Still using the nose-length as the module, a larger circle was drawn to define the limits of the chin, round to the top of the head, including the coiffure or Virgin's hood. In our examples, the archangel's hair and virgin's hood follow these lines perfectly, giving these masterworks their hieratic quality.

Hence, through the system of the three circles, invisible lines were traced out that served as guides for the visible contours. This allowed artists to render the figure in the uniquely Hieratic style of the Byzantine empire. The hieratic nature of this style is indicated *by the use of the circle* – that simple, perfect shape which brings into harmony all the random shapes contained within its limit. More than that, the Byzantine artists chose, as the centre of the circle, the point just above the eyebrows – known in wisdom traditions from east to west as the third eye – the Eye of the Divine.

All of these Sacred Codes gave the Byzantine face its distinct Hieratic Style. But, as Sendler laments, *"The schema of the three circles was used in many icons to design the face, up until the beginning of the 18th century. Afterward, this schema seems to have been lost. Instead, the naturalist influence of Western art came to dominate."*[30]

VII. Byzantine Proportions of the Figure

A close examination of Byzantine frescoes has shed some interesting light on the artists' working methods.[31] After inscribing the halo in the plaster, a vertical axis was marked with a cord or rope, impressing its length in the still-wet stucco. This vertical line, as we will see later, finds its equivalent in the West *in the plumb line* – that invisible line of balance which gives the figure stasis and movement.

In his *Painter's Manual*, Dionysius of Fournos mentions the use of the compass and cord, but here used for icon painting rather than stuccoed frescoes:

How to put haloes on icons:

When you draw a figure on an icon, put in the halo with a pair of compasses, and apply gesso to the area as when you first prepared the panel: take a cotton thread dipped in gesso so that it is full of it, and put it round the halo on the mark made by the compasses.[32]

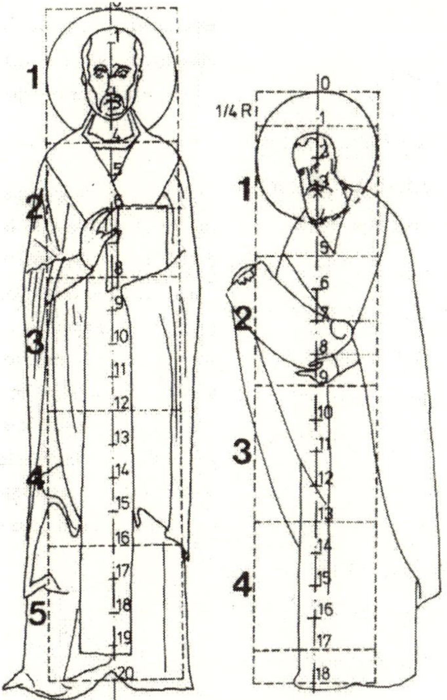

Fig. 5.14 - Left: 5 halo measures
Right: 4 haloes plus 2 x ¼ measure

In a passage cited earlier, Dionysius told his apprentices to take up their compass and mark "*the proportions of the figure and describe their haloes.*" In his study, *The Art of Harmony: Principles of Measuring and Proportioning in Byzantine Wall Painting*, Vladimir Mako demonstrates that the halo, when used as the module, determines both the proportion of figures and their harmonious placement in Byzantine compositions.

This is particularly true of large-scale compositions, where the fresco may take up the entire wall of a church. In this case, the smaller module of the nose-length was increased to the larger module of the halo.

After measuring numerous examples, Mako determined that the halo was circumscribed by a square then subdivided into four horizontal parts, which were marked along the length of the figure. This series of larger and smaller measures harmoniously subdivided the figure, allowing for the precise placement of its various features.

Typically, the figure stood 4 or 5 haloes tall, while the second square down from the top marked out the line for the bend in the elbows. Here, a forearm could be raised in a specific holy gesture or hold a book against the chest. Lower squares marked out the lengths of the sleeves or the folds in drapery, thus indicating the knees and feet.

In this way, the squared circle of the halo, measured down the vertical axis 'to mark the proportions' (Dionysius) gave the figure a constant linear rhythm, descending its entire length. A half or quarter of the square could then be added to the left or right to give the figure a harmonious width.

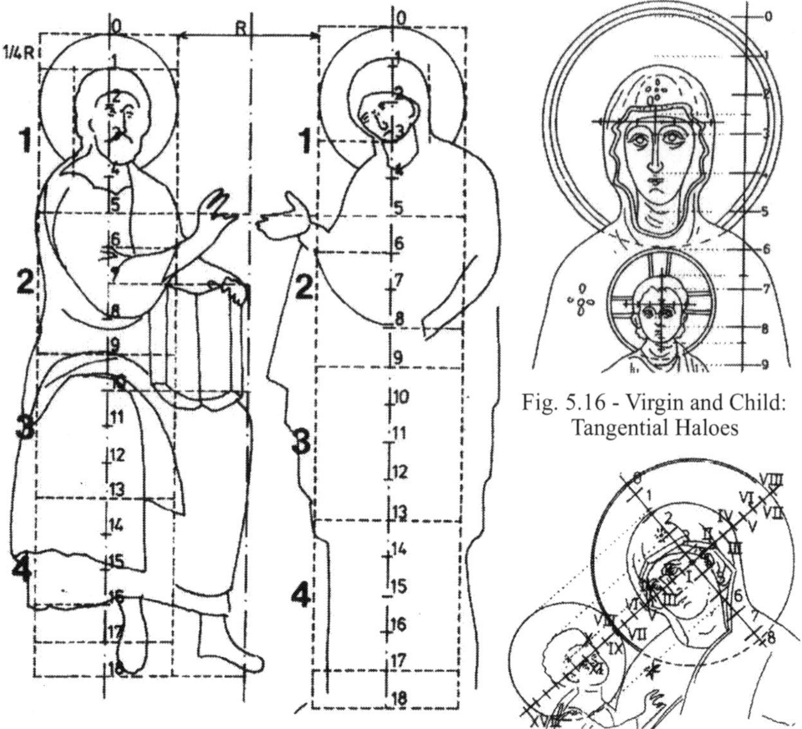

Fig. 5.15 - Christ and the Virgin: 1 Halo Measure apart

Fig. 5.16 - Virgin and Child: Tangential Haloes

Fig. 5.17 - Virgin and Child: Tangential Haloes

What is more, the distance between two figures, such as Christ and the Virgin (Fig. 5.15), would be determined by their haloes. Either they stood half a halo measure or a full halo measure apart. Or, in the case of the Virgin and Christ Child (Figs. 5.16 and 5.17), their haloes touched at the circumference, forming tangential circles.

More fascinating still is the case of the Virgin cradling the lifeless Christ, deposed from the cross. Through deep compassion, their haloes have intermingled so that the centre of his lies on the circumference of hers and *vice versa*, thus forming the *vesica piscis*.

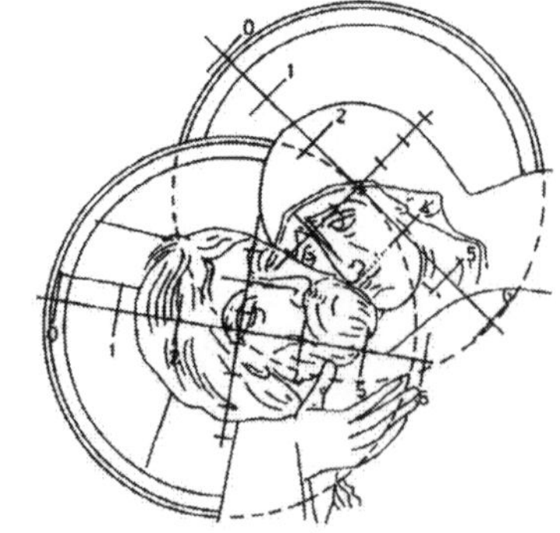

Fig. 5.18 - Virgin and Deposed Christ: Intersecting Haloes

As a nimbus of light, the halo manifests that circular prism which expands in our field of vision when light pierces through a crack in the darkness. From the rainbow body of the Buddha to the aura of the transfigured Christ, the halo has always reminded us that we are in the presence of a luminous being.

But the halo is more than just a symbol. Its circular aspect lends visual perfection to every feature delineated within its bound. In Byzantine compositions, this measure of perfection extends, linearly and horizontally, in every direction to harmonize the figures as a whole. Through these Sacred Codes, the Byzantine artists eventually developed entire compositions based on Hieratic principles, harmonically uniting the smallest features of the face with the entire length and breadth of the holy basilica.

VIII. Gothic Proportions of the Face

Little is known about Villard de Honnecourt. But his sketchbook offers tantalizing speculations into the life and wanderings of this Mediaeval craftsman. Born around 1200 in the Picardy region of northern France, he was most likely an architect or stone mason. Page after page of his notebooks reveal a fascination for the geometry underlying sculpted figures, ornaments, towers and tombs. In his journeys through France and Switzerland he drew the maze at Chartres, the rose-window at Lausanne; the towers of Laon and the traceries of Reims. Nothing eluded his observation and imagination: basilisks, boars, eagles and insects – he drew them all, including a lion *"drawn from life."* (pl. 47).

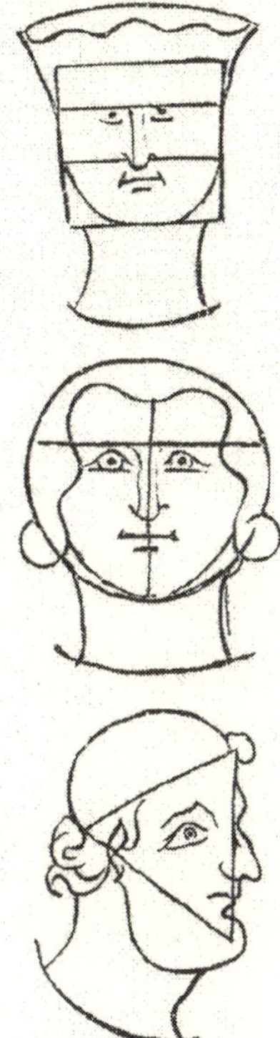

Fig. 5.19 - Villard de Honnecourt: Proportions of the Face

The thirty-three parchment pages of *The Medieval Sketchbook of Villard de Honnecourt*[34] offer a rare glimpse into the thoughts and working methods of a Gothic artisan. Of particular interest to us are plates 34 to 37, which form a thematic unit. At the bottom of the page showing the proportions of the face, he writes, *"Here begins the method of representation as taught by the art of geometry, to facilitate the work."* (pl. 35) And on the last page of this series, he adds, *"On these four pages are figures of the art of geometry, but to understand them one must be careful to learn the particular use of each."* (pl .37)

The page on facial proportions (Pl. 35 - see Fig. 5.19) shows how the square, circle and triangle add grace and perfection to a human face. The square, divided thrice horizontally, gives the three proportions already determined by the Byzantines: from the top of the nose to its tip (as the middle measure), with the same distance again to the hairline (the upper measure), and once more to the chin (the lower measure). As with the Byzantines, *the hairline* forms the uppermost measure.

The face in the circle, by contrast, stresses the symmetry of the two halves, while the triangle is prominent in the profile. It is no co-incidence that Honnecourt chose these three basic shapes, since all constructions *ad quadratum* (from the square) and *ad triangulum* (from the triangle) originate in the circle, as the two major modes taught to Mediaeval masons. Not just sculptures, but entire cathedrals were built from these Euclidean postulates, which engendered two specific grid patterns (which we will pursue in detail in Ch. 13). In plate 27 of his Sketchbook, for example, Honnecourt designed the ground plan of a cruciform church using the *ad quadratum* method (Fig. 14.25).

As we can see in plate 37 (Fig. 5.20), the same grid of orthogonals and diagonals, usually used in architectural planning, appears here to design the face. Villard is exploring the relationship of the parts to the whole. Once more, the basic three-part division of the face is used, but now he has added diagonals to determine the placement of the eyes and nose, while a fourth square a the top and two on the sides to define the coiffure.

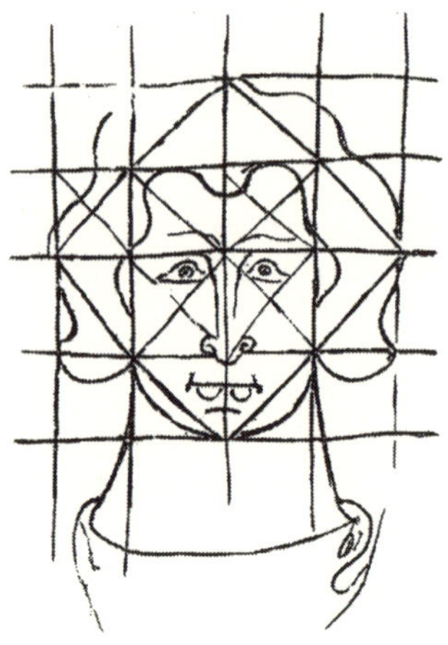

Fig. 5.20 - Villard de Honnecourt: Proportions of the Face *Ad Quadratum*

IX. Gothic Proportions of the Figure

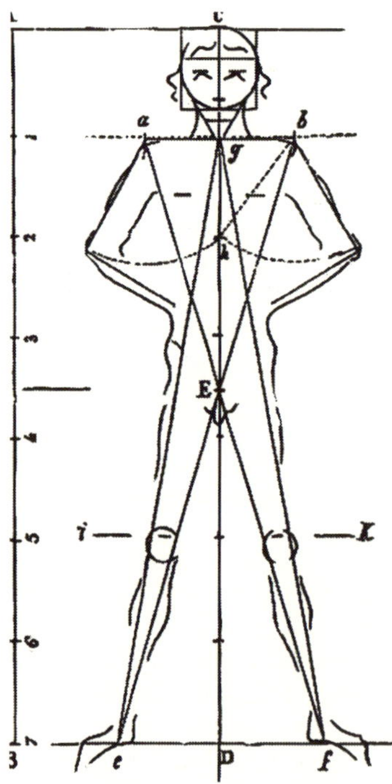

Fig. 5.21 - Viollet-le-Duc: Gothic Proportions of the Figure based on Villard de Honnecourt

Honnecourt also drew the figure as a whole (Fig. 5.21), and gave an intriguing geometrical schema for determining the placement of the limbs. In the pages nearby, he demonstrated how this underlying armature shifts with the figure's pose, transferring the balance of its weight and force (Fig. 5.22). While these drawings offer no clear measure of the figure, Eugène Viollet-le-Duc used Honnecourt's sketches to determine anew the lost Canon of Mediaeval proportion.

During the Gothic Revival of the 19th century, Viollet-le-Duc headed many of the most important restorations to abbeys and cathedrals, which lay in desolate ruin after the French Revolution. Among others, he restored the Basilica of Saint-Denis (this first truly Gothic church), the Basilica of Mary Magdalene at Vézelay and Notre Dame de Paris (adding the famous spire between its two towers).

His knowledge of Gothic architecture was profound, and he actively 're-created' (rather than restored) many statues now found on the facades of these famous buildings.

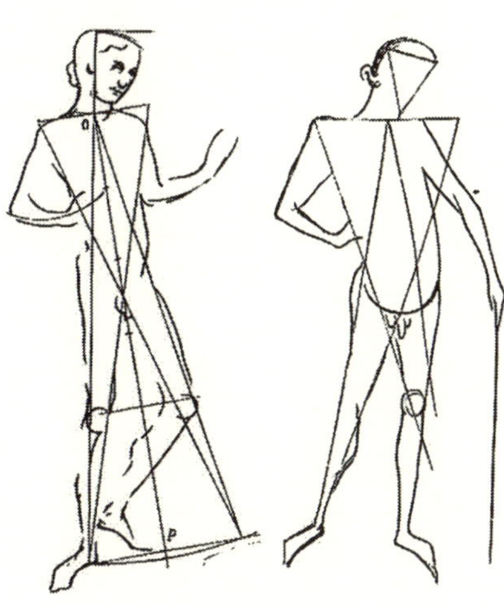

Fig. 5.22 - Viollet-le-Duc: Balance and Movement of the Figure based on Villard de Honnecourt

In his article on 'Sculpture' for the *Dictionnaire raisonné de l'architecture française du XIe au XVIe siècle* (Dictionary of French Architecture from 11th to 16th Century) he published his lost Canon of Medieval proportions, based on Honnecourt's sketch:

"By comparing the tracings of this figure with those found in manuscripts, stained glass, bas-reliefs and statues, we are able to recognize how this geometrical schema gave to figures of the 13th and 14th centuries, not only their proportion, but also the graceful accuracy of their gestures and movements... This canon of proportions, roughly sketched by Villard, has been clarified using the best possible statues, particularly those within the western facade of Reims cathedral."[35]

Viollet-le-Duc then goes on to explain how the human figure (see Fig. 5.21) stands 7 measures high, the module of that measure being the head and neck. Below this point is Honnecourt's geometric schema, based on 2 inverted triangles (*afg* and *beg*) which cross along the axial vertical (CD) at E. This midpoint of the axial vertical (E) lies at the pubis, which is 3½ measures above the feet and below the top of the head.

The two inverted triangles begin at the shoulder line (*ab*) which is two-ninths of the total height. The axial vertical (CD) crosses the shoulder line (*ab*) at its midpoint (*g*), which is located at the pit of the neck. *"Having established the basic shapes of the canon,"* Viollet-le-Duc wrote, *"we may see how the sculptors* [*imagiers*] *gave movement to the figures."*[36]

In a new diagram based on Honnecourt (Fig. 5.22), he demonstrates what happens when the figure transfers its weight to the left. The *b-e* diagonal of triangle *beg* now becomes the *new* axial vertical, while the old axial vertical (CD) becomes a diagonal descending *to the right*. Hence, the shoulders and torso follow this shift in balance, as the shoulder line (*ab*) tilts down to the left and up to the right. The head, to maintain balance, nods to the right.

We have in this example the first indications of that *contrapposto* movement which would become the hallmark of the Italian Renaissance, though scholars tend to refer to it by the French word *torsion* to distinguish it from the later Italian 'twist' (see for example Roland Recht's 'Torsion et hanchement dans la sculpture gothique'). In its roots, Gothic sculpture owes much to Byzantine painting (from whence it obtained its Hieratic qualities), while also absorbing Humanist qualities from the Classical Greek canon by way of Romanesque sculpture.

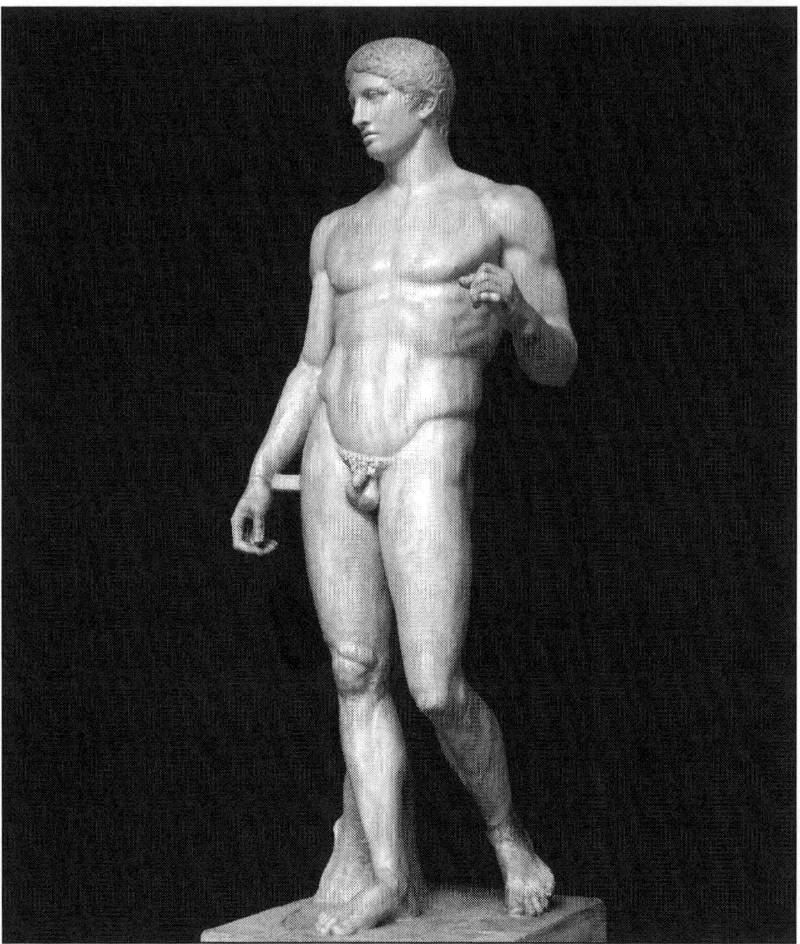

Fig. 6.1 - Polykleitos: *The Doryphoros* or *Spear Bearer,* 440 BCE (Roman copy)

Viollet-le-Duc was all-too-aware of this Humanist and Hieratic distinction when we wrote:

"Sculpture in antiquity proceeds from two different principles, which create two different types on the whole. First of all there is hieratic sculpture, and then there is that type of sculpture which takes, as its starting point, the imitation of nature. This type tends to develop, rise to a certain height, then descend so far into realism that it becomes decadent. The peoples of the East, such as India, Asia Minor and Egypt, practiced the first type of sculpture, which continually preserved its sacred forms. It was only the ancient Greeks who practiced that annoying second type, beginning with models from the earlier civilizations and, through their precise observation of nature, gradually progressed in the direction of absolute beauty."[37]

With this distinction in mind, we may now consider Proportion from the Humanist perspective, following its development from Classical times to the Renaissance.

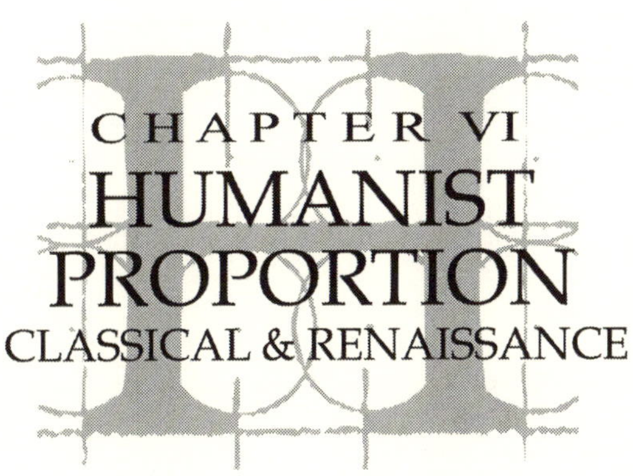

CHAPTER VI HUMANIST PROPORTION CLASSICAL & RENAISSANCE

I. The Doryphoros

For the greater part of Western history, the Canon of Polykleitos has held sway over all discussions of beauty and proportion. 'The Canon' was both a text and a sculpture that demonstrated the aesthetic theory of Polykleitos, a 4th century BCE sculptor whose works, like the Disc Bearer and the Spear Bearer, exemplified the Classical Greek style at its height. Alas, both the text and its accompanying sculpture, created around 440 BCE, have been lost for the greater part of two thousand years.

However, tantalizing fragments of Polykleitos' original text were preserved by later writers like Galen, Lucian and Plutarch. Meanwhile, even though the original bronze sculpture was lost, a Roman copy (Fig. 6.1) was found in Herculaneum and conserved at the Archaeological Museum in Naples. But, it was not identified as a copy of Polykleitos' famous statue until 1863.

Since then, the *Doryphoros* or Spear Bearer has generated a lot of scholarly debate concerning the actual proportions developed by Polykleitos in his Canon. What the surviving texts reveal, first and foremost, is that Polykleitos used a part of the body as a module which, through a common ratio progression, developed the harmonious proportions of the parts to the whole.

Galen writes:

"But beauty [resides...] *in the proper proportion* [*symmetria*] *of the parts, such as for example that of finger to finger and all these to the palm and base of hand, of those to the forearm, of the forearm to the upper arm and of everything to everything else, just as described in the Canon of Polykleitos. For having taught us in that work all the proportions of the body, Polykleitos supported his treatise with a work of art, making a statue according to the tenets of the treatise and calling it, like the treatise itself, the Canon. So then, all philosophers and doctors accept that beauty resides in the due proportion of the parts of the body."*[1]

When considering the proportion of a statue, we must begin with the module, the first unit of measure, which is continually multiplied to measure out larger and larger parts of the body, until we reach the height of a man as a whole. This is the proper meaning of *symmetria*, which is often translated as 'proportion' but better translated as 'the commensurability of parts to the whole'.

According to Euclid, a *ratio* (Gr. *logos*) is the relation of one measure to another, such as 1:2. So, if we take the hand as the module of measure, and then discover that the forearm is 2 times the length of the hand, we say that they possess a 1:2 ratio.

A *proportion* (Gr. *analogia*) is a *comparison of two ratios* that share a common term. So, in the case of 1:2 = 2:4, the 2 is the 'common mean' which allows for a comparison between the 'extremes' of 1 and 4. As we shall see in our chapters on Composition, there are different types of mean, such as the arithmetic, geometric or harmonic mean.

In the case of the geometric mean, the ratios on either side may be reduced to the same fraction. So, in the proportion 1:2 = 2:4, the right side may be divided by 2, to show that it also equals 1:2. To increase the magnitude on the right side, the ratio on the left side was simply multiplied by 2.

This multiplication creates a geometric *progression*, where each number in the series is multiplied by a constant value. The geometric proportion 1:2 = 2:4 generates a geometric series that begins with 1, 2, 4, and progresses indefinitely, as the series 1, 2, 4, 8, 16, 32... Each successive term is calculated by multiplying the previous term by a constant value which, in this case, is 2.

Returning to the hand and forearm, we may expand the ratio into a proportion by examining the upper arm. In a geometric proportion, the three parts are related as 1:2 = 2:4, which may be simplified to 1:2:4. Now the forearm is twice the length of the hand, and the upper arm is twice the length of the forearm. The *measures* have grown larger, but the ratio has remained the same. All these comparisons are based on the *first* measure, the hand, which is the module.

As Gregory V. Leftwich has noted in his paper, 'Polykleitos and Hippokratic Medicine': *"Important scholars have suggested that the famous proportions of the Canon followed a modular system, a fractional system, an arithmetic mean, a geometric mean and the golden section."*[2] Alas, Polykleitos could have used any of these means to establish his proportional systems. It all depends on what part of the body we establish as the module, what other part we compare it to (for the ratio), and how we create a progression (for the proportion).

One way to create a geometric progression is to use root rectangles (which we shall encounter in depth in our chapter on Dynamic Composition). To make a root rectangle (see Fig. 6.2), we begin with a square, then draw a diagonal with a straight edge, and use a compass to transfer the length of the diagonal down to the base of the square. The new rectangle that results is called a root rectangle, because the ratio of its shorter side to its longer side is $1:\sqrt{2}$. (As we shall see later, there is also a $\sqrt{3}$ rectangle, $\sqrt{4}$ rectangle, $\sqrt{5}$ rectangle, and so on).

Root rectangles have the unique property of recursiveness. This means that, in the case of the √2 rectangle, two smaller √2 rectangles may be inscribed within it, and two more within those, and so on, for infinity. In this way, the √2 rectangle creates a geometric series, based on the ratio of 1:√2 (which, arithmetically, produces the irrational number ratio of 1 : 1.41421..., rounded off to 1 : 1.5). It is possible that Polykleitos used a root rectangle progression in his Canon.

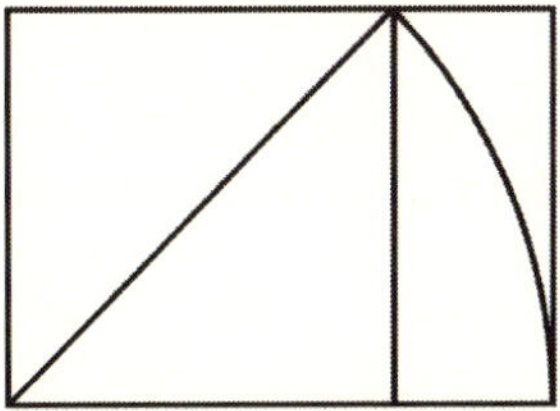

Fig. 6.2 - Construction of a Root 2 Rectangle

But, another rectangle with recursive properties is the Golden Rectangle. It is created in a way similar to root rectangles (see Fig. 6.3), except we first bisect the square and then draw the diagonal from *the midpoint* of the base up to the corner. Using a compass, we transfer the length of this diagonal down to the base. The resulting Golden Rectangle produces the Golden Mean, a ratio of the shorter side to the longer side expressed as 1:ϕ (or 'phi' – named in honour of the Greek sculptor Phidias, who is said to have used the Golden Mean in his works).

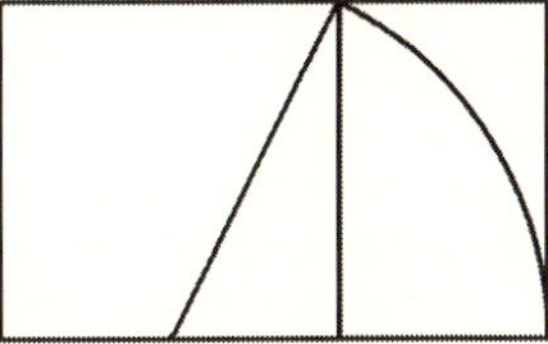

Fig. 6.3 - Construction of a Golden Rectangle

'Phi' is an irrational number: 1.6180339887498948482... so the Golden Mean is often shortened to 1 : 1.6. When we inscribe a square in the Golden Rectangle, a smaller Golden Rectangle results – and so on, *ad infinitum*. This recursive property generates a series of proportions which Polykleitos may have also used in his Canon.

II. The Canon of Polykleitos as the Root Two Square

In 1975, Richard Tobin measured out the Doryphorus through a root rectangle progression, which he described in his article '*The Canon of Polykleitos*'[3] for *The American Journal of Archaeology*. Tobin began by constructing a theoretical canon, using the third phalange of the little finger as the smallest unit of measure. After drawing a square around this part, he followed the procedure for creating a √2 rectangle (arcing the diagonal to the base) except the new resulting shape was made into another square rather than a rectangle (Fig. 6.4).

Thus, a geometric progression of squares was created, using as their ratio 1 : √2. To measure out the proportions on a statue, Tobin came up with the expedient method of the knotted cord. Once the sculptor worked out the simple geometrical construction on paper, he could knot a cord at each point in the √2 progression, and use it as a plumb line or measuring device while sculpting (Fig. 6.4).

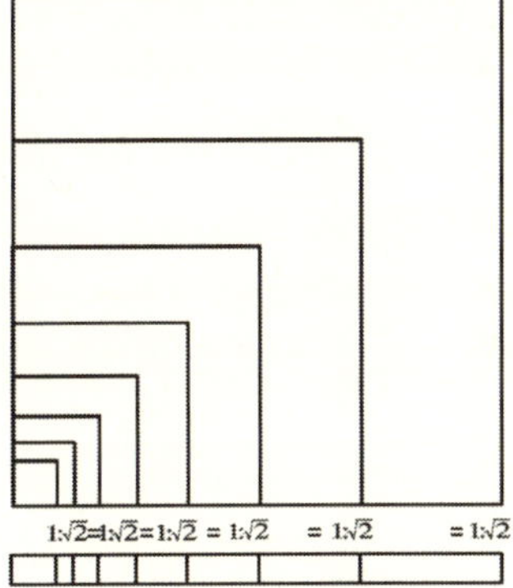

Fig. 6.4 - Root 2 Progression in the Square, producing Measures for the Knotted Cord

Beginning with the third phalange of the little finger, his progression followed this ratio when measuring one phalange to the next in the little finger, then the little finger to the palm and wrist, then this to the hand, the hand to the forearm and the forearm to the arm as a whole (Fig. 6.5).

By establishing a correspondence between the forearm (EF) and the head (GH), he was able to transfer this progression to the body, beginning with the head.

The new progression appeared as follows:

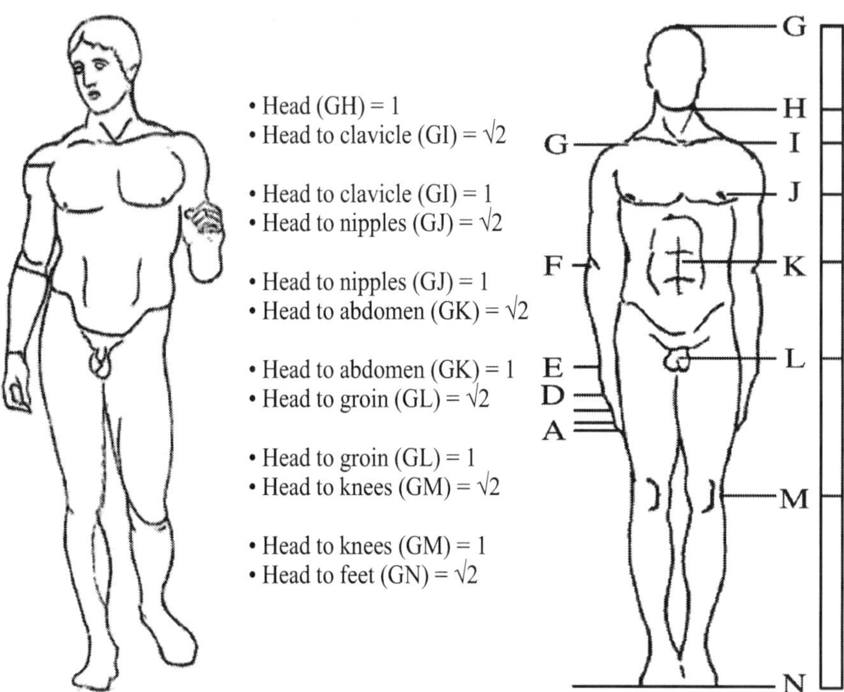

Fig. 6.5 - The Canon of Polykleitos, based on a 1 : √2 Progression

This canon established a constant geometric progression in the measure of the smaller parts to the greater, beginning with the third phalange of the little finger and progressing step by step to the arm. Transferring this progression to the body as a whole, he began another geometric progression with the head, and progressed step by step to the entire human figure. In all, he established six measures in the arm and seven in the figure.

Next, Tobin applied this canon to a hypothetical statue, supposing that the length of the phalange for the little finger is 1.65 cm. After obtaining the measures of this hypothetical statue, he compared them to the actual measures of the Doryphoros as recorded by A. Kalkmann in his 1893 work, *Die Proportionen des Gesichts in der Griechischen Kunst* (Proportions of the Face in Greek Art -1893).

All the measurements matched up, with both figures standing 199.5 cm tall. However, there was a 3 cm discrepancy in the head, which may have resulted from the difference in pose. Polykleitos must have enlarged the head by 3 cm, Tobin claims, to correct the slight loss in height of the *contrapposto* figure, due to its bend. By adding 3 cm to the head, the bent figure measures to the full height of an erect figure, following the proportional canon.

III. Classical Greek Proportions of the Face

Tobin was also able to apply the √2 Canon to the face. By using the distance from the bottom of the chin to the mouth as the square module, he was able to geometrically progress through the features of the face, up to the hairline. Referring to the bottom of the chin as the base, we arrive at the following list of proportions:

- From base to mouth (AB) = 1
- From base to tip of the nose (AC) = √2

- From base to tip of the nose (AC) = 1
- From base to dip in the nose (AD) = √2

- From base to dip in the nose (AD) = 1
- From base to eyelids (AE) = √2

- From base to eyelids (AE) = 1
- From base to hairline (AF) = √2

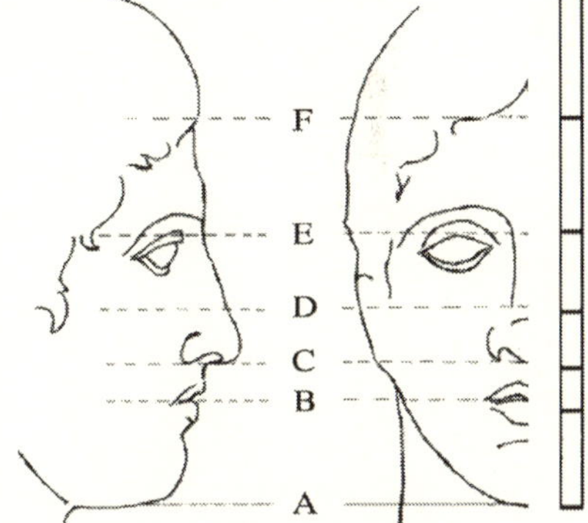

Fig. 6.6 - The Canon of Polykleitos: √2 Progression in the Face

IV. The Canon of Polykleitos as the Golden Ratio

The Golden Ratio has fascinated artists since time immemorial, and it was only a question of time before it would be applied to Polykleitos' Canon. Research on the role of the ϕ ('phi') ratio in human proportion began with Leonardo, but reached its most complete expression with Adolf Zeising's 1854 publication *Neue Lehre von den Proportionen des menschlichen Körpers* (New Theory of the Proportions of the Human Body). Zeising saw the Golden Ratio as *"a ground-principle of all formative striving for beauty and completeness in the realms of both nature and art, and which permeates, as a paramount spiritual ideal, all structures, forms and proportions ...which finds its fullest realization, however, in the human form."*[4]

In his *Neue Lehre*, Zeising discovered the role of the ϕ ratio in crystallography, plant growth (phylotaxis), animal anatomy and, indeed, the disposition of the entire cosmos. He also applied it to Classical sculptures like the *Apollo Belvedere*, *Knidean Venus* and Polykleitos' *Diadumenos* (the Diadem Bearer). But, since the *Doryphorus* had not yet been re-discovered, that task would fall to G.D. Grimm in 1933, who called upon Zeising's work in his *Proportionality in Architecture.*

In Fig. 6.7 below, I have reproduced the diagram from the 1854 edition of Zeising's *Neue Lehre*, and added my own notations on the left. The human figure is divided into four major sections: the head, torso, navel to knees, and below the knees. These stand in a ϕ relationship to each other, so that the torso, to the head and torso, equals 1 : 1.6. The navel to knees also stands in a 1 : 1.6 ratio when combined with the torso above or the legs below the knees.

Within each section, Zeising makes finer calculations (right side of Fig. 6.7) by dividing each section into 5 parts, which stand in a symmetrical relationship to each other as ABBBA or BABAB, where A = 1 and B = 1.6 in the ratio of A:B. Zeising uses the Fibonacci number of 21 as his starting unit to create the following proportions:

- Within the head:
  A = 21 and B = 34
  (in a ABBBA relationship)

- Within the torso:
  A = 34 and B = 55
  (in a ABBBA relationship)

- From navel to knees:
  A = 55 and B = 89
  (in a BABAB relationship)

- Below the knees:
  A = 34 and B = 55
  (in a BABAB relationship).

In this way he is able to show how all the five smaller parts within the four sections are related by the ϕ ratio, while the figure as a whole totals 987 units (144 for the head, 233 for the torso, 377 for the navel to knees, and 233 for below the knees). Since the lower two sections (navel to knees and below the knees) amount to 610, this means that the figure, from navel down (610) to the entire length of the figure (987) stands in the Golden Ratio of 1 : ϕ or 1 : 1.618033...

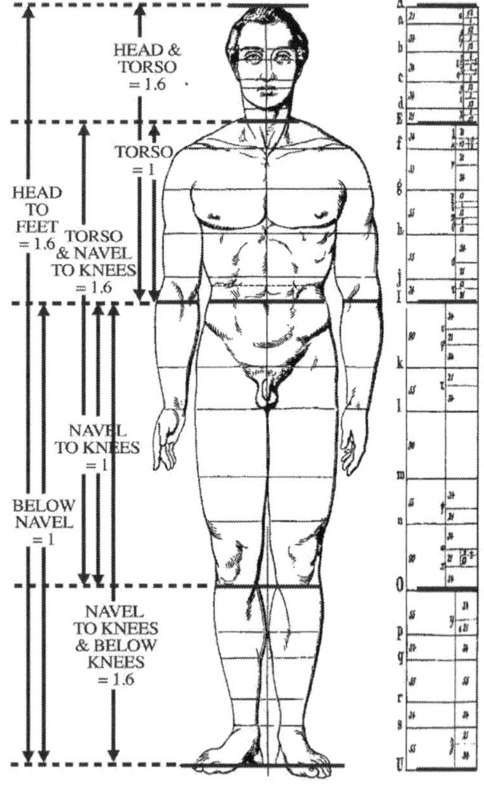

Fig. 6.7 - The ϕ Ratio in the Human Figure
From Adolf Zeising's *Neue Lehre* - 1854

When the statue of the Doryphoros came to light in 1863, researchers were able to apply Zeising's Golden Ratio to Polykleitos' Canon. The first to do this was the Russian architect G. D. Grimm in his 1935 book *Proportsionalnost' v arkhitekture* (Proportionality in Architecture). In 1981, György Doczi also

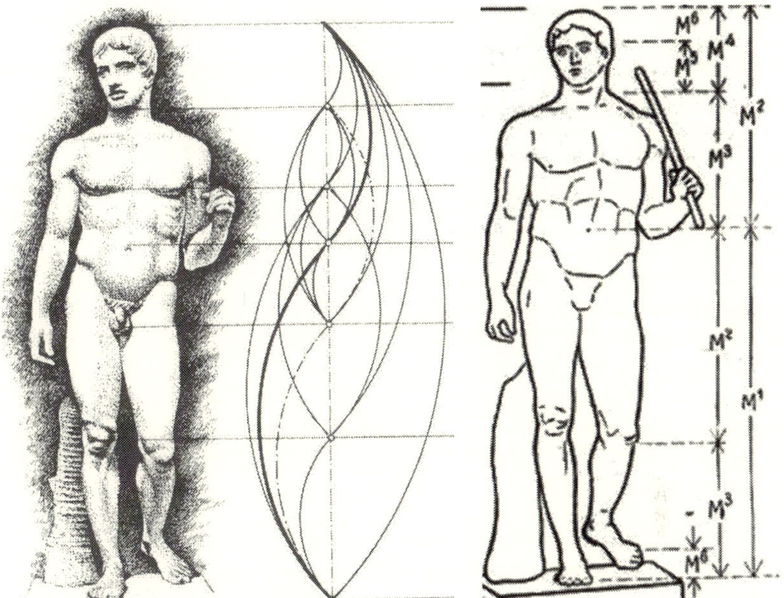

Fig. 6.8 - The ϕ Ratio in the Human Figure
From György Doczi's *The Power of Limits* - 1981

Fig. 6.9 - From G. D. Grimm's
Proportionality in Architecture

applied the ϕ ratio to the statue in his book *The Power of Limits: Proportional Harmonies in Nature, Art and Architecture*. However, Doczi's diagram (Fig. 6.8) inscribes ϕ rectangles within √5 rectangles, creating a system that is fairly complex (and so, will not be considered here).

In Grimm's diagram (Fig. 6.9), he uses only ϕ rectangles, building upon Zeising's work. Grimm begins with the entire length of the figure as ϕ or 1.6, which he progressively divides by the Golden Mean. Proceeding in this manner, we arrive at the following:

The Whole Figure:
- From navel to feet (M1) = 1
- From top of the head to feet (M1 + M2) = 1.6

The Lower Body
- From navel to knee (M2) = 1
- From navel to knee, and below the knee (M2 + M3) = 1.6

The Mid Body:
- From navel to knee (M2) = 1
- From navel to knee, and the torso from neck to navel (M2 + M3) = 1.6

The Upper Body:
- The torso from neck to navel (M3) = 1
- The torso from neck to navel, and the head (M3 + M4) = 1.6

The Head:
- The top of the eye brows to the chin (M5) = 1
- The whole head (M4) = 1.6

In 1914, Theodore Cooke published his richly illustrated volume, *The Curves of Life,* a book which became another landmark in the study of the Golden Mean. Cooke was particularly concerned by patterns of growth in Nature, and found logarithmic spirals in such diverse examples as sulphur crystals, sea shells, pine cones, ram's horns, the clouds, the seas and even the nebula of our neighbouring Andromeda galaxy.

In the final chapter of his book, he developed the Phi Progression, based on the Fibonacci Sequence. Back in 1202, Leonardo of Pisa (nicknamed Fibonacci) had noticed that the recursive nature of the Golden Rectangle generated a unique spiral (Fig. 6.10). When he measured the progression of squares in the spiral, he saw that they began at a ratio of 1:1, then advanced to 1:2, then 2:3, 3:5, 5:8 and so on. Each ratio *approximated* the Golden Mean, and the whole series *converged* with ever-greater accuracy towards 1 : ϕ. This generated the famous Fibonacci Sequence, where each successive term is the sum of the two previous terms: 0, 1, 1, 2, 3, 5, 8, 13, 21...

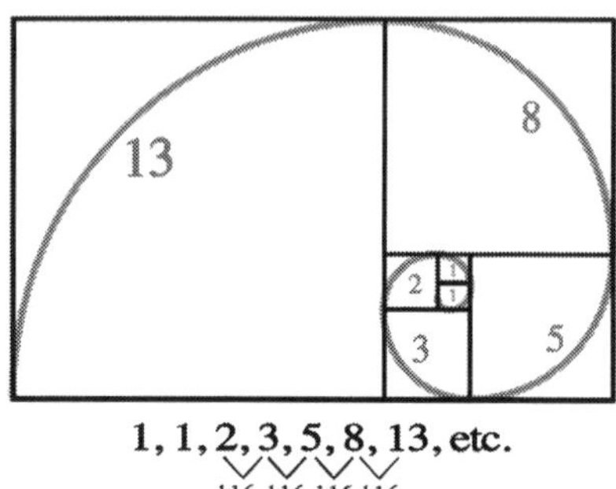

Fig. 6.10 - The Fibonacci Spiral and Sequence

The Phi Progression developed by Cooke also converged to 1 : ϕ, but did so *with greater accuracy* than the Fibonacci Sequence. It also created a spiral with finer curves for modelling growth in Nature. To generate the Phi Progression, Cooke used successive powers of ϕ, as follows: $\phi^1, \phi^2, \phi^3, \phi^4, \phi^5, \phi^6, \phi^7$ etc. Each of these has a corresponding value based on the Fibonacci Sequence:

$$\phi^1 = \phi$$
$$\phi^2 = 1 + \phi$$
$$\phi^3 = 1 + 2\phi$$
$$\phi^4 = 2 + 3\phi$$
$$\phi^5 = 3 + 5\phi$$
$$\phi^6 = 5 + 8\phi$$
$$\phi^7 = 8 + 13\phi$$

As we can see, the Phi Progression generates 'a double Fibonacci Sequence'. *"The most significant fact,"* Cooke writes, *"about the ϕ series is that it gives a double Fibonacci series, and in the ϕ series the ratio of any two successive numbers is not merely approximate, but exact, for the constant ratio is $\phi = 1.618034$."*[5]

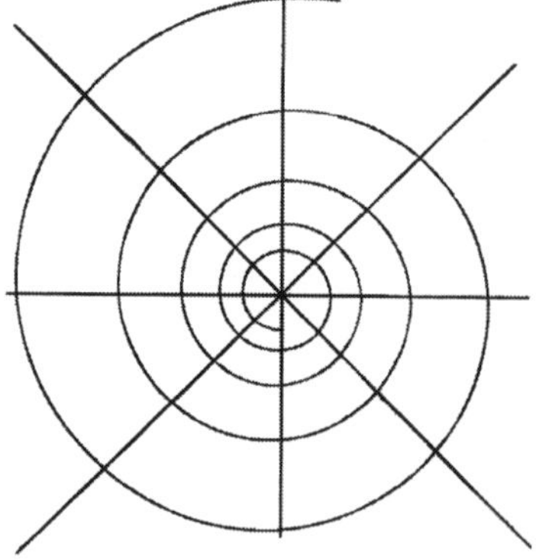

Fig. 6.11 - The Phidias Spiral by Cooke

Where the Fibonacci Sequence *converged* with ever-greater accuracy towards 1 : ϕ, the Phi Progression meets it every time.

The Phi Progression also creates a logarithmic spiral (Fig. 6.11) different from the Fibonacci Spiral. In this spiral, which Cooke calls the Phidias Spiral (he actually writes "Phedias Spiral"), the curve begins at 1 on the radius and

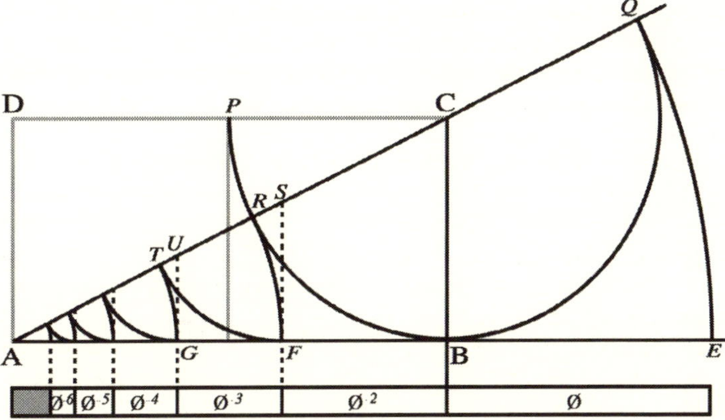

Fig. 6.12 - Construction for The Seven Powers of Phi

- Begin with a double square ABCD and draw a diagonal to create the right angled triangle ABC. Extend the baseline and diagonal beyond the triangle.
- From centre C, draw arc PQ using side CB of the triangle as the radius.
- From centre A, draw arcs QE and RF down to the baseline, from the points where the previous arc cut the diagonal.
- Draw perpendicular SF at F to mark the ϕ distance
- Repeat the operation above, now using S as the centre to draw arc TF using the side SF of the smaller, similar triangle as the radius.
- From centre A, draw arc TG down to the baseline, from the point where the previous arc cut the diagonal.
- Draw perpendicular UG at G to mark the ϕ distance.

then progresses to ϕ^1, ϕ^2, ϕ^3, etc. As a result, the third length on each radius (i.e. each of the eight rays going out from the centre) is always equal to the previous two.

The *"seven powers of phi"*[6] are generated through a simple geometrical construction, given above in Fig. 6.12.

Cooke applies the Phi Progression to Botticelli's Venus and to 'An Artist's Model' (Fig. 6.13) which he describes as "a tall slender Swiss." To generate the progression, he begins *with the nose-length* (from the centre of the brow to the tip of the nose) as 1. Above the brow to the top of the head is the first ϕ measure, repeated below from the tip of the nose to the cleft of the neck. The Phi Progression then increases as follows:

- ϕ^2 – from the cleft of the neck to the nipples
- ϕ^3 – from the nipples to the navel
- ϕ^4 – from the navel to the tips of the fingers
- ϕ^5 – from the tips of the fingers to the feet

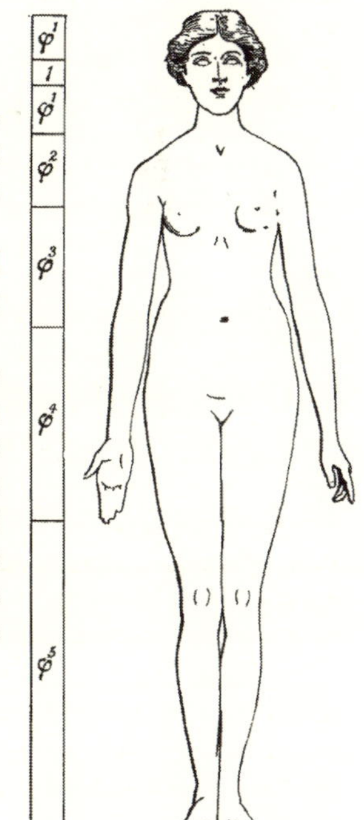

Fig. 6.13 - The Phi Progression applied to Human Proportion

Cooke concludes his study of human proportion with the words, *"It may be urged that ϕ proportions are as likely to be found all over a well-formed human body as they are in other living forms, and therefore that their occurrence in paintings of the human form is only natural."*[7]

V. Lysippos' New System of Proportion & the Statue's Surrounding Space

It would be a mistake to believe that Polykleitos' system of proportion (*symmetria*) held sway over all of Greek statuary. The names of other great sculptors have come down to us through time, such as Phideas, Myron, Skopas and Praxiteles. On the whole, Greek sculptors preferred to cast their statues in bronze, but it is through Roman copies in marble that most of their legacy has come down to us through time.

One such marble of great importance is Lysippos' *Apoxymenos* or 'The Scraper' (Fig. 6.14), which depicts an athlete scraping sweat from his body. In his *Natural History,* Pliny noted that Lysippos distinguished himself *"...by making his heads smaller than the old sculptors used to do, and his bodies more slender and firm, to give his statues the appearance of greater height. He scrupulously preserved the quality of 'symmetry'* [proportion] *by the new and hitherto untried method of modifying the squareness* [quadrata] *of the figure of the old sculptors."*[8]

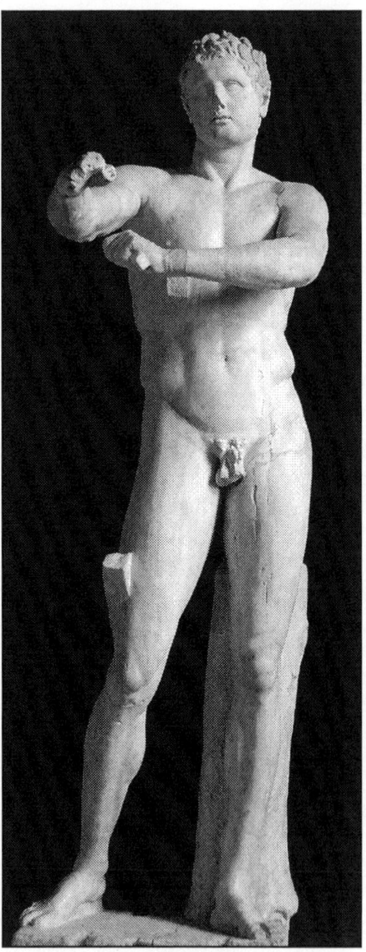

Fig. 6.14 - Lysippos: *Apoxymenos*

Where the *Doryphorus* of Polykleitos stands seven heads tall, the *Apoxymenos* of Lysippos stands eight heads tall. This change in proportion made the figure appear, as Pliny said, taller, 'more slender and firm'. As court sculptor to Alexander the Great, the influence of Lysippos was widespread (his famous 'Head of Alexander the Great' was reproduced and disseminated throughout the empire). By introducing a new style and proportion into Greek sculpture, Lysippos helped to usher in 'the Hellenistic period' of Classical Art.

Another innovation introduced by Lysippos is noticeable in the outstretched arm of the *Apoxymenos* (Fig. 6.15). Sculptors from Egyptian times to Polykleitos generally respected the rectangular shape of the block, containing the figure within it. But Lysippos, according to J. J. Politt in his *Art and Experience in Classical Greece*, *"...was willing to let his figures break out of the neat spatial cube in which the stable figures of Polykleitos could be contained. It is perhaps this innovation which Pliny is referring to, among other things, when he tells us that Lysippos altered the squarish or block-like statures (quadratas staturas) of the figures of his predecessors, since in another passage he specifically singles out the works of Polykleitos as being quadrata."*[9]

The squarish (*quadrata*) or block-like statures (*quadratas staturas*) of ancient sculpture is one of its most characteristic features, making it appear 'Hieratic'. By drawing on four sides and then cutting into the block, ancient Egyptian and Babylonian craftsmen gave their deities their 'squarish' proportions. Such a practice continued, it seems, from Archaic Greek Kouros sculptures up to the time of Polykleitos – until Lyssipos abandoned it, introducing 'a new and hitherto untried method'.

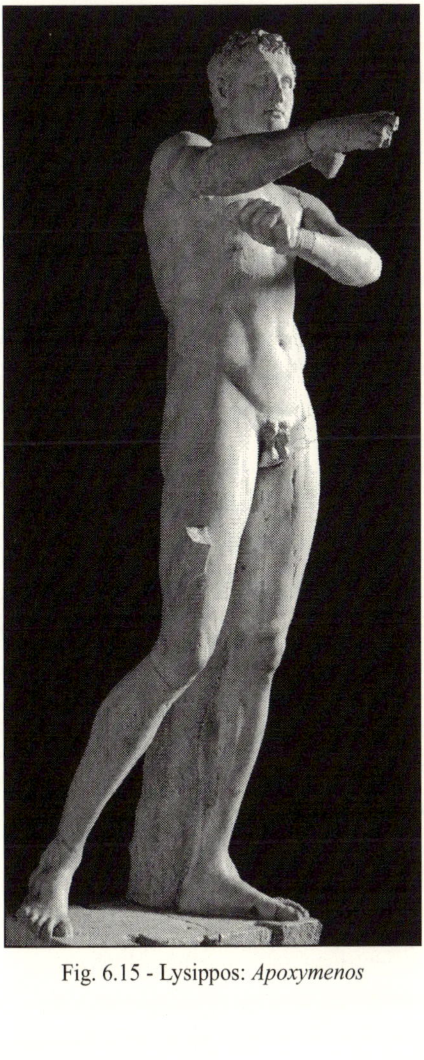

Fig. 6.15 - Lysippos: *Apoxymenos*

Hence, even a sculpture like Polykleitos' *Doryphorus* was probably conceived in four aspects – the front, back and two side views – which were drawn onto the block's four cardinal aspects in squared grids that guaranteed 'the Canon' its famous proportions. According to Rhys Carpenter in *Greek Sculpture: A Critical Review*:

"If Pliny was to record Varro's criticism that the Polykleitan figures were all "four-square" (quadrata), the complaint was based on the entirely accurate observation that only the four cardinal aspects had been the sculptor's concern."[10]

What Lysippos altered was not only the proportion of the statue, but its surrounding space. Previously, the Hieratic statue was carved to be viewed from a distinct angle. When approached reverently from the front, it manifest its divine proportions, thus commanding its surrounding space (the temple). This was true, not only for Egyptian and Babylonian statuary, but most of Greek sculpture, from the Archaic Period (Kouros statues) to Classical times (Myron, Polykleitos).

But, with Lysippos' *Apoxymenos* in the Hellenistic Period, the viewer is free to walk around the statue, viewing it from any angle that he chooses. In the words of J. J. Politt, *"In the Apoxymenos this torsion and the bold thrusting of its right arm out into what might seem to be the viewer's space asserts a new spatial independence for the statue. It does not 'pose' for the viewer like a figure in a painting; rather it challenges him to move through space and explore many angles of vision in order to understand it fully."*[11]

Although the *Apoxymenos* has ended up in the Vatican Museum, it originally stood (according to Pliny) in the Baths of Agrippa, until the emperor Tiberius had it placed in his royal bedroom. Such a mundane setting seems appropriate for the statue of a nude athlete. But it is not only the subject matter which makes it Humanist in style – its very stance and execution invite a more Humanist gaze, thus creating *a de-sacralized space around it.* The statue's surrounding space is determined by the ambulant human viewer rather than the stilled divine statue. In Humanist art, *it is we who view* the statue; in the Hieratic tradition, *the statue gazes at us*... We enter the hallowed space surrounding the statue and share in the divinity's all-commanding gaze.

VI. Vitruvius – Geometry & Proportion

Four hundred years after Polykleitos' Canon, the Roman architect Vitruvius recorded his theory of proportions in the third book of *De Architectura* (The Ten Books on Architecture). *"No temple can be put together coherently without symmetry and proportion,"* Vitruvius wrote, *"unless it conforms exactly to the principle relating the members of a well-shaped man."*[12]

When Vitruvius' work was rediscovered in 1414, Renaissance architects like Bramante, Alberti and Martini took this very much to heart. Alas, the passage in Vitruvius on the proportions of 'a well-shaped man' are confusing if not contradictory. Since antique copies of *De Architectura* were not illustrated, different Renaissance editions offered different solutions to the enigmatic puzzle of 'Vitruvian Man'. We today look back at Leonardo's famous rendition of Vitruvian Man as a *fait accompli*. But at the time, it offered a daring solution to one of history's greatest conundrums.

The contradictions in Vitruvius' work began when he inscribed the human figure in a square and circle thus:

"*The navel is naturally placed in the centre of the human body, and, if in a man lying with his face upward, and his hands and feet extended, from his navel as the centre, a circle be described, it will touch his fingers and toes.*

It is not alone by a circle, that the human body is thus circumscribed, as may be seen by placing it within a square. For measuring from the feet to the crown of the head, and then across the arms fully extended, we find the latter measure equal to the former; so that lines at right angles to each other, enclosing the figure, will form a square."[13]

By locating the centre of the body *in the navel* (and not the pubis), Vitruvius laid a trap for many artists who wished to work out the accurate proportions of the human figure. Worse yet, he suggested that both a square and a circle can enclose the human figure in this manner. Hence, when Francesco di Giorgio Martini illustrated the Vitruvian Man in his own *Trattato di Architectura* (c. 1481), he roughly inscribed the circle in the square (see

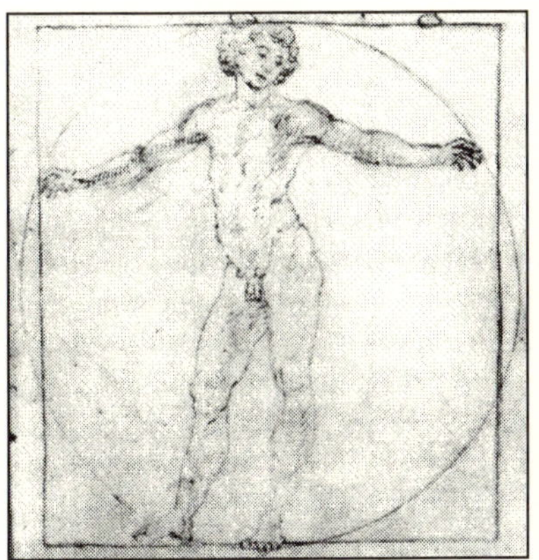

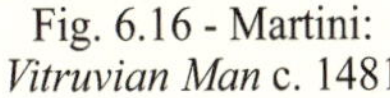
Fig. 6.16 - Martini:
Vitruvian Man c. 1481

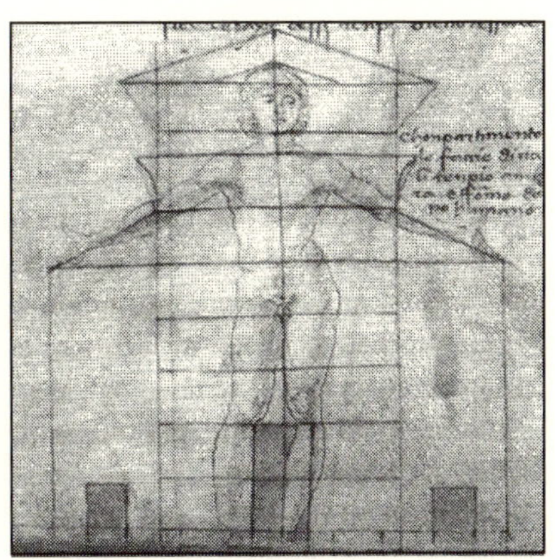

Fig. 6.17 - Martini:
Nine Face Human Proportion c. 1481

Fig. 6.16). In other illustrations to this fascinating treatise, Martini shows how temples and churches may conform, in Vitruvius' words, 'to the members of a well-shaped man' (Fig. 6.17).

Martini's construction of the human figure is proportionally consistent throughout the treatise, and follows Cennini's construction in *Il libro dell'arte.* There, the centre of the human body occurs at the pubis, and Martini has so-drawn his Vitruvian Man so that the pubis – not the navel – forms the centre of the square and circle. But, aside from enclosing a man within the squared circle, Martini had no interest in constructing a proportional figure consistent with Vitruvius' instructions.

Elsewhere in the *Trattato di Architectura* Martini draws the human figure as a proportional model for a column or the elevation of a church. In each case, he follows Cennini's construction from *Il libro dell'arte*, which was written in the late 13th century. Cennini's *Libro* (The Craftsman's Handbook) bears many similarities to Dionysius of Fournos' *Manual*, including the Byzantine author's canon of human proportions. In Chapter LXX of the *Libro*, Cennini describes his canon as follows:

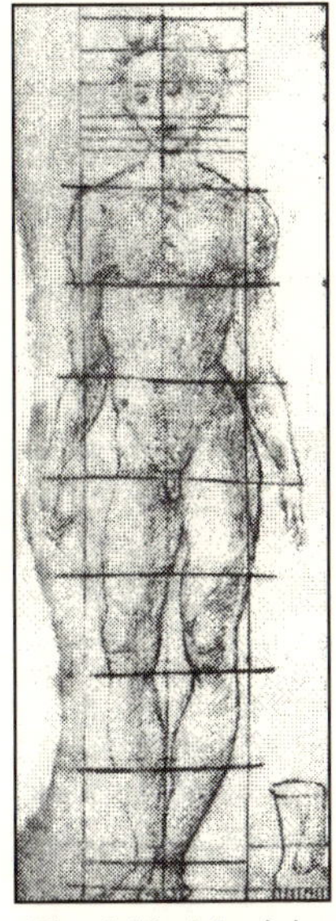

Fig. 6.18 - Martini:
Column Proportion

"The Proportions Which a Perfectly Formed Man's Body Should Possess. I will give you the exact proportions of a man... First, as I have said above, the face is divided into three parts, namely: the forehead, one: the nose, another; and from the nose to the chin, another... The throat, one measure long... From the pit of the throat to that of the chest, or stomach, one face. From the stomach to the navel, one face. From the navel to the thigh joint, one face. From the thigh to the knee, two faces. From the knee to the heel [ankle] *of the leg, two faces. From the heel* [ankle] *to the sole of the foot, one of the three measures... The whole man is eight faces and two of the three measures in length* [up to the hairline. Adding one third from the hairline to the top of the head, we get nine faces.]"[14]

Thus, we see that Martini's figures (Figs. 6.17-18) have 3 divisions in the face, and the face itself is the module which repeats 9 times over the length of the figure (8 times with the facial-measure, plus ⅓ for the feet, neck and top of the head). We are back in the Byzantine sphere of proportion, but this time with Renaissance nudes in a *contrapposto* stance.

VII. Da Vinci's Vitruvian Man

On one of the random pages of the *Codex Arundel*, Leonardo recorded a powerful experience which could only have arisen in a dream:

"Having traveled a certain distance through overhanging rocks, I came to the entrance of a large cave and stopped for a moment, struck with amazement, for I had not suspected its existence. Stooping down, my left hand around my knee, while with the right I shaded my frowning eyes to peer in, I leaned this way and that, trying to see if there was anything inside, despite the darkness that reigned there. After I had remained thus for a moment, two emotions suddenly awoke in me: fear and desire. Fear of the dark, threatening cave; and desire to see if it contained some miraculous thing."[15]

This passage portrays, in the manner unique to dreams, Leonardo's unbridled curiosity for the strange and miraculous, which only fear of the unknown could hold in check. His approach to the human figure reflects this fear and fascination combined, since the mystery of man's composition led him to extensive dissections and anatomical research. Combining this with detailed measures of the human frame, he envisioned a grand treatise (never compiled) on 'The Universal Measure of Man'.

Fortunately for the history of humanity, Leonardo did complete one drawing (Fig. 6.19) which offered up his own vision of Vitruvian Man. When faced with the contradiction of the circle and the square, especially in relation to man's centre, Leonardo devised a brilliant solution. Rather than inscribing one shape in the other, he gave them the same base. By spreading the arms and legs, he shortened the figure enough to actually locate the centre of the circle in the navel. Meanwhile, the pubis remained the centre of the square.

Across the figure, Leonardo drew straight segments to measure out the proportions offered by Vitruvius. But, where Vitruvius gave ten basic measures, Leonardo added another twelve. Citing Vitruvius,[16] the most important ones may be described thus:

• FACE – "*A third part of the height of the face is from the bottom of the chin to the bottom of the nostrils; the nose from the bottom of the nostrils to the line between the brows, as much; from that line to the roots of the hair, the forehead is given as the third part.*" Hence, the classic three part division of the face.

• FACE – "*the face from the chin to the top of the forehead and the roots of the hair is a tenth part* [of the whole body]." Hence, the figure stands 10 faces tall.

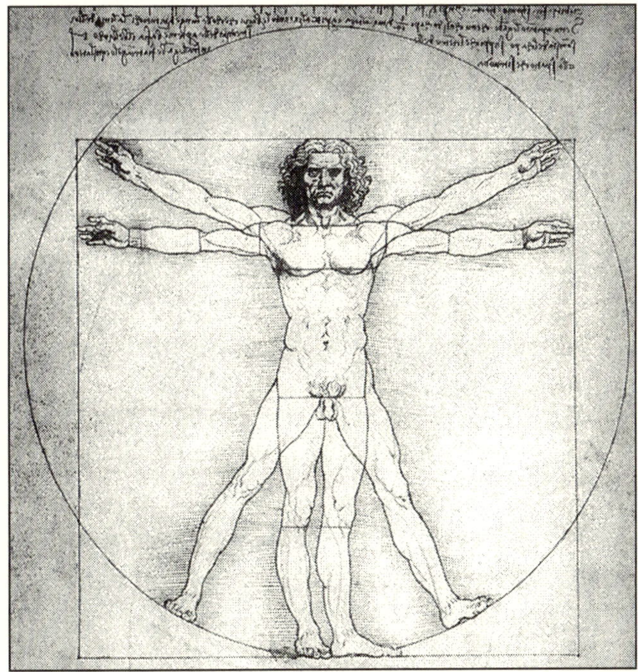

Fig. 6.19 - Leonardo da Vinci: *Vitruvian Man* c. 1487

• HEAD – "*The head from the chin to the crown, an eighth part* [of the whole]." Hence, the figure stands 8 heads tall.

• BODY – "*The cubit* [is] *a quarter* [of the whole body], *the breast also a quarter... from the middle of the breast to the crown, a fourth part.*" Hence, from head to foot, the whole figure stands 4 cubits tall, divided at the nipples, pubis and knees. This means (not shown) that each quarter of the body may be divided into 2 heads. After the top of the head, the dividing lines are located at the collar bones, nipples, indent above the navel, pubis, mid-upper leg, knee, mid-lower leg and base.

• HEIGHT & WIDTH – "*Measuring from the feet to the crown of the head, and then across the arms fully extended, we find the latter measure equal to the former.*" Hence, the figure is as wide as it is tall.

One of most important measures worth recalling here is that Leonardo's figure stands 8 heads tall. If the face is used as the module, his figure stands 10 faces tall. While this was above average height for the Byzantines and Hindus, who preferred 9 faces, the Hindu *daśatāla* proportion did allow 10 face-lengths (*tālas*) for Brahma, Vishnu and Shiva. For the next five hundred years, writers on iconometry (the measure of the human figure) would argue over whether the ideal figure stands 8 or 9 heads tall.

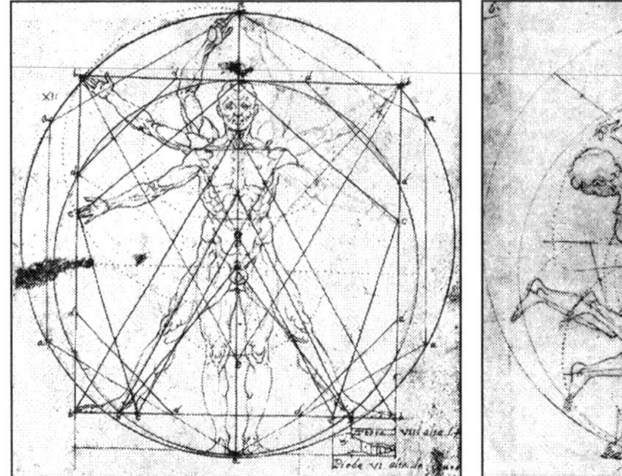

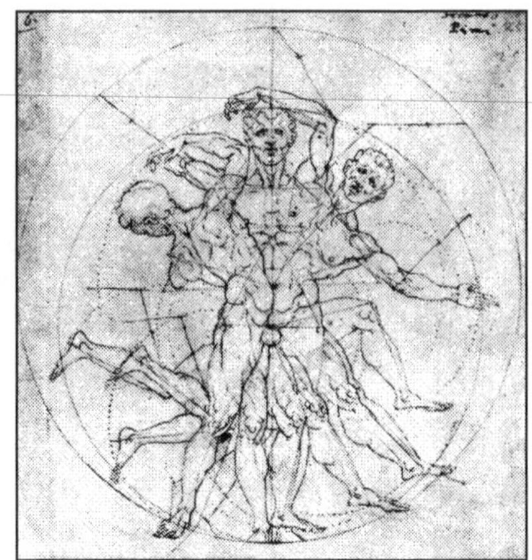

Fig. 6.20 - After Leonardo da Vinci: *Codex Huygens* 16th century

VIII. The Circle & the Square

One reason for the enduring appeal of the Vitruvian Man is its iconic simplicity: Man, 'the measure of all things', stands within the perfect circle and square. As an architect whose principle tools were the compass and set-square, Vitruvius was naturally drawn to these two perfect shapes.

Indeed, he refers to these two shapes time and again in his treatise. The ideal city should not be square, but circular, like the cosmos itself, revolving like an immense armillary sphere. Nevertheless, each Roman city was divided into quadrants through the *cardo* and *decumanus*, the cross in the circle, indicating the four cardinal directions.

Thus the city, like the temple, gains its measure through man – the man inscribed in the circle and square. Man is the microcosm, and his shape reflects the greater cosmos. *"Man, called the little world,"* Martini wrote in his treatise, *"contains in himself all the general perfections of the cosmos."*[17] Leonardo echoed this sentiment when he wrote, *"Man is a model of the world."*[18]

The man in the squared circle – *Homo ad circulum et ad quadratum* – becomes like an archetype, a glyph for our dual nature – terrestrial like the square and celestial like the circle. Although its original intention was to show Man's hieratic relationship to the cosmos (the circle), it is Man who stands squarely at the centre of all things.

While Vitruvian Man has indeed become an icon of Humanism, Leonardo explored far more resonant shapes for humanity than just the circle and square. In the little known *Codex Huygens*, image after image appears of man inscribed in the pentagon, hexagon and triangle (Fig. 6.20). This 16th century codex is not by Leonardo's hand, *per se,* but his drawings, designs and measurements (now lost) were scrupulously copied by Carlo Urbino, who set them down in this folio volume of 128 pages. Of particular interest is a drawing (Fig. 6.21) showing the Eight Head Canon constructed through concentric circles.

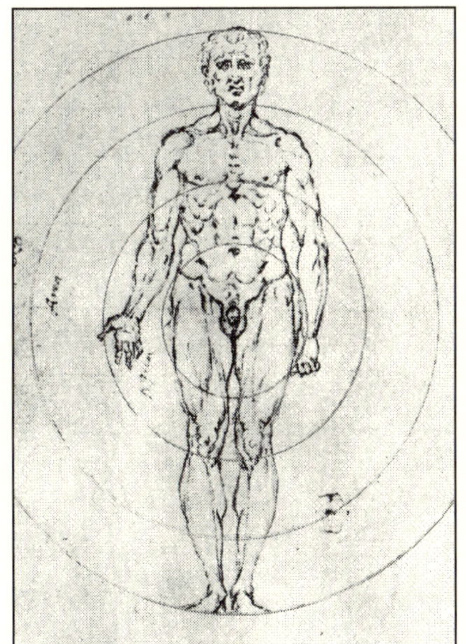

Fig. 6.21 - After Leonardo da Vinci: *Codex Huygens* - The Eight Head Canon

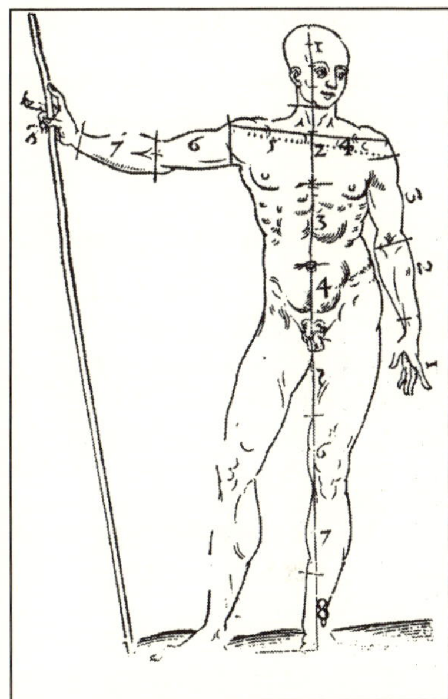

Fig. 6.22 - Jean Cousin the Elder: *Art of Drawing* - The Eight Head Canon

Leonardo's graceful hand and curious mind are everywhere in evidence, displacing the human frame in an endless variety of postures and positions to determine their movements and lines of action. These drawings are *proportion in motion*, the stop-action study of anatomy in time. As an exploration of man's *moto actionale*, they investigate both the kinematic forces at work in the body (will / repose) and the kinetic forces (muscle tension / gravity) which keep it in balance.

As such, these drawings by Leonardo bring us, in the West, to that same spirit of creation which moved the sculptors of the East to portray Shiva Nataraja in a continuous display of human movements frozen in time. Like the East, we accept the multiple hands and heads as a suitable convention for transcending linear time. Each hand gestures at a different segment in time, yet we behold them all as present here and now.

As segments, they no longer show the spatial measure of the human figure (proportion), but its temporal measure (kinematics). Within each segmented moment, a new form of grace and harmony arises.

IX. The Eight Head Canon

Jean Cousin the Elder (c. 1490 – 1560) is best known for his reclining nude *Eva Prima Pandora* in the Louvre (Fig. 19.3). But he was also the first French painter to become a true Renaissance man: Cousin was a master geometer in his youth who turned to glazing (the windows of Sainte Chapelle in Vincennes), etching and engraving (the 1596 Le Clerc Bible), as well as being the first French painter to use oils. He also wrote several treatises on Painting of which one, *Le Livre de Perspective*[19] (The Book on Perspective – 1560) was published in his lifetime.

His post-humous writings were later published under the title *l'Art de dessiner*[20] (*The Art of Drawing*), which went through many editions and became a standard text for the French Academy. In the text, Cousin lays out an Eight Head Canon which is as elegant as it is simple (Fig. 6.22). As late as 1890, the French Academician Paul Richer would write in his *Anatomie Artistique* that *"Of all the authors who have written on this subject* [of proportion], *the most clear, the most precise and without contradiction is Jean Cousin, who's little book is still widely used in our schools."*[21]

As these chapters on Proportion come to a close, I think it necessary to distill the many different systems down to one simple formula that can be used by the artist. The one measure that presents itself most readily is the Eight Head Canon (a measure which may also be called the Ogdoadic Proportion, since it divides *one* figure into *eight* equal parts). In the *Codex Huygens* and his drawing of Vitruvian Man, Leonardo also proposed the Eight Head Canon, as did Desiderius Lenz at the very outset of these investigations.

These two artists could not be further from each other in their aims, since Leonardo sought out a system that best aided the artist to imitate Nature (*mimesis*), while Desiderius sought instead God's ultimate plan in designing the Ideal human form. The former was supremely Humanist; the latter, intensely Hieratic – yet both arrived at the same conclusion.

The beauty and simplicity of the Eight Head Canon is that it allows the artist to quickly determine three to five reference points ('landmarks') for the figure, dividing it into four equal parts. If we imagine that, for the sake of simplicity, we are drawing a free-standing nude, then we would first make two quick strokes on our page to mark the top of the head and the bottom of the feet, thus determining the figure's overall length.

The next step is to mark the halfway point which, since Egyptian times, has been recognized as the pubis. The upper half of the body may be divided into two again at the nipples, and the lower half just below the knees. This simple proportional device, which follows the NPK measure (Nipple – Pubis – Knees), may be called the Tetradic Proportion, since it quickly divides one whole figure into four equal parts.

One afternoon by chance I came across a drawing from the School of Raphael that was on auction at Christies (sale 9747, 5 December 2013 – Fig. 6.24). Whoever this artist was, we can see that even in Renaissance times they used the expedient method of the Tetrad, dividing the figure in four at the nipples, the pubis and (just below) the knees.

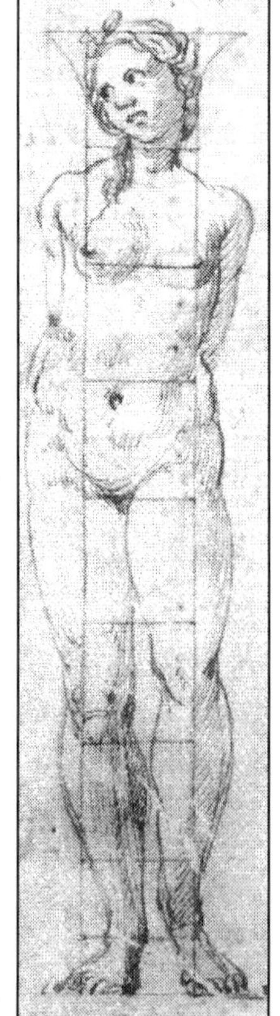

Fig. 6.23 - Fra Giocondo da Verona: Eight Head Canon

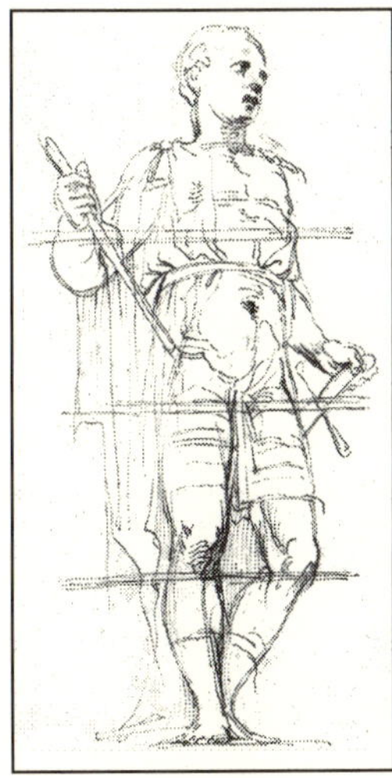

Fig. 6.24
School of Raphael:
Tetradic Proportion

An expedient method for drawing the face comes to us from Michelangelo. We are fortunate in having drawings by Michelangelo which preserve some of the lessons in facial proportions which he taught to his students. In one such drawing, he left a message for Antonio Mini (an assistant who remained with him for eight years), saying: *"Draw Antonio Draw Antonio and Don't waste time."*[22] In another, for his 14-year old apprentice Andrea Quaratesi, he wrote, *"Andrea abbit patientia"*[23] – Andrea, have patience.

From numerous examples, we can see that Michelangelo's method of teaching was to divide the face in three, then subdivide it into nine, and add a tenth part for the top of the head. We find these markings in his drawings for an Ideal face, both in profile and the frontal view. At times, he also drew a skull beside the head, to show its underlying structure, and he roughed in some basic geometrical shapes like triangles.

In the drawing reproduced here (Fig. 6.25), the original marks are barely visible, but can be clearly seen in a good reproduction. Michelangelo first drew a vertical line and cut it in three to determine the Greater Thirds, then these in three for the Lesser Thirds, and finally added the Halves.

The Greater Thirds divide the face into the three basic sections known to us from Byzantine, Gothic and early Renaissance art: the BNM measures of the Brow (hairline to eyebrows), the Nose (eyebrows to the bottom of the nose), and the Mouth (the bottom of the nose to the bottom of the chin). We recall that, from Ancient Egypt to the Renaissance, the nose-length has been used as the basic measure for the three-part (triadic) division of the face.

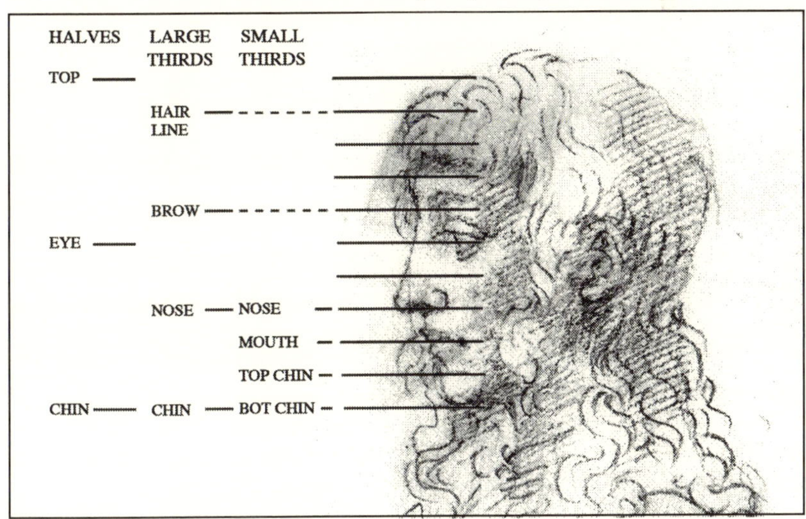

Fig. 6.25 - Michelangelo: Ennead Proportion of the Face

The Lesser Thirds divide each of the three parts into three more, for a total of nine. Concentrating on the bottom third of the face, we divide it into three smaller sections which give us two important marks: the line for the mouth (one mark down from the bottom of the nose), and the line for the top of the chin (one mark down from the mouth).

Concentrating on the middle third of the face, we also divide it into three, giving us the mark for the eyes, one down from the brow. This is specifically *the centre of the eyes*, where the pupil is located. Finally, we may divide the upper third of the face into three, solely for the purpose of adding one more, lesser third above the hairline, to give us the top of the head. As a result, we now have ten divisions for the entire head.

To obtain the Halves, which divide the head equally from the top of the skull (not including the hair) to the bottom of the chin, we count down five marks to the pupil of the eye, which lies *exactly at the half-way point* of the head.

Since this system divides the face into nine, it may be called the Ennead Proportion of the Face. However, since it also divides the entire head into ten equal parts, it may also be called the Decadic Proportion of the Head. For reasons of simplicity, I refer to it as the BNM measure.

In the NPK division of the Figure and BNM division of the Face, we have two simple systems which have many precursors throughout history. During figure drawing, these may be used to mark out basic reference points ('landmarks'), keeping in mind that each figure is unique when we draw 'from Nature'.

Meanwhile, for most of art history, whether working in the Humanist or Hieratic Style, artists have sought to draw the face and figure in their most perfect, harmonious and beautiful of shapes, following the Sacred Codes of Proportion and Pose, rather than toiling away at *mimesis* (copying from Nature). The measures of the face and figure discussed here are certainly not the only proportions to have arisen over time, but each of them, in their own unique way, strives to create *an Ideal face and figure*, thus elevating, ennobling and perfecting the human form.

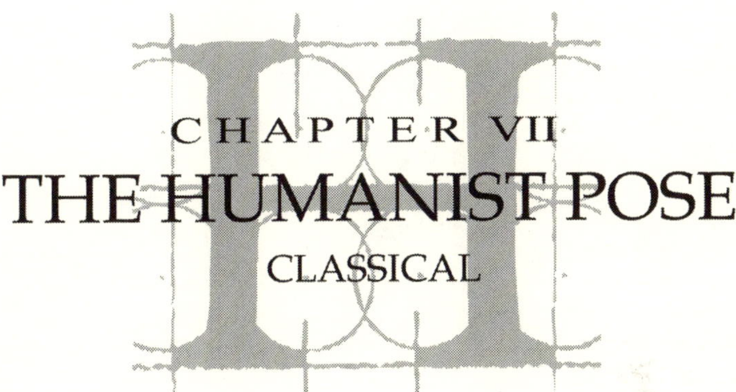

CHAPTER VII
THE HUMANIST POSE
CLASSICAL

I. The Last Judgement

I have stayed in Rome several times over the course of my life, and each time I have never failed to visit the Sistine Chapel to initiate myself deeper into the mystery of Michelangelo's vision. But finally, in the Fall of 2006, I had to admit to myself, while staring at his magnificent *Last Judgement*, that I was really seeing nothing. The distance, darkness and most of all the distractions from the crowds were just too overwhelming...

So, I bought myself a decent reproduction and, back in my studio in Paris, I spent an entire weekend in deep meditation upon that image. Using the techniques described earlier, I 'entered through' the image three times. Each successive journey opened my eyes to new ways of seeing – new Sacred Codes – which were unique to Humanist works of art. Toward the end, I released all attempts at understanding and experienced Michelangelo's epic vision in its full glory, as a monumental revelation and *apokalypsis*.

After years of just 'looking' at the image, I felt that I had finally pierced the veil and actually 'seen' *The Last Judgement*. What I saw was the energy and dynamism, the *contrapposto* movement, the rise and fall that gives the Humanist Style its unique power.

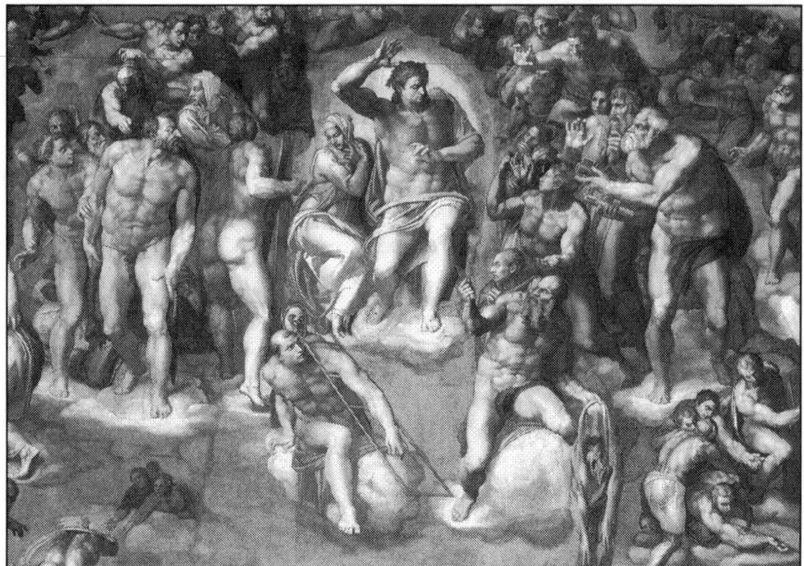

Fig. 7.1 - Michelangelo: *The Last Judgemen*t 1541 (Detail)

At first I had some difficulties, as I was used to meditating on *Hieratic* images, with their calm static figures and symmetrical compositions. I was used to focussing my gaze on one fixed point. But here, my gaze was in continuous motion, excitedly following the flow of movement from one figure to the next. I realized that I had to learn 'to read' the narrative movement, to learn the Sacred Codes unique to the Humanist Style.

Thus began a seven-year journey into the principles underlying Humanist art in both the Classical and Renaissance periods. As I shared each new insight with my fellow artists, they too saw the value of these discoveries. For our knowledge of these codes has been lost, and a new Sacred Art is now ready to remember and integrate their dynamic principles. By balancing Hieratic codes with Humanist ones, a more dynamic yet contemplative art may emerge in our epoch.

When I began my meditation on Michelangelo's image, I naturally sought out its *Hieratic* codes: the balanced composition, the symmetrical armature, and the central figure of Christ at the summit. As I came to focus upon Christ's dynamic pose, I could even make out 'The Hidden Sign of the Hieratic' – the triangle encompassing his upper body, such that, the saviour's eye was enclosed by a smaller triangle at the apex.

In a moment that made my heart stand still, this triangle expanded – descending through the entire composition – until I saw the luminous aureola around Christ like an immense Eye of God, with a plethora of figures streaming outward in rays of vision that actively created and consumed the layers of the cosmos.

Those to the left ascended and returned to the Divine source of light and vision; those on the right fell from God's sight or were repelled by demons to descend into darkness and blindness. This rise and fall flowed through the whole fresco, with Christ's two passionate gestures – one hand upturned, the other lowered – as an all-decisive movement at the source of this luminous flux and cosmic swirl.

Following the diagonal lines of armature, Christ appeared at the apex of an immense triangle and, just beneath him, two figures turned their heads to gaze upon the saviour – their lines of sight following the exact angle of the diagonals. Through my studies in iconography, I knew that these two were St. Lawrence with his ladder-like grid-iron and St. Bartholomew with his flayed skin (bearing Michelangelo's tortured features).

But, I also saw a deeper significance to their poses. As they turned their heads to gaze upon Christ, they seemed to be saying: you must shed the flesh (Bartholomew's flayed skin) and ascend the ladder of vision (Lawrence's grid-iron) to behold Christ, not through eyes of the flesh, but in a higher state of vision...

Slowly, over the course of those three meditations, all the figures in the fresco revealed to me their allegorical meanings. But to read them, to read the divine unfolding of the narrative, I had to understand the Sacred Codes which Michelangelo had acquired from Classical culture and revived in this masterpiece. I had to see the invisible lines of armature, and how the energetic movement of the figures flowed over and around them.

This created two distinct classes of invisible lines: those relating to Composition and those relating to Figuration. The former, we could say, are a class of diagonals and orthogonals emerging from the perfect triangle and square. The latter, creating sinuous volumes and stylistic contours, are a class of curves emanating from the perfect circle. All these shapes – the circle, triangle and square – appear in Michelangelo's armature as axes for individual figures or areas for their groupings.

In Chapter 18, I shall return to *The Last Judgement* and demonstrate how *all* these invisible lines interact and fuse, when Figuration and Composition finally come together to express the *istoria*, the narrative movement through the painting that may finally result in a moment of understanding, revelation and epiphany.

For now, we must begin with the figure.

II. Invisible Lines of Gravity and Force

In order to understand Michelangelo's figures, I did what any good apprentice does – and started copying. I chose as my subject one of Michelangelo's *ignudi* – those twenty garland-bearing Nature Spirits who frolic above the thrones of the Prophets and Sibyls in the Sistine Chapel ceiling (Fig. 7.2). As I was drawing, I became increasingly aware of the forces at work within a single figure – indeed, within each limb.

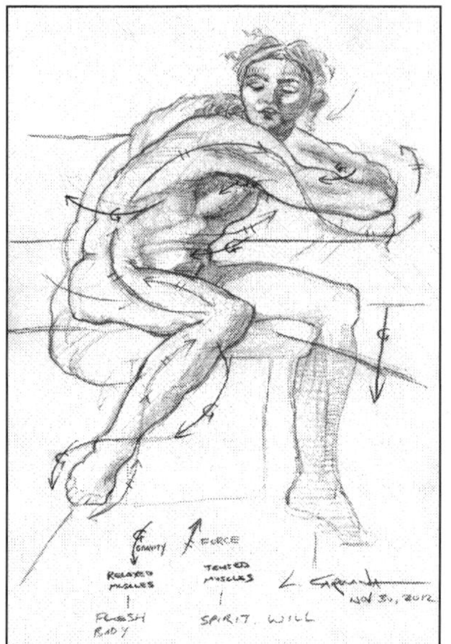

Fig. 7.2 - L. Caruana:
Study of Michelangelo, Ignudo 2012

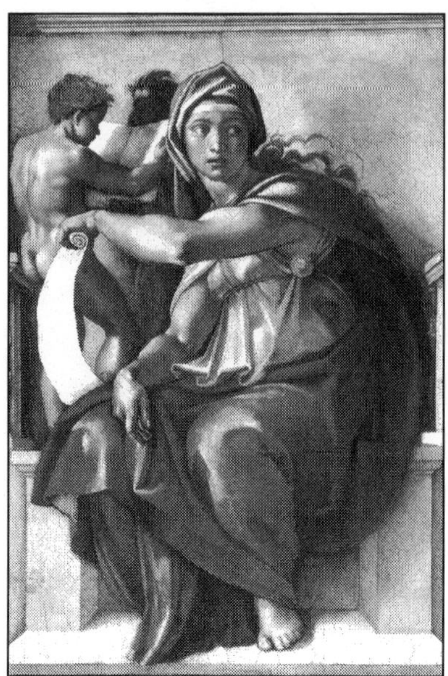

Fig. 7.3 - Michelangelo:
Delphic Sibyl 1509

Basic anatomy teaches us that muscles are attached to the bone: when the muscles on one side flex, those on the other side relax. The flexed muscles shorten and pull against the bone, which moves like a lever against another bone at the joint. In this way, force and movement are generated throughout the human body.

As I drew Michelangelo's *ignudo*, I began to feel with my pencil the hard, sharp curves of the tensed muscles – each volume ending abruptly to clearly emphasize the break from one hard muscle group to the next. For the relaxed muscles, on the contrary, my pencil moved with a fluid movement, softly defining their rounded contours, with gentle transitions between the muscle groups.

Afterward, I began drawing the 'invisible' lines of force and gravity – the force (F) moving upward along the tensed muscles, as the *ignudo* pushed against the ground with his right foot; the gravity (G) descending along the relaxed muscles, pulling his limbs down to earth. The lines of force, quite naturally, followed the sharp contours of the tensed muscles, while the lines of gravity followed the soft contours of the relaxed muscles.

But, the more I contemplated the drawing, the more I began to see the spiritual ramifications of all this. The tensed muscles manifest the *striving of the will*, the inner animation of spirit and soul, while the relaxed muscles manifest *the torpor of the body*, the lassitude of the flesh. All these forces were at play in each limb, while adding to the overall thrust and movement of the figure as a whole.

The flowing helical lines of will and repose possessed a certain beauty, and I thought it a pity that these graceful curves would remain forever unseen.

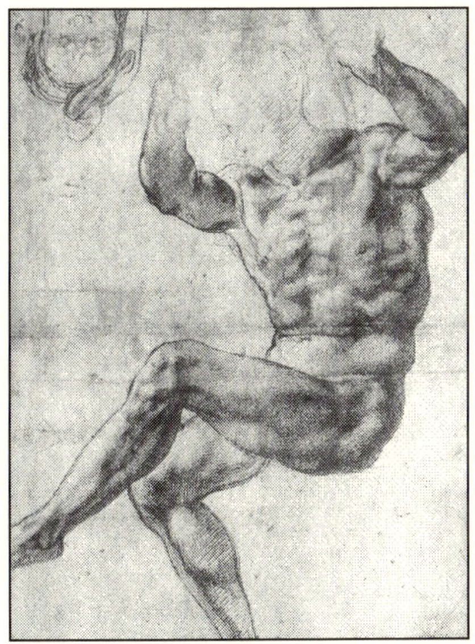

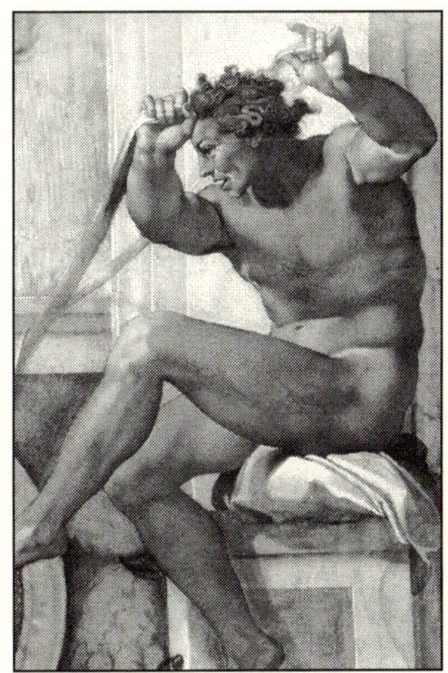

Fig. 7.4 - Michelangelo: *Ignudo - Preparatory Drawing and Fresco,* 1509
Balancing Anatomy and Style; Nature and the Ideal

Then it struck me – I had seen these lines somewhere before... Flipping through the book on Michelangelo, I came across his Delphic Sibyl (Fig. 7.3), a figure which had mesmerized me many times in the past.

And there it was...

Although the pose of the Sibyl was laterally reversed, the force and movement were the same. Michelangelo *had indeed drawn the invisible lines – and translated them into drapery!* The pleats and folds commenced along the contours of flexed muscles, then billowed and flowed as they moved round the contours of relaxed muscles, typically obscuring them.

But the movement of these folds *traced out and preserved* the invisible lines of will and repose. I felt, with this small discovery, like I had uncovered one of those secrets which the master of a *bottega* only imparted to his sworn apprentices...

III. Anatomy & Style

As I continued to copy and learn from Michelangelo, another important insight rose before my eyes. We are fortunate to have a preparatory drawing for another *ignudo,* (Fig. 7.4) and here we can see Michelangelo's profound mastery of anatomy: every muscle, whether tensed or relaxed, is drawn with great accuracy and care.

But, when we compare this drawing to the final image frescoed on the ceiling (Fig. 7.4), we discover that many of the anatomical details – the distinct muscle groups with their individual volumes and shadows – have been massed together and simplified. There is the point at which anatomy comes into conflict with style. Or – to be more precise – when the imitation of Nature comes into conflict with the Ideal.

While anatomy, like science, pursues accurate observation from Nature, it risks ignoring the artist's quest for the Ideal. That Ideal becomes manifest in the graceful contours and flowing lines which simplify and stylize the figure to its most essential archetypal shape – like an Egyptian figure in profile that emanates its holiness as a single 'hiero-glyph'.

This is not to say that the artist can forget anatomy altogether. Rather, anatomy must first be mastered and then overcome. The accuracy of anatomy, with its odd groupings of muscles and tendons, must be tempered by the stylistic quest for simplified shapes and beautified proportions.

To express these same thoughts in different terms: we must learn to combine the Humanist quest for Nature with the Hieratic Ideal of a more sacred style. The Hieratic, by itself, pursues a stylistic line that totally glosses over anatomy. We can see this in the art of Hinduism, Buddhism and ancient Egypt, where individual muscle groups are mainly ignored.

But, at the opposite extreme, Western art (before it abandoned figuration completely) became progressively more Nature-based, from the Realism of Caravaggio and Naturalism of Courbet to the Hyperrealism of the 20th century. No nuance of the flesh was left unseen or unexplored. Hence, while Renaissance artists mastered muscle under skin, later artists like Rembrandt, Rubens and Boucher went so far as to master the anatomy of fat!

The academies, by promoting the Greek stylistic ideal, hoped to keep the excesses of anatomy in check. From Classicism to Neo-Classicism, the nude remained stylized in pursuit of the Ideal. But, from the beginning, the academies saw Greek Classicism as the *only* style worthy of emulation. Oddly, the Hieratic styles of other cultures was regarded more as 'idol' than 'ideal'...

If I keep coming back to Michelangelo, Blake, Moreau and Fuchs, it is because they are among the few Western artists who were not afraid of idols, of moving beyond the dominant sphere of Classical Greece to integrate Hieratic styles from *all* cultures of the past. They achieved, as much as any Western artist could, a fusion of the Humanist and Hieratic Styles.

IV. Humanist Life-likeness & the Hieratic Ideal

On January 14th in the year 1505, Michelangelo was at the home of his friend Guiliano de Sangallo when an urgent message arrived from Pope Julius II: *"Some excellent statues have been dug out of the ground in a vineyard near the Church of Santa Maria Maggiore."*[1] At once they mounted and rode out to the vineyard, where a large marble statue stood partly unearthed. The tragically heroic figure, accompanied by his two sons, was arching powerfully from his pedestal, as the threesome fought vainly to disentangle their limbs from the writhing coils of twinned serpents. Familiar with the *istoria* from his reading of Pliny, de Sangallo cried aloud, *"It is the Laocoön!"*[2]

It is difficult for us today to imagine the impact which Classical sculpture had upon Renaissance painters. For artists like Michelangelo, a statue like the *Laocoön* (Fig. 7.5) or the fragmented *Torso of the Belvedere* revealed new and unimagined forms of expression. While writers like Marsilio Ficino

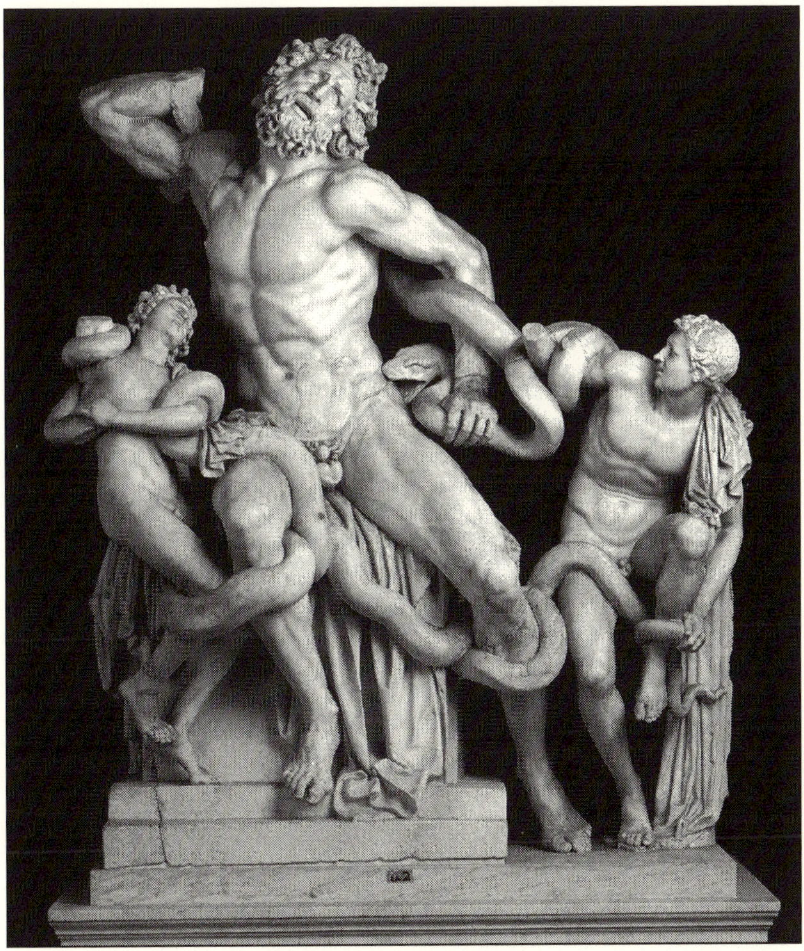

Fig. 7.5 - Agesander, Athenodoros and Polydorus: *The Laocoön* 31 BCE

and Giovanni Pico were reviving the Platonic, Hermetic and Neo-Platonic worldviews, their brethren artists like Michelangelo, Leonardo and Raphael were creating an entirely new Christian art, infused with the artistic principles of the Classical world.

Indeed, our current view onto the Classical world is so deeply influenced by Renaissance aspirations that we can hardly separate one from the other. Our on-going researches (including my own) into Classical art are the natural extension of Renaissance dreams and ideals. Both cultures shared an emerging fascination for Man, and Humanity's accomplishments as a form of creation that rivaled even the Divine creator...

This new worldview is generally called Humanism, and the art it engendered is Humanist in style. It is a passionate style, dynamic and fluid, that contrasts sharply with the stilled and contemplative art of Egypt, India and Tibet which (among others) I have come to call Hieratic. Nevertheless, in the art of the Classical world, the Hieratic and Humanist styles mingled for the longest time, and it was only during the late Hellenic Period that a purely Humanist style of art emerged (before Classical culture collapsed completely).

There are three basic periods of ancient Greek art: the *Archaic Age*, which lasted from c. 800 – 500 BCE, during which the many *Kouros* and *Kore* figures appeared. Then, from 500 – 323 BCE the *Classical Age* of Greek sculpture surged into form, with many recognizable masterpieces by Phidias, Myron and Polykleitus (while the works of Praxiteles became a bridge to the next era). Toward the end, from 323 – 31 BCE, the *Hellenistic Age* bore witness to late masterworks by Lysippos, Skopas, Agasias and the collaborative effort known as *The Laocoön*.

Two distinct currents moved through all of Greek culture, whether in its art or philosophy.

On the one hand, there was the Hieratic striving for *the Ideal*. In their art, artists attempted to rise up, in a visionary soul ascent, to the higher realm of divinely-inspired forms and subsequently render that vision through *stylized images* that resonated with the ideal shapes and archetypal forms (the Platonic *eidé*) of the heavenly realm.

On the other hand, there was the Humanist striving for *Life-likeness* (*to zotikon*). Now, artists attempted to closely observe, understand and copy Nature with a rational and scientific curiosity, following Aristotle's dictum that 'Art is an imitation of Nature' (Aristotelian *mimesis*). In sculpture, the human figure acquired startling anatomical accuracy, and the purely symbolic and impassive gestures of divine figures gave way to the more passionate, tragic and heroic gestures (*ethos*, *pathos*) of mortal human beings.

This dual tendency, which we also saw in the preparatory drawing and final fresco of Michelangelo's *ignudo*, runs through all of Greek history. At times, the stylized figure acquires anatomic precision; at times, that precision is sacrificed in favour of smooth and graceful lines.

V. Humanist Life-likeness

The Greek fascination with the body, and more particularly the nude figure, has always troubled historians. As the first culture to openly depict the nude with anatomic accuracy, they seem to be celebrating the body (*soma*) above all else. And certainly, there were many Greek practices to support this view. Their society celebrated the warrior's courage and athlete's skill. From banquets to baths, a homo-erotic sensuality seemed ever-present, and was extolled with Epicurean fervor. The Dionysian Mysteries encouraged ecstatic abandon through inebriation, dancing, trance, intoxication and orgiastic rites.

For this reason, Greek sculpture is overrun with warriors and athletes, ephebes and cup-bearers, prancing satyrs and dancing maenads. Everywhere, the human physique is lovingly reproduced in finest detail: veins bulge, muscles flex and eyes open wide with wonder. This meticulous rendering of the human form manifest the Greek fascination for 'life' (*zoé*), for 'likeness' (*mimesis*) and their unique combination of 'Life-likeness' (*to zotikon*).

Time and again in Greek literature, statues are celebrated for their living quality. An epigram from *The Greek Anthology* states: *"The Bacchante is of Parian marble, but the sculptor gave life to the stone, and she springs up as if in Bacchic fury."*[3] In a mime by Herodas, one character says, *"You could expect the sculpture to speak, if you did not see that it was made of stone."*[4] And in a Satyr play by Aeschylus, another character says of his statue: *"...All it needs is a voice!"*[5] From this glyptic striving for Life-likeness comes the myth of Pygmalion, that legendary sculptor who rendered such a beautiful and vivid image of a woman in stone that he fell in love with his creation. Finally, in answer to his prayers, Aphrodite breathed life into her image.

But we would be sorely mistaken if we thought that the artist's striving to create a living *homoioma* (likeness) or *mimema* (imitation) fulfilled some deep desire for Naturalism or Realism. Rather, a sculpture had 'the appearance of life' (*to zotikon phainesthai*) because it captured a likeness of the human figure, in both its body and soul. The fifth century revolution in Greek sculpture paralleled a similar revolution in Greek philosophy, where *psyche* and *soma* (soul and body) emerged as two opposing forces momentarily united by *zoé*, the omnipresent life-force.

The word *soma*, in the Homeric epics, meant only a life-less figure or corpse. Once it was animated by *psyche*, it gained movement and life. As Plato says in the *Cratylus*: *"The name psyche meant to express that the soul, when in the body, is the source of life, and gives the power of breath and revival, and when this reviving power fails then the body perishes and dies."*[6]

One of the greatest challenges of the Greek sculptor was to somehow infuse a statue with this invisible and elusive essence. The soul, Plato decided, became evident in the *willful direction* of the body, in the body's capacity for 'self motion': *"We shall feel no scruple in affirming that what is precisely the essence and definition of soul is, to wit, self-motion. Any body that has an eternal source of motion is soulless, but a body deriving its motion from a source within itself is animate or besouled."*[7]

Hence, although the soul itself remained invisible, sculptors could render its willful workings (*erga*) through the tremor of the limbs and their stirring movement into life.

VI. The Hieratic Ideal

The striving for the Ideal (Plato's archetypal image, idea or form – singular *eidos*, plural *eidé*) emerges in Greek sculpture as a direct result of the Platonic philosophy, which had its roots in Orphic, Pythagorean and Pre-Socratic thought, as well as its subsequent influence on Hermetic, Gnostic, Theurgic and Neo-Platonic thinking.

All of these philosophies share an Emanationist worldview, where the Divine One separates and expands into the entire creation while remaining fundamentally unified at the source. The cosmos is a many-stepped pyramid, with an eye at its summit, that is actively seeing and manifesting the hierarchy of creation on various levels. Those levels furthest from the source lack knowledge of the original love, light and sacrifice which holds the all together.

In the Emanationist worldview, it is particularly the body, trapped in the lower world of ignorance, desire, passion and forgetting, that shrouds the soul and hinders its perception. The physical world is a world of Becoming, fleeting and illusory. Only in rare moments of vision and realization does the soul rise up, beyond the earthly veil, and enter the timeless realm of Being. It sees, in a land of perfect shapes and ideal forms, the higher world – the domain of the *eidé* and archetypes.

In Plato's *Phaedo*, Socrates says: *"For we live in a hollow of the earth* [... but] *if a man could come to the top of it, and get wings and fly up, he could peep over and look, just as fishes here peep up out of the sea and look round at what is here, so he could look at what is there, and if nature allowed him to endure the sight, he could learn and know that this is the true heaven and the true light..."*[8]

What the more contemplative soul beholds at the height of 'the soul ascent' is the world of Being, a timeless realm of stillness and perfection: *"When she* [the soul] *examines by herself, she goes away yonder to the pure and everlasting and immortal and unchanging ...and there she rests from her wanderings."*[9]

But the soul is continually held in check by the body, which Plato characterizes as a kind of cloak or garment (Plato, *Phaedo* 87b. – see the tale of Cebes' weaver.) Due to the body's passions, the soul staggers like one drunken and suffers the drowsiness of sleep:

"Then it [the soul] *is dragged by the body towards what is always changing, and the soul goes astray and is confused and staggers about like one drunken..."*[10]

Just as Michelangelo portrayed in *The Last Judgement*, the soul must peel away the bodily garment and ascend the ladder of vision – an ascent through the seven heavenly spheres to the Empyrean (which we shall examine in depth in Chapter 27 on Theurgy).

For Plato, as for Pythagoras, the higher dimension was a world of number – of perfect geometrical shapes and constant circular measures in time. For this reason, a work of art measured out into constant shapes and balanced proportions (*symmetria* – 'the commensurability of parts to whole') would harmonize with the higher spheres. Although art is a mere shadow, a semblance of the original – the figures here below, when carefully idealized and proportioned, could become clear reflections of the higher forms – of the Gods good, beautiful and true.

Indeed, when the Demiurge fashioned this world, he made all that is beautiful and true by keeping his eye on the eternal archetypes, the Ideal forms. As Plato describes in the *Timaeus*:

"The work of the creator, whenever he looks to the unchangeable and fashions the form and nature of his works after an unchangeable pattern, must necessarily be made fair and perfect."[11]

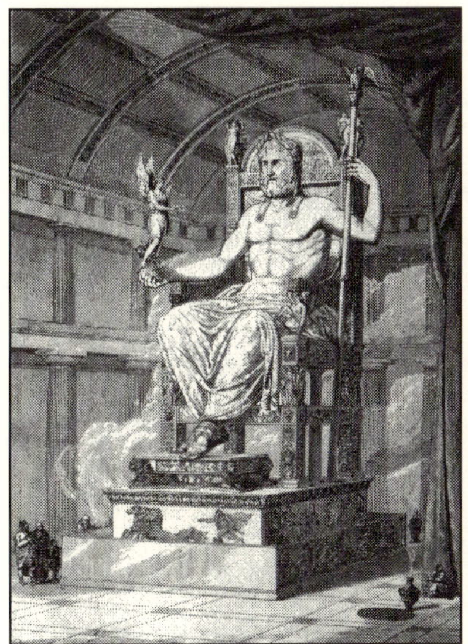

Fig. 7.6 - Phidias:
The Chryselephantine Zeus at Olympia

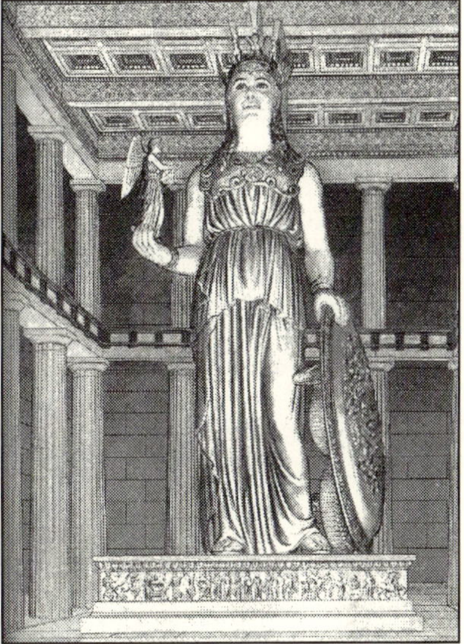

Fig. 7.7 - Phidias:
The Athena Parthenos in the Parthenon

VII. Hieratic & Humanist Art in the Classical Period

During the Archaic Period (c. 800 – 500 BCE), the Greeks erected statues of young nude men (*kouroi*) and robed women (*kore*) which share the same Hieratic stillness and sacred proportions as Egyptian statuary (See Fig. 4.14, Ch. IV). Whether as deities, commemorated athletes or funerary monuments, these life-size and monumental statues stood rigidly with one foot before the other, hands at their sides, smiling impassively with a noble expression called 'the archaic smile'. Their anatomy was basic, indicated by shallow lines that simplified and stylized the contours.

In *The Emergence of the Classical Style in Greek Sculpture*, Richard Neer writes:

"Most discussions of kouroi *note their peculiar timelessness. They are oddly intermediate, neither walking nor standing still. Frozen and immobile, weight distributed with perfect evenness over both legs, ...the* kouros *in fact seems somehow outside time. Indeed, it seems almost as if the conventions of the* kouros *type were designed specifically to convey this sense of what the archaeologist Dieter Metzler called 'perpetuity',* die ewiger Dauer.*"*[12]

This timeless aspect, 'frozen and immobile', gives Archaic Greek statuary its Hieratic quality. But even in the Classical period (500 – 323 BCE), when a more Humanist Style sprang to life, the Hieratic tendency survived. For example, Phideas (480 – 430 BCE) was considered one of the greatest artists of the Classical world. Pliny the Elder praised him as *"unequalled'* and *"before all others,"* adding that his statuary was *"...of such exquisite beauty, that it received its name from its fine proportions."*[13] He was called 'the god maker' due to his famed creation of the chryselephantine Zeus at Olympia and the Athena Parthenos in the Parthenon.

The statue of Zeus was a seated colossus some 13 metres tall, while the free-standing Athena reached to the roof of the Parthenon. Following the custom of the Archaic period, these votive statues were 'chryselephantine' in character, with skin carved from ivory (*elephantinos*) and drapery gilded in sheets of gold (*chrysos*). Jewels and semi-precious stones adorned their armor while coloured glass made their eyes flash bright ('bright-eyed' was an epithet of Athena, just as 'wide-seeing' was an epithet of Zeus). So precious were these materials that Lachares, the tyrant of Athens, stripped away Athena's gold to pay his troops, and both statues were eventually pillaged and perished over time.

Had these Hieratic masterpieces survived, our impression of the Classical style would no doubt be different. From contemporary descriptions and coins, we know that the Athena Parthenos wore a tunic cinched with entwining serpents, bore a breastplate of the Medusa, and was crowned with a sphinx flanked by two griffons. Apparently, her left knee was slightly bent, shifting her weight to the upraised right hand supporting a statue of *Nike* (Victory). With her left hand she either grasped a serpent-entwined spear or rest it upon a massive shield.[14]

The lost statues by Phidias attest to the fact that the Hieratic Style survived well into the Classical period. Although Athena's angled knee suggests a slight *contrapposto* bend, the commanding gaze, ornamental attire and symbolic hand gestures – combined with their monumental size, beautiful proportions and chryselephantine adornments – make these statues Hieratic works of the highest order. They were deemed dwelling places of the Gods; receptacles worthy of the Deities' immense and indwelling power.

VIII. The Emergence of the Humanist Style

Around 480 BCE, a noticeable shift in the glyptic art occurred. The statue which most clearly manifests this new Humanist tendency is the Kritian Boy, prized for its early expression of Classical anatomy, style and pose.

Attributed to the sculptor Kritios, the Kritian Boy reveals a naturalistic striving for *Life-likeness* (*to zotikon*) hitherto unseen in the Greek world. Suddenly, the simplified anatomy of the *kouros* gives way to a more subtle and refined *mimesis* of the human form. The delicate balance, graceful poise and elongated curves of the limbs reveal, for the first time, that 'Classical Beauty' by which Greek sculpture became so renowned.

Kritian Boy manifests many of the features unique to the Classical Style, such as the angular prominence where nose meets brow, the enlarged eyes with well-defined ridges for upper and lower lids, the bow-shaped lips and spherical chin. His physique is well-defined, with muscles smoothened into compact volumes defined by graceful lines.

In the hollow below the ribs and the hump above the pelvis, we also have the first indications of the 'athlete's girdle' – an essential component of Classical anatomy. As Neer remarks:

"The 'athlete's girdle' [is] *a continuous line formed by the iliac crest and the inguinal ligament, or meeting of thigh and torso. This line does not exist on a real human body, even a well-toned one. The iliac crest is real, and*

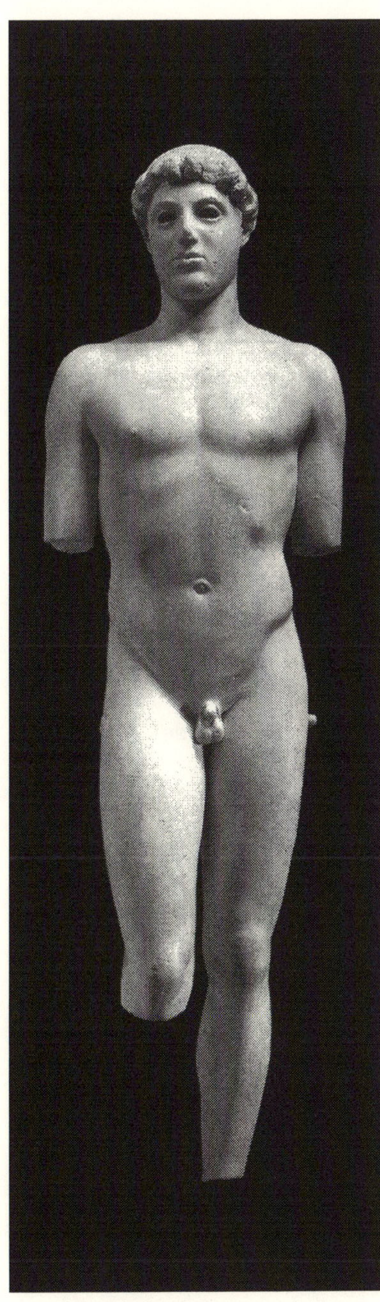

Fig. 7.8 - Kritios:
The Kritian Boy c. 480 BCE
from the Acropolis

the inguinal ligament is real, but their assimilation into a single, continuous arc is not. It is a stylization to which Greek sculptors were addicted. They were addicted, presumably, because the line made a pleasing effect."[15]

Neer also notices that, in Greek sculpture *"...the genitalia of many Classical males are simply too short. Men are sexually immature relative to their physiques."*[16]

Certainly this is the case with the Kritian Boy. In the first daring attempt of the Classical period to observe, understand and copy (*mimesis*) human anatomy, Kritios has, in part, achieved a faithful rendition of the youthful figure – a *Life-likeness* (*to zotikon*) that heralds the Humanist Style. But, at the same time, he has surrendered to the Hieratic impulse for *stylization* – subtly altering human anatomy to achieve the continuous arcs and elongated curves so characteristic of Classical Beauty. For the next five hundred years, this classical architecture of the human body (the *cuirasse esthétique*) will be continually refined – but anatomical likeness will always be tempered by the stylistic quest for the Ideal.

In the upward thrust of the youth's left hip we also have the first stirrings of that *contrapposto* movement which will become the hallmark of the Humanist Style. Here, it is still in its infancy, as both heels (the feet are missing) remain pressed to the ground and the shoulders hang at an even balance. This 'one-part bend' of the hips (as distinguished from the two-part bend of hips and shoulders in the *contrapposto*) is often referred to as 'moderate ponderation'.

With this revolutionary advance in the pose, a new life-force has entered Greek statuary. Suddenly, all the parts of the body move as one, with a rudimentary S-curve ascending the figure. That dynamic flow of energy in an otherwise stilled statue brings new life to the glyptic art. Henceforth, the human figure will gesture, breathe, raise the head and arc the torso to express anger, grief, sorrow and elation.

"One of the distinguishing features of the art of the Classical period," J. J. Politt remarks in *Art and Experience in Classical Greece, "was that it broke away from the emotional impassivity in Archaic art."* And he adds, *"Early Classical artists begin experimenting with the representation of conscious inner life."*[17]

This inner life expressed itself, in Greek culture, through certain distinct characteristics:

"Ancient Greek psychology," Politt continues, *"recognized two forces at the root of human emotional expression – ethos, a man's 'character' as formed by inheritance, habit, and self-discipline, and pathos, his spontaneous reaction to experiences in the external world."*[18]

When, much later in Greek sculpture, the Knidean Venus (Fig. 9.17) will modestly hide her sex, this is *ethos*. And when the Laocoön (Fig. 7.5) will raise his arm in suffering, that is *pathos*. In his *Poetics,* Aristotle gave birth to both concepts, seeing Greek drama as the stage for revealing a man's fundamental character (his *ethos*), and for expressing the passion and suffering (*pathos*) resulting from his contest with Fate.

Indeed, Aristotle dedicated the greater part of his *Poetics* to defining the language and terminology for Humanity's tragic contest with Fate – a major theme that traverses most of Classical mythology, drama and statuary. To summarize Aristotle: a play, like a work of art, is an imitation (*mimesis*) of human actions (*praxis*) which utilizes plot (*mythos*) and character (*ethos*) to portray humans 'just as they are in real life' (*to zotikon*) whether for better (comedy) or for worse (tragedy).

Alas, Aristotle's writing on comedy never survived through time. In his writing on tragedy, he said that a well-constructed plot (*mythos*) involves a sudden change (*catastrophe*) or reversal (*peripeteia*) of fortune, causing the main character to experience both suffering (*pathos*) and a profound realization *(anagnorisis*) about their over-reaching pride (*hubris*) or tragic flaw (*hamartia*), for they have transgressed the ordinance of Fate (*moira*) as decreed by the gods. During that dramatic moment of self-recognition *(anagnorisis*), the audience responds 'with fear and pity' (*di heleou kai phobou*), indeed with deep empathy and terror, for this dramatic enactment of human tragedy has become a transformative experience, a kind of ritual cleansing and awakening (*catharsis*).

In the opening paragraphs of the *Poetics*, Aristotle says, *"For even dancing imitates character* [ethos], *emotion* [pathos] *and action* [praxis] *by rhythmical movement* [rhythmos]*."*[19] And he adds the much-used phrase, *"It is the same with painting."* Whether we speak of dance, painting or sculpture, 'art imitates nature' – specifically *human* nature, by portraying human figures in action (*praxis*), such that their stilled movements (*rhythmoi*) or poses (*schemata*) evoke, not only the passions (*pathos*) born of a certain temperament or character (*ethos*), but also a profound moment of realization, understanding and epiphany (*anagnorisis*).

Anagnorisis, in Aristotle's words, *"...is a change from ignorance to knowledge."*[20] It is particularly during this latter moment of 'recognition' that art achieves its highest expression. When a tragic human figure, such as the Laocoön, oversteps the order established by the gods, he must suffer accordingly – and his action portrays that pivotal moment when Humanity dramatically awakens to a higher, Hieratic design for existence.

Classical Greek sculpture did not arise in isolation, but as an integral part of that culture's sacred tradition as expressed through poetry, music, dance, drama and art ('cultus' – at the root of 'culture' – means the ritual practices attending a deity). The Kritian Boy, lest we forget, was unearthed in 1866, among a cache of sacred artifacts in the environs of the Parthenon. Classical sculpture expressed Humanist suffering and awakening within this Hieratic context – as statuary and narrative friezes adorning sacred temples and portraying mythic scenarios extolling the supreme power of the gods.

IX. The Doryphorus

Around 440 BCE, at the height of the Classical Period, Polykleitus cast his famous sculpture of the Doryphorus or Spear Bearer. Not only did 'the Canon' become the model and measure for a new system of Proportion; it also revolutionized the Pose in Greek sculpture.

Xenophon's *Memorabilia*[21] (c. 371 BCE) offers us a rare testimony of how Polykleitus' accomplishment was viewed by his countrymen. The text offers a dialogue between Socrates and a certain sculptor named 'Kleiton' who is most probably Polykleitus himself.

"At another time he [Socrates] entered the workshop of the sculptor Kleiton, and in course of conversation with him said:
Socrates: You have a gallery of handsome people here, Kleiton, runners and wrestlers... But how do you give the magic touch of life [*to zotikon*] to your creations, which most of all allures the soul of the beholder through his sense of vision?

As Kleiton stood perplexed, and did not answer at once, Socrates added: Is it by closely imitating the forms of living beings that you succeed in giving that touch of life to your statues?
Kleiton: No doubt.
Socrates: It is, is it not, by faithfully copying the various muscular contractions of the body [*soma*] in obedience to the play of gesture and poise, the wrinklings of flesh and the sprawl of limbs, the tensions and the relaxations, that you succeed in making your statues like real beings – make them 'breathe' as people say?
Kleiton: Without a doubt.

Socrates: And does not the faithful imitation of the various affections of the body, when engaged in any action, impart a particular pleasure to the beholder?
Kleiton: I should say so.
Socrates: Then the threatenings in the eyes of warriors engaged in battle should be carefully copied, or again you should imitate the aspect of a conqueror radiant with success?
Kleiton: Above all things.
Socrates: It would seem then that the sculptor is called upon to incorporate in his ideal form the workings and energies also of the soul?"

The dialogue breaks off here, but within Socrates' typically one-sided discourse, the greatest aesthetic questions of the age were aired and debated. First of all, Socrates questions whether the sculpture is pure *mimesis*, concerned chiefly with the two-fold task of 'faithfully copying the various muscular contractions' and 'the faithful imitation of the various affections of the body' – which is to say that the body's anatomy and, beyond that, the bodily expression of feeling give the sculpture its true *Life-likeness* (*to zotikon*) by 'closely imitating the forms of living beings'.

But, at the end, Socrates moves beyond the body to discuss the soul, and suddenly declares that the sculpture – in its Ideal form (*eidos*) – expresses 'the workings and energies of the soul'. Here, we have the typically Platonic distinction between body and soul, where the passions (affections) belong *to the body,* as a hindrance and distraction for the higher seeking of the soul. The greatest art, we surmise by the end of the dialogue, does not just imitate the nature of the body, but manifests, in a more Ideal form, the workings (*erga*) of the soul.

How does it do this? Through a closer reading, we discover that the artist 'makes the statue breathe' through 'the play of gesture and poise' which results from a clear depiction of 'the tensions and the relaxations'. We have in this dialogue the first clear explication of how the Greeks viewed the fundamental principles at work in any great sculpture.

A great statue must demonstrate 'the tensions and relaxations' – the counter-balancing movements *of will and repose,* which are themselves the greater expressions of *the soul and the body* – with the soul striving for the higher world of the Ideal forms, while the body sinks to a more relaxed state of sleep or repose. That sleep or repose is the body's natural inclination to immerse itself in the world of Becoming – in the fleeting and ever-changing world of the senses, where 'the soul goes astray and is confused and staggers about like one drunken.'

Images of warriors and athletes celebrate the soul's successful expression of courage and skill through bodily movements that are graceful and powerful. In contrast, the 'drunken faun' is the archetypal Greek image of the soul who surrenders to bodily pleasure, intemperance, sensuality and excess. The satyr staggers about, without balance or grace, to eventually tumble into intoxicated sleep.

Returning to Polykleitos' *Doryphoros,* what makes this sculpture so unique is that it gives equal expression *to will and repose*. This is the *contrapposto*,

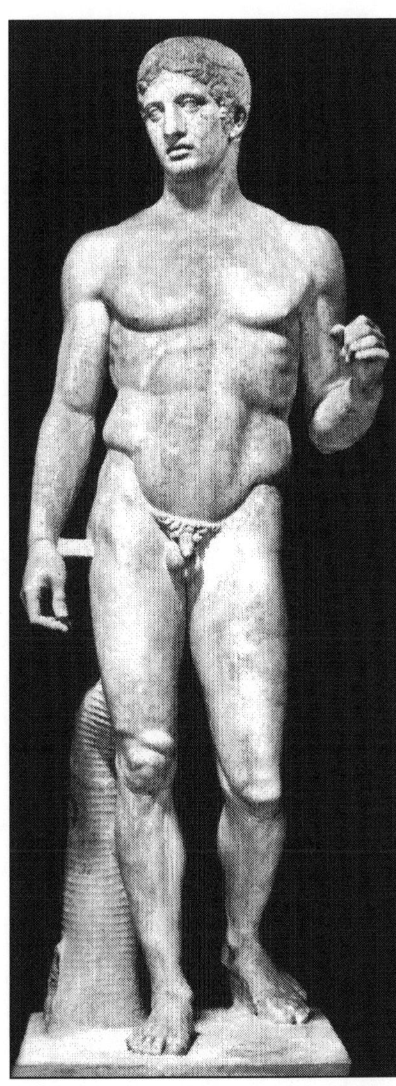

Fig. 7.9 - Polykleitos: *The Doryphoros* or *Spear Bearer,* 440 BCE (Roman copy)

the *chiastic* principle, which infused countless figures with new life during the Classical Period and eventually breathed a new spirit into Renaissance art.

Contrapposto means, literally, 'the counter poise' – a counter balance of opposing forces within the body. The term is a Renaissance invention, just as our modern designation of *chiastic* principle (from the Greek letter χ or 'chi') describes the two opposing axes – one straight, one curved – which keep the body in dynamic counterbalance. The Greeks themselves simply described this phenomenon as the *'schema'* or pose. The various *'schemata'* of Greek sculpture expressed *'the tensions and relaxations'* in the figure, through its 'play of gesture and poise'.

This all begins with the simplest of conventions – to raise the back heel. With this *shift in balance*, a play of opposites courses through the figure: from left to right, above and below, the physique shifts in its movement and rest, resulting in limbs straight and curved. As one hip pivots up; the same shoulder sags down. Like a serpent, an invisible S-curve of energy ascends the body, winding round the central axis in a two-part bend that traverses the invisible plumb line – beginning at the weight-bearing foot, crossing at the pubis, and ending at the watchful eye. Horizontals at the soles, knees, hips, shoulders and eyes tilt this way and that, perpendicular to the serpentine movement. Half the body sinks in sleepful repose while the other half, animated by the will, awakens with energy and life, which finally explodes through a single expressive gesture or soulful glance of the eye.

I have spoken before of the hieroglyphic quality of certain poses: how the human figure holds together like a sacred letter or glyph within the divine alphabet. If the sitting Buddha inscribes the delta – Δ – and Christ crucified, the tau – T – then the *Doryphoros* is the chi – χ. In her book, *Fifth Century*

Styles in Greek Sculpture, Brunilde Ridgway has commented at length on 'the Chiastic principle' which she differentiates from the *contrapposto*. In the chi (χ), two opposing axes are created – one straight, one curved – which keep the body in dynamic counterbalance.

Is the Doryphorus stepping forward or standing still? For centuries this question has been debated, but the curious quality that gives the statue its endless mystery is that – it is actually caught in a pregnant moment of 'suspended action'. This is the *rhythmoi*, the 'stilled movement' that gives the statue's *schema* (or pose) its enduring and unique quality. In the words of J. J. Pollit:

"A dancer, moving in time with music, performed specific 'steps' (called eremiai*) in which the body was held for an instant in characteristic positions. The positions were* 'rhythmoi', *'patterns' isolated within continual movement. A single, well-chosen rhythmoi could convey the whole nature of a movement."*[22]

It is surely in this sense that 'the pose' (*schema*) may be best understood: it is *an arrested movement*, combining repose with the intention of action. In his study of *The Nude*, Kenneth Clarke remarks upon the unique quality given off by *"the naked body of an athlete, standing poised between movement and repose."*[23] Indeed, no better word than 'poise' may be used to describe the graceful and delicate balance of a dancer – stopped in mid-motion – which a statue must also possess.

Kenneth Clarke goes on to say about Polykleitus, *"His first problem was to find some means by which the figure should combine repose with the suggestion of potential movement... Polykleitus invented a pose in which the figure is neither walking nor standing, but simply establishing a point of balance."*[24]

In a stilled symmetrical figure from the Hieratic tradition, such as a standing Osiris or sitting Buddha, that 'point of balance' lies mid-way up the invisible plumb line. But with a Humanist figure, the situation is different. As the flexed limbs dynamically balance one another, they create *a new invisible line* – a *curving* line which, if it were to be drawn, would weave *around* the invisible plumb line, respecting its central point of balance with dynamic curves moving above and below, and from side to side.

In the world of dance, the word that best describes this more dynamic form of balance is *aplomb*. According to the *Dictionnaire de l'Académie française*, the term originally came from the world of dance, but expanded to encompass the figure in painting. A well-drawn figure possesses *"la juste pondération des figures"*[25] – 'the proper balance of the parts' – presumably, on either side of the *ligne de plomb* or plumb line. So as long as the weight of the body is distributed evenly on either side, the dancer or sculpted figure, momentarily holding a dynamic pose, will possess the graceful balance of *aplomb*.

X. Persistence of the Hieratic Style

While statues like the Doryphorus and Kritian Boy brought a new Humanist vitality to Classical Greek art, they also preserved certain Hieratic qualities. Most authors emphasize the Humanist innovations, such as the *contrapposto* pose. But Richard Neer, in *The Emergence of the Classical Style in Greek Sculpture*, stresses that the *Kouros*' original pose, as an Archaic trait, persisted well into the Classical period.

In a passage quoted above, Neer described the pose of Archaic *kouros* figures as *"oddly intermediate, neither walking nor standing still."* This mid-point between motion and stasis creates *"...a continuity between Archaic and Classical* [periods, where] *the celebrated rhythmos of the Classical statue, its chiastic interplay of flexed and relaxed, motion and stasis,* [may be viewed] *as a variation on a traditional theme... The slight torsion of Classical contrapposto, such that one shoulder and one hip pivot toward the beholder while the others pivot away, has no counterpart in Archaic work. But* [we may] *see it as the extension and amplification of the traditional, Archaic play of contraries. Contrapposto ratchets up the tensions internal to the kouros pose, makes the play of motion and stasis ever more emphatic, even as it extends that play to govern even the smallest details of the figure."*[26]

Nevertheless, statues from the Classical period did create a sense of time that is manifestly different from the Archaic era. *Kouros* figures possess a "*peculiar timelessness*" that is unique to Hieratic art; they seem to exist in a Platonic world of forms *"outside time."* Meanwhile, the inventions of Kritios and Polykleitos exist in a *'frozen moment'* – an arrested movement or 'pose' that is stilled, yet is still occurring in linear-historical time.

Neer wonders about the *"...preference in Classical Greek art for the depiction of a pregnant moment ...a movement, a gesture, that has either just now slipped into the past or will, any second, come to be. Rhythmos is a real phenomenon,"* he says, but adds that the arrested movement is *"...a gesture that seems to include both the immediate past and the immediate future."*[27]

In this sense, the pose of Classical sculptures exist in a linear-historical measure of time that is decidedly Humanist. Man, the measure of all things, experiences time according to his own mortal measure. In Greek sculpture he stands upon a stage – and rails, suffers or triumphs through stilled gestures to express his bitter encounter with Fate.

In his *Description of Greece* (10.24.1), the 2nd century writer Pausanius mentions two inscriptions carved on the Oracular Temple at Delphi: GNOTHI SAUTON and MEDEN AGAN. The first – *Know Thyself* – sums up the Greek *ethos*, the necessity of understanding one's own character and temperament. But the second – *All Things in Moderation* – summarizes instead the Greek attitude toward *pathos*, of the necessity of avoiding excess passion and maintaining an inner harmony and equilibrium.

As Socrates said above, a statue must do more than 'imitate the forms of living beings' by 'faithfully copying muscular contractions in the body.' Instead, this faithful rendering of the nude figure, its anatomy and *Life-likeness* (*to zotikon*), must be tempered, through the artist's sensitivity and skill (*techne*), to 'incorporate in his ideal form the workings and energies of the soul'.

This faint tremor of intention gives Classical statues their psychological depth. We sense the *psyche* – the stirrings of the soul – as that invisible force inciting the body into action. Through their graceful poise and *aplomb*, Classical statues manifest this delicate balance between action and inaction. In their stilled steps (*rhythmoi*), they achieved a *contrapposto* pose (*schema*) where will and repose counterbalance one another to express the figure's deepest inner strivings in an as-yet unmoved movement.

This is the attribute which gives Classical sculpture its unique beauty: their balanced temperament, inner consideration and calm restraint. But, as Classical art progressed into the Hellenic period, the soul's inner equilibrium was sacrificed in favour of greater expression. To exaggerate certain movements, bodies shifted off balance to dramatically enact humanity's more tragic deeds, exploits and afflictions.

XI. The Hellenistic Era

A sculpture like *The Laocoön* (Fig. 7.5) epitomizes the new Hellenistic spirit in Greek sculpture. The subject is supremely tragic: the temple priest and his two sons must suffer the coils of twin serpents as just retribution for offending the gods. Laocoön's offence has come down to us variously, but in one account (by Servius), he was punished for acting impiously in the gods' sanctuary, committing sacrilege before its sacred image.

The statue is attributed to Agesander, Athenodoros and Polydorus, three Rhodian sculptors working in the Pergamese style around 31 BCE. As it now stands in the Vatican, Laocoön's upper arm is bent, but most likely that arm extended in a heroic diagonal to grasp the serpent (as depicted by Blake in his annotated engraving).

The painful contortions of the three figures created such a profound impression on Renaissance artists that a new term was needed to describe this extreme torsion and overarching *flexus*: the *figura serpentinata*. Unlike the Doryphorus' lateral bend in the two-part *contrapposto*, now the pelvic twist hinted at by the *Belvedere Torso* could be experienced in its full flower: along the main diagonal created by the extended arm and leg, the opposing arm and leg, in their angular flexion, create *an upward spiral* of agony that finally explodes in the Laocoön's anguished features.

In simple terms, a *contrapposto* statue is best viewed form the front, where the lateral tilting of the shoulders and hips creates a flat S-curve of energy. This basic S-curve (the two-part bend) may be augmented by additional C-curves through further tilts of the head, knees and feet (three-part bend, four-part bend, etc).

A *serpentinata* statue, on the other hand, is best viewed from multiple angles, since the shoulders and hips turn *crosswise* (torsion), creating a helical spiral of energy. The energetic movement rises upward like a twisting vine or coiling serpent.

Sculpture in the Hellenistic Age is characterized by brave new explorations in thematics and pose: from childhood (*The Boy with a Goose*) to old age (*The Old Drunk Woman*), from the tragically noble to the comically grotesque. At times, the Ideal is exaggerated to Herculean proportions (*The Farnese Hercules*), while the quest for Naturalism and *Life-likeness* (*to zotikon*) results in a stark and disturbing Realism (*The Old Market Woman*).

The Classical Age tried to tame the opposing forces of *psyche* and *soma* through *contrapposto* poses that balanced their will and repose. But in the Hellenistic Age, these opposing forces became detached and unleashed. The clearest exemplars of these polar extremes are *The Borghese Gladiator* and *The Barberini Faun*.

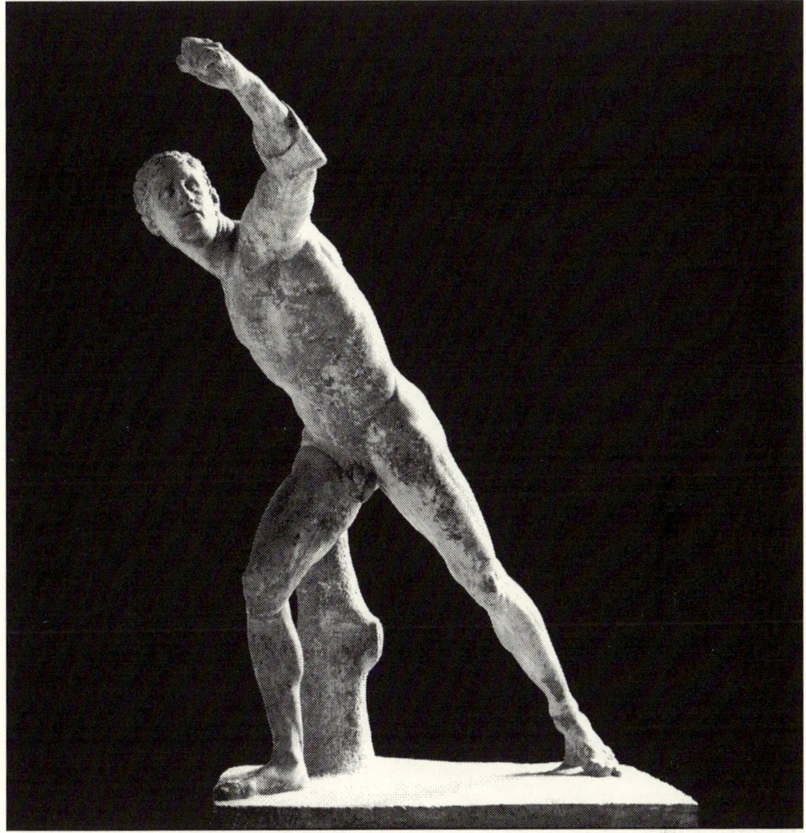

Fig. 7.10 - Agasias: *The Borghese Gladiator* 100 BCE

The marble that has come down to us, of a Swordsman or Gladiator carved by Agasias around 100 BCE (Fig. 7.10), epitomizes that linear burst of energy called 'the heroic diagonal'. The shield once strapped to his upraised arm is now gone, as is the short sword once held in the lower right hand poised to strike. But his extended left arm and left leg form a clear axis around which his angular limbs will soon unleash their coiled power. In the next moment, the shield will come down and the blade arc up to strike home. But for now, he stands poised to act, his muscles stretched and tendons strained, frozen in deep anticipation of the mortal blow.

Once housed in the Villa Borghese and now in the Louvre, *The Borghese Gladiator* has always been renowned for its anatomical accuracy. Each muscle is delineated with greatest care and carved with life-like precision, creating countless bulges and bumps that forego all attempts at stylized lines or Ideal forms. Instead, every fibre and muscle is tensed to express the immense burst of energy that will soon explode across his limbs. In no part of his physique do we find signs of relaxation or repose. Instead, this image is the archetype *of the force of the will* – and more so, *of the soul* in its undaunted courage to overcome the body's trembling, and make one final strike into the heart of its mortal threat.

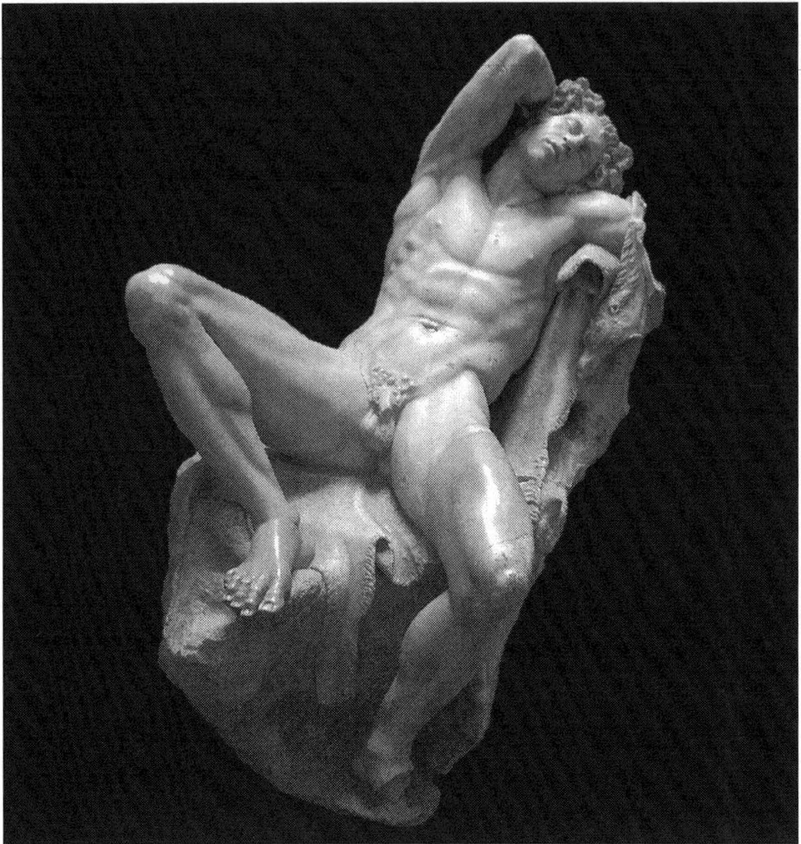

Fig. 7.11 - *The Barberini Faun* c.100 BCE

The Barberini Faun (Fig. 7.11) was carved in the Pergamese style around 100 BCE, and rediscovered in Rome around 1620. After several restorations (parts of the hands, head and right leg were missing), it passed from the Palazzo Barberini in Rome to Munich's Glyptothek. Although the faun lacks his customary horns and hoofs, the drunken abandon and overtly sexual pose attest to his Dionysian character.

In startling contrast to *The Borghese Gladiator*, the languid limbs and stupefied slumber of *The Barberini Faun* bear witness to his *bodily surrender*. Through careless intoxication or perhaps the benumbing milk of the opium poppy, he has succumbed to troubled dreams. Almost every muscle of his well-toned physique has been carved long and flat, then polished smooth to accentuate his *relaxed and lifeless torpor*. Never was a more fitting image carved for the blind surrender of the soul to the body's appetites, pleasures and over-indulgences.

Only in the faint and uneasy tensing of the brow do we sense that this faun's self-induced dreams may fail to soothe his dull and restless soul.

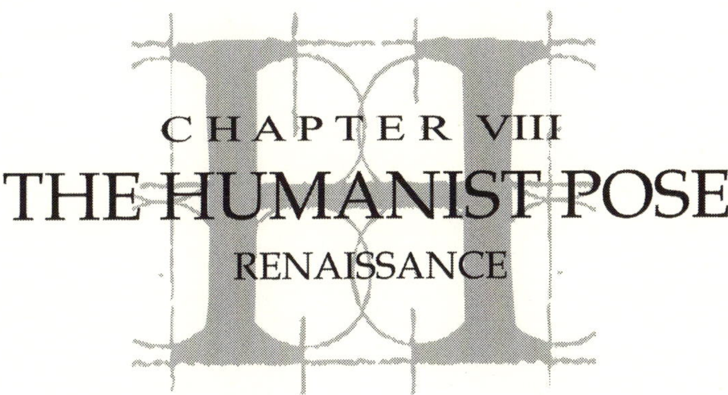

CHAPTER VIII THE HUMANIST POSE

RENAISSANCE

I. The Garden of San Marco

One day in 1475, the fifteen year old Michelangelo, who was still in the third year of his apprenticeship with Ghirlandaio, truantry avoided the master's studio and wandered toward the Garden of San Marco – a plot of land on the Piazza San Marco where Lorenzo the Magnificent had cultivated his antique treasure grove. Amid terraced slopes shaded by tall trees there lay scattered the Duke's prized collection of archaic statues, marbles and bas reliefs, some bordering the winding paths, others sheltered under the white-columned *loggia*.

Under the watchful guidance of Bertoldo, the garden's master sculptor, young Michelangelo carved his first marble – a faun's head copied from fragments of the antique. The workmanship so impressed Lorenzo de Medici that, in Condivi's words, 'he resolved to help and encourage such genius'. *Il Magnifico* invited the young artist to enter his court, giving him a room in his house, a salary of five *scudi* a month, and the key to the garden's gates.

Michelangelo passed the next three years of his life in that fabled treasure grove where Florence's finest (Leonardo had frequented the garden ten years before) wrested the secrets of Classical form from its fragments and remains. *"And not only were these things pleasant to the sight,"* Vasari wrote of the garden's statuary, *"but they became a school and academy for young painters and sculptors."*[1]

In the Villa Medici, Michelangelo sat at table with Marsilio Ficino and Pico della Mirandola, learning first-hand the Platonic, Hermetic and Neo-Platonic worldview from Florence's finest philosophers. Other times, Lorenzo invited the young artist into his private chambers to show him his rare collection of intaglio gems and original paintings by Fra Angelico, Uccello and Van Eyck.

So talented did Michelangelo become that, in 1495, he made a *Sleeping Cupid* that was sold to Cardinal Raffaele Riario in Rome, who bought it thinking it was an antique. When the deception was revealed, the Cardinal sent for the artist and subsequently commissioned a large statue of *Bacchus* (Fig. 8.1). The 21-year -old created a masterpiece through the hitherto-untried method of a Classical nude figure poised *utterly off-balance* due to his frenzied drinking. A few moments more and his Bacchus would topple, like *The Barberini Faun,* in total surrender to his unrestrained revelries.

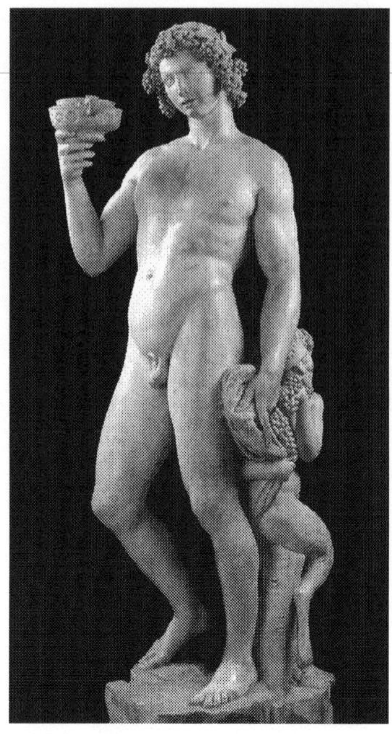
Fig. 8.1 - Michelangelo: *Bacchus* 1497

Alas, other pieces by Michelangelo from this period, such as his *John the Baptist* and colossal *Hercules*, have not survived. But he soon produced two of his most memorable pieces while still in his late twenties: the great marble *Pietà* in Rome and the free-standing *David* in Florence.

II. The Renaissance Revival of Classical Beauty

What these two statues reveal, aside from Michelangelo's rare gift for carving, his unusual temperament and extraordinary genius, is that the artist possessed *a thorough-going understanding of Antique principles – la maniera antica* as it was then called. His *David* (Fig. 8.3) epitomizes the Renaissance revival of Classical Beauty. In this pensive youth poised between action and inaction, the gentle *contrapposto* arches the tensed hip *up* and the relaxed shoulder *down* to create a powerful S-curve of energy that explodes in the glance of an eye. The statue's anatomy is subordinated to style, and the opposing forces of will and repose course up and down his perfectly-balanced figure, which is caught in a pregnant moment of suspended action. From the accentuated eye down to the inner ankle of the weight-bearing foot, the plumb line becomes an ever-constant fulcrum for the counterbalance of flexed limbs. Michelangelo had studied well the antique statues in the Garden of San Marco, and applied their Classical principles to his pondering colossus.

His *Pietà* (Fig. 8.4) pursues these same principles, but now the forces of will and repose are distributed equally over the ensemble of figures. Recently deposed from the cross, the body of Christ slumps lifeless in the Virgin's arms – deprived of all will, his spirit resting, his soul surrendering unto death. It seems that the Virgin too, in deep compassion for her son, has slumped lifeless under her burden. Yet, through a slight tremor of the will,

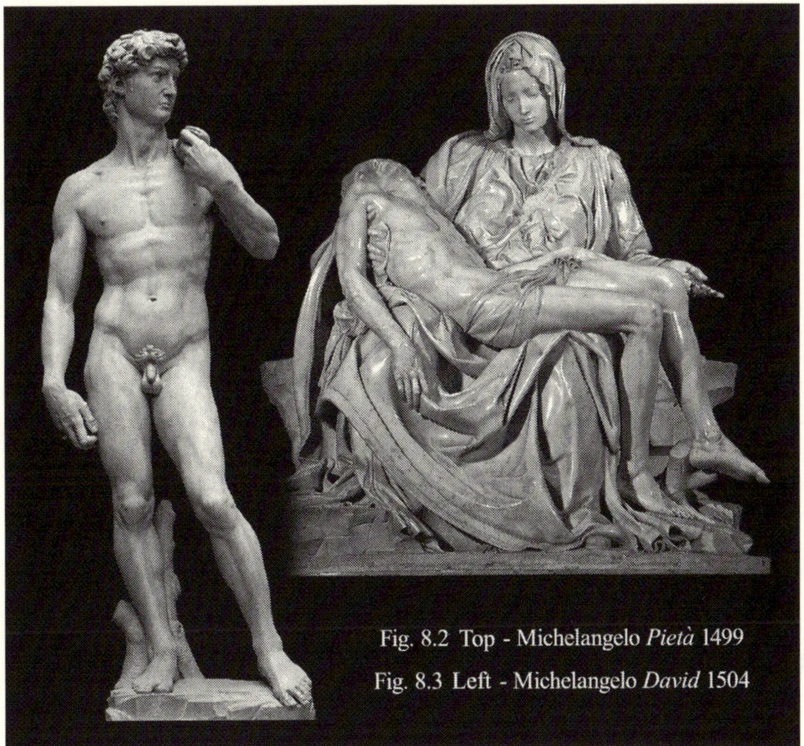

Fig. 8.2 Top - Michelangelo *Pietà* 1499

Fig. 8.3 Left - Michelangelo *David* 1504

she bows her head and gestures willingly, in loving surrender and acceptance of his sacrifice. In this ensemble of figures, the play of motion and stasis, as death and acceptance, balance one another in a paused moment of tranquil suffering.

In his treatise *On Painting*, Leon Battista Alberti gave voice to the same silent principles underlying the art of his contemporaries. In the first part of his treatise he introduced the key concept of the *istoria* – the story or theme that gives a work of art its soul-stirring power. In the second part, he finally furnished his contemporaries with an example, citing a (now-lost) sarcophagus in Rome:

"An istoria is praised in Rome in which Meleager, a dead man, weighs down those who carry him. In every one of his members he appears completely dead—everything hangs, hands, fingers and head; everything falls heavily. Anyone who tries to express a dead body – which is certainly most difficult – will be a good painter, if he knows how to make each member of a body flaccid... The members of the dead should be dead to the very nails; of live persons every member should be alive in the smallest part. The body is said to live when it has certain voluntary movements... that is, motion and feeling. Therefore the painter, wishing to express life in things, will make every part in motion."[2]

In Alberti's unmistakable style (of Italian embellishments on Latin prose), we have the true Renaissance expression of those same Classical principles that Xenophon expressed in his *Memorabilia*. A dead body should 'hang with its members flaccid' – that is, in utter and complete *repose* – while a living body should express 'motion and feeling' through *the intentions of the will.* Due to its 'voluntary movements' ('self-motion'), the painted or sculpted figure will 'express life', and hence, manifest that soulful and Life-like quality (*to zotikon*) so cherished by the Greeks.

Alberti presents the *mortuus languidus* as a kind of challenge, and many Renaissance artists rose to the occasion, because the tragic Greek theme of *The Fallen Warrior* or *The Death of the Hero* translated well into Christian altarpieces of *The Crucifixion* or *The Deposition from the Cross.* And the underlying philosophy – of the soul's striving for the body's release – also translated well from Neo-Platonism to Christian theology. It was Michelangelo, above all, who returned to the *Pietà* theme repeatedly at the end of his life, to express his tormented vision of the soul's striving for liberation from *il carcer terreno* (as Michelangelo called it in a poem), *the earthly prison.**

In Michelangelo's poetry, this striving becomes the quest for Ideal Beauty – of the soul's visionary ascent to the higher forms, the realm of Ideas, which our bodily senses cloud and obscure:

"As a sure guide to me in my vocation, the Idea of Beauty
Which is a mirror and a lamp to both my arts
Was bestowed upon me at birth.
Whoever conceives otherwise is mistaken.
This Idea alone lifts my eyes to those high visions
Which I set myself to carve and paint here below.
If men of rash and foolish judgement drag sense-ward the Beauty
Which moves and transports every right Intelligence to heaven
It is because weak and wavering eyes, and even eyes not fixed on things above,
Cannot pass from the mortal to the Divine,
For without grace, it is a vain thought that one may rise thither."[4]

III. The Prisoners at Death's Doorway

The clearest examples of Michelangelo's self-tormenting schism comes with the *Two Slaves,* carved in 1513 as part of the funerary monument to Pope Julias II. Now housed in the Louvre, these larger-than-life statues seem to rise, conscious and alive, from their heavy pedestals. Originally, Michelangelo had planned some sixteen to twenty *Prigioni* (Prisoners), chained to herms (squared pillars tapering to the head of a god), and flanking Death's doorway. According to his biographer Condivi, *"...in a niche were herms. Fettered to these, on certain socles which rose from the ground and projected outward, were other statues, Captives as it were... prisoners of death."*[5]

*"In order to return where it came from, the immortal form came down to your earthly prison."[3]

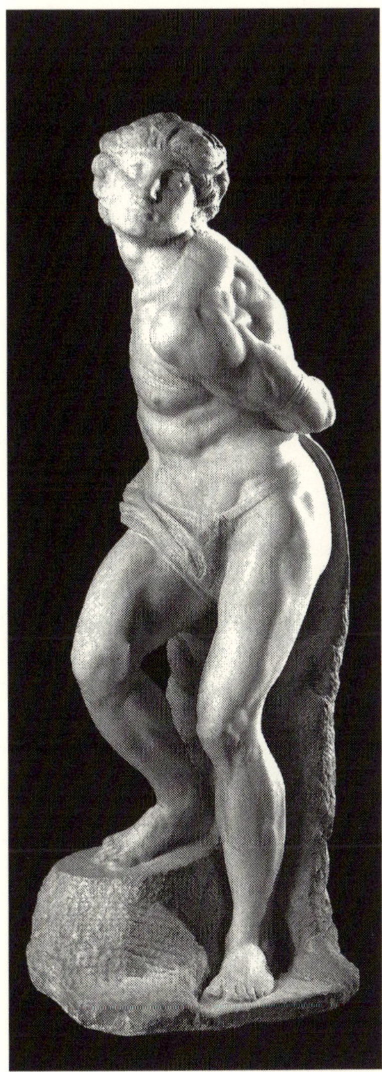

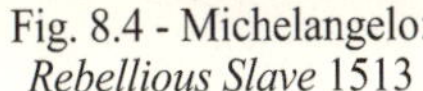

Fig. 8.4 - Michelangelo: *Rebellious Slave* 1513

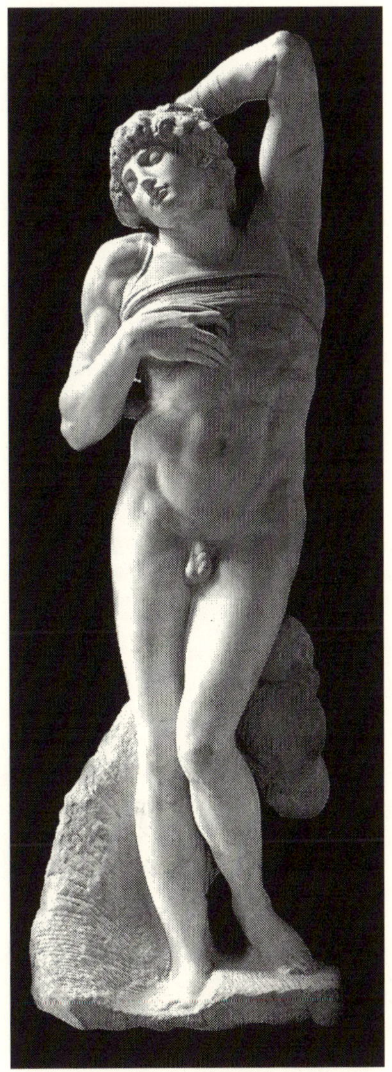

Fig. 8.5 - Michelangelo: *Dying Slave* 1516

Each manifests its own attitude toward death – and yet how different are the Two Captives which have come down to us through time... The first, called *The Rebellious Slave,* strains with all the strength *of the will* against his restraining bonds. Like *The Borghese Gladiator*, an undaunting determination, fearless and true, struggles against the shackles of the flesh, to liberate the soul from its entrapment in matter and time. His powerful twist ends in an upturned head with eyes opened wide, staring heavenward with hopes of redemption.

By contrast, *The Dying Slave* surrenders to death, his limbs bent loosely in erotic abandon and hypnotic *repose*. His *contrapposto* curve ends with an upturned arm, the Classical sign (from Niobids to the Laocoön) of mortal suffering. Yet, like *The Barberini Faun*, his sensuous curves and slumbering attitude indicate a complete lapse of the will – of the soul giving itself over to the dull and heavy burden of the flesh. Like his brother, he too tilts his head heavenward, but heavy lids shield his eyes from higher vision. He dies in deep sleep, surrendering to sensory illusion and trapped in a world of fading forms and earthly shadows.

In another poetic stanza, Michelangelo wrote:

"Had my soul not been created God-like
It would still seek no more than outward beauty
The delight of the eyes;
But since this fades so fast, my soul soars beyond
To the eternal Form."[6]

In their contrasting poses, the two *Prigioni* take the opposing forces of *psyche* and *soma* to their polar extremes, making one the utter and complete expression *of the will*, and the other, the laxity and surrender *of bodily repose*. In this sense, they manifest the same Hellenistic exaggerations as *The Borghese Gladiator* and *The Barberini Faun*. But, in some of the more powerful figures from *The Last Judgement*, Michelangelo has successfully balanced these two attitudes. More than that, he has used the contrasting forces of will and repose to create an energetic tension that transcends the confines of the individual figure and explodes in a gesture or glance. This can be seen most clearly in the two great figures flanking Christ, of John the Baptist on the left and St. Peter on the right.

IV. The Power of a Gesture or Glance

As Vasari noted, "[in The Last Judgement] *may be seen marvellously portrayed, all the emotions that mankind can experience... Moreover, anyone in a position to judge will also be struck by the amazing diversity of the figures, which is reflected in the various and unusual gestures... The Last Judgement must be recognized as the great exemplar of the grand manner of painting.*"[7]

If we cast our gaze once more upon the upper portion of this fresco (Fig. 7.1), we remark how the Baptist and the Saint are turning towards Christ in a most dramatic manner. Meditating on these figures as if they were statues carved entirely in marble, we note how each has placed his weight upon one foot, which becomes the central axis (or plumb line) for the figure's dramatic turning. Meanwhile, the heel of the hind foot rises slightly, creating a ¢-shaped movement around the central axis. Situated an equal distance from Christ, these two appear to be mirrored reflections. Yet, each moves and expresses its energy in a different manner.

John the Baptist (Fig. 8.6) is being restrained by another figure. With the right foot forward, he strives with all his might to turn to the right and

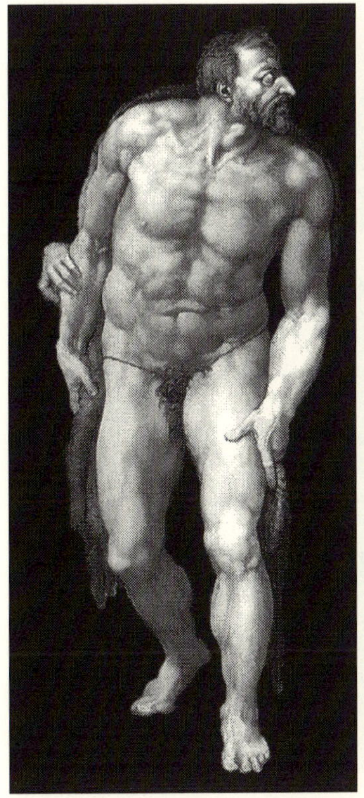

Fig. 8.6 - Michelangelo: *John the Baptist*
Detail of The Last Judgement 1541

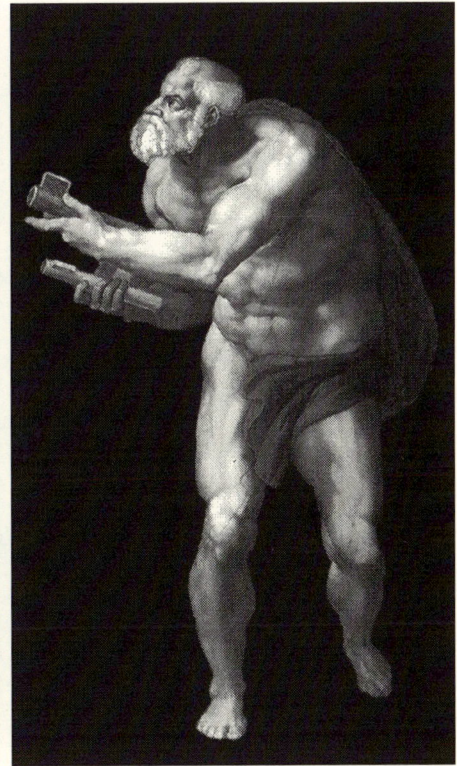

Fig. 8.7 - Michelangelo: *St. Peter*
Detail of *The Last Jadgement* 1541

'see' the Christ. To emphasize this glance, the Baptist's eye was rendered disproportionately large. Meanwhile, the hips shift laterally one way while the shoulders tilt laterally the other. Michelangelo has focussed all of the body's energy and torsion in such a way that the twisting *contrapposto* movement *explodes in a glance.* Instinctively, our eye ascends the energetic tensions in the figure, from weight-bearing foot to glancing eye, to transcend the figure on a horizontal line of vision that ultimately comes to rest upon Christ.

Meanwhile, with St. Peter (Fig. 8.7), his intense glance is accompanied *by a powerful gesture,* as the saint holds up two keys, one silver, one gold. In Dante's *Purgatorio*, an angel unlocks Peter's Gate with two such keys – the silver signifying the soul's remorse, and the gold a token of God's forgiveness. Both, Dante says, are necessary for the soul's salvation. Standing just above the damned, with a terrified St. Paul at his shoulder, St. Peter seems to be *offering* the keys to Christ – beseeching him to take salvation into his own hands.

To create St. Peter's powerful gesture, Michelangelo has resorted to the extreme twist of the *Figura Serpentinata.* Moving beyond the *lateral tilting* of the Baptist's *contrapposto,* Saint Peter's shoulders *turn cross-wise* to the pelvis, creating an acute torsion that pushes figurative expression to its limits while still maintaining a degree of balance and repose. To offer the keys, the arm opposite the weight bearing leg *crosses over* the central axis in a serpentine spiral that pushes the energy *beyond the gesture*, carrying our gaze in a horizontal line of vision, once more, toward the Christ.

The expression *Figura Serpentinata* comes to us through Gian Paolo Lomazzo, an Italian painter who turned to writing when he lost his sight in 1571. His seminal work, *Idea del tempio della pittura* (The Idea of the Temple of Painting – 1590) was intended, in fact, as an introduction and summary of an earlier work called *Trattato della pittura* (A Treatise on Painting – 1584) published six years before. *The Idea of the Temple of Painting* appeared forty years after Michelangelo's *Last Judgement*, during a time when the *cinquecento* or High Renaissance was already in decline. Lomazzo's writings became, for the newly-emerging period of Mannerism, what Vasari's writings were for the Renaissance.

Typical of Mannerism, Lomazzo's writings stressed the linear quality and stylistic expression of a figure, preferring 'grace' rather than well-structured proportion. To this end, he promoted Michelangelo's *figura serpentinata*, preferring its spiralling movement and intense expression to the lateral bend and balanced tension of the *contrapposto*. In one section Lomazzo wrote:

"It is said that Michelangelo gave this piece of advice to Marco da Siena, his student – that the figure should always be pyramidal, serpentine, and bend one, two or three times. It seems to me that the whole secret of painting is contained in this precept, since the figure achieves its greatest grace and elegance when shown in movement – what the painters call the figure's fury. To represent this movement, there is no better form in Nature than the fiery flame..."[8]

Following up on the idea of the pyramid and the flame, Lomazzo wrote, *"There are two sorts of pyramids, one straight, ...the other in the form of an undulating flame. Which is to say, the figure should manifest the shape of a right-facing S, or its opposite, and in this way it will possess beauty."*[9] Returning to the idea of the serpent, Lomazzo wrote, *"All movement should be represented in such a way as if the body had the form of a serpent, which is the way Nature had intended it."*[10]

Through John the Baptist's *contrapposto* and St. Peter's *figura serpentinata*, Michelangelo demonstrated his profound understanding of Classical principles – *la maniera antica* – and how these had moved past the world of Antique sculpture and into the realm of Renaissance painting. For sculpture is primarily concerned with the figure, with the forces of will and repose that animate the stone. But painting subordinates the figure to a whole series of other concerns, such as composition and armature, *istoria* and narrative.

Through these expressive gestures and glances, the energetic tensions of will and repose transcend the confines of the individual figures and explode in a burst of energy that directs our eye across lines of armature to create *a narrative movement* through the painting. This is what gives Renaissance art its unique power. Instead of the single and stilled focus of Hieratic art,

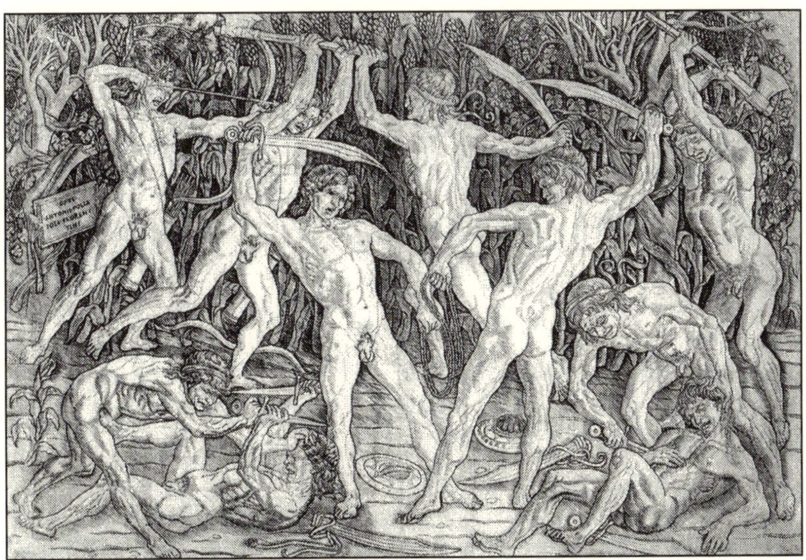

Fig. 8.8 - Pollaiuolo: *Battle of the Nudes* c. 1465

which directs the eye towards calm meditation on a central divine figure, in Humanist art the eye is encouraged to rove and scan from figure to figure, in a deliberate unfolding of the painting's narrative or *istoria*. Ultimately, with the fusion of Humanist and Hieratic Styles, we will encourage the wandering eye to come to rest on a stilled and contemplative point at the centre. But for now, we wish to understand how the eye may be deliberately directed around the painting, moving from figure to figure.

V. Complementary & Opposing Figures

"That figure is most praiseworthy," Leonardo wrote, *"which, by its action, best expresses the passions of the soul."*[11] For the Renaissance artist, the highest aspiration was to create human figures that, through dramatic action and outbursts of emotion, expressed the soul's inner workings. But, once that energy had moved beyond the confines of a single human figure, it manifested its dynamic movement in new relationships, engaging complementary or opposing figures.

An early but important example of this is Antonio del Pollaiuolo's *Battle of the Nudes* (Fig. 8.8) where five figures with headbands are opposing five figures without such an adornment. The two central figures epitomize this new *contrapposto* conflict, where energy is transferred *from one figure to the other.* The composition carefully preserves a balanced symmetry, wherein the 'heroic diagonals' of the central couple follow a large V or inverted triangle, which is inscribed overtop the central upright triangle (Fig. 8.9).

Over this basic armature (which we will investigate later as The Harmonic Armature), Pollaiuolo has arranged his central figures, which pull against

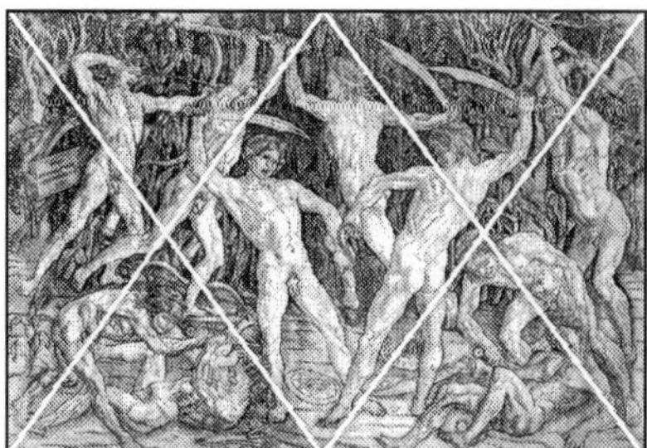

Fig. 8.9 - *Battle of the Nudes* Armature

one another (linked by chained hands) even as they stand poised to strike each other down. In the two smaller triangles at the base, pairs of figures to the left and right form self-contained circuits of dynamic energy, trapped in mortal combat. To the far left and right, standing figures (one with a stretched bow, the other with an upheld axe) form inward-facing columns or brackets for the composition – a standard device from antique sarcophagi. Finally, the figure at the apex of the central triangle (raising his sword) draws our attention decidedly to the left, to engage his opponent with the upheld club.

All in all, ten separate figures are carefully arranged around the armature, drawing our attention in a large circle around the central triangles that form a basic diamond shape.

By the time we reach Leonardo's *Battle of Anghiari*, this genre of 'dynamic battle scene' had become well-established. The two basic triangles – one upright, the other inverted – are still present, but Leonardo has arranged his six warriors and four horses with a coiling *serpentinata* transfer of energy that goes far beyond any *contrapposto* conflict devised by Pollaiuolo. Our eye still follows a large circle around the basic diamond shape, but now the countless spirals in the helmets, breast plates and horses' manes invite our gaze to pause and dwell upon all the details.

Rather than portray two figures divided in strife, the artist could also seek to unite them in love. The upper right portion of Michelangelo's *Last Judgement* was severely criticized upon its unveiling, because it depicted the Saints embracing – men kissing women, and men kissing men. But, for once, Michelangelo had abandoned his *terribilità* temperament, and celebrated the *contrapposto* joining of two figures in love. Renaissance artists like Mantegna (*Parnassus*) and Botticelli (*Primavera*) delighted in depicting this shared passion and joy, the joined movement of all-uniting love, by interlacing their dancing muses and prancing nymphs. In these works, figures move harmoniously together, delighting the eye in a circuitous dance around the composition.

VI. Alberti's *Della Pittura* – Book I: Bodies, Members & Planes

In a certain sense, artists from all traditions (whether Humanist or Hieratic) have always depicted scenes from sacred texts, mythology or literature. What makes the *istoria* unique is that it seeks to create *a narrative movement* within the composition – using the dynamic transfer of energy from figure to figure as the essential driving force for the narrative unfolding. Hieratic art, which tends towards stilled figures in hierarchal structures, lacks this dynamic movement.

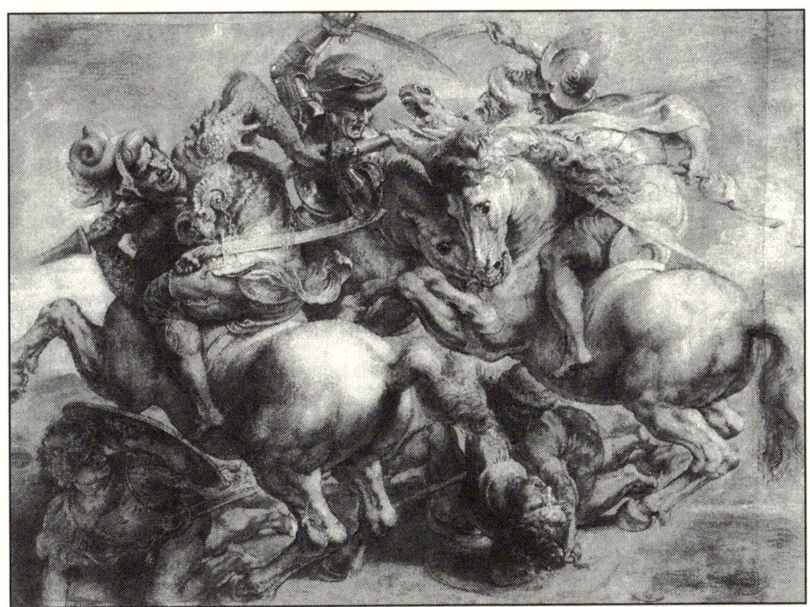

Fig. 8.10 - Rubens: Copy of Leonardo's lost *Battle of Anghiari* from 1505

In his seminal text *Della Pittura* (On Painting - 1435), Alberti introduced the key concept of the *istoria* (Latin: *Historia*; Italian: *Istoria* or *Storia*) as the narrative idea that holds the figures together in a composition, giving a definite meaning and purpose to their emotive expression.

Alas, the author's explication of the *istoria* is never clear and precise. Rather, he introduces the *istoria* as part of a much greater and far-reaching plan – to elevate the craft of Painting to the same level of nobility as Poetry, History, Rhetoric, Grammar and Ethics – all of which constituted the *Studia Humanitatis* or 'Humanist Curriculum' of the newly-emerging Renaissance.

As we shall see next chapter on The Academy and the Guild, painting in the early Renaissance was still considered a craft. To elevate this pictorial art to the same status as poetry, Alberti had to give it a solid theoretical foundation, on par with Cicero's and Quintilian's texts on Rhetoric, which gave the *ars poetica* its philosophical dignity and intellectual prestige.

In this regard, he was joined by other important Renaissance writers, such as Giorgio Vasari (*Le Vite de' più eccellenti pittori, scultori, ed architettori* – The Lives of the Most Excellent Painters, Sculptors and Architects -1550), Ludovico Dolce (*Aretin: Dialogo della pittura* – Aretin: A Dialogue on Painting -1557) and, somewhat later, Gian Paolo Lomazzo (*Idea del tempio della pittura* – The Idea of the Temple of Painting - 1590).

The great aesthetic question of the day concerned the *paragone* (or 'comparison') – which of the arts, among painting, sculpture, architecture, poetry and music, was superior to the rest? Leonardo spilled a lot of ink championing painting over sculpture (much to Michelangelo's chagrin). But what made painting superior to the others, or at least of equal rank to poetry, was its narrative capacity – the *istoria*.

Ut Pictura Poesis – a maxim by the Latin poet Horace – became the catchphrase and rallying cry of Renaissance artists and writers: *"As is poetry, so is painting.*" Whatever qualities made poetry great, so too did painting possess those qualities in abundance. This becomes clear in the arguments Alberti, Vasari and Dolce developed for their defence of painting as a noble art.

Alberti begins his argument in Book I of *Della Pittura* by analyzing the component parts of painting. Just as the Rhetoricians divided their language into clauses, phrases and words, so does Alberti divide the painter's language into three parts: bodies, members and planes. Planes, in particular, may be further reduced to basic geometrical shapes, such as squares or cubes; triangles or tetrahedra; circles or spheres.

The 'body' is the figure delineated in a painting, whether it be human, animal, vegetable or mineral. The 'members' of the body are its constituent parts, such as the head or limbs. And we perceive the 'planes' when light falls upon the members – causing some planes to fall into shadowy shapes, while others become well-defined forms in the light.

As such, each plane has an 'outline' (*Circumscriptione*) which defines its basic geometrical shape, whether flat or voluminous. In one section, the plane appears to be flat: *"As the movement of the outline is changed, the plane changes both name and appearance so that it is now called a triangle, now a quadrangle and now a polygon."*[12] In another section, the plane may also be voluminous: *"Some planes are flat, others are hollowed out, and others are swollen outward and are spherical."*[13]

All of this geometry is necessary because Alberti wishes to ultimately introduce linear perspective, as a rational measure for ordering planes in space.

VII. Alberti's *Della Pittura* – Book II: Circumscription, Composition & Reception of Light

In Book II, Alberti expands his argument by analyzing the three steps necessary for the creation of a painting. *"Painting,"* he says *"is composed of circumscription, composition and reception of light."*[14] Once again, the author has taken his cue from the Latin Rhetoricians, who divided the art of oratory into five basic steps: *inventio, dispositio, elocutia, memoria,* and *pronunitiatio*. These 'Five Canons of Classical Rhetoric' may be summarized as follows:

- *Inventio* (the invention) – the orator develops the ideas or arguments for his discourse.
- *Dispositio* (the arrangement) – he arranges these parts into an ordered sequence or outline.
- *Elocutia* (the style) – he selects word order and ornamentation for the stylistic expression of his ideas
- *Memoria* (the memorization) – he uses mnemonic techniques to memorize his discourse.
- *Pronunitiatio* (the delivery) – he pronounces his discourse, paying close attention to gesture, pacing and emphasis.

For Alberti, the art of painting follows the same canonical steps as Classical Rhetoric. Although Book II mentions only three of these steps – *circonscriptione*, *compositione*, and *receptione di lumi* – later in Book III he also speaks of invention (*inventio*), memory (*memoria*) and style (*maniera* as *elocutia*).

Ludovico Dolce, in his *Dialogue on Painting (*1557) also divides painting into three parts, and his division follows even more closely the order of the Latin Rhetoricians. For Dolce, painting is a process of invention (*inventio*), design (*disegno*) and colouring (*colorito*):

"The whole sum of painting is, in my opinion, divided into three parts: invention, design and colouring. The invention [inventio] *is the fable* [favole] *or history* [istoria] *which the painter chooses on his own or which others present him with, as material for the work he has to do. The design* [disegno] *is the form he uses to represent the material. And the coloring* [colorito] *takes its cue from the hues with which nature paints (for one can say as much) animate and inanimate things in variegation."*[15]

It is worthwhile to examine some of these key concepts, since they ultimately shed light on the *istoria*.

In Alberti, the first step of painting – *circonscriptione* – is basically the drawing stage, when 'bodies, members and planes' are all delineated through outlines:

"Circumscription describes the turning of the outline in the painting... circumscription is nothing but the drawing of the outline... that is, a good drawing [disegno]. *"*[16]

Despite the simplicity of this passage, Alberti has much more in mind. First of all, the Italian word for drawing – *disegno* – also means 'design'. In this sense, Alberti's first step (*circonscriptione*) is equivalent to Dolce's second step (*disegno*) – both require a degree of, not just drawing, but planning and design.

Instead of *disegno*, Alberti uses the more technical term *circonscriptione* because he wishes to emphasize the geometrical 'outlining' of the basic shapes that constitute 'bodies, members and planes'. But, *circonscriptione* is *disegno*; Alberti advises his artist 'to draw' and, more than that, 'to design' his figures according to certain 'rules of mind':

"Never take the pencil or brush in hand," Alberti says, *"if you have not first constituted with your mind all that you have to do and how you have to do it... and that hand will proceed most rapidly which is well guided by a certain rule of the mind."*[17]

These 'rules of mind', it turns out, have to do with the construction of the figures, particularly in terms of proportion, the pose, and perspective.

The first 'rule of mind' concerns the constant measure of one 'member' to the next in the 'body', thus granting the figure its proper proportion:

"A thing to remember: to measure an animate body take one of its members by which the others can be measured. Vitruvius, the architect, measured the height of man by the feet. It seems a more worthy thing to me for the other members to have reference to the head... Thus one member is taken which corresponds to all the other members in such a way that none of them is non-proportional."[18]

The second 'rule of mind' concerns the figure's expression of will and repose in the pose:

"[The diligent artist] *will remember how graceful are the hanging legs of him who is seated; he will note in standing persons that there is no part of the body which does not know its function."*[19]

Finally, the figures will be spatially arranged through perspective, a system which treats the painter's canvas as a 'glass' (often called Alberti's Window). When the painter stands in a certain place before this glass, pyramidal rays of vision pass through it, connecting his eye with the outline of planes. After a long technical explanation of perspective (which, alas, was far from complete, leaving many of his contemporaries in the dark), Alberti writes:

"Some will say here of what use to the painter is such an investigation? I think every painter, if he wishes to be a great master, ought to understand clearly... that they circumscribe the plane with their lines. When they fill the circumscribed places with colours, they should only seek to present the forms of things seen on this plane as if it were of transparent glass. Thus the visual pyramid could pass through it... Each painter demonstrates this when, in painting this plane, he places himself at a distance as if searching the point and angle of the pyramid from which point he understands the thing painted is best seen."[20]

What Alberti does not say is that linear perspective, for the first time in history, unified pictorial space in an entirely novel way – through the convention of perceiving (supposedly) parallel lines as converging in the distance onto a common 'vanishing point'. This unified the painting's interior space in a way hitherto unknown and untried in art history. Perspective (from the Latin *perspicere* – 'to look through') allowed the artist's vision to 'pass through' the canvas, as if, through a window, gathering all the figures together into one cohesive compositional space.

VIII. Alberti: *Compositione & Istoria*

In Alberti's first step of painting – *circonscriptione* – the artist 'draws and designs' (*disegno*) the bodies, members and planes according to certain 'rules of mind' pertaining to proportion, the pose, and perspective. This first step then segues into the second – *compositione* (composition). But, in the same paragraph where he defines composition, Alberti also mentions, for the very first time, the concept of *istoria*:

"Circumscription [circonscriptione] *which pertains not a little to composition, remains to be treated. For this it is well to know what composition is in painting. I say composition* [compositione] *is that rule in painting by which the parts fit together in the painted work. The greatest work of the painter is the* istoria. *Bodies are part of the istoria, members are parts of the bodies, planes are parts of the members. Circumscription is nothing more than a certain rule for designing* [disegno] *the outline of the planes, since some planes are small as in animals, others are large as those of buildings and colossi."*[21]

In this important passage we have both a definition of *compositione* ('the rule by which the parts fit together') and its dependence upon the *istoria*, as a broader category for subsuming bodies, members and planes in the composition. But the *istoria* is more than that. In a later passage, Alberti comes closest to defining what the *istoria* is:

"The fame of the painter and of his art is found in the following – the composition of bodies... All bodies should harmonize in size and in function to what is happening in the istoria. *The* istoria *which merits both praise and admiration will be so agreeably and pleasantly attractive that it will capture the eye of whatever learned or unlearned person is looking at it and will move his soul."*[22]

Here, *compositione* is not only 'the rule by which the parts fit together' in painting, but also *the harmonious organization* of those parts, *according to the istoria*. Already during the first step of *circonscriptione*, 'the parts fit together' through their disposition in perspectival space. But during the second step of *compositione*, the artist must also use his figurative imagination to compose them *harmoniously*, according to the requirements of the *istoria*.

The most important function of the *istoria* is 'to capture the eye of the beholder' and 'move his soul'. Through its narrative direction, *the istoria guides the eye around the composition*; and through its subject matter or theme, the figure's gestures acquire sufficient meaning *to move the spectator's soul*. In this way, the *istoria* takes the energy erupting in a single figure's gesture or glance and directs it around the painting according to the narrative unfolding. This is what makes painting – *Ut Pictura Poesis* – like epic poetry: they share a well-defined narrative development.

"I strongly approve in all istoria," Alberti writes, *"that which I see observed by tragic and comic poets. They tell a story with as few characters as possible. In my judgment no picture will be filled with so great a variety of things that nine or ten men are not able to act with dignity."*[23]

It is not only the narrative (the Aristotelian *mythos*) which makes painting the sister art of poetry, but also its portrayal of character (the Aristotelian *ethos*). Like Epic Poetry, a major work of art will have a great many characters, in variety and abundance:

"That which first gives pleasure in the istoria *comes from copiousness* [copia] *and variety* [varieta] *of things... I say that* istoria *is most copious in which in their places are mixed old, young, maidens, women, youths, young boys, fowls, small dogs, birds, horses, sheep, buildings, landscapes and all similar things... However, I prefer this copiousness to be embellished with a certain variety, yet moderate and grave with dignity and truth."*[24]

The risk of depicting such a wide variety of figures is that the composition might fall into chaos and confusion – leaving the eye to err and wander aimlessly (*"It is not composition but dissolute confusion* [dissolutus],*"*[25] Alberti laments). As such, the greatest challenge for the Renaissance artist was to achieve *varieta e compositione* – to portray an abundant variety of characters (*varieta*) *and* still preserve a high degree of harmony and cohesion in the composition (*compositione*), so that all accord well with the *istoria*. Such a major work of art, successfully executed, expressed *la maniera grande* – the grand style.

In this way, Renaissance painters were able to rise above the status of mere craftsmen, and share with poets the noble aims and rhetorical devices for 'moving the spectator's soul':

"For their own enjoyment," Alberti concludes, *"artists should associate with poets and orators who have many embellishments in common with painters and who have a broad knowledge of many things whose greatest praise consists in* the invention... *Poets, rhetoricians and others equally well learned in letters... will give new* inventions *or at least aid in beautifully composing the* istoria.*"*[26]

After comparing painters to poets and orators, Alberti mentions 'the invention' (*inventio*) – the first of the Five Canons utilized by rhetoricians, and the first of three steps in painting described later by Dolce. For Dolce, we recall, cited the three steps of painting as invention (*inventio*), design (*disegno*) and colouring (*colorito*). And he went on to say that *"The invention* [inventio] *is the fable* [favole] *or history* [istoria] *which the painter chooses..."*[27]

The starting point for any great work of art, in Renaissance times, was *the invention* – that initial sketch of figures disposed here and there, each with its unique pose, gaze and expression, but all variously composed in such a way as to convey – in a purely pictorial manner – the *istoria.*

Once *the Invention* was complete, the artist would labour hard to perfect the individual parts – drawing and designing (*disegno*) the gestures of the hands, observing the character of each unique face, and developing the interaction of figures within the whole. The outlines (*circonscriptione*) gave the figures their basic disposition in space, respecting the laws of proportion, pose and perspective. Through armature (though Alberti never mentions *la trame* or armature explicitly), a more harmonious composition (*compositione*) was attempted, respecting the requirements of the *istoria.*

"When we have an istoria *to paint,"* Alberti writes, *"we will first think out the method and the order to make it most beautiful; we will make our drawings and models of all the* istoria *and every one of its parts first of all... We will force ourselves to have every part well thought out in our mind from the beginning, so that in the work we will know how each thing ought to be done and where located. In order to have the greatest certainty we will divide our models with parallels."*[28]

Among other methods described here, Alberti also mentions how the artist will 'make models' – meaning the jointed wooden figures or manikins used by many artists to pose their figures – and then 'divide our models with parallels', meaning either their correct proportions or the square grids used for transferring the initial drawing.

Once the underdrawing was complete, the artist proceeded with the third step of painting. First, an ink wash would help determine the distribution of light and shadow (*receptione di lumi*). Next, the painter would grind his pigments, mix them in oil or egg tempera, and lay down an even glaze of colour (the *imprimatura*), upon which the volumes were developed in lead white (again: *receptione di lumi*). Finally, with costly pigments, he would glaze the figures multiple times to develop their rich chromatic hues (*colorito*).

IX. Vasari on Memory & Design

Memoria, as we saw, was the fourth Canon of Classical Rhetoric. By visualizing a series of inscriptions on architectural edifices, or imagining key words inscribed on the feathers of a six-winged cherub,[29] poets and orators were able to memorize and recite long epic poems or political speeches.

In painting, the art of memory (*ars memoriae*) was no less valued or praised. In his *Lives of the Most Excellent Painters, Sculptors and Architects,* Giorgio Vasari commended the young artist to commit to memory all the forms and principles of art, in order to aid the drawing and design. For example, in one passage Vasari wrote: *"By drawing on paper, the mind is filled with beautiful conceptions, and one learns to make by memory* [fare a mente] *all the objects of nature, without having to keep them always before you."*[30]

The importance of *Memoria* in drawing brought with it a whole new debate – already raised in Classical times – as to whether art was 'an imitation of Nature' (*mimesis*) or a striving for the Ideal (*eidos*). The great artists of the past, such as Polykleitus, tempered anatomical accuracy with the stylistic ideal. But, to accomplish this, the Renaissance artists had to, first, *draw from memory*, which takes examples from *both* Nature *and* the Imagination. Once again, Vasari:

"The best thing is to draw men and women from the nude and thus fix in the memory by constant exercise the muscles of the torso, back, legs, arms and knees, with the bones underneath. Then one may be sure that, through much study, attitudes in any position can be drawn by help of the imagination without one's having the living forms in view."[31]

For an artist to *invent* (*inventare*) a *design* (*disegno*) that composes multiple figures in the *istoria*, he could not, of course, depend upon a whole studio of nude models posed in some battle scene. Rather, through constant practice (beginning as an apprentice in early youth), he studied anatomy, poses and proportion, committing all of these to memory. The apprentice also studied antique models and casts to acquire the Classical Style, which 'improved upon Nature' through Ideal stylization. Again, Vasari:

"He who has not drawn much nor studied the choicest ancient and modern works cannot... improve the things that he copies from life, giving them the grace and perfection in which art goes beyond the scope of Nature."[32]

Here, Vasari is touching upon the debate, aforementioned, of art as 'an imitation of Nature' (*mimesis*) or as a striving for the Ideal (*eidos*). For the new scientific spirit of the age, as exemplified by Leonardo, sought nothing more than to accurately observe and understand the principles of Nature. But the Neo-Platonic spirit, as exemplified by Michelangelo, renounced the evidence of the senses and sought instead those higher forms, seen only by the soul in vision.

"All our knowledge has its origin in our perceptions,"[33] Leonardo wrote in his Notebooks, adding elsewhere: *"The eye, which is called the window of the soul, is the chief means whereby the understanding may most fully and*

abundantly appreciate the infinite works of Nature."[34] Leonardo's Notebooks are filled with sketches and remarks on the nature of vision, flight, motion, mechanics, optics, perspective, anatomy, astronomy and human character.

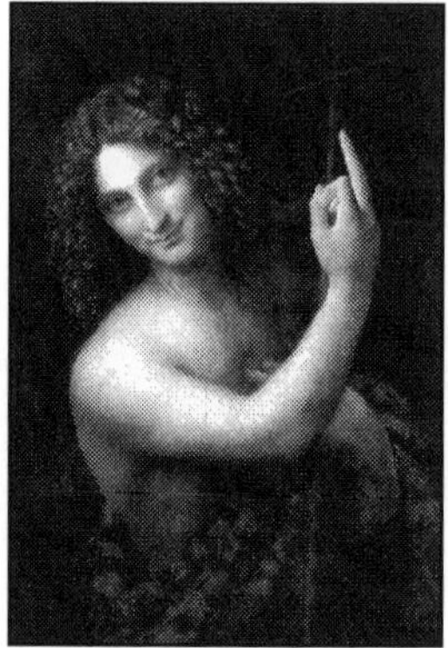

Fig. 8.11 - Leonardo
John the Baptist

"Now do you not see," he asks of the artist in his (never completed) Treatise on Painting, *"that the eye embraces the beauty of the whole world? ...It has measured the distance and size of the stars... it has given birth to architecture and to perspective and to the divine art of painting. Oh excellent thing, superior to all the others created by God! ...Owing to the eye, the soul is content to stay in its bodily prison, for without it such bodily prison is torture."*[35]

For Michelangelo, on the contrary, the eye must see beyond its bodily prison, and seek out *"the eternal form."* In a poem already quoted above, he wrote, *"this Idea alone lifts my eyes to high visions."*[36]

And in another poem, he declares:

"As my soul, looking through the eyes
Draws near to beauty as I first saw it
The inner image grows, while the other recedes,
As though shrinkingly and of no account."[37]

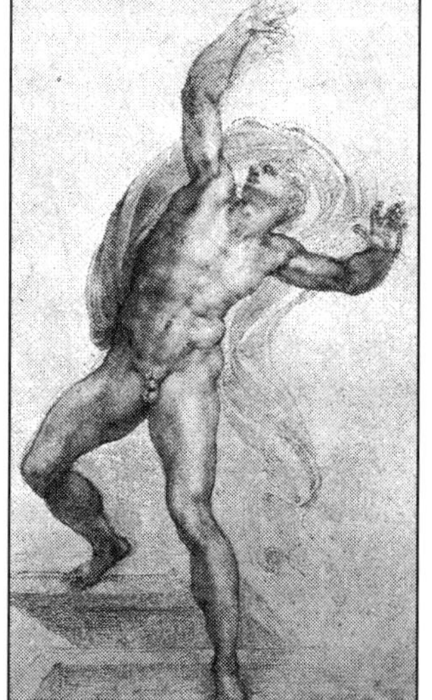

Fig. 8.12 - Michelangelo
The Risen Christ

Here, the soul alone beholds the higher beauty, like a Platonic 'remembering' (*anamnesis*) of the heavenly archetypes (*eidé*) first witnessed when the soul still dwelt with the Divine. In life, the lower images perceived by the senses, 'recede, as though of no account'.

For Vasari also, art finds its inspiration in the mind's ideas, the inner conceptions that guide the *disegno* of a painting:

"Seeing that Design, the parent of our three arts, Architecture, Sculpture and Painting, has its origin in the intellect and draws out from many single things a general judgment, it seems like a form or idea of all the objects in nature. Afterwards, when it is expressed by the hands and is called Design, we may conclude that Design is none other than a visible expression and declaration of our inner conception and of that which others have imagined and given form to in their ideas."[38]

Through the art of memory, drawing *becomes* design. When Vasari writes above that 'Painting draws out from many single things, a form or idea of all the objects in nature,' he is referring to the manner in which artists hold in their memory many different images of natural beauty, but compose a higher beauty by combining the best features of each. Alberti said something similar when he wrote, *"Complete beauties are never found in a single body, but are rare and dispersed in many bodies."*[39]

Most likely, Vasari and Alberti had in mind *The Dissertations* of Maximus of Tyre, a 2nd century Roman rhetorician, who wrote: *"Painters gather beauty from every detail of every human body, they collect them artistically from different bodies into one representation and in this manner they create one beauty which is healthy, fitting and internally harmonized. In reality you would never find a body precisely like a statue, since the arts aim at the greatest beauty."*[40]

Aristotle is often credited with the expressions 'Art improves upon Nature' and 'Art represents life, not as it is, but as it ought to be.' In fact, what he wrote in his *Poetics* was much more general: *"Since the poet represents life, as a painter does, or any other maker of likenesses, he must always represent one of three things—either things as they... are; or things as they ...seem to be; or things as they ought to be."*[41] Nevertheless, writers from Classical times could not resist attributing to Aristotle the sentiment that 'Art amends Nature.'

The classic example of this 'Ideal imitation' comes from Pliny the Elder. All the Renaissance writers – Alberti, Vasari, Dolce and Bellori – included this famous anecdote in their writings. In his *Natural History*, Pliny recites the tale of Zeuxis, a famed Greek painter who was commissioned by the people of Agrigentum to make an image of Juno for their temple. "[Zeuxis] *made an inspection of the virgins of the city, who were nude, and selected five in order that he might represent in the picture that which was the most laudable feature of each."*[42]

In *De Inventione*, Cicero elaborated upon Pliny's story, adding that the painter used this approach, *"For he did not believe that it was possible to find in one body all the things he looked for in beauty, since Nature has not refined to perfection any single object in all its parts."*[43] It falls upon art to do this, to 'amend Nature' and elevate it to the Ideal.

Thus, Michelangelo wrote, in another poetic fragment, of his life-long pursuit of that *"...Art which, if a man bring it with him from Heaven, subdues and surpasses Nature."*[44] And in a letter to his friend Castiglione, Raphael wrote of his *Galatea* in the Farnesina: *"To paint a beauty I need to see many beauties, but since this is a dearth of beautiful women, I use a certain idea which comes into my mind."*[45] Throughout the Renaissance, the imitation of Nature was tempered by the artist's quest for an ever higher Ideal.

X. Raphael & Apollonian Art

Of the three great artists who crowned the High Renaissance with their works, we have spoken much of Michelangelo and Leonardo, but have yet to mention Raphael. If Leonardo embraced all of Earth's beauty and Michelangelo strove for a more heavenly archetype, then Raphael remains a great mystery. His art is all over the place, absorbing influences from his master Perugino in Umbria, then emulating Leonardo and Michelangelo after his arrival in Florence, to finally find his own voice through the great *Stanze* in Rome. In his short thirty-seven years he managed to blaze a glorious path through the history of art.

As the Renaissance was superseded by the Mannerist style, the influence of Michelangelo and Leonardo could still be keenly felt. Artists like Cellini, Fiorentino, Pontormo and Bronzino went to stylistic extremes to outdo the late exuberance of these two great prodigies, whose *Resurrected Christ* (Fig. 8.12) and *John the Baptist* (Fig. 8.11) celebrate, with Dionysian abandon, the artists' unique flair, temperament and genius.

Raphael's figures maintain, by contrast, an Apollonian calm and majesty, even in the extremes of spiritual suffering. For this reason, once the stylistic extremes of Michelangelo and Leonardo had been exhausted by Mannerist and Baroque artists, it was Raphael's more serene and harmonious influence that held sway over Academic painting for the next three hundred years. Instead of striving to create an exceptional or individual style, Raphael's more classical manner came to represent, for the academies, the definitive 'cultural style' for all of Western Art.

His *School of Athens* offers to any inquisitive artist endless hours of rewarding contemplation and countless lessons on how a single figure (such as Raphael himself) may gaze outward at the viewer and draw him into the painting, only to guide his eye around its interior space, from one compositional grouping to the next. Ultimately, my gaze always comes to rest upon the statue of Apollo (Fig. 8.13) who surveys the entire scene from his niche high above.

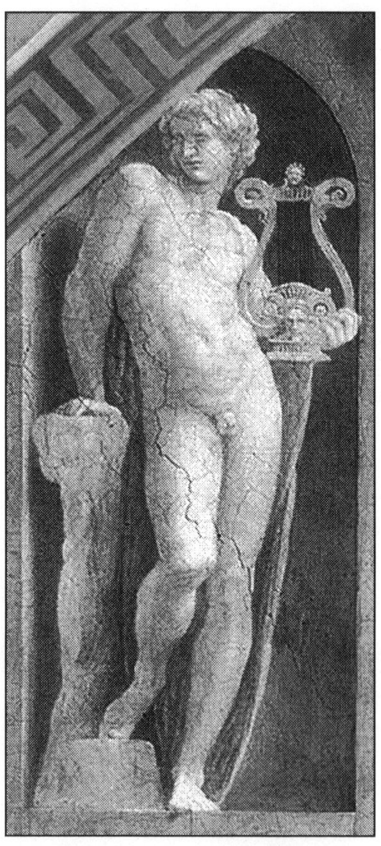

Fig. 8.13 - Raphael: *Apollo*
Detail from *The School of Athens*

Raphael has scrupulously obeyed the principles of the pose acquired during his youth: an invisible *ligne de plomb* perfectly ascends Apollo's figure, from the weight-bearing foot, through the navel, to the outward glancing eye. Around this axis, the figure bends no less than *four times* (knees, hips, shoulders, and head – not counting the feet, which follow the knees). Despite the continuous bends of this sinuous pose, Apollo remains relaxed and at ease, shifting this way and that to delicately place one hand on a serpent-entwined column while balancing a lyre in the cleft of his left hip.

This motif of Apollo upholding the *cithara* (an eight-stringed lyre) comes from Classical Antiquity, where colossal statues of *Apollo Citharoedus* (Apollo the Cithara Bearer) celebrated the god as a Patron of the Arts and 'Leader of the Muses' (*Apollo Musagetes*). The serpent is a reference to Apollo's Sanctuary at Delphi – where the solar god slew the primaeval serpent Python and thereafter established his Delphic Oracles through soothsaying priestesses and *prophetai*.

It was at Delphi, we recall, that two sayings were inscribed: *Know Thyself* and *All Things in Moderation*. Apollo upholds the *cithara* or lyre because its resonant tones remind us of the Delphic philosophy: to knowingly seek out Harmony and moderation in all that we do. Raphael's art epitomizes this Apollonian temperament: it is peaceful and concordant, balanced and well-ordered, seeking out harmony and unity in all aspects of creation. It was ultimately these values that he bequeathed to those artists who, through their Academy training, preserved Classical and Renaissance principles while pursuing new forms of expression.

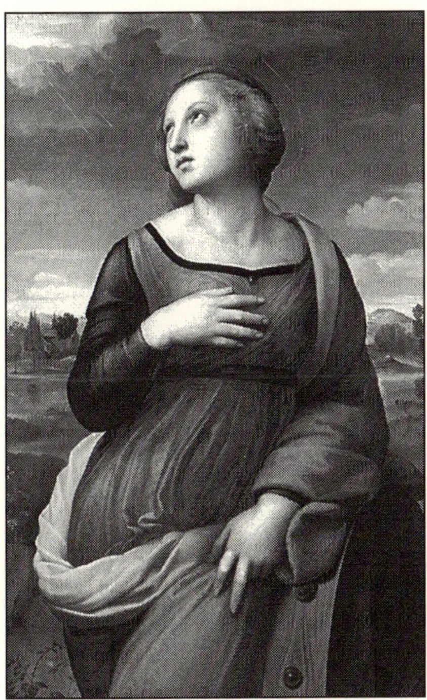

Fig. 8.14 - Raphael:
St. Catherine of Alexandria 1508

Among Raphael's myriad graceful figures, I have also spent many long hours gazing at his *St. Catherine of Alexandria,* (Fig. 8.14) contemplating her mysterious gestures and pose. Leonardo, it seems, was obsessed by spirals, just as Michelangelo always respected the *quadrata* blocks from which his figures were hewn. But Raphael revered the circle, along with its ovoid form of the ellipse. We can see this in the faint halo surrounding St. Catherine's head, causing her features to expand outward with a convex bulge, reaching to the outer limits of an invisible sphere.

Meanwhile, her figure seems safely ensconced within some greater unseen ovoid. Each limb and extremity is held close to the body, and all – shoulders, neck, hands and hips – possess extreme roundedness and volume. If the artist can take away one lesson from this figure, it is to always respect the egg-like shapes and volumes in the human form.

But the most intriguing aspect of this figure is her expression of energy. Clearly, a *contrapposto* twist has caused the left hip to shift forward and the right shoulder to fall back. Through this upward thrust of energy, her eye turns skyward and suddenly all the passion and ecstasy in her soul is released through a transcendent glance that rises to the heavens. Kenneth Clarke called it *"the glance towards a more radiant world."*[46]

A closer inspection of Raphael's art reveals that in many of his works (from the early *Coronation of the Virgin* painted in Perugia to the Vatican *Transfiguration* left unfinished at his death), this heavenly glance persists. It gives Raphael's work *"sa verticalité, sa dimension verticale"* (as the French painter Pierre Peyrolle often expressed it to me – its 'verticality or vertical dimension'). Through this upward glance, our vision mounts, transcending the composition, to glide and soar in the invisible heights beyond even the pictorial frame.

What gives Raphael's art its enduring mystery, from this perspective, is the transcendent gaze – forever seeking what is higher, unseen and unknown.

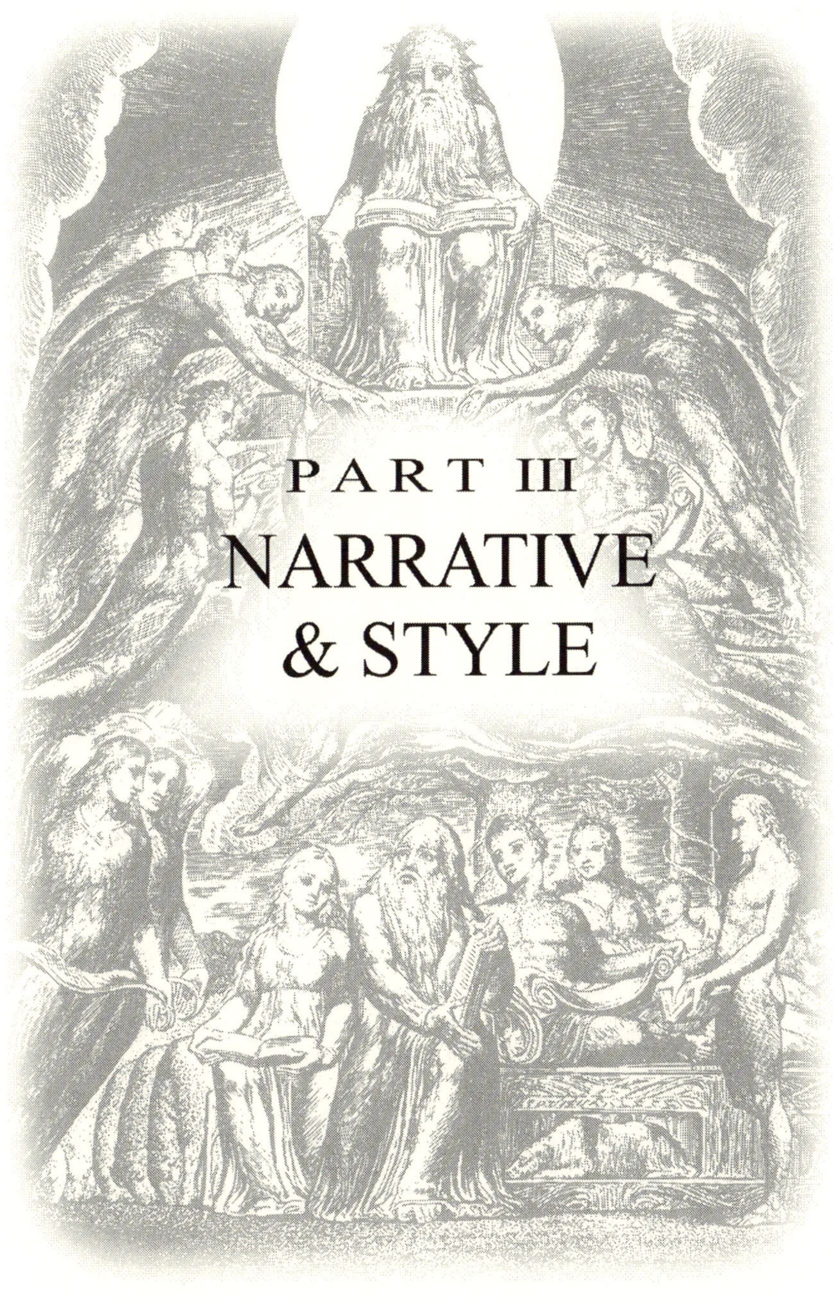

PART III
NARRATIVE & STYLE

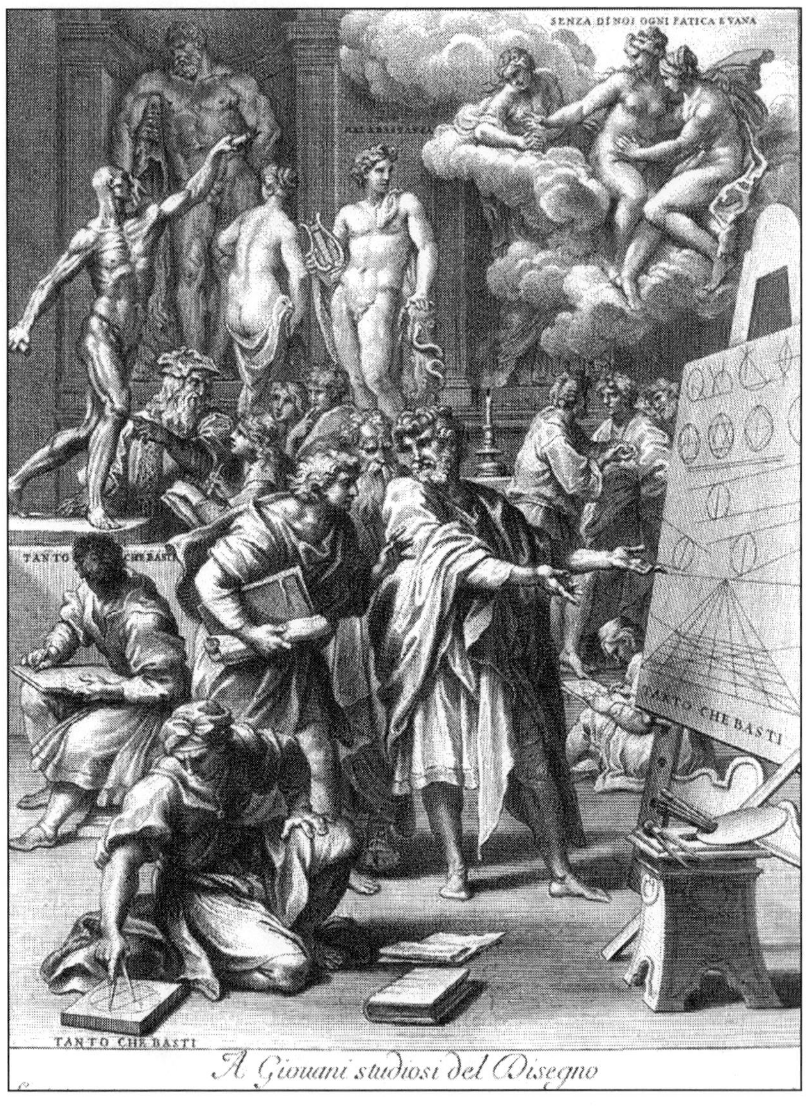

Fig. 9.1 - Carlo Maratta: *A Giovani studiosi del Disegno* 1682
Engraved by Nicolas Dorigny

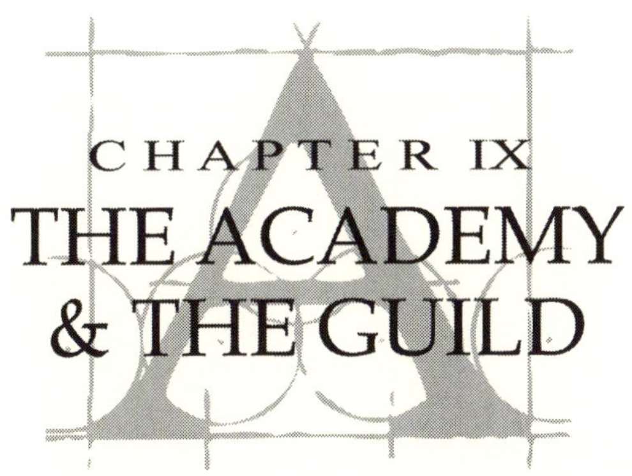

CHAPTER IX THE ACADEMY & THE GUILD

I. The Vienna Academy of Visionary Art

Every summer for the past nine years, I have taught painting at *The Visions in the Mischtechnik Seminar*, held in the hilltop village of Torri Superiore, Italy. Surrounded by terraced slopes of mimosa trees and olive groves, the villagers live in a single labyrinthine structure, founded in the 14th century, composed of a hundred and sixty-two vaulted chambers on five levels. Fallen into ruin and since restored, the town's thick limestone walls and winding narrow passages make it the ideal place for the pursuit of visions.

By the summer of 2012, attendance at the seminar had reached capacity, and I began contemplating a more ambitious scheme. Fortunately, a space had opened up in the Palais Palffy, across from the Hofburg Palace in the centre of Vienna. With the help of colleagues and friends, The Vienna Academy of Visionary Art opened its doors in September of 2013. After three years, it moved to a larger space in the Otto Wagner building at Döblergasse 2, the former premises of the Wiener Werkstätte in Vienna's alternative and artistic 7th district. While transmitting time-honoured techniques, the Academy explores sacred and visionary approaches to painting.

To better understand Western painting methods, I began researching the history of academies – from their roots in the Renaissance workshops to their eventual decline in the 19th century. Having assisted Ernst Fuchs in his studios in Monaco and Castillon, I had learned painting in the older and more traditional way of 'master and apprentice'. But ten years prior, in 1990, I had also spent a year as a guest student at *die Akademie der bildenden Künste* in Vienna, which gave me a good taste of more modern academic practice. All of these experiences allowed me to formulate a clearer picture of academies – their past and possible future.

Without a doubt, academies have played a pivotal role in Western art, defining much of its style, aesthetic and ideals. Before we delve deeper into narrative groupings of figures, we should understand how Western artists learned their craft over the past five hundred years.

II. The Workshop & the Guild

In 1563 the first 'Academy' was founded in Florence, called the *Accademia des Disegno*. Although it was not an academy in the strict sense that we think of one today, it brought together artists with the common interest of elevating painting to the status of 'art' rather than 'craft'. This distinction between art and craft is vital for understanding Renaissance culture, since it gave rise to the institution of the *accademia.*

Sometime in the early 1400's, Cennino Cennini wrote his *Libro del Arte* (translated as The Craftsman's Handbook), wherein painting was still treated as a craft practiced by merchants, tradesmen and artisans. Yet, by 1435, Alberti had written his *Della pittura* (On Painting), where he argued that painting is, rather, the noble production of artists touched by genius.

Alberti's treatise, which was published in Latin (*De pictura*) as well as the vernacular Italian (*Della pittura*), was intended as a textbook for Vittorino da Feltre's new academy in Mantua, the Casa Giocosa, an educational institution for princes and courtiers.[1] This, in itself, was surprising, since most painters of the day studied at 'the Abacus school,' an institution run by the Silk Guild to teach commercial arithmetic and applied geometry.[2]

...But, no Latin. Latin was the language of nobility and the educated class, yet none of the great Renaissance artists could read Pliny or Virgil in the original. Since they associated with courtiers, some painters like Leonardo and Mantegna struggled to master the language later in life.[3] But, most Florentine artists attended the Abacus school to gain practical and commercial skills before apprenticing under their master in his '*bottega'* or workshop. Leonardo apprenticed under Verocchio, Michelangelo (rather bitterly) under Ghirlandaio, and Raphael (so it seems) under Perugino.

In *The Intellectual Life of the Early Renaissance Artist*, Francis Ames-Lewis notes that *"...most Renaissance painters and sculptors came from the artisan class, and often were brought up in family workshops* [where they...] *gained experience working in specialized materials or techniques down the generations."*[4]

And so, rather than being 'educated' in an *accademia* setting, most Renaissance artists that we know were 'trained' in a *bottega.* The ideal training, according to Cennini, began when the novice endeavoured to *"find a master; and they bind themselves to him with respect for authority, undergoing an apprenticeship in order to achieve perfection."*[5] He should also, Cennini says, conduct himself humbly *"...by decking* [himself] *with this attire: Enthusiasm, Reverence, Obedience and Constancy."*

Entering the workshop at ten or eleven years of age, the apprentice should *"...begin as a shop boy studying for one year, to get practice in drawing on the little panel; next, to serve in the shop under some master to learn how to work at all the branches which pertain to our profession... for the space of a good six years. Then to get experience in painting... for six more years..."*[7]

By the time the apprentice completed his 12-year training, he was in his early twenties, and still considered a journeyman. Only the Guild could

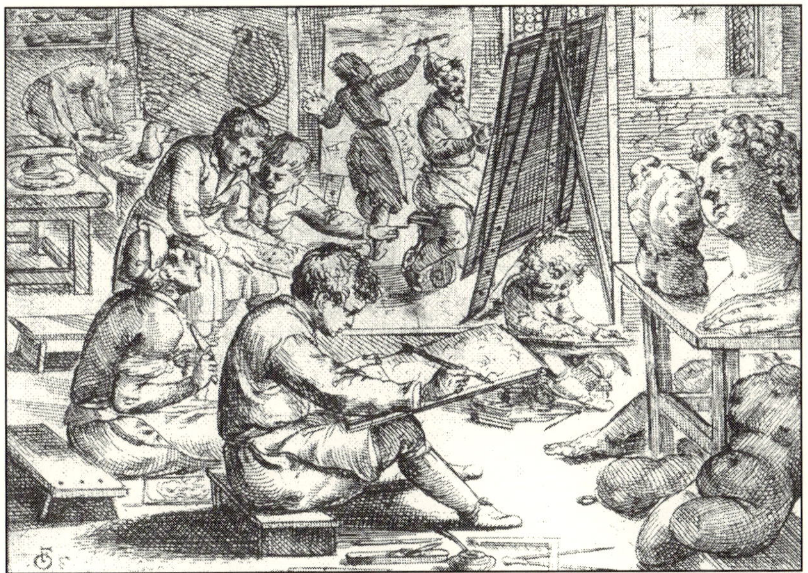

Fig. 9.2 - Odoardo Fialetti: *The Artist's Studio* 1608

confer the title of master on an artist – a coveted title, often passed down from father to son, extending the family lineage of the *bottega.* To become a sworn member of the Guild, one had to submit a painting deemed worthy of a 'masterpiece'.

Of the seven great Guilds (*arti maggiori*) in the early 1400's, Florentine painters belonged to *Arte dei Medici e Speziali*, the Guild of Physicians, Apothecaries and Spice Merchants (because painters, like their alchemical brethren, mixed powders and pigments). The Guilds established the rules of trade, regulated prices and maintained standards of quality. Only Guild members could practice their trade within a certain city or state. Since the Guilds had their origins in religious fraternities, they also ran charitable organizations (supporting the families of deceased brethren) and sponsored the feast of their patron saint (Florentine painters belonged to *The Company of St. Luke*).

Hence, the master's *bottega* was the real training ground for Renaissance artists. After learning to grind pigments, mix glue (and sweep the floor), the novice started drawing, as Cennini noted, 'on the little panel'. Paper and parchment were expensive, so the young artist made his first drawings on a re-usable boxwood panel, wiping it clean with a rag (Fig. 9.2).

When sufficiently skilled, he graduated to silverpoint, a metal stylus that leaves a fine line on paper – once the ground is painstakingly prepared with four or five layers of lead white, ground bone, and earth pigment (*terra verde*) mixed in glue size (a simpler recipe called for ground bone and spittle).[8] Silverpoint cannot be erased, nor does its line vary in thickness, while shading can only be achieved through fine hatching. *"For these reasons, it served perfectly as the preliminary training-ground of the workshop apprentice."*[9]

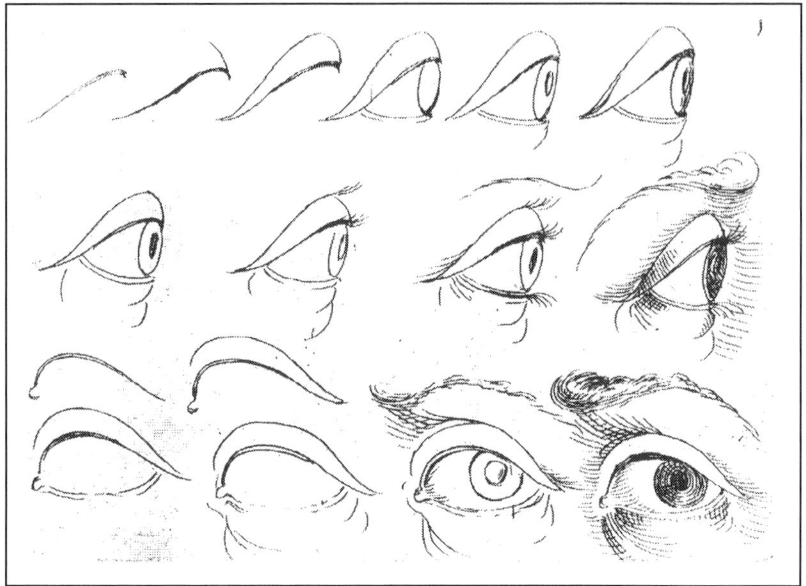

Fig. 9.3 - Odoardo Fialetti: *Drawing an Eye* 1608

After a year in silverpoint, the apprentice graduated to drawing in black ink (ferrous sulphate in iron gall or carbonated lamp black in gum arabic) with a sharpened goose quill. Cut on both ends to different thickness, the goose quill responded to pressure and delivered a variety of lines. Even a brush could be used to render shadows in ink wash.

Toward the end of the 14th century, black chalk was introduced – a delicate balance of earth pigment (carboniferous shale) and clay (too much clay and it smeared; too little, and the line would not hold.[10]) Red chalk (haematite and clay) did not come into prominence until the sixteenth century, when Leonardo and Michelangelo used it to great effect.[11]

The apprentice learned to draw by copying from statues, casts and copper engravings – thus acquiring the Classical Style much-praised in the newly-emerging Renaissance (Fig. 9.3). A good number of apprentice drawings survive which show how young artists also learned to draw 'from life' by sketching *each other* – standing, sitting, draped, semi-nude, posing or going about their daily business.

Since animals – especially exotic animals – were hard to come by, novices copied 'pattern drawings' collected in 'model books' – late Gothic reference manuals for artists, such as the *Codex Escurialensis* preserved in Madrid. To capture the delicate folds of drapery, 'linen soaked in glue' was carefully arranged over a studio mannequin. These jointed figures were popular in Renaissance *botteghe*:

"The three-dimensional models available in the painter's workshop were of several types: jointed wooden lay-figures or manikins, models in wax, clay, plaster or bronze, and of course the live model – usually the studio apprentice himself. By studying this range of models, the apprentice-painter gained

experience ... of the human form, both active and at rest, and the awareness of classical precedent in representing form, expression and movement."[12]

Most of all, the apprentice learned to draw by copying the drawings of his master. According to Savonarola, who wrote of this practice in 1493, the student copied in order to acquire his master's style: *"What does the pupil look for in the master? I'll tell you. The master draws from his mind an image which his hands trace on paper and it carries the imprint of his idea. The pupil studies the drawing and tries to imitate it. Little by little, in this way, he appropriates the style of his master."*[13]

Not only was the student expected to learn the Classical style of Antiquity, he also had to acquire the unique style of his Master, so the workshop could produce a line of paintings in the Studio's trademark *'maniera'* or style. Skilled apprentices were highly valued, and Masters went out their way to attract talented protégés.

In an agreement signed October 30th, 1467, the Paduan painter Francesco Squarcione listed some of the valuable skills which his studio offered to the aspiring artist (noted in square brackets). Squarcione agreed:

"...to teach [a new apprentice...] *the principle of a plane with lines drawn according to my method* [perspective], *and to put figures on the said plane* [composition], *and place objects, namely a chair, bench or house* [perspectival shapes], *and get him to understand these things, and teach him to understand a man's head in foreshortening... and teach him the system of the naked body* [the nude], *measured in front and behind* [proportion], *and to put eyes, nose, mouth and ears in a man's head at the right measured places* [facial proportion]... *and always keep him with paper in his hand to provide him with a model,* [life drawing] *one after another, of various figures* [the pose] *in lead white* [reception of light], *and correct these models for him, and correct his mistakes as far as I can..."*[14]

All of these skills, which Alberti and Vasari also mention in their writings, were coin and currency for the artist of that age. As the Renaissance progressed, the skill level expected of masters grew dramatically. Yet, no *bottega* would willingly share its knowledge and secrets with another *bottega*, for fear of losing economic advantage. And so we may be surprised to learn that 'perspective' (which Squarcione proudly mentions in his list) remained a guarded secret for most of the 15th century...

As late as 1506, Dürer wrote during his trip to Italy, *"I want to ride to Bologna to learn the secret of the art of perspective, which a man is willing to teach me."*[15] (*"ich bin noch 10 Tagen hier fertig; darnach würde ich nach Bologne reiten um der Kunst in geheimer Perspective willen, die ich einer lehren will."*[16]) Although Brunelleschi had worked out the theory of perspective as early as 1413 (in a painting – now lost – of the Florentine Baptistery), and had communicated it (secretly?) to artists like Masaccio (*The Trinity* - 1427) and Donatello (*The Feast of Herod* - c. 1427), the schema was not written down until Alberti published *Della Pittura* in 1435.

Alas, Alberti's explanation was sorely incomplete, so that artists like Jacopo Bellini were still *"grappling with Alberti's incomplete explanation,"*[17] in 1450, as evidenced by a pen & ink *Nativity* drawing by Jacopo's hand. Thirty years later, in 1480, Piero della Francesca wrote *De prospectiva pingendi* (On Perspective for Painting - c. 1474), completing Alberti's schema, and giving perspective a mathematical foundation – but his treatise remained unpublished for the next three hundred years.

Perspective, proportion, composition... the rules governing all of these skills were never written down, but demonstrated and passed on from master to apprentice. As the *quattrocento* (1400's) gave way to the *cinquecento* (1500's), the status of the artist changed dramatically, and so the humble *bottega* soon ceded place to the more noble *studiolo*.

III. From Bottega to Accademia: The Italian Academies

As artists increasingly saw themselves as practitioners of a liberal art, so too did their workplace transform from a *bottega* (shop, literally 'box') or *stanza* (room) to a *studiolo* (studio). The studio suggests *a place of study* where, as we saw with Francesco Squarcione's list of skills, a whole curriculum of studies was drawn up for the young apprentice. This new emphasis on study led to the creation of the first *accademia*, a gathering place for artists to share their knowledge of geometry, perspective, anatomy and proportion.

The Florentine *Accademia des Disegno*, it should be noted, was founded one year before the death of Michelangelo (in 1564), in a time when Leonardo (d. 1519) and Raphael (d. 1520) had long since departed. Its role, it seems, was to preserve the knowledge which had almost perished with these masters.

The statutes of the Florentine *Accademia* show that the main aim, rather than painting *per se*, was *"the setting of a standard, bodied forth by masterworks."*[18] And, what is more, *"the definition of a stylistic norm, the 'correct' style of modern Florence to which all the young artists were expected to conform."*[19] Hence, the transmission of 'style' – particularly the Classical style – seemed to be the foremost aim and ambition of the earliest academy.

In the *trecento* (1300s'), the works of Renaissance painters like Duccio di Buoninsegna and Simone Martini still bore strong traces of the Byzantine age. The *maniera bizantina,* as it was called, evoked the Sacred in the venerable tradition of the Hieratic Style, through stillness, symmetry and centeredness. But the works of antiquity, recently discovered and brought to light, possessed a lively dynamism and movement, celebrating human anatomy, gesture and expression, as the *new* Humanist expression of the Sacred. The *maniera antica,* as mastered by Leonardo, Michelangelo and Raphael, became the new language of expression – the new *style* – for this emerging Humanism. *"Abandoning the old style,"* Vasari wrote, "[the High Renaissance artists] *reverted to the imitation of classical art with all their skill and wit."*[20]

The scant evidence of the Florentine *Accademia* shows that late Renaissance artists were interested in two specific areas of painting: in 1563, lectures on *"geometry"* were instigated; and the same year they also added lectures on *"anatomy."*[21] This would suggest that they were still struggling with the complex relationship of figuration ('anatomy') and composition ('geometry').

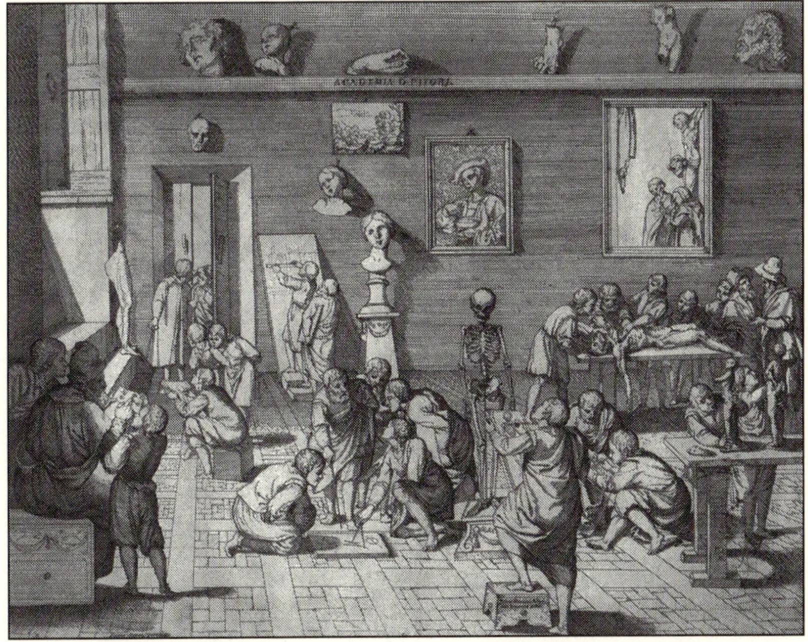

Fig. 9.4 - Pierfrancesco Alberti - *Accademia di Pittura* c. 1600

Calling it the *Accademia des Disegno* manifest their strong emphasis on drawing and design (*disegno*) rather than painting (*dipingere* or *colori*, which remained the task of the masters in their studios). *Disegno* stressed *the lines* of a painting (whether visible or invisible), the theme (*istoria*), invention (*inventio*) and interior design; how the figures, in their proportions, poses and perspective, came together (*compositione*) into a harmonious whole. And finally, how all of this was delineated in the Classical Style, following all the principles rediscovered from Antiquity.

By the late 1500's, academies had sprung up in all the major courts of Italy. The most important were the *Accademia di San Luca* in Rome, and the private school of the Caracci brothers in Bologna called the *Accademia de' Carracci*. For the first time, instructional engravings emerged (Odoardo Fialetti's *True Method and Order for Drawing All Parts and Members of the Human Body* - 1608, Fig. 9.3). Another engraving by Fialetti (Fig. 9.2) shows the apprentices in the Master's *studiolo* sitting near his easel and drawing. They are drawing *from casts* – emphasizing once more the acquisition of *la maniera antica*.

An engraving by Pierfrancesco Alberti (Fig. 9.4) dated to the early 1600's depicts an *Accademia di Pittura* (inscribed on the upper shelf as ACADEMIA D' PITORI). An older man with a crutch leads a younger man into the academy where (from left to right) a master painter points out to a younger apprentice Fialetti's instruction for drawing an eye in the Classical manner. Then, another young apprentice, observed by two more, draws the cast of a leg into his 'little panel'. In the background, two assistants with a ruler work out the architectural design for a painting while, in the main foreground, another master with four young apprentices points out the geometrical design made with a compass (inspired by Raphael's *School of Athens*). To the right, more artists are making drawings from a skeleton while, in the background, a dissection takes place. Above them on the shelves are a variety of antique casts suitable for copying. All in all, this was the ideal vision of an Italian *Accademia* in the early 1600's.

By 1682, Carlo Maratta was able to draw an image of *"A Giovani studiosi del Disegno"* (later engraved by Nicolas Dorigny - Fig. 9.1) where, once again, a student is making a geometrical design with a compass on a tablet. In the middle plane, an artist is gesturing towards a demonstration of perspective while, in the background, artists make copies of the statues from antiquity, some emphasizing anatomy while others, the ideal nude (including a reversed version of Raphael's *Apollo Citharoedus*). Maratta, who was one of the last artists descended from Raphael's workshop, has stressed in his allegory the Apollonian dictum "All Things in Moderation" (*Meden Agan*) through the words *Tanto che Basti* ('as much as is needed') which appear no less than three times in the engraving.

IV. The French School

In 1648, the *Académie Royale de Peinture et de Sculpture* (later called the *Académie des Beaux-Arts*) was founded in Paris by royal charter. With huge financial support from both royal and private patronage, 'The French School' came to dominate the teaching of painting for the next two hundred years.

What characterizes the French School of painting, or 'Academic painting' as a whole, is its emphasis on historical and allegorical subjects. Recalling Alberti's emphasis on *istoria*, *varieta* and *compositione*, these epic paintings aspired to large narrative compositions with a 'copious variety' of figures, executed in *la grande manière.*

One of the greatest theorists of the day, André Félibien, created a hierarchy of genres, citing Allegorical painting as the highest type, accompanied by historical, mythological, religious and literary painting as typical of *grand genre* paintings, since they conveyed an important moral or intellectual message. These were followed by portraits, scenes of every day life (*scènes de genre* – what we now call 'genre painting') and the *petit genre* of landscapes, animal painting and still lifes.

This emphasis on History Painting (as it is generally called, from the French *histoire*, as a translation of the Italian *istoria*), lasted from the 1600's to the late 1800's, from Poussin and Le Brun through David and Ingres to Bouguereau and Moreau (the *'last'* of the academy painters). Respecting the Italian *accademia* tradition, all these French artists looked back to the Renaissance, and to Raphael in particular, as the true guardian of the hidden rapport between figuration and composition.

Basing its *Cursus Studiorum* on the *Accademia di San Luca* in Rome, the French Academy taught students to draw *by copying*, primarily from statues, casts and master drawings (later 'engravings'), but also with the aid of *le modèle vivant.*[22] Once students completed a drawing from the nude model, they were expected to redraw it *"with the antique in view."*[23] The drawing from life, to be made complete, had to be drawn once more and idealized, *"giving the figure the character of a particular ancient statue."*[24] As such, the long years of copying from statues and casts was to not only facilitate the skill of drawing, but to impress in the memory the *maniera antica*: the unique lines that bridged the nose, shaped the lips and curved the eyes according the Classical style.

It may surprise us to learn that, *"the academy was never conceived as a replacement for the workshop* [i.e. master's studio]. *A student learned neither to paint nor to model in the academy but did so, rather, in the workshop or studio of his master, with whom he still lived as before the age of the academy."*[25] Hence, painting itself remained the domain of the master's studio.

Each of the professors maintained a large studio, which sent *les élèves* (accepted students) to the academy for theoretical courses, while preparing *les aspirants* (aspiring students) for the entrance exam. To compete, *les aspirants* had to be less than thirty years of age, recommended by a professor – and male.[26] To win a place at the academy, they had to pass an *épreuve* of their drawing skills, rendering a live model in natural day light for the duration of six two-hour sessions.

Once accepted, the student's course of studies focussed primarily on *la Copie*:

"*The courses were given by the twelve professors, according to a system of rotation, and each month the students followed a different course."*[27] In general, *"the academic year was divided into two semesters – the summer from April to October, where students worked by natural daylight from 7am to 2pm, and the winter trimester during which they drew from 9am to 2pm in artificial lamplight...*

"The lessons were based essentially on la Copie, *done in pencil, alternating between Nature and the Antique. The live models posed for a period of two weeks... In addition to the practical courses, the academy taught Anatomy and Perspective (two times a week), as well as History, Archaeology, Literature and the History of Art (once a week). The academic year was punctuated by a multitude of bi-weekly and monthly competitions*."[28]

The student's only hope for advancement came by winning medals (first, second or third place) in the seemingly endless round of *concours* (competitions). Held twelve times a year, the Copying Competitions (*concours d'émulation*) gave students the task of faithfully copying in pencil (*crayon*) antique statues and the live model. The Special Competitions (*concours spéciaux*) tested them on Anatomy, Perspective, Historical Landscape and Historical Composition. Finally, private patrons created competitions on the Painted Figure (*figure peinte*), Painted Half-figure or Torso (*demi-figure peinte ou torse*), and the Expressive Head (*tête d'expression*).[29]

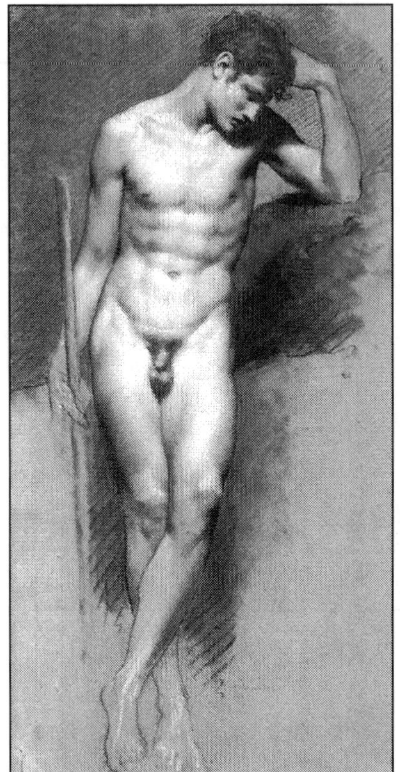
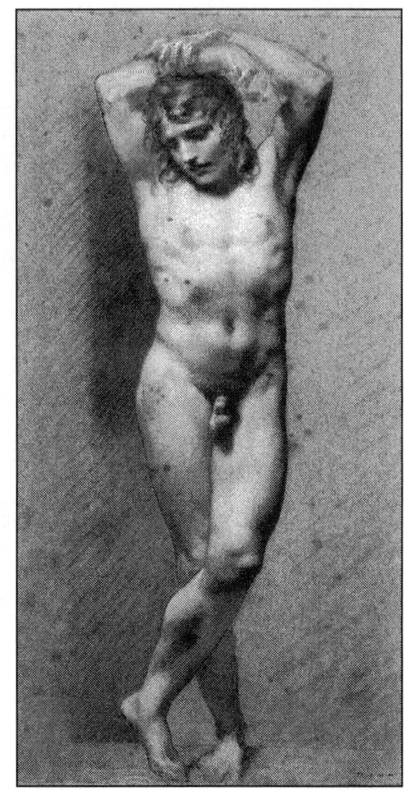

Fig. 9.5 - Pierre-Paul Prud'hon - *Académies* c. 1800

V. The Nude

A slight mystique still surrounds the artist and the nude. I can well-remember the hushed tones and dark atmosphere of the *Anatomische Saal* at the *Akademie* in Vienna, where I first began drawing the figure from life in 1989. To enter this rounded theatre, where the nude model was posed on the dais, required a high degree of piety and respect. We have tried to maintain this atmosphere in our own Figure Drawing Classes, held once a week since its inception at The Vienna Academy of Visionary Art.

This mystique was much stronger during the time of the French Academy. In the statutes of 1655, *"the academy was given a monopoly on life drawing,"* so that, by ordinance of the king, *"posing the model anywhere else* [was] *expressly forbidden."*[30] Indeed, in later years, any drawing from a nude model was referred to, simply, as an *académie*.

Although the academies gave their students a thorough grounding in anatomy, the *modèle vivant* was never intended to be rendered 'naturally' but rather, in his true state of grace as *le Nu idéal*. The average man resembled

Adam in his fallen state, naked and ashamed. This was called the *nuditas naturalis*. But the Classical hero, as a child of the gods, lived in a true state of innocence and grace. This was the *nuditas virtualis*.

From its inception, *"the life class was supervised by the twelve man governing board, each responsible for posing the model for one month."*[31] These twelve men, who were in fact twelve masters, each with his own studio, pored over the classical lexicon of sculptures to pose the model in an attitude that recalled the *nuditas virtualis* from a more remote Golden Age of art. The pictorial erudition and aesthetic discernment of these *savants* was legendary.

As it turns out, the model they posed was exclusively male. The female nude model was not permitted in the academies at all. It was only in the late 1800's, just before the complete collapse of the academy system, that the female nude model was allowed into the drawing theatre.[32] In 1896, women themselves, as fellow artists, were finally admitted to the *Ecole des Beaux-Arts*.[33]

How, we wonder, did they draw the female figures that appear so often in their paintings? While we may assume that the artists snuck into brothels at night and brought 'the painted women' back to their studios by dawn – no such possibility existed for those artists competing for the *Prix de Rome*.

To gain the glory of a five year pension at the Villa Medici in Rome, the ten competing artists (who, after two previous *épreuves,* had been narrowed down from a field of hundreds) were *"...locked into their 'loges'* [academy studios] *from seven in the morning till eight at night,"* with no access to references *"for a period of seventy-two days to bring the composition to completion."*[34]

Without access to models of any sort, these competing artists depended upon – as Vasari had advised – the art of memory (*ars memoriae*) to render their male and female forms. Only in the late eighteenth century did *"...a new legislation authorize the students to take to their loges* [a cast of] *the Venus de Medici or Crouching Venus, the Apollo* [Belvedere] *or the Antinous – so as never to lose sight of the most beautiful forms."*[35]

To enter the competition for the *Prix de Rome*, the artists had to prove sufficient merit through medals already won in previous *concours*, such as the Historical Landscape, Historical Composition and (the most difficult and detested of all) Perspective.[36]

The *Prix de Rome* competition began when the *histoire* for that year was solemnly announced: *The Death of Vitellius* (1847), *Ulysses Recognized by his Wet-nurse* (1849) or *Zenobia Found on the Banks of the Araxes* (1850). The competitors had twelve hours to develop a figurative composition (without reference materials or sources - Fig. 9.7) that would serve, significantly unaltered, as the foundation for their painting over the next seventy-two days[37] (Figs. 9.6 - 9.9). In each case, a specific human emotion carried the scene (*l'expression*), and the painting was judged primarily for its *théâtralité*[38] – its theatric ability to evoke *the passions of the soul*, thus moving the spectator.

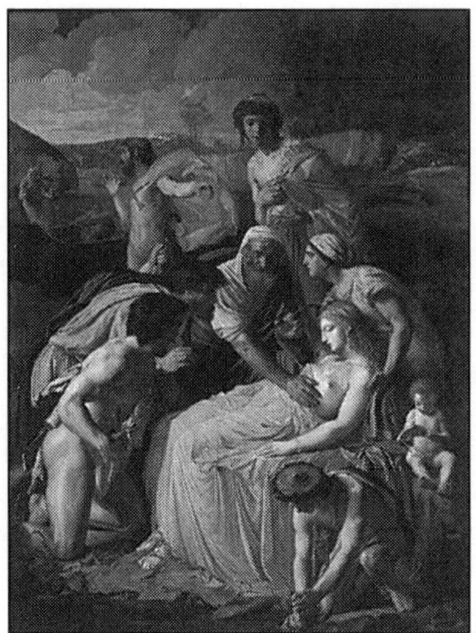

Fig. 9.6 - Emile Levy:
Zenobia Found on the Banks of the Araxes 1850
Honourable Mention

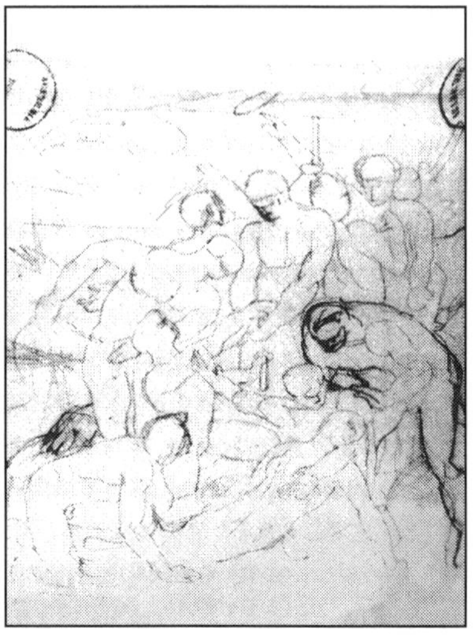

Fig. 9.7 - Paul Baudry
Foundation Drawing:
Zenobia Found on the Banks of the Araxes 1850

VI. The Classical Canon

Those fortunate few who won the *Prix de Rome* were housed in the Villa Medici for five years and had one major responsibility: to learn the style of Antiquity through direct acquaintance with the original statues. Like the young Michelangelo, they had been handed the key to the Garden of San Marco (my expression is figurative – the garden no longer existed) in order to 'wrest the secrets of Classical form from its fragments and remains'. One of their chief duties, in fact, was to send back well-rendered copies of Antique statues and Renaissance paintings for their poorer brethren, whose only access to these canonical works came through engravings.

Following an edict already laid down in the first *Accademia des Disegno* in Florence, each academy thus established a collection of 'master works', the noblest and most ideal models of the Classical style. The *Académie des Beaux-Arts* in Paris spared no expense in making life-sized casts of the *Laocoön* or the Farnese *Hercules* in Rome and transporting them back to France.[39]

Eventually the *Musée du Louvre*, as Europe's first public art museum, opened in 1793. Napoleon took the zeal for collecting antiquities to its limits and, between 1798 and 1815, seized Rome's greatest classical statues (including *The Laocoön* and the *Apollo Belvedere*) to display them in the Louvre – appropriately re-named the *Musée Napoleon*. (They were returned in 1815 under the terms of the Treaty of Vienna[40]).

This valued collection of copies constituted 'the Canon', the most beautiful examples of the Humanist style, for the students to contemplate,

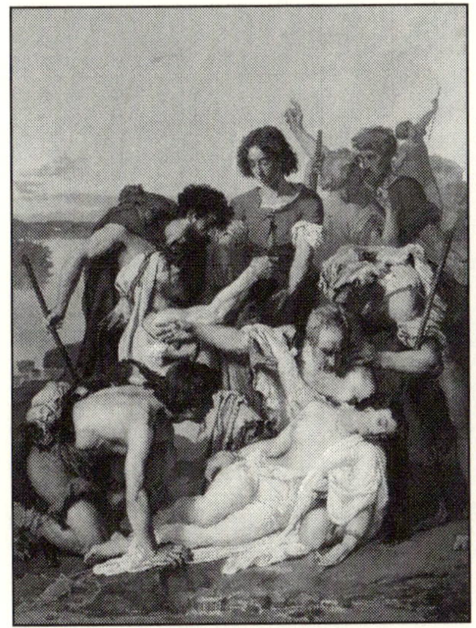

Fig. 9.8 - Paul Baudry:
Zenobia Found on the Banks of the Araxes 1850
Prix de Rome - Shared First Prize

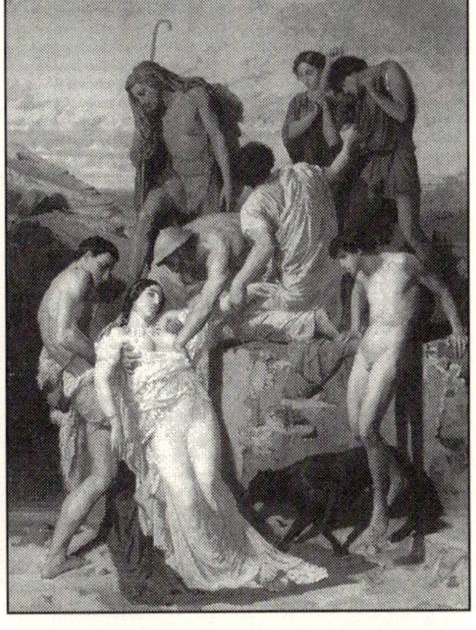

Fig. 9.9 - William-Adolphe Bouguereau:
Zenobia Found on the Banks of the Araxes 1850
Prix de Rome - Shared First Prize

draw and emulate. Indeed, 'the Canon' was upheld as the 'ideal forms' of Western Art, descended from a long-lost Golden Age of Classical culture. In its earliest phase, the Canon was composed of a specific series of statues which, over its three hundred years of existence, was amended with each new archaeological discovery.

According to Vasari, the Classical Canon consisted of *"the Laocoön, the* [Farnese] *Hercules, the great torso of Belvedere, as well as the Venus* [de Medici], *the Cleopatra* [actually *Sleeping Ariadne*], *the Apollo* [Belvedere] *and countless others."*[41] In later years, this Canon was amended [42] to include (more or less) the following:

- The Laocoön (Fig. 7.5)
- The Farnese Hercules (Fig. 9.16)
- The Belvedere Torso (Fig. 9.19)
- The Venus de' Medici (Fig. 9.14)
- The Sleeping Ariadne (Fig. 9.12)
- The Apollo Belvedere (Fig. 9.10)
- The Venus de Milo (Fig. 9.11)
- The Knidean Venus (Fig. 9.17)
- The Crouching Venus (or Lely Venus) (Fig. 9.18)
- The Doryphoros (or Spear Bearer) (Fig. 7.9)
- The Antinous Belvedere (or Lantin) (Fig. 9.13)
- The Borghese Gladiator (Fig. 7.10)
- The Dying Gladiator (or Dying Gaul) (Fig. 9.15)
- The Barberini Faun (Fig. 7.11)
- The Apoxymenos (or Scraper) (Fig. 6.13)

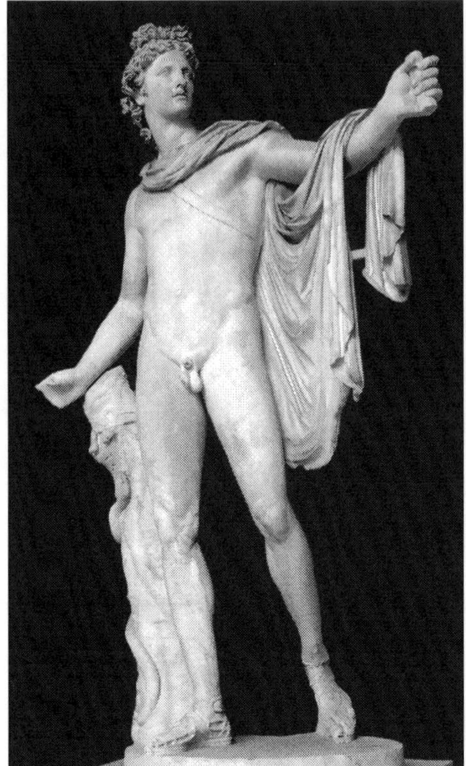

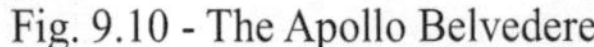

Fig. 9.10 - The Apollo Belvedere

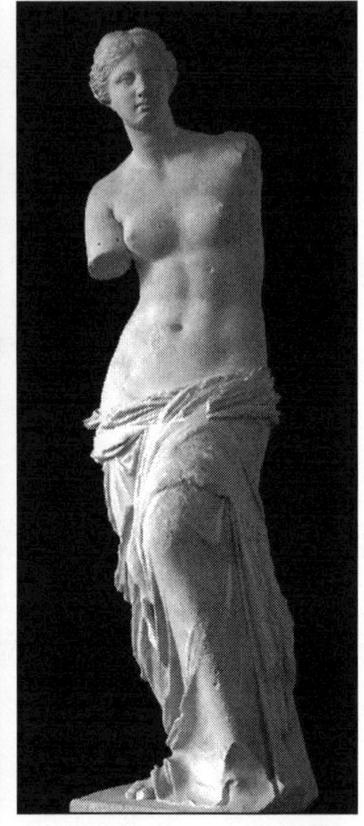

Fig. 9.11 - The Venus de Milo

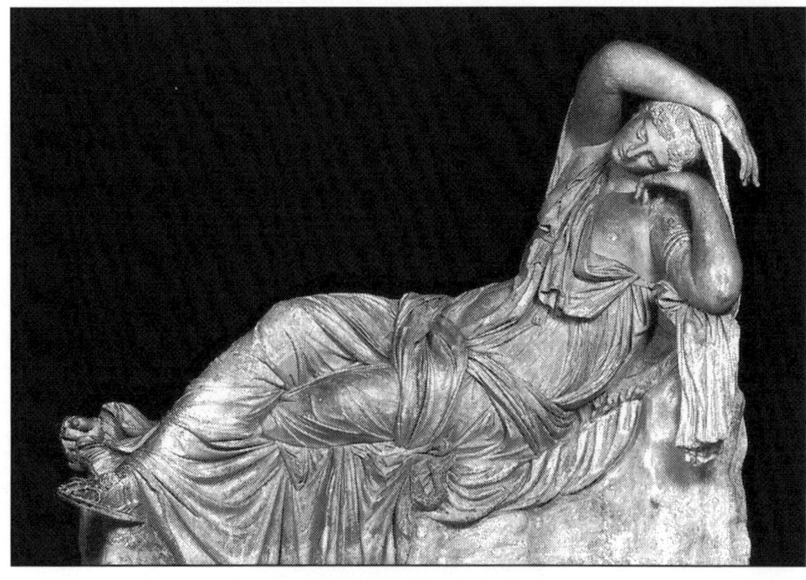

Fig. 9.12 - Sleeping Ariadne

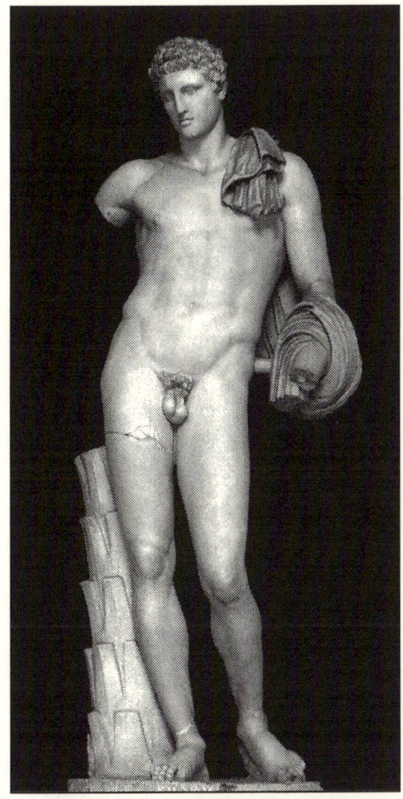

Fig. 9.13 - The Antinous Belvedere

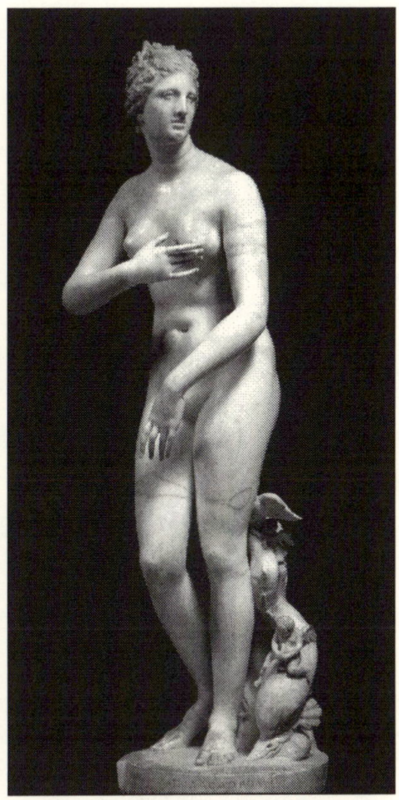

Fig. 9.14 - The Venus de' Medici

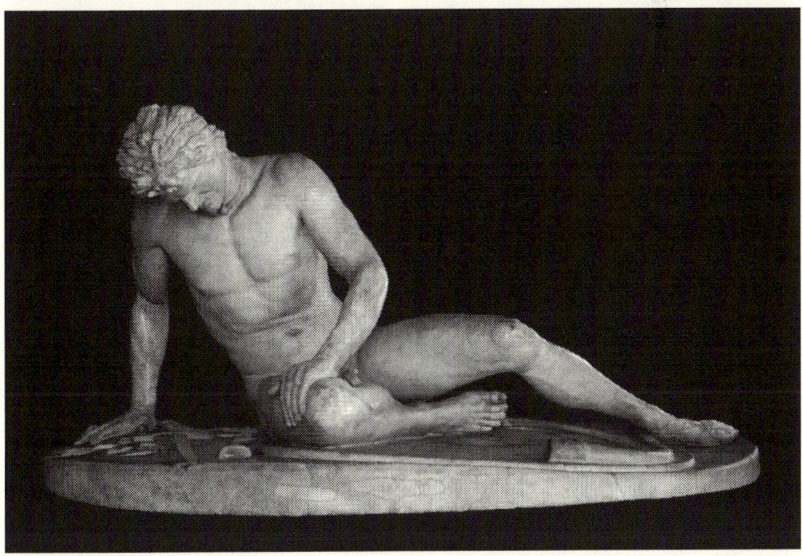

Fig. 9.15 - The Dying Gladiator (or Gaul)

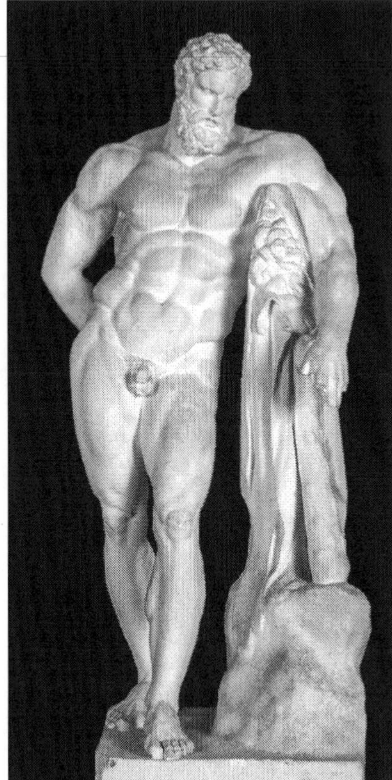

Fig. 9.16 - The Farnese Hercules

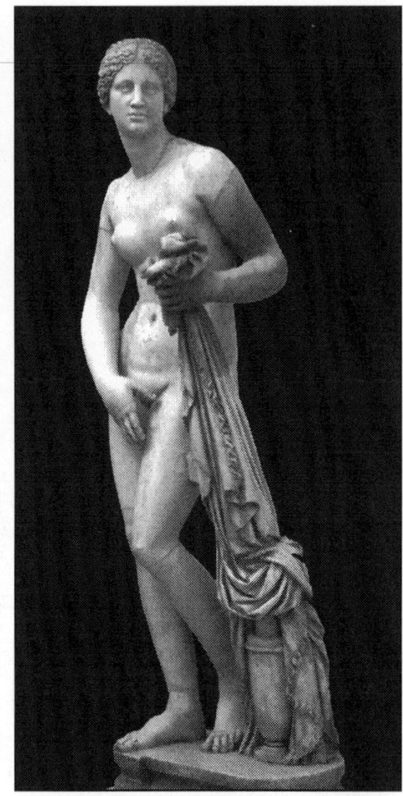

Fig. 9.17 - The Knidean Venus

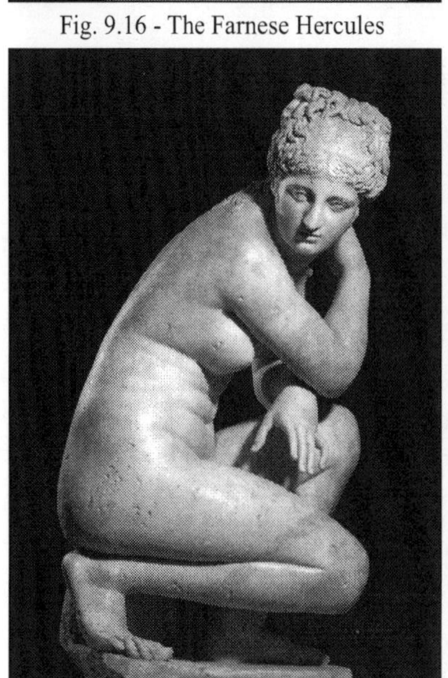

Fig. 9.18 - The Crouching Venus

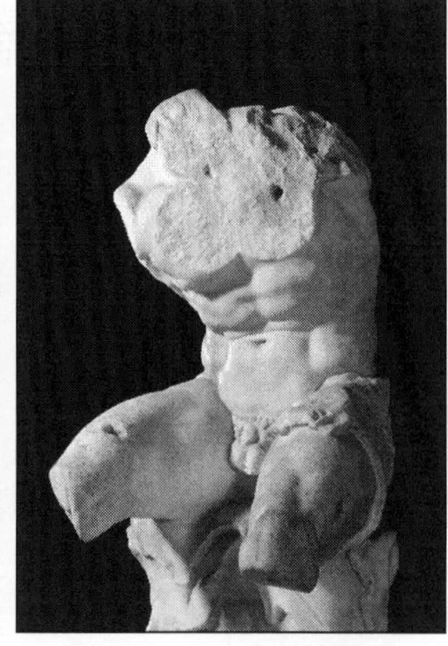

Fig. 9.19 - The Torso Belvedere

VII. Anatomy & Proportion

In 1889 an artist named A. Lemaistre, a student of the *École des Beaux Arts* in Paris, left behind his impressions of the Anatomy Class taught by Professor Matthias Duval:

"The class which the students frequented most assiduously was the course on Anatomy... Imagine the hour was a quarter to one. As bright light streamed through the large bay windows, the heads of the students formed circles within circles, descending row on row. Below, the space reserved for the professor was occupied by a single heavy table, with a rotating display of anatomical parts or even a partly dissected cadaver. Two large plaster casts stood on either side: one of the Borghese Gladiator, the antique statue most-renowned for its anatomic exactitude, the other, an écorché *of the same, now without its skin.*

In one corner stood a skeleton; along the walls were more écorchés, *each in a different position, all flanking a statue of Castor and Pollux... Suddenly, one o'clock arrived and the door to the laboratory opened wide... Thunderous applause greeted the professor. Then, silence reigned – the silence of the cloisters, which none dared disturb."*[43]

If artists like Michelangelo and Leonardo had to learn anatomy through secretive or clandestine dissections, wary of the ever-watchful eye of the church, by the time of the Academy, dissection and anatomy had become integral skills in every young artist's training.

By the late 19th century, Artistic Anatomy had become a reputable field of study, with its own textbooks, faculty and department (*la Chaire d'Anatomie-Morphologie*). Today, there is no shortage of books offering 'Anatomy for Artists' but many fall short of the original French *Académie* texts, such as Paul Richer's *Anatomie artistique* (1890), *Physiologie artistique de l'homme en mouvement* (1895) and *Morphologie de la femme* (1920), not to mention the more recent *Anatomie Artistique de l'Homme* (1959) by Arnould Moreaux.

Even for those who cannot read French, the diagrams tell their own unique tale of muscles, tendons and bones in movement. In 1971, Robert Beverly Hale translated Richer's *Anatomie artistique* (1890) into English, then went on to publish his own *Anatomy Lessons from the Great Masters* (1977) and *Drawing Lessons from the Great Masters* (1989) – two valuable books from America's own master of anatomy, whose many informative lectures are preserved on film. Now, in the digital age, we have 3D animation with layers and transparencies to image the human body.

Although early anatomical works like Andreas Vesalius' famous *De humani corporis fabrica* of 1543 show us 'the flayed man' in movement, it is not until the late 1800's that academicians like Paul Richer and Matthias Duval developed 'Artistic Anatomy' as a discipline apart from Scientific Anatomy. Artistic Anatomy is not only concerned with the layout of the human body, but the dynamic tension and repose of the actual muscles involved in the various poses. At the same time, they examined the layout of the head, limbs and torso, comparing the parts to the whole, treading gently into the time-honoured domain of proportion.

In *Les canons du corps humain au XIXe Siècle* (Canons of the Human Body in the 19th Century - 2004), Claire Barbillon makes a detailed analysis

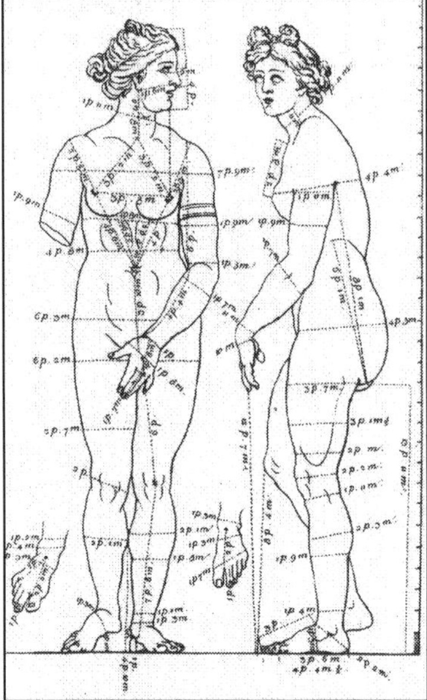

Fig. 9.20 - Iconometry of The Venus de' Medici - 1894

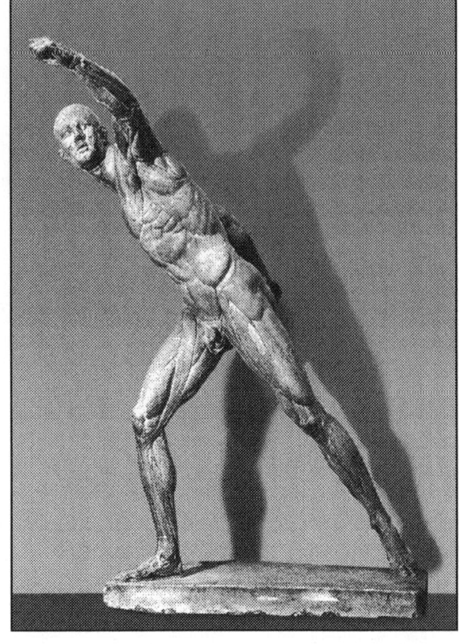

Fig. 9.20 - Galbert Salvage: *Écorché of the Borghese Gladiator* 1804

of the different systems of proportion that arose when the *Académie* system was at its height. We today may find it hard to imagine the lengths to which scholars went to determine these proportions.

For example, in the raging field of Iconometry (the measure of the human figure), researchers recorded hundreds of measurements from canonical statues, particularly the Apollo Belvedere and the Venus de Medici, beholding these two as the ideal male and female figures (Fig. 9.20).

Abraham Bosse was the first with his *Representation of Diverse Human Figures with Measures taken from Antique Statues in Rome* (1656), followed by Gérard Audran's *Proportions of the Human Body Measured Against the Most Beautiful Figures from Antiquity* (1683). Audran, whose work was reprinted for the next 200 years, established that most statues varied between 7 and 8 heads high, usually falling short of 8 heads.

This procedure of minutely measuring hundreds of parts of hundreds of statues was taken up in the 19th century by Frédéric Compte de Clarac (1826) and Johann-Gottfried Schadow (1835), recording their results in large tomes with line diagrams, all the measurements of the statues duly indicated. Despite this immense effort, none were able to derive a consistent canon from their data:

"Schadow accumulated measures without being able to deduce a synthetic formula, and finally renounced the idea of any one single canon,"[44] Barbillon writes.

Perhaps the most eccentric artist to emerge from this strange period, which mixed the exactitude of science with the pursuit of art, was Jean Galbert Salvage (1770 – 1813). A graduate of the Montpellier Medical School

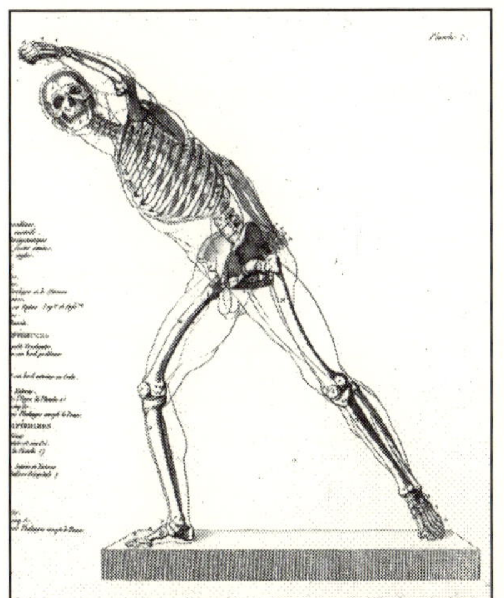

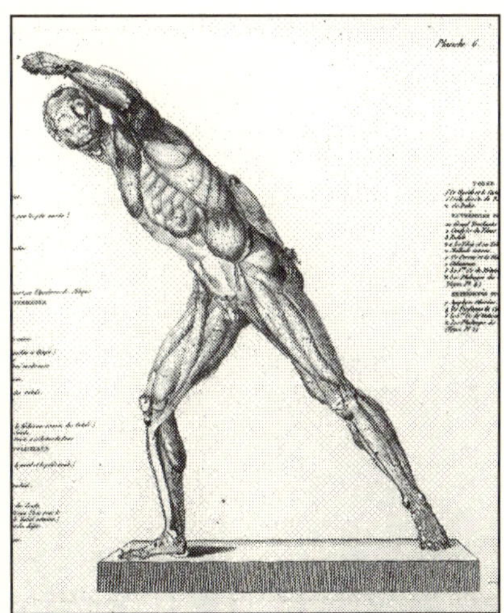

Fig. 9.21 - Plates from Galberta Salvage: *Anatomie du gladiateur combattant*

who served as a surgeon in the Medical Corps, he turned to drawing while teaching at the Val-de-Grâce hospital in Paris. In the Musée Napoleon (as the Louvre was then called), he became obsessed with *The Borghese Gladiator*, conceiving a unique project:

"The figure known as the Gladiator was the one that struck me the most; its attitude, its elegant carving, its movement, its action, everything in this statue showed me the fruits of science and the genius of art. It was in one of these moments of admiration that I conceived the plan for a book that unites both the exact study of anatomy and its application to the progress of art."[45]

His first act was to obtain a cast of the Gladiator, which he received from the Musée Napoleon after two years of bureaucratic delays. Through his tenure at the Val-de-Grâce, he was also able to obtain the cadavers of at least three healthy young men (killed in duels), which he dissected, preserved and then posed in the form of the Gladiator so as to make plaster casts. *"Owing to them, I was able to analyze the movement of this antique statue,"*[46] he later wrote. The first result of his labours was an *écorché* of the Borghese Gladiator, which was exhibited at the Salon of 1804 with much success (Fig. 9.20).

Spurred on by the success of his *écorché*, he commenced the first plates of his great work, *Anatomie du gladiateur combattant, applicable aux beaux arts* (Anatomy of the Fighting Gladiator, Applicable to the Fine Arts – 1812 – Fig. 9.21), which would be published one year before his untimely death by consumption in 1813. Due to his obsession with the project, Salvage lost his post at the Val-de-Grâce, but survived by taking out subscriptions to deliver his work to private collectors in several installments (his repeated requests for government funding were interminably delayed).

To survive, the artist also found employment for a time with J.-L. Moreau de la Sarthe, illustrating the fourth volume of *l'Art de connaître les hommes par la physionomie* (The Art of Knowing Men by their Physiognomy – 1806), where Salvage rendered precise anatomical diagrams for the muscles at work behind expressive human emotions (or *Têtes d'Expression*), using his own head as the model.

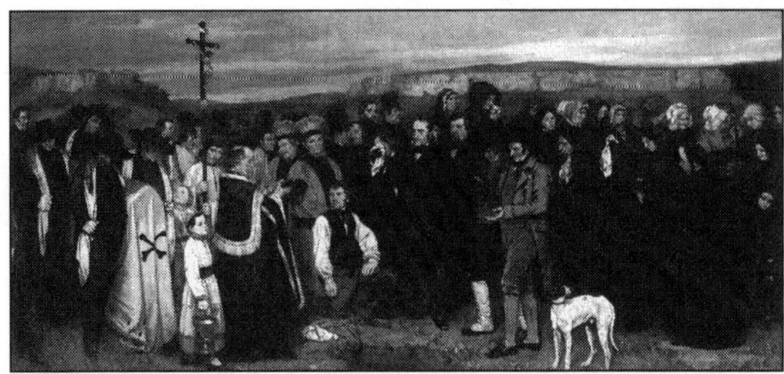

Fig. 9.22 - Gustave Courbet: *The Burial at Ornans* 1849 - 50

Falling into debt and increasingly in ill health, Salvage managed to complete the text and forty-five coloured plates to his precious book which, as its subtitle proclaimed, *"...treats the bones, muscles, mechanisms of movement, proportions and character of the human body."* In its finely engraved drawings we behold the Borghese Gladiator from the four cardinal directions, at the subdermal level of muscles and bones, and *"...in a context that encompassed movement, the body at rest, proportion, age, temperament, moods and passions."*[47]

Salvage's drawings are unique, insofar as they treat a classical work of art from the standpoint of 19th century science. At one and the same time, his antique figure expresses the Platonic striving for an artistic Ideal (*eidos*), and the Aristotelian pursuit of accurate observation from Nature (*mimesis*). Salvage's system of proportion, incidentally, results in the ogdoadic division of the human form, or Eight Head Canon.

The precision and beauty of Salvage's work remains unparalleled, and attests to the rare spirit of an age which is no longer upon us. The artist created his work during the Napoleonic era, a post-revolutionary period when the arts and academy in France were thrown into much tumult and eventual collapse.

VIII. The Academy in Decline

After the French Revolution of 1789, the *Académie des Beaux-Arts* was abolished by law, particularly through the machinations of its greatest opponent, the painter Jacques-Louis David. When reconstituted in 1795, the *Académie des Beaux-Arts* became an administrative institution, while the newly-formed *Ecole des Beaux-Arts* was responsible for teaching. As before, the masters' studios (*ateliers*) provided the real training in painting, while the *Ecole* directed the competitions (*concours*) and the *Académie* organized the exhibitions (*les salons*).[48]

Each faculty member of the *Ecole des Beaux-Arts* continued to run his own studio as a commercial enterprise that produced paintings from state commissions while preparing students for the academy's entrance exams. By the mid-1800's, nude models, even female nudes, were allowed to pose in the masters' studios. During the reforms of 1863, the masters' studios were moved directly into the *Ecole des Beaux-Arts* and so 'painting' was

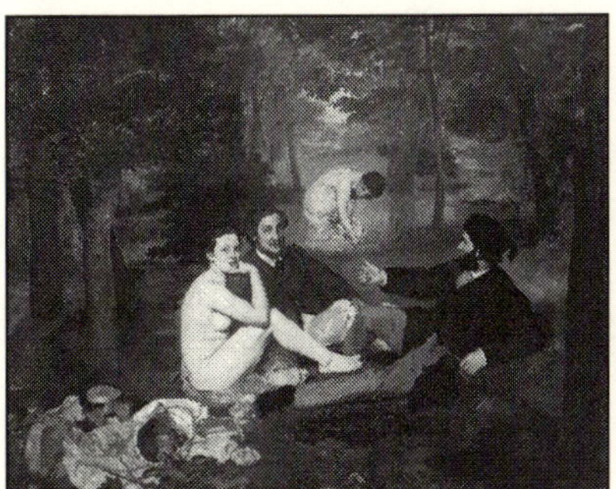

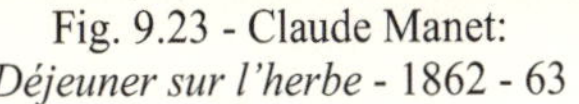

Fig. 9.23 - Claude Manet:
Déjeuner sur l'herbe - 1862 - 63

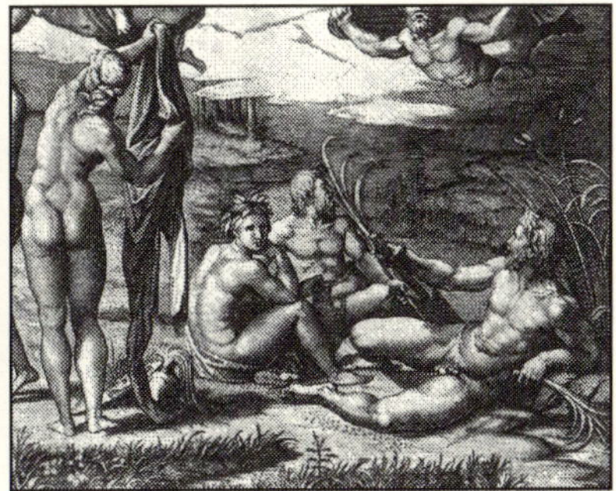

Fig. 9.24 - Raphael:
Judgement of Paris (detail) 1510
Engraving by Marcantonio Raimondi

finally taught at the academies. It is worth remembering, in this regard, that academies only started to teach 'painting' *in the last half of the 19th century*.

But, the death knoll of the Academy system had already been sounded. As taste in painting changed, the academies were increasingly criticized for their rigidity and theatricality. At the Salon of 1850-51, Gustave Courbet exhibited his huge and provocative *Burial at Ornans* (Fig. 9.22), polarizing viewers between those who championed its stark Realism and those who preferred the reigning Classicism of Couture and Gérôme. Thirteen years later, Manet also managed to scandalize the public through his *Déjeuner sur l'herbe* (Fig. 9.23), exhibited at the Salon des Refusés in 1863. Manet intentionally based his figures on a Raphael engraving (Fig. 9.24), in parody of academic practice, while his female nude, provocatively gazing at the public, was a far cry from the *le Nu idéal.*

Manet's work inspired a small group of genre painters, who began to exhibit themselves independently of the Salons under the name of *Les Impressionistes*. Their work, depicting colourful scenes of every day life, contrasted sharply with the allegories and histories of academic painting, which had increasingly come under fire as *Art Pompier* (literally, 'Fireman Art', since the helmets of classical figures resembled the headgear of French firemen or *pompier*). Through their novel approach of selling work directly to the public via private galleries and independent exhibitions (rather than through commissions generated by the Salons), the Impressionists changed the financial and commercial structure of modern art.

As state patronage of the arts declined, the age of art speculation began, so that today Contemporary Art is nothing more than an investment commodity in an art market controlled by profiteers (posing as curators and collectors), while the artist's main line of business has become provocation, publicity and political intrigue.

If I may summarize Contemporary Art with one word, I would say it is a *kallophobic* art – it fears beauty...

And so it falls to us today, as Visionary artists, to rediscover the lost aims of art and restore painting to its former purpose: to spiritually enrich a culture through authentic works of vision, skill and, yes, beauty. Forgoing the fleeting vanities of materialist culture, we must seek out art's eternal role, to create works of style, artistry and grace that strive – Ad Sacrum – *Toward the Sacred.*

Such an art has emerged time and again in history, as evidenced by the temple art and statuary from both East and West. Such a spiritual renaissance, in our own times, may be accomplished, in part, by academies that revive our knowledge of Sacred Codes – of the principles underlying drawing, design, and painterly execution. But it may also be accomplished, in part, by those artists who aspire to a higher ideal, of the eternal quest to 'see unity' and so behold the Divine in a work of art, thus transfiguring humanity through our collective visions of oneness.

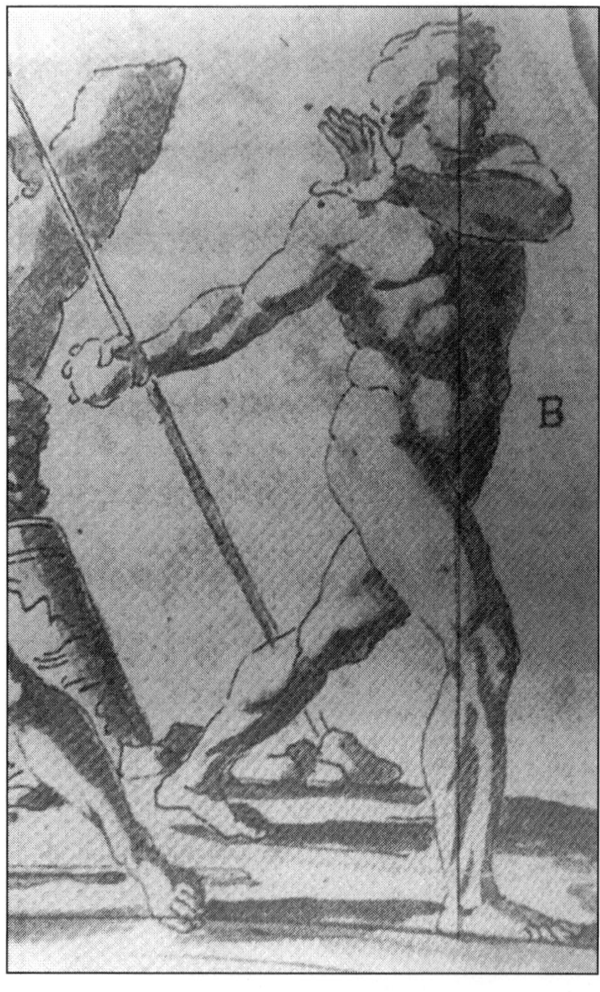

Fig. 10.1 - Example of the Plumb Line
in a Drawing by Nicolas Poussin (1594 - 1665)

CHAPTER X
NARRATIVE GROUPINGS OF FIGURES

I. Rubens' Theory of the Figure

In 1773 a curious text appeared, called (to give it its full title): *Théorie de la Figure Humaine, considerée dans ses Principes, soit en Repos ou en Mouvment* (The Theory of the Human Figure, Considered in its Principles, either in Repose or in Movement). Its text and original designs were attributed to none other than Peter Paul Rubens (1577 – 1640). Although the work's authorship has long been debated, its authenticity was recently established by Nadeije Laneyrie-Dagen[1].

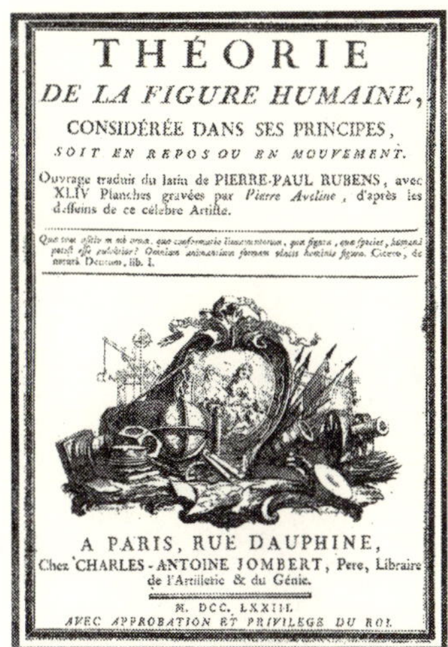
THÉORIE
DE LA FIGURE HUMAINE,
CONSIDÉRÉE DANS SES PRINCIPES,
SOIT EN REPOS OU EN MOUVEMENT.
Ouvrage traduit du latin de PIERRE-PAUL RUBENS, avec XLIV Planches gravées par *Pierre Aveline*, d'après les desseins de ce célèbre Artiste.

A PARIS, RUE DAUPHINE,
Chez CHARLES-ANTOINE JOMBERT, Pere, Libraire de l'Artillerie & du Génie.
M. DCC. LXXIII.
AVEC APPROBATION ET PRIVILEGE DU ROI.

Fig. 10.2 - Title Page of Peter Paul Rubens' 1773 Text

In his treatise, Rubens begins by associating the human figure with the perfect geometrical shapes of the square, circle and triangle (as well as their 3D homologues the cube, sphere and tetrahedron), and then proclaims, *"The virile form is the true perfection of the human figure"*[2] – 'virile' meaning 'male'.

He goes on to say, *"His beauty, according to the perfect Idea, is the unmediated work of the Divine, who created him alone, according to his own principle."*[3] Although Man is a mirrored reflection of the Divine, Rubens illustrates instead his beastly aspect, demonstrating in one plate after another how some men bear a striking resemblance in their physiognomy to lions, horses and bulls...

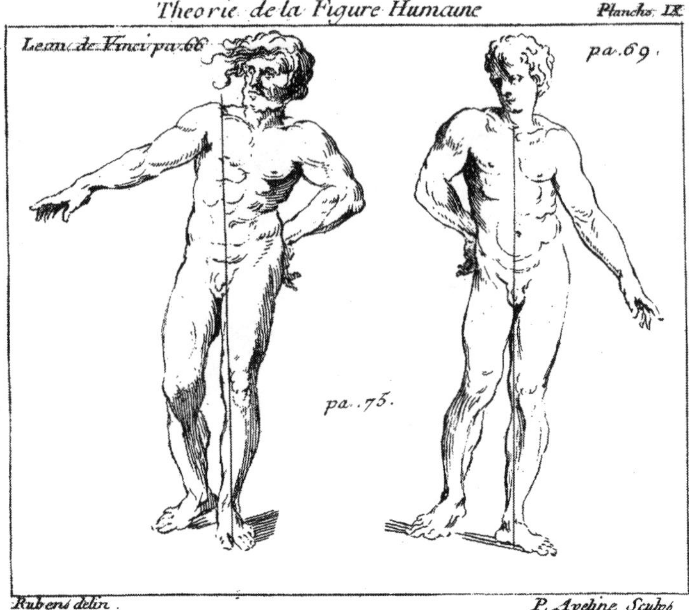

Fig. 10.3 - Illustration by Peter Paul Rubens: For a male figure in repose, the plumb line extends from the base of the throat to the middle of the lower leg

Citing the statues of Antiquity, Rubens then elucidates the principle human poses for movement and repose. Beginning with repose, he stresses the importance of balance – *"A figure is in repose when its balance is perfectly sustained."*[4] And he adds, *"Repose, or the privation of movement, comes from a balanced ponderation around the centre."*[5]

For the standing figure in repose, he remarks, *"We admire above all the attitudes of those figures which appear to have just come to a stop, or those which seem just about ready to leave their state of repose and begin to move"*[6] – thus echoing the Classical principle of *rhythmos* or 'arrested movement' where, as we saw, the antique statue seems to be forever poised between movement and repose.

He cites the *Antinous Belvedere* (Fig. 9.13) as a prime example where *"...the members are disposed with such art that we believe the figure is going to pass from movement to repose."*[7] By comparison, the *Apollo Belvedere* (Fig. 9.10) *"...appears to want to abandon its state of repose and begin to move."*[8]

In another section entitled 'Ponderation' he examined what happens when the figure *moves away* from the vertical plumb line, which he renders explicitly in each example, calling it *la ligne perpendiculaire.*[9] He decides that *"In the human figure, movement is born through the imbalance of weight."*[10] And so, in one drawing after another, he illustrates how the figure's inclination or movement *away* from the vertical plumb line *creates movement.*

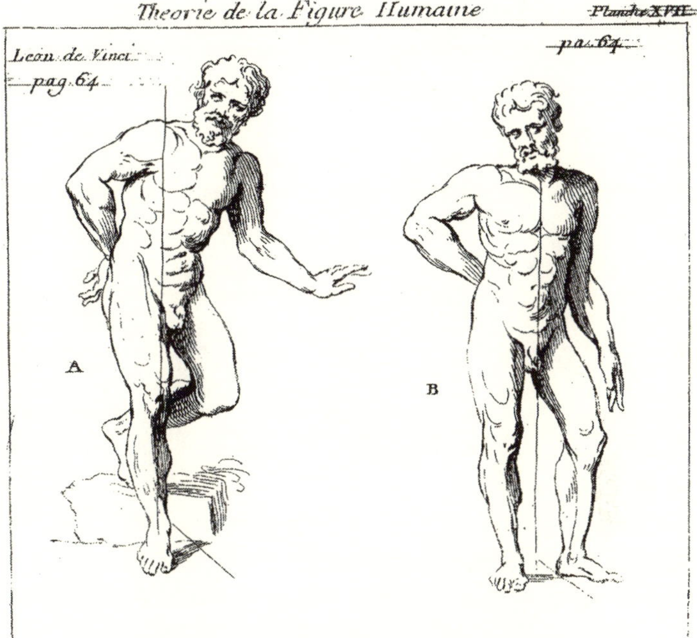

Fig. 10.4 - Illustration by Peter Paul Rubens:
"Movement is born through the imbalance of weight"

Regarding the exact location of the plumb line, Rubens notes that, in standing statues, it extends from *"the base of the throat"* to *"the middle of the lower leg"* (in men) or from the base of the throat to *"the inside heel of the weight-bearing foot"* (in women).[11] Rubens' *Theory of the Human Figure* confirms that, for the academically trained artist, the Classical principles established in antiquity persisted up until the eighteenth century.

In another intriguing section called 'Of the Various Antique Statues', he goes on to cite, with amazing breadth and erudition, the lexicon of poses exemplified by the Canon. All academically-trained artists were expected to know, and to cite in their art, specific poses from the Canon. We may take, as but one example, the figure of Venus from a Hellenistic relief (now lost) known as the *Letto di Policleto...*

II. The Policleto Venus

One of the first, great archaeologists of the Renaissance was Lorenzo Ghiberti (1378 - 1455), who was not only a great sculptor (he created the bronze doors of the Florence Baptistry) and a great writer (his *Commentari* offer a rare, autobiographical view onto the art of the early Renaissance), but also a great collector. Among the many masterpieces of antiquity which he had amassed in his collection was a marble relief which he attributed to Polykleitus, calling it *il Letto di Policleto* (The Bed of Polykleitus).

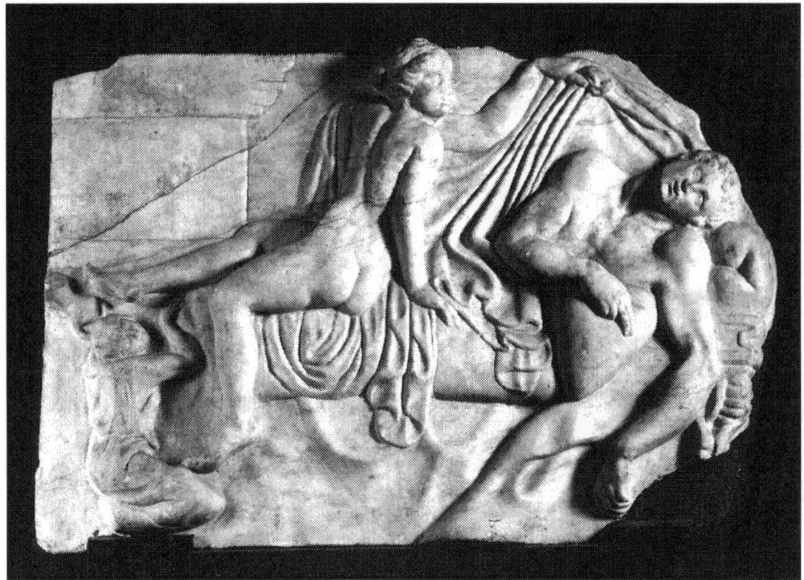

Fig. 10.5 - A 16th century copy of the lost *Policleto Venus*

After Ghiberti's death, the *Letto di Policleto* passed to other hands – an event which Vasari recorded in his *Lives* (referring to the statue as 'the bed of Polycretus'): "[Ghiberti] *bequeathed many relics of antiquity to his family, some in marble, others in bronze. Among these was the bed of Polycretus which was a most rare thing...*"[12] Two hundred years later, the relief ended up in Prague, a prized addition to the vast collection of Emperor Rudolf II, until it vanished from history during the Swedish Sack of 1630.[13]

The subject of the statue remains a mystery. Most likely, Venus is about to depart from the bed of her slumbering lover. The work has been titled variously *Venus Enticing Vulcan* or just *Venus and Cupid*. Her pose offers us a rare example of Classical Beauty, composed in a twisting diagonal that is strongly charged with erotic overtones.

Despite its disappearance, the statue was preserved in several lesser copies (Fig. 10.5). More interesting still, the erotic pose of the 'Policleto Venus' (as I will call it here) inspired some of the greatest artists of the Renaissance.

Around 1515, when the 85-year-old Giovanni Bellini painted his first female nude (the half-length *Lady with a Mirror*), he was also inspired to paint his first full-length nude in *Orpheus and Eurydice* (Fig. 10.8), basing it on the Policleto Venus. Thirty-eight years later, in 1553, Titian revived the pose for his *Venus and Adonis* (Fig. 10.6), where the nude goddess is now turning to hold onto her lover before he departs for the hunt. Both Titian and Giorgione had apprenticed under Giovanni Bellini, and both painted the first, overtly erotic, 'reclining female nudes' (Giorgione's *Sleeping Venus* of 1510 and Titian's *Venus of Urbino* of 1538). One wonders if their master Bellini had not introduced them to the *Letto di Policleto*, inspiring the *belle donna* motif into Venetian art.

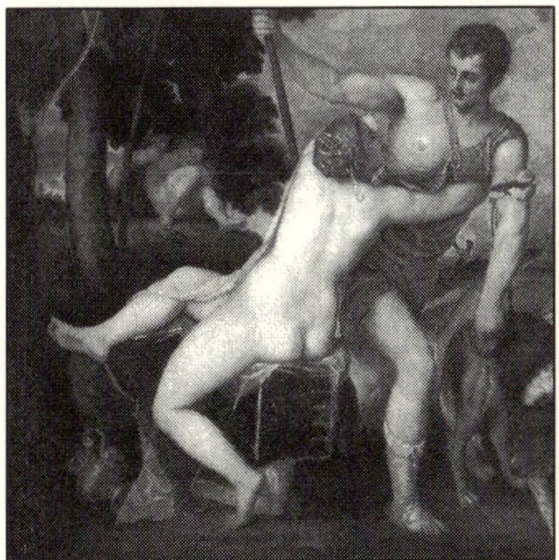

Fig. 10.6 - Titian:
Venus and Adonis (detail) 1553

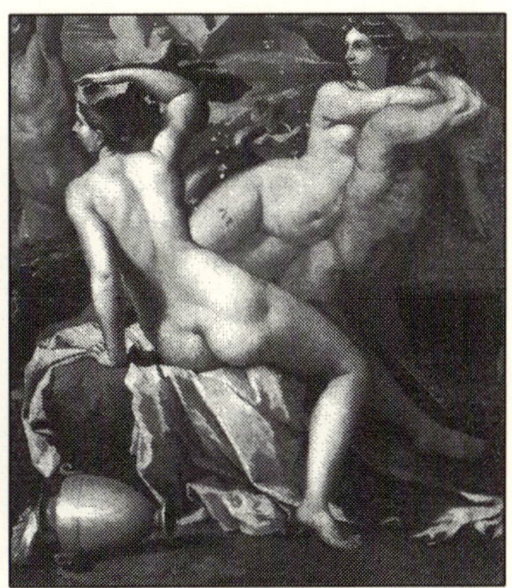

Fig. 10.7 - Poussin:
The Birth of Venus (detail) 1635

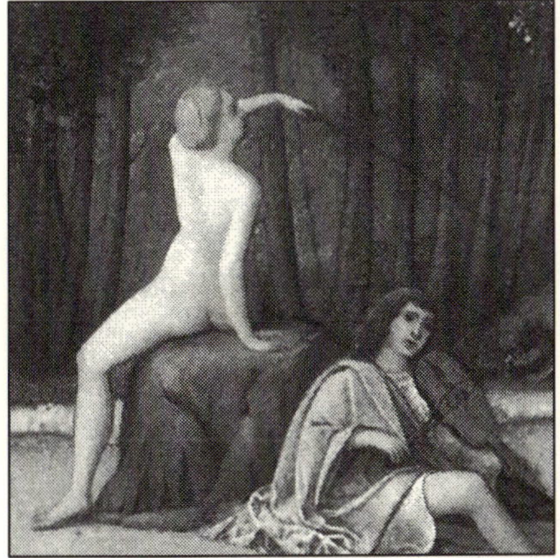

Fig. 10.8 - Giovanni Bellini:
Orpheus and Eurydice (detail) c. 1515

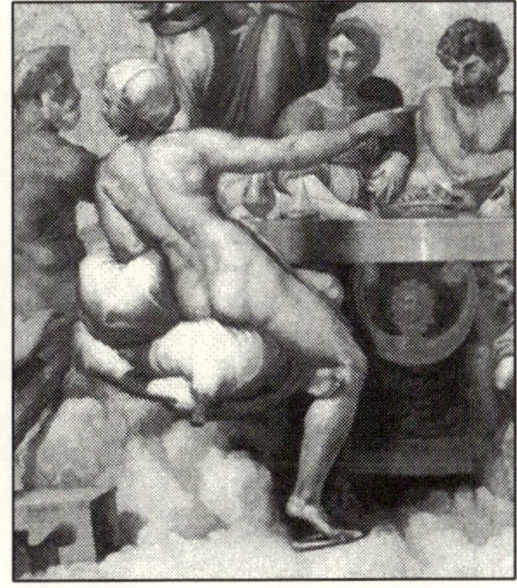

Fig. 10.9 - Raphael: *The Wedding Banquet of Cupid & Psyche* (detail) 1517

In the last years of his short life, Raphael turned to the *Policleto Venus* as his inspiration for the central nude figure (reversed) in *The Wedding Banquet of Cupid and Psyche* (Fig. 10.9), one of the two great frescoes on the ceiling of the Villa Farnesina. As Vasari remembers it, Raphael *"...was not able to give much attention to his work* [at the Villa Farnesina], *on account of the love that he had for his mistress; at which Agostino* [the villa's owner] *fell into such despair, that he so contrived by means of others, by himself, and in other ways, as to bring it about, although not only with difficulty, that this lady should come to live continually with Raphael in that part of the house where he was working; and in this manner the work was brought to completion."*[14]

Finally, in 1635 Cardinal Richelieu commissioned Nicolas Poussin to paint a series of four *Bacchanals* for his chateau in the Loire Valley. In the bottom right of the first *Bacchanal* painting (called variously *The Birth of Venus* and *The Triumph of Neptune* - Fig. 10.7), the *Policleto Venus* again appears, in perfect counterpoint to another nude being carried off by a satyr.

In all four cases, the nude Venus inclines in a twisting diagonal, flexing her left leg while turning her head to the right. It is this *serpentinata twist* that gives the figure its erotic energy, even if the placement of the arms may vary from artist to artist. These four examples show how Renaissance artists recognized certain poses as 'archetypes' – as Ideal shapes or forms for the expression of certain emotions. In this way, the human figure becomes a recognizable cypher or glyph for the innermost workings of the soul.

III. Expression – Passions of the Soul

The first head of the *Académie des Beaux-Arts* in Paris was Charles Le Brun, court painter to the king and close friend of Nicolas Poussin. Had not Poussin lived and worked in Rome, he would probably have been the Academy's first director. Instead, Le Brun worked hard to transmit Poussin's knowledge of Italian art to the French court by instigating a series of lectures. In 1668 Le Brun delivered the first of seven lectures in the *Grande Salle* of the Academy, taking his examples from the *Cabinet des Tableaux du Roi*, the King's personal collection. The first lecture elucidated a painting by Raphael; the last, a painting by Poussin. We shall return to these celebrated *Conferences* shortly.

The next year, Le Brun delivered a new series of lectures, this time under the title: *Expressions des Passions de l'Ame* (The Expressions of the Passions of the Soul), which was published in three versions [15] and became a standard resource for all academies.

Le Brun begins by saying, *"A passion is a movement of the sensitive part of the soul, which is designed to pursue that which the soul thinks to be for its good or to avoid that which it believes to be hurtful. ...Since most of the passions of the soul produce bodily actions, we ought to know what the actions of the body are which express the passions."*[16]

Rather than depict the actions of the body (the pose), Le Brun illustrated his lecture with a series of facial expressions – creating a 'Codification of the Passions' that was to be passed down from generation to generation in the Academies. *"There are many wise men who have written on the passions,"*[17] Le Brun notes and, though he does not cite their names explicitly, he clearly has the works of Aquinas and Descartes in mind. He begins with Aquinas, who distinguished between *simple* passions that follow a *concupiscent* appetite, and *complex* passions that follow an *irascible* appetite:

"The ancient philosophers, having given two appetites to the sensitive part of the soul, place the simple passions in the concupiscible appetite, and the wilder and mixed passions in the irascible."[18]

According to Aquinas, the *concupiscible* appetite creates *simple* passions because it moves in two simple directions: it is either attracted to what is beneficial or repelled by what is harmful. The *irascible* appetite is more complex, and gives rise to *mixed* passions, because it is attracted to the beneficial, even though it may be harmful, or repelled by the harmful, even though it may be beneficial. Le Brun then lists Aquinas' passions, where five are 'simple' and six are 'mixed':

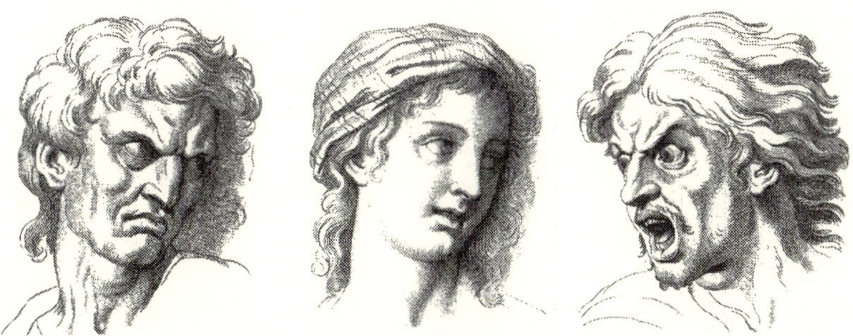

Fig. 10.10 - Nicolas Poussin *The Passions of the Soul*
Right to Left: Hatred, Admiration, Fear

"For they [the old philosophers] *maintain that Love, Hatred, Desire, Joy, and Sorrow are contained in the former* [simple passions], *and that Fear, Courage, Hope, Despair, Anger, and Fright belong to the latter* [mixed passions]. *"*[19]

He contrasts this to Descartes, whose recently-published treatise, *Les Passions de l'Ame* (The Passions of the Soul – 1649) added Wonder to the list of simple passions: *"Others* [i.e. Descartes] *add to them Wonder, which they place first, followed by* [Aquinas' five simple passions of] *Love, Hatred, Desire, Joy, and Sorrow, and from these they derive the others which are mixed, such as Fear, Courage, and Hope."*[20]

Descartes never listed nor enumerated the complex passions, though Aquinas counted them (as we saw above) as six. By combining Aquinas with Descartes, Le Brun is able to arrange feelings into a list of six simple passions and five mixed passions, though he adds, *"There are several other* [mixed passions] *which I shall not discuss here, but will content myself with showing you some drawings of them."*[21] In the end, he renders some twenty-three passions in all.

And so the Codification of the Passions begins. *"Wonder is the first of all the passions,"*[22] he exclaims. But our inability to sustain wonder leads to the contrary feelings of Love and Hate, or Joy and Sorrow, while Desire stands in the middle. Love, like Joy, is 'attracted to what is beneficial' (Aquinas) while Hatred, like Sorrow, is 'repelled by what is harmful' (Aquinas). Le Brun's list of Simple and Mixed Passions runs as follows:

The Simple Passions:
• Wonder – *"...a surprise for objects rare and extraordinary."*
• Love – *"...joins voluntarily to objects which appear agreeable."*
• Hatred – *"...separates from objects which appear harmful."*
• Desire – *"wishes for those things which seem agreeable."*
• Joy – *"an agreeable emotion which consists in the enjoyment of a good."*
• Sorrow – *"a disagreeable emotion which consists in the discomfort of an ill."*

The Mixed Passions

- Fear – *"anticipates threats."*
- Hope – *"expects to obtain what it desires."*
- Despair – *"expects to not obtain what its desires."*
- Courage – *"resists evil."*
- Anger – *"withdraws from injury while rousing itself against the cause."*[23]

In 1759, the Compte de Caylus sponsored the first *Concours* on the Expressive Head (*Tête d'Expression*) where the Passions of the Soul were to be drawn, modelled or painted in the form of 'a head' by competing academy students. Professor Dandré-Bardon, the first director of the *Concours*, chose as its subject 'Wonder mixed with Joy'. The results were deemed to be so *minable* that no prize was awarded. Nevertheless, a charter of rules was drawn up, and the *Concours* survived – held each year for the next hundred and forty-one years, until its demise in 1900.[24]

The question of *decorum* (*bienséance*) quickly entered into the debate around the model and the passions. At the instigation of the Compte de Caylus, the model for the *Tête d'Expression* had to be a woman, preferably an actress who possessed beauty, character and good morals:

"The truth is, if we wish to represent the passions clearly, we must look toward the character of the face that expresses them. If the character is noble and beautiful, then the passion will be noble; but if it is base and common, then the passion will be vulgar."[25] For this reason, Prof. Dandré-Bardon established that, *"The model must be of good morals, of high social standing or nobility, and possess a beautiful physiognomy."*[26]

The rules of *decorum* further dictated that certain passions were deemed inappropriate to women: *"This is not to say that women are not susceptible to the same passions as* [men], *but whether all passions are appropriate to them. If we are pleased to see Faith, Desire, Fear, Suffering and tears as those expressions which embellish their beauty, then we are shocked when they present to us a character expressing Hate, Spite, Anger, Extreme Despair or Fury. Such violent expressions of the soul disfigure their beauty. For this reason, the professors have chosen, since the inauguration of the prize, to present only those feelings which are soft or mixed* [des sentimens mixtes et doux]."[27]

When we read the list of different passions proposed each year for the *Concours*, or look at the resulting paintings that have come down to us through time, we may confirm that only 'soft or mixed' feelings were expressed: Pain mixed with Joy (1823), Surprise mixed with Fear (1827), Contemplation (1831), Melancholy (1843 – won by François-Léon Bénouville, Fig. 10.11), and Disdain (1850 – won by Bourguereau, Fig. 10.12).

It may strike us as odd that the French Academy gave so much attention to the Codification of the Passions, as well as to the Canonical history of the Pose. To reduce the infinite variety of expressive human movements to a set number of conventional gestures strikes us today as unnatural and contrived. Indeed, even within the academy, and especially during their annual Salons, there were *"...all kinds of critics who denounced the weakness of the expressions and the theatricality of the gestures* [la faiblesse des expressions et la théâtralisation des gestes]"[28]

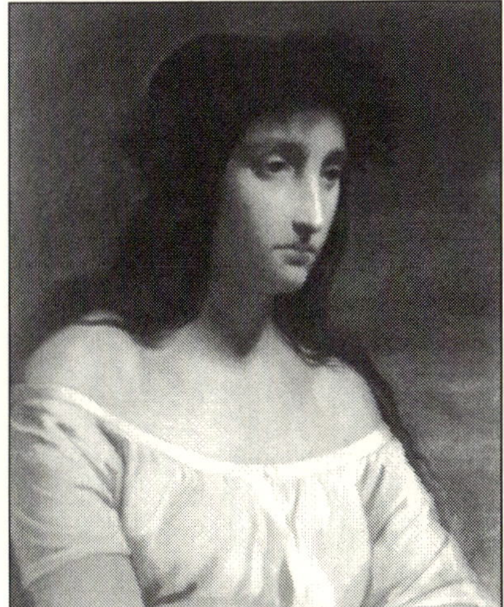

Fig. 10.11 - François-Léon Bénouville: *Tête d'Expression - Melancholy* (1843)

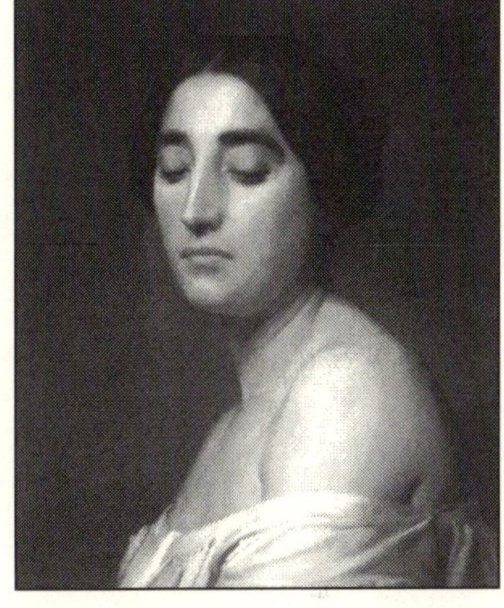

Fig. 10.12 - William-Adolphe Bouguereau *Tête d'Expression - Disdain* (1850)

Meanwhile, any painter who aspired to *la grande manière* was dependent upon pose and expression, as a kind of language, to clearly transmit their ambitious narrative programme (*l'histoire*). When we turn to Hieratic Art (as we shall in the next chapter), we will discover in Hindu and Buddhist art that numerous manuals for artists conventionalized the pose and facial expression into a clearly codified language. But in Humanist Art, the flow of passion and energy could not, it seems, be simply contained by a well-crafted figure. With the collapse of the academies, that energy would soon break free of its constraining bonds, and strive for a greater Naturalism (Courbet) or Poetic Symbolism (Moreau).

IV. Félibien: the *Histoire* in *Grande Manière* Painting

In History Painting, it is primarily the *histoire* (narrative) or, more generally, the *sujet* (subject) which constructs a meaningful relationship between the figures, allowing us to consider them in the context of the whole. But the Composition also does this, in a more visual way, as does the Disposition and even the Invention. All these terms helped to define the chief aim of academic painters: to construct a painting in the grand-manner. What is *la grande manière?*

Not only did André Félibien do us the great service of preserving Poussin's letters and recording Le Brun's lectures, he also wrote key texts on History Painting, becoming a kind of Alberti or Vasari for the foundation of the French Academy. In his *Principes de l'Architecture, de la Sculpture, de la Peinture* (Principle of Architecture, Sculpture and Painting – 1676), he begins by saying, *"In a painting* [le tableau], *there are three things to consider: the Composition, the Drawing and the Colouring* [la Composition, le Dessin, & le Coloris]. *"*[29] He is not far from Ludovico Dolce here, who gave Invention (*inventio*) as the first principle, followed by Drawing (or Design – *disegno*) and Colouring (*colorito*).

Indeed, when Félibien defines Composition, he mentions Invention in the same breath: *"The Composition, which some call the Invention, brings together a number of different aspects, such as the disposition of the figures, the choice of attitudes, including the appropriate drapery, ornament, place, architecture and landscape, as well as the movements of the body and the passions of the soul in all their diverse expressions."*[30]

The Drawing, as the second principle, is responsible for the design of the figures in their respective poses: *"The aim of Drawing* [le Dessin] *is to represent the figure through the use of line... Drawing renders the figure in its pose, as well-balanced on a central point (due to its own weight, or the weight of another), but absolutely firm in all the actions, which imitate all the diverse movements given to us by Nature."*[31]

The Colouring, as the third principle, is not just the application of colour, but includes the *clair-obscur*, the contrasts of light and darkness: *"The Colouring* [le Coloris] *has as its object the colour, light and darkness."*[32]

The successful execution of the *clair-obscur* (or *chiaroscuro* in Italian, the 'light-dark') gives the painting the character of a Classical relief, and so is called *le grand relief*: *"If the light gives a certain accent to the fore-most figures while gently receding over the masses, diminishing little by little until it softly diffuses into a darkness without colour, then we say that it is executed in grand relief."*[33]

Last of all, the Colouring itself must remain harmonious: *"If, among the lights and shadows, we find true natural colours mixed with such agreement and sympathy that no part seems separate but all are integrated and unified, as if the painting had been painted in one sitting with one palette of colours, then we say that it is well-coloured."*[34]

The three principles of art come together as the painting's manner or style (*manière*) which, if the Invention is well-designed, becomes a painting in the Grand-manner:

"From these three principles we derive what is called 'the Manner' [Manière]... *As such, in the composition of a history* [histoire], *when the figures are well-disposed in groups, with a good choice of attitudes according to the necessities of the subject, and the general plan of the landscape conforms to Nature, so that nothing in regard to the expression* [l'expression] *seems to be lacking, then we say it is 'well-invented'* [bien inventé]. *If, finally, all the parts come together in a great design* [sont desseignées grandes], *appearing neither uncertain nor excessive but well-executed with force and clarity, then we say that it is well-designed in the grand-manner* [est bien desseigné et de grande manière]."[35]

V. Grouping of Figures in History Paintings

In his inaugural lectures for the *Académie des Beaux-Arts*, Charles Le Brun cited Raphael and Poussin as the two great practitioners of *grande manière* painting. So important were these 1667 lectures that they were transcribed and, two years later, published by André Félibien under the title of *Conférences* (Lectures). In 1831, the Swiss painter Johann Heinrich Füssli, as an elected Professor at The Royal Academy in London, delivered a similar series of lectures on Raphael and Poussin, which were preserved in volume II of the three-volume opus *The Life & Writings of Henry Fuseli.* Although these lectures are separated by two centuries, they attest to the consistency and continuity of certain academic principles. Both texts are invaluable for the light they shed on those principles, which treat the complex problem of Composition and Figuration in a large-scale work of art.

Raphael's *School of Athens* (Fig. 10.13) and Poussin's *Gathering of Manna in the Desert* (Fig. 10.16) are upheld as the two great exemplars of History Painting. Raphael's masterpiece has withstood the test of time, while Poussin's painting seems of little interest today, perhaps to only a small handful of specialists and *connoisseurs.* I must admit that I needed fifteen years in France to finally gain some appreciation for Poussin's genius – and then, it was only because of the huge impact of his work on French Painting as a whole, and on Gustave Moreau in particular. We cannot begin to understand Academic Painting – and Gustave Moreau as the last great painter to emerge from that tradition – without acknowledging Poussin, who transmitted the ambitions of Renaissance painting (especially Raphael) to the French Academy, particularly through the lectures of Le Brun.

In one of his rare letters, sent from Rome on the 28th of April 1639, Nicolas Poussin advises the purchaser of the *Manna* painting, M. Chantelou, to *"...read the* histoire *in the painting, to determine if each part is appropriate to the subject."*[36] The remainder of the letter makes clear that Poussin assumes his purchaser *already knew* 'how to read' the painting – a task which seems rather daunting to us today...

In another letter, Poussin explains the best distance from which to view a painting:

"The painting must be placed in the gallery... with sufficient distance to allow it to be seen at an eye's glance [coup d'oeil]*."* And he repeats, *"From the same point and distance, we should be able to see* [the whole painting] *with a single glance of the eye* [on doit regarder d'un seul coup d'oeil]*."*[37]

This first *coup d'oeil*, it turns out, is the first reading of the painting – we take in the entire 'perspective', beholding the whole *at a glance.* After that, we begin the second reading, which is to examine the parts one by one – an exercise that Poussin calls 'prospective' in contrast to 'perspective'.

In the same letter he explains that there are two ways of looking at a painting:

"You must know that there are two ways to see objects. The first views them simply, the second considers them with attention. To see simply is to receive in the eye, quite naturally, the form and resemblance of the thing seen. But to consider something with attention... we make a distinct effort to search out the best way to know and understand the object. This requires the use of reason, and which I call 'prospect'."[38]

In his lecture of 1831, Johann Heinrich Füssli remarks that, *"By breadth the artist puts us into immediate possession of the whole, and from that, gently leads us to the examination of the parts according to their relative importance."*[39]

This distinction between the whole and the parts leads us to one of the great paradoxes of reading. In the 19th century, Friedrich Schleiermacher introduced the concept of 'the hermeneutic circle' which states that, during the act of reading, the parts can only be understood in relation to the whole, and the whole can only be understood in relation to the parts. He meant this for words in a sentence, or sentences in a paragraph, or even paragraphs on a page – but it also holds true for figures in a composition: to read the parts of the painting (the figures), we must first see them in the context of the whole (the composition), but to read the whole of the painting (the composition), we must first see it part by part (the figures). Both are equally necessary and, in Heidegger's words, both are 'equiprimordial' (*gleichursprünglich*).[40]

This sheds an important light on the process of reading. It is wrong to assume that reading is a purely linear, word-by-word understanding of the text. Although the eye may scan a sentence linearly, it 'reads' by understanding the words in relation to the whole sentence, and vice versa. To read a painting, then, is to continually scan the figures, but their meaning will not emerge until each is compared with the others and with the composition as a whole. More than that, the figures need not be confined to a single linear scan 'from left to right' but may be approached and assembled in a variety of ways.

VI. Reading the Painting: Temporal Disposition from Left to Right

If we 'cast a glance' at Raphael's *School of Athens* or Poussin's *Manna*, our eye quickly takes in *the composition as a whole*, noting the basic triangular disposition of figures in both paintings: at the apex appears the central pair, followed by two groups to the left and right. This triangular disposition of figures suggests an invisible's armature, like a massive X drawn from corner to corner, with the apex of the triangle at the centre of the X.

If we interpret that same basic triangle from the viewpoint of *perspective*, then the main pair is 'in the middle plane' close to the central vanishing point on the horizon line, while the left and right groups are 'in the foreground' closer to the corners (there is also a 'background plane' of architecture in Raphael, and the landscape in Poussin).

Once our eye has taken in the painting's triangular composition 'at a glance', it begins a 'prospective' (Poussin) observation of the parts – tracing a path through the various groups of figures. In his analysis of Poussin's *Manna*, Le Brun calls this 'a journey through the landscape': *"...the eye should be able to journey* [se promener] *through all of the desert's expanse."*[41]

Whether it travels to the right or left does not really matter – it will have to travel around the entire composition two or three times before 'the parts' are understood in relation to 'the whole'. That whole, as we noted earlier, is held together, not just by the composition, but the *histoire*. Particularly during the period of History Painting, long detailed titles were provided to aid in reading the painting's *histoire*.

The School of Athens (Fig. 10.13), as it has come to be known, was probably titled *Causarum Cognitio*. It appears in the *Stanza della Segnatura* in the Vatican, with a tondo above it depicting the allegorical figure of

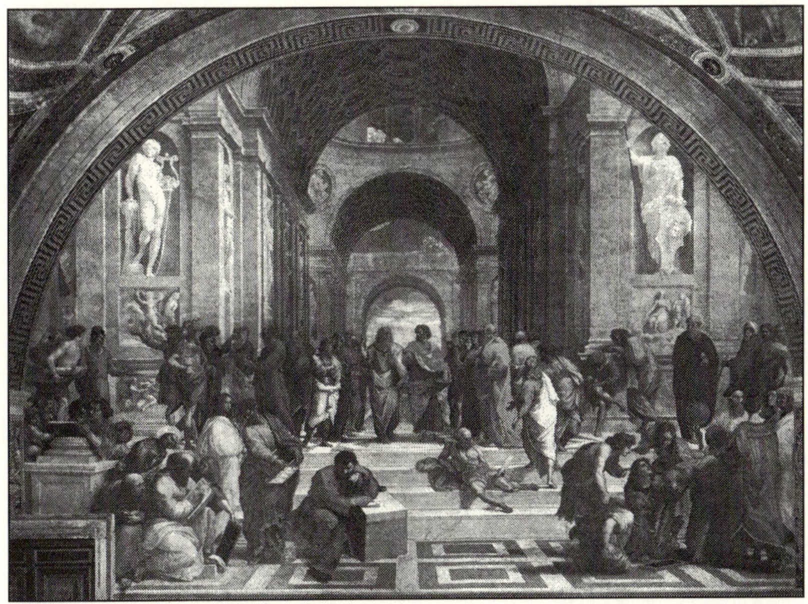

Fig. 10.13 - Raphael: *The School of Athens* 1511

Philosophy accompanied by two putti. These two hold tablets inscribed with the words *Causarum Cognitio* – literally 'Knowledge of Causes' or more generally, 'Seek out Knowledge of First Causes'. If *Causarum Cognitio* is the true title, then this panorama of ancient Greek philosophers, who are standing before a veritable Temple of Philosophy, demonstrates how each great thinker was, in his own way, a seeker after first causes.

For Poussin's work *Les Israélites recueillant la manne dans le désert* (The Israelites Gathering Manna in the Desert – 1638, Fig. 10.16), the *histoire* comes directly from the *Book of Exodus,* chapter 16, where Moses and Aaron led the Israelites away from Egypt and into the desert. There, they began to suffer from starvation until the Lord rained down *manna* (bread chips) in the morning.

The simplest way to translate this *histoire* into a painting would be to establish a temporal reading 'from-left-to-right' where something happens 'before' on the left and 'after' on the right. Poussin has done this, since the group in the left foreground is still in a state of suffering (*before* the miracle), while the group in the right foreground are joyfully gathering up the manna (*after* the miracle). In the centre, the Israelites are kneeling in gratitude before Moses and Aaron, while Moses points heavenward to indicate that it is the Lord who has sent down the miraculous manna.

In *The School of Athens*, a similar 'temporal' reading is possible, since the philosophers on the left half lived *before* Plato (423 – 347 BCE – he is in the centre on the left, pointing skyward), while those on the right half lived *after* Aristotle (384 – 322 BCE – he is in the centre on the right, with his hand held out earthwise). This is especially true of the two main groupings in the foreground, which surround *Pythagoras* on the left (570 – 495 BCE – the kneeling bald-headed philosopher writing into a book) and *Euclid* on the right (c. 365 – 275 BCE – bending over a slate with a pair of compasses in hand). We shall come back to these groupings around Pythagoras and Euclid in due time.

Socrates, who preceded Plato as his teacher, appears in the middle plane to the left, as the bald, pug-nosed philosopher (in profile) debating with the man in armour. Many of the renowned Pre-Socratic philosophers, such as Parmenides (standing to the right of Pythagoras and pointing into an open book) and Heraclitus (sitting pensively at the writing block) also pre-date Plato. Meanwhile, the two figures holding globes above Euclid are thought to be Strabo (64 BCE – 24 CE) and Ptolemy (100 – 170 CE), while Plotinus (204 – 270 CE) stands above them, pointing downward – all of these philosophers post-dating Aristotle by hundreds of years.

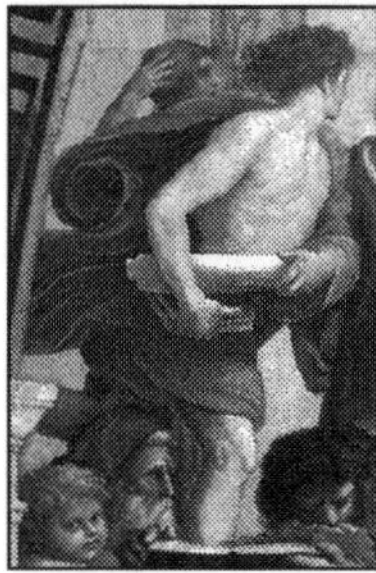
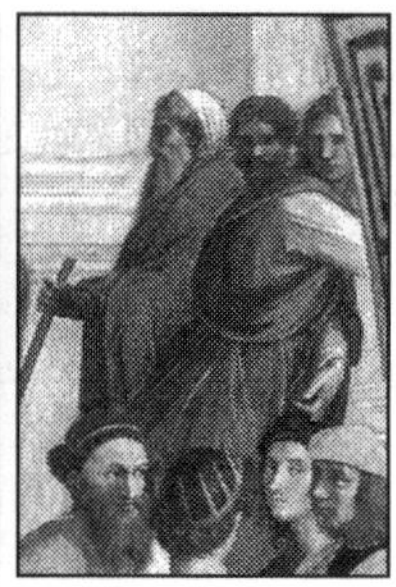

Fig. 10.14 - *School of Athens* (detail)
Figures Running In and Out

More fascinating still are the two figures at the extreme right and left of Raphael's fresco (Fig. 10.14). The mysterious figure on the left is running *into* the composition while his homologue on the right (glancing backward) is running *out of* it. These actions encourage the eye to move *from left to right*, reading the historical course of philosophy as a linear development over several hundred years, from the Pre-Socratic to Neo-Platonic eras.

Less noticeable, but equally important, are the two sets of figures to the right and left of the groupings around Plato and Aristotle (Fig. 10.15). To the left, two philosophers (one bearded, one barely visible) are *emerging from* the perspectival depths of the Temple of Philosophy – that symbolic edifice with its rounded arches converging onto an infinitely-distant point in the vast blue sky. Meanwhile, on the right, two philosophers (one with a bald head, the other not) are *walking towards* the arch and its distant skies – to that metaphysical place where First Causes are sought.

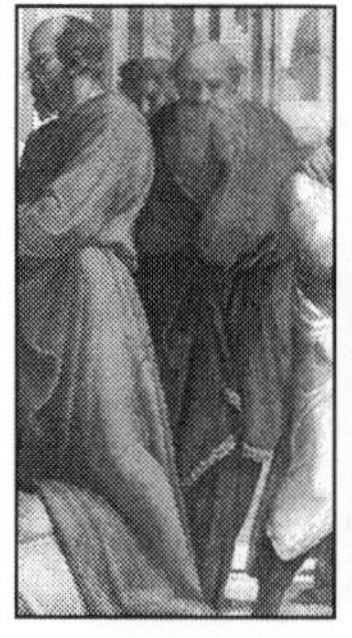
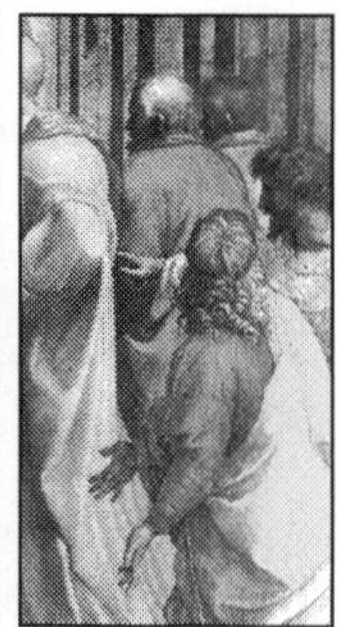

Fig. 10.15 - *School of Athens* (detail)
Pairs of Philosophers Entering
and Leaving the Temple of Philosophy

In this way, the artist translates the *istoria* into a *temporal* arrangement of figures, guiding our eye from left-to-right to read the groupings as so many incidents transpiring 'before-and-after'. Le Brun remarks that, even though the incidents may seem to transpire 'before-or-after' the main event, the scene in a painting actually transpires 'in a single moment':

"Since the painter has only a single moment in which to represent the main event of his subject, he is bound, at times, to join several events together, including the incidents that preceded [or followed] *the main event."*[42]

Hence, even though several incidents are 'joined together', the scene depicted in the painting does not lose its 'unity of action'. As Le Brun noted: *"There is nothing in Poussin's picture which could, we may say, disturb the unity of action."*[43]

The expression 'unity of action' comes from Aristotle, who recommended in his *Poetics* that a drama take place in one location only (unity of space), over the course of a day (unity of time) and with one main plot (unity of action). Nevertheless, Aristotle intended this for Tragedy alone, holding that Epic poetry (and *Grande Manière* painting aspires to Epic status) could take place over much longer periods of time: *"...for Tragedy endeavours, as far as possible, to confine itself to a single revolution of the sun... whereas the Epic action has no limits of time."*[44]

This distinction eventually led to the Cortona-Sacchi Debate of 1636, held at the *Accademia di San Luca* in Rome, where the Academy's director, Pietro da Cortona, argued that a complex composition with many figures aspired to Aristotle's vision of Epic Poetry, creating multiple episodes and sub-plots over an unlimited period of time. Andrea Sacchi argued, on the contrary, that a simple composition with fewer figures fulfilled Aristotle's vision of Tragedy, with the main action transpiring in a single time and place. Both artists created frescoes for the ceilings of the Palazzo Barberini, and Sacchi's composition strikes us today as no less convoluted, baroque and ornate as Cortona's.

The painters of the French Academy, like their Italian brethren, were acutely aware of Painting's relationship to Poetry (*Ut Pictura Poesis* we recall, *As is poetry, so is painting*). Aristotle's *Poetics* prescribed the rules of Poetry – or, to be more precise, Poetic *Drama*, since his classic work was primarily concerned with Theatre in its two major forms: Tragedy and Comedy (the latter text of Aristotle, *On Comedy*, being lost). Likewise, painting in the *Grande Manière* aspired to a distinct *théatralité*, creating a strong link between Painting and Theatre (*Ut Pictura Theatrum* as one researcher[45] has described it – *As is theatre, so is painting*).

VII. Theatre of the Passions

While describing a drawing by Raphael (for *The Death of Ananias*), Füssli remarks upon the theatrical effect of the composition:

"At the first glance, and even before we are made acquainted with the particulars of the subject, we become partners of the scene. The disposition is amphitheatric, the scenery a spacious hall, the heart of the action is the centre, the wings assist, elucidate, connect it with the ends."[46]

In a similar way, Le Brun notices that the landscape in Poussin's *Manna* has a theatrical purpose: *"The scene occurs in the middle of a plane, surrounded by mountains which take the form of an amphitheatre."*[47]

Poussin, as is well-known, went to certain extremes to compose his paintings in a theatrical manner. In fact, he constructed a small stage in his studio, dividing the floor plan into various levels of scenery, and populating it with small wax figures, dressed in fine linen, which he posed according to the necessities of the *histoire*. As Anthony Blunt explains:

"When he first began to plan a composition, he first read all that was relevant to the subject, whether in the Bible or in Plutarch or in Ovid, so as to be able to visualize the story [histoire]. *At this stage he made a rough sketch to record his first idea* [la première idée] *of how it might be represented. He developed his conception in further sketches, and he would then proceed to the next step which was much more unusual.*

"He made little wax figures, about nine inches high, representing the individual characters taking part in the action, and for these he made draperies of fine linen, and then arranged them on a miniature stage, the floor of which was squared like a chessboard and which was equipped with means of controlling the lighting and a slot at the back for a drawing to supply the landscape or architectural background. He would then make a drawing of the group as it appeared on the stage..."[48]

This elaborate process allowed him to harmoniously arrange his compositions according to Alberti's directive that *"the* istoria *comes from copiousness* [copia] *and variety* [varieta] *of things... in which in their places are mixed old, young, maidens, women, youths, young boys... buildings, landscapes and all similar things..."*[49]

Observing Poussin's *Manna* painting, Le Brun also marvelled at *'the breadth and variety'* of his figures:

"For those who take the time to view the perspective of this painting, Poussin has perfectly rendered the mountainous landscape as a series of uneven perspectival planes, situating his figures on the most elevated of the terraced slopes to give his disposition of figures a great degree of breadth and variety [de jeu & de variété]. *In this way, his composition accommodates a large number of figures within its relatively small confines."*[50]

This is precisely the kind of stage necessary for the narrative to unfold in a theatrical manner. The painting offers a 'copious variety of things' so that the eye may move from figure to figure and experience a large range of emotions through the diverse characters, male and female, old and young. At first, such 'passions of the soul' may be experienced randomly and without order. But, with the aid of the composition and *histoire*, they may eventually fall into their intended narrative sequence.

Returning to Poussin's *Manna*, Le Brun wonders at *"...how the author of this painting has so admirably brought the figures to life, giving them such a diversity of movements, so that all their various actions and expressions have specific causes that relate directly to the principle subject."*[51]

And he cautions us, *"But to enter into the particular state of each figure and understand their actions, not only in terms of what they are doing but what they are actually thinking, we must examine their movements very closely."*[52]

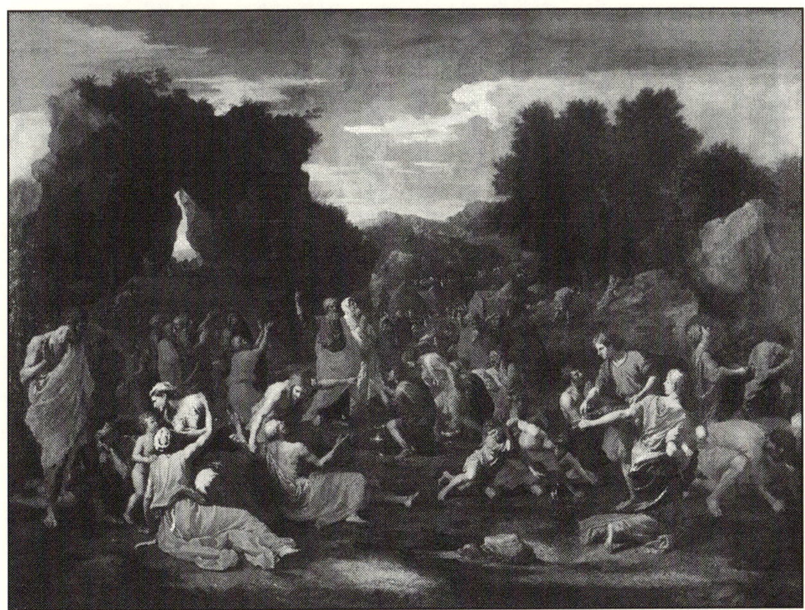

Fig. 10.16 - Poussin: *The Israelites Gathering Manna in the Desert* 1638

Thus begins a much closer reading of the parts in relation to the whole, but now at the level of painterly expression and dramatic feeling in relation to the narrative development. This, we discover in Poussin's letter to his friend and fellow artist, Jacques Stella, was exactly what he intended by his *Manna* painting:

"In my painting for M. de Chantalou, I've found the right distribution of figures and the right attitudes to express the misery and hunger which the Israelites have suffered, but also the joy and exultation which they have found in the desert. Add to this the wonder that has touched their hearts and the respect and reverence they feel for their leaders – all expressed through a mixture of men, women and children of different ages and temperaments. Such things, I believe, will not fail to please those who know very well how to read them."[53]

As this letter suggests, there are three main 'passions of the soul' which Poussin wished to express through his groupings of figures: misery, joy and wonder. We recall that Sorrow (i.e. misery), Joy and Wonder were three of the six 'Simple Passions' listed by Le Brun and illustrated with specific facial expressions in his Canon of the Passions. Through his composition, Poussin has expressed each one of these simple 'passions of the soul': Sorrow (or misery) in the left group, Joy in the right group, and Wonder in the middle. He has achieved this through *a copious variety* of 'men, women and children of different ages and temperaments', as he proudly proclaims to Stella about his painting for M. de Chantalou.

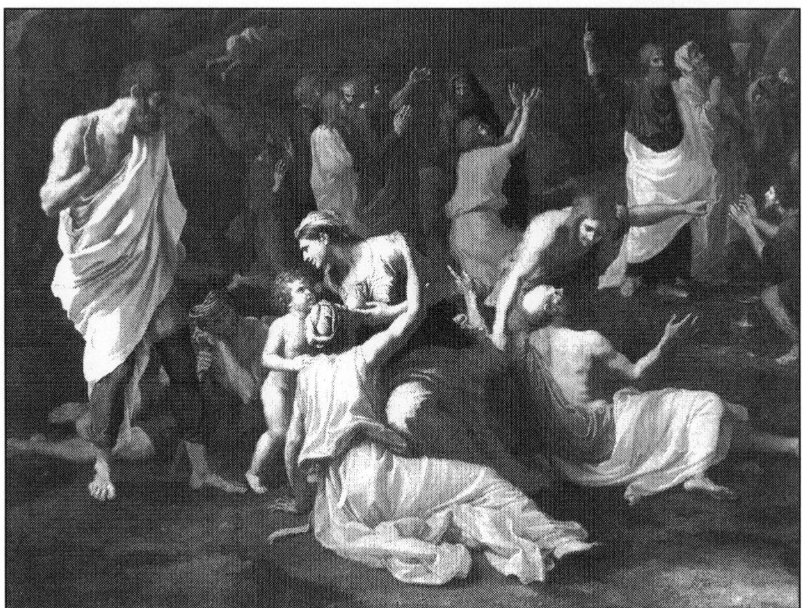

Fig. 10.17 - Poussin: *Gathering Manna in the Desert* - Left Group: Misery

It was precisely M. de Chantalou, the purchaser of *Manna*, who Poussin wrote to directly in April of 1639, saying *"...read the* histoire *in the painting, to determine if each part is appropriate to the subject."*[54] Poussin began this important letter with the words:

"As for the rest, if you consider the painting as a whole, and call to mind my first letter, where I promised to render all the figures in their various movements, then I think you will easily recognize which ones are wasting away with hunger or marvelling with wonder, which are feeling pity or acting out of charity, and which are acting out of dire necessity, or strong desire, or finding consolation. Because in the seven figures on the left you will find all that is written here, when you read the histoire in the painting, to determine if each part is appropriate to the subject."[55]

When we compare the letter with the group appearing on the left (Fig. 10.17), we are surprised to discover that Poussin has indeed rendered seven figures that express each of these seven passions. At the centre of the triangular grouping appears a kneeling mother who (*acting out of charity*) has taken her breast from the mouth of her own child (*strong desire*) and offered it instead to her starving elderly mother (*acting out of dire necessity).*

To their left, a bearded man recoils (*marvelling with wonder*) while raising his right hand and gazing down at the motherly act of charity. Below him in the shadows, a feeble man with crutch (*wasting away with hunger*) also turns his upper body to gaze upon the mother's offering. To the right, a young man (*feeling pity*) raises up an elderly man. As the young man points to the falling manna on the right, the elderly man (*finding consolation*) opens wide his arms to express gratitude and reverence for the miracle wrought by Moses and Aaron.

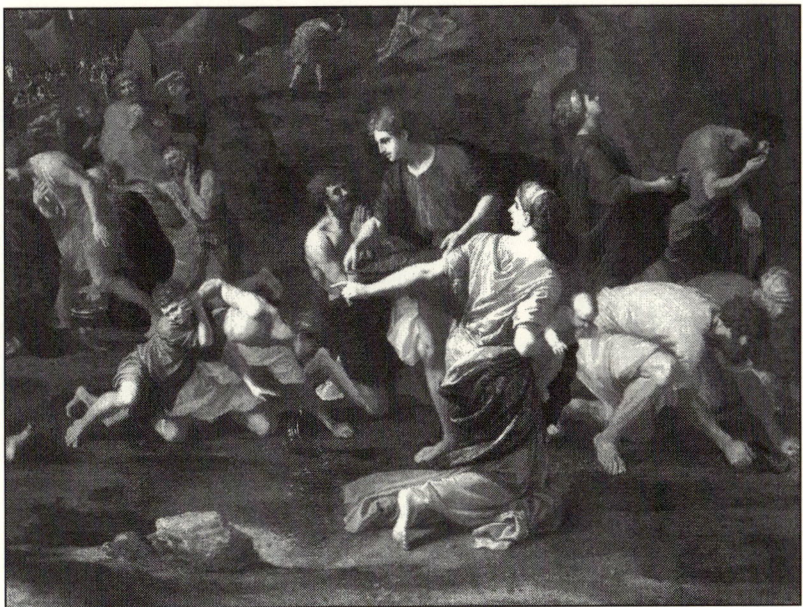

Fig. 10.18 - Poussin: *Gathering Manna in the Desert* - Right Group: Joy

The triangular grouping on the left thus becomes a self-contained unit which announces seven specific passions through sculptural groups in carefully-contrived poses and expressions. Since this group is encountered *first* in the temporal reading 'from-left-to-right' (*before* the fall of manna), it *announces* those passions (like a musical prelude or the overture of an opera) which are then *developed and expanded* through the groups of figures to the right and in the centre.

Returning now to the group on the right (Fig. 10.18), we see how the central figure of a kneeling mother and child *also expresses wonder* as she turns to gaze upon Moses and Aaron. But, to her left, a young man and a child struggle over a tipped bowl of manna (*strong desire*) while a man just behind her (*acting out of charity*) steps forward with a pan, to bring manna to the elderly man on the left. Others behind her kneel and gaze heavenward to express the group's ruling Simple Passion: *Joy and exultation* for the manna that has fallen.

Finally, on the middle plane in the centre, smaller groups of figures around Moses and Aaron raise their hands and fall to their knees to collectively express the culminating feeling of Wonder – '*the wonder that has touched their hearts and the respect and reverence they feel for their leaders.*'

VIII. The Codification of the Passions & the Canonical History of the Pose

To read and experience these passions, we examine the sculptural groups particularly in light of their specific *poses and expressions*. In his lecture on Poussin's painting, Le Brun does this with extraordinary erudition and discernment. For example, when he describes the expression of wonder in the man on the far left, he says:

"This great painter does not dispose his figures simply in order to fill the space of his painting, but rather, renders them so admirably as to make us believe that they are moving, whether through the actions of the body or the movements of the soul. He shows us how the [bearded] *man* [on the far left] *represents a person struck with awe and wonder. He has recoiled with one arm raised and the other pressed close to his body because in moments of great surprise all the bodily parts withdraw in response to that wondrous event which imprints its image upon the mind – an image so great in awe and wonder that we feel no fear or trepidation... Thus his eyes open as wide as possible to better discern and marvel at the greatness of the woman's charity."*[56]

Reading this, we clearly recall Le Brun's *Expressions of the Passions of the Soul* where *"Wonder is the first of all the passions."* As a Simple Passion, Wonder remains unmixed by fear or trepidation. Indeed, Le Brun describes the man's face as he would a *tête d'expression*.

The same is true of Le Brun's description of the poses, which he likens to statues drawn from the Antique Canon:

"What makes this painting so excellent and well-considered is that Poussin has derived all the proportions of the figures from the finest Antiquities, which suit his subject perfectly... the old man has the same proportions as the Laocoön [...while] *the woman who gives her breast to her mother holds the same pose as Niobe* [...and] *the young man has the same proportions as the* [Apollo] *Belvedere."*[57]

To render a 'well-considered' painting in the Grand-Manner, the poses are derived from 'the Canonical history of the Pose' and the expressions are clearly delineated, as in Le Brun's 'Codification of the Passions,' so the *histoire* may be clearly read, part by part, in light of the whole.

Returning to the poses in the left group, we note how all the figures are arranged within the confines of a triangle. There is, however, a circular flow of energy contained within that triangle, beginning primarily with the woman offering her breast to her elderly mother. These three receive the most emphasis through light, contrast and colour, while forming a statuesque arrangement worthy of Michelangelo's *Pietà*. The two men on the left, by gazing in wonder upon the charitable mother, keep our eye fixed on that inner pyramidal arrangement of three figures while amplifying the emotions. Meanwhile, the two men on the right, by pointing and looking away, offer our gaze a passage out of the left group.

The same holds true for the group on the right, where the kneeling woman with a child (she too receives the most light, contrast and colour) turns to gaze upon Moses and Aaron, thus offering our gaze a line of vision out of her triangular formation. Although our gaze may wander back and forth between the various groups, eventually a greater narrative order is established through the *histoire*.

Another narrative technique used by Academy painters was to arrange groups of figures through *contrast* – a contrast that arose within a single set of figures, or between two groups of figures. Le Brun noted such a contrast in the pairing of the old man and young man, situated to the right of the charitable mother in the left group:

"In the case of the old man gazing upward with arms raised, and the young man pointing across to the falling manna, the artist wanted to depict two very different spiritual states. Because the young man is so overcome with joy by the falling manna that he doesn't even think about its cause. But the old man, who is wiser and more prudent, is raising his eyes to heaven in order to show adoration and praise for the source of that Divine Providence which has spread manna upon the earth."[58]

By that same token, the groups to the right and left contrast one another in their emotional tone, since the left group expresses Sorrow while the right group expresses Joy. It is precisely these contrasts, whether in the pairing or the groups, which allow the narrative to develop *in a dramatic manner*. As Le Brun concludes about Poussin's painting:

"Through his knowledge and understanding, the painter has shown that he's also, in truth, a poet, having composed his work according to the rules of poetry as seen in a work of theatre. To portray his story [l'histoire] *in the best possible way, he's made sufficient use of those elements necessary to poetry, moving from misfortune to joy. In the various actions accompanying his groups of figures, we find the sequence of episodes that serve to create the 'peripeteia', as it is called, the 'turning point' where the Israelites are freed from their misery and returned to a happier state."*[59]

Le Brun is certainly correct in his observation. But his analysis of the narrative ends at the *peripeteia* – the reversal or turning point where Sorrow turns to Joy. As we have seen in Poussin's letter to Jacques Stella, there is also a third movement, expressed by the central group of worshippers around Moses and Aaron, where Joy turns to Wonder.

This is the culmination of the drama, which Aristotle called the *anagnorisis* – a profound moment of realization and understanding, a sudden epiphany resulting in *"a change from ignorance to knowledge."*[60] At that moment, according to Aristotle, the main character acknowledges a higher force at work in his existence, a knowing recognition of Divine Providence.

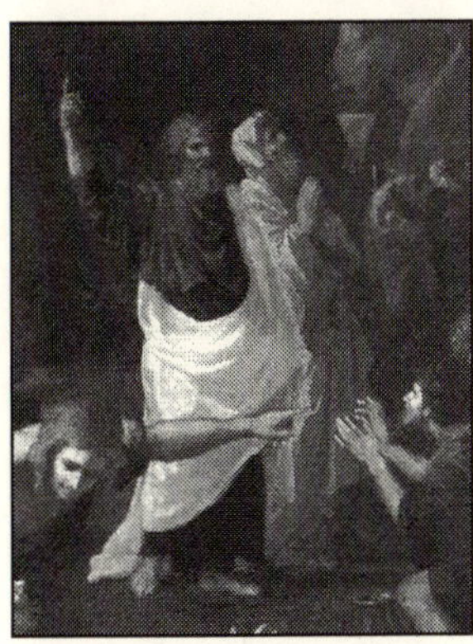

Fig. 10.19 - Poussin: *Gathering Manna* (detail) Moses and Aaron

In Poussin's painting, the central figures of Moses and Aaron express this in two possible ways. Aaron, the prophet and high priest, *gazes* heavenward with piety and awe; Moses, the leader and law-giver, *gestures* dramatically by pointing to the skies. Either way, our vision is led upward to the invisible and transcendent source of the manna falling in the desert.

Through his *Manna* painting, Poussin demonstrates his mastery of Invention – of the ability to compose figures in a variety of ways so as to convey the *istoria*. He has done this, as we saw, through a left-to-right reading that temporally arranges the groups into 'before and after' episodes in the narrative. And, he has done this in a more theatrical manner, by evoking the various passions of the soul, through a variety of sculptural poses and expressions, that move from group to group and develop the dramatic feelings from suffering to joy to wonder, like so many episodes in an epic poem.

In a painting 'well-considered in the Grand-Manner', our eye is led around the composition, experiencing an abundance of figures ('a copious variety of things') with a range of canonical poses and expressions to evoke all the passions of the soul. Once the eye makes several turns around the painting, examining the parts, it will eventually form a narrative order for these episodes, according to the *histoire*. At a glance, the parts support the whole and the whole supports the parts. But in a final movement, our eye will eventually come to rest upon a single central point, to experience wonder and awe in the acknowledgement of a higher, transcendent source which has inspired the dramatic unfolding, breathing meaning and life into the painting's narrative.

IX. One Great Doctrine: The Platonic & Aristotelian Accord

Nicolas Poussin was a French painter who spent most of his working life in Rome. Through his *Manna* painting (1638) and other admirable works, he was able to transmit a knowledge of Renaissance principles to the newly-founded *Académie Royale de Peinture et de Sculpture* (founded in 1648), particularly through the intermediaries of Le Brun and Félibien.

But even as late as 1831, in his lectures at The Royal Academy in London, Johann Heinrich Füssli was able to re-iterate these principles, citing Raphael's *School of Athens* as his prime example. For Füssli, Raphael's fresco unifies the disparate groups of figures into a harmonious whole:

"The School of Athens [seems to offer] *an arbitrary assemblage of speculative groups. Yet, if the subject be the dramatic representation of Philosophy as it prepares for active life,* [then] *the parts of the building are not connected with more regular gradation than those groups. Archimedes and Pythagoras, Plato and Socrates, Aristotle and Democritus... in different degrees of characteristic modes, tell one great doctrine, that, fitted by physical and intellectual harmony, man ascends from himself to society, from society to God. For this, group balances group, action is contrasted by repose, each weight has its counter poise; unity and variety shed harmony over the whole."*[61]

In Füssli's mind, the figurative groups are no less integrated into the composition than are the arches and columns into the architectural edifice. His metaphor is apt, since it suggests that the same laws governing harmony in architecture – weight, balance, counter poise – also govern groupings of figures in a composition.

When we turn to Raphael's composition, we find that, indeed, group balances group and action is contrasted by repose. We have already taken note

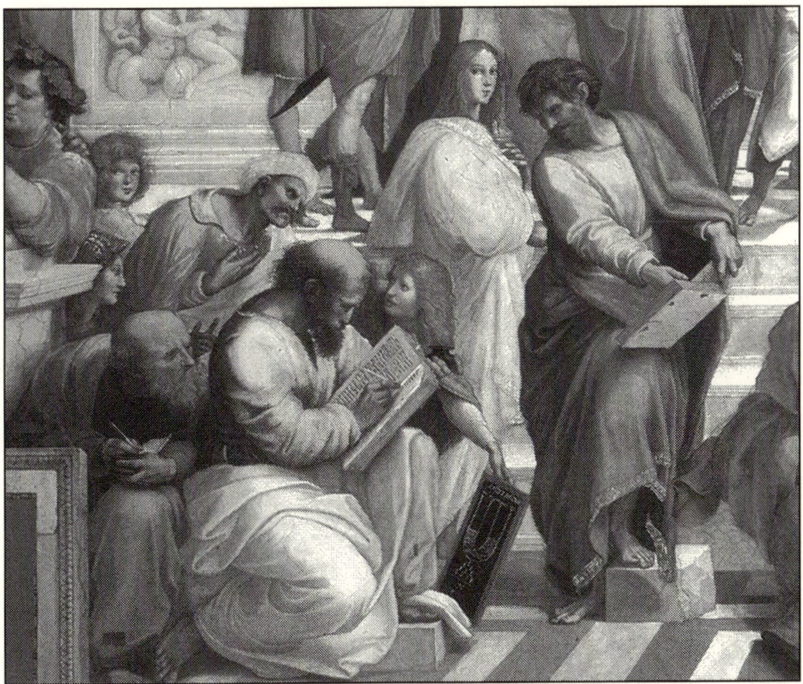

Fig. 10.20 - Raphael: *School of Athens* - Left Group Around Pythagoras

of the two groups in the foreground, where Pythagoras on the left balances Euclid on the right. These two philosophers dominate their configurations because each performs *a vigorous action*: Pythagoras *kneels* to scribble a new discovery in his book; Euclid *bends over* to inscribe a circle in the tablet. At least three, if not four of the figures around Pythagoras *react* to this action; the same is true of Euclid, whose action provokes *a circle of reactions* in the four figures around him.

Thus, the principle figures *willfully initiate an action*, which courses through their bodies, only to be released through the power of their gesture or glance. That energy is picked up, echoed and amplified by the lesser figures around them. This transfer of energy also occurs at the level of sight: at least three of the figures around Pythagoras *turn to scrutinize* the writing in his book, just as two or three of the figures around Euclid *marvel* at his tablet. As such, not only the gestures but *even the gaze* of the principle figures is amplified by the lesser figures around them.

Through this method, a circle of energy cycles through the group, which is otherwise contained by a static triangle in the armature. With the configuration around Euclid (Fig. 10.21), our eye is led *out* of the circle by the young man, who is looking *away* and gazing upward to the right. Following his line of sight along the diagonal of the armature, we pass the

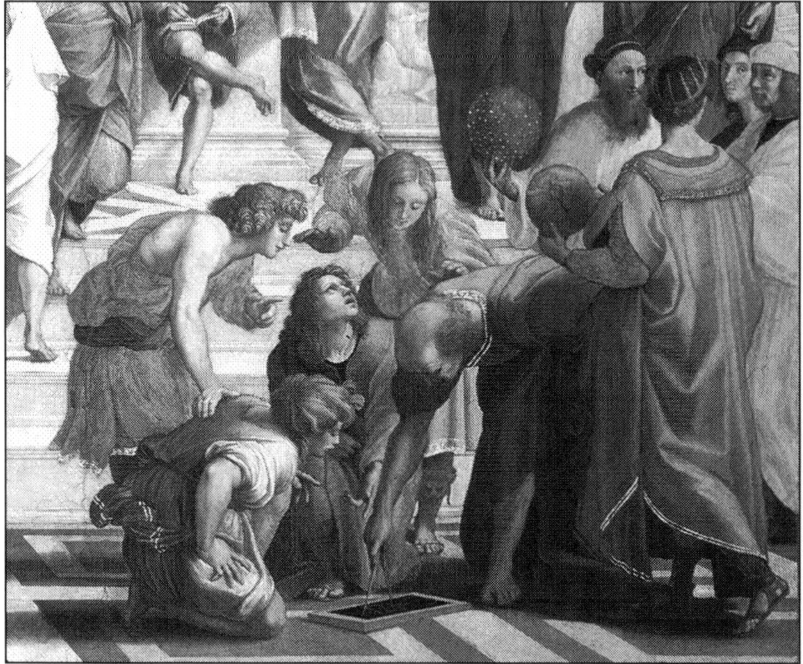

Fig. 10.21 - Raphael: *School of Athens* - Right Group Around Euclid

geographer and astronomer with their globes (Strabo and Ptolemy, who are also turning to the right) until our eye finally lands upon Apelles hidden in the corner – who is none other than Raphael himself.

In the case of the configuration around Pythagoras, we have no specific path to draw our sight out of the circle. Nevertheless, the graceful youth in white robes, who is standing at the apex of the configuration, shares with Raphael the same disturbing quality: *he is staring directly at us.*

The reason why the direct gaze seems so disturbing in this fresco is because we are standing before a Humanist work of art, where energy dynamically moves from figure to figure through lines of sight or dramatic action along the armature. Yet, in more ancient, Hieratic works of art, *the deity gazes directly at us,* transfixing our regard and inviting extended contemplation. That is why our wandering eye, in Raphael's fresco, suddenly comes to a standstill. It is confronted by the more ancient Hieratic Gaze, a sacred and holy power that is usually only attributed to divinities, saints and door guardians.

In order for energy to keep moving through a painting, the lines of sight must travel along horizontals or diagonals – along those very lines which, invisibly, zigzag through the painting as its armature. Faces turned at a three-quarter angle (which are typical for the Humanist Style) offer us these more dynamic lines of sight to follow. The heavenly glance, as we saw with Raphael's St. Catherine, leads the eye instead in a vertical ascent out of the picture plane. By contrast, other types of gaze momentarily hold and fix our regard.

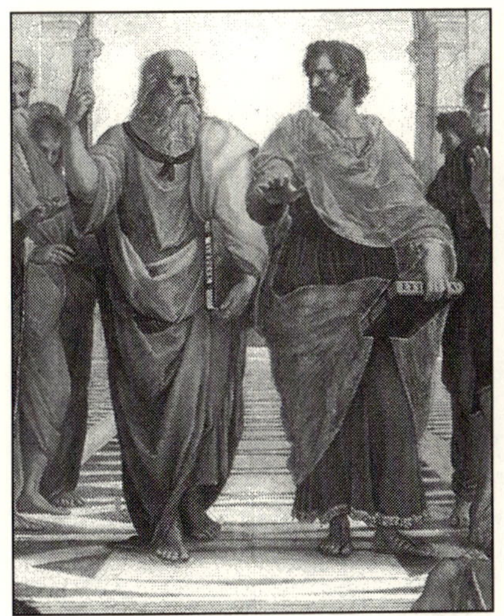

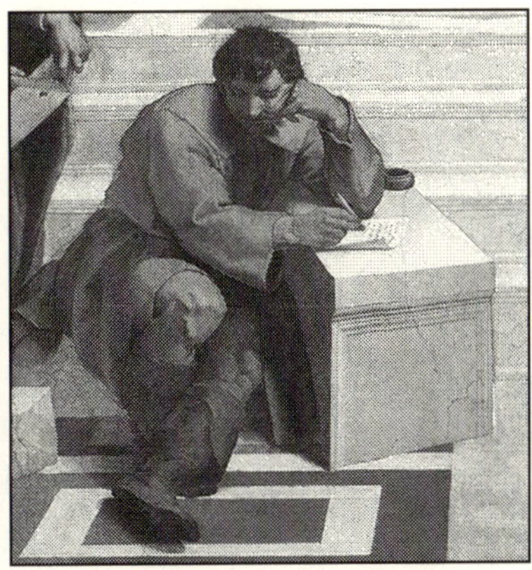

Fig. 10.22 - Raphael: *School of Athens*
Left: Plato (Leonardo) and Aristotle
Right: Heraclitus (Michelangelo)

This is certainly the case with the pondering Heraclitus (Fig. 10.22), who is self-contained in his pose and self-absorbed in his reveries. We know from Raphael's original *cartone* (Fig. 25.1) that no such figure was planned for this part of the composition but, after Raphael gained a clandestine glance of the unfinished ceiling in the Sistine Chapel, he added this portrait of Michelangelo. His inward-turned gaze fixes our glance upon him, cycling our sight in an infinite figure-8 that courses through his seated *serpentinata* pose (an invention used by Michelangelo for his Sistine Prophets and Sibyls). The pensive figure, though added late, certainly helped to balance Raphael's composition, completing the triangular configuration on the left and offering some counterweight to the sprawled figure of Diogenes, on the stairs to the right.

With the central pair of Plato and Aristotle (Fig. 10.22) – each turning to the other with their gazes interlocked – our wandering eye again comes to a standstill, cycling round on a fixed point. This was certainly Raphael's intention, and their two figures invite our extended contemplation. Through their stance, attributes and gestures, these two figures allegorically express the entire theme of the fresco.

Aristotle to the right stands in a three-part *contrapposto*, but both his feet are planted firmly on the ground. He holds his book at an even level, and his fore-shortened arm reaches outward, in perfect alignment to the vanishing perspective. His book, *The Ethics*, is concerned with human conduct and moral virtue, while Plato's volume, *The Timaeus*, pursues more lofty themes on the creation of the cosmos. Aristotle's attitude and bearing, indeed his entire philosophical outlook, are grounded on the horizontal and earthly plane, on Philosophy as a rational and scientific investigation *into Nature*. All our human endeavours are 'an imitation of Nature' (*mimesis*), and a striving after *Life-likeness* (*to zotikon*).

Plato, by contrast, is aligned to the vertical. He holds his book upright, and raises his left heel to add extra force to the upward thrust of his right hand.

Neither walking nor standing, he is simply establishing a point of balance – poised between movement and repose. For an eternally-stilled moment, he is pointing upward, indicating the higher invisible world of the *eidé* – the original ideas, forms and archetypes from the timeless realm of Being.

If Plato and Aristotle are gazing at each other, it is because their opposing philosophies have finally reached a common accord. Through the Renaissance writings of Marsilio Ficino and Giovanni Pico della Mirandola, the great union, the *concordia platonis et aristotelis* was finally achieved. And through the Art of Painting, Raphael wished to similarly express this *concordia* and final union.

As we shall see in Chapter 16, the lower left of the fresco and especially the tablet in front of Pythagoras holds the key to the Harmony of Forms. And as we shall see in Chapter 25, the lower right of the fresco and especially the tablet inscribed by Euclid holds the key to the Geometry of Space and Time.

Thus, the entire left half of the fresco, overseen by Apollo and inspired by Plato, reveals *the Ideal Philosophy*, the world of the higher Forms, governed by harmony and poetry. The entire right half, by contrast, is overseen by Athena, the Goddess of Wisdom, and her faithful servant Aristotle, who rationally and empirically pursues *the Natural Philosophy*, with its structures of Space and Time governed by astronomy, geometry and perspective.

Through this magnificent fresco, Raphael brings these different worldviews into one harmonious accord. From a single point at the centre of this panorama, vision flows outward in a stream of human forms, moving over and around the invisible lines that define space and time, achieving the mysterious fusion of armature and perspective in a highly symmetrical composition that is static in parts, and yet, also intensely dynamic. The tension of will and repose, which animated a single figure in Greek sculpture, now explodes its bounds and animates entire groups, moving dynamically through the composition to express the Renaissance striving for balanced harmony and the union of opposites.

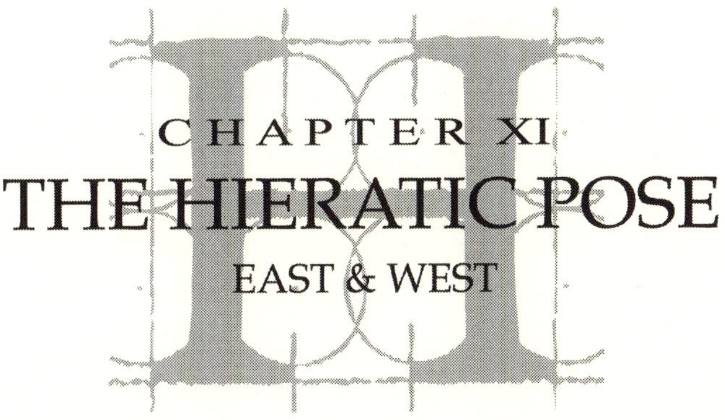

CHAPTER XI
THE HIERATIC POSE
EAST & WEST

"In the early days of Christianity, in the period of the illusionistic styles of Late Antiquity, artists were held by the followers of the new religion to be deceivers, and a painter would find himself named together with a harlot, brothel-keeper, a drunkard, an actor and an athlete. An echo of this view of the artist is heard in the iconoclasts's accusations that the painters were in league with demons who induced them to fashion false appearances.

"Parallel to the development of a [Byzantine] *church art founded on theology and dogma, this view of the artist necessarily had to undergo a fundamental change. The painters of sacred images came to be looked upon as spiritually qualified persons with a special relationship to the hidden things that they could reveal in their art."*

Hjalmar Torp[1]

I. Icons & Iconoclasm

While gazing upon an icon, we tend to forget that Byzantine art almost never existed at all.

In 726, the Byzantine Emperor Leo III destroyed the icon of Christ above the entrance to the Imperial Palace. This symbolic act was accompanied by a decree, co-signed by the Patriarch of the Eastern Church, calling for the destruction of *all* icons and the persecution of *anyone* who venerated them as holy. This iconoclastic movement caused much bloodshed and destruction over the next century, as the decrees were variously repealed and re-enforced until *The Seventh Ecumenical Council* of 787 and the final 'Triumph of Orthodoxy' declared by Theodora, regent of the throne, in 843.

In this way, the theology of the icon was forged by Saints and Church Fathers, who risked their lives in defending the veneration of Christ and the Virgin in images. At its core, Byzantine theology has several concepts which Western thinking can only describe as 'mystical'. Such is the case with *theosis* (deification), meaning that each individual, and the creation as a whole, is on the path towards a total union with the Godhead, by gradually becoming divine.

This process of becoming, or *metamorphosis*, is best exemplified by Christ during the Transfiguration – in which he appeared both in his human likeness and as a being of pure Light. Through prayer, purification and contemplation (*theoria*), certain unique individuals have achieved *theosis*, and are recognized as such, calling them Saints. Their faces glowed with the same light as the transfigured Christ, and so they are depicted with haloes.

The icon itself has a similarly unique status. There is, for example, an icon of Christ's face appearing on a veil, which is called the *Acheiropoieton – "the icon not made by human hands"* (Fig. 5.10). It is similar to the Western tradition of the Shroud of Turin or Veronica's Veil, but much older.

According to the 7th century legend, King Abgar of Odessa sent an emissary to Palestine, begging Christ to come and heal him of his leprosy. The emissary, who was also an artist, could not even reach Christ due to the huge crowds, so he attempted to draw him instead. He failed to capture a true likeness *"because of the indescribable glory of His face, which was changing through grace."*[2]

Upon seeing the artist-emissary, Christ bade him approach. Then the Saviour washed his face and wiped it with a piece of linen, leaving the imprint of his features on the cloth. The emissary brought this back to King Abgar, who received it and was healed.

This image of Christ became known as the *Mandylion* or Image of Odessa, a holy relic that was venerated for centuries until it disappeared during the Sack of Constantinople in 1204. It resurfaced at Sainte Chapelle in Paris under Louis IX, only to disappear completely during the French Revolution of 1789.

Similar legends accompany many of the holy relics of Byzantine Christendom – from portraits of the Saints to *The Virgin Hodegetria,* a much venerated icon of 5th century Constantinople that was reportedly painted by Saint Luke himself. These 'portraits from life' are considered to be *prototypes,* and constitute the Canon of Byzantine iconography.

As Leonid Ouspensky notes, *"The Orthodox Church has never accepted the painting of icons according to the imagination of the painter or from a living model, which would signify a conscious and total break from the prototype... In order to avoid falsehood and a break between the image (icon) and its prototype, iconographers use old icons and manuals as models."*[3]

These Painter's Manuals appeared mostly in Greece (as *hermineia*) and Russia (as *podlinniki*). *The Painter's Manual of Dionysius of Fourna* is the best known example today, written in 1730 by a painter monk of Mount Athos. Meanwhile, St. Alipy of the Caves is considered the Father of Russian iconography. I was fortunate to visit his cell at the cave monastery of Kiev Pechersk Lavra. With only a slender tallow held in the cleft of my upturned hand, I reverently walked the dark and narrow passages where this 11th century icon painter prayed in solitude and where his relics still remain.

II. Byzantine Codes

"In its coded language, the icon speaks to us,"[4] Leonid Ouspensky writes in his two volume work, *Theology of the Icon,* which is one of the modern classics of Byzantine iconography (alongside *The Meaning of Icons* co-authored with Vladimir Lossky). Being an icon painter himself, Ouspensky had a rare gift for translating the icon's deeper meaning into words.

When early Christians attempted to portray Christ, they first used Roman models. But *"the new content could not be clothed in the old forms of antiquity,"*[5] Ouspensky writes. A unique style was required, authentic to Christianity. Much of this new style was forged during the Iconoclastic period, when opponents of icons claimed that the Holy could not be properly portrayed in images. To depict the Holy in human form, they said, was to debase it, since all of humanity is fallen.

In defense of the icon, the Seventh Ecumenical Council proclaimed: *"Although the Catholic Church represents Christ in His human form (morphe) through painting, it does not separate his flesh from the Divinity which is joined to it... When we make the icon of the Lord, we confess His deified flesh, and we recognized in the icon nothing except an image representing a resemblance to the prototype. It is for this reason that it receives its name* [as an icon or likeness]*; it participates only in this, and is therefore venerable and holy."*[6]

Hence the icon, Ouspensky explains, *"...does not represent the corruptible flesh, destined for decomposition, but transfigured flesh, illuminated by grace, the flesh of the world to come."*[7] Indeed, *"The deification* [theosis] *attained by the saint constitutes the beginning of the cosmic transfiguration* [metamorphosis]*,"*[8] he says. *"The final goal of creation is its transfiguration."*[9]

When we behold the image of Christ in an icon, it is not the Divinity in its imperfect human form, but the human form transfigured and made perfect through Christ's theosis: *"The divine image was re-instated in man in the perfect life of Christ. He destroyed the power of original sin by His freely-accepted passion and led man to realize the task for which he was created: to achieve divine likeness. In Christ, this likeness is realized to a total perfect degree by the deification of human nature. Indeed, the deification* [theosis] *represents a perfect harmony, a complete union of humanity and divinity."*[10]

It is for this reason that Byzantine painters never attempted to portray Christ, the Virgin and the Saints as recognizably human with natural features. Similarly, *"The aim of the icon is not to provoke or glorify in us a natural human feeling. It is not 'moving', not sentimental. Its intention is to attune us to the transfiguration of all our feelings."*[11]

We in the West have been trained by the Humanist tradition to treat artworks as moving images of our Human comedy or tragedy (Aristotle's basic definition of *mimesis* in the Poetics). We seek similitude, sympathy and *catharsis*. But the Byzantine artists followed a different tack, avoiding accurate depictions of Humanity and favouring a Hieratic 'likeness' (*eikon*) of a higher ideal (Plato's *eidos*) – of a Humanity fully perfected, transfigured, and deified.

It is for this reason that geometry and style are so important in Byzantine art. The underlying sacred geometry and the clear linear outlines offer us the essential shapes and archetypal traits that make up the *prototype* – the divine image and first-ever depiction of the Holy figure.

III. Byzantine Contemplation:
Hesychasm & Theoria

Only the rarest of individuals, like saints and holy fools, may be granted a vision of the Holy Face. But, over the course of the icon's history, certain monastic painters have also achieved this vision. Although icon painters never signed their works, the names of a few great artists have come down to us through time, such as the Holy Andronik, Daniil the Black and Andrei Rublev...

The Eastern Orthodox church has a long tradition of *hesychasm* (literally "keeping still"), which is the monastic practice of inner prayer and contemplation aimed at *theosis*, the holy revelation. While creating an icon, the icon painter should also practice some form of prayer and meditation, which may include visual contemplation: *"For we speak of it* [the icon] *from contemplation,"* says St. Simeon the New Theologian, *"therefore what we relate should be called a record of what has been contemplated."*[12]

And Ouspensky corroborates: *"An icon cannot be invented. Only those who know from personal experience the state it portrays can create images corresponding to it, which are truly 'a revelation and evidence of things hidden.'...No artistic fantasy, no perfection of technique, no artistic gift can replace actual knowledge, drawn from 'seeing and contemplating.'"*[13]

This unique practice of 'contemplation', which the Byzantines referred to by the Greek term *theoria*, is a higher form of 'seeing'. For a few moments, our flesh may be perfected, our vision transfigured, so that we see the world with the Divine Eye.

In one rare 15th century text, the author describes a collaboration between Daniil the Black (c. 1360 – 1430) and Andrei Rublev (c. 1360 – 1430) with another painter named the Holy Andronik. Although the text is long, it is worth citing in full, since it suggests that these artists engaged in a higher form of seeing:

"Holy Andronik was radiant with great virtues and with him were his disciples Savva and Alexander, and wonderful and famous icon painters Daniil and his pupil Andrei [Rublev], *and many other similar people, who had such virtue and such care for fasting and monastic life that would make them worthy of God's grace, and only to ascend to divine love, never worrying about earthly cares, but always raising their mind and thought to the immaterial and divine light, always raising their sensible eye to the eternally painted images of Christ our Lord and His Most Pure Mother of God and all the saints, as if seated on thrones at the very feast of the most radiant Resurrection of Christ and beholding before them the divine and most-holy icons, which they ceaselessly look upon; and thus they were filled with divine joy and radiance."*[14]

It is the words, *'which they ceaselessly look upon,'* that strikes a strong chord in me. It suggests a form of meditation or contemplation that led these artists to practice a form of 'sacred seeing': *'raising their sensible eye to the eternally painted images.'* Although this text was written in the fifteenth century, Joseph of Volokolamsk probably had an earlier text in mind.

Indeed, Pseudo-Dionysius wrote in the fifth century, *"In sensible images, if the painter looks without interruption at the archetypal form, neither distracted by any other visible thing, nor dividing his attention towards anything else, then he will, so to speak, duplicate the person painted and will show the true in the similitude, the archetype in the image, the one in the other, except for their different essences."*[15]

The *'archetype in the image'* appears to the icon painter who *'looks without interruption... neither distracted... nor dividing his attention.'* In Buddhist culture, a prolonged meditation upon a sacred image has long been accepted as a form of worship and personal illumination. But could not these same forms of image-contemplation have been practiced in the West?

IV. The Byzantine & Buddhist Traditions: Shared Sacred Codes

When we search for an art-form that makes the same impression on us as Byzantine icons, then we will find it, unequivocally, in Buddhist thangkas. Suddenly, it all make sense. Both of these traditions use the same Sacred Codes, since both are directed toward the same spiritual end: to transform the viewer's gaze into a more contemplative state of vision.

This begins with the all-important marking of a 'centre' for the painting – a centre which will draw our eye towards one point, to focus it into a more contemplative mode of seeing. From that centre, a series of verticals and horizontals are then constructed, to form a grid for the balanced and axial placement of the main figure, whose centre is determined by proportional measure.

In *The Craftsman's Handbook*, Cennino Cennini describes the Byzantine practice of creating an orthogonal grid from a central point in space. The relevant passage is titled: *'The Method and System for Working on a Wall, that is, in Fresco.'* Since his instructions are somewhat vague, I have created a diagram (Fig. 11.1) and added information in square brackets. To draw his curves, Cennini used a large wooden compass, and to draw his straight lines he used a string dipped in charcoal, which was then snapped against the wall to leave its mark. Essentially, Cennini drew a large X to mark the centre of space, then derived a horizontal line from the vertical plumb line by drawing its perpendicular bisector.

"Then when the plaster is dry, take the charcoal, and draw and compose according to the scene or figures which you have to do; and take all your measurements carefully, snapping [diagonal] *lines first, getting the centers of the spaces* [by snapping an X from corner to corner to create A]. *And the* [vertical] *line* [CB] *which you snap through the center to get the level* [line DE] *must have a plumb bob at the foot* [to make it perfectly vertical].

"And then put one point of the big compasses on [A, at the centre of] *this* [vertical] *line, and give the compasses a half turn on the under side* [to form arc B]. *Then ...swing the other semicircle on the upper side* [to form arc C]. *And you will find that* [when you draw more arcs from B and C onto the right and left of the horizontal line], *you make a little slanted cross on the right* [and left] *side, formed by the intersection of the* [arced] *lines* [at D and E]. *From the left side apply the* [horizontal] *line to be snapped, in such a way that it lies right over both the little crosses* [at D and E]; *and you will find that your line is horizontal by a level. Then compose the scenes or figures with charcoal, as I have described. And always keep your areas in scale, and regular."*[16]

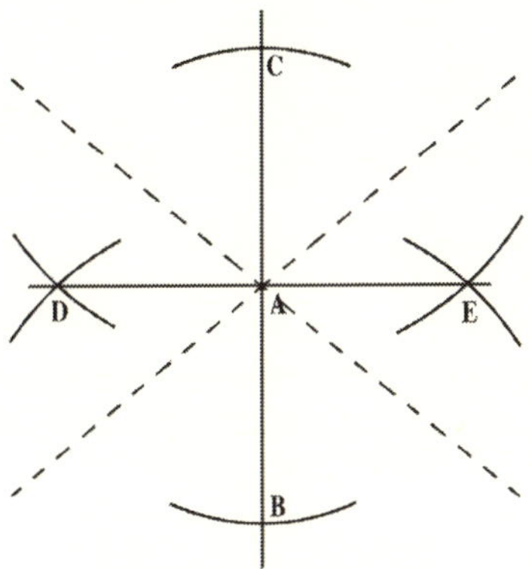

Fig. 11.1 - Ceninni's Method for Determining the Centre of a Wall

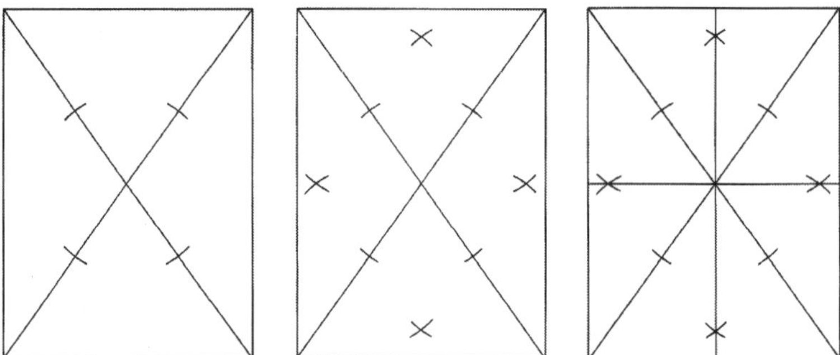

Fig. 11.2 - Tibetan Method for Determining the Centre of a Thangka

In the case of Tibetan Thangka painting, an almost identical procedure is followed (Fig. 11.2). In *Tibetan Thangka Painting: Methods and Materials*, David and Janice Jackson observed three thangka painters and described their procedure in detail:

"The first two of the eight major lines were the diagonals – lines drawn from one corner of the canvas to its diagonal opposite. These two lines enabled the establishment of the vertical and horizontal, and thus had to precede them. To lay down these lines they only needed a chalk line or 'marking string' (thig krud)... devised by rubbing a length of string with a little pigment powder.

"...Next the artist determined the vertical and horizontal axes. As above, he used a marking line, but he could also use a compass (skor thig). ...To establish the vertical axis, the artist began by determining four points on the diagonal lines that were equidistant from the intersection.

"...Next – and here a compass was helpful – the artist drew eight arcs of the same radius in the empty quadrants between the diagonals, using each of the four equidistant points as the focus of two arcs... Then, by connecting these points of intersection with the centre point of the canvas using a chalk line, the artist established the horizontal and vertical axes."[17]

As we saw in Chapter 5 on Hieratic Proportion, the standing figure in both the Byzantine and Buddhist traditions share the same basic proportion of nine face-lengths (Figs. 5.5 and 5.9). They also divide the face into three equal parts (Figs. 5.8 and 5.10). Byzantine artists draw the halo from a small semi-circular dip between the eyebrows – a point resembling the hair whorl or *ūrṇā* between the eyebrows of the Buddha. Most thangka artists use the point atop the hairline to draw the halo, though some sculptors and painters have used the *ūrṇā* – just as the Byzantine artists use the dip between the eyebrows.

The pose of the Seated Buddha is called variously the *padmāsana* (lotus position) or *vajraparyanka asana* (adamantine throne posture). As we have seen, the exact centre of this figure is found *at the heart* (Fig. 11.4). This means that a Seated Buddha may be placed at the exact centre of a thangka, such that, *the heart* becomes the centre of compositional space and the main focal point of meditative vision.

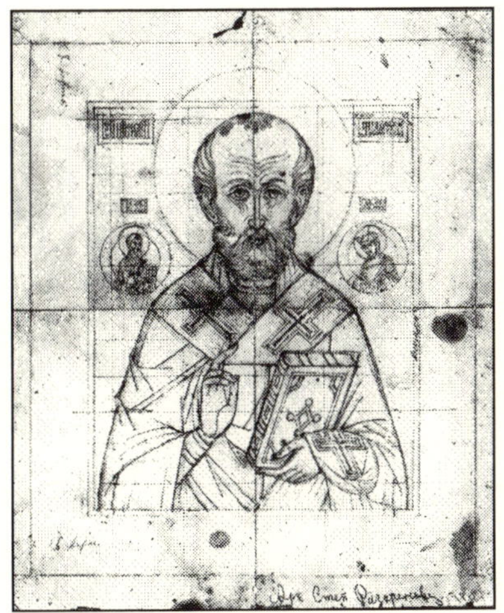

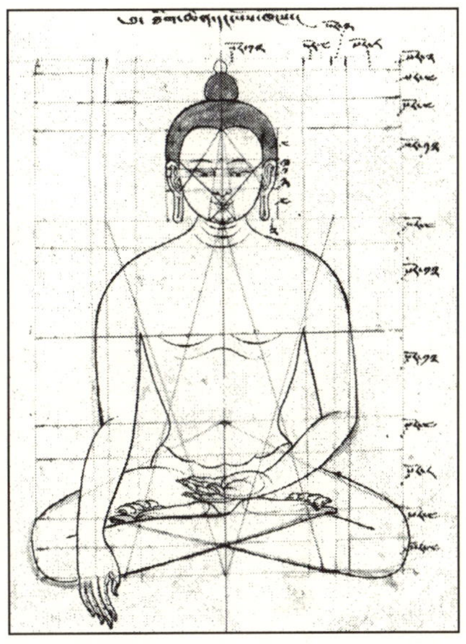

Fig. 11.3 Left - Byzantine Saint: Icon Pattern for Half-length Pose

Fig. 11.4 Right - Boddhisattva Thangka Pattern for Lotus Position

Many Byzantine icons portray Christ, the Madonna and the Saints in a half-length pose – which shares the same compositional format as the Seated Buddha. As we shall see in the Ch. 16 on Rectangular Composition, an icon of *Elijah the Prophet* from the Novogorod school (Fig. 16.9) *gives the heart* a central position – but this is located within the lower square of the rectangular frame. Most half-length icons place the centre of the figure higher up, around the pit of the neck (Fig. 11.3).

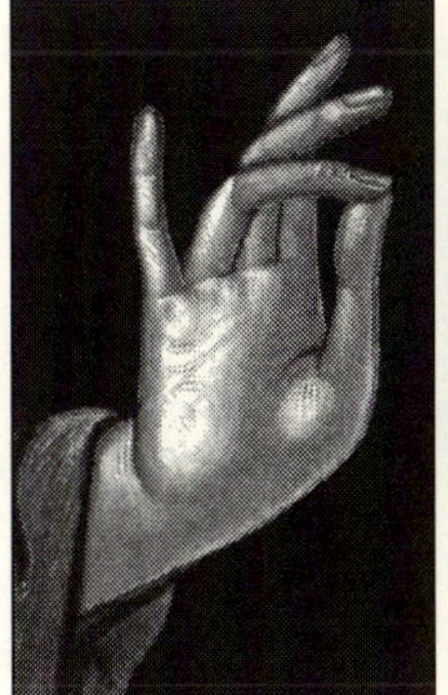

Fig. 11.5 - Hand of Byzantine Pantocrator

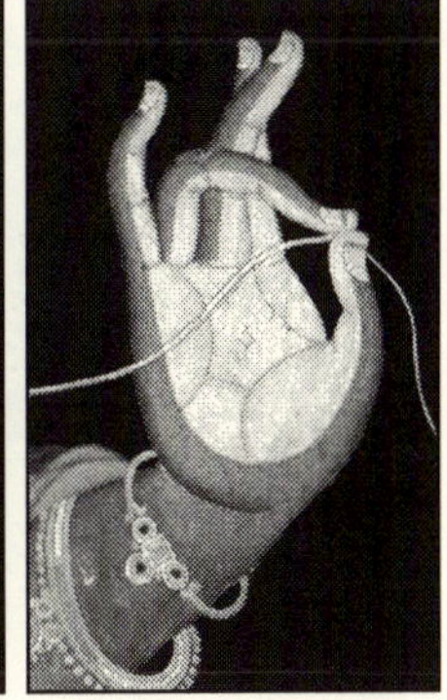

Fig. 11.6 - *Vitarka* mudra of Buddha

Icons of Christ Pantocrator and thangkas of the Meditation Buddha share the same Hieratic symmetry, where a perfectly stilled and balanced figure engages the viewer with *a direct gaze* of the eyes. With his right hand (fig. 11.5), the Pantocrator touches his third (and sometimes fourth) finger to his thumb, thus offering us his benediction while also signing his name (since the fingers spell out IC XC – the first and last letters of Jesus Christos – IHCOYC XPICTOC). The similarity of this gesture to the Buddhist *vitarka mudra* (fig. 11.6) is striking, where the Buddha holds up his right hand and touches his first finger to his thumb, signifying the teaching of the Word or *dharma*.

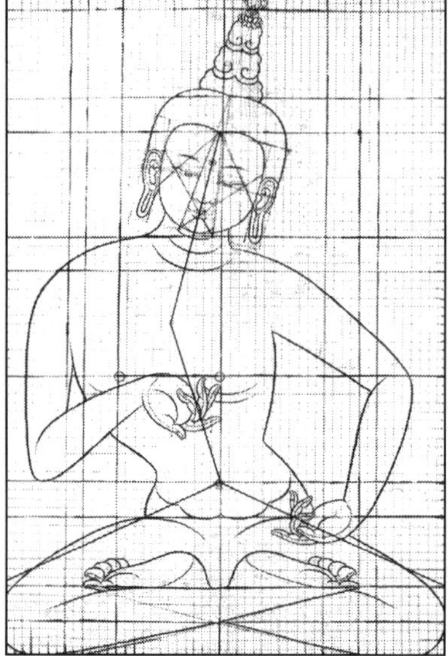

Fig. 11.7 - Two-Part Bend in the Seated Buddha

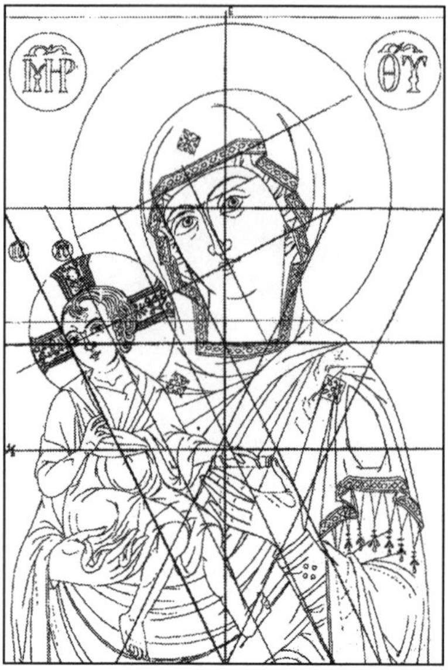

Fig. 11.8 - Two-Part Bend in the *Madonna Constantinopolitana*

The Bible held in the left hand of the Pantocrator (Fig. 11.9) similarly emphasizes the teaching of the Word. Such a symbolic object, in the iconography of thangka painting, becomes a ritual implement such as the thunderbolt (*vajra* or *dorje*), dagger (*kila* or *phur bu*), bell (*ghanta* or *dril bu*) and, yes, book (*pustaka* or *glegs bam*). More important than these symbolic objects and gestures are *the gaze* – a directly frontal gaze which attracts the viewer's wandering eye and fixes it into a more contemplative form of vision.

V. The Byzantine & Buddhist Two-Part Bend

Other half-length figures in Buddhist and Byzantine art assume a slight two-part bend rather than maintaining strict symmetry. In the examples given here, the plumb line is clearly drawn. With the Seated Buddha, the diagonals of the two-part bend are delineated, such that the bottom diagonal deviates from the plumb line at the navel, changes direction near the heart, and returns to the plumb line at the tip of the hair line (Fig. 11.7).

In the reconstruction of armature lines from the *Madonna Constantinopolitana* at Padua,[18] the heart of the Madonna is located at the centre of the lower square. From this point, the main diagonal (ascending to the upper right) changes direction at the pit of the neck, and returns to the plumb line at the mouth. Note however that the right eye of the Madonna lies close to the junction of the main vertical with the top of the square. Located close to the centre-point of the halo, it captures our gaze and fixes it into a stilled stare (Fig. 11.8).

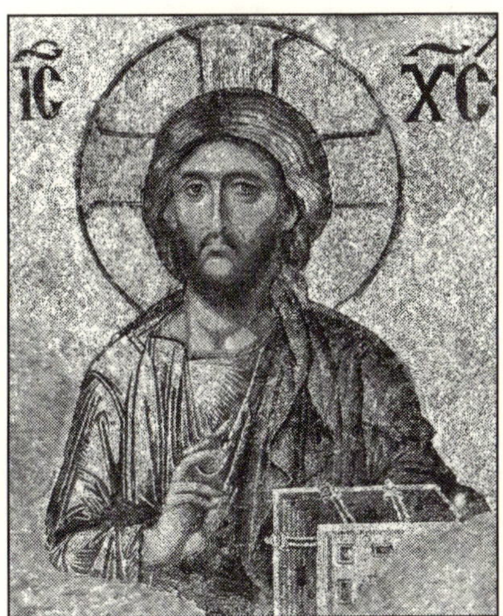

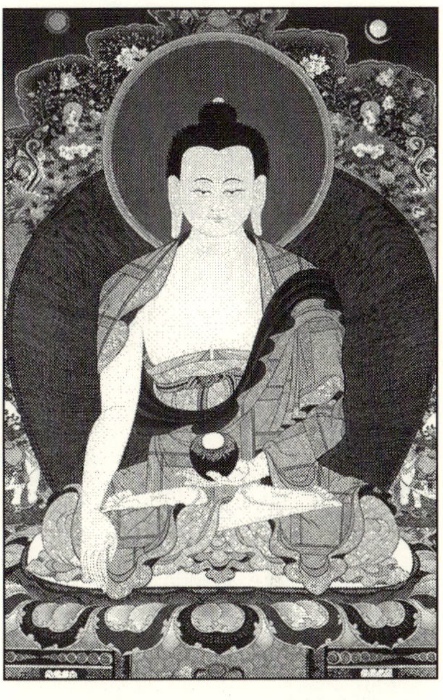

Fig. 11.9 (Left) - *Christ Pantocrator* 1261
Deësis Mosaic from Hagia Sophia

Fig. 11.10 (Right) - *Shakyamuni Buddha*
Romio Shrestha 2002

Stylistically, Byzantine and Buddhist art share a linear quality, depicting only the outlines and most essential traits of the figures. A select number of symbolic colours fill the well-defined shapes in a fairly flat manner. The five primary colours of thangka painting are white (*dkar*), red (*dmar*), blue (*sngo*), yellow (*ser*) and black (*nag*),[19] though gold highlights also appear. In Byzantine icons, gold is the principle colour (*chromata*), followed by royal purple, blue, red, white, green and brown.

If we compare descriptions of icons by Leonid Ouspensky with descriptions of thangkas by Robert Beer, we are struck by the similarity of language: both emphasize the timeless quality, the unique sense of space, and the overall light and atmosphere. Regarding icons, Ouspensky writes:

"The icon is a revelation of eternity in time,"[20] And he elaborates, "*It is the new order in the new creation. That is why what we see in the icon is so unlike what we see in ordinary life. The Divine Light permeates all things, so there is no source of light, which would illuminate things from one side or another; objects cast no shadows, for no shadows exist in the kingdom of God. All is bathed in light."*[21]

Compare to Beer on thangkas:

"*An image of divine grace has been captured and held in a stolen or frozen moment in time... Whether dynamic or static, visions of the divine are infinite, reflecting that pure, still moment of 'seeing'... Objects appear as self-illuminated and composed of the five precious substances of gold, silver, coral, pearl and gemstones."*[22]

In neither Byzantine nor Buddhist art does the painting's space aspire to linear perspective of the Renaissance type, nor to the naturalistic depiction

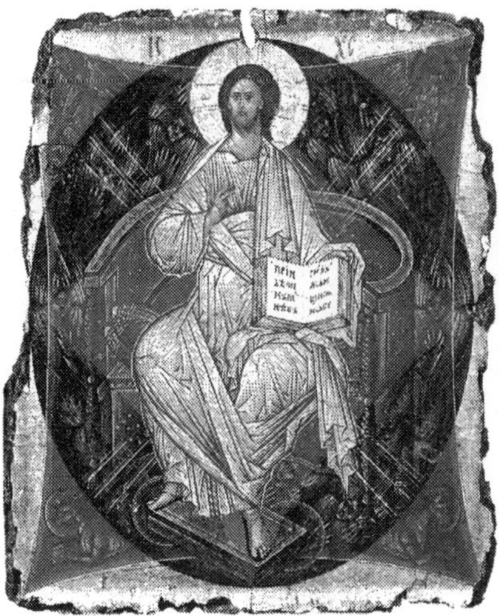

Fig. 11.11 - Andrei Rublev:
Christ in Majesty 1408

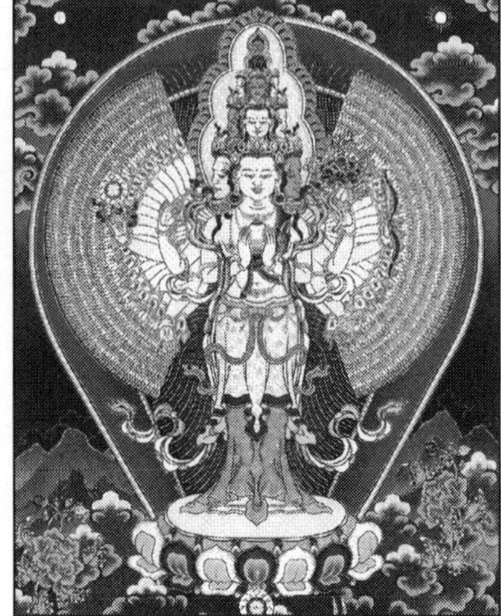

Fig. 11.12 - Nick Dudka:
Avalokiteshvara 2003

of volume. Ouspensky writes: *"In the icon, space and volume are limited to the surface of the panel and must not create an artificial impression of going beyond it."*[23] Instead, *"...people, landscape, architecture, animals... all are centered on the spiritual content and act as one harmonious whole."*[24]

Likewise, Beer writes on thangkas:

"As breathtakingly majestic as the external world appeared, it was still a pale reflection of the internally visualized worlds of the deities' paradise realms... Here, in a landscape which was lit up from within, perspective, scale and shadow lost their logical solidity. A distant mountain peak possessed the same clarity and importance as a foreground flower... the same meticulous detail and clarity was applied to each component. Yet the whole is always more than the sum of its parts."[25]

In icons, drapery should not fold like real clothing, but play a more symbolic role, as a garment of light. While speaking of a saint's drapery, Ouspensky notes that it *"...becomes in some way the image of his vestment of glory, of his 'robe of incorruptibility'* [which is shown in] *the severity of the often geometrical forms, in the lighting and in the lines of the folds."*[26]

In a similar way, the Buddha's vestments are also symbolic of his light nature, especially in the case of the *dharmaogakāya* or *chos sku* form of the Buddha, where his body is fully transfigured into 'clear light' (*prabhāsvara* or *od gsal*). The delightful curving folds seem to be moved by invisible winds and, in the words of Robert Beer, *"exhibit a fluent vocabulary in the language of line."*[27]

Last of all, we may speak of the consecration of the finished work. When a thangka is finished, the artist writes the mantra of the deity on the back. Likewise, the last stage of painting an icon is to write the abbreviated name of the divine figure (the *siglum* or *nomina sacra*), such as O ωN or O ΩN for *He who Is*, meaning God; IC XC for Christ; and MP θC for the God-bearer *Meter Theotokos* or MP ΘY for the Mother of God *Meter Theou*, both meaning the Virgin Mary: *"There is always the name of the depicted person on the icon,"* Christopher Schönborn writes in *God's Human Face. "The act of inscribing the name on the icon, as it was understood then, constitutes the consecration of the icon."*[28]

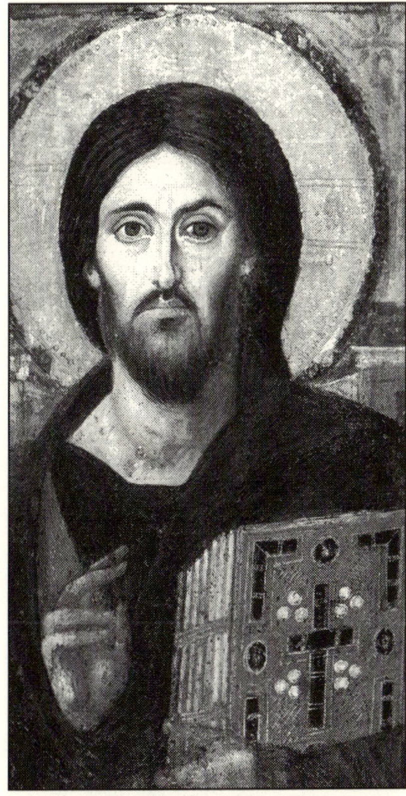

Fig. 11.13 - *Christ Pantocrator* 5th c.

One of the most intriguing icons to come down to us through time is the *Christ Pantocrator* from the Sinai desert (Fig. 11.13). Dated to the 5th century, it is one of the few icons from Constantinople to survive the iconoclastic period, since it was preserved among the rich collection of codices, icons and manuscripts housed in the remote Monastery of St. Catherine's in the Sinai desert.

The extraordinary artist who painted it was a master of encaustic, that technique of heated bees' wax used most notably in the Fayum mummy portraits of Roman-dominated Egypt in the first to fourth centuries. What makes this icon so unique, aside from its early date, is the juxtaposition of two distinct yet related styles. The right of Christ's face has all the naturalism and life-likeness of the Fayum mummy portraits: delicate brushstrokes, voluminous modelling and soft contrasts create a most vivid and Humanist impression through loose hair, an errant gaze and the corners of the eye, brow and mouth rising to a slight smile. Meanwhile, the left side of Christ's face has all the stillness and severity of the Byzantine style: the flat, linear contours, absence of shadow and sharp geometric shapes that create a stylized and archetypal Christ whose rigid features, direct gaze and symbolic hand gestures possess all the gravity and mystery of the Hieratic style.

It seems as if the artist were aware of these two different styles and fused them to express Christ's dual nature: at once, touchingly frail and human while also being majestic, all-powerful and godlike. He is, at once, the Son of God and the Son of Man. The artist accomplishes this through a fusion of the Hieratic and Humanist Styles.

VI. The Hindu-Hellenistic Fusion of Styles

When visualizing a statue of Vishnu, Brahma or the Buddha, we typically see a symmetrically balanced figure, calm and stilled, with multiple hands holding distinctive *mudras* or symbolic attributes. But not all figures from the Eastern tradition are static and symmetrically balanced. Wrathful deities (Buddhist *Yama* or *Mahakala*) and celestial spirits (Hindu *apsaras* or *gandharvas*) assume dynamic poses that strike fear or pleasure in the hearts of their beholders. Even deities such as Durga slaying the Water Buffalo Demon assume powerful energetic poses.

While the static, symmetrically balanced poses seem typical of the Hieratic Style, it would be misleading to identify these more dynamic poses as Humanist. Rather, these energetic figures 'play' at portraying their myths, rising above the realistic expression of Humanist emotion, and manifesting a higher, Hieratic calm, detached from all worldly engagement. They know that this life is *maya* – a play of appearances – and so, like dancers, their stylized movements dramatize the tragi-comic episodes of their myths.

In this sense, even the more dynamic poses from the Hindu and Buddhist traditions should be perceived as Hieratic. By stylizing their movements into conventionalized iconographic gestures, the emotions expressed are 'read' rather than experienced. Their ultimate purpose is to direct the heart and mind to a higher place of inner stillness, dispassion and quietude.

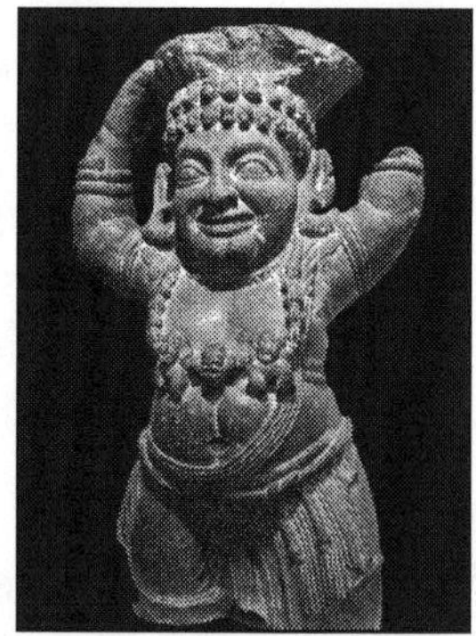

Fig. 11.14 - *yakṣa* c. 3rd c. BCE

A quick review of Eastern art reveals that, historically, the dynamic pose in Hindu sculpture may have come from the West, from ancient Greece, when Alexander the Great crossed the Khyber Pass into the north-west tip of India. Though his invasion of north-west India remained brief, a door had opened between the Hindu and Hellenistic worlds, creating a turning point and fusion of cultural styles.

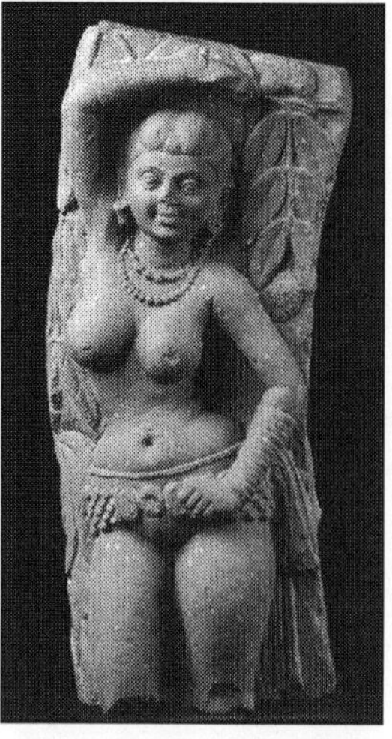

Fig. 11.15 - *yakṣi* c. 3rd c. BCE

After the Indus Valley statues and reliefs of the Bronze age (3300 – 1300 BCE) the first recognizably Hindu sculptures emerged in the 3rd century BCE in the Mauryan style, depicting fertility figures like stout *yakṣas* and sinuous *yakṣis*. Often found as gate-keepers and door guardians, the male, dwarf-like *yakṣas* (Fig. 11.14) supported lintels, while the voluptuous female *yakṣis* (Fig. 11.15) entwined a slender arm round coiling vegetation.

The 3rd century also witnessed the emergence of Buddhist art, such as the Great Stupa of Sanchi, with its carved gates and reliefs (from the 1st c. BCE Satavahana period) bearing narrative scenes, *yakṣis* and *yakṣas*. However, no actual image of

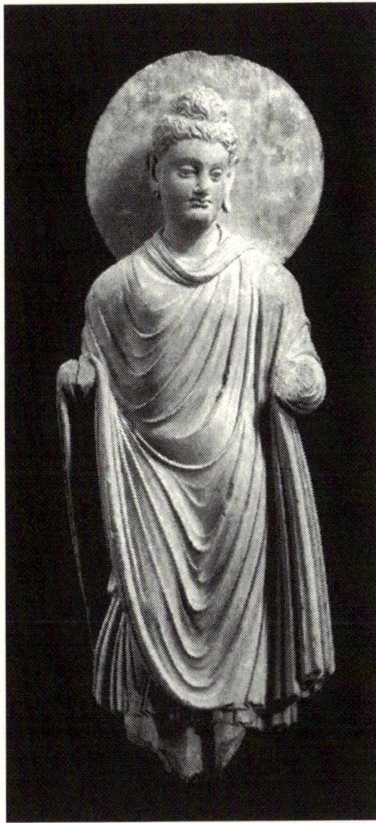

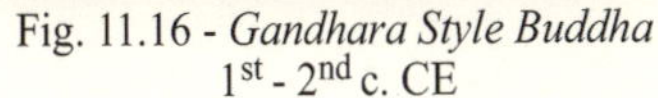

Fig. 11.16 - *Gandhara Style Buddha*
1st - 2nd c. CE

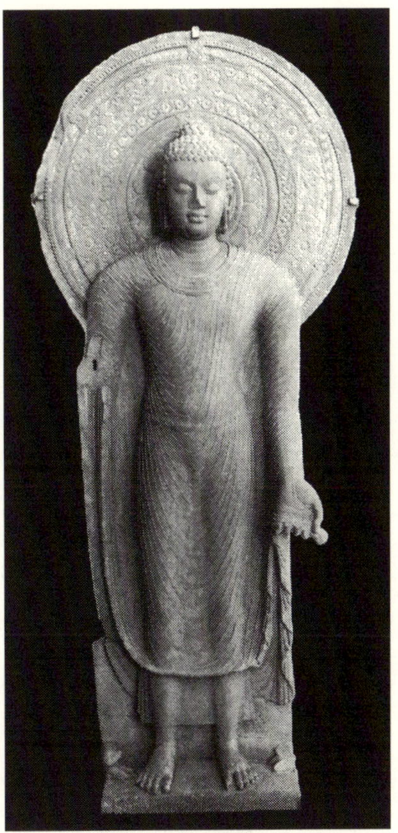

Fig. 11.17 - Yasadinna:
Mathura Style Buddha - 5th c. CE

the Buddha appeared ('aniconism') during this period. Instead, an empty space was left for him in the reliefs.

Once Alexander the Great invaded India in 327 BCE, the first actual representations of the Buddha appeared, bearing undeniable traces of Greek influence: delicate folds in the drapery, fine wavy hair and a slight *contrapposto* twist to the Buddha's erect stance. This Hindu-Hellenistic fusion appeared most clearly in the Gandhāra style (1st and 2nd centuries). From a perfectly circular halo, the Buddha's form flows out with sinuous curves. In the contemporary Mathurā style, the circular halo is still present, but the Buddha's form emerges with straight and stout proportions that echo back to the *yakṣas* of the Mauryan style.

The first real flowering of Hindu divine images took place in the Gupta period (4th – 7th centuries), the "Classical" period of Hindu sculpture with the Kailashnatha rock cut temple in Ellora (6th – 8th centuries) and the great Trimurti statue carved from the caves of Elephanta island (5th – 8th centuries). Now the familiar pantheon of Hindu deities emerged in their multi-armed splendour: Brahma, Vishnu and Shiva; Saraswati, Lakshmi and Parvati. Buddhist and Jain art also flourished during this period at places like Ellora and Ajanta.

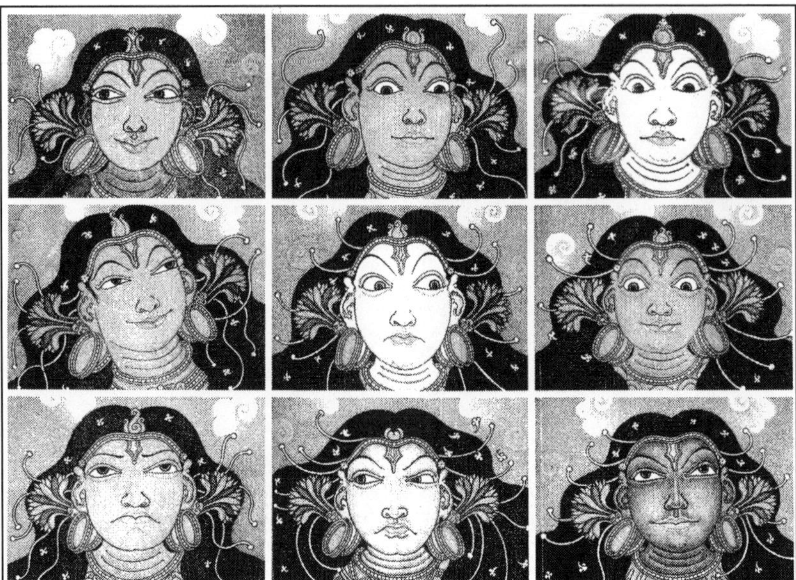

Fig. 11.18 - The Nine *Rasas* or Principle Passions

After the Gupta period, regional rulers became the patrons of the arts, leading to the construction of the Khajuraho temples under the Chandellas (11th century), the solar chariot of Surya at Konārak (13th century) and the Hampi temples in the south (16th century) during India's "Mediaeval" period.

Indian art, from its inception, was a *Gesamtkunstwerk* – a 'total art' involving the interplay of architecture (*vāstu*), sculpture (*shilpa*), music (*sangīta*) and dance (*natya*). To understand the pose of a statue, one had to understand dance, and dance was the dramatic expression of music and mythology. Over three hundred 'Manuals for Sculpture' (the *Shilpa Śāstras)* have been preserved from as early as the 8th century, and these go hand in hand with the many 'Manuals for Dance' (e.g. the *Nātyaśāstra* of Bharata).

The *Shilpa Śāstras* are an extra-ordinary compilation of detailed knowledge, which far exceed any Sculptors' Manual from the West. Aside from iconographies and descriptions, they offer modulated canons of proportion (*mānas*) and anatomies of poses (*bhangas*) to aid the artist.

VII. The Nine Principle Passions

When Charles Le Brun gave his lecture on *Les Expressions des Passions de l'Ame* in 1727 he carefully enumerated the six simple passions and even drew their canonical forms. Nevertheless, Western art never achieved that same formal rigour and discipline as the Eastern tradition for elaborating the passions (*rasa*) in art. According to the 7th century Sanskrit text, the *Vishnudharmattara*, there are nine principal passions for Hindu painters: the erotic (*srngara*), comical (*hasya*), pathetic (*karuna*), heroic (*vlra*), furious (*raudra*), fearful (*bhayanaka*), loathsome (*vibhatsa*), supernatural (*adbhuta*) and peaceful (*ianta*).[29]

These correspond, more or less, to the eight primary *rasas* cited by Bharata in his Manual for Dance, the *Nātyaśāstra*. Indian dance, like Indian sculpture, is a highly structured iconographical display of set movements that embody specific emotions (*rasas*). To understand the poses of Hindu sculpture, we must turn to the Manuals of Dance for a more precise explanation of human movement and expression.

Indian dance is a hieratic art in the sense that the dancers ritually re-enact the myths of the gods. Understanding intrinsically that all is *maya* or illusion, the dancer's movements display nothing more than the eternal 'play' (*lila*) of deities in time, leading us away from our attachment to the passions (*rasas*) so as to finally experience release (*mokṣa*).

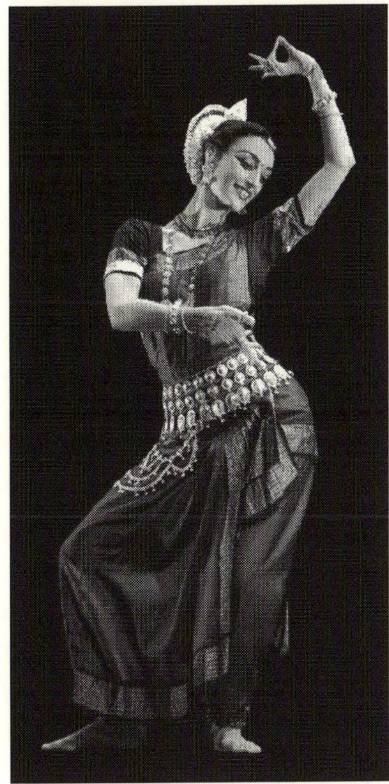

Fig. 11.19 - Odissi Dancer: Frozen Movement

Although dancers move through time, they continually freeze their movements into certain set poses (*bhanga*), glances (*drsti*) and hand gestures (*hastabhinaya* or *mudra*) which have become elaborated over time into a set iconography of the passions (*rasas*). Each apprentice-dancer learned these postures from childhood, while different lineages developed iconographic variations that expressed their unique traditions.

In her study on the role of dance in sculpture, Nilofar Haja writes: *"Just as the Indian dancer aims at attaining the perfect pose, the moment of perfect balance after a series of movement in time, so too does the Indian sculptor try to capture* [...and] *arrest the rapturous intensity and abandon of dance movement."*[30]

The *brahmasutra,* the 'plumb line' of a Hindu sculpture, also plays a key role in dance as the vertical line of balance. The Indian dancer must constantly maintain a sense of poise, limiting his or her movements to specific measures (*cari*) in space (through the body's balance) and in time (with the music). The transition from one static pose (*bhanga*) to another around the vertical axis (*sutra*) constitutes the essence of Indian dance.

Through this intimate relationship between the plumb line (*sutra*) and the pose (*bhanga*), Hindu sculpture has documented Indian dance for more than 1600 years. Long before the *Nātya śāstras* existed, sculptors were writing in stone the Manuals for Dancers. Nilofar Haja writes:

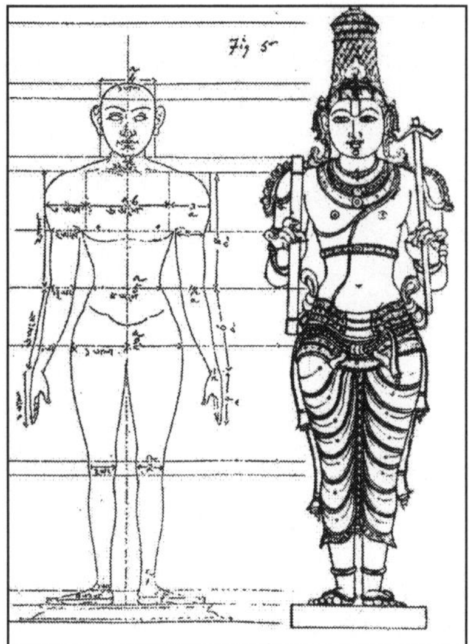

Fig. 11.20 - The *Samabhanga* or No Bend

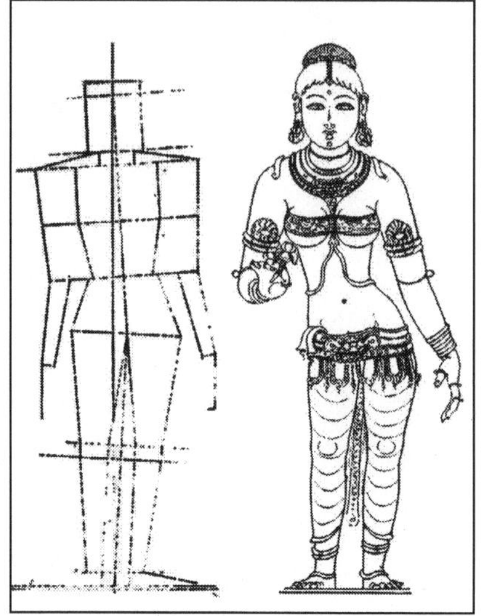

Fig. 11.21 - The *Abhanga* or Slight Bend

"Even though the Indian dancer can use space more freely than the Indian sculptor, the emphasis is always on the pose [bhanga] *which the dancer attains through a series of movements; and neither in these movements nor in the final pose (karana) does the dancer deviate from the prescribed limitations of the plumb line (sutra) and the relative distance of the different parts of the body in a given bhanga."*[31]

In this sense, the Hieratic pose of the Hindu stone-carver resembles the Humanist pose of Classical Greek sculptor. For the stilled pose (*karana*) of the Hindu parallels the arrested movement (*rhythmoi*) of the Greek, which J. J. Pollit called *"patterns isolated within continual movement."*[32]

Both Greek and Hindu sculpture capture the *unmoved movement*, where the figure freezes in a moment 'just before' or 'just after' the intended action, so as to express a distinct *rasa* or 'passion of the soul' through a gracefully balanced but dynamic pose that is centered with precision, poise and *aplomb* on the *brahmasutra* or plumb line.

VIII. The Hindu 'Contrapposto'

Just as Hellenistic culture developed a series of variations on the dynamically-poised figure, from moderate ponderation to *contrapposto* to the *figura serpentinata*, so did Indian culture witness the creation of no less than three different types of *bhanga* or 'bend'.

This is especially true of the *Odissi* (or *Orissi*) form of classical dance, one of the oldest forms, originating in the state of Odisha (former Orissa), south of Bengal. In his short book entitled *Some Notes on Indian Artistic Anatomy*, the Bengali artist Abanindranath Tagore (nephew of the famed poet

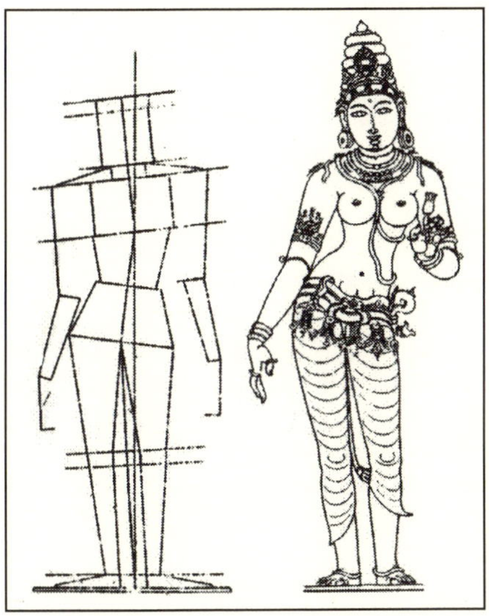

Fig. 11.22 - The *Tribhanga* or Three-Part Bend

Rabindranath Tagore) attempted to revive a knowledge of India's different classical poses.

Having first set out the *návatāla* system of proportion, he goes on to say that, *"Indian images are given the following four different bhangas, that is flexions or attitudes: the Samabhanga or Samapada (equipoised); Abhanga (a slight bhanga flexion), Tribhanga (Tri – thrice) and Atibhanga (Ati – extreme)."*[33] He then illustrates these with diagrams and describes them in detail.

Summarizing his commentaries, we may arrive at the following four types of poses (*bhanga*) for Hindu figures.

• *Samabhanga* – There is no bend. The *sutra* or 'plumb line' bisects the entire figure in two, passing straight down from the hairline, through the navel, to the heels. Standing firmly poised on both legs without inclining in any way, images of Buddha, Surya and Vishnu typically follow this rigid schema of vertical symmetry, while gesturing (*mudras*) with multiple hands and holding their attributes (Fig. 11.20).

• *Abhanga* – A slight bend. The head and heels are still bisected by the *sutra* or plumb line, but the navel is slightly displaced. With a bend at the hips (or genital line – *meḍra*), all the horizontals in the upper half tilt one way (navel, heart, neck, hairline), while the horizontals in the lower half tilt the other way (knees). This slight disturbance in vertical symmetry is typical for sages, holy men and Bodhisattvas. When the two-part bend becomes more pronounced, the pose is called *Dvibhanga* (Fig. 11:21).

• *Tribhanga* – A three-part bend. Now the heart (*hṛdaya*) and heals are bisected by the sutra or plumb line, while the hairline and genitals (*meḍra*) are both displaced to one side. Typically, the plumb line passes through the left or right eye of the face. A three part zigzag is formed, with the figure bending at the heart horizontal (*hṛdaya*) and the genital horizontal (*meḍra*). All horizontals above the heart and below the genitals (neck, hairline; knees) tilt one way, while those between (the navel), tilt the other way. Goddesses often appear in *tribhanga*, as do the small *shaktis* flanking *samabhanga* statues of Vishnu. Krishna dancing on the Kalinga serpent in another fine example (Fig. 11.22).

• *Atibhanga* – An extreme bend or accentuated twist. This is a more extreme form of *tribhanga*, where the spiralling S-curve is considerably enhanced. Examples include Durga slaying the demon, Ugra Nrusimha tearing apart the demon, and Shiva Nataraja, the Lord of Dance (Fig. 11.23).

The parallels between Hindu poses and those already encountered in the West seem too interesting to ignore. The slight bend of the *Abhanga* posture resembles to a startling degree the 'moderate ponderation' of the Kritios Boy, just as the thee-part *Tribhanga* resembles the classical *contrapposto* of the Doryphorus. Beyond this, the more extreme *Atibanga* finds its parallel in the *figura serpentinata* of Michelangelo and later Mannerist sculptors (Giambologna, Bernini), where a spiralling twist is added to the lateral bends of the *contrapposto*. Strangely, as the twist in Western poses became more exaggerated, the expression also became more stylized, giving Mannerist art the same stylized theatricality of Hindu dance and sculpture.

Eventually, this Mannerism led to the formalized repertoire of movements known as "ballet" in the West, an extremely stylized form of dance patronized by King Louis XIV (an avid dancer), leading to the establishment (by royal charter in 1661) of the *Académie Royale de Danse*. In ballet, as in the *Odissi* form of classical dance, each pose between movements is carefully named and choreographed. Eventually, in the works of artists like Edgar Degas and Gustave Moreau (who, incidentally, were close friends in their youth), the poses of French ballet became fixed in paint and immortalized for all time. This is especially true of Degas, but Moreau's series of *Salome* paintings should not be forgotten here.

In *A Celebration of Life*, Nilofar Haja writes: *"The Indian dancer, like the Indian sculptor, does not lay much emphasis on the muscles of the human body but takes the joints and the fundamental bone structure as its basics..."*[34]

This observation is of extreme importance. While Indian sculpture may have gained its *contrapposto* movement from the Hindu-Hellenistic fusion of the Gandhāra period (1st and 2nd centuries), it never attempted to convey movement in the 'natural' or Humanist manner of the Greeks. There was never the slightest emphasis on muscles, or their anatomy of tension and repose.

Rather, Hindu sculptors always delineated the head, limbs and torso with gently rounded contours, maintaining their Hieratic style. It is this quality which makes Hindu sculpture so unique, and a class apart from the Hieratic styles of the Egyptians and Babylonians, who never translated the *contrapposto* into their sacred art.

IX. The Dancer in the Sphere

My knowledge of Indian dance has been greatly enhanced through my cousin, Joanne Camilleri. Since we are the same age, we have known each other from the cradle, and have formed a deep kinship, perhaps due to the fact that she never had a brother, nor I, a sister. Both Maltese in origin, born in Toronto, we shared the same strange *wanderlust* and artistic temperament. Years would sometimes pass before we could meet up again and compare notes from our wanderings.

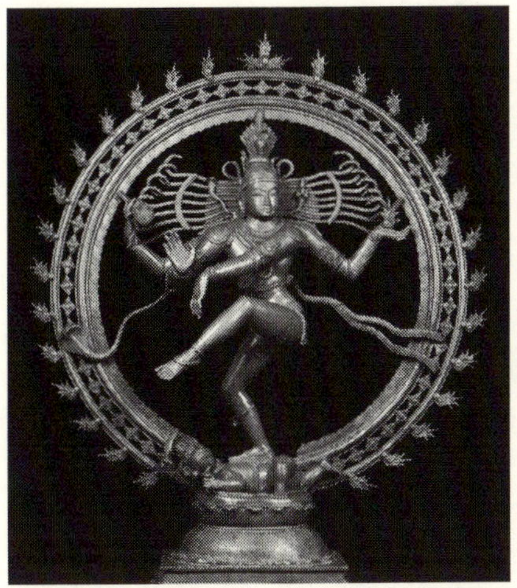

Fig. 11.23 - *Shiva Nataraja* - The Lord of Dance

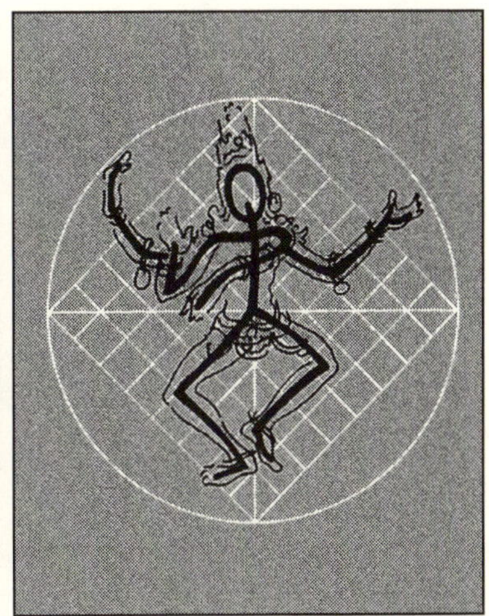

Fig. 11.24 - Kapila Vatsyayan: Shiva Diagram

While I wandered mostly around Europe to study classical techniques of painting, she lived variously in Pakistan, India and Saudi Arabia, learning classical forms of eastern dance. Beginning with ballet as a child, she expanded into the Classical *Kathak* dance of Northern India and *Raqs Sharqi* of the Middle East ('belly dancing'). Now that she has her own school of dance, I was able to catch up with her one cold Canadian winter and, in the warmth of her studio, she explained to me the intricacies of these ancient dance forms.

A deep inner awareness of the body's centre of balance is vital for each of the dancer's moves. That centre is located at the navel and forms an imaginary sphere around the dancer. Balancing on one leg, the dancer may pivot and turn, sensing the outer limits of this sphere with her outstretched hands or feet.

While the *brahmasutra,* the vertical line of gravity traversing the body, remains an important reference for the rigid style of Classical dance, the sphere and its centre offer a more practical reference point for dynamic dancing. This sphere, in its 2D form of the circle, can be seen very clearly around Shiva Nataraja, the Lord of Dance (Fig. 11.23).

While two of his four hands are evenly balanced along the vertical *brahmasutra*, the other two counterbalance the opposite movements of his upper and lower body. Because he is in perfect balance, the centre for all movement and energy has shifted upward along the supporting leg and become focussed in his navel. From here, energy spirals outward in a coil, which we see two-dimensionally as the S-curve. Forever frozen in the *atibhanga* pose, if he were to begin moving, his outstretched limbs would trace out the contours of an invisible sphere.

Following this inspiration, classical dance scholar Kapila Vatsyayan has reconstructed Shiva's movements in her book *The Square and the Circle of Indian Arts*, situating the god of destruction in the centre of a circle inscribed with squared orthogonals while other lines radiate outward from his navel at the centre[35] (Fig. 11.24).

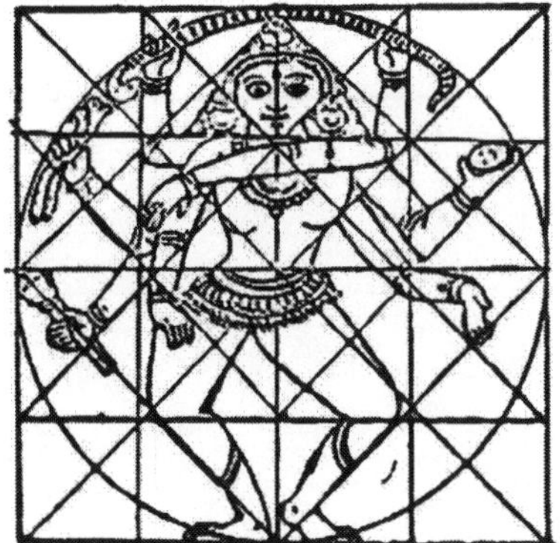
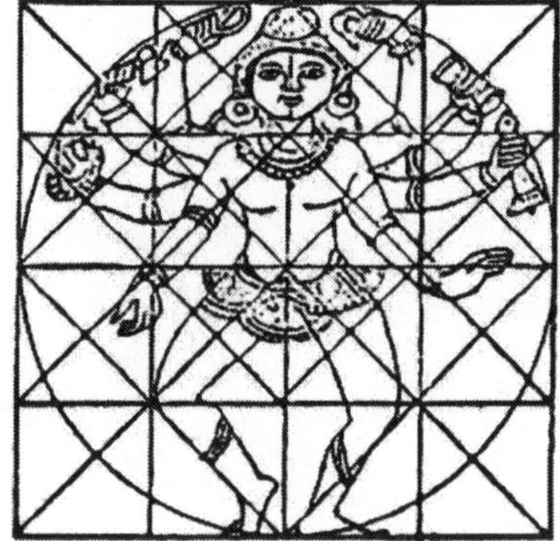

Fig. 11.25 - Shilp Siddanthi Sri Siddalinga: Shiva Diagram

In a drawing by the late 19th century artist Shilp Siddanthi Sri Siddalinga Swamy of Myore, the movements of Hindu sculptures are also regulated by orthogonals and diagonals inscribed within a circular armature, and all meet, once more, at the navel (Fig. 11.25).

All of these drawings bear a strange resemblance to the images designed by Leonardo da Vinci in the *Codex Huygens* (Fig. 6.19). Here, a geometrical shape lent grace to the human form, not only in space, but in time. Instead of a static armature for a standing figure, a new series of geometric shapes traced out the lines of movement. New harmonies began to appear through the perfect shapes inscribed in the circle.

In the best plates of the *Codex Huygens*, the circle is always there, as the outer extension of an invisible sphere. With the navel as the centre of all energy and motion, Leonardo's figures twist and turn while reaching out to the invisible sphere that defines the outer limits of balance. One more step, one slight stirring beyond this bound, and the figure would come tumbling down, out of balance and dis-'graced'. The sphere with its rotational axis (*sutra*, plumb line) assure that man moves in harmony with the higher spheres.

In this way, we return to the very beginning of these chapters, where a sphere was imagined around King Thutmosis III to stylize and perfect the amorphous shape of a human head. The human body is also a twisting mass of articulated limbs, bending this way and that around a vertical torso. But, the moment we situate those movements within a perfect sphere, a certain harmony begins to adhere. The bounding circle lends grace to the contours, while any square or triangle we care to inscribe (as orthogonals and diagonals) allow for the 'play' of visible movements around these invisible lines.

The numerous lines described in these chapters – geometry, proportion, grids – are eventually erased and become hidden to everyday sight. The viewer never sees them though he or she may sense the harmony they impart. But the artist, as craftsman and artisan, guards this secret knowledge, passing it along from one generation to the next. Sometimes, centuries may pass and the Sacred Codes are forgotten. But, underlying the artist's work, they remain hidden in plain sight. By contemplating these works and sharing our knowledge, we may begin to remember and restore those harmonizing lines which grant beauty and unity to every work of art.

CHAPTER XII
THE FUSION OF HUMANIST & HIERATIC STYLES

I. The Old Masters & the New

One evening after a hard day's work, Fuchs and I paused to look and actually 'see' the advances we had made to his large *Triumph of the Unicorn* painting, where a new combination of colours had been added to the angels descending on either side. I was struck by the strong vibration of orange and green – something I had seen in Michelangelo's work – and I commented as such. *"Yes,"* Fuchs replied, *"I was so happy to see the Sistine Chapel restored. It shows just how much of a colourist he was."* Then he turned to me, gazing over his glasses, and said, *"I'm a student of Michelangelo, you know..."*

Another evening, this time at the *Brasserie Quai des Artistes* below his studio in Monaco, we were having an animated conversation about learning and tradition. *"The apprentice must submit himself to a greater authority,"* he said, *"to carry on the tradition, which is greater than either the master or apprentice. The master was once an apprentice himself, who learned from his master. Each forms the link in a chain that goes back in time, unbroken. Each must submit to the greater tradition."*

These words, more than ten years later, continue to resonate with their oft-unheeded truth. If I find myself returning time and again to the works of Michelangelo, Blake and Moreau, it is not only because my master was the student of these masters. Rather, it feels like a deeper kinship, an unspoken lineage, had already linked these artists from the very beginning.

Another conversation springs to mind, this time with Kuba Ambrose, who had also assisted Fuchs a few years after me. During a late-night conversation in Vienna, he and I shared in whispered tones some of our more interesting visionary experiences. Remembering one such visionary encounter, he recalled how Michelangelo had spoken to him directly. The voice said: *'Don't put the Old Masters on a pedestal. There is no separation between the old masters and the new. You are one of us, but you have the advantage of still being alive now.'*

As such, all the Sacred Codes rediscovered from the past have no real value, unless they continue to resound today – in new relationships, styles and expressions... clothing the eternal in our present mode and manner. As our world today approaches greater unity, we must learn to combine codes from East and West, revive the past and marry it to the present, to see a greater oneness in all that we do.

As these chapters on The Figure draw to a close, I would like to examine how Michelangelo, Blake, Moreau and Fuchs approached the human form – its proportion, pose and placement in the composition – to better understand how these four masters continually inspired one another, forming links in a Golden Chain dedicated to the eternal beauty of the embodied soul.

II. The Somnambulist & the Sibyl

Of all the sibyls and prophets lining the Sistine Chapel ceiling, the Delphic Sibyl (Fig. 12.1) has called me back to her time and again, whispering her mysterious oracles in my ear as I gazed upon her enigmatic visage. Indeed, it was after a lengthy meditation on her graceful form that I first 'saw' and understood the distinction between Humanist and Hieratic Styles.

On the one hand, her billowing cloak and *contrapposto* motion express all the dynamism of the Humanist Style. And yet, is it mere co-incidence that her scroll curves so gently thus, to complete a perfect circle round her triangular pose? – And why are these two shapes inscribed so perfectly in a square or rectangular space?

Is she in motion, or sitting perfectly still? Gustave Moreau, recognizing this strange quality, once remarked, *"Toutes les figures de Michel-Ange semblent être fixées dan un geste de somnambulisme idéal."* Which is to say, *"All of Michelangelo's figures appear frozen in the idealized gesture of a somnambulist... I must find the reason for this self-absorbed revery, where the figures appear as if asleep, or transported to worlds beyond the one we inhabit."*[1]

When we focus our regard on her face (Fig. 12.2), the expression is no less intriguing. On the one hand, her face has the epic proportions, the perfect symmetry, and holy stillness so characteristic of a Hieratic visage. Like an Egyptian bust, each facet and proportion have been measured and carved with perfect precision. And yet, she is turning her head, glancing leftward, as if, overcome by awe and uncertainty. A Humanist emotion enlivens this otherwise timeless face and eternal gaze.

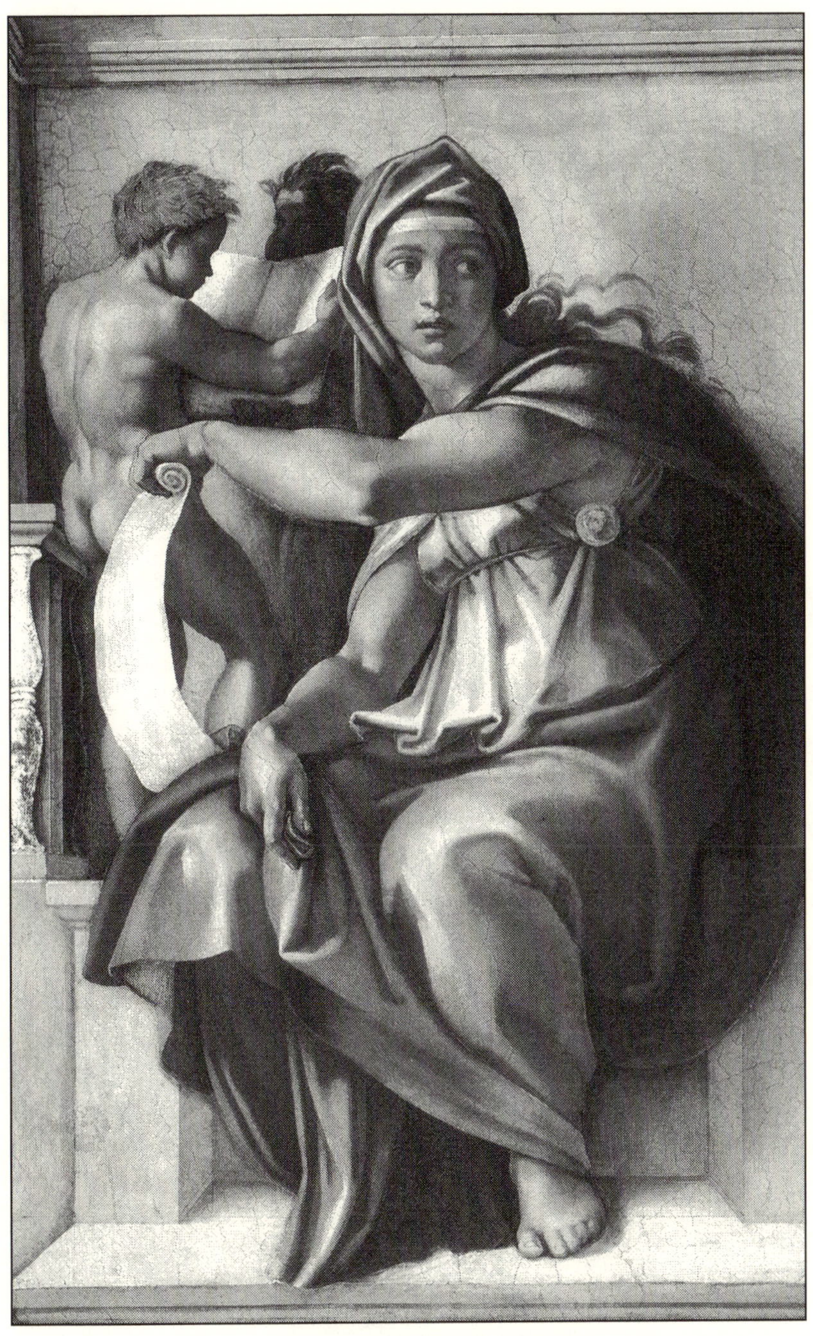

Fig. 12.1 - Michelangelo: *The Delphic Sibyl* 1509

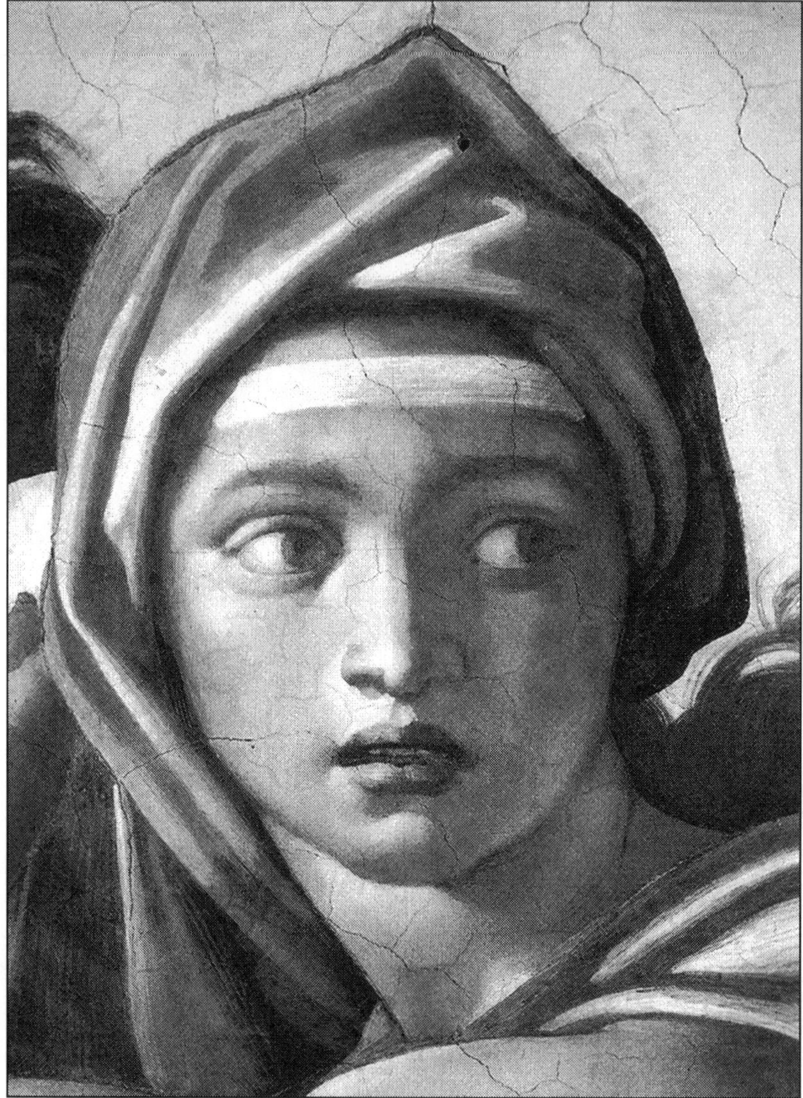

Fig. 12.2 - Michelangelo: *The Delphic Sibyl* (Detail) 1509

Michelangelo has mastered the Sacred Codes that underpin the Humanist Style – the forces coursing through her body and exploding in a glance; the draperies tracing out invisible lines of gravity and motion. But something far more ancient inheres – the monumentality, stillness and geometric proportion of the Hieratic Style. Somehow, he has combined these two, to make an image that transcends its own time, regressing far into the past while extending onward to our own era, and even, no doubt, beyond.

III. Blake & 'The Eternal Principles that Exist in All Ages'

I would not imagine for a moment that Michelangelo, Blake and Moreau form the only links in a chain that ultimately transcends history. The world of vision is a world without time, transpiring in the eternal now. Many such artists have pierced the veil and painted that timeless and immutable realm: Bosch, Grünewald, Rossetti, Burne-Jones, Delville and Dali (to name only a few...).

But if there ever was an artist anachronistic to his own time, yet a constant visitor to visionary worlds, it was William Blake. *"All his life,"* Peter Ackroyd writes in his biography of Blake, *"he spoke of 'lost originals' as if he were reaching beyond his own civilization to the simplicity and grandeur of a remote past."*[2]

This fascination with the art of past eras began during Blake's apprenticeship, when the master engraver Basire set his young apprentice to engraving plates for Jacob Bryant's *A New System, or An Analysis of Ancient Mythology.*[3] Over the course of many months, the young Blake traced out images and designs from Egyptian, Babylonian, even Mithraic art. The presence of these epic styles – their monumentality, constant profiles and profound stillness – re-appeared time and again in Blake's later work.

That same year, Basire sent his young apprentice to Westminster Abbey, to sketch gothic figures for plates to Richard Gough's *Sepulchral Monuments in Great Britain.*[4] Surrounded by the tombs of poets and kings, the artist had a vision: *"The aisles and galleries of the old cathedral,"* Blake later recalled, *"suddenly filled with a great procession of monks and priests, choristers and censer-bearers."*[5]

At the same time, the Gothic style – with its long flowing lines, sweeping drapery, and energetic spirals and swirls – forever left its mark on Blake's art. *"Let them look at Gothic Figures & Gothic Buildings,"* Blake wrote, *"& not talk of Dark Ages or any Age. Ages are all equal. But Genius is always above the Age."*[6]

In Gothic art, Blake had found his hidden prime of styles. As Ackroyd remarks, "[Later in life] *he knew instinctively that he should return to that 'true Art Calld Gothic in All Ages' an art of form and outline, which are themselves lineaments of the spirit; he believed he had rediscovered the art that expressed 'the eternal Principles that exist in all ages.'"*[7]

But most of all, Blake's style evoked the antiquities of Greece, which he clearly admitted when he wrote that *"the purpose for which alone I live is... to renew the lost Art of the Greeks."*[8]

Despite these constant echoes and combinations of Ancient, Gothic and Antique styles, Blake's manner was undoubtedly his own. His vision gave him access to that same trans-temporal world once beheld by the ancients. *"All religions are one,"*[9] he declared, and the art of different epochs simply traced their different styles over the same timeless revelation: *"Vision or Imagination is a Representation of what Eternally Exists."*[10]

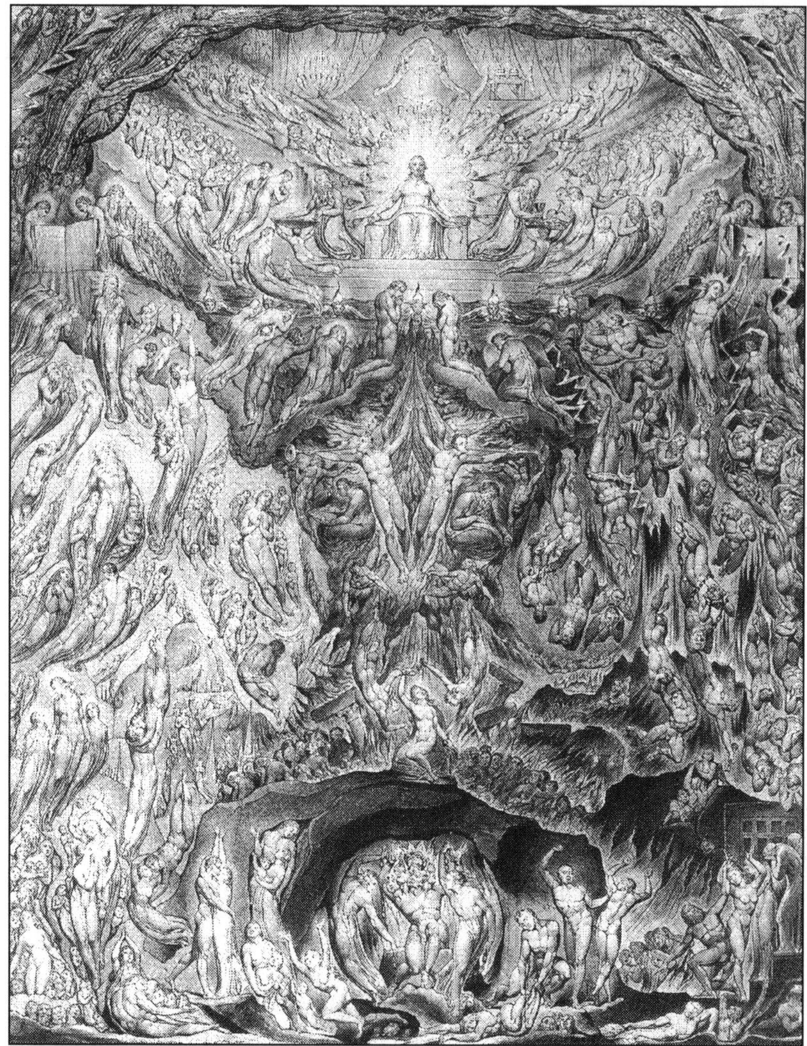

Fig. 12.3 - William Blake: *A Vision of the Last Judgement* 1808

IV. A Vision of the Last Judgment

In 1803, Blake moved to new lodgings at 17 South Molton Street in London, renting two rooms where he and his wife would remain for the next seventeen years.[11] Four years later, he commenced *A Vision of the Last Judgment*, a major work where, as Ackroyd explains, *"his reverence for medieval sacred art and his devotion to Michelangelo were displayed in a painting reputed to be seven feet by five feet and to contain more than one thousand figures."*[12]

Over time, Blake was to become obsessed with this image: *"He drew or painted this sacred subject at least seven times, and he kept the last one by him until his death. He worked upon the final version for some seventeen years, and at the end it was so blackened with overpainting that little of it remained visible."*[13]

Ultimately, the artist's masterpiece disappeared and was lost to the vagaries of time. Fortunately for us, a smaller ink and watercolour version survived (Fig. 12.3) and is now preserved at Petworth House in West Sussex. Fifty years later, a manuscript was discovered by William Michael Rossetti (brother of the famed Pre-Raphaelite Dante Gabriel Rossetti), where Blake described his large, lost work in detail. Though we can only imagine the magnitude and complexity of the large version (his manuscript describes scores of figures), the ink and watercolour rendering still ranks among the best and most majestic of Blake's works.

At first, I was only able to find minute reproductions of this epic work in books (for which I apologize here, given the size-limitations of these pages). Finally, after much searching, I procured a large giclée from Petworth House, and spent many wondrous hours deep in meditation, 'entering through the image'.

To my amazement, Blake describes *his own experiences* in this regard, in his manuscript on the Last Judgment:

"If the spectator could enter into these images in his imagination, approaching them on the fiery chariot of his contemplative thought; if he... could make a friend and companion of one of these images of wonder, which always entreat him to leave mortal things ... then would he meet the Lord in the air, and then he would be happy."[14]

At first glance, Blake's indebtedness to Michelangelo is obvious. But, the longer we look, the more we come to understand how Blake, in his own inimitable style, is clarifying and advancing Michelangelo's original design. In his Last Judgment, Blake has given equal respect to figuration and composition, where Michelangelo emphasized figuration above all. And Blake has grouped his figures dynamically in ways Michelangelo could never have imagined possible.

The emphasis on composition allowed Blake to create strong symmetries both vertically and horizontally: those rising on the left find their dark mirror in those falling on the right. Where, with Michelangelo, we could compare John the Baptist and St. Peter as lateral reflections of each other, in Blake's symmetrical composition, numerous such comparisons arise, both horizontally and vertically, which have much to teach us of the Sacred Codes operating in Blake's world.

To the far left and right of Christ are two books, one inscribed with the names of the saved and the other, marked in black streaks with the number of the damned. Before each book stands an angel, whose stance is well-worth examining in detail.

The bearded angel on the left (Fig. 12.4), like Michelangelo's Baptist, is turning to gaze upon Christ the Judge. All the force and torsion in his body spiral round to focus their energy upon his powerful gaze. The eye, as with

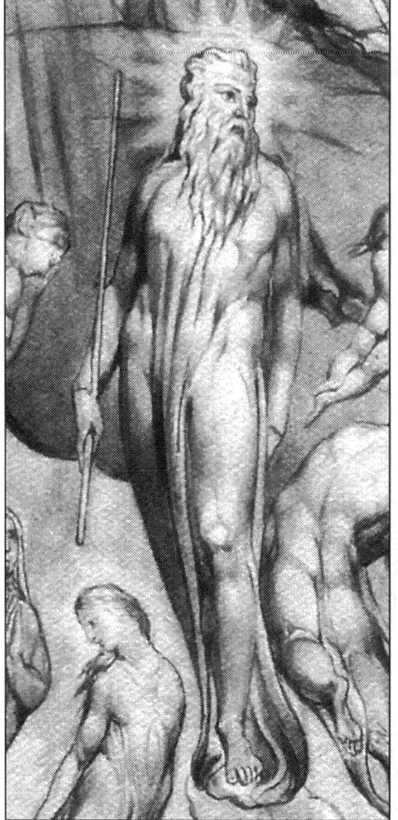

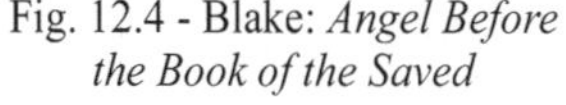

Fig. 12.4 - Blake: *Angel Before the Book of the Saved*

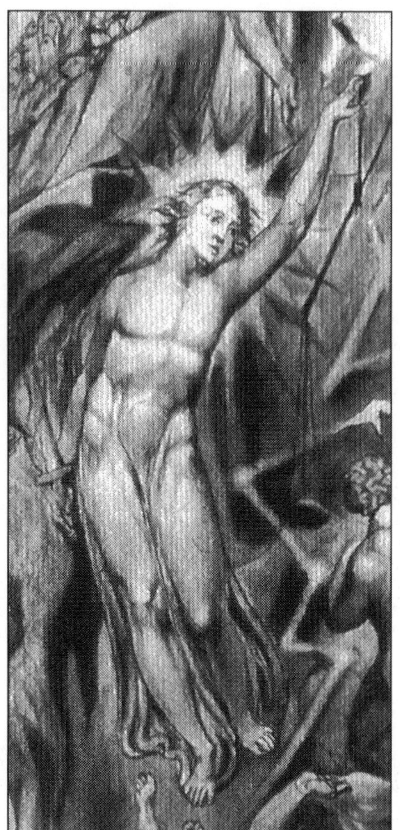

Fig. 12.5 - Blake: *Angel Before the Book of the Damned*

Michelangelo's *David*, is located exactly at the top of the plumb line, just as the weight-bearing foot is located at its bottom.

But, in this unique *contrapposto* twist, the back leg crosses behind the forward leg, and the opposite upper shoulder also twists back, until these two are in line with each other. In our hieroglyphic language of poses, the figure forms a ¢ shape, with the back leg and back shoulder spiralling round the plumb line descending from eye to foot.

Contrast this to the other angel (Fig. 12.5), who turns away from Christ to raise the scales with his extended arm. This figure does not twist, but bends itself laterally, like an extreme version of the *abhanga* – the two-part bend. The plumb line is still there, descending from eye to foot, but now the lateral bend of body, including the weight-bearing foot, form a massive C around the invisible plumb line, rendering the same basic glyph: ¢

V. The Contrapposto of Grouped Figures

"Energy is eternal delight,"[15] Blake wrote. Having mastered the movement of energy in a figure, he was free to explore its movement between multiple figures in motion. Thus, we may compare the two couples below,

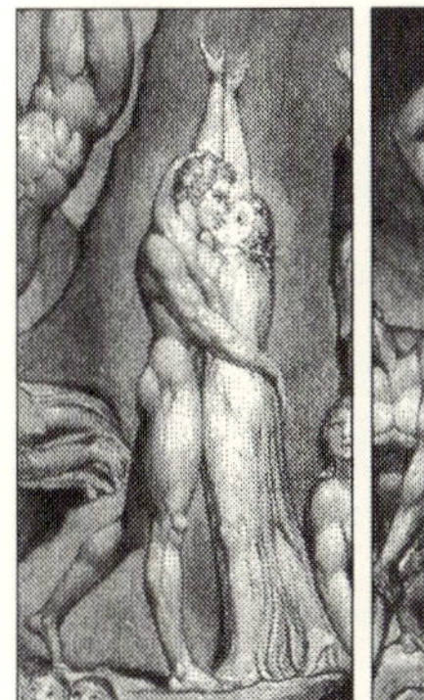

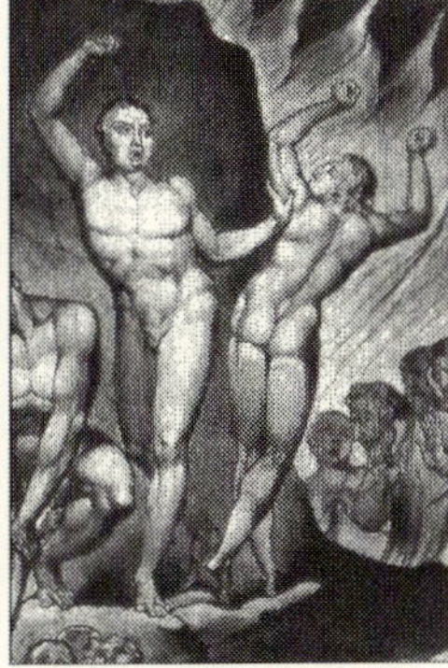

Fig. 12.6 - Blake: *Couples Joined as One or Divided by Strife*

laterally flanking the hell hole (Fig. 12.6).

The couple on the right consists of two figures caught in strife. In both, the energy spirals upward through their *contrapposto* pose, and is released in their angered gaze and upraised arm – so as to swing and strike at one another. This is pure hatred, as a passion of the soul, leading to conflict and division. Those who see the world in this manner are already, unbeknownst to themselves, living in the depths of hell.

Meanwhile, the couple on the left consists of two figures embracing in love. They are so closely entwined that the spiral of energy winds round their twinned figures, binding them as one. They gaze steadfastly into each other's eyes, their lips joined, their hands pointing upward to the heavens. These passions of the soul, as ecstasy and love, lead straight to union with the Divine. Already, though sunk in the bowels of hell, they are living a heavenly existence.

"The Last Judgment," Blake says, *"and its vision is seen by the eye of every one according to the situation he holds."* And he adds, *"The nature of my work is visionary, or imaginative... The Last Judgment is one of these stupendous visions. I have represented it as I saw it."*[16]

But Blake's vision and inventiveness, it seems, knew no limits. If energy may pass from one figure to another, then why allow gravity to limit this exchange, nailng their feet to the ground? Just above the hell hole sits the Whore of Babylon. To her extreme right and left, two more contrasting couples emerge, except now they float and sink with no gravity to restrain them. (Fig. 12.7)

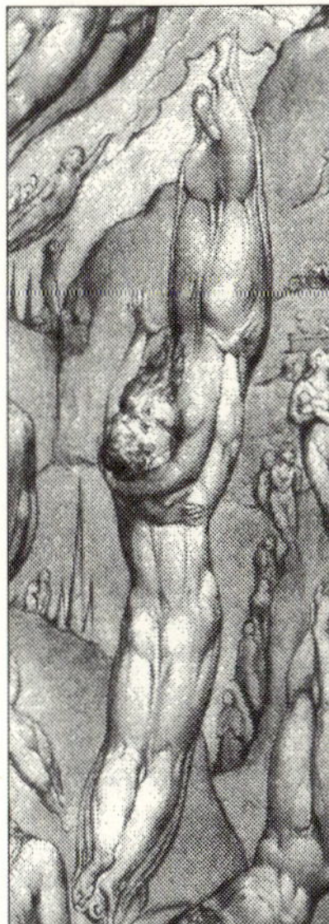

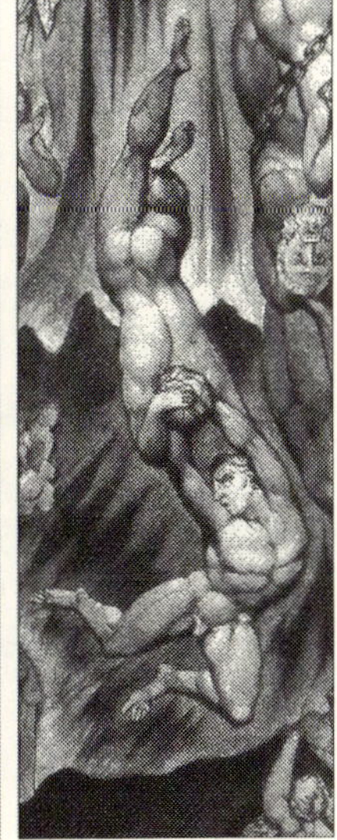

Fig. 12.7 - Blake: *Couples in Union or Conflict*

In the couple on the right, a soul is being dragged hellward with great force and commotion. The spiral of energy that vertically descends their forms offers a violent twist and contortion, joining them through conflict and opposition. In the couple on the left, the powerful union of their lips and limbs is able to lift them heavenward, a purely vertical ascent of two figures bonded as one.

A prolonged scrutiny of all of Blake's figures reveals his unique manner of grouping human forms so their energy and movement flow together. The invisible lines of force and gravity re-emerge, at times, in his long swirling draperies. But even his nude figures seem to fly and twirl on these invisible winds.

The main reason for this, I believe, is his inheritance from the Gothic, which may descend as far back as the serpentine weavings and knotwork of Celtic patterns. As an Englishman, Blake was a natural heir to these patterns, which he translated through Michelangelo and the Greeks into the dynamic interweaving of energy in human forms.

This is clearly evident in the binding angel to the right of the Seven-headed Beast (Fig. 12.8). If *contrapposto* may be called a bi-lateral tilt and *serpentinata* a more dramatic twist, then this pose needs a new vocabulary. The angel has firmly planted his foremost foot in the frontal position. Meanwhile, the back foot with heel raised is in perfect profile. As we trace the movement around the figure, we notice *a complete 180° turn*, until the upper body appears in profile *opposite* to the foot. But, his raised arm turns *another* 180°, making *a 360° twist* in all. Despite the difficulty of such a turning, the angel appears perfectly balanced, poised and graceful.

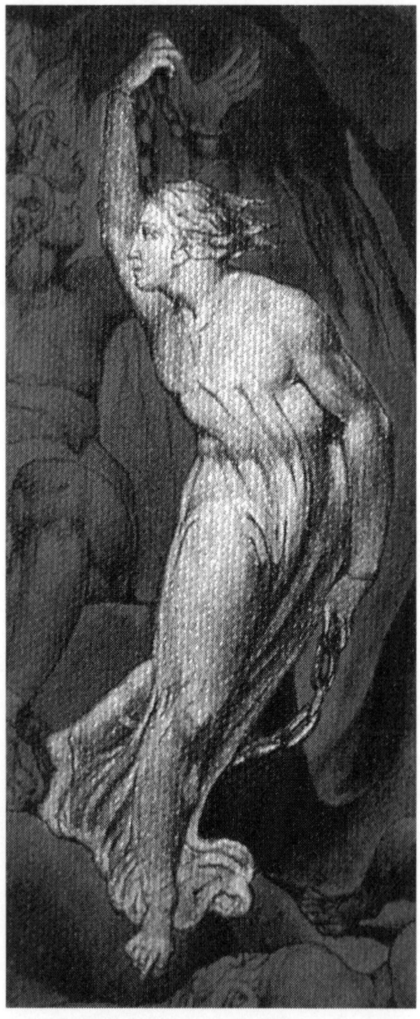

Fig. 12.8 - Blake: *Angel on the Right Binding the Seven-Headed Beast*

At the centre of the watercolour are the angels who sound the first four trumpet blasts (Rev 8:6). And at their feet are two lesser figures so small that we may almost miss them (Fig. 12.9). Yet, a closer examination reveals the extremes to which Blake could variously twist and turn the human figure without losing beauty and ease. Both are descending from the heavenly realm and turning their faces, one upward, one down. With arms outstretched, they point in different directions. Yet, how powerful is the swirling movement coursing through their sinuous figures. From uppermost

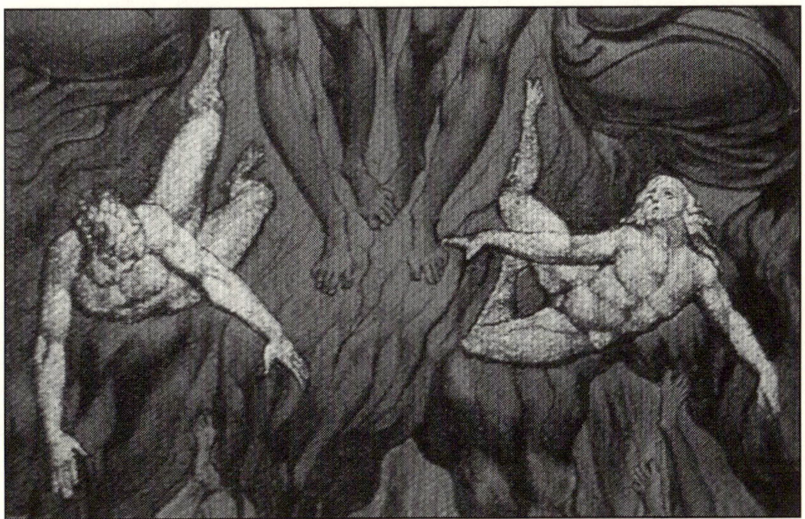

Fig. 12.9 - Blake: *Two Smaller Angels Below the Four Trumpetting Angels*

foot to glance of the eye, we can trace the movement of energy through their spiralling figure, which is seen from such a foreshortened angle as to make the most Baroque or Mannerist artist envious. Yet Blake has executed these ornamental figures with complete artistry and mastery.

"The old heavens and the old earth are passing away," the artist wrote in his description of the Last Judgment, *"and the new heavens and the new earth descending."* At the apex of this composition sits the Saviour, who does not raise his hands in judgment, but opens a scroll, which contains *"the word divine of revelation,"* Blake wrote.[17]

This Christ sits at the apex of a huge triangle, which is itself inscribed in the squared space of the painting's rectangular frame. And the aureole around Christ, circular and luminous, forms once more an immense Eye of God, uniting all the figures below in a singular vision of darkness overcome by the light.

"All things," Blake wrote *"are comprehended in these eternal forms in the divine body of the Saviour, the true vine of eternity... who appeared to me as coming to judgment among His saints, and throwing off the temporal, that the eternal might be established. Around him were seen the images of existences according to a certain order, suited to my imaginative eye."*[18]

VI. The Timeless Style that Preceded History

Before leaving the Last Judgment, I must also comment upon Blake's manner of rendering anatomy. If, as we saw before, Michelangelo had simplified anatomy to preserve the Classical style, then Blake has evolved and perfected this mannerism. Without a doubt, he knows where each muscle and tendon rises and falls. But Blake has chosen instead to emphasize the stylistic outline, simplifying its curves while rounding and flattening all volumes to the shallow shadows of *bas relief*. This is what gives his figures their monumental quality, reminding us of the 'flat and wide' figures of ancient Egypt and Babylon, carved in low relief. Yet, they twist and turn with Gothic grace and the fluidity of the ancient Greeks.

Ultimately, what makes Blake resemble Michelangelo, or Fuchs resemble Blake, is their shared fascination for combining styles from different epochs. But this tendency to transcend individual eras is not simply a stylistic exercise. Rather, it is their entry into the timeless realm of Vision – which grants them direct knowledge and acquaintance of the trans-temporal style.

"In my Brain are studies & Chambers fill'd with books & pictures of old, which I wrote and painted in ages of Eternity before my mortal life,"[19] Blake wrote, underlining his acquaintance with the timeless style that preceded history. It is a style which seeks beauty and the ideal as its highest attainments. But, *"knowledge of Ideal Beauty is Not to be Acquired,"* Blake wrote, *"It is Born with us."*[20]

It is no wonder that he called his works *"visions of eternity."*[21] Each form and figure was rendered in that eternal, epoch-transcending style of the true visionary:

"The man who never in his Mind & Thoughts traveld to Heaven Is No Artist,"[22] Blake decided. And, in what is perhaps his most stirring declaration, he wrote:

"And I know that This World Is a World of IMAGINATION & Vision. I see Every thing I paint In This World, but Every body does not see alike... To Me This World is all One continued Vision of Fancy or Imagination."[23]

VII. Moreau & the Academy: Idealizing the Figure

The Musée Gustave Moreau in Paris was one of the first of its kind – an artist's studio bequeathed to the state, with all the artist's studies, sketches and unfinished works left intact. Moreau went to great pains to construct the large wooden frames which open like immense books onto his innumerable studies. And he spent the last years of his life renovating the building and supervising the hanging of his paintings (which have remained, ever since, in the order he arranged them). The museum offers a unique view into the working methods of an Academy painter who transcended his own times through the sheer originality and profundity of his vision.

If an artist like Blake seemed to effortlessly toss off hundreds of figures in diverse poses due to his god-given inspiration and imagination, Moreau typified the diligent artist who, despite an immense talent, had to work and rework each figure, succeeding through sheer, dogged perseverance and perspiration. His *atelier* reveals numerous working methods for creating a well-posed figure – many preserved from his years of Academy training under François-Édouard Picot. This member of the *Académie des beaux-arts* had, himself, studied under Jacques-Louis David, and had won the *Prix de Rome* (second place) in 1811, allowing him to sojourn in the Villa Medici.

Moreau entered Picot's *atelier* in 1846 at the age of twenty, and won his first medal (for Composition) one year later. He began competing for the *Prix de Rome* in 1848, and was admitted to the *loges* in 1849 (along with William-Adolphe Bouguereau, Émile Lévy and Paul Baudry), but the prize went to Gustave Boulanger for his *Ulysses Recognized by his Wet-nurse* (Moreau's version was stolen from the museum in 1986). Although Moreau never won the *Prix de Rome*, he travelled through Italy for two years (1857 - 59), staying at the Villa Medici and making copies of the Renaissance masters (particularly Raphael, Michelangelo, Veronese and Poussin).[24]

Upon his return, he began participating in the *Salons*, where his *Oedipus and the Sphinx* made a huge impression in 1864, winning a medal before being purchased by Prince Jérôme Napoléon. Moreau continued to participate in the Salons for the next sixteen years, submitting two paintings per year, garnering critiques and generating commissions until 1880, when he decided to work in solitude. He also refused commissions by the State to decorate, among others, the Sorbonne. Nevertheless, writers like Charles Baudelaire, Théophile Gautier and J.-K. Huysmans began to celebrate the reclusive artist, and younger painters like Odilon Redon, Fernand Khnopff and Jean Delville sought him out for encouragement. He was elected *professeur chef d'atelier* at the *École des beaux-arts* in 1892, six years before his death on April 18, 1898.

Although Moreau was trained as an academic artist and participated in the Salons, he saw himself as a reformer of History painting, destined to return *le grand art* to its former glory. His dual striving for feminine beauty and spiritual ideals caused him to be labelled as a Symbolist or Decadent artist. In *Gustave Moreau: History Painting, Spirituality and Symbolism*, Peter Cooke describes him as *"a sensual spiritualist, marked by sincere religious and ascetic aspirations, but obsessed by the beauty of the female body."*[25] Without a doubt, the human form as an expression of a higher, ideal beauty obsessed Moreau for much of his creative life.

An inventory of the museum after his death revealed no less than eighty plaster casts: antique hands, heads, torsos and feet, but also entire figures, such as the Venus de Milo, Dancing Faun and Ares Borghese. His collection also included nine *écorchés* (one by Houdon, whose pose directly inspired Moreau's *Young Man and Death*)[26] and six Michelangelos (whose face of The Dying Slave re-appears in Moreau's *Head of Orpheus*).[27]

"I've often regarded and copied from the Antique,"[28] Moreau wrote. It was common practice at the Academy to *"faire la bosse"* – to draw hands and feet from molds of Classical Greek statues. Meanwhile, other sketches demonstrate how he also drew from the *modèle vivant*. But we would be mistaken if we thought that these life drawings were made for the sake of anatomical accuracy.

Rather, what the drawings reveal is the gradual 'idealization' of the human form, moving beyond Nature to a higher and more sacred archetype. Above all, what Moreau pursued in drawing after drawing was the ideal pose, which he described as *"cet aspect immobile et inquiétant de la fixité – that disquieting and immobile aspect of stillness."*[29]

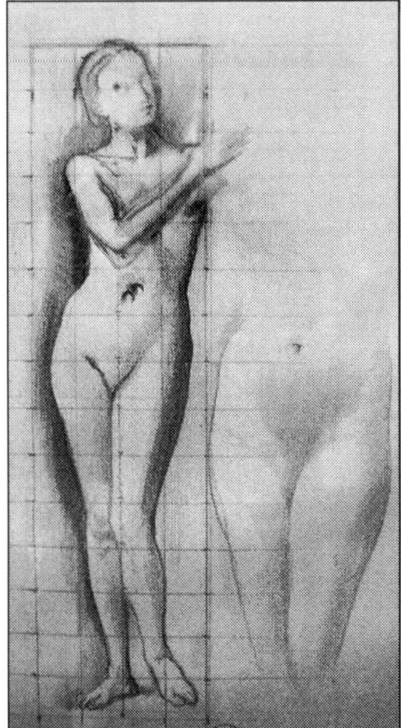

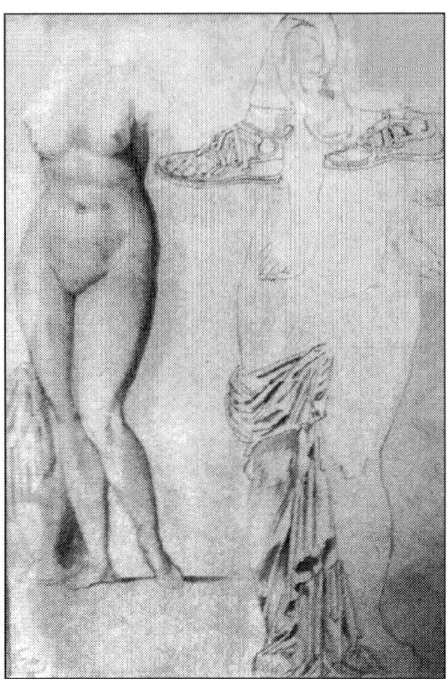

Fig. 12.10 - Gustave Moreau: *Female Figure from Life (cat. 3380) and Idealized (cat. 3409)*

On one of my many visits to the Musée Gustave Moreau, I came across a series of five drawings he made for a Classical nude, two of which I have reproduced here. Moreau drew the model from life at least three times (cat. no's 3380, 3382 and 3407), searching for the most harmonious pose. Twice, he squared off the drawing (*"la mise au carreau"*) to recopy it elsewhere.

In the drawing I have reproduced here (cat. 3380), we can see the *mise au carreau* but, more interesting still, the grid (4 squares x 15 squares) is developed *from the plumb line*, which clearly passes through the middle of the figure, from the eye to the weight-bearing foot. As well, he has drawn *an extra horizontal at the pubis*, and labelled this *"la moitié juste"* – meaning *"exactly half-way."*

Following his Academy training, Moreau has laid out the two main axes for all figures: the median or plumb line (*"ligne de plomb"*) for the vertical axis (from eye to weight-bearing foot) and the transversal or half-way line (*"la moitié juste"*) for the horizontal axis (at the pubis). Utilizing the Cartesian co-ordinate system invented by René Descartes, the remainder of the figure was then measured off and numbered.

In the life drawing that he did not square off (cat. 3382 – not reproduced here), he nevertheless drew the vertical plumb line through the figure. Understanding the figure's pose in relation to the plumb line was, it seems, a necessary part of his Academy training.

Returning to the first drawing (cat. 3380), we can see on the right that Moreau has already begun *an idealized version of the live model.* Where his slender model has rather thin legs and boney hips, in the ideal version, he has rounded out the contours, adding softer volumes.

In the next drawing (cat. 3409), he has accentuated the curves even more, so that the broad arc of the hips now unites the upper and lower portions of the figure. The pose and placement of the feet remain identical (respecting the plumb line), but the figure has now been fully 'Hellenized' and stylized to the Classical ideal. Moreau has even added a Grecian urn to the left, and begun working out the draperies and sandals to the right.

VIII. Moreau: Finding that First Idea

Due to the immense number of preparatory drawings, we are able to reconstruct some of the artist's working methods. In his notebooks, Moreau wrote long lists of possible subjects for a painting. Among the 14,000 drawings preserved at the *Musée* (only 5,000 are displayed), we find numerous *ébauches* or 'first sketches', which are endless variations on a given theme, working out the possible poses, compositions, and arrangements of light and shadow. Moreau delighted in using different media: mostly graphite, but also black or red chalk (*sanguine*), watercolour, and gouache. Rough pencil lines, exploring different lines for the figure, were gone over and finalized with ink.

After much searching, Moreau arrived at *la première idée* – the 'first idea' which contained the basic germ and outlines of the painting in miniature. Then began a period – which could last up to four or five years – where he researched and developed all the separate elements of the painting: sketching out the exact pose, drawing the model from life, then refining it stylistically.

Numerous pictorial resources were consulted for the drapery, landscape, architecture and animals. Some of these were drawn from life; others traced from books and transferred directly onto the canvas. Before painting he also made 'abstracts' which showed the general outlay of light and shadow in relation to colour.

Once Moreau was satisfied with his drawing of a certain figure, it was squared off and enlarged, then transferred onto the *carton* – the cartoon or complete drawing on paper. This full-size *carton* was finally transferred to the canvas. In the beginning Moreau did all these laborious steps himself. Later in life, he hired assistants (Henri Rupp, Joseph Paÿ) and drew directly onto the canvas. Indeed, his later works reveal a much looser method, where objects or figures were sketched directly onto the canvas, either tracing their contours in black paint or highlighting their volumes in white.[30]

Another interesting discovery I made at the museum was Moreau's extensive use of wax models (Fig. 12.12). At least fifteen such mannequins have survived, many depicting figures from Moreau's greatest works: *Salome, Prometheus* and *Young Moses*, among others. In 2010 an exhibition on these models was organized (*Gustave Moreau: l'Homme aux figures de cire*), with an accompanying catalogue that delved into the forgotten art of *modelage* for Academy painters.

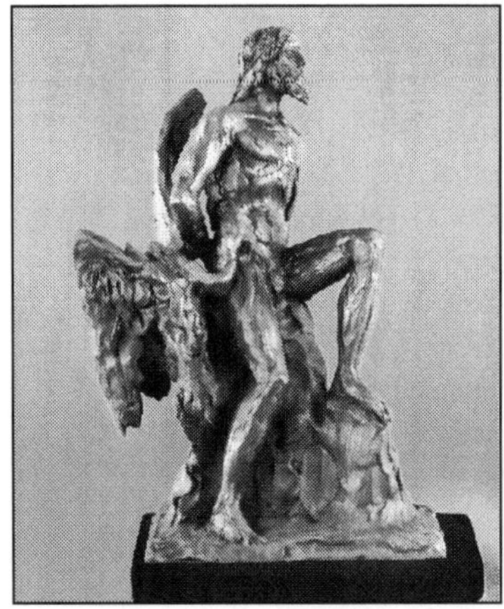

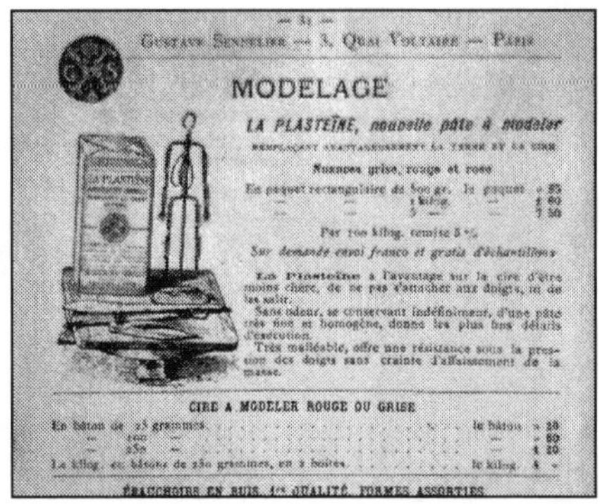

Fig. 12.11 - Right: *Sennelier* Ad for Armature
Fig. 12.12 - Left: Moreau Wax Model for *Prometheus*

Sennelier on the Quai Voltaire specialized in fabricating the wire supports (Fig. 12.11) which, as the advertising of the day proclaimed, could be modelled with wax (*cire*) or the newly-invented 'plasticine' (*"la plasteïne – nouvelle pâte à modeler"*[31]). Wax models were ideal for viewing the figure from difficult angles: foreshortening, odd perspectives, aerial views etc. The *armatures articulées* were specifically designed to move like the human body – the shoulders and hips well-articulated for *contrapposto* bends and *serpentinata* twists.

In a fascinating passage from his notebooks, Moreau recounts his rather unique approach to painting: *"...The work, the endless research, myself evolving through sheer effort, this constant pursuit of the rarest and finest, the invisible in art; the chance discoveries from the tools themselves, the skills of the craftsman, the enlarging, simplifying, and idealizing each day a little bit more, the innermost aims, dreams and conceptions worked and reworked to infinity, finding that first idea, the mind's inner spectacle, the infinite combinations of figures and forms, the sacred language, the unseen ideal emerging from the material seen."*[32]

Moreau was undoubtedly a Visionary artist. But, in his quest for the higher ideal, he was never satisfied with a single pose or representation. He painted five versions of *Leda and the Swan*, and each one was entirely different. The same is true of *Salome, Europa* and *Oedipus*. His subjects were drawn from Christianity and Greco-Roman lore, but he was neither a true Academic artist nor a painter of Histories. At the time of his death Moreau was grouped with The Symbolists.

In a recent monograph, Peter Cook writes about 'Gustave Moreau and the Re-invention of History Painting'. While Moreau was keenly aware of Poussin's heritage and Grand-Manner painting (*"le grand art"* he called it), he sought instead to create a more poetic and allegorical style that avoided theatrical gestures or grandiose displays of feeling in favour of a more 'contemplative immobility' to reveal the figure's 'inner awareness':

Fig. 12.13 Right - Gustave Moreau: *Oedipus and the Sphinx* 1864

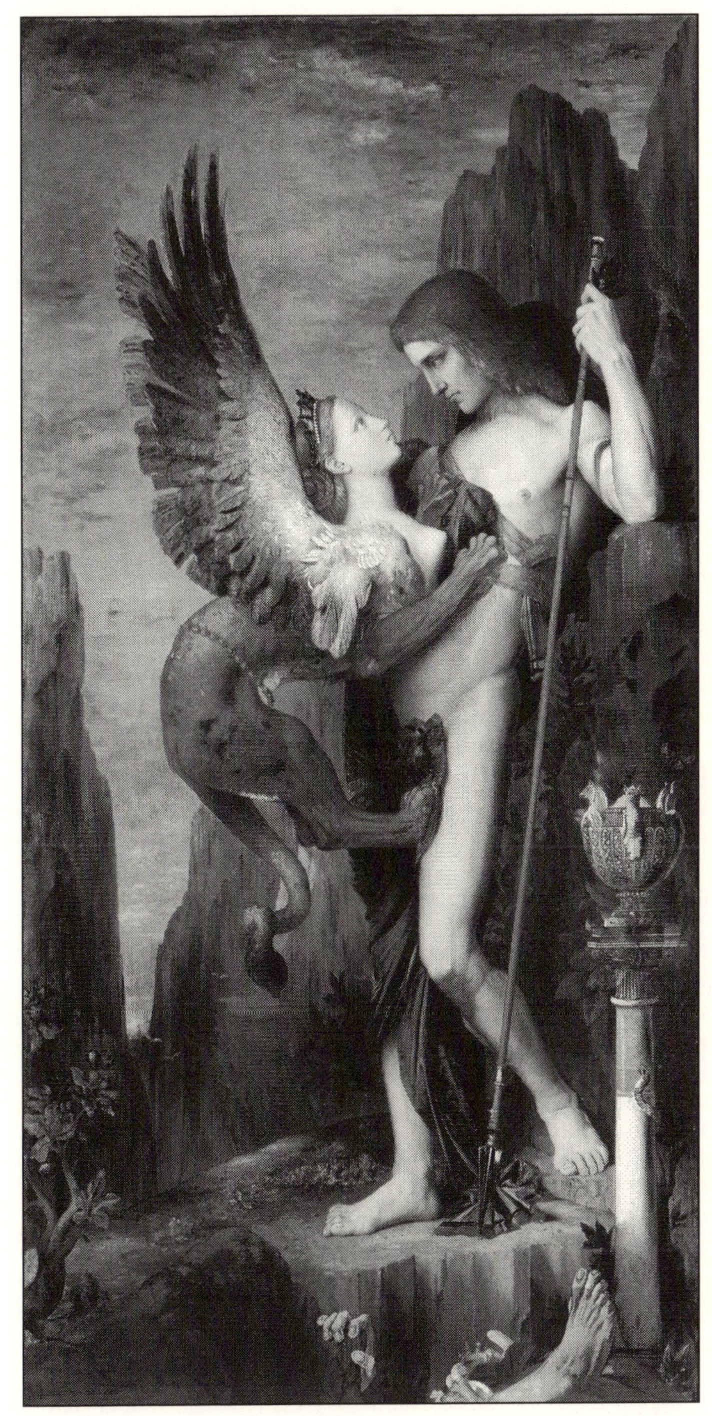

"Without a doubt I'm interested in the expression of human feeling and passion," Moreau wrote, *"but these movements of the soul interest me less than the visible manifestation of a figure's inner realizations [les éclairs intérieurs]."*[33]

For this reason, Moreau sought to portray stilled and statuesque figures that, in his words, forego *"the action and movement of the body in favour of a more contemplative immobility. [préférer l'immobilité contemplative du corps humain à l'action et au mouvement de ce corps]."*[34]

By the late 19th century, many Academic artists had turned against Poussinesque compositions with their complex temporality, multiple groupings and 'copious variety' of figures. Instead, they responded to Gotthold Ephraim Lessing's call, in his essay 'The Laocoon', for a single dramatic action which, suggestive of the past and future, became 'the pregnant moment'.

"Painting, in its coexistent compositions," Lessing wrote, *"can use but a single moment of an action, and must therefore choose the most pregnant one, the one most suggestive of what has gone before and what is to follow."*[35]

This was most amply manifest in the sculptural grouping of *The Laocoön*, and many of Moreau's most memorable works from the 1860's salons combine two figures into a single sculptural image, where a contemplative immobility expresses the hero's inner realization or *éclair intérieur*. This is true of his *Prometheus*, *Head of Orpheus* and especially *Oedipus and the Sphinx* (Fig. 12.13). For Moreau, this gave Grand-Manner painting a more poetic and allegorical significance:

"Great art [le grand art] *is the art of lofty poetic and imaginative conceptions—an art improperly called, in the case of painting, 'History Painting,' which is nonsense, because great art does not find its elements, its means of expression in history. It finds them in pure poetry, in high imaginative fantasy, and not in historical facts, unless they are allegorized (symbolized)."*[36] (The word *symboliser* has been added, showing that Moreau hesitated in his choice of the term).

In his later years, Moreau returned to the multi-figured History Paintings of his youth (*The Suitors*, *The Daughters of Thespius*) and expanded their canvases, adding architecture, ornament and emblems to transform the principle narrative or *histoire* into a more symbolic 'allegory'. Returning to André Félibien's hierarchy of genres, Moreau now promoted Allegorical painting as the highest type of *grand genre* painting, above historical, mythological, religious or literary painting because it conveyed a higher spiritual message.

Moreau's *œuvre* arose at a pivotal time in history. Edgar Degas was a friend of his youth (accompanying him on his Italian sojourns), while Henri Matisse and Georges Rouault were his students from his final days as a professor at the *École des Beaux-Arts* in Paris. As Modernist movements like Impressionism (Degas), Fauvism (Matisse) and Expressionism (Rouault) rejected and revolted against Academic painting, Moreau's art showed that there was indeed a path for art to follow, from the High Renaissance through French History Painting and beyond the sterility of Academicism into the twentieth century.

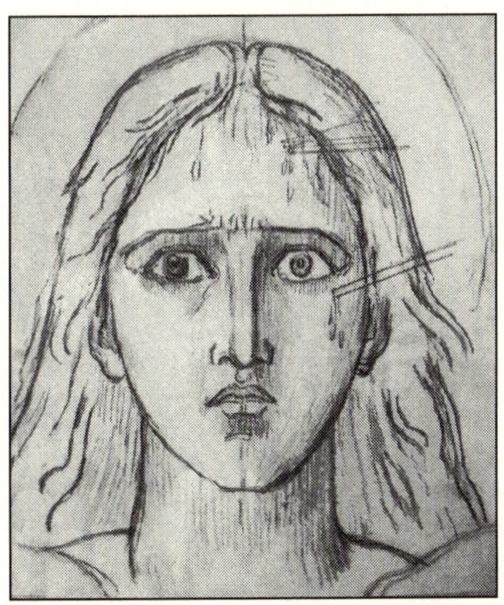

Fig. 12.14 - Moreau: *Sketch for St. Sebastian*

By elevating History Painting to Symbolism, Allegory (and ultimately, Visionary Art), 19th century artists like Moreau and Burne-Jones forged new links in a long chain, which 20th century artists like Delville, Dalì and Fuchs augmented with passion, dedication and genius. All their works, so mythic and poetic, extend Allegorical painting into new spiritual domains. In their own way, these great artists became Moreau's true heirs, upholding the Sacred Art of Painting.

But, after his death, Moreau's *œuvre* soon fell into obscurity – judged as a bizarre example of an Academic painter overcome by opium abuse (read chapter V. of Huysmans' *À rebours*). Like a time capsule, his museum protected his art from the vagaries of fashion. It was only in 1961 that a retrospective at the Louvre, organized by the Musée National d'Art Moderne, saved Moreau's work from total obscurity.[37] André Breton and Georges Bataille hailed him as a proto-Surrealist. Today, we do no different in regarding him as a Visionary. His art has now transcended its own age and begun to address new eras and epochs.

One reason for this is his universality. Unlike many of his contemporaries, Moreau searched beyond the standard Greek canon to the art and statuary of other cultures. In 1997, the important exhibition and catalogue *l'Inde de Gustave Moreau* showed how the artist had sought out and traced numerous Hindu and Buddhist designs (from the *Magasin Pittoresque* or Samuel Bourne's photos) for his large *Triumph of Alexander the Great*, which portrays the Macedonian king's conquest of India. Similarly, for his painting of *Young Moses* as a child floating down the Nile, Moreau delved deep into Egyptian architecture and ornament. His *Salomé Tatouée* bears many motifs borrowed from French Gothic and Romanesque sculpture. Fragments of Japanese woodcuts, Persian miniatures and Medieval *Book of Hours* – they all make their appearance in his work.

If we pause to admire his quick sketch for the face of St. Sebastian (cat. 3958 - Fig. 12.14), we ask ourselves – where have we seen this face before? Like the face of the Delphic Sibyl, there is a Hieratic simplicity, cutting each facet and reducing each line to its utmost, essential curve and volume (while resonating harmoniously with the halo's perfect circle).

An Egyptian sculptor would be proud of this handiwork. And yet, the Humanist style still shows through: the blood on his brow, the agony of the arrows, as he gazes with awe and uncertainty into his own imminent sacrifice. Sebastian, not yet martyred, is on the path to enlightenment, his death and transfiguration leading to own apotheosis...

Through the combination of Humanist and Hieratic Styles, both the sacred and mundane aspects of his transfiguration come to the fore. He is, like all saints or avatars of Christ, an image of man and humanity now made divine.

IX. Fuchs: The Hidden Prime of Styles

In 1966, Ernst Fuchs wrote a series of texts, and even published parts of his Working Diary, which cast a clear light onto some of his thoughts and working methods at the time. They offer a rare glimpse into the artist's state of mind while he accomplished some of his greatest works, such as *Job and the Judgment of Paris*, *The Triumph of Christ* and the *Anti-Laocoön*.

The two ideas which emerge most forcefully are the Dark Glass and the Hidden Prime of Styles. We will elaborate upon the Dark Glass in the next volume. For now, it is the Hidden Prime of Styles which speaks most eloquently of the fusion of Humanist and Hieratic Styles.

After citing Blake several times and even reproducing his *Vision of a Last Judgment*, Fuchs goes on to express his passion for Moreau:

"...the 'discovery' of Gustave Moreau was the transparency of the sphinx. I made his closer acquaintance only in the decisive year of... 1960. After having seen some colour reproductions of his picture Jupiter and Semele, I visited the Musée Gustave Moreau near Montmartre and here I found traces of the hidden prime of styles, the primeval realm, undertones of the deepest sphinx-like level. The transparency of the adjoining paradise realm shines through all of his pictures... Especially in his picture Jupiter and Semele I again saw the dark glowing blue of my dreams and the gleaming of the innumerable sparkling stones. This man had to have had the same experiences as myself. ...in his later pictures... were ornaments and architectures as they were before all epochs of the style."[38]

'The sphinx', as we shall see, is Fuchs' image for the Hidden Prime of Styles – a riddle, an endless enigma, which can never be fully divested of its mystery, and never completely resolved in time. Instead, the insoluble mystery leads Fuchs on a meandering quest through all of history – his own personal history and the entire history of art – in search of his Philosopher's Stone. At times, his narrative seems to lose its thread entirely, as if his mind were constructing a convoluted labyrinth (out of long Germanic sentences) to protect the mysterious beast at its core. Nevertheless, there is much beauty and genius in his 'stream of consciousness' prose.

In the clearest and most elaborate passage, he describes this timeless style in the form of a vision:

"I saw the entire history of art like a bundle of tablets, which, cut and coined by the square hand of the original angel, lay in the lap of astonished mankind – which now in time made the eternal treasure, plate by plate, advancing from age to age, the model of its creation. ... The artist, the artifex, who in veneration pressing this bundle of tablets against his front (like Moses the tablets of Law), receiving the abundance of the seals, is the only person (in his time) who, like the angel, is able to dive below the times... Almost all of those who dive down... into the 'hall of the simultaneousness of all images' have seen the sphinx of the enigma, 'of the beginning' cower near that first tablet whose signs nobody can read any more today... There on the base of

the [sphinx] *image where all shadows gather together... the gate is hidden through which... the tablet bundle of images has come unto man and his time. From there the images were taken into his (man's) history; recognized by a few as to their origins, they were the icons and models of the styles of their respective times."*[39]

What emerges in this passage is a vision of the Hidden Prime of Styles as that single primordial style which preceded all history, including those culturally recognizable styles of later times, such as the Egyptian, Hindu or ancient Greek. Nevertheless, what makes these historical styles so special is that each seems to echo, in its own unique way, that archetypal or 'first' style which has *"its pre-existence in a meta-historical realm."*[40]

In the styles of certain artists as well, the 'traces' of the Hidden Prime may still be detected. Fuchs speaks of Bosch, Blake, Monsu Desiderio, and Moreau as *"the truly old masters with their meta-historical connection."*[41] They are the ones who have dived down into 'the hall of the simultaneousness of all images' and re-emerged with 'the tablets' – their paintings (or *tableaux* in French) – which bear the signs and seals of 'the sphinx' with her insoluble enigma, the Hidden Prime of Styles.

Meanwhile, even Nature herself may mysteriously reveal traces of the Hidden Style, which Fuchs calls in German, the '*verschollener Stil'*:

"A secret art whose traces I have discovered with almost all people and cultures, but also in nature itself – there where the primæval world appears... like a notion, a memory of the submersed culture of a long passed, unmeasured time which preceded history."[42]

For Fuchs, the history of art – both in its cultural styles and the styles of individual artists – is strangely a-historical. It is not a question of tracing the influence of one epoch on another, or seeing how this artist inspired that. Rather, all artists or epochs – if they are truly Visionary – possess a deeper 'meta-historical' connection:

"The awareness of many apparent influences which one tries to prove [about a certain style] *should rather be understood as a reference to the ultimate incomparability of this style, and should help to re-discover the meta-historical tendency to the original motivation... 'before time'* [which] *must rather be considered the root of the many stylistic trends."*[43]

X. Cultural Styles as Temporal Reflections of the Eternal

While working with Fuchs in Monaco, I wrote *The First Manifesto of Visionary Art* (2000). It was a strange time, in which I was absorbing more working methods, insights and ways of seeing than I could possibly understand or consciously assimilate. When I take the time to re-read the manifesto today, I am startled by some of its passages, which echo with a distinct urgency to express the new ideas I had encountered. For example, to describe the timeless state of vision which produces images in the Hidden Style, I wrote:

"In the process of beholding the Sacred as a timeless and eternal Unity, the visionary artist frees himself momentarily from his inherited spiritual tradition, its particular symbols and style of expression. During that momentary epiphany, his vision partakes of the universal, *sans* cultural perspective: it acquires a stilled, more timeless, even eternal way of seeing.

"Think of the strange stare manifest in sculpted visages of Babylonian or Greek gods: their elongated eyes, opened wide, absorbing a vision without horizon. They are beholding the eternal.

"But, the moment the artist attempts to render this expanded vision, he is caught once more in the currents of his own time, its style of rendering bound by perspective and finite perception. The resulting image betrays his age's fashion, its preference for a certain line, form, and proportion, while still revealing – above and beyond it – the timeless shape, the divine symmetry, briefly glimpsed, from the higher world."[44]

In another passage, I cite Fuchs while describing cultural styles as 'temporal reflections' of the eternal:

"Visionary art is as ancient as the shaman's first etchings on cavern walls or the mysterious spirals carved on megalithic stones. Our art manifest itself among the Egyptians, Mesopotamians, Minoans, and ancient Greeks. In Middle America, it uprose among the Aztecs, Mayans and Olmecs. Towards the East, it reached a high degree of refinement in Hindu and Buddhist art.

"Indeed, in all these earlier cultures, it acquired an almost 'pure' form of expression, as the depiction of the Creation, the Cosmos and its Gods, the sacred hero and his death and rebirth – all of these appeared spontaneously and alive in a unique cultural style, whose visual language was near-perfect in its expressiveness.

"Each of these cultural styles seemed to emerge 'fully-formed' in history, with a complete symbolic vocabulary and complex pictorial expression. Each manifest, at one and the same time, a distinctively epic or monumental quality and, transcending this, a more universal and timeless quality.

"As Fuchs noted, *'A work of art is simply a monument to the temporal within eternity. Art alone can confer and transmit to other ages an enduring validity of what is trapped within its own era.'*[45]

"In our ancient, more epic works of art, a momentary vision was seen, then seized, and finally set into time-resistant stone, which has preserved its hidden message into our present times. The task awaiting us, while beholding such a work, is to open ourselves up to its forgotten spiritual message, thus broadening our vision beyond its own cultural horizon and spiritual inheritance."[46]

When I read these words today, I re-live the epiphanies they attempt to describe. Yet, what I had not yet done is recognize the important divide between Hieratic and Humanist Styles. Although I included the Greek style among the many cultural styles that are 'Visionary' I had not yet seen that the Greek was Humanist while the others were Hieratic.

Meanwhile, if we try to determine what specifically characterizes the Hidden Prime of Styles, we find this same vague tendency: it seems to be Hieratic, but may also appear in Humanist works. At first, Fuchs found evidence of the Hidden Style in the Phantastic art of his favourite artists: *"This style is the Gordian knotted navel from which all styles are delivered. I found its traces above all in so-called 'Phantastic Art'. Its emblematic writing which through the times and the different cultures became visible to me."*[47]

As he made drawing after drawing in 1966, the lineaments of this style became more evident. For example, after drawing the double-headed eagle

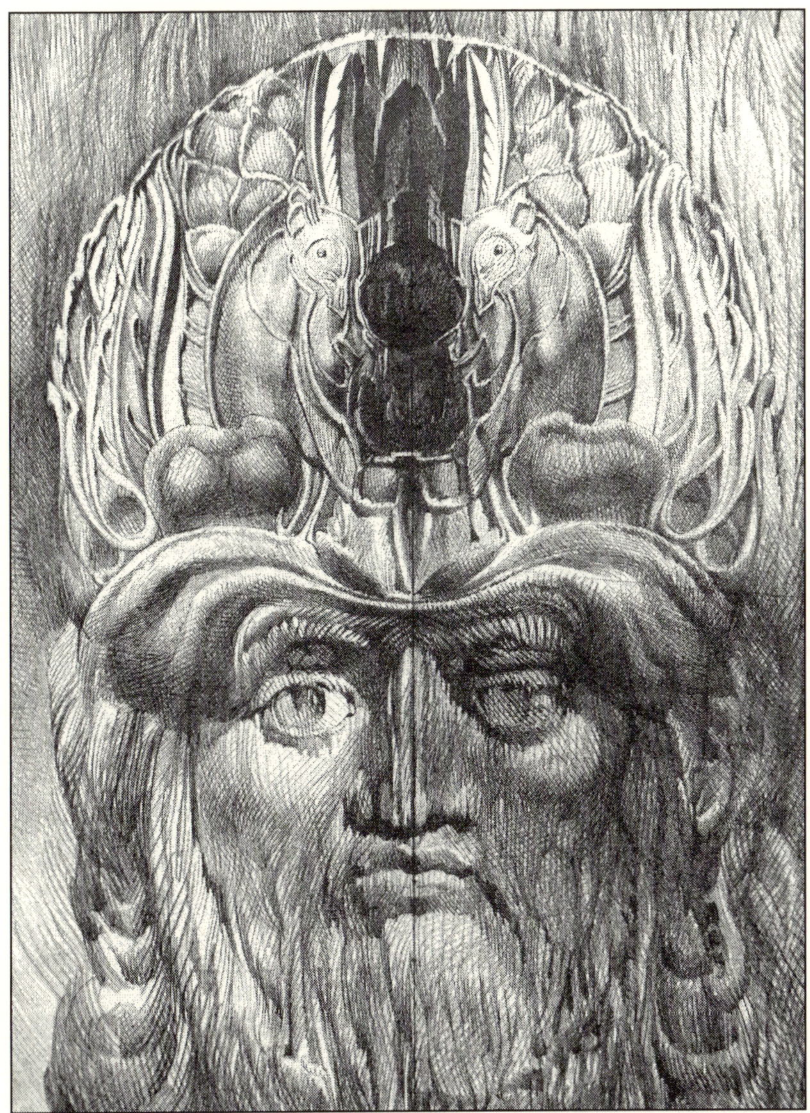

Fig. 12.15 - Ernst Fuchs: *Head of the Angel of History*

above *Job and the Judgment of Paris*, he seemed to recognize the Hidden Style, above all, in symmetry:

"The symmetrically spread motive had appeared 'compulsively' again and again since 1961 as a 'stylistic characteristic' of my celestial images and had been registered with me as the 'symbol of the double eagle.' ... I discovered the characteristic of symmetry which I loved so much as the first sign of the hidden prime of styles everywhere in the early history of art."[48]

Another quality is the *"thick-set square proportions"*[49] which give certain figures their monumentality. *"Many of my figures appeared in square proportions... as with William Blake."*[50]

Yet another quality is the 'serpentine line' which we have already explored before, as that "[curving] *line which searched flexibly, in a wave-like dance, for the straight line."*[51] Above all, this tendency becomes clear in the *Anti-Laocoön* and the architecture of *Job and the Judgment of Paris*, where he finds evidence of *"the pure serpentine style, everything wound and dramatized."*[52] In yet another passage, he describes how *"the hidden prime of styles became visible with full precision – all pictures were traversed by flowing lines streaming into each other."*[53] And he gives, as the clearest example (beside his own telephone doodles), the strongly linear drawings of the Jugendstil period.

As we shall see next volume in our discussion of the Dark Glass, images in the Hidden Style also 'glow from within'. Under the effects of hashish, he first rendered *"the jewel-like forms* [where] *everything in the picture became like precious stones or at least seemed covered with jewels."*[54] And later, in his description of Gustave Moreau's work (cited above) he "*found traces of the hidden prime of styles"* in, above all, *"the dark glowing blue... and the gleaming of the innumerable sparkling stones."*[55]

Time and again, he mentions 'the transparency' of Moreau's work, which he describes as *"the transparency of the adjoining paradise realm* [which] *shines through all of his pictures."*[56] This transparency, which he also saw in the Shroud of Turin (recognized by the Pope in 1958 as a proper devotional image of Christ), came to permeate many of his works in the early 60's.

The defining qualities of The Hidden Prime of Styles would thus appear to be five-fold: symmetry, square proportions, serpentine lines, glowing from within and transparency. The first two are clearly associated with the Hieratic Style. Serpentine lines, when gently rounded, are also Hieratic, but becomes more Humanist when their curves express a more dynamic energy and movement in time. The last two are more painterly qualities, and have less to do with style.

In a drawing such as *Adam, Eve and the Tree of Knowledge* (Fig. 12.16), we can see that Fuchs had a clear grasp of the human figure – as Classically idealized by the ancient Greeks. Both Adam and Eve have transferred their weight onto one foot, allowing the body's energy to traverse their *contrapposto* movement and find its final release in a gesture or glance. Although the volumes have been rendered in pencil, their outlines have been emphasized in ink. This stress on the silhouette shows a clear concern for the stylistic line.

As such, Fuchs clearly understood the Humanist Codes of Western art, inherited from the Renaissance and Ancient Greeks. But many of his figures betray other influences, beginning with the Gothic elongation of Grünewald and Dürer, and expanding into the static figures with strong profiles typical of the Babylonians (Samson engraving 1960, King Solomon 1963, Lohengrin 1977)

The latter are clearly Hieratic. But when I asked him about this, noting the strong Babylonian influence on his style, he replied, *"You know, the first time I saw a Babylonian stele, I was astounded by the similarity to my own work. I said to myself 'so that's where it comes from. They were seeing the same vision as me.'"*

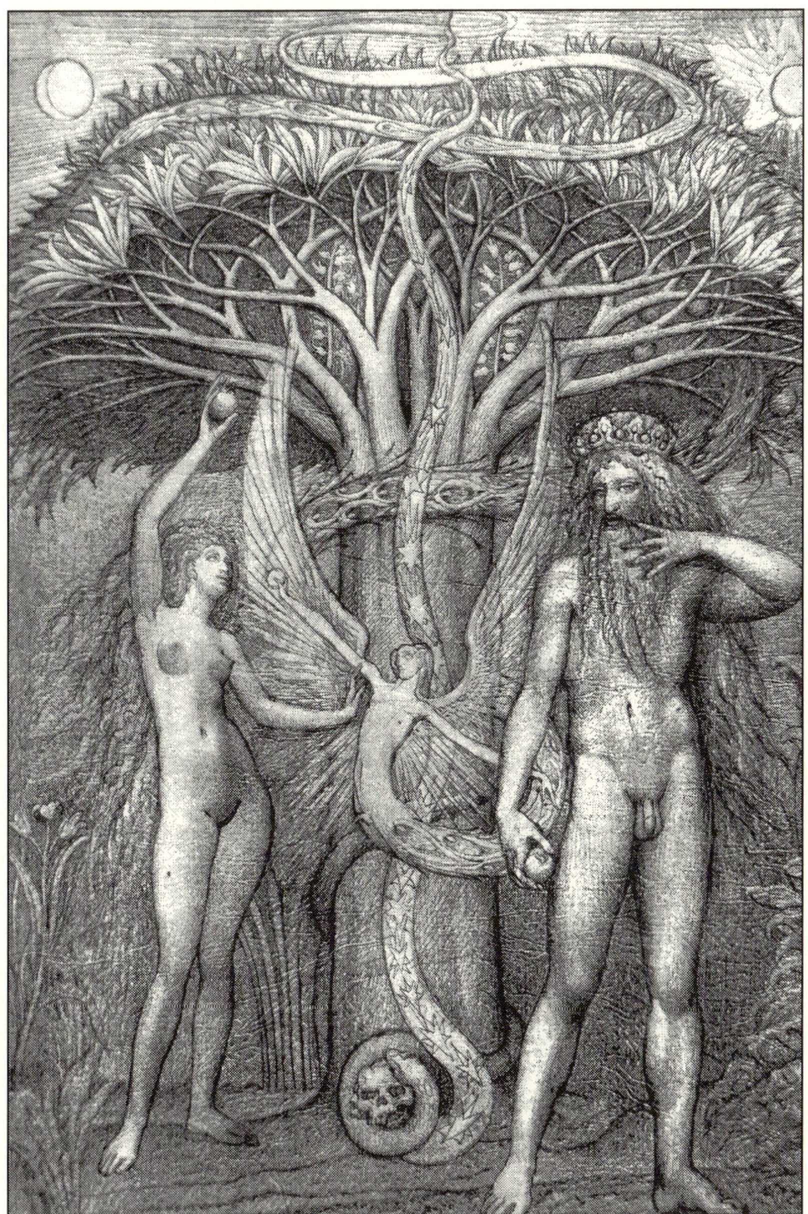

Fig. 12.16 - Ernst Fuchs: *Adam, Eve and the Tree of Knowledge* 1974

The style of the Egyptians, Mayans or Babylonians are, first and foremost, Visionary styles. They relay the strange quality of figures seen in a state of vision. We then define these Visionary styles through their historical and geographical emergence, calling this one Egyptian and the other Babylonian. But all are, in truth, delineations of the higher hieratic world.

XI. Fuchs: Hieratic & Humanist Styles

Having met him many times in my dreams, my first *real* encounter with Ernst Fuchs occurred at the Apocalypse Chapel in Klagenfurt. Since that summer of the year 2000, I have returned to the chapel often. It is, in many ways, a summation of his life's work, his mature style, and Fuchs' own Sistine sanctuary. It offers the apprentice endless opportunities for 'seeing' and understanding the Sacred Codes underlying his art. I once spent an entire night in the chapel alone, journeying through his vision of the Apocalypse. It was an unforgettable experience, and taught me many lessons about spectral colour and the creation of form.

On one wall stands The Angel of History, who appears in the tenth chapter of the Book of Revelation: *"Then I saw another mighty angel coming down from heaven, wrapped in a cloud, with a rainbow over his head, and his face was like the sun, and his legs like pillars of fire. And in his hand was a small scroll that had been opened. He stood with his right foot on the sea and his left foot on the land."* (Rev 10:1)

When we pause to meditate upon the original drawing for the angel's face (Fig. 12.15), we feel as if transported into another sphere of seeing. So many Sacred Codes, derived from the Hieratic Style, lend this face its immense spiritual power: the broadening and widening of the features, the epic symmetry, the serpentine lines in the headdress that compress and expand, dancing round the volumes they create, the jewel-like quality of the eyes and ornamentation, the softly rounded volumes, the enigmatic expression. There is something truly epic, monumental and timeless about this statuesque figure.

Behind the altar of the Apocalypse Chapel, another image appears (Fig. 18.28) depicting the twelfth chapter of The Book of Revelation, where a woman *"clothed with the sun, with the moon under her feet"* (Rev 12: 1) has given birth to a son, who will rule over all nations. But a battle breaks out in heaven, as the Archangel Michael fights the dragon with seven heads, who sought to devour the child in the hour of his birth. It is a powerful image, which we shall return to time and again.

For now, it is the features of the Archangel Michael (Fig. 12.17) which demand our attentive gaze. There are so many Sacred Codes which link this face to the Angel of History: the broadened features, softly rounded volumes, large jewel-like eyes and other-worldly gaze, as if he is contemplating the eternal.

But now, Humanist Codes have also been introduced: the tilt of the head (which gains its energy from the figure as a whole), the three-quarter angle, the wind-swept movement of the highlights in the hair. Above all, there is the tortured brow and down-turning of the lips which, combined with his contemplative gaze, enliven this Hieratic figure with a powerful Humanist expression of pain and compassion. It is, as if, the angel regrets having to destroy one of God's creations, even if it is evil incarnate.

The face of the Archangel has that same enigmatic quality as Moreau's St. Sebastian and Michelangelo's Delphic Sibyl: combining Hieratic features with a Humanist expression to evoke our own innermost spiritual torments and aspirations. It is this what makes their faces so unique.

As we gaze upon their features, as if, gazing into a Sacred Mirror, it is our own more human emotions which link us, ultimately to these higher spiritual beings. For a few rare moments, our heart swells with suffering and compassion, which transfigures our existence, making us one with the sibyls, saints and angels. Through an extended contemplation, as we 'enter through' their images, we experience once more the ancient epoptic moment of revelation: One are all the gods, angels, sibyls and saints, and we are one with them.

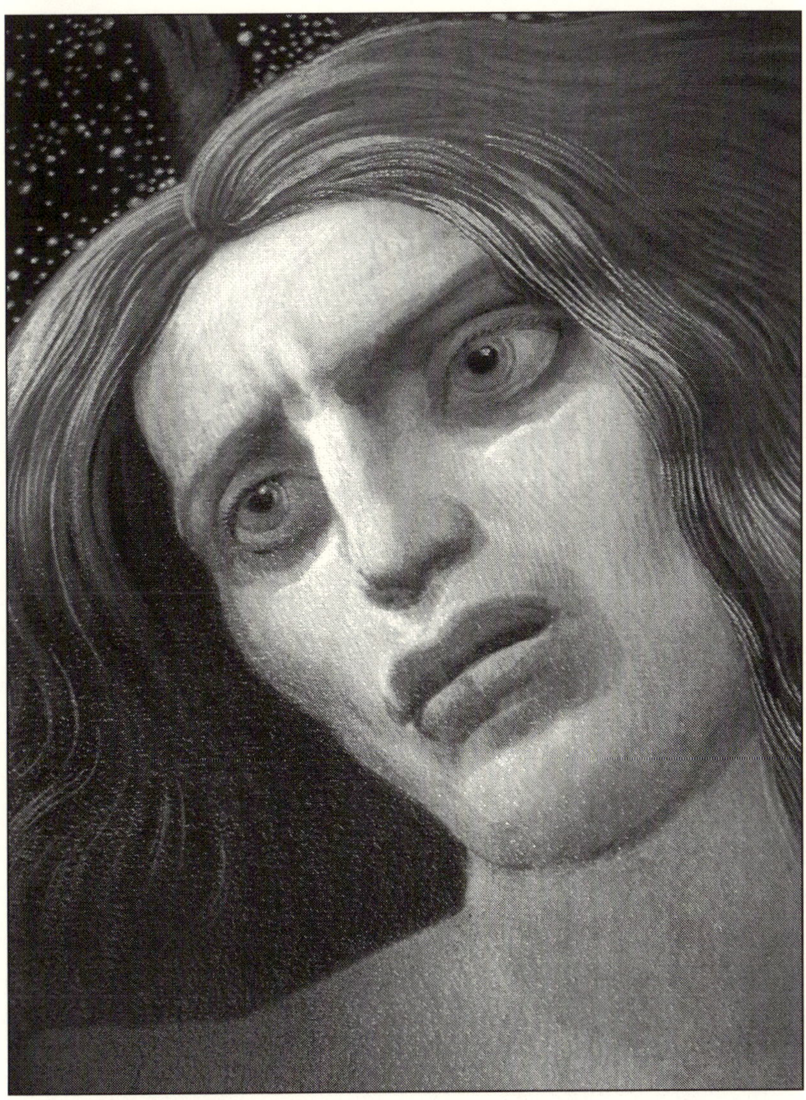

Fig. 12.17 - Ernst Fuchs: *Archangel Michael* (Detail) c. 2008

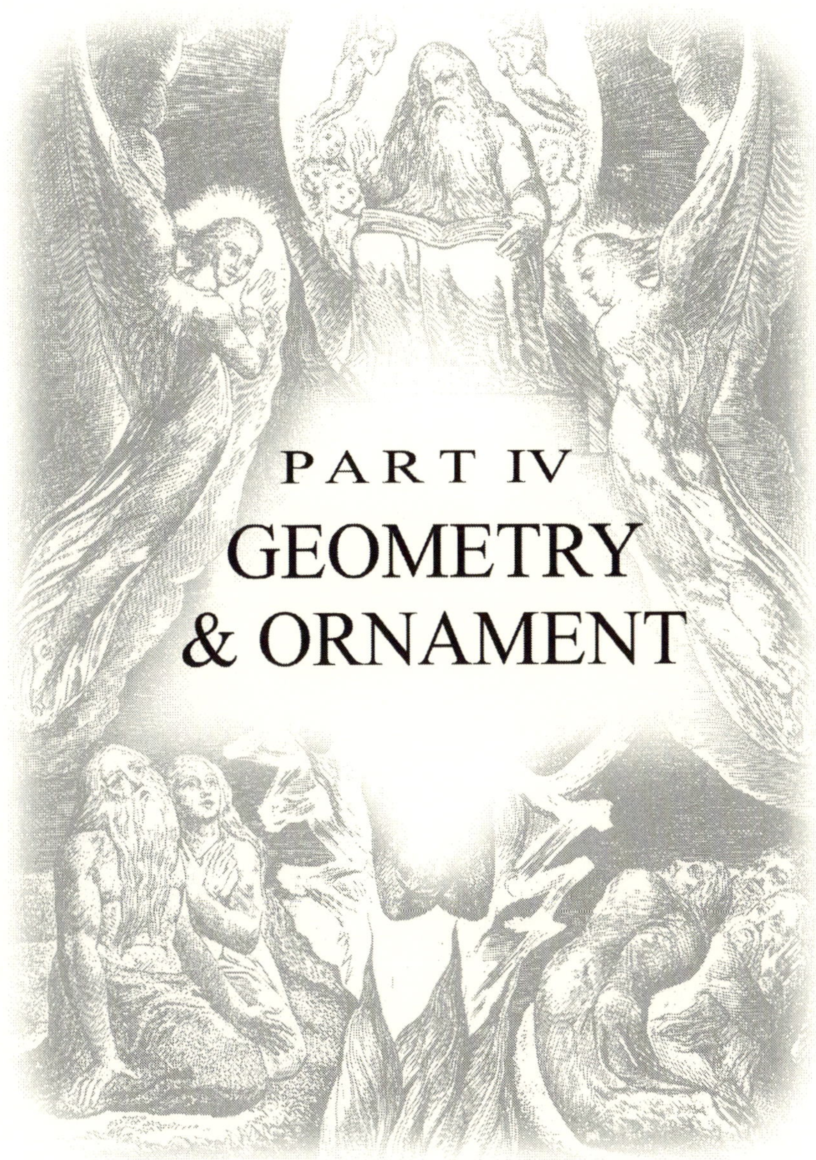

PART IV
GEOMETRY & ORNAMENT

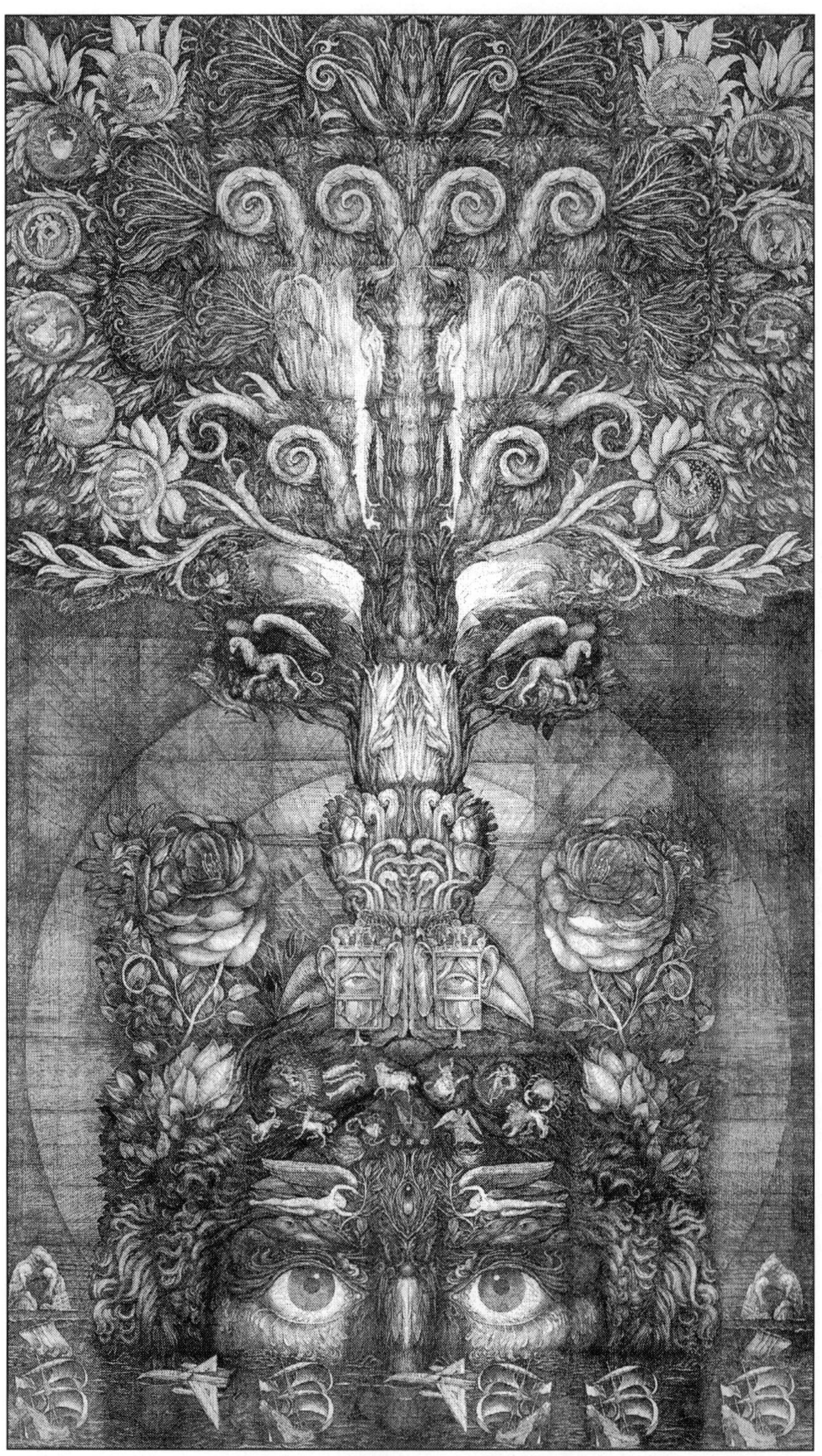

Fig. 13.1 - Ernst Fuchs: *Chronos* 2000

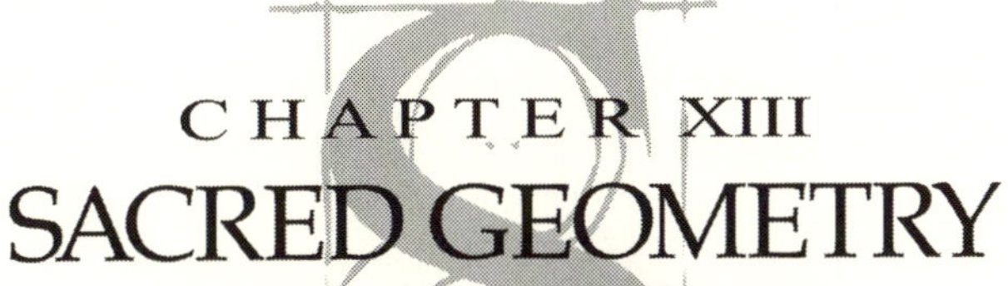

CHAPTER XIII
SACRED GEOMETRY
THE FOUNDATIONS OF HIERATIC COMPOSITION

I. Expanding Vision

While working with Fuchs, there were Sacred Codes in certain paintings which were staring me in the face for hours and days – but I did not see them until years afterward. When I finally recognized them for what they were, I wondered how I could have been so blind – they were sitting in front of me *all that time*. But, I did not see them because they were a 'new way of seeing' which I had not yet learned.

New ways of seeing always involve 'seeing unity' but at a different level of the painting's development. For example, while trying to unify colours, the artist should not have to unify the composition at the same time – that should have been worked out in the drawing stage, through many hours of 'seeing unity' at that level. The *Mischtechnik*, as Fuchs once remarked to me, necessarily divides up the stages of a painting's elaboration, allowing the artist to concentrate on aspects like line, tonality and colour separately.

From its first *imprimatura* until very late into the glazing process, I worked for a year on the large painted version of the drawing reproduced here (Fig. 13.1). I was so focussed on learning the progress of different glazes and how their colours interacted – that I did not really think about the drawing stage.

Yet, there is something decidedly odd about the composition. Odd... yet familiar. The strangeness, of course, is that Fuchs has divided the composition into many small squares. The familiarity, is that he has done that in most of the works that I saw while working with him, which encompasses a large part of his late masterworks.

I knew he had divided the *Chronos* composition into small squares because he had left his sketchbook in the studio, and this contained page after page of ink drawings that were precisely the smaller drawings which make up this larger composition. As he explained to me, he drew them sitting in the back of a car (!) while being driven each day to *Magic Flute* rehearsals (a 1996 production for which he designed the costumes and decor). Thus, *Chronos* is a collage, and all the smaller elements that make up the composition are perfect compositions onto themselves, like small reflections of the greater whole.

In this way, the Sacred Code emerges, which I only recognized years later... Through the grid of squares, each smaller part becomes a perfectly rendered microcosm in the whole. There is unity in both the whole and the parts, as each smaller part expands outward geometrically, to become harmoniously connected with all the others in the totality. The grid of squares in this painting aids the eye *to harmoniously expand its circle of focus* to encompass more and more perfectly recognizable shapes.

II. Pattern & Composition

But we must distinguish between 'the pattern' and 'the composition'. The Pattern is the grid of squares, which remains geometrically consistent throughout the surface of the painting. The Composition is a distinct selection of larger shapes that emerge from the underlying pattern.

In Tribal cultures, the Pattern is an important Sacred Code – whether etched on pottery or stitched on tapestry, it calls forth the presence of the Sacred. The Pattern recalls the visionary realm, and the visionary realm is often one of patterns because it manifests the unity of the parts in the whole. By creating patterns *within* patterns, it manifests different levels of unity – the unfolding of the One into its different layers of complexity in multiplicity.

The most obvious example of this is the Flower of Life (Fig. 13.5), which consists of interlocking circles which expand outward from a single centre. This design manifests the fundamental unity underlying all of creation, and the progression of the One into the many, with no inherent loss of unity, since the circle re-emerges at a higher level and its oneness is sustained. It does this geometrically through the regular expansion of circles in space.

My own experience of Pattern in Tribal culture was sudden and profound. The first time I had ever really experienced open-eye visions for an extended period (more than six hours) was after ceremoniously ingesting ayahuasca. My first open-eye visions were of patterns – the exact same *'kene'* patterns which Shipibo-Conibo women stitch onto their clothing and tapestries. In my case, I was gazing at one such pattern on the *vegetalista's* clothing when it expanded across my entire field of vision. I saw the web of life which embraces all living things in the womb-like matrix of the ancient Goddess. I was so moved by this visionary pattern that I painted its every detail in a work called *The Vine of the Dead.*

In later journeys with the plant, I spent many timeless moments marvelling at the synesthetic translation of an *icaros* (or shaman's song in the Shipibo-Conibo tradition) into complex patterns of glowing light, incredibly bright and complex. Seemingly impossibly, these filled my entire field of vision, while moving diagonally in a slow 'stop-start' motion. The patterns were formed from precise geometrical shapes, distinguished by strong glowing colours of different hue and vibration. Some resembled Navajo weavings, others were so complex as to resemble sacred writing.

What is so unique about Fuchs' *Chronos* painting is that, even though it possesses Composition, it gives equal emphasis to Pattern – which is usually reserved for Tribal cultures. Nevertheless, Fuchs had managed to create a large coherent composition from these small square drawings, each a world onto itself.

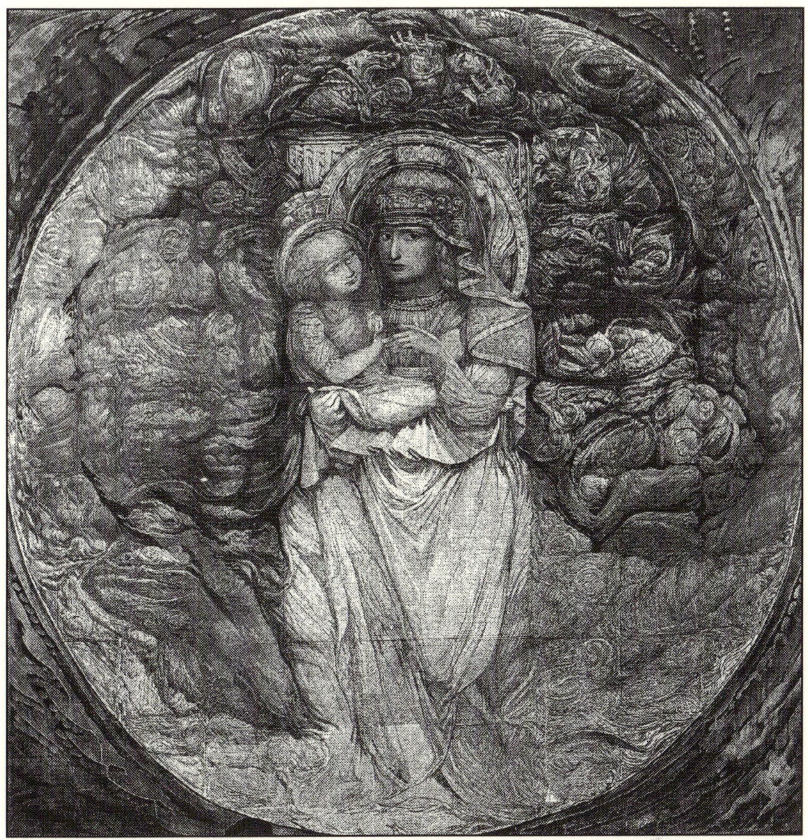

Fig. 13.2 - Ernst Fuchs: *The Virgin of the Apocalypse* 1988

By the time we had laid down several glazes, reworking the volumes in white casein after each coloured glaze, the underlying square pattern had receded from view. The grid became yet another layer of 'unseen lines' which nevertheless influence the movement of the forms.

It is for this reason that I also worked on several paintings in the Apocalypse Chapel – and failed to notice that *they too* possessed underlying square grids. This is especially true of *The Virgin of the Apocalypse* and *The Angel of History*. It was only years later, when I came across the original drawings, that I 'saw' how Fuchs had also created these compositions through a collage of many small square cards.

When we focus upon *The Virgin of the Apocalypse* (fig. 13.2), the halo and face of the Christ child are clearly composed *within* the space of a perfect square. The same is true of the Madonna's hand, head, shoulder and so on, so that her face lies *exactly at the centre* of a 3 x 3 square (called the 'magic square' in sacred geometry). The square's outer limits are clearly drawn and accentuated through the contrast of light and dark. Thus, the face of the Goddess, as a unity, appears at the very centre, while her body expands outward harmoniously through space, with the aid of these constant square measures.

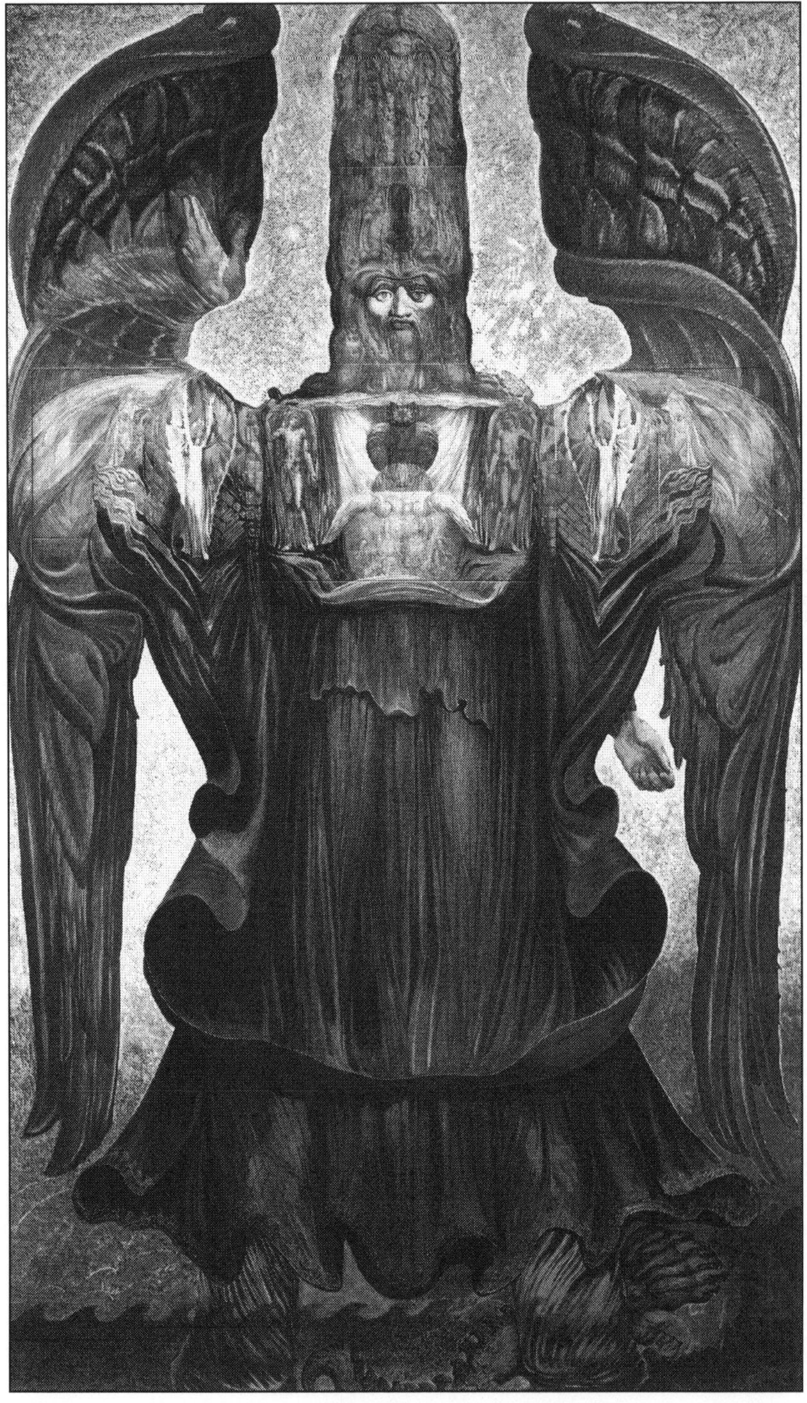

Fig. 13.3 - Ernst Fuchs: *The Angel of History* 1992

A close look at *The Angel of History* (Fig. 13.3) shows the same technique, as do his large masterworks, *Job and the Judgement of Paris* (Fig. 18.23) and *The Triumph of Christ*. In the case of these latter drawings from the mid-sixties, Fuchs explained to me once that he began drawing from *one point* and the image just kept on expanding. Thus, *The Triumph Of Christ* began with the unicorn's eye, he said, and *Job and the Judgement of Paris* with the central figures. Fuchs kept adding rectangular sheets around the latter composition to constantly increase its size.

An examination of Moreau's work reveals that he often did the same thing. Many of the major works in the *Musée Gustave Moreau* were fully painted, then the canvas was restretched and expanded to incorporate new elements in a larger outlaying composition. This is true of *The Argonauts*, *The Pretenders*, *The Daughters of Thespius* and especially *Jupiter and Semele*. Over time, the artist's circle of vision *expanded* to encompass more and more elements on its periphery. At the same time, he was plunging *deeper* into the original centre.

III. Sacred Geometry – *Ad Triangulum*

It is not by mere co-incidence that Blake (and many others before him) depicted the Divine Creator bending down to measure out the cosmos with a pair of compasses. Plato is reported to have said, *"God ever geometrizes."*[1] And the feminine figure of Wisdom says in the Book of Proverbs: *"The Lord possessed me in the beginning of his way, before his works of old... When he prepared the heavens, I was there: when he drew a circle upon the face of the depth."* (Prov 8:22-27).

If an artist wishes to create a harmonious cosmos in their work, then they must begin with a compass and straight rule in hand. Gothic masons were initiated into their craft by demonstrating a knowledge of certain key geometrical constructions.

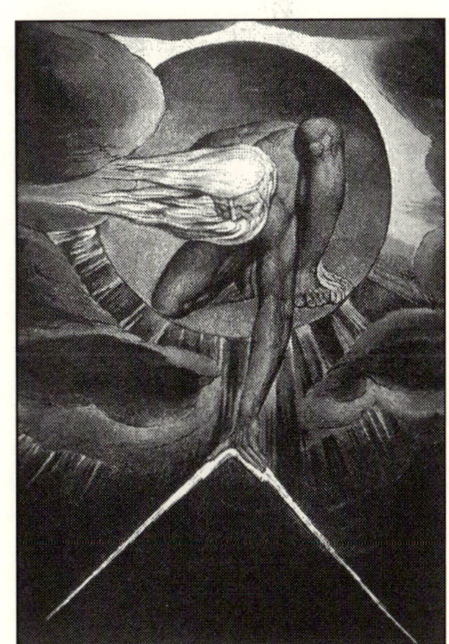

Fig. 13.4 - William Blake: *The Ancient of Days* 1794

This is also true of painting, as evidenced in Pierfrancesco Alberti's engraving from the early 1600's (Fig. 9.4), where we saw how young artists at the *Accademia di Pittura* had to compose geometrical shapes on their tablet. Carlo Maratta's image of the *studiosi del disegno* (Fig. 9.1) showed, as well, a young artist in the left foreground, inscribing a hexagram in a circle. This image is clearly inspired by Raphael's depiction of Euclid in *The School of Athens* (Fig. 10.21), where the Greek geometer inscribes an interesting and mysterious variation of the hexagram on his tablet. The memorization and construction of such shapes, as we shall see, formed part of the apprentice's initiation into his craft.

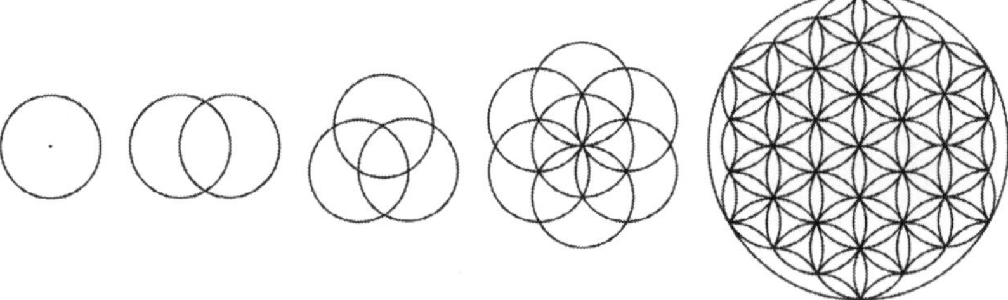

Fig. 13.5 - From Circle to Vesica Piscis, Tripod of Life, Seed of Life and Flower of Life

Sacred Geometry is nothing less than the attempt to create the world – a perfect world, one that existed before the Fall; a world without flaw, which will exist again when heaven comes down to earth as the New Jerusalem. Each Gothic cathedral manifests the heavenly kingdom on earth, as a perfect *'ordo et equilibrium'* (in the words of Bernard de Clairvaux). This is true of *all* temples from *all* traditions – they manifest sacred space as a perfectly ordered and harmonious cosmos.

Hence, the starting place of Sacred Geometry is the starting place of all creation – *Omnis ab Uno* – the harmonious self-multiplication of the One into the many ('All from One'), both in space and in time. For the Visionary artist, a blank canvas offers the possibility of re-living the creation, of inscribing a circle on the face of the depths and harmoniously arranging space in accord with the divine will. Like the *artifex principalis*, the artist strives to continually expand the creation while maintaining a unity of the parts in the whole.

Opening his perception to Divine Sight, the Visionary Artist sees vision as the active creation of the world, rather than the passive reception of it. To make a point in the middle of space is to establish a centre for the Divine Eye, from whence all vision will flow forth. And to draw a circle around that point is to express the infinite possibilities of shape and form that may emerge in the surrounding visual space.

With compass in hand, the next stroke cuts the perfect circle into meaningful parts – but where to begin? From the matrix of this circle, an infinite variety of shapes may emerge, to measure out the surrounding space in regular proportions. For the ancient Babylonians, the next stroke was clear and decisive. Using the same measure of the compass, the sharp tip was placed on the side of the circle, and a second circle was drawn through the centre of the first, creating the *vesica piscis*. Originally one, the first circle had now become two (Fig. 13.5).

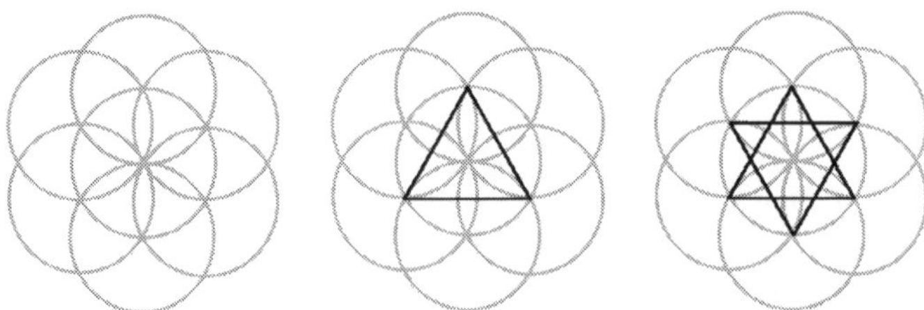

Fig. 13.6 - The Emergence of the Triangle and Hexagram from the Seed of Life

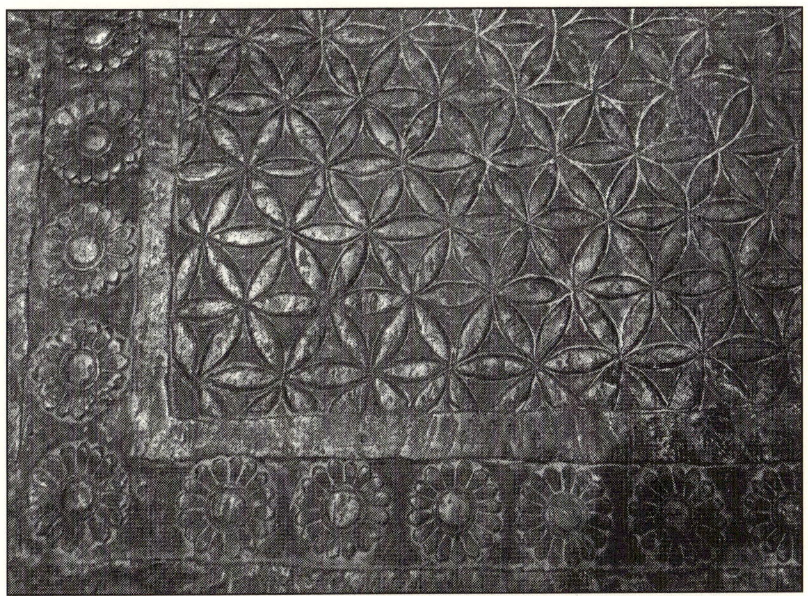

Fig. 13.7 - Threshold Stone to Chamber 1 of Ashurbanipal's Palace in Nineveh, c. 645 BCE

Repeating this procedure, with the sharp tip on the upper intersection of the two circles, another circle was drawn through the centres of the other two, thus creating the Tripod of Life. From the new intersection on the primordial circle, this procedure was repeated, drawing more circles around the primordial circle, until six circles were evenly distributed around the first, creating the seven-circled Seed of Life (Fig. 13.5).

From here, the circles could be multiplied in all directions, forming the Flower of Life, with nineteen circles in its hexagonal arrangement. A series of *six-petalled* flowers appear within its circumference (Fig. 13.5). Returning to the circle at the innermost centre of the Flower and Seed of Life, three points of the six-petalled flower were connected with a straight rule to inscribe *the first of all regular polygons* in the circle – *the triangle*. In fact, two triangles could be inscribed, one upright and the other inverted (the 'turned triangle') to create *the hexagram* (Fig. 13.6).

In Ashurbanipal's Palace in Nineveh, the Threshold Stone to Chamber 1 (Fig. 13.7) shows how the Assyrians were indeed aware of the Flower of Life construction. Meanwhile, the Stela of Ur Nammu (Fig. 13.8) depicts a six-pointed star above the crescent moon: a star which could only have been created with a knowledge of the hexagram. The stela is at least 4,000 year's old.*

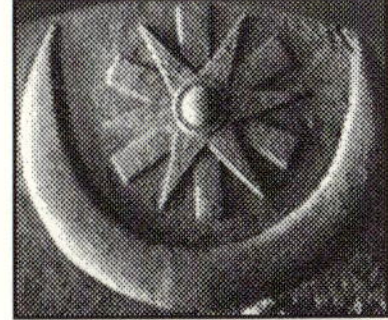

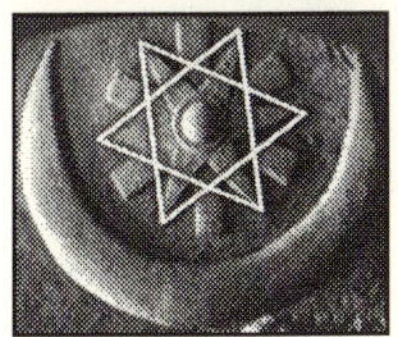

Fig. 13.8 - Stela of Ur Nammu c. 2030 BCE

*Despite frequent claims that The Flower of Life in The Osirian Temple at Abydos is 6,000 years old, it probably dates from the 1st century CE (though accurate dating is difficult).

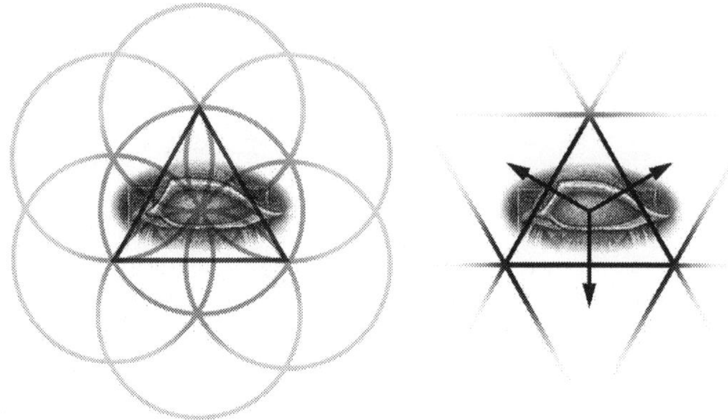

Fig. 13.9 - The Emergence of the Triangle from the Circle, and its *Ad Triangulum* Measure of Space in Extramission Vision

But, more importantly, Babylonia's entire system of measurement was sexagesimal – based on 60 units – a system that clearly emerges from the Seed of Life and its *six-fold* division of the circle. We today still use the sexagesimal division to measure out all of time and space, whether that be the circular year of 360 days (plus 4 and quarter interstitial days added) or the 360 degrees of our circular horizon.

The Seed of Life makes a hexagonal grid of circles, where each hexagon may be evenly divided into a hexagram of two opposing triangles. If we focus back down to the primordial circle at the centre of creation, and visualize the hexagram within its circular confines, then we arrive at *a six-fold division of space*, with each angular division of space being 60°, to make a total of 360° (Fig. 13.10).

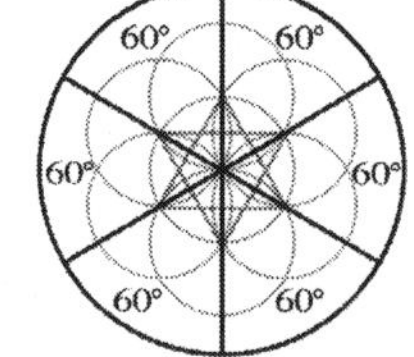

Fig. 13.10 - Six-fold Division of Space to 6 x 60°

What the ancient Babylonians discovered, sometime back in the dawning mists of time, was the Divine or Hieratic division of space *into triangles*. The Seed of Life's hexagonal grid is, in fact, *a grid of perfect equilateral triangles*, which measures out space (to use the term of the Gothic masons) in a manner that is distinctly *ad triangulum* – from the triangle.

When we visualize the Divine Eye as that central point from which vision flows – actively creating all space and time – then the triangle emerges as the first sacred shape to measure out its endless expanse. This singular triangle surrounding the Eye of God may, in fact, be multiplied infinitely in all directions, forming an *ad triangulum* grid (Fig. 13.9) which creates three distinct dimensions in axonometric perspective. To visualize Islamic patterns or Gothic ornaments within that grid is to carve out sacred shapes in a Hieratic space that is divinely-triangular.

From the circle, the triangle was the first of all regular polygons to emerge. But a whole variety of regular polygons may arise within the Seed of Life. Each of these polygons is called 'regular' because, by definition, its outermost points may be inscribed in a circle. When we geometrically construct a regular polygon, a whole matrix of circles is needed to determine the specific points which are then connected by lines into fixed shapes.

Typically, we recognize a regular shape by noting the number of sides, but it also possesses an equal number of points (vertices). Instead of a many-sided shape, we may visualize each regular polygon as a star with multiple rays reaching out to so many distinct points an equal distance from the centre. Each reveals how the One at the centre self-multiplies into the many, and how the space surrounding the Divine Eye crystallizes into a different shape of sacred and harmonious proportions. As the rays multiply, so too do the number of outermost points, creating star bursts on the order of 1:3 (triangle), 1:4 (square) and so on. The crystallized shapes most typical of Hieratic art are:

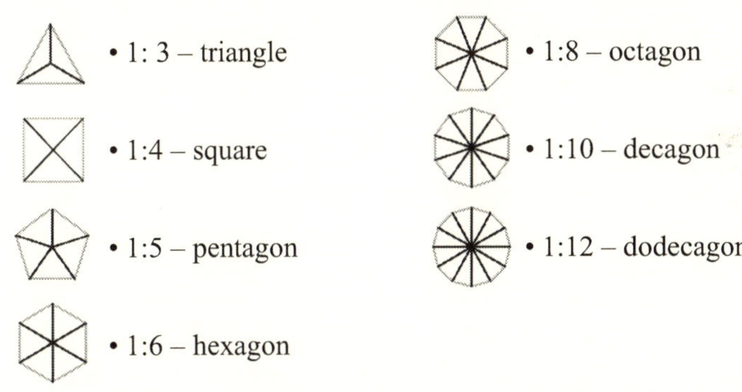

Once we move beyond the dodecagon, the shape becomes so consistently uniform as to be almost indistinguishable from the circle. (For this reason, many Colour Wheels use the dodecagon, since twelve is the greatest number of coloured shapes that we can conveniently hold in our mind).

IV. Sacred Geometry – *Ad Quadratum*

In the above list, we are missing the movement from one to two (1:2). In a line segment, the mid-point is equidistant from the ends, giving us a spatial visualization of the primordial movement from one to two – but a line segment is not a regular polygon. Nevertheless, the line segment does play a key role in another measure of space, which the Gothic masons called *ad quadratum* – from the square.

Aside from the Babylonian division of space into six 60° triangles to form an *ad triangulum* grid, a second division of the primordial circle was discovered in ancient times, creating another, distinct grid measure. *To divide space into the square,* the first geometers began by cutting the primordial circle *with a line segment* (Fig. 13.11).

Proceeding, then, with a straight rule rather than a compass, a vertical line is drawn *through* the centre of the primordial circle, dividing it into two

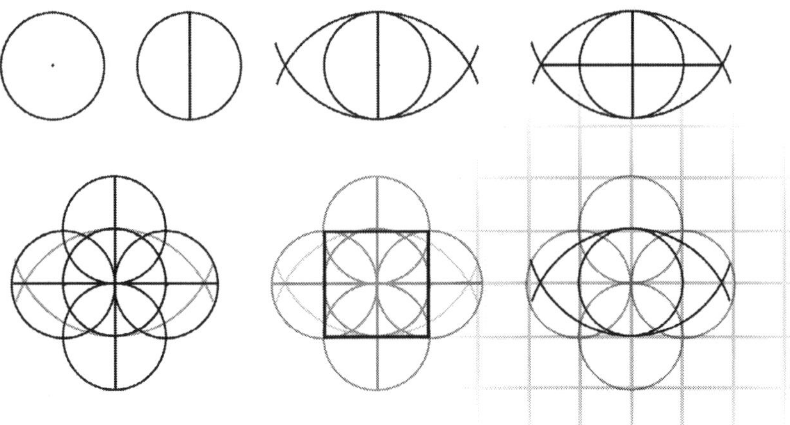

Fig. 13.11 - The Emergence of the Square from the Circle, and its *Ad Quadratum* Measure of Space

equal halves. Expanding the compass to the entire height or diameter of the circle, the sharp tip is placed at the bottom (where the circle is intersected by the vertical) and a semi-circular arc is drawn from the top to both sides. The same procedure is repeated, now with the sharp tip at the top, to draw another semi-circular arc from the bottom to both sides, thus completing an *oculus* or eye-like shape around the primordial circle. Through this construction, we may imagine that the Divine Eye has, in fact, momentarily been visualized.

With a straight rule, a horizontal line is now drawn from one corner of the eye to the other, dividing the original circle into four equal parts. Returning the compass to its original size, four circles are now drawn, each with its centre on one of the four cardinal points, and its circumference passing through the centre of the original circle. As a result, the central circle now contains *four petals*, whose outermost tips may be connected to form a square.

This procedure of 'squaring the circle' may be repeated indefinitely, forming an infinite *ad quadratum* grid of large squares. More lines may be drawn through the centre of each four-petalled flower, to create a finer mesh of squares, dividing each circle into four equal parts (like an *Irish Cross*). Returning then to the primordial circle at the centre of creation, we see that the Divine Eye *has envisioned a different space,* with a different shape as its measure (Fig. 13.12). From the centre, space has emerged as a squared circle, with a cross at its centre, so that all things now exist in a *four-fold division of space,* each quadrant measuring out a 90° angle of the whole (totalling 360°).

This *ad quadratum* division of space closely resembles our own experience of the world, where the horizon traverses our vision laterally, and gravity makes us stand vertically, so that our eye is constantly viewing Nature through crossed lines in the circle. Indeed, we shape our whole environment with this measure, constructing cubic buildings and quadratic furniture, to more easily navigate our earthly existence. In this sense, the *ad quadratum* grid delineates a space that is human, all-too-human... Nevertheless, this measure still provides us with a link to the higher realm. Even as the square

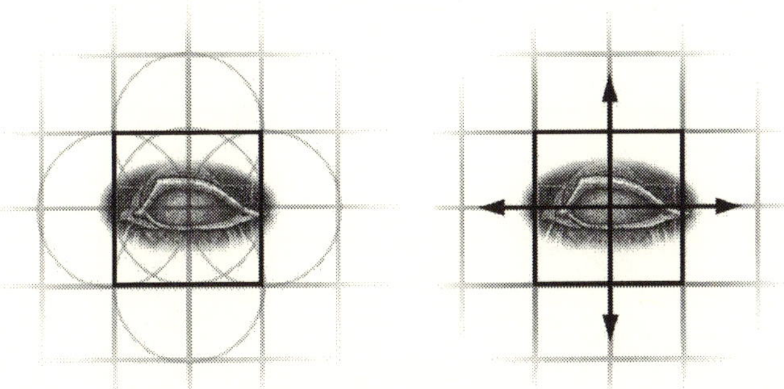

Fig. 13.12 - The *Ad Quadratum* Measure of Space in Extramission Vision

gives shape to our worldly experience, so may we attempt to transcend it, by gaining entry into the *ad triangulum* realm of the Sacred.

When we look at sacred architecture, we come to realize that a great variety of cultures carved out their temples in *ad triangulum* space. This is true of the pyramids, pyramidions and obelisk-peaks of Egypt, the ziggurats of Babylonia, the Maya pyramids and their unique triangular corbelled arches, Buddhist temples such as Borobudar in Java, Hindu temples of the Chola Empire, Gothic spires and the triangular pediments atop Greek temples.

Although sacred architecture must make concessions to gravity by incorporating vertical columns and rectangular doorways in *ad quadratum* space, the uppermost levels often aspire to more mystical measures, like the upward-pointing triangle or heavenly circle. The Middle Ages witnessed a revolution in sacred architecture, when Gothic architects *rounded the triangle* into the pointed or 'ogival' arch. This geometrical construction led to such Gothic innovations as the ribbed vault and the flying buttress – all of which gave Gothic architecture its unique style. Meanwhile the circular stained-glass window or *rosace* lay at the heart of the cathedral's elevation, giving each steepled facade its true centre.

The Renaissance is famed for its hemispheric domes, of which Brunelleschi's ribbed octagonal dome over the Duomo is one of its greatest achievements. Brunelleschi, a *cognoscente* of antiquity, was inspired by the great dome of the Parthenon from ancient Rome, and indeed, domes of the hemispheric type were the hallmark of Roman architecture, which found countless variations in the Byzantine, Russian, Persian and Ottoman empires. The dome, imitating the vault of the heavens, measures out sacred space according to the Hieratic circle or sphere.

V. Pythagoras & Plato

Much of the life and thought of Pythagoras (c. 570 – 495 BCE) remains shrouded in mystery. His work has come down to us in fragments through oft-quoted sayings and designs. The most mysterious of his designs, without a doubt, is the Tetractys ('fourfold'), which yields multiple readings and interpretations.

The followers of Pythagoras regarded the Tetractys as sacred, and prayed to it with the words:

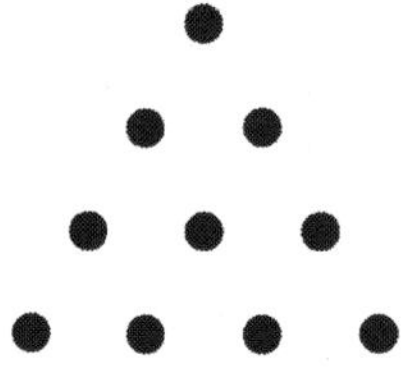

Fig. 13.13 - The Tetractys

"Bless us, divine number, thou who generated gods and men! O holy, holy Tetractys, thou that containest the root and source of the eternally flowing creation! For the divine number begins with the profound, pure unity until it comes to the holy four; then it begets the mother of all, the all-comprising, all-bounding, the first-born, the never-swerving, the never-tiring holy ten, the keyholder of all."[2]

It is evident that the design begins with the One (or Monad) at the top, which expands into two (the Dyad), then three (the Triad) to end with four (the Tetrad) which, taken together, make ten (the Decad). The transitions from one to four form the foundation of Pythagorean-Platonic harmony: the 1:2 *diapason*, the 2:3 *diapente* and the 3:4 *diatessaron*, which become harmonic ratios that not only govern the motion of the celestial spheres, but echo their eternal harmonies here below, through music in time, and painting in space (as we shall see in our chapters on Composition).

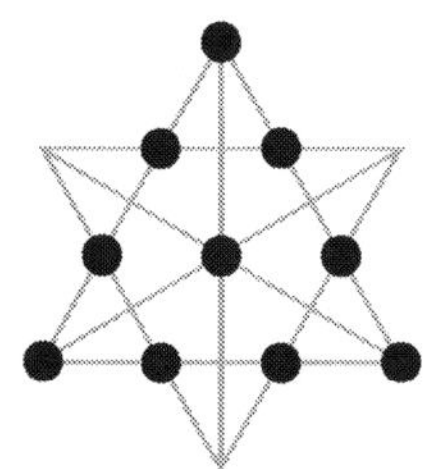

Fig. 13.14 - The Tetractys Drawn from the Hexagram in *Ad Triangulum* Space

When we attempt to draw the Tetractys (which the Pythagoreans surely did as part of their initiation), we soon become confused if we think sheerly in terms of *ad quadratum* space. In fact, the only way to properly draw a Tetractys is to imagine an invisible grid *of triangles*, which emerges most quickly from the hexagram. So, with the hexagram firmly in mind, all ten points may be marked out in *ad triangulum* space (Fig. 13.14). The drawing of the Tetractys is, in part, an initiation into a different, more Hieratic conception of space, visualizing its measure in triangles rather than squares.

In his *Timaeus*, Plato constructs an elaborate model of the cosmos to explain how the Divine Craftsman or Demiurge created this world in an orderly and harmonious manner. The basic constituents of the cosmos are the Four Elements, earth, water, air and fire. At a finer level, the Four Elements are, themselves, composed out of the Platonic Solids (Fig. 13.15), where the cube gives shape to the basic particles of earth, the icosahedron to water, the octahedron to air and the tetrahedron to fire (*Timaeus* 55d). Later, in an apocryphal dialogue called the *Epinomis*, Plato's pupil Xenocrates added the dodecahedron for the fifth element, the aether.

The Five Platonic Solids are the only regular convex polyhedra that may exist in three-dimensional space. In other words, if a point expands outward to a sphere, assuming a regular 3D shape, then this may only occur in five possible ways: as the tetrahedron (four triangles), the cube (six squares), the octahedron (eight triangles), the dodecahedron (twelve pentagons) and the icosahedron (twenty triangles).

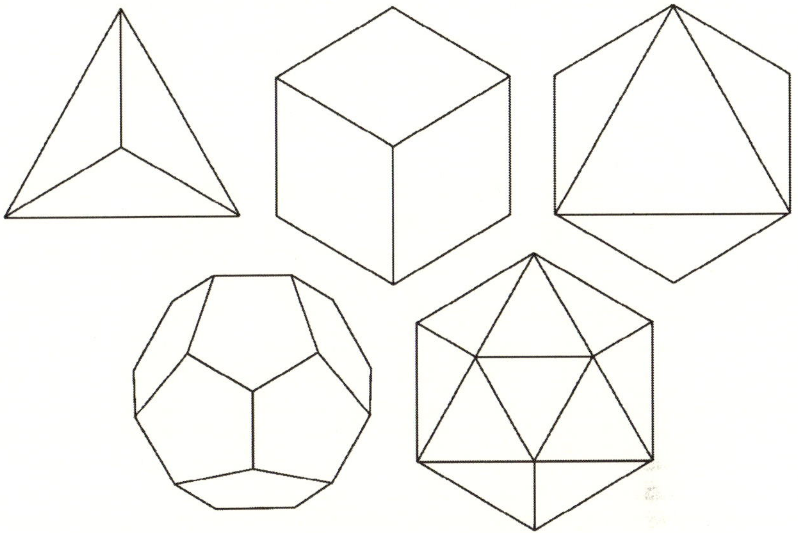

Fig. 13.15 - The Five Platonic Solids: The Tetrahedron, Cube, Octahedron, Dodecahedron and Icosahedron

If an initiate into the Mysteries wanted *to draw* these five shapes on a flat surface, they would have to resort, once more, to an *ad triangulum* grid, which creates the illusion of 3D space through axonometric perspective. Again, the easiest way to proceed is to draw a hexagram. However, we have to distinguish between the hexagram and the turned hexagram. Both of these shapes, when inscribed in the circle, divide 360° space into 60° sextants.

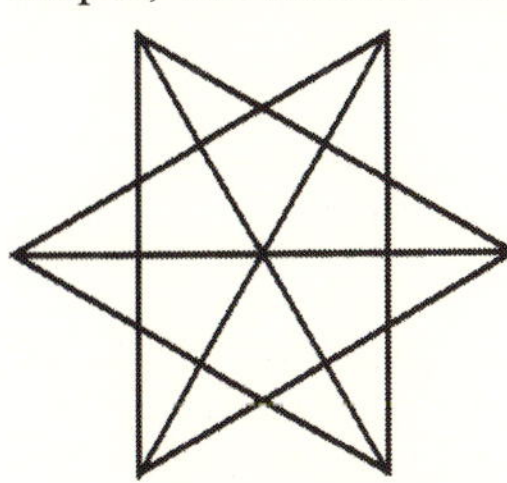

Fig. 13.16 - The Turned Hexagram

But, when we look at the three basic lines crossing through the centre, we notice that the turned hexagram (Fig. 13.16) has a central line oriented *toward the horizon*, while the regular hexagram (Fig. 13.17) has a central line oriented *toward the vertical* (the line of gravity or plumb line). If we try to use the turned hexagram as a template for our spatial grid, the diagonals of illusory depth would run *at a 60° angle to the horizon line*. This is not the ideal choice.

The easiest way for an initiate to draw the Five Platonic Solids on a flat surface is to begin with the *regular* hexagram. But (and this is a crucial observation), we must imagine, nevertheless, an *invisible* horizon line (a *fourth* line) cutting through the three central lines of the regular hexagram, to visualize the three axes of axonometric perspective against this horizon line. The diagonals of illusory depth will thus appear *at a 30° angle to the horizon line.*

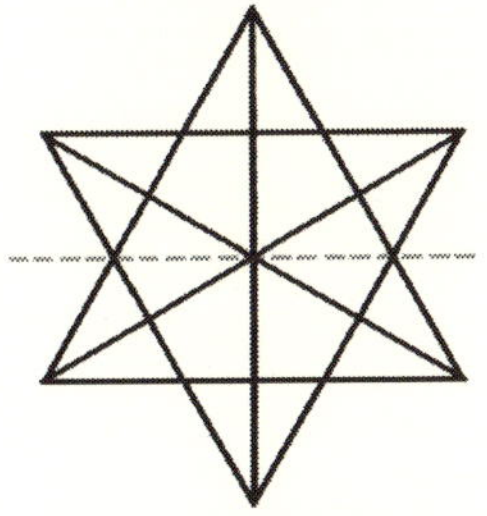

Fig. 13.17 - The Regular Hexagram with Horizon Line

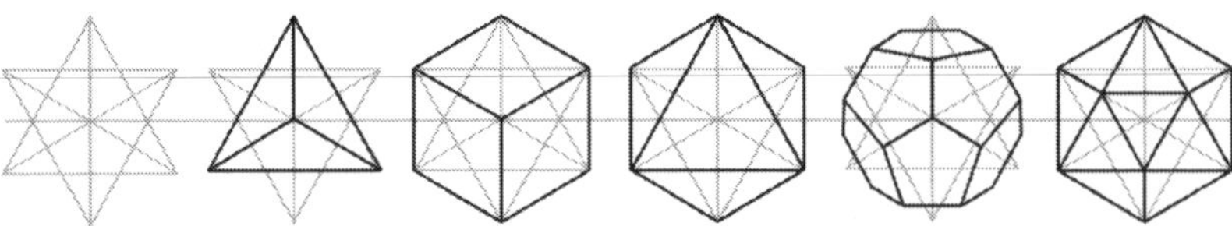

Fig. 13.18 - Regular Hexagram Guide Lines Creating
the Five Platonic Solids in Axonometric Perspective

Having lightly sketched the three axes and horizon line of the *regular* hexagram (these are all 'invisible lines' for the apprentice to memorize), the Five Platonic Solids (Fig. 13.18) can then be drawn in their *ad triangulum* sacred space. In all cases, the invisible horizon line *cuts through the centre*, allowing us to visualize the polyhedron as a 3D shape in perspectival space, where the outer edges converge on the horizon and other important points project up or down, forward or back.

As we shall see in our chapter on Hieratic Perspective, these Platonic Solids are arranged in *axonometric* perspective, which is *object-centered*, compared to Renaissance *linear* perspective, which is *viewer-centered*. Due to axonometric perspective, the Platonic Solids may take shape *equally in all directions, from a central point* in space (using an *ad triangulum* grid). The active visualization of these shapes proceeds, as if, from the Divine Eye at the centre of all creation. Meanwhile, linear perspective imitates what the *human* eye normally perceives, adjusting the diagonals according to *the viewer's* distance point from the horizon. It is a more Humanist form of perspective.

Returning to Plato's *Timaeus*, the Athenian philosopher sought out the most basic and fundamental 2D shapes from which to compose his Platonic Solids which, in turn, composed the Four Elements. These primordial shapes, we must remember, were created by the Divine Craftsman in the realm of the *Eidé* or Ideas (the Platonic forms or archetypes). From these eternally stilled and perfect shapes (existing in a higher realm of pure Being), the Demiurge then fashioned material imitations of them in time (existing in the lower realm of Becoming). These primordial 2D shapes, originating in the higher sphere, are thus absolutely perfect, sacred and Hieratic.

Plato does not fail to notice that the tetrahedron (four triangles, making fire), the octahedron (eight triangles, making air), and the icosahedron (twenty triangles, making water) are mostly made up of *equilateral triangles*, while the cube (six squares, making earth) derives from *the square* (Fig. 13.19). Since he only has Four Elements, Plato ignores the aether, with its dodecahedron of twelve pentagons, which Xenocrates later added in the *Epinomis*.

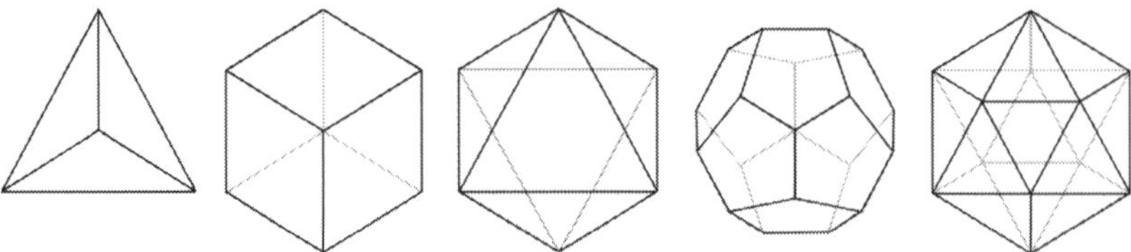

Fig. 13.19 - The Tetrahedron, Cube, Octahedron, Dodecahedron and Icosahedron:
The First, Third and Fifth made of Triangles; the Second made of Squares

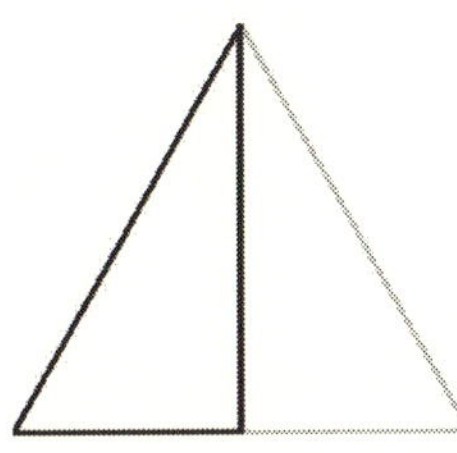

Fig. 13.20 -
The Platonic Half-equilateral

The two most basic and fundamental shapes, Plato decides, are *the equilateral triangle* (divided in two) and *the square* (divided in two). The first creates two smaller right-angled scalene triangles (which Plato simply calls *half-equilaterals* – Fig. 13.20), and the second creates two smaller right-angled isosceles triangles (which he calls *half-squares* - Fig. 13.21). After further discussion, he decides that, ultimately, the equilateral triangle is 'the most perfect shape' (Timaeus 53c, d).

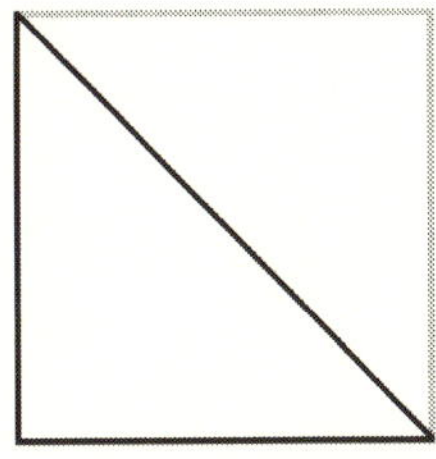

Fig. 13.21 -
The Platonic Half-square

The reason why Plato reduces the Platonic Solids to scalene and isosceles triangles is that he wants to demonstrate the mechanism and geometry behind the transformation of one element to another. By breaking down the Elements and their component Solids to their most basic geometrical shapes (the triangles), these can be re-composed into other Solids and Elements. But water, air and fire are composed of triangles that are *half-equilateral*, while earth is uniquely composed of triangles that are *half-square.*

The earth then, as the lowest and most mundane of the four, cannot be re-composed into the other three, while the upper three can variously transform and metamorphose. In a long difficult passage he demonstrates how this occurs geometrically. The upshot of all this is very important for our understanding of pictorial space in Sacred Geometry.

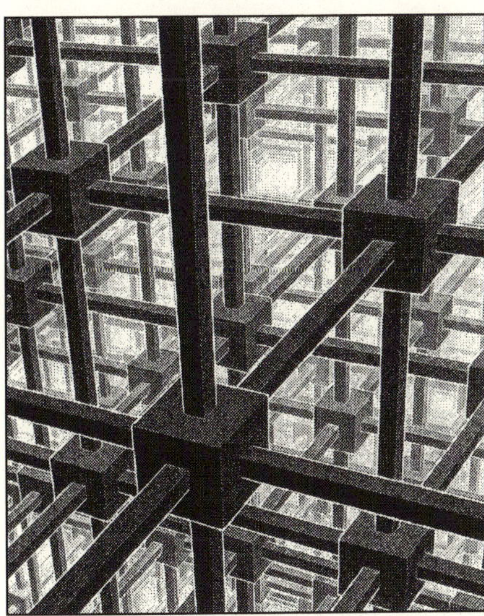

Fig. 13.22 - M. C. Escher:
Cubic Space Division 1953

First of all, the *Timaeus* constructs a cosmology where *the square* (composed of half-squares) holds a unique place as the basic geometrical shape *of Earth*, the lowest of the Four Elements. The *ad quadratic* or cubic division of space, then, is typical for human perception and the Humanist visualization of space. Indeed, most people can visualize a 3D lattice of squares and cubes, to measure out their spatial field (Fig. 13.22). Aristotle referred to this in his *Physics* as 'the six directions': up, down, left, right, forward and back (*Physics*, III, 5, 205b 24) which he saw as absolute, and present in all of Nature, not just human perception.

Meanwhile, the *equilateral triangle* (composed of half-equilaterals) is the 'most perfect shape', composing the higher Elements of Water, Air and Fire. The *ad triangulum* or *tetrahedral division of space* is where the Divine Creator visualizes *the higher shapes*, the tetrahedra, octahedra and icosahedra that structure the higher Elements. Only sacred craftsmen of great skill and imagination can visualize a 3D lattice that fashions and carves out these much more complex shapes.

For example, 3D space may indeed be visualized as an infinite lattice *of tetrahedra* (touching point to point). Or, as an infinite lattice *of octahedra* (touching edge to edge). Or, these two *may be combined* into a lattice that Buckminster Fuller called the Isotropic Vector Matrix (Fig. 13.23). But it is only in certain rare cultures and periods of history, like Islamic and Gothic art, that craftsmen rise to such lofty heights.

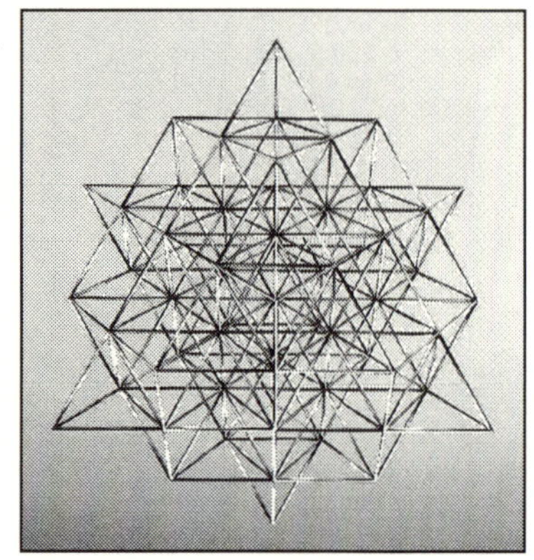

Fig. 13.23 - Isotropic Vector Matrix

Second of all, Plato's *Timaeus* gives us *two primordial triangles*, the half-equilateral and the half-square, both of which possess a horizontal base. If these two primordial triangles are multiplied infinitely in 2D space, then the half-equilaterals form an *ad triangulum* grid (with orthogonals running through it), while the half-squares forms an *ad quadratum* grid (with diagonals running through it). The diagonals in the *ad triangulum* grid possess *a 60° incline*, while the diagonals drawn into an *ad quadratum* grid possess *a 45° incline* (Fig. 13.24). When we turn to pictorial space and its harmonic division into regular polygons (which is to say, armature), this distinction will become crucial.

Plato recognized as early as the 3rd century BCE the existence of *ad triangulum* and *ad quadratum* grids (which would only receive these names in the 11th century Gothic period). These grids underlay the design of all ornament and art from most ancient times to the present day.

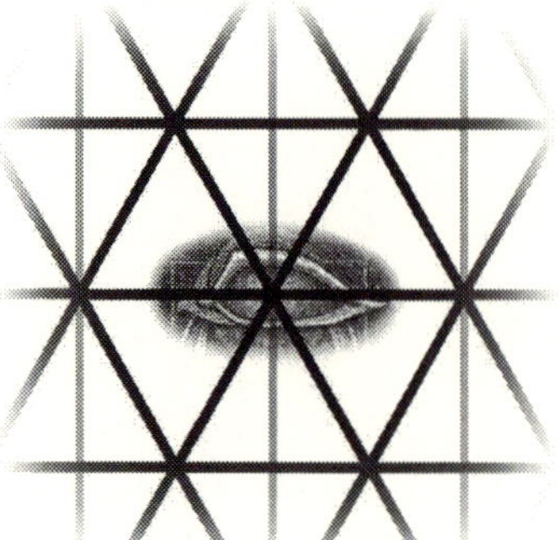

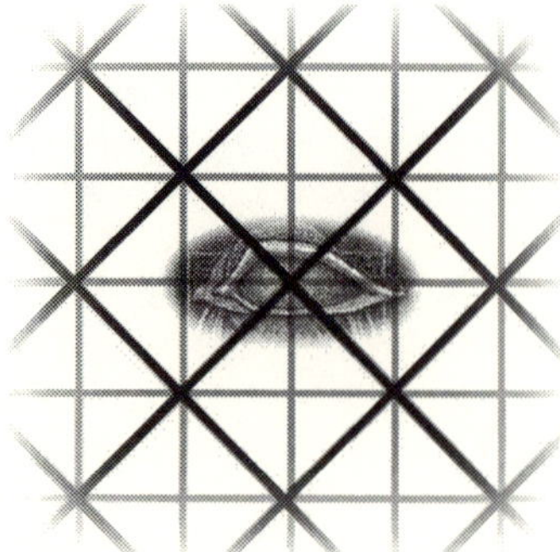

Fig. 13.24 - 60° *Ad Triangulum* and 45° *Ad Quadratum* Grids

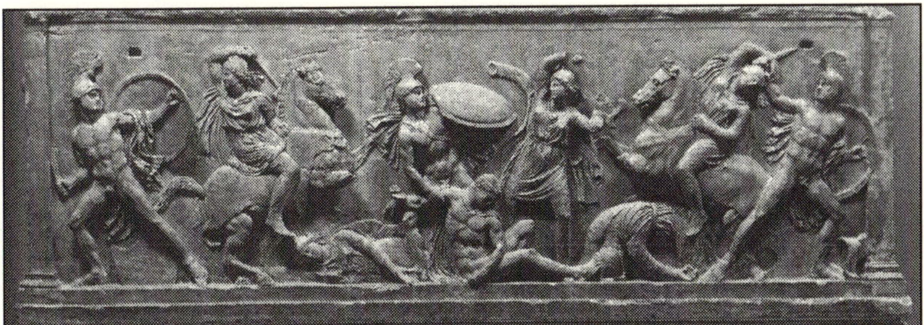

Fig. 13.25 - Greek Sarcophagus: *Battle Between the Greeks and Amazons* c. 330 BCE

VI. The Armature of a Roman Sarcophagus

I have spent many hours standing in front of a Greek Sarcophagus in Vienna's *Kunsthistorishes Museum*, marvelling at its organization of pictorial space. To allegorically portray the death of its recipient, the frieze depicts the *Battle between the Greeks and Amazons*. Such large marble sarcophagi depicting the *Amazonomachy* are typical of Greek and Roman funerary monuments.

The *istoria* comes from Homer's *Iliad*, where the Greek hero Bellerophon briefly engages the Amazons: *"Then he* [Bellerophon] *massacred the Amazons, women who rival men."* (Bk. VI, line 187). In this composition, three male warriors (all nude) fight to protect their fallen comrade in the centre, while two equestrian and one standing Amazon (all clothed) retaliate, though two of their sisters have fallen. To organize the nine figures in this long frieze, the ancient craftsman resorted to underlying geometrical lines and shapes.

These invisible lines of armature are commonly referred to, in other European languages, as the *charpente* (French), *trame* (Italian), or *Bildkonstruktion* (German). From ancient friezes to modern painting, a great tradition has grown around the harmonious construction of pictorial space through underlying lines which, alas, have vanished with time...

As we can see in this example, the bounding pictorial space is basically rectangular. During the Classical and Renaissance periods, there was a distinct preference for rectangular frames. Although square and circular compositions were not unknown during the Renaissance (the *tondo* or round painting witnessed a brief resurgence in Michelangelo's day), the newly-discovered *linear perspective* created a distinct preference for the rectangle, which aided in the construction of perspectival space. This is so characteristic of Classical and Renaissance art, that we may speak of armatures in *rectangular* frames as *Humanist* Compositions.

Meanwhile, Medieval works of art manifest a distinct preference for square frames. These were often inscribed with an invisible circle, where a variety of regular polygons could be inscribed: triangles, pentagrams, hexagrams, turned hexagrams, octagrams and turned octagrams. When we examine the geometric shapes underlying the Gothic style, it quickly reveals its Moorish roots. To truly understand Gothic compositions and their harmonious division of space, we will first have to turn to Islamic art and

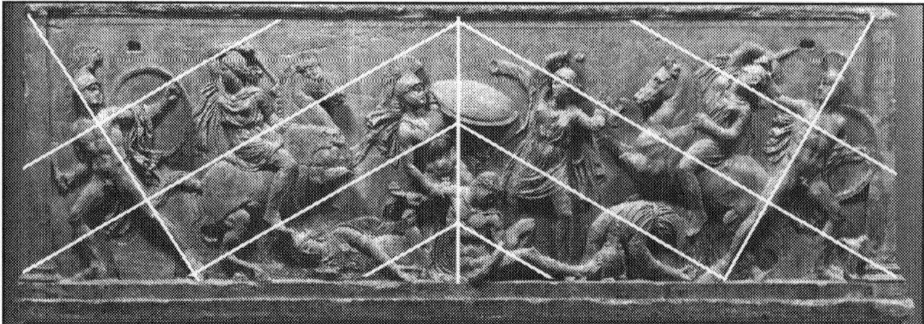

Fig. 13.26 - Greek Sarcophagus: *Battle Between the Greeks and Amazons* c. 330 BCE

ornament. All these examples will encourage us to speak of *square* frames as typical for *Hieratic* Compositions.

Returning to the Greek Sarcophagus (Fig. 13.26), we can immediately sense the presence of a wide isosceles triangle, ascending from the bottom corners and meeting at the central apex. Passing through the dynamic movement of the rearing horses, these corner diagonals lead the eye upward to the apex, where it may then descend along the main vertical to the principle figure in the composition. More diagonals, parallel to the first, give the composition the overall appearance of a Greek pediment, such as the frieze above the Parthenon.

Meanwhile, two bracketting figures at the extreme left and right assume 'the heroic diagonal', twisting around two diagonals that extend from the base of their out-thrust legs to the top right and left corners.

When we take out a protractor and measure these principle diagonals, we arrive at some interesting conclusions. First of all, the heroic diagonals are perpendicular to the wide isosceles triangle, crossing it at a 90° angle. As for the wide isosceles triangle itself, it ascends from the horizontal base at an angle of 30°. As a result, the heroic diagonals ascend at a 60° angle.

All of this would suggest that the craftsman was thinking in terms of an *ad triangulum* division of space. As we can see in Figure 13.27, the 60° heroic diagonals create two half-equilateral triangles from the sides of the composition (derived from the angle of the bracketting figures). If we extend an *ad triangulum* grid from these diagonals, we arrive at a constant measure of pictorial space. From the bottom of the warriors' out-thrust legs, two full equilateral triangle rise to the top of the third register then descend again,

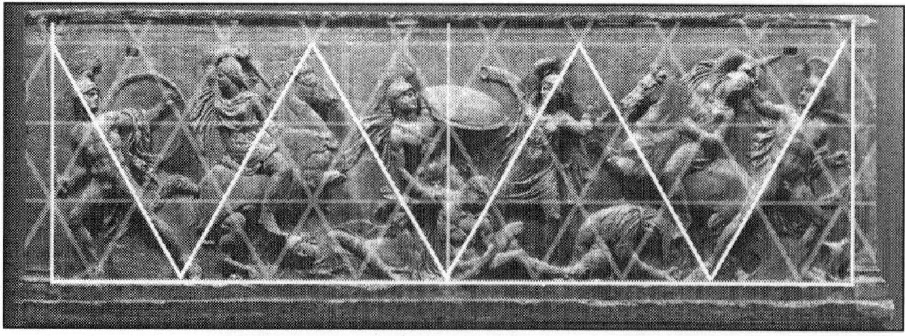

Fig. 13.27 - Greek Sarcophagus: *The Battle Between the Greeks and Amazons* c. 330 BCE

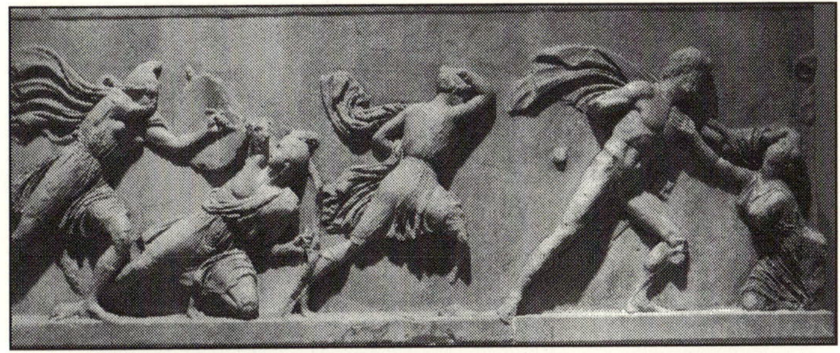

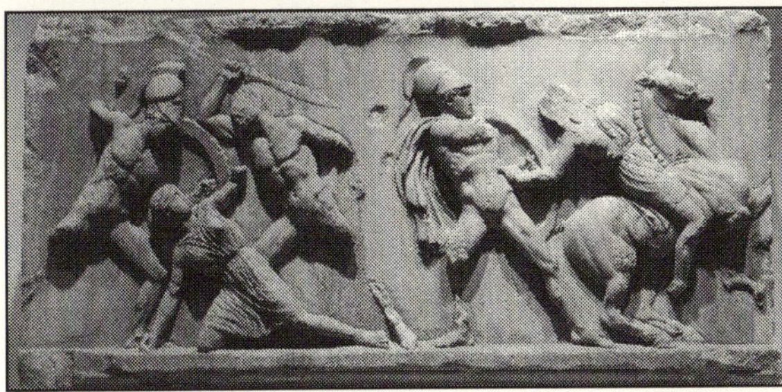

Fig. 13.28 - Mausoleum at Halicarnassus: Two Panels Depicting *The Battle Between the Greeks and Amazons* 350 BCE

meeting at the half-way point at the bottom. Finer triangular divisions give us the three horizontal divisions (these horizontals are part of the *ad triangulum* grid), where the tops of all the figures fit within the upper register, and the fallen Amazons fit within the bottom register.

VII. The Mausoleum at Halicarnassus

According to Antipater of Sidon, the *Mausoleum at Halicarnassus* was one of the Seven Wonders of the Ancient World. Built in 350 BCE to house the remains of Mausolus (from whence the word 'mausoleum' comes to us), it employed four of Hellenia's most renowned sculptors: Leochares, Bryaxis, Timotheus and Skopas. The two blocks reproduced here (Fig. 13.28) are taken from a long frieze which depicts, appropriately enough, the *Amazonomachy*. Once again, the heroic diagonal is in full evidence, inviting a reconstruction of the possible lines underlying the compositions.

A quick glance (or *coup d'oeil...*) at both compositions suggests that the heroic diagonals are, indeed, different. In the bottom example, the sculptor has resorted once more to the 60° diagonal, suggesting an *ad triangulum* measure of his space (Fig. 13.29). And indeed, at least three if not four of the figures follow this angle of inclination, as the diagonals rise to both the left and right.

In the top example, the inclination of the figures is much stronger. Measurement reveals an angle of 45° from the base (Fig. 13.29). This is very important, since it suggests that the sculptor began with an *ad quadratum* measure of space, drawing 45° diagonals into the square lattice. For the purpose of clarity, I have not traced out the *ad quadratum* grid, but only the diagonals at a 45° angle.

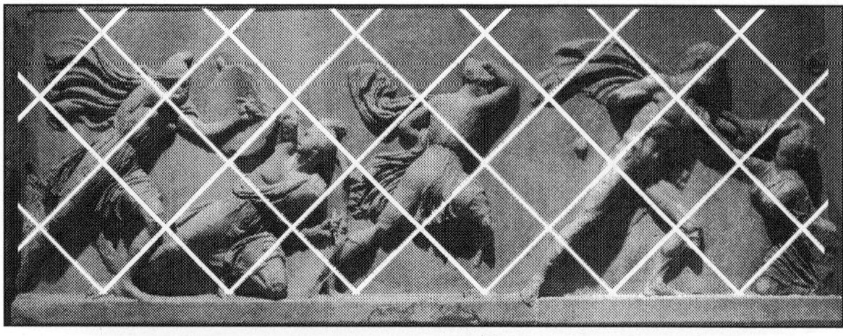

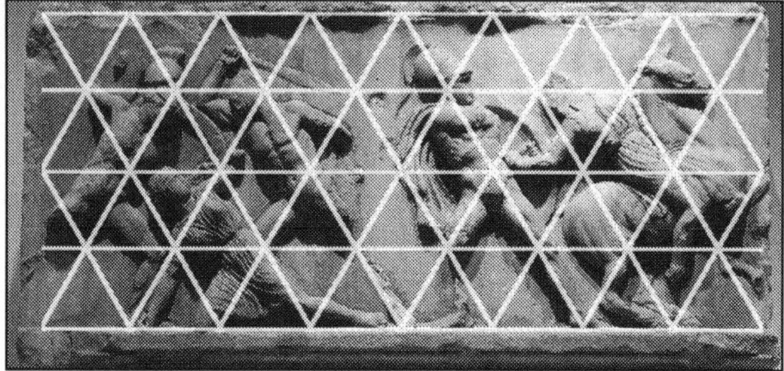

Fig. 13.29 - Mausoleum at Halicarnassus - 350 BCE
Top: 45° *Ad Quadratum* Diagonals; Bottom: 60° *Ad Triangulum* Diagonals

Which brings us to a very important point: *ad triangulum and ad quadratum grids are mutually exclusive*. There is no way to superimpose these two grids so that their lines meet up in a consistent manner. If an artist begins at the centre of their composition and marks out an *ad triangulum* grid, then he or she will not be able to mark out an *ad quadratum* grid that meshes with it.

In our initial construction of these grids, we noted that the *ad triangulum* grid emerges from a hexagonal matrix of circles generated by the Seed of Life. The central circle has *six petals*. Meanwhile, the *ad quadratum* grid divides the circle into two and then four parts, creating a flower with *four petals*. Even if both operations were to be carried out from the same centre (using, for example, different coloured lines), the two grids would not line up (except perhaps after every tenth circle, very far outside the picture plane).

This means that, when an artist begins a composition, they can only visualize it in a space that expands from the centre *in one of these two possible grids*. The triangles will generate 60° diagonals; the squares, 45° diagonals. In our active visualization and creation of the cosmos, only certain types of shape may emerge naturally and unforced from certain types of grid. As we shall see in our next chapter, other kinds of grid are indeed possible, such as the radial grids of Islamic art. But the curvilinear motifs that arise within their matrix will always be guided by invisible lines – to ensure them a higher order, harmony and beauty...

CHAPTER XIV
HIERATIC PATTERN & DESIGN IN ISLAMIC & GOTHIC ART

I. The Two Pens & Seven Principles

Over the years that we have met, A. Andrew Gonzalez and I have had many revealing conversations. In 2011, while walking through the stoney hilltop town of Eze in southern France, we discussed the spiralling motifs in his work. He related with great feeling a profound experience he had in the Black Rock desert at Burning Man, where the outlying mountains were covered with a cursive mystical script, like Kufic characters, that also appeared to him on human skin. He has since spent many years trying to recapture some of those mysterious glyphs in the heavenly architecture and graceful figures of his ethereal paintings.

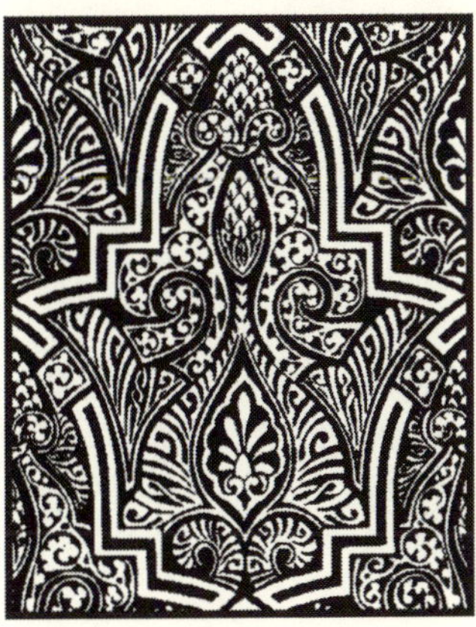

Fig. 14.1 - Alhambra Ornament from Jacob von Falke: *Aesthetik des kunstgewerbes* 1883

The relationship between entheogenic visions and Islamic art has long fascinated Western culture, and may be seen in such diverse places as the hookah-smoking *Odalisque with Slave* (1839) by Ingres to the Moorish architecture in Mati Klarwein's *Turkish Delight* (1970). The similarity between Islamic designs and entheogenic visions is startling, once recognized. Nevertheless, their shared motifs may be due to the fact that both portray the Sacred realm in its geometric aspect, its mysterious calligraphy and swirling vegetal forms.

In their book *Symmetries of Islamic Geometrical Patterns*, Abas and Salman speak of three major motifs in Islamic art.[1] First of all, there are Calligraphic

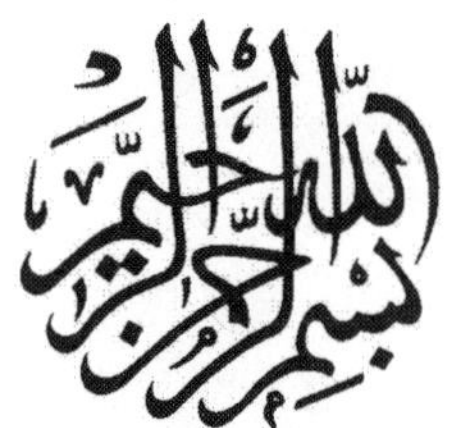
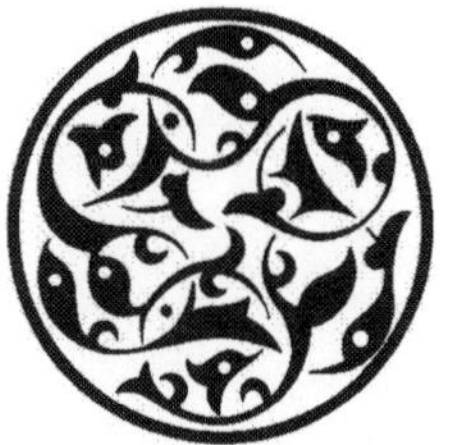
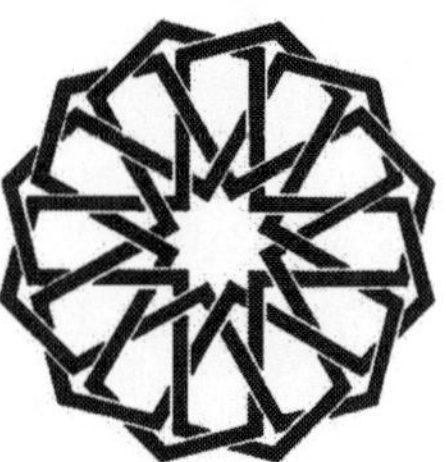

Fig. 14.2 - Islamic Calligraphy, Arabesque and Geometric Tessellation

compositions created from the letters of divine names (Allah, Mohammed) or from passages in the Koran. Second, there are Arabesques, which Titus Burckhardt describes as, *"sinuous and spiral forms more or less related to vegetable motifs."*[2] And last are the well-known Geometric Tessellations. *"The first,"* Burckhardt goes on to say, meaning Arabesques *"is all rhythm and fluidity and continuous melody, whereas the second* [of Tessellations] *is crystalline in nature: the radiating of lines from multiple geometrical foci recalls snowflakes or ice; it gives the impression of calm and freshness."*[3]

Today, scholars of Islamic Ornament consider the word *Arabesque* to be an out-dated but generally useful term – a broad category that encompasses the fourfold modern taxonomy of Calligraphic, Vegetal (or biomorphic), Geometric, and Figural motifs, practised in major historical centres like the Persian (Safavid), Ottoman and Moghul empires. The depiction of God and the prophets (especially the Prophet Mohammed) was forbidden by *Sharī-ah* law, but Persian and Moghul Miniatures abounded nevertheless in figural motifs.

Two major competing courts in the 16th century were the Safavid court of Shah Tasmasp I and the Ottoman court of Sultan Süleyman, each with its own court scriptorium (*kitābkhāna*) where painters (*naqqāsh*) and calligraphers (*khattat*) worked on illuminated manuscripts, carpet designs, and a variety of palace decorations. The Safavid artists of Tabriz continued to depict human figures until the 1544 victory of Sultan Süleyman over Shah Tasmasp I, forcing the Shah to dismiss most of his court poets, painters, and musicians, in accord with the aniconic edicts of the *Treaty of Amasya* (1555), and due, as well, to the Shah's own vaunted 'repentance' (*tawba*), despite the fact that he had studied painting in his youth and practiced as well as patronized the art.[4]

Just as Early Renaissance artists struggled to achieve the status and nobility of court poets (*Ut Pictura Poesis* – 'As is poetry, so is painting'), so did Islamic painters struggle for recognition with calligraphers, in a land where the Word of the Prophet was praised and esteemed above all else. Nevertheless, 'Abdi Beg Shirazi's 1543 poem 'The Excellence of Art' (in his *Rules of Alexander*) introduced the Theory of the Two *Qalams* or Pens:

"What is this key [of art] *? The tip of the qalam* [pen].
The qalam is an artist and a painter
God created two kinds of qalam:
The one, ravishing the soul, is from a plant
And has become the sugar cane for the scribe;
The other kind of qalam is from the animal,
And it has acquired its scattering of pearls from the fountain of life."[5]

Here, the painter's brush, which is made of animal fur, has the same weight and power as the poet's pen, made from the reed of plants. And, just as Calligraphy was recognized to have six known styles (*naskh, thuluth, muhaqqaq, rayhani, tawqi'* and *riqa'*), Painting was found to possess seven styles in all – which became known as 'The Seven Principles of Painting' (*haft aṣl-i naqqāshī*).

In the same poem, 'Abdi Beg Shirazi writes, *"Painting has seven principles; It is like the sky, which has seven spheres."*[6] That the artist has his eye fixed on the higher ideal, the upper world of Platonic forms called the *alam al-mithal* in the Sufi tradition, is confirmed by Mir Sayyid-Ahmad, who wrote of painters: *"They follow God's craft from the compass of the spheres to the surface of the earth. With their gazes fixed on creation, they take an image from every proto-type."*[7]

'Abdi Beg Shirazi did not actually name the seven principles of painting. But in 1557, the court poet Qutb al-Din Qissakhvan recorded each of the seven modes: *"As in calligraphy, which has six styles, in this* [painter's] *technique, seven 'styles' are to be found: islamī, khaṭā'i, farangī, faṣṣalī, abr, dāq, girih."*[8]

However, the only Persian artist known to have written a technical treatise on par with, say, Cennini's *Libro dell'arte*, was Sadiqi Beg Afshar in his *Canons of Painting* (Qānūn al-ṣuvar - 1597). And here, the list of seven styles is slightly different: *"First come islimī and khaṭā'i. You may then take as your third and fourth abr and vāq. This leaves nīlūfar and farangī as your fifth and sixth. And with these in mind, do not overlook the seventh, band-i-rūmī."*[9] Thus, in Sadiqi Beg Afshar"s *Canon*, *islamī* becomes *islimī*, *faṣṣalī* is replaced by *nīlūfar*, and the last, *girih*, becomes *bandi-yi rūmī*.

There is no simple translation for any of these terms, since they are referring to regional styles as well as to actual content. But in general, the Seven Principles of Painting are:

• *Islimī* – The Islamic Style, which encompasses vegetal motifs like the split palmette scroll

• *Khaṭā'i* – The Cathayan or Chinese Style (*'chinoiserie'*) from the Mongol invasion of Persia (Ilkhanate Dynasty, 1219 – 1335), including Asian motifs like lotus scrolls or cloud bands inhabited by angels, dragons, phoenixes and auspicious animals

• *Farangī* – The Frankish or European Style, including naturalistic vegetation, animal and human forms

• *Faṣṣālī* – Ruled and compartmentalized shapes (like the margins and lay-out of Persian Miniatures)

• *Abr* – Vague, cloud-like and marbled textures (like the end pages of Persian Miniatures)

• *Vāq* (also called *dāq* or *vāq vāq*) – Vegetal scrolls with animal or human heads (often found in Persian rugs)

• *Girih* – Geometric interlace or strapwork, also called *girih-i rūmī* or *girihbandi-yi rūmī,* meaning 'Anatolian knot'

In Sadiqi Beg Afshar's *Canons of Painting* (1597), the Timurid term *islimī* (vegetal scroll) becomes *islamī* to emphasize its religious origins in Islam. *Islimī* vegetal scrolls, in the Ottoman context, are called *rūmī*, which means, 'from the lands of Rum'– the former Roman territories (Anatolia and the Balkans) conquered by the Ottomans. Thus, *Rūmīyān* means 'Ottoman' in style. Sadiqi Beg Afshar also mentions *nīlūfar*, which means lotus flowers, a popular motif that originated either in Egypt or Asia.

For now, we are interested in the geometric interlace called *girih* or *girih-i rūmī*. In our next chapter on Ornament & Form, we shall encounter the *islimī* palmette scrolls, as well as the *vāq* scrolls with their animal or human heads. Finally, in our chapters on Hieratic Perspective, we shall delve deeper into *faṣṣālī* – the ruled and compartmentalized shapes of Persian Miniatures.

II. Interlace Patterns: the Breath of the Compassionate

Research into the methods and texts of Islamic craftsmen reveals that even an illiterate artisan, given a compass and straight rule, could develop the complex multiplication of shapes typical of *girih* patterns, tilings and tessellations. Their history is long and unclear, rooted in the Pre-Islamic cultures of Sassanian Persia (224 – 651) and the Byzantine empire (657 BCE – 1453). At the same time, the nomadic tribes of Arabia, Persia and Afghanistan developed many of the more recognizable motifs in their textiles and 'Oriental rugs'.[10]

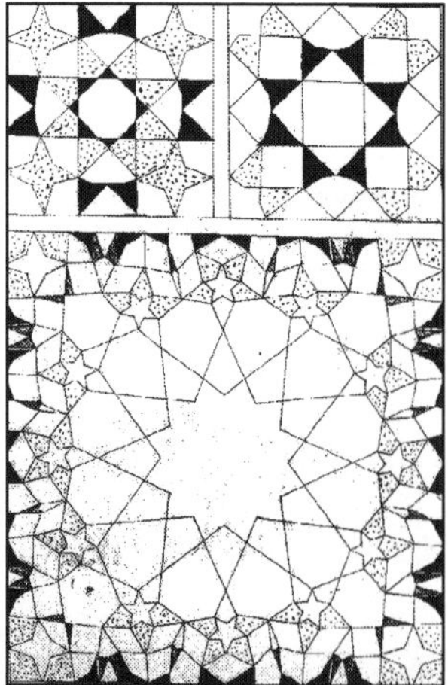

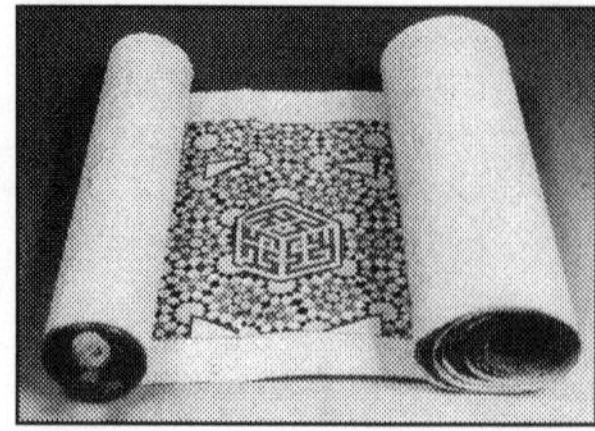

Fig. 14.3 - Examples of *girih* patterns from the Topkapi Scroll

The earliest Handbook for Craftsmen dates back to the first part of the 16th century (while Islamic patterns themselves date back to the 9th century). The most important is the *Topkapi Scroll,* (Fig. 14.3) recently discovered in the Topkapi Palace Museum Library in Istanbul. The complete scroll (c. 30 m. long) portrays 114 different geometric patterns for Timurid ornaments. These are drawn in multiple colours (mostly black and red ink) to distinguish the shapes and underlying grids. Most lattices are square or triangular, and covered with interlaced polygons, though some grids are radial (a quarter circle) for decoration on vaults. Sometimes, only one design is drawn and its repetition assumed.[11]

Other fragmentary handbooks exist, such as the *Tashkent Scrolls* discovered in Bukhara in the 1930's, providing more models of geometric tessellations. All of these scrolls lack text, and modern scholars believe they were created by master craftsmen as models for the transmission of their designs. However, the famed mathematician Abu 'al Wafa' al-Buzjani (940 – 998) did write a text called *A Book on those Geometric Constructions which are Necessary for a Craftsman* (*Kitab fima yahtaju ilayhi al-sani'*

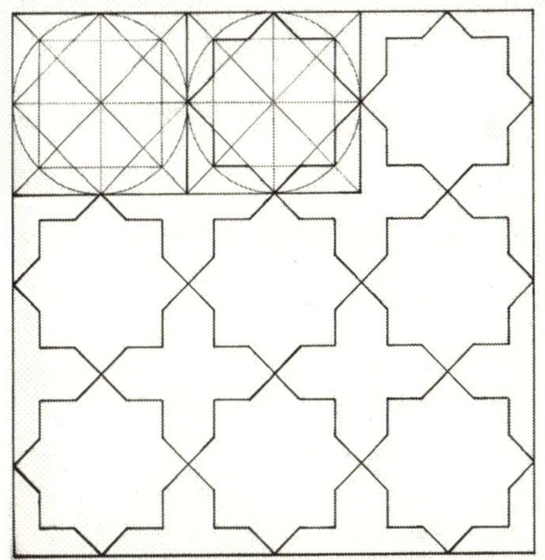

Fig. 14.4 - Construction of the *Girih* Pattern Called 'the Breath of the Compassionate'

min a'mal al-handasa) suggesting that mathematicians may have contributed to the elaboration of *girih* geometry.[12]

An example of how a *girih* is created can be seen in Fig. 14.4. Beginning with no tools other than a compass and straight rule, the craftsman first drew the basic armature for his motif in red ink. Within this armature, more construction lines were added in red ink, referencing specific points in the armature and connecting them. Finally, by isolating certain shapes or line segments and tracing them out in black ink, he created the *motif.*

As with most *girih* patterns, the motif has emerged within a square area called *the pattern cell.* To repeat his motif, he then drew a *lattice*, a grid of squares in red ink. By repeatedly copying the pattern cell into the lattice, he created the larger *girih* pattern. Sometimes, the craftsman wove the connecting lines under and over each other; other times his pattern cell was fudged, flipped, or rotated as it moved along the lattice. One motif could also alternate with others, joined by improvised bridges.

In Islamic culture, the Octagram is called *Khatem Sulemani*, meaning Solomon's Seal, and it constitutes one of the most basic and pervasive motifs in their sacred tradition. The *girih* pattern in Fig. 14.4 has been called 'the Breath of the Compassionate' (*nafas al-rahmân*) because its alternating cross and octagram motifs are, in fact, truncated and stellated squares. The cross, which cuts *into* the square, expresses the inhalation of breath while the octagram, which *extends* the square, expresses the exhalation. The pattern manifests the Sufi doctrine of 'the renewal of creation at each instant' (*tajdīd al-khalq bi'l-anfās*). As Seyyed Hossein Nasr writes, *"At every moment the universe is absorbed in the Divine Centre and manifested anew in a rhythm of contraction (qabḍ) and expansion (basṭ)."*[13]

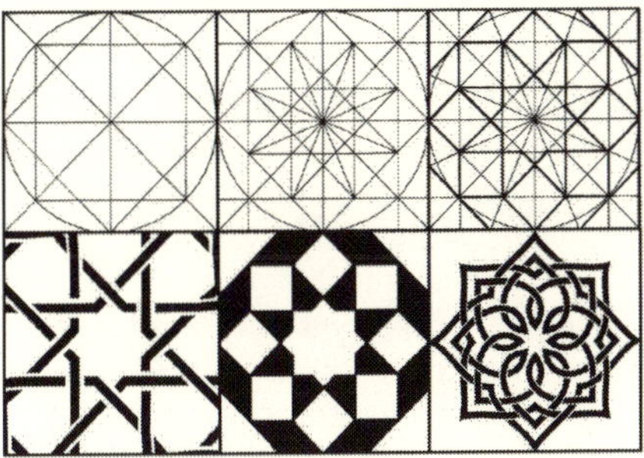

Fig. 14.5 - Construction of the Eight-pointed Star Octagram from the *Khatem Sulemani*

In the next example of a *girih* pattern (Fig. 14.5), we can see how the number of construction lines has increased, as has the complexity of the resulting motif. In the first row, the basic armature is expanded to form a Maltese Cross, from which the eight-pointed Star Octagram emerges. In the second row, we can see how a variety of motifs can arise from this same structure: overlapping strapwork, black and white tiling, or a curvilinear rosette.

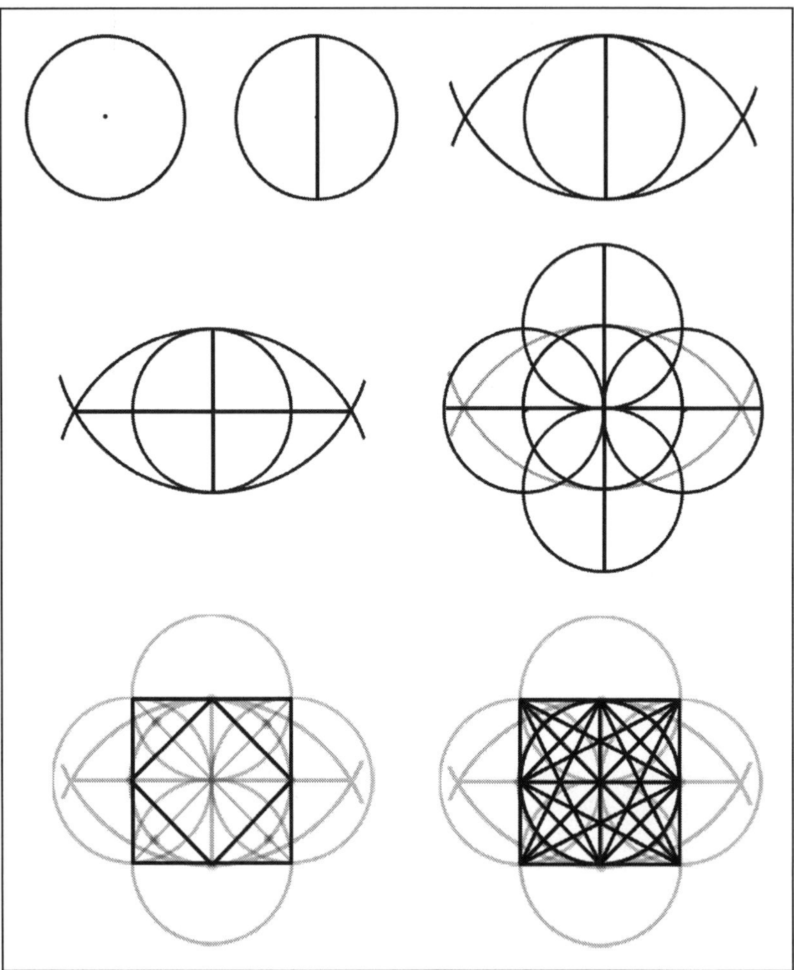

Fig. 14.6 - Armature Construction for the Pattern Cell

The black and white tiling was so universally appealing that it transcended Islamic culture to appear time and again in Gothic and Renaissance art.

The basic armature of the pattern cell is created according to the geometrical steps[14] given in Fig. 14.6. We have already met with the four-petalled flower and its *ad quadratrum* measure of space. Specific points within the circular matrix are identified and connected to generate the square and its polygonic star, which forms a basic armature for square pattern cells.

One of the more unique properties of this armature is that it generates *seven distinct ratios* through the polygonal star at its centre, beginning at 1:2 and ascending to 1:8 (Fig. 14.7). In other words, a vertical line drawn through specific points in the armature will divide the whole line (1) into an equal number of parts (indicated at the top as 2, 3, 4... 8). The geometric shapes on the vertical line (circle, triangle square etc) mark the points of the harmonic ratios, given at the bottom as the ○halves, △two-thirds, □three-quarters etc.

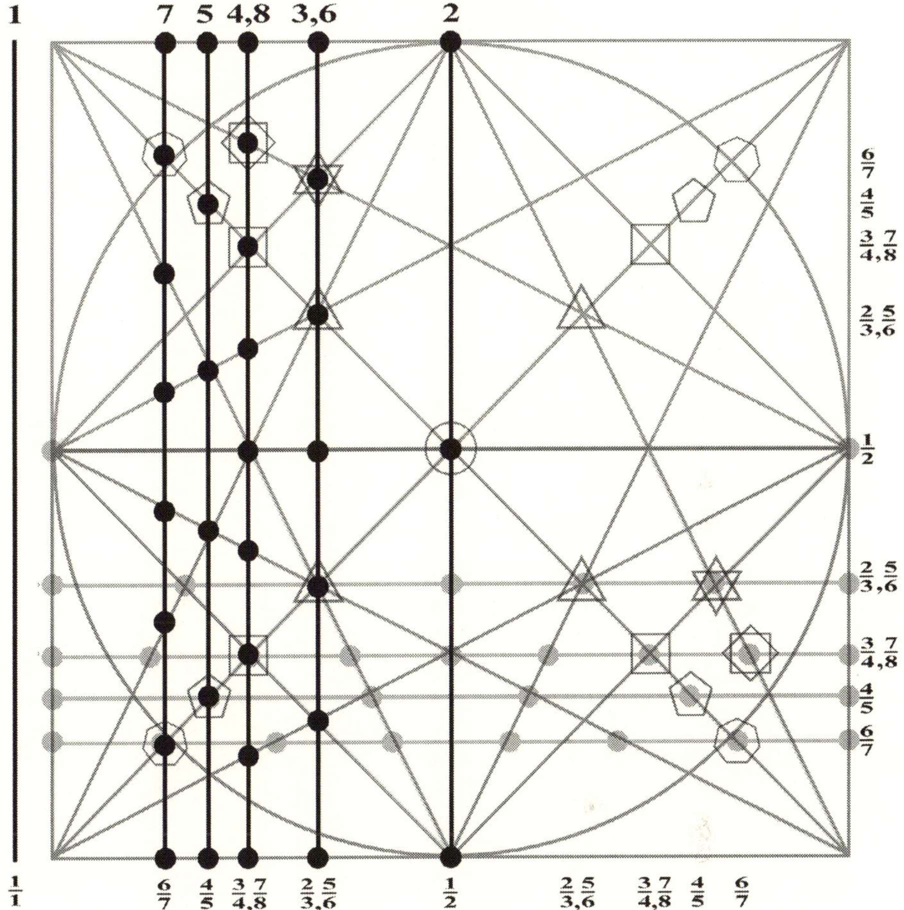

Fig. 14.7 - Seven Ratios of the Armature for a Square Pattern Cell

The same operation may be carried out in a *horizontal direction*, dividing up the whole square *into grids* of smaller squares that increase exponentially. Hence, when the division of the vertical line at 2 is also carried out horizontally, we have a grid of $2^2 = 4$ squares. When the division of 3 is carried out in both directions, it creates a grid of $3^3 = 9$ squares, and so on – forming ever finer grids of 4, 9, 16, 25, 36, 49 or 64 squares. However, the five-sixths pentagon and seven-eighths octagram, which do *not* lie on the X main diagonals, must be carefully re-located on the horizontals – the five-sixths hexagram on the thirds horizontal, and the seven-eighths octagram on the quarters horizontal.

Due to these measures, the basic armature generates *girih* motifs which possess Hieratic harmonies and proportions. In the Pythagorean-Platonic tradition, it is particularly the *diapason* ○halves, the *diapente* △two-thirds and *diatessaron* □three-quarters that reverberate with the whole (1), echoing the divine harmonies of the cosmos.[15]

III. Reading Islamic Patterns

As our eye falls upon an Islamic Pattern, its circle of focus widens to absorb the ever-increasing complexity of shapes on the periphery. Fig. 14.8 reveals three types of *girih* pattern and their underlying grids. By focussing on the central rosette and counting the number of petals, we may detect the Sacred Code, the underlying matrix of six, four or five circles, as well as their inset triangles, squares and pentagons that create their spatial grids.[16]

In the top row of *girih* patterns, the central rosettes have six, eight and ten petals respectively. In the first column, the hexagonal rosette (with a 12-pointed star in the middle) reveals the six-petalled Seed of Life, which generates regular polygon and star shapes like the triangle (3), turned triangle (3) and their combination in the hexagram (6) or dodecagram (12). All of these exist in *ad triangulum* space.

In the second column, the octagonal rosette reveals the four-petalled flower of interlacing circles, which generates all four-pointed shapes and their multiples, like the square (4) and turned square (4) or their combination in the octagram (8), dodecagram (12) and hexadecagram (16). All of these exist in *ad quadratum* space. (The dodecagram, I would like to note here, exists in both *ad triangulum* and *ad quadratum* space).

In the third column, the decagram rosette reveals the five-petalled flower of circles at its heart, which generates the pentagon (5) and turned pentagon (5) as well as their combination in the decagram (10). We are tempted to say that these shapes exist in *ad pentagonum* space (i.e. 'from the pentagon'), but pentagons may *not* be laid out side by side to create a consistent grid measure for their space (nor can a grid of five-petalled flowers be drawn from one circle in the centre). Instead, the decagram rosette invites us to examine *radial grids,* which we shall in the following sections.

But first, we should also note that the triangle, square and pentagon manifest their own harmonic ratios. As we can see in the bottom two rows, the equilateral triangle generates the *half-equilateral,* which manifests a $1:\sqrt{3}$ ratio; the square generates the *half-square*, which manifests a $1:\sqrt{2}$ ratio; and the pentagon generates a unique isosceles triangle, which manifests the ϕ (phi) ratio, an irrational number that may be expressed as $(\sqrt{5} + 1) / 2$. We shall examine these ratios later in this chapter, in our exposition on Gothic art. For now, let us note that fundamental ratios based on $\sqrt{3}$, $\sqrt{2}$ and ϕ underlie the three most basic geometrical shapes of Islamic patterns.

IV. Harmonic Pattern in Space: Wallpaper Groups

There are three basic ways in which Islamic craftsmen may arrange their patterns in space: as a frieze, a wallpaper group, or a radial point system. A 'frieze' repeats the pattern cell's motif in *one direction* only. A 'wallpaper group' arranges the motif in *two directions*, but these need not be perpendicular, as with a grid of squares. Instead, the pattern cell may be rhombic, hexagonal etc. and their lattice appear more angled. The last group, the radial point system, takes a basic rosette shape and expands it outward from the centre, in as many directions as there are rays within the core star shape (e.g. 10 directions for a decagram). First, we shall concentrate on wallpaper groups, and turn our attention to radial space thereafter.

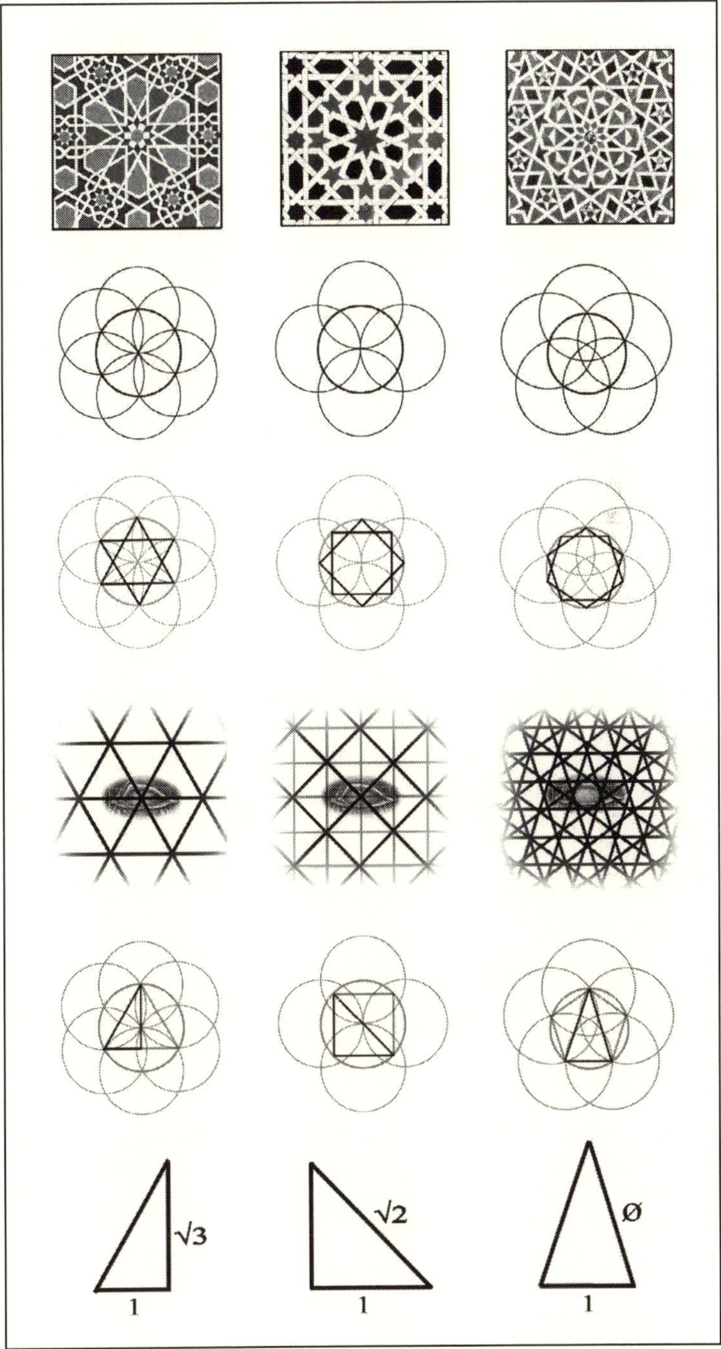

Fig. 14.8 - Types of Rosettes, Their Geometries, Grids and Ratios

The Alhambra in Granada Spain seems to summarize in one walled palace all the visionary beauty and geometry of Islamic art. Like a book rendered in glazed tiles, it contains the seventeen basic geometrical patterns which crystallographers later described as 'wallpaper groups'. Briefly, these groups are made up of a pattern cell and the lattice which governs its repetition. Within each pattern cell is a motif, such as the *girih* designs we have encountered thus far. The number of motifs is seemingly infinite, but there is a mathematical limit to how many kinds of pattern cells can be harmoniously repeated in Euclidian planar space in two directions. Pattern cells take on the appearance of five basic shapes:[17]

□ square ▭ rectangular
⬡ hexagonal ◇ rhombic
▱ parallelogram

All of the seventeen wallpaper groups use these simple polygons to create their lattices. This is because they can be laid out beside each other, like 'tiles', and constantly expand in all directions with no gaps between them. The pattern cell and its motif can be variously flipped, fudged and rotated within the expanding latticework. Their movements from one cell of the lattice to another are called 'mappings' or 'projections'. The simplest is to just repeat the same motif in a new cell, or flip it so its neighbour appears like a mirror reflection. But, master craftsmen will perform two or even three projections on a single motif. The basic projections are the following:

- Translational – repeating the same motif
- Rotational – spinning the motif 60°, 90°, 120° or 180°
- Reflective – flipping it like a mirror image
- Glide reflective – flipping it like an angled mirror image.

Below, Figure 14.9 shows the seventeen pattern cells, marked with their centres of rotation and axes of reflection, which allow for their various projections within the lattice.[18]

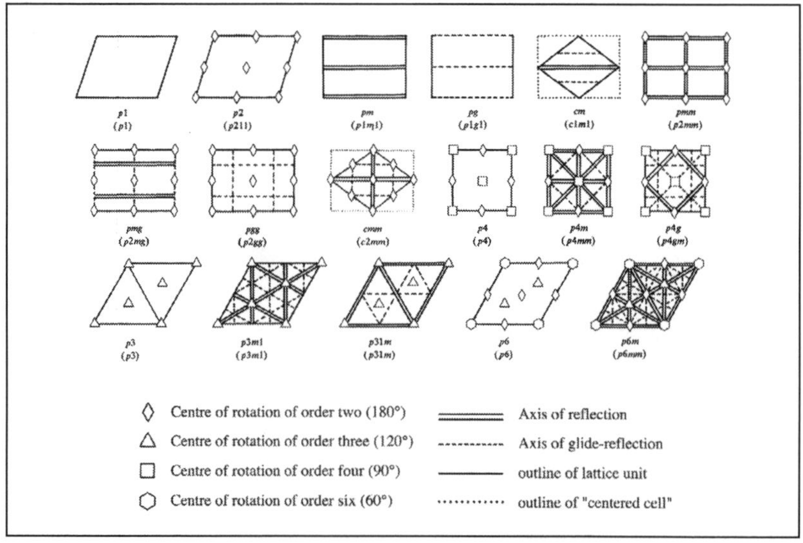

Fig. 14.9 - The Seventeen Pattern Cells

In *Symmetries of Islamic Geometrical Patterns*, Abas and Salman show Islamic designs for all seventeen wallpaper groups. Fig. 14.10 gives seventeen examples from Owen Jones' *The Grammar of Ornament*, and shows what happens when a motif in a pattern cell is projected in two directions within the lattice.[19]

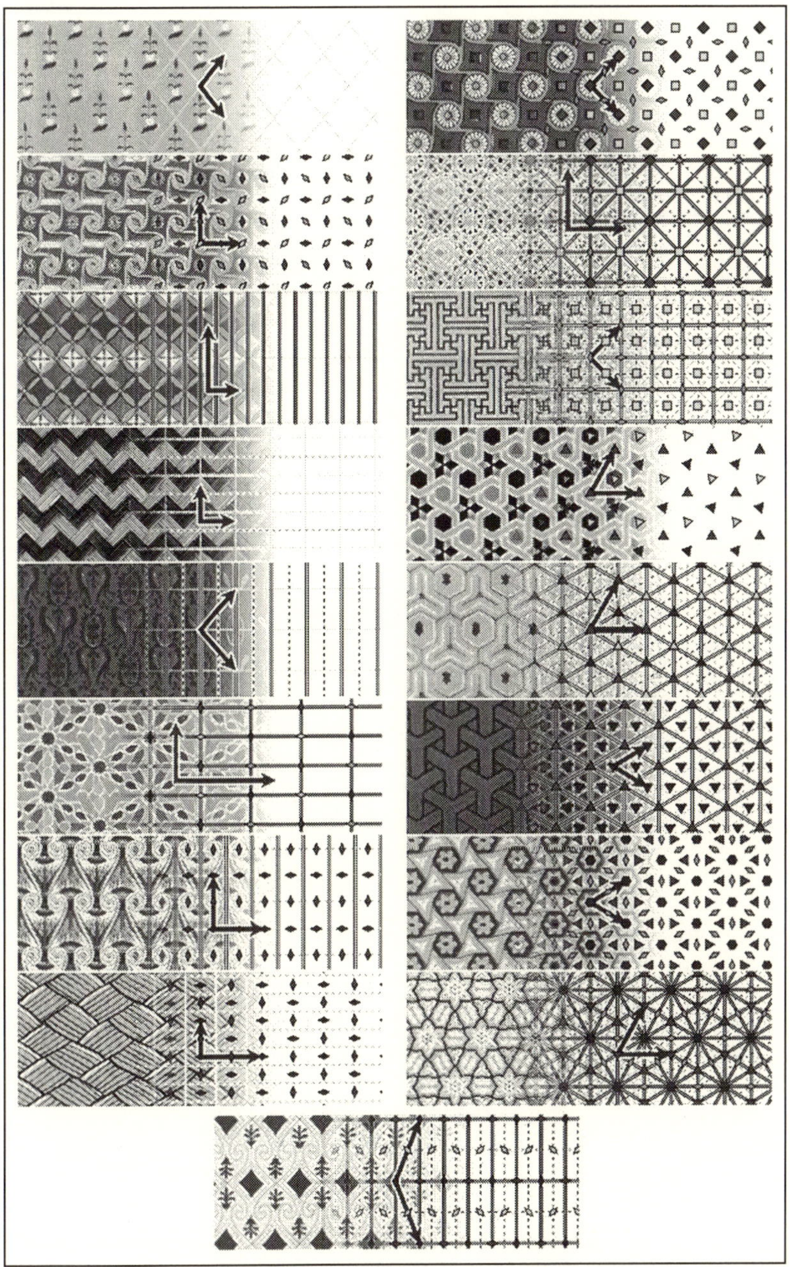

Fig. 14.10 - Examples of the Seventeen Wallpaper Groups

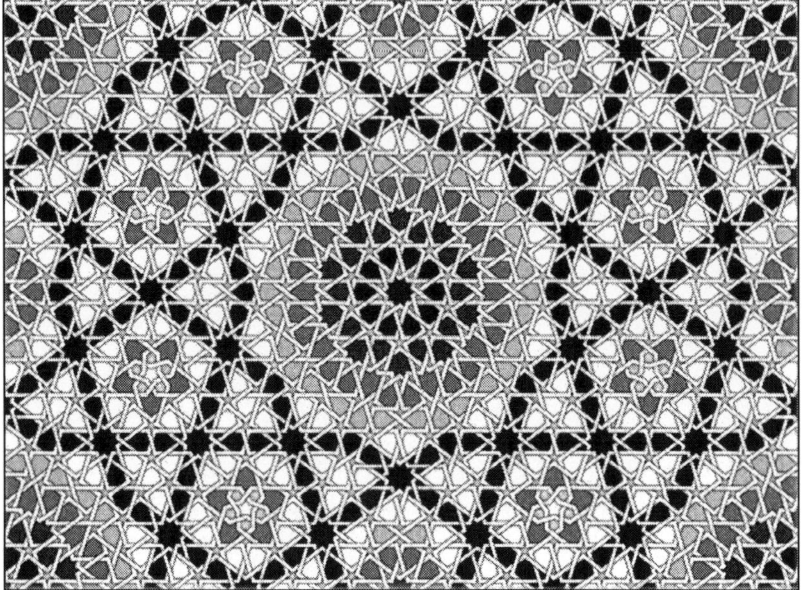

Fig. 14.11 - Islamic Pattern Exploring Five Axes of Planar Space

V. Rosettes and Radial Space

When we meditate for some time on the design in fig. 14.11, it seems to posses both unity and diversity. At first glance, the greater underlying pattern is not easy to detect, because the eye is focussing on the innermost *rosette*, which is a shape *far too complex* for the mind to immediately grasp and encompass. In fact, this rosette may double or triple the basic polygon of the spatial grid, then progressively rotate it to form the radial star pattern.

But, as our focus expands, the eye begins to recognize the major axes of the larger pattern. The rosette at the centre appears once more at a higher level, and within each petal we may detect an upright or inverted pentagon. These smaller motifs, called *furmah,* help the eye to mark out the basic shapes and axial directions of the radial space. The pentagonal *furmah* tells us that the core rosette is a pentagon and inverted pentagon, combined to form a ten-pointed decagram.[20] In Fig. 14.12, the five major axes of its radial space have been accentuated.

If we return to row 4 of Fig. 14.8, we will notice how all three measures of space possess a 180° horizon line. In *ad triangulum* space, the larger pattern emerges through shapes that follow the horizontal axis, as well as the diagonals running at 60° angles to it, which stem from the grid of upright and inverted triangles. In *ad quadratum* space, the larger pattern emerges through lines that follow the 180° (horizon) and 90° (gravity) axes of the square grid, as well as the 45° diagonals of the turned square grid.

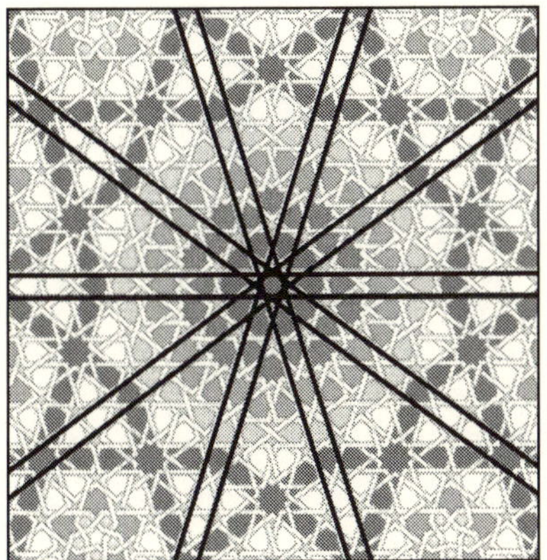

Fig. 14.12 - The Five Axes of Space Created by the Decagram Star

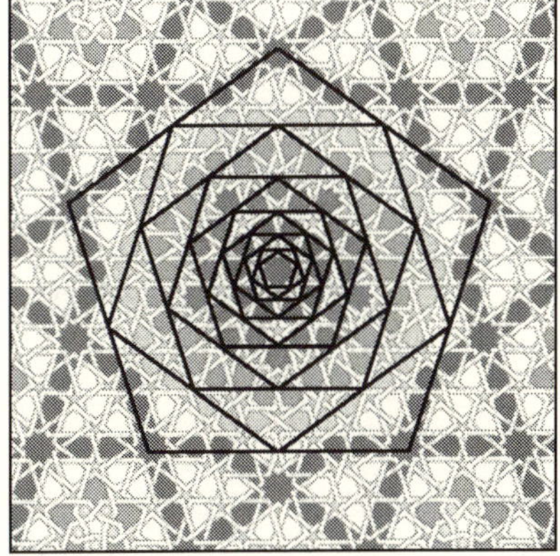

Fig. 14.13 - Expanding the Spatial Measure through Nested Pentagons

In Fig. 14.12, we can see that the horizontal axis persists, in the form of a flat double line, to aid the viewer in orienting his way through its axial space. Added to this are four more double lines which, angled to the horizontal axis, create the five principle axes of radial space. Due to the decagram at their core, two sets of diagonals run at 36° angles to the horizon, and two more run at 72° angles (i.e. 2 x 36°). These five axes provide the Islamic craftsman with the basic grid of his so-called *ad pentagonum* space, since all the shapes within it will follow one of these five axes.

But, we have yet to explain how the pattern grows outward from the centre. As in fig. 14.4, it is indeed possible to take a star shape and simply repeat it in a square grid (a wallpaper group), creating Islamic patterns of great beauty. But, in Fig. 14.11, the space is organized in a different manner. Turning to Fig. 14.13, we can see how a series of nested pentagons (upright and inverted) expand the space while respecting the five axes of *ad pentagonum* space. (We could also have drawn these as a series of inset decagrams).

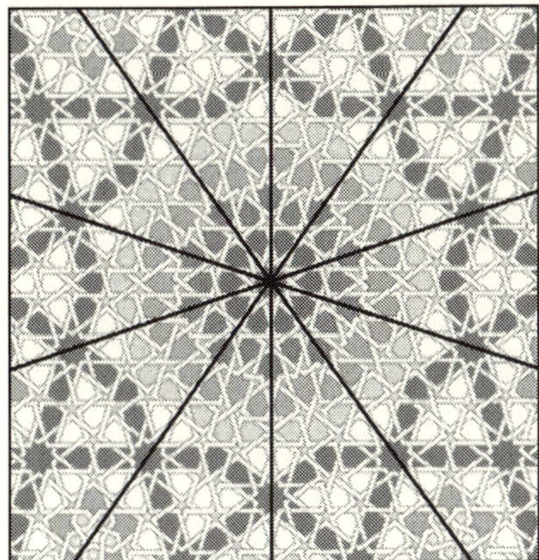

Fig. 14.14 - Ten Part Division of 360° Radial Space into 36° Slices

From these nested pentagons, the Islamic craftsman is able to draw five more lines which divide the radial space into ten equal slices (Fig. 14.14). The pattern motif in each slice is identical to its neighbour, being one tenth of the whole, and hence, a 36° slice of the 360° radial space. We can see this method in practice in one section of the Topkapi Scroll (Fig. 14.15), where the slice of a radial design has been preserved.

Thus far, we have only touched the surface of Islamic Patterns, which can become exceedingly complex. There are, for example, semi-regular tesselations, where two different pattern cells may combine to create even more complex grids (of which, eight known types exist). Or, we can break out of our 'regular polygon' way of thinking and embrace 'a-periodic patterns'. In Moroccan tile, artisans combine up to three hundred small terracotta pieces called *Zallig* (or *Zellige*) to create colourful interlocking mosaics with either regular polygonal or a-periodic designs. Although their master craftsmen (called *maâlems*) have created these designs since the 14th century, it was only in the 1970's that the West came to understand and appreciate their complexity through the mathematics of Roger Penrose and the woodcuts of M. C. Escher. Today, Islamic patterns are an important field of research in computer graphics, where 'shape grammar modelling' allows geometers to map and generate a bewildering variety of Islamic patterns.[21]

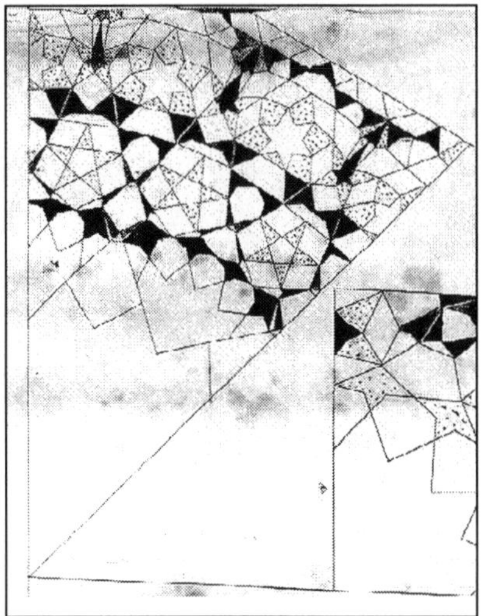

Fig. 14.15 - Radial Design from the Topkapi Scroll

In Fig. 14.11, we can appreciate the complexity and underlying unity of a single *girih* pattern. The master craftsman who created this design had to abandon his usual *triangula* and *quadrata* ways of thinking, to conceive of patterns and shapes within the five axes of his *pentagona* space. We note that the decagram rosette at the centre appears once more at a higher level, organizing the complex variety of shapes into one unified design.

All of this reveals how Islamic art contains patterns within patterns – some visible and others invisible. Their art is a multi-layered lattice-work of intermeshing grids with increasing layers of unity and complexity. It is especially interesting to note that, as the design's complexity increases, the basic circle also comes to the fore. In fact, it is reminding us that, beyond the layer upon layer of geometrical forms, all these visible and invisible designs have their origin *in the circle*. And the core decagram, like all the other regular or star polygons, was created from the matrix of the circle.

The circle, let us not forget, is the image *par excellence* of Divine Unity. When Islamic designs become focussed down onto their centre, they seem to momentarily break apart their abstract quality, and become true images of the Sacred. This is especially true of *girih* patterns because of their star and rosette shapes, which appear like the primordial light bursting forth at the beginning of time.

One of the great scholars of Islamic geometric patterns, S. Jan Abas wrote of these star shapes:

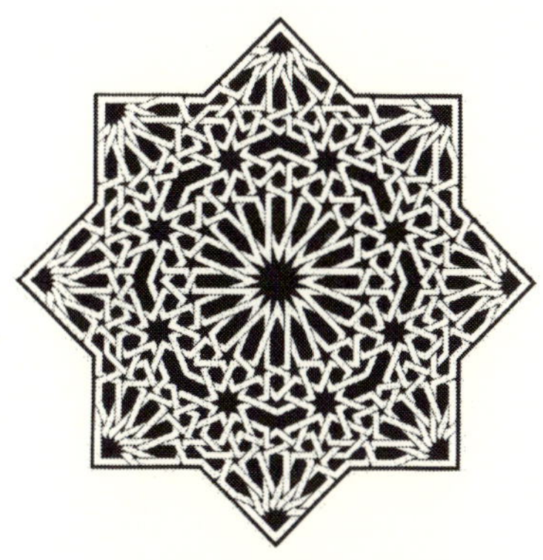

Fig. 14.16 - *Nur* Star-burst:
The Crystallization of God's Light

"The only material image of God that the Koran offers is that of Nur, meaning light. "God is the light of the heavens and earth", it proclaims. [Koran 24:35] *Since stars produce the light of heavens, it is not at all surprising that Muslim artist should produce art containing star shapes for sacred buildings."*[22] In this sense, *girih* patterns are nothing less than the *crystallization* of God's Light – the fractalline explosion of luminous polygonal shapes that reveal, nevertheless, the one true light at their origin.

Islam is dominated by the principle of *Tawhid* or 'Oneness' which can be variously interpreted as strict Monotheism (*lā 'ilāha 'illā l-Lāh – There is no god but Allah)* or the mystical experience of divine unity. For the Sufi's, *Tawhid* evoked the *Wahdat al-Wujud* – the 'Unity of Existence', and their goal was to wed the individual with the Divine in inseparable union. In its most mystical sense, Islamic art and religion are inspired by the unseen unity which underlies the infinite web of existence.

VI. Sacramental Geometry of the Gothic Cathedral Builders

The actual transmission of Islamic craftsmanship to the Gothic cathedral builders remains shrouded in mystery. Certainly, the Christian pilgrimages and crusades, coupled with the 500 year-long Muslim expansion into Sicily, Malta and the Iberian peninsula (called *al-Andalus* from 722 - 1236) provided many opportunities for architects and masons to exchange their knowledge of craft.

As well, by the Late Middle Ages there was a large and fashionable demand by the courts of Europe for embroidered *'damask'* tapestries (from Damascus), *'mousseline'* silks (from Mosul) and all sorts of filigree glass, gold and silver work – all bearing Islamic motifs and workmanship. The artisans of Europe quickly adapted these design-methods into their own areas of specialty.

In a seminal essay called *'The Geometrical Knowledge of Mediaeval Master Masons'*, Lon R. Shelby revealed that most masons could not read, nor make mathematical calculations, nor understand Latin. Instead, *"...technical knowledge required in design and construction was transmitted from father to son, from master to apprentice, from learned journeymen to those who were less learned in the craft traditions."*[23]

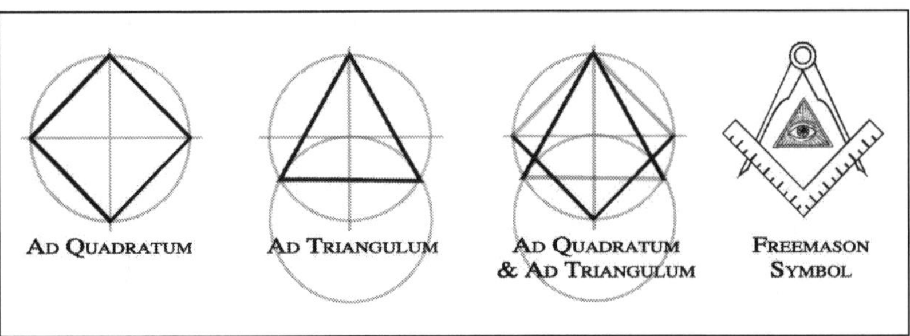

Fig. 14.17 - *Ad Quadratum* and *Ad Triangulum* Measures of Space Symbolized by the Compass and Set-square in the Freemason Insignia

The two basic tools of Gothic design are the compass and the straight edge. Already in the 3rd century BCE, Euclid stated in his *Elements* that all constructions were to be made with just these two instruments. As we have already seen, Islamic craftsmen also constructed their designs in this manner. In later times, the straight edge was modified to become the L-shaped set-square. Freemasons then used the interpenetrating compass and set-square as their insignia. As Fig. 14.17 shows, the hidden geometry behind these two symbols reveals their *ad quadratum* and *ad triangulum* measures of space.

The compass and straight edge have played fundamentally different roles in the history of Western art, particularly from the standpoint of harmony and proportion. Although both tools have always been used, their measures have dominated different periods of history. In the Classical period, Pythagoras measured harmony through the whole number units of the ruler, while Plato preferred the geometric constructions of the compass that resulted in irrational numbers like square roots. This opposition persisted in art and architecture, since the Gothics continued to favour geometry, while the Renaissance revived an interest in arithmetic.

Pythagoras preferred the metrical norms of the ruler because it gave him *whole number* ratios, such as the 1:2 *diapason*, 2:3 *diapente* and 3:4 *diatessaron* that were implicit in the Tetractys. Indeed, the famed Pythagorean Theorem was derived from the Egyptian knotted cord – a primitive ruler made from a rope with twelve equally-spaced knots.

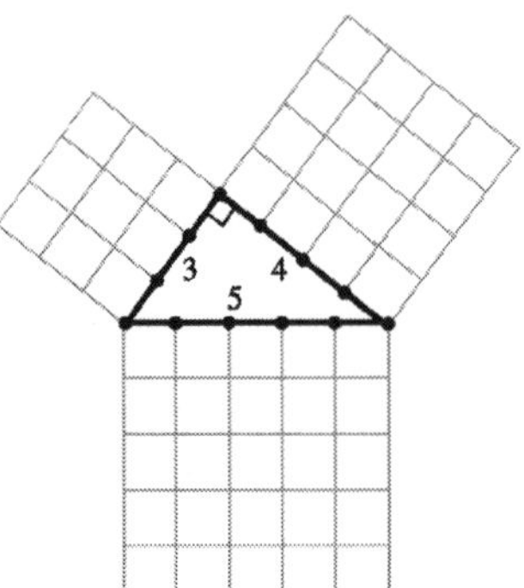

Fig. 14.18 - The Pythagorean Theorem Derived from the Egyptian Knotted Cord

In Egypt, the knotted cord was used to make a right-angled triangle with sides measuring three, four and five. The 3-4-5 triangle lies at the heart of the Pythagorean Theorem, since the measure of the hypotenuse (the side opposite the right angle) equals the sum of the remaining sides, when all are squared (i.e. $A^2 + B^2 = C^2$). In the 3-4-5 triangle, $3^2 + 4^2 = 5^2$ or $9 + 16 = 25$. By applying the square root, the value of the hypotenuse may be calculated to 5.

Through the Pythagorean Theorem, the Pythagoreans also came across square roots with irrational numbers, but these were called *alogon* or 'unutterable' because irrational numbers did not fit into their whole number view of the universe. As Karl Popper notes,

"The discovery of the irrationality of the square root of two... destroyed the Pythagorean programme of 'arithmetizing' geometry... The tradition that this discovery was first kept secret is, it seems, supported by the fact that Plato still calls the irrational at first 'arrhetos' *i.e. the secret unmentionable mystery."*[24]

In his *Timaeus*, Plato not only enshrined the whole number harmonic ratios of Pythagoras, but also the *irrational number* ratios arising from half-equilateral and half-square triangles. We recall that Plato's Demiurge constructed the Four Elements from four of the Five Platonic Solids: earth from cubes, water from icosahedra, air from octahedra and fire from tetrahedra. These, in turn, were constructed from two types of triangle, the half-square and half-equilateral.

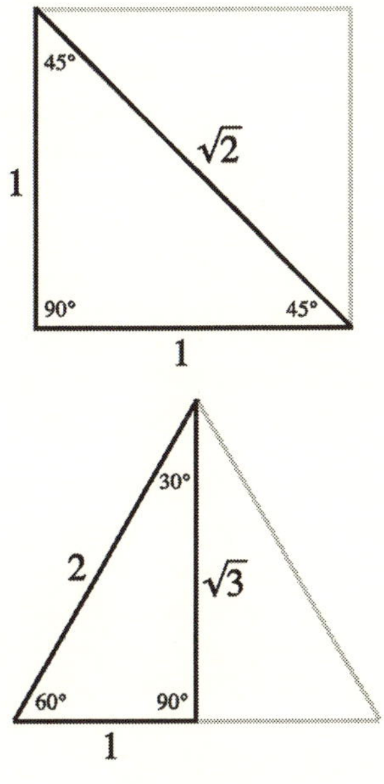

The half-square is a right-angled triangle constructed from angles measuring 45°- 45°- 90°. Using the Pythagorean Theorem, the shorter sides measure out to a length of 1 and 1 while the longer side measures out to √2. Hence, the ratio of the base to the hypotenuse is 1:√2 or 1:1.4142135... – an irrational number.

The half-equilateral is a right-angled triangle constructed from angles measuring 30°- 60°- 90°. The ratio of the base to the perpendicular is 1:√3 or 1:1.7320508... – another irrational number. As Richard Padovan writes in *Proportion: Science, Philosophy, Architecture*:

"The irrational square roots of 2, 3, and 5, together with the offspring of √5, the golden section, provide one of the two constituent principles on which architectural proportion is based. The other principle is founded on the harmonic division of the octave [i.e. the 1:2 *diapason*, 2:3 *diapente* and 3:4 *diatessaron*], *which we have seen was also a Pythagorean discovery. These two schools can be traced through history up to our own day."*[25]

Fig. 14.19

It was particularly the Gothic period which enshrined the irrational square roots of 2 and 3 in their architecture, since the √2 half-squares lay at the heart of all *ad quadratum* measures while the √3 half-equilaterals gave rise to all *ad triangulum* measures. Although the Middle Ages did not calculate the *arithmetic* values of their geometrical constructions as square roots or irrational numbers (the 1:√2 ratio, for example, was simplified to 5:7),[26] Gothic architects constructed their harmonious proportions through a compass and straight rule – through *geometry* rather than arithmetic.

In contrast, Renaissance architects revived the harmonic proportions of Pythagoras, based on whole number ratios. Architects like Alberti and Palladio read deeply into the writings of the 1st century BCE Roman architect Vitruvius, who preserved Pythagorean ratios in his work. Vitruvius declared that proportion lay in the relation of the parts to the whole, which he called *symmetria,* literally "with measure". More specifically, a 'module' was required, a constant measure, to design a building.

This is why Vitruvian Man gained such great importance during the Renaissance, since the parts of a man formed the module for the parts of a building – all the parts fitting harmoniously into the whole through arithmetic proportion. In Vitruvius' words:

"The planning of temples depends upon symmetry: and the method of this architects must diligently apprehend. It arises from proportion (which in Greek is called analogia*). Proportion consists in taking a fixed module, in each case, both for the parts of a building and for the whole, by which the method of symmetry and proportion is put into practice. For without symmetry and proportion no temple can have a regular plan; that is, it must have an exact proportion worked out after the fashion of the members of a finely-shaped human body."*[27]

Vitruvian Man (Fig. 6.18) showed the relationship of the part to the whole, since he stood eight heads tall (8:1) or ten faces tall (10:1). With his arms outstretched, he was as wide as he was tall (1:1) – hence the relationship of man to the square and to the circle.

Following Vitruvius, the Renaissance architect Alberti decided, in his *De re aedifactoria* (On the Art of Building – c. 1450) that the ideal shape for a Renaissance church is the circle, followed by the square, hexagon, octagon, decagon and dodecagon, then the square plus one-half, the square plus one-third and the square doubled. These last three rectangles are, respectively, the 2:3 *diapente*, the 3:4 *diatessaron* and the 1:2 *diapason* (which we shall examine in detail in Ch. 16).

With all these measures, Renaissance architects depended primarily upon the ruler, since it gave a module which was arithmetically expanded into whole number harmonic ratios (1:2, 2:3, 3:4). By contrast, Gothic architects depended primarily upon the compass, and a straight rule with no measures, since their geometrical constructions transferred arcs and diagonals through the compass (witness the Gothic arch), resulting in irrational numbers like the $\sqrt{2}$ and $\sqrt{3}$.

In *The Changing Concept of Proportion*, Rudolf Wittkower writes:

"Two different classes of proportion, both derived from the Pythagorean-Platonic world of ideas, were used during the long history of European art: while the Middle Ages favored Pythagorean-Platonic geometry, the Renaissance and post-Renaissance periods preferred the arithmetical side of the same tradition.

"The reason for this can only be indicated here. Many of the geometrical proportions cannot be expressed by integral numbers or simple fractions, i.e., they are incommensurable or irrational. Thus the hypotenuse of the right-angled isosceles triangle is related to the shorter sides as 1:√2...

"Irrational proportions would have presented a dilemma to Renaissance artists, for the Renaissance attitude to proportion was determined by a new organic approach to nature, which aimed at demonstrating that everything was related to everything by integral number.

"By contrast, the medieval quest for ultimate truth behind appearances was perfectly answered by geometrical configurations of a decisively fundamental nature."[28]

In another seminal work on proportion called *Architectural Principles in the Age of Humanism*, Wittkower offers an example:

"The contrast between Villard de Honnecourt's [Fig. 5.21] *and Leonardo's* [Fig. 6.18] *proportioning of figures is a typical one: the mediaeval artist tends to project a pre-established geometrical norm into his imagery, while the Renaissance artist tends to extract a metrical norm from the natural phenomena that surround him."*[29]

VII. The Turned Square: Roots & Square Roots

Where Renaissance architects like Alberti moved from the circle to the square to three types of harmonious rectangle, Gothic architects moved from the circle to various types of triangle, as well as the square, pentagon and their derivatives. Again, Wittkower:

"The equilateral triangle, the right-angled isosceles triangle, the square, the pentagon, and derivative figures like the octagon and decagon formed the basis of medieval aesthetics. The evidence is overwhelming that many medieval churches were built ad quadratum or ad triangulum. Also, the doubling or halving of the area of a square which Plato explained in his Meno in order to exemplify the incommensurability of the sides of two such squares... received a wide application during the Middle Ages, particularly in the construction of the tiers of Gothic spires."[30]

Since 'the doubling or halving of the area of a square' forms a fundamental principle in Gothic art, we should examine it in detail. It arises from an important construction called the *quadrature* or 'turned square'. In Plato's *Meno*, Socrates demonstrates this construction to a slave boy, because he wishes to show to his friend Meno that knowledge is acquired through recollection (*anamnesis*) rather than learning. Knowledge by recollection suggests that the soul has access to certain eternal truths, from its sojourn in the higher realms, before birth became our forgetting.

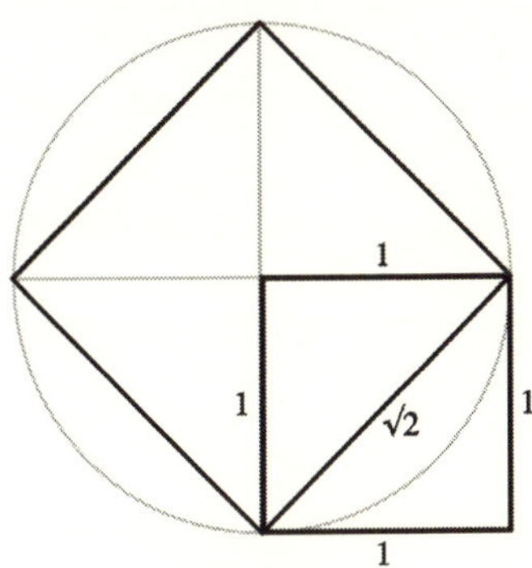

Fig. 14.20

The task is to draw a square with an area double that of the first square. Socrates begins with a small square (Fig. 14.20, bottom right) and draws a diagonal, with the result that two triangles or half-squares give half the volume. By constructing a large turned square from the diagonal of the first, it becomes evident that the four half-squares of the larger turned square are double in area to the two half-squares of the first.

The lesson is important because it also teaches us the meaning of arithmetic terms like square and root, rational and irrational numbers. To construct the large turned square from the diagonal of the smaller, we must use a compass to draw a circle, which has a radius equal in length (1) to the side of the smaller square. By extending the sides of the smaller square to form a cross within the circle, the larger turned square can be drawn within the circle.

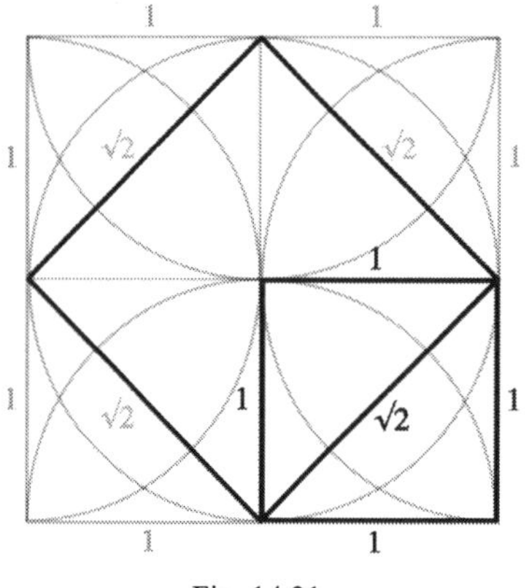

Fig. 14.21

In Fig. 14.21, a compass is used to inscribe more arcs, which again transfer the length (1) of the smaller square, to form an even larger square with sides of the length 1 + 1 = 2. By counting the half-squares and adding them together, it becomes evident that the area of the small square is 1, the area of the turned square is 2, and the area of the largest square is 4.

The largest square shows us that, in arithmetic, any number multiplied by itself is called *the square* because, to calculate the area of the square, one side of the square (2) is multiplied by the other side of the square (2) to give the area of the square (4). Hence, $2^2 = 4$.

The inverse of that operation is called *the square root* because the 'root' is the number or side-length (Fig. 14.22) that was multiplied by itself to generate the area of the square. Returning to the largest square, we recall that it has an area of 4. So, the square root of the area 4 is $\sqrt{4} = 2$, the length of its sides. These operations are all fairly simple in the case of the largest square because the arithmetic delivers rational 'whole number' results.

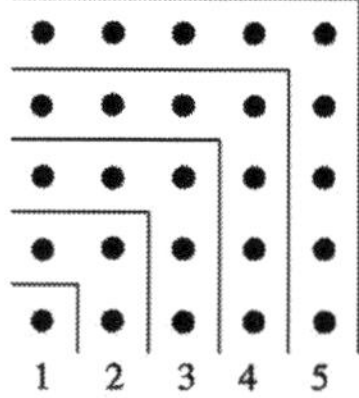

Fig. 14.22

But, in the case of the turned square (Fig. 14.21), the geometry creates arithmetic results that can only be described with irrational numbers. We know that the area of the turned square is 2, but the only numbers we have to calculate its area is to say that one side of the turned square ($\sqrt{2}$) multiplied by the other side of the turned square ($\sqrt{2}$) equals 2. We can write this as $\sqrt{2} \times \sqrt{2} = 2$ or as $\sqrt{2}^2 = 2$. The *square* of $\sqrt{2}$ is 2 and the *square root* of 2 is $\sqrt{2}$. The closest we can come to calculating $\sqrt{2}$ as a rational number is to write it as 1.4142135..., but that number actually goes on for infinity, and so is irrational.

Irrational numbers are the result of diagonals and arcs generated by a compass and straight rule in geometry. God ever geometizes, but humans have only (thus far) come up with irrational numbers to arithmetize that geometry.

VIII. Out of the Centre of the Circle

To transmit their knowledge of craft, Gothic architects and masons *demonstrated by drawing*. We today think that arithmetic measure is necessary for geometrical construction, but Sacred Geometry is visually self-evident: a series of diagrams, if properly arranged, suffice for the transmission of craft.

This is why so few Medieval texts are found on Gothic building and design. One of the exceptions is Hanns Schmuttermayer's *Fialenbüchlein* (Pinnacles Booklet - 1487), published in the dying days of Gothic architecture. In his preface, Schmuttermayer mentions three key elements of Gothic design:

"By the Grace of Almighty God (I have written this little book)... for the edification and instruction of our fellow men and all masters and journeymen who use the high and liberal art of geometry, so that their feeling speculation and imagining can be better subjected after memorization, to the true basis of measured work, and be allowed to take root. Fundamentally, this art is more freely and truly planted and developed out of the centre of the circle, together with its circumference, correct rules, points and settings out."[31]

Schmuttermayer emphasizes *geometry* as the foundation of Gothic design. He stresses *imagining* and *memorization* as the way geometrical designs are transmitted. And most importantly – all geometrical constructions *are developed out of the centre of the circle*. As we saw last chapter, the circle has been, since Babylonian times, the sacred beginning for all creations in space.

In the second part of his preface, Schmuttermayer makes a few more key points:

"I explain these matters not because I wish for my own honour, but more to praise the fame and reputation of the old-timers, our fore-runners, rule-makers and inventors of this high art of building construction which has its original true base in the level, set-square, triangle, dividers and straight-edge, and which is now pursued with precision, subtlety, higher understanding and deeper reckoning... I have not discovered such by myself but have received it from many other great and famous masters, such as the Junkers of Prague, Master Ruger and Nicholas of Strasbourg..."[32]

Here, the importance of transmission is emphasized, the lineage of knowledge going back to the *old-timers* and *fore-runners* – the Old Masters. These could very well have been Islamic craftsmen, but they too had their sources in Persian and Byzantine cultures, going all the way back to the Greeks, Egyptians and Babylonians. In all of these cultures, the basic tools of the compass (dividers) and the straight-edge were used, supplemented by others like the set-square, triangle and knotted cord.

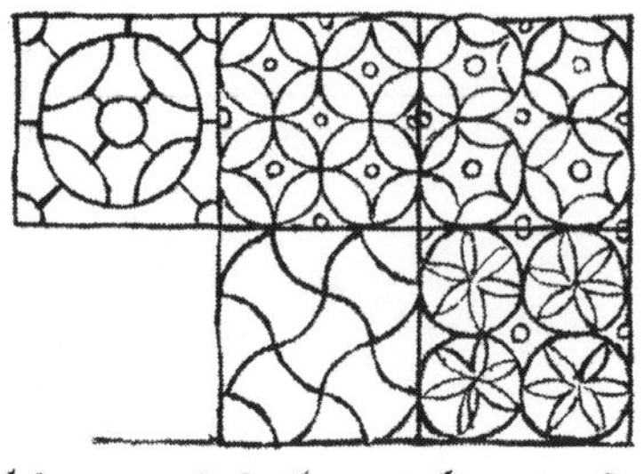

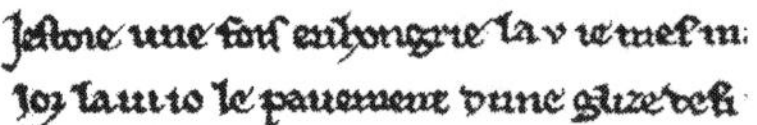

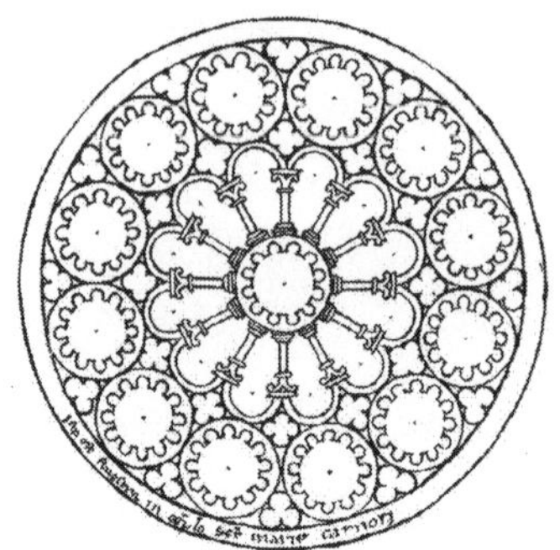

Fig. 14.23 - Honnecourt's Paving Design and Chartres Rosace

IX. *Ad Quadratum* and *Ad Triangulum*

Among the 250 drawings in Villard de Honnecourt's *Sketchbook*, plate 29 depicts the *rosace* of Chartres' west facade. Above it, Honnecourt made a sketch of tile pavings, and relates *"Once when I was in Hungary where I remained for a long time, I saw the paving of a church with this design."*[33] It is typical of Honnecourt's ever-searching stylus to draw pages of seemingly random images (much like Leonardo in his Notebooks) which are nevertheless obliquely related. No explanatory text is given to connect the images. Rather, for architects and masons their correspondence was 'visually self-evident'.

In the case of this page, the seemingly insignificant paving tiles reveal Honnecourt's thorough familiarity with circular grids. This drawing, out of context, could be mistaken for the pattern design of an Islamic craftsman. Of particular interest are the circular designs in the bottom right square, which show the six-petalled circles unique to the Flower of Life.

Although he has not bothered to measure these out with a compass, their shape alone suffices for him, as a kind of glyph, to remember the basic hexagonal grid of circles memorized during his youthful years of *compagnonnage*, apprenticing himself to his art. Meanwhile, the other designs are based on four and five-petalled flowers of circular grids. As Fig. 14.24 shows, a four-petalled flower can divide a circle into twelve equal parts which form the twelve petals of the Chartres *rosace*. From floor tiles to stained glass, the same geometrical patterns underlay the design of all Gothic monuments.

In *'Medieval Architectural Design Methods 800 – 1560'*, François Bucher examines cathedral plans from Paris, Nuremburg and Vienna, remarking that *"...square schematism was a practical approach long before 1230 when it was systemized once more in Villard de Honnecourt's workings years."*[34]

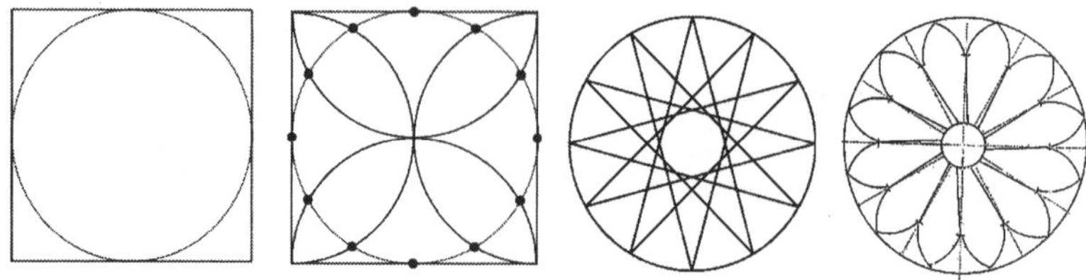

Fig. 14.24 - Construction of twelve-petal *rosace* from the four-petal flower of circles

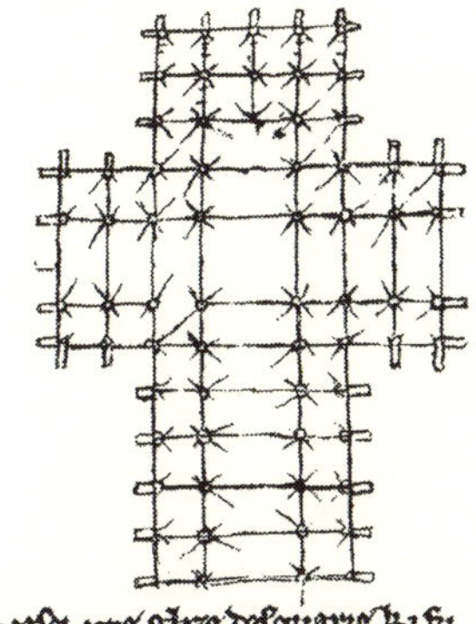

Fig. 14.25 - Honnecourt: Design of a Square Church

As an example, he refers to Plate 27 of Honnecourt's *Sketchbook* (Fig. 14.25), showing the floor plan of a Cistercian church, with the comment: *"This is a square church designed for the Cistercian Order."*[35]

The square grid drawn by Honnecourt was typical of Gothic design, and of all plans drawn *ad quadratum* – 'from the square'. The other important grid for Gothic design was *ad triangulum* – 'from the triangle'. As Bucher notes, *"Building ad triangulum comes in as a distinct second to construction ad quadratum."*[36] While most floor plans were based on the square schema, the triangular grid was used instead in the elevation for the windows' mullions, traceries and trefoils.[37] (See, for example, Fig. 14.32).

In his essay, Bucher makes the (much-contested) claim that the floor plan alone was sufficient for a cathedral's construction, and that the elevation could be geometrically worked out by the masons according to the architect's basic design: *"At the Regensburg Meeting of Lodges in 1459,"* Bucher recalls, *"it was decreed that 'No one was to teach how to derive the elevation from the plan' to anyone outside the masons' guild."*[38]

On the floor plan, the foundation of the towers, nave, transept and aisles were worked out *ad quadratum*. And, as they rose to the heavens, the towers often underwent the 'quadrature' or 'turned square': *"The rotation of the square became the main practical and aesthetic key for Gothic architecture and its parts, including even glazed pavement designs,"*[39] Bucher notes. (See, for example, Fig. 14.29).

Thus we return to the most pervasive motif in Islamic art, the *Khatem Sulemani* or Octagram (Fig. 14.26 - left), which appears in so many Muslim creations. The Octagram is nothing less than 'the turned square' – which Bucher calls 'the key' for Gothic Architectural design. Meanwhile, the rotation of the triangle, creating the Hexagram (Fig. 14.26 - right) was used by Gothic masons and goldsmiths for the design of liturgical instruments, baptismal fonts, reliquaries and pulpits.[40]

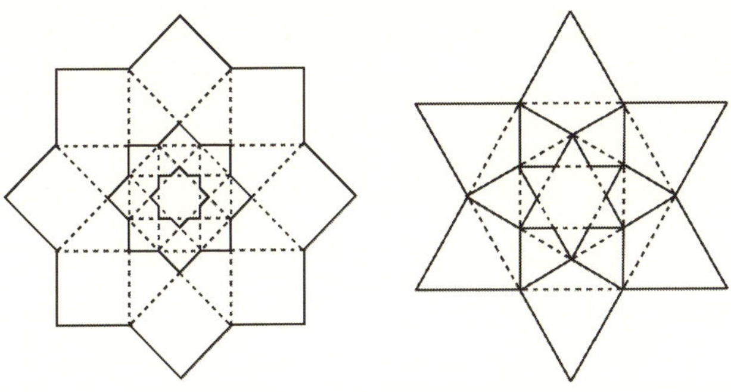

Fig. 14.26 - The Turned-square Octagram and Turned-triangle Hexagram

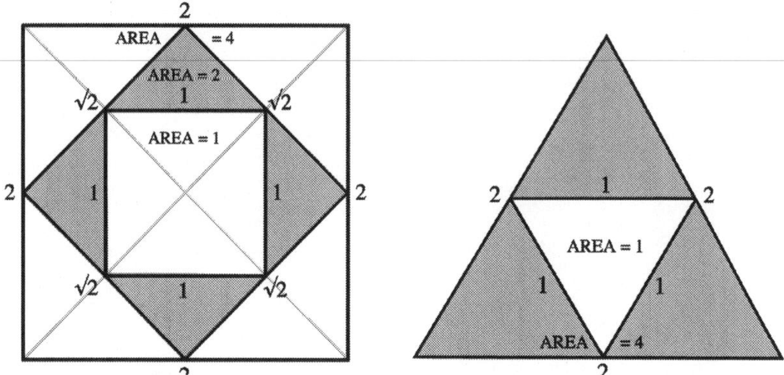

Fig. 14.27 - Quadrature or Turned-square and Triangulature or Turned-triangle

But it is particularly in floor tiles that we may see the recursive designs of turned-square Octagrams, or turned-triangle Hexagrams, which reflect the ever-expanding square and triangular measures of the building's sacred space.

The quadrature or turned square (Fig. 14.27 - left) was a key geometric construction in Gothic architecture because of the harmonious proportions it brought to the ever-expanding space. In a series of nested squares and turned squares, the *area* increases at a geometric rate with the common ratio of 2, generating proportions like 1:2:4. Meanwhile, the *side-lengths* increase at a geometric rate with the common ratio of √2, generating proportions like 1 : √2 : 2. The value of √2 is 1:1.4142135... or roughly 1.5, which is roughly half-way between 1 and 2. So, the area increases at a precise rate of 1:2 (the *diapason*), and the side-lengths increase at an approximate rate of 1:1.5. (the 2:3 *diapente*). Geometrically speaking, both progressions express Pythagorean harmonies.

In the case of triangulature or the turned triangle (Fig. 14.27 - right), the area increases at a geometric rate with a common ratio of 4, generating proportions like 1:4:16:64. Meanwhile, the side-lengths increase at a geometric rate with a common ratio of 2, generating proportions like 1:2:4:8. So, the area increases at a rate of 1:4 (the *diatessaron* quarters) and the side-lengths increase at a rate of 1:2 (the *diapason*). These progressions also express Pythagorean harmonies.

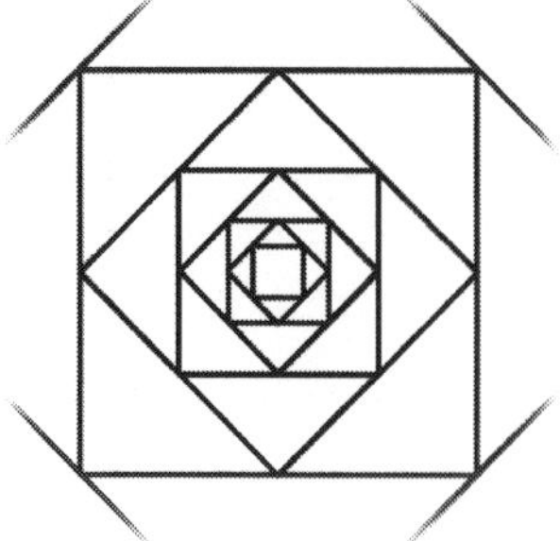

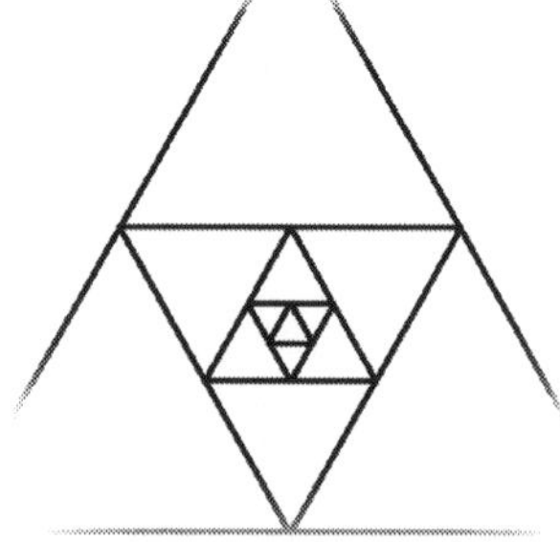

Fig. 14.28 - Quadrature and Triangulature of Sacred Space

In this way, the pervasive use of the triangle and the square allowed Gothic artisans to achieve a perfectly harmonious relationship of the parts to the whole. Each block, carefully measured and carved, was fit one beside the next, and all arranged according to the hidden lines and latticework of their sacramental geometry. As Bucher notes:

"Perhaps the main reason for the longevity of the Gothic style lies in the visually nearly imperceptible inter-relationships of complex forms derived from each other through a strict geometric process. To exaggerate one might say that a single finial [i.e. end ornament] *preserved from a crumpled tower could suffice for a reasonably close reconstruction of the total structure, provided its position within the structure were known."*[41]

X. Quadrature, Armature & Ornamental Markers

In *The Geometry of Creation* (2011), Robert Bork investigates the Gothic design process by analyzing most of the 600 or so architectural drawings still extant, of which 442 are found in Vienna and pertain to the south spire of its Stephansdom, the tallest masonry structure in Europe upon its completion in 1433. According to Bork:

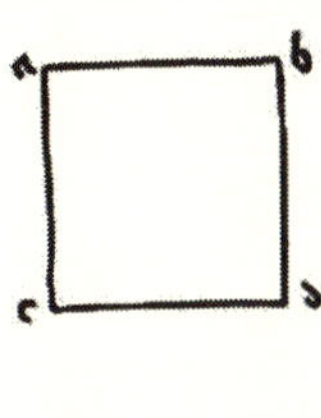

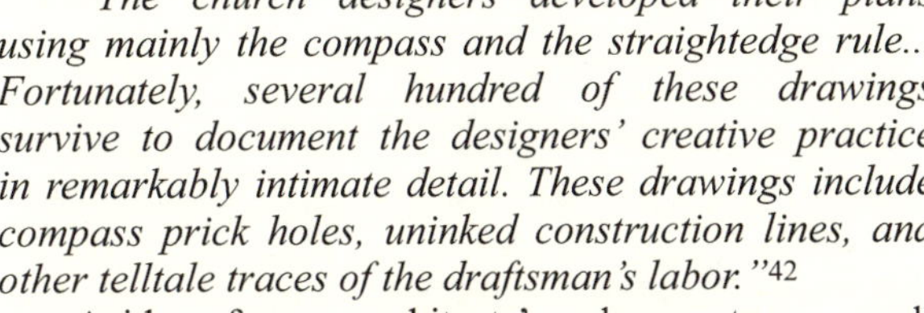

"The church designers developed their plans using mainly the compass and the straightedge rule... Fortunately, several hundred of these drawings survive to document the designers' creative practice in remarkably intimate detail. These drawings include compass prick holes, uninked construction lines, and other telltale traces of the draftsman's labor."[42]

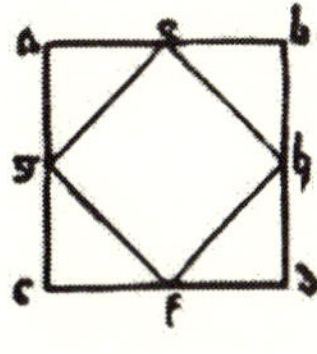

Aside from architects' plans, two small booklets, Matthäus Roriczer's *Büchlein von der Fialen Gerechtigkeit* (Booklet Concerning Pinnacle Correctitude – 1486) and Hans Schmuttermayr's *Fialenbüchlein* (Pinnacles Booklet – 1487) reveal certain design methods, particularly in the creation of the pinnacles and gablets which, as Bork notes, are "*...paradigmatic products of the Gothic design method. Both authors* [Roriczer and Schmuttermayr] *agree that the first step in designing a pinnacle should be to establish a square as its basic ground plan. Next, a series of progressively smaller rotated squares should be inscribed within the original square, in a sequence often called 'quadrature'.*"[43] We can see this in Fig. 14.29, which is an illustration from Roriczer's *Booklet* that shows the *quadrature* construction of a pinnacle, when viewed from above.

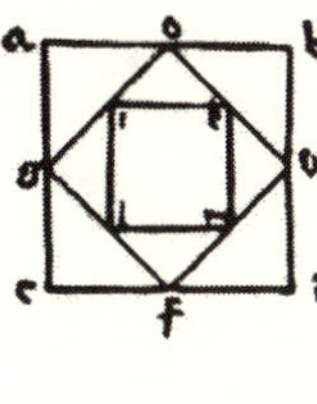

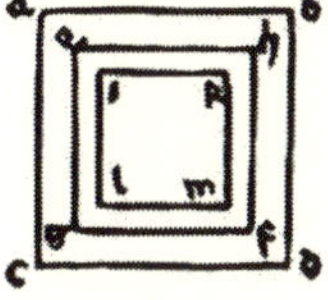

Fig. 14.29

But the clearest example of this design process comes to us from Villard de Honnecourt's drawings for the plan and elevation of the Laon tower (Fig. 14.30). Although Honnecourt drew the plan and elevation separately, I have laid them out vertically to show their

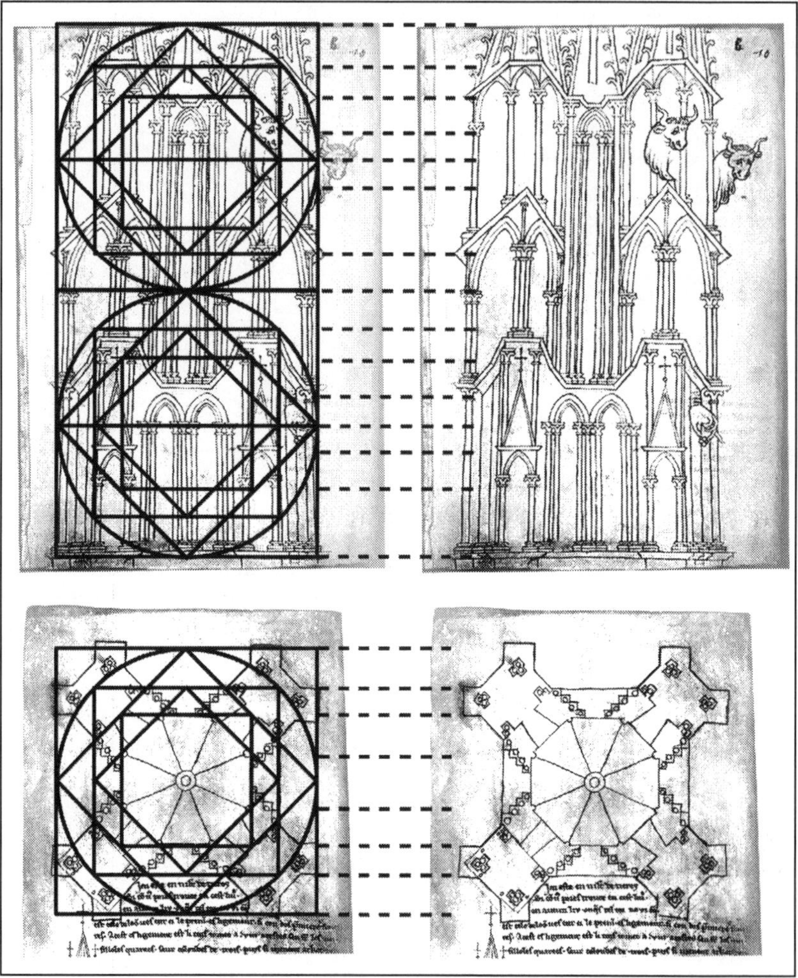

Fig. 14.30 - Left: Bork's Heavy Black Lines Explaining the Quadrature Design
Right: Honnecourt's Original Drawing of the Laon Tower - Plan and Elevation

profound inter-locking relationship. Honnecourt did not *design* the Laon tower, but his drawings indicate an insider's knowledge of the design process.

The tower's architect began with a square that set the outer limits of the buttresses with their turned tabernacle foundations (Fig. 14.30 - bottom). A circle was inscribed in this outer square, and an octagram (a square and turned square) was inscribed in the circle, to set the limits of the tower proper. Next, another octagram was inscribed in the first to create the octagon inside the tower. Through this process of *quadrature* – inscribing squares and turned squares one within the other – the resulting octagrams get smaller by a factor of $\sqrt{2}$. This same geometrical proportion determines the thickness of the tower walls, which are equal to the space between the nested octagrams.[44]

In the frontal-view of the tower (Fig. 14.30 - top), we can see how the elevation was derived from the ground plan through a process called *Auszug* in German or 'pulling out'. *The same geometrical proportions in the ground plan are used again in the elevation.* Honnecourt's drawing stands exactly two squares high (1:2), with two significant markers at the halfway point of each square (1:4 and 3:4). At the 1:4 mark Honnecourt has drawn 'the Hand of God', an ornament that does not appear in the Laon tower, and at the 3:4 mark he has drawn two bulls.

"Seemingly capricious decorative details in the drawings," Bork writes, *"actually call attention to key points in these armatures. Gargoyles, grotesques, and tracery elements were all used as signposts or aide-memoires that would help to make the drawings geometrically legible to the designers and their colleagues."*[45]

We see in this way how certain ornaments in the drawing relate to specific geometric proportions, such as the 1:2 *diapason* and 3:4 *diatessaron.* By following the horizontal dotted lines from the armature on the left to the facade on the right, we can see how numerous other proportions from the *quadratura* correspond to the heights of the columns and their capitals.

In his conclusion to *The Geometry of Creation*, the author writes:

"*The most frequently encountered governing figures in Gothic drawings were squares, equilateral triangles, and octagons, all of which can be easily constructed with compass and rule. The unending variety with which such figures could be combined, though, shows that simple terms like 'ad quadratum' and 'ad triangulum' provide a grossly insufficient vocabulary for the description of Gothic design options. The dialog between all these polygons and their circumscribing circles plays such an important role in Gothic design, meanwhile, that terms like 'octature' and 'hexature' deserve to be recognized alongside the more well-established term 'quadrature.'*"[46]

All of these geometrical constructions constitute Sacred Codes for the harmonious measure of sacred space. Yet, we would be wrong to suppose that polygons form the *only* basis for Gothic design. In order to draw a grid of squares or triangles – *ad quadratum* or *ad triangulum* – the defining limits of these shapes must first be marked upon *an underlying grid of circles.* Although the words *ad circulum* are never mentioned in the surviving texts, the emergence of the triangle and the square *'from the circle'* is the true and most primary construction. As Schmuttermayer recalled in 1487, the liberal art of geometry is *'developed out of the centre of the circle.'*

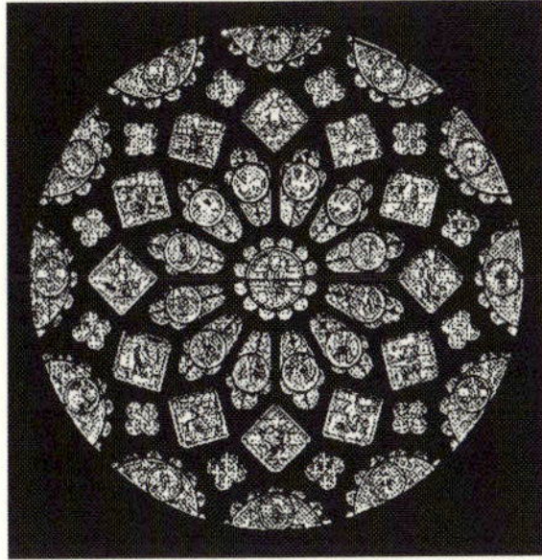

Fig. 14.31
North Rosace - Chartres

Just as the phrase *ad circulum* is never spoken, neither is it *depicted* in a sacred work of art. Rather, it recedes into invisibility, as another Sacred Code underlying and unifying sacred space. Where it *does* appear, most of all, is in *the forms* – the countless curvilinear forms that make up the endless arabesques, traceries and trefoils decorating the cathedral's facade.

And it appears, above all, in the central rose window (Fig. 14.31), where the Divine Unity manifests itself in a luminescent exfoliation of perfectly harmonized colours and shapes. What the *girih* star designs are to Islamic art, so is the *rosace* to the Gothic. In the East, the *Wahdat al-Wujud* or 'Unity of Existence' reveals itself in a sharp lightning burst of crystalline shapes, spreading outward as the divine light – or *Nur* – overtaking the darkness. In the West, the celestial rose unfolds in a scintillating latticework of stained glass, and all the figures, like dew drops, receive their light and circular form within the radiant petals of the *Unio Mystica*.

XI. The Harmonic Armature from the Circle

While Gothic design is primarily based on geometry rather than arithmetic, it would be wrong to presuppose that the Gothic era did not venerate the same Pythagorean-Platonic harmonies as the Renaissance, which is to say, the *diapason* halves, *diapente* thirds and *diatessaron* quarters.

In the first book of Michael S. Schneider's five volume opus *Constructing the Universe*,[47] he retraces a method (which I will expand upon here) used by Gothic masons to construct an 'ogival' or pointed arch (Fig. 16.16). This arch, we must remember, lies at the very heart of the Gothic style, and reveals their deeply mystical conception of the creation as the harmonious expansion of the One into the many.

The mason began, like the Divine Creator, by *'drawing a circle upon the face of the depth.'* (Prov 8:22-27). This is the main circle at the top of the Gothic arch, and it is called the *oculus* or 'eye' because it actively sees and creates the All. The point at the centre of the *oculus* symbolizes the source of divine vision, which creates all shapes by visualizing them into existence. And, like the archetypal 'eye in the triangle', the outer circle of the *oculus* will eventually be surrounded by the curved triangle of the ogival arch.

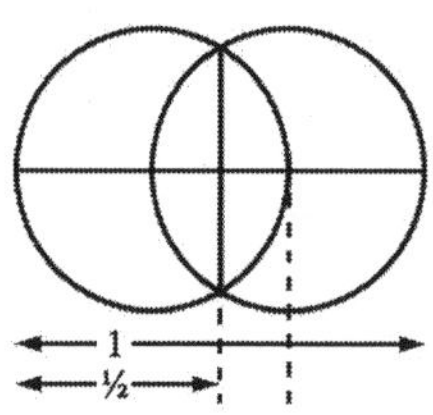

Fig. 16.17
1:2 *Diapason*

In the next step, the One becomes two, as two circles of the same measure are inscribed again, below the first, in the form of the *vesica piscis*. As we can see in Fig. 16.17, a vertical line drawn straight down from the centre of the first circle divides these two circles at the point of their intersection (called the mandorla). And so, a horizontal line drawn from the limit of these circles to the point of their intersection gives us the first of all harmonies, the *diapason* ratio of 1:2. Through the *vesica piscis*, the One has actively visualized its own harmonic division into two, sounding it out visually and musically, as the two-in-one 'halves'.

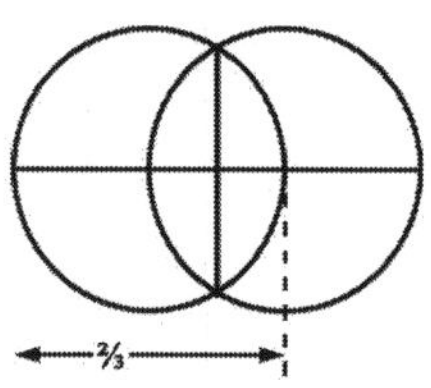

Fig. 16.18
2:3 *Diapente*

Meanwhile, the centre of each circle lies on the limit of the other, creating the second of all harmonies, the 2:3 *diapente* (Fig. 16.18). A horizontal line, drawn from the limit of one circle to the centre of the other, measures out this new harmony of the three-in-one 'thirds'. As we can see in Fig. 16.16, the intersection of the two circles (the mandorla) also creates the measure for the smaller circle in the *oculus*, which lies at the exact centre of the six-petalled flower.

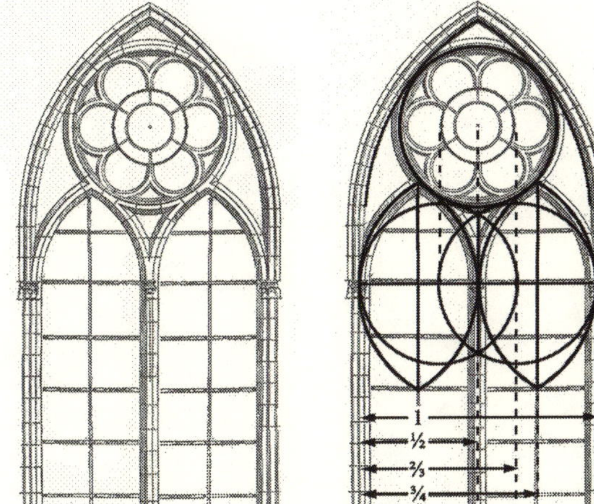

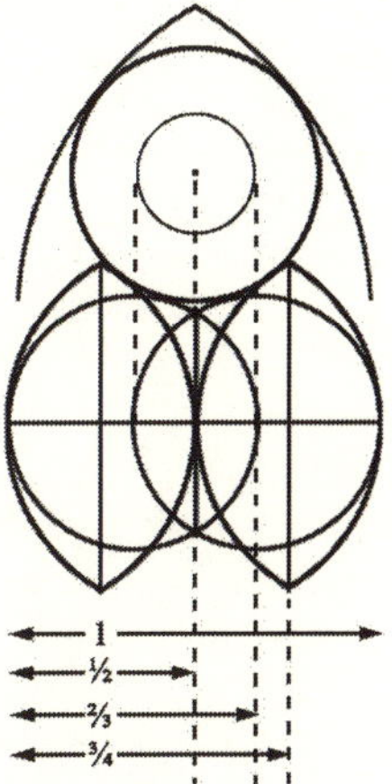

Fig. 16.16 - Harmonic Construction of the Gothic Ogival Arch

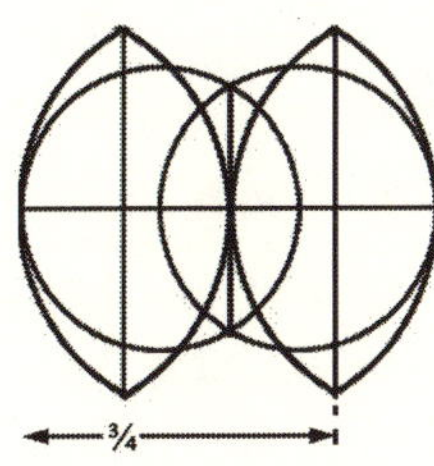

Fig. 16.19
3:4 *Diatessaron*

Still imitating the Divine Creator, the mason then spread his compass to the entire width of the *vesica piscis* and used that measure to draw four arcs (like double mandorlas), and vertical lines through each mandorla to divide the entire width into the four-in-one 'quarters'. As a result, the Divine One has now created the third of all harmonies, the 3:4 *diatessaron*. As we can see in Fig. 16.19, a horizontal line drawn from the limit of one circle to the vertical through the other, reveals this new harmonic measure in space and in sound.

Fig. 16.16 shows how the architecture of the Gothic window follows a metaphysical geometry, in which the primordial circle measures out, first the *oculus*, and then the *vesica piscis* (two more circles of the same measure) to determine the entire width of the arch. *That measure* is used to draw the triangular arcs *of the ogival arch* surrounding the *oculus* – that is, the measure of the divine triangle. Meanwhile, the arcs of the double mandorla are used to trace out the smaller ogival arches of the two slender windows below. These windows become a visual manifestation of the 1:2 ratio, the harmonic division of Divine sight, from one measure in space to two. At the same time, the traceries of these slender Gothic windows manifest the 3:4 ratio, the harmonic division of divine sight from three measures to four.

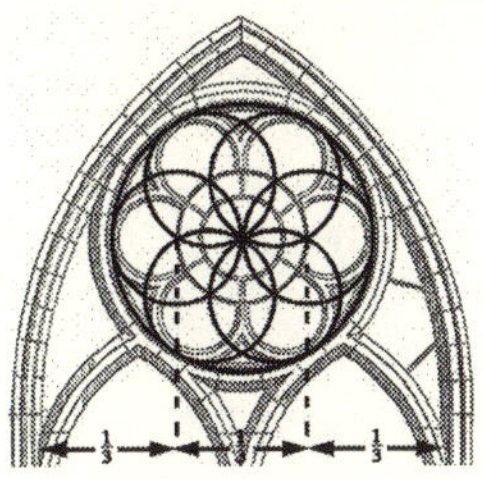

Fig. 16.20
3:4 *Diatessaron*

The 2:3 division in the Gothic arch may not be obvious at first glance. But, the width of the intersection of the *vesica piscis*, we may recall, created the measure for the smaller circle in the *oculus*. This circle lies at the exact centre of the six-petalled flower, which was created by drawing the smaller circle *seven* times. Like the seven days of creation, or the seven heavenly spheres, these seven small circles measure out the Seed of Life, which exfoliates as a six-petalled flower at the very centre

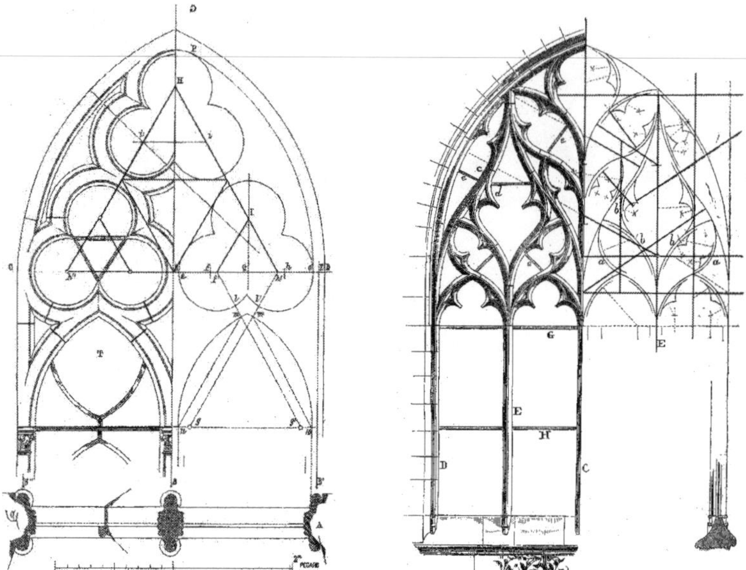

Fig. 14.32 - Ogival Arch with Trefoils   Fig. 14.33 - Rayonnant Arch

of the *oculus*. Indeed, if the six-pointed hexagram were traced into the flower, we would have the matrix for the three main axes of *ad triangulum* space.

In this way, the small circle gives us the 2:3 ratio, the harmonic division of divine sight from two (the *vesica piscis*) to three (the smaller circle arising from their intersection). This small circle, at the heart of the three-sided triangle, divides the entire width of the arch into three equal parts.

Traced out time and again on the façades of Gothic cathedrals, the ogival arch reveals the harmony of all creation, expanding *ad circulum* in the ratios 1:2, 2:3 and 3:4.

XII. Flamboyant Curves & the Hidden Prime

Although the *ogival* arch characterizes the Gothic style, its design did not remain static during its 500 year history. In his *Dictionnaire raisonné de l'architecture française du XIe au XVIe siècle* (Dictionary of French Architecture from 11th to 16th Century), Viollet-le-Duc traces out the stylistic development of its stone tracery.[48]

Beginning with Fig. 14.32, we can see how an *ad triangulum* grid was used for this part of the cathedral's elevation. All of the *trefoils* (the three-leaf clover shapes) are created by drawing small circles round the three end-points of the small triangles. Meanwhile, these smaller triangles are, themselves, parts of a larger triangle, which shows the *triangulature* process – inscribing ever larger triangles or inverted triangles around the first central triangle.

The *trefoils* are themselves symbolic of the Holy Trinity, the Three-in-One deity. The arch – which is an *ogival* arch – is constructed by drawing circular arcs from each corner of the base. The ogival arch is nothing other than a triangle reaching out to the curves of a circle.

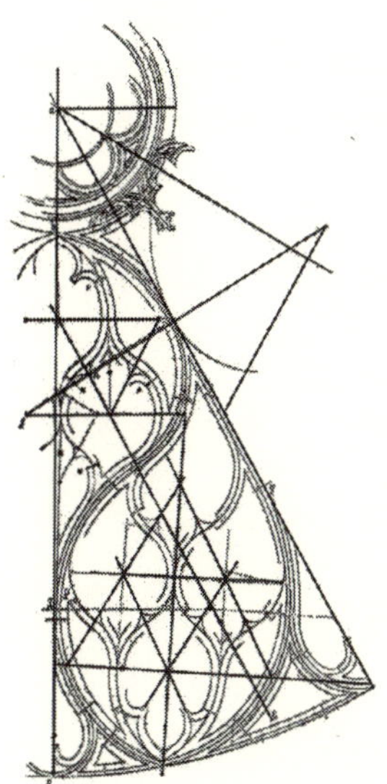

Fig. 14.34
Flamboyant Arch

What we see, in the end, are the visible arcs and circles drawn from invisible triangular grids. What we do not see is that the triangles themselves, at one point, were constructed *within circles*, so the circles we see here are but the visible parts of a much larger, invisible grid of unifying circles (*ad circulum*).

In the next two diagrams (figs. 14.33 and 14.34), we can see how Gothic design evolved from the *Rayonnant* style (c. 1240 – 1350) to the *Flamboyant* style (c. 1350 – 1500). Over the centuries, the curling branches in the traceries transformed into undulating flames (*flamboyant* means 'flaming'). At the same time, the relationship of the curves to the straight lines became far more complex.

If we look closely at Fig. 14.34, we can see that the stonemason has still placed his compass on certain fixed points (determined by a triangular grid that looks more like a ◇ rhombic grid). But, after having traced out his arcs, he freely draws the mouchettes, daggers and cusps so characteristic of the flamboyant style. These designs, though expressive, still work within well-defined geometrical shapes.

We are reminded of Viollet-le-Duc's remark: *"Style is the manifestation of an ideal founded upon a principle."*[49] And, what Fuchs called the "[curving] *line which searched flexibly, in a wave-like dance, for the straight line,"*[50] The geometry of straight lines, with their shapes and grids, provides *the principle* which underlies the Gothic style. Indeed, this same principle underlies all carefully-conceived curvilinear styles, from ancient Egypt to Jugendstil – that Jugendstil so dear to Vienna, and to Fuchs in particular.

Meanwhile, as one of the five marks of 'the Hidden Prime of Styles' this principle creates styles that ultimately *transcend* history. Alas, as eternal or 'meta-historical' styles, they are forever being displaced by more fashionable 'mannerisms'. As François Bucher so passionately remarked about the Late Gothic: *"The Renaissance was to reject these* [Gothic geometrical] *games with a vengeance, very much as the Bauhaus was to reject Art Nouveau."*[51] Caught within a post-post-post Modernism, we are still living in the *Bauhaus* age of abstract, straight-lined buildings, deprived of all curvilinear ornament.

With these thoughts in mind, we turn to Ornament, its history and its principles, since ornament holds the key to the art of curving serpentine lines round straight lines in armature. However, all this is nothing more than a prelude to our greater task: of determining how figures move in relationship to armature – and indeed, how Figuration as a whole relates to Composition.

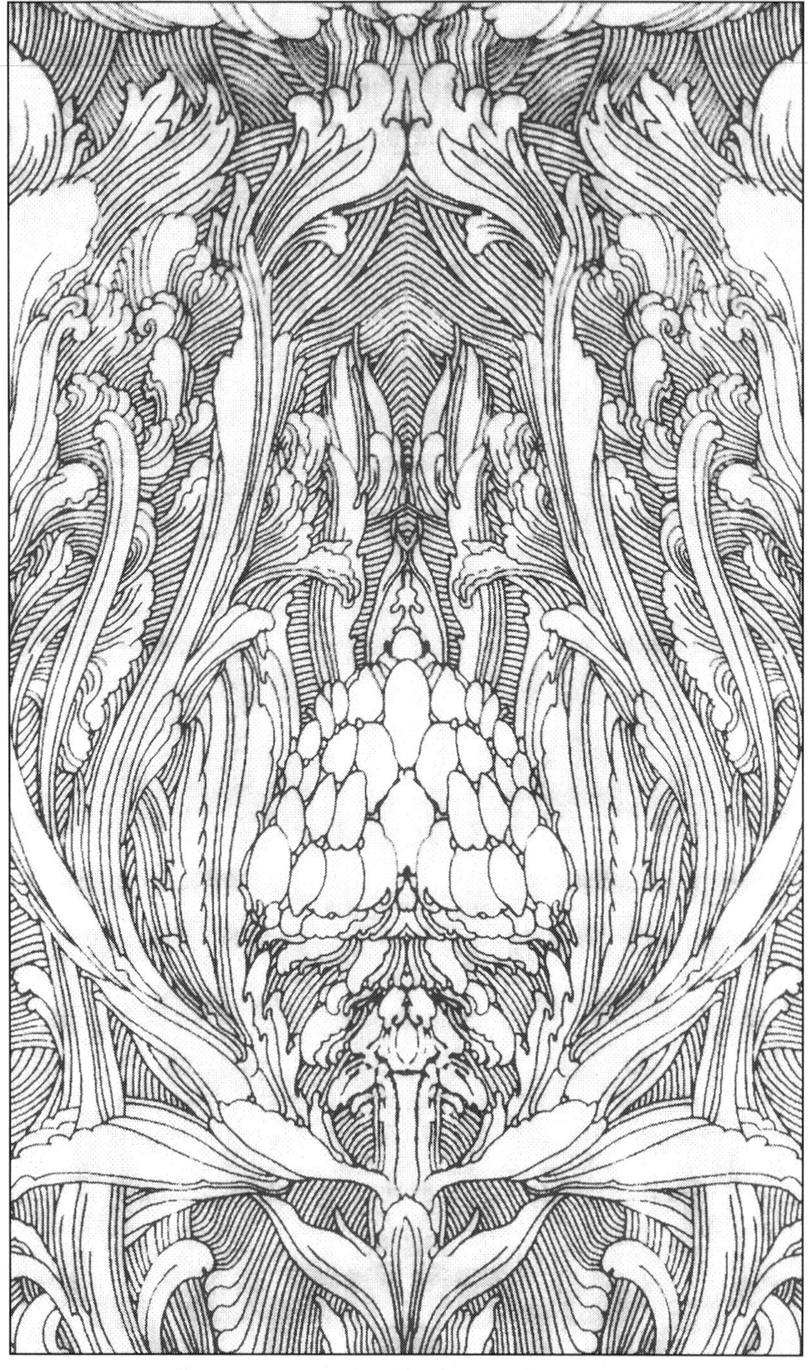

Fig. 15.1 - Ernst Fuchs - Floral Design for Wallpaper

CHAPTER XV
ORNAMENT & FORM

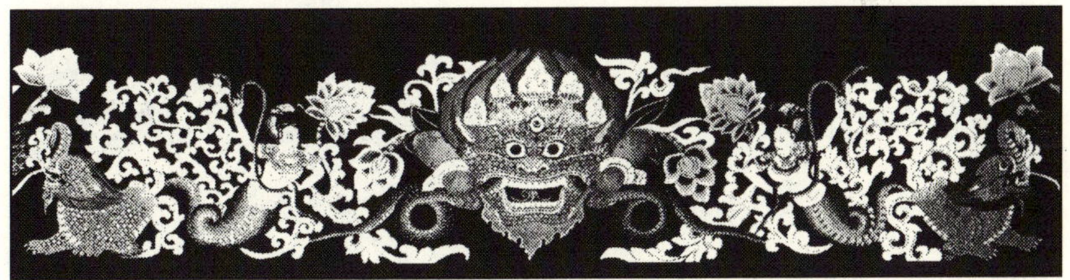

I. The Wandering Eye & Fixed Gaze

As we gaze upon a sacred work of art, our ultimate aim is to seek a stilled point of focus where the deity, as the divine source of vision, may activate our own sacred seeing. With eyes wide and attentive, we surrender our passive human sight to the more active, creative and transformative gaze of Divine Vision. But, before that moment of true contemplation, our eye tends to wander, curious and entranced, through the myriad of lesser beings calling for our attention. Like an array of recessed statues on a temple facade, the ornaments surrounding a sacred painting serve to prepare our vision, to cleanse and purify it, through images of fear or protection, wrath or bliss.

The *Kīrtimukha* is an ornamental image that adorns the gateway to many a Hindu temple or Buddhist thangka. Also called 'The Face of Glory' it is the creation of Lord Shiva, who called forth the all-devouring beast from his own Third Eye to combat a dangerous demon. When the demon begged for mercy, Shiva restrained the beast he had created and bid it to devour itself, which it did, leaving only the upper part of its body remaining. Shiva henceforth affixed the Face of Glory on the lintel of his temple gateways, to repel any impious soul who dared to enter his holy sanctuary.

Fig. 15.2 Above - Romio Shrestha: Kīrtimukha Border of a Buddhist Thangka

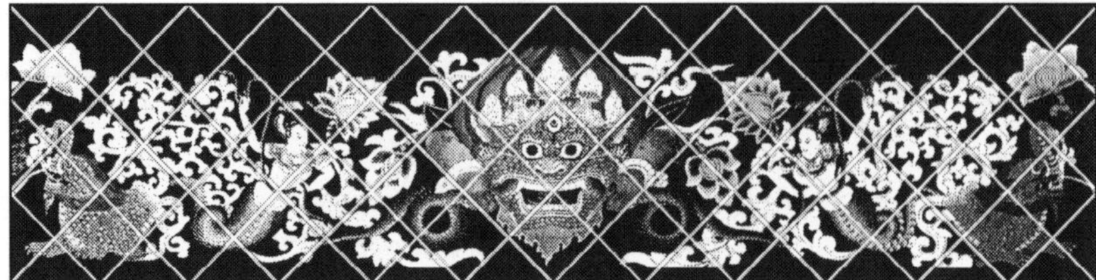

Fig. 15.3 - Romio Shrestha: Kīrtimukha Design with *Ad Quadratum* Armature

In the example given here (Fig. 15.3), the Face of Glory forms part of a decorative frieze bordering a thangka produced in the studio of Nepalese painter Romio Shrestha. I have added the grid of 45° diagonals that underlies the design. This image reminds us of certain key principles underlying Ornament in general.

In a sacred work of art, ornamental figures express Divine Vision in either its positive or negative aspect. The blissful figures, whether in the form of angels, heraldic animals or sacred plants, manifest the playful multiplicity of Divine Seeing. In truth, God is One, absolute and complete in itself. Yet it reflects upon itself by actively seeing and transfiguring itself into the vast variety of living forms that populate its surrounding space. In ornament, each blissful figure opens its eye and 'sees' as an expression of that Divine Sight which is gazing upon itself, now as this Solar Falcon gliding on outspread wings (Fig. 15.4), now as this acroterion palmette with leaves and volutes arrayed around a single centre (Fig. 15.5).

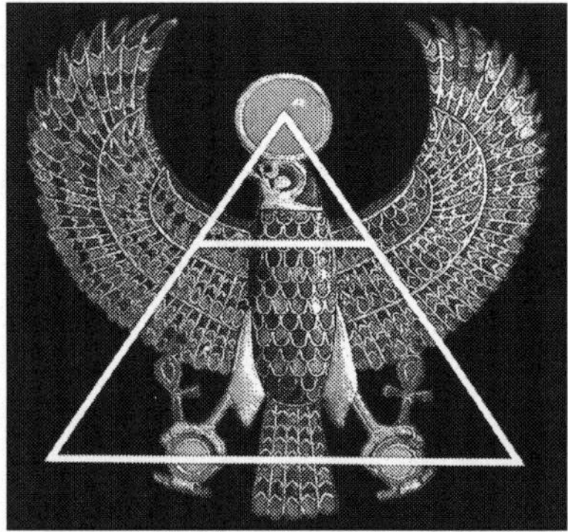

Fig. 15.4 - Egyptian Horus Falcon

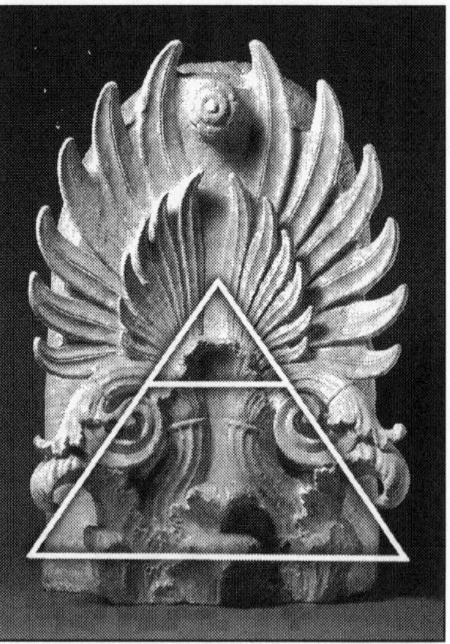

Fig. 15.5 - Greek Acroterion c. 325 B.C.E

With a more meditative gaze, we are able to contemplate each ornament and increasingly activate our divine way of seeing. That is why ornaments possess so much structure and symmetry: they are so designed as to fix our regard, to hold it and awaken it to the Divine Eye that is imminent in each shape, awaiting activation.

The Hidden Sign of the Hieratic does not underlie every ornament. But the tell-tale signs of order, geometry and armature suggest that it is strikingly

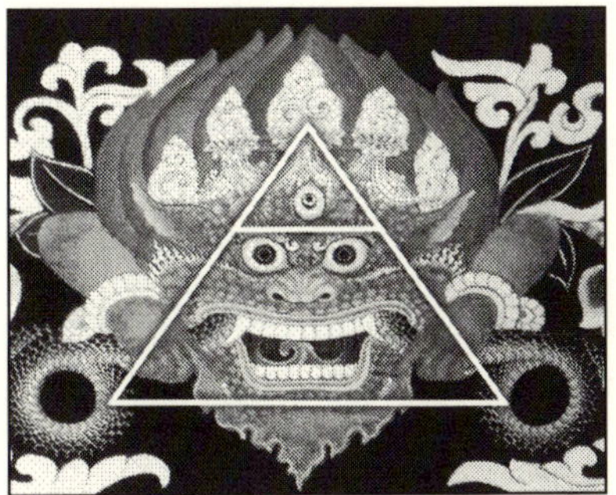

Fig. 15.6 - Shrestha: Kīrtimukha

present in many, where the plant forms express the growth, opening and expansion of Hieratic Vision through the waxing movement of their leaves, and heraldic animals manifest the Divine Eye as surrounded by powerful limbs and outspread wings that allow it to move – and see itself move – in the graceful form of a falcon, lion or unicorn.

If the blissful figures of ornament prepare us by gradually cleansing and purifying our sullied human sight, then the wrathful figures serve a much different purpose. The Face of Glory (Fig. 15.6) is a typical example of an apotropaic figure (lit – *'those turning us away'*). Such faces evoke our greatest fears, forcing us to confront even our fear of death. But a small detail, such as an ornament on their crown or a mark on their forehead, reminds us of their hidden higher origin. Like angels with fearful faces, they may test our faith or inner knowledge of what lies beyond, and our readiness to confront the unknown.

In China, the *T'ao t'ieh* (Fig. 15.8) serves the same purpose, as does the head of the Gorgon (Fig. 15.7) in the West: to ward off the Evil Eye and neutralize its malevolent power. By tradition, any human can possess the evil eye, when he or she casts a gaze so filled with envy or possession that it casts a curse upon the very object of its desire.

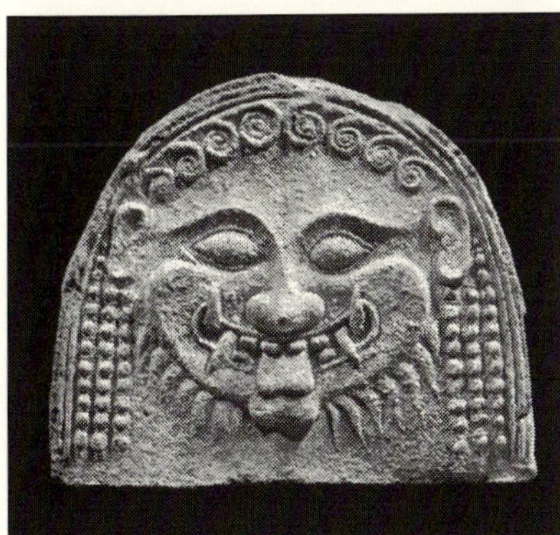

Fig. 15.7 - Greek Gorgon

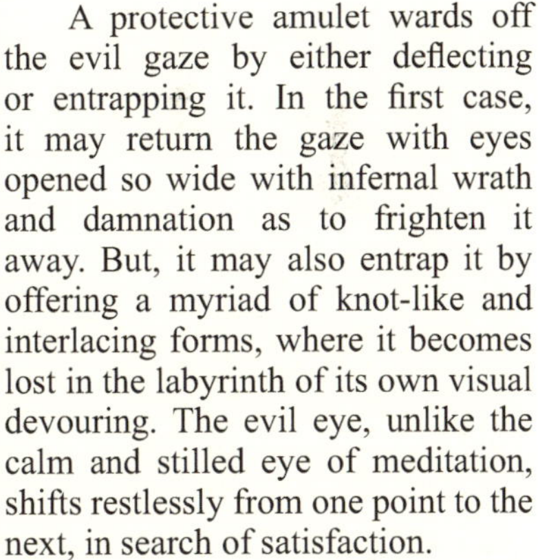

A protective amulet wards off the evil gaze by either deflecting or entrapping it. In the first case, it may return the gaze with eyes opened so wide with infernal wrath and damnation as to frighten it away. But, it may also entrap it by offering a myriad of knot-like and interlacing forms, where it becomes lost in the labyrinth of its own visual devouring. The evil eye, unlike the calm and stilled eye of meditation, shifts restlessly from one point to the next, in search of satisfaction.

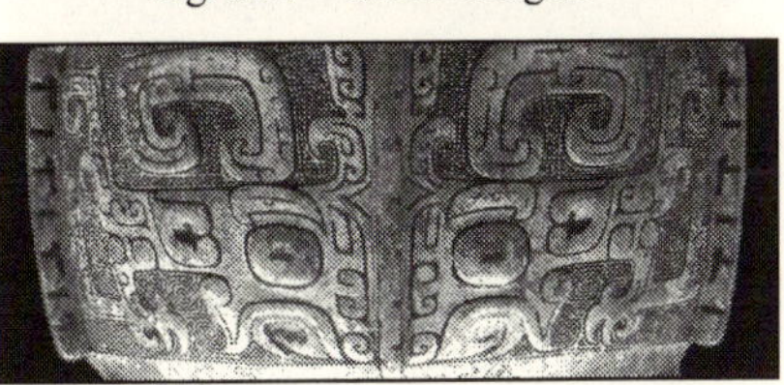

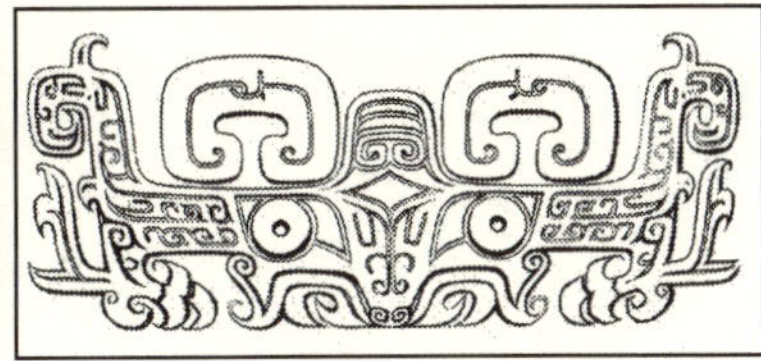

Fig. 15.8 - Shang Dynasty Bronze Vessel with C-horns, round Eyes, Claws of T'ao t'ieh

We can see this in the ornamental frieze atop Romio Shrestha's thangka, where the Face of Glory is surrounded by swirling forms of energy. The Kīrtimukha opens its eyes wide with anger to frighten away any form of seeing that has no peace or divinity in its heart. But the leonine face is also surrounded by watery or plant-like forms emerging from the mouths of the two *makaras*, to the far left and right of the frieze. We shall meet with these bizarre creatures later in this chapter.

For now, our gaze may wander, captivated and entranced, by the sinuous, coiling movement of those slender curving shapes, which move very much in the manner of serpents. Indeed, the feminine *apsaras* hold serpents in their hands, and the Kīrtimukha is furiously devouring the heads of two more.

In other ornamental friezes atop thangkas or temple doorways, it is the almighty eagle Garuda who grasps *naga*-serpents in its claws or triumphantly devours them. As the winged vehicle of Brahma, Garuda is a heavenly emissary, a conquering force of divine energy. Kīrtimukha, though less beautiful than Garuda, is an emissary of Shiva's divine power. Their purpose is to tranquilize and defeat the serpent-power, which is here symbolic of the ever-hungry, ever-devouring gaze of those spirits who have become lost in the illusion of their own lust and desire.

In this way, ornaments have the power to either subdue our errant gaze by entrapping its wayward course in labyrinthine corridors, or to attract and finally transfigure it by focussing our eyes onto a fixed point and activate a more sacred way of seeing.

II. Fuchs' Complementary Forms

I first met Amanda Sage at Ernst Fuchs' Apocalypse Chapel in Klagenfurt. We assisted Fuchs at roughly the same time – she in Vienna and myself in Monaco. Occasionally we worked together at the large studio in Castel Caramel, but it was only years later, when we co-taught at Torri Superiore (during the *Visions in the Mischtechnik Seminars*), that we were able to sit down and really compare notes. We discovered that Fuchs had repeated, time and again, certain key phrases that encapsulated his working methods.

The phrase that related most to the drawing stage was deceptively simple: *Always seek out complementary forms*.

We can see this in the ornamental designs (Fig. 15.1) which Fuchs developed for his wallpaper and textiles. (Amanda Sage also demonstrates this principle admirably through the energy lines in her work). Whenever two curving lines meet, they should cross each other at *dynamic angles*, not too slight and not too straight, but in an organic and energetically interesting way.

Ornament is not only the stylistic line; it is also the intimate knowledge of *forms*. Throughout time, certain motifs have recurred, due to their structural and organic beauty. This is especially true of the acanthus leaf, which appears time and again in ornament, from Corinthian capitals to Islamic *rūmī* designs. At the top of Fig. 15.9 is a reproduction from M. Meurer's *Vergleichende Formenlehre des Ornaments und der Pflanze* (Comparative Study of Ornamental Forms and Plants - 1908) and below it is a detail from

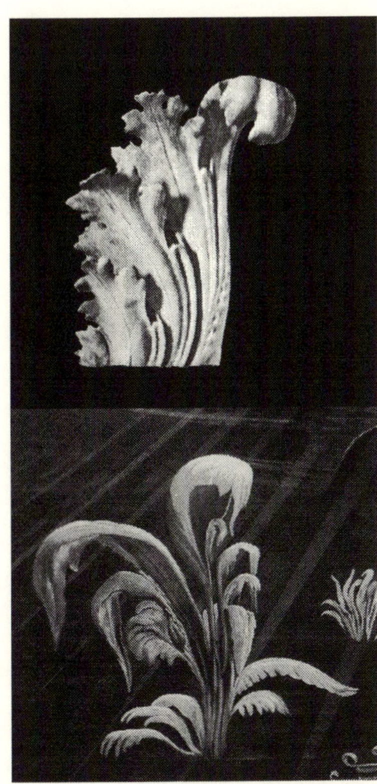

Fig. 15.9 - Top: Acanthus from M. Meurer's *Vergleichende Formenlehre* - 1908
Bottom: Floral Design from Ernst Fuchs: *Paradiso* - 2010

Ernst Fuchs' *Paradiso* painting (which I spent many hours working on as an assistant). The resemblance between the two forms is startling, yet Fuchs has captured, beyond its basic morphology, the growth pattern of the acanthus – its graceful, swan-like movement. Moritz Meurer called this the *Ursprungsform* – the structural logic of the plant's organic shape due to its symmetry, bifurcation pattern, growth stages, phyllotaxis and evolutionary history ('phylogenesis').

As Owen Jones noted, geometry can also aid in the creation of ornamental forms, through the creative interplay of straight and curving lines. Originally published in 1856, using the newly-invented chromolithography to capture in colour the textiles and ornaments of nineteen different cultures, Owen Jones' *The Grammar of Ornament* was prefaced with thirty-seven propositions, as *"certain general laws"*[1] for the construction of ornament. Proposition 8 states: *"All ornament should be based upon geometrical construction."*[2] And Proposition 10 adds, *"Harmony of form consists in the proper balancing, and contrast of, the straight, the inclined and the curved."*[3]

Jone's final chapter is dedicated to those forms arising from Nature herself, since *"True art consists in idealizing, and not copying, the forms of Nature."*[4] He recalls the Nile Lily at the root of Egyptian ornament, and the Acanthus leaf so dear to the Greeks, and states that each culture must bring forth its own ornaments, according to set principles, given the flora and fauna of its own environment. *"Artists should,"* he says, *"by an attentive examination of the principles which pervade all the works of the past, and which have excited universal admiration, be led to the creation of new forms, equally beautiful."*[5]

III. The Language of Ornament

An exhaustive history of ornament has yet to be written, since the subject does not lend itself easily to any simple chronological or geographical narrative. In *The Language of Ornament,* James Trilling prefaces his work with the statement that *"Ornament is a key to the otherwise secret life of styles and cultures."*[6] The author offers a few historical sketches, but soon admits that no complete history of ornament may be made.

One reason is that *"...ornament does not evolve within strict categories of time and place, but reflects the interaction and transformation of cultures through migration, trade, conquest and the spread of religions... Styles diverge and converge, exhaust and renew themselves."*[7] Scholars have traced the diffusion of certain motifs from one culture to another, but their fusion with a variety of other local traditions, called *syncretism*, creates both hybrids and entirely new designs.

"Diffusionism is the assumption," Trilling writes, *"that artistic styles and other forms of cultural expression are transmitted from one society to another, changing as they go but preserving a core of similarity."*[8] That core of similarity, however, may mislead us into believing in a direct source of transmission, when really it is a phenomenon of the same motif arising in different places under the same conditions.

The prime example of this is Rudolf Wittkower's 1939 article 'The Eagle and the Serpent: A Study in the Migration of Symbols', where he traces the motif of 'the eagle in combat with the serpent' from Mesopotamia to Europe, Asia, and the Pacific Islands, then onto Aztec and the indigenous New World cultures. But, one can also observe in Nature the universal truth that eagles do indeed eat snakes, and so the wide-spread dispersion of this symbol may be due to common occurrence rather than cultural transmission.

Or, if C. G. Jung is correct, this same configuration may be an archetype arising from our Collective Unconscious, and more the result of shared dream-motifs than disseminated mythology. Yet again, such images may be the result of Visionaries entering the same subtle realms of the Sacred, and returning with authentic accounts of what they have witnessed. A history of ornament should integrate all these different approaches, while recognizing that the mysterious core of ornament remains timeless – an eternal creative play of the divine imagination.

One of the earliest and most erudite historical studies, becoming a landmark in the field of ornamentation, was Alois Riegl's 1893 opus *Stilfragen: Grundlegungen zu einer Geschichte der Ornamentik* (Questions of Style: Foundations for a History of Ornament). As Riegl traverses history from Paleolithic times to the Renaissance, he analyzes four main types of design: the Geometric Style, Heraldic Style, Vegetal Ornamentation and Arabesques. Underlying the development of different styles is a creative urge, which Riegl calls *Kunstwollen* (the will to art), which drives artistry to evolve new motifs while remaining independent of determining factors like materials, periods or conventions.

The temporal style of each culture is written into its ornament. It is a language, with its own grammar and syntax, of which Trilling laments: *"Ornament should once again speak for itself, as it did universally for thousands of years. The problem is that few people* [today] *remember the language of ornament well enough to enjoy it, let alone use it creatively."*[9]

In ornament, different cultural styles meet and their motifs transform from one period of history to the next. In this sense, ornament is the main place where the Hidden Prime of Styles happens – the sudden emergence of a unique linear style that moves us beyond a single historical epoch, into the trans-temporal realm of the Hidden Prime, that timeless and eternal style underlying all of history. For Fuchs, the Hidden Prime emerges most clearly in the serpentine line, which dances in counterpoise to the straight line. Over the course of ornamental history, these two lines alternate, as one comes to the fore while the other sinks, out of fashion, into invisibility and obscurity.

In this chapter, I will attempt a brief history of ornament, by following this idea of the 'style' as the alternating pursuit of the straight and serpentine line...

IV. The History of Ornament: A Sketch

The first 30,000 years of ornamentation, and of art in general – we tend to forget – constitute the Era of the Goddess. From the wandering tribes of the Paleolithic age to the first settlements of the Neolithic era, pendants, statues and figurines of the Goddess attended our earliest ancestors. As She who gives and receives all life, the Goddess is associated with the moon, serpent, bull and tree, as symbols of her ever-dying and rising power. The V, whether inverted (the chevron) or in its tri-line form, recalls her vulva, the womb of all creation. Rows of dots in red ochre recall her blood. Her plaited hair and tissued garments gave rise to interwoven motifs like zig-zags, meanders and nets.

From Paleolithic caves to the first free-standing stone circles, her life-engendering spirals, S- and C-scrolls have been found engraved in pottery. She is the Mistress of the Beasts, standing between two rearing stags, and the Goddess of the Fields, holding aloft her two shafts of wheat. At times, she becomes the Twins, the sisters of light and darkness, who alternate like the lunar cycle: one queen reigning luminous, the other obscured, as Empresses of life and death. The labyrinthine spiral, contrasting this light and darkness, manifests the two-in-one power of generation and decay.

Finally the Bronze Age saw the rise of city-states like Sumer and Akkad, and with these towering cities came the mighty Thunder God – who brought forth writing, mathematics, monumental architecture and weapons of iron and steel. From cuneiform script to hieroglyphs to the first Phoenician letters (which Philo of Byblos said were 'serpent tracks'), writing evolved into the countless styles of ornamental script. For writing, lest we forget, *is* ornament – its calligraphy and typography offering endless possibilities for style and design

Each empire of the ancient world signified its kingship through emblematic flora and fauna. In Babylon, the symbolic Tree of Life pushed forth palmettes or pine cones from its branches, while rams reared up on either side and the waters of life streamed from its roots. The king wore the horned crown of the bull, and his royal insignia included the eagle, lion and dragon. In Egypt, the Pharaoh was the Lord of the Two Lands, who knotted together the lily and papyrus, symbols of the Upper and Lower Kingdoms. He wore 'the two ladies' on his brow, the rearing *Wadjet* cobra of the north and the crouching *Nekhbet* vulture of the south. The Nile lily, depicted as alternating between nascent bud and open flower, symbolized eternal Egypt's life-renewing power.

In ancient Greece, the palmette emerged as its most emblematic foliage. Based on the Egyptian lily and the Babylonian Tree of Life, it appeared at the apex and outer edges of Greek pediments, as the *acroterion*, the crowning beauty of their architecture. The palmette was seconded only by the acanthus leaf, which appeared on the capitals of Corinthian columns.

The evolution of the Greek column, as recounted by Vitruvius in his *De Architectura*, became a paradigm for the history of ornament: the ever-recurring contest between the straight and serpentine line. The Doric column came first, and manifest the divine ratio of 6:1, the height of King Dorus in comparison to his foot. This 'masculine' column epitomized simplicity, austerity and the straight line, with its unadorned capital, no base, and long wide fluting that emphasized strength and stability.

Next came the Ionic column, of feminine slenderness, 8:1, with the narrow fluting of a woman's robes and two spiralling volutes in the capital, topped by a small frieze of egg-and-dart motifs. Last came the Corinthian column, roughly 10:1, with an ornate acanthus-leaf capital crowned by verdant helices, flourons and volutes beneath a flat abacus. It epitomized the luscious and fanciful style of the curving line, with its swirling dynamic energy and movement.

This contest between the straight and serpentine line cycled through history, as age after age gave preference to either audacity or simplicity. The Romans, like all military cultures, preferred the simplicity and restraint of the straight line, especially in their architecture, though this was relieved by the cornucopia, garlands and grotesques of their ornament. The Byzantines pursued a lavish programme of ornamentation, with their marbled mosaics, interlacing five-circled *quincunx* designs and the 'medallion style' of their silk tapestries (embedded with the emperor's two-headed eagle). Likewise, Islamic culture courted the most sublime intricacy and complexity with their *rūmī* leaf designs, climbing sinuously round polygon tilings and geometric latticework.

But, Romanesque architecture of the 10th century signalled a return to the straight line with the austerity of their heavy barrel vaults and thick flat walls. Cistercian architecture, according to Bernard of Clairvaux, should forgo 'the strange shapes' and 'ridiculous monstrosities' of ornament. Only in their illuminated texts and liturgical metalwork, encrusted with enamel, ivory and precious jewels, did Romanesque artisans pursue Irish interlace and Celtic knotwork, weaving serpents, babwyns and whole bestiaries into their designs.

The Romanesque soon gave birth to the Gothic, with its cathedrals resembling entire forests carved in stone: climbing vines, verdant foliage, and gargoyles crouched upon tall steeples. Their sculptural facades, like an immense book, iconographed all of Biblical history. From flying buttresses to ogival arches, the Gothic style celebrated Nature's serpentine line without losing sight of Her underlying geometry.

The Renaissance disdained these Gothic excesses and called for a return to the Greek and Roman canon, with sharp edges and smooth square surfaces to clearly expose their measured proportions. This love of the straight line lasted until the Baroque period, when the curving line burst forth with fresh abundance. Baroque and Rococo architects used ornament to celebrate deceit through *trompe l'oeil* designs and *faux* finishes. Their extravagant decors abounded with *coquille*-shell moldings, stucco curlicues and airy *ajouré* carvings to let light pass through the gilded scrollwork.

The Neo-Classical period simplified the excesses of the Baroque, returning to Vitruvian principles of order, balance and harmony. But, by the end of the 19th century, the Neo-Gothic, Pre-Raphaelite and Symbolist movements called for a renewal in the arts and crafts, giving rise to William Morris & Co, the Wiener Werkstätte, Jugendstil and Art Nouveau, where artists like Mucha, Gaudi and Klimt extolled Nature's spirals and her fluid graceful lines. Adolf Loos' 1913 manifesto *Ornament und Verbrechung* (Ornament and Crime) called for the end of all ornament, and his cry was echoed by *Die Form Ohne Ornament* (Form Without Ornament – 1924) a declaration by the Weimar Bauhaus to promote functionalism *as* form.

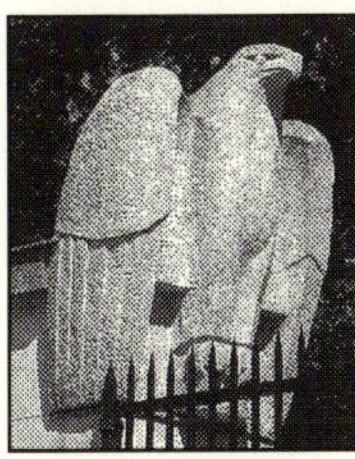
Fig. 15.10 - Vienna Hofburg Eagle

But, as Fuchs noted in *Architectura Caelestis*, the lone voice against the rule of the straight line was Rudolf Steiner, whose domed Goetheanum of 1919 (in natural wood) expressed the most graceful and oneiric curves. Alas, this architectural masterpiece was torched to the ground, and the National Socialists soon embarked on an ambitious programme of Fascist architecture in key locales like Vienna (where pairs of eagles still adorn the entrance to the Hofburg), Munich (the *Haus der Kunst*) and Nuremberg (the vast Rally Grounds filmed in *The Triumph of the Will* and still standing today), with Speer and Hitler's Berlin (*Welthauptstadt Germania*) to be its crowning achievement, before the city was bombed to near-oblivion in 1945.

Alas, the most expedient solution for re-building Europe after WWII was to promote the efficient, functional and ornamentless architecture of Adolf Loos (whose work was championed by Le Corbusier, Gropius and Mies van der Rohe) with its barren square facades, quickly built, lacking in all charm or imagination.

The call for a return to the curving line came with Friedensreich Hundertwasser's *verschimmelungs-manifest gegen den rationalismus in der architektur* (Manifesto on Going Moldy against Rationalism in Architecture – 1958), with photos of the artist bending a ruler in his hands. Finally, Ernst Fuchs' *Architectura Caelestis* (1966) convicted Adolf Loos of his own proper crime. Not only did ornament have a rich and complex history, but a long hidden history, arising from an underlying creative force, timeless and a-historical, which he called the Hidden Prime of Styles.

From the art of the Gothics to the Hindus and Mayans, the serpent emerges as an ever-recurring motif in ornament. Although Fuchs clearly promoted the curving line over the straight, he recognized the importance of the straight line as an invisible rule to aid in the craftsman's designs. Curvilinear forms are organized by clear geometric shapes which grant order and proportion to each element. The combination of these two lines – straight and curved, seen and unseen – leads to what Fuchs called 'the serpentine style'.

V. The Islamic Half-Palmette

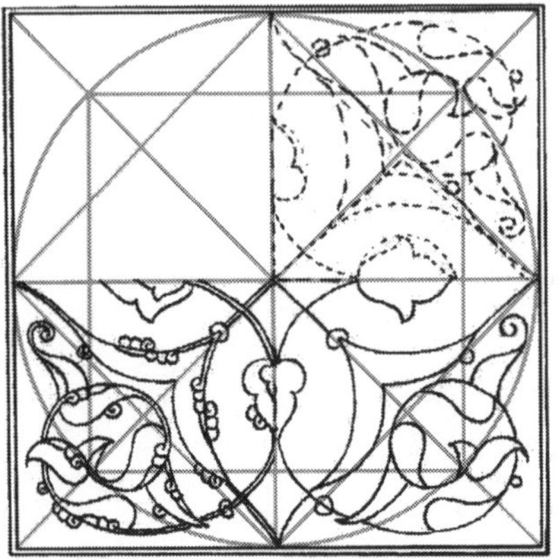

Fig. 15.11 - From Armature to Islimi Design

One of the finest exemplars of the serpentine style, where vine leaves climb, wrap and weave round invisible grids, are the *islimī* designs of the Persian and Ottoman Empires, emerging from Anatolia around the 10th century. In their finely-carved palaces and mosques, these tiled mosaics evoke the Heavenly realms, where Birds of Paradise frolic within the Tree of Life.

The main motif is the *islimī* or *rūmī,* a slender curling leaf in profile, derived from the full-face palmette cut in half (Fig. 15.12, below right). Various forms of embellishment are added to the half palmette, such as three or four seed-like circles called *chintamani* (an Ottoman term derived from the Sanskrit for the 'auspicious jewels' accompanying Hindu figures). As well, Lotus flowers (*nīlūfar* - Fig. 15.12, below left), tulips (*naqṣ-i lāle*) and grapes (*naqṣ-i engür*) may also appear in the interlacing patterns.

The Islamic palmette originates either in the acanthus leaf, the grape vine, or a combination of both. The full-face palmette forms a large curving medallion

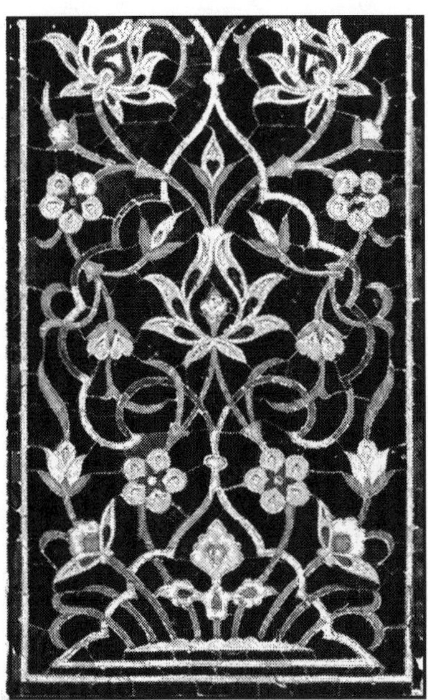

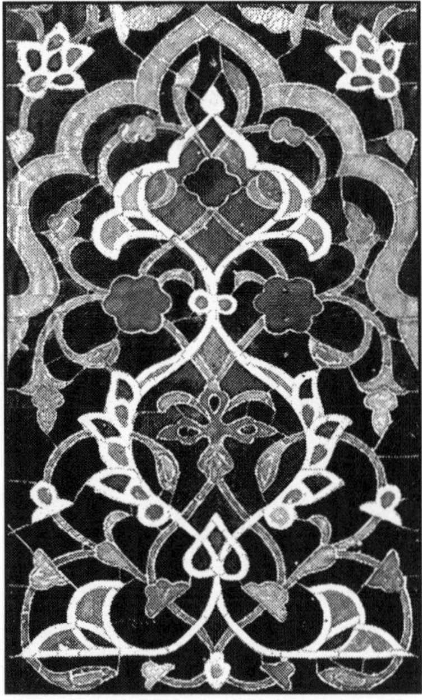

Fig. 15.12 Left - Lotus Flowers (*nīlūfar*) in Timurid Mosaic, Transoxiana, 15th c.
Right - Palmettes (*islimī, rūmī*) in Samarkand Mosaic, Transoxiana, 1660.

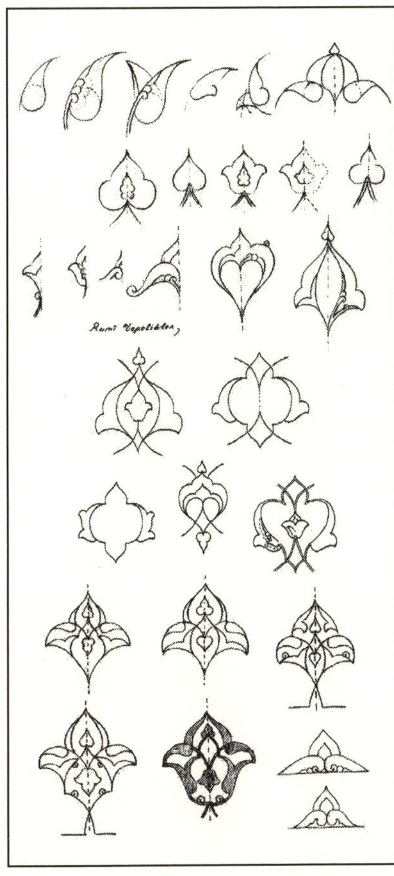

Fig. 15.13 - Above: *rūmīs,* Below: *tepelik*

called a *tepelik* (Fig. 15.13), a central point of focus for the climbing stems of the *rūmīs* to variously weave and spiral round. Both the *tepelik* and the *rūmīs* are traced over geometric grids that eventually disappear from view.

As we can see in the four quadrants of Fig. 15.11 (opposite), the artisan first drew the basic armature in red ink, of an octagram and X in the squared circle. In the next quadrant, he lightly traced out the *islimī* design, which respects the basic shapes of the armature while weaving in and out of it. In the third quadrant, he simplified the design in black ink. Finally, the artisan expanded his basic shapes, widening the stems and adding *chintamani* dots to the *rūmī* and *tepelik* palmettes.

So detailed and refined were the artisans' designs that poets praised their handiwork to the heavens, saying the palace walls resembled *'the mirror of Alexander the Great, that mirrored the cosmos.'*[10] The craftmen's industry was also recognized when, for example, the Selimiye Mosque of Edirne was praised with the words: *"many peerless masters expended eye-straining effort..."*[11]

V.I Motifs in Transformation: From Islamic to Gothic

In his fascinating study Le *Moyen-Âge Fantastique: Antiquités et Exotismes dans l'Art Gothique* (The Fantastique in the Middle Ages: Antiquities and Exoticisms in Gothic Art – 1981), Jurgis Baltrušaitis traces the genealogy of Gothic ornament to its Islamic roots. Although Gothic art, in its own time, was called the *Opus Francigenum* – 'the French work' – its decorative elements were attributed to Moorish (hence the term *moresque*) and Arabian (hence *arabesque*) sources.

The Lithuanian scholar (who studied at the Sorbonne and wrote in French) focusses his study on those *fantastique* creatures that often accompany Gothic ornament – not just heraldic lions or grotesque gargoyles, but ever more bizarre and visionary creations. He begins, naturally enough, with the

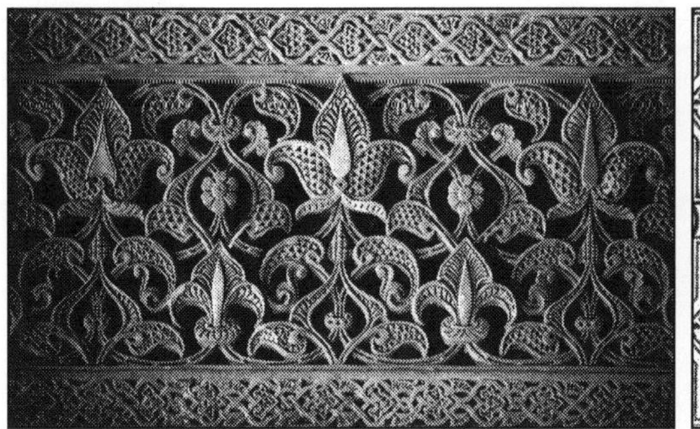

Fig. 15.14 - Islamic Frieze with *Rūmī* and *Tepelik* Motifs

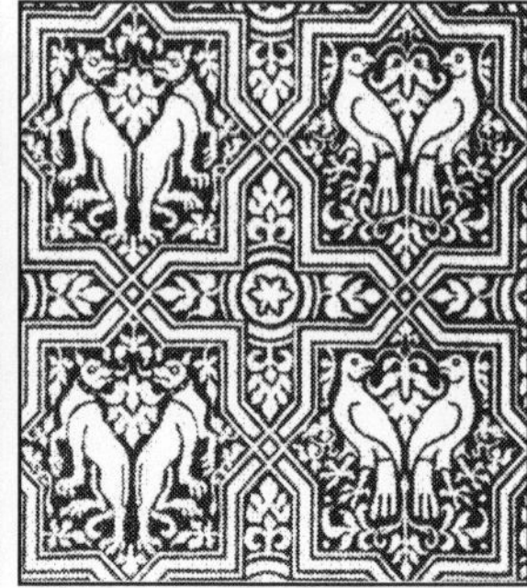

Fig. 15.15 - Heraldic Medallions

straight-edge patterns adorning Gothic cathedrals, which clearly have their origins in *girih* interlace and the *Kufic* 'square-style' of Islamic calligraphy.[12] Even the cruciform and barbed quatrefoil of Gothic facades (see next section, Fig. 15.23) derive from Fatamid designs of the first Cairo palaces.[13]

But Baltrušaitis' investigation soon leads him to the spiralling vines and floral motifs that rhythmically meander to break up the monotony of geometric abstraction. These vegetal and animal motifs, which he calls *rūmī* and *arabesques*, are harmoniously integrated into the tilings in two possible ways: either they *follow* the pattern (as an open-ended *frieze*) or they are *enclosed* within it (as *medallions*).

In the example of a frieze (Fig. 15.14), the vegetation *becomes* the pattern, with its constant interlacing C- and S-swirls in the foliage. Meanwhile, in the example of the medallions (Fig. 15.15), the geometric tiling remain, while the heraldic animals *are inserted into* the pattern – as new decorative motifs within the medallions. The *girih* pattern in this example should be familiar – it is the Breath of Compassionate (Fig. 14.4) based on the *Khatem Sulemani* or Octagram.

These recurring C- and S-curves (I would like to remark) manifest a certain life-force that flows through all of creation – empowering the elements (earth, air, fire and water) and enlivening the movements of flora and fauna. From the Bayeux Tapestry to Ernst Fuchs' engravings (Figs 15.16 - 17), we can see the same C- and S-curves in lions and unicorns, where the beast turns its head to devour its own tail. This *ouroboros* motif is prevalent in ornament, where life-devours-life in the æviternal cycle of death and rebirth.

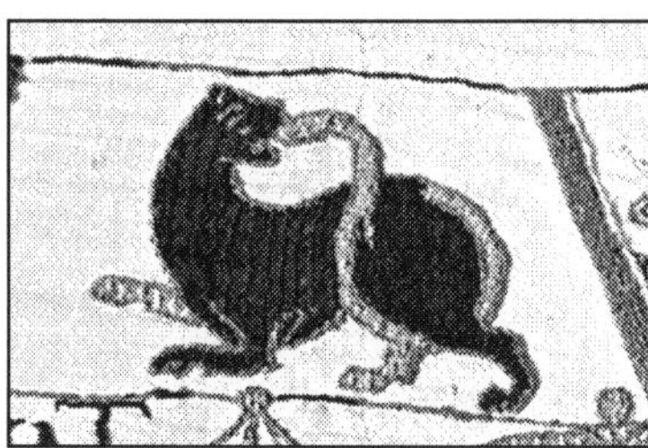

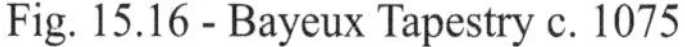

Fig. 15.16 - Bayeux Tapestry c. 1075

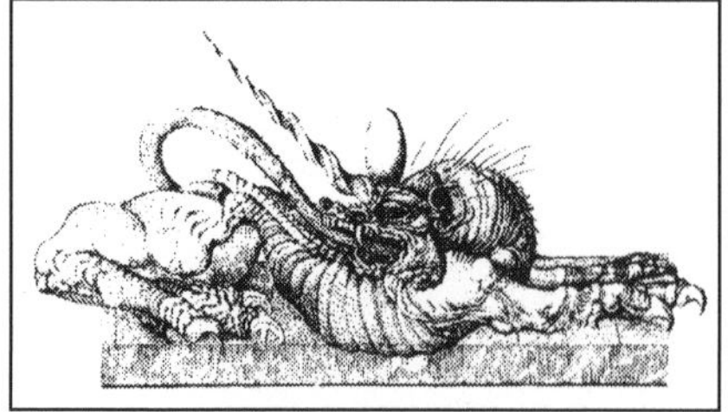

Fig. 15.17 - Ernst Fuchs: *Unicorn* 1952

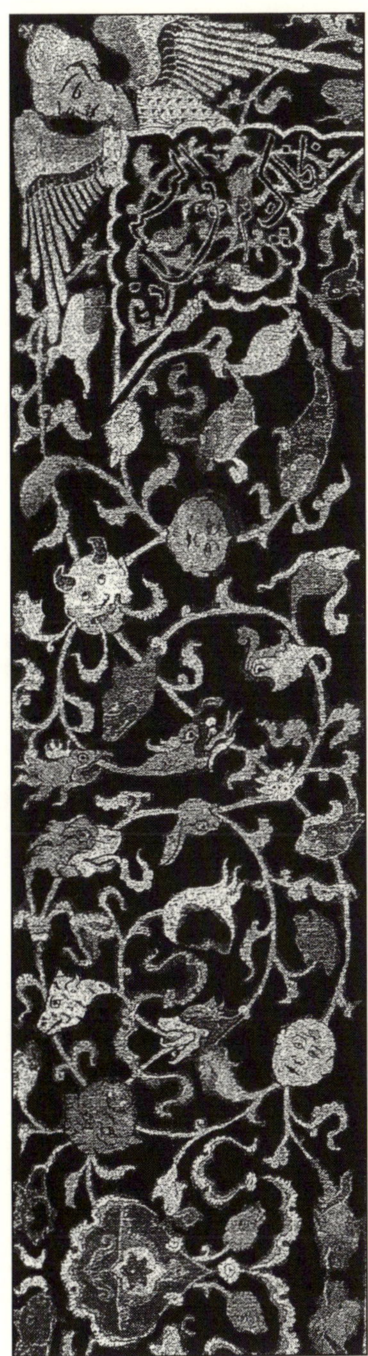

Fig. 15.18 - Detail of *Vāq* Carpet (*Derakht-e Gūyā*) 1529

Baltrušaitis notes that, once an abstract pattern becomes interlacing vegetation, it may undergo some interesting transformations. Specifically, the coiling *rūmī* metamorphoses into snakes. As the patterns interlace, the serpents intertwine. In Persian Manuscripts, they acquire the heads of foxes, rabbits and donkeys. A detail from a Persian carpet shows this *vāq* or 'talking tree' theme (another of the Seven Principles of Painting), where the swirling branches acquire both human and aquatic heads, devouring one another in the cycle of life. By the time these motifs reach Gothic illuminers, a fully human body emerges from the vegetation, such as winged angels and armoured knights.[14]

The same is true of the heraldic beasts from Islamic art; once they reach Europe, they undergo some startling transformations. Gothic cathedrals are overrun with basilisks, manticores and amphisbaena (a serpent with heads on each end). The imagination of the Gothic mason knew no limits.

Of particular interest are the two facing lions typical of heraldry. At Dijon cathedral, their bodies are united under a single head (a *cephalopagus*). Interestingly, this Gothic motif can also be found in other cultures, such as Egypt, India and even Mayan culture. We shall meet with it again.

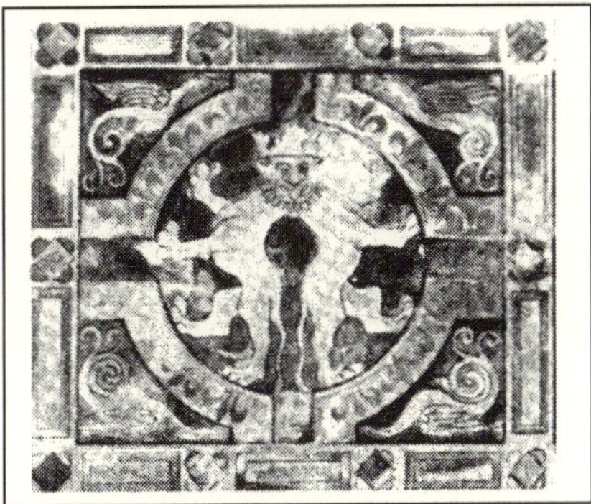

Fig. 15.19 - Lion Cephalopagus, Dijon Cathedral c. 1325

VII. Geometry Generates Form

The Sketchbook of Villard de Honnecourt gives us some indication of how these fantastic creatures were conceived. In the thematically related section (plates 34 – 37) titled *"Here begins the method of representation as taught by the art of geometry,"*[15] we discover that it was not only the geometry of human proportion that Honnecourt sought to explore, but also the way geometrical shapes may generate certain forms. We see this, for example, in plate 35, where a pentagram underlies the form of an eagle.

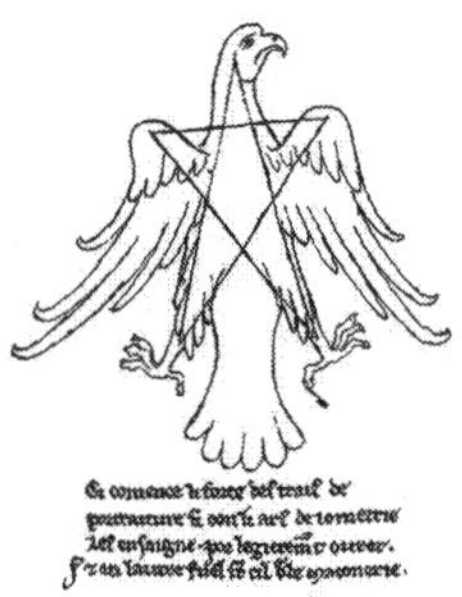

Another example is offered by the Archimedean spiral (a spiral which expands at an arithmetic rate), which he drew on pl. 39. From this shape, Honnecourt generated a pelican piercing its own breast (as an emblem of Christ – pl. 1), a curling branch of vegetation (as a choir stall – pl. 53), and a winged serpent whose head rests upon its wings (pl. 11). These different drawings show how, in the Gothic imagination, vegetal and animal forms are continually inspired by Nature's underlying geometry of spirals.

On yet another page, Honnecourt drew a Gothic window from Reims cathedral and, immediately above it, the Virgin and Child (Fig. 15.21). It is surely no co-incidence that the form of one perfectly echoes the form of the other, with the Virgin's eye situated at exactly the same place as the centre-point of the poly-lobed circular *oculus* (a Gothic term for the circular tracery in the window – *oculus* meaning 'eye').

When we include the armature of invisible circles which helped create the Gothic window (Fig. 15.23), we understand why both the Virgin and Child are turning to the left, each moving in accord with its own circle. In the end, the Gothic window offers the general geometrical shape outlining the Virgin and Child, while *the invisible circles describe their movement and attitude*. Both the window and the Virgin share the same invisible armature based on the circle.

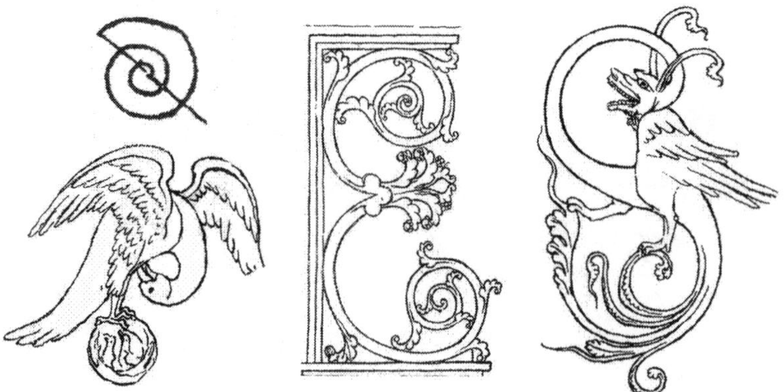

Fig. 15.20 - Villard de Honnecourt: Designs based on the Archimedean Spiral

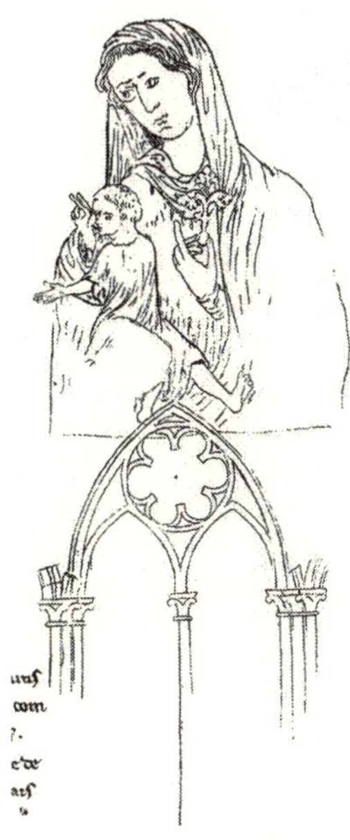

Fig. 15.21 - Honnecourt: Sketchbook Plate 19

In Mediaeval art, the quatrefoil, specifically the barbed quatrefoil, served as the basic frame and compositional device for untold thousands of figures decorating cathedrals, from the Twelve Signs of the Zodiac to the Seven Stages of a Man's Life. It came in two basic types (Fig. 15.22), the cruciform quatrefoil (from the four-petalled flower) and the barbed quatrefoil, with each square and turned square in the *quadrature* expanding its pictorial space at rate of √2. To establish the five circles, its X and + divide the composition into halves and quarters. Meanwhile, new lines and variations may continually be added, offering the craftsman a never-ending matrix of possibilities. The shape itself breeds abundance.

All the examples given here are taken from the north transept portal of Rouen cathedral.[16] The first three panels (Fig. 15.24) tend to manifest rigid and well-structured compositions, but the following three panels (Fig. 15.25) grow progressively more creative and dynamic. The basic armature becomes a fixed shape for the mason's vision to focus upon as he creatively imagines different kinds of compositions, ranging from static to dynamic.

In the first example, we see *God Resting on the Seventh Day of Creation*. The artist has used the + cross in the armature to imagine God along the central vertical axis. *A strict symmetry reigns*, both vertically and horizontally. Nevertheless, the ◇ turned square gently influences the composition, as do the circles.

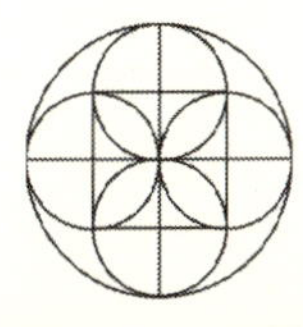

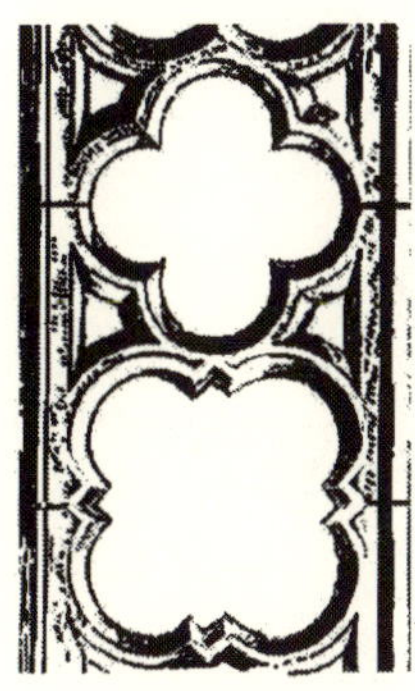

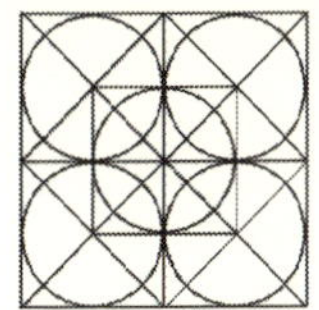

Fig. 15.22 - Cruciform and Barbed Quatrefoil

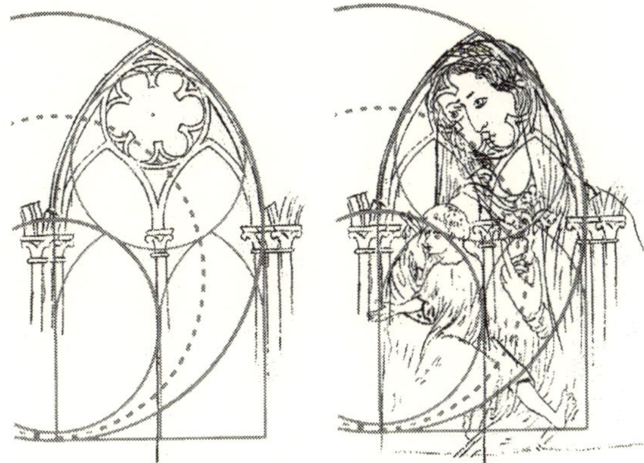

Fig. 15.23 - Armature Construction for Ogival Arch and Virgin and Child

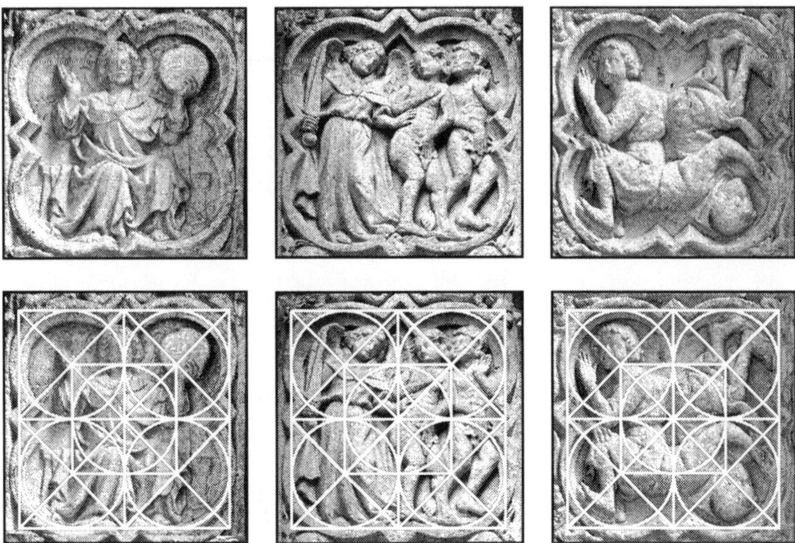

Fig. 15.24 - Rouen Cathedral: The Creation, The Expulsion, and The Tumblers

In the second example, we see *The Expulsion of Adam and Eve from Paradise*. The + cruciform division of space is still prominent and, indeed, *this four-fold division of space becomes the dominant compositional feature of all Gothic art*. We could say that Gothic sculpture is primarily conceived *ad quadratum*.

The mason has used the + cross in the armature to imagine Adam and Eve on one side of the central axis and the angel on the other. Now, the influence of the ◇ turned square is felt more strongly: it influences Eve's posture – her raised hand and bent leg, as well as the angel's leg and the general turning of the figures towards each other, so that Adam and the angel's heads twist along the diagonal axis. Note the gentle 'torsion' (Gothic *contrapposto*) as the couple's lower bodies move in one direction and the upper bodies turn in the opposite.

With the third example, the mason begins to break free from rigid forms and creatively experiment. In this unique composition, the bodies of the two *Tumblers* can be read in different ways: either as contrary figures vertically back to back, or as contrary figures horizontally front to front. A small inner □ square has helped the mason to imagine this visual trope, as did the large X.

In *The Woodchopper* (the first panel of Fig. 15.25), the ◇ turned square has come to dominate the composition. The source for the subject is not clear: a man is recoiling from an oak tree which he has struck with an axe. The mason has made thorough use of the diagonals from the ◇ turned square to bend the figure at the waist, creating a distinctive K glyph within his pose.

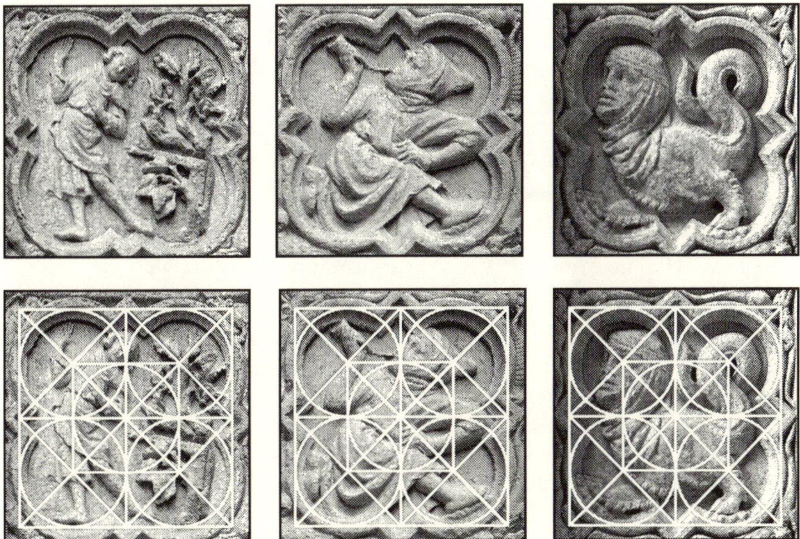

Fig. 15.25 - Rouen Cathedral: The Woodchopper, The Dancing Monk and The Cockatrice

In the next example, we see *A Dancing Monk Blowing His Horn*. To imagine the strongly contorted and twisted figure, the mason has made thorough use of an X drawn from corner to corner. The / right-diagonal provides the axis for his body while the \ left-diagonal guides his foot and trumpet-bearing arm. This figure is an excellent example of how the half turn of a + cross to an X *creates a more dynamic composition*, in contrast to the regular symmetry of the upright + cross.

The last example – *A Cockatrice with a Nun's Head* – shows how the four circles of the barbed quatrefoil may inspire the mason to a more circular design. In all these examples, it is the basic geometrical shape, such as the ○ circle, □ square, ◇ turned square, + cross or X which creates a kind of scaffolding for the mason's imagination, to freely elaborate the figure and its curvilinear composition in a visionary way.

The simple framing device of a barbed quatrefoil allows for the construction of a fairly complex armature. But complex armatures can confuse the imagination, simpler ones inspire it. The experienced artisan knows how to select simple but inspiring shapes, depending on the required subject matter, and move the figure within it.

The main figure may follow these shapes, while other elements wrap themselves around it in a kind of counterpoise. The geometrical armature insures that 'complementary forms' (Fuchs) are created. But its primary function is to create sacred space through the harmonious relationship of parts to the whole. The various triangles, squares and circles relate the figure to its bounding medallion, but also to the Gothic cathedral as a whole, since its plan and elevation are constructed according to the same *quadratura* principles and *ad quadratum* patterns.

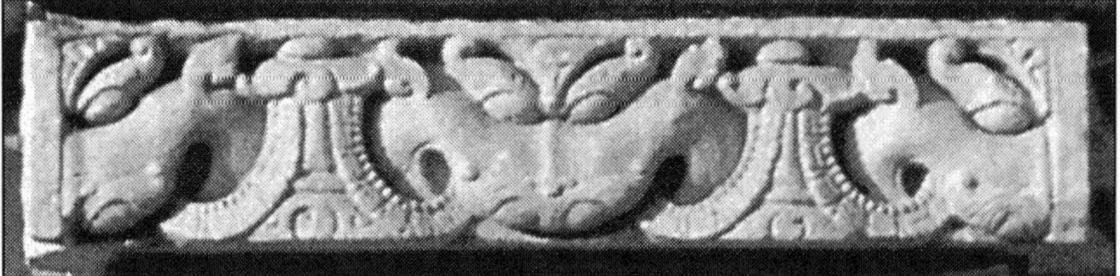

Fig. 15.26 - Khajuraho Temples: Makara Frieze, 11th century

VIII. The Makara: Visionary Creature from the Depths

All the decorations on the exterior of a Gothic cathedral or Hindu temple are nothing but waves upon waves of door guardians flanking the central portal. And when we encounter them once more within, they play the same role, as layers upon layers of door guardians flanking the central altar or statue, where the Holy takes form. If we regard them with fear – they become monstrous forms of our own passions and emotions, blocking further passage due to our fear of death and too-strong attachment to this life. But when we regard them with love, they transform into the infinite variety of the Holy One's creation, all beckoning and welcoming us to union with the Divine.

During my visionary journey at Khajuraho, I became increasingly intrigued by a decorative figure which, I later learned, is called a *makara*. The makara's face appears repeatedly on long decorative friezes (Fig. 15.26) and is found throughout Hindu architecture. At first, I perceived it as a single face viewed from the frontal position.

But, in the inner sanctum of the Devi Jagadambi temple, I came across the motif (already mentioned above) of the *cephalopagus* – two lions united under a single head (Fig. 15.27). Suddenly it became clear to me that the makara was not only a single face viewed from the frontal position, but two faces in profile, conjoined so as to form one visage (see again Fig. 15.26)

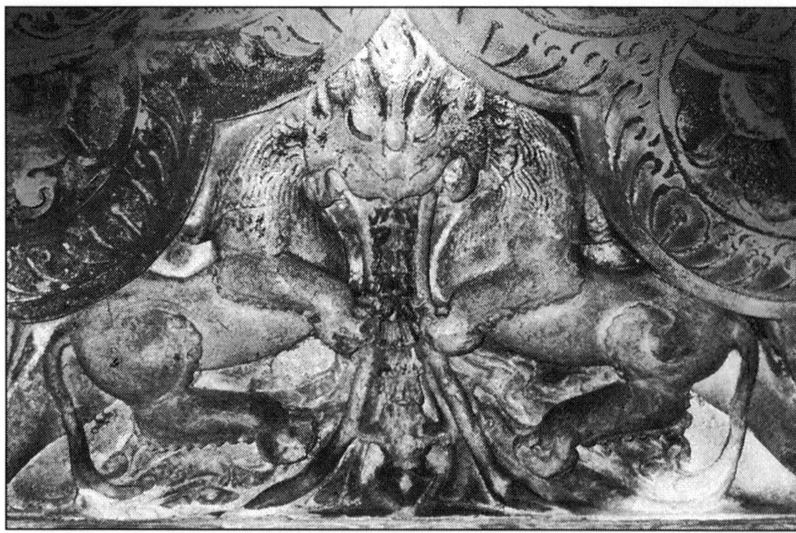

Fig. 15.27 - Khajuraho Temples: Lion Cephalopagus, 11th century

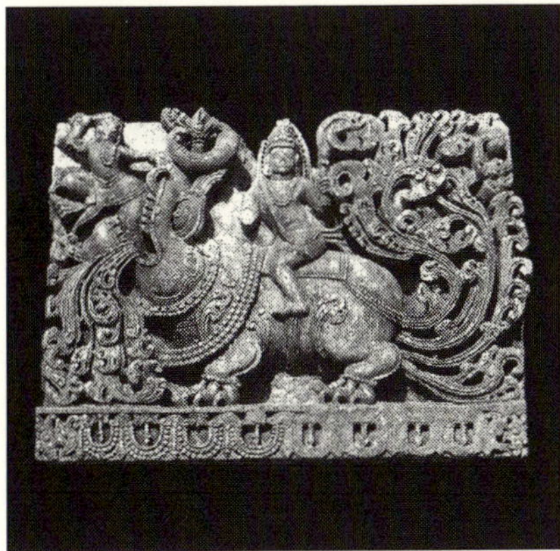

Fig. 15.28 - Hindu Makara in Profile

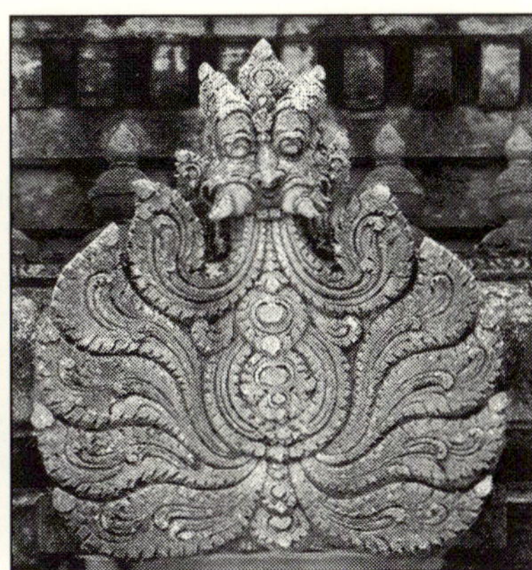

Fig. 15.29 - Makara Pouring forth Maya

In *Yaksas*, Ananda K. Coomaraswamy notes that the makara dates from the Mauryan period (c. 300 BCE), but only emerged atop ornamental gates (*toraṇa*) in its well-known frontal form (resembling the Kīrtimukha or 'face of glory') during the Gupta period (4th – 7th centuries).[17] Like the gargoyles of Gothic art, sometimes it was also used as an ornamental drainage system.

But, more often it was depicted in profile in *bas reliefs* as a horned creature, part lion, part crocodile, that spewed forth torrents of water from its open mouth (Fig. 15.28). *"The makara is obviously a symbol of the waters,"* Coomaraswamy writes, *"more specifically of the Essence in the Waters, the principle of life."*[18] Aside from water, curling scrolls of vegetation may emerge from its open mouth, as well as animals or dwarf-like figures with garlands of pearls in their hands.

Although the true meaning of the makara remains lost to history, for me, the mysterious essence spewing forth from its mouth (Fig. 15.29) is clearly *maya*, both the source of life and the ocean of appearances. In a similar sense, it is *chitta*, the ever-expanding mind substance which continually metamorphoses from vegetation to animals to dwarfs to 'the ten thousand things'.

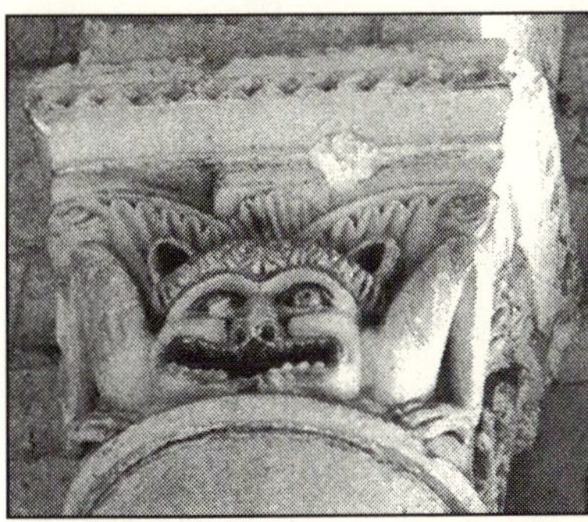

Fig. 15.30 - Gothic Capital with Makara
Notre Dame de Cunault, Loire c. 12th c.

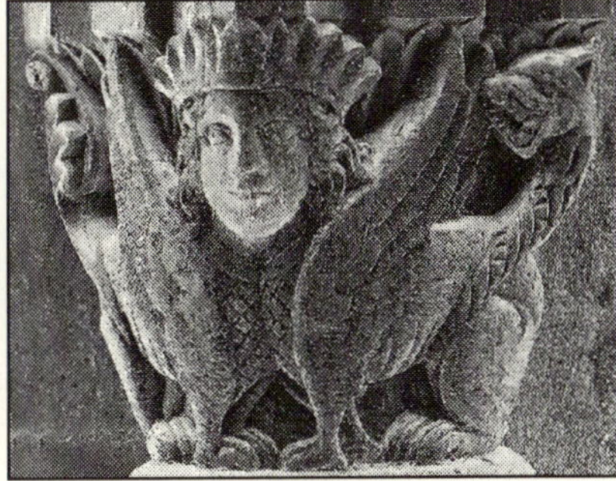

Fig. 15.31 - Gothic Figure Straddling Block
St Savin, Vienne c. 1050

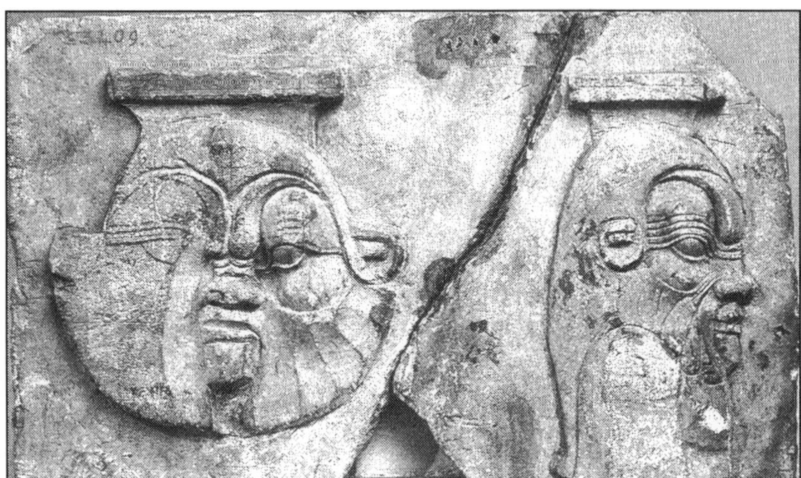

Fig. 15.32 - Egyptian Dwarf God Bes, whose Face combines Two Profiles in the Frontal View

Upon my return to France, I started to find examples of the makara motif in a surprising number of different cultures, from ancient Egyptian (Fig. 15.32) and Mayan art (Fig. 15.38) to Gothic sculpture (Fig. 15.30). Did their artisans use the same Sacred Codes to construct these apotropaic images? Or perhaps, they entered the same Visionary sphere, leaving authentic records of their encounters...

In Gothic masonry, the makara motif often appears at *the corner* of blocks or capitols, uniting profiles on either side (Fig. 15.31). This mythic motif has taught me many interesting lessons about how geometry may generate new forms, particularly ones that straddle multiple dimensions.

The makara uses its symmetry to combine two recognizable motifs in our vision. If its design is approached from the standpoint of an Islamic craftsman, then the face was first drawn in profile, filling one cell of a square pattern. Then, that same motif was 'flipped' symmetrically in the next cell. Due to the symmetry we are able to read the profiles as *one* central view, and hence, 'see unity' in the face. Once this principle is grasped, it becomes a Sacred Code for the construction of far more complex motifs, using rotations, reflections and glides to create the new decorative designs.

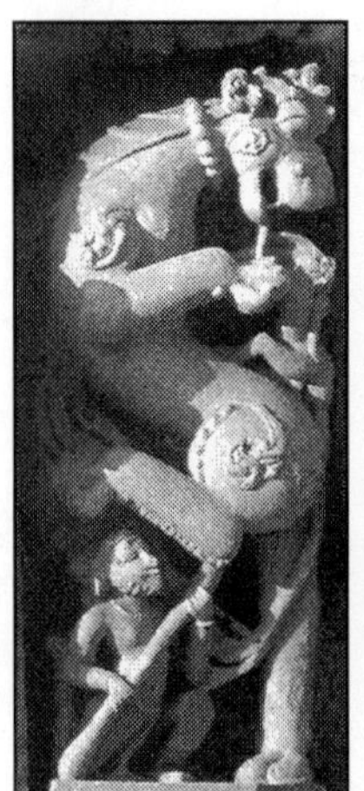

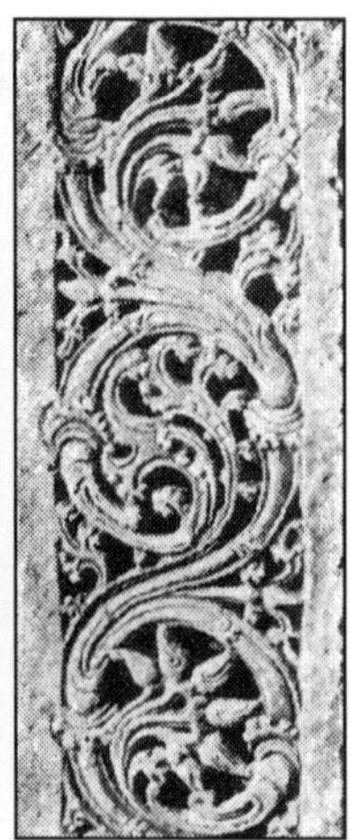

Fig. 15.33 - Hindu Vyala and Vegetal Frieze

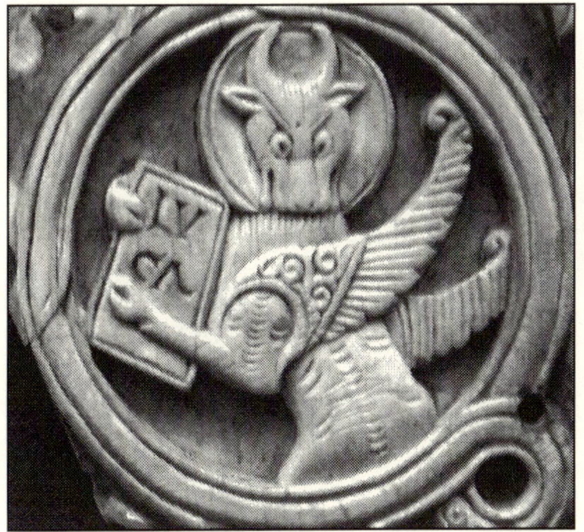

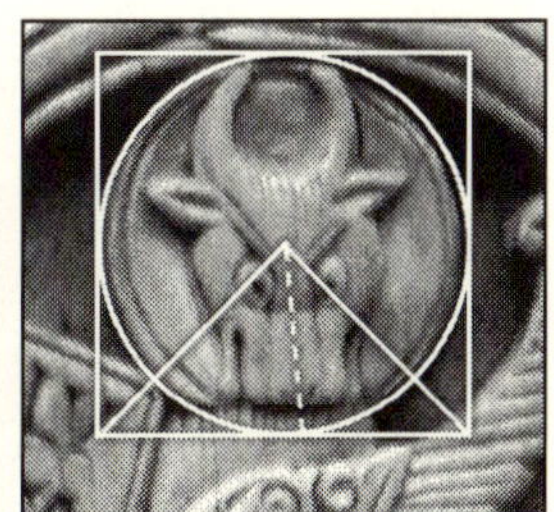

Fig. 15.34
Left: Winged Bull
of St. Luke the Evangelist
Gothic Ivory c. 1100

Above; The Armature of a
circle and triangle helps
to combine two profiles
laid out vertically

In Hindu temple ornament, for example, the lion guardian (*vyala* or *gajabidala*) and vegetal frieze (Fig. 15.33) follow this same principle, flipping the C-curve as it advances, to form a continuous S-pattern.

One afternoon in the Cluny museum in Paris, I made a most fortuitous discovery – a Gothic makara (Fig. 15.34) as the winged bull of Luke (hence the LVCA on the Bible). After meditating upon this image, I came to understand the principles underlying its construction.

Like the Hindu makara, it brings together two faces in profile, but this time the profiles are laid out *vertically* rather than horizontally. If the design is approached from the standpoint of an Islamic craftsman, then half the face was first drawn horizontally in profile (like the Hindu makara). But, it was then *rotated 90° to a vertical position*, before being 'flipped' symmetrically to the neighbouring cell. The craftsman has added a 'rotation' to his list of projections.

Was this planned out? Or rather, did the ivory carver begin with an underlying geometrical shape and develop his curvilinear form around it? If so – what shape? What *charpente*?

I return to the triangle inscribed in the squared circle (my Trimorphic Matrix Subocularis, which here exists in a slight variation). We can see from the halo that a circle played an important role in the figure's design. Then, from the centre of the circle – its mark just happens to exist at the place of the 'third eye' – the artisan drew a triangle, which is no longer visible.

What remains visible is the way the curvilinear profiles wrap themselves around the invisible rays of the triangle. As the form progressively takes shape, descending from the third eye at the centre – the triangle divides the face in two, while the circle holds it together as one. Through this armature, 'seeing unity' is preserved, and the figure holds together as a sacred sign of divine sight. (I have used this same technique to design the four beasts of the evangelists on the lintel of my painting *Vishnu-Christ Avatar* - Fig 3.4).

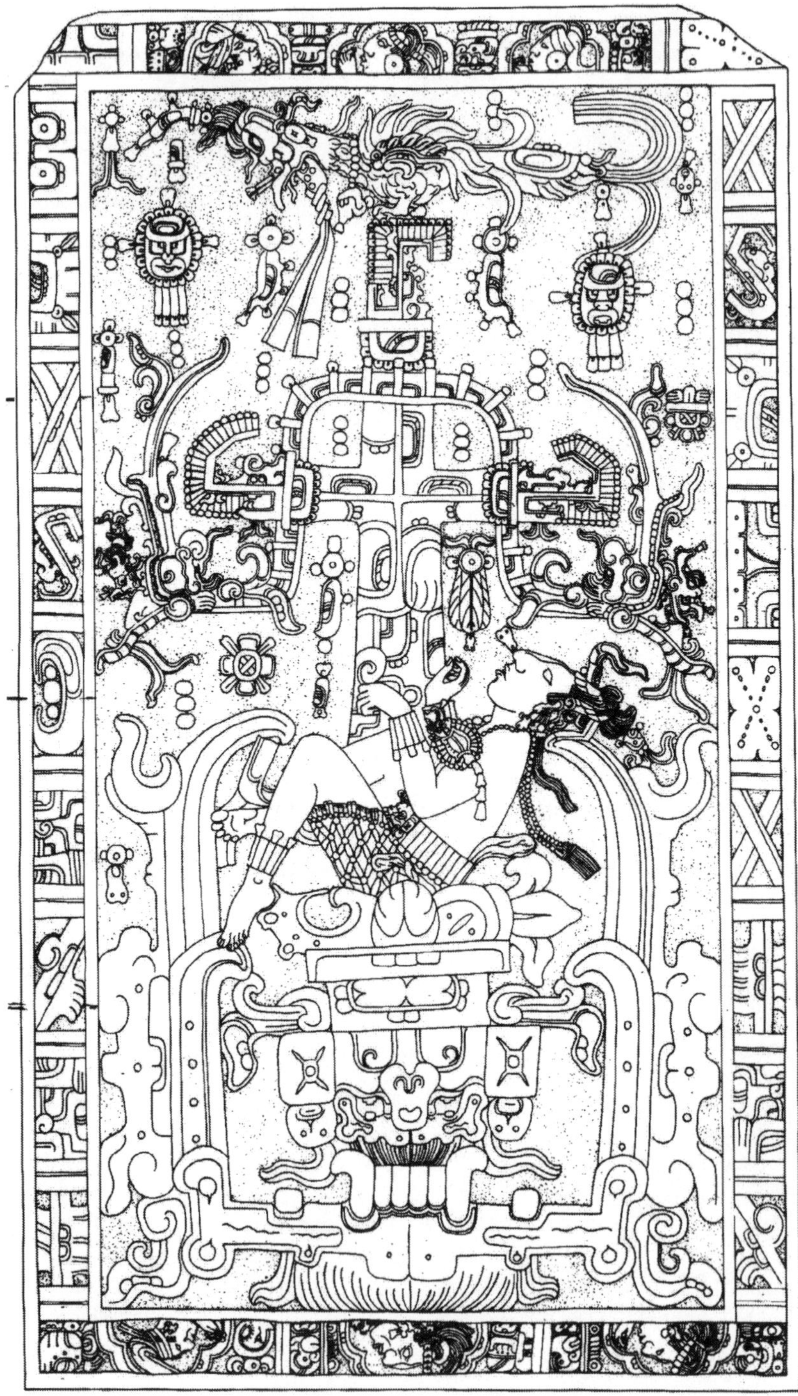

Fig. 15.35 - Pacal's Sarcophagus Lid, Palenque Mexico c. 688

IX. The Mayan Vision Serpent

Anyone who has entered the Visionary world particular to tryptamines (mushrooms, ayahuasca, DMT) knows that it is a multi-dimensional world where figures may warp, morph and expand into a kaleidoscopic variety of shapes. During one particular journey, I saw a frightening face multiply exponentially across my field of vision, from 4 to 16 to 256 faces – while still staring straight at me, transfixing my regard. As Visionary artists, it is our duty to seek out the Sacred Codes which underlie these omni-directional ways of seeing.

Fortunately for us, at least one advanced civilization has left behind the marks and signs of entheogenic experience – the Mayans, who are known for their sacramental use of mushrooms (*teonanácatl*), morning glory seeds (*ololiuqui*) and probably peyote (*peyotl*) as well. Along with their ancestors, the Olmecs, and their descendants, the Aztecs, the Mayans created a unique visual world with its own rules and codes.

In the Spring of 2006, I journeyed through Mexico, Guatemala and Honduras for three months, making an intense study of Meso-American culture. Although my backpack was strained by the weight of heavy books, I never regretted the extra effort: the recent findings of Linda Schele, Karl Taube and Claude-François Baudez opened my eyes to the visual complexity of the Mayan style.

At first glance, even a masterpiece like Pacal's sarcophagus lid at Palenque (Fig. 15.35) seems utterly foreign and indecipherable to our eyes. It is no wonder that, like so many others, I was first exposed to it as a Mayan astronaut at the controls of his interstellar spacecraft... The decipherment of Mayan art and glyphs has progressed rapidly in the last two decades, allowing us to recognize their rich mix of ornament, figures and hieroglyphs.

As Linda Schele notes, Pacal's sarcophagus lid depicts *"The instant of Pacal's death and his fall into the under world* [Xibalba]*"*[19] symbolized below by the 'quadripartite sun monster' within the huge jaws of the 'underworld serpent' (to be explained momentarily). Above him rises the cruciform 'world tree' with serpent heads on the ends of its three branches. A 'double-headed serpent bar' is draped around the arms of the cruciform tree, while the 'celestial bird' at its summit symbolizes the heavenly realm.

As I travelled deeper into Mayan territory, my eyes became accustomed to recognizing their strange visual language. Since their culture used hieroglyphs, they could 'read' their visual motifs with the same ease that we read typography. In a Mayan figure, numerous hieroglyphs are integrated into the figure's design, while also co-existing as independent blocks of script in the composition.

As an example, let us begin with one of the most pervasive motifs in Mayan art – the vision serpent. In Pacal's sarcophagus lid, there are no less than six serpent heads – the clearest being the amphisbaena or W-shaped 'serpent bar' draped over the tree, with a head on each end (and a small deity – one with a bright mirror, one with a dark obsidian mirror – emerging from each of the gaping jaws).

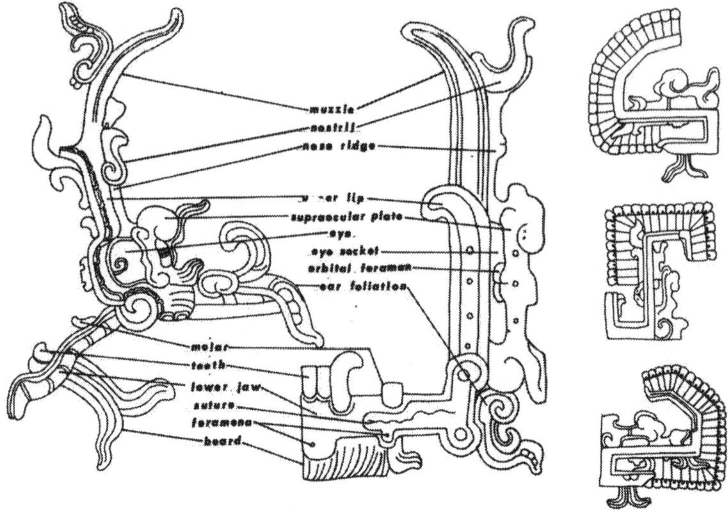

Fig. 15.36 - Linda Schele: Iconography of the Mayan Serpent

In Linda Schele's diagram (Fig. 15.36), she points out each distinctive shape or glyph (like the letters of a word) that make up the head of a Mayan vision serpent. Just as we play with the shapes of letters in typography and calligraphy, so did they play with the forms of their glyphs.

The serpent is the 'angel' of Mayan culture. And like our 'angel of the annunciation', the vision serpent appears as a messenger from the other world, opening its mouth so an ancestral spirit may emerge with a divine message or oracle.

When it appears in the heavens (and atop gates in temples), the serpent with a head at either end becomes the Celestial or Cosmic Serpent (Fig. 15.37). One head (marked with the sign of Venus and 'cross-banded eye') signifies life or rebirth, while the other head (marked with a skeletal jaw and 'quadripartite sign' of the sun) symbolizes death and transformation. (In the underworld section of my painting *The Pearl*, these two heads of the Cosmic Serpent can be seen).

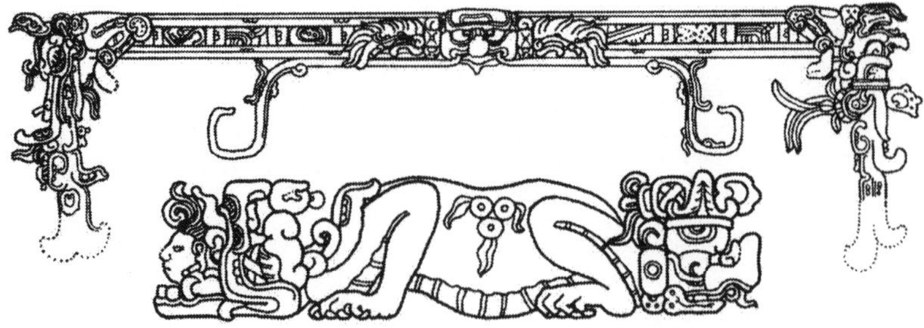

Fig. 15.37 - Cosmic Serpent with Heads of Venus (left) and Death (right)

Seen from the perspective of the Earth, Venus has a 584-day cycle, appearing as 'the morning star' for 263 days where it *leads* the sun out of the underworld; then disappearing for 50 days before re-appearing as 'the evening star' for another 263 days where it *follows* the sun into the underworld, and finally disappears once more for 8 days before beginning a new cycle.[20]

In this scheme of things, the Cosmic Serpent symbolizes the path of Venus and the sun, not just through the heavenly overworld of the day sky, but also through the hellish underworld of the night sky. Just as, in ancient Egypt, the souls of the dead accompany the sun god Re on his journey through the netherworld, so in Mayan culture, Pacal's soul is about to accompany the sun on its night journey.

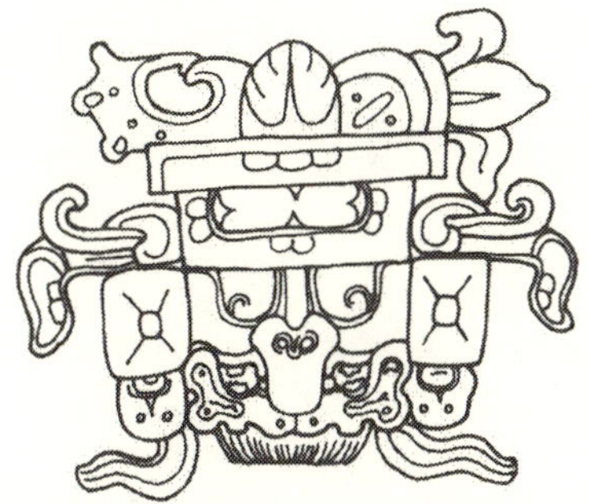

Fig. 15.38 - Quadripartite Sun Monster

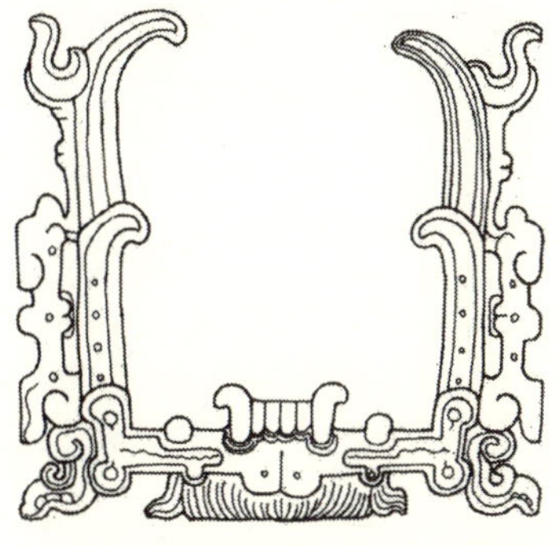

Fig. 15.39 - Jaws of the Underworld Serpent

This is made clear by the quadripartite sun monster (Fig. 15.38) within the huge jaws of the 'underworld serpent'. The deathly head of the sun which appears (in profile) on one end of the Cosmic Serpent now appears below Pacal (in frontal view) with its skeletal jaw and 'quadripartite sign' in its crown (crossed bands, stingray spine and shell in a sacrificial bowl embossed with the sun's quatrefoil 'kin' glyph – except in Pacal's version, the crossed bands are replaced by the 'cimi' glyph of death and transformation). Together with the 'dead' or night-sun, Pacal is entering the gaping jaws of the Cosmic Serpent.

Those jaws are depicted separately in another diagram. If we wish to learn the Sacred Codes of Mayan culture, we must meditate on this image for some time. We can see on the left and right the distinctive glyphs that make up the head of a Mayan vision serpent *in profile*: the eyes, ridges and nostrils. And below we can see the glyphs that make up the serpent's lower jaw in *frontal* view.

To depict Pacal's fall into the jaws of death, the Mayan craftsman has skillfully split the serpent's head in three parts. In essence, he has performed a projection similar to the Gothic artisan of the winged bull – except he has started from the bottom and worked his way up.

If the design is approached from the standpoint of an Islamic craftsman, then the serpent's face was first drawn horizontally in profile, then rotated 90º to a vertical position, then 'flipped' symmetrically to the neighbouring cell. But this time, the symmetrical projection (in contrast to the winged bull of Luke) does not fold the vertical profiles *inward* to join at the foreheads, but *outward* to meet at the jaw. For this reason, the jaw may be added at the bottom.

The jaw itself brings us back to the Hindu makara, since it can be interpreted as the meeting of two jaws in profile or as a single jaw in the frontal view. Which makes us wonder about the 'quadripartite sun monster' just above it (Fig. 15.38). As an image that appears at the threshold between this world and the next, could it not also be constructed like the Hindu makara? Could this skull in the frontal view also be two faces joined in profile? (Hence the dividing line at the centre of the jaw). Does it become, in this way, the Mayan version of the makara?

It is indeed strange that the Cosmic Serpent also appears (e.g. Copan altar 41) in the form of the Cauac monster or crocodile, which Schele notes when she writes, *"the body may be rendered as crocodilian or as a band of symbols."*[21] We recall that, according to Coomaraswamy, the Hindu makara is also 'part crocodile'. Indeed, in ayahuasca visions, crocodiles also appear in a role similar to serpents (see, for example, Jan Kounen's 2004 film *Renegade / Blueberry*). With the makara, we seem to be in the presence of a unique form or ornament that transcends cultural epochs, emerging from the timeless realm of vision.

Through their unique construction, the jaws of the Cosmic Serpent show that the Mayan craftsman was thinking in multiple dimensions. Or rather, he had possibly seen this serpent from a multi-dimensional point of view, in a visionary state.

As a masterpiece of Mayan art, it should not surprise us to discover that the composition of Pacal's sarcophagus lid follows a square armature composed of ϕ (phi) and root rectangles. In a recently-published study, *The Shapes of Sacred Space: A Proposed System of Geometry used to Lay Out and Design Maya Art and Architecture* (2010), Christopher Powell finds a stunning number of cases where the ϕ and root rectangles (to be explained in detail next chapter) create armatures for both the floor plans of temples and the lay out of stele.

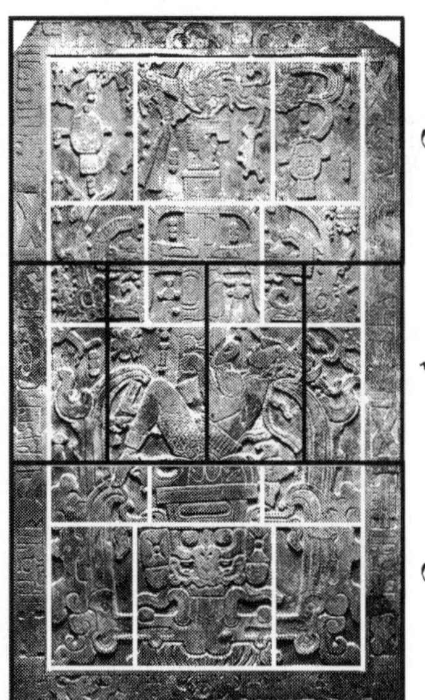

Fig. 15.40 - Geometric Armature of Pacal's Sacrophagus Lid

In the case of Pacal's sarcophagus lid, the frame consists of a vertical √3 rectangle which is divided into three horizontal rectangles (in black lines): a √4 rectangle in the middle, and two ϕ rectangles at the top and bottom. This creates a basic division of the composition into three parts, with the arms of the cross at the upper dividing line and the crown of the 'quadripartite sun monster' at the lower dividing line. In her iconographic interpretation, Schele noted the three-fold division of the scene into Overworld, Middleworld and Underworld.[22]

Powell goes on to subdivide the rectangle inside the frame into a whole series of ϕ rectangles (in grey lines), following geometric constructions found in Mayan architecture and art. The lines of the armature consistently mark out compositional sections within the greater whole. As Powell notes, *"A master draftsman laid out the arrangements and subdivisions of the work surfaces before outlining the compositional content."*[23]

Although evidence for armatures is scant in Mayan culture (no 'square grids' of the Egyptian type have been found), a mural at the famous Tepantitla palace in Teotihuacan (substructure 3, zone 2) shows engraved traces of 15 circles which equally measured out the wall space.[24] A list of Aztec construction tools has been discovered, which includes the plumb line (*temetztepilolli*), level (*quamniztli*), compass (*tlayolloanaloni*), and set-square (*tlanacazanimi*).[25] As masters of astronomical alignment and temple construction, we should not be surprised to find that the Mayans carefully laid out the compositions in their stele.

The division of the compositional space into squares and rectangles brings us back to Fuchs and his *Chronos* painting. As there, so here, each minor composition expands through its harmonious geometrical shape to become part of the greater totality. While focussing on any one point, our vision may expand through these constant measures.

More than that, the composition allows for the flow of curvilinear forms around fixed shapes. The 'wave-like dance of a curving line around an invisible straight line' is especially prevalent in Mayan art, giving it a recognizable 'psychedelic' quality. (There are many 'Mayan' qualities to some of Fuchs' paintings – a case in point being the serpent pillars in his *Job and the Judgment of Paris*, Fig. 18.23, which seem directly inspired by the serpent pillars of Chichen Itza).

The highly-stylized 'world tree' is, like the vision serpent, a seminal motif in Mayan art. In its cruciform shape, it appears three times on major stele at Palenque, and its appearance in the Great Goddess mural at Tepantitla is highly evocative of entheogens. As Linda Schele notes, the tree in Pacal's sarcophagus lid is covered with *"Nen or 'mirror' signs* [which] *mark it as a thing of brilliance and power."*[26] At the end of each branch are sacrificial bowls with beaded blood scrolls; and from these, bejeweled vision serpents emerge, marked with jade as especially holy.

As a 'vision tree' the luminous plant above Pacal offers him a glimpse of the Upper World, where the bird of paradise awaits in the top branches – a realm which Pacal hopes to enter at the end of his long underworld journey through Xibalba.

In all then, Pacal's sarcophagus lid offers us an image of a king at death's threshold, witnessing a vision of the afterlife. As his body falls into the underworld realm, he gazes upward at the Vision Tree, gesturing to it with hieroglyphic 'hand signs', and watching it exfoliate into a beatific vision of shimmering magnitude. In wavy patterned lines, it takes shape as the archetypal tree, the first and original tree, at the centre of a briefly-glimpsed and long-awaited paradise.

X. Byzantine Form in Multiple Dimensions

In Ch. 5 on Hieratic Proportion, we noted how Byzantine craftsmen first drew a series of circles along a vertical axis and then constructed the figure in accord with their measures. This Byzantine technique should remind us that Hieratic figures are not depicted in a single perspectival view. The head, the body, the feet – each are viewed separately from *a perfect frontal view*, then laid one atop the other, block by block. We do not see the feet as if we were 'looking down' at them – as we would from a single perspectival view. This convention is so accepted in our culture that we hardly even notice it.

But, this same technique may be used to construct a face from the three-quarter angle, and slowly we become aware of how we are indeed viewing the same object *from multiple angles simultaneously*. The Byzantine construction of the face from the three-quarter angle, as described earlier (Fig. 5.12), placed the sharp point of the compass between the eyebrows. But other methods were commonly used, and the Byzantine Madonna depicted here offers another example.

In his *Manual of Painting*, Dionysius of Fournos describes the steps for drawing a face in the three-quarter angle. He begins by drawing a vertical line down the centre, and measuring out the nose-length.

"Then," he writes, *"take half the measure of the nose and mark one eye in the larger part of the face* [here, the right eye]. *Do not draw the pupil in the middle of the eye, but a little to the side towards the ear. Then take the* [full] *measurement of the nose with the compass. After that, set one point of the compass in the iris of the larger* [right] *eye and strike this measurement to the other part of the face and mark the other* [left] *iris. And thus, circle the other eye in the smaller part* [of the face]*, only make this* [left eye] *a little rounder and smaller than the first, and a little lower."*[27]

In the example offered here (Fig. 15.41), the artist has indeed used this technique. Beginning with the nose measure, this length has been divided in half and used to mark the placement of the right eye from the central vertical. Then, taking the *full* nose-length as his compass measure, he has

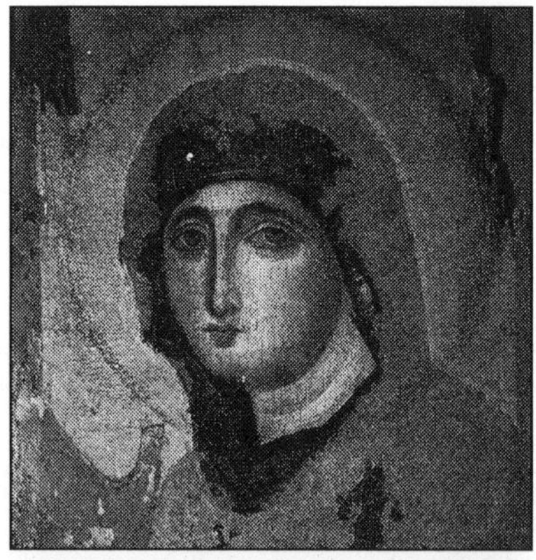

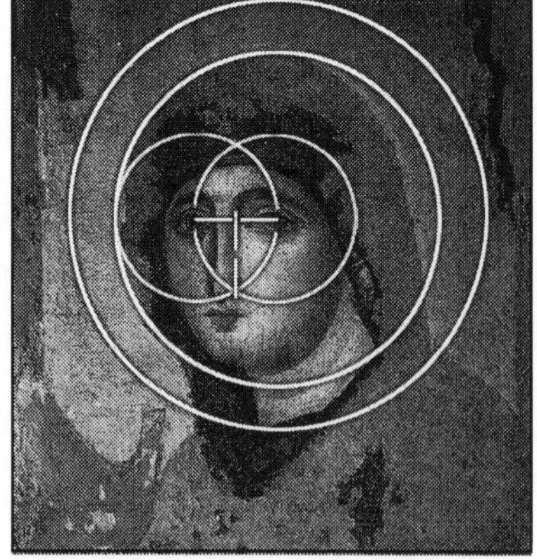

Fig. 15.41 - *Madonna di San Sisto*, Rome
Originally from Constantinople, c. 500

drawn a small circle with its centre on the right eye, and its circumference marking the placement of the left eye. After this, another small circle of the same size is drawn around the left eye (creating the *vesica piscis* on the cross formation), and this determines the outer limit of the Madonna's veil. Thus, returning to the right eye as the centre, a larger circle is drawn for the curve of the veil. Expanding the compass once more, a final circle is drawn for the halo – which is centered, once more, on the right eye.

This type of construction creates a three-quarter angle face that places a great amount of emphasis on the right eye, since it lies exactly at the centre of three circles. But something more is happening. While the left side of her face definitely appears to us from *the frontal view*, ('*make this* [left eye] *a little rounder and smaller than the first'*) the right side seems to extend further to the right, drawing out the features *in the profile view* ('*Do not draw the pupil in the middle of the eye, but a little to the side towards the ear'*). We are, in essence, seeing half the face in the frontal view (left circle) and half in profile (right circle) then putting these together and uniting them in our vision (the two outer circles).

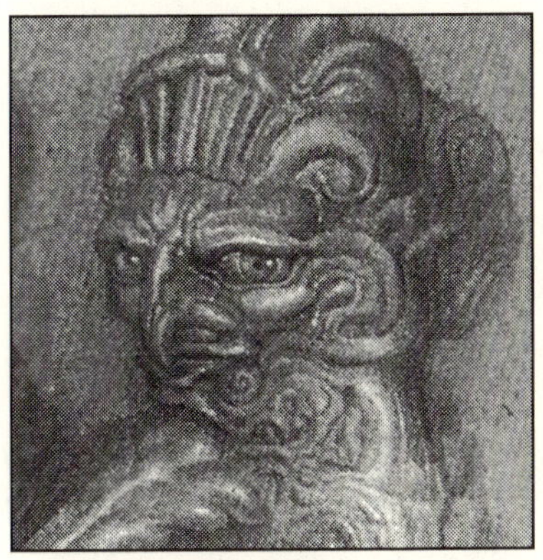

Fig. 15.42 - Ernst Fuchs:
Tree of Paradise 1963 - 72
Detail: Bird atop the right branch

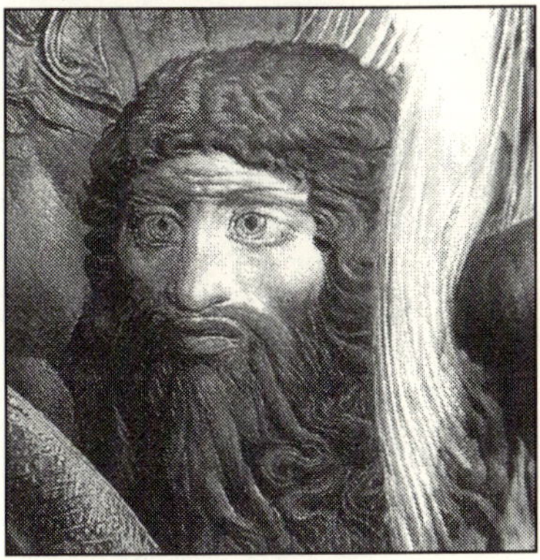

Fig. 15.43 - Ernst Fuchs:
Detail: *Adam Mysticus* 1977 - 82

As a result of this construction, the eye that straddles the three-quarter angle *becomes elongated.*

This stylistic device, of the three-quarter angle elongation of the eye, began to intrigue me, since I came across so many instances of it. It exists, for example, in the distinctive style of Khajuraho sculpture (see Ch. 3), but also in the works of Ernst Fuchs.

Indeed, I first became aware of the Sacred Code underlying its construction while meditating on Fuchs' *Tree of Paradise* (Fig. 15.44 over – a Mayan-inspired 'vision tree' if there ever was one...), particularly the bird which sits atop the right branch (Fig. 15.42). But it also appears in the face of *Adam Mysticus* (Fig. 15.43). Fuchs always manifest a decided preference for profiles in his work, but here he seems to have consciously *combined a frontal view and a profile*, so the right eye manifests a distinct elongation.

This new way of seeing first appeared to Fuchs in a dream. In the essay 'The Hidden Prime of Styles' from his book *Architectura Caelestis*, he recounts a dream where a colossus

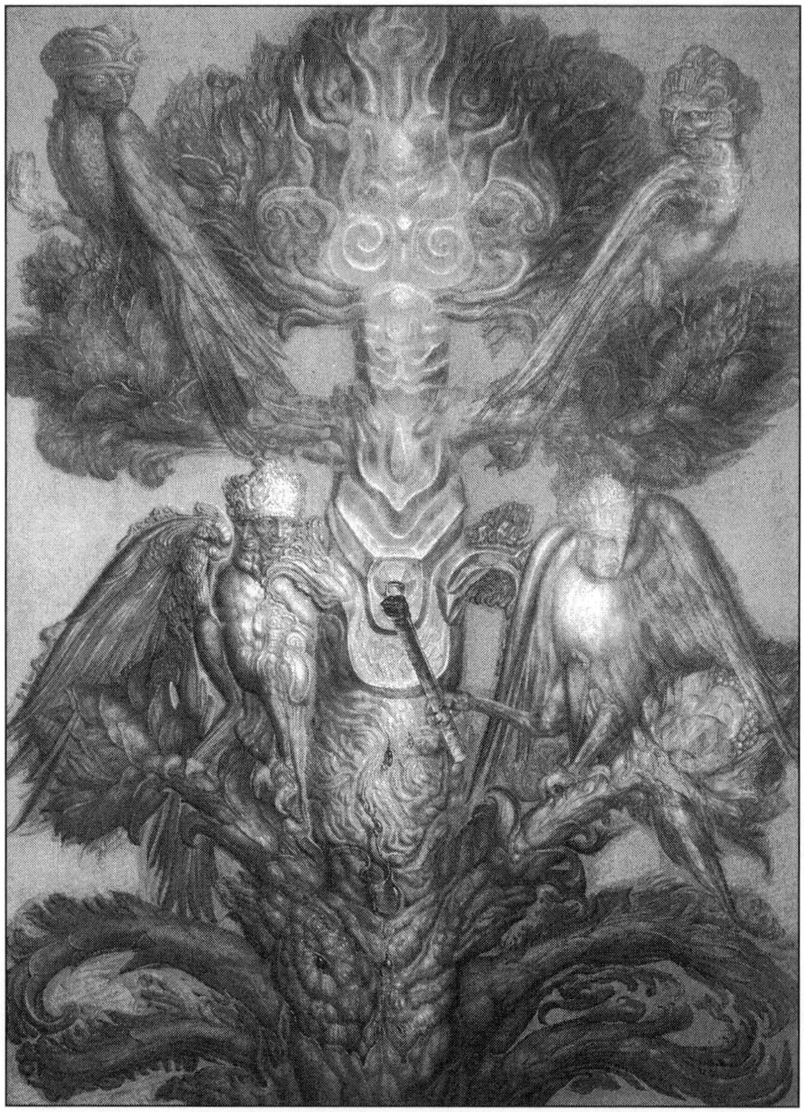

Fig. 15.44 - Ernst Fuchs: *Tree of Paradise* 1963 - 72
(For the armature of this work, compare to Figs. 1.2 and 30.4)

rose from the sea at night: *"A colossal huge round head emerged... his face was turned towards me, his pair of eyes, round and strongly arched towards the outside, were directed at me – power and strength radiated from his sight."*[28] But the same colossus also appears in the dream as square: *"I saw that he was as high as wide – like an ashlar, powerful – but round."*[29]

An 'ashlar' describes the solid square block which masons used to carve out their sculptural or architectural figures. As soon as this particular feature of the Hidden Prime of Styles began to emerge in his work, Fuchs wrote that

"Many of my figures appeared in square proportions." And he added *"...which I knew from my dreams."*[30]

When we focus on the face of the right bird of *The Paradise Tree* (Fig. 15.42), we seem to be gazing at an ashlar or solid block from a perfect three-quarter angle, so that the vertical edge (where the two sides meet) passes directly through the eye facing us. Meanwhile the squared sides of the block, rather than receding into the distance, *flatten out* to the sides. The block is not seen from a single perspectival view (as with Renaissance perspective, when both sides diminish as they recede into the distance), but from multiple perspectives simultaneously.

When the eye does indeed 'straddle the angle' – breaking past one side of the block (frontal dimension) and turning to the other side (profile dimension) – *it becomes elongated*, as we can clearly see in the Khajuraho style of Hindu sculpture as well. Just as the circles in the Byzantine Madonna overlap through the *vesica piscis*, here the two squared sides also seem to overlap – it is difficult to distinguish where 'the frontal view' ends and 'the profile view' begins. We are far indeed from the three-quarter angle as developed during the Renaissance. Rather, in this new way of depicting the three-quarter angle, *both the frontal and profile views are preserved.* This Sacred Code *combines* the Hieratic profile with the Hieratic frontal view, allowing us to view the face from two angles simultaneously.

In this context, it is worth noting that Babylonian sculpture – one of the greatest Hieratic Styles of the past – *had no three-quarter angle.* When we look closely (Fig. 15.45), we notice that the eye looks well-placed from the frontal and profile view, but fails to straddle the angle effectively in the three-quarter view. In ancient Babylon, Hieratic faces were depicted *in either* the frontal or profile view.

This is due to the manner in which the sculptor approached his task. By drawing a grid on four sides of the block and then cutting into the design (Fig. 4.15), ancient Egyptian and Babylonian craftsmen gave their deities a certain 'squarish' proportion. Even in ancient Greece, the squarish (*quadrata*) or block-like shape (*quadratas staturas*) of their sculpture was preserved, giving it a Hieratic quality. Only Lyssipos, with the out-stretched arm of his *Apoxymenos* (Fig. 6.14), abandoned this practice and introduced a more Humanist style of sculpture to the Hellenistic period.

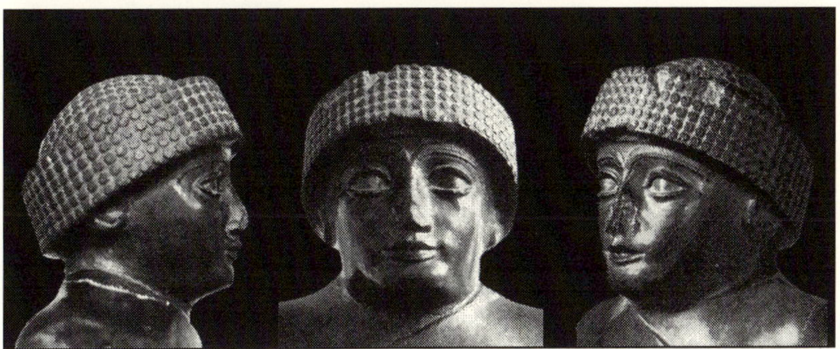

Fig. 15.45 - Sumerian Statue of King Gudea c. 2140 B.C. E, diorite.

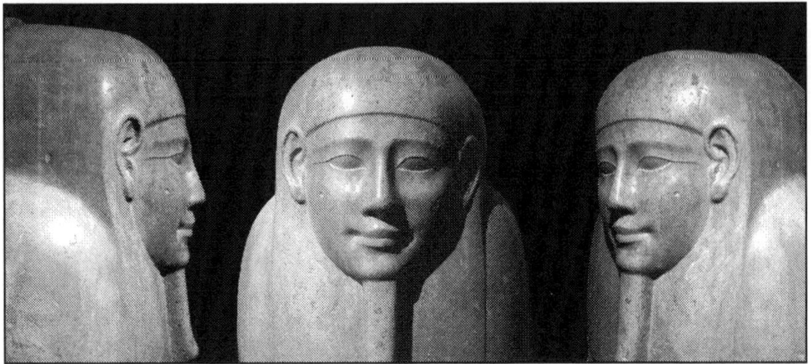

Fig. 15.46 - Egyptian Sarcophagus, Ptolemaic Period

By drawing a grid onto the sides of the block, ancient sculptors were also able to play with proportions. In the *Kunsthistorisches Museum* in Vienna, I came across a large Egyptian sarcophagus (Fig. 15.46) in which the proportions of the face were clearly altered. By increasing the horizontal spacing in his grid, the Egyptian craftsman was able to *broaden the face,* giving it a more epic and monumental quality. Yet, from the side angle, the proportions of the profile were perfectly preserved. The artist had achieved a graceful and refined distortion of the human face, while preserving its harmonious proportions.

XI. Modernist Ornament: the Formless Form

One of the key advances in painting, which marked the birth of Modernism, was Picasso and Braque's development of Cubism. Here too, the figure is viewed from multiple dimensions. And yet, what is entirely lacking in Cubism is the attempt to *harmoniously integrate* the parts in the whole – to create a composite figure that is seamlessly complete.

Instead, Picasso's figures appear fragmented, ugly and disjointed. It is for this reason that we often refer to Picasso's figures as 'monsters' (*les monstrueux*). Knowing this, the elder Hieratic cultures reserved this technique for frightening faces and grotesques which, as threshold guardians, prevented unprepared souls from entering the higher sacred realm. But, when we turn to Fuchs' ornamental figures, even the most grotesque mask manifests a distinct beauty and style. James Trilling noted this when, in the final chapter of *The Language of Ornament,* he acknowledged Fuchs and Giger's work as the culmination of ornamental history.

After analyzing Adolf Loos' rejection of architectural ornament in *Ornament und Verbrechung*, Trilling realized that *"...he did not practice what he preached. Under cover of his own diatribe against ornament, Loos introduced a new ornamental style, using the 'natural' patterns of stone and wood."*[31] We can see this in the green marble of his seminal building on Vienna's Michaelerplatz (now called *das Looshaus*), where the eidetic patterns in the stone serve as decoration to break up the monotony of the straight lines. Following Loos, Modernist architects sought out marble or wood as a kind of 'non-ornamental ornament', where our eye is free to wander and imagine all manner of creatures in the swirling flux of the material.

"This branch of modernist ornament," Trilling notices, *"flirts with the sinister and monstrous. The fact that instead of recognizable (albeit fantastic) subject matter, it depicts the very opposite, the refusal of matter to take a recognizable shape, suggests that the twentieth century has its own distinctive breed of monsters to deal with."*[32]

And so, after a review of over 30,000 years of ornament, Trilling culminates his erudite study with images by Fuchs and Giger:

"Surrealist and Visionary painters such as Max Ernst and Ernst Fuchs reinforce this trend in ornament, bringing indeterminacy to life with meticulous craftsmanship. More recently, the Swiss artist H. R. Giger, an avowed admirer of Fuchs, has allowed the almost-forms of his predecessor to crystallize into images of unearthly beings and bizarre technologies. Many of his paintings express a repulsive sexual sadism, but his best work is as brilliantly ornamental as it is nightmarish."[33]

Yet, I think it mistaken to elevate Fuchs and Giger's work to this level, simply because they overcame the bankruptcy of Modernism through 'meticulous craftsmanship'. Granted, they possessed the craftsman's deep respect for the working material, elucidating the random forms inherent in the *matière* through 20th century psycho-analytic techniques like *pareidolia*, active imagination and Rorschach's ink blots. But both were also passionately engaged with the history of art – with creating works in a trans-temporal dialogue with their predecessors.

Fuchs spoke to me of this during an interview I made with him in June of 2001:

"You know, the way I understand it, art is also the discovery of all the artists who have come before you... and that, they are in you... so you have to revive them. This resurrection of the arts that goes on, I think, from generation to generation. If you think of Michelangelo, when he saw the Laocoön, he didn't see an old piece of greek sculpture. He saw his own art, on an eternal level...

"The artist responds to something that he is. It awakens, and comes to life – by looking at art. And that's what I think has been very important in all the periods that I've passed through. I know what inspired me. I even know what I wanted to repeat – just to see if I was good enough. It becomes a kind of 'conjuring', if you will. You see somebody doing a trick, and you have no idea how he did it. You stand in front of a painting and wonder: how did he do that? And then you go home and you try and you try. And suddenly – you got it! That's really something – to discover an artist who was living maybe centuries before you, by doing what he was able to do."[34]

Through these words, we come to understand how technical mastery opens up a trans-temporal dialogue, where each well-executed painting engages in discourse with another artist from another age. Much of Fuchs' work was carried out in dialogue with Michelangelo, Blake and Moreau. And, on the level of ornament, it was particularly Moreau's work that Fuchs admired most, as is clear when he wrote: *"Here were ornaments and architectures as they were before all epochs of style."*[35]

Moreau's obsession with ornament was extreme, and it reflected, in part, his fascination with other, more exotic cultures, integrating them into his own timeless vision. To give but one example (Fig. 15.47), the ornament at the

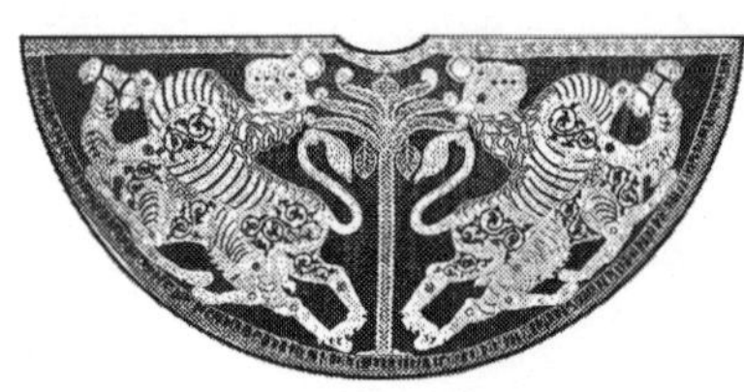

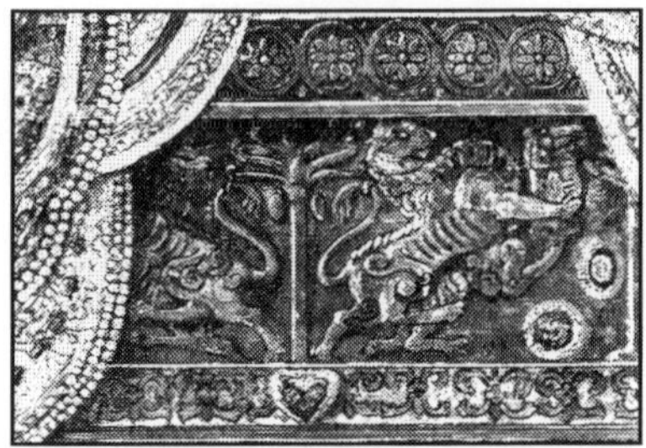

Fig. 15.47 - Left: Coronation Mantle of Roger II, Byzantine, 12th c.
Right: Gustave Moreau: *Jupiter and Semele* Detail of Throne Ornament

foot of the throne in *Jupiter and Semele* is inspired by the Coronation Mantle of Roger II. This 12th century masterpiece of Byzantine embroidery (3.4 m wide, now in the Vienna Schatzkammer) depicts the Tree of Life, flanked by the symbolic motif of the Lion triumphing over the Camel.

Arising from the Palace of Persepolis in Persia, the tree symbolizes the eternal source of life; this life-force becomes channeled through different heraldic beasts at different points in history. During this epoch, the life-force of fierce leonine strength is triumphing over the camel's gentler, life-preserving and nomadic nature. In ornament, each fantastic archetype (the gryphon, the phoenix, the unicorn) emanates a unique form of *animal power*, which the artists may tap into and manifest in their own creative flow.

A closer look at Moreau's *Jupiter and Semele* reveals how the ornaments in the celestial architecture form one continuous descent through the entire hierarchy of being – from angels to satyrs to humans, animals, vegetation and minerals. Each link in the chain offers a unique symbol and reflection of their heavenly source. In the Middle Ages, this chain was called the *Catena Aurea* – the Golden Chain of Being,[36] and the whole of creation could be contemplated, rung by rung, as a ladder of vision leading to its divine maker.

The experienced craftsman knew every sort of plant and herb, every precious mineral and stone, as well as their complex correspondences. When Moreau, in his *Jupiter and Semele*, needed green pillars to complement the yellows and blues in Jupiter's throne, he naturally called upon emerald as its substance. Like the theurgists and alchemists of ancient lore, the eternal craftsman treats each allegorical element, metal, plant and animal as a sigil, reflecting the divine movements in the heavens. All may be linked and harmonized into the *harmonices mundi*, a microcosm of the divine cosmos.

Today's artists have the duty to revive ornament, and the Sacred Codes underlying its construction and transmission. Often, this requires a different way of seeing – one that rises above the paucity of our times, where the imagination is impoverished, the Sacred is profaned, and ornament is abolished. The figures of ornament, when properly understood, frolic and thrive in a garden of heavenly delights, a paradise regained, where blissful creatures co-exist in harmony. Birds of paradise devour fruits from the tree of life, which endlessly regenerates and blossoms anew. Not only does the lion lay down with the lamb, but devours it playfully and painlessly, in a world without suffering, where life endlessly cycles round in God's eternal play of the creative imagination.

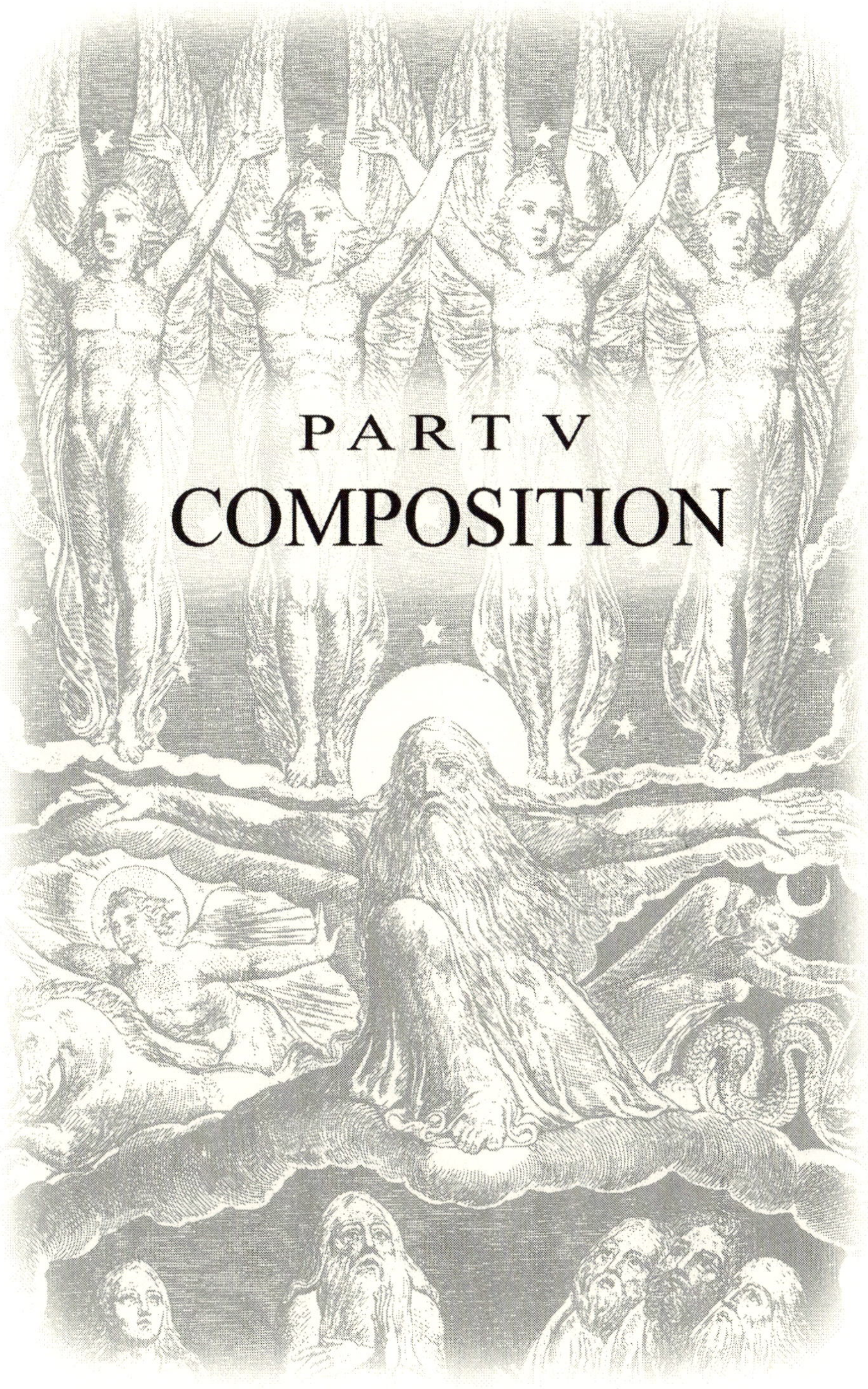

PART V
COMPOSITION

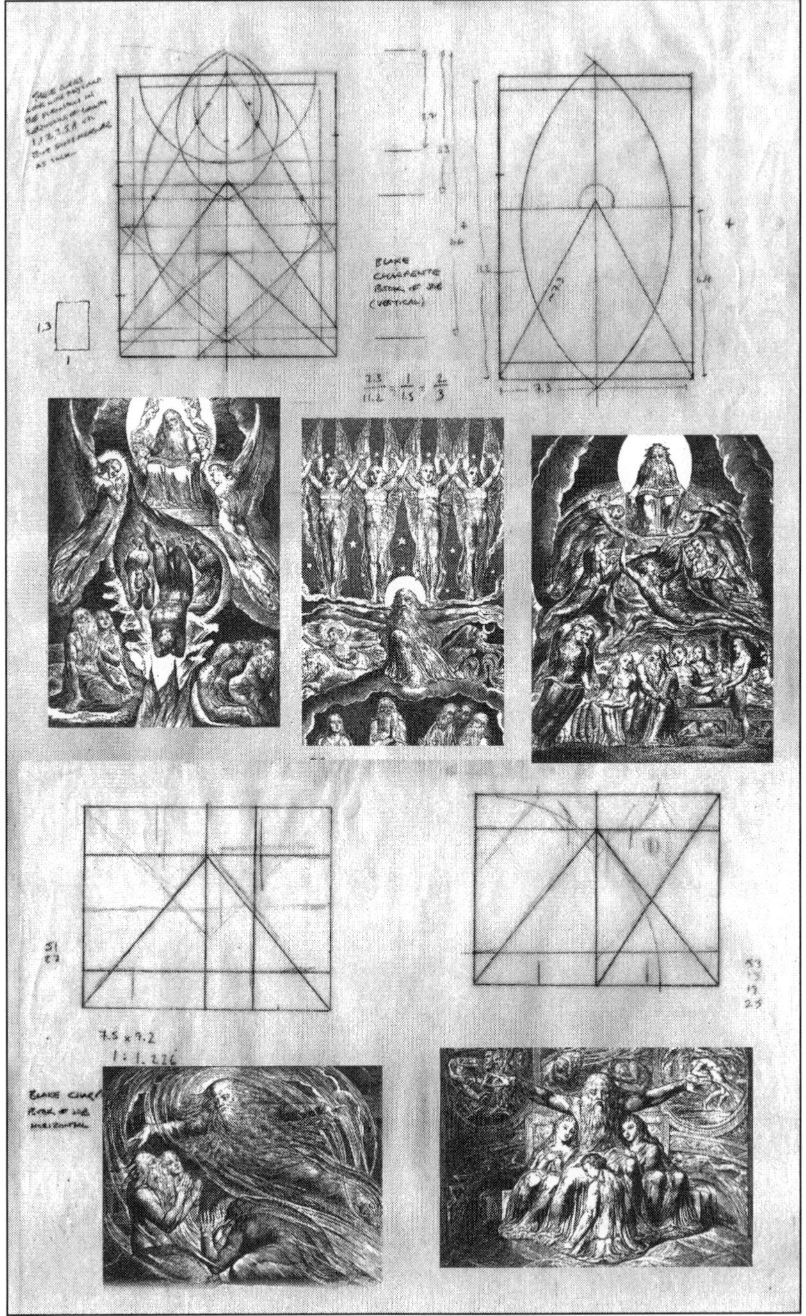

Fig. 16.1 - L. Caruana: Armature Studies of William Blake's *Book of Job*

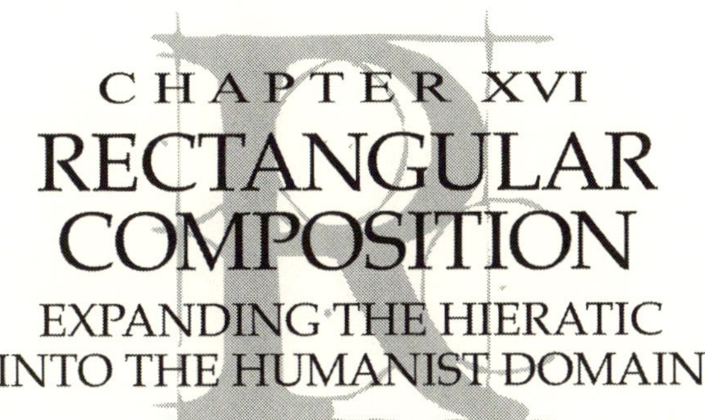

CHAPTER XVI
RECTANGULAR COMPOSITION
EXPANDING THE HIERATIC INTO THE HUMANIST DOMAIN

I. *Contemplatio*: To Mark Out Space for Holy Signs

Like a temple, a painting may become a 'template' of the cosmos – a place that we can enter into, to 'con-template' our place in the greater scheme of things. The Latin word *contemplatio,* derived from 'temple' or *templum*, means 'to mark out a space for seeing augers and other holy signs'. For the artist, the Composition of a painting is this 'marking out' of hallowed space where sacred seeing occurs.

To enter a temple's sacred space is to undertake a soul journey through many doors and unexpected passages, penetrating into the deep inner sanctum where the deity awaits. Likewise with a painting, many guardian-images or guides may be encountered on the periphery as the eye slowly wanders, captivated and entranced, to the main point of focus, inviting a more prolonged meditation.

The organization of space in painting has occupied artists for centuries, if not millennia. Alas, the harmonious lines of composition, once drawn, are eventually covered over and lost to view. Although ateliers and academies were created to preserve this hidden knowledge, much has been lost over time. Hence we are compelled to rediscover for ourselves the Sacred Codes of composition.

When we think of a composition today, we immediately think of the rectangle as the basic starting point. Although the rectangle has a long history in Hieratic art, going back in time through Mayan, Byzantine, Buddhist and Egyptian cultures, the rectangle would not exist, geometrically speaking, were it not for the square. To understand composition within the rectangle, we must first have a thorough grasp of the square and its inner harmonics.

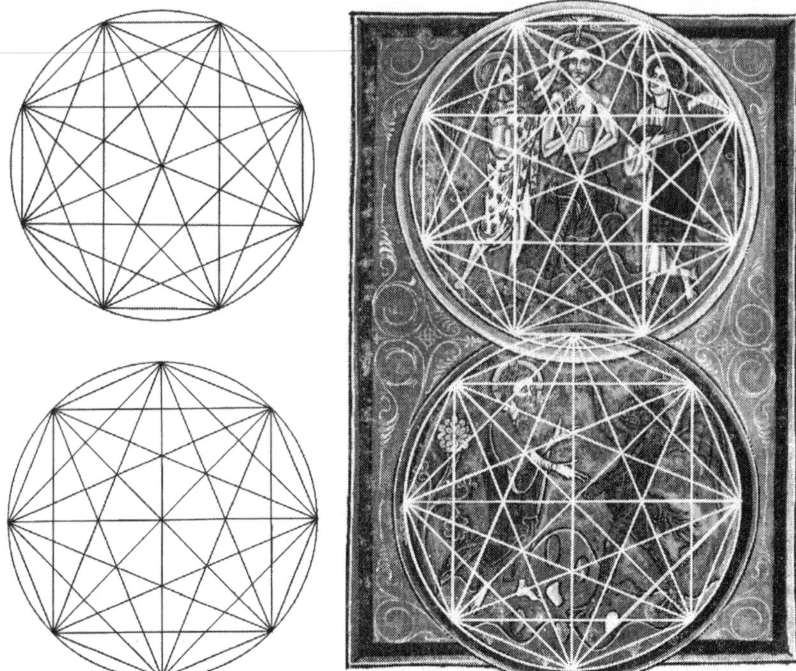

Fig. 16.2 - Above: Octagram Armature for *The Baptism of Christ*
Below: Turned Octagram Armature for *The Temptation*
From *The Psalter of Louis and Blanche de Castille* c. 1220

As we have seen with the barbed quatrefoil, the square was an important compositional device during the Gothic period. However, it would be more precise to say that the square inscribed in the circle – *ad circulum* – was the point of departure. This naturally leads to 'the turned square' or *quadrature* which Bucher called 'the key' for Gothic architectural design. But, the turned square, as we have noted, has its roots in Islamic design, as the *Khatem Sulemani* or Octagram of so many Islamic tilings.

In his book *Charpentes: La Géométrie Secrète des Peintres* (The Painter's Secret Geometry – 1963), Charles Bouleau recognized the Islamic roots of Gothic art: *"The men of the Middle Ages knew how to use a compass, and it is through geometry that they tried to reach their ideal. The geometry that was practiced by the Arabs quickly spread through the Occident and was widely taught by the 13th century. We see it, in greater or lesser scale, in the art of ornament, with purely geometrical tracings derived from Arab designs: the arcs of interpenetrating circles and their resulting polygons."*[1]

As a key example of Gothic armature, Bouleau gives us none other than the Octagram inscribed in the circle, and demonstrates how it was used in thirty-two of the medallions from *The Psalter of St. Louis and Blanche de Castille* (c. 1220).[2] The illuminer who made these medallions used his armature in two ways: as a □ square combined with a ◇ turned square (the

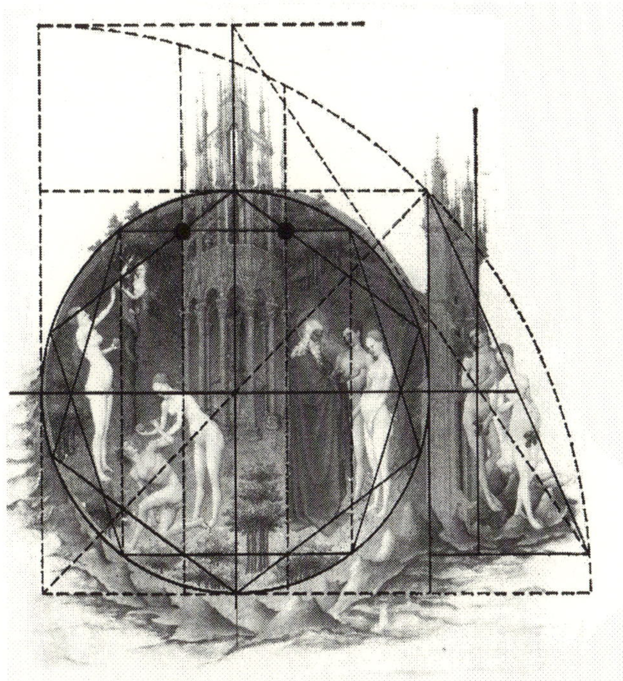

Fig. 16.3 - Decagram Armature for *The Fall From Paradise*
From Les Frères Limbourg: *Les Très Riches Heures du Duc de Berry* c. 1416

regular octagram), or as these two turned 45° (the turned octagram) so two points appear at the top and bottom, rather than a flat line. In Fig. 16.2, the upper medallion uses the regular octagram while the lower one uses the turned octagram.

In the upper medallion of *The Baptism of Christ*, it is the vertical lines that dominate, with the figures of John the Baptist and the angel following the two main verticals, giving the composition a static and hieratic quality. Meanwhile, in the lower medallion of *The Temptation*, it is the diagonals that come to the fore, marking out the lines of movement for the limbs, creating a more dynamic composition.

But, for the Gothic illuminers, the turned square was not the only regular polygon that could be inscribed in the circle. For *The Fall From Paradise* in *Les Très Riches Heures du Duc de Berry* (Fig. 16.3), a similar armature was made with the pentagon and turned pentagon, inscribing a decagon in the circle. As Bouleau shows,[3] the upper points of intersection of the two pentagons provided the artist with the two precise points for determining the width of the ornate architecture above the Celestial Fountain (the source of the four streams in Eden, offering the waters of life). A square drawn round the main circle provides the placement for the ornate gateway that lead out of paradise. Is it mere chance that the artist chose the circle as the basic shape for the paradise realm, while the square becomes the doorway to our fallen earthly existence?

And, following this logic, what are we to make of the space outside the square? By using the square's diagonal (bottom left to top right), the artist has drawn an arc to the bottom right and upper left corners. This arc clearly defines the limit of the Gothic spires atop Heaven's Gate and the Celestial Fountain.

At the same time, it extends the square's measure to become two rectangles, one extending upward vertically, and the other extending horizontally to the right. These rectangles (which, as we shall see, are called Root rectangles), measure out the mundane, earthly and (I dare say) Humanist space outside of the paradise realm, which is defined by the Hieratic squared circle.

All regular polygons, from the triangle and square up to the dodecagon are considered to be Hieratic shapes because they emerge from the matrix of the perfect circle. They bear the imprint of the Divine Maker, and crystallize the expansion of sacred space into regular shapes with their endpoints equidistant from the centre.

But the rectangle is different. Although each one has a centre (the intersection of two diagonals), the sides are of different lengths, creating ratios on the order of 1:2, 2:3 and 3:4. Or, they create a ratio of 1 to an irregular number, such as root rectangles of the type $1{:}\sqrt{2}$, $1{:}\sqrt{3}$ etc.

The ratio of the sides of a square are always 1 : 1. But the ratio of the sides of a rectangle will be $1 : x$, where x is *some other number,* always greater or lesser than one. Constructing the most harmonious rectangle *geometrically*, and measuring its ratio *arithmetically*, has been the constant pursuit of artists throughout history. Indeed, it is a mystery that calls into question the very relationship of geometry to arithmetic, since certain harmonic rectangles may only be measured *approximately*, with irrational numbers.

II. Constructing the Rectangle

This is not to suggest that rectangles are not Hieratic. Rather, what rectangles represent is *the expansion of the Hieratic into the Human domain*. Whether we refer to the Pharaoh in Egyptian times, the Messiah in Judaeo-Christianity or the Avatars of Vishnu in Hinduism, the incarnation of the supreme Deity into human form remains a cultural constant. In other traditions, this Primordial Man has been called Adam Kadmon (Kaballah), Puruṣa (Rg Veda) or Pigeradamas (Gnosticism). And the basic shape of the *Anthropos* (despite Renaissance depictions of Vitruvian man) is the rectangle.

We are seeking, like Desiderius Lenz before us, those higher rectangles which the Divine Craftsman created, as the matrix for *"...the normative human pair as it emerged from the mind of God."*[4] From Pacal's sarcophagus lid to the Shroud of Turin, the rectangle has symbolized the embodiment of the Hieratic in Humanist form – the sacred measure of our Divinely Human prototype.

With the aid of a compass and straight rule, we may draw a perfect square within a grid of circles. From that 1:1 square, a variety of rectangles may emerge, some totally irregular, others becoming increasingly regular and harmonious. We shall begin our examples with those irregular rectangles which are recognizable, nevertheless, in French canvas sizes. From there, we may proceed to Byzantine rectangles, which use the *rabattement* (the 'folding' of one side to the base) to increase their regularity. After that, we will pursue two main types of regular rectangles.

Of these, the first type is constructed *arithmetically*, principally through the measures of a straight rule. We shall call these *harmonic rectangles* because of they produce whole number ratios with harmonic properties (1:2, 2:3, 3:4). In ancient Greece, philosophers like Pythagoras and Plato were the first to note these harmonies, which were transmitted to the Gothic Era via Plato, Vitruvius and Boethius. Harmonic rectangles then experienced a resurgence during the Renaissance, since they measure out space with the same consonances that may be heard in music and the harmony of the spheres.

The second type is constructed *geometrically* with a compass and straight rule. These include the various *root rectangles* (√2, √3, √5) as well as the *golden rectangle* (ϕ or 'phi'). As we have seen, the construction of a root rectangle results when we fold the diagonal of the square down to the base (Fig. 16.4 gives the example of a root 2 rectangle). The extension of the square to this new measure forms a root 2 rectangle with the ratio 1:√2. In the *Timaeus*, Plato placed √2 and √3 at the heart of his cosmology. These root rectangles became prominent in the Byzantine era, and during the Gothic period √2 led to the *ad quadratum* measure, just as its complement √3 led to the *ad triangulum* measure.

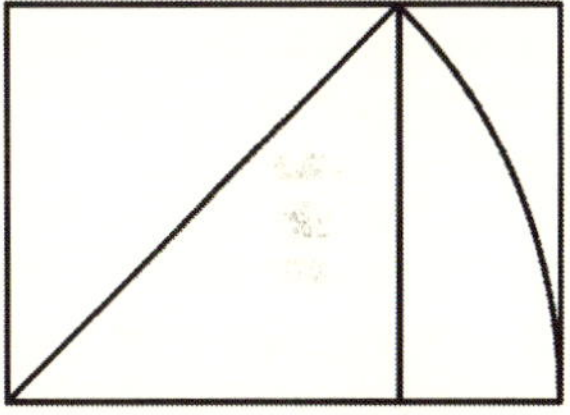

Fig. 16.4 - Construction of a Root 2 Rectangle

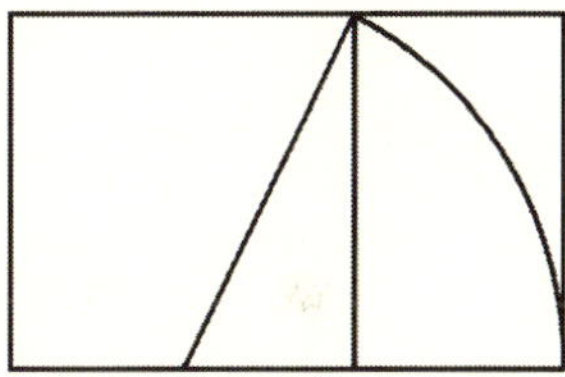

Fig. 16.5 - Construction of a ϕ ('phi') or Golden Rectangle

The construction of the ϕ rectangle (1: ϕ) is similar (Fig. 16.5), except the diagonal *from the midpoint of the base* is folded down to create the new measure for the ϕ rectangle. The Golden Rectangle has been known throughout history, but experienced a resurgence in the Renaissance and again in the 20th century.

When the sides of these rectangles are measured arithmetically, they give ratios with *irrational* numbers, so that 1 : √2 actually equals 1 : 1.4142135... while 1 : ϕ equals 1 : 1:1.618... These irrational number ratios should not mislead us into thinking that their rectangles are somehow less elegant or harmonious. Rather, the incommensurability of their ratios tells us that the diagonal (from the triangle) transferred by the arc (from the circle) had an important role to play in their construction. So our arithmetic can only measure *approximately* what was constructed through geometry *precisely*.

Harmonic rectangles with their arithmetic construction shall come to dominate this chapter, just as root rectangles, with their geometric construction, shall come to the fore in the exposition on Dynamic Composition next chapter. All of these rectangles offer a variety of methods for the harmonious organization of *contemplative* space.

III. Irregular Rectangles in Standard French Canvases

While living in Paris, I became intrigued by the quaint and curious tradition in France of offering pre-established canvas sizes. Since the mid 1700's, a definite system has been put in place, with sixty standard canvas sizes defined by pre-set numbers. The list of sizes is printed on little cards and widely distributed (Fig. 16.6). The artist need only specify that she wants a F6, P8 or M10, and the ready-made canvas is handed over.

The F stands for *Figure* (portrait) or a vertical composition, while the P stands for *Paysage* (landscape) and the M for *Marine* (seascape) – both being horizontal compositions (the latter a bit shorter). By tradition, the *Tondo* (circle), *Carré* (square) and *Double Carré* (double square) are also offered.

The logic behind the numbering system and corresponding sizes is a mystery lost to time. For example, a F6 canvas is 41 cm x 33 cm – a ratio that can be reduced neither to a simple fraction nor a harmonic ratio. The same is true of the vast majority of the 60 standard canvas measures on offer: *all are irregular rectangles.* Yet, artists like Monet and Van Gogh have created masterworks from these standardized yet irregular canvas sizes.

In *The Art of Impressionism: Painting Technique and the Making of Modernity*, Anthea Callen digs into the mystery, seeking the source of standard French canvas sizes. In 1684, the artist Roger de Piles made a remark in one of his writings about *"une toile de 20 sols"*[5] (a canvas of 20 *sous* or pence), leading Callen to suggest that the numbering system was based, in fact, on the old *sous* prices for canvases.

As for the measures, their present lack of harmony may be attributed to the fact that they were first created in the Pre-Napoleonic era of *pieds et pouces* (feet and inches), then 'rounded off' when Napoleon enforced the

N°	FIGURE	PAYSAGE	MARINE	N°	FIGURE	PAYSAGE	MARINE
0	18 x 14	18 x 12	18 x 10	15	65 x 54	65 x 50	65 x 46
1	22 x 16	22 x 14	22 x 12	20	73 x 60	73 x 54	73 x 50
2	24 x 19	24 x 16	24 x 14	25	81 x 65	81 x 60	81 x 54
3	27 x 22	27 x 19	27 x 16	30	92 x 73	92 x 65	92 x 60
4	33 x 24	33 x 22	33 x 19	40	100 x 81	100 x 73	100 x 65
5	35 x 27	35 x 24	35 x 22	50	116 x 89	116 x 81	116 x 73
6	41 x 33	41 x 27	41 x 24	60	130 x 97	130 x 89	130 x 81
8	46 x 38	46 x 33	46 x 27	80	146 x 114	146 x 97	146 x 89
10	55 x 46	55 x 38	55 x 33	100	162 x 130	162 x 114	162 x 97
12	61 x 50	61 x 46	61 x 38	120	195 x 130	195 x 114	195 x 97

CARRÉ et DOUBLE CARRÉ						
40 x 30	70 x 35	120 x 60	25 x 25	40 x 40	60 x 60	120 x 120
50 x 25	80 x 40	150 x 50	30 x 30		80 x 80	130 x 130
60 x 30	100 x 50	20 x 20	35 x 35	50 x 50	100 x 100	150 x 150

Fig. 16.6 - Card with French Canvas Sizes
From Maison Gattegno, Rue de la Grande Chaumière, Paris

Revolutionary Metric system (centimetres) by law in 1812. When the ratios for Figure canvases are adjusted back to *pouces*, they *approximate* simple rational ratios.

But, the real basis for standard canvas sizes in France, Callen decides, is commercial rather than aesthetic: *"It can be shown that all standard canvas sizes fitted neatly, in a logical jigsaw, into the most common pre-industrial loom-widths of 1 metre and 1.40 metres."*[6] As such, there seems to be no harmonious foundation for the measures of standard canvas sizes in France.

Meanwhile, the author André Béguin states in *Dictionnaire technique de la Peinture* that F and M canvases are based on the ϕ ratio, while P canvases are based on the root rectangles, but 'these relationships are only approximative.'

In America, standard canvas sizes are measured in inches, such as 16" x 20", 18" x 24" etc. All of them may be reduced to simple ratios of 2:3, 3:4 and 4:5, which easily produce harmonic ratios in their bounding rectangles.

IV. Byzantine Armatures

In *l'Icon: Image de l'Invisible*, Egon Sendler offers a diagram (Fig. 16.7) of the methods used by Byzantine icon painters for the construction of rectangles.[7] All are derived from the square, using the basic technique of 'folding the diagonal'.

When the sharp end of the compass is placed on D and an arc is drawn from E to J, the ϕ rectangle appears. Likewise, an arc with centre A drawn from F gives a root 2 rectangle.

But, an arc with centre B drawn from C gives a new, hitherto unconsidered rectangle of the irregular dimension 9:10.

Likewise, an arc with centre I (the centre of the square) drawn between E to F (the top corners of the square) gives, at its uppermost point, a rectangle of 5:6. By using the intersection of CD with the diagonal GB to give us point H, we can draw another arc from centre C to create a regular rectangle of 4:5. Last of all, if we draw two arcs to make a root 2 rectangle, one with centre A drawn from F, and one with centre B drawn from E, then *the point of intersection* of these two arcs gives us a 3:4 rectangle.

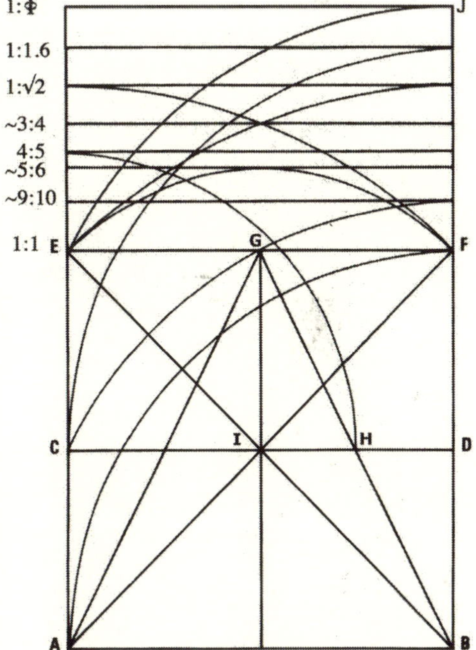

Fig. 16.7 - Rectangle Construction for Byzantine Icons

The icon of *The Annunciation* by Andrei Rublev (Fig. 16.8) gives a clear example of how the artist decided on a root 2 rectangle as the basic shape for his composition. The foreground figures of the angel Gabriel and the Virgin fit evenly into the square, while the extension of the diagonal creates the background plane for the architecture.

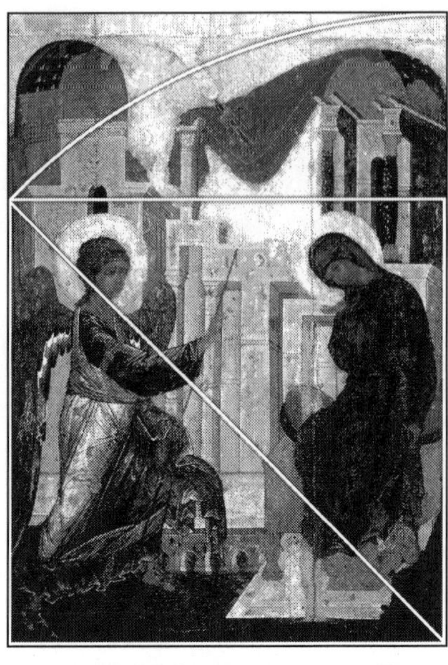

Fig. 16.8 - Rublev: *The Annunciation* 1405

The icon of *Elijah the Prophet* from the Novogorod school (Fig. 16.9) shows the basic armature used for many Byzantine works of the 'portrait' type. The first and most important step in Byzantine painting was to determine the placement of the halo. To do this, the artist followed a well-known technique called the *rabattement* or 'infolding'. This consists of taking the shorter side of any rectangle (here, the baseline AB) and *folding it in* to the longer side (point C or D), thus creating *a square* (ABCD) within the rectangle. We shall return to the *rabattement* time and again, since it is, as Bouleau says, *"un schéma fondamental"*[9] for the making of armatures.

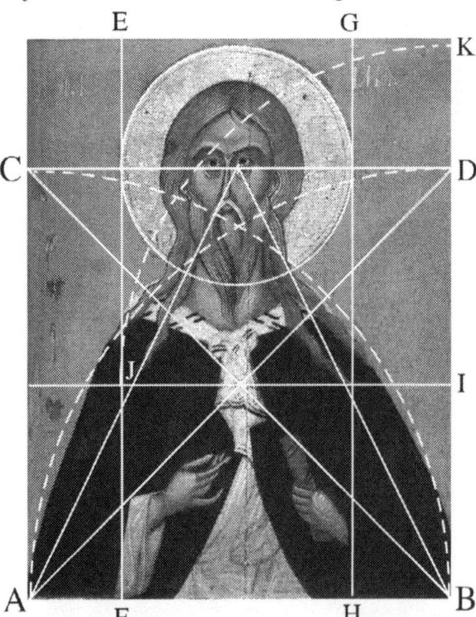

Fig. 16.9 - *Elijah the Prophet* early 15th c.

Two interesting features immediately rise before our eyes. First: that the artist has used the arcs of the *rabattement* to delineate the basic shape of Elijah's black robe. Second: that the top of the square determined by the *rabattement* creates the segment CD, such that, its midpoint serves as the centre of the halo's circle. Thanks to the *rabattement*, the icon painter has determined the halo's placement in the rectangle.

"To better understand the composition of an icon," Egon Sendler writes, *"one must first study the halo, which is of great importance for the geometric structure. It is likewise of great importance for the compositional*

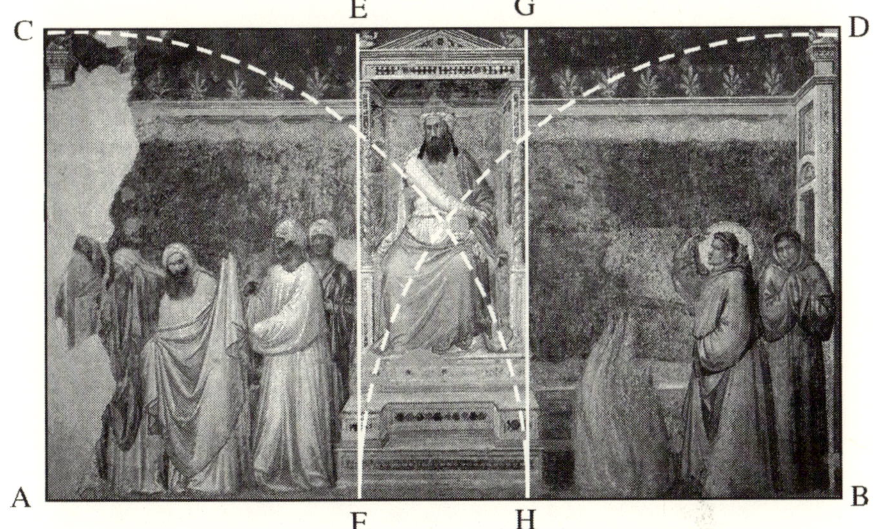

Fig. 16.10 - Rabattement in Giotto's *Saint Francis Before the Sultan* 1325.

schema because, in all icons, the halo constitutes the centre around which the subject matter is constructed."[10]

By drawing two verticals (EF and GH) from the halo's outermost measure, the artist has determined the outer limits of the hair and the placement of the hands. The angle of the hands is further determined by the square's diagonals (AD and BC) and the placement of the white drapery at the square's midpoint. Finally, by using the technique of 'folding the diagonal', the artist drew an arc with centre I from J up to K, to measure out the rectangle's height, which happens to approximate a 3:4 rectangle.

Byzantine art lies at the foundation of all Gothic and Renaissance works. We should pause here to recognize how the Byzantine artist has 'seen unity' in the construction of his work. The centre of the halo (which is often found in *the eye* of a three-quarter figure, or between the eyebrows at *the third eye* of a frontal figure) is the unifying point of space for this rectangular composition. *From that point*, all the remaining features of the Saint – the head, body and hands – are geometrically determined, thus making them integral parts of an organic whole. All the lesser points lead our eye inexorably to the centre point, and when we gaze upon that centre point, we behold the Saint *as unified and whole,* a holy image of Divine unity in human form. From the circle at the top of the triangle, the hieratic human form flows into existence.

In Giotto's fresco of *Saint Francis Before the Sultan* (Fig. 16.10), Charles Bouleau offers another clear historical case of *rabattement*.[11] To determine the placement of the sultan's throne, Giotto drew one arc with centre A from C to H, and another arc with centre B from D to F. The resulting verticals EF and GH place the sultan's throne in a harmonic relationship to the whole. The space created by the overlap of 2 squares (CGHA and EDBF) is, Bouleau notes, an important compositional device that results from the *rabattement*.

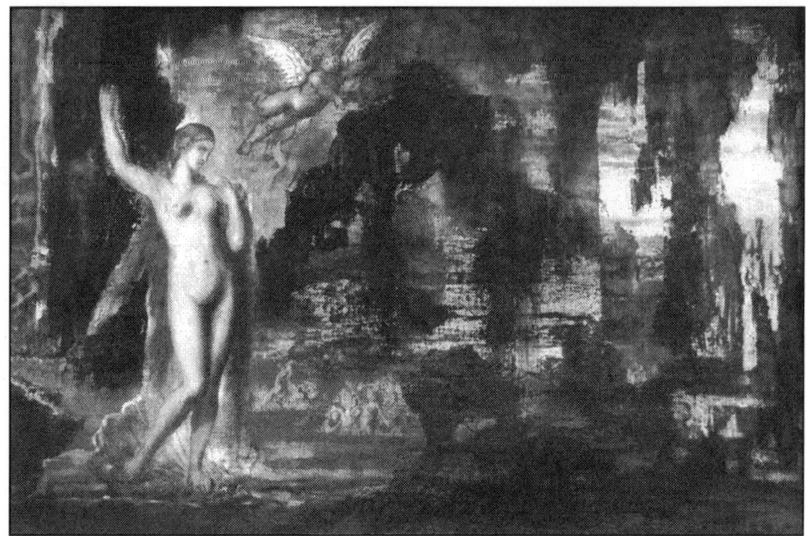

Fig. 16.11 - Gustave Moreau: *Study for Pasiphae*

IV. The Harmonic Armature for All Rectangles

During one of my many visits to the *Musée Gustave Moreau*, my eye was caught by a painterly sketch for *Pasiphaé* (Fig. 16.11). What caught my attention was the large black pyramidal shape dominating the background, and a similar inverted shape created by the negative space. So, I photographed it and, once I returned to my Paris studio, I laid out the basic Harmonic Armature overtop (Fig. 16.12).

Sure enough, Moreau's rough painterly strokes followed these lines intuitively, as if the artist had already visualized the basic armature in his mind. Not only do the pyramidal shapes follow the *charpente*, but so does Pasiphaé's figure: her tilted head, bent knee and raised arm following the diagonals, while the winged cherub ascends along the corner diagonal.

I did not detect any underlying construction lines, and tend to believe that the Harmonic Armature was so basic to Moreau's way of seeing that it was simply ingrained. To better understand the basic Harmonic Armature, let us examine it step by step.

Given any rectangle – whether regular or irregular – the artist makes three basic operations that determine the halves, the thirds and the quarters (Figs. 16.13 - 15). These may refer to specific harmonic *points* in the painting, or to their vertical and horizontal *dividing lines*.

The first step, of *drawing the diapason halves* (1:2), is to draw two intersecting diagonals from the opposite corners, like an X. Their point of intersection indicates the exact centre of the rectangle. A vertical or horizontal line drawn through this point neatly divides the compositional space into halves.

This first step forms the basis of all Hieratic symmetry, and artists from Buddhism to Byzantium have been known to make the initial X of corner-to-corner diagonals (Figs. 11.1 & 11.2) to locate the sacred centre of the painting's holy ground.

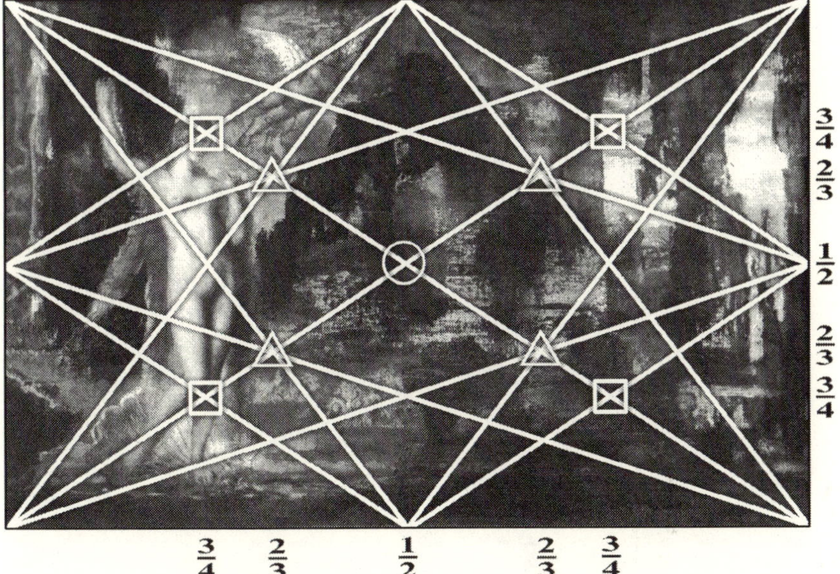

Fig. 16.12 - Harmonic Armature over Moreau's *Pasiphae*

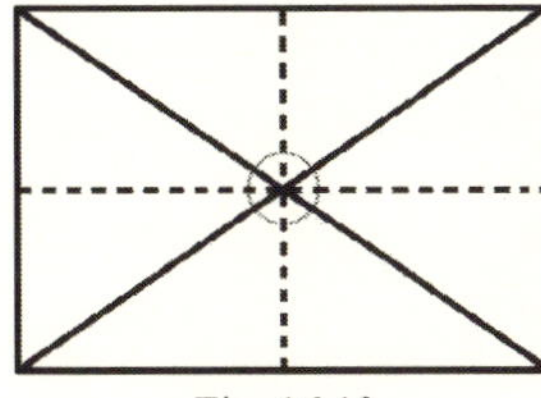

Fig. 16.13
1:2 *Diapason* Halves

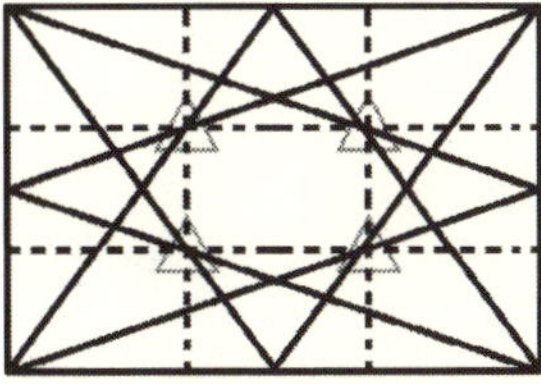

Fig. 16.14
2:3 *Diapente* Thirds

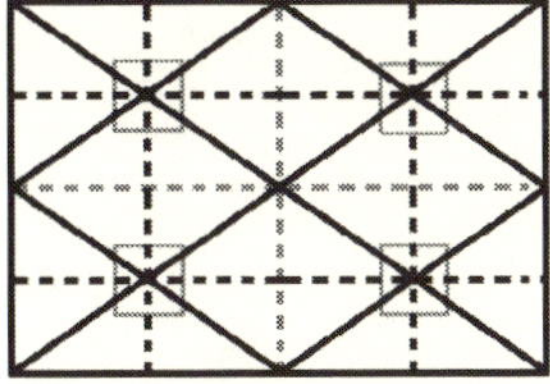

Fig. 16.15
3:4 *Diatessaron* Quarters

When vertical and horizontal lines are drawn through the midpoint, the rectangle is divided into *four* lesser rectangles, each of the same proportion as the greater bounding rectangle.

The second step, of *drawing the diapente thirds* (2:3) is to draw four sets of double diagonals, two on the vertical axis – ∨ ∧ – and two on the horizontal axis – > <. The first two sets of diagonals – ∨ ∧ – begin at the corners and end at the *midpoint* of the upper and lower frame. The second set of two diagonals – > < – begin at the corners and end at the *midpoint* of the right and left frame.

At the four points where these particular diagonals intersect, the *thirds* of the rectangle appear. Hence, vertical and horizontal lines drawn through these points will quickly divide any rectangle into *nine* smaller rectangles, each of the same proportion as the greater bounding rectangle.

The third and final step, of *drawing the diatessaron quarters* (3:4) is to draw four diagonals from midpoint to midpoint of each side, resulting in a ◇ rhombus shape. Now, at the four points of intersection between these ◇ diagonals and the diagonals of the halves (X), the *quarters* of the rectangle appear. This

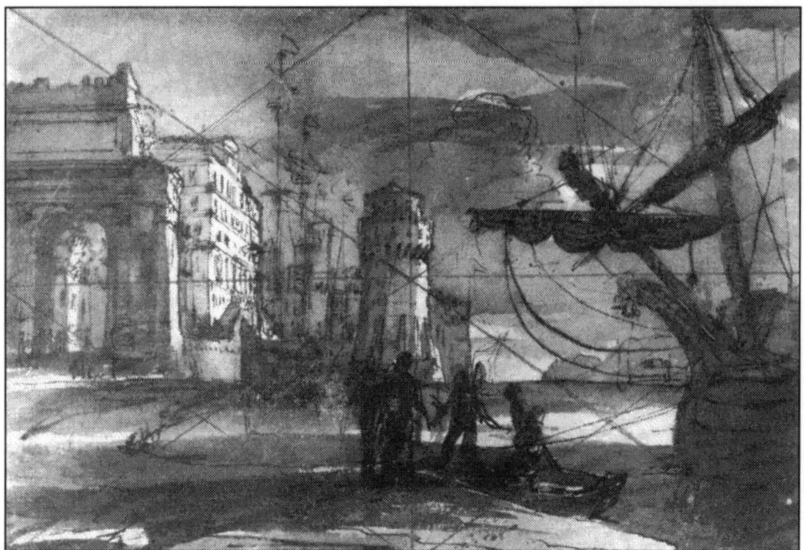

Fig. 16.16 - Drawing by Claude Lorrain with Harmonic Armature.

means that vertical and horizontal lines drawn through these points (while maintaining the original + through the midpoint) will quickly divide any rectangle into 16 smaller rectangles of the same proportion as the greater bounding rectangle

I spent many years trying to procure a copy of Charles Bouleau's classic study *Charpentes: La Géometrie Secrète des Peintres* (The Painter's Secret Geometry – 1963). Finally, after scouring *les bouquinistes* on the banks of the Seine, I found a first edition in the original French and made some important discoveries in its pages (After being out of print for many years, the English edition has recently been re-issued by Dover).

Bouleau's work is a precious resource. In most cases, he attempts to *reconstruct* the invisible lines of armature which have vanished over time. The rare exceptions are three ink washes by Claude Lorrain and a pencil drawing by Anne-Louis Girodet, where the artists' *original* construction lines are still in evidence.

According to Bouleau, ten such drawings by Lorrain are extant, of which three appear in his book. In all three cases, Lorrain has used a simplified version of *the Harmonic Armature*, showing only the halves and quarters, while ignoring the thirds. *"For the most part,"* Bouleau notes, *"Claude* [Lorrain] *would indicate only the essential lines, and drew a few such strokes to serve as reminders... He knew the divisions well enough to find them without effort. By using the diagonals as his starting point, he could find all the points instinctively."*[12]

In the drawing reproduced here (Fig. 16.16), Lorrain has placed the tower on the half, and the luminous facade of the building on the left falls on the upper three-quarter. Though the thirds are not shown, the horizon line and the slender mast of the distant ship on the left fall on the two-thirds. Typical for Mannerist art, the dark ship in the right foreground serves as a *repoussoir* to draw the eye into the composition. The ship's dark sails and bowsprit follow the diagonals of the construction lines.

It is worth recalling the history of armatures as presented thus far. In the barbed quatrefoil, we saw the importance of the basic □square and its + cross division for static compositions, while the ◇turned square combined with the X division created more dynamic compositions. The □square and ◇turned square, as the quadrature and 'key' to Gothic design, we recall, had its origin in the *Khatem Sulemani* or Octagram of Islamic art. Its *girih* pattern, such as 'the Breath of the Compassionate', emerged from a square pattern cell with seven standard ratios.

How far have we progressed really? Except for the fact that these cardinal shapes are now inscribed in a rectangle rather than a square, *the same basic divisions of space occur,* with their Pythagorean-Platonic harmonies of the *diapason* halves, *diapente* thirds and *diatessaron* quarters. The simplified Harmonic Armature, as drawn by Lorrain, uses the same basic +, X and ◇ divisions of space as used by Gothic masons. Had he drawn five circles at the intersections of the diagonals, he would have been right back to the barbed quatrefoil of his French ancestors...

V. The Monochord

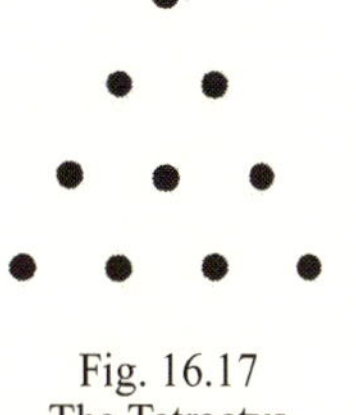

Fig. 16.17
The Tetractys

The notion of harmony based on the halves, thirds and quarters extends back in time to the 5th century BCE philosopher Pythagoras of Samos (c. 570 – 495 BCE). His curious construction of the *Tetractys* has survived from antiquity, and its interpretation has intrigued philosophers for millennia.

Visually, we can see the emergence of the many from the One as it expands, row on row, into the dyad, triad and tetrad, making ten in all. But what binds these ten together as one? For Pythagoras, it was *the law of harmony* which manifest itself in the heavens through planetary motion and, musically, through the harmonic progression of the 1:2 *diapason*, the 2:3 *diapente* and the 3:4 *diatessaron* (Fig. 16.17).

A curious instrument called the monochord has existed since antiquity for the sole purpose of exploring harmony. The monochord had a single string and a moveable bridge, allowing the philosopher to test the relationship of different string lengths to different harmonic tones. With the open string as the fundamental note (Oneness or wholeness), a second harmonic note would sound if the bridge was moved to half the string's length (1:½, which is the same as 2:1), or to two-thirds of its length (1:⅔, which is the same as 3:2) or to three-quarters of its length (1:¾, which is the same as 4:3). Each of these notes resounded harmonically *in relationship to the open string's fundamental tone.*

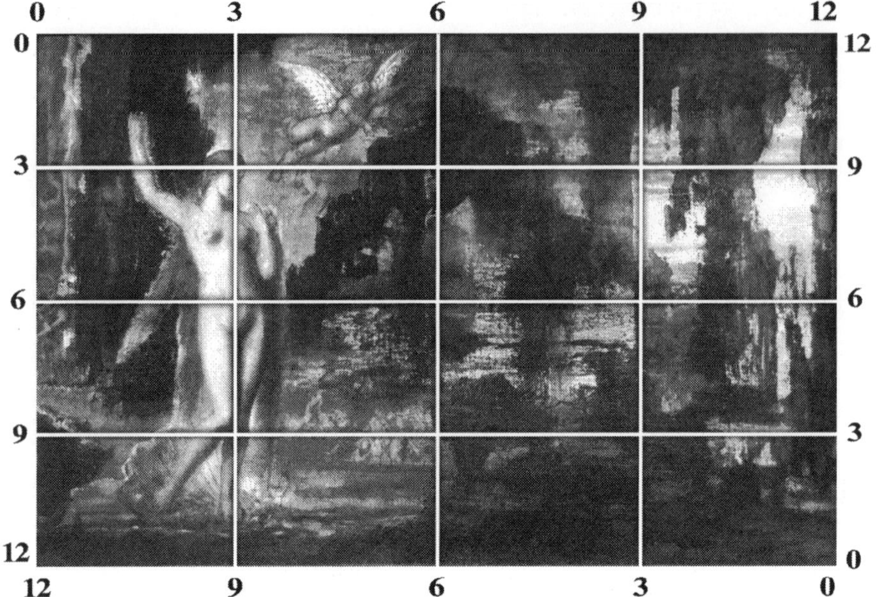

Fig. 16.18 - Pasiphae Resounding a 3:4 *Diatessaron* Note within the Whole Space

Which is to say, each new division of the whole resounded harmonically *with the original Oneness*. The One divides progressively and harmoniously into 2 (at the 1:2 point), then into 3 (at the 2:3 point) and into 4 (at the 3:4), as demonstrated by the *Tetractys* – "*the root and source of the eternally flowing creation.*"

The monochord is a unique instrument because it demonstrates, both audibly and visually, how harmony relates to the sound of different string lengths – *and to the sight of different line segments.*

When Gustave Moreau placed his Pasiphaé (Fig. 16.18) at the *diatessaron* three-quarter point (baseline 9) along the horizontal axis, he was dividing it at one of the most harmonic points along its entire length (12). If that horizontal axis was a monochord string, and Pasiphaé were the bridge dividing it at the three-quarter point, then the note struck at that division would resound harmonically in relationship to the whole – in relationship to the whole horizontal space of the painting.

But the surface of a painting has two dimensions, not one. Pasiphaé also divides the vertical space of the painting, through the vertical axis traversing her figure. That line is divided, once again, at the *diatessaron* three-quarter intervals – by her head, when measured from the baseline up (right 9); and by her knees, when measured from the topline down (left 9).

The most expedient way of determining the three-quarter points, *on both* the vertical and horizontal axes, *is to use the diagonal*. And this is what Moreau has done – not through careful measure, but intuitively. The gentle inclination of her forehead, the delicate turning of her knee – both of these occur at two of the most harmonious points in the painting's space. When our eye falls upon them, it relaxes its searching gaze, feeling a sudden sense of harmony and peace with the surrounding space as a whole. For a few precious moments, the unity of the parts in the whole is experienced, and beauty – personified by Pasiphaé herself – is felt in our very soul.

VI. Pythagoras & Harmony

Although Pythagoras of Samos was a great philosopher who gathered round him many brilliant disciples (the *Pythagorikoi*), over time a series of legends accrued to this 'long-haired' vegetarian who would sit for days in silent meditation, and occasionally utter 'symbolically oracular sentences' like *"All things accord in number,"* and *"The beginning is the half of the whole."*[13] His great sensitivity to harmony earned him the epithet 'Son of Apollo'.[14]

According to Iamblichus, who wrote 'On the Pythagorean Way of Life', contemplation works best *"...when one perceives beautiful figures and forms, or hears beautiful rhythms and melodies... From these, he* [Pythogoras] *obtained remedies of human manners and passions, and restored the pristine harmony of the faculties of the soul."*[15]

Explaining in greater detail the healing power of harmony, Iamblichus relates, *"For his disciples, he* [Pythagoras] *arranged and adjusted what might be called 'preparations' and 'massages', divinely contriving the mingling of certain diatonic, chromatic and enharmonic melodies, through which he easily switched and circulated the passions of the soul in a contrary direction, whenever they had accumulated ...sorrow, rage, pity, over-emulation, fear, manifold desires, angers, appetites, pride, collapse or spasms. Each of these he corrected by the rule of virtue, attempering them through appropriate melodies, as through some salutary medicine."*[16]

Although Iamblichus is writing in the 3rd century, he *"often quoted verbatim very ancient sources, not presently available,"*[17] Algis Uždavinys notes in *The Golden Chain: An Anthology of Pythagorean and Platonic Philosophy.* It is curious that Iamblichus lists ten specific 'passions of the soul' (possibly eleven, depending on how we count 'collapse or spasms').

The Pythagorean cosmos also had ten planetary spheres. According to his disciple Philolaus (quoted by Stobaeus in his *Anthology* I. 22. 1d), the Pythagorean cosmos had a primordial fire at its centre, and another fire at its periphery, with the cosmic spheres rotating between these two extremes:

"Philolaus has located the fire in the middle, the centre... Besides, he locates a second fire, quite at the top, surrounding [the cosmic framework of] *the world. The centre, says he, is by its nature the first; around it, the ten different bodies carry out their choral dance. These are: the* [starry] *heaven, the* [five visible] *planets, lower the sun, and below it the moon; lower the earth, and beneath this, the counter-earth..."*[18] The 'counter-earth' (*Antichthon*) is another Pythagorean curiosity, never fully explained...

But, the correspondence of the ten planetary spheres with the ten 'passions of the soul' suggests that Pythagoras had the unique ability to 'tune in' to specific planetary harmonics and play those consonances that 'attuned' the listener to the Divine source. These harmonies brought unity and wholeness, which 'attempered' the passions of the soul – reversing the planet's negative influence and *circulating the soul's passions in a contrary direction.*

These healing harmonies, though sensed by him, lay above all sight and hearing. According once more to Iamblichus, Pythagoras would soothe the passions of his disciples, *"...through certain peculiar chords and modulations, produced by either simply striking the lyre, or adapting the voice.* [Actually, it was] *not through instruments or physical voice that Pythagoras affected this; but by the employment of ...his intellect on the sublime symphonies of the world, he alone apparently hearing and grasping the universal harmony and consonance of the spheres ...arranged with reference to each other in a certain musical ratio."*[19]

It is in this sense that we must approach the harmonic ratios of 1:2, 2:3 and 3:4. When Aristotle writes of the Pythagoreans, *"they considered the principles of numbers as the principles of all things, and the whole universe as a harmony and a number,"*[20] he does not mean musical theory or mathematical science, in their empirical sense. Rather, harmony and number exist higher up, beyond all hearing and seeing. Like the Platonic *eidé*, these harmonic ratios emanate their soul-calming consonances from the eternally divine sphere, and our music and art can do no more than compose, convey, and resonate the healing power of 'attunement' from the divine source.

VII. The Harmony of Space & Sound

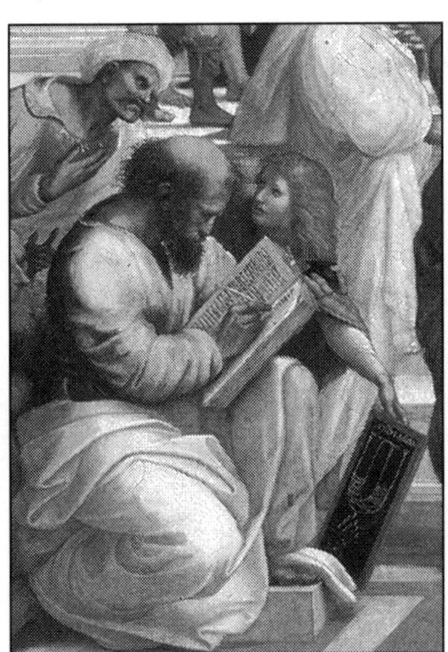

Fig. 16.19 - Pythagoras of Samos

In Raphael's *School of Athens,* Pythagoras is portrayed on the lower left, gazing at a tablet held by a sibylline child (Fig. 16.19). I have reproduced the design on the tablet both in the original Greek version and an English translation (Fig. 16.20) to better understand its mysterious message.

At the base we can clearly see the *Tetractys* laid out in a series of vertical 'I's rather than dots, and their total of 10 is inscribed in the line below with a curving Roman numeral 'X'. Above it is a diagram from the 6th century Neo-Platonic philosopher Boethius, which portrays the mysterious relationship of the *Tetractys* to the *harmonious* division of the One into the many.

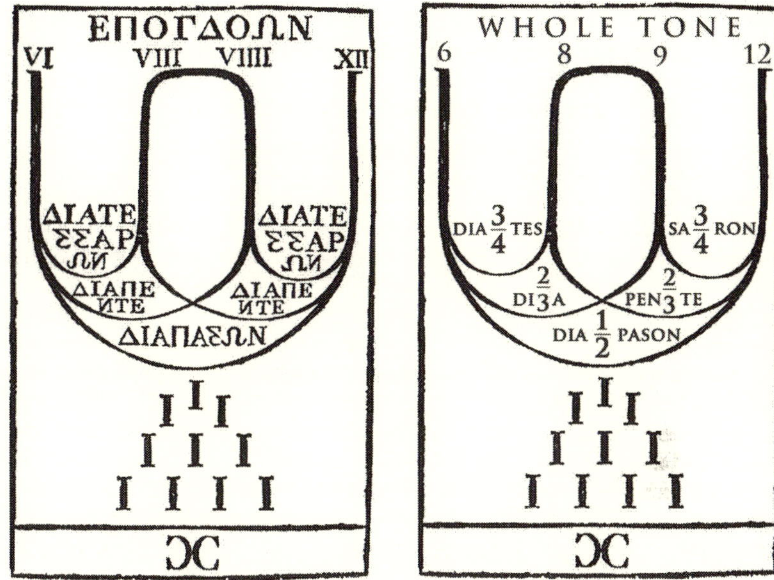

Fig. 16.20 - Pythagoras' Tablet From Rapahel's School of Athens

In fact, the diagram portrays the four-stringed lyre or tetrachord, and each vertical line surmounted by a number (6, 8, 9, 12) is one of the four strings. The Greek words show the harmonic relationship between the different strings, as follows:

- ¾ or 3:4 – *Diatessaron* – literally, *"across four"* or the musical *fourth*
- ⅔ or 2:3 – *Diapente* – literally, *"across five"* or the musical *fifth*
- ½ or 1:2 – *Diapason* – literally, *"across all"* or the musical *octave*

Since the ratios, expressed as fractions, have different denominators at their base, they may all be related to each other in whole number ratios if their denominators are expanded to *twelfths*. That is the reason for the numbers at the top, which are the lengths of the strings *expressed as fractions of 12*. They should be read as 6:12, 8:12, 9:12 and 12:12.

The names *diatessaron* ('across four'), *diapente* ('across five') and *diapason* ('across all') give their numbers as fractions *of eight* because the 'octave' has *eight* notes (which, in the diatonic Dorian scale are E', D, C, B, A, G, F, E). The *diatessaron* is called a musical 'fourth' because it is the fourth note (B) in the series of eight, just as the *diapente* is called the musical 'fifth' because it is the fifth note (A) of eight. To avoid confusion between eighths and twelfths, I call them by their Greek names, referring to them as the half *diapason*, two-thirds *diapente* and three-quarters *diatessaron*.

In the tetrachord, all the strings are the same length, but produce different tones because they are wound and stretched ("tuned") with different tensions, producing different tones. If the strings were not wound, stretched and tuned, but laid out side by side to their true length, they would appear as in Fig. 16.21. This shows the true relationship between harmonic notes and string lengths (i.e. line segments) as expressed by the tetrachord.

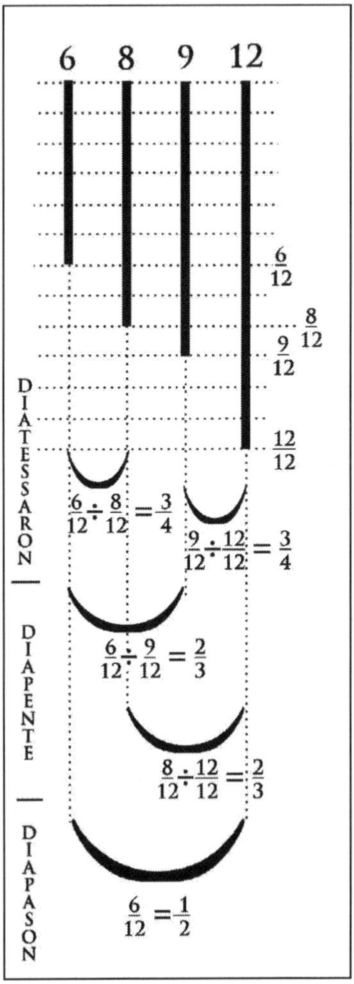

6 8 9 12

$\frac{6}{12}$ $\frac{8}{12}$ $\frac{9}{12}$ $\frac{12}{12}$

DIATESSARON

$\frac{6}{12} \div \frac{8}{12} = \frac{3}{4}$

$\frac{9}{12} \div \frac{12}{12} = \frac{3}{4}$

DIAPENTE

$\frac{6}{12} \div \frac{9}{12} = \frac{2}{3}$

$\frac{8}{12} \div \frac{12}{12} = \frac{2}{3}$

DIAPASON

$\frac{6}{12} = \frac{1}{2}$

Fig. 16.21 - The Tetrachord

The 12 string on the far right is the open string or fundamental tone. The 6 string on the far left is half its length and produces a note one octave higher. As we can see at the bottom of the diagram, the *diapason*, the movement of 1:2, manages to divide the original Oneness *into two parts* with no loss of unity, since it resounds harmoniously a second time, but at a higher pitch (the octave). We may call the mysterious harmony of the *diapason* (1:2 or 6:12), the dyad, since it preserves unity in duality – in the initial separation of 1 into 2, expressed in string lengths as 1:½, and in the *Tetractys* as rows of dots from 1:2.

The harmonic division of dyad into the triad, moving from 2:3, occurs at the next level, with the *diapente*. As Fig. 16.21 shows, it happens on the tetrachord twice, in the interval between the 6 and 9 string, and in the interval between the 8 and 12 string. In other words, the 6 string is two-thirds of the length of the 9 string, producing a higher note which resounds harmoniously with it. And the same is true of the 8 string, which is two-thirds of the length of the 12 string, producing another consonant tone. Raphael has also shown us this in Pythagoras' Tablet (Fig. 16.20) through the U-shaped lines which locate the ⅔ *diapente* twice, between the 6 and 9 strings, and again between the 8 and 12 strings.

In this way, the original Oneness (the 12 string) divides a second time, with no loss of unity, *into three parts* – resounding harmoniously with the 8 string at two-thirds of its length. At the same time, the movement within the *Tetractys*, with its rows of dots expanding from 1:2 to 2:3, is expressed by the consonance between the 6 and 9 strings. The mysterious harmony of the *diapente* is expressed by the interval of 2:3 *twice*, as 6:9 and 8:12, which is shown in the tetrachord as string lengths from 1 to ⅔, and in the *tetractys* as rows of dots from 1:2 to 2:3.

Finally, the harmonic division of the triad into the tetrad, moving from 3:4, occurs at the upper level, with the *diatessaron*. Again, as Fig. 16.21 shows, this happens twice on the tetrachord, in the interval between the 6 and 8 string, and the 9 and 12 string. Now, the 6 string is three-quarters of the length of the 8 string, and the 9 string is three-quarters the length of the 12 string – each shorter string producing a higher note which resounds harmoniously with the longer. In Raphael's diagram (Fig. 16.20), the ¾ *diatessaron* also appears twice, once between the 6 and 8 string, and again between the 9 and 12 string.

In this final step, the original Oneness (the 12 string) divides a third time, with no loss unity, *into four parts* – resounding harmoniously with the 9 string at three-quarters of its length. At the same time, the movement within the *Tetractys*, with its rows of dots expanding from 1:2 to 3:4, is expressed by the consonance between the 6 and 8 strings. The *diatessaron* division of the One is expressed by the interval of 3:4 *twice*, as 6:8 and 9:12, and is shown in string lengths as 1:¾, and in the *Tetractys* as rows of dots from 1:2 to 3:4.

In this manner, the mysterious relationship is made manifest – of the harmonious division of the One into the many, which occurs both mathematically in the *Tetractys*, and musically in the tetrachord.

But for us, as artists, what is of greater interest is the translation of string lengths into line segments, since they show the harmonious relationship of different line segments *to each other*. Not only is the relationship of the half to the whole (½:1) a harmonic one, or of the thirds to the whole (⅔:1) and the quarters to the whole (¾:1), but so is the relationship of the half to the two-thirds (½:⅔) and of the two-thirds to the three-quarters (⅔:¾). Each bears a harmonious relationship both to the whole *and to each other*.

VIII. Alberti & Extended Harmonic Rectangles

It is this realization that prompted Leon Battista Alberti (1404 – 1472) in his *De re aedificatoria* (On the Art of Building in Ten Books – 1452) to explore the harmonious dimension of room sizes, which also translate into canvas dimensions. Alberti took the original Pythagorean ratios and multiplied them to create, what we may call, 'extended harmonic rectangles'.

In Book IX, Ch 6, he begins by saying:

"I affirm again with Pythagoras [...that] *the very same numbers that cause sounds to have that* concinnitas [harmony], *pleasing to the ears, can also fill the eyes and mind with wondrous delight.*"[21]

Beginning with the three harmonic ratios of Pythagoras, Alberti extends these to create a total of nine. Although he begins with the Greek names for the ratios, he tends to use the Latin terms (*sesquialtera*, *sesquitertia)* most of the time. To avoid confusion, I will continue to add the Greek terms with their associated ratios. Alberti writes:

"We define harmony as that consonance of sounds which is pleasant to the ears... The names of the consonants are as follows: the [2:3] *diapente, also called the* sesquialtera; *the* [3:4] diatessaron, *also called the* sesquitertia; *then the* [1:2] diapason, *which is* double; *and the* [1:3] diapason diapente, *which is a* triple, *and the* [1:4] disdiapason, *which is called* quadruple."[22]

Having defined his terms, Alberti divides his rooms into three basic types, which may be followed in Fig. 16.26:

"To begin with the area, since it is determined by two dimensions: an area may be either short, long, or intermediate.

"The shortest of all is the [1:1 square or] quadrangle *with all four sides of equal length, whose angles are all matching right angles.*

"After this come the [2:3 diapente or] sesquialtera, *and another short area is the* [3:4 diatessaron or] sesquitertia. *So these three relationships, which we call 'simple,' apply to the short area.*

"There are three appropriate to the moderate area as well, the best of which is the double [square or 1:2 diapason], *followed by that composed of a* double [2:3 diapente or] sesquialtera. *This latter is constructed as follows: having established the lesser dimension of the area – for example, four* [i.e. a 4 x 4 square] – *construct the* [2:3 diapente which is 4:6 or the] sesquialtera, *making the length six; to this add another* [2:3 diapente], *making the length nine* [i.e. 4:9]... *Another intermediate area is the* double [3:4 diatessaron making 9:16, or the] sesquitertia, *constructed by precisely the same method: this produces a width of nine to a length of sixteen...*

"For a longer area use the following method: either the double square *is enlarged by a* [2:3 diapente or] sesquialtera *to become a* triple [1:3], *or the* double *is enlarged by a* [3:4 diatessaron or] sesquitertia *so that the proportions are three to eight: alternatively, dimensions should be chosen to make the proportions one to four."*[23]

As can be seen in Fig. 1622 opposite, Alberti arrives at nine different ratios, which may be listed as follows:

SHORT:
- 1:1 – *Square* (*Quadrangle*)
- 2:3 – *Diapente* (*Sesquialtera*)
- 3:4 – *Diatessaron* (*Sesquitertia*)

MODERATE:
- 1:2 – *Double 1:1 Square* or *Diapason*
- 4:9 – *Double 2:3 Diapente* (*Double Sesquialtera*)
- 9:16 – *Double 3:4 Diatessaron* (*Double Sesquitertia*)

LONG:
- 1:4 – *Quadruple 1:1 Square* or *Enlarged Diapason*, also called *Disdiapason*
- 1:3 or 3:9 – *Triple 1:1 Square* or *Enlarged 2:3 Diapente* (*Enlarged Sesquialtera*) also called the *Diapason Diapente*
- 3:8 – *Enlarged 3:4 Diatessaron* (*Enlarged Sesquitertia*) also called the *Diapason Diatessaron*.

The logic behind Alberti's schema is far from clear, but our quest for understanding will lead us deeper into the nature of harmony. In each type, Alberti begins with a certain kind of square (single, double, quadruple), followed by a certain kind of *diapente* or *diatessaron,* which he multiplies (short), 'doubles' (moderate) or 'enlarges' (long).

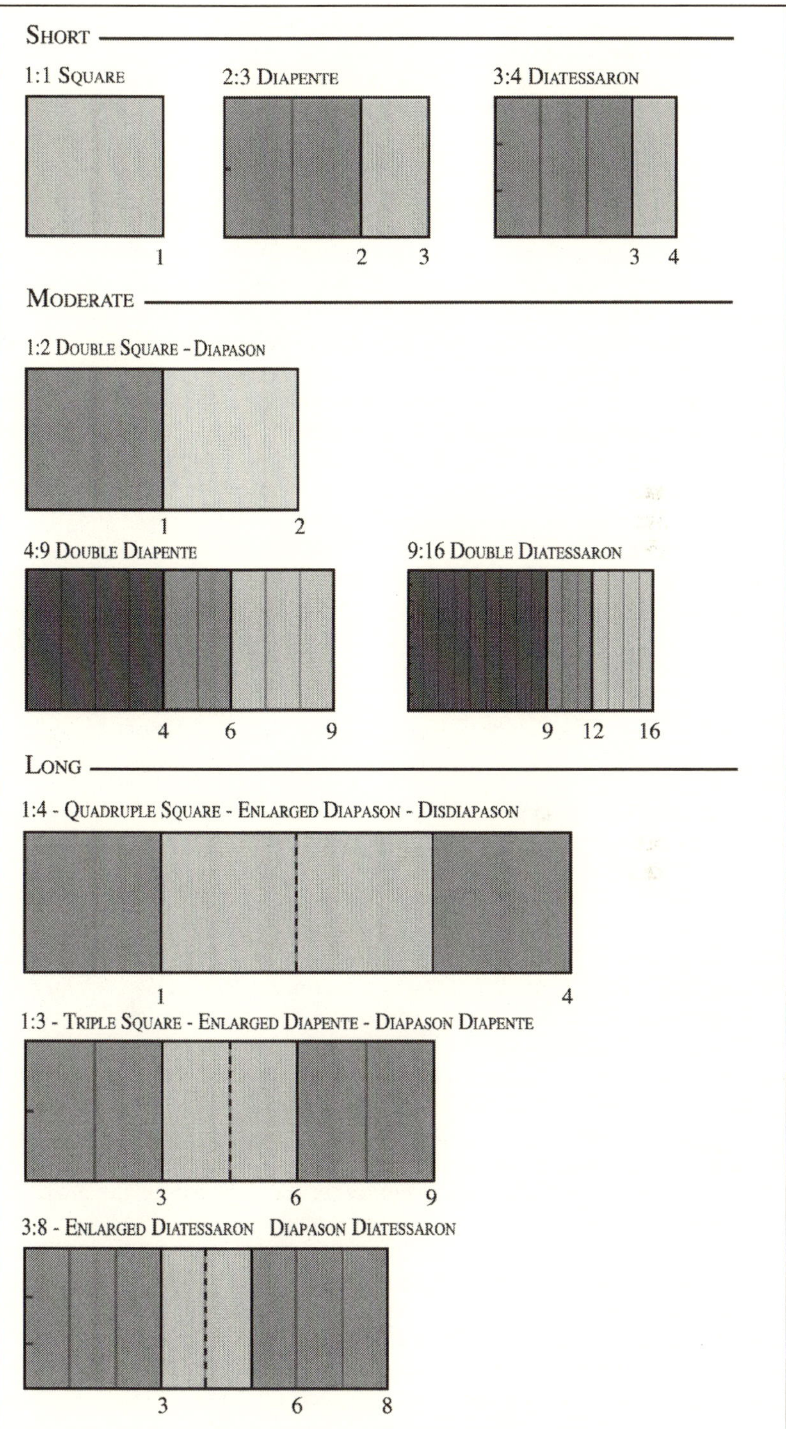

Fig. 16.22 - Alberti: Extended Harmonic Rectangles

With the short type, he first gives the 1:1 square. Next, he multiplies the 1:1 square by the ⅔ ratio to obtain the 2:3 *diapente* rectangle. After that, he multiplies the 1:1 square by the ¾ ratio to obtain the 3:4 *diatessaron* rectangle.

With the moderate type, he begins with a 1:1 square and multiplies it by the ½ ratio, making the 1:2 *diapason*. For the 4:9 rectangle, he begins with the 1:1 square and multiplies it *twice* by the ⅔ ratio, first making a 2:3 *diapente* rectangle, then multiplying it again by the ⅔ ratio to make a 4:9 *double diapente* rectangle. The same is the case with the 9:16 rectangle, where Alberti begins with the 1:1 square and multiplies it *twice* by the ¾ ratio, first making a 3:4 *diatessaron* rectangle and then a 9:16 *double diatessaron* rectangle. In these last two cases, the shape is not only multiplied *twice* by the ratio, but multiplied *in both directions*. With all the others, Alberti expands them in one direction only.

With the 'long' type, Alberti could explain things more easily by saying that he is mirroring each to extend it. This 'mirroring' may be thought of as 'making a 1:2 *diapason*' out of each – doubling it laterally. So, the 1:2 *diapason* is mirrored to make a *diapason-diapason* or quadruple square (1:4), which he calls the *disdiapason*. Next, the 2:3 *diapente* is mirrored (2:6) to make a *diapason-diapente* or triple square (1:3 or 3:9). Finally, the 3:4 *diatessaron* is mirrored (3:8) to make a *diapason-diatessaron* or 3:8 rectangle.

Throughout the schema, Pythagoras' musically harmonious ratios are preserved. Alberti has simply begun with the 1:1 square and multiplied, doubled or enlarged it through the 1:2, 2:3 and 3:4 consonances. While these expansions may not work musically with string lengths, they still produce rectangles with a distinct *concinnitas* (harmony) that 'fills the eyes and mind with wondrous delight.'

IX. Examples of Alberti's Extended Rectangles

The Neo-Classical period of French painting offers the clearest examples of how harmonic rectangles were used. Anne-Louis Girodet (1767 – 1824) was a *Prix de Rome* painter who had studied under David, and his original sketch (Fig. 16.23 left) for *Hippocrates Refusing the Gifts of Atarxerxes* (Fig. 16.23 right) offers us a rare glimpse into *Académie* working methods.[24] First of all, Girodet chose a 3:4 *diatessaron* rectangle because it offered up perfectly *square* divisions of space (*ad quadratum*) with 45° diagonals.

Using the bottom two-thirds, Girodet has constructed a flat frieze of figures in the manner of the Classical Greeks. The most important figure – Hippocrates on the left – appears exactly at the three-quarter point on the horizontal axis (baseline 9). Like Moreau's Pasiphaé, this figure strikes a strong *diatessaron* note within the painting's horizontal space (12). Meanwhile, on the vertical axis, Hippocrates' head appears at the *diapason* half (left 6) and his lower hand on the *diapente* two-thirds (left 8).

The 45° diagonals form a perfect △ triangle or ◇ diamond around Hippocrates, isolating him from the crowd of Atarxerxes' emissaries. His leg clearly follows the 45° diagonal, as do the limbs of many other figures in the painting, creating constant rhythms in space. As an exception, Hippocrates' arm refusing the gift dramatically breaks this visual rhythm, following the horizontal axis that lies at exactly the *diapason* half (left 6). Indeed, the main action of 'refusing the gifts' transpires almost exactly at the centre of the

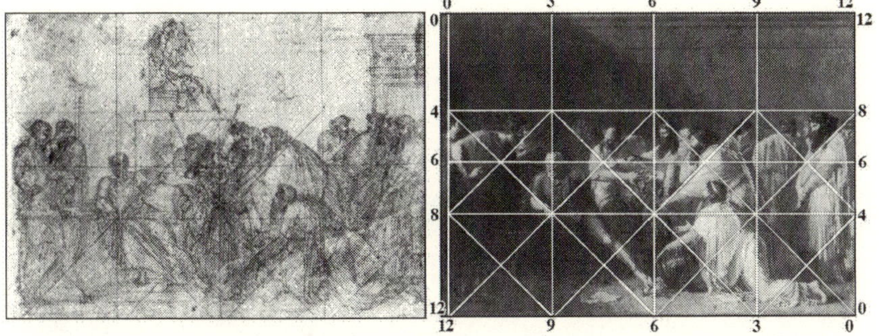

Fig. 16.23 - Girodet: *Hippocrates Refusing the Gifts of Atarxerxes* 1792

painting, where the horizontal and vertical halves meet (6 and 6). The grid of perfect squares helps to emphasize this half *diapason* note struck right at the painting's centre.

"Composition," Alberti has said, *"is that rule of painting by which the parts of the things seen, fit together in the painting."*[25] In Girodet's composition, the notes struck at the three-quarter *diatessaron* point (Hippocrates) and at the half *diapason* point (refusing the gifts) are not only resonant with the whole (the rectangular frame) but *with each other*. If we refer to the tetrachord in the last section, then it is not only the half note (baseline 6) which strikes a *diapason* (6:12) with the whole string (baseline 12), or the three-quarter note (baseline 9) which strikes a *diatessaron* (9:12) with the whole string (baseline 12) – but the half note (baseline 6) which strikes a two-thirds *diapente* (6:9) with the three-quarter note (baseline 9), since 6 is two-thirds of 9. The placement of 'Hippocrates' and his hand 'refusing the gifts' are in a harmonious relationship with each other.

As Bouleau shows in *The Painter's Secret Geometry,* the dimensions of the rectangle need not be regular for the Harmonic Armature to be applied. Instead, each side of an *irregular* rectangle may be divided into equal parts (like 9ths, 12ths or 16ths), and a harmonic division is applied to each side. As an example, Bouleau analyzes Titian's *Presentation of the Virgin in the Temple*, finding that *"the musical proportions are applied with great assurance; the architecture, the perspective and the position of the infant Virgin on the steps are established by the diapason-diapente ratio of 3:6:9."*[26]

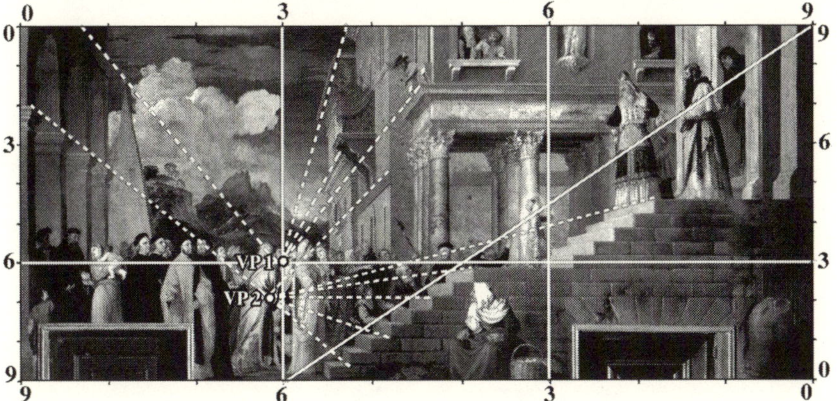

Fig. 16.24 - Titian: *Presentation of the Virgin at the Temple* c. 1538

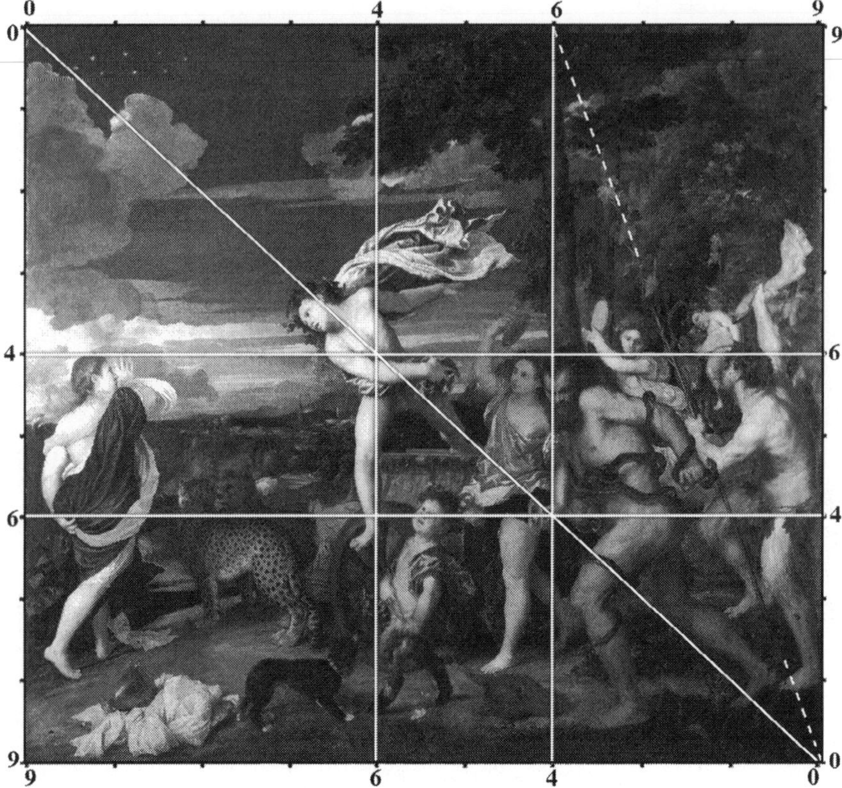

Fig. 16.25 - Titian: *Bacchus and Ariadne* 1523

Indeed, in Fig. 16.24, the key figure of the infant Virgin does stand close to the topline 6 and left 6 (i.e. the 2:3 *diapente*) measured from the top left (0,0), while her mother, St. Anne, awaits at the bottom of the steps at the baseline 6 (again, the 2:3 *diapente*) measured from the bottom right. Bouleau has drawn a diagonal from the top right corner (9,9) to the baseline 6, showing that the steps follow this diagonal, as does the infant virgin's gaze.

Titian uses the crossing of the vertical at baseline 6 and the horizontal at left 6 to establish the vanishing point (VP1) for the perspective of the upper architecture. However, as we shall see in our chapter on Humanist Perspective, Venetians like Tintoretto, Veronese and Titian sometimes used *multiple vanishing points* in their paintings. Bouleau ignores the second vanishing point, (VP2) which is located close to the first, and is used principally for the perspective of the stairs.

In a second example (Fig. 16.25), Titian's *Bacchus and Ariadne* follows the 4:6:9 proportion of the *double diapente*, where the main figure of Bacchus appears on the crossing of the main diagonal (0,0 - 0,0) with the baseline 6 vertical. The tree straddles the vertical at topline 6, and it is surely no mere coincidence that the thrysus staff of the satyr (on the far right) follows exactly the diagonal (marked by a dotted line) from the bottom right corner (0,0) to the topline 6. All these 6:9 ratios consistently express the 2:3 *diapente*, as does the 4:6 ratio of the tree (baseline 4) to Bacchus (baseline 6).

X. Proportion: the Geometric, Arithmetic & Harmonic Means

With harmonic measures like 3:6:9 (*double diapente*) or 4:6:9 (*diapason-diapente*), we are moving from the domain of ratios to 'proportion' as it is properly understood. For a ratio has only two terms, such as 4:6 or 6:9. But a proportion is a *comparison of two ratios*, expressed as 4:6 = 6:9 ('four is to six as six is to nine') and shortened to 4:6:9 ('four is to six is to nine'). In the example of the 4:6:9 *diapason-diapente*, the 4 and 9 form the 'extremes' of the proportion, while the 6 gives us 'the mean'. It is the *mean* which allows us to compare one ratio to another.

The Greek mathematician Pappus of Alexandria (c. 290 – c. 350) listed ten kinds of mean, of which the most important are the *geometric*, *arithmetic* and *harmonic*. If we wish to truly understand harmony and proportion, we must make a brief foray into arithmetic, with its translation of geometric lengths into measures and numbers.

A proportion may be expressed in the form A:B=B:C, where A and C are the extremes and B is the common mean. To calculate the mean, we may visualize the process through Fig. 16.26 below. Here, we can see that the arithmetic, geometric and harmonic means are so constructed as to give a middle term that is half, two-thirds or three-quarters between the extremes, depending on their magnitudes.

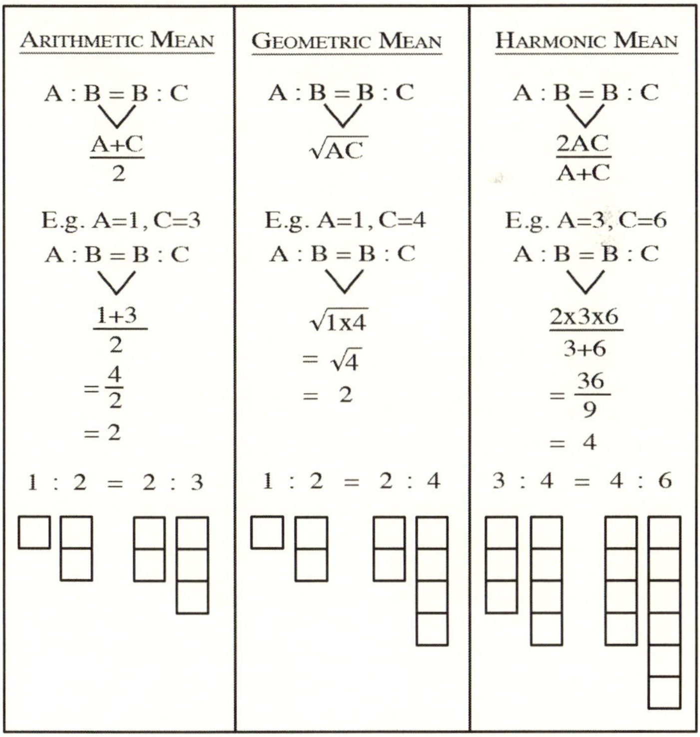

Arithmetic Mean	Geometric Mean	Harmonic Mean
$A : B = B : C$	$A : B = B : C$	$A : B = B : C$
$\frac{A+C}{2}$	$\sqrt{AC}$	$\frac{2AC}{A+C}$
E.g. A=1, C=3	E.g. A=1, C=4	E.g. A=3, C=6
$A : B = B : C$	$A : B = B : C$	$A : B = B : C$
$\frac{1+3}{2} = \frac{4}{2} = 2$	$\sqrt{1x4} = \sqrt{4} = 2$	$\frac{2x3x6}{3+6} = \frac{36}{9} = 4$
$1 : 2 = 2 : 3$	$1 : 2 = 2 : 4$	$3 : 4 = 4 : 6$

Fig. 16.26 - Three Types of Means for Calculating Harmonic Proportions

In a rectangle of the 4:6:9 type, the common term 6 between the extremes of 4 and 9 may be calculated through one of the three means, in this case, the *geometric* mean, since it gives us a whole number. So, in the proportion A:B=B:C, where A=4 and C=9, we may calculate B through the equation B=√(AC). Since AC = 4x9 = 36 and since √36 = 6, therefore B = 6.

By creating a proportion such as 4:6=6:9, we are able to compare two ratios. When the 4:6 ratio on the left is divided by 2, it gives us 2:3. And when the 6:9 ratio on the right is divided by 3, it also gives us 2:3. That means 4 is two-thirds of 6, and 6 is two-thirds of 9 – both sides share the same harmonic ratio of the 2:3 *diapente.* When we look at the 4:6:9 rectangle, the length of 0 to 4 is two-thirds of the length from 0 to 6; and the length of 0 to 6 is two-thirds of the length from 0 to 9. This is what makes the figures placed at these points so harmonious *with each other* and with the rectangle as a whole.

When we look at a rectangle of the 3:6:9 type, the means is calculated differently, and the comparison of ratios also differs. In this case, we use the *arithmetic* mean to obtain a middle term in whole numbers. So, in the proportion A:B=B:C, where A=3 and C=9, we may calculate B through the equation B = (A+C) / 2. Since A+C = 3+9 = 12 and since 12/2 = 6, therefore B = 6.

Through the proportion 3:6=6:9, we are able to compare two ratios. When the 3:6 ratio on the left is divided by 2, it gives us the 1:2 *diapason.* And when the 6:9 ratio on the right is divided by 3, it gives us the 2:3 *diapente.* This time, the ratios are *not* the same. Nevertheless, *both* are harmonic. When we look at the 3:6:9 rectangle (which Bouleau called a *diapason-diapente* rectangle), the length of 0 to 3 is one-half the length of 0 to 6; and the length of 0 to 6 is two-thirds the length from 0 to 9. Any figures placed at these points will be harmonious *with each other* and with the rectangle as a whole.

The logic behind Alberti's schema has now become more transparent. In Fig. 16.27, I have reproduced his short, moderate and long rectangles, but now I have also included the arithmetic to calculate their ratios, the means to calculate their proportions, and the type of harmonic ratio (*diapason, diapente* or *diatessaron*) underlying each side of their proportions.

But this invites the question: does Alberti's schema cover *all* the Extended Rectangles which may be created by multiplying Pythagoras' three harmonic ratios?

With his Extended Rectangles of the *Long* type, Alberti has shown us what happens when each of the three types is multiplied by the 1:2 *diapason*:

1:2 x 1:2 –> $\frac{1}{2} \times \frac{1}{2} = \frac{1}{4}$ Hence a 1:4 rectangle — 1 : 2 = 2 : 4
Through the geometric mean, a 1:2:4 rectangle results — 1 : 2 = 1 : 2

1:2 x 2:3 –> $\frac{1}{2} \times \frac{2}{3} = \frac{2}{6} = \frac{1}{3} = \frac{3}{9}$ Hence a 1:3 or 3:9 rectangle — 3 : 6 = 6 : 9
Through the arithmetic mean, a 1:2:3 or 3:6:9 rectangle results — 1 : 2 = 2 : 3

1:2 x 3:4 –> $\frac{1}{2} \times \frac{3}{4} = \frac{3}{8}$ Hence a 3:8 rectangle — 3 : 6 = 6 : 8
Through no known mean, Alberti's 3:6:8 rectangle results — 1 : 2 = 3 : 4

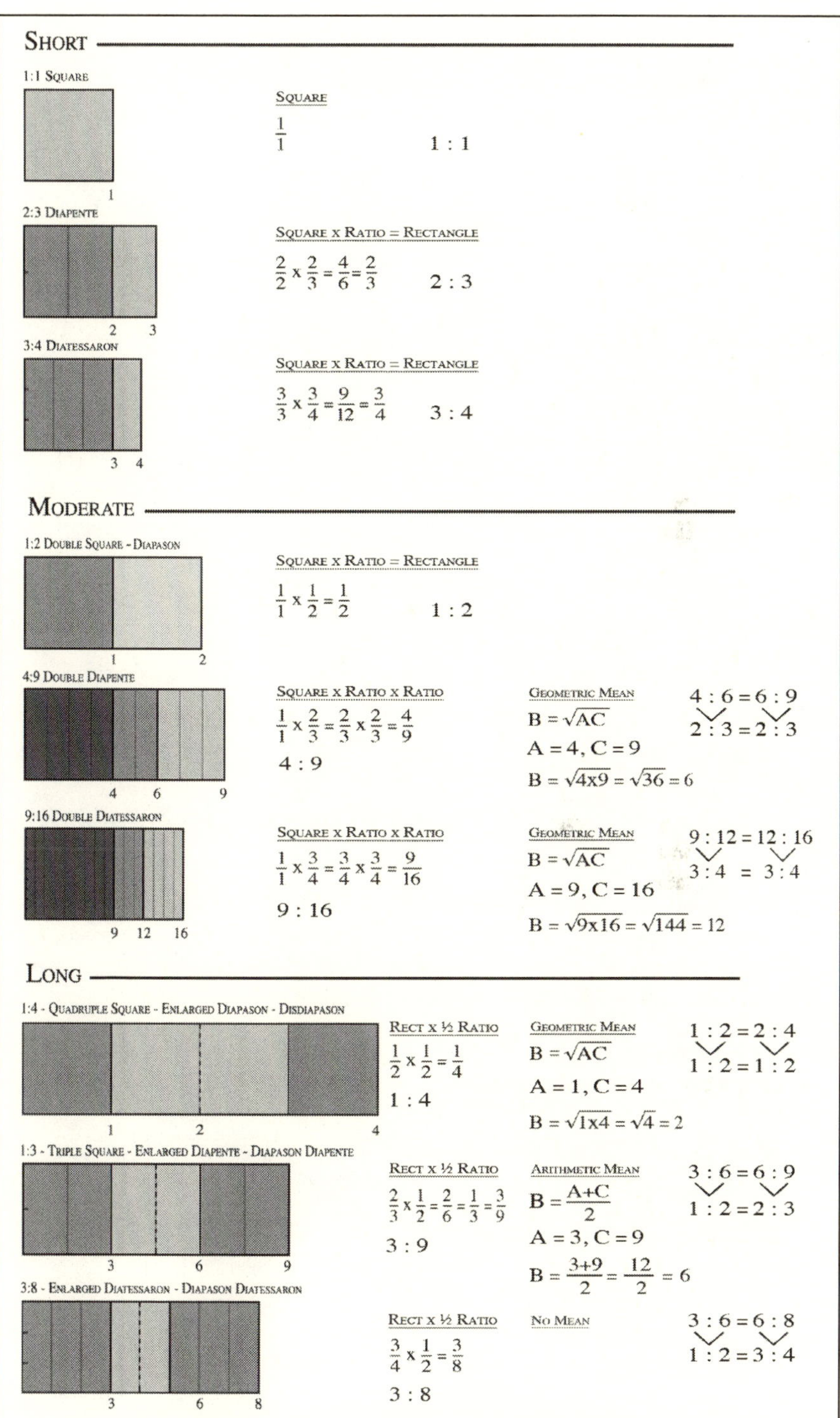

Fig. 16.27 - Alberti's Extended Harmonic Rectangles
With their Ratio Calculations, Means and Underlying Harmonic Ratios

It is worth noting that, for the 3:8 diapason-diatessaron, there is no way of calculating the middle term of 6 through any of the ten means listed by Pappus. Nevertheless, in a 3:6:8 rectangle, the lengths of 3:6 show the harmony of the ½ *diapason* while the lengths of 6:8 show the harmony of the ¾ *diatessaron.*

With his Extended Rectangles of the moderate type, Alberti has shown us what happens when the 2:3 *diapente* and 3:4 *diatessaron* are multiplied by themselves:

2:3 x 2:3 –> $\frac{2}{3}\times\frac{2}{3}=\frac{4}{9}$ Hence a 4:9 rectangle
Through the geometric mean, a 4:6:9 rectangle results — 4 : 6 = 6 : 9 / 2 : 3 = 2 : 3

3:4 x 3:4 –> $\frac{3}{4}\times\frac{3}{4}=\frac{9}{16}$ Hence a 9:16 rectangle
Through the geometric mean, a 9:12:16 rectangle results — 9 : 12 = 12 : 16 / 3 : 4 = 3 : 4

This means that, the only combination which Alberti has *not* tried is the 2:3 *diapente* multiplied by the 3:4 *diatessaron.* Through their multiplication, these ratios create two more types of Extended Rectangle *not covered* by Alberti:

2:3 x 3:4 –> $\frac{2}{3}\times\frac{3}{4}=\frac{6}{12}$ Hence a 6:12 rectangle
Through the harmonic mean, a 6:8:12 or 3:4:6 rectangle results — 6 : 8 = 8 : 12 / 3 : 4 = 3 : 4
Through the arithmetic mean, a 6:9:12 or 2:3:4 rectangle results — 6 : 9 = 9 : 12 / 2 : 3 = 3 : 4

Both of these (Figs 16.28 - 29) may be called diapente-diatessaron rectangles, where the 6:8:12 rectangle results from the harmonic mean; and the 6:9:12 rectangle from the arithmetic mean.

6:8:12 Diapente-Diatessaron

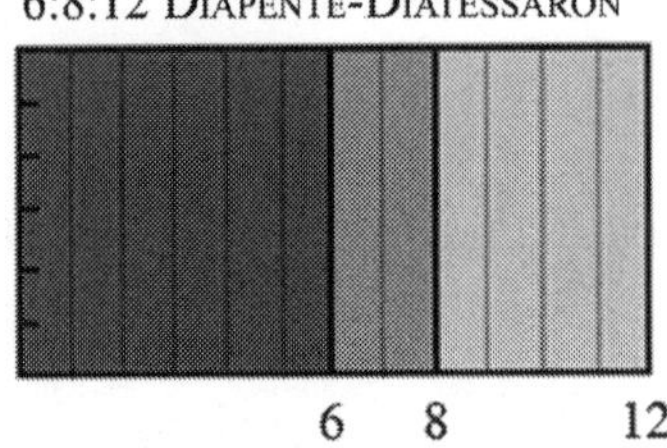

Fig. 16.28 - 6:8:12 Rectangle
From the Harmonic Mean

6:9:12 Diapente-Diatessaron

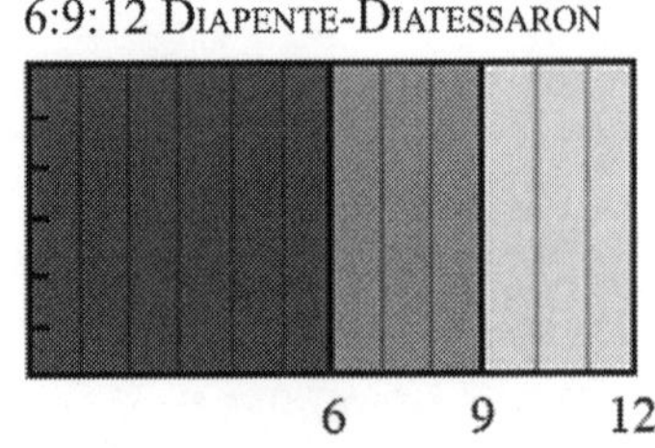

Fig. 16.29 - 6:9:12 Rectangle
From the Arithmetic Mean

XI. Harmonic Proportions of the Lambda

Alberti did not create his harmonic proportions; he acquired them from more ancient sources, such as Vitruvius' *De Architectura libri decem* (*Ten Books on Architecture* – c. 15 BCE) and Boethius' *De musica* (On Music, c. 510), which made extensive use of Plato's *Timaeus* (c. 360 BCE). All these texts survived Antiquity and were known to the Gothic period as well as the Renaissance.

It is particularly the *Timaeus* which, thanks to Marsilio Ficino's translation and commentary, had a major impact on the Renaissance revival of Pythagorean-Platonic harmony. In his dialogue on the Creation, Plato has the world's creator or Demiurge fabricate the World's Soul – the eternal realm of the ideal forms or *eidé* – which will then impart its order onto the chaos of the World's Body – the material realm of earth, water, air and fire. The Demiurge does this by seeking out those harmonies and proportions which govern the celestial motions and the music of the spheres.

Throughout the *Timaeus,* Plato calls upon the philosophy of his predecessors, Pythagoras and the Orphics. The *Orphicum Fragmenta,* which is a collection of Orphic writings dating back to the 6th century BCE, asked the primordial question: *"How may I have all things one and each one separate?"*[27] In other words, how was the world created, such that, the divine One divided itself into many parts, yet with no loss of its unity? How was unity preserved at each level?

For Pythagoras, the answer lay in harmony, number and proportion. When the low E' of the diatonic Dorian scale re-sounded an octave higher with the high E, these two notes manifest a Sameness, a Difference, and a third quality (which Plato simply called Existence, but elsewhere identified with the common mean of a proportion) which manifest their deeper unity. Though separated by an octave (their Difference), they shared the same note (E' and E, their Sameness) brought about by a deeper and more fundamental bond (their common Existence or mean).

In the *Timaeus*, Plato writes about proportion and the fundamental role of 'the mean' as the unifier of 'the extremes': *"Two things cannot be rightly put together without a third; and there must be some bond of union between them. And the fairest bond is that which makes the most complete fusion of itself and the things which it combines, and proportion is best adapted to such a union. For whenever, in any three numbers... there is a mean... then the mean becoming the first and last, and the first and last both becoming the mean, they will all of them of necessity come to be the same, and having become the same with one another will all be one."*[28]

To seek out the mean, the Demiurge creates a long strip which he divides into lengths that correspond to the squares and cubes of the first three numbers, 1, 2 and 3. Of these, Pythagoras considered 2 to be the first female number and 3 to be the first male number, while the 1 remained androgynous. Their squares and cubes generate the even series 2, 4, 8 and the odd series 3, 9, 27. According to tradition, Pythagoras laid out these seven numbers in the form of the Greek letter *lambda* – a famous configuration that has traversed all of history, and called Plato's Lambda (See Fig. 16.30, next page).

In the next step, the Demiurge places more numbers between these, which act as the intervals or means to re-unify that which was separated: *"After this he filled up the double intervals* [that is, between 1, 2, 4, 8] *and the triple* [that is, between 1, 3, 9, 27...] *so that in each interval there were two kinds of means, the one* [...being the harmonic mean] *and the other being* [the arithmetic mean]*."*[29]

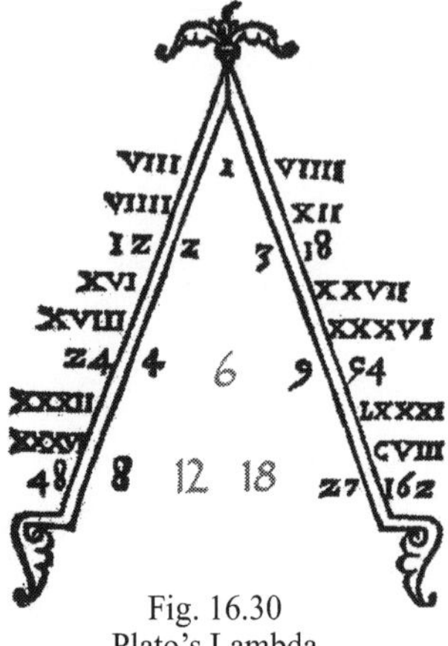

Fig. 16.30
Plato's Lambda

The purpose of this long and rather complicated passage is to determine the Pythagorean proportions that lie at the root of both musical harmony and the motion of the heavenly spheres, which Plato explains in detail in section 36a of the *Timaeus*.*

The intervals between the even series of female numbers and odd series of male numbers are 6, 12 and 18. In his *Introduction to Arithmetic* (*Arithmetike eisagoge*), a follower of Plato named Nicomachus of Gerasa (60 – 120 CE) turned the lambda on its side and expanded it into a triangle which reveals the fundamental proportions underlying both musical harmony and the motion of the spheres[30] (Fig. 16.31).

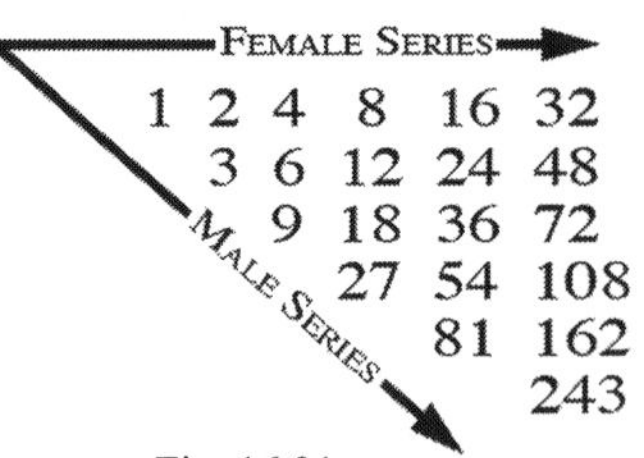

Fig. 16.31
Nicomachus' Table

In the top row are the female series created by the ratio of 1:2 (the *diapason*), and in the bottom row (diagonally descending) are the male series created by the ratio of 1:3. After the 1, we come upon the vertically descending column of 2 and 3, making the 2:3 *diapente* ratio. And from the 3, we may read it in an ascending diagonal to the 4, making the 3:4 *diatessaron* ratio.

If we take the same arrangement of numbers but shift the rows just slightly, then a variety of harmonic relationships rises before our eyes (Fig. 16.32). Now, beginning with the 1:2, we can see that all pairs of numbers in the horizontal rows express the 1:2 *diapason*. So, 2:4, 3:6 or 9:18, when reduced, form the 1:2 ratio. Next, with the 2:3, we can see that all pairs of numbers descending diagonally to the right express the 2:3 *diapente*. Thus, 4:6, 6:9 and 8:12, when reduced, form the 2:3 ratio. In the opposite direction, beginning with 3:4, all the numbers ascending diagonally to the right express the 3:4 *diatessaron*. As such, 6:8, 9:12 and 12:16, when reduced, form the 3:4 ratio.

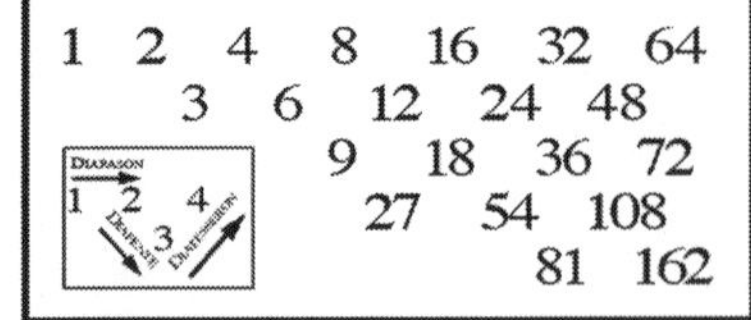

Fig. 16.32
Variation on Nicomachus' Table

*For an in depth analysis of this passage, I recommend Ernest G. McClain's *Pythagorean Plato: Prelude to the Song Itself* (1984) and Joscelyn Godwin's *The Harmony of the Spheres* (1992) – a sourcebook of texts with commentary.

But, more importantly, when various triads of numbers are read in certain directions, they reveal their middle term to be the arithmetic, geometric or harmonic mean of a proportion.

To find the arithmetic mean, we locate any number and create a triad with the two numbers diagonally above it, forming an inverted triangle. So, if we locate the number 3, then the 2 and 4 create the arithmetic proportion 2:3=3:4, expressed simply as 2:3:4. The same is true of 9, which creates the arithmetic proportion of 6:9:12. And so on.

To find the geometric mean, we locate any number and create a triad with the two numbers on either side, forming a horizontal line (or a diagonal line, whether ascending or descending, but only in the first three rows). So, if we locate the number 2, then the 1 and 4 create the geometric proportion of 1:2:4. The same is true of 4:6:9 or 9:12:16.

Last of all, to find the harmonic mean, we locate any number and create a triad with the two numbers diagonally below it, forming an upright triangle (but only in the first three rows). Now, if we locate the number 4, then 3 and 6 create the harmonic proportion of 3:4:6. The same is true of 6:8:12 or 9:12:18

Through Nicomachus' table, we are able to understand, at a much deeper level, the logic behind Alberti's schema. Those same proportions which relate to the harmonies of music and the celestial spheres also relate to Alberti's extended rectangles. In all the proportions offered here, one of the three types of means brings together the extremes in a way that shows the deeper unity (Existence) which underlies their Sameness and Difference.

XII. The Geometric Creation Myth

To better understand this unifying power of proportion, we may return to Alberti's schema and add some missing shapes, to reveal the 'geometric creation myth' that lies at its core (Fig. 16.33). Plato does not recount this creation myth explicitly, but it follows logically from various passages in the *Timaeus*.

To begin, Plato describes the process of generation, where the Father or male principle contributes the form *(eidos)*, while the Mother or feminine principle contributes the material, from which the Child, as 'the intermediate' principle, is engendered. Alas, the ordering of these three principles is a bit confused, requiring a careful reading. Plato writes:

"But the forms [eidé] *which enter into and go out of her* [Nature, the Mother] *are the likenesses of eternal realities* [from the Father], *modelled after their patterns in a wonderful and mysterious manner... For the present we have only to conceive of three natures: first* [the Child], *that which is in process of generation; secondly* [the Mother], *that in which the generation takes place; and thirdly* [the Father], *that of which the thing generated is a resemblance naturally produced. And we may liken the receiving principle to a mother, and the source or spring to a father, and the intermediate nature to a child."*[31]

By 'intermediate nature', Plato clearly has in mind the mean which unifies the opposites or extremes in a proportion. The Child has this unifying power because it is created in the image of both the Father and the Mother. Its form is modelled after the Father, who is 'the source and spring' of all eternal forms (the *eidé*), and its material nature comes from the Mother, who is 'the receiving principle' and *genetrix* of all material shapes that are a 'becoming in time'.

In the beginning of the geometric creation myth, there is only one: the divine One, perfect in shape, of the ratio 1:1. Although called by the name of Father, it is neither male nor female, since the Pythagorean number 1 is androgynous. Its shape expresses its 1:1 ratio, being a perfect square.

In the next step, the One reflects upon itself, becoming two: the seer and the seen, the thinking and the thought, the Father and the Mother. Geometrically, its shape becomes the double square, with a ratio of 1:2. In this way, each square being 1:1, they reflect each other but, being two, their two shapes express the 1:2 rectangle – the *diapason*. By creating the Pythagorean number 2, the second square manifests the feminine principle, the Mother who receives and engenders.

Together, these two create the first Child, who is 'the intermediate nature', the means which unifies the opposite extremes. Geometrically, this is the 2:3:4 rectangle, *which is* the 1:2 rectangle – resembling its parents – except the ratio of its side has now been doubled (from 1:2 to 2:4) to incorporate *the arithmetic mean* of 3. In the proportion 2:3=3:4, the Child is the common mean of 3 which mediates between the Father and Mother. By creating the Pythagorean number 3, the Child manifests the masculine principle, like the Father. This Child is the Son.

But, the Son has a twin, similar to itself yet different in gender: a sister. Geometrically, this is the 3:4:6 rectangle, which is also a 1:2 rectangle – she too resembles her parents – except the ratio of its side has been tripled (from 1:2 to 3:6) to incorporate *the harmonic mean* of 4. Now, in the proportion of 3:4=4:6, this second Child becomes the common mean of 4, which also mediates between the Mother and Father. But, by creating the Pythagorean number of 4, this Child manifests the feminine principle, like its Mother, being an even number. The second Child is the Daughter.

In *The Republic*, Plato writes: *"And all children born in which their fathers and mothers were procreating will regard one another as brother and sister."*[32]

While still in their infancy, Children remain androgynous, though called by a male or female name. But as they become adults, they take on their true gender roles, resembling the Mother or Father. The Son, as the 2:3:4 rectangle, identifies itself with the masculine number 3, and so manifests the 2:3 rectangle uniquely – the *diapente*. The Daughter, as the 3:4:6 rectangle, identifies herself with the feminine number 4, and so manifests the 3:4 rectangle uniquely – the *diatessaron*. Each of these emerges from the 1:2 *diapason* of their parents, and reveals their roots through the mysterious Pythagorean equation: one half equals two-thirds times three-quarters.* The equation expresses the fundamental unity of the trinity: from the 1:2 Parents, the 2:3 Son and 3:4 Daughter emerge.

As we have already seen with Alberti and Nicomachus, new generations of harmonic rectangles arise from combinations of these three. Each new Child resembles its progenitors, being a geometric, arithmetic or harmonic

* $\frac{1}{2} = \left(\frac{2}{3} \times \frac{3}{4}\right) = \left(\frac{6}{12}\right) = \frac{1}{2}$

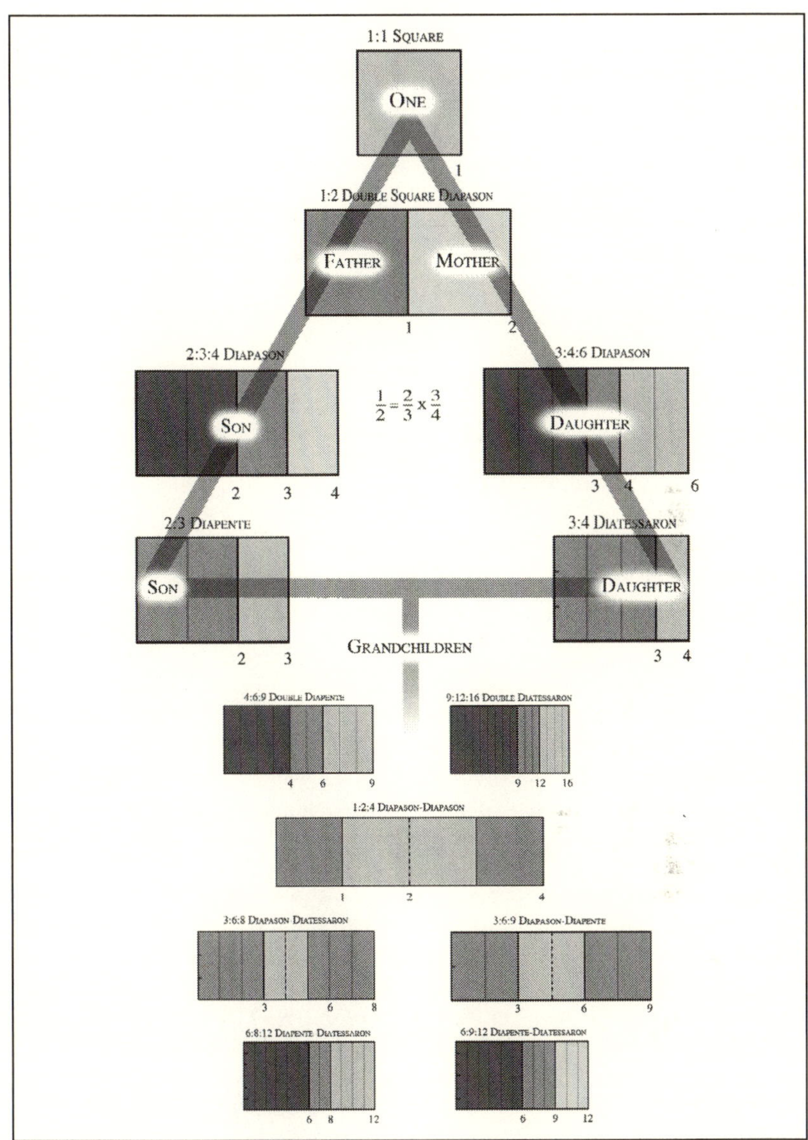

Fig. 16.33 - The Geometric Creation Myth

mean from the 1:2 Parents (the *diapason*), the 2:3 Son (the *diapente*) or the 3:4 Daughter (the *diatessaron*). As their grandchildren, the next generation expresses all the possible combinations of these three fundamental harmonic ratios.

We can see this, first of all, in Nicomachus' table (Fig. 16.31). As we read it from left to right, we recall how, from the 1:2 Parents, the 2:3:4 Son (with 3 as the arithmetic mean of 2:4) and the 3:4:6 Daughter (with 4 as the harmonic mean of 3:6) were the first to emerge.

From here, the next generations (which are not reducible to an existing proportion i.e. 4:6:8 and 6:9:12 are reducible to 2:3:4, and so discounted) are the grandchildren 4:6:9 (with 6 as the geometric mean of 4:9) and 9:12:16 (with 12 as the geometric mean of 9:16) – both of which Alberti has already listed as Extended Rectangles of the moderate type: the double diapente and double diatessaron.

Nicomachus' table does not offer us any more generations, but Alberti's schema does. With his Long type of Extended Rectangles, he multiplies all three harmonic ratios by the 1:2 Parents (the *diapason*), creating as its grandchildren the diapason-diapason (1:2:4). diapason-diapente (3:6:9) and the diapason-diatessaron (3:6:8).

The last of the possible combinations, not mentioned by Alberti, are the two diapente-diatessaron rectangles, 6:8:12 and the 6:9:12, which result when the 2:3 Son (the *diapente*) comes together with 3:4 Daughter (the *diatessaron*).

XIII. The Decline of Proportion in Art

The harmony of the cosmic spheres, being ideal, lies beyond all hearing and seeing. But, through music and painting, its consonances echo down to the sublunar realm. Though mathematically similar, the harmony of music and painting differs. Indeed, comparisons between the two occurred throughout history, yet each experienced its own evolution.

The harmony of music, for example, began in ancient Greece with the seven-stringed heptachord – a divine instrument of Mercurial invention championed by Apollo, whose seven strings sang the harmony of the seven cosmic spheres. In essence, two tetrachords were combined (each had four strings that spanned the intervals from the whole note to the 3:4 *diatessaron*) with a middle string between them (the *mese*) that fused the two into a harmonic scale.

Pythagoras added an eighth string to create the full octave (the eight notes of the diatonic scale). Unfortunately, the single string of a monochord cannot simply be divided into eight equal parts and struck at each interval (1/8, 2/8, 3/8 etc) to make a harmonic series of notes. The greatest harmony between two notes is heard at the 1:2 *diapason*, that is, between the whole string and half string, which is called musically the fundamental and the octave. The next interval of greatest harmony comes with the 2:3 *diapente*. From there, Pythagoras calculated the remaining intervals in a variety of mysterious ways.

It is particularly the lambda in Plato's *Timaeus* (as interpreted by Nicomachus of Gerasa) that reveals Pythagoras' calculations. The seven terms of the series 1, 2, 3, 4, 8, 9, 27 contain all the ratios necessary to calculate the diatonic scale. This begins with the 1:2 *diapason* which has, as its arithmetic mean, the 2:3 *diapente* and, as its harmonic mean, the 3:4 *diatessaron*. From there, the 8:9 whole note may be calculated in a different manner.

Instead, we calculate that the 1:2 *diapason* minus the 2:3 *diapente* leaves the 3:4 *diatessaron* i.e. 2/1 – 3/2 = 4/3. Continuing in this direction, the 2:3

diapente minus the 3:4 *diatessaron* leaves the 8:9 whole note (3/2 – 4/3 = 9/8). From there, the calculations became more and more complex (4/3 – 9/8 = 32/27 etc) while the interval between notes became less and less harmonious. In the end, Pythagoras left our culture with a diatonic musical scale that functioned well unto the Middle Ages.

Greek music was mainly *melodic*, expressing harmony in a series of single notes that formed a lyrical phrase. But, as music progressed in the Middle Ages, harmony came to be expressed *chromatically* in notes sounding simultaneously together (chords, polyphony). Because the major third (81:64) and minor third (32:27) were considered dissonant in Pythagorean tuning, they prevented the formation of triads and chords until their pitches were slightly tempered by musicians.

This lead to the creation of a more open tuning system called Just Intonation. Then, for instruments to accord with each other, Just Tuning was adjusted again in the 15th century to Equal Temperament. With his *Well-Tempered Clavier,* J. S. Bach demonstrated the expressive range of Equal Temperament, and it was soon taken up by Classical composers like Haydn, Mozart and Beethoven, who created huge symphonic masterpieces by according the entire orchestra with the tuning of a single piano.

Thanks to these advances in harmony, music reached untold heights of expression in the Classical Period of Haydn, Mozart and Beethoven (1750 – 1820), and continued to explore harmony well into the 21st century. Today, musicians are expanding the relation of harmony to proportion through studies in cymatics and the lambdoma – a new form of keyboard that forgoes Equal Temperament in favour of expanded Pythagorean tuning.

What, then, of painting?

We have seen that Renaissance artists like Raphael and Titian championed harmony, composing their works with balance and proportion. Through the intermediary of Poussin, that knowledge was then passed on to the *Académie Royale de Peinture et Sculpture* in Paris, as records of a lecture by Charles Le Brun demonstrate:

"M. Le Brun also reminded the Académie of an observation he had made some time before on all the works of M. Poussin... He said that M. Poussin, conforming to the harmonic proportion which musicians observe in their compositions, desired that in his pictures all things should contain reciprocal harmonies and should conspire to the same end."[33]

Le Brun's *confrère* at the Academy, André Félibien, expanded on this idea:

"The soul that loves proportion and equality takes more pleasure in the sounds of instruments and the accents of voices, in which the numbers are whole, and in which there is less dissonance. So also painting, of which the whole beauty consists of symmetry and fine proportion."[34]

The preparatory drawings by Claude Lorrain and Anne-Louis Girodet clearly demonstrated an awareness of proportion. But, in the last decades of the 1600's, a debate broke out that shook the very foundations of the Academy. Called *la Querelle des Anciens et des Modernes* ('the Quarrel of the

Ancients and Moderns'), it was provoked by Claude Perrault (1613 -1688), a polymath at the court of Louis XIV who defended his architectural changes to the Louvre through a series of footnotes in his 1673 translation of Vitruvius. Perrault accepted that beauty and proportion come to us from the ancients, but *"this imprints on our imagination an idea formed solely of prejudice and custom, in which received opinion binds us without our realizing it."*[35]

For François Blondel (1618 - 86), the first director of the *Académie Royale d'Architecture*, this was heresy. In a series of lectures published in 1675 as *Cours d'architecture* (Course of architecture), he argued that proportion emanates from a higher sphere, and we perceive its consonances due to ideas divinely implanted in our minds. Beauty is not a question of taste or preference, but something sublime, absolute and unchanging.

The debate spread across Europe to England, where the Irish philosopher Edmund Burke championed the 'Modern' view on harmony by inquiring into beauty as the result of human psychology rather than divine inspiration. In the concluding pages of his *Changing Concept of Proportion*, Rudolf Wittkower writes:

"When we turn to pages of Burke's Enquiry into the Origin of our Ideas of the Sublime and the Beautiful *(first published in 1757), we find ourselves face to face with an emotional and subjective aesthetic theory. Burke categorically refutes the Pythagorean-Platonic notion, which the Renaissance had fully embraced, that beauty resides in certain fundamental and universally valid proportions – in other words, that mathematical ratios as such can be beautiful. He denies that beauty 'has anything to do with calculation and geometry.'"*[36]

Burke's aesthetics had a major impact on the Romantic movement, as Wittkower observes:

"Romantic artists and their progeny clearly had no use for the shackles of intellectual number theories which would appear to endanger their hard-won freedom. And it may be said at once that we have not yet outlived the freedom for which the eighteenth century prepared the way."[37]

In other words, once painting liberated itself from harmony based on proportion, it never looked back. As the heirs of Romantic aesthetics, artists today still believe that balance and composition are more a matter of taste or feeling than mathematical measure. Yet, we have certainly lost a lot along the way. Compared to the complexity of musical harmony, the painter's sense of proportion seems rudimentary at best. Only with colour, perhaps, has painting explored new avenues of harmony (as we shall see in Volume III).

While armature and proportion may have faded over the course of art history, certain artists continued to call upon its Sacred Codes. This is certainly true of Blake, Moreau, Dalì and Fuchs, who explored different harmonic armatures in their works. As Moreau demonstrated with his *Pasiphaé* painting, the artist works best when a knowledge of proportion is so deeply ingrained that it becomes intuitive. Then, like a musician, he may pursue his ideal forms with free-flowing melodic lines full of harmony, beauty and grace.

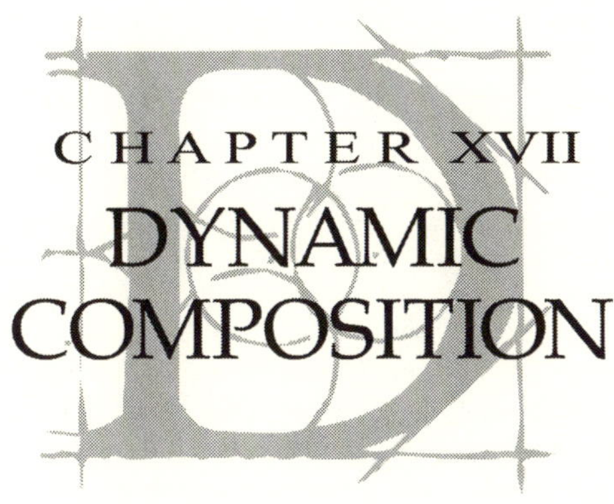

CHAPTER XVII DYNAMIC COMPOSITION

I. The Temple of Painting

In 1590, Giovan Paolo Lomazzo wrote a long meandering treatise called *The Idea of the Temple of Painting*. In it, he envisioned an ideal temple where seven giants of the Renaissance – among them, Mantegna, Titian, Raphael, Leonardo and Michelangelo – stand as gargantuan pillars or caryatids upholding the arced dome of the temple where light streams in through a circular aperture at its summit.

Each statue is made of a different metal, corresponding to one of the seven visible planets in the heavens, and allegorical figures at the base of each statue allude to different facets of the artist's temperament, such as the saturnine brooding of Michelangelo or the venusian beauty of Raphael.

In this 'memory theatre of the mind', each of us must visualize ourselves as standing in the centre of the temple, surrounded by these titans of painting who represent different stylistic 'types'. As such, we ourselves, as artists, may recognize our own particular stylistic expression as a unique combination of these seven celestial and artistic influences.

Behind the pillars are the walls of the temple, and these are divided horizontally into friezes that represent the seven parts of painting: proportion, movement, colour, light, perspective, composition and form.

As Jean Julia Chai writes in her introduction to Lomazzo's work:

"*Universal lighting from above indicates a divine presence that filters down the walls, through the parts of painting, into the seven chosen masters of the Temple. The Neo-Platonic belief in a descending cosmic influence implies a harmonious correspondence between every link in the chain. This means, from an aesthetic point of view, that harmony is necessary among all the parts in order for painting to receive beauty or grace from above, ultimately resulting in the coherent expressive styles of all the governors.*

"While not talismans, ...the statues nonetheless possess a certain aura, derived from traces of the divine, channeled into them by the flow of planetary influence that relates and unifies all of painting according to these seven styles."[1]

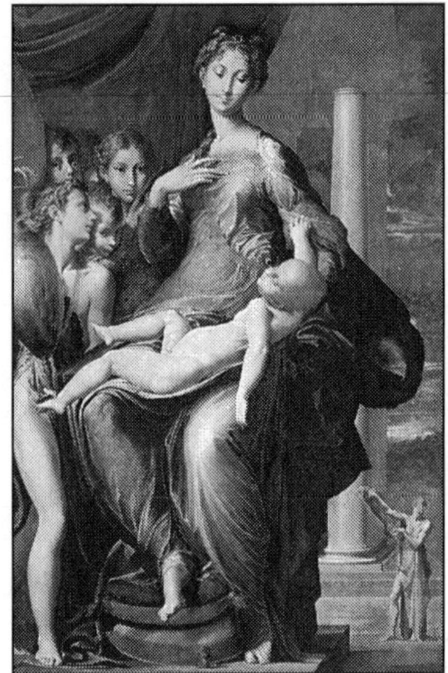

Fig. 17.1 - Parmigianino: *Madonna with the Long Neck* 1535

Lomazzo's *Idea del tempio della pittura* (Idea of the Temple of Painting – 1590) reflects the Mannerist preference for a painterly style that is flamboyant and exaggerated. The word 'mannerism' derives from the Italian *maniera*, meaning 'style'. Mannerist artists, such as Bronzino, Tintoretto and Parmigianino (whose unfinished masterpiece *The Madonna with the Long Neck* epitomizes the Mannerist preference for grace, style and elongation of the figure over the rigid proportions of Classicism – Fig. 17.1) tended to be intellectually astute and artistically-gifted prodigies that pushed the High Renaissance beyond its balanced temperance and moderate good taste into the flair, excesses and conceits of the Baroque period.

Following Lomazzo's precepts, sculptors like Cellini, Bernini and Giambologna (Jean Boulogne) portrayed the figure as 'a fiery flame' with undulating S-curves and out-thrust limbs that broke it forever out of the *quadrata* square block of Classicism. Like a satellite, the viewer had to orbit around Giambologna's *Astronomy* (Fig. 17.2) to appreciate its spiralling energy and view its *serpentinata* twist from numerous angles.

Compositionally, they introduced movement, lines of force and hard diagonals, eventually forgoing balanced and centered compositions in favour of dynamic, asymmetric arrangements with highly-contrasting forces and an over all dis-equalibrium. None of this occurred immediately, but gradually grew to more extremes as the 16th century gave way to the 17th century, and artists like Rubens and Goya came to prominence.

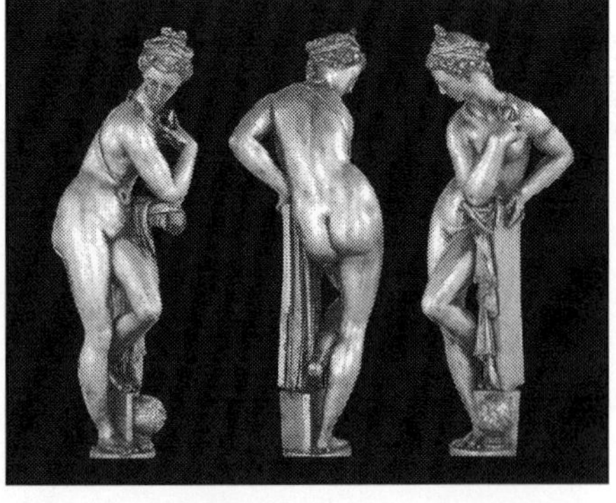

Fig. 17.2 Giambologna: *Astronomy* c. 1575

II. Dynamic Composition in the Renaissance

The roots of Mannerism and the Baroque may be found, compositionally speaking, in *Quattrocento* Renaissance artists like Sandro Botticelli and Andrea Mantegna. As astute students of Alberti, they introduced greater movement and variation into their compositions while maintaining a distinct preference for harmony and proportion.

As Charles Bouleau discovered in his *Secret Geometry of the Painters*, the key to deciphering their compositions lay in Alberti's doubling of certain harmonic ratios. If we return to the 'moderate' rectangles of the previous

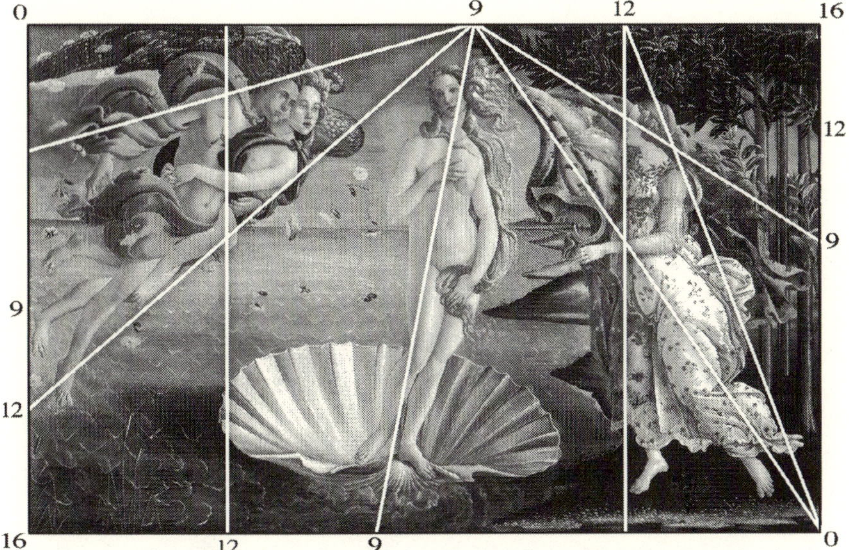

Fig. 17.3 - Sandro Botticelli - *The Birth of Venus* 1486

chapter, we recall that the 4:9 *double diapente* and the 9:16 *double diatessaron* were created by multiplying the square two times by the same harmonic ratio.

Through the geometric mean, the 4:6:9 proportion became one of the main keys for maintaining harmony in dynamic compositions. The other important key, also derived by the geometric mean, was the 9:12:16 proportion.

Taking Sandro Botticelli's *Birth of Venus* as a prime example, Bouleau demonstrates[2] how the dynamic angle of the central figure is determined by marking out the 9:12:16 proportion along the sides of the frame. By drawing a line from the baseline 9 to the topline 9, the space of the rectangle is harmoniously divided *by a dynamic diagonal.*

Indeed, had Botticelli decided to draw a perfect vertical from the baseline 8 to the topline 8, he would have placed Venus along the *diapason* half, which is the harmonious note that resounds in all Hieratic works of perfect symmetry. Instead, he replaced this static vertical with a more dynamic diagonal, which maintains harmony nevertheless by striking a three-quarter *diatessaron* note along the top and bottom horizontals (9:16). Almost off-balance, her figure wraps around the *diagonal* plumb line.

Botticelli does not begin with a 9:16 rectangle, nor does Bouleau use a square grid to determine the measures of the sides. Instead, *all* the sides of Botticelli's rectangle are divided into 16 equal parts, resulting in a fine grid of 256 (16 x 16) rectangles, each a smaller version of the bounding rectangle. Like the Harmonic Armature, the 4:6:9 or 9:12:16 proportions may be applied to *any* rectangle, regular or irregular, while dividing its space harmoniously.

From the topline 9 (again, a three-quarter *diatessaron* note), Bouleau draws a 'fan' (*eventail* in French) to other harmonious points on the sides of the rectangle (9, 12, *etc*), thus dividing the space with more harmonious diagonals. Botticelli's figures convincingly fall within these construction lines, respecting their dynamic yet harmonic division of pictorial space.

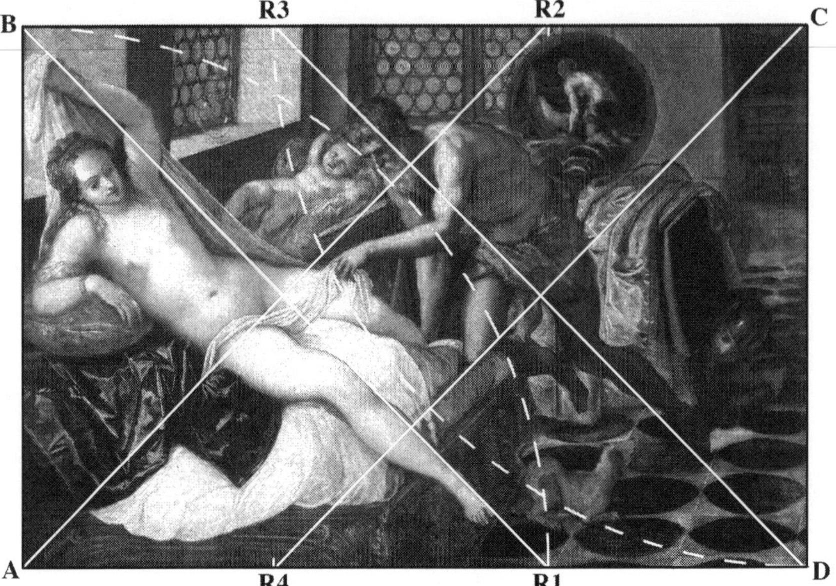

Fig. 17.4 - Tintoretto - *Venus, Mars and Vulcan* 1551

III. Dynamic Composition in the Mannerist & Baroque Period

As painting became more theatrical during the Mannerist and Baroque periods, the figures balanced more precariously to emphasize their dramatic action. Likewise, the compositions lost their regular measure and centeredness, inviting the eye to race across the diagonals and around their swirling figures.

In Tintoretto's *Venus, Mars and Vulcan* (Fig. 17.4), we have a clear example of how a Mannerist painter constructed[3] his rather banal comedy of the ugly husband (Vulcan) coming home to his beautiful wife (Venus) while the handsome lover (Mars) hides under the bed (in the shadows to the right). Although the subject is based on a Greek myth, we are hardly in the realm of Hieratic art, but have now descended into the follies and foibles of the Humanist condition.

Rather than measuring out the *diapente* 9ths or *diatessaron* 16ths of each side of his painting to obtain the diagonals, Tintoretto has used the more expedient method of *rabattement*. Through the infolding of the shorter side to the longer side of the rectangle (dotted curves), he has obtained four points (R1 – 4). For example, beginning with side AB, he has used center A to arc B down to R1 – and so on.

Then, from each of the four corners (A, B, C and D), he has drawn diagonals to each of the four points determined by *rabattement* (R1 – 4). The B to R1 diagonal clearly gives the artist an axis for the voluptuous movement of Venus as she lazily coils a linen cloth round her nude form. Likewise, Vulcan follows the D to R3 diagonal as he modestly drapes a kerchief over her

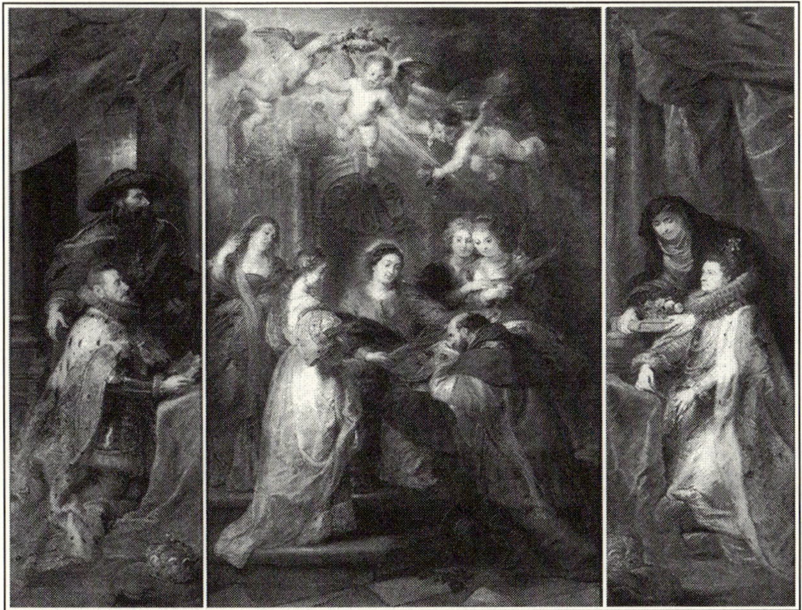

Fig. 17.5 - Rubens - *Ildefenso Altarpiece* 1630

sex. This diagonal also divides the light and shadow of the painting, leaving Vulcan and Mars in the upper right shadows, with Venus well-lit in the lower left. Meanwhile, the opposite diagonals (A to R2 and C to R4) determine the space of the painting, as the perspective lines of the beds clearly follows the C to R4 diagonal. (For the perspective of this painting, see Fig. 23.33).

Most important is the ◇ parallelogram near the centre created by the crossing of the four diagonals. In many dynamic compositions, this ◇ parallelogram creates a centralized area for the principle gestures or actions (such as Vulcan draping the kerchief).

Progressing historically from Mannerism to the Baroque period, we find in Rubens' *Ildefenso Altarpiece* (Fig. 17.5) a similar example of diagonals created through the *rabattement*.[4] If we gaze for a moment at the painting without the armature marked in, we immediately sense the presence of strong diagonals rising up from the bottom corners of the main panel, as well as a ◇ parallelogram around the Virgin, who is presenting St. Ildefenso with a holy vestment upon which her image appears. In the wings, we see the donors of the altarpiece (Isabella Clara Eugenia on the right, attended by her patron saint, St. Elisabeth of Hungary, and Archduke Albrecht on the left, attended by St. Albrecht). Again, diagonals rise up from the bottom corners, where the faldstools are covered with drapery in rich deep red hues.

The painting's armature (Fig. 17.6, over) shows that the main diagonals (in white) ascend from the bottom corners of the wings to the top of the main panel, and from the bottom corners of the main panel to the top of the wings. Where they cross the border between the main panel and the wings, we find the points of *rabattement* for the main panel, each marked with an R.

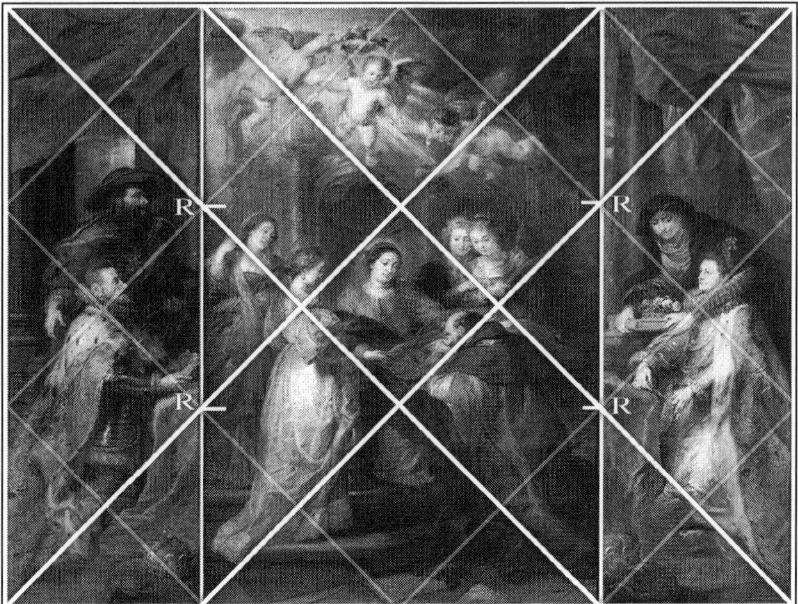

Fig. 17.6 - Rubens - *Ildefenso Altarpiece* 1630

The main action takes place within the central ◇ parallelogram. When we fill in the remaining diagonals (in grey) and count the x's, we notice that Rubens began with a 2:3 (*diapente*) vertical rectangle in the main panel, which became a 3:4 (*diatessaron*) horizontal rectangle for the altarpiece as a whole. The diagonals run at 45° angles, creating a series of turned squares (*quadrature*) within the invisible *ad quadratum* grid.

More interesting still, the cherubs at the top of the painting straddle the orthogonals and diagonals. Like the ornamental figures in Honnecourt's drawing of the Laon Tower (Fig. 14.30), they are *visible reminders of the invisible armature* underlying the altarpiece.

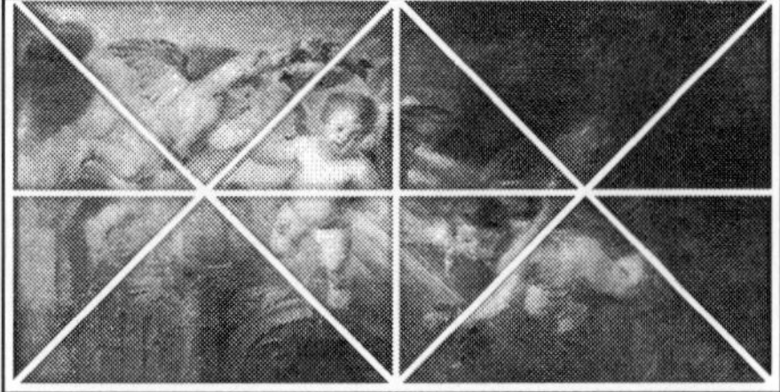

IV. Harmonic Proportion & Root Rectangles

In *De Vita Pythagora* ('On the Pythagorean Way of Life'), Iamblichus recounts how a student of Pythagoras named Hippasus suffered the gods' wrath and was drowned at sea because he revealed $\sqrt{2}$ to be an irrational number.

Pythagoras bequeathed to history a system of Harmonic Proportion based on the whole number ratios 1:2, 2:3 and 3:4. But, when confronted by geometric constructions with ratios in irrational numbers, he dismissed them as unbecoming to the divine creation. It was left to Plato and his *Timaeus* to enshrine *both whole and irrational numbers* in the divine scheme of creation.

He did this, as we have seen, in the half-square where the ratio of the base to the hypotenuse is 1 : √2 (or 1:1.4142135...) and in the half-equilateral where the ratio of the base to the perpendicular is 1 : √3 (or 1: 1.7320508...).

To better understand root rectangles and their relationship to Harmonic Proportion, let us begin with the most perfect of all shapes, the circle.[6]

Proceeding *ad circulum*, we inscribe a square within the circle (Fig. 17.8, next page). If we give the square a quarter turn and divide it in half, we soon become aware of the isosceles triangle (or Platonic 'half-square') within – a right-angled triangle with two lesser angles of 45°.

Fig. 17.7:

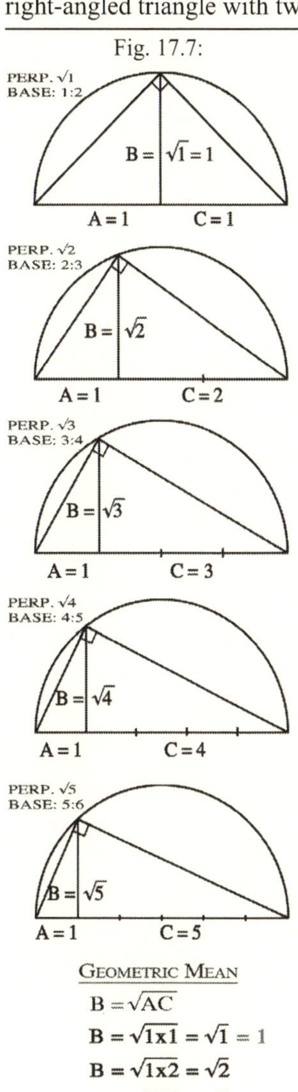

If we focus on the upper semi-circle with its right-angled triangle (Fig. 17.7, left), we can eventually recognize one of Euclid's laws: that any triangle inscribed in a semi-circle, with its base running the entire diameter of the circle, will be a right-angled triangle (Euclid *Elements* Bk 3, Theorem 31). Euclid referred to this as *Thales' Theorem*, attributing it to the Pre-Socratic philosopher Thales of Miletus (c. 624 – c. 546 BCE), a pre-cursor of Pythagoras.

If we look at the base of the isosceles triangle, we notice that it is equally divided in two parts, creating *a diapason ratio of 1:2*, a ratio which describes part of the base to the whole.

Meanwhile, a proportion arises between the length of the perpendicular B and the parts of the baseline, A and C. In the proportion A:B = B:C, the extremes A and C vary in their length according to the length of the mean B, which is the perpendicular. This may be calculated using the geometric mean, B = √(AC), where A and C are the lengths of the divided parts of the baseline and B is the length of the perpendicular. So, if A = 1 and C = 1, then B = √(1x1) which equals √1 which equals 1.

Continuing in this manner, we may construct a whole series of root triangles, by dividing the baseline into equal parts, to show the relationship of Harmonic Proportion to root rectangles. In the next example, the baseline is divided in three parts and the perpendicular is shifted to the left, *creating a 2:3 diapente ratio* in the baseline. When the value of the perpendicular B is calculated according to the geometric mean, it becomes √2.

Next, the baseline is divided into four parts and the perpendicular is shifted again to create *a 3:4 diatessaron ratio* in the baseline. The value of the perpendicular is √3.

With the √4 triangle, the baseline has a 4:5 ratio. We have not yet encountered this ratio in the diatonic scale of Pythagorean tuning, but it is a musically harmonious ratio that produces *the major third note* in relation to the fundamental. The value of the perpendicular is √4.

Last of all, with the √5 triangle, the baseline has a ratio of 5:6, which is *the minor third note* in musical harmony. The value of the perpendicular is √5.

In Fig. 17.8, we have simply expanded the semi-circle into a full circle once more, and laterally flipped the inverted bottom triangle. The result is the creation of all five root rectangles from their right-angled root triangles. This diagram shows the fundamental relationship between root rectangles and Harmonic Proportions.

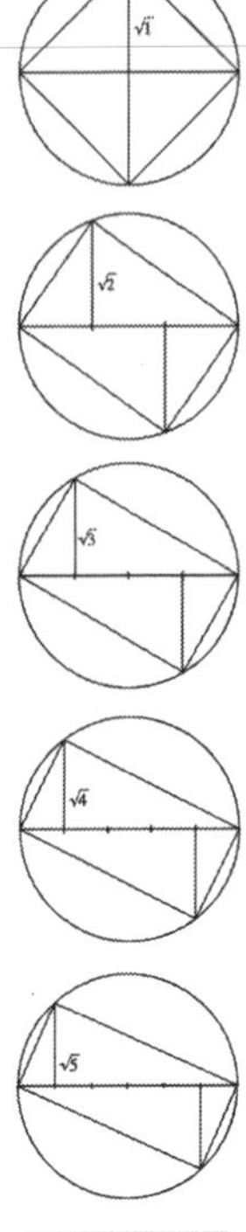

Fig. 17.8

V. Root Rectangles

Although evidence for the construction of root rectangles dates back to Egyptian times, it was Jay Hambidge, through the publication of his two books *Dynamic Symmetry: The Greek Vase* (1920) and *The Elements of Dynamic Symmetry* (1926), who revived an interest in them in the 20th century. While Hambidge provides ample evidence of their use in Greek vases, very few art historians have followed his lead and analyzed compositions for evidence of root rectangles.*

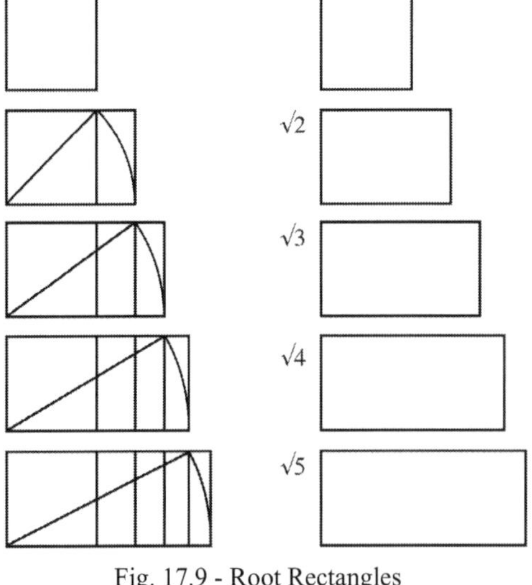

Fig. 17.9 - Root Rectangles

Yet, their construction is intuitive, and invites interesting possibilities and variations for the artist. As we have seen, the root 2 rectangle is made by 'folding' the square's diagonal measure down to the base, then extending the baseline to create the root 2 rectangle. The same procedure is repeated to create the other root rectangles (Fig. 17.9). Thus, a new diagonal is drawn in the root 2 rectangle, then arced down to the base and the baseline is extended to create the root 3 rectangle – and so on up to root 5 or more.

*Notable exceptions are Michael S. Schneider's *Constructing the Universe* series and Karyl M. Knee's *The Dynamic Symmetry Proportional System is Found in Some Byzantine and Russian Icons of the Fourteenth to Sixteenth Centuries.*

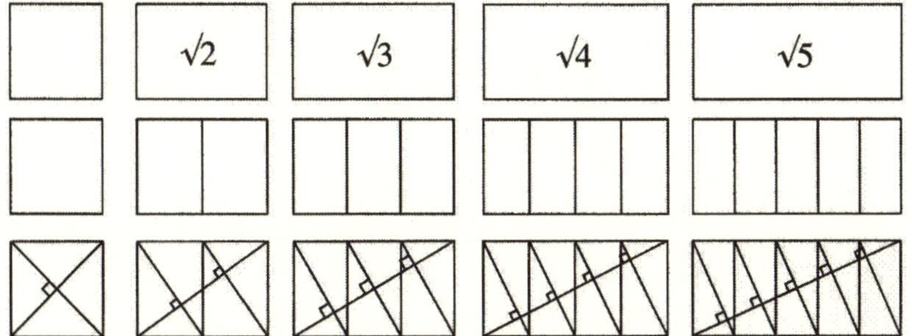

Fig. 17.10 - Recursive Root Rectangles

One interesting property is that a root rectangle, when divided by the number of its root, produces an equal number of smaller root rectangles (Fig. 17.10). So that a root 2 rectangle, for example, produces two more root 2 rectangles within it, and each of these will produce two more, *ad infinitum.*

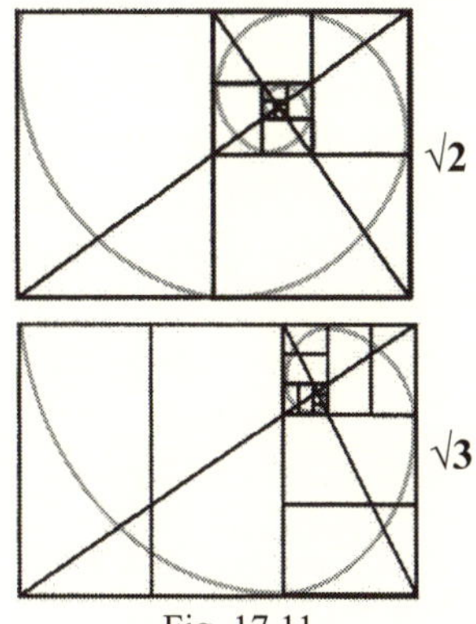

Fig. 17.11

The diagonals created by the greater and smaller root rectangles meet at right angles. But, more than that, they meet at the place where the ever-smaller root rectangles undergo a recursive regression down to infinity (using the outermost rectangles only). As such, these points are extremely powerful within the overall composition. A curving spiral can also be drawn through the recursive root rectangles, to create a dynamic movement through the composition, which terminates at the power point at the centre of the spiral.

Although the verticals and horizontals play important roles in root rectangles, it is particularly their diagonals and their recursive property which give root rectangles their *dynamic* character. Indeed, Hambidge calls his entire enterprise 'dynamic symmetry'.

Root rectangles can also be created *within* the square (Fig. 17.12). Using the technique of *rabattement*, two arcs are inscribed in the square by 'folding the sides' down to the base. When the main X diagonals are drawn from each corner of the square, we draw a horizontal at the place where the arcs and diagonals meet to give us the root 2 rectangle. This process is repeated within the root 2 rectangle, using the original arcs of the square but adding new diagonals within the root 2 rectangle. At the place where the new diagonals meet the arcs, the horizontal for the root 3 rectangle is drawn – and so on.

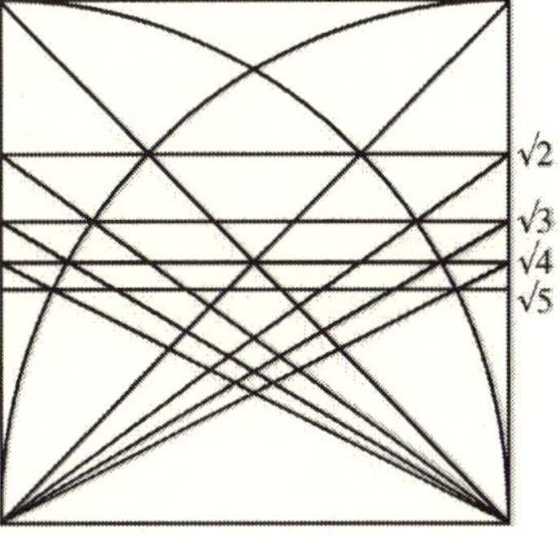

Fig. 17.12 - Construction of Root Rectangles in the Square

Root rectangles have a number of interesting relationships with other rectangles. For example, the root 4 rectangle is the equivalent of the 1:2 *diapason* rectangle or double square (Fig. 17.13). The arithmetic also proves this, since the ratio of the sides of a root 4 rectangle is 1:√4, which is the same as 1:2, the *diapason*.

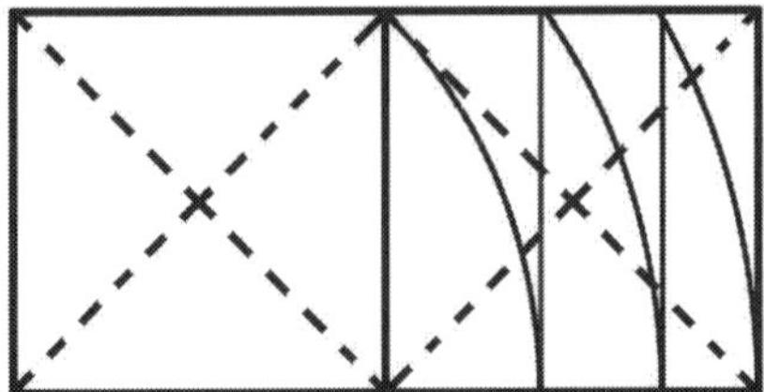

Fig. 17.13 - 1:√4 = 1:2 Rectangle

Meanwhile, the root 5 rectangle is the equivalent of 2 phi rectangles overlapping at their common square (Fig. 17.14). Commonly used in triptychs, this figure may be drawn quickly by passing an arc over the square's upper corners.

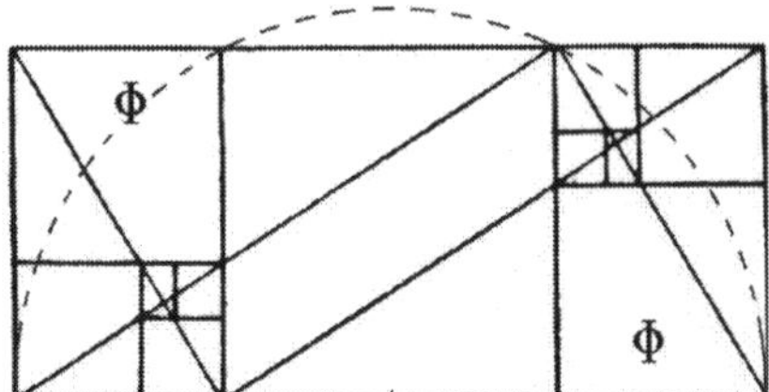

Fig. 17.14 - √5 = 2 ϕ Rectangles

In *The Shapes of Sacred Space: A Proposed System of Geometry used to Lay Out and Design Maya Art and Architecture* (2010), Christopher Powell analyzes Maya art and finds a non-co-incidental number of cases where ϕ and root rectangles occur. We have already seen an example (Fig. 15.40) in our chapter on Ornament as to how Pacal's sarcophagus lid reveals several root 3 and root 4 rectangles.

In lintel 24 of Yaxchilan[7] (now in the British Museum) the well-known *Vision Quest of Lady Xoc* (Fig. 17.15) transpires within a root 2 rectangle. Her husband Shield Jaguar appears on the left, holding a flaming torch while she pulls a thorn-lined rope through her tongue as part of a blood-letting ritual. The flaming torch upheld by Shield Jaguar roughly follows the diagonal of the √2 rectangle construction.

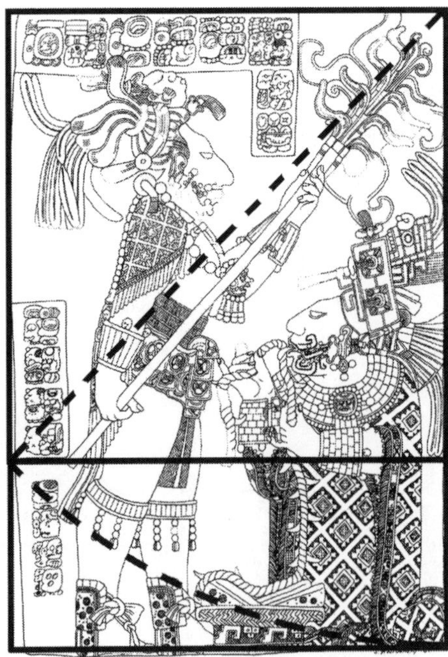

Fig. 17.15 - *Vision Quest of Lady Xoc* c. 725

My own researches have brought me to Mantegna's *Christ on the Mount of Olives* (Fig. 17.16) which gives us a clear example of a root 2 rectangle in the Renaissance period. To begin, Mantegna constructs square ABCD within his composition through *rabattement*.

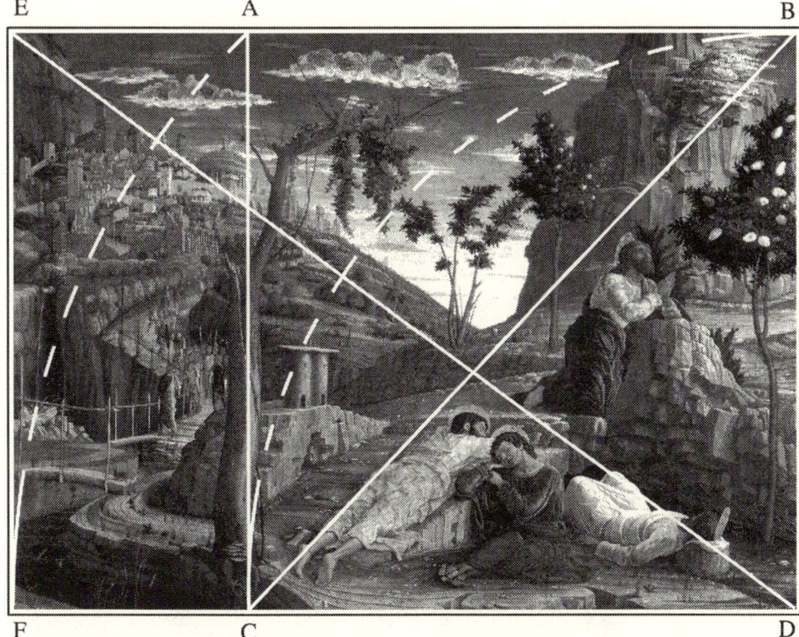

Fig. 17.16 - Mantegna: *Christ on the Mount of Olives* c. 1459

This gives him the strong diagonal CB ascending from the base of the tree to the top right, which clearly contains Christ and the three sleeping disciples. The tree, meanwhile, marks the limit of the square ABCD.

Drawing arc AF down from the top left of the square, he measures out his root 2 rectangle, and then draws diagonal ED across it, defining the steep descent of the landscape. The disciples fit neatly as a pyramidal group within the triangle formed by the two diagonals.

The *Pectoral of Mereret* (Fig. 17.17) dates from the 12th dynasty. Through a knowledge of root rectangles, we are able to reconstruct some of the Sacred Codes that guided the ancient craftsman in his construction of this masterful artifact.[8] Within the rectangle ABCD, he began the construction of the Harmonic Armature, first drawing the X diagonals (dotted lines) AD and CB for the 'halves', then the ∧ diagonals CED for the 'thirds'. Where these 'halves' and 'thirds' meet near the top, he drew his main verticals GH and IJ as well as the main horizontal KL.

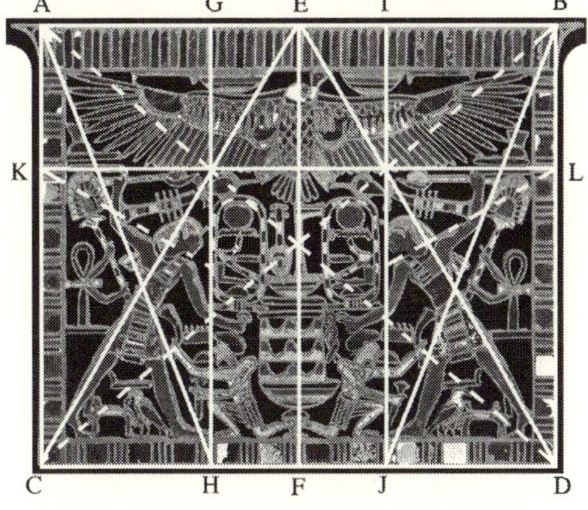

Fig. 17.17 - Pectoral of Mereret c. 1839 BCE

The result was rectangle KLCD, which is a root 3 rectangle with three smaller root 3 rectangles inscribed within it. Each of these smaller rectangles defines the space for the figures within: the central cartouche and, to the left and right, the pharaoh in a stance of victory over his enemies.

The legs and raised fore-arm of the pharaoh neatly follow the diagonals, and even the raised upper arms follow the diagonals KD and LC within rectangle KLCD. But it is principally the diagonals of the pharaohs' bounding root 3 rectangles which serve as the central axis for these dynamic figures, (like early examples of 'the heroic diagonal'), giving them movement and life.

VI. The Golden Rectangle

During a trip to Colorado in May of 2013, I stayed in the studio of David Heskin and Aloria Weaver. I was surrounded by their paintings that manifest, in a subtle and delicate way, the complex intricacies of armature, space and sacred geometry. Aloria Weaver shared her husband's passion for geometry, and her latest painting, *Guardian of the Golden Mystery*, offered much to ponder on the armature of recursive ϕ rectangles.

During a late-evening gathering of artists in their home, David began a spontaneous composition on the guitar – and it was then that I had a rare glimpse into the dizzying depths of genius that underlay all his works.

It was a form of music which I had never heard before – chords upon chords – each a unique fingering far beyond the standard C, F and G7 chords of Western music. And each progression was leading somewhere distant and new, yet never losing sight of the most ethereal harmony. The performance – in the midst of people talking – was far from perfect, but I could understand and follow his ongoing quest for more obscure and time-transcendent notes, like the distant seeking and remembering of the famous 'lost chord' which King David played to please the Lord...

In 2005, Michael S. Schneider wrote about Sacred Geometry:

"As I study this subject, I have to say that there appears to be a secret design language at work in great art, probably only taught within temples, guilds and among groups of artists, from mouth to ear and hand to eye. Some teachers are known, like Luca Pacioli who taught Leonardo da Vinci, but most will never be identified. We can only see what they and their students left for us. From studying great art, one can discern a few of the 'rules' at work when composing with this timeless language of geometry."[9]

Schneider's five volume opus *Constructing the Universe* is a valuable resource for the artist, since he seeks out the Sacred Codes of geometry from all cultures and all times.

The construction of the ϕ rectangle – drawing a diagonal *from the midpoint of the base* to the top corner, then arcing the diagonal down to create the new baseline – is so naturally intuitive that it has probably existed from most ancient times. As with root rectangles, its construction is the natural result of playing with a compass and straight rule.

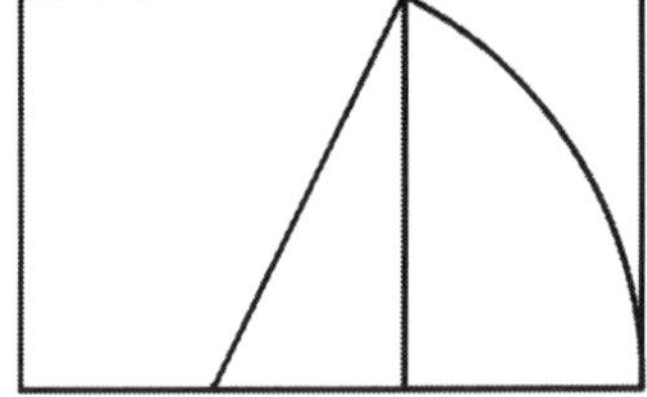

Fig.17.18 -Construction of ϕ Rectangle

Euclid mentioned the ϕ rectangle in the thirteenth and final book of his *Elements*, and Luca Pacioli, after writing his *De divina proportione* (1509), revived an interest in it during the Renaissance. Johannes Kepler gave it a special place in his work. By folding in the long side of a ϕ rectangle, Kepler created a right-angled triangle with sides measuring 1, ϕ and ϕ^2 that has come to be known as the Kepler triangle (Fig. 17.19).

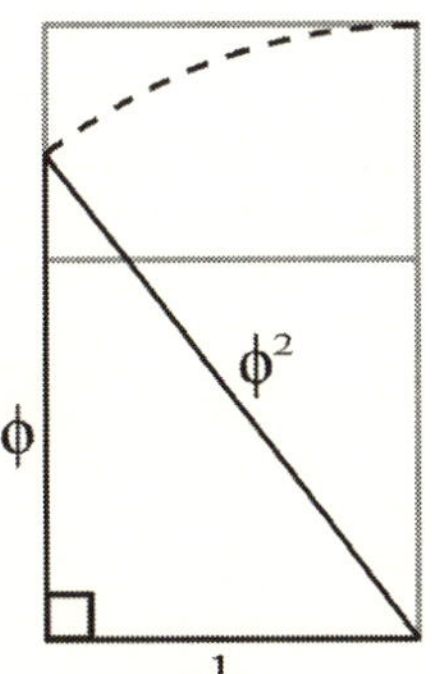

Fig. 17.19
Construction of the Kepler Triangle from a ϕ Rectangle

Following Pacioli, Kepler called ϕ the *sectio divina* and *göttlicher Schnitt*.[10] The term 'Golden' first appeared in Germany in the 1830's, when Kepler's *göttlicher Schnitt* became the *goldene Schnitt*. German writers like Adolf Zeising (1810 - 1876) and Gustav Fechner (1834 - 1887) explored ϕ in relation to aesthetic theory, while Englishmen like Theodore Cooke and D'Arcy W. Thompson pursued its logarithmic spiral in patterns of growth.

In the 20th century, a new interest began thanks to Jay Hambidge's *Dynamic Symmetry* and a series of works by Mathila Ghyka, including *Esthétique des proportions dans la nature et dans les arts* (1927) and *Le nombre d'or: Rites et rythmes pythagoriciens dans le dévelopment de la civilisation occidentale* (1931), summarized in a short English edition called *The Geometry of Art and Life* (1946). Ghyka's work had a major impact upon Salvador Dalì, among others.

When the diagonal is arced down to the baseline to create the ϕ rectangle, the ratio of the base of the square to the base of the ϕ rectangle is an irrational number – 1.6180339887498948482... shortened to 1.6 or ϕ.

This is the Golden Ratio, also called the Golden Section or *sectio aurea* in Latin. The Golden *Proportion* compares two ratios, but in this case it is entirely unique because it is able to reduce the three term proportion down to only two terms. Thus far, we have written proportions with three terms, as A:B = B:C where the extremes A and C find their common mean in B. But, with the Golden Proportion, A:B = (A+B):A; and there is no need for C.

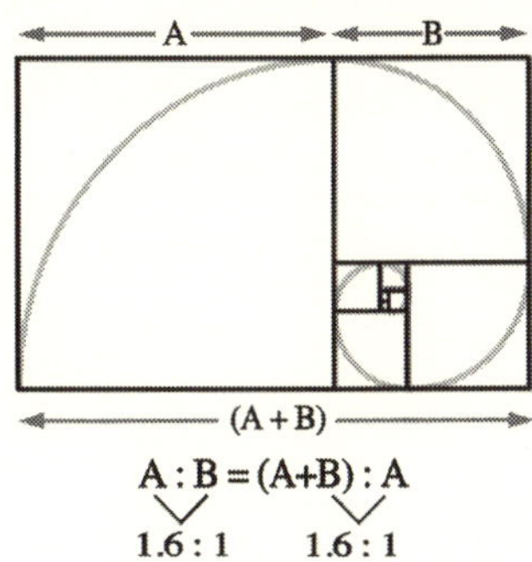

Fig. 17.20 - The Two Terms of the Golden Proportions in the ϕ Rectangle

When we look at the ϕ rectangle, we can see this unique relationship (Fig. 17.20). The ratio of A:B occurs in the ratio of the side of the larger square A to the side of the smaller square B. The ratio of (A+B):A occurs in the ratio of the side of the ϕ rectangle (A+B) to the side of the larger square A. On *both* sides of the proportion, the ratio of 1.6:1 or ϕ occurs. Since the ϕ rectangle is recursive, this ratio repeats with the ever smaller ϕ rectangles that spiral downward.

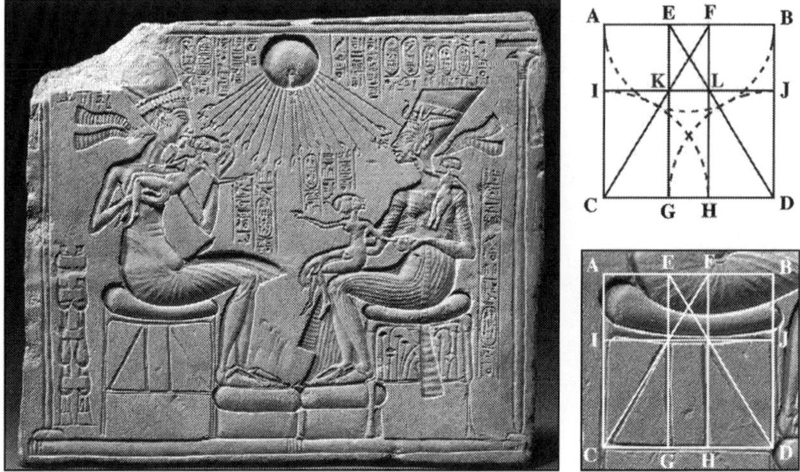

Fig. 17.21 - ϕ Rectangle in *Tell el-Amarna Stele* with Akhenaten and Nefertiti 1340 BCE

VII. The Golden Rectangle in Art

In this altar panel from the Amarna Period (Fig. 17.21), the pharaoh Akhenaten is depicted with Nefertiti and their three daughters – all being blessed by the hands of the sun. Akhenaten is sitting on a throne which betrays a most interesting geometrical construction.

Below, Fig. 17.22 shows the geometrical steps for dividing a line segment into the golden section, using only a compass and straight rule. One begins by constructing a square from the vertical line, drawing a series of arcs. With the aid of a triangle, one draws three adjacent arcs and then draws a horizontal line where the two lower arcs meet the sides of the square. The result is a horizontal line bisecting the original vertical line at the 1:1.6 ratio.

If we focus on the fourth step in this sequence, we can see how the same geometrical construction appears in Akhenaten's throne. As demonstrated in the lower right diagram of Fig. 17.21, Akhenaten's throne is indeed a ϕ rectangle IJDC, which is divided into smaller overlapping squares and ϕ rectangles through the *rabattement* of the sides CI to H, and DJ to G.

Using the same three circular arcs as step four below, the upper right diagram in Fig. 17.21 shows how the horizontal IJ divides the original square at the height of 1:1.6. Meanwhile, the verticals EG and FH are drawn from the points where the lower circular arcs touch the base at G and H, creating two interpenetrating ϕ rectangles – one that is AFHC and one that is EBDG.

The diagonals CF and ED are, in fact, diagonals that cut across each of the interpenetrating ϕ rectangles. Meanwhile, all we see in Akhenaten's throne are CK and LD. Nevertheless, in the ϕ rectangle IJDC that forms the throne, there are two smaller ϕ rectangles, IKGC and LJDH (each marked by a diagonal). The pharaoh is sitting on a series of ϕ rectangles.

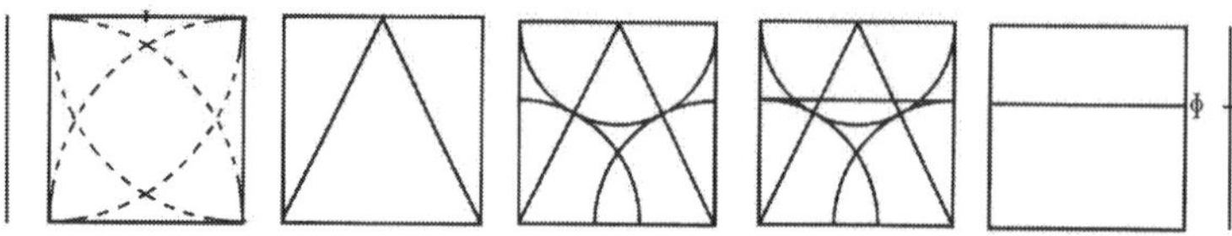

Fig. 17.22 - Construction of ϕ Ratio in a Line, using only a Compass and Straight Rule

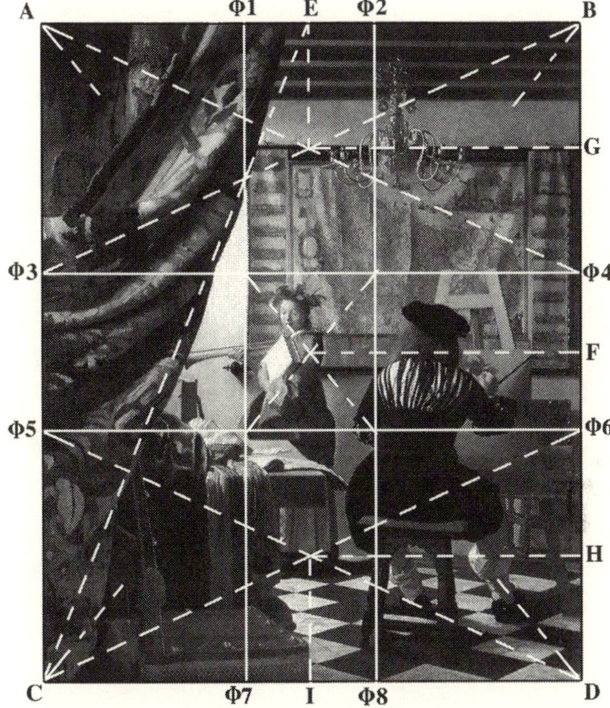

Fig. 17.23 - Vermeer - *The Artist in his Studio* c. 1662

Even when he was pursued by creditors, Vermeer never let go of *The Artist in his Studio* (Fig. 17.23). This canvas, his largest work and most likely a self-portrait, is Vermeer's visual statement on the Art of Painting, and its composition has piqued the curiosity of scholars and artists for generations.

In *Charpentes: La géométrie secrète des peintres*, Charles Bouleau offers a fairly original application of the golden section.[12] Usually, it is assumed that the bounding rectangle of a painting will be a ϕ rectangle, and so the continuous division of its interior space into ever-smaller squares and ϕ rectangles will result in the harmonious arrangement of the parts. (We shall see this next chapter in Moreau's *Jupiter and Semele* - Fig. 18.17).

But, just as Bouleau applied the 9:12:16 progression to *all* the sides of Botticelli's *Birth of Venus*, so does he apply the 1:1.6 progression to all the sides of Vermeer's painting. The results are intriguing, to say the least. Vermeer began with an irregular rectangle (4.25 : 5) and marked the ϕ ratio of 1:1.6 along the entire lengths of the horizontal and vertical sides. Looking at the top of the painting, A to ϕ2 = 1 and A to B = 1.6. In the opposite direction, B to ϕ1 = 1 and B to A = 1.6. Likewise, looking at the left side, A to ϕ5 = 1 and A to C = 1.6 while C to ϕ3 = 1 and C to A = 1.6.

Immediately we note that the vertical ϕ1 to ϕ7 coincides with the left of the map against the wall, and the ϕ3 to ϕ4 horizontal co-incides with the top of Vermeer's easel. What is more, if we draw X diagonals above and below, then the top of the map matches the half horizontal at G and the floor line of the room matches the half horizontal below at H.

If the entire rectangle ABDC is divided by X diagonals (only partly shown) then the horizontal line F at half the painting's entire height marks the top of the little painting on Vermeer's easel. Likewise, the vertical line EI marking half the painting's width gives us the diagonal for the curtain (CE), and the corner of the small table in the foreground below at I.

The ϕ ratio has consistently allowed for the harmonious placement of objects within Vermeer's composition, yet there are no ϕ rectangles drawn in this particular armature. Hence, it is important to remember that the 1 : 1.6 progression can be applied to the sides of *any* rectangle, be it a ϕ rectangle or an irregular one.

Although Bouleau mentions many other kinds of construction, the most important are the *rabattement*, the Harmonic Armature of halves, quarters and thirds, the 4:6:9 or 9:12:16 progressions, and the ϕ ratio of 1:1.6, which he calls *le nombre d'or*. All of these may be applied to the sides of *any* rectangle, regular or irregular. Add to this the construction of root rectangles, and the artist has a formidable range of geometrical shapes to create both static and dynamic compositions.

However, all of these geometric constructions should be understood as *principles* of painting. Once the artist has mastered them, he or she need not cling to them. Rather, they should encourage the artist to explore new and untried geometrical relationships within their composition, searching them out intuitively and expanding on them creatively. In Visionary Art, numbers and shapes have a mystical significance, and the artist should respond to those mysterious ciphers with artistry, invention and imagination.

VI. Conclusion

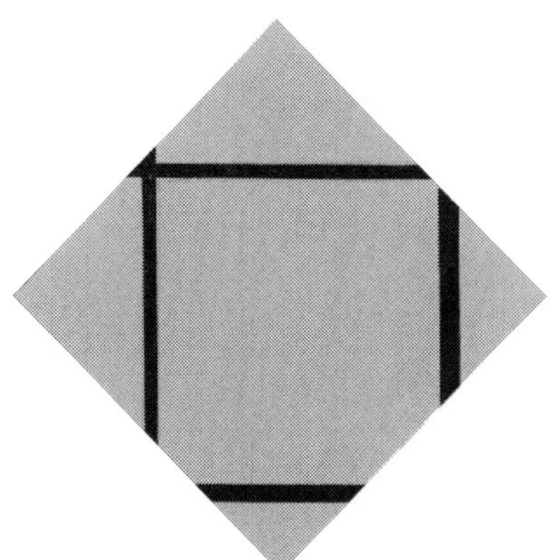

Fig.17.24 - Mondrian: *Lozenge with Four Lines and Grey* 1926

In a work from his second Paris period (Fig. 17.24), we can see how Mondrian laboured hard to preserve the hidden lines of composition in his painting.[13] As demonstrated in Fig. 17.25 opposite, he began with the large □ square ABCD and gave it a 45° turn to the ◇ rhombic position, then drew the lines AC and EF such that they crossed at the ϕ ratio of 1:1.6 on each line.

In the second step, the whole arrangement was rotated back 45° to its original □ square position, and reduced until the two compositions, when superimposed, met at the place where the diagonals crossed at the ϕ

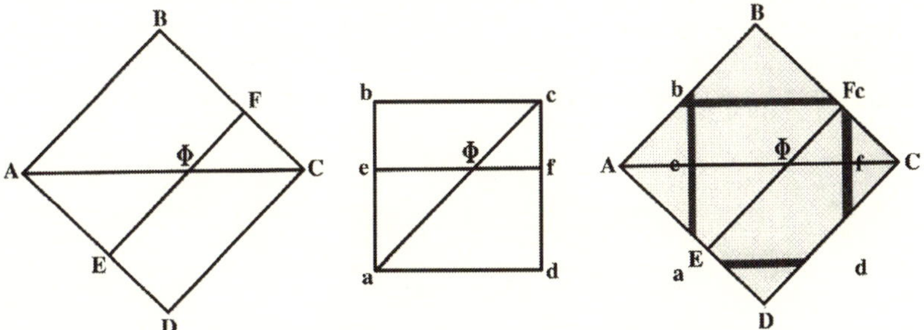

Fig.17.25 - Mondrian: Construction with ϕ Ratio

ratio. These crossing diagonals, visible in the third step, were then erased or overpainted, becoming invisible in the final painting (Fig. 17.24).

With the death of the Academy system in the late 1800's, Figuration became increasingly obsolete, with its complex demands of style, pose, anatomy and proportion. As the late 19th century took its first cautious steps towards abstraction, the figure lost its Classical unity and coherence. The Sacred Codes of Figuration were lost, seemingly forever.

Meanwhile Composition experienced a kind of Renaissance all its own in the works of Abstract and Formalist painters (like Mondrian). Thanks to the writings of Father Desiderius and Matila Ghyka, geometrical construction witnessed a resurgence in the compositions of Cezanne, Matisse, Picasso, Gris, Villon and his *Groupe de Puteaux* painters (whose members like Duchamp, Gleizes, Picabia and Kupka published a revue and organized exhibitions on *La Section d'Or*). Yet, it was only Dalì who attempted to marry the hidden lines of Composition with the long-lost knowledge of Figuration.

In the following chapter, we shall pursue the relationship between Composition and Figuration in depth, attempting to revive some of the artistic principles that inspire their dynamic interaction. I have found evidence of these, particularly, in the works of Michelangelo, Blake, Moreau and Fuchs. Yet, I believe that many Visionary artists today are capable of rediscovering and reviving that complex relationship.

Any form of art, be it Humanist or Hieratic, becomes stale and lifeless if it only follows set rules. But the invisible lines of Figuration and Composition, when combined in an imaginative way, offer endless opportunities for the creative artist. So as long as the eyes of the artist remained fixed on a higher ideal, this rare combination may be achieved through the more timeless pursuit of 'seeing the higher'.

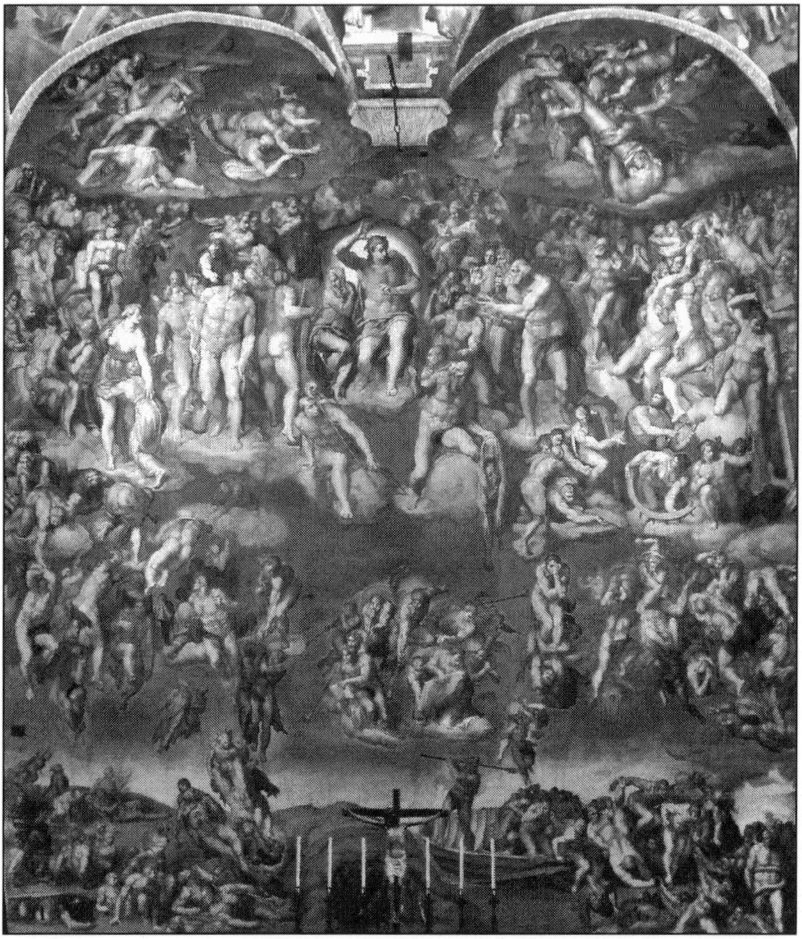

Fig. 18.1 - Michelangelo: *The Last Judgement* 1541

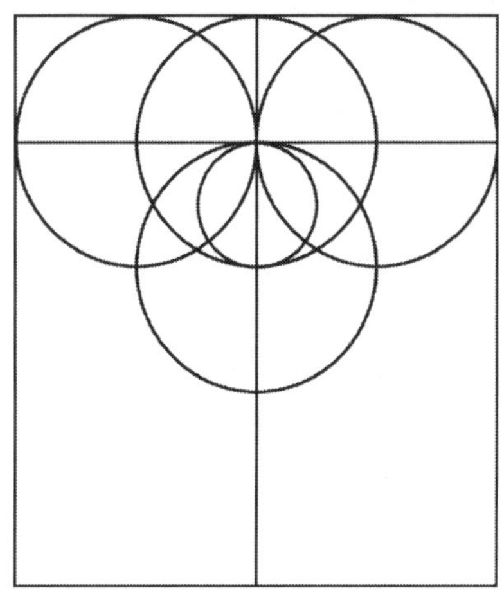

Fig. 18.2 - Armature, Stage 1: *Ad Circulum*

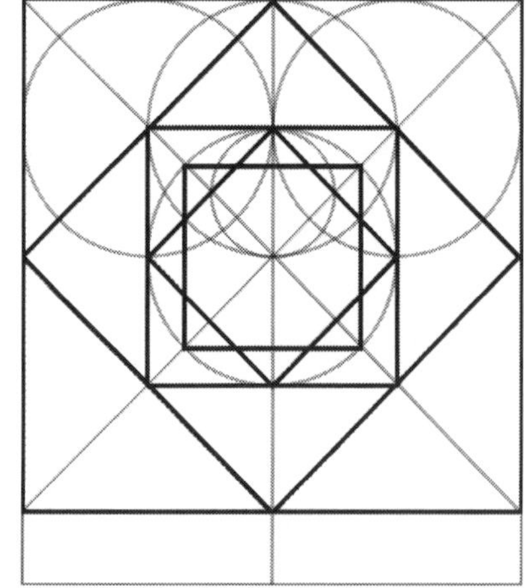

Fig. 18.3 - Armature, Stage 2: *Ad Quadratum*

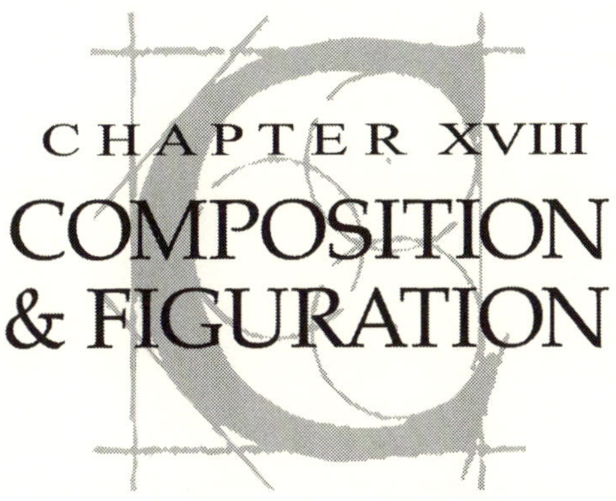

CHAPTER XVIII
COMPOSITION & FIGURATION

I. Composition of Michelangelo's Last Judgment

When Michelangelo began planning *The Last Judgment* (Fig. 18.1) around 1534, he had to decide how to divide up the west wall of the Sistine Chapel. The existing space already had squarish proportions with two round lunettes at the top. Beginning *ad circulum*, he completed the semi-circles of the lunettes, drawing two immense circles which touched at the vertical line of symmetry down the middle of the wall (fig. 18.2).

Like a double *vesica piscis*, he then drew the same size circle between them, its centre on the vertical line of symmetry and its circumference touching the centres of the lunette-circles. Below this, he drew another circle of the same size, like a vertical *vesica piscis*. He could have continued drawing an entire grid of circles, but these four sufficed for his foundation.

The overlap of the two circles in the vertical *vesica piscis* gave him the space for an *oculus* or 'eye' atop the mural, which was completed with a small circle where Christ and the Virgin would appear.

Proceeding *ad quadratum* (Fig. 18.3), Michelangelo then drew a □ square with its uppermost corners determined by the centre-points of the two lunette-circles. This square perfectly enclosed the circle in the middle. He had now 'squared the circle'.

Using the method of the *quadrature*, he inscribed a small □ square and ◇ turned square within the middle circle, creating an octagram. Outside the first □ square, he drew a large ◇ turned square, and outside it he drew a larger regular □ square – one which determined the limits of his fresco at the top and two sides. At the bottom, it determined the horizon line behind Charon's barque.

By drawing a large X from the corners of the outermost square, he was able to determine the centre of his pictorial space, (not including the area below the horizon line). The centre of this square heavenly space appeared just below Christ's foot.

The X and ◇ turned squares gave Michelangelo a series of 45° diagonals, of which the two most important were the two triangles, (Fig. 18.4) one with its apex above Christ's raised hand, and the other with its apex below his lowered hand.

Many of the figures followed the 45° inclination of these diagonals, particularly the risen souls in the lower left of the fresco. The risen cross in the upper left lunette, and the pillar of the flagellation in the upper right lunette, follow the 45° angles of the large ◇ turned square.

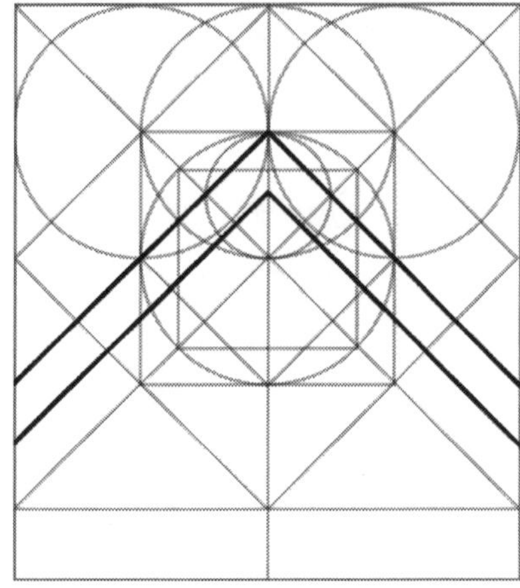

Fig. 18.4 - Armature, Stage 3: Triangles

The two squares touching the middle circle (one inside; the other outside) provided the vertical axes (or plumb lines) for John the Baptist's and Peter the Apostle's *contrapposto* movements, while the horizontal line formed by the top edge of the inside square provided their lines of sight to Christ.

As an architect and draughtsman, Michelangelo would have surely been familiar with the *quadrature* method, where each square and turned square doubles the area of pictorial space. Thus, if the innermost turned square has a value of 1, the surrounding squares and turned squares increase the fresco's area at a rate of 1:2:4:8.

Christ appears on the vertical line of symmetry (Fig. 18.5), which is to say, on the line which divides pictorial space at the 1:2 *diapason*. The square surrounding the middle circle has four corners which mark the 3:4 *diatessaron* points. And the square inscribed within the middle circle has four corners which mark the 2:3 *diapente* points. These are of great significance in Michelangelo's fresco, since the heads of John the Baptist and Peter the Apostle fall close to the upper two *diapente* points, while the angel of mercy (bending down to lift up two souls) and the condemned soul covering one eye fall close to the lower ones. In this way, a Pythagorean-Platonic harmony reigns over the entire disposition of figures, forming a cohesive and unified whole.

The armature offered here is my own invention, seen and sketched after meditating on the image. I do not present it as a *fait accompli*, but more of an *ébauche* – a sketch to orient the viewer through its harmonic divisions of space.

After meditating on Michelangelo's fresco for many hours on several occasions, I became convinced that this image holds the key to the relationship of Figuration to Composition. But the lines of armature, once drawn, must fall away into invisibility. Their role is to divide the whole into harmonic parts, yet the resulting lines, whether orthogonal or diagonal, should be treated lightly and creatively. The triangular shapes help to group figures into

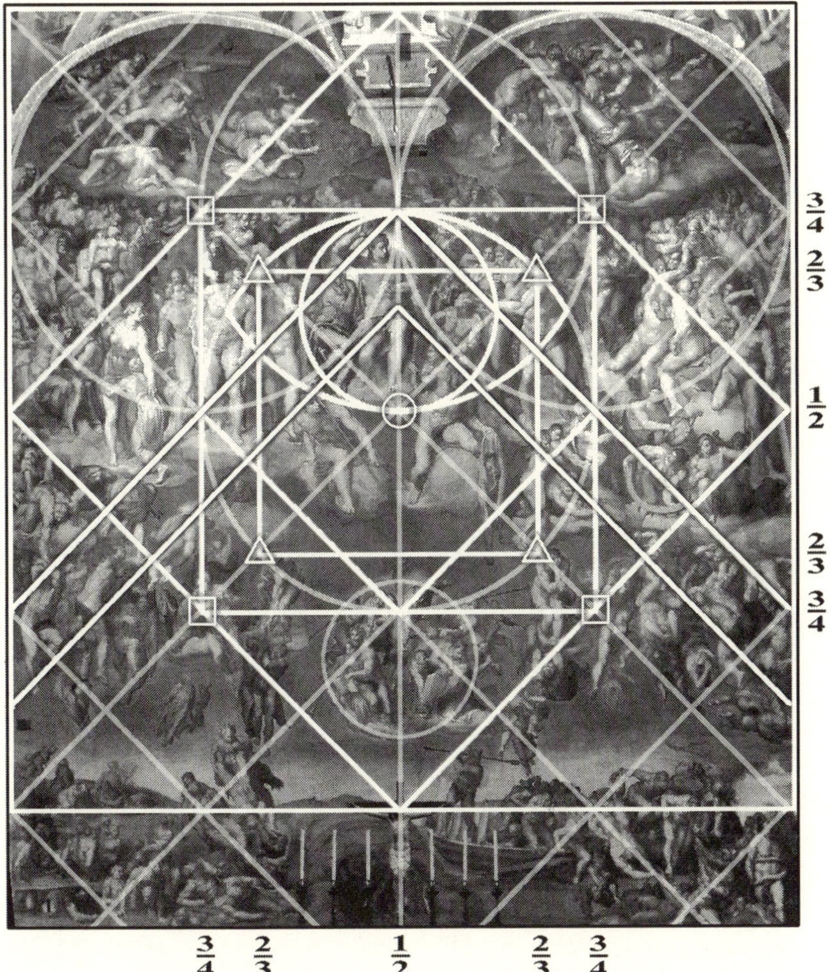

Fig. 18.5 - Michelangelo: *The Last Judgement* with Armature

masses, while the vertical axes provide plumb lines for the figures' energetic movement.

In Michelangelo's Revelation, the movement in Christ's raised and lowered hands flows through all the figures, at once attracting and repelling them like the opposing forces of an immense cyclone. The dynamic energy of his *contrapposto* movement works in swirling counterpoise to the straight lines of the armature. Like crystalline shapes, the squares and turned squares expand outward from the centre, while rings of resonant energy echo throughout the fresco in response to his momentous gesture. With ever-expanding vision, we behold the newly-risen souls, whose arcing torsos and tortuous limbs turn away or toward the blinding epiphany of the saviour.

In Gothic representations of the Last Judgement, such as the majestic figure sculpted over the main doorway of Notre Dame in Paris, Christ sits in judgement *with both hands* raised: *"He shows His wounds,"* said Vincent of Beauvais, *"to bear witness to the truth of the gospel and to prove that He was in truth sacrificed for us."*[1] And the Golden Legend adjoined: *"His scars show His mercy, for they recall His willing sacrifice, and they justify His anger, by reminding us that all men are not willing to profit by that sacrifice."*[2]

In the west facade of Notre Dame, (facing the setting sun), the Hieratic Christ (Fig. 18.6) sits in perfect stillness, frozen for all time in a gesture that raises both wounded hands, showing forth his mercy and anger equally to the saved and the damned – who rise and fall in accord with the scales of the Archangel Michael before him. The Humanist Christ (Fig. 18.7) of Michelangelo, by contrast, is frozen in mid-motion: forcefully raising up his right hand to reveal his mortal wound, while lowering his left hand in mercy and forgiveness.

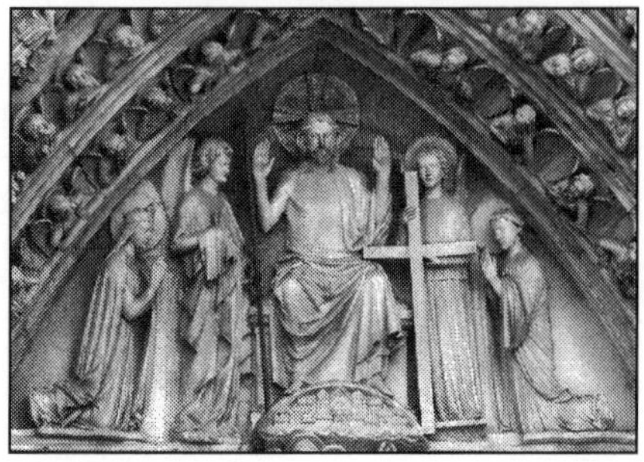
Fig. 18.6 - Notre Dame - *Last Judgement* c. 1240

These two gestures initiate an explosion of reactions throughout the swirling ranks of figures below. The saved, as if drawn by the lowered hand of healing and love, rise to the upper regions – some afloat on invisible winds; others borne by weightless angels. The damned, unable to bear the sign of sacrifice in his raised right hand, twist and turn away, repelled by strife and dragged by demons to Charon's awaiting craft, then herded like beasts to their fiery holocaust.

We are immediately reminded of that other masterpiece of the Renaissance: Leonardo's *Last Supper* (Fig. 24.12). Here too, Christ's sudden announcement that *"One of you will betray me,"* initiates a wave of fear and denial in the faces of the apostles, which breaks in both directions across the altar of their repast, rising and falling with each three-fold grouping of figures. In Michelangelo's masterpiece, the three hundred figures form an immense circle, rising and falling round Christ as they all react in different groupings to his momentous gesture.

Christ is raising his right hand in judgement – that is the whole message of this altarpiece, as manifest through the *contrapposto* movement. He is shifting his weight onto the forward leg and, rather than letting it lag behind, it is tensing, moving, rising upward, expressing a higher will: that the damned bear witness to the wound in Christ's hand. Through this act of the Son, the decree of the Father is made manifest: all of this is God's will.

For myself, the immense Eye of God – staring at us from the top of the armature – reveals Michelangelo's profoundly visionary nature. All of the figures in this fresco pour forth like watery tears, giving shape and form to the active, all-creative vision of the Divine Eye. Supreme sight, like rays of

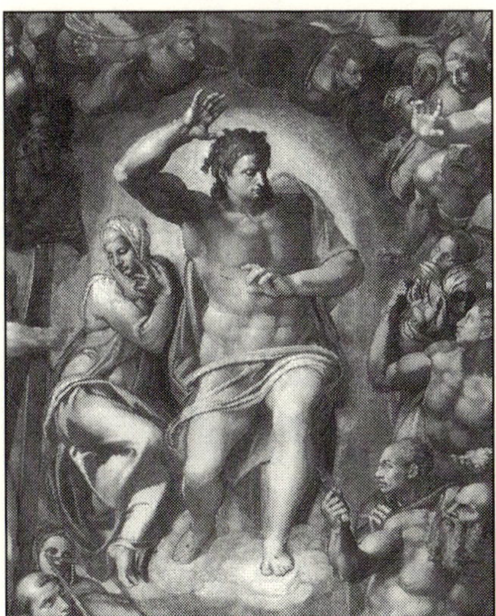

Fig. 18.7 - Michelangelo: Christ of *The Last Judgement* (detail)

light, projects outward in diagonal lines, creating the immense triangles of pictorial space. And the watery tears of life, assuming human shape, flow out and around these invisible shafts of light, some rising in remembrance, others falling in forgetfulness.

As I said previously, the moment I became aware of this stupendous vision, my heart stood still... That same eye would re-appear, time and again, in major works by Blake (*The Vision of the Last Judgment*) and Fuchs (*The Virgin of the Apocalypse*). Here within this armature was the triangle inscribed in the squared circle, and above it the Divine Eye that manifest the Hidden Sign of the Hieratic.

Lest we forget, Michelangelo consciously evoked the *Belvedere Torso* in his Christ, imagining the lost arms and legs, extending them beyond the fragmented remains, to fully express the contrary movements of judgement and forgiveness. At the centre of this Renaissance masterpiece, he enshrined a Classical Greek fragment. The figure of Christ is poised between movement and repose.

Meanwhile, the figures of St. Peter and John the Baptist use the armature's verticals as central axes for their *contrapposto* and *serpentinata* movements: each glance, gesture and stance moving like so many invisible lines of energy, coiling serpentwise to express their holy reverence. It is the serpentine dance of the curving line round the invisible straight line...

These fundamental principles, so potently manifest in Michelangelo's work, were to transcend his own epoch and re-appear – recognizable yet renewed – in the works of his successors. They are Sacred Codes, fairly unique to Western Art, exhibiting the dynamic relationship of Figuration to Composition. The Humanist figure, expressing all the agonies and ecstasies of the soul, works in perfect counterpoise to the symmetry and stasis of the Hieratic composition. We shall see these again in Blake, Moreau and all those Western artists aware of our Humanist inheritance and the Hieratic revival.

II. Composition of Blake's Last Judgment

When we meditate for some time on Blake's *Vision of the Last Judgement* (Fig. 12.3), we are suddenly struck by the recognition that *two eyes* reflect our worldly gaze. The Divine Eye above shines with the love and light of Christ, who gazes at us from its very centre, as the absolute incarnation of

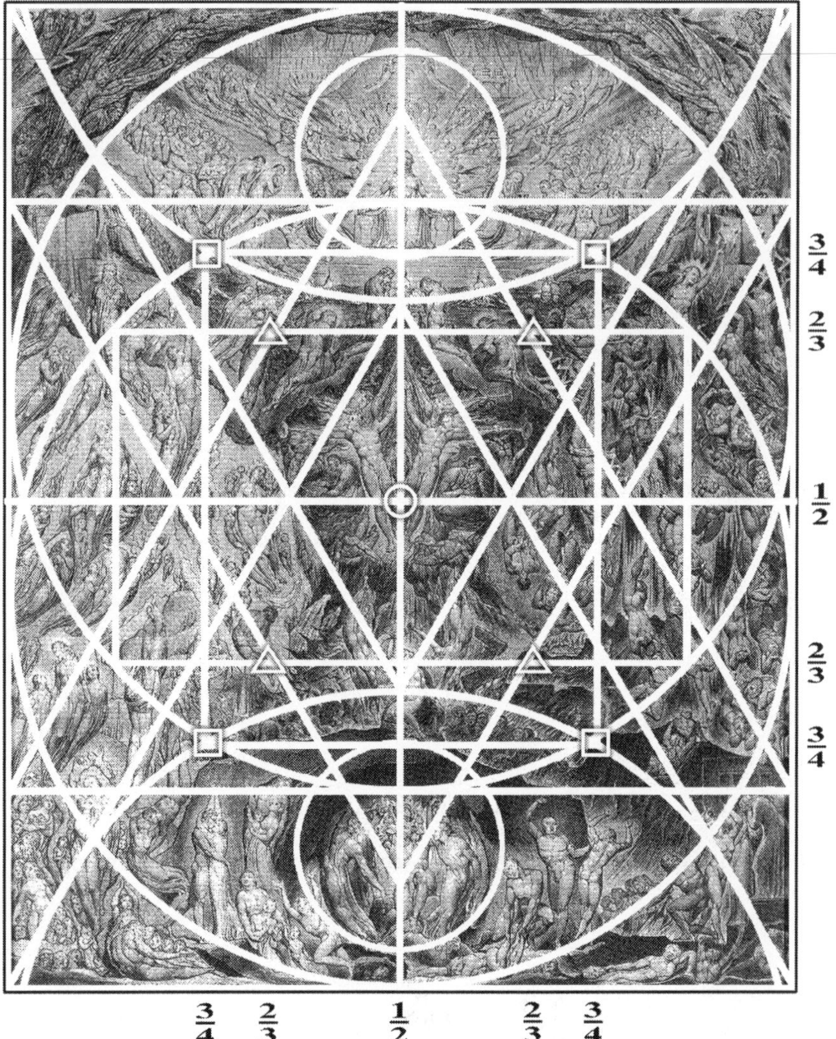

Fig. 18.8 - Blake: *A Vision of The Last Judgement* 1808 - with Armature

peace, clarity and stillness (Fig. 18.13). To form the upper and lower lids of this eye, Blake has lovingly rendered the surrounding angels with arms raised, to glorify him; with open mouths, to sing his divine praise; and with eye-encrusted wings, to reflect the One's all-inclusive gaze.

The lower eye, at first glance, is harder to detect, since its outer shape is broken and distorted by the caverns of Hell and its all-consuming flames. But, just as the Divine Eye above showers all the figures with rays of loving unity and joy, so does the Demonic Eye below inspire all the figures above it with hatred, strife and division. At its centre, the seven-headed Beast (Fig. 18.10) fractures demonic vision into seven sets of wandering eyes, like the seven wandering planets called Archons by the Gnostics, who darken our

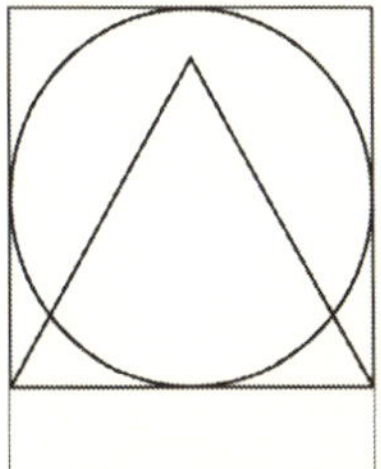 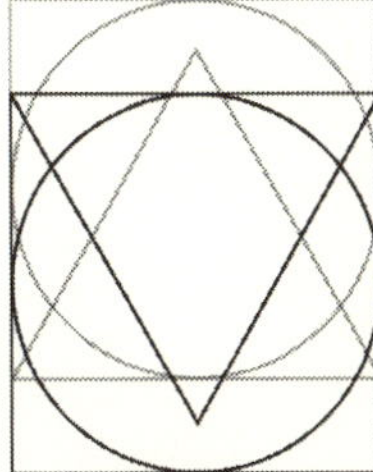 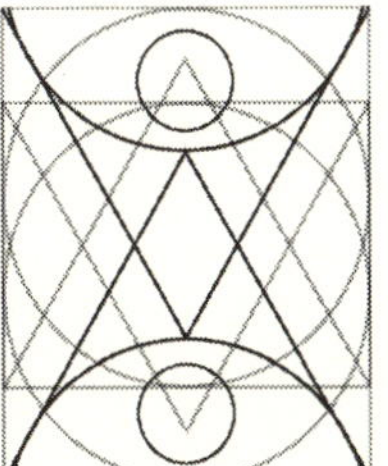 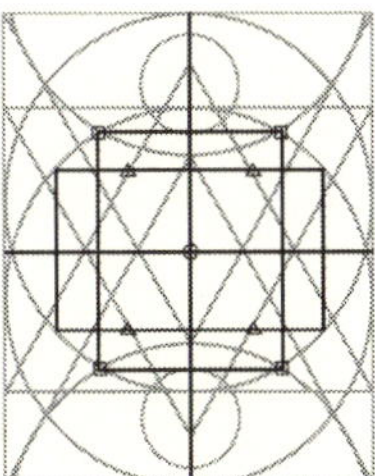

Fig. 18.9 - The Construction of Blake's Armature: Steps 1 - 4

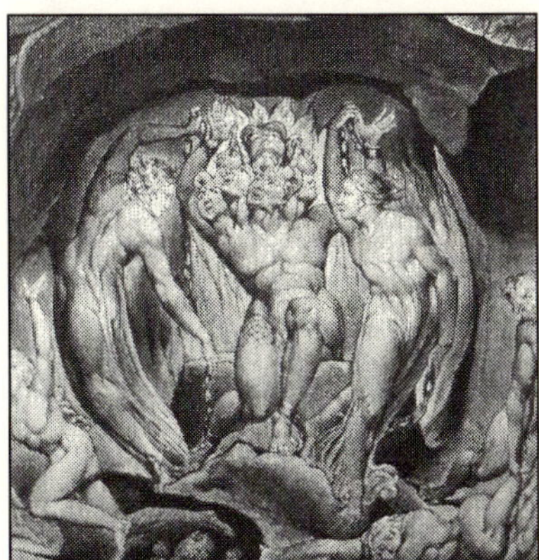

Fig. 18.10 - The Seven-Headed Beast

worldly gaze and distract it with delusion (Saturn), envy (Jupiter), wrath (Mars), and pride (the Sun), followed by lust (Venus), greed (Mercury) and, last of all, inconstancy (the Moon).

This gives a frightening new interpretation to Blake's words, already quoted above: *"The Last Judgment and its vision is seen by the eye of every one according to the situation he holds."*[3] The eye demonic and eye divine are not situated outside of history at the end of time, nor do they lie outside of us in some heavenly or hellish sphere.

Rather, it is we ourselves who open our eyes and submit our sight to one of these two opposing visions in our soul. Where we turn our gaze, how we act upon it – these reflect our 'situation in the world' and what vision of the Creation we ultimately choose to manifest. The Revelation and Last Judgment are transpiring every day, here and now, within our very soul.

To render this dual vision, Blake called upon the most basic shapes of the square, circle and triangle. Starting from an irregular rectangle (51 cm x 39.5 cm, roughly 4:5), he used the *rabattement* to draw an even square at the top, then inscribed an equilateral triangle and perfect circle in the square (Fig. 18.9 - Step 1) in an arrangement which I have previously described as the Trimorphic Matrix Subocularis. This gave him the basic armature for the upper portion of his composition.

Next (Step 2), he simply turned this arrangement upside-down, so the lower square could begin at the bottom and its inverted triangle manifest the dark gaze of demonic vision. As the third diagram shows (Step 3), he inscribed two more triangles, each with its base on the top and bottom of the rectangle. At their apices, he drew semi-circles which completed the eyes suggested by the existing circles. Within each eye he drew a smaller circle, which can clearly be seen in the light surrounding Christ and the cave surrounding the seven-headed Beast.

Last of all (Step 4), he added a series of orthogonals which served to harmonize his composition. First, the main + axes as the *diapason* halves, which create constant symmetry both laterally and vertically. Then, a horizontal rectangle (inscribed in the intersection of the two circles) which marks the △ *diapente* two-thirds. The Angels before the Book of the Saved and the Book of the Damned (Figs. 12.4 - 5) appear at the upper corners of this horizontal rectangle, while the Couples in Union or Conflict (Fig. 12.7) appear at its bottom corners – which is to say, two-thirds up and down the length of the entire composition. Finally, at the points where each large circle intersects with each half circle, a vertical rectangle was inscribed, marking the □ *diatessaron* quarters.

At the bottom right of the horizontal rectangle, the demon dragging a soul to the depths of Hell (Fig. 18.11) bears closer scrutiny. When we examine the figure in the absence of armature, his pose – awkward and orthogonal – strikes us as rather odd. Why is his back leg branching out horizontally in contrast to his upright torso? But, when the figure is seen in relationship to the armature, we suddenly understand how Blake has twisted the demon *to move energetically with the corner* of the rectangle. The lines of Composition – long since erased – have inspired the process of Figuration.

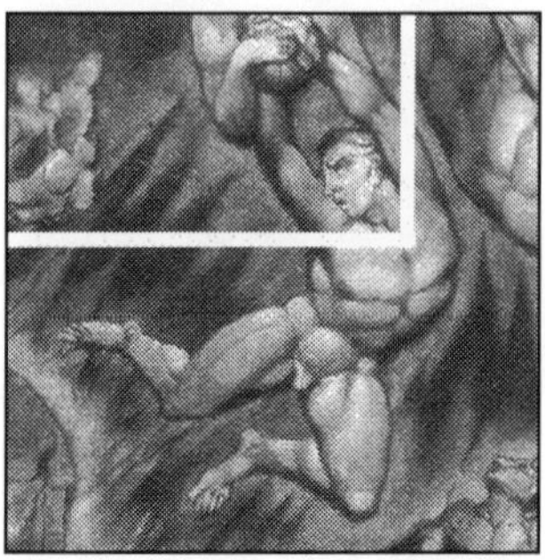

Fig. 18.11 - Lower Corner Demon

The same curious process is at work near the rectangle's upper right corner (Fig. 18.12). This figure does not twist around the corner of the armature. Rather, all the strange energy and motion of his flight seem to be inspired by the meeting of orthogonals: his legs horizontal, his upper torso vertical, as this fallen soul twists to gaze back at the forsaken Christ. Only Blake, it seems, could create a figure like this.

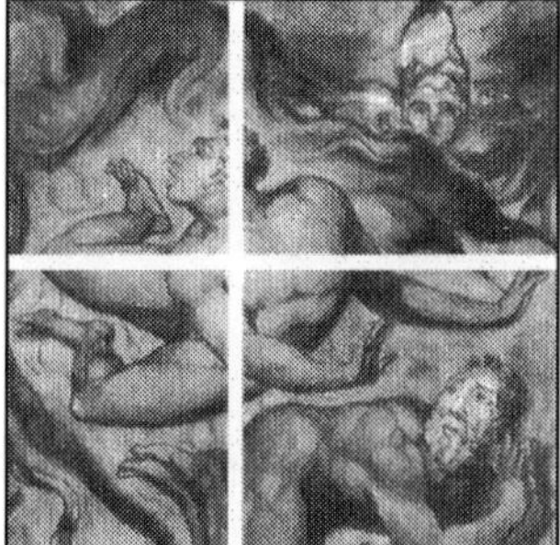

Fig. 18.12 - Upper Corner Figure

And yet, Blake's biographer Peter Akroyd was surely not wrong when he astutely observed how this composition revealed Blake's *"...reverence for medieval sacred art and his devotion to Michelangelo."*[4] These figures have been specifically designed to emphasize the greater lines of the composition. Like the ornamental figures in Honnecourt's Tower of Loan (Fig. 14.30) and the cherubs above Rubens' *Ildefenso Altarpiece* (Fig. 17.6), they become visible reminders of the invisible armature.

Thus, in the complex relationship of Composition to Figuration, sometimes it is the figure that will come to the fore, sometimes it is the armature. An experienced artist will allow space for both, and take delight in the creative interplay of the parts in the whole. The Greek word *harmonia*, lest we forget, is based on *harmozo* – "to fit things together." If something has harmony then all the pieces fit with balanced accord.

Through his use of the equilateral triangle in the circle and square, Blake's armature differs from Michelangelo in one crucial aspect: whereas Michelangelo's half-squares create 45° angles in *ad quadratum* space, in

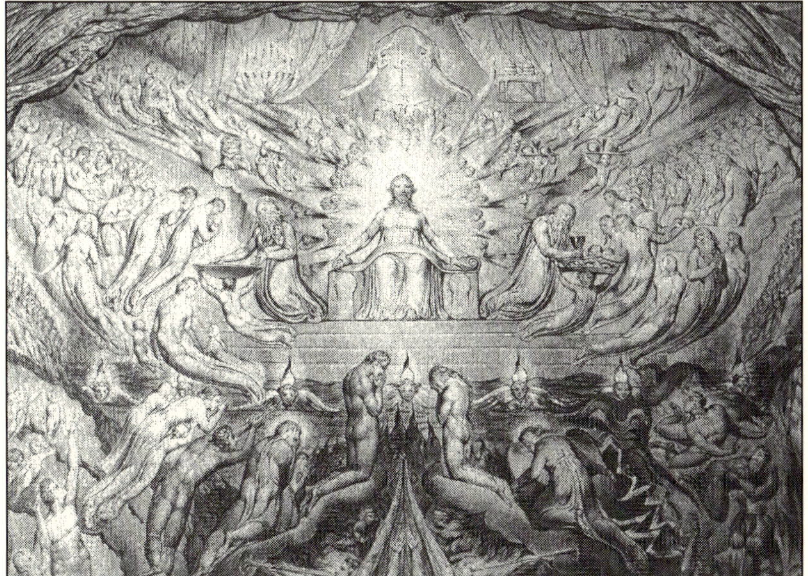

Fig. 18.13 - Blake *A Vision of The Last Judgement* Upper Portion

Blake's watercolour it is the 60° angles of the equilateral triangle that come to the fore, creating an *ad triangulum* measure of space. Vision streams outward from the Divine Eye along these diagonals, while the figures pour forth like tears from the corners of eye, assuming dynamically rounded shapes. From the demonic eye below, it is not a watery light but darkened tongues of flame that blaze upward, creating jagged shapes that cast zigzag shadows on the cavernous rock, thus illuminating the hell realms with their own dark light.

Delineated in a visionary manner entirely unique to Blake, the black flames with their zigzag shadows mount to the very throne of God where, like lightning streaks, they carve arcane letters onto the Book of the Damned. Behind this book, the Council of Twenty-four Elders recede into the distance, a series of profiles in frighteningly steep perspective. They gaze upon Christ who, contrary to Michelangelo's *contrapposto* figure, sits in perfect stillness – his Hieratic pose a stable and symmetric triangle, with hands like open compasses upon the scroll. This is not Christ the Judge, but the Word of God.

To his left and right, angels bear the sacraments of redemption: left, the bread and wine of the Eucharist, which transfigures death into new life through surrender and sacrifice; right, the bronze font of Baptism, filled with holy water that reflects the new image and name of the initiate, who is equally cleansed and born again by the water of life. Before the holy throne, our patriarchs and most ancient forebears bend their knee in prayer: Abraham with Isaac, Moses with his tablets of the Law, and the last who are first, Adam and Eve. With the sensibility of a poet, Blake renders each figure as a symbol and allegory, all to be read with increasing wonder and awareness. Here is the remembrance and recognition that awakens us through *gnosis*.

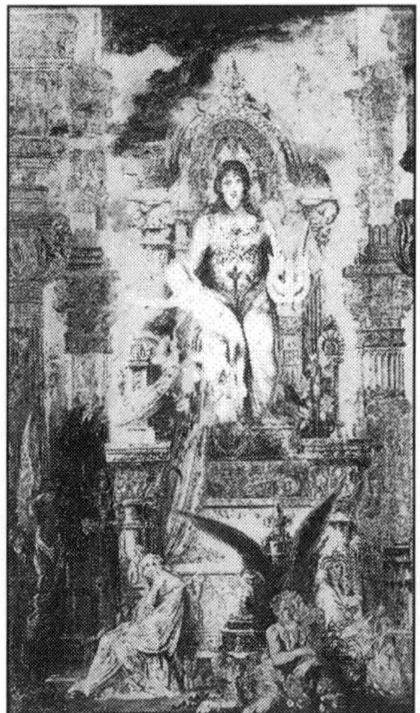

Stage B

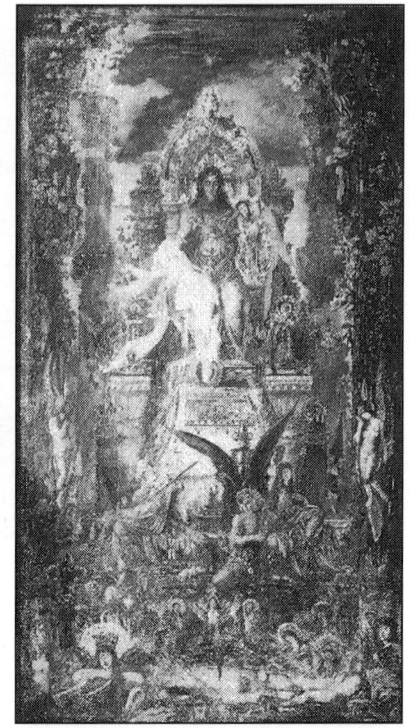

Stage C

Fig. 18.14 - Photo Documentation of Four Stages of Development: 1889 - 1895

Stage B (Inv.16036) - Stage C (Inv.16195)
Stage D (Inv.16038) - Stage E (Inv.16037)

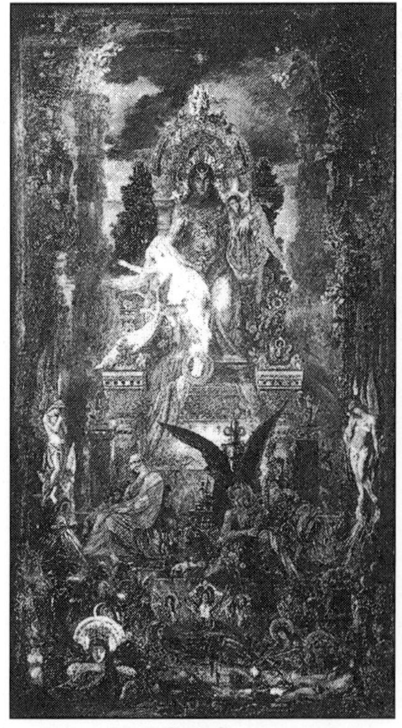

Stage D

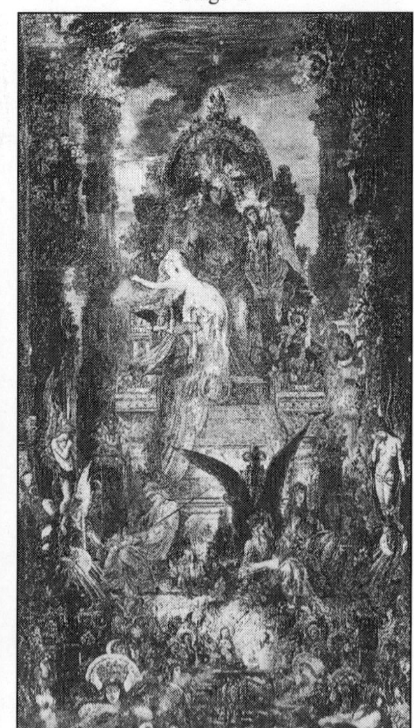

Stage E

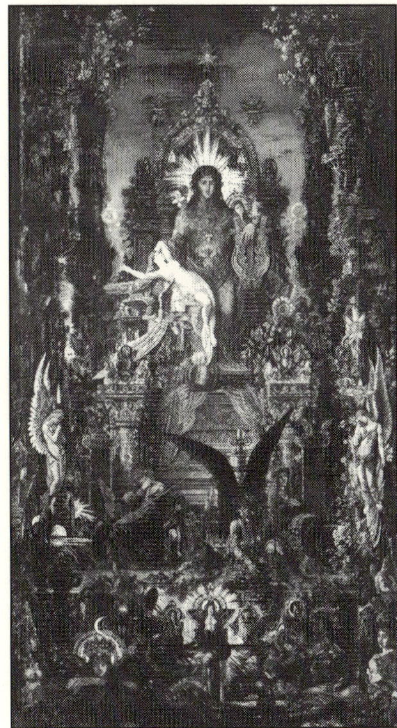

Fig. 18.15 - Moreau: *Jupiter & Semele* 1895

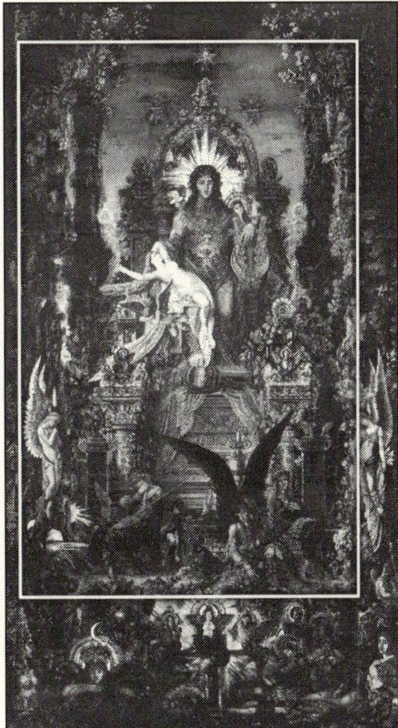

Fig. 18.16 - Enlargement

III. Composition of Moreau's Jupiter & Semele: The Original Smaller Version

During the six years that Gustave Moreau worked on *Jupiter and Semele* (Fig. 18.15), he enlarged the canvas (Fig. 18.16) to incorporate more figures on the bottom and outer edges. The alterations to the canvas can be clearly seen today, and are documented through a series of photographs taken at the time[5] (Fig. 18.14). By laying down *charpentes* over the original and expanded versions, we may discover how the artist coped with the alteration in composition, and indeed, why he made the enlargement in the first place.

Beginning with the original smaller version (Stage B), it is interesting to note that Moreau chose a ϕ rectangle as his starting point (Fig. 18.17 - over). As we have seen, this rectangle has the unique property of infinite self-replication: when a square is inscribed, a smaller ϕ rectangle results – a recursive process that can be repeated *ad infinitum*. Moreau has used the golden rectangle especially to develop the architecture, which he described as 'towering', 'colossal' and 'with neither foundation nor summit.'

The most important division occurs between the throne and its dais, which is decided by the large square inscribed (*rabattement*) in the framing ϕ rectangle. In the smaller ϕ rectangle that results below, a series of smaller rectangles to the lower left decide on the placement of the left emerald column as well as the width and height of its capital. The series of rectangles to the lower right decide on the placement of the Shiva lingam. The height of both

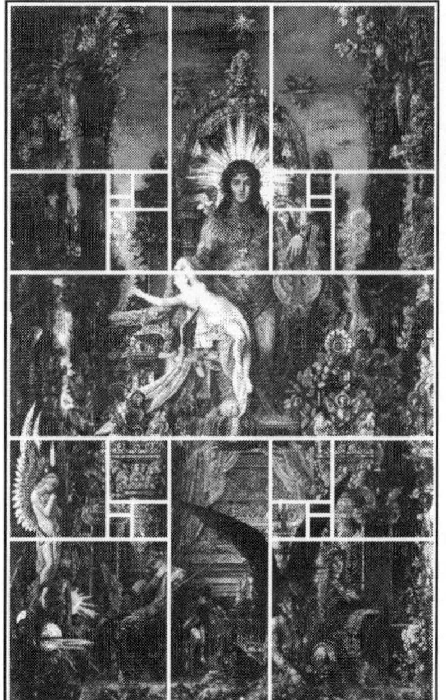

Fig. 18.17 - Recursive ϕ Rectangle Division

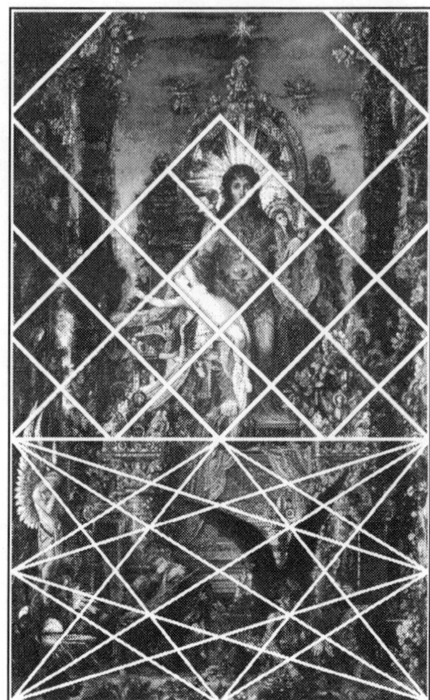

Fig. 18.18 - Armatures

female allegorical figures – Death to the left and Suffering to the right – is determined by the squares inscribed in golden rectangles.

The series of smaller rectangles on the above left help determine the width of Jupiter's throne and the placement of the columns, as do the smaller rectangles on the right. It makes sense for Moreau to use golden rectangles for the harmonious division of space *in architecture*, since architecture is comprised mostly of vertical and horizontal measures.

But the arrangement of the figures follows a different logic (Fig. 18.18). Now it is the diagonals that group the figures, flora and ornaments into recognizable patterns. The main square of the rectangle is divided in the Neo-Classical manner reminiscent of Girodet and much favoured by *Académie* painters. Because they are inscribed in perfect squares, the diagonals lean at 45°, evenly dividing the space into halves and quarters.

The most important diagonal, obviously, is the one which forms the diagonal axis \ of Semele's figure. But, Moreau could not ignore the painting's symmetrical axis which crosses Semele's diagonal axis at her hips. And so, her lithe figure deftly *arcs around* the meeting of these two lines, forming the delicate curve of her hips.

In counterpoint to the fluid line of Semele's figure is the arced drapery which shoots out to the lower left, following the cross-diagonal / (an excellent example of Complementary Form). Semele's gaze, as well, sharply follows another / diagonal straight into Jupiter's face – her all-decisive gaze that leads the soul to its ultimate liberation in the light or its return to the darkness deep below. Her hand, stretched out horizontally, indicates the falling stars of light on the left, which are souls falling back into Hecate's realm of darkness, death and distraction.

Semele's dynamic figure, with its curving *contrapposto*, brings a sharp note of life, movement, and Humanist expression into what is otherwise a perfectly static and Hieratic composition. Her strong declaration of feeling contrasts sharply with the languid repose (like 'somnambulists') of all the figures below. This effect is created by curving her figure around the armature, so two types of invisible line come into play – the invisible lines of Figuration (will and repose) coursing through her body, and the invisible lines of Composition (armature) relating that movement to the painting as a whole.

Meanwhile, Jupiter himself is a case in point, and his figure is worth examining more closely. He is wide awake, with an intense gaze that is almost indecipherable. With one hand he indicates the lyre – the importance of harmony – and with the other he upholds a lily and stylized sceptre.

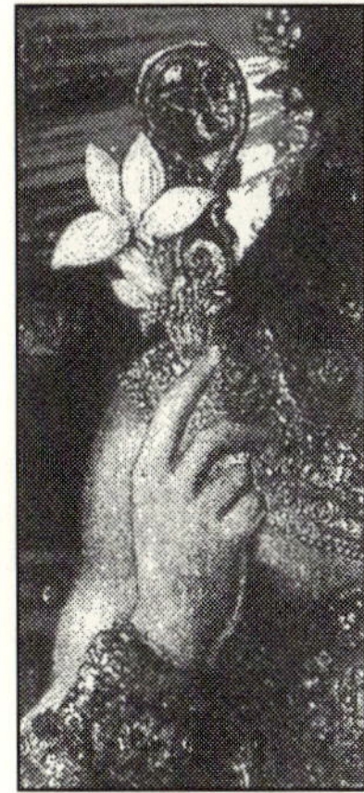
Fig. 18.19

If we focus in on the hand (Fig. 18.19), we can see how it acquires its hieratic quality, like the *mudra* of a Hindu deity. When surrounded by a rectangular form and other regular shapes, the hand acquires its own perfect harmony and symmetry. Although it is a human form with irregular curves and contours, Moreau has so shaped them as to become well-ordered and resonant with their surrounding perfect but invisible shapes.

Which brings us to another realization. Although the armature offered here shows the basic lines of composition – ever finer lines and armatures may be inserted into the larger pattern. For example, when we focus on the flowers above the right pillar (Fig. 18.20), we can see that the 45° diagonals offer the basic bounding shape, which may be subdivided into ever finer shapes, allowing for the harmonious grouping of the details.

In these flowers, there is a constant interplay between geometrical shapes (△ triangles, ◇ rhomboids) and the free development of vibrant living forms – like a steady rhythm that supports the lyrical development of a melody in music. All of Moreau's forms, whether vegetal, animal or human, have this dual quality of careful composition and lively expression.

The recursive quality of the ϕ rectangle reveals the fractal nature of reality, of the reflection of the whole in each part. In Moreau's *Jupiter and Semele,* the golden rectangles can be inscribed, one in the next, throughout the painting's space. Theoretically, the ratio of 1:1.6 could be used repeatedly throughout the painting to determine the size of one level of ornament to the next, beginning with the smallest figures and expanding at a constant rate, to link each level of ornament to the others and to the whole.

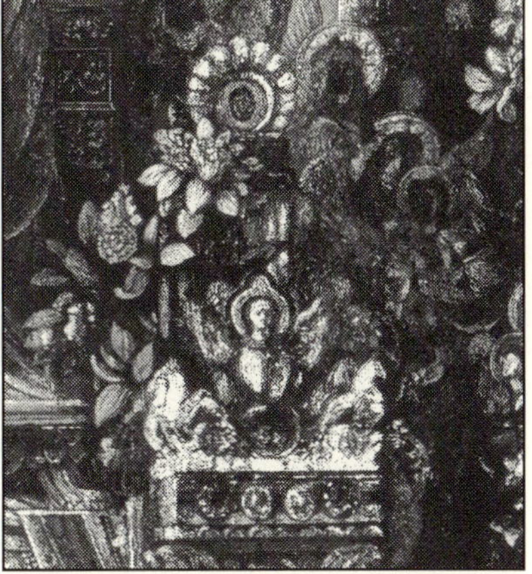
Fig. 18.20 - Flowers Above Right Pillar

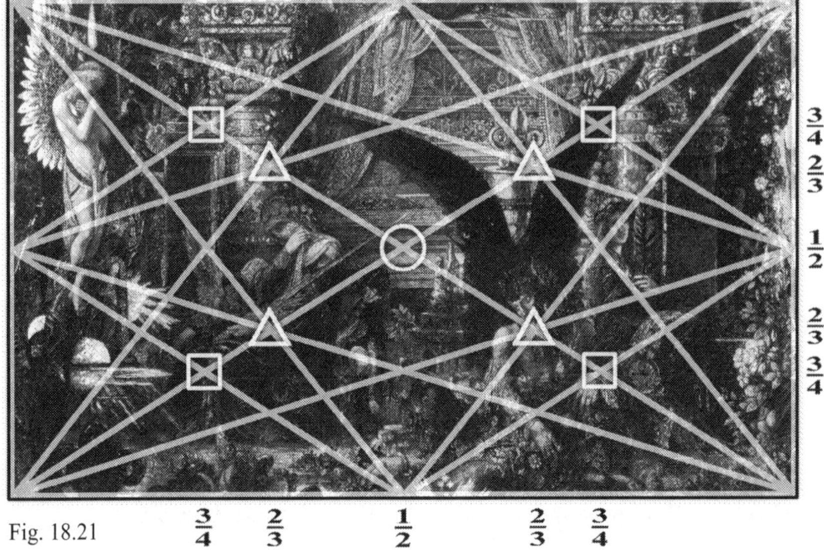

Fig. 18.21

IV. Composition of Moreau's Jupiter & Semele: The Original Smaller Version – Lower Section

In the smaller version (stage B), the golden rectangle below is best divided into diagonals through the Harmonic Armature (Fig. 18.21). Now, liberated from the confines of the square and its 45° diagonals, the artist is free to develop an entire composition within the harmonious space of the Golden Rectangle.

Given the choice of halves, thirds and quarters, Moreau has elected to place the most important figure – the reclining Pan – at the △ *diapente* two-thirds mark, both vertically and horizontally. Musically speaking, the figures in the square above strike their resonant notes at the *diapason* halves and *diatessaron* quarters. In harmonic contrast, the figures in the rectangle below strike a series of new notes at the △ *diapente* thirds.

One of the clearest signs, allegorically speaking, of Moreau's sensitivity to spatial and musical harmony appears in the lyre, perched in perfect counterpoise to Semele's writhing figure. In the iconography of Greek art, the lyre is the emblem of Apollo, father of the muses. Attributing the lyre to Jupiter is unheard of – except in Moreau's painting. But the artist had to include the lyre to stress how art and harmony are the true path to divine enlightenment. Where Raphael painted a diagram of the tetrachord to express the importance of harmony, Moreau has painted the lyre.

Returning to the lower rectangle, we can see how the △ *diapente* two-thirds are also emphasized through the placement of the Shiva lingam, left emerald pillar and the general positioning of Death, who fits perfectly into the scalene triangle with its apex on the upper left △ two-thirds mark. Her sword follows the exact angle of the ○ *diapason* main X diagonal, while one wing of Jupiter's eagle follows the upper diagonal of the △ *diapente* thirds (the other wing follows the 45° diagonals above – showing that, as Jupiter's mount, he is partly resonant with the upper world.)

Moreau's skillful interweaving of figures in the armature reveals his great sensitivity to the eternal question in art: of how to keep Composition and Figuration in constant harmonic balance. In the composition as a whole, the square in the upper portion gives a more symmetrical and Hieratic quality to the heavenly realm of Jupiter, while the rectangle below creates a more dynamic and Humanist quality in the earthly realm ruled over by Pan.

V. Composition of Moreau's Jupiter & Semele: The Final Larger Version

Sometime between the Winter of 1890 and the Spring of 1892, Moreau felt compelled to alter the proportions and think through everything anew. So, he had the canvas expanded to its final shape – a double square (Fig. 18.14 - Stage B→C). By establishing a centre-point in the coiled serpent just below Jupiter's foot, he re-measured the canvas in all directions to create the double square.

The first and most immediate result of this alteration was that now – finally – Jupiter appears along the symmetrical axis of the painting, giving the composition a stronger Hieratic emphasis. Indeed – everything appears more symmetrical: the four pillars of the heavens and their central throne, while the lone angel on the lower left now has a counterpart on the right.

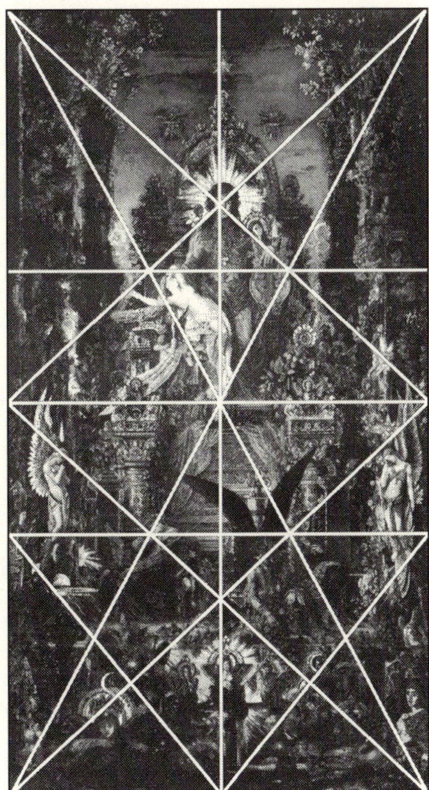

Fig. 18.22 - Final Version, with Armature

It is worth noting that these two angels, though they appear within the lower rectangle, bow their heads and move their feet *in accord with the 45° diagonals from the upper square.* Like Jupiter's eagle, they too are moved by the music and attuned to the spatial harmony of the higher plane. Moreau calls them 'two hierophants' who *"...flanking the throne with outspread wings, bow their heads with hallowed reverence before the god."*

With Jupiter's face now at the exact centre of the upper square, both vertically and horizontally, his figure acquires a more epic and monumental quality, as the summit of an immense pyramid (diagonals still at 45° angles) with its base the bottom of the throne. The double square makes the architecture appear more massive and colossal.

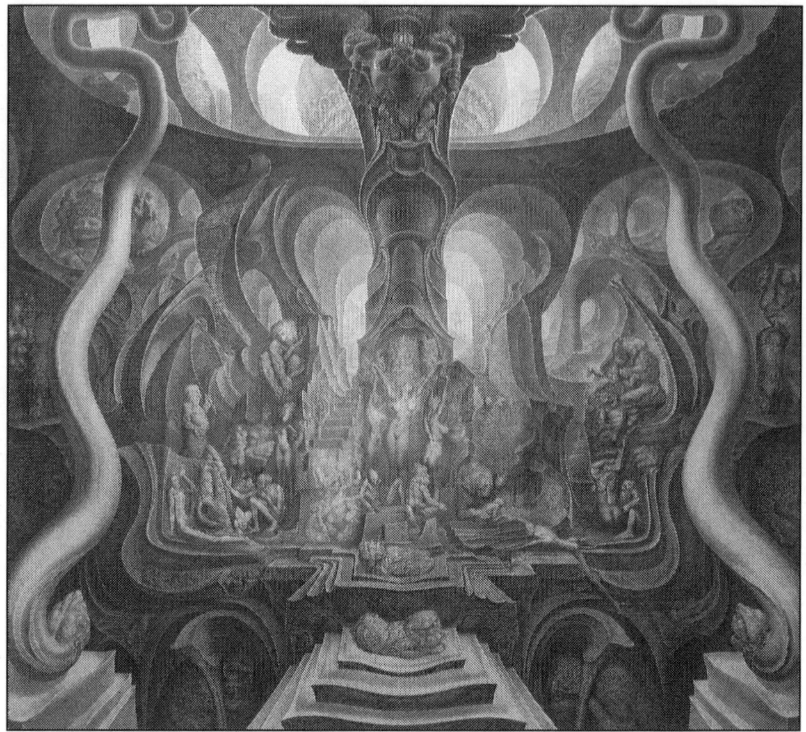

Fig. 18.23 - Ernst Fuchs: *Job and the Judgement of Paris* 1966

Moreau's choice of the double square is interesting. Throughout history, the double square has fascinated architects because it is the only rectangle that is both static (Alberti's 1:2 *diapason* rectangle) *and* dynamic (equivalent to a $\sqrt{5}$ rectangle). Plato described the main temple of Atlantis, dedicated to Poseidon, as 1:2 in proportion (*Critias* 116d). In Solomon's Temple, the *Hekhal* (House of the Holy) was 1:2 in proportion, leading to the 1:1 Holy of Holies in the innermost sanctum (*1 Kings* 6:17). And finally, the King's Chamber of the Great Pyramid at Giza, according to W. M. Flinders Petrie, was also 1:2 in proportion.[6]

The main reason for the enlargement, it seems, was to achieve a more symmetrical disposition of figures – and hence, a more Hieratic and monumental composition. But the extension below (an extra 40 cm.) also allowed the artist to explore new territory in the depths. It is no longer Pan that forms the dark complement to Jupiter, but Hecate – the Goddess of gateways, cross roads and the liminal zone between life and death. Along with the Moon on the left, these two powerful Goddesses now counterbalance the patriarchs Jupiter and Pan.

The addition of Hecate's realm to the painting brings an entirely new reading to the overall composition, since it is now clearly divided into three realms rather than two: the heavenly realm above, the middle realm of regeneration, and the dark underworld. We shall journey through these three realms next chapter, following the narrative movement through the painting.

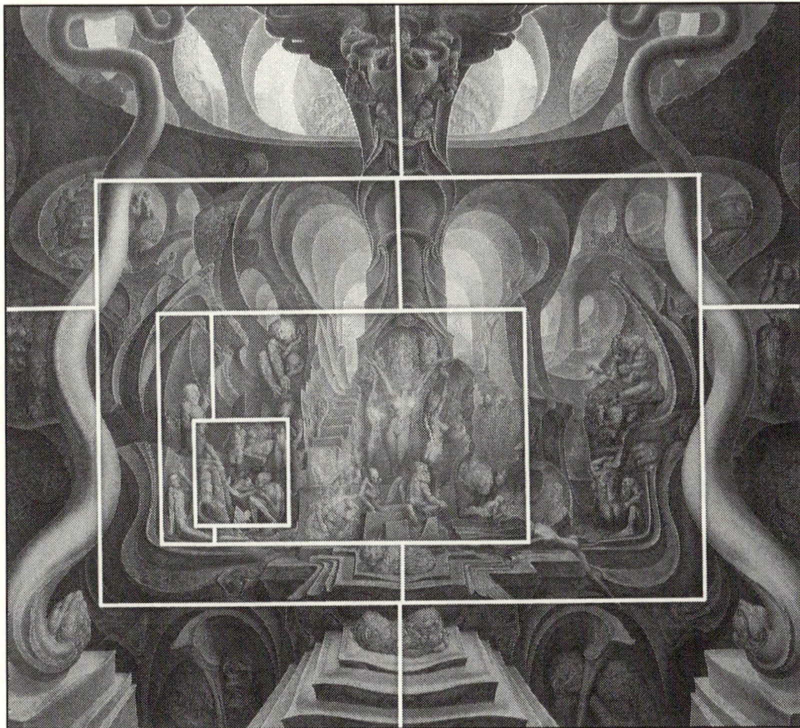

Fig. 18.24 - Ernst Fuchs: *Job and the Judgement of Paris* - Five Stages of Development

VI. Fuchs' Job & The Judgment of Paris

In 1965 Ernst Fuchs began *Job and The Judgment of Paris* (Fig. 18.23), a large grisaille (127 cm x 148 cm) now on exhibit in the Ernst Fuchs Museum in Vienna. Like Moreau's masterpiece, it underwent several enlargements before it reached its final form. Five distinct phases of development can be seen, as shown through the cut lines on the paper which are still distinctly visible, and enhanced in Fig. 18.24.

Fuchs began with a small drawing of *Job* (the crouching figure inside the small square on the lower left), a fact which he explained to me one evening at Castel Caramel. This may be called version 1 (v. 1). This small drawing was then incorporated into the rectangular composition of *The Judgement of Paris* marked ABDC in Fig. 18.25. This rectangle (54.5 cm x 40 cm) approximates the standard A2 size of art paper found throughout Europe. A2 art paper has the proportions of a √2 rectangle. We may call this √2 rectangle composition, version 2 (v. 2).

Despite the rectangular shape of the paper, Fuchs centered his composition in a square drawn toward the right side of the √2 rectangle. To approximate a square, he may have simply held corner B while flipping corner D up to E. A more precise technique transfers the length of BD to BE with the aid of a large compass (*rabattement*).

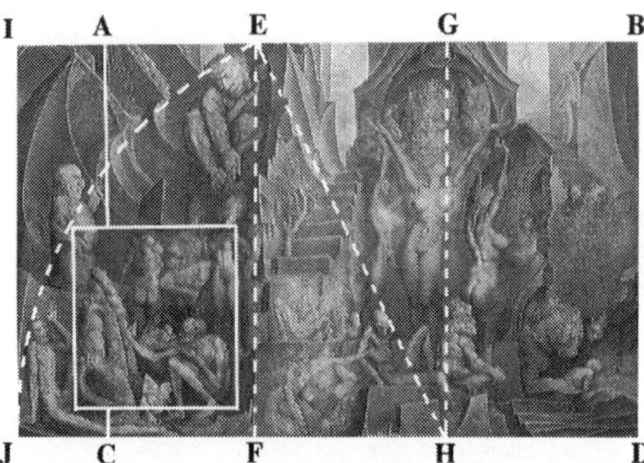

Fig. 18.25 - V. 2 as √2 Rectangle; V. 3 as ϕ Rectangle

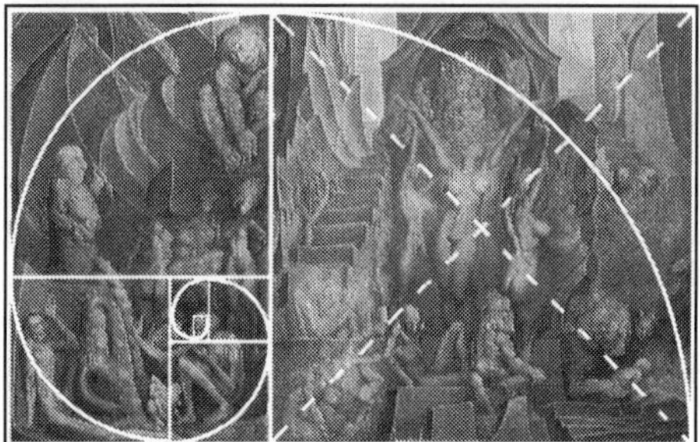
Fig. 18.26 - V. 3 as ϕ Rectangle

He quickly became dissatisfied, it seems, with the proportions of the √2 rectangle, and so decided on another shape. From point H, which lies at half the square's base, he arced the diagonal HE down to J and created a ϕ rectangle, adding on a strip of paper on the left, marked IACJ. This Golden Rectangle of IBDJ (64 cm x 40 cm) became the third version (v. 3).

The addition of this strip on the left explains, at least in part, why the figure in the bottom left corner (a portrait of his master, Albert Paris Gütersloh) has his leg bent in such an odd position. Once again, 'Geometry generates Form' as the figure is drawn, like a corner ornament, to fill the space left by this alteration.

With a Golden Rectangle as his frame, Fuchs was now free to explore its unique properties on the left side of his composition (Fig. 18.26). Since ϕ rectangles are recursive, they create logarithmic spirals that infinitely regress down to four possible points. Is it mere co-incidence that one of these spirals regresses to the figure of Job on the lower left? Indeed, the spiral seems to begin at his face, then curl round his body, while his extended hand points in the direction of the curve...

Having expanded the √2 rectangle into a ϕ rectangle, Fuchs decided to enlarge his composition once again (Fig. 18.27), creating a much larger and more spacious arrangement. The fourth version (v. 4) emphasizes architecture over figures, with more space for the development of his fluid forms.

I cannot say how he arrived at this larger rectangle (106 cm wide and 73 cm tall). But, he has made certain compositional constructions which can be clearly identified. If we use the technique of *rabattement* to fold the sides down to the base (CA→CF and DB→DE), we are struck by the fact that the stepped dais for the sphinx ends at these points (E and F).

Fuchs is using the same technique as Giotto in his fresco of *Saint Francis Before the Sultan* (Fig. 16.9). The result is to create two overlapping squares, AHFC and GBDE with the common space between them as the area for a new architectural construction – in Giotto, the Sultan's throne; in Fuchs, the sphinx's dais.

Once the paintings interior space has been defined by the two verticals (GE and HF), then the diagonals IG and HJ may be added, which incline

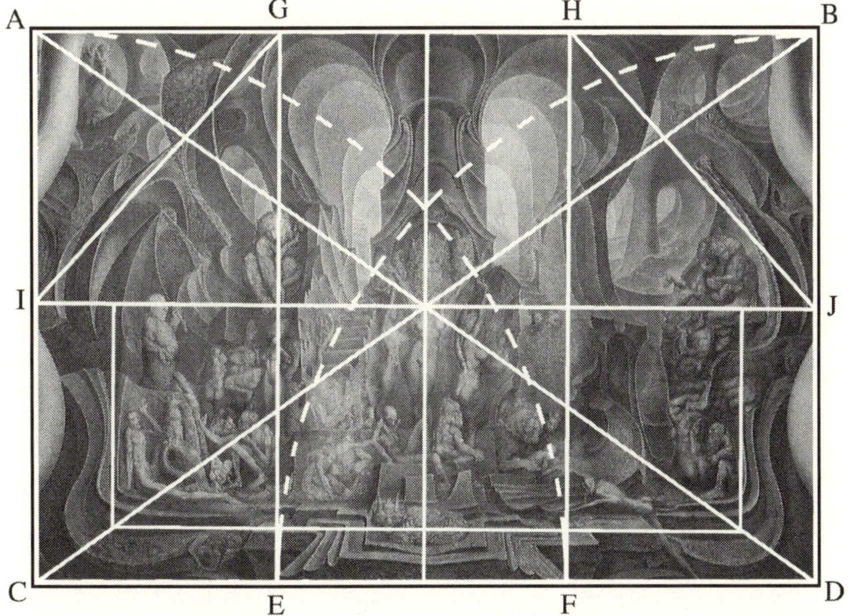

Fig. 18.27 - V. 4 with *Rabattement* of CA→CF and DB→DE to form dais at E and F.

at 45°. Through the addition of the main X diagonals and + orthogonals Fuchs is able to develop his famous 'dance' of curving lines around straight lines, which is a hallmark of the Hidden Prime of Styles. In the architecture we can see him develop *"the pure serpentine style, everything wound and dramatized,"*[7] as the curving lines *"...search flexibly, in a wave-like dance, for the straight line."*[8]

In the upper portion, the fluid architecture wraps around the diagonals (GI and HJ, AD and CB), while below, the architecture moves in waves around the L-shaped corner orthogonals.

If we return to Fig. 18.24, we can see that v. 4 has shifted the rectangle, which contains *The Judgment of Paris*, into the central position (just as Moreau had done with Jupiter in *Jupiter and Semele*). The small square with *Job* (the starting point of the drawing) is now relegated to a more minor place in the overall composition. On the right, Fuchs has quickly developed a conglomeration of figures to counterbalance the carefully conceived figures on the left. The sphinx below and the high luminous archways above fit perfectly into the new space provided by the larger rectangle.

Finally, in the completed composition, version 5 (v. 5 – Fig. 18.23) Fuchs has expanded the architectural space into another horizontal rectangle (1:1.15) which could easily be mistaken for a square. The space below (22 cm high) creates a new foreground for the base of the serpent columns and another sphinx on a stepped dais below. Above, the capital of the central column is adorned with a two-headed eagle (or *Doppeladler*) which, on closer inspection, actually has four if not five heads.

For Fuchs, this heraldic device was a mirror image of *"the symmetrically spread motive* [which] *had been registered with me as the 'symbol of the double eagle.' "*[9] Indeed, if v. 4 corrected the composition of v. 3 to create *lateral* symmetry, now v. 5 was correcting v. 4 to assure it of *vertical* symmetry. If diagonals are drawn from corner to corner of the new v. 5 rectangle, then the exact centre of the composition now lies *on the face* of the main figure, Paris, standing behind the three goddesses. Let us not forget that *symmetry*, like the serpentine style, is also a hallmark of the Hidden Prime of Styles.

As for the serpent columns which now appear on the sides, Fuchs saw them as epitomizing all he sought to achieve in architecture:

"Job and the Judgment of Paris has now found its final size," he wrote in his journal on March 5, 1966, *"It is the banned conquered snake which carries the vaulting of hades. It personifies the serpentine style in all clarity... The pushing, accelerating force moves up through the tense bending of the snake pillars, carrying the vault."*[10]

In this manner, Ernst Fuchs was able (like Moreau) to continuously expand his composition, while seeking out new harmonies and exploring the compositional possibilities of each new space. Compositions that began with dynamic rectangles from the Humanist tradition (the $\sqrt{2}$ and ϕ rectangles of v. 2 and v. 3) eventually gave way to a more Hieratic symmetry, both horizontally (v. 4) and vertically (v. 5). Nevertheless, the final composition, in its harmonic movement, strikes a careful balance between dynamism and symmetry – between the Humanist and Hieratic approaches to composition...

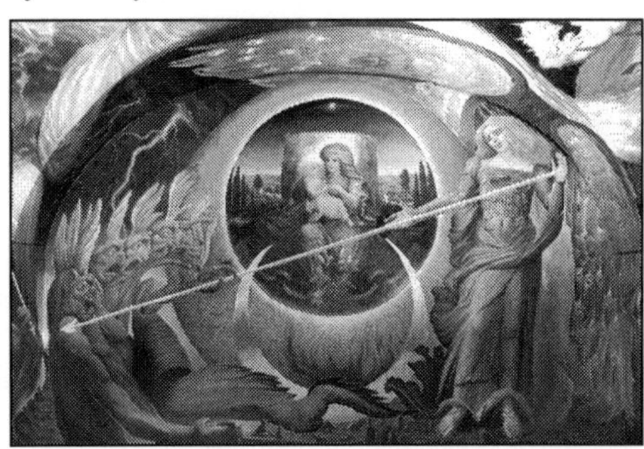

Fig. 18.28 - Ernst Fuchs: *The Virgin of the Apocalypse*
Apocalypse Chapel, Klagenfurt Austria

While working with Ernst Fuchs at his Apocalypse Chapel in Klagenfurt, I became keenly aware how his art was echoing the Sacred Codes of other great masters. The influence of Michelangelo and Blake on his figures was felt almost immediately. But, it was only after some time that I came to see a much deeper kinship between these artists, which existed in the timeless sphere of Visionary seeing.

That intuition was confirmed one profound evening in the summer of 2008, when I spent the entire night alone in the chapel, journeying through its Apocalypse. On my headphones was Fuchs' *Mystiche Gesänge*, where he chants a series of poems that he wrote specifically to accompany the paintings, creating one massive *Gesamtkunstwerk* on the Apocalypse: *"Es ist alles aufgeschrieben... jedes Zeichen! Jedes Wort!"* he enunciates time and again – It is All Written... Every Sign. Every Word.

When my gaze fell upon *The Virgin of the Apocalypse* (Fig. 18.28), tears fell upon my cheeks as I suddenly recognized the Eye of God framing the entire scene. This whole Revelation was streaming forth from the Eye of God, and Fuchs was following in the footsteps of his masters, rendering the Apocalypse as an immense outpouring of vision from the Divine Eye...

CHAPTER XIX
THE NARRATIVE MOVEMENT THROUGH COMPOSITION

I. The Musée Gustave Moreau: Secrets to the Eternal Craft of Painting

Over the past few years, Gustave Moreau has appeared to me several times in my dreams. One morning, just before waking, I dreamt that I was in the *Musée Gustave Moreau* in Paris, walking up the grand spiral staircase that leads to his large *Jupiter and Semele* painting, which appears majestically in the vestibule of the top floor.

To reach it, one must pass through an entryway created by two self-portraits – one on the right of the young Moreau and another on the left of the elder Moreau – contemplating each other across the aeons of time. Stepping past these two self-portraits and their interlocked gaze, I beheld Moreau's *Jupiter and Semele* like no painting I had ever seen before, whether in real life or in my dreams.

The painting, in its composition and design, seemed so perfect and harmonious that it radiated a field of divine energy. In a strange moment that made my heart stand still, I could somehow 'see' through the painting and the wall behind it to an Egyptian-styled tomb where the remains of Gustave Moreau, like an ancient Pharaoh or Mediaeval *gisant*, were reposing.

He had been sepulchered *just behind this painting*, and its perfect proportions – like the proportions of an ancient pyramid – were emanating a field of energy so harmonious and pure that *nothing within its confines would ever experience corruption or decay*. His corporeal remains, I felt, would be immaculately preserved for all time.

Since that dream, I have never been able to view his painting in quite the same way. It always seems to radiate a field of divine energy, harmoniously ordered and immaculate... Meanwhile, the work itself seems to harbour countless secrets to the eternal craft of painting.

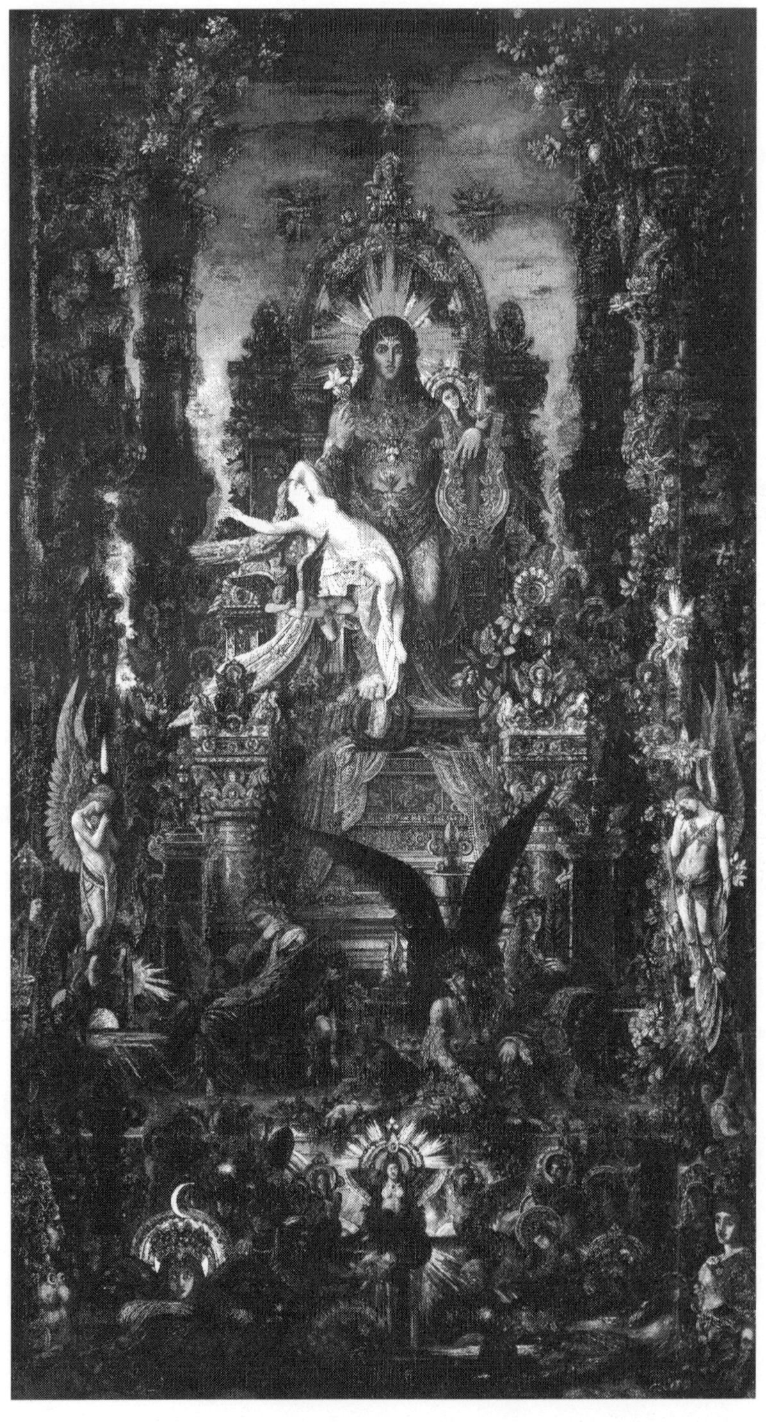

II. The Narrative Movement: Creating the Cosmology through Light & Darkness

In his last masterpiece, Moreau shows a profound understanding of how to guide the meditative eye through a work of art so as to construct a narrative. This narrative reading is allegorical, where each figure has a symbolic role to play in the unfolding of the *histoire* – including the soul-moving epiphany at the end. However, we would be misled into thinking that there is only *one* narrative unfolding. Rather, the artist gives our eye choices and presents options for where we may freely direct our gaze. As the eye quickly moves around the painting, it absorbs figures and constructs narratives, based on the most prominent and salient points created by the artist. I have detected three basic compositional readings, though many more, of course, are possible.

Since the Renaissance, artists have constructed pictorial space as so many *parallel planes* arranged through greater or lesser shades of contrasting light. At first glance, *the eye will naturally go to the place with the greatest contrast*. However, that strong opposition may be created in two possible ways – through *the strongest contrast of light and dark*, or through *the strongest vibration of saturated colours*. In Moreau's painting, the halo around Jupiter's head creates the strongest vibration of colour, while the central grouping of Jupiter and Semele creates the strongest contrast of tonality.

In the first reading, we begin with the strong white figure of Semele, who sharply contrasts with the mid-tones of Jupiter. From there, the eye is immediately drawn downward to the second sharpest contrast in the painting – Jupiter's black eagle against the mid-tones of the throne. Indeed, in the first version of Moreau's painting (before it was enlarged), the black eagle was certainly conceived as the key-element to counterbalance Semele in the composition. Appearing both vertically and horizontally opposite her, the graceful curve of its wings offers a dynamic counterpoint to her twisting figure. A photo of the painting in its early stages reveals that the eagle was the *only* figure at the bottom of the composition, with no sign of Pan whatsoever.

From above to below and from side to side, Semele and the eagle counter-balance one another, not only spatially, but also through their strong contrasts of light and darkness, *as her strong white light finds its equal and complement in the eagle's deep black shadow*. This dynamic correspondence of light-and-dark-extremes draws our eye in a quick circle around the painting.

This first reading establishes two major points of interest in the painting: an 'Above' with Jupiter and Semele, and a 'Below' with the eagle, and Pan residing in its shadow. If we take the time to read these figures allegorically, then we may come away with such simple contrasts as 'Jupiter's divine realm of light above' and 'Pan's earthen realm of generation below.' On the mythic level, we have established *a basic cosmology* – a stage for the unfolding of some eternal drama, which the narrative *histoire* will provide (I remind my reader at this point that the French word *histoire*, from the Italian *istoria*, is often translated as the *history*, but is better understood as the painting's *narrative*).

Fig. 19.1 Left - Gustave Moreau: *Jupiter and Semele* 1895

In the second reading of the composition, our eye begins once again with the sculptural group of Jupiter and Semele, and this time it traces a counter-clockwise movement through *the most luminous figures* – Semele, then the winged Hierophant on the left, then Hecate glowing below, and finally the winged Hierophant on the right, before returning once more to the place where we began. In all, four diagonal movements of the eye create a diamond shape in the composition, following the 45° angles of the diagonals in the armature.

Given the plethora of figures in the composition and the immensity of its theme, the artist has not yet given us sufficient information to piece together a narrative. Rather, he is still building his cosmos, still establishing the setting. Now, we realize that there is *a third realm*, lower than Pan's earthen realm of generation. This is Hecate's underworld, where all figures *glow from within* – illuminated by a different light, like Hecate's red blaze and the Moon's eerie blue penumbra. The two Hierophants, left and right, may be read at this point as threshold guardians, standing at the earthen realm of generation, mid-way between Olympus above and Erebus below.

It is only upon a third reading, where we focus down onto the smaller figures and their allegorical meaning, that the narrative emerges. We have already attempted such a reading at the start of this volume; but now we are more prepared to go into the details and read them closely, aided by the painting's Sacred Codes. (At this point, the close observer may wish to re-read Moreau's own text, cited in the first chapter).

Creating the Narrative Movement through the Composition

At the outset of the *histoire*, our eye naturally falls upon Semele and the graceful arc of her figure (Fig. 19.2). Through the codes of the Humanist Style, we feel – deep in our soul – how her lithe figure offers two lines of movement: a downward movement of 'repose', which descends from the eye (and upturned elbow) to her relaxed knee and upper foot; and an upward movement of 'the will', which pushes up from the lowermost foot to rise through her body and find release in her outstretched arm and powerful gaze.

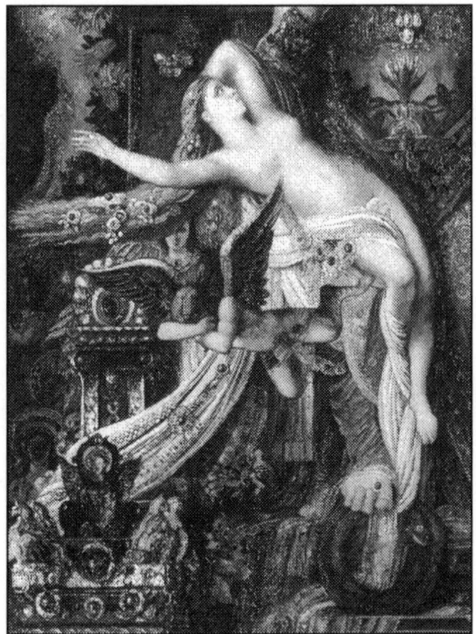

Fig. 19.2 - Semele

Through our analysis of the armature, we have seen that her graceful curving form 'dances' in a serpentine motion around a 45°

diagonal (drawn into the Golden Rectangle of the first version). But her outstretched arm follows a horizontal line while her legs follow a vertical line – both of these, orthogonals. Moreau's knowledge of the female nude and its history of poses was profound. Here, he has consciously fused two well-known poses: the Reclining Nude and the Standing Nude.

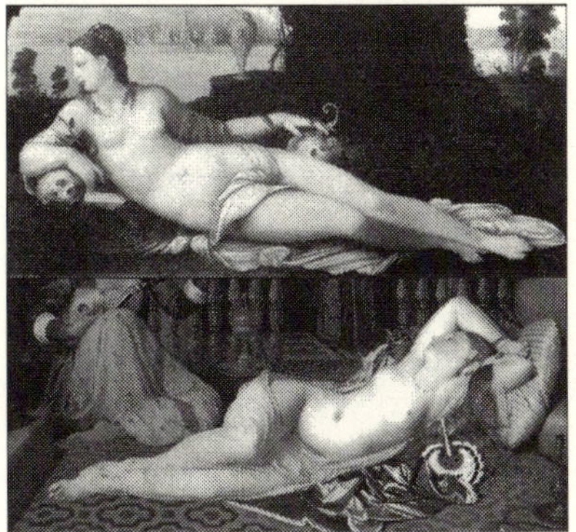

Fig. 19.3 - Reclining Nudes: Cousin & Ingres

The Reclining Nude (Fig. 19.3) is the image *par excellence* of the female figure *in repose*: an elbow tucked below or above the head, the legs resting with one knee upon the other – for example, Jean Cousin's *Eva Prima Pandora* of 1550 (top) or Ingres' *Odalisque with Slave* of 1839 (bottom), both French masterpieces inspired by *The Sleeping Ariadne* (Fig. 9.12) of the Classical Canon. Like a hieroglyph, the Reclining Nude curves the female form *around the horizontal line* – which may be 'L' shaped, an arc, or simply a flat line.

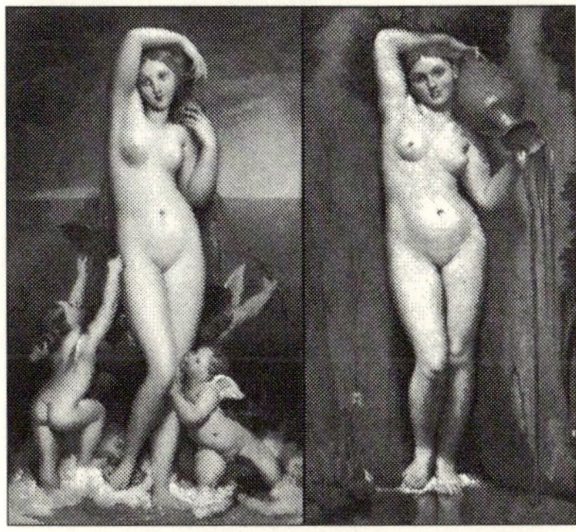

Fig. 19.4 - Standing Nudes: Ingres

Meanwhile the Standing Nude (Fig. 19.4), through its attitude and gestures, expresses *an act of the will*. Like a different hieroglyph, it curves the female figure *around a vertical line* – for example, Ingres' *Venus Anadyomene* of 1848 (top) or *The Source* of 1846 (below), both of which are based on the *Venus de Milo* (Fig. 9.3) of the Classical Canon. Moreau has quite consciously *fused* these two poses to create Semele's unique *diagonal* figure, which echoes these historical precedents.

His intimate knowledge of Humanist poses allows him to create a figure symbolic *of the viewer's soul*. This is borne out by the symbol of the blue butterfly just above Semele's head. The Greek word *psyche* means both 'soul' and 'butterfly', and the human soul has been symbolized by this winged creature since Late Antiquity. But, more than that, the butterfly undergoes a metamorphosis, symbolic of *the soul's death and rebirth*, which the Greeks referred to by the term *metempsychosis* – meaning *the soul's transmigration* from one life to the next. This, as we shall see, is the main theme of Moreau's painting.

III. Moreau's Vision of Death and Rebirth

If our eye descends Semele's figure to her foot and the drapery just beneath it, it eventually lands upon the curling green serpent which Jupiter is treading upon (Fig. 19.5). This serpent appears *at the very centre* of the larger composition (at the crossing of the X diagonals), dividing the 1:2 rectangle into upper and lower squares – the upper realm of Jupiter's divine light and the lower realms of Pan's earthen darkness and Hecate's glowing underworld. The serpent's curling movement is symbolic of the cyclic journey from one realm to the other – of the soul's passage from heavenly existence to earthly incarnation and possible incarceration in the underworld, before rising once more to its original heavenly abode.

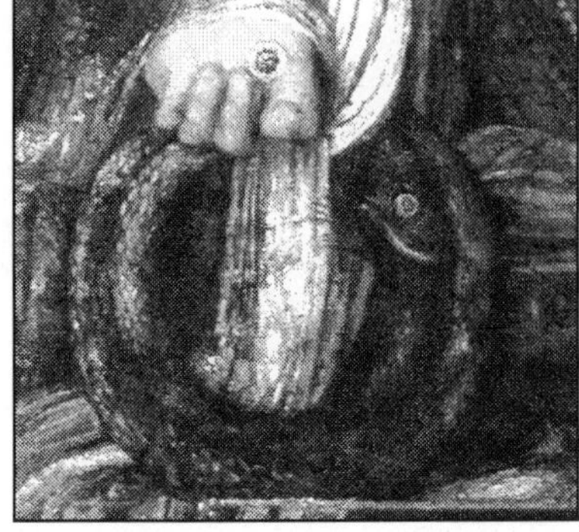

Fig. 19.5 - The Green Serpent

All of the energy and movement in Jupiter's and Semele's figures *originates at this point*, which anchors their feet, allowing for the explosion of 'the will' to course upward through their Humanist and Hieratic forms. Semele's movement, as we have just noted, explodes in her gesture and her gaze – both of them teeming with passion and expression.

As we follow her gaze into Jupiter's eyes, the key moment in the *histoire* is experienced: not yet prepared to see and visually embrace Jupiter's divine overflowing, Semele becomes 'thunderstruck' with awe and fear. Mortally afraid, she turns away. In Moreau's words, she *"...dies and yet regenerates – purged in the holy fire and purified by the sacred overflowing – and with her, a cloven-hoofed angel, the Spirit of Earthly Love."*

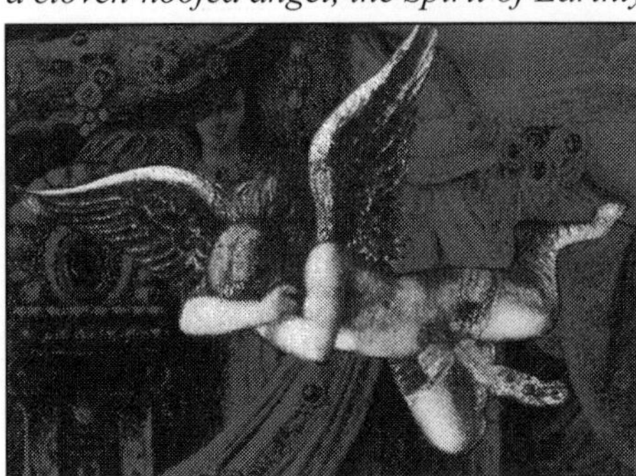

Fig. 19.6 - The Cloven-Hoofed Angel

Just below Semele – his dark wing contrasting sharply with her light drapery – appears a small winged figure: the 'cloven-hoofed angel' who falls, blinded, from the sight of Jupiter's glory. The multiple sketches in the *Musée Gustave Moreau* attest to the fact that the artist laboured hard over this figure for many hours, if not days. In his first sketches, the cherub appears as a fallen angel, but in later sketches Moreau added hooves, making it *an angel transforming into a satyr* as it falls to the middle realm of generation.

Through these details, we are led to understand that, in the eternal cycle of *metempsychosis*, the fallen angels become those spirits that animate all of Nature, such as the *"dryads, satyrs and fauns,"* mentioned by the artist in his description of the painting. As *"denizens of the water and woods... all*

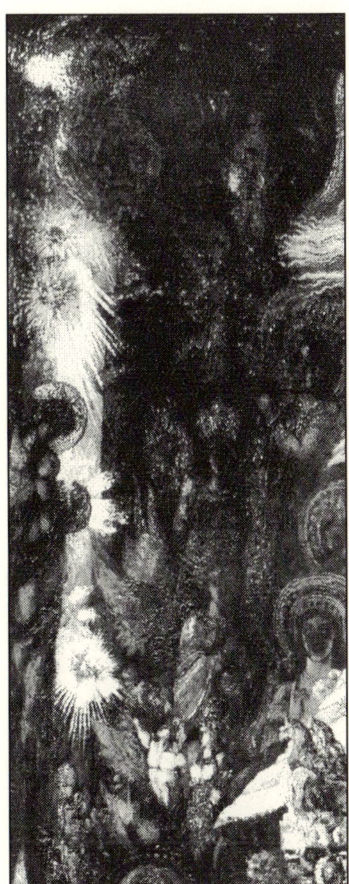

Fig. 19.7 - Repelling Angel

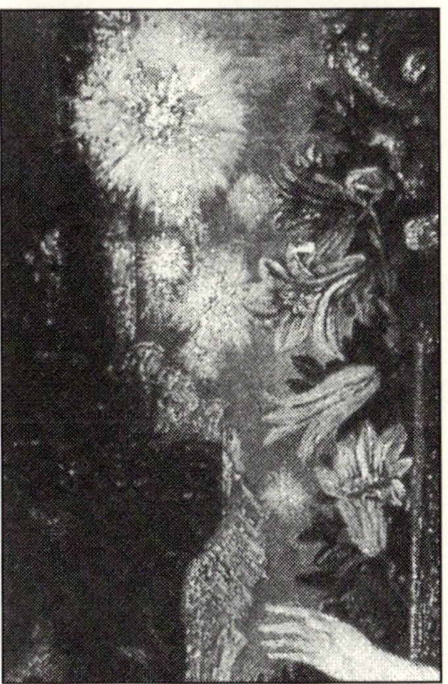

Fig. 19.8 - Falling Stars of Light

are overcome by ecstasy, love and joy." This fallen angel, now a satyr like Pan, symbolizes *"the Spirit of Earthly Love,"* and descends, like the vegetation around the left pillar, into the realm of generation.

Although the fallen angel is shielding his eyes, our glance follows this downward diagonal movement. It follows *the arc of brightly illuminated drapery*, which curves around the 45° diagonal of the first armature (a Golden Rectangle). It also makes a dramatic leap through perspectival planes, moving from Semele in the middle ground to the extreme foreground. Our eye naturally follows this dramatic curve to the Hierophant on the lower left, with his head bowed. But, if we take the time, through a prolonged gaze and meditation on the painting, to examine some of the finer details, we are soon struck with awe and wonder...

In fact, the powerful arc of drapery leads our eye to *a small winged figure*, which is granted a high degree of illumination compared to the darker figures around it (Fig. 19.7 - bottom). With an outstretched hand, this small angel is barring entrance to those falling souls who wish to enter the middle realm of generation. Just as two sphinxes below, at the extreme bottom right and left of the painting, *"stand as guardians to this herd and their heavenly ascent,"* so here does another small sphinx, behind the angelic guardian, repel any soul who wishes to enter the realm of generation, if it is not sufficiently prepared.

Where do these falling souls come from? When our eye follows Semele's outstretched arm, we are amazed to discover *stars of light* in the heavens, just above her hand (Fig. 19.8). I have previously described these luminous sparks as 'souls falling back into Hecate's realm of darkness, death and distraction.' These light-beings re-appear, to the left of Semele's hand, as small sparks of light *becoming entrapped in matter* (Fig. 19.7). They become embedded in the transparent

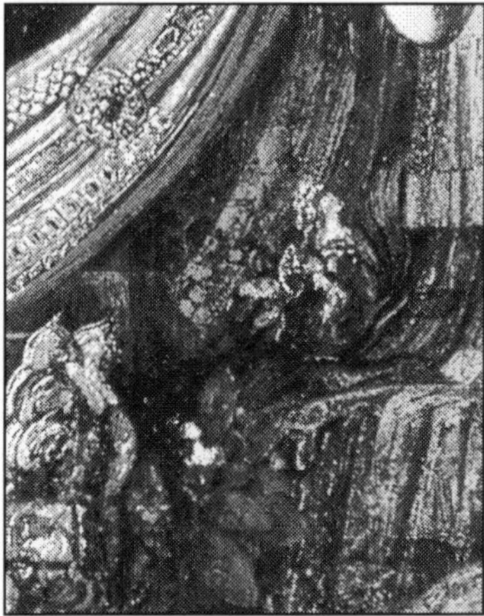

Fig. 19.9 - Small Beings in Ornament

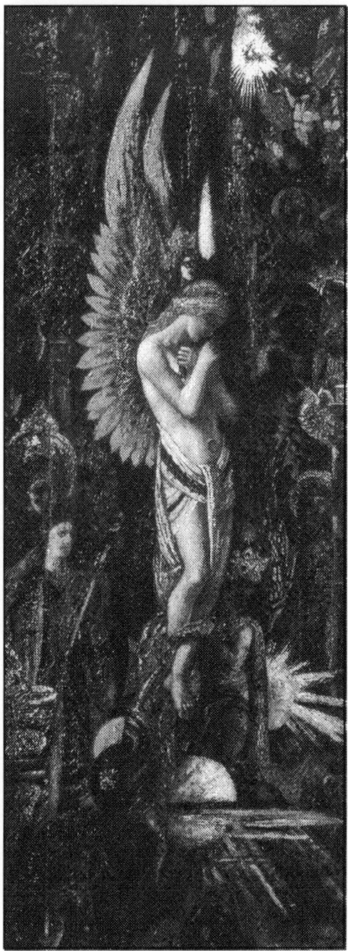

Fig. 19.10 - Left Hierophant

jewel-like figures that adorn the columns – providing all the jewels with their *inner glow*. A close examination of the ornaments in this celestial architecture reveals that all the enhaloed beings are 'glowing from within' – particularly the large angel to the left, barely visible, which glows a deep transparent red.

When I first discovered these elements, I thought I surely must be dreaming. But the ornamental figures 'glowing from within' (small as they are and difficult to see...) constitute important figures in the painting's deeper reading. For example, if we allow our eye to wander into the space just below the fallen angel-satyr and the arc of drapery, we discover *more small beings* (Fig. 19.9). Ostensibly, they belong to the ornamental figures of the bejewelled column to the left. But they are emerging from – or merging into – those bejewelled ornaments. We behold small human figures merging with the orange-and-red ruby flowers, or interlaced in the creeping green vegetation that (as I said before) descends the left column into the realm of generation.

All the small figures close to Semele and the angel-satyr are, in fact, luminous sparks from the Divine god-head that have – like Semele herself – turned away from the divine visage and fallen into the world of matter, multiplicity and becoming. They fall into the ornaments around his throne, as translucent angelic beings. In Moreau's words, *"The eternally Sacred expands into the all."* Some enter Pan's realm of generation; others descend further, into Hecate's darkness below.

This downward movement brings our eye, eventually, to the Hierophant on the left (Fig. 19.10). As noted previously, Moreau took great pains to wrap this figure around the armature with a *contrapposto* movement that *"bows his head"* to the higher realm. Meanwhile, his wings *glow from within* – a deep red colour – relating him to the ornamental angels in the columns. A flame rises above his head (in contrast to the star above the head of the Hierophant opposite) and a green serpent wraps itself around his feet – the serpent of death and regeneration. He bows his head with the knowledge that he – and all who pass through the gateway he guards – enter the cycle of *metempsychosis*. Beneath him, the glowing planetary spheres and small angel gazing into darkened shadows draw our eye deeper into the depths. Like sparks of light descending into darkness, we fall through the seven heavenly spheres, absorbing their qualities during our descent.

Pan's Middle Realm of Generation

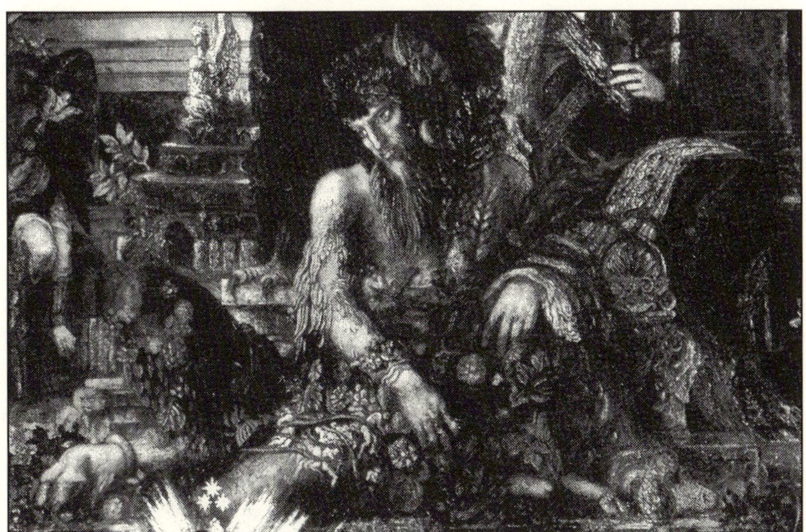

Fig. 19.11 - Reclining Pan with Beheaded Ram and Vegetation Springing from his Loins

Following the Wisdom Traditions of the Orphics, Gnostics and Neo-Platonists, Moreau has portrayed our innermost *psyché* as a spark of light trapped in the cavernous darkness of the lower world. From Plato's upper world of pure Being, with ideal forms and archetypes, they have descended into the realm of nature, matter and Becoming. Although, from a certain point of view, the middle realm of generation may be seen as a place of "*Earthly Love*" where vegetation flourishes and satyrs frolic with "*ecstasy, love and joy,*" Moreau's allegorical figures suggest otherwise.

If we now follow the gaze of the left Hierophant – a gaze which clearly descends the 45° angle of the main diagonal in the bottom square – we soon discover the allegorical figures of Death on the left and Suffering to the right, with Pan in the middle, shaded by Jupiter's eagle (Fig. 19.12). The cloven-hoofed Pan (Fig. 19.11), who is usually portrayed as a lusty satyr dancing with nymphs while playing on his pipes, here appears sad and defeated: *"a symbol of our earthly predicament."* In a *contrapposto* reclining pose, he *"lowers his brow in sad remembrance of our enslaved and exiled state."* The body, as much as it may offer us the passions and pleasures of the flesh, also encloses our soul in darkness, death and suffering, diverting its attention from the Good, Beautiful and True.

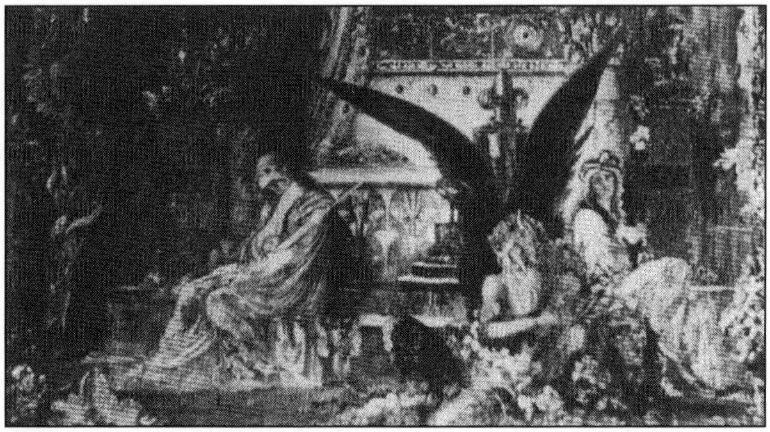

Fig. 19.12 - Early Version of *Jupiter and Semele* with Pan's Arm at a Different Angle

A closer examination reveals that Pan's arm and upraised knee – following the 45° angle of the armature – create a *contrapposto* motion away from his defeated gaze. As the photos of the painting's progress show (Figs. 18.14 and 19.12), Moreau altered Pan's arm when he added the bottom section so it would parallel the underworld's main 45° diagonals, thus leading the viewer's eye downward. Following the movement of this hand, we discover a beheaded ram or goat (the life-giving sacrifice), with bejewelled fruit and vegetation spurting from its severed neck (the head lies nearby, next to its out-stretched hoof). The sloughed-off skin of a serpent (as the bodily shroud of *metempsychosis*) is wrapped around Pan's fore-arm, while more minute figures (like those beneath the angel-satyr above) desperately cling to Pan's breast or struggle, trapped, in the rich vegetation that sprouts from his loins. The entire composition, in this earthly realm of generation, is crowned by a Shiva lingam – the ancient Hindu symbol of fertility.

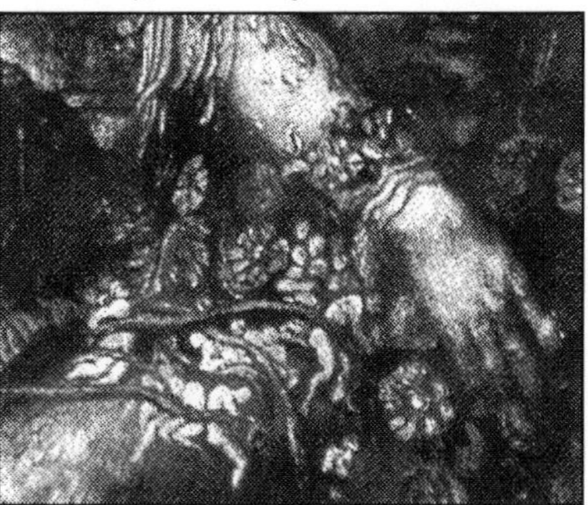

Fig. 19.13 - Vegetation from Pan's Loins With Small Figures Emerging

How does Moreau present our soul's death and suffering? The allegorical figure of Death to the left is not a veiled Grim Reaper or dancing skeleton of the *Totentanz* variety. Rather, Death is seen *from a higher point of view* – of the eternally Divine's deep and lasting regret that Death must continue to bloody her sword until all beings have been liberated from the cycle of *metempsychosis.*

Her entire body collapses, lifeless. Only her upraised hand betrays deep and lasting regret. With a white veil, she wipes away the tears from her face – that same white veil, studded with jewels, which swathes Semele's form and cascades down the steps of Jupiter's throne, veiling Death then descending between her knees to her feet – *where it transforms into a transparent flow of jewels, white and blue in hue.* These jewels are stained by the life-blood

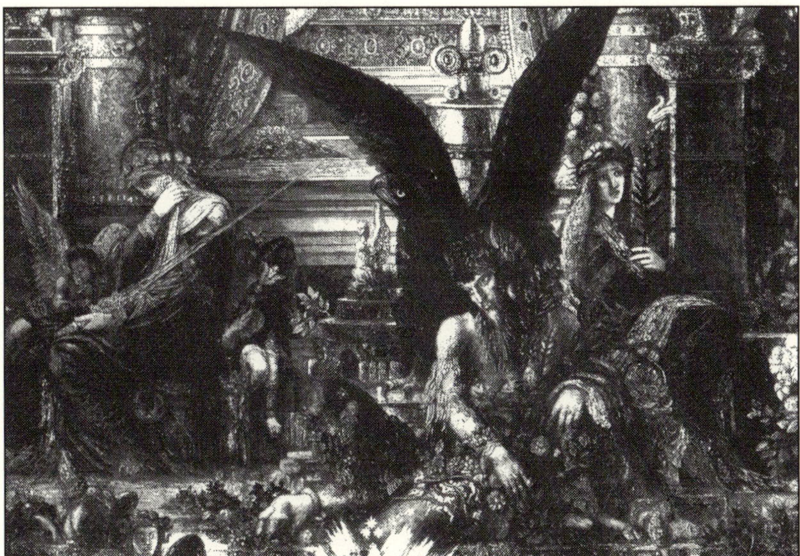

Fig. 19.14 - Death (left), Pan (centre) and Suffering (right) with Eagle and Shiva Lingam

of her sword and, in the underworld, transform into a glowing stream of red liquid. Flanking Death on either side are two small angels – one with red wings, the other blue – the latter holding a lily entwined by two serpents (the caduceus of rebirth) while gazing downward at the hourglass of Time.

The allegorical figure of Suffering on the right also holds a sprouting lily in her hand and *raises her head* – in a gesture contrary to Death. Her entire being and bearing express *awakening* – the sudden realization that all human suffering eventually brings truth and understanding. Eventually, we may follow her redemptive gaze upward. But, for now, we focus on the crown of thorns on her head, the Christian symbol of suffering, revelation and redemption.

But wait! The drops of blood on her brow also transform into ruby red drops. Like the life-blood staining the sword of Death, these descend over her shoulder in a stream of *glowing red jewels*. Mingling with the acanthus ornament at Pan's elbow, they pulsate with life. Past the feet of Suffering, her life-blood flows into the underworld, where it clusters like fruit in gem-like formations. Indeed, the whole underworld in Moreau's painting, despite the darkened hues, *is brightly glowing from within*, with an abundance of opalesque reds, oranges, greens and blues. The artist has glazed these, like the Gothic artisans of stained glass, a great number of times to achieve that gem-like luminescence.

Death, Pan and Suffering, with the Eagle (gazing upward) and the Shiva lingam, form a triangular composition all their own. At its centre, Pan's powerful gaze (empowered by his reclining *contrapposto* pose) leads our gaze *out of* this triangular composition – following the main diagonal of the bottom square in the 1:2 rectangle – past the female face of the Moon to the Sphinx in the lower left corner. This Sphinx, in profile, contemplates the Sphinx opposite. Her sister and counterpart, across in the right corner, turns to us in a three-quarter view. With one eye, she gazes back at her sister, with the other she gazes upward and away from this dark underworld.

Between the gazes of these two sisters, Hecate's realm unfolds in the darkness.

IV. Hecate's Realm of Darkness

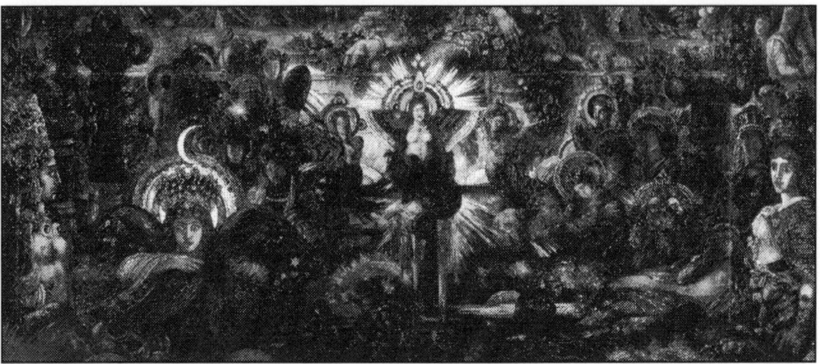

Fig. 19.15 - Hecate's Underworld, bounded by two Sphinxes, with the Moon (middle left)

Through a prolonged meditation on the painting, gazing deep into the smaller figures and details, a new level of narrative has emerged – where sparks of light become trapped in the cycle of *metempsychosis*. While some may enter the middle realm of generation, others fall past the Hierophant on the left, descending through the seven heavenly spheres to enter the darkened realm of Hecate's underworld (Fig. 19.15). The frightening truth of this realization is borne out by the presence of *a single spark of light*, entering the underworld, which appears just above the allegorical figure of the Moon with a crescent crowning her head (Fig. 19.16).

Hecate and the two angelic beings to her right and left (Fig. 19.17), react in different ways to the presence of this single spark in the underworld. Hecate – she of the oblique gaze – has not yet noticed the spark. Instead, she is turning one eye to the angel on the right, who attempts to look away, but is caught in the goddess's gaze – as if, caught in the gorgon's frightful stare. Those who gaze upon the Medusa, we recall, are so petrified with fear that they immediately turn to stone. In this case, the angel gazing upon Hecate is *transformed into transparent jewels*, which cling like glowing beryls, ambers and jaspers on her wings and serpentine figure (which rests upon a red gryphon).

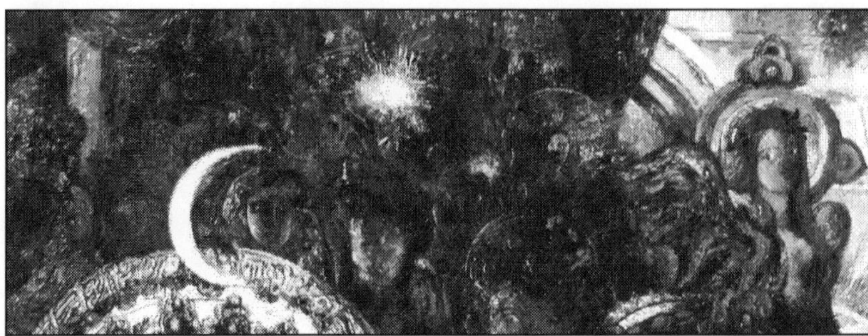

Fig. 19.16 - A Single Spark of Light, noticed by an Angelic Being (right)

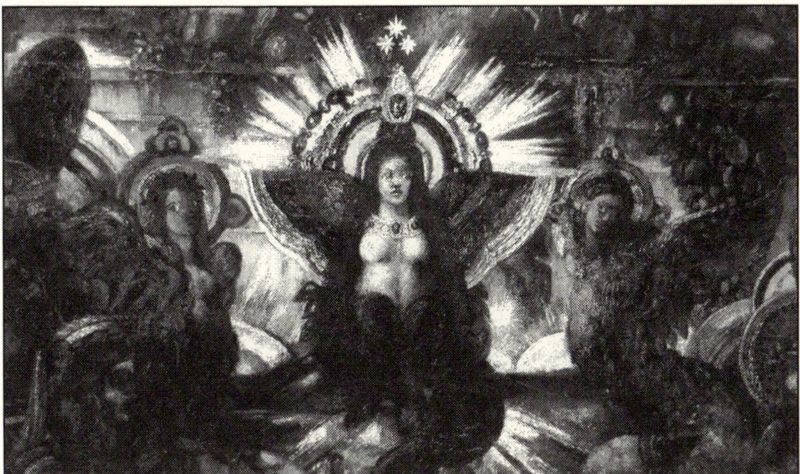

Fig. 19.17 - Hecate of the Oblique Gaze, flanked by Two Jewel-Encrusted Angels

Meanwhile, the angel to the left of Hecate *glances away from the goddess*, and casts her gaze instead upon the newly-arrived spark of light (Fig. 19.16). She seems to react with fear – afraid of the moment when the newly-arrived soul will gaze upon Hecate and their eyes will meet – for then its light will also sink into stone, becoming a glowing, ornamental gem, like all the other denizens of the underworld. Moreau has carefully glazed these figures countless times so that their countenances glow like ornaments in stained-glass.

Indeed, he has cloistered each colour (*cloisonné*), surrounding it in black – like the lead *calmes* or curving frames of each stained-glass medallion. Following the codes of the Mediaeval *glaziers*, who heated silica and mixed it with metallic oxide powders, Moreau has used red (*selenium ruby*), orange (*silver stain*), green (*copper oxide*) and blue (*cobalt*) as the four principle and symbolic colours of his inner-glowing underworld.

One glance at Hecate gives us these four elemental colours. The halo behind her head is red, and this same red glow flows like blood below, mixing into the planetary spheres and forming ruby red jewels. Like the life-blood staining Death's sword, like the same life-blood crowning Suffering's brow, this sanguine flow transforms into ruby red jewels in the underworld, which glow with the inner light of anguish, agony and pain – borne from our spirit's separation and fall from its once-divine state.

That glowing red colour, we remark, begins above in Jupiter's halo, and flows down as beads of blood on Semele's hip (she bore the infant Dionysius in her womb before she died). Staining the angel-satyr's wings, it descends into the middle realm of generation. More dramatically, the glowing red illuminates transparent fruits and other ornamental figures on the column on the left, where sparks of light sink into stone.

The orange and green also begin above, as the semi-circular arc of gemstones adorning Jupiter's throne (just behind his red and orange halo). Hints of their glowing light appear beneath the falling angel-satyr, but they reach their true strength and glory in the lap of Pan. From the abundance of

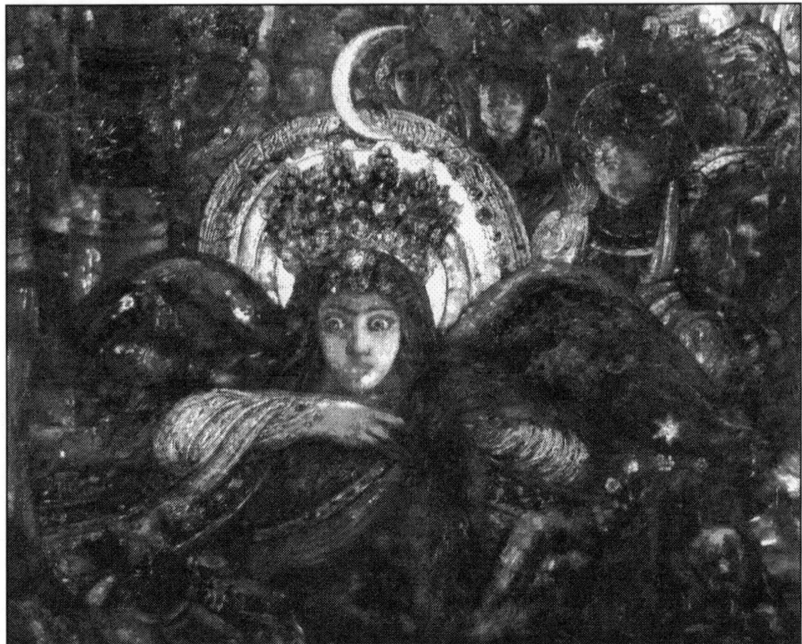

Fig. 19.18 - The Moon, with tears in her eyes, gazes downward

vegetation springing from his loins, the orange glow covers the floor of the middle realm before descending in a liquid flow of jewels to the underworld. Here, it receives new life, as the golden glow around Hecate, and in the planets illuminating her realm. It is symbolic of the divine light, whether above in Olympus or below in Erebus.

Likewise, the green glow descends as foliage from Pan, but finds its strongest light and power in the green snake that not only entwines Hecate's legs but actually forms the lower part of her serpentine body. Green, associated with the snake and vegetation, becomes the force of transformation, the ever-cycling life-force that moves from death to rebirth, from suffering to "ecstasy, love and joy". Green is symbolic of the soul's transmigration.

Blue, the hue of the sky above, adorns the cloaks of Death and Suffering, and colours countless ornaments in the underworld before receiving its greatest treatment in the halo, jewels and eyes of the Moon.

This allegorical figure appears on the lower left, crowned with the crescent, and surrounded by a halo which casts its darkening blue glow upon all of the underworld creatures (Fig. 19.18). Her oblique gaze – with one eye staring at us and the other staring downward – suggests that even lower and darker realms exists, beyond the border of the underworld. Tears fall from her wide blue eyes, and her entire manner and mean suggests that blue is symbolic of deception, mirage and illusion in the underworld.

Aside from *"the silent Moon"*, Moreau mentions *"Erebus and Night"* in his letter to Léopold Goldschmidt. *Erebus*, meaning "the Darkness of the Underworld", is first mentioned in Hesiod's *Theogony*, where he appears as one of the five most primordial beings in the cosmos' creation, a child engen-

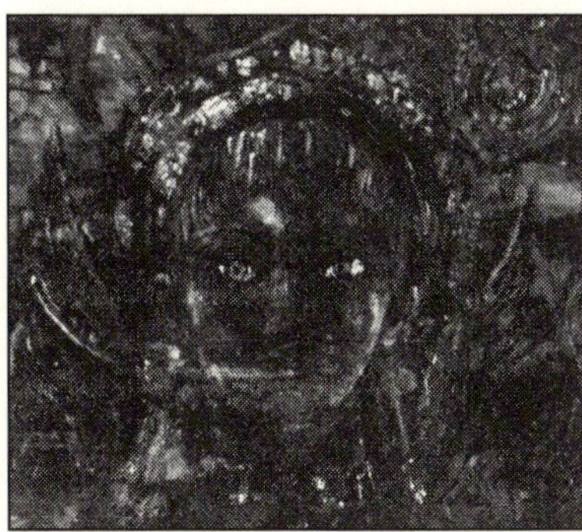

Fig. 19.19 - Night

dered by *Chaos*. "Night", as *Nix*, also appears in Hesiod's *Theogony,* where she becomes the consort of *Erebus*, and gives birth to *Hypnos* (Sleep) and *Thanatos* (Death). All of these allegorical figures appear at the bottom of the painting in the darkest blues and browns of the underworld – gazing out at us with their fear-inspiring, hieratic stares. Night, I surmise, appears as a dark female visage, just below Hecate's outpouring of blood (Fig. 19.19). She stares directly at us, with a bejewelled sceptre and crowned with a diadem, but her face is so dark as to be almost invisible.

As our meditative gaze gets lost in the darkness, we encounter ever-stranger and more bizarre creatures – *"hydras, lemures and griffons"* Moreau writes – those *"beings of mystery and shade* [who] *mingle in the depths."* One of the most curious is the reclining female figure at the bottom right, emblematic of Sin, with the Demon of Lust (Fig. 19.20). Her nude form, curving and voluptuous, is swathed in a stream of ruby-red jewels that pass over, around and between her legs – suggesting that this underworld being revels erotically and luxuriously in the anguish, agony and pain of others, which she experiences as ecstasy. Below her a stream of ruby red hues, like glowing lava, flows in a serpentine fashion into the depths.

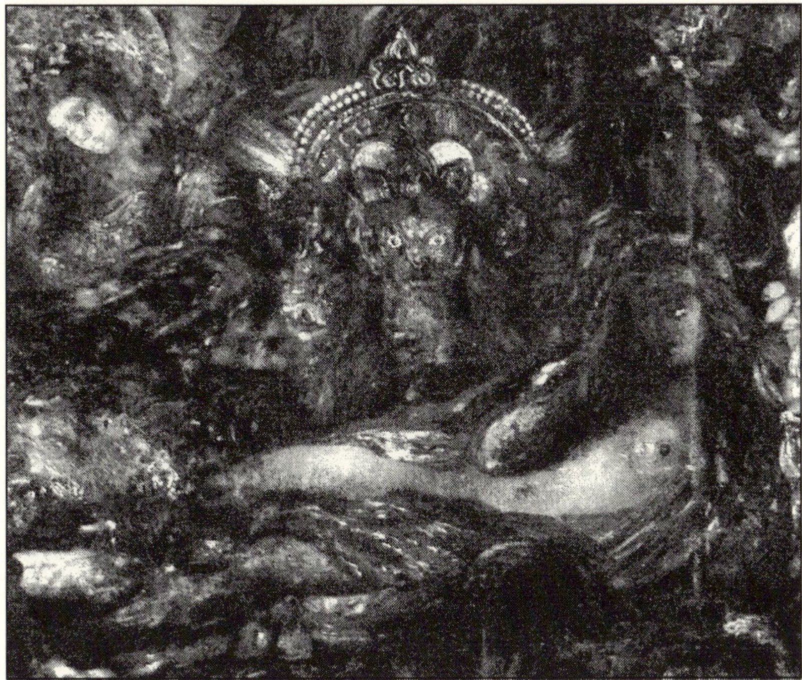

Fig. 19.20 - Reclining figure of Sin, and the Three-Headed Demon of Lust

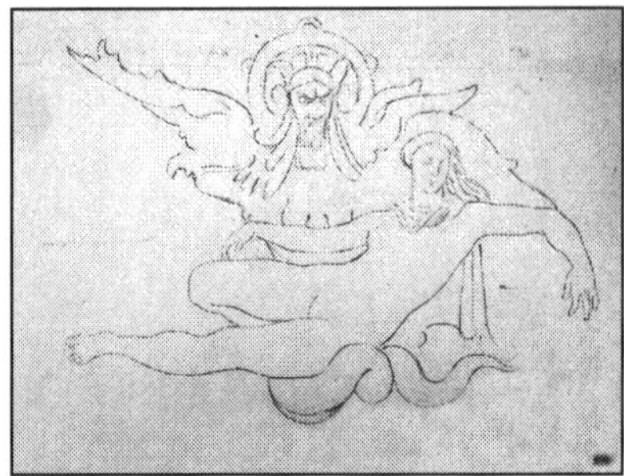

Fig. 19.21 - *Cartone* for Lust

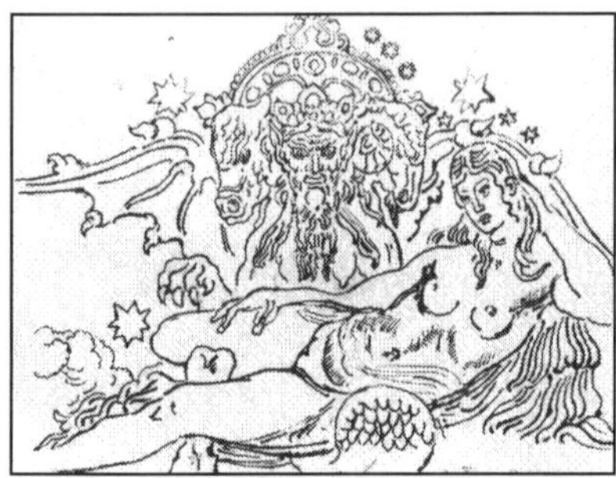

Fig. 19.22 - Sin with the Demon of Lust

A *cartone* at the Musée Gustave Moreau (cat. 807)[1] gives us the outlines for this feminine figure, as well as the serpentine deity above her, who clearly has wings, breasts and a serpent's tail. His bearded visage is crowned with a halo and curling ram's horns. Given the size of the *cartone* (84 x 110 cm), Moreau had envisioned this composition (based on opposing triangles) as an independent work, portraying the theme of 'Lust'.

Instead, it found its way into *Jupiter and Semele*. In a smaller but more elaborate drawing,[2] the serpentine deity now clearly has bat wings and three heads: the head of a crowned and bearded male, flanked by a bull's head to the left and a ram's head to the right. A similar three-headed deity is depicted in J. Collin de Plancy's 1863 book *Dictionnaire Infernal*[3] where it bears the name of Asmodeus. This Persian deity, which appears as a lusty devil in the biblical *Book of Tobit* (6:13), has traditionally been classified as one of the seven demons ruling over the seven deadly sins – specifically, as the Demon of Lust.

At the feet of the reclining nude another spark of light appears, trapped in the underworld. Even more bizarre is the figure above *Asmodeus* – an important figure we would surely miss if we were not meditating upon each design and detail. In the shadows we behold a female visage, enhaloed and crowned – and *flowing from her right eye is a flood of ruby red tears,* which cover half her face before they descend into the darkness below (Fig. 19.23). Do the anguish, agony and pain of our separation from God become a veil a tears that blind us from our true, exiled and darkened state? What is the means of escape from this terrible place?

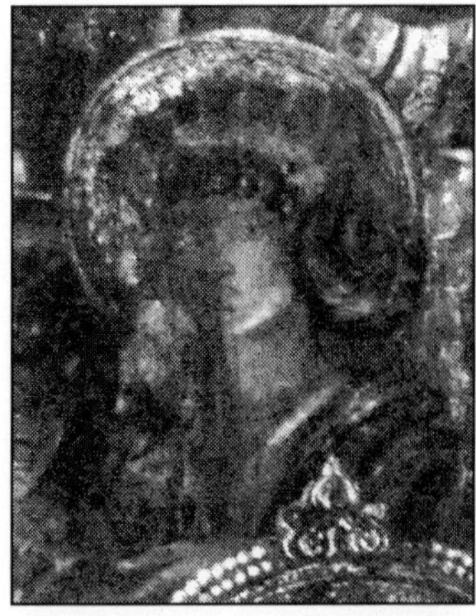

Fig. 19.23 - Woman with Ruby Tears

"The two great sphinxes," Moreau writes, *"stand as guardians to this herd and their heavenly ascent."* And he ends his descriptive text with the mysterious observation that they *"...contemplate each other with a smiling*

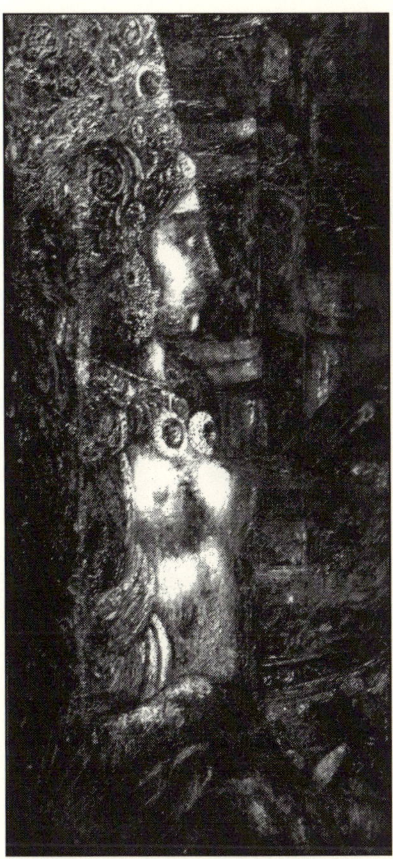

Fig. 19.24 - Left Sphinx
In Profile - Gazing Across

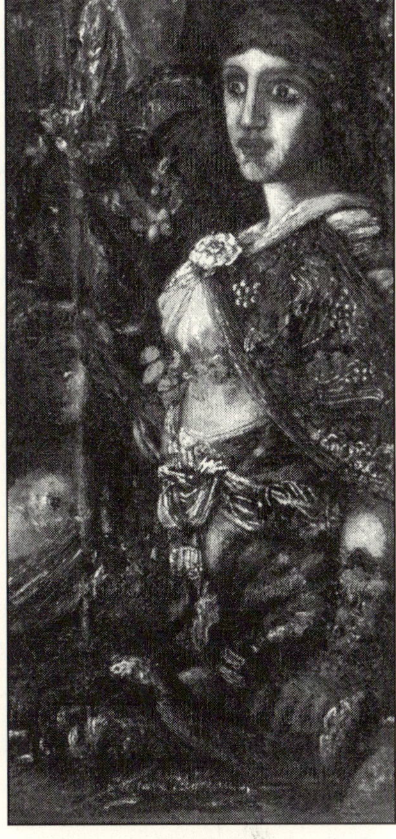

Fig. 19.25 - Right Sphinx
In 3/4 View - Gazing Across and Up

and hieratic stillness." While it is true that the sphinx on the left, *in profile*, stares directly at her counterpart; the sphinx on the right, *in a three-quarter view*, turns one eye back to her sister while *gazing upward* with the other (Figs. 19.24 and 19.25). Meanwhile, with a leonine paw, she grasps yet-another green serpent – thus demonstrating her mastery over the lord of *metempsychosis* (Moreau's signature appears just below this sphinx). Through her upward-turned gaze, our own contemplative gaze may escape Hecate's petrifying glance and begin the *"heavenly ascent"*.

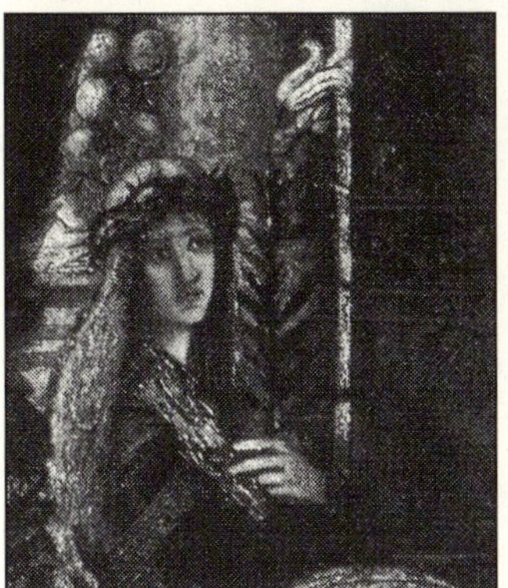

Fig. 19.26 - Suffering

Rising upward, we encounter the Pre-Raphaelite figure of Suffering (Fig. 19.26). Awakening to the redemptive nature of suffering, she turns her head *at a three-quarter angle* and, glancing upward with one eye, she offers our vision another line of ascent.

V. The Soul Ascent

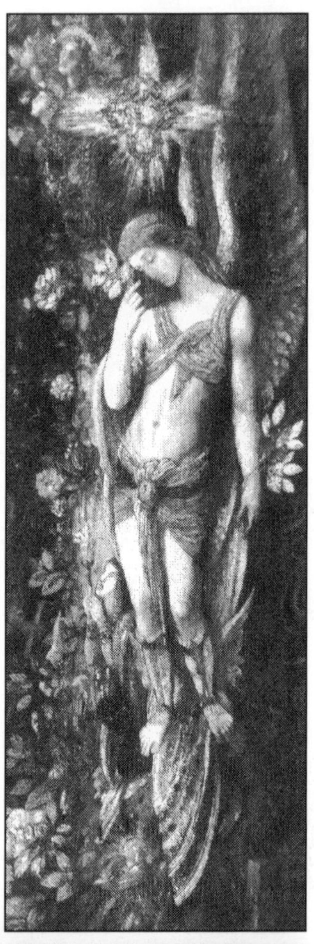

Following the 45° diagonal of the armature, our eye rises to the Hierophant on the right (Fig. 19.27) who, like his brother, curves in a *contrapposto* manner to *"bow his head"* along the armature line of the upper world diagonal. Though his eyes are pressed shut, he holds a blue flower in hand and, below to the left, an angelic figure at his knees clasps a virgin white lily – the symbolic flower of purity, also held in the hands of Suffering – while gazing passionately upward. Having understood the true nature of suffering, this angelic figure leads our vision ever upward – past the Hierophant's threshold to the figures at the right of the throne.

Crowning the emerald column of Jupiter's throne, an arrangement of ornamental flowers appears (vegetation – the ever-cycling life-force of death and rebirth - Fig. 19.28). And in its shadow, winged beings hide themselves from Jupiter's commanding gaze. In the darkness, they unite and fuse with the figures in the columns, as timeless ornaments in the celestial architecture. Stilled and sphinx-like, with open eyes, they shall gaze for all time at the spectacle of Becoming – of the soul's eternal cycle of rising and falling.

Fig. 19. 27 Right - The Right Hierophant
Fig. 19.28 Below - Ornamental Flowers with (on the right) an Angel Gazing at Jupiter

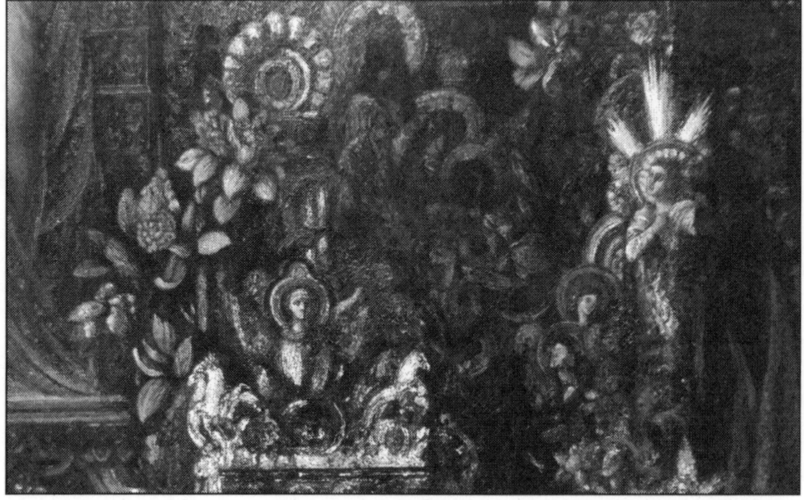

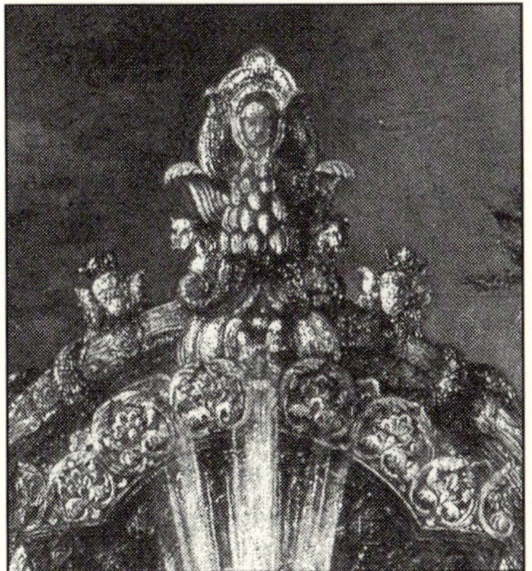
Fig. 19.29 - Many-Breasted Artemis

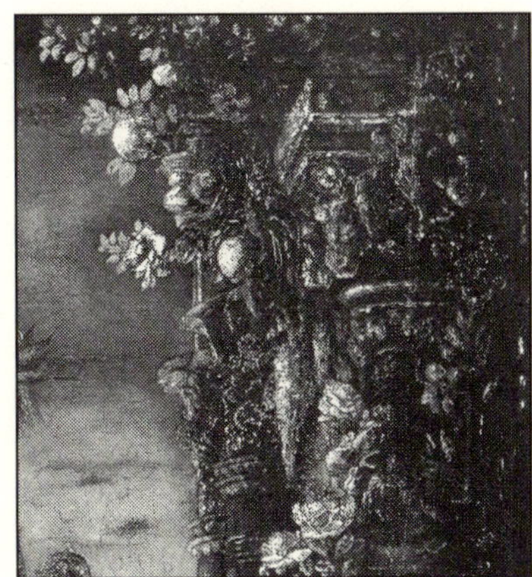
Fig. 19.30 - Column Capitals with Poppies

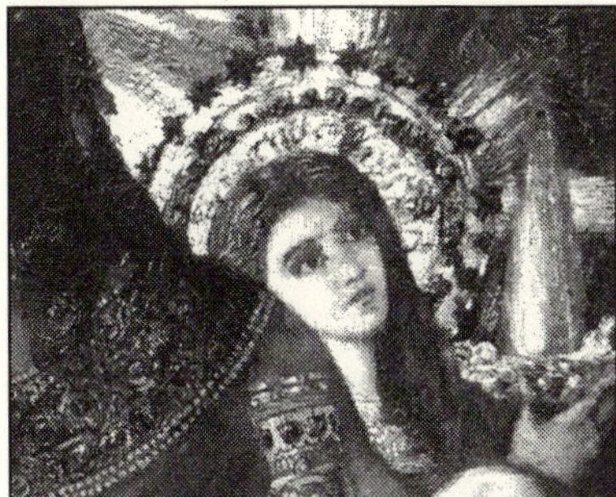
Fig. 19.31 - Upward-Gazing Angel

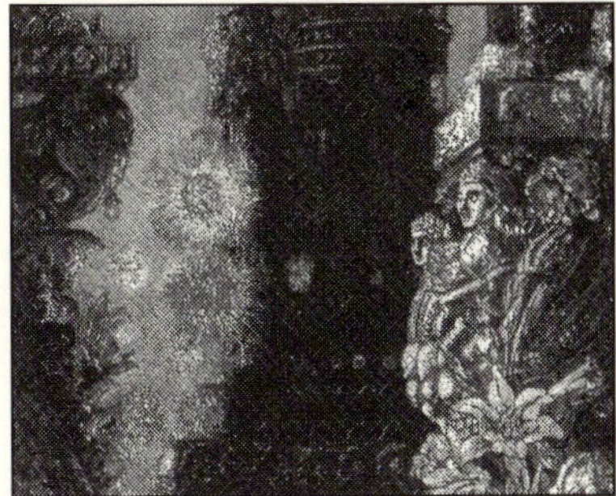
Fig. 19.32 - Rising Sparks of Light

Meanwhile, in the light on the right, other figures emerge as luminous angels (Fig. 19.28). Indeed, one angel in their midsts, resplendent with a shimmering halo of light, turns her eyes upward and *willingly gazes into the all-powerful visage of Jupiter*. This creates another 45° diagonal line of sight, following the main diagonal that cuts through the upper square.

For a few precious moments, if not an eternity, our gaze rests upon Jupiter's visage. But above the god's shoulder, to the right, another winged angel (Fig. 19.31) gazes *yet higher*, to the *"towering colossal architecture,"* where so many luminous souls have now integrated themselves into the stonework. To the right of the upward-gazing angel, we see them as yellow sparks of light (Fig. 19.32), which now rise up to become living ornaments, jewels and arabesques, joining with vegetal swirls as the *"...sacred flora, quivering and alive, against the sombre blue solitude of the sky."*

Flowers of all kinds – morning glories, orchids, but especially poppies – shoot forth from the capitals (Fig. 19.30), each of the four columns displaying a different epoch of ancient history: Babylonia, Egypt, Greece and Rome. The ornaments adorning Jupiter's throne are more oriental in character: the elephant-headed capitals (Fig. 19.32) remind us of the Buddhist stupa at Sanchi. They are topped by Hindu deities, sitting cross-legged on lotus blossoms. At the apex of Jupiter's throne (Fig. 19.29) appears the many-breasted Artemis, our Lady of Ephesus.

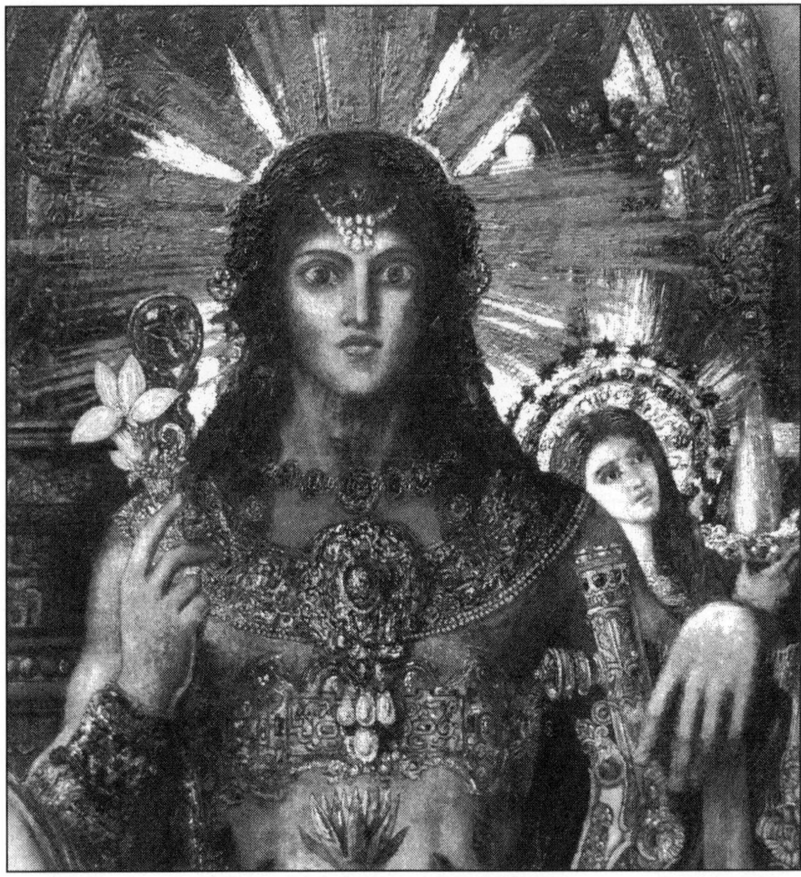

Fig. 19.33 - The Mystery of Jupiter's Gaze

Jupiter himself (Fig. 19.33) rests one hand on the lyre (guarantor of harmony), while upholding a white flower (whether lotus or crocus) and a jewelled silver sceptre resembling a *thrysus*. His forehead is adorned with pearls, and more ornaments appear, as if, on each of the *chakra* centres – from heart to throat to third eye and crown. Most stunning of all, an Egyptian scarab rises from his sacral chakra and spreads its wings, uniting with a blossoming Nile Lily above the solar plexus (Fig. 13.35). These symbols evoke the eternal mystery of the entire painting: of the soul's transmigration and *metempsychosis*, moving beyond the cycle of Death and Rebirth to a final perfect Awakening.

One of the greatest enigmas in Moreau's painting is the mystery of Jupiter's gaze. At first glance, his visage appears to be Hieratic – his features gracefully carved (like an Egyptian statue) in a fully frontal position, while the god stares at us directly with his azure blue eyes. But, upon closer inspection, this is only true of the *right half* of his countenance. The *left side* is slightly turned to the three-quarter angle, and his eye rises (amplified by the angel to the right) to an upward-turning gaze, which leads our own vision ever higher into the celestial architecture.

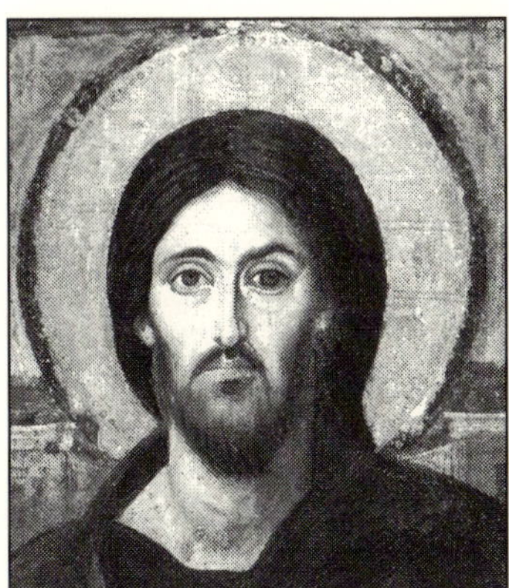

Fig. 19.34 - *Christ Pantocrator*
St. Catherine's Monastery, Sinai

We are immediately reminded of the 5th century icon of *Christ Pantocrator* from St. Catherine's Monastery in the Sinai (Fig. 19.34). There too, one side of Christ's face (in this case, the right) had a more Humanist expression – his eye glancing away and aloft – while the other side of his face manifest a Hieratic stillness – his eye engaging us directly with its eternal gaze. The ancient encaustic master had fused two historical styles to express Christ's humanity and divinity.

The three-quarter angle, we have noted in this treatise, was refined during the Renaissance for its more Humanist expression of feeling, passion and movement. The frontal view of the face, meanwhile, fixes our regard with a contemplative immobility characteristic of the a Hieratic gaze. This basic Sacred Code is implicitly at work throughout Moreau's composition. The two sphinxes at the bottom *clearly manifest these two types of regard*, since the sphinx on the lower left is posed in a Hieratic profile, and can do no more than contemplate her sister in a strictly horizontal line of sight. But the sphinx on the right, we note, turns her head in a more Humanist three-quarter angle, to liberate our sight from the underworld along its ascending diagonal.

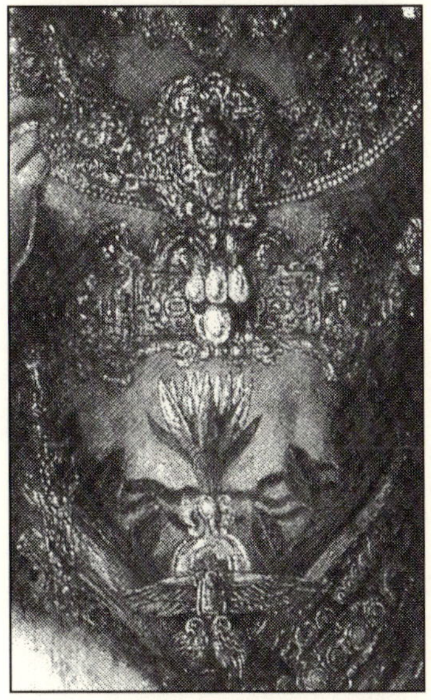

Fig. 19.35 - Chakra Ornaments

As the artist places figures around the armature, he must be aware of the *histoire* that binds them all together into a narrative composition. He must be aware of the various lines of sight that transfer our gaze from one figure to the next. The Hieratic gaze differs from the Humanist glance in certain key ways. When the Hieratic face appears in a frontal view, the eyes of the deity engage the viewer directly, locking them in a fixed regard. *It invites stilled contemplation.*

The Hieratic face in profile is capable of directing our vision across the composition, horizontally or diagonally, but in a slow movement that typically runs back and forth between the seer and the seen. Meanwhile the Humanist face, particularly in its three-quarter angle, moves our eye more energetically, sometimes horizontally, but more often diagonally, *creating a dynamic narrative movement throughout the composition.* (In certain rare instances, such as Raphael's *St. Catherine*, the gaze may be directed *straight upward*, in a perfectly *vertical* movement).

As we have just witnessed in our reading of *Jupiter and Semele*, it is principally *the diagonal movement along the lines of armature* that moves our eye around the composition, creating the *histoire*. Each time a figure dramatically turns, *contrapposto*-style, to release a burst of energy (through a gesture or a glance), our eye follows that energetic movement, which Moreau carefully places *along the lines of armature*. In *Jupiter and Semele*, this movement begins with Semele and the falling angel-satyr along a diagonal leading to the Hierophant on the left. Following his bowed head (in profile), we descend diagonally again to Death and Pan, who redirect our eye downward once more to the bottom left sphinx.

The Moon, were we to follow her gaze, would lead us yet further deeper into the depths. Instead, following the Hieratic gaze of the sphinx on the left, we cut across Hecate's underworld, absorbing the various glances and regards – especially Hecate's oblique gaze – until the liberating sphinx on the right leads our eye back upward. From the allegorical figure of Suffering, our eye rises ever higher, to the Hierophant on the right. At his knee an angel, clutching a lily in her hands, gazes passionately upward and, above the Hierophant, another shining angel gazes directly into Jupiter's divine visage. We follow this angel's gaze until our eye comes to a rest, in stilled contemplation, upon the divine visage. But, an even higher movement is made possible, by Jupiter and the angel at his shoulder, who grant us access to even higher celestial realms.

Should our eye come to rest on Jupiter's visage, we find ourselves in full circle – back at the decisive moment when Semele first gazed upon the god and turned her face away from his overwhelming epiphany. If the soul finally feels prepared to engage the god's gaze directly, then it may surrender itself and become fully absorbed in the act of Divine Seeing – at once seeing and being seen by the god who beholds the whole creation as his own self-expanding and re-absorption into oneness.

Indeed, Moreau himself described Jupiter as an *"apparition of divine light."*[4] This deity appears in the full effulgence of his glory – half golden, half scarlet – the unseen source of all light and life, exploding in a flash of yellow and red hues. Then, like a jewel, the light crystallizes; it solidifies into a material image – triangular in shape, human in form – the emperor or king, seated upon his pyramidal throne. All the ornaments adorning his throne, from the stepped dais to the pillared canopy, are themselves extensions of divine matter stamped with form: the *eidé* and ideal shapes that carve out a malleable and ever-metamorphosing substance which, as a 'becoming-in-time', momentarily assumes the stable, eternal shapes of the heavenly archetypes. All the figures, including Semele herself, are a manifestation of the god's one true Light.

Humanist art of the Western tradition teaches us to gaze upon a painting and move our eye around its salient features, thus creating a narrative movement that, in its highest form, transcends the *histoire* and becomes an allegory, symbolic of our suffering and redemption. Hieratic art, in contrast, teaches us to gaze upon a painting and fix our regard onto a single, stilled point, thus creating a contemplative state of calm that, in its highest form, transcends all seeing to become a total absorption in the Divine.

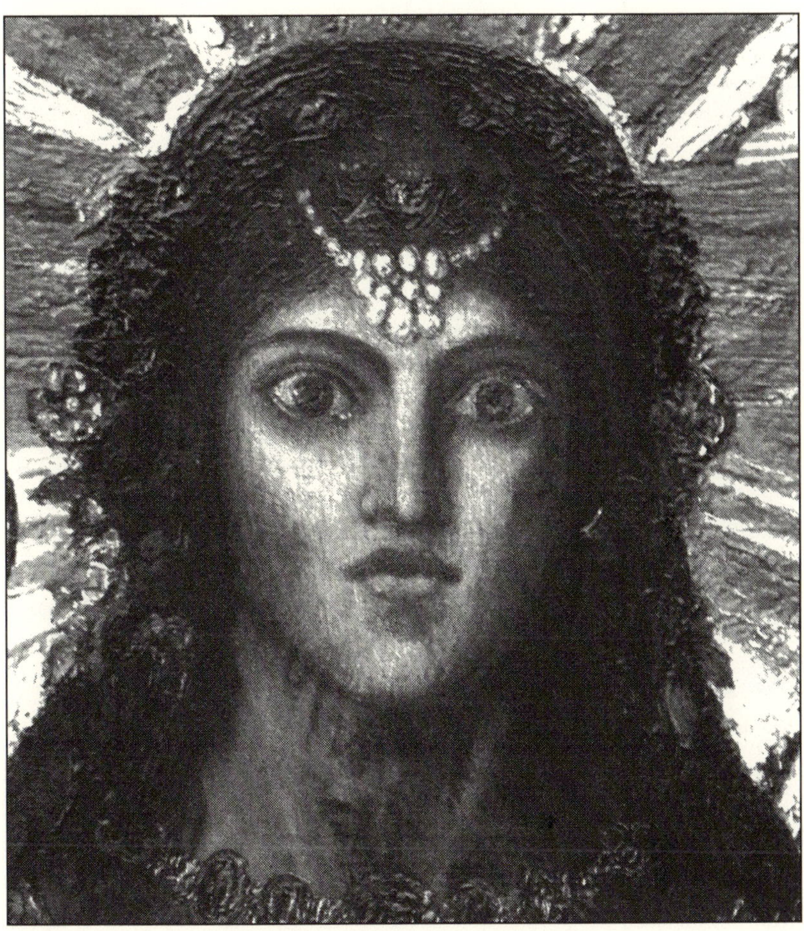

Fig. 19.36 - Jupiter as Tutelar Deity

Moreau's *Jupiter and Semele*, as a Visionary work of art, fuses these Humanist and Hieratic traditions; it shows us a new way of looking at a Western work of art. Emerging at the apex (and indeed, at the end) of our Western academic tradition, it invites us to follow its narrative unfolding, developing the *histoire* through allegorical actions, through the theatricality of the poses, the symbolic gestures, and all the passions of the soul. But, remembering a Hieratic tradition (half Gothic, half Byzantine) sadly neglected in the West, his art also invites us to slow our roving eye and fix it upon the central figure – as this painting's propitiatory or tutelary deity. Anticipating the re-emergence of Sacred Art – its migration from the East and re-integration in the West – Moreau's painting invites us to engage its central image and gaze upon it as if it were a temple statue or thangka. Through extended meditation and contemplation (which we shall investigate in depth in Part V), we approach this painting as a Moreauvian Altarpiece, and experience its intended epiphany as a portal to the Divine.

VI. The Forgotten Master

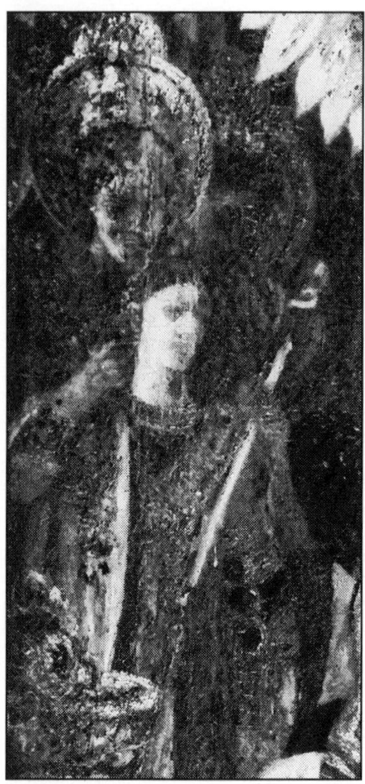

Fig. 19.36 - Self-Portrait of the Artist with his Parents?

Although we have examined a multitude of small figures in this composition, there remains one which has, as yet, eluded our speculation. That is the small figure hiding in the shadow of the left Hierophant. What makes this figure so entirely unique is that *he is staring directly at us*. Moreau has not forgotten the Sacred Code that states the craftsman may include a likeness of himself in his work. From the Renaissance onward, the artist has always appeared, uniquely, with a gaze directed straight at us.

He wears a bejewelled cloak and grasps a ruby red sceptre. Behind him, two spectral figures hover over his shoulder. Moreau points to the one on the left – which receives more volume and light. Meanwhile, the one on the right hands him the sceptre while receding into the darkness. These are, I believe, his parents – his father (on the right), who died when Moreau was thirty-six year's old, and whose inheritance allowed the young man to become an independent artist (Indeed, the family residence at 14 rue de la Rochefoucauld, purchased by his father in 1852, eventually became the artist's studio and, finally, the Musée Gustave Moreau). And his mother (on the left), who lived with Moreau all of his life and was deeply immersed in all his personal and artistic endeavours (as evidenced by the large correspondence left between them, until her death in 1884, five years before he began *Jupiter and Semele*).

The young Moreau, without his characteristic beard, gazes out at us confidently – this entire masterpiece is the creation of his active and fertile imagination. In the end, Moreau's *Jupiter and Semele* is a masterpiece of the same order and magnitude as Michelangelo's *Last Judgment* or Blake's *Vision of the Last Judgement*. Like these past masters, he is depicting the entire creation, the entire unfolding of history, as a stilled and timeless vision where the soul falls from or rises to the eternally Sacred.

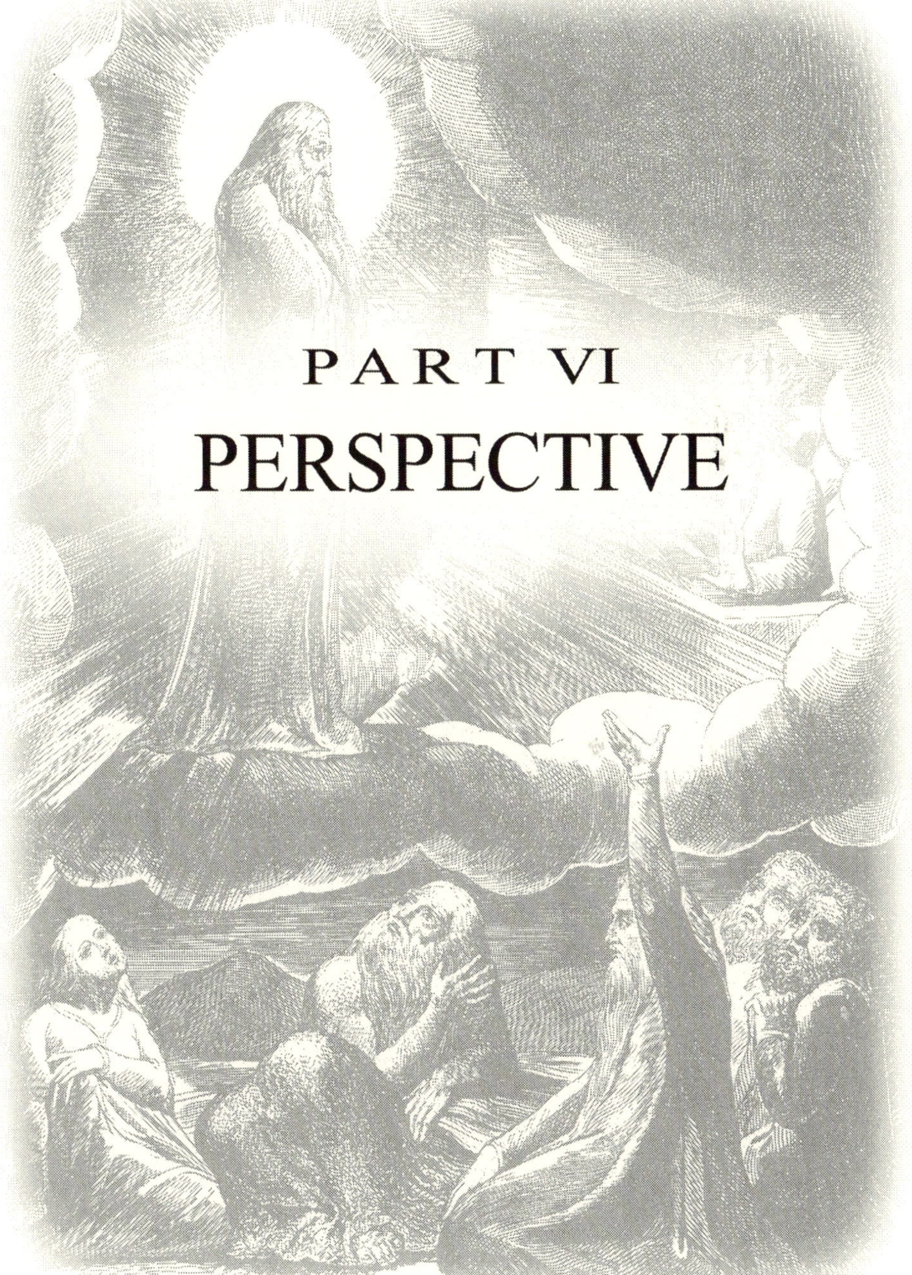

PART VI
PERSPECTIVE

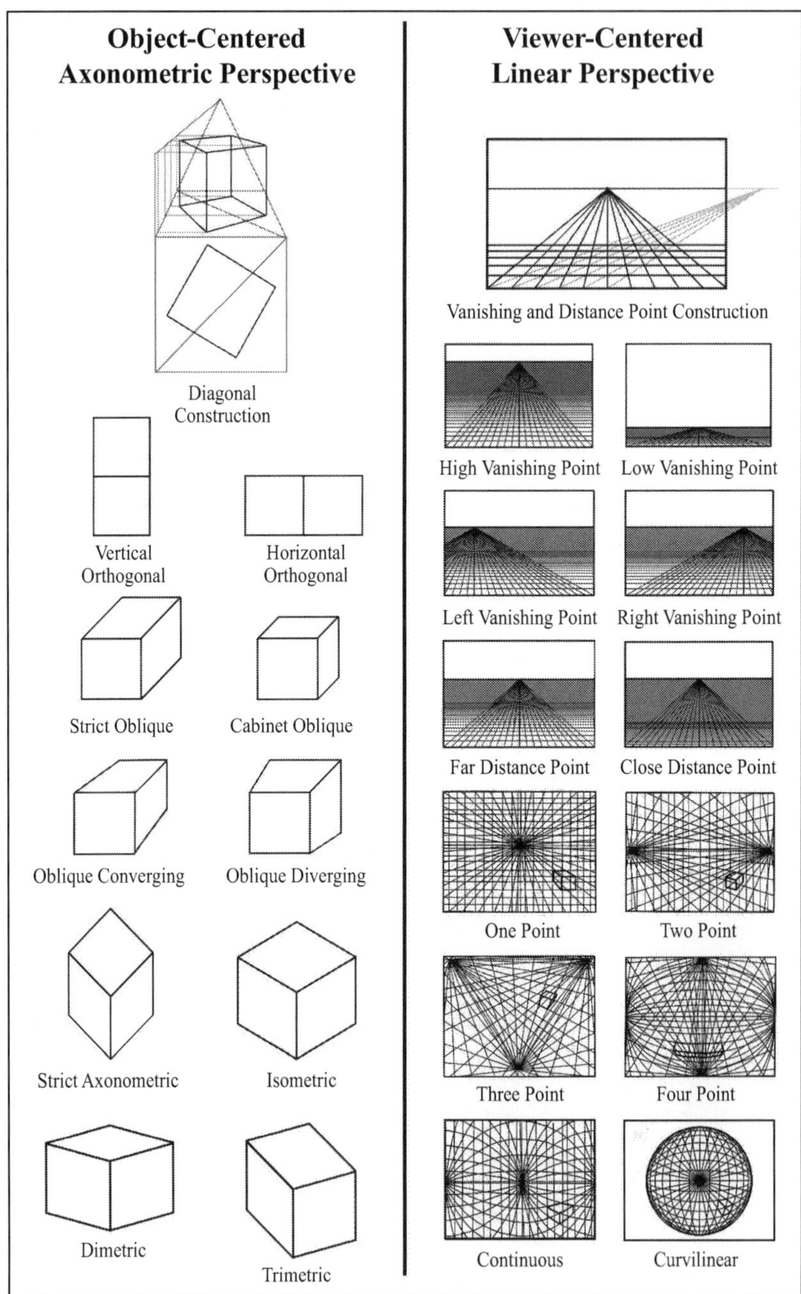

Fig. 20.1 - Types of Perspective

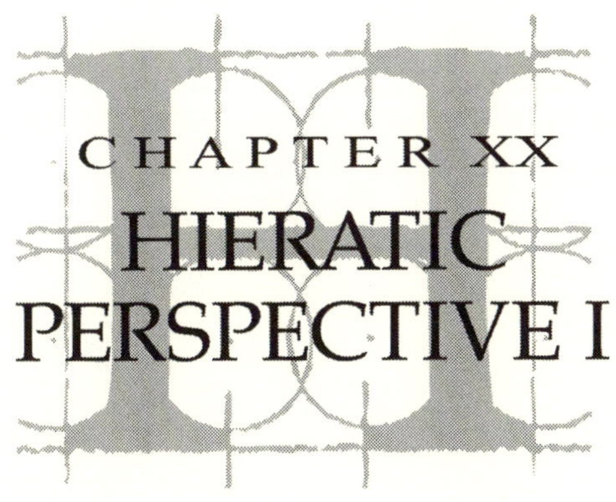

CHAPTER XX HIERATIC PERSPECTIVE I

I. Perspective, the Viewer & the Concept of Space

If we wish to study perspective from its earliest stages, we may go back as far as 40,000 years, to Paleolithic cave painting. For perspective is, quite simply, the representation of 3D shapes on a 2D picture plane. To 'compress' the visual object, and make it viewable from a distinct angle in pictorial space – has been the artist's task for millennia, and craftsmen have developed numerous systems of perspective to achieve that end.

Along the way, science has developed equally numerous systems of geometry that parallel and partially explain the art of perspective. I have no choice but to fall back upon this terminology, even though it is often confusing, if not plainly contradictory (for example, the converging diagonals in linear perspective are called 'orthogonals'). Indeed, the whole study of perspective, I have come to realize, is a deep labyrinth, full of obfuscation and ambiguity, both in science and in art. Yet, it continues to fascinate and delight, because of the sheer challenge it presents.

I shall begin these chapters with the study of Hieratic perspective, but a knowledge of Humanist perspective will naturally be assumed. For our Humanist perspective, with its convergence of parallel lines onto a single vanishing point, has become so deeply ingrained in our way of seeing, that it is difficult for us to imagine other systems as equally valid and meaningful. As Visionary artists, our first task is to rediscover the invisible lines of Hieratic perspective, with its oblique angles and axonometric grids, since they engender a more spiritual outlook from a very different point-of-view.

I have found Dubery and Willats' *Perspective and Other Drawing Systems* to be a clear introduction to this complex subject, and a great stimulation to my thinking. At the outset, they make the essential distinction between *object*-centered perspective and *viewer*-centered perspective. What is unique about Western linear perspective is that it is *viewer*-centered: the object and its spatial grid are constructed to be visualized from the *observer's* point-of-view. For this reason, we are quite justified in calling linear perspective a *Humanist* endeavour.

By contrast, axonometric perspective is constructed with *the object* in mind: the object becomes the centre from which the spatial grids are constructed. We have seen this already in our visualization and drawing of the Pythagorean Tetractys and the Five Platonic Solids. These shapes give rise to perspectives transcending the strictly Humanist viewpoint – to a more universal and even divine perspective which we may call Hieratic.

The study of Optics adds a further distinction to the viewer-centered / object-centered dichotomy. The Renaissance was the first epoch in history to develop the *intromission* theory of vision – that vision is the passive reception of shapes that imprint on our eye. In most theories of Optics prior to that, the eye actively cast its vision onto objects, recognizing their unique shapes in space.

Building upon the *extramission* theory of vision, divine craftsmen viewed their task as 'seeing with the Divine Eye' – participating in the active visualization of each object's ideal or perfect shape, from the centre to the circumference. Each object, the moment it was visualized, also imparted this defining shape to its surrounding space; as triangles and squares, they expanded into entire grids, which measured out those spaces while extending them in multiple directions. This is especially true of ornament and Islamic Patterns, but extends to all the symmetrical compositions – Buddhist, Christian, Maya – so typical of Hieratic art.

So, in Humanist linear perspective, we focus on the shape of a particular object and its surrounding spatial grid collapses as it enters the eye. In Hieratic axonometric perspective, we focus on the shape of a particular object and that shape expands into its surrounding spatial grid.

All these lines, shapes and grids contribute to a distinct *conceptualization* of space. From our contemporary Western point of view, space *is a void* where Euclidian lines and Cartesian co-ordinates measure out its extension in multiple dimensions (this may go so far as to include non-Euclidean and Hilbert spaces). But, in the Platonic and Aristotelian tradition still dominant before the Renaissance, the universe was *a finite plenum or fullness* – an immense sphere filled with the four elements, continually shifting places in the aether (the fifth element, also a substance). Above these, the seven planets and outer empyrean of stars sparkled like so many jewels, set into a series of spheres within spheres – the whole *Orbium Cœlestium* as a set of nested spheres moved in circular motions by the First Mover or *Primum Mobile* (see Fig. 27.8).

In this model of the cosmos, *everything had its place*, as elements and aether shifting places in the *plenum* – and the existence of a void was categorically denied. It was only in 1637 that Descartes re-defined space as a co-ordinate grid of matter extended in three directions, which Newton transformed, fifty years later, into an infinite but *empty* grid – a unified and homogeneous space fundamentally *devoid of matter* – where time and space became a measurable field in which objects appeared and events occurred.

From the Humanist point-of-view, Hieratic art in the Islamic, Persian and Byzantine traditions seem dense, convoluted, and overwrought with details. These artists, we are told, suffered from a *horor vacuii* – a fear of empty space. In fact, these craftsmen *had no concept of space* as we know it.

Instead, the art of these traditions reveals a different worldview, prior to our Humanist understanding of space, optics and perspective.

To create a Hieratic work of art, these craftsmen saw the world with the Divine Eye, actively participating in its on-going creation. In the painting, each element occupied its own unique place, actively created and shaped the moment it was seen. Painting became a glimpse into the higher world, where the luminous archetypes existed eternally in the mind of God. Sometimes, the only indication of 'space' was a golden ground filled with God's infinite light.

Other times, these artists envisioned spatial grids measured out by flat Islamic patterns or oblique lines of perspective which denied a single human point-of-view. For, Humanist perspective condensed our vision to an accurate, scientific reproduction *of the material world* – giving us one visual perspective at one point in time. Instead, craftsmen sought out systems that accurately reproduced visions *of the spiritual world*, which transcended a single human viewpoint and presented the world from multiple points of view simultaneously – a more eternal and timeless viewpoint that can only be described as omnipresent, infinite and divine.

For us today as Visionary artists, we must rediscover the older modes of seeing and shaping space. Rather than viewing the earlier Hieratic conceptions as primitive and flawed, we should engage them fully with our vision, attempting to see anew how Egyptian, Chinese, Persian and Byzantine artists painted and perceived sacred space. At the same time, we must pursue a deeper understanding of our own Western perspective (as we shall in the following chapters), since the Renaissance Humanist view unified our perception in ways hitherto unseen.

Ultimately, all these different methods and constructions must be understood as the infinite play of perception shared by humanity and divinity. As the mind of God actively creates all it sees, it also shapes those forms in a grand array of spatial measures which we too may witness and conceive. No one measure is true since all participate in the endless variety of grids, patterns and shapes which may divide unified sight into an ever-finer crystallization of space surrounding the Divine Eye.

II. Typology of Perspective

• Linear and Axonometric Perspective

In Fig. 20.1, I have differentiated between two basic types of perspective, calling the *viewer*-centered perspective *linear*, and the object-centered perspective *axonometric*. In fact, *all* systems are axonometric (meaning they attempt to 'measure' – *metreo* – an object via its axes – *axon*) and *all* are linear (constructed with *linea* or 'lines'). But, by convention, we may use these names to refer to two very different ways of viewing objects in space.

The object in question will be a 3D cube with a front, side and top. This cube is drawn onto a flat 2D plane (the paper or support) that is basically square or rectangular. Due to the horizontal and vertical edges of our paper, the cube is oriented toward a horizontal 'baseline' and a 'main vertical' (the two dimensions of our flat surface). The cube is the simplest object for us to visualize in space, and may be turned to show the bottom instead of the top, or the left side instead of the right; but no more than three faces will be visible at any given time. Meanwhile, a variety of objects, whether regular or irregular, may be visualized within the cube, so that we can reference this 3D shape from three basic angles. In our case, that object will be a human skull viewed from the front, side and top.

Sometimes, 'invisible lines' may be extended from the edges of the cube to form parallel lines, repeated in all directions, to reveal the underlying grids that support the shape in space – such as the square (*ad quadratum*) or triangular (*ad triangulum*) grids already encountered in these pages.

• Linear Perspective

During the Renaissance, artists made the world-turning move of converging parallel lines onto a common vanishing point. This form of linear perspective has been called a variety of names: artificial perspective (*perspectiva artificialis*), natural perspective, artist's perspective (*prospectiva pingendi*), convergent perspective etc. It comes in a great variety of types, from 1-point to 5-point, from worm's eye view to bird's eye view, and may include curvilinear perspective as well. In different systems, the diminishing horizontals may recede at different rates, due to different methods of construction. We shall pursue them all in Ch. 22 and 23.

• Axonometric Perspective – Orthogonal

In strict geometrical parlance, I should speak of axonometric *projection* rather than perspective, but craftsmen throughout history have considered these angled views to be *perspectives*. Axonometric perspective (also called planimetric) encompasses a great variety of types, beginning with orthogonal (also called orthographic) perspective, which *only uses lines at right angles* (only horizontals and verticals) *with no diagonals to represent depth*. Surprisingly, this system served craftsmen well for a period of 40,000 years, from Paleolithic cave painting and a variety of Tribal cultures all the way through Egypt and Mesopotamia to our own day.

It has been used by architects from time eternal to plan out temples and other dwellings from two basic angles: the ground plan and elevation. These plans may be laid side-by-side or one-above-the-other, and cross-referenced. Since orthogonal perspective uses just two axes, there are two basic types:

1a. *Horizontal* Orthogonal perspective – the front and side of the cube are arranged horizontally, *side-by-side* (Fig. 20.2).

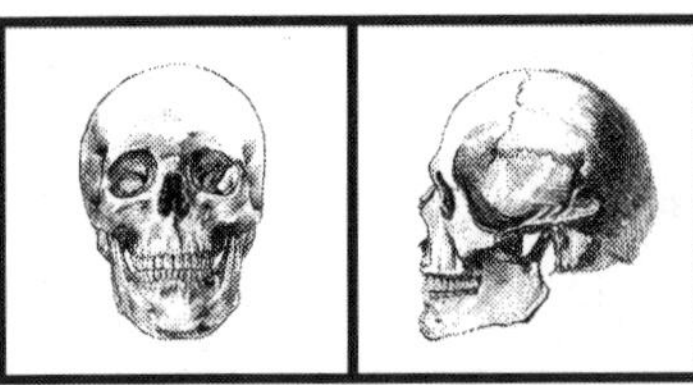

Fig. 20.2 - Horizontal Orthogonal

1b. *Vertical* Orthogonal perspective – the front and top of the cube are arranged vertically, *one-above-the-other* (Fig. 20.3). (In an architectural plan, the front and *bottom* of the cube are used, as the elevation and *ground plan*).

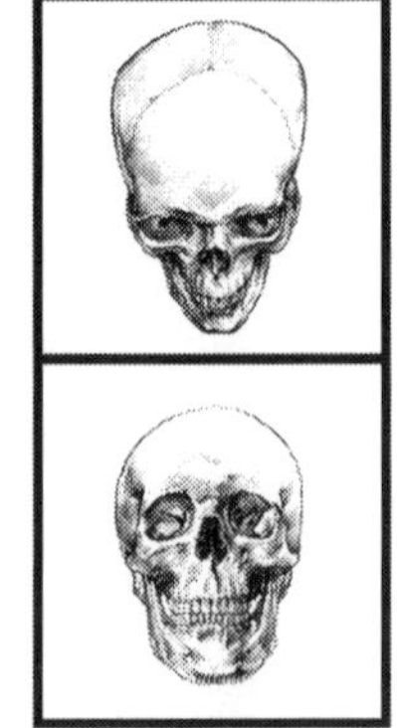

Fig. 20.3
Vertical Orthogonal

• Axonometric Perspective – Oblique

Another form of axonometric perspective is called oblique. In oblique perspective, *the front face only uses lines at right angles* (only horizontals and verticals), *while the top and side faces are diagonal* to the baseline. In some cases, the diagonals for the top and sides *remain parallel*; in other cases they either *converge or diverge*. The angle of the diagonal (from the baseline) may vary, but is usually 45°. The length of the diagonal may also vary, to allow different types of measurement for the receding side. This gives rise to four basic types:

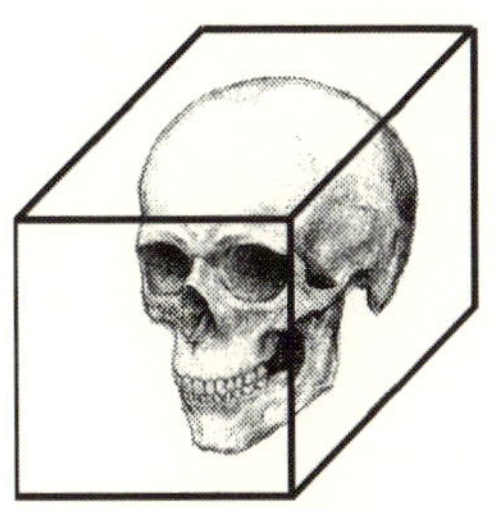

Fig. 20.4 - Axonometric Strict Oblique

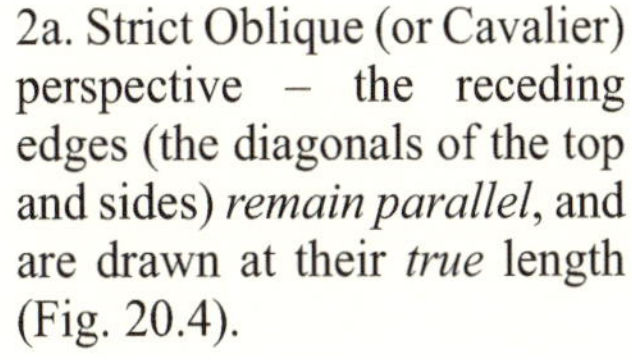

2a. Strict Oblique (or Cavalier) perspective – the receding edges (the diagonals of the top and sides) *remain parallel*, and are drawn at their *true* length (Fig. 20.4).

2b. Cabinet Oblique perspective – the receding edges *remain parallel*, and are drawn at *half* their length (Fig. 20.5).

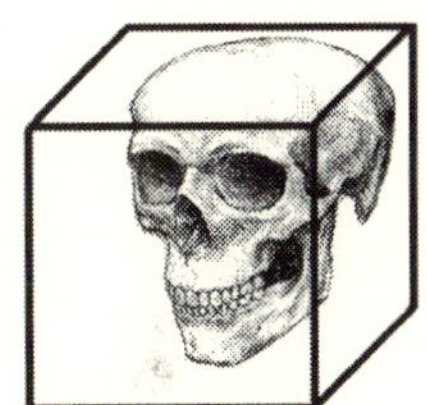

Fig. 20.5 - Axonometric Cabinet Oblique

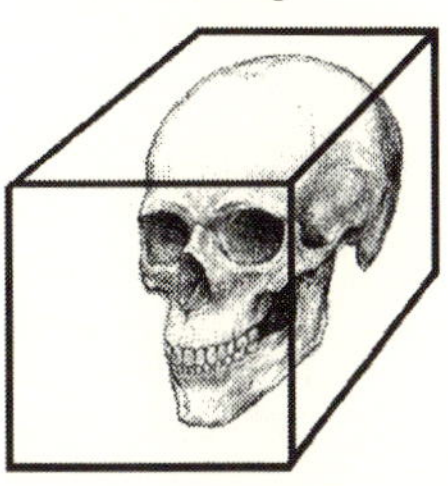

Fig. 20.6 - Axonometric Oblique Converging

2c. Oblique Converging perspective – the receding edges do not remain parallel, but *converge* Fig. 20.6).

2d. Oblique Diverging perspective – the receding edges do not remain parallel, but *diverge* (Fig. 20.7).

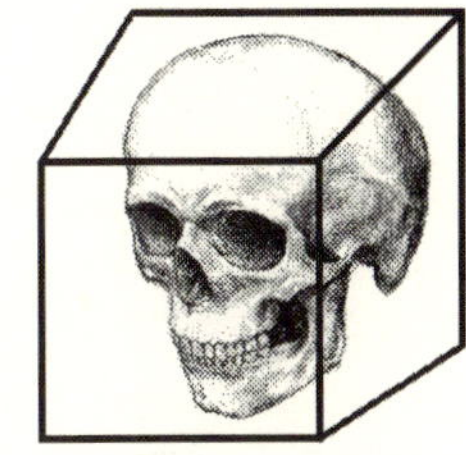

Fig. 20.7 - Axonometric Oblique Diverging

The first two types (Strict and Cabinet) are used by architects and craftsmen to accurately measure out the receding side of a cubic object in their plans. As long as the receding edges *remain parallel*, the measures will hold true. Oblique perspective is often encountered in Chinese, Persian and Byzantine works of art, where their furniture and architecture recedes with parallel lines.

The third type (Oblique Converging) is found in Early Renaissance paintings, with their first bold attempts to converge parallel lines onto a common vanishing point. Instead, these artists converged their lines onto *a common area* of the painting, or onto a common *vertical line*. So, when they drew furniture or architecture, each cubic shape converged *onto its own* vanishing point, but not onto a common vanishing point shared by all cubic shapes. This only happened with true linear perspective.

The last type (Oblique Diverging) is mostly found in Byzantine icons, where it is called Reverse Perspective. Contrary to our accustomed way of seeing things, the diagonals of the cubic shapes *diverge* in the distance rather than converge. (Or – to say the same thing – they converge onto a point *in front of* the object).

Oblique perspective, in its broad variety of types, was the main form of perspective until the Italian Renaissance, and reached a high level of sophistication in Chinese, Persian and Byzantine art. All these traditions used some form of oblique perspective, combining it with (what we shall consider next as) strict axonometric and isometric perspectives.

We must continually bear in mind that, in oblique perspective, *the front face of the cube is always drawn as a square*, with its bottom on the baseline and its edges vertical, so *it faces us directly*. In the next two types of axonometric perspective, the front face of the cube may *turn away from the baseline*, and be drawn as a parallelogram.

• Strict Axonometric Perspective & Isometric Perspective

When the front face of the cube turns away from the baseline, we begin to view it in either strict axonometric perspective or in isometric perspective. In both cases, the 3D cube turns laterally 45°, so we see it at an exact three-quarter angle. At the same time, it tilts downward, though the degree of tilt may vary, revealing more or less of the top face. Nevertheless, the receding diagonals *always remain parallel.*

3a. In strict axonometric perspective (also called 'military projection'), the receding diagonals run *at a 45° angle to the baseline* (Fig. 20.8).

3b. Meanwhile in isometric perspective the receding diagonals run *at a 30° angle* to the baseline (Fig. 20.9).

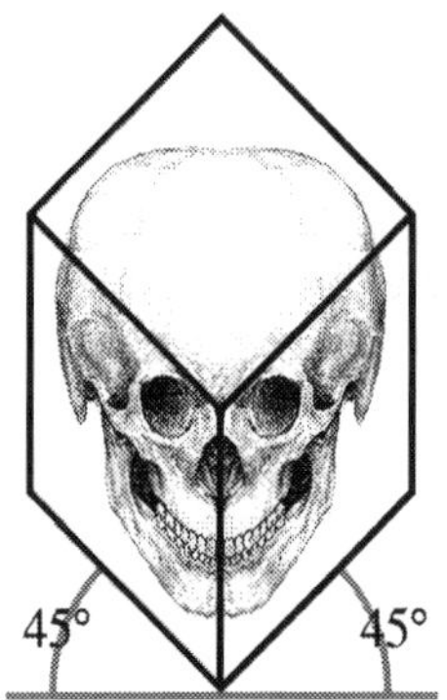

Fig. 20.8 - Strict Axonometric

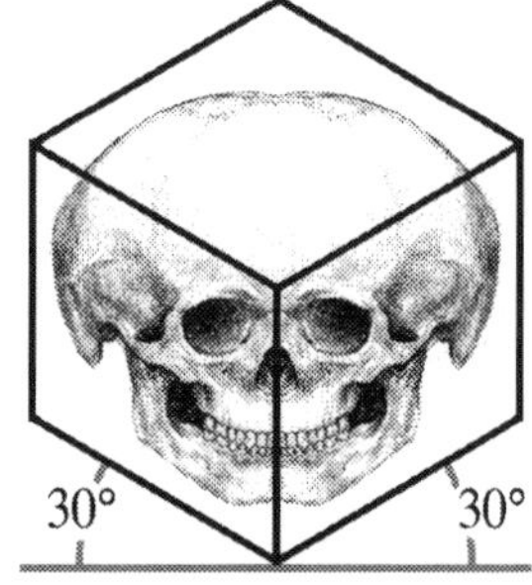

Fig. 20.9 - Isometric Perspective

Axonometric and isometric graph paper are sold to architects, as a convenient means for orienting their designs. A close look at axonometric graph paper (Fig. 20.10) reveals a basic *ad quadratum* grid, where the diagonal axes run *at 45° to the baseline.* The vertical axis also appears, while the horizon line is assumed and remains invisible. Meanwhile, isometric graph paper (Fig. 20.11) takes an *ad triangulum* grid and gives it a quarter turn, so that the triangles run vertically. The two diagonal axes now run *at 30° to the baseline* which, like the horizon line, *is assumed* and remains invisible. Because this is an *ad triangulum* grid, all the lines on the paper *run at a 60° angle to each other.*

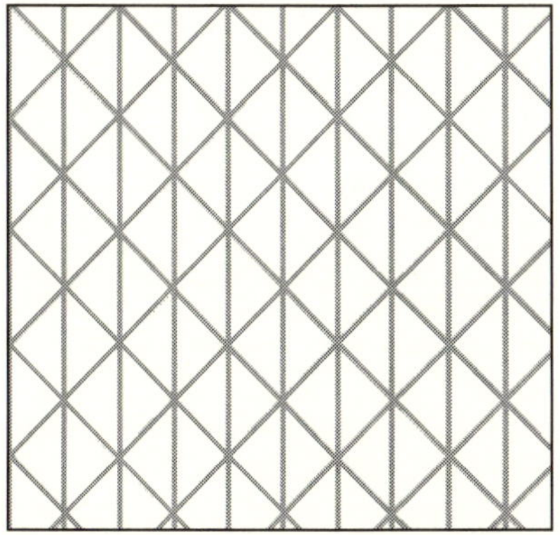

Fig. 20.10 - Axonometric Graph Paper with *Ad Quadratum* Grid turned 45° to Baseline

Fig. 20.11 - Isometric Graph Paper with *Ad Triangulum* Grid turned 30° to Baseline

We recall that, while drawing the Platonic Solids, axonometric and isometric grids were used to orient the receding diagonals toward an invisible horizon line which, passing through the exact centre, allowed the shapes to emerge equally in all directions. Rather than a human eye passively observing the convergence of a shape (intramission theory of vision in linear perspective), the Divine Eye was actively creating the shape, which grew outward from the centre (extramission theory of vision in axonometric perspective).

There is a certain irony in the way Humanist and Hieratic perspectives operate. In Humanist linear perspective, the receding edges of a shape *converge* onto a common vanishing point, so that parallel lines undergo *a triangular mapping in space*. The square contracts into the triangle. In Hieratic axonometric perspective, the receding edges *remain parallel*, so that the diagonals undergo *a quadratic mapping in space*. The triangle expands into the square.

• Isometric, Dimetric & Trimetric Perspective

The last types of axonometric perspective fall under the category of isometric, and are called *dimetric* and *trimetric*. If we return to our cube in isometric perspective and measure the interior angles of the foremost corner (Fig. 20.12), we notice that they add up to 360° (120° + 120° + 120° = 360°). At the same time, the angle at the baseline remains at 30° on either side, which we may express as 30-30 (isometric means 'equal measure').

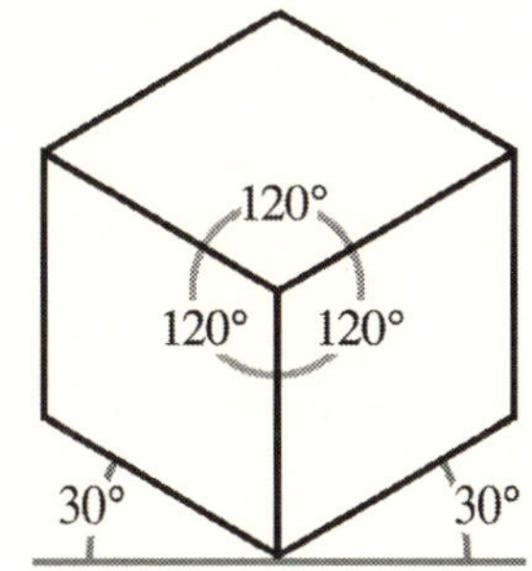

Fig. 20.12 - Isometric Perspective

In dimetric and trimetric perspective, the interior angles always add up to 360°, but the angles at the baseline may vary. In *dimetric* perspective, the baseline angles *remain equal*, but may be inclined at, say, 15-15 or 40-40. As a result, *at least two* of the interior angles remain equal, while the third varies to make a total of 360°. So, in our example, the baseline angles are 15-15, and the interior angles are 105° + 105° + 150° = 360° (Figs. 20.13 - 14).

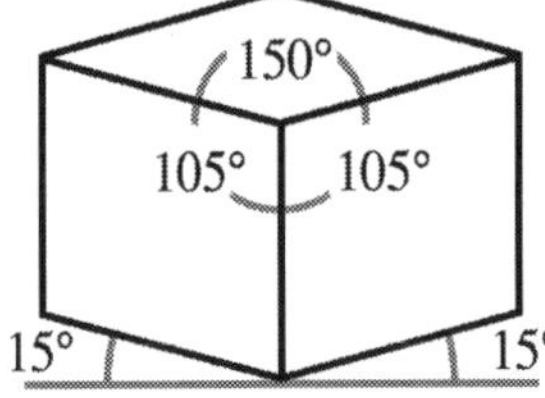

Fig. 20.13 - Dimetric Perspective

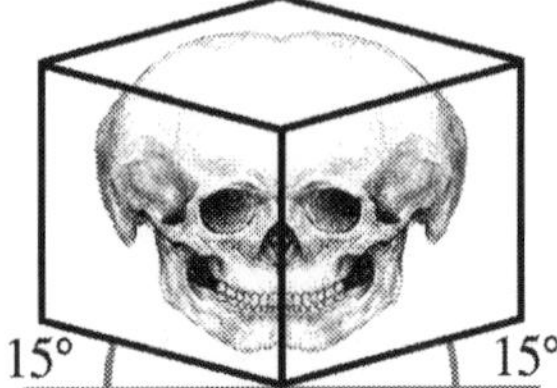

Fig. 20.14 - Dimetric Perspective

In *trimetric* perspective, the angles along the baseline *are not equal*. As a result, the interior angles *differ*, but will still add up to 360°. So, in our example, the baseline angles are 15-45, and the interior angles are 105° + 135° + 120° = 360° (Figs. 20.15 - 16).

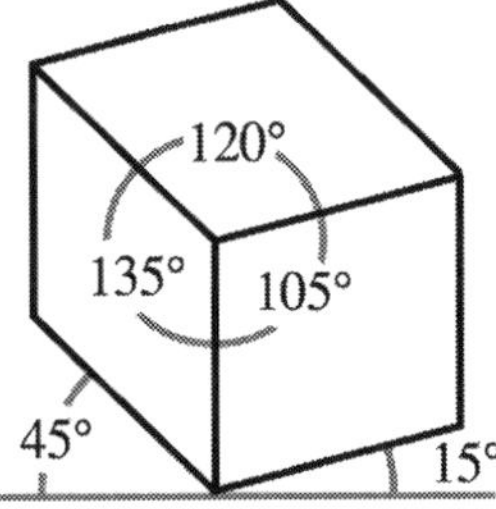

Fig. 20.15 - Trimetric Perspective

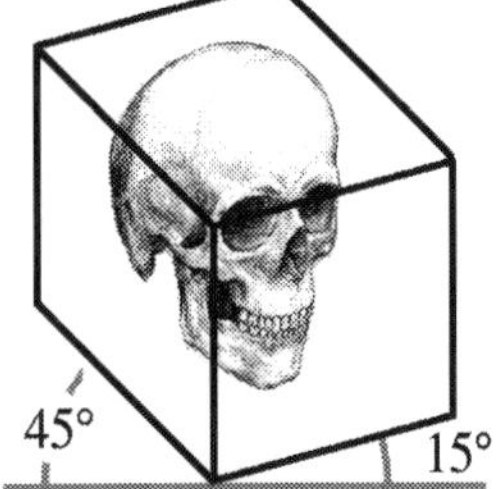

Fig. 20.16 - Trimetric Perspective

To summarize, there are three basic types of axonometric perspective: one, *orthogonal*, with no diagonal lines; two, *oblique*, with diagonals, but the front face remains strictly orthogonal to the baseline (four types); and three, *strict axonometric* or *isometric* (two types), where the front face is diagonal to the baseline.

III. Orthogonal Perspective & Ancient Egypt

In 1820, a young Greek named Yanni d'Athanasi discovered the Tomb of Nebamun (c. 1350 BCE), the richly-decorated burial chamber of a New Kingdom scribe from Thebes named Nebamun ('My Lord is Amun'). Working for the British Consulate, d'Athanasi chiselled out many of the most beautiful scenes and shipped them directly to England, where they are now on display in a special room of the British Museum. D'Athanasi died without ever revealing the tomb's whereabouts.

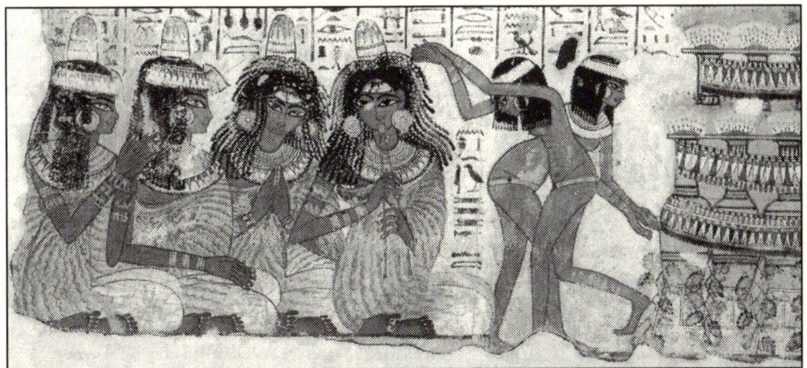

Fig. 20.17 - *Nebamun's Banquet Scene* c. 1350 BCE

The scenes which have come down to us (Fig. 20.17) show hunting marshes, sacred pools, and a banquet with musicians and dancers – a scene that offers a surprising departure from the usual Hieratic depiction of figures in Egyptian art. Not only do the two dancers on the right overlap, but they move their bodies with sinuous delight. To the left of the dancers, two musicians turn their heads to each other, their flying braids falling before and behind their ornamental pectorals. A close look at their nose and eyes reveals something rarely encountered in Egyptian art – faces suggestive of the three-quarter view.

This banquet scene reminds us that, for most of its three thousand year history, Egyptian art followed *a strictly canonical form of representation*, especially for the human figure. This has become so well-known as to be almost cliché: the head, arms and lower body turned in profile while the upper body remains in a frontal view. Out of respect for the hieroglyphic significance of many sacred gestures (*hai* – hands raised in rejoicing; *iakbyt* – hands raised in mourning; *dua* – hands raised in praise), the human figure followed this strictly canonical form, *which displays the body in orthogonal perspective* (Fig. 20.18).

In our chapter on Hieratic Proportion, we saw how Egyptian craftsmen used square grids to measure out the figure in exact proportions. From the top

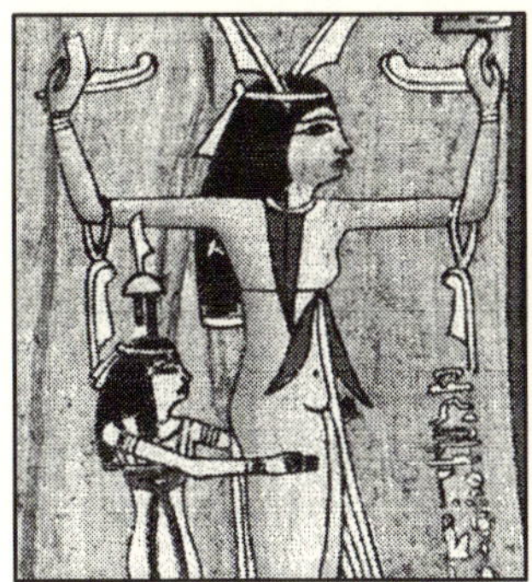

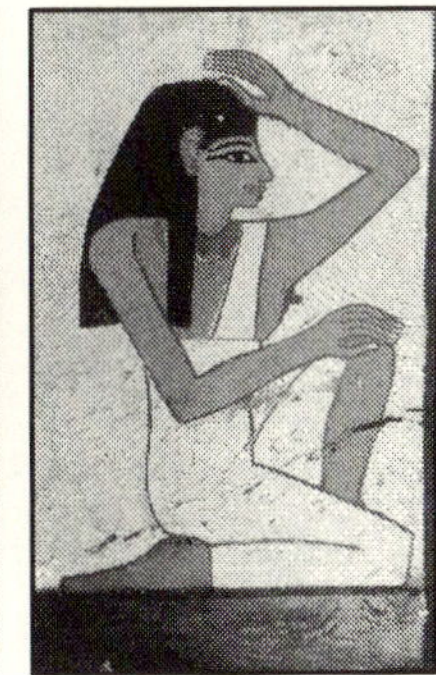

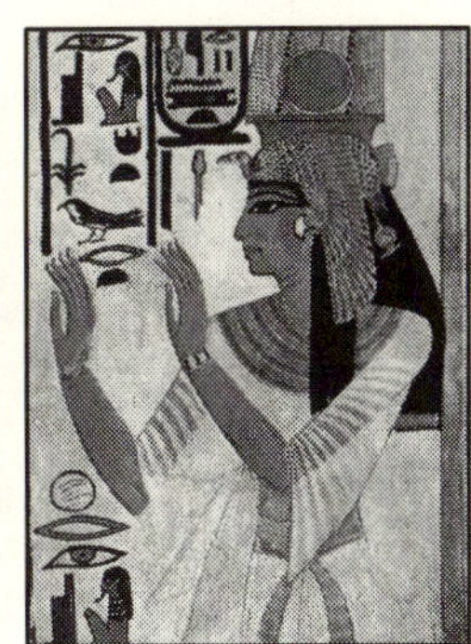

Fig. 20.18 - *Hai* - Rejoicing *Iakbyt* - Mourning *Dua* - Praise

of the shoulders to the navel, a distinct section of the grid was reserved for the upper body *in frontal view*. The remainder of the figure, *in profile view*, was laid out in sections, one-above-the-other, to create the figure as a whole in *vertical* orthogonal perspective.

This same approach was used for the composition of entire scenes: either a grid of squares or a series of vertical and horizontal lines were marked on the surface, and the figures were arranged within this orthogonal space. Both axes – the horizontal and the vertical – were used to great effect.

Horizontal registers allowed the artist to depict unified compositions in orthogonal space, but they also allowed for a *temporal* movement through several compositions unified by mythic narrative, such as the opening of the eye and mouth ritual (Fig. 26.5) or the sun passing through the twelve hours of the night, symbolized by Atum-Re's solar barque passing through the twelve gates of the Netherworld. *The Books of the Afterlife* inscribed on the walls of the Pharaoh's tombs were, in fact, immense maps of the netherworld, fully charted for navigation. Though divided into different registers and scenes, then inscribed on different walls extending across the entire length of the Pharaoh's burial chamber – their spatial and temporal dimensions were, in fact, fully unified.

On the vertical axis, the rule of 'hierarchal importance' reigned, where deities and royal figures were scaled to larger proportions than their acolytes and attendants. To the Western eye, large means *closer* in space – closer to *the viewer* from *his* perspectival view onto the scene. Egyptian art had no such viewer, since all scenes transpired in a sacred space created by orthogonal perspective. As such, a figure that occupied more of the vertical grid was greater in size and status. Horizontally, scenes could be read (like hieroglyphs) from right-to-left or left-to-right, but the right side of the composition was always reserved for figures of greater importance.

In Spell 126 of *The Book of Coming Forth by Day* (commonly called *The Book of the Dead*), we behold four baboons and four flaming braziers arranged around the dreaded Lake of Fire (Fig. 20.19). This image, taken from the famous *Papyrus of Ani*, was probably drawn by Ani himself (a scribe who appears with his wife throughout the book). Ani has chosen to depict the Lake of Fire from above, while the baboons and braziers appear in profile view, mirroring each other above and below. To the right and left, the braziers appear sideways, but facing in opposite directions.

Using orthogonal perspective, in both the vertical and horizontal directions, Ani has unified his top and profile views into one spatial measure. His disregard for linear perspective (with its singular view onto space) has allowed him, instead, to create a kind of mandala, where the baboons appear side-by-side symmetrically (like guardians), but also mirror each other vertically (like reflections in the pool). Such a Hieratic composition, with its delicate balance and multiple symmetries, would be impossible to achieve in linear perspective.

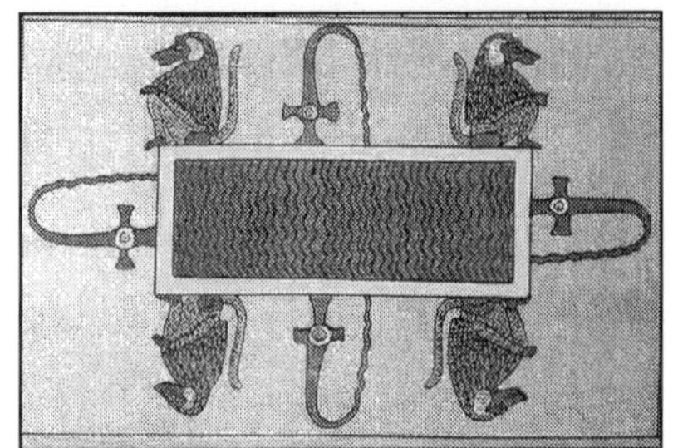

Fig. 20.19 - Lake of Fire
From *The Papyrus of Ani* c. 1250 BCE

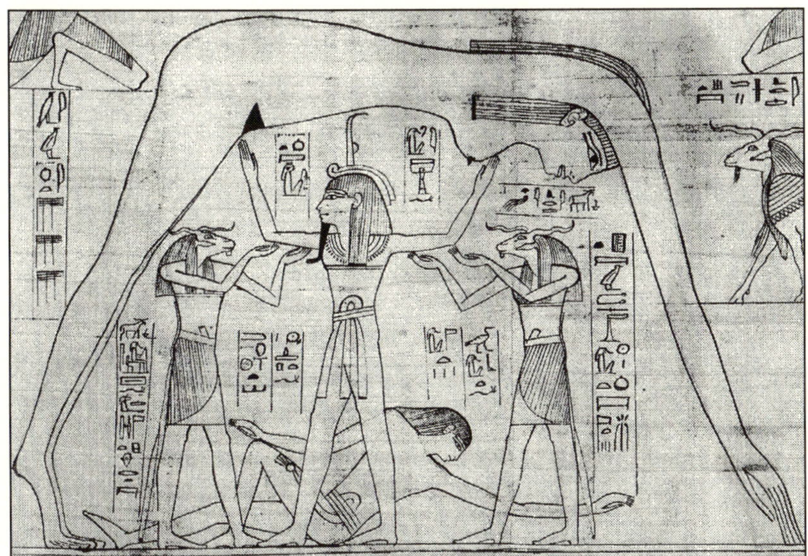

Fig. 20.20 - The heavenly *Nut* above, earthly *Geb* below, with *Shu* between them

The same is true of the Egyptian depiction of the Creation (Fig. 20.20). In *Temple of the Cosmos*, Jeremy Naydler offers a strikingly new interpretation of this well-known Egyptian motif. During the Middle Kingdom, the Coffin Texts frequently depicted Shu, the god of the middle realm, separating the sky goddess Nut from her consort, the earth god Geb. This arrangement has been read as an image of the Creation, when the Earth and Sky, originally united, were separated by Shu.

At the same time, this scene also depicts, according to Naydler, the three realms of being to which all humans have access:

"Egyptian cosmology is based on the division of the manifest cosmos into three qualitatively distinct domains... They are three orders of being:

1. The spiritual or heavenly (Nut)

2. The intermediate (Shu)

3. The physical or earthly (Geb)

The psychic nature of Shu's intermediate realm is hinted at by the fact that Shu's arms are often portrayed as being supported in their life-giving gesture by ram spirits [...which] *take the form of ba birds, or soul birds. The hieroglyph of the ram in fact has the sound value of 'ba'. Their frequent depiction in the intermediate region occupied by Shu is an indication that this was understood on one level as symbolizing the realm of soul, which is intermediate between spirit and matter."*[1]

Whenever we gaze upon this image we are confronted, in fact, by a symbolic reflection of our own tripartite being. Like Geb, we have our material aspect, which the later Greeks and Gnostics called our body, the *somatic* level of being. Like Nut, we also have our spiritual aspect, which was called spirit or the *pneumatic* level of being. And between them is our soulful aspect, which the Greeks and Gnostics called our *psychic* level of being. Hence, *soma, psyche, pneuma.*

This Hieratic image, engraved upon black alabaster coffins in the Middle Kingdom, symbolized the occupant's tripartite nature. Ancient craftsman created this symbol through the careful arrangement of figures in orthogonal space. Its simple symmetrical structure, like an emblem or medallion, gives it an archetypal shape that engraves itself upon our memory. Left and right, above and below – all of these orthogonal axes are used to compose a mnemonic device that has survived in our cultural memory for more than four thousand years.

IV. China: Oblique Perspective

What we in the West call axonometric perspective had already been used by artists in China for a period of fifteen hundred years. Axonometry first came to Europe in the 17th century when missionaries returning from the East described a novel approach for military planning. Father Claude François Millet Deschales, a Jesuit mathematician and missionary, published in 1677 his important treatise *L'Art de Fortifier, de Défendre et d'Attaquer les Places* (The Art of Fortifying, Defending and Attacking Spaces), which he subtitled: *Following the Methods of the French, Dutch, Italians and Spaniards*.

The Jesuit neglected to mention the role of his Muslim brethren, since he had sojourned in the Ottoman Empire for a period of nine years in his youth. After Millet Deschales' publication, a whole slew of Jesuit tracts emerged, dedicated to this new form of perspective which allowed military engineers to avoid blind spots and false measures in their designs. Thus, the axonometric perspective of Persian miniatures and Chinese brush scrolls ultimately found its place in the West among defence strategists and military engineers.[2] Already familiar with *ad quadratum* and *ad triangulum* grids from the Gothic period, they simply turned their grids to re-orient cubic shapes toward the diagonal (Fig. 20.10).

Evidence of oblique perspective in Chinese painting extends as far back as Chinese painting itself – to the murals on the tombs of the Han dynasty emperors from the early 2nd century CE (Fig. 20.21). The court painter Gu Kaizhi (c. 344 – 406), who is considered to be the founder of Chinese scroll painting, wrote three treatises on the art, including one entitled *On Painting* where he described the use of *ruled lines* for organizing pictorial space. As Christopher W. Tyler and Chien-Chung Chen note in their study, 'Chinese Perspective as a Rational System': *"The Chinese tradition of oblique orthographic perspective extends back nearly 2000 years."*[3]

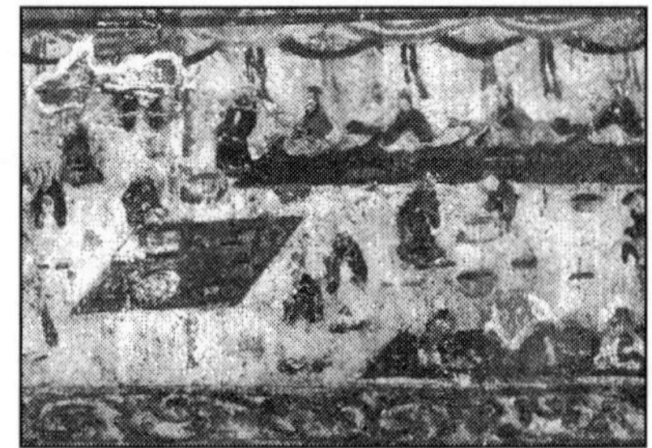

Fig. 20.21 - *Banquet of an Emperor*
Eastern Han Dynasty 25-220 CE

In their most typical use of oblique perspective, Chinese painters depicted furniture and other cubic shapes with the front face orthogonal to the baseline, while the sides receded in parallel diagonals – thus in Strict Oblique

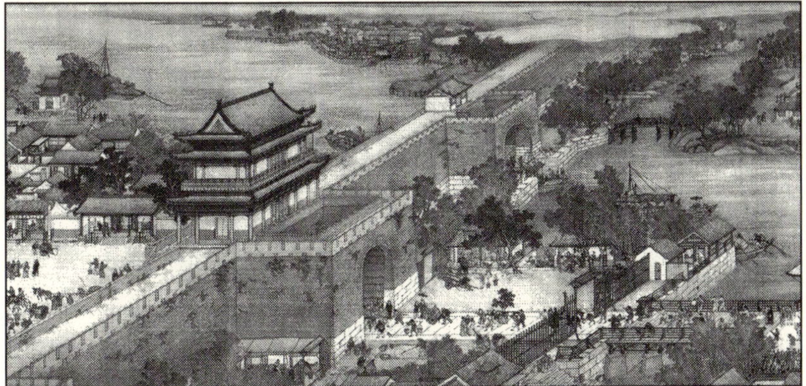

Fig. 20.22 - Zhang Zeduan: *Along the River During the Qingming Festival* c. 1130

perspective. One reason for this perspectival method is the nature of Chinese painting itself. From its inception, Chinese painting consisted of delicate brushwork on paper or silk scrolls, some of which were hung vertically as 'wall scrolls', but most of which were designed horizontally as 'hand scrolls'.

Hand scrolls were unrolled from right to left and 'read' like books. They could be several metres long, and depict a single story unfolding along a continuous landscape, which opened out in an on-going sequence of narrative scenes. Oblique perspective was ideal for this purpose, since it allowed *a continuous reading of the landscape*, without convergence onto any one fixed point or point-of-view. Like our first-generation video games (game designers are now at the forefront of research into oblique perspective), parallel diagonals allow the landscape to roll past our eye in one continuously unified space.

Perhaps the finest example of this technique is the epic scroll *Along the River During the Qingming Festival* (*Qing Ming Shang He Tu*). Painted by the imperial court artist Zhang Zeduan (1085 – 1145), it is the Chinese equivalent of Brueghel the Elder's panoramic views onto Netherlandish peasant life (painted 300 years later). Only 25 cm tall and over 5 metres long, the Song Dynasty scroll takes us on a leftward journey along the Bian river, from the verdant countryside with its harbour and fishing boats, past the immense Rainbow bridge at the centre, to the gated capital city of Bianjing (modern Kaifeng), with its market stalls and bustling commercial streets (Fig. 20.22).

Along the way, the oblique perspective never changes but always orients the landscape to a 30° diagonal. The horizon line is not shown, lying atop the visible limits of the scroll, offering a more distant and aerial view onto this vast panorama of 12th century Chinese society.

V. China: Converging & Diverging Oblique Perspective

Over time, Chinese artists expanded their repertoire to include not only Strict Oblique, but also the Converging and Diverging types of Oblique perspective. A prime example is the 10th century silk painting *The Night*

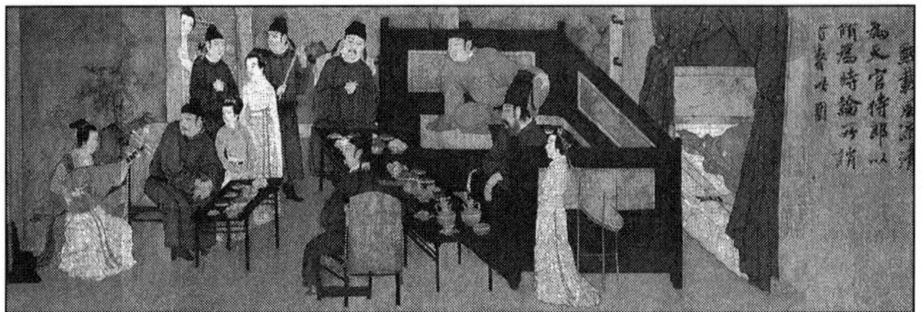

Fig. 20.23 - Gu Hong-zhong: *The Night Revels of Han Xizai* c. 950

Revels of Han Xizai, a scroll 30 cm tall and 3 metres long painted by Gu Hong-zhong (c. 937 – 975) and preserved in a 12th century copy. It depicts five scenes in the court life of minister Han Xizai, beginning with a view onto the minister and his guests enjoying a concert with a Chinese lute (*pipa*) player (Fig. 20.23).

In their analysis of this picture, Tyler and Chien-Chung note Gu Hong-zhong's tendency to create *"patches of oblique parallel perspective with angles that are inconsistent across the scene."*[4] In other words, though the diagonals on the right side are parallel with each other, the diagonals on the left create a separate set of parallels that give the impression of *convergence* within the scene, and even of *divergence* within certain types of object. They elaborate:

"There is a form of convergence in this example, however, in that the food table at the left with the man turning is angled on the other oblique [thus opposite to the obliques on the right]*, which is quite a rare occurrence in Chinese painting... Remarkably, although the two sides of the tabletop are parallel, the legs are painted with a strong divergence of their parallels; the back legs are substantially longer than the front legs. ...Thus, we must conclude that, in this early period, Gu Hong-zhong had a set of particular rules for his perspective constructions, largely consistent with the oblique orthographic scheme but with some idiosyncratic deviations that followed their own rules within local objects."*[5]

Although Gu Hong-zhong was able to *converge* two oblique perspectives in one scene, his discovery (which would lead Renaissance artists to develop linear perspective) went unnoticed, and was rarely repeated in Chinese painting. In the curious table on the left, Gu Hong-zhong also used a form of Oblique Diverging perspective, a system much-favoured by Byzantine icon painters for more than a thousand years. Yet again, this discovery went largely unnoticed, and was never systemized in Chinese painting. Rather, the Converging and Diverging forms of Oblique perspective became a part of Gu Hong-zhong's unique style.

Tyler and Chien-Chung also notice Gu Hong-zhong's 10th century use of an optical illusion that has recently become known in the West as Shephard's illusion (Fig. 20.25). When the same parallelogram is viewed in different directions, such as a table top oriented either lengthwise or sideways, we

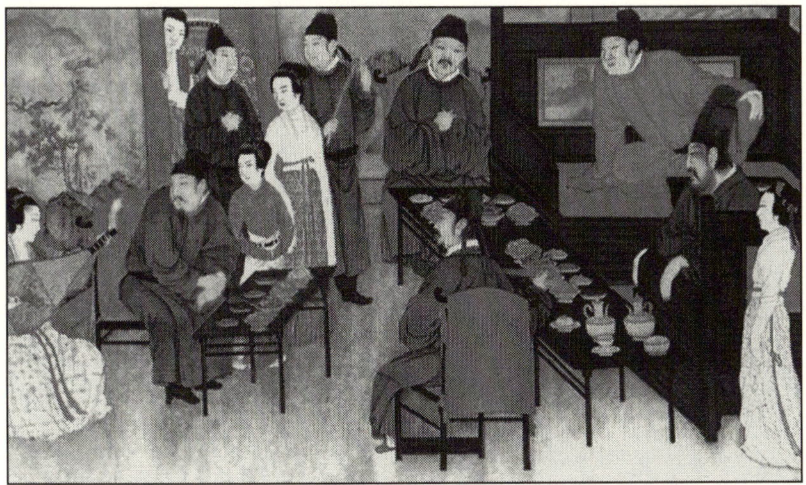

Fig. 20.24 - Gu Hong-zhong: *The Night Revels of Han Xizai* (Detail)

view the lengthwise orientation as longer, and the sideways orientation as wider, even though the parallelograms are identical. Thus, the chair in the centre foreground of Gu Hong-zhong's painting (Fig. 20.24) appears wider, and the table on the left appears longer, even though their top surfaces are almost identical in shape and size. What is more, the chair appears larger and the table smaller, because we view the chair as closer to us. Artists accustomed to Axonometric perspective adjusted the size and width of their furniture according to the illusionistic needs of the scene.

From three millennia of Egyptian history to another two thousand years of Chinese dynasties, axonometric perspective served the royal craftsmen well in their harmonious design of pictorial space. Yet, our history of Hieratic Perspective has only just begun, as Persian, Byzantine and Buddhist painters advanced axonometric methods far beyond their predecessors – creating works of extraordinary beauty and complexity, while still respecting their orthographic and oblique rulings.

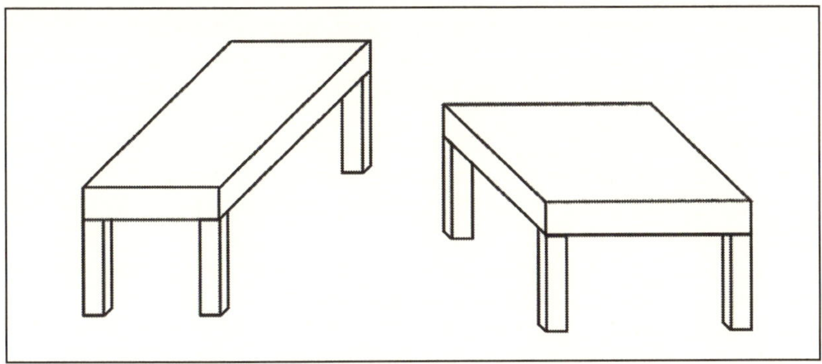

Fig. 20.25 - Shepherd's Illusion: The Two Parallelograms are Identical in Size

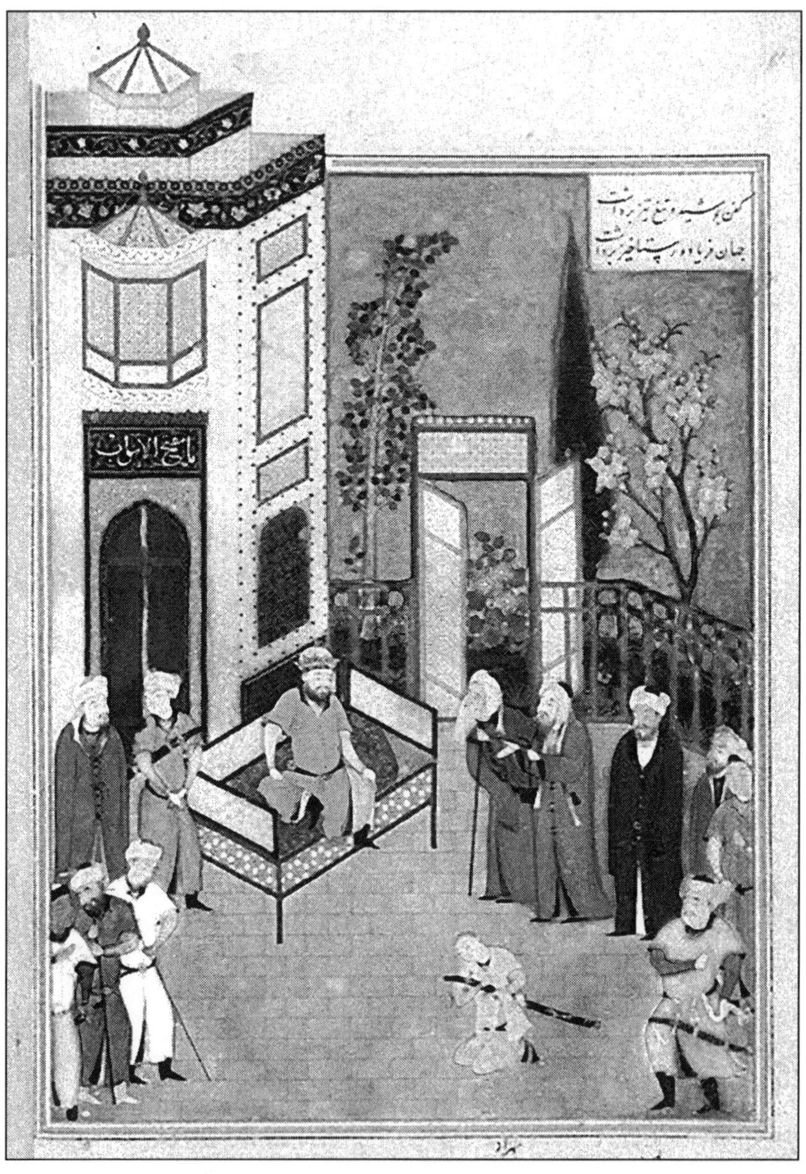

Fig. 21.1 - Kamāl ud-Dīn Behzād: *Khusraw and Shirin* in The Khamsah of Nizami
The Elders plead with King Hormuzd to forgive his son Khusraw

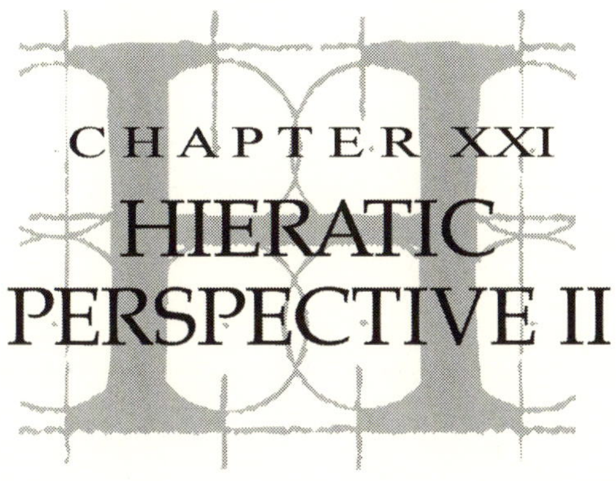

CHAPTER XXI HIERATIC PERSPECTIVE II

I. Persian Miniatures: The Influx of Different Cultural Styles

In the early 13th century, Genghis Khan sent his Mongol army into Persia, defeating the Shah in his capital city of Samarkand. The Mongol Emperor's grandson, Hulagu Kahn, created a new court in the capital, establishing the century-long Ilkhanate dynasty (1219 – 1335). Hulagu Kahn's mother and wife were both Nestorian Christians, while he and his ruling descendants became Tibetan Buddhists. But the majority of their subjects were Muslim, and the court eventually converted to Islam with its seventh ruler, Mahmud Ghazan, in 1295.

The Ilkhanate dynasty brought many Chinese arts and methods to Persia, including the technique of painting on paper and silk – and thus the Persian Miniature was born. As the court travelled back and forth between their summer and winter palaces, the portable book, with its poetry and plates, became a favourite travelling companion. In the Ilkhanate court, local Persian craftsmen (who were steeped in the Baghdad School of painting) adopted elements of the new Chinese style, including steep mountainous landscapes, fluid line-work in the clouds – and Axonometric perspective.

In 1381, the Turco-Mongol conqueror Timur (known is the West as Tamerlane) invaded Persia as part of his much broader campaign to establish an empire equalling that of Genghis Kahn. The Timurid Empire (c. 1370 – 1467) extended from modern-day Turkey through Iraq, Iran and Afghanistan to Pakistan and northern India. This brought a fresh wave of Chinese influence into Persia, and the Persian Miniature experienced its Classical Age. Illuminated texts began to combine Persian poetry and calligraphy with Islamic patterns and Asian painting techniques, which spread westward to the Ottoman Empire and eastward to the later Moghul Empire of Northern India.

It was particularly the city of Shiraz that produced the best-known 'Classical style' of miniatures from the Timurid period, illustrating poems by Sufi poets like Saadi, Khajoo Kermani and Hafez. The Shiraz style is noted for its symmetrical compositions, strict rulings and frieze-like narratives.

The other important centres of book production were located in the capitals of Herat and then Tabiz, where the renowned artist Kamāl ud-Dīn Behzād (c. 1450 – c. 1535, also known as Kamaleddin Bihzad) headed the imperial atelier (called the *kitabkhāna*) and brought the art of the Persian Miniature to new heights of expression. Behzād freed up the strict compositions of the Classical period, creating open spaces and a narrative flow through complex visual patterns and expressive human gestures.

In 1501, the first indigenous Persian rulers returned to power since the fall of the Sassanian Empire in 651. This Safavid Dynasty revived Persian power throughout the region, and gave birth to a new age of Persian Miniatures. In the city of Tabriz, a new style emerged, detaching itself from Asian influences and seeking inspiration in Armenian and Byzantine models. Under Reza Abassi (1565–1635), the Safvani school of painting came to prominence, producing stand-alone plates for *muraqqa* or albums, often depicting a single beautiful youth or reclining maiden in a floral landscape.

In the early 1500's, the exiled Mughal emperor Humayun found refuge in Tabriz, where he discovered Persian Miniatures in the workshop of Behzād. With the help of the Safavid emperor, Humayun regained power and subsequently brought two Safavid artists with him to Dehli. Thus began the art of the Mughal Miniature, which subsequently flourished under three succeeding generations of Mughal emperors. The original Persian style was modified by local craftsmen to include Hindu, Jain and Buddhist motifs. As rich patrons of the arts, the Mughal rulers brought the once-Persian Miniature to new heights of refinement.

Throughout its long history, the Persian Miniature witnessed a continual influx of different cultural styles, blending them together to create a unique art form that arose only in history's most epic periods and cultures, rivalling the Egyptian Books of the Afterlife, the Mayan Codices, and the Illuminated Texts of the European Middle Ages.

II. Persian Armature & Orthogonal Perspective

In the Topkapi Palace Museum in Istanbul, a unique page was discovered in a *muraqqa* album from the Timurid period. It consisted of a *arzadasht* or 'report' from Ja'far Tabrizi, the director of the atelier, and grants us a brief glimpse into the daily of life of a Persian Miniaturist. Tabrizi reports:

"Amir Khalil has finished the waves in two sea scenes of the Gulistan and will begin to apply color. Mawlana Shihab has applied gold to the frontispiece illumination, four cartouches, and the finials of the frontispiece... Khwaja Ata the ruling maker has finished Mawlana Sa'duddin's Tarkh... Mawlana Muhammad Mutahhar has finished writing 25,000 verses of the Shahnama."[1]

He goes on to add that, *"Khwaja Abdul-Rahim is busy making designs for the binders, illuminators, tent-makers and tile-makers,"* while *"Mawlana Ali is designing a frontispiece illumination for the Shahnama. His eyes were sore for a few days."*[2]

We learn from this report that miniatures were produced by a number of craftsmen specializing in different tasks. The 'ruling maker' laid out the page, the gilder outlined cartouches, while the calligrapher wrote lines of text. Most important was the head of the atelier, who 'designed' the whole composition. Others then traced out the figures in ink and painted them in gouache. Some added Islamic patterns, while others touched them up in gold. It was a complex operation that not only produced books, but created the designs for carpets, tapestries, 'tent-makers and tile-makers'. No wonder Mawlana Ali's eyes were tired...

Ja'far Tabrizi's report mentions '*Khwaja Ata the ruling maker'*, suggesting that invisible lines of armature structured the composition. We recall that one of 'The Seven Principles of Painting' (*haft aṣl-i naqqāshī*) mentioned by Qutb al-Din Qissakhvan was *faṣṣālī*, meaning 'ruled and compartmentalized shapes' – such as the margins and lay-out found in Persian Miniatures. Particularly in the Shiraz style of the Timurid Empire, a Classical symmetry reigned, with strict rulings for the compositional layout and calligraphed cartouches.

In her 1949 study on *Shiraz Painting in the Sixteenth Century*, Grace Dunham Guest analyzes twenty-five plates from *The Khamsa* of Nizami in the Smithsonian's Freer Collection. The *Khamsa* (or *Quintet*), also called *Panj Ganj* (*The Five Jewels*) is a series of five epic poems on war, courtly love, spiritual allegory and ascension. Guest concentrates on the allegory of *The Seven Beauties* (*Haft Paykar*), where Prince Bahram-e Gur visits the seven pavilions of seven princesses promised to be his wives.

He visits each pavilion on a different day, and each pavilion is a different colour. Within, a princess of a different race tells a tale, related to the pavilion's planetary mood, colour and feeling. In the end, the framing story becomes a Sufi allegory on the journey of the soul through the *Hasht-Bihisht*, the 'eight paradises' which encompass the seven planetary spheres and the eighth sphere of the stellar firmament.

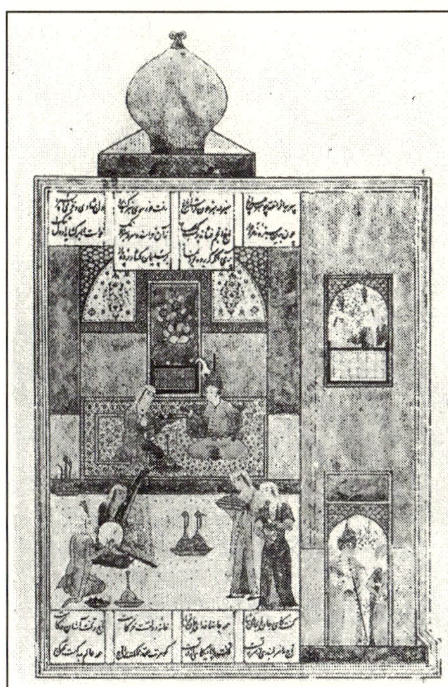

Fig. 21.2 - Prince Bahram-e Gur Visits the Green Pavilion

Calling upon a 1936 study by the Viennese art historians Emmy Wellesz and Kurt Blauensteiner ('Ilustrationen zu einer Geschichte Timurs' in Wiener Beiträge zur Kunst- und Kulturgeschichte Asiens X, 1936), Guest reveals the armature that Shiraz painters drew to organize their pictorial space: *"The excellence in composition... is due to an 'inner order' based upon a mathematically controlled plotting of the page design as a whole."*[3]

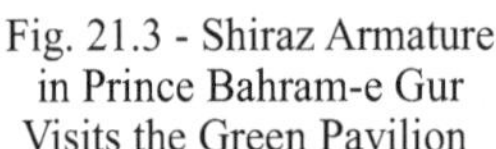
Fig. 21.3 - Shiraz Armature in Prince Bahram-e Gur Visits the Green Pavilion

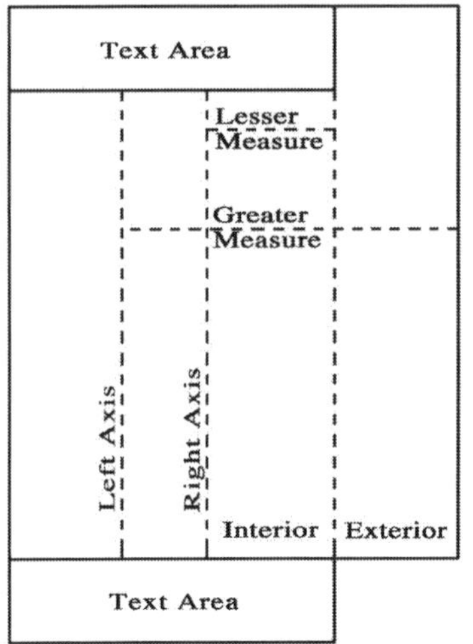

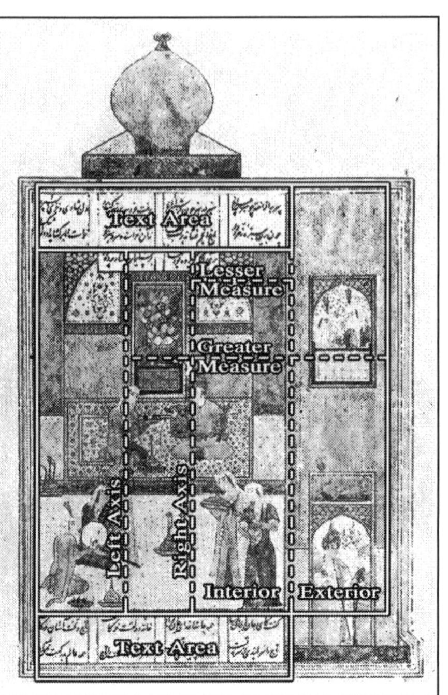

In the Shiraz armature (Fig. 21.3), we note that the text areas (or 'cartouches') above and below are fixed. Between them lies a space dedicated to the *interior scenes*, while to the right, an extra space is added for the *exterior scenes*. These share a common *horizon line* called 'the greater measure'. Within the interior space are two verticals: *"On, or between these inner axes, are placed the principal figures of the main scene,"*[4] Guest notes.

At the same time, there is "*the repetition of the two principal measures repeated in a kind of counterpoint throughout the design, appearing in height and width of avians, doors, and windows length and width of carpets, and so on... This deliberate contrapuntal scheme of recurring measures* [creates] *a harmonious and rhythmically ordered structure... the survival of a system which characterizes the best works of the Timurid period as late as the end of the 15th century."*[5]

In *Bahram-e Gur Visits the Green Pavilion*, (Fig. 21.3), the dimensions of the main doorway, along with its decorative frame, are repeated in the dimensions of the carpet (along with its decorative frame), even though the rectangular shape is turned horizontally. Meanwhile, the door and window in the exterior space have different dimensions, which are repeated in the wall space to the left and right of the main door. Through this contrapuntal play of two principle measures, the artisans created a rhythmically harmonious space.

In the example given here, the two main figures on the carpet (the Green Princess and Bahram-e Gur) fall exactly upon the left and right vertical axes of the armature, while their court of servers and musicians below form a balanced pyramid, leading our eye to the main doorway that is symbolic of Bahram-e Gur's soul ascent from this planetary gateway to the next. (For this reason, the door is framed by a dome with star shapes). Framed by the cartouches above and below, the whole interior scene displays Hieratic symmetry, which is only offset by the exterior scene, to provide some contrapuntal relief.

The Classical style of Shiraz painting gradually evolved during the Timurid period. As Guest notes: *"The static ratio of 2:2 employed by Timurid artists was succeeded by a more rhythmic ratio of 2:3 or sometimes 3:5, contrapuntally employed in the basic composition."*[6]

In the *Haft Paykar*, the armature remains the same in plate after plate, as Bahram-e Gur visits pavilion after pavilion, though sometimes the armature is flipped laterally. Its constant measures provide architectural continuity to the ever-evolving panoply of figures, geometric designs and graceful movements in the slender cypresses and flowering magnolias.

From the standpoint of perspective, Classical style Shiraz paintings are less daring than the later Herat and Tabiz counterparts. The carpet and the wall, with their flat rectangular shapes, are a good example of Vertical Orthogonal perspective – the same system used by the Egyptian scribe Ani two thousand years earlier. Indeed, the whole space in the plates *is orthogonal*, with no attempt to offset the exterior areas through diagonals.

III. Persia: Isometric & Dimetric Perspectives

The *Hasht-Bihisht* or 'eight paradises' was not only a literary theme in Timurid culture, but also extended to architecture. When the Emperor Timur died in 1405, he was entombed in Samarkand in a specially built mausoleum called the Guri Amir (Fig. 21.4). His octagonal sepulcher, with eight sides reflecting the eight paradises of the afterlife, became the archetype for some of the greatest monuments in Timurid and Moghul architecture, from the Hasht Bihisht Palace in Isfahan to Humayun's tomb in Dehli and the Taj Mahal in Agra.

As Wolfram Kleiss notes in 'Safavid Palaces', the octagonal shape (called *Hasht-Bihisht*) also emerged as a common shape for garden pavilions, occasionally expanding to sixteen-sided hexadecagons, or reducing down to a four-sided square. A prime example is the Rose Garden pavilion in Isfahan which, alas, no longer exists (Fig. 21.5).

At the same time, the six-sided hexagon, which often appeared in Islamic tilings, became a common shape *for interiors*. The inner walls of Timur's tomb, for example, are covered with hexagonal designs, and the *muqarnas* – a honeycomb vault of interlocked niches, projecting and receding – was another architectural innovation that began with the Guri Amir.[7]

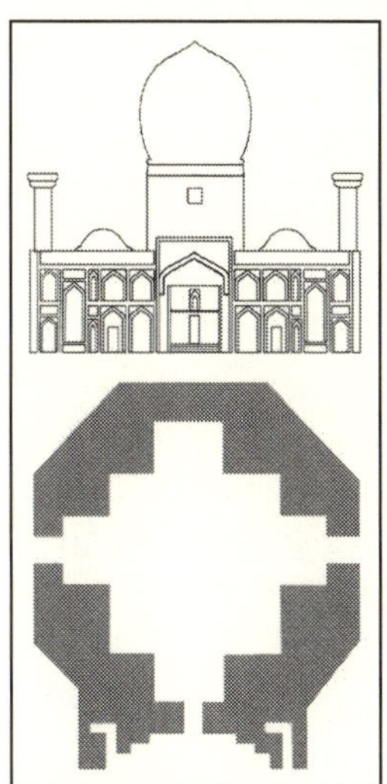

Fig. 21.4
The Guri Amir

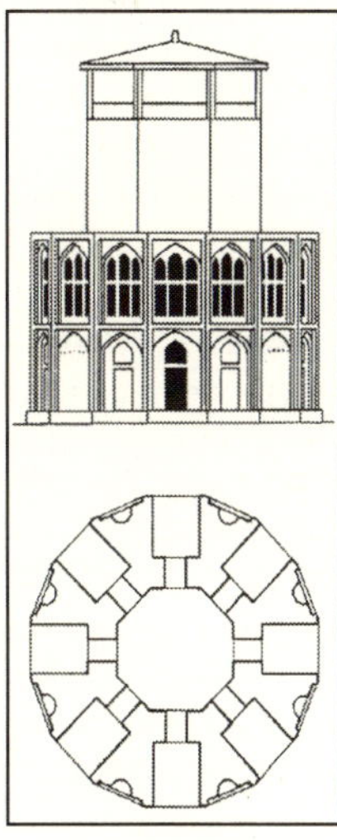

Fig. 21.5
The Rose Garden Pavilion

This posed an interesting problem for Persian Miniaturists, particularly when it came to representing their interior and exterior spaces. For octagonal and hexagonal architecture, when viewed in orthogonal perspective, appears rectangular. It is only when the flat top is placed *above* the flat sides, in Vertical Orthogonal perspective, that we realize the sides refer to a hexagonal shape.

We can see this in Behzād's treatment of the tower in his illustration for Nizami's love story *Khusraw and Shirin* (Fig. 21.1 - head of chapter). Though only two sides are shown to us, we can infer from the balcony (or *balkaneh* in Persian) and the pointed roof that the tower is most likely hexagonal in shape. Meanwhile, in the courtyard, King Hormuzd sits upon a rectangular throne with parallel diagonals in Axonometric perspective.

If we take the time to measure the angle of the throne's diagonals, we discover that they both run at 30° angles to the baseline (the floor is a grid of rectangular tiles in perfect Orthogonal perspective). With its two sides receding at equal angles, the throne offers us a perfect example *of Isometric Perspective in Persian Miniatures*.

Indeed, *all* the diagonals in Behzād's painting run at 30° angles. But the tower is viewed from the exterior, as a convex object, while the courtyard is seen from the interior, as a concave space. To distinguish between exterior and interior views, Behzād came up with a brilliant solution: all exterior angles recede *upward,* while interior angles recede *downward*. For this reason, one door of the garden's gateway opens *into* the courtyard while the other door opens *out* to the garden.

One of the greatest Sufi poets was Nur ad-Dīn Abd ar-Rahmān Jāmī, known simply as Jami. One of his works, the *Baharistan* or *Gardens of the Spring*, involves an allegorical journey through eight gardens. In this illustration to 'The Rose Garden of the Pious' (Fig. 21.6), an atelier of Timurid artists has tackled a similar problem of interior and exterior spaces. But here, they have indicated an interior space *within* an exterior space *through ascending diagonals only*. To create an interior concave space, the receding diagonals *converge* (Oblique Converging perspective); to create an exterior convex space, the receding diagonals *diverge* (Oblique Diverging perspective).

If the interior and exterior spaces are indeed rectangular, then the diagonals may be said to converge or diverge. But the roof suggests a hexagonal tower, such as the one in the Tabriz School illustration to *Khusraw and Shirin* (Fig. 21.7), meaning that both scenes are consistently viewed in Isometric perspective. Since the diagonals actually recede at 25° and 40° angles respectively (and not 30°), we may technically refer to this space as Dimetric perspective.

The compositions as a whole follow the balanced symmetry of Classical Shiraz paintings, with their familiar carpets and doorways arranged in Vertical Orthogonal perspective. But, unlike *Bahram-e Gur Visits the Green Pavilion* (Fig. 21.1), the exterior space is now clearly indicated by diagonals, where parallelograms give a more dynamic shape to the windows and doors.

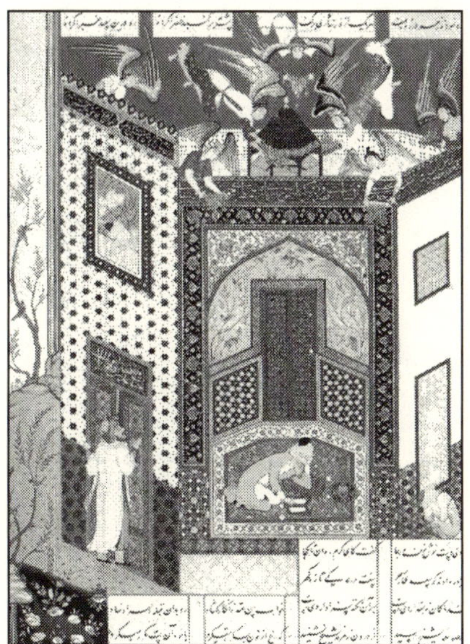

Fig. 21.6
The Rose Garden of the Pious
from Jami's *Gardens of the Spring*
Timurid, 1553

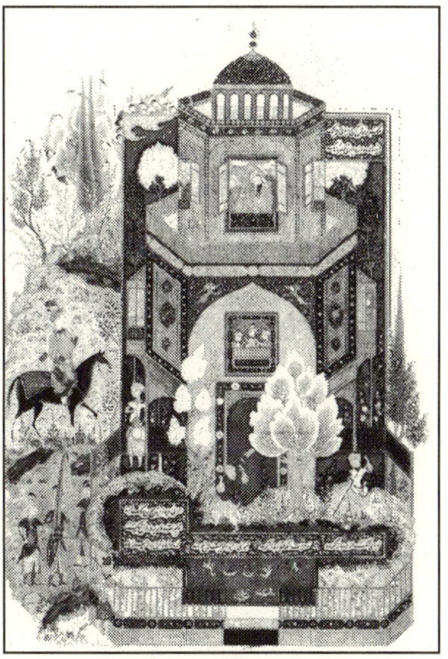

Fig. 21.7
Khusraw and Shirin
from Nizami's *Khamsa*
Tabriz School, 15th c.

IV. Behzād & Multiple Axonometric Perspectives

The complex Islamic patterns appearing throughout Persian Miniatures should remind us that these artists were master geometers. The disposition of 2D space was carefully organized through harmonic lines of armature, which proportionally divided up the painting into areas of calligraphed texts, Islamic patterns and ornamental architecture, while still allowing open spaces for pleasure gardens.

It should not surprise us that these master geometers also organized their 3D space through a complex use of Axonometric perspective, calling upon Orthogonal, Oblique and Isometric systems in ways that Gu Hong-zhong would never have dreamed of...

Behzād's *Seduction of Yusuf* (Fig. 21.8) is a masterpiece of the Persian Miniature. Not only is his use of Axonometric perspective daringly complex, but his organization of pictorial space leads the eye through the painting on a carefully-designed allegorical journey.

Poets did not hesitate to celebrate the greatest artists with praise, and Kamāl ud-Dīn Behzād was compared to Mani in one such ode. Mani (c. 216–274) was a 2nd century Persian Gnostic, the fabled founder of Manichaeism, who combined Judaeo-Christianity and Hindu-Buddhism with his native Zoroastrianism. Considered a prophet in the Sassanid period, Mani taught a strictly dualist worldview, preaching of a final battle between light and darkness. According to legend, he was born lame, and was reputed to be as fine an artist as a prophet. In the eyes of the poets, he became the first Persian Miniaturist, the prototype of the artist as spiritual practitioner and prophet.

For this reason, the historian Khwandamir praised Behzād by comparing him to Mani:

"With a brush like Mani's, felicitous in his works,
Excellent in character, praiseworthy in his manners,
Most accomplished of all artists in the world,
Acknowledged master in his craft,
Behzād, unique in his age, in whose time
Mani has been relegated to fable."[8]

Behzād's *Seduction of Yusuf* illustrates a poem called *Yusuf and Zulaikha* by Amir Khusrow (1253–1325), and is part of a large work called the *Hasht-Bihisht* or 'Eight Paradises'. Using Nizami's allegory of *The Seven Beauties* (*Haft Paykar*) as the frame story, Khusrow recounts the well-known tale of *Yusuf and Zulaikha,* which originally appeared in *The Quran* and *The Bible* (*Joseph and Potiphar's Wife*), and was made popular in a version by Jami.

The prophet Yusuf is blessed with such divine beauty that he incurs the wrath of those who cannot tolerate God's face on earth. After his brothers throw him into a well, he is sold into slavery and becomes a servant in the house of Zulaikha. She falls in love with him and chases him through the seven chambers of her house. He resists her at every turn, and their love becomes an allegory of the soul's unfulfilled longing for divine beauty.

In Behzād's treatment of the poem, each of the seven chambers is indicated by a doorway, dispersed on three levels in a complex space. Leaving aside its 3D Axonometric perspective, we may concentrate our gaze, first of all, on the flat 2D space of the picture plane. A close look at the Islamic patterns reveals that *all* the geometric and floral designs are based on the hexagon – and hence, operate in *ad triangulum* space. Meanwhile, most of the spatial divisions – the floors, walls and doors – are orthogonal, operating in *ad quadratum* space. Already, at this level, two different spatial grids are used to differentiate space.

All the *ad triangulum* grids have one vertical line and two diagonal lines running at 30° to the baseline (but at 60° to each other). The *ad triangulum* grid thus becomes an invitation to divide up the 3D space both Orthogonally (at right angles) and Isometrically (at 30° angles to the baseline). And indeed, this is what Behzād does.

However, it remains unclear whether the external structure is square or hexagonal. The small tower at the top appears hexagonal (angled at 15° Dimetric perspective), but another small tower above the balcony is square (angled at 30° Isometric perspective). The diagonals for the balcony and the right side of the building – suggesting 'exterior' space – ascend at a 30° angle. But the balcony projects *forward* in space while the right side of the palace *recedes*, in a paradoxical use of Parallel Oblique perspective.

Meanwhile, *all* the interior diagonals also run at a 30° angle, suggesting a more consistent use of Isometric perspective. But, contrary to Behzād's rule of descending interior diagonals in his *Khusraw and Shirin* painting, now *all* the diagonals *ascend*, whether interior or exterior. They consistently ascend at 30° (Isometric perspective).

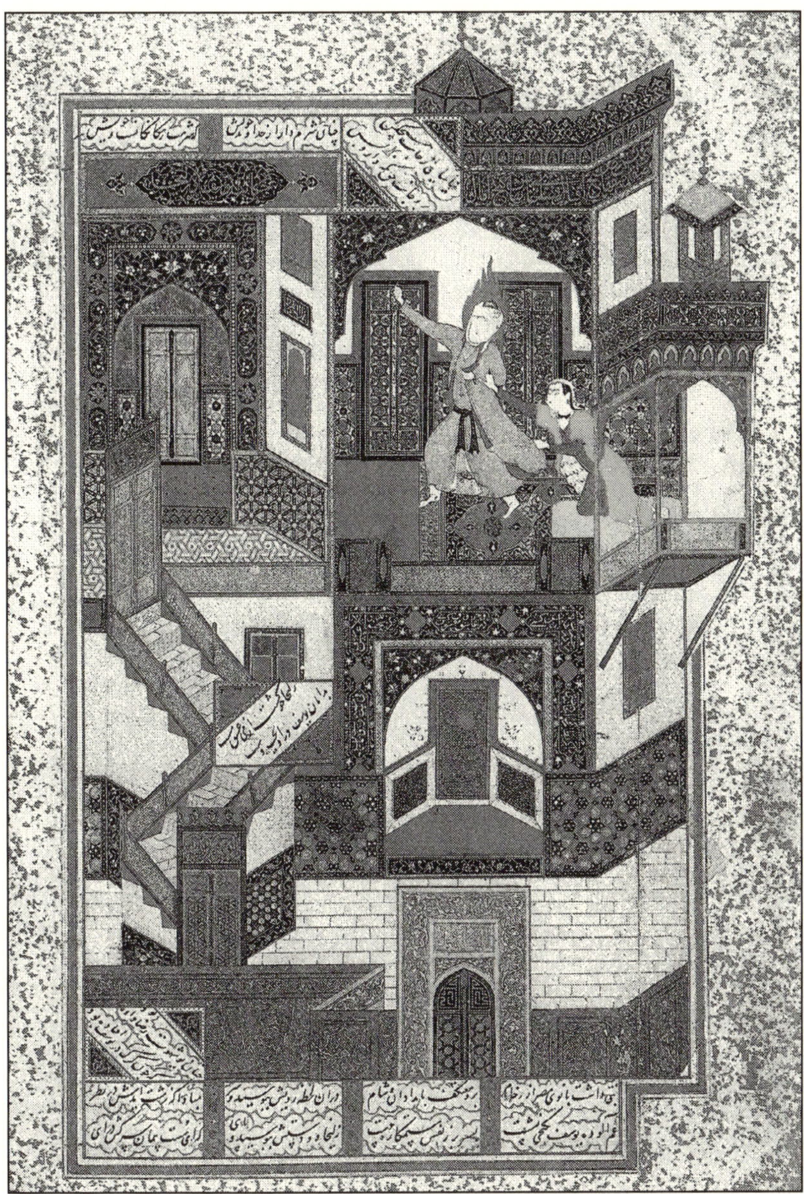

Fig. 21.8 - Kamāl ud-Dīn Behzād: *Seduction of Yusuf* 1488

The exception is the stairs, which ascend at a mixture of 45° and 50° angles (the three calligraphed cartouches – one above, one below and one half-way up the stairs – also run at 45° angles). Six of the seven doors are orthogonal, except for one at the top of the stairs, which is a parallelogram oriented at 30°. That door leads to an interior space (the room on the top left) which also has one wall set to the interior diagonal (at 30°). This interior wall is a curious counterpart to the exterior wall on the right, creating balance and symmetry, with Yusef in the middle.

Despite this complex use of diagonals to indicate 3D space, we should not forget the Orthogonal perspective that runs throughout the *ad quadratum* space. Yusef is standing on a flat carpetted floor that connects, in Vertical Orthogonal perspective, to the flat patterned doors and walls behind him. Indeed, *all* the right-angled floors, walls and doors relate to each other in Horizontal or Vertical Orthogonal perspective.

Through this complex use of multiple Axonometric perspectives, Behzād and the members of his atelier reveal themselves to be master geometers, playing with *ad triangulum* and *ad quadratum* patterns in both 2D and 3D space.

V. The Hieratic Space of Persian Miniatures

When philosophers look closely at Persian Miniatures, they soon discover that a more sacred or Hieratic form of space emerges through Axonometric perspective. In their writings, both Iffet Orbay Grignon and Seyyed Hossain Nasr contrast this Hieratic space to the more profane or mundane space of Humanist perspective.

For example, in his *'Remarks on the Concept of Pictorial Space in Islamic Painting'* Iffet Orbay Grignon writes:

"The illusion of coherently receding depth on a flat surface was successfully created only at some expense: In Renaissance painting, the infinite character of space is paradoxically confined within the spatial unit of the picture. Infinity, where all parallel lines are imagined to meet, corresponds to a precise point in the picture, that is to the vanishing point, which was often dissimulated by the painters. All orthogonals in the picture plane converge toward that point and, hence, define the visual limits of the pictorial space. Since the precise location of the vanishing point on the picture plane is geometrically determined in reference to the viewer's location, this point becomes, so to say, the symmetrical counterpoint to the viewer's eye: The infinite space finds itself unified and contained within the gaze of a single viewer. In contrast to this paradox of Western painting, it can be argued that Islamic and Chinese painting achieve more directly the suggestion of an unlimited space."[9]

So, what happens, we may ask, when the viewer-centered perspective is forgone in favour of object-centered perspective? Grignon continues:

"Depicted objects that cannot be unified in the sight of a single viewer cancel a unique perception of a depicted space; in other words, space cannot be derived from the order of objects seen at once, but it has to be explored pictorially. This can be achieved by shifting our gaze, to look at the objects depicted with respect to different viewpoints... Thus, by its very structure depending upon multiple viewpoints, the two-dimensional miniature painting represents space by implication of movement [...that is] *often sustained by the narrative composition."*[10]

This narrative movement of the eye through pictorial space is admirably demonstrated by Behzād's *Seduction of Yusef.* As with the modern graphic novel, the first place the eye goes is *to the text,* in order to read the gist of the story. In Behzād's atelier, an artisan equivalent to 'Khwaja Ata the ruling maker' arranged the calligraphed cartouches so that our eye begins at the top, then dips diagonally (45°) to the scene of Yusef pursued by Zulaikha. Halfway up (or rather, *down*) the stairs, another diagonal cartouche is read, followed by the final cartouche at the bottom.

From there, the eye makes the journey *back up the painting*, beginning with the door at the bottom, which appears to be a gateway into a walled garden running around the palace. Visually, we undergo an allegorical journey through the seven doors, navigating Behzād's complex pictorial space by focussing our gaze into the space created by each object, *entering* one doorway and *ascending* to the next. The beautiful Islamic patterns may give us reason to pause and admire the arabesques, floral motifs, and holy sayings calligraphed round each doorway. Like Zulaikha, we pursue divine beauty through each of the seven heavenly realms symbolized by a celestial doorway. The whole becomes a visual narrative, a re-enactment, of the mystical soul ascent.

In *'The World of the Imagination and the Concept of Space in the Persian Miniature'* the Sufi philosopher Seyyed Hossain Nasr expands upon the notion of Axonometric perspective as sacred space. "*To conceive of space which is more than physical space and whose experience certain types of sacred art seek to make possible through their techniques and symbolism, there must exist a discontinuity between the space created by this art and the physical space in which man lives in his profane life..."*[11]

In contrast to Western Humanist art, the Islamic art *"...did not betray the two dimensional nature of the surface by making it appear as three dimensional, as was to happen through the application of rules of* 'artificial perspective' *the* perspectiva artificialis *during the European Renaissance."*[12]

Rather, *"by conforming strictly to the non-homogeneous (or heterogeneous) and qualitative conception of space, the Persian miniature succeeded in transforming the plane surface of the miniature to a canvas depicting grades of reality, and was able to guide man from the horizon of material existence, and also profane and mundane consciousness, to higher states of being and consciousness, to an intermediate world with its own space, time, movement, colours and forms, where events occur in a real but not necessarily physical manner. This world the Muslim philosophers of Persia have called the 'imaginal world' (mundus imaginalis) or the 'alam al-khayal."*[13]

This brings us to the concept of the *mundus imaginalis,* which the French philosopher Henri Corbin was so instrumental in bringing to the West. In Sufi philosophy, this intermediate realm is sometimes called the *alam al-mithal*, meaning the realm of 'idea-images' or 'similitudes' resembling Plato's *eidé* or archetypes. Other times, it is called the *alam al-khayal*, meaning 'the realm of the imagination'.

Seyyed Hossain Nasr acknowledges Corbin's contribution, and attempts to place the *mundus imaginalis* in its greater Sufi context:

"Regarding the 'alam al-mithal or 'world of imagination' we must make this clear. It is summarized in five principal states which the Sufis call the five

'Divine Presences' (al-hadarat al-ilahiyyah):
- the physical world (mulk)
- the intermediate world (malakut)
- the archangelic world (jabarut)
- the world of the divine Names and Qualities (lahut)
- the Divine Essence or Ipseity itself (Dhat, also called hahut)

"The worlds above the intermediate world (malakut) are above forms and formal manifestations, whereas the intermediate world (malakut), which corresponds to the world of the imagination, possesses form but not matter in the ordinary Peripatetic sense... This world [the mundus imaginalis] *possesses, likewise, its own space, time, and movement, its own bodies, shapes, and colours. In its negative aspect, this world is the cosmic labyrinth of veils which separate man from the Divine, but in its positive aspect it is the state of paradise wherein are contained the original forms, colours, smells, and tastes of all that gives joy to man upon the earth.*

"The space of the Persian miniature is a recapitulation of this space and its form and colours are a replica of this world... The space is depicted in such a way that the eye roves from one plane to another, moving always between the two-dimensional and the three-dimensional. But the miniature does not allow the eye to 'fall' into the three-dimensional pure and simple. If it were to do so it would cease to be a depiction of the malakut and would become simply a replica of the mulk. By remaining on another plane, and yet possessing life and movement of its own, the miniature is able to have a contemplative dimension and create an aspect of joy, so characteristic of the Persian spirit."[14]

In our allegorical reading of Behzād's *Seduction of Yusef*, we had a brief glimpse of how '*the eye roves from one plane to another, moving always between the two-dimensional and the three-dimensional.'* Each Persian miniature, as a *mundus imaginalis* conjured by Sufi allegory, has the narrative potential to lift our soul through the cosmic spheres, traversing the 'eight paradises' of the *Hasht-Bihisht* and ultimately transcending them.

VI. Mughal Miniatures

When the exiled Mughal emperor Humayun brought two Safavid artists with him to Dehli after regaining his throne in 1555, the Persian Miniature witnessed a resurgence under Humayan's son, Akbar (1542 -1605) and Akbar's son Jahangir (1605 – 1625), who assembled large ateliers of Hindu, Jain, Buddhist and Persian artisans. In the royal ateliers at Fatehpur Sikri and Lahore, Mughal Miniatures illustrated both Persian allegories (like the *Khamsa* of Nizami) and Hindu epics (like the *Ramayana* and *Mahabharata*).

The example given here is attributed to Faizallah, a third generation court artist who fled the royal atelier after turmoils in Dehli, to settle in the provincial atelier of Awadh (Lucknow). Dated to c. 1765, *A Palace Complex with Harem Gardens* (Fig. 21.9) shows that, by this time, Linear Perspective had become known to miniature artists. But, rather than converging his orthogonals onto a single vanishing point, Faizallah has created a hierarchy of planes – three in all – with vanishing points on three parallel horizon lines.

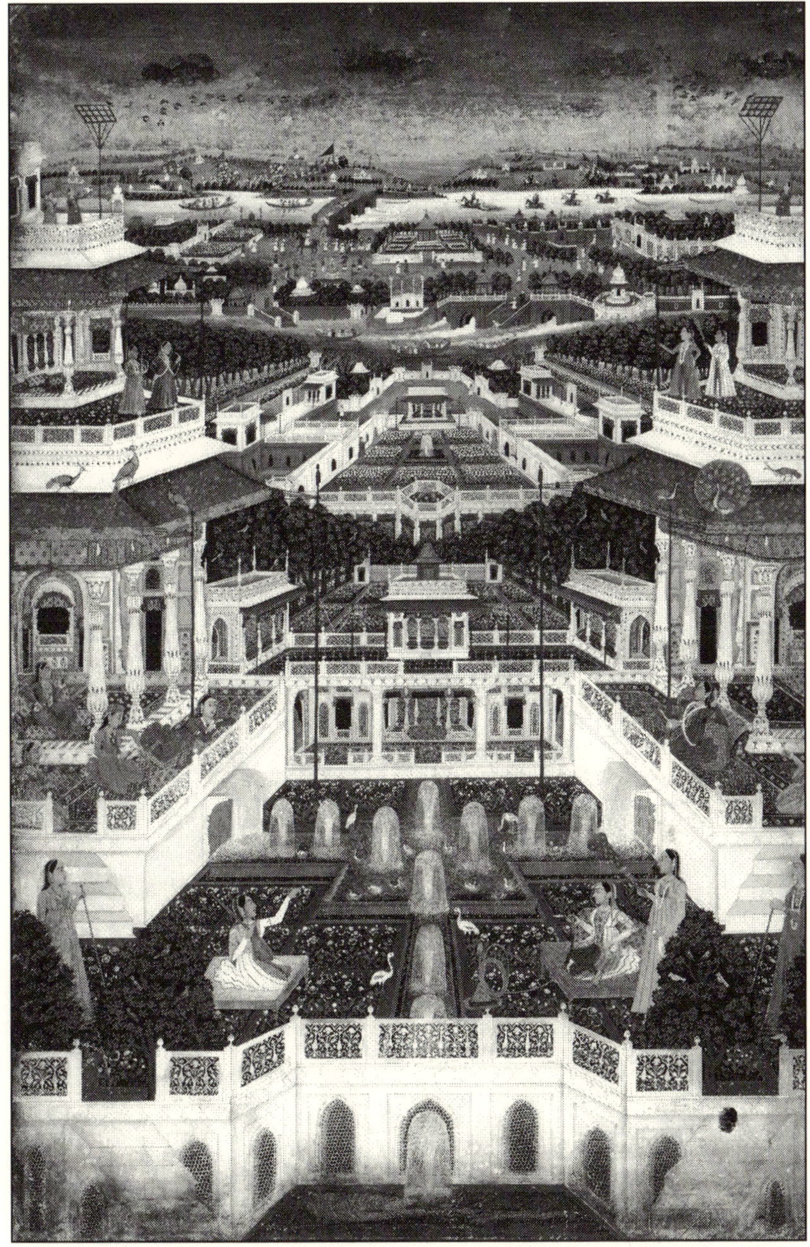

Fig. 21.9 - Faizallah: *A Palace Complex with Harem Gardens* c. 1765

As we enter through the garden gates below, our eye is free to explore the first level of pleasure gardens, with courtesans playing musical instruments around the fountains and reflecting pools. The higher we ascend, the greater the vista in our vision. Like the princesses and peacocks on high terraces and rooftops, we gain an unobstructed view across two rivers and into the infinitely distant hills.

Not all Moghul Miniatures used this technique, but Faizallah's work attests to the increasing experimentation that results when different cultural traditions converge.

VII. The Byzantine Measure of Space

Although I have left Byzantine icons till the end, we must bear in mind that the Byzantine Empire extended from the 5th century to the fall of Constantinople in 1453 (at the hands of their Muslim invaders, the Ottoman Turks). During that time, the Byzantines themselves destroyed many early examples of their art (during the first Iconoclast Period of 730 – 787 and the second Iconoclast period of 814 – 843). Fortunately some icons, dating back to the 6th century, survived (particularly in the desert monastery of Saint Catherine in the Sinai), and the Byzantine style continued to evolve in Greece, Russia and Eastern Europe, up until the present day.

Due to the Silk Route (3rd – 15th century), early Byzantine artists would surely have been exposed to Chinese scroll painting and Persian Miniatures. I have already noted the Buddhist influence on Byzantine icon painting. However, the uncommon form of Oblique Diverging perspective (also called Reverse perspective) strangely persisted in Byzantine painting, as a unique and unparalleled phenomenon.

To see into a Byzantine work of art, we must first orient ourselves within its pictorial space. Byzantine architecture and ornament offer us a first glimpse into how that culture measured and organized space according to geometrical constructions.

In his pioneering study of early Byzantine churches, the Vienna-born architect and scholar Hans Buchwald determined two distinct but related geometrical constructions. The floor plans of some churches, especially those constructed between 1230 – 1265 in the Lascarid period, used *root rectangles* (particularly $\sqrt{2}$ and $\sqrt{3}$ rectangles) to determine the size of the narthex (or porch) in relation to the nave (the central interior). This is true, for example, of the Latmos churches 4 and 8 at the Ikis Ada monastery in modern Turkey (Fig. 21.10), the Church of the Virgin at Sikelia, and the Church of St. John the Baptist at Cahlkios, both on the Greek island of Chios.[15]

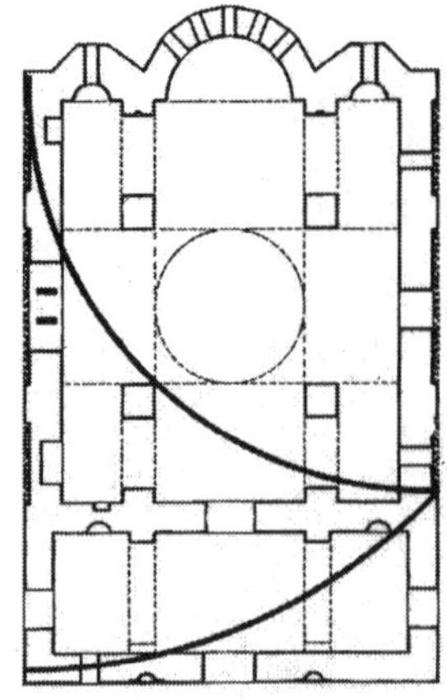

Fig. 21.10 - Latmos Church 8
Based on Root 2 Rectangle

The other main construction is, what Buchwald calls *the quadratura* – meaning a geometric progression of squares, such that, the turned squares framing the regular squares determine the expansion of the floor space, moving outward from the four pillars under the main dome to the narthex and exterior walls:

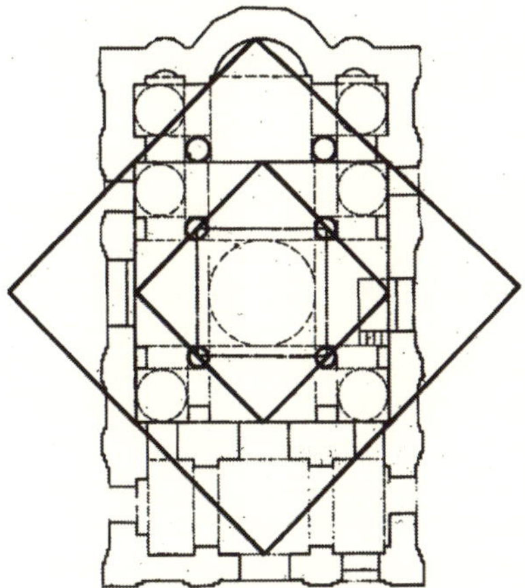

Fig. 21.11 - Sardis Church E Based on the *Quadratura*

"I have suggested," Buchwald writes, *"that the plan of Church E in Sardis, probably constructed about 1230 – 1245,* [Fig. 21.11] *was controlled by a geometric configuration known as the* quadratura. *The* quadratura *is a method of relating the dimensions of building parts to each other using a system of diagonally inscribed squares...*

"The basic unit of the quadratura *in Church E is a square which defines the locations of the four columns underneath its major dome...* Quadratura *creates a proportion of 1:2 – each square is either half or double the size of the next parallel square. The diagonal squares help determine the proportion but are not used as architectural dimensions."*[16]

When we turn to Byzantine ornament, we can see immediately that the *quadratura* also played a key role in the construction of many designs. Figure 21.12 is an interlacing ornament (called a *cosmatesque*) from St. Mark's Basilica in Venice. It clearly depicts the *quadratura* interlaced with the *quincunx* – a design of four semi-circular *eyelets* surrounding a main circle or *guilloche*. The *quincunx* often appears on the inlaid floors of Byzantine churches because its five circles reflect the lay-out of the church's five domes – a central dome with four smaller domes forming a Greek Cross – as in, for example, St. Mark's Basilica in Venice (Fig. 21.13).

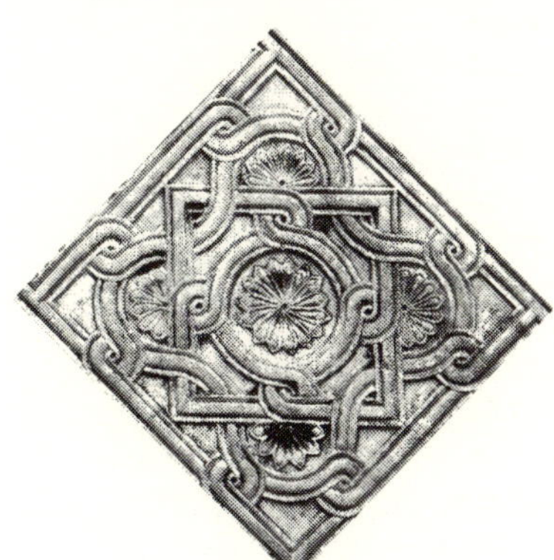

Fig. 21.12 - Quincunx Ornament from St. Mark's Basilica, Venice (turned 45°)

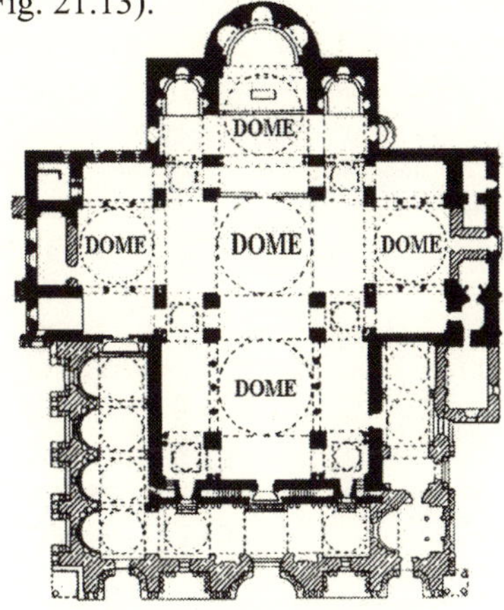

Fig. 21.13 - Floor Plan of St. Mark's Basilica, Venice

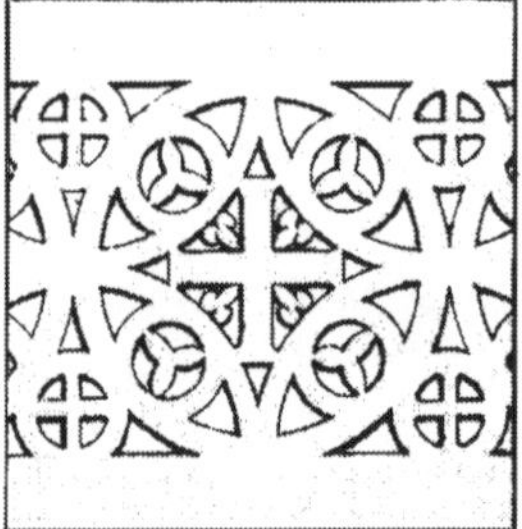

Fig. 21.14

Figure 21.14 shows the Greek Cross as well as the grid of circles (we can still make out the four-petalled flower) which is divided by orthogonals to create *ad quadratum* space. In fact, the Greek Cross rests upon the intersections in the *ad quadratum* grid. If diagonals were to be drawn through the eye-shaped petals, then the *quadratura* would also appear in this design.

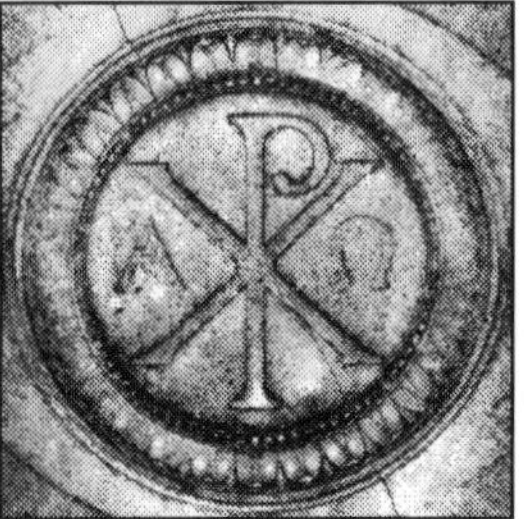

Fig. 21.15

Figure 21.15 depicts the *chi rho,* the monogram of Christ which combines the first two letters of his name, XPICTOC. In Revelation 22:13, Christ says, *"I am the Alpha and Omega, the First and the Last, the Beginning and the End."* Hence the Alpha (A) and Omega (Ω) flanking the *chi rho*. To carve out this design, the mason had to trace a vertical line for the *rho* (P) and two diagonals for the *chi* (X).

Last of all are two ornaments (Fig. 21.16) from Hagia Sophia (the patriarchal basilica of Constantinople, capital of Byzantium). In the upper design, the *quincunx* appears once again in combination with the *quadratura*. This basic shape reminds us how closely related Gothic ornament is to the Byzantine, since we are not far away here from the *barbed quatrefoil*. In the lower design, a web-like device unites the Greek Cross (+) with the Chi (X). The geometry manifest in this last ornament offers us the basic template (✳) for many Byzantine designs.

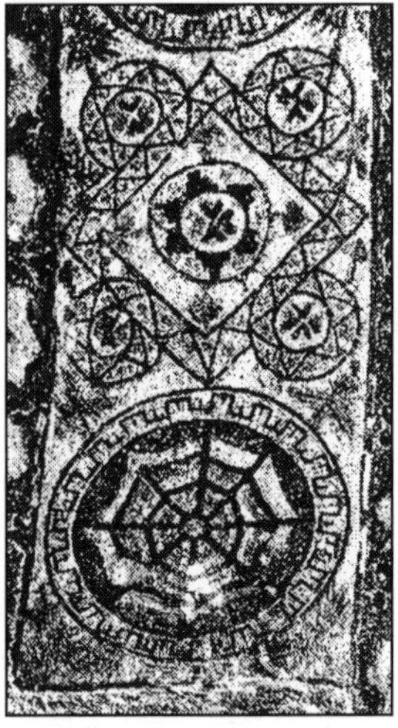

Fig. 21.16

All of these ornaments are constructed through the combination of two grids: an *ad quadratum* grid of squares and, superimposed on top of it, a *quadratura* grid of turned squares, related to it at a 45° angle. With these two grids we have the entire dimensional space of Byzantine art. These two grids may be reduced down to a motif which I will call 'the Byzantine Armature' (Fig. 21.17). It consists of the square (□) and turned square (◇) inscribed with a Greek Cross (+) and a Chi (X). As a basic armature, it need not remain square but can be re-adjusted into a variety of rectangles.

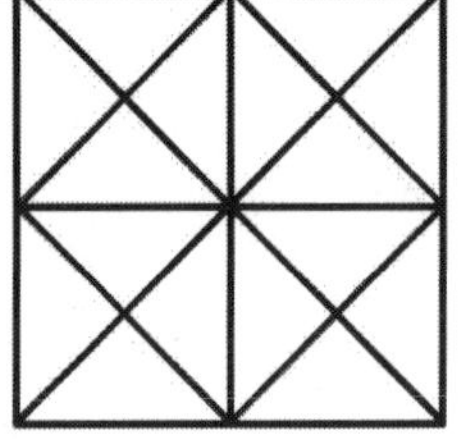

Fig. 21.17
The Byzantine Armature

Returning now to Byzantine icons, we soon become aware how the two geometrical constructions identified by Buchwald in church design also underlie many holy images. Andrei Rublev's *Annunciation* of 1405 (Fig. 16.8) has already furnished us with a fine example of the first construction. Essentially, *root rectangles*

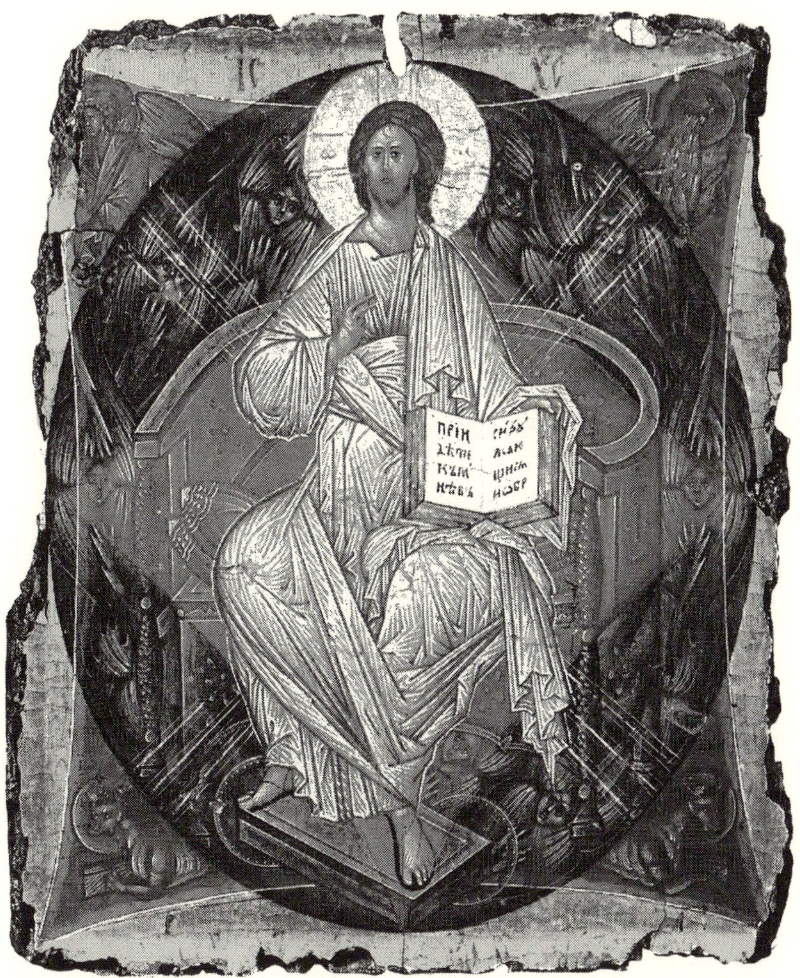

Fig. 21.18 - Andrei Rublev: *Christ in Majesty* (*Spas v Silah*) 1408

use the diagonal of the square to extend its space, by arcing the diagonal beyond the square's limits to form the rectangle. It is the circular extension *of the diagonal* that creates the new spatial measure.

In Andrei Rublev's *Christ in Majesty* (Fig. 21.18), we have a clear example of the Byzantine Armature. Once again, the diagonals play a key role in the spatial construction of this image. The icon shows the full-length figure of Christ Pantocrator, enthroned in his full glory. To express the radiant burst of light around Christ, Rublev has used the Chi (X) within a turned square (◇) that is, itself, inscribed in a rectangle or square (□). Rendered in bright red, the squares are separated by a green oval, where winged cherubs attend the glorified Christ. In the four corners, the four beasts of the evangelists (Luke's bull, Mark's lion, Matthew's angel and John's eagle) *face outward*, each an aspect of Christ's divine vision, *gazing in the four divisions of space and time*

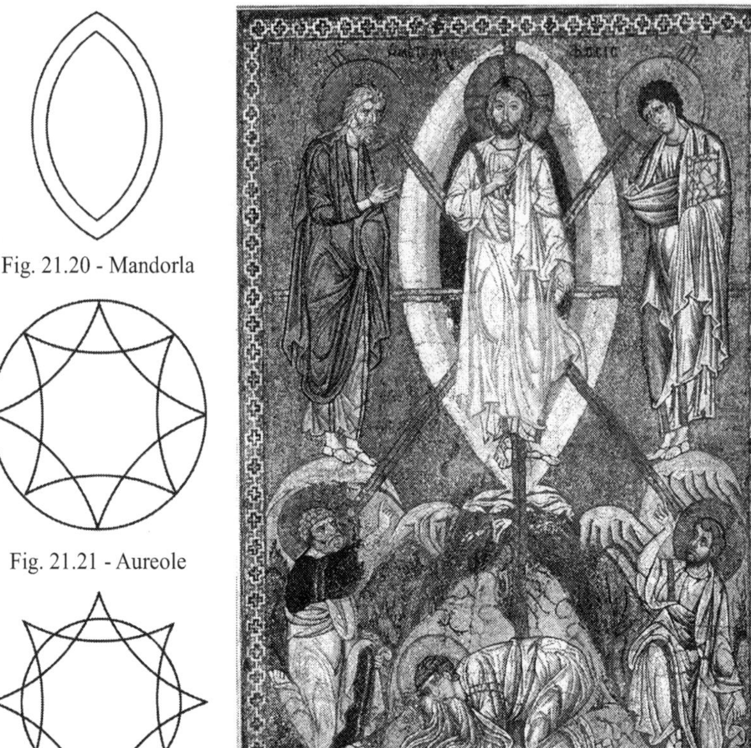

Fig. 21.20 - Mandorla

Fig. 21.21 - Aureole

Fig. 21.22 - Aureole

Fig. 21.19 - *The Transfiguration* Louvre, Late 12th c.

The open book in the hands of the Pantocrator reveals the text: EGO EIMI TO PHOS TOU KOSMOU – *I am the Light of the World.* In icons of *The Transfiguration,* (Figs 21.19) we have a direct vision into the divine light, and behold the geometrical shapes it assumes around the elevated Christ. Some icon painters depict this light as a *mandorla* (Fig. 21.20). Although *mandorla* (from the Greek *amugdalé*) refers to its 'almond' shape, the *vesica piscis* plays an obvious role in its construction. Christ exists in the intersection of two worlds, spiritual and material.

More than that, the *vesica piscis* suggests that the light and image of the transfigured Christ emerge directly from the Eye of God. We can see this in the earliest surviving depiction of *The Transfiguration,* preserved in the desert monastery of Saint Catherine in the Sinai (Fig. 21.23). Here, the dome above the apse *creates an ocular shape*, with Christ emerging from the very centre of the Divine Eye. Behind him, rays of light and vision flow outward, *spreading in eight directions* – creating the orthogonals and diagonals of the Byzantine Armature (✳).

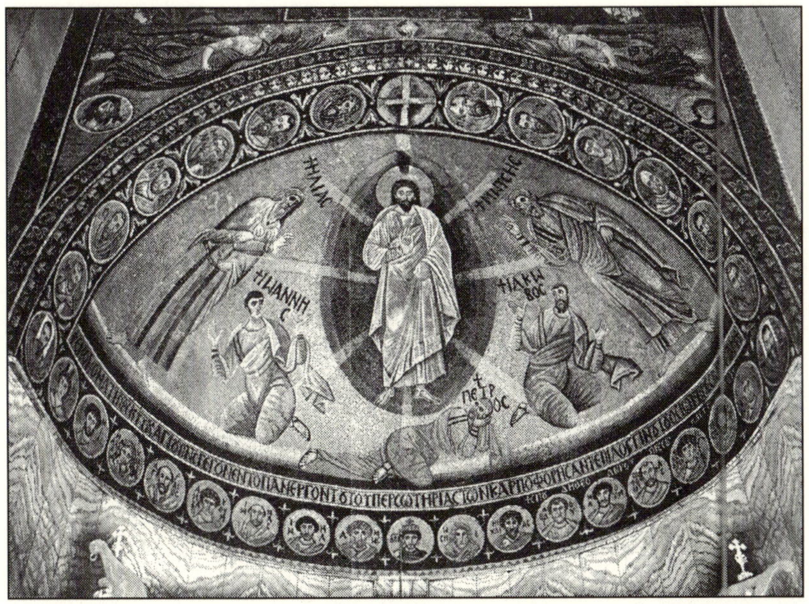

Fig. 21.23 - *The Transfiguration* Saint Catherine's Monastery 565 CE

Following this same logic, the *aureole* (Figs. 21.21 - 22) surrounding the transfigured Christ often assumes the shape of the *quadratura* – the square and turned square in a circle, giving the Divine Light its enduring eight-pointed shape. In this sense, the *quadratura* is not simply a geometrical construction, but acquires a more mystical significance, as the archetypal Byzantine shape of sacred light in space.

VIII. Byzantine Perspective

When we turn to the question of Byzantine perspective, we should not be surprised to discover the key role which these shapes play in the construction of pictorial space. The Byzantine Armature, as we have already noted, is a motif derived from two square grids: one an *ad quadratum* grid of orthogonals, the other, a *quadratura* grid of 45° diagonals. Each grid may be understood as a measure of dimensional space. When the artist draws a cubic shape in his furniture or architecture, *the orthogonals* measure out the sides oriented to *the flat picture plane*, while *the diagonals* measure out the sides verging toward *the background depths*. Unlike Renaissance linear perspective, there is no need for a horizon line or the convergence of rays onto a single vanishing point.

Rather, the turned square (◇) and its inset Chi (X) provides the basic angles for *diagonal depth*. We can see this clearly in Andrei Rublev's *St. Matthew* (Fig. 21.24), where the gospel writer's seat and writing block in

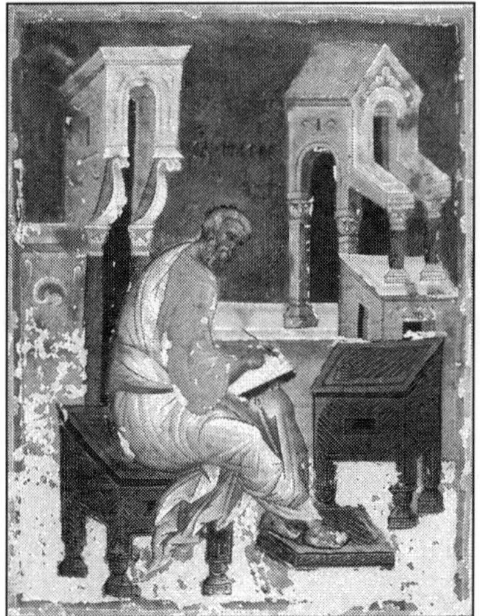
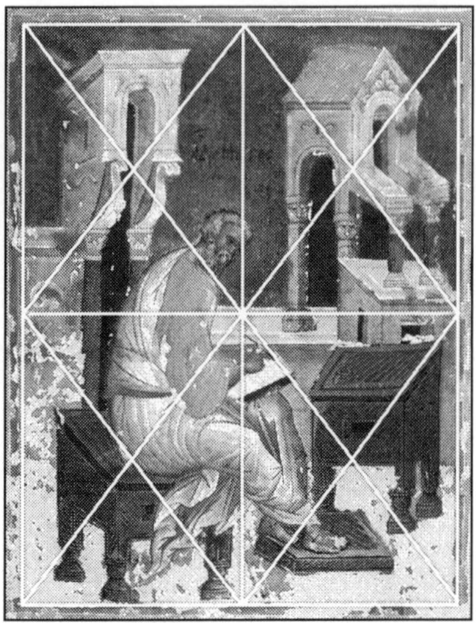

Fig. 21.24 - Andrei Rublev: *St. Matthew* c. 1400

the lower half possess diagonals that clearly follow the orientation of the turned square. The same is true of the architecture in the upper half: all of the orthogonal faces remain flush with the flat picture plane while the diagonal faces follow the turned square to indicate depth. The Byzantine Armature provides all the lines necessary for the creation of a harmonious composition *in both two and three dimensions*.

As an armature, these lines need not be followed rigorously, but provide a general schema for orienting the direction of diagonal depth. It is worth noting that *all* the objects in Andrei Rublev's *St. Matthew* have the front face orthogonal to the baseline, making them consistent examples of Oblique perspective. But, in the case of the writing block and footstool, the diagonals *do not remain parallel but diverge*, giving them the added distinction of Diverging Oblique perspective.

The most common term for this, beginning with Oscar Wulff (*Die umgekehrten Perspektive und die Niedersicht* – 1907) is Reverse Perspective. Under this name, it has been minutely analyzed by Russian theorists like Pavel Florensky,[17] Lev Zehgin,[18] and Boris Uspensky.[19]

Zhegin notes at least three different types of Reverse perspective, depending on the position of the horizon line and vanishing point in relation to the object:

- Reverse Perspective – the vanishing point is below the object's baseline
- Hidden Reverse Perspective – the vanishing point is above the horizon line
- Intensely Converging Perspective – the vanishing point is below the horizon line and above the object

The problem with this typology is that it assumes the existence of a horizon line and vanishing point – something which seems highly unlikely with Byzantine icon painters (who rarely drew a horizon line in their paintings). But, Zhegin's typology does give us another angle onto Reverse

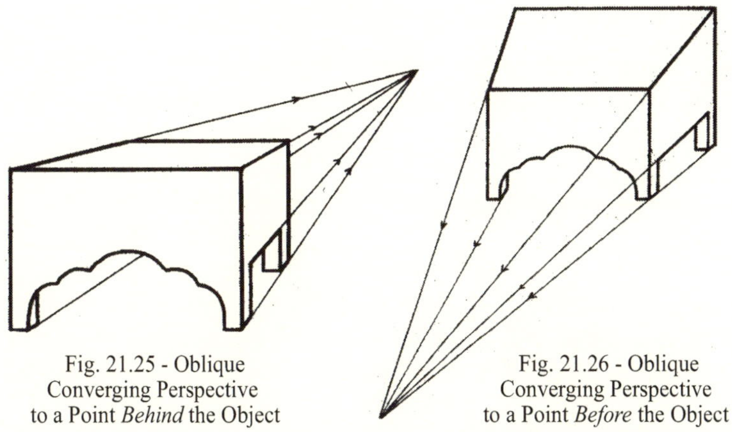

Fig. 21.25 - Oblique Converging Perspective to a Point *Behind* the Object

Fig. 21.26 - Oblique Converging Perspective to a Point *Before* the Object

Perspective. Although we have characterized St. Matthew's writing block as an example of Oblique *Diverging* perspective, its diagonals may also be read as *converging* before (or below) the object's baseline (Fig. 21.26).

In this case, the Reverse Perspective in the bottom half of the painting is simply the result of the artist trying to follow the Byzantine Armature. The diagonals of the architecture in the upper portion also converge to a central point at the top of the picture plane (Fig. 21.25) – yet we find this less disturbing, since the construction now aligns with our own preference for linear perspective. With the objects in the lower half, the artist had no choice but to converge his lines to a central point at the bottom, if he hoped to follow the Byzantine Armature. And indeed, the lines of Matthew's chair and writing block do converge *exactly on the baseline*, either on or near its midpoint.

IX. Byzantine Perspective

I do not wish to underestimate the importance of Reverse perspective (i.e. Oblique Diverging perspective), since it gives objects a very original spatial orientation, elevating Byzantine art to a singular and unique status in the history of Axonometric perspective. But, like the Persian Miniaturists, Byzantine icon painters used a wide variety of Axonometric systems, from Parallel Oblique to Converging or Diverging to Isometric and Dimetric.

As will happen with such a broad variety of systems, the angle of the diagonal is not always consistent, and so the space lacks homogeneity from the Viewer-centered standpoint. But Axonometric perspective is Object-centered. If the artist uses a variety of systems in one painting (not *just* 30° Isometric, or *just* 45° Strict Axonometric), then the grid emerging from each object *will be unique to that object*, and not homogenous over the whole space of the composition.

When we were initiated into drawing the Five Platonic Solids in Axonometric perspective, we learned that the active visualization and creation of these shapes proceeds, as if, from the Divine Eye at the centre of

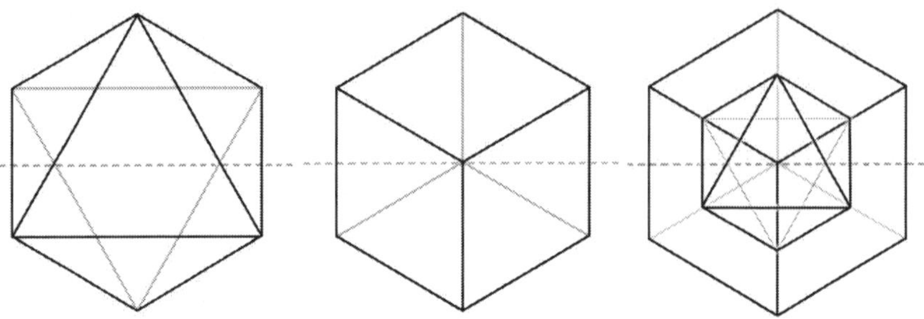

Fig. 21.27 - Octahedron Fig. 21.28 - Cube Fig. 21.29 - Octahedron in Cube

each shape. By focussing our vision onto a point at the exact centre of the 3D shape, we were able to visualize an imaginary horizon line from whence to orient our vision. That central point is the origin of the spatial measure in Object-centered perspective.

In the case of the octahedron (Fig. 21.27), we visualized four sides of the pyramid rising above the central point, and four sides of an inverted pyramid descending below it. In the case of the cube (Fig. 21.28), the foremost corner of three sides moved to the foreground, while the backmost corner of three more sides receded to the background – even though these two corners occupied the same point in space. In fact, it was only our perspective which had changed.

With our eye fixed on the object's central point, its 'depth' may be visualized as above or below, in front or behind (Fig. 21.29). This is what makes Object-centered perspective so unique, and so inconsistent with Viewer-centered perspective, which creates a single homogenous (but empty) space, in which all objects appear and events occur.

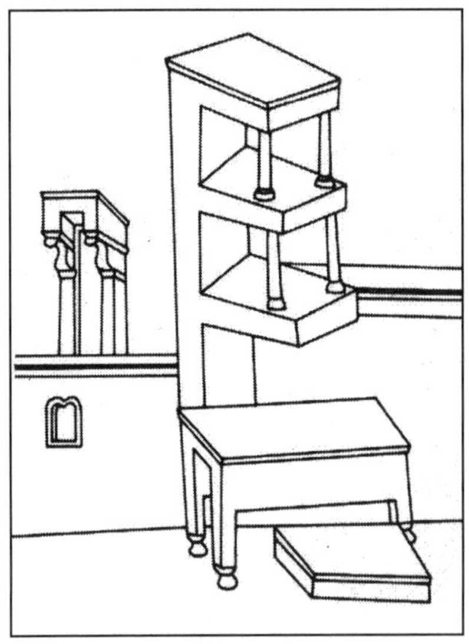

Fig. 21.30 - Byzantine Architecture

Turning to an example of Byzantine Architecture (Fig. 21.30), we note that a variety of Axonometric perspectives are used, each arising from the object in question. If we attempt to relate all of the shapes to each other, in a single homogeneous space, we will soon become lost and confused. But, by treating each individual object as centered in itself, then we may read its shape in *object-centered* Axonometric perspective: some have their sides oriented above or below its central point (like octagons), others have sides oriented toward or away from it (like cubes). The objects are not oriented toward a common horizon line, but each emerges in our vision as a single cohesive shape.

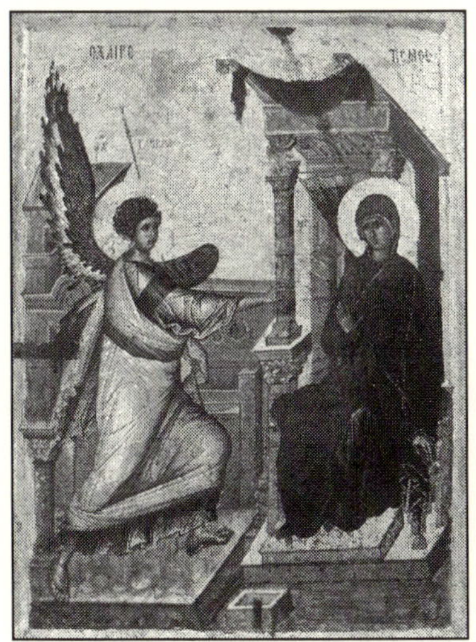

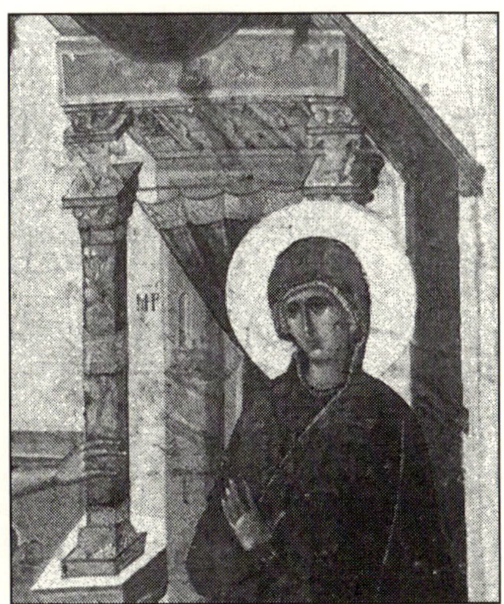

Fig. 21.31 - *The Annunciation,* Constantinople Early 14th Century - All and Detail

The Byzantine icon is constructed in the same manner and spirit as the Holy text that inspires it. When we gaze at the architecture surrounding the Virgin in *The Annunciation* (Fig. 21.31), we discover a construction called the *Ciborium* or *Baldachin* – a shrine composed of four columns rising from her throne, and above her head, a roofed canopy hung with curtains (called the *tetravela*). In the preceding sentence, I just spoke of the columns and the roof as two separate elements composing the *Ciborium.*

Likewise, the icon painter has perceived the *Ciborium*'s columns and roof as two separate objects, each conceived and painted within its own Axonometric perspective. Like words in a sentence, these objects are placed side by side (or one atop the other) to form the *Ciborium.* The only space is the luminous *plenum* of the golden background. The Virgin and Angel, the throne and the Ciborium – all these unique objects, each in their singular perspective, combine to form the holy icon, which translates the text, word by word, image by image: *"God sent the angel Gabriel to Nazareth, a town in Galilee, to a virgin... The angel said to her, "Do not be afraid, Mary; you have found favor with God. You will conceive and give birth to a son."* (Luke 1:26).

X. Byzantine Space

Fig. 21.32

It remains for us to describe a type of Byzantine perspective that transcends all the categories defined thus far. The writing block shown in Fig. 21.32 is a unique example of Reverse Perspective which we have characterized as Oblique Diverging. As a result of its divergence, we are able to see, not just three, but *four sides* of the object. It is this feature of Reverse Perspective which has so fascinated Russian philosophers of the past century like Florensky, Zehgin and Uspensky.

In her recent book, *Space, Time, and Presence in the Icon: Seeing the World with the Eyes of God*, Clemena Antonova summarizes the researches of these scholars, giving the Russian definition of Reverse Perspective as: *"The simultaneous representation of different planes of the same image on the picture surface, regardless of whether the corresponding planes in the represented object could be seen from a single point of view."*[20]

This definition frees Reverse Perspective from the Viewer's singular standpoint. But, at no point does Antonova revert to Object-centered perspective or speak of Axonometric measures. Rather, the 'simultaneous representation of different planes' allows her to speculate on the nature of the viewer who can see an object from multiple points-of-view simultaneously.

After an in-depth analysis of Byzantine theology, she is not able to find many theologians interested in God's spatial capacity to be omnipresent, or in multiple places at one time. But, many Byzantine theologians did write about God's *eternal* nature, not as His limitless extension over linear time, but as a timeless and ever-present Being. In this sense, the viewer of the Byzantine icon can be *none other* than God, and through its unique perspective, the icon elevates our sight to divine vision:

"*Probably not all, but an overwhelming number of icons have been done in 'reverse perspective'... The main principle of 'reverse perspective' is understood not as the turning around of the laws of linear perspective (as in the widely accepted view), but as the representation of the 'simultaneous planes' of an object, i.e., planes which cannot be seen from a fixed position at one moment of time.*

"The viewer's perception of an icon, defined in these terms, can be compared to the 'vision' of a God, who exists beyond time and to whom, therefore, all aspects of the objects in the world would appear at once, simultaneously. In other words, such a divine being would have no point of view in space. The transcendental nature of icons, frequently remarked upon but almost never convincingly explained, is interpreted here as founded on a spatial construction which allows the beholder to experience a form of divine vision which transcends the human constraints of space and time."[21]

And so, by acknowledging the existence of *"a timelessly eternal God to whom all moments in time exist simultaneously* [and who is] *able to see all points in space simultaneously,"* she concludes, *"An icon is constructed in a way that it could appear to divine vision."*[22]

XI. Buddhist Perspective

In Fig. 21.33, a curious detail from a 19th century *thangka* shows a monk, surrounded by disciples, painting an image of the Buddha on a stretched canvas. Most likely, the monk is a previous incarnation of Dudul Dorje, the 13th Karmapa of Tibet. A close examination of the image reveals a variety of perspectival systems, from orthogonal to axonometric. Interestingly, the bench upon which the artist sits is rendered in *reverse perspective*, with its vanishing point in front or below the object.

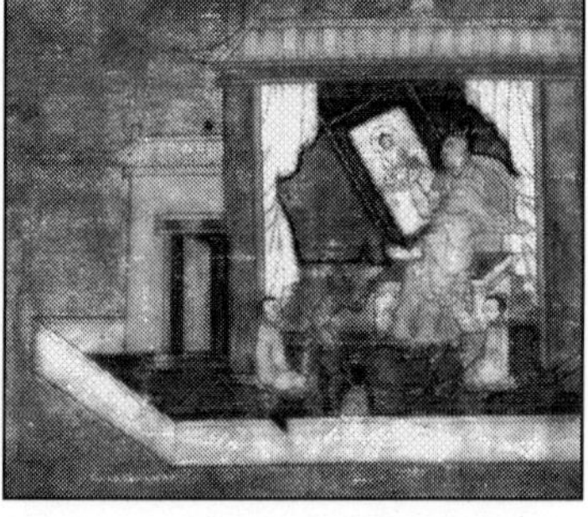

Fig. 21.33 - Dudul Dorje 19th c. Detail

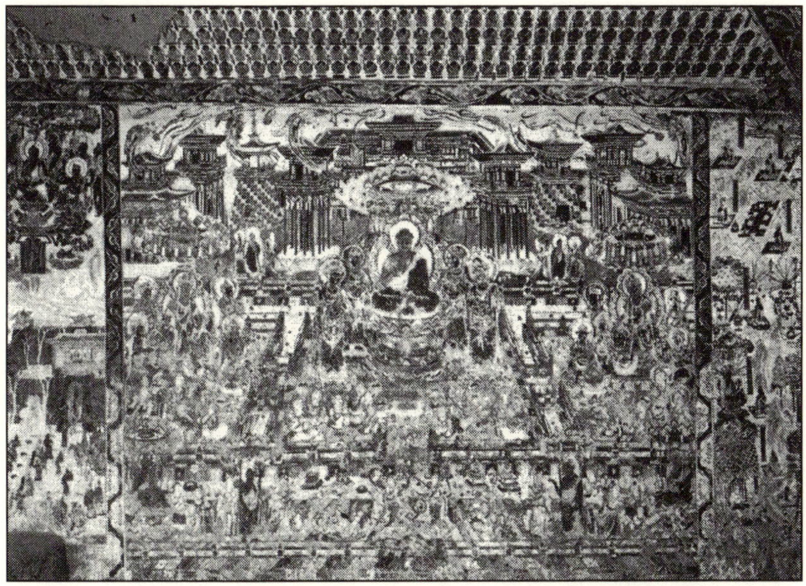

Fig. 21.34 - *The Western Paradise of Amitabha,* Late 7th c.
Cave 217 of the Mogao Caves, Dunhuang, China

When we turn our attention to Buddhist perspective, particularly in Tibetan *thangka* painting, we must soon admit that no system readily presents itself. Artists employed a variety of axonometric systems, using whatever angle or inclination seemed best-suited to the object's visual representation. Perhaps it is for this reason that research on Buddhist perspective is rare if not non-existent. The many surviving manuals of painting address questions of proportion and composition, but never speak of perspective.

The word *thangka* comes from Tibetan, meaning 'a thing that one unrolls.' Since *thangkas* are painted on a perishable material, it is difficult to establish when the first *thangkas* were created. From Tibet itself, the earliest *thangkas* date to the 11th century. But the famous Mangao Caves at Dunhuang preserve even earlier examples.

Located above the Dachuan river in China, the 'caves of a thousand Buddhas' preserve examples of Buddhist art from the 4th to the 14th century. Particularly the Library Cave, which was sealed off in the 11th century and only rediscovered in 1900, preserved a cache of silk paintings, textiles and prints – as well as nearly 50,000 manuscripts (including long-lost works like the Nestorian Jesus Sutras).

Located on the Silk Route, the Mangao Caves were an important centre of pilgrimage, with carved statues in elaborately painted shrines, libraries and meditation chambers. The style of art found in surviving *thangkas* and frescoed on the walls reveals a cross-cultural influence, mixing Chinese with Indian, Tibetan and Uyghur painting styles.

When we turn to an example (Fig. 21.34), we are surprised to find such great refinement in so early a work. In the middle of the 'Western Paradise' with its different levels of heaven, the bodhisattva Amitabha sits in perfect tranquility. To display the various heaven realms (Sanskrit *Sukhāvatī,* Tibetan

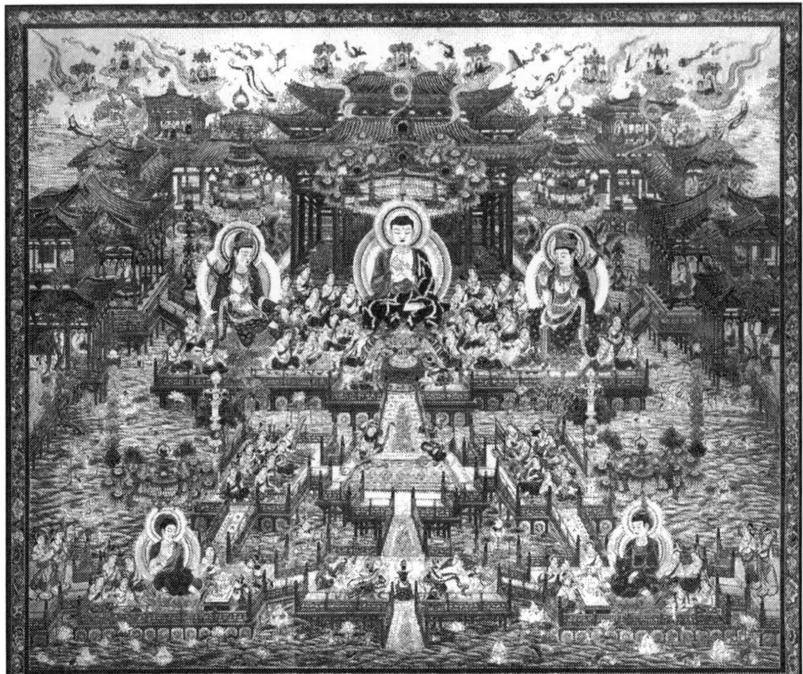

Fig. 21.35 - Modern Version: *The Western Paradise of Amitabha*

Dewachen, meaning "Land of Bliss"), the artist has used converging lines of perspective. As we can see in a modern version (Fig. 21.35), there are no less than ten parallel horizon lines, with their hierarchy of vanishing points falling on the central vertical to give the composition a perfect symmetry.

Like the Mughal Miniature *A Palace Complex with Harem Gardens* (Fig. 21.9), here too we are able to read the painting's depth through the simple formula: bottom = foreground; top = background. As our eye moves from the bottom to the top, and from foreground to background, we have the sensation of rising ever higher and higher over the scene.

But the perspectival lines in this painting serve only to enhance the composition. All of the diagonals serve to encase Amitabha within a series of perfect triangles. Although the *shri yantra* (Fig. 21.36) with its series of interlocking triangles is *not* used to form the foundation of this perspective, the purpose remains the same: to guide the eye, through a series of diagonals, towards a meditative centre – where the titular deity (Sanskrit *iṣṭadevatā*, Tibetan *yidam*) reflects to us our true, hidden nature as a fully enlightened being.

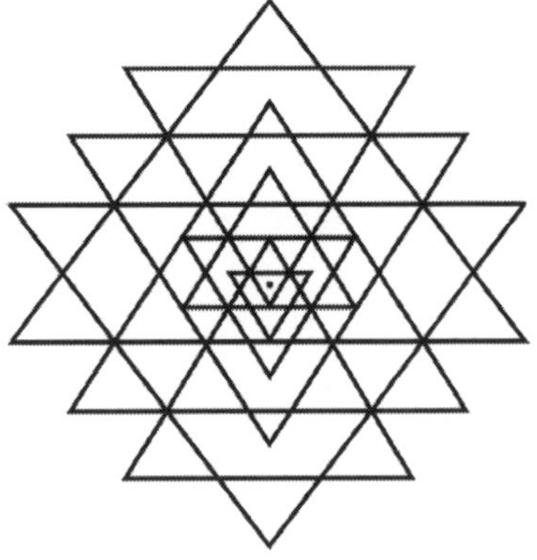

Fig. 21.36 - Shri Yantra

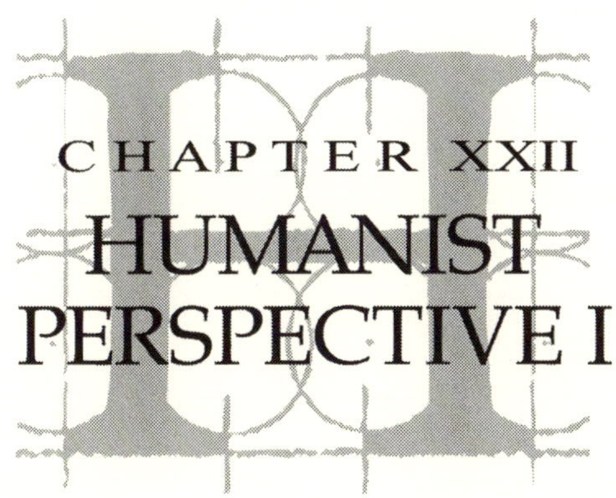

CHAPTER XXII
HUMANIST PERSPECTIVE I

I. What is Linear Perspective?

I have often wondered what linear perspective would look like to the Egyptian scribe Ani, or to Gu Hong-zhong or Behzād. Then again, I did have such an experience while under the influence of ayahuasca. It was a difficult journey, and despite my attempts to 'go with the flow', the insane visions unfolding before my eyes were all-too-much. For a moment, I had to look away, in a vain attempt to ground myself. Sitting in the darkness, I shifted my posture, changed my breathing pattern, and glanced to the lower left.

At that moment I saw it... 'It' was an oblong object glowing in deep blue and green hues, which had clearly materialized from another time and dimension. To this day, it lies beyond the powers of language to describe it. For the object, though vaguely oblong and orthogonal, held itself together in a conceptualization of space that utterly baffled me...

Whatever it was, 'it' began to grow. Within seconds, it became a vortex of energy sheering dimensional space into ever-finer slices of spectral light, spinning in a stop-start, stop-start motion that spliced time at ever-increasing speeds. To my horror it, metamorphosed into a frightening entity that overwhelmed me by its sheer multiplicity and complexity – I could not tolerate so many dimensions opening up before me at once...

Another time, another journey, I rose from my place after five hours of full-on visions. The simple act of standing, gaining balance, and taking a few uncertain steps plummetted me back to my childhood, and the very first time I stood or took an infant step. But the room around me, which resembled a chapel, was entirely transparent to a golden clear light, like an immense orb or luminous sphere with glowing orange shadows, etched with faint traces

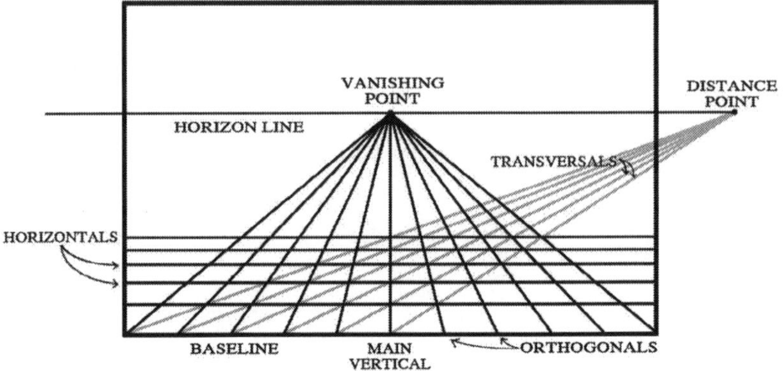

Fig. 22.1 - Linear Perspective

of the room's geometric shape. I realized or somehow remembered how the entire spatio-temporal co-ordinate system which I had acquired as a child was a *construct* – and that the three dimensions of space surrounding me now were nothing more than a veil, falling before my infinite vision.

Since then, I have often wondered about the shifts in time and space that occur in visionary states. Once, at Kalakmul in Guatemala, I gazed upward at a Mayan pyramid and marvelled at its monumental stature – so vast, towering, epic and ever-present. Its unique shape seemed to *carve out* a 'Maya space and time' far beyond our Western spatio-temporal notions. Another time, an increased awareness of detail allowed me to view the distant Morvan peaks from my hilltop farmhouse in Bourgogne as a Netherlandish painting – each remote lake and village minutely-rendered in finest detail. The sweep of the panorama and the atmospheric depth were utterly breath-taking...

To speak of linear perspective we must begin by summarizing its basic construction, particularly from the standpoint of the practicing artist. In Fig. 22.1 we have the simplest construction: a tiled floor of even squares presented in one-point perspective. The tiles are assumed to be square, so the baseline is divided into equal measures, beginning at the mid-point and ending exactly on the two bottom corners of the frame (in practice, these measures will extend beyond the frame).

Parallel to the baseline, a horizon line is drawn (anywhere, but here it is two-thirds up from the baseline). From the equal measures on the baseline, a series of converging lines called 'orthogonals' are drawn to a point on the horizon line, called 'the vanishing point'. In this example, the vanishing point lies exactly above the midpoint of the baseline, creating a 'main vertical' or 'centric line'.

Next, the measures of the receding squares must be worked out. Another point, called the 'distance point' is placed somewhere left or right of the vanishing point (here, it lies outside the picture frame) and a series of 'transversals' are drawn from the distance point to the equal measures on the baseline. For greater precision, another distance point may be placed an equal distance on the other side, and more traversals drawn from it.

A series of 'parallels' or 'horizontals' are then drawn by observing where the transversals cross the main vertical, and drawing a horizontal line at

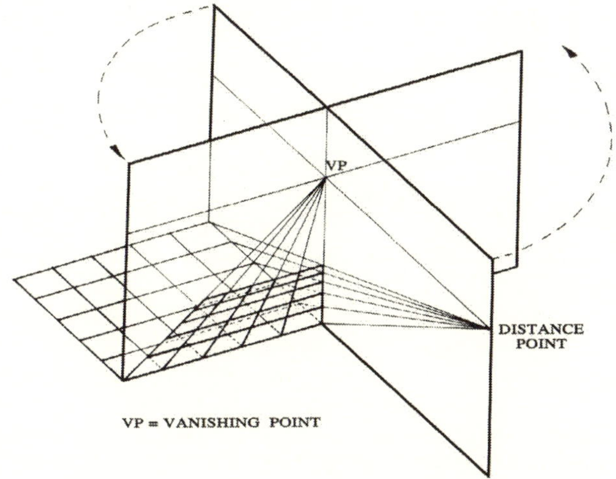

Fig. 22.2 - Viewer-Centered Linear Perspective

each point. These lines should cross *all* the intersections of transversals with orthogonals, but the main vertical is used as the reference line.

As we can see in Fig. 22.2, linear perspective is a Viewer-centered perspective, which is calculated from the position *of the viewer* in relation to the frame. To properly *see* the painting's perspective, the viewer should stand exactly before the vanishing point, with one eye level to the horizon line, and as far back from the surface as the distance point is from the vanishing point. This is demonstrated by our diagram, where the distance point, normally off to the side of the painting, is swung around to the front, to demonstrate how perspective really works. The distance point *is* the viewing point.

In Fig. 22.3 we have an axonometric view of what is actually happening in linear perspective. Although the orthogonal floor lines A, B and C are parallel and go on for infinity, they are projected onto the picture plane in such a way as to converge at H on the horizon line. As the sight-lines of the viewer (V) fall upon the grid of squares in floor p q r s, they pass through the picture plane p q t u, where the floor's horizontals are projected onto the picture plane as a receding series of horizontals. On the floor, these horizontals parallel each other and recede to infinity, but on the picture plane they merge at the horizon.

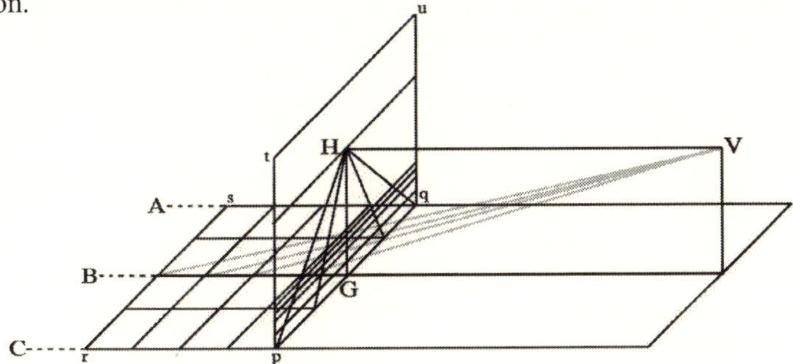

Fig. 22.3 - Linear Perspective Construction (Axonometric View)

Linear perspective breaks the fifth postulate of Euclid's *Elements*, where parallel lines, by definition, do not meet. But Euclid himself was aware of perspectival convergence, and in the sixth proposition of his *Optics,* he noted that parallel lines *appear* to meet in the distance (we will examine this below). For most artists, linear perspective was a 'workshop construction' without need of foundations in Euclidian geometry. But Humanists like Brunelleschi, Alberti, Leonardo and Piero della Francesca took a deep interest in Euclid, and investigated perspective, not just as a studio practice, but in the venerable lineage of Optical Geometry. For us, both the optical theory and the studio practice will absorb our attention.

II. Linear Perspective: Early History

It is still openly debated whether the ancient Greeks and Romans had a working knowledge of linear perspective. Several texts, like those of Lucretius and Vitruvius, seem to imply that they did.

In *De Rerum Natura* (On the Nature of Things), the Roman poet and philosopher Lucretius (c. 99 BCE – c. 55 CE) made the following observation:

"And though dimensions of a colonnade are the same throughout, and it is standing supported from one end to the other by equal columns, yet when we look down at its entire length from the top portion, it gradually shrinks down to the tip of a tapering cone, joining roof and floor and all things on the right and on the left, until it brings everything together at the apex of the cone and disappears."[1]

And in *De architectura* (*The Ten Books on Architecture*), the Roman architect Vitruvius (c. 70 – c. 15 BCE) described three basic ways of drawing up the plan of a building: through *ichnogaphia* (the ground plan), *orthographia* (the elevation), and *scaenographia* (the perspective):

"A ground plan is made by the proper successive use of compasses and rule, through which we get outlines for the plane surfaces of buildings. An elevation is a picture of the front of a building, set upright and properly drawn in the proportions of the contemplated work. Perspective is the method of sketching a front with the sides withdrawing into the background, the lines all meeting in the centre of a circle [ad circinique centrum]*."*[2]

Scaenographia – the word Vitruvius uses for perspective – is related to 'scenography', the art of painting scenery for the theatre. In a later passage, Vitruvius describes how scene painters create the illusion of perspective:

"Agatharcus, at the time when Æschylus taught at Athens the rules of tragic poetry, was the first who contrived scenery, upon which subject he left a treatise. This led Democritus and Anaxagoras, who wrote thereon, to explain how the points of sight and distance ought to guide the lines, as in nature, to a centre [certo loco centro]*; so that by means of pictorial deception, the real appearances of buildings appear on the scene, which, painted on a flat vertical surface, seem, nevertheless, to advance and recede."*[3]

In both these passages, Vitruvius speaks of lines converging to 'the centre of a circle' (*ad circinique centrum*), suggesting that some form of linear perspective was understood and used in the Classical Period.

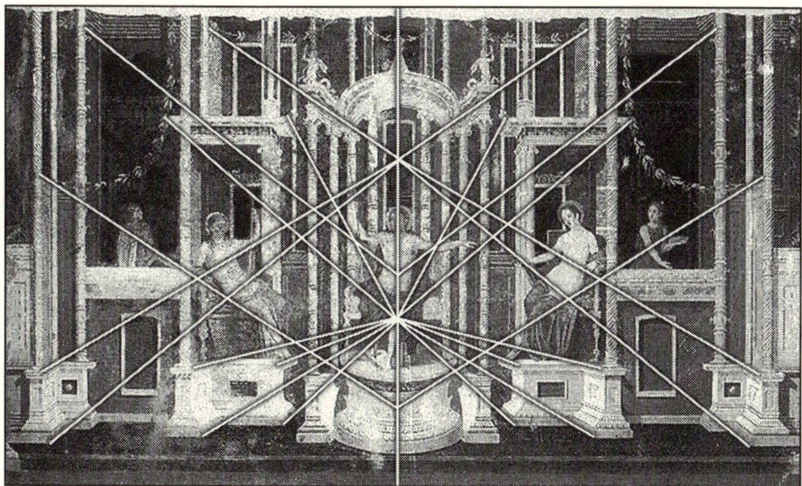

Fig. 22.4 - *The Contest Between Venus and Herperus* House of Apollo, Pompeii, c. 60 BCE
Watercolour Copy by Mastracchio 1841

But, when we search through Greek and Roman art for examples, the story becomes far more complex. In the case of Greek art, alas, not a single work by their greatest painters, such as Apelles, Zeuxis or Parrhasius (Pliny mentions scores of Greek painters in Book XXXV Ch. 36 of his *Natural History*) has survived through time. The scenes on Greek vases offer the occasional table or chair, but not much in terms of architectural perspectives. That leaves us with Roman frescoes, particularly in the Second Style, which have survived on the walls of Roman villas.

The 19th century scholar of Antiquities August Mau defined four basic styles of Roman wall painting, of which the Second Style, also called the Architectural or Illusionistic Style, specialized in representing *scaenographia* and architectural settings. The best-known examples come from The House of Apollo (Pompeii c. 60 BCE), the Villa of Oplontis (60 – 50 BCE), the Villa of Publius Fannius Synistor (60 BCE), and the Room of the Masks in the House of Augustus (Rome 30 BCE).

Our first example, taken from The House of Apollo (*Domus M. Herenulli Communis*) in Pompeii (Fig. 22.4), shows *The Contest Between Venus and Herperus*, with Apollo sitting in judgement between the two deities. In this painting, many of the orthogonals do in fact *converge* onto a common point, but not consistently. Some converge above, some below, and some remain parallel. Instead, they all fall somewhere *along the main vertical* of the composition, which is extremely symmetrical in its conception. This gives rise to a type of perspective called *axial* or 'fishbone' perspective.

Our second example comes from the *Villa of Publius Fannius Synistor* (also called the *Villa Bascoreale*) just north of Pompeii (Fig. 22.5). At first glance, we may be led to believe that the lines of perspective converge onto a common vanishing point, or at least along the main vertical. But, when we

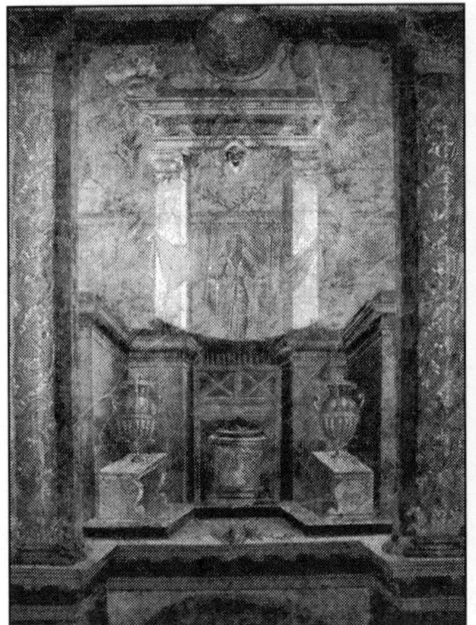
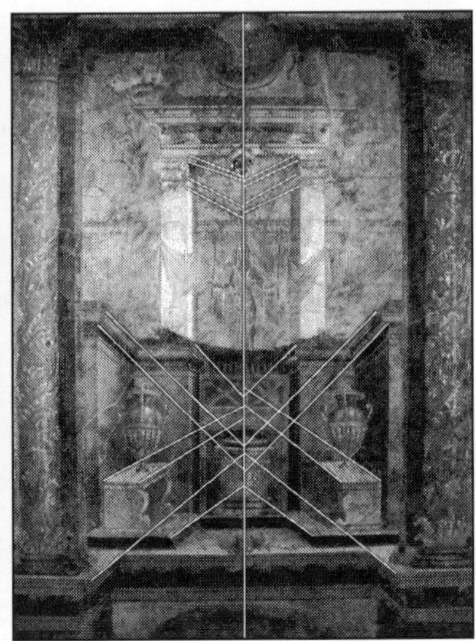

Fig. 22.5 - *Villa of Publius Fannius Synistor* North of Pompeii c. 50 BCE

trace out the orthogonals, we discover that a form of Oblique perspective was used. Rather than converging, the orthogonals *remain parallel* as they meet along the main vertical.

In his study *'Perspective Systems in Roman Second Style Wall Painting'*, Philip Stinson reviews many such examples and concludes:

"Analysis of Second Style wall paintings... reveals two major types of perspective, convergence and parallel, which are organized together in compositions along a central vertical axis. Convergence perspective is typically found in the upper areas of wall paintings. Parallel perspective is found in the lower areas... Another important feature is the manner in which orthogonals appear to recede precisely to a point but actually fall within a small area."[4]

Stinson goes so far as to re-construct the methods of the fresco painters from *"the few examples of underdrawings that are exposed and accessible."*[5] He discovers that, first, the basic underdrawing or *sinopia* (the word comes from its reddish brown pigment) was transferred using a square grid. Then, *"converging lines were either drawn against a straight edge of some kind or snapped against the red plaster using a cord."*[6]

The convergence of lines to a circular area rather than a definite point may have been due to the fact that *"an assistant might have held a cord in place in the general area of a convergence centre."*[7] To prepare the wall for the fresco, a layer of wet plaster was then applied, and this may have also obscured some of the architectural lines. For whatever reason, it seems that *"painters strove for 'near convergence' to points on the wall surface."*[8]

In my own researches into Roman wall painting, I have also come across cases of Oblique Diverging perspective, such as this example from the Villa of Publius Fannius Synistor (Fig. 22.6). Since much of the Byzantine style is derived

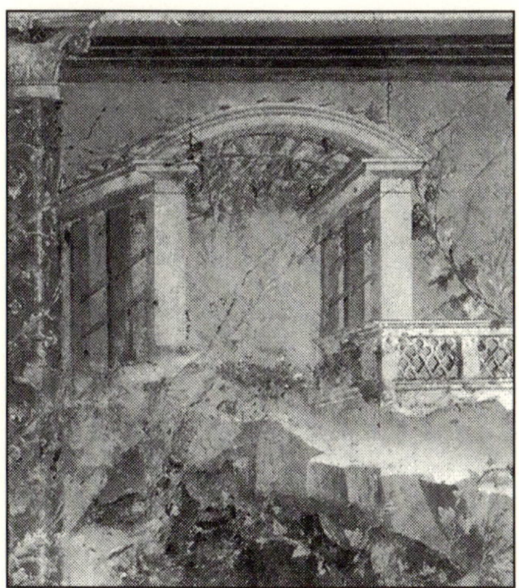

Fig. 22.6 - *Villa of Publius Fannius Synistor*

from Roman art, it seems quite possible that Byzantine Reverse Perspective originated from Roman examples like these. Both cultures used *a wide variety of perspectival systems*, from parallel to converging to diverging...

"The use of different perspective systems," Stinson remarks, *"reflects the role of painters in crafting the complex form of perspective found in Second Style wall painting."*[9] As a result, *"multiple facets of perspective could come into harmony... Interestingly, convergence perspective all but disappears with the coming of Third and Fourth Style wall painting."*[10]

And so it appears that, though Roman culture had many forms of perspective, including a system of converging orthogonals that approximated linear perspective, they did not set much store by it, or hold it in such great esteem the way we do – as heirs of the Renaissance way of seeing...

III. The Legend of Linear Perspective

When the 4th century philosopher Boethius translated the Greek word *optiké* into Latin, he chose the word *perspectiva*.[11] For most of the Middle Ages, *Perspectiva* meant the study of Optics and how the eye sees. Indeed, the Latin verb at its root, *perspicere* means *to perceive* but also, more literally, *to look into* or *see through*. It was this sense that emerged during the Renaissance, when painters saw the canvas as a kind of window or veil for the viewer to *peer through*. This new, painterly sense of Perspective was called *prospectiva pingendi* or *perspectiva artificialis*, to distinguish it from the traditional study of Optics, which was then called *perspectiva communis* or *perspectiva naturalis*.

Although Boethius had translated parts of Euclid's *Elements* into Latin during the fifth century, it was only during the first half of the twelfth century that Euclid's two most important works, *The Elements* and *The Optics*, were fully translated and began to exercise their influence over European thinkers like Bacon, Witelo and Peckham, who wrote the most important treatises on Optical Geometry. By the time of the Renaissance, Euclid's *Optics* held sway over all developments in linear perspective.[12]

Without a doubt, the convergence of parallel lines onto a common vanishing point was an epochal moment in the history of Western Art. It forever redefined the way in which we would perceive space. Henceforth, all the receding diagonals would direct our vision towards a unifying point in the centre of our vision. At the same time, the frame became a kind of window which we could peer through, plunging our vision into the painting's spatial

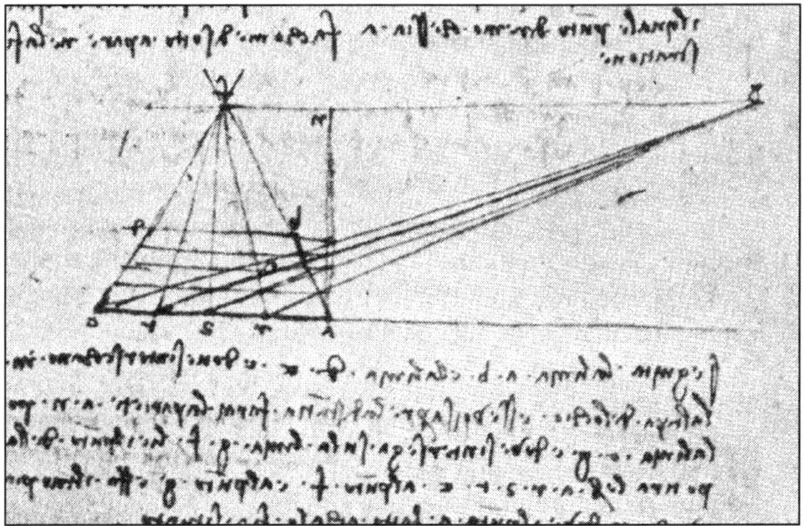

Fig. 22.7 - Leonardo Da Vinci: Linear Perspective Diagram in his Notebooks

depths. Pictorial space became, not only the flat 2D space of the composition, but the deep 3D space of perspective, creating a whole new level of harmony for painters to pursue. The artist's task of harmonizing 2D space with 3D, and composition with perspective, was not an easy one, and so we shall pursue this task in depth in subsequent chapters.

Over the last five hundred years, a myth of sorts has emerged to explain the momentous discovery of linear perspective. From Manetti,[13] we learn that Brunelleschi discovered perspective around 1413, demonstrating his technique with a mirror and painting of the octagonal Baptistery in Florence. From Vasari,[14] we gather that Brunelleschi's secret was passed along to artists like Masaccio, Masolino, Ghiberti and Donatello, whose frescoes and reliefs exhibited a clear working knowledge of linear perspective.

Then, in 1435 Alberti penned his classic work, *Della Pittura* (On Painting), which offered the first written exposition of the technique (without diagrams), which he called *la costruzione legittima.* Piero della Francesca expanded perspective and gave it a firm mathematical foundation in his treatise *De prospectiva pingendi* (On Perspective for Painting - c. 1474), a work which remained unpublished, though it was included (uncredited) in Luca Pacioli's *De divina proportione* (On Divine Proportion -1498).

While this outline is essentially true, linear perspective had a much longer and 'unwritten' history as a workshop method used by practicing artists to organize the interior space of their works. Throughout the Middle Ages, Italian artists painted in the Byzantine style, using a variety of perspective systems, from parallel Oblique to diverging and converging. Each *bottega* had its methods, passed on from master to apprentice. At the same time, monasteries and universities (the first European *universitas* was founded in

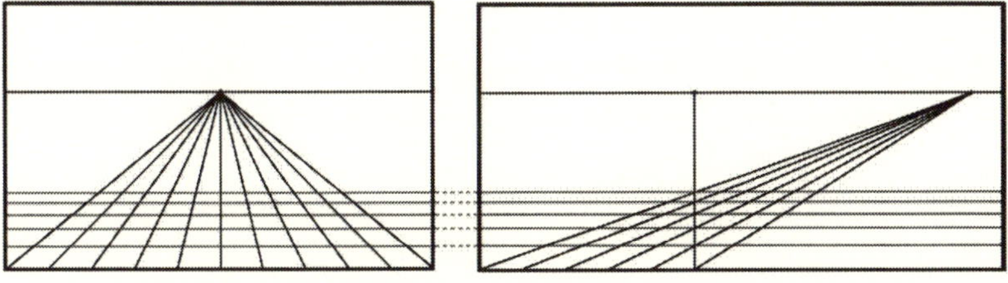

Fig. 22.8 - Vanishing Point Construction Fig. 22.9 - Distance Point Construction

Bologna in 1088) produced scholarly works in Optics and Geometry. Writers like Alhazen, Bacon, Witelo and Peckham provided a more theoretical picture of vision in space, based especially on Euclid's *Elements* and *Optics*. All these approaches are necessary if we wish to have a more complete picture of linear perspective.

Even though Leon Baptiste Alberti only dedicated four pages of *Della Pittura* to the *costruzione legittima*, his work achieved a rare synthesis of workshop methods and scholarly knowledge. For the Visionary artist, Alberti offers an Ariadne Thread through the dense labyrinth of Humanist Perspective. His approach is worth examining in detail, since it sheds much light on the invisible lines and geometric constructions which underlie much of our present way of seeing.

IV. Alberti's Vanishing Point Construction

Figure 22.7 shows a diagram from Leonardo's notebooks, where the basic construction reviewed at the head of this chapter was drawn for, what appears to be, *the very first time*. In his treatise, Alberti never drew his *costruzione,* but we know from his description that *two*, and not one, constructions were needed to create the illusion of perspectival space.

The first construction (Fig. 22.8), which we will call *the Vanishing Point construction*, converged all orthogonals onto a common point on the horizon line. The second construction (Fig. 22.9), which we will call *the Distance Point construction*, was drawn *on a separate piece of paper,* and determined the rate of diminution in the horizontals.

Repeatedly in his exposition, Alberti writes, *"In all this discussion, I beg you to consider me not as a mathematician but as a painter."*[15] Nevertheless, his work continuously calls upon his reading of Euclid's *Optics* and *Elements*. Beginning his discussion with geometry, Alberti observes that *"vision makes a triangle."*[16] Whether sight lines proceed *from* the eye (at the apex of the triangle – Extramission theory of vision) or proceed *to* the eye (from the plane at the base – Intromission theory of vision) remains vague. Alberti acknowledged Euclid's Extramission theory of vision when he wrote, *"Among the ancients there was no little dispute whether these rays come from the eye or the plane. This dispute is very difficult and is quite useless for us. It will not be considered."*[17]

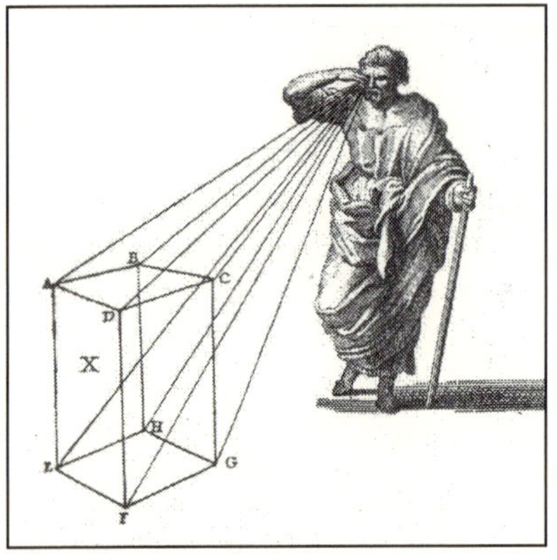

Fig. 22.10 - The Visual Pyramid with Extrinsic, Median and Central Rays

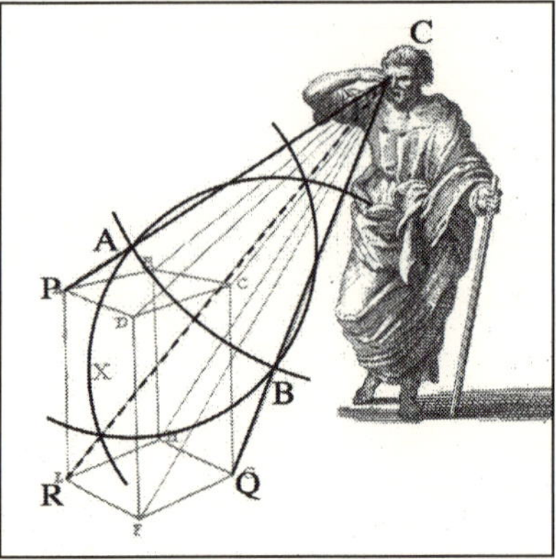

Fig. 22.11 - Determining the Centric Ray By Bisecting the Angle

He goes on to say that three types of rays connect the eye to the scene (Fig. 22.10). At the extremes of our vision, the extrinsic rays reach outward to the outermost limits of a shape (Alberti's circumscription of the plane). Between these are the median rays, which give us its colour and surface texture. And exactly at their centre, dividing the angle of vision in two, is the centric ray.

The centric ray may be determined by the Euclidian method of Bisecting the Angle (Fig 22.11). By drawing the arc AB from centre C, we create the two points A and B on the extrinsic rays CP and CQ. Centering our compass on point A and then B, we draw two more arcs, and the centric ray CR bisects the angle as it crosses through the intersections of these two arcs.

Alberti called the angle of vision 'the Visual Pyramid': *"It is time for me to describe what this pyramid is and how it is constructed by these rays. I will describe it in my own way. The pyramid is a figure of a body from whose base straight lines are drawn upward, terminating in a single point. The base of this pyramid is a plane which is seen. The sides of the pyramid are those rays which I have called extrinsic. The cuspid, that is the point of the pyramid, is located within the eye where the angle of the quantity is."*[18]

So, when artists draw a tiled floor, their flat picture plane becomes a kind of 'transparent glass' – a window or veil, quadrangular in shape – that cuts the Pyramid of Vision, projecting linear traces of the visual rays onto a flat surface. At the outer limits of the picture plane, the extrinsic rays reach to the outer limits of the floor's visible perimeter. Within the frame, the centric ray reaches to the central vanishing point on the picture plane and on the horizon.

Thus begins the Vanishing Point construction of *la costruzione legittima. "I will tell what I do when I paint... First of all... I inscribe a quadrangle of right angles, as large as I wish, which is considered to be an open window through which I see what I want to paint.* [Next] *I divide the baseline of the rectangle into as many parts as it will receive... Then, within this quadrangle, where it seems best to me, I make a point which occupies that place where the central ray strikes. For this it is called the centric point... The centric point being located as I said, I draw straight lines from it to each division placed on the baseline of the quadrangle."*[19]

V. The Vanishing Point Construction & Workshop Methods

Although Alberti has succeeded in putting into words – for the first time – the Vanishing Point construction, it was already known by artists for centuries before as a workshop method. The Basilica of St. Francis of Assisi, which dates back to 1288, has interiors frescoed by Cimabue, Simone Martini, Pietro Lorenzetti and the young Giotto. All these *trecento* artists used some form of convergent orthogonals in their works. The ceiling of the basilica offers an intriguing mystery, since it could have been painted by *any* of these artists.

If indeed it *was* the young Giotto, then he had succeeded in painting one of the earliest examples of convergent orthogonals. Instead, the ceiling is attributed to 'the Isaac Master'. Whoever he was, he painted the Church Fathers in the vault and the Life of Isaac in the clerestory around 1290. Twice in the vault, he depicted four scenes as triangular compositions converging to a common centre. In a total of eight scenes, the vertical orthogonals converge – not to an exact point but, *certo loco centro,* to a common circular area (Fig. 22.12). Alas, the frescoes were destroyed when the entire ceiling collapsed during a major earthquake in 1997.

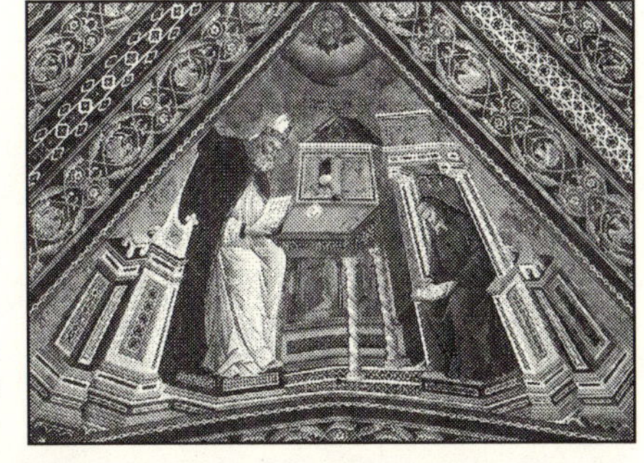

Fig. 22.12 - The Isaac Master: *St Jerome* c. 1290

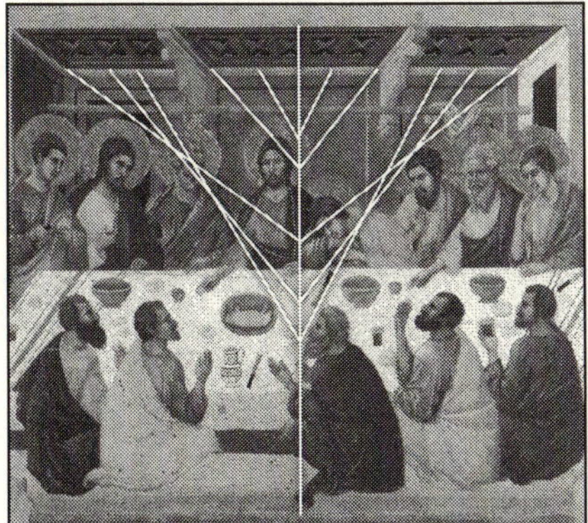

Fig. 22.13 - Duccio: *The Last Supper* c. 1310

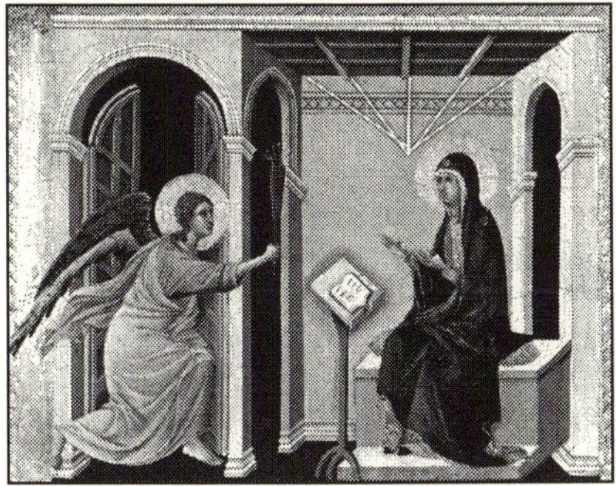

Fig. 22.14 - Duccio: *Annunciation*

According to Vasari, the Renaissance began with Cimabue, Duccio and Giotto, who were the first to evolve beyond the *maniera bizantina* by adding a sense of volume, movement and spaciousness to their art. Duccio di Buoninsegna's *Last Supper* (Fig. 22.13), dated to c. 1310, shows the ceiling orthogonals converging to *the main vertical*, creating Axial or 'fishbone' perspective. But his *Annunciation of the Virgin's Death*, (Fig. 22.14) dated to the same period, has the ceiling orthogonals converging onto a small circular area (*certo loco centro*) that could be considered a point.

Giotto's *Arena Chapel* in Padua, painted around 1305, is recognized as revolutionary in its spatial conception, its cohesive use of light and its linear narrative. Also called the *Cappella degli Scrovegni,* certain scenes in its unified space were designed to be viewed *from a single human viewpoint.* But, as J. H. Brown notes in *'Unscrambling Giotto's Perspective'*, a variety of constructions were used. Brown lists these as:

"1. Orthogonals and diagonals obey no consistent projection scheme;
2. Objects diminish eccentrically with respect to distance;
3. Architectural impossibilities abound;
4. Perspectival and parallel projections are co-mingled."[20]

Whether we consult John White's authoritative study on the history of Western Perspective called *The Birth and Rebirth of Pictorial Space* or Kirsti Andersen's more geometrical analysis of 'The History of the Mathematical Theory of Perspective' called *The Geometry of an Art*, the results are largely the same: Ambrogio Lorenzetti (c. 1290 – 1348) is credited as the first artist to clearly use the Vanishing Point construction. This can be seen in his *Annunciation* (Fig. 22.15) where the tiled floor shows a consistent geometrical construction. Although Ambrogio's older brother Pietro was also active as a painter, everything about Ambrogio's style *marks him as unique*, suggesting that he was a true Humanist. Lorenzetti painted his panel in 1344, demonstrating a knowledge of the Vanishing Point construction almost a century before Alberti's publication in 1435.

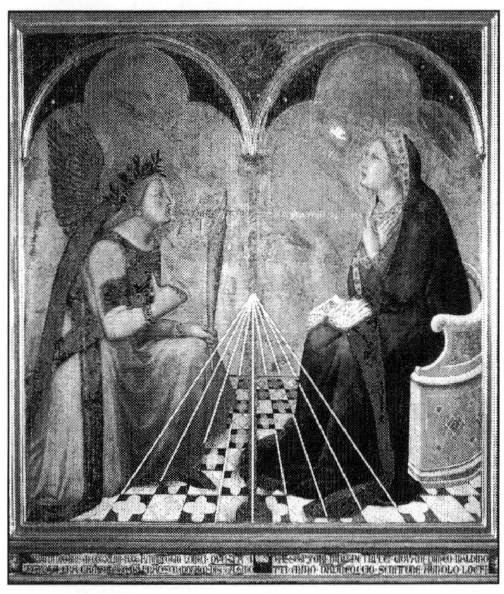

Fig. 22.15 - Ambrogio Lorenzetti: *Annunciation* 1344

VI. The Vanishing Point Construction & Euclidean Perspective

To this day the Library of St. Mark in Venice preserves Alberti's copy of Euclid's *Elements*, underlined and annotated in Alberti's own hand. Having studied the document, Metrovic notes in his paper 'Leon Battista Alberti and Euclid' that, *"Alberti's work on the manuscript was systematic and thorough. He made substantial efforts to compare it with other manuscripts and correct, in his hand, the scribe's omissions. This must have been a very labour-intensive task."*[21]

One reason why Alberti was so interested in Euclid is that his work provided all the geometry necessary to construct linear perspective:

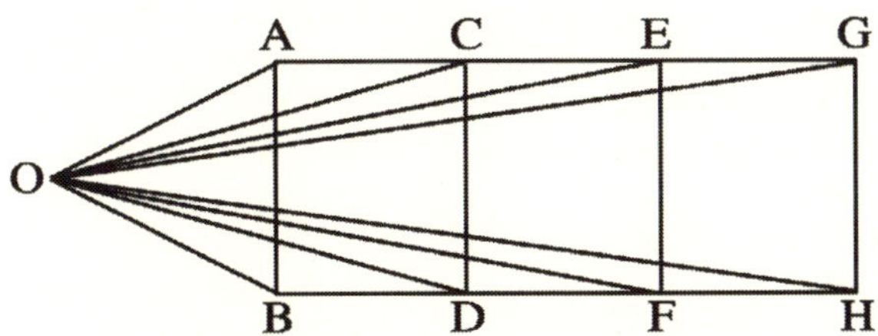

Fig. 22.16 - Euclid's Optics - Proposition 6

"The quantification of visual experience is indeed one of the central problems of Alberti's treatises about the visual arts. In De pictura *and* Elementa picturæ *the problem is framed in its classic form as a discussion of the geometrical construction of perspective and its fundamental principles... The knowledge of mathematics that enabled Alberti to formulate this programme was largely derived from his studies of Euclid's* Elements. *The Greek mathematician's* Elements *and* Optics *contain all the mathematical knowledge necessary for the geometrical construction of perspective."*[22]

Although Euclid never set out to write a treatise on Perspective *per se*, his study of Geometry (*The Elements*) and especially his *Optics* (called *De Visu* or *De Aspectibus* in Latin) continually call upon perspectival notions. In his *Optics*, Euclid deduces fifty-eight geometrical *propositions* (or theorems) from seven original *postulates* (or axioms). It is particularly propositions 6 and 10 that form the foundations to linear perspective – proposition 6 for the Vanishing Point construction; and proposition 10 for the Distance Point construction.

Let us focus for now on the Vanishing Point construction. Proposition 6 of Euclid's *Optics* says, *"Parallel lines, when seen from a distance, appear not to be equally distant from each other."*[23] To illustrate this, he provides a diagram of the visual angle, viewed from above (Fig. 22.16), where the eye, situated at point O, is looking at two parallel lines, the horizontals AG and BH. Between these are a series of perpendiculars, marked AB, CD, EF and GH, which continue onto infinity. When Euclid measures *the angle of vision* for each of these (O+AB, O+CD, O+EF, O+GH), he notices that O+AB appears wider than O+CD, and that O+CD appears wider than O+EF, and so on. *"Therefore,"* he says of the parallels AG and BH, *"lines equally distant from each other will no longer seem to be parallel."*[24] As these lines get further from the eye, the angle of vision *narrows*, and so the parallel lines *appear* to converge.

VII. Euclidean & Renaissance Perspective

When we look at the world through Euclidean Perspective, there are two fundamental principles which may strike us, as heirs to the Renaissance manner of seeing, as questionable and strange. The first is his Extramission theory of vision, and the second is his visual cone. As mentioned in Ch. III, *the very first* of Euclid's seven postulates (or axioms) in his *Optics* assumes "*...that rectilinear rays proceeding from the eye diverge indefinitely."*[25] This more active way of seeing leads to, what Euclid calls in postulate two, the visual cone: *"The figure contained by a set of visual rays is a cone, of which the vertex is* [located] *at the eye and the base* [is located] *at the surface of the objects seen."*[26]

Like the Extramission theory of vision, the visual cone is an important Euclidean notion which seems at odds with our Renaissance way of seeing. Alberti described perspective as a view seen through a window, giving rise to the term 'Alberti's Window'. This term reflects our Humanist view of perspective as a panoramic view through a square opening, a view that extends to either end of the visible horizon.

By contrast, 'Euclid's Cone' describes perspective as a series of visual rays which extend from the eye to the outer limits of the object's shape or silhouette. Euclid is firm about this point, as the third postulate makes clear. Here, he assumes *"...that those things upon which the vision falls are seen, and that those things upon which the vision does not fall are not seen."*[27]

This leads to a crucial difference between Euclidean perspective, which uses the *angle axiom*, and Renaissance perspective, which uses the *distance axiom*. By limiting his geometry to the visual cone – beginning in the eye and ending at the outer limits of the object – Euclid makes his calculations *from the angle of vision*, while Renaissance perspective bases its calculations *on the distance* between the viewer and the object.

In postulates four, five and six, Euclid lays out three more axioms that show how the visual cone conforms to our perspectival way of seeing. These three propositions state:

"4. That those things seen within a larger angle appear larger, and those seen within a smaller angle appear smaller, and those seen within equal angles appear to be of the same size;

"5. That things seen within the higher visual range appear higher, while those within the lower range appear lower;

"6. And, similarly, that those seen within the visual range on the right appear on the right, while those within that on the left appear on the left."[28]

These last three postulates establish three main axes of measurement – larger from smaller, higher from lower, and left from right – while basing all these measurements *on the angle of vision*. As we shall see, Renaissance perspective, from Alberti onward, based its measurements on *the size of the object*, and *the distance* between the object and the viewer.

Hence, there are three basic measures which we must take into account while speaking of linear perspective: the angle, the distance, and the size of the object (Fig. 22.17). Since Renaissance perspective cuts the angle of vision with a plane, we may also speak of *the distance between the picture plane and the viewer,* and the *apparent size* of the object on the picture plane. In all these cases, Euclid's perspective is based on the *angle* axiom, while Renaissance perspective is based on the *distance* axiom.

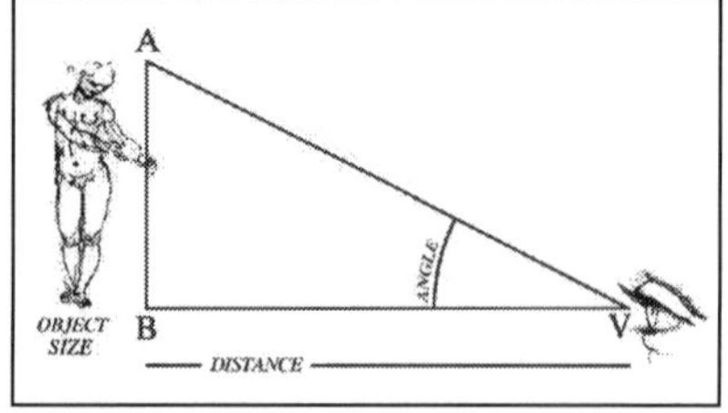

Fig. 22.17 - Euclid's Angle of Vision Determined by the Distance and Object Size

In his very influential work, *Perspective As Symbolic Form*, Erwin Panofsky stated that Classical Greek perspective is 'diametrically opposed' to Renaissance perspective, because Euclidean perspective measures the angle of vision, while Alberti's perspective measures the distance and object-size:

"Because it conceived of the field of vision as a sphere, antique optics maintained, always and without exception, that apparent magnitudes (that is, projections of objects onto that spherical field of vision) are determined not by distances of the objects from the eye, but rather exclusively by the width of the angles of vision. Thus the relationship between the magnitudes of objects is, strictly speaking, expressible only in degrees of angle or arc, and not in simple measures of length. Indeed Euclid's Eighth Theorem explicitly pre-empts any opposing view... This is diametrically opposed to the doctrine behind modern perspectival construction..."[29]

Panofsky's argument had a huge impact on the history of perspective (influencing scholars like John White, author of *The Birth and Rebirth of Pictorial Space)*. However, in his article *'Euclid's Optics and its Compatibility with Linear Perspective'*, C. D. Brownson has recently shown that no such 'diametrical opposition' exists. In fact, from the mathematical point of view, measures made from the angle and from the distance are perfectly compatible.

In the *Optics*, Euclid does not calculate the angle of vision with specific measures because the field of trigonometry – meaning 'triangle measures' – did not come into existence for at least another century, with the work of the astronomer Hipparchus of Nicea 180 – 125 BCE. Instead, Euclid compared the ratio of one angle to another. In order to prove the compatibility of Euclidean angle measures with Alberti's distance measures, Brownson uses trigonometry.

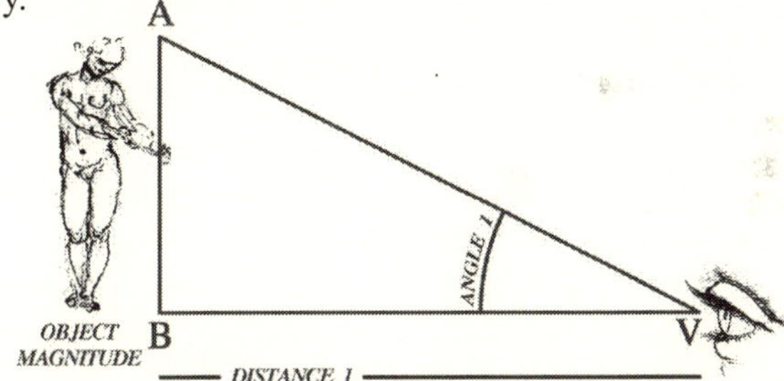

Fig. 22.18

In trigonometry, the angle may be calculated if we know the measures of the adjacent and opposite sides of a right angle triangle. Brownson begins with a very simple example of the visual triangle, which we have represented in Fig. 22.18 as triangle VAB, with the angle 1, the object AB (the figure on the opposite side) and the distance 1 (the ground as the adjacent side). To calculate angle 1, we measure the length of the opposite side and divide it by the adjacent side, calling that ratio 'tan a' or 'tangent of angle 1'.

If the opposite side is 150 cm and the adjacent side is 260 cm, for example, then 150 divided by 260 gives us 0.577. That is the angle in radians, which measures the circumference of the circle mathematically as 2π. To convert the angle to degrees (the Babylonian measure of a circumference as 360 degrees), we must use a conversion chart that multiplies each radian by 180 over π, arriving at an angle of 30 degrees.

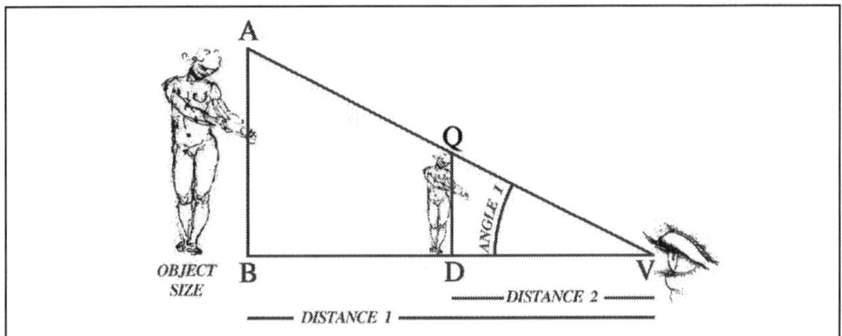

Fig. 22.19 - Comparing Euclid's Angle Measure with the Distance Measure

Panofsky mentioned Euclid's eighth theorem as the proposition which *"explicitly"* shows the incompatibility of the angle axiom with the distance axiom. Brownson calls upon *this very proposition* to demonstrate, on the contrary, that they are entirely compatible. Euclid included a diagram with proposition 8 to prove something quite different. But Brownson uses this example because it allows us to treat one of Euclid's two verticals as the picture plane. As a result, we can compare the angle measure with the distance measure – for an object *as it appears* on the picture plane.[30]

In Fig. 22.19 we have the same situation as Fig. 22.18 except now we have added the picture plane QD. The object AB appears on the picture plane as the smaller figure QD (which reaches to its full height). The angle measure is still angle 1, but the picture plane QD creates a new measure on the ground, called Distance 2, which reaches from the eye at V to the bottom of the picture plane at D.

To discover if the angle measure and the distance measure give us the same results, we have to make two separate calculations, one that measures angle 1 without knowing the apparent height of figure QD (using trigonometry), and one that measures the apparent height of figure QD without knowing angle 1 (using similar triangles). Then, these two calculations can be compared to see if they give rise to the same result.

To calculate angle 1 (without knowing the apparent height of figure QD), we simply revert to the calculation already made in Fig. 22.18, since *the angle of vision does not change* when cut by the picture plane. We measure the length of the figure AB and divide it by distance 1 to get 'tan a' or 'tangent of angle 1'. Since AB is 150 and distance 1 is 260, that gave us an angle of 30°.

To calculate the apparent height of the figure QD on the picture plane (without any reference to the angle), we use the 'similar triangles' proportion, comparing the sides of triangle VQD with triangle VAB. If two sides (AB and QD) opposite the same angle are parallel, then their ratio is equal to the ratio of the two adjacent sides (BV which is distance 1, and DV which is distance 2). From Fig. 22.18, we already know the measures of triangle VAB, so that AB is 150 and distance 1 is 260. To calculate the apparent height of QD, let us assume that the picture plane is half the distance between the viewer and the object, making distance 2 equal to 130. This gives us the proportion:

$$\frac{QD}{150} : \frac{130}{260} \quad \text{Therefore } QD = 75$$

So, we know that the apparent figure stands 75 cm tall on the picture plane, which is 130 cm away from the viewer. If the ratio of 75:130 gives us a visual triangle with a tan angle that equals 30°, then the two methods of calculation are the same. In fact, 75 divided by 130 equals 0.577 radians. Using the conversion chart that multiplies each radian by 180 over π, we arrive at an angle of 30°.

Despite Panofsky's claim, the Euclidean angle method and the Albertian distance method are not 'diametrically opposed'. As Brownson remarks, *"Euclid's diagram itself suggests that his angular method of determining size of appearances and linear perspective's method are compatible."*[31] The final result of all these observations and calculations is that Alberti (or Brunelleschi) could have derived the Vanishing Point method from Euclid.

VIII. Alberti's Distance Point Construction

In the next section of *Della Pittura*, Alberti determined the rate of diminution in the horizontals, a process which I have called the Distance Point construction (Fig. 22.20). *"Prendo uno piccolo spatio,"* he says, "*I take a small space"*[32] – meaning that he drew it, most likely, on a separate piece of paper:

"Know that a painted thing can never appear truthful where there is not a definite distance for seeing it... In transverse quantities, where one [parallel horizontal] *recedes behind the other, I proceed in this fashion. I take a small space* [prendo uno piccolo spatio] *in which I draw a straight* [horizontal base] *line and this I divide into parts similar to those in which I divided the baseline of the quadrangle.*

"Then, placing a [distance] *point at a height equal to the height of the centric* [vanishing] *point from the baseline, I draw* [transversal] *lines from this* [distance] *point to each division scribed on the first* [base] *line. Then I establish, as I wish, the distance from the eye to the picture. Here I draw, as the mathematicians say, a perpendicular... The intersection of this perpendicular line with the others* [transversals] *gives me the succession of the transverse quantities* [i.e. parallel horizontals]. *In this fashion I find described all the parallels, that is, the square... pavement in the painting."*[33]

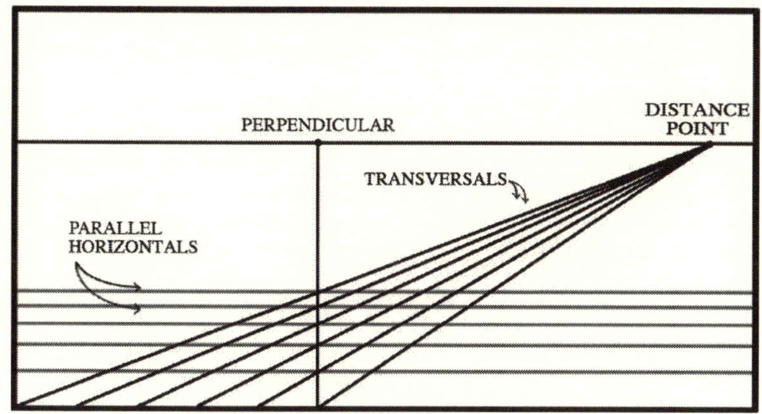

Fig. 22.20 - Distance Point Construction

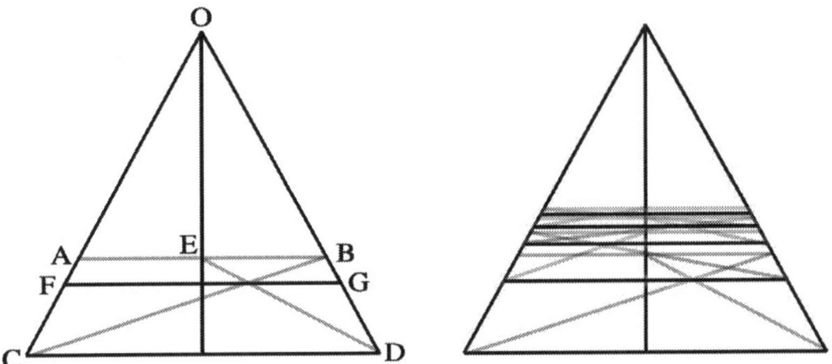

Fig. 22.21 - The Two-Thirds Method of Receding Horizontals

In this account, Alberti is aware how the viewer's distance from the picture plane (the perpendicular) relates to the Distance Point. By laying the sheets of his Vanishing Point and Distance Point constructions side-by-side, Alberti would have joined up their lines to complete his perspectival diagram.

IX. The Distance Point Construction & Workshop Methods

When Alberti wrote *Della Pittura* in 1435, a number of workshop methods were already in use to calculate the receding parallels. Alberti himself mentions one, the 'two-thirds method', which he criticizes as inaccurate:

"Some would draw a transversal line parallel to the baseline of the quadrangle. The distance which is now between the two lines they would divide into three parts and, moving away a distance equal to two of them, add on another line. They would add to this one, another and yet another, always measuring in the same way so that the space divided in thirds which was between the first and second always advances the space a determined amount... I can say those who would do thus, even though they follow the good way of painting in other things, would err. Because if the first line is placed by chance, even though the others follow logically, one can never know certainly where the point of the visual pyramid lies. From this no small errors arise in painting."[34]

We can reconstruct this method using the procedure described in Ch. 16 (Fig. 16.14) for constructing the *diapente* thirds in a rectangle, except here we are using a triangle. To find the two-thirds point in a perspectival construction (Fig. 22.21), we draw triangle OCD with a main vertical descending from O, and draw the horizontal AB at an arbitrary distance from the baseline. Then, we draw the diagonals CB and DE, and where these two cross establishes our two-thirds point. So, the horizontal FG is drawn through this point, and the process is repeated, drawing the next diagonal through GE. The result is given in the second diagram in Fig. 22.21.

Another method comes to us from some early drawings by Raphael. In his article *'Raphael's Annunciation Predella panel and a perspective drawing'*,[35] Eun-Sung Kang compares a perspective drawing from the British Museum

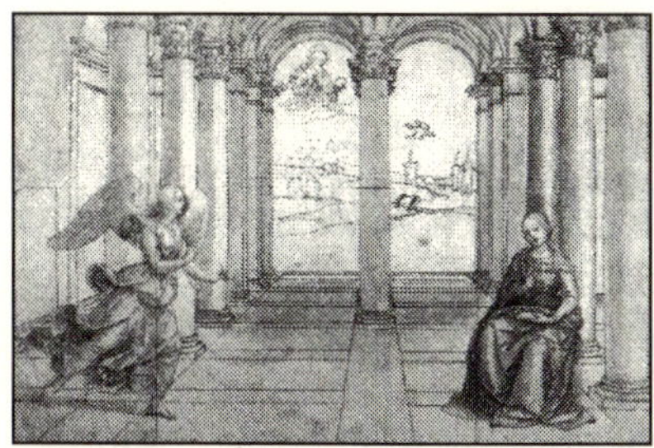

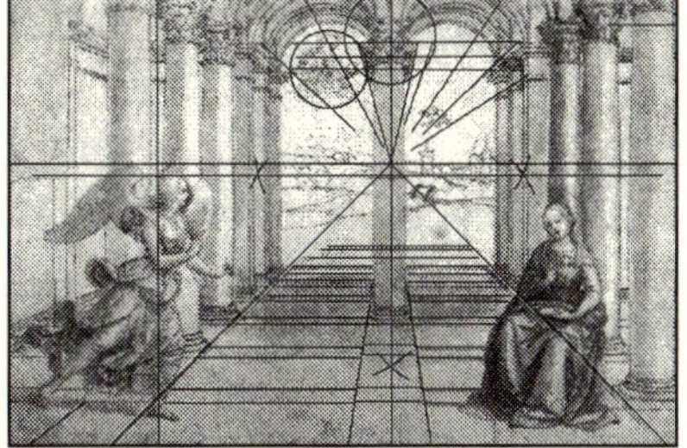

Fig. 22.22 - Raphael: Louvre *Cartone* - Original and Overlay with Stylus Impressions

('B.M. drawing') with another drawing from the Louvre ('Louvre *cartone*'), which is an underdrawing, drawn in full-scale and pricked with holes for transfer, of the Madonna and angel Gabriel in an architectural setting. Both drawings served as preparatory sketches for an *Annunciation* panel dated to c. 1503, now in the Pinacoteca Vaticana in Rome.

Raphael's *cartone* offers a good example of the artist's working method, since he was apt to impress lines with a stylus onto the paper, using only the depth impressions to guide his initial chalk drawing, which was then finished in pen and ink and tinted in a brown wash. A reconstruction of the stylus incisions in the Louvre *cartone* (Fig. 22.22 right) reveals careful measures with a compass, as Raphael tried to work out the recession of horizontals in the tiled floor using a distinct method.

The B.M. drawing, which is a study for the head and hand of the angel in the *Annunciation* panel, reveals *more stylus incisions on the back.* A comparison of this perspective construction with the Louvre *cartone* shows that Raphael had worked out a variation for the receding horizontals, using the same method, which is shown in Fig. 22.23.

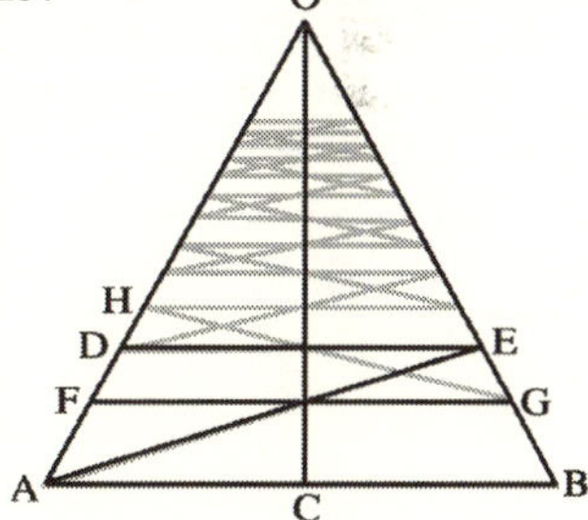

Fig. 22.23 - Raphael's Method

First, the triangle OAB is drawn with main vertical OC. At an arbitrary distance from the baseline, the horizontal DE is drawn, and the diagonal AE. Where it crosses the main vertical, the new horizontal FG is drawn. This process is repeated, drawing the diagonal GH through the point where DE crosses the main vertical. Through this geometrical construction, Raphael was able to establish a diminishing rate for his receding horizontals.

It is still debated whether Raphael apprenticed in Perugino's workshop (Vasari says he did) or headed his own atelier, which he had inherited from his father upon the latter's death in 1494 (Raphael was eleven year's old at the time). Whether Raphael learned this method from his father or picked it up from Perugino must remain unknown. But it is interesting to note that, despite Alberti's description of the *costruzione legittima* in 1435, the young Raphael was using a different method as late as 1506.

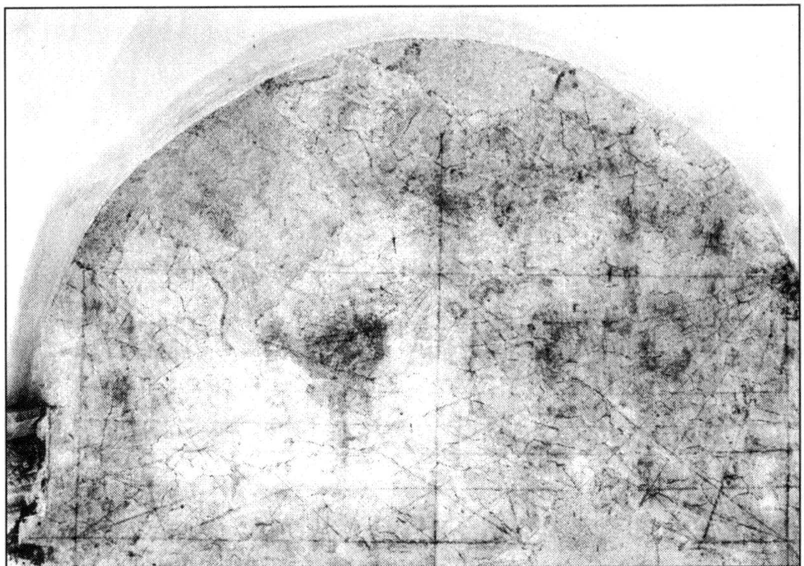

Fig. 22.24 - Uccello - Sinopia of Lunette with Construction Lines

In his description of the 'two-thirds method', Alberti begins by saying *"Some would draw a transversal line parallel to the baseline."* His use of the word 'transversal' here is odd, unless he meant a horizontal used to establish the first transversal, as was the case in Raphael's method. Later on, he says *"the first line is placed by chance,"* which is certainly the case in Raphael's method. Although Raphael used transversals to establish his receding horizontals, the result – interestingly enough – is that *his horizontals recede at a rate of two-thirds* – the same measure mentioned by Alberti.

The final workshop method considered here is described by Samuel Y. Edgerton in his article *'Alberti's Perspective: A New Discovery and a New Evaluation.'*[36] After examining several paintings with similar perspectival schemas, Edgerton suggests that a workshop method called Bifocal perspective was in use well before Alberti. What is unique about the Bifocal Construction is that the distance point is placed *exactly* on the frame of the painting. Although Edgerton offers several examples with redrawn construction lines, in the case of the lunette by Paolo Uccello from the cloister of San Martino all Scala, no such reconstruction is necessary – the fresco has become so damaged over time that *the sinopia with its perspective lines remains in tact* (Fig. 22.24).

This lunette for a *Nativity* scene (now preserved in the Uffizi in Florence) is dated to c. 1446 (i.e. ten years after the publication of Alberti's *Della Pittura*). From Fig. 22.25, it is clear that Uccello began with the Vanishing Point construction, drawing a main vertical in the arch with a central vanishing point on the horizon line (Alberti's centric ray and centric point). Then, on the right and left where the horizon line meets the limits of the lunette, he used the Distance Point construction – *twice* – to draw transversals descending to the baseline. From the main vertical, he measured out the receding horizontals.

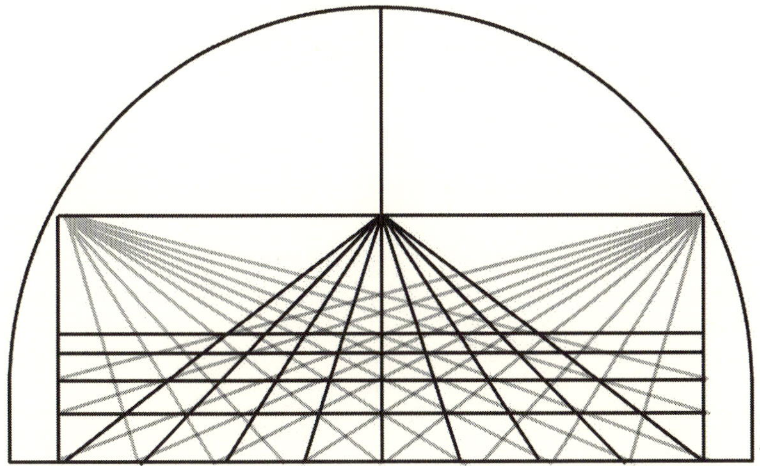

Fig. 22.25 - Reconstruction of Uccello's Lunette with Bifocal Construction

"The bifocal construction," Edgerton remarks, *"is a supposed proto-perspective workshop method presumed by many art historians as an explanation for the apparently accurate projection of diminishing checkerboard floors as well as for oblique (two point) perspective compositions by some artists long before Brunelleschi's invention."*[37]

This would suggest that Alberti was simply recording in writing a pre-established workshop method. Certainly in the case of Neroccio di Landi's lunette of *The Annunciation* (Fig. 22.26), an overlay of the construction lines reveals the bifocal construction, with the distance point established on the outer frame of the lunette. But this example also post-dates Alberti's treatise.

X. The Distance Point Construction & Euclidean Perspective

After comparing Alberti's Distance Point construction to proposition 10 of Euclid's *Optics*, Edgerton suggests that *"Alberti's perspective* [was] *a synthesis of Optical Geometry and older workshop practice."*[38]

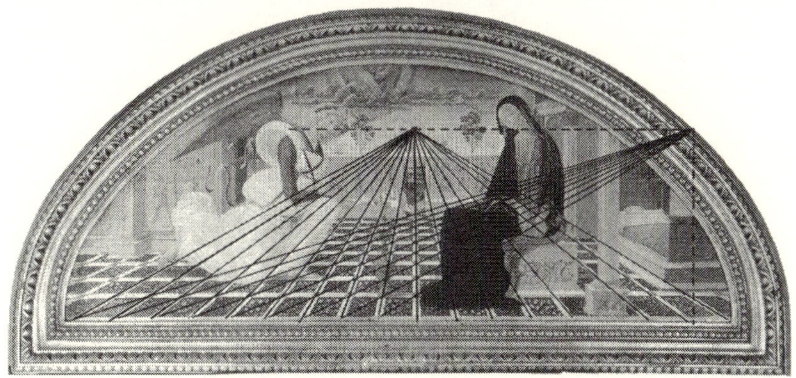

Fig. 22.26 - Reconstruction of Uccello's Lunette with Bifocal Construction c. 1475

For many scholars, proposition 10 of Euclid's *Optics* has gone down in history as *the* inspiration for Alberti's *costruzione legittima*. Euclid writes: *"In the case of flat surfaces lying below the level of the eye, the more remote parts remain higher."*[39] To illustrate this, he draws a diagram of the visual angle, viewed from the side (Fig. 22.27), where the eye at O casts its visual rays OF, OG and OH onto the flat plane EH. At some point along this flat plane, "*let the perpendicular"* AD, he says, *"be drawn."*[40] Although Euclid never describes AD as the picture plane, it clearly corresponds to the picture plane in Alberti's Distance Point construction, where he says, *"Here I draw, as the mathematicians say, a perpendicular."*[41]

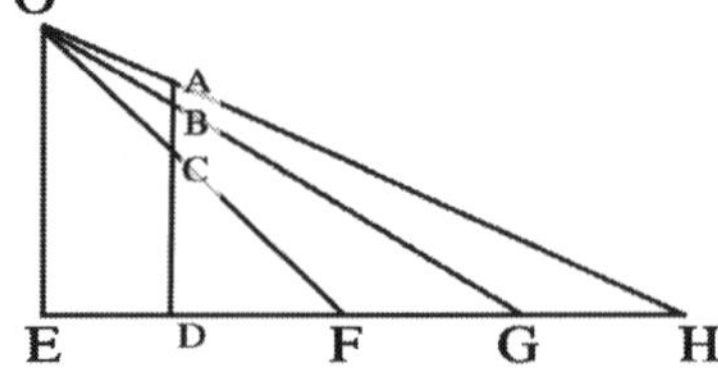

Fig. 22.27 - Euclid's Optics: Proposition 10

With the perpendicular in place, Euclid can establish that the more remote section GH of the flat plane appears higher up on the perpendicular, as BA, while the closer section FG appears lower down, as CB. Through proposition 10, Euclid is offering a unique diagram for the Distance Point construction, which is separate from his diagram for the Vanishing Point construction of proposition 6. The Distance Point construction views the visual angle *from the side*, while the Vanishing point construction views the same visual angle *from above*. It is only when we mesh these two visual angles, one from the top and one from the side, that linear perspective is born.

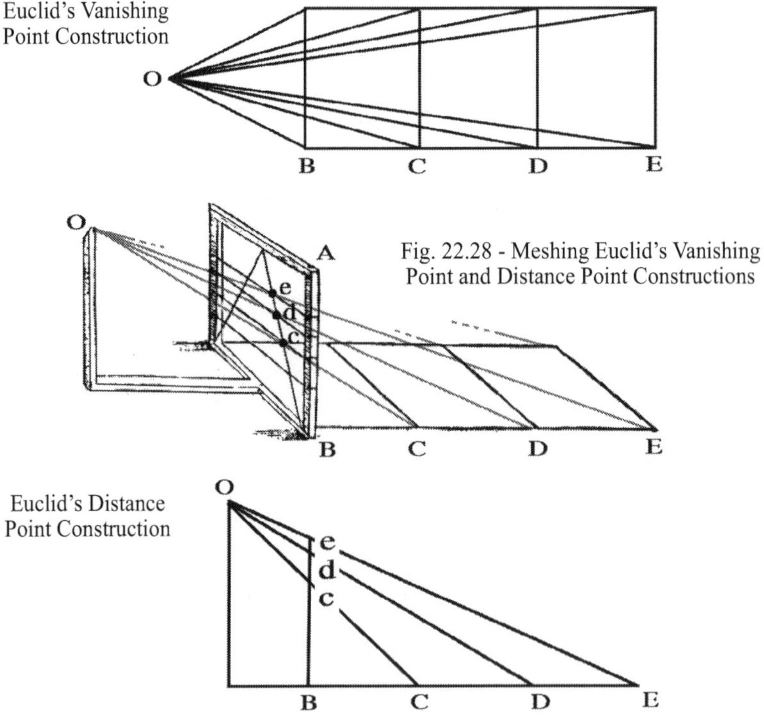

Fig. 22.28 - Meshing Euclid's Vanishing Point and Distance Point Constructions

We can see this in Fig. 22.28, where these two constructions are combined in an axonometric view. Vision from the eye at O passes through the perpendicular AB with the result that points C, D and E on the baseline appear as points c, d and e on the picture plane. *Neither* Euclid *nor* Alberti conceived of an axonometric view that would allow them to visualize the two constructions *as one*. In his proof of linear perspective (Fig. 22.29), Piero della Francesca did combine the two constructions, but not in axonometric perspective. Instead, the eye at A was represented twice.

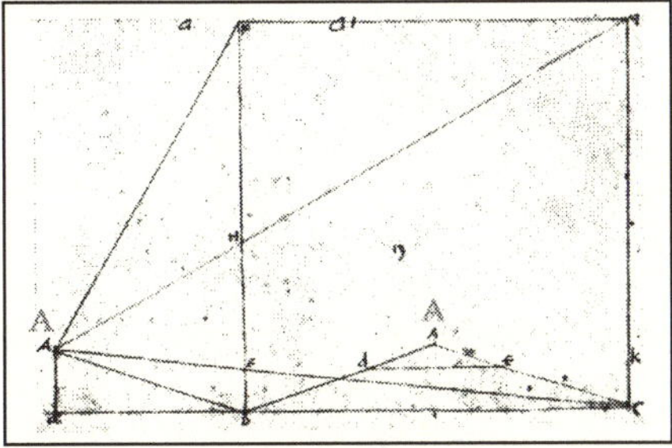

Fig. 22.29 - Piero's Proof of Linear Perspective

XI. The Parameters of Perspective

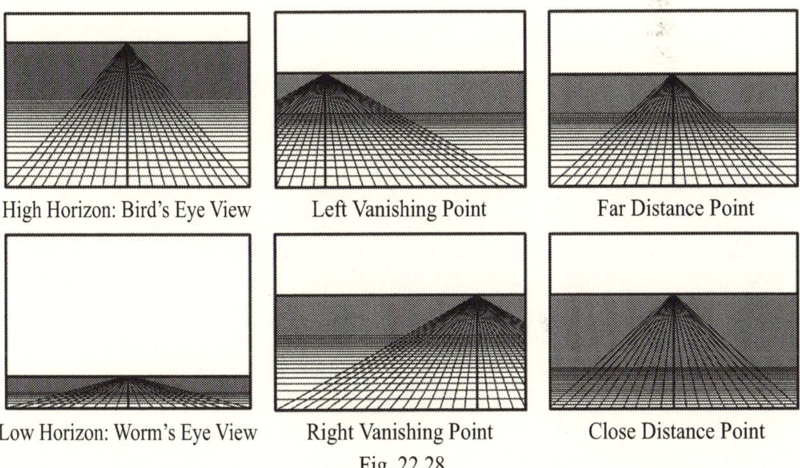

High Horizon: Bird's Eye View | Left Vanishing Point | Far Distance Point

Low Horizon: Worm's Eye View | Right Vanishing Point | Close Distance Point

Fig. 22.28

During the Renaissance, artists learned to see linear perspective as the play of a few key parameters: the horizon line, the vanishing point, the distance point, the viewing point, the frame and the visual angle. Normally, these operate in tandem, but at times, in opposition, so a paradox can arise.

For example, the height of the horizon line from the baseline determines the height of the viewer's perspective through the picture frame (or 'window') onto the scene. A higher vanishing point gives a higher, bird's eye view, and a lower vanishing point gives a lower, worm's eye view (Fig. 22.28).

If the vanishing point is shifted along the horizon line to the left, then the viewer also shifts to the left of the window, and sees less to the left, but more of the scene to the right. Of course, the same is true in the opposite direction.

If the distance point is moved further away from the central vanishing point, then the spectator's ideal viewing point moves further back from the picture: his angle of vision through the frame becomes narrower, with less panoramic breadth. The closer the distant point, the closer the ideal viewing point comes to the frame, and the greater the angle of vision. We shall

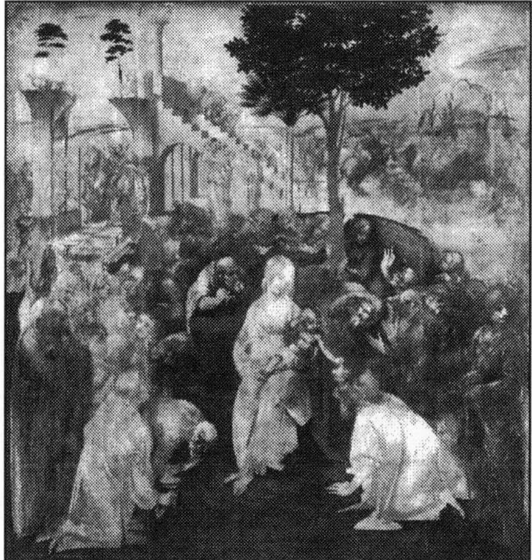

Fig. 22.29 - Leonardo: *Adoration of the Magi* - Bird's Eye View

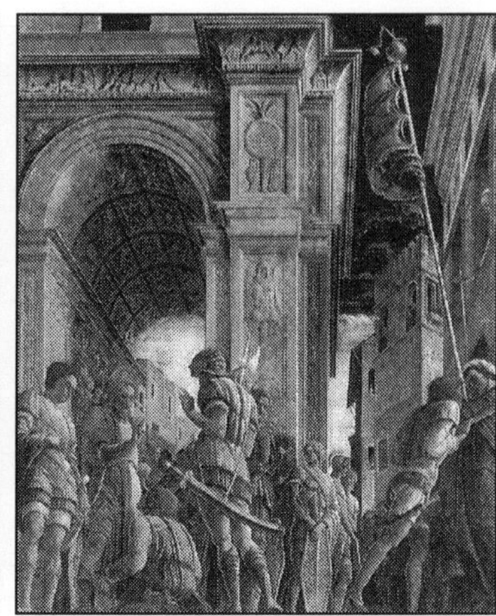

Fig. 22.30 - Mantegna: *St. James led to his Execution* - Worm's Eye View

investigate this play of distance point and viewing angle more closely in the next chapter, where it will be recognized as Leonardo's Paradox.

Throughout the Renaissance, perspective was surprisingly one-pointed. Examples of two and three point perspective are actually quite rare. Instead, the single vanishing point was shifted to alter our view into the five-sided 'perspective box', with its back, two sides, top and bottom. The picture plane becomes, in fact, the sixth side of the box (or cube), invisible and open to our view. Architecture often gave shape to the box, with its tiled floors, regular arches and receding colonnades. Like their ancient Roman counterparts, Renaissance artists viewed pictorial space as a proscenium stage, with a clear view onto the floor, backdrop and angled flats near the wings.

For Alberti, each side of the perspective box (or cube) could be thought of as a plane. As the vanishing point moved and our angle of vision shifted, the shape of each plane altered accordingly (that shape, like a parallelogram, was the 'circumscription of the plane'). As one plane expanded in our vision, the opposite plane contracted.

Let us illustrate this with a series of examples.

In Leonardo's *Adoration of the Magi* (1481), we can see how a higher horizon line gives us a bird's eye view (Fig. 22.29). By raising the horizon line, Leonardo has increased the depth of the ground plane, allowing us to see three distinct sub-planes: the background plane (with its carefully calculated perspectival view of arched stairways), the middle plane (marked by two trees), and the foreground plane, where the magi offer their gifts to the infant Christ. Our view in this painting, we could say, extends from the foreground to infinity.

Contrary to this, Mantegna's *St. James led to his Execution* (c. 1455) lowers the horizon line down to the baseline, offering us a worm's eye view (Fig. 22.30). Now, it is the upper plane that has increased in depth, providing a detailed view of the coffers in the barrel vault. On the upper right, the extreme angle of the cornice races – *precipitoso* – to the horizon line. The angled tower in the background gives us a rare glimpse of two-point perspective – so uncommon in Renaissance painting. Mantegna has obviously taken delight in foreshortening his figures from this angle (his *Lamentation of Christ* being the epitome of Renaissance *scorcio* or foreshortening). Alas, this painting was destroyed when the Ovetari Chapel in Padua was struck by an Allied bomb in 1944.

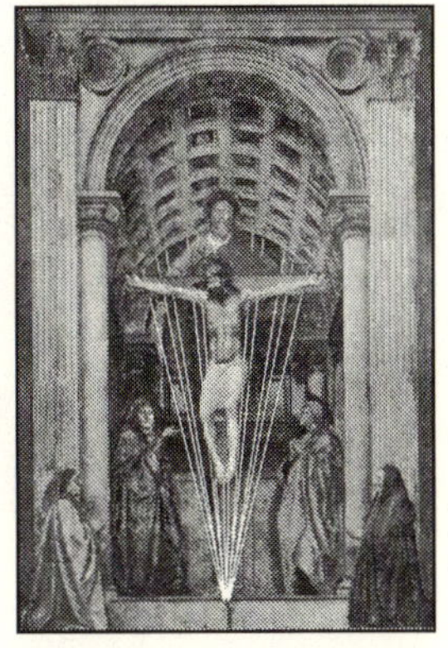
Fig. 22.31 - The Holy Trinity

These examples may be multiplied endlessly. Masaccio's *Holy Trinity* of 1427 (Fig. 22.31) is generally recognized as the first painting to use linear perspective. But it also lowers the horizon line down to the baseline, viewing the entire scene from an extremely low angle. Jacopo de' Barbari's *Portrait of Pacioli* (Fig. 23.14) does just the opposite, raising the horizon line to the very top of the painting. In all these examples, the vanishing point has remained fixed *on the mid-point* of a raised or lowered horizon line. But, in the next two examples, the artists have shifted the vanishing point to the extreme left and right (while keeping the horizon line roughly in the middle).

Paolo Uccello's *Miracle of the Host* (c. 1465) consists of a series of horizontal compositions which formed the predella to an altarpiece. The first scene (not shown here) offers a fairly conventional view into a room, like a five-sided perspective box. But the second scene, which is to its right (Fig. 22.32), shifts the vanishing point to the right side of the painting, so one internal wall of the room is now seen from the outside. This shift in perspective moves the viewer outside the room, but we can still see through the fourth wall to the occupants within (where 'Jews' are committing sacrilege to the host – a fairly anti-semitic picture...). All of the orthogonals, we note, converge into the middle of the crowd trying to break down the door. The

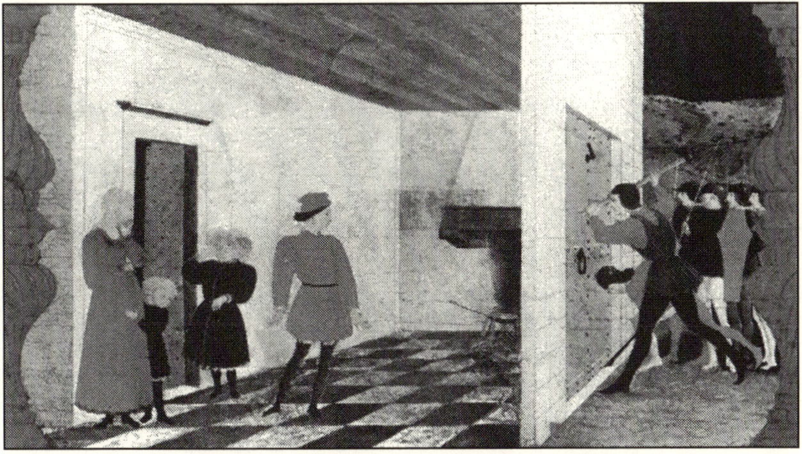
Fig. 22.32 - Uccello: *The Miracle of the Host* c. 1465
Shifting the Vanishing Point to the Right

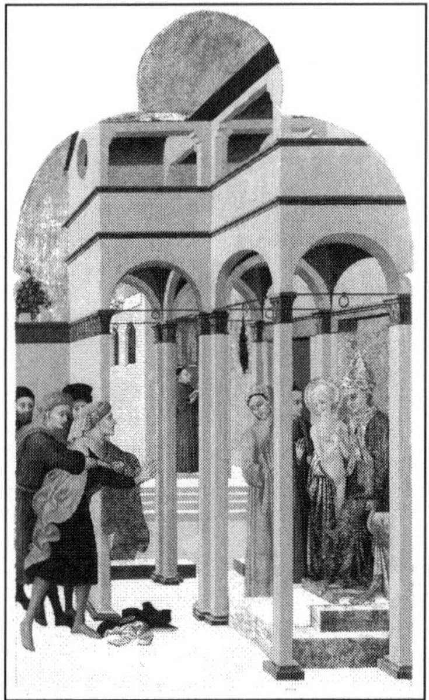

Fig. 22.33 - Sassetta: St. Francis Renouncing his Earthly Father c. 1440 Shifting the Vanishing Point to the Left

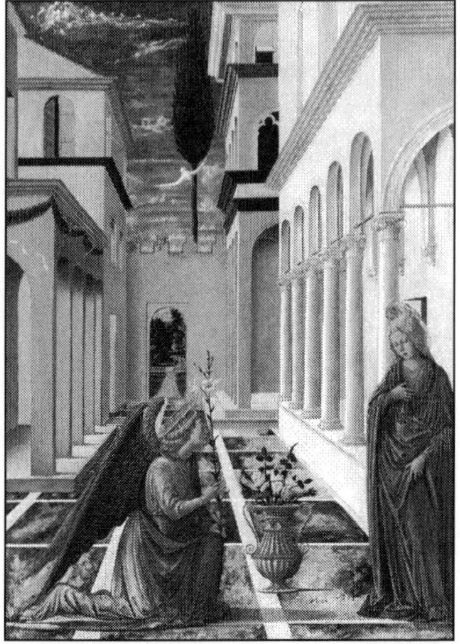

Fig. 22.34 - Crivelli: Annunciation Close Distance Point (Bifocal Construction) With Narrow Frame

composition reminds us of Euclid's diagram to proposition 10 (Fig. 22.27), since Uccello's interior wall cuts through the converging orthogonals, like the perpendicular picture plane through Euclid's angle of vision.

Sassetta's *St. Francis Renouncing his Earthly Father* (Fig. 22.33) belongs to the Siena School of painting, which was renowned for its labyrinthine approach to pictorial space, mixing interiors and exteriors through arched doorways and narrow passages. In this example, the vanishing point lies beyond the left of the frame, offering us a wide angle view onto the right. From this example we learn that, the further left the vanishing point goes, the wider becomes our angle of vision onto the opposite side. The right side of the perspective box now has multiple depths, while the left side has disappeared completely.

So far, we have only moved the *vanishing point*, whether up or down, left or right. When we move the *distance point*, it is the angle of vision that changes. In theory, the viewer's angle should get narrower, the further away we move the distance point from the central vanishing point, (since the viewer stands further from the frame), and the opposite: the viewer's angle should get wider, the closer we move the distance point to the vanishing point (since the viewer stands closer to the frame).

In practice, the change in viewing angle is actually quite negligible. If the horizon line with its central vanishing point is kept in the same place, and only the distance point is moved further or closer, then all that changes, really, is *the compression* in the grid of receding parallels: the first row of tiles looks taller with a close distance point, and shorter with a far distance point.

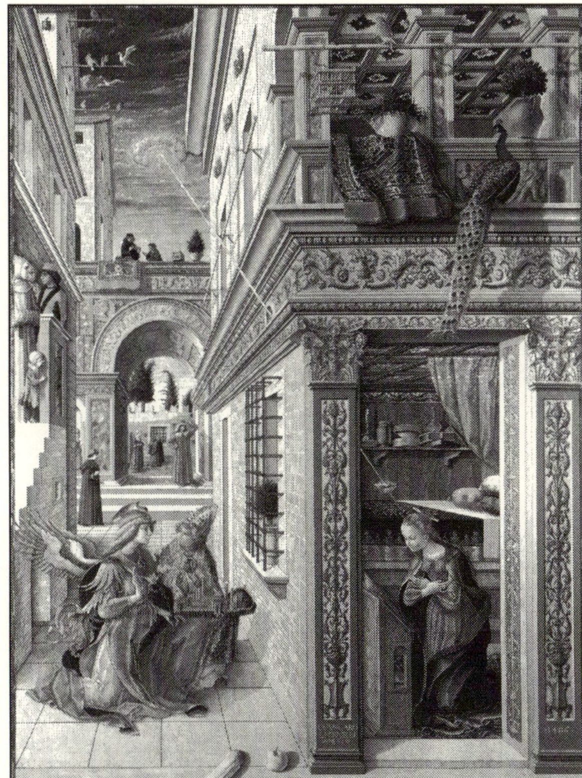

Fig. 22.35 - Master of the Barberini Panel: Annunciation, c. 1435
Far Distance Point with Narrow Frame

If the artist really wants to change the angle of vision, then they have to change *the shape of the frame*. And so, quite obviously, a narrow frame gives a narrow angle of view, and a wide frame gives a wide angle of view. Let us illustrate this with more examples.

The viewing angle in both Crivelli's *Annunciation* (Fig. 22.34) and the *Annunciation* by the Master of the Barberini Panel (Fig. 22.35) is fairly narrow. When we follow the transversals, we discover that the distance point in the Barberini is actually quite far out from the side. Meanwhile, Crivelli followed the Bifocal workshop construction, keeping the distance point on the edge of the picture frame. In theory, the viewing angle should be wider in Crivelli's painting, but the difference is actually quite negligible. Since both artists have used a narrow rectangular frame, it is *the frame* which gives us the impression of a narrow viewing angle. The impression of great depth comes about by placing the sides of the building close to the vanishing point, so the columns and windows recede – *precipitoso* – at a steep rate.

In the Prato Cathedral, Fra Filippo Lippi painted a series of frescoes in the chancel, including *The Funeral of St. Stephen* (Fig. 22.36) and *The Feast of Herod* (Fig. 22.37). In both works, Lippi extended the width beyond the borders of the painting. For *The Funeral of St. Stephen,* he extended the columns of the hall *into the next fresco* on the right. For *The Feast of Herod,*

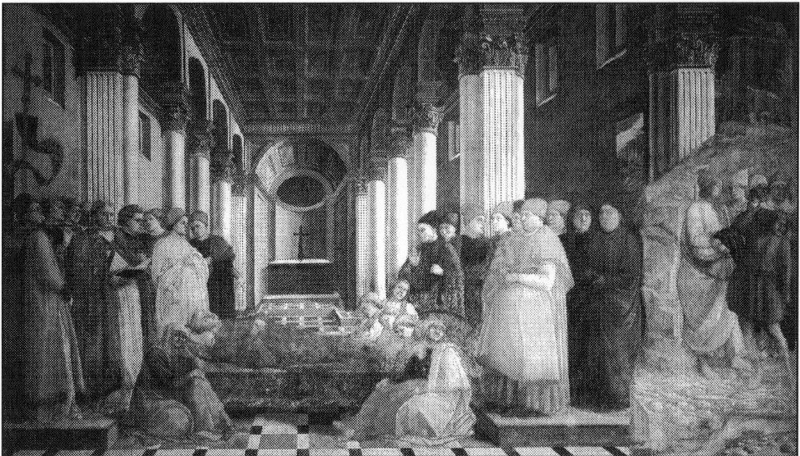

Fig. 22.36 - Lippi: *The Funeral of St. Stephen* - Close Distance Point with Wide Frame

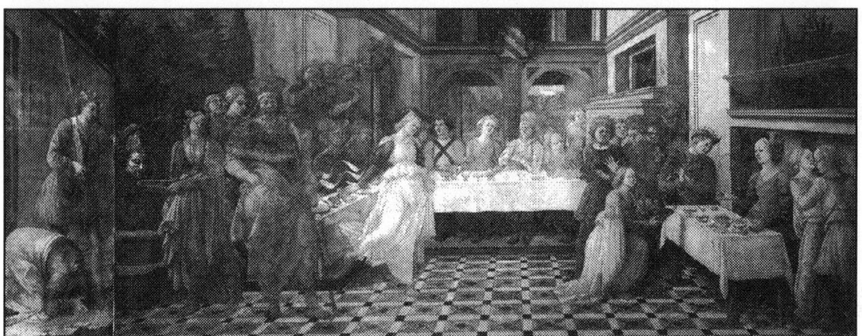

Fig. 22.37 - Lippi: *The Feast of Herod* - Far Distance Point with Wide Frame

he depicted the beheading of John the Baptist *on the adjacent wall*, so the head is handed *across the corner* onto the awaiting platter.

When we follow the transversals, we see that Lippi tried to push the distance point to the limit of the frame (above) and even beyond it (below). Theoretically, the further out the distance point is, *the narrower* the angle of vision. As we can see in the architecture, the angle of vision is indeed quite narrow, with those *precipitoso* cornices rushing to the horizon line (not unlike the two previous *Annunciations*). What has changed with these paintings is *the frame*. By orienting his long rectangles toward the horizon, Lippi has *widened* our angle of vision.

XII. The Symbolic Placement of the Vanishing Point

Since many of the lines in a painting, especially in architecture, direct the eye towards a central vanishing point, Renaissance artists had to struggle with the question – *where* to place that point in the composition, in a meaningful or symbolic way. Compositions with a central figure, like Christ crucified or the Virgin and Child, did not pose such a problem. The entire space of *The Funeral of St. Stephen,* for example, converges to the cross on the altar. But scenes with two central figures, like *The Annunciation*, posed greater difficulties.

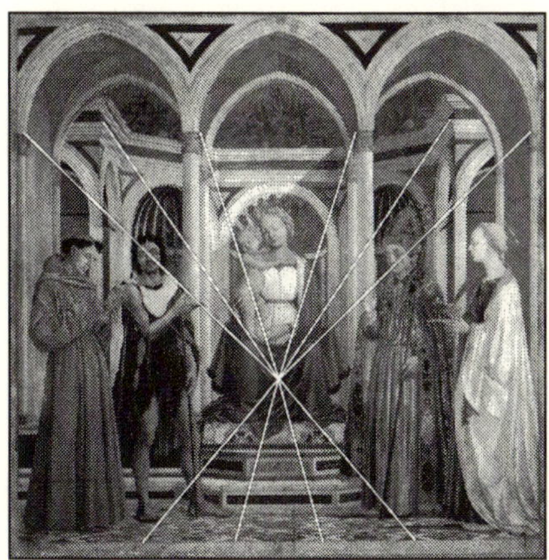

Fig. 22.38 - Veneziano: *St. Lucy* Main Panel
Vanishing Point on the Virgin's Womb

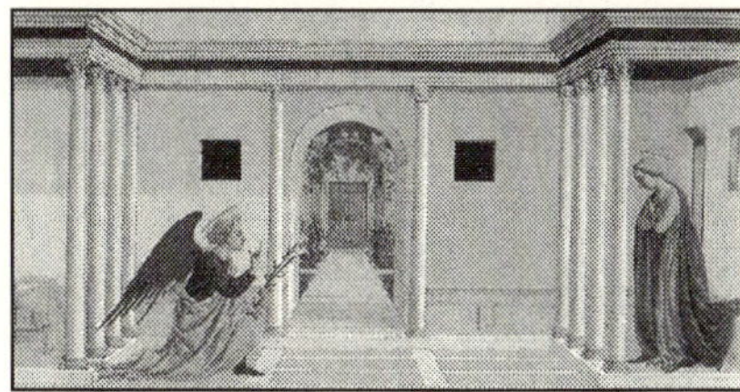

Fig. 22.39 - Veneziano: *St. Lucy* Predella
Vanishing Point on the Closed Door and Garden

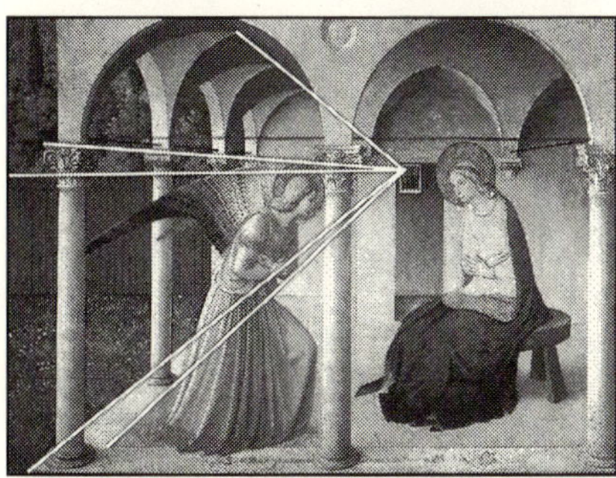

Fig. 22.39 - Fra Angelico
Vanishing Point on the Small Barred Window

After examining a number of altarpieces, John F. Moffit was able to establish that, in many scenes of the Annunciation, *"the vanishing point is emphatically placed upon a 'closed door'* (porta causa – *Ezekial 44:1-2), itself placed at the far end of the* hortus conclusus *('closed garden'), both figures of speech conventionally alluding to the virginity of Christ's mother."*[42] The Master of the Barberini panel (Fig. 22.35) has done just this, where all the orthogonals in his *Annunciation* converge to a closed garden just beyond the doorway.

Moffit concentrates his study on Domenico Veneziano's *St. Lucy Altarpiece* (c. 1445), and particularly the *Annunciation* (Fig. 22.39) which served as its predella (i.e. bottom horizontal painting). Beyond the wide angle of the Roman courtyard, we have a narrow view through a doorway into an enclosed garden (*hortus conclusus*), where we can glimpse, at the end, a bolted door (*porta clausa*). Another famous example is Fra Angelico's *Annunciation* in San Marco (Fig. 22.39), where the portico creates a perspective that leads our eye to a narrow doorway and, just beyond it, a small barred window with a view onto a luscious but enclosed garden.

Curiously, the convergence of pictorial space, in some pictures, comes to fruition in the Virgin's womb. Moffit has remarked upon this in his 'case for Uterine Perspective' in the main panel of Veneziano's *Saint Lucy Altarpiece* (Fig. 22.38). A close inspection reveals that the artist was a master geometer, measuring out hexagonal patterns in the floor and octagonal shapes in the throne and architecture around the Virgin. All these shapes are carefully projected in one-point perspective to a vanishing point located, surprisingly, just below the Virgin's womb. Given the symbolism of the *hortus conclusus* and *porta clausa* in the *Annunciation* predella below, it seems quite likely that Veneziano intended a symbolic meaning here: of the Virgin as Christ's throne, canopy and church – and her womb as the creative matrix of all shapes in perspectival space.

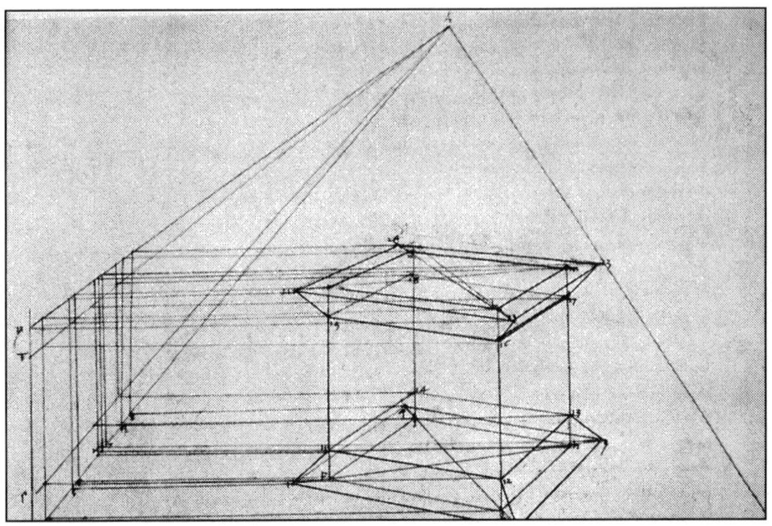

Fig. 23.1 - Piero della Francesca: Cubic Shape in Two-Point Perspective

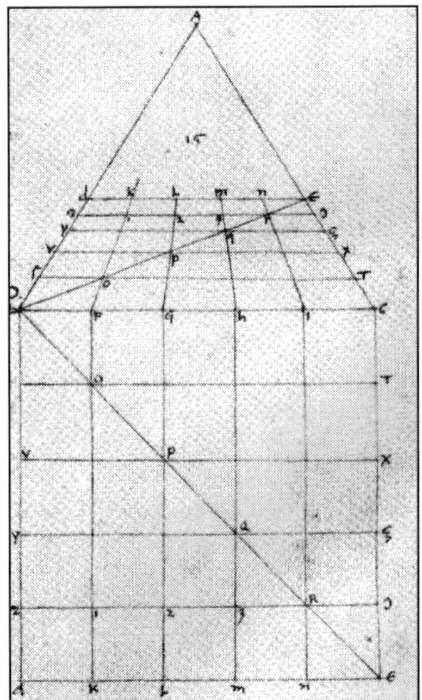

Fig. 23.2 - P.d. Francesca: Diagonal Construction Grid

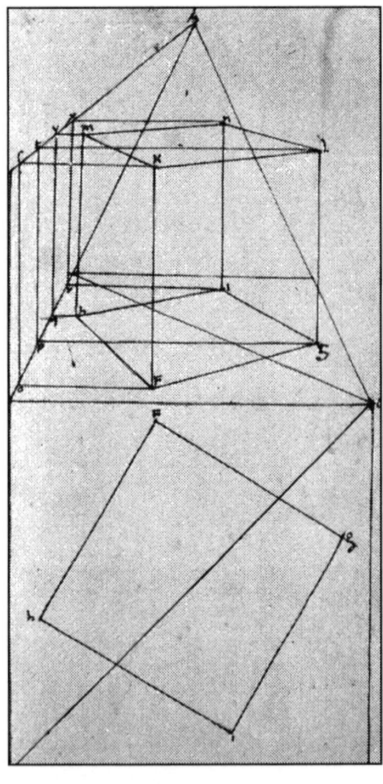

Fig. 23.3 - P.d. Francesca: Diagonal Construction of Cube in Two-Point Perspective

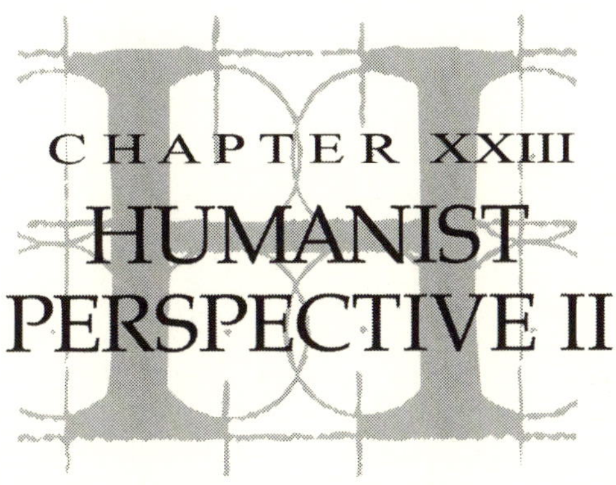

CHAPTER XXIII
HUMANIST PERSPECTIVE II

I. Piero della Francesca & the Diagonal Construction

The art of Piero della Francesca (1415 – 1492) offers a unique combination of human tenderness and rigorous precision. There is a delicate expression of piety and stillness in each of his figures. Yet, they stand in architectural spaces that reflect his love of precise measure, proportion and perspective.

Piero's contribution to the study of perspective was enormous. With Alberti, artists had gained a view through a window onto a perspectival space that was essentially one-pointed. When called upon to draw a cube, artists could only draw it so that the bottom was parallel with the baseline, and its sides converged to a single vanishing point. Piero offered artists a different construction (Fig. 23.2), one that allowed the cube to veer away from the baseline (Fig. 23.1), so its sides could converge to two or even three points.

More than that, Piero showed artists how to use the cube to draw a variety of polyhedra in perspective – from the five Platonic Solids to several of the Archimedean Solids... a task that had never been accomplished before.

As J. V. Field has noted, *"Piero's perspective treatise is essentially a workshop manual designed to teach the apprentice to draw a series of objects in perspective."*[1] Divided into three books, *De Prospectiva Pingendi* (On Perspective for Painting – 1475) shows the artist how to progress from drawing a variety of flat polygons in perspective (triangles, squares, hexagons) to three dimensional polyhedra, using a method that has been called variously the Circumscribed Rectangle construction (Elkins) or, more commonly, as the Diagonal Construction (Andersen).

So, let us now retrace the steps necessary for drawing a cube with no edge parallel to the baseline.[2] In section XV of Book I, Piero establishes the Diagonal Construction.[3]

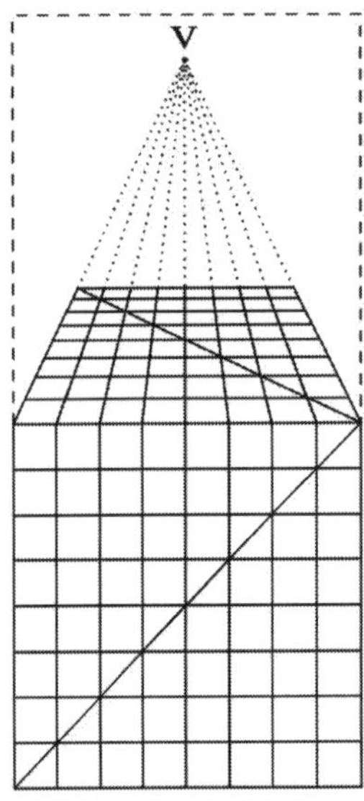

Fig. 23.4
The Diagonal
Construction

In the upper part of Fig. 23.4, he draws a grid of squares 'in a perspectival view' (*degradato*), like a tiled floor in one-point perspective. A diagonal cuts the orthogonals, as a transversal guide for the receding horizontals (Piero does not refer to this diagonal as the Distance Construction, but it is). In the lower portion, he draws the same grid of squares, now viewed from above in orthogonal perspective, with a diagonal that mirrors the first.

This Diagonal Construction, in its elegance and simplicity, allows for the expedient translation of the most complex shapes, whether regular or irregular, from orthogonal to linear perspective. Before continuing, I must pause to admire how beautifully this diagram illustrates the relationship of Humanist and Hieratic perspective. From below to above, we see the triangular mapping of space that occurs when parallel lines converge in our vision, as with linear perspective in the Humanist tradition. And from above to below, we see the quadratic mapping of space that occurs when the converging parallels of our vision remain parallel, as with Orthogonal perspective in the Hieratic tradition.

The next two procedures involve the drawing of the cube in two of its aspects: the base and the elevation. Both procedures use the same operation: a rectangular mapping which allows us to re-locate points from the orthogonal grid to the perspectival one. To simplify our working space (Fig. 23.5), we remove the grids, leaving us with the square ABCD (with diagonal CB) and its homologue ABC′D′ (with diagonal C′B), a perspectival square converging to the vanishing point V.

We can now begin with the basic operation, which we shall call the Rectangular Mapping. In the first book of *De Prospectiva Pingendi,* Piero describes this in section XXV. Given point p on the orthogonal space of ABCD, how may we re-locate that point, as p′, in the perspectival space of ABC′D′?

From point p we draw a vertical line to point r on the baseline AB, and a horizontal line to point q the diagonal CB. Then from

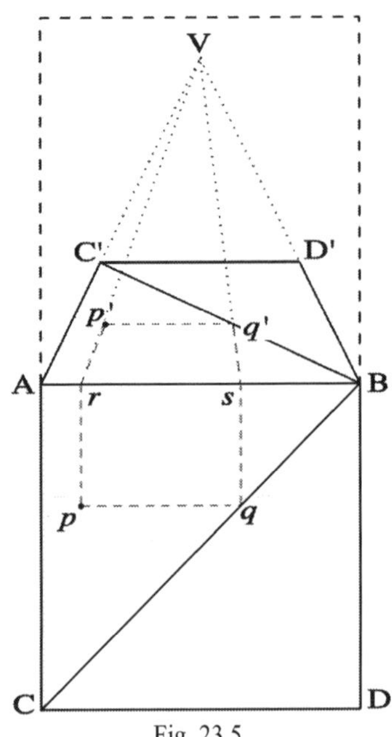

Fig. 23.5

point q, we draw another vertical line to point s on the baseline AB, creating the rectangle pqrs with point p in one corner.

With that rectangle in place, we are ready to re-locate point p in perspectival space by mapping its rectangle. From point r on AB, we draw a line to the vanishing point V. From point s on AB, we draw another line to the vanishing point V. Where that line crosses the perspectival diagonal C′B at q′, we now draw the horizontal line p′q′ which becomes the reflection of pq. Through our Rectangular Mapping, we have re-located p in orthogonal space to p′ in perspectival space.

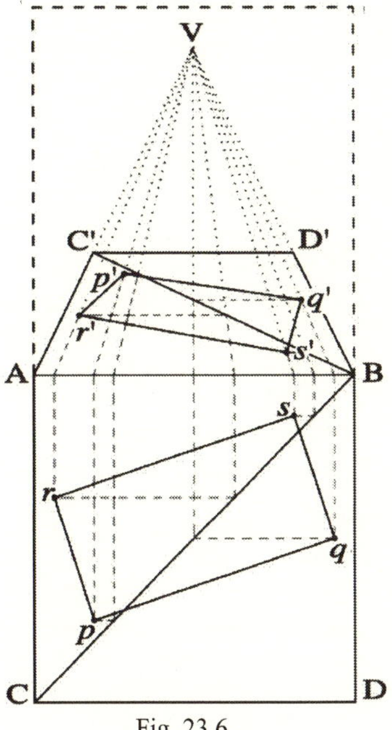

Fig. 23.6
The Ground plan
Construction

With this operation in mind, we may now draw a cube with no edge parallel to the baseline. Two constructions are necessary, which we will call the Ground plan construction and the Elevation construction.

In the Ground plan construction (Fig. 23.6), we begin by turning our ground plan 180° so its baseline is now at the top. If this were the plan of a building, with its facade drawn at the bottom, then that facade would now be facing up. In this case, the square ground plan of our building is not parallel to the baseline, but set at an oblique angle. We mark the corners of the square as pqrs.

Using the Rectangular Mapping for each point in orthogonal space, we re-locate the points pqrs to the points p′q′r′s′ in perspectival space. The diagonals guarantee that the plan will be flipped into perspectival view. Our Ground plan construction is now complete.

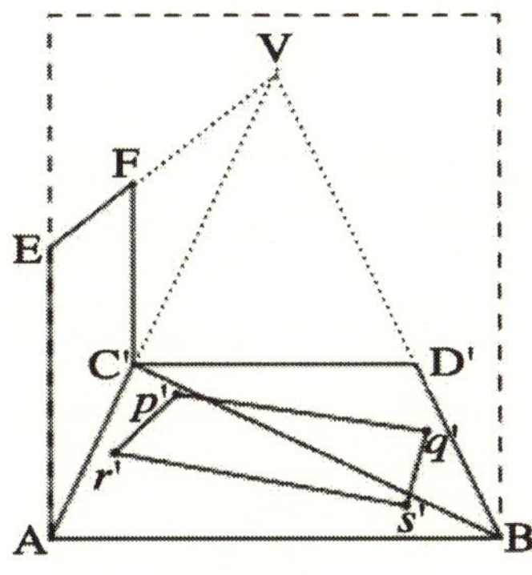

Fig. 23.7
The Elevation
Construction
- The Wall -

To see the whole cube in perspective, we begin with the Elevation construction (Fig. 23.7). Piero describes this in the second section of Book II of *De Prospectiva Pingendi*. Since we no longer need the ground plan, it is left out in our diagram. On the left, we must first construct a vertical reference plane or 'wall' AEFC′. To do this, we decide on the height of the cube and mark it with point E on the left, then draw line EA. From E we draw a line to the vanishing point V. Then from C′ we draw a vertical up to that line, to get point F. We now have our wall.

In the next step, the Rectangular Mapping is used to determine points p″ q″ r″ s″ from p′ q′ r′ s′, but this time using the vertical reference plane for the rectangles. In essence, we want to map the bottom of the box to the top, using the plane AEFC′ as our reference.

So, let us begin with point s′ to obtain point s″ (Fig. 23.8). We draw a horizontal line from s′ to the wall, stopping where it meets the bottom line AC′. From there, we draw a line up the wall to its top at line EF. Then we draw a horizontal line to the right. We may now draw our solid line from s′ to s″, since this will be the one edge of our cube.

This procedure is repeated in Fig. 23.9. Using the Rectangular Mapping, we re-locate the remaining bottom points p′ q′ r′ to their homologue top points p″ q″ r″. By connecting those points, we draw the remaining edges of our cube, which is oblique to the baseline, yet in perspective.

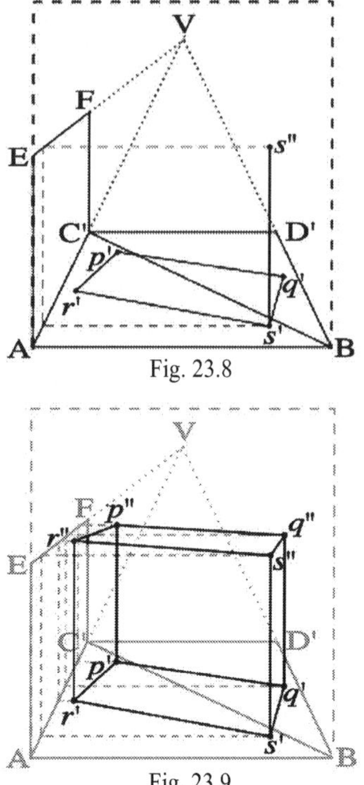

Fig. 23.8

Fig. 23.9

II. Piero della Francesca & Archimedean Solids

Aside from leaving us a rich collection of paintings, Piero della Francesca wrote three treatises during his lifetime, before finally going blind in 1487. The first, *De Prospectiva Pingendi* (On Perspective for Painting – 1475) covered topics like the visual ray, foreshortening and curvilinear perspective. The second, *Trattato d'Abaco* (Abacus Treatise) was a typical text for apprentice painters studying at the Abacus school, and covered practical problems in arithmetic and geometry. The last, *Libellus de Quinque Corporibus Regularibus* (The Little Book on the Five Regular Solids) was written in the last decade of his life, and contained a lifetime's reflections on solid geometry.

It is a unique feature of Piero della Francesca's thinking that he was able to see the relationship of various shapes by truncating or inscribing one within another. In the *Lebullus*, this begins with planar shapes, like regular polygons, and is extended to regular and irregular polyhedra in three dimensions.

Early in the treatise, he cuts the corners of a triangle to form a hexagon, and repeats the operation on a square to form an octagon (Fig. 23.10). Through this method, he is able to show how hexagons may be inscribed in triangles, and octagons in squares. We have already seen how, in Islamic and Gothic

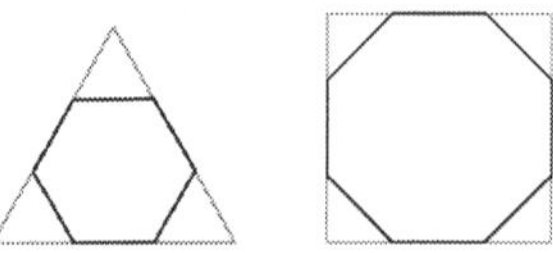
Fig. 23.10 - Truncated Triangle and Square

ornament, turned triangles create hexagons, and turned squares create octagons (Fig. 14.26). But Piero extends these two-dimensional examples into the third dimension.

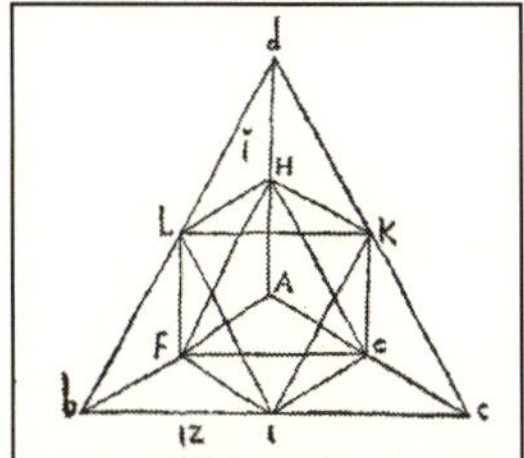

Fig. 23.11

In Book II of the *Lebullus*, he introduces the Five Platonic Solids, and proceeds to truncate each of them, so that the corners of the tetrahedron, for example, may be cut to reveal the octahedron within it (Fig. 23.11).

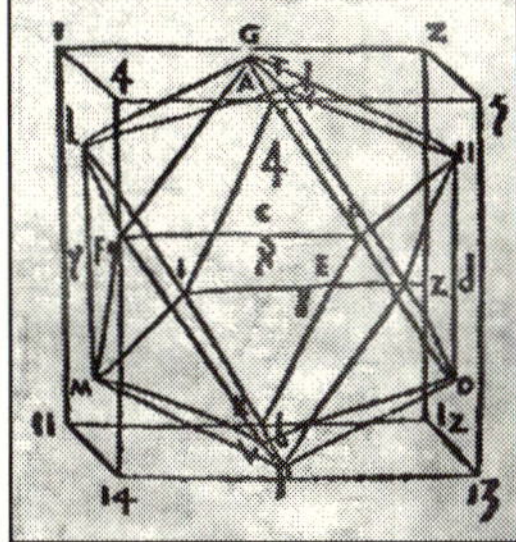
Fig. 23.12

This allows him, in Book III of the *Lebullus,* to begin inscribing one shape within another. In section three of Book III, he demonstrates how easily an octahedron may be constructed inside a cube, by matching each of its six vertices (or 'tips') to the centre of each cube face (Fig. 23.12).

Piero also inscribes a tetrahedron and icosahedron in a cube, then performs more complex operations, such as inscribing an octahedron in a tetrahedron. He ends with a dodecahedron inside an icosahedron.[4]

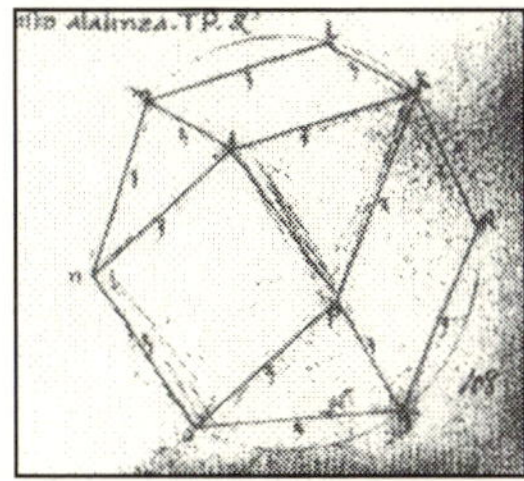
Fig. 23.13

In Book IV of the *Lebullus*, titled 'On the Irregular Bodies', Piero does what no artist or geometer had done since the time of the Ancient Greeks – he rediscovers the Archimedean Solids. The Platonic Solids, we recall, are five regular convex polyhedra which repeat only one polygon on their faces (e.g. the four triangles of a tetrahedron or the six squares of a cube, etc). Archimedean Solids may combine *two or more* polygons on their faces, while remaining perfectly regular as convex polyhedra.

In his *Synagoge* (Collection – c. 340 CE), Pappus of Alexandria (c. 290 – 350 CE) described thirteen such polyhedra (without diagrams), and attributed them to the Greek mathematician Archimedes (c. 287 – c. 212 BCE). Piero della Francesca had no access to this text, but re-discovered six of them for himself. Five of these were truncated versions of the Platonic Solids, and the sixth was the cuboctahedron (Fig. 23.13). This latter is considered one of the most elegant and important Archimedean Solids, since it combines only triangles (8) and squares (6), alternating in all directions. When cut along its axis of symmetry, this 14-sided shape yields a perfect hexagon.

Not only did Piero re-discover these Archimedean Solids (which he called 'Irregular Bodies'), but he also *drew them for the first time* in Western history. Some he drew in perspective, others as axonometric.

In his dedication of the *Libellus* to Guidobaldo (son of Federigo da Montelfeltro, the Duke of Urbino), Piero asked that the *Libellus* be placed along side his other manuscript, *De Prospectiva Pingendi,* in the court library of Urbino. Piero wanted the two manuscripts to be viewed side-by-side and compared.[5]

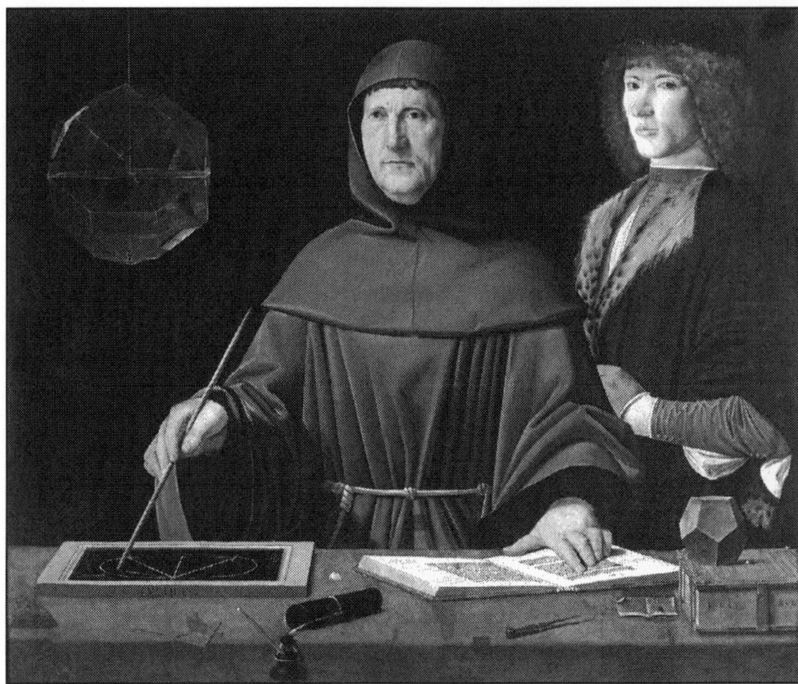

Fig. 23.14 - Jacopo de' Barbari: *Portrait of Fra Luca Bartolomeo de Pacioli* 1495

Piero's two major treatises come together harmoniously with his operation of inscribing polyhedra in the cube. In *De Prospectiva Pingendi*, he described how to draw a cube in perspective. In *Libellus de Quinque Corporibus Regularibus*, he described how to inscribe a polyhedron in the cube. By comparing both manuscripts, Renaissance artists could, henceforth, draw any Platonic or Archimedean Solid in perspective.

The first one to do this was Leonardo da Vinci, in his illustrations for Pacioli's *De Divina Proportione* (On Divine Proportion – 1509). In his study of the Golden Ratio, the Franciscan friar and mathematician Luca Pacioli re-discovered two more of the thirteen Archimedean Solids, the icosidodecahedron and rhombicuboctahedron (Fig. 23.15). While studying geometry with Pacioli in 1496, Leonardo made perspectival drawings of the polyhedra, which were eventually incorporated in *De Divina Proportione* as woodcuts.

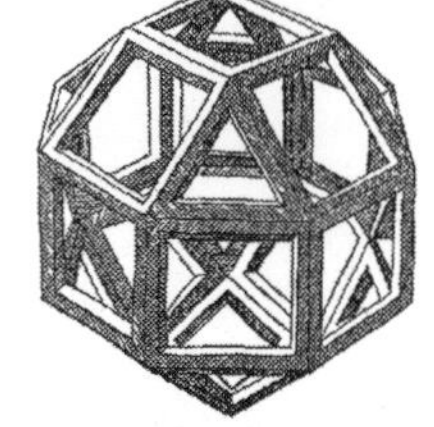

Fig. 23.15 - Rhombi-cuboctahedron

Pacioli was justly proud of his rediscovery of the rhombicuboctahedron, as a portrait of him shows (Fig. 23.14). Painted by Jacopo de' Barbari in 1495, the portrait shows the Friar with one hand pointing to Euclid's *Elements* (Book XIII, proposition 12) and with the other he is drawing a Euclidean construction (Book XIV proposition 8) with a long chalk onto a tablet. That long chalk, we may mention here, leads directly to the painting's vanishing point, which is high up, above Pacioli's head. Hence the elevated view onto the table top, with its carefully arranged compass and set square. On the right, a wooden dodecahedron sits upon a copy of Pacioli's first book. And hanging from a thin thread on the left is a crystalline vessel, half-filled with water, in the form of a rhombicuboctahedron.

Like Piero della Francesca's cuboctahedron, Luca Pacioli's rhombicuboctahedron combines only triangles (8) and squares (18), alternating in all directions. When cut along its axis of symmetry, this 26-sided shape yields a perfect octagon. For this reason, it was investigated by Bramante and Raphael – as we shall see when we return to *The School of Athens* in our chapter on Perspective and Proportion.

III. Leonardo da Vinci's *Trattato della Pittura*

Scattered throughout Leonardo's Notebooks are thousands of drawings and remarks which he hoped to gather together one day into a cohesive work, briefly titled *De Pittura* ('On Painting'). That task was left to his apprentice, Francesco Melzi, who compiled the *Libro di pittura* (Book on Painting – 1540), an illustrated manuscript that was never published. A condensed version, the *Trattato della Pittura* or *Treatise on Painting* was published in France in 1651, and was widely read as Leonardo's original work (by Poussin, Félibien and others) until Melzi's more comprehensive version (which contains passages *not found* in Leonardo's surviving Notebooks) was re-discovered in the Vatican Library in 1817 (now called the Codex Urbinas[6]). Leonardo's outline for his project included chapters on Light and Shade, Colour, Proportion – and at least three kinds of Perspective. Thanks to Lomazzo and Cellini, we know that Leonardo had composed a single comprehensive *Discorso* on perspective, but it was lost during his final years in France.

Leonardo's painting shows an initial fascination with linear perspective, which waned over time as other forms of perspective came to the fore in his work. This is seen in the Notebooks as well, where observations from Nature vie with his more theoretical researches into Optics and Geometry.

In his plans for *De Pittura*, Leonardo wrote:

"There are three branches of perspective... Linear Perspective, the Perspective of Colour, and the Perspective of Disappearance."[7]

In another Notebook from 1513, he writes:

"Perspective, as bearing on drawing, is divided into three principle sections; of which the first treats of the diminution in size of bodies at different distances. The second part is that which treats of the diminution in colour in these objects. The third [deals with] *the diminished distinctness of the forms and outlines displayed by the objects at various distances."*[8]

One of Leonardo's later editors, Jean Paul Richter, attempted to reassemble the artist's remarks on painting into an authoritative work called *The Notebooks of Leonardo da Vinci* – 1883, with chapters dedicated to, respectively, Linear Perspective (*prospettiva liniale*), the Perspective of Colour (*prospettiva de' colori*) and the Perspective of Disappearance or Distinctness (*prospettiva de' perdimenti*) – to which Richter added a fourth: Aerial Perspective (*prospettiva aerea*).

As painters, we are deeply indebted to Leonardo for this reminder that Perspective consists of more than just lines. In the second and third volumes of Sacred Codes, I will explore the play of light and shadow over volumes, and their translation into colour. For now, I will let Leonardo speak for himself, briefly, on each of these forms of Perspective.

In the case of Linear Perspective, Leonardo was one of the first Renaissance artists to state explicitly that visual rays enter the eye *from the object* (Intromission Theory). This allowed him to examine 'the visual pyramid' from a much different perspective:

"Perspective is a rational demonstration by which experience confirms that every object sends its images to the eye by a pyramid of lines; and bodies of equal size will result in a pyramid of larger or smaller size, according to the difference in their distance, one from the other."[9]

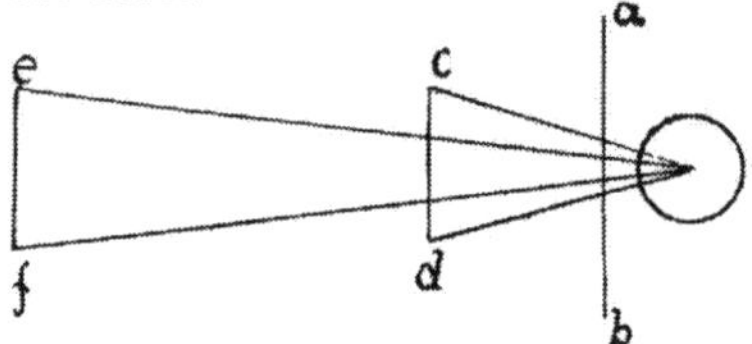

Fig. 23.16 - Leonardo's Intromission Visual Pyramids

As we can see in the diagram illustrating this remark (Fig. 23.16), Leonardo is basically re-stating Proposition 6 of Euclid's *Optics,* where the angle of vision narrows as parallel lines of equal height (ef, cd) increase their distance from the eye. Except, where Euclid spoke of the angle of vision as "*rectilinear rays proceeding from the eye* [that] *diverge indefinitely."*[10] (Proposition 1 of *The Optics*), for Leonardo "*every object sends its images to the eye by a pyramid of lines."*

In Fig. 3.1 from Ch. 3, Leonardo has shown this explicitly, where the object is now shooting out images of itself 'by a pyramid of lines' in all directions, and (at the top) in a variety of distances:

"Every opaque body fills the surrounding air with an infinite number of its images, which by means of infinite pyramids infuse the representation of this body, all in all and in every part."[11]

The second form of perspective, *prospettiva de' colori* or perspective of colours, shows distance through *a loss of* colour – its variety and vividness:

"All colours at a distance are indistinguishable in shadow,"[12] Leonardo writes. And to the young painters, he says:

"Take care that the perspective of colour [la prospettiua de' colori] *does not disagree with the size of your objects, that is to say: that the colours diminish from their natural* [vividness] *in proportion as the objects at various distances diminish from their natural size."*[13]

The third form of perspective, *prospettiva de' perdimenti,* which is perspective of disappearance or distinctness, blurs the edges of objects as they recede in our sight:

"An object will appear more or less distinct at the same distance, in proportion, as the atmosphere existing between the eye and that object is more or less clear. ... You must diminish the definiteness of the outline of those objects in proportion to their increasing distance from the eye of the spectator."[14]

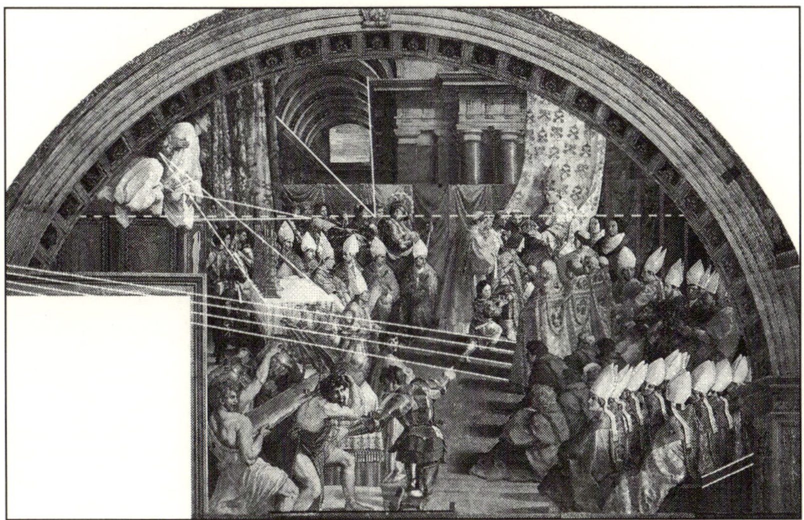

Fig. 23.17 - Raphael: *The Coronation of Charlemagne* 1516

Last of all is *prospettiva aerea* or aerial perspective:

"There is another kind of perspective which I call aerial... You know that in an atmosphere of equal density, the remotest objects seen through it, as mountains, in consequence of the great quantity of atmosphere between your eye and them – appear blue and almost of the same hue as the atmosphere itself. Hence, you must make the nearest building... its real colour, but the more distant ones make less defined and bluer."[15]

IV. Beyond One-Point Perspective

With several rare exceptions, Renaissance artists did not seem to grasp the concept of two-point perspective until the 1600s. (A notable exception is Uccello's lunette for the *Nativity* c. 1446, where the scant remains of the fresco suggest that he used the bi-focal distance points as vanishing points for the furniture. Other examples include Giotto's *Christ Before the Caïf* of 1305 and Lorenzetti's *Allegory of Good and Bad Government* of 1338).

A curious example is Raphael's fresco of *The Coronation of Charlemagne* of 1516 in the Vatican (Fig. 23.17). All the other frescos in the *Stanze* show a masterful grasp of one-point perspective. But the tables on the left and the Bishops' pews on the right suggest that Raphael was trying to orient his space onto two lateral vanishing points. The barrel arch in the background gives a plausible horizon line, and the stairs to Charlemagne's throne may indeed converge to a distant vanishing point on the left of that horizon line. But the table on the left is oriented to another vanishing point that is much higher up. Compared to the other frescoes in the Stanze, *The Coronation of Charlemagne* seems be a rare experiment in conceptualizing space in a much different manner.

The first theorist north of the Alps to publish a work on perspective was Jean Pèlerin (c. 1445 – c.1524), a well-travelled diplomat for Louis XI, who published his work under the name of Viator ('the voyager'). His *De Artificiali Perspectiva*[16] (Artificial Perspective – 1505) appeared a decade before Raphael's *Coronation of Charlemagne* fresco. Unlike Italian theorists on perspective, Viator offered few explanations and concentrated instead on numerous examples that showed his basic construction in operation.

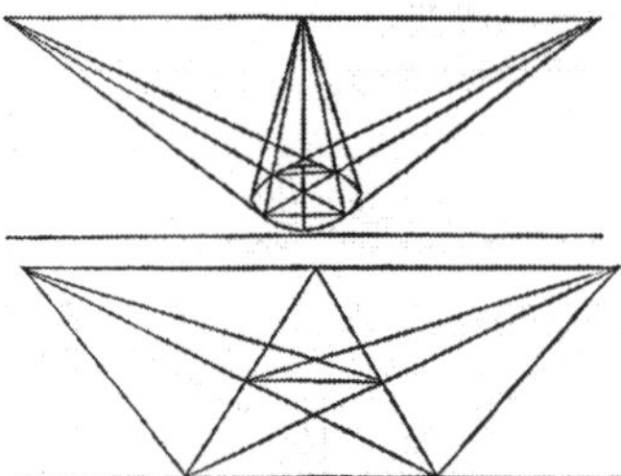

Fig. 23.18 - Viator's Construction

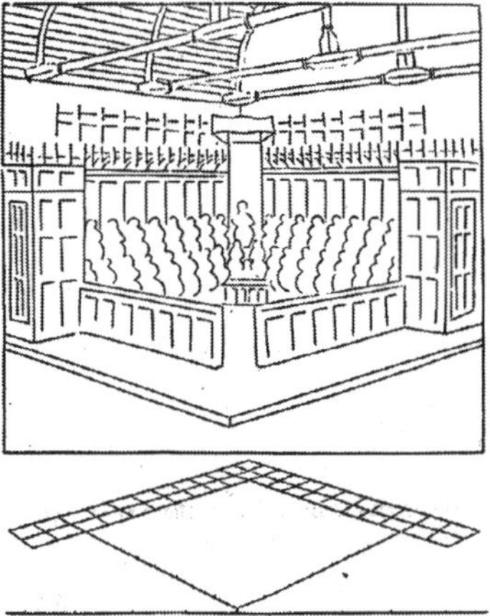

Fig. 23.19 - Viator's Two-Point Perspective

Viator's *De Artificiali Perspectiva* is historically important for two reasons. He was the first to publish diagrams of linear perspective *with two equal distance points* – diagrams that are memorable for their elegance and simplicity (Fig. 23.18). And, he was the first to give an example of a scene oriented *to two-point perspective* (Fig. 23.19). To do this, he simply treated the two distant points as vanishing points. This shift in perspective may seem obvious to us today, but at the time it was clearly revolutionary.

Indeed, artists did not implement two-point perspective for at least another fifty years. In fact, it is difficult to find the first clear case of two-point perspective for the pictorial space of a painting. The clearest examples come from the North, in the paintings of Pieter Brueghel the Elder (1525 – 1569), whose *Fight Between Carnival and Lent* of 1559 displays a functional knowledge of two-point perspective for the layout of the town square, just as his *Peasant Wedding* of 1566 clearly shows this for the interior of the barn where the wedding is celebrated.

One would expect to find earlier examples in the work of Albrecht Dürer (1471 – 1528), who lived a generation before Brueghel. Instead, the perspective in his pictorial space remains fixedly one-pointed. The important exceptions are his depictions of *isolated objects*. We can see this with the chair in his engraving of *St. Jerome in his Study* (Fig. 23.20) dated to the year 1514.

When the orthogonals are extended, we discover that the central vanishing point (CVP) is located – rather unusually – toward the right edge of the picture frame. This steep one-point perspective of the interior space causes the left orthogonals to come streaming into the room like beams of light through the trellis window. Meanwhile, the orthogonals for the chair (in the right foreground) fall upon two lateral vanishing points (LVP), with the one on the right located far outside the picture frame. Dürer has used these lateral vanishing points to orient the direction of his chair – a clear case of an object in two-point perspective.

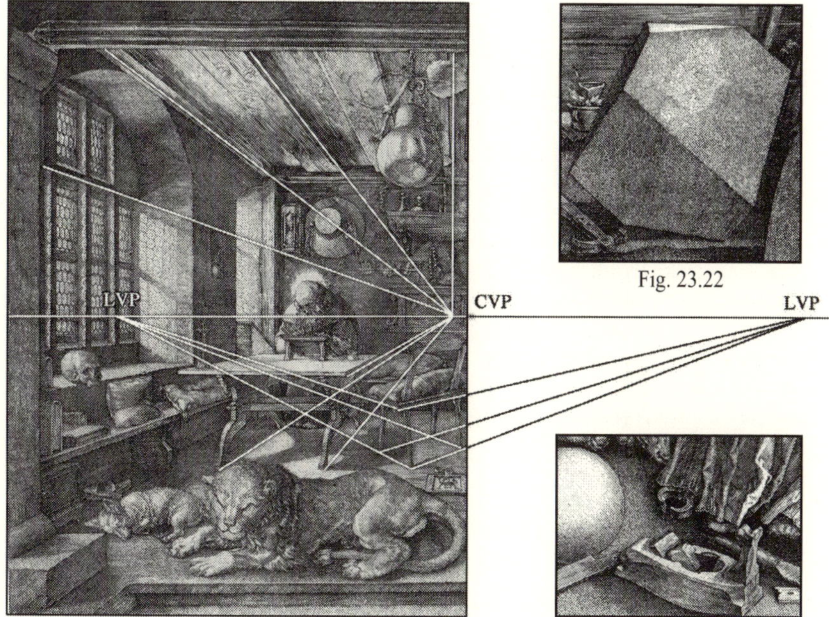

Fig. 23.22

Fig. 23.20 - Dürer: *St. Jerome in his Study* 1514

Fig. 23.21

In that same year of 1514, Dürer also engraved his famous *Melancholia*. The profusion of mysterious objects in the painting may cause us to ignore the woodworking tools at the bottom, where the hand plane (Fig. 23.21) is also oriented in two-point perspective. Instead, our sight tends to gravitate towards the curious eight-faced geometrical solid (Fig. 23.22), which may or may not be a truncated triangular trapezohedron. In fact, the actual shape and perspectival orientation of this polyhedron has been debated for centuries.

Nevertheless, it demonstrates Dürer's profound knowledge of geometry, which emerged with the publication of his *Four Books on Measurement* (*Underweysung der Messung mit dem Zirckel und Richtscheyt* – literally: *Instructions for Measuring with Compass and Ruler)* printed in 1525, just three years before the artist's death. In these four books, Dürer demonstrated his thorough grasp of regular polygons (book II) and complex polyhedra (book IV), as well as the linear perspective constructions he had learned during his second Italian journey of 1505 to 1507. It was most likely Luca Pacioli, in Bologna, who showed him Piero della Francesca's treatise on perspective, but Dürer also met and remained in correspondence with Raphael, Giovanni Bellini and (through Lorenzo di Credi) Leonardo da Vinci. How we can only dream of being present at such meetings...

V. Multiple Vanishing Points

Since the appearance of Alberti's *Della Pittura* in 1436, literally thousands of books have been written on perspective. From its roots in Optics and Geometry, the study has diverged in numerous directions, from mathematics and CGI to psychology and art history. Curiously, artists' books

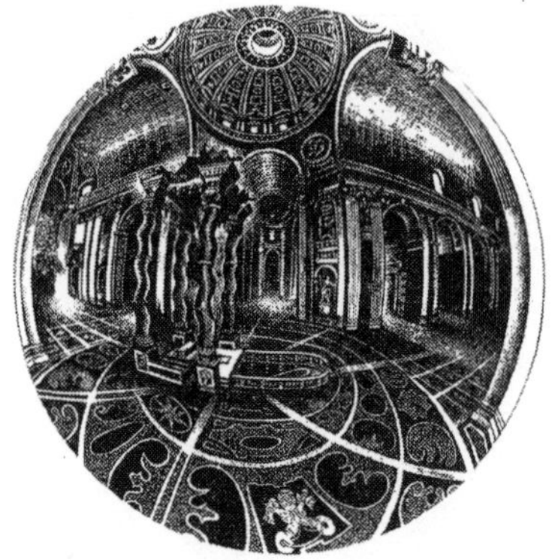

Fig. 23.27 - Dick Thermes: *Interior of St. Peter's Basilica*

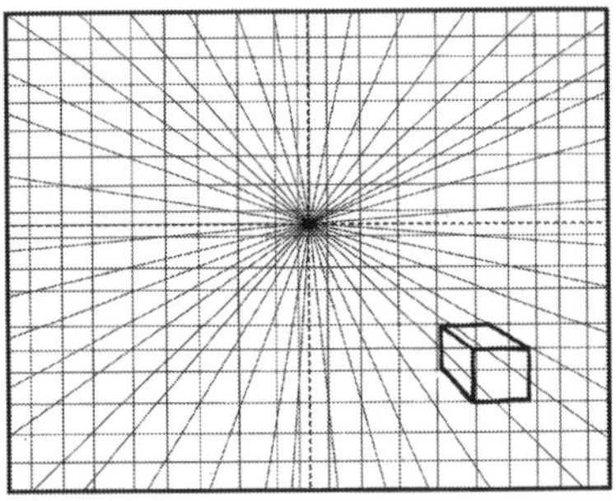

Fig. 23.23 - One-Point Perspective

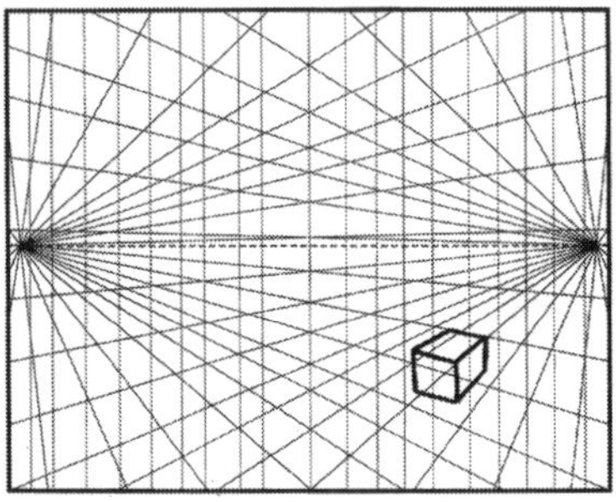

Fig. 23.24 - Two-Point Perspective

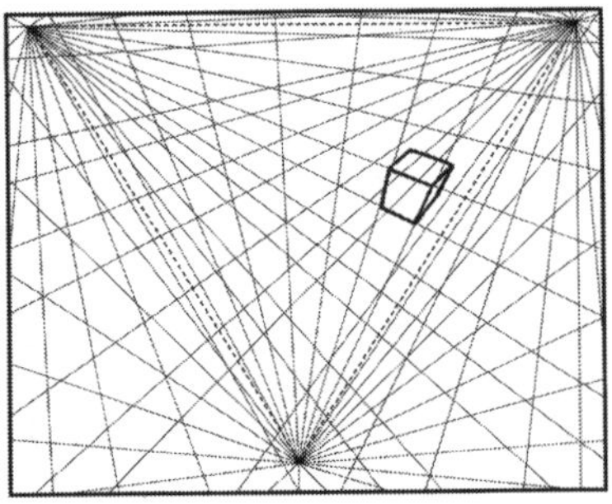

Fig. 23.24 - Three-Point Perspective

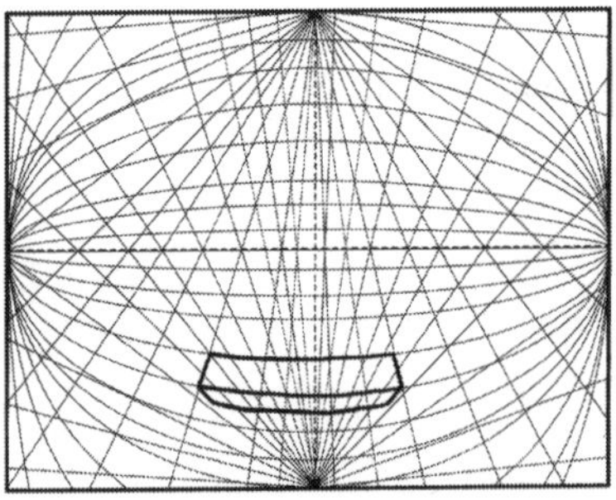

Fig. 23.25 - Four-Point Perspective

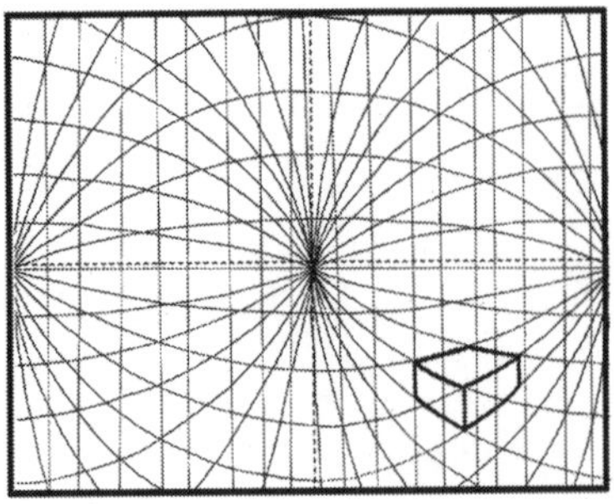

Fig. 23.26 - Continuous Perspective

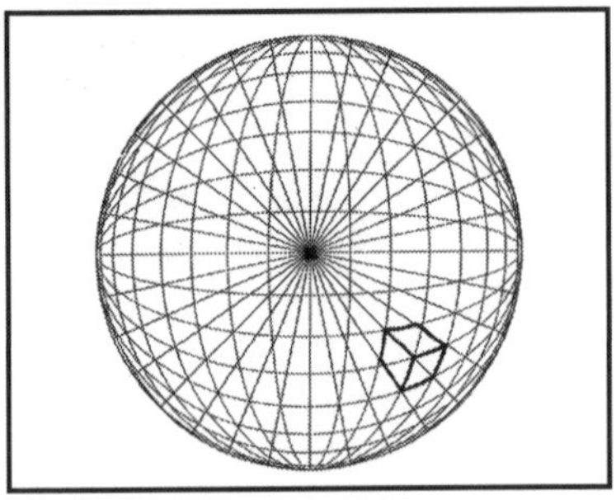

Fig. 23.26 - Curvilinear Perspective

on perspective always seem to concentrate on the one-to-five-point schema, which may be summarized in a series of diagrams, complements of Dick Termes.[17]

As Termes shows, one-point rectilinear perspective (Fig. 23.23) keeps the front face of the cube orthogonal to the picture frame, so all horizontals remain parallel to the baseline. By contrast, the front face of the cube turns away in two-point rectilinear perspective (Fig. 23.24) so two sides of the cube converge onto the lateral vanishing points. Until now, the verticals have always remained parallel. But in three-point rectilinear perspective (Fig. 23.25), the verticals also converge onto a third vanishing point. Depending on the view, this may be located below the horizon line (bird's eye view) or above it (worm's eye view). (For the worm's eye view, Fig. 23.25 must be turned around). In the example given here, the horizon line has shifted to the top and the cube is hovering in space with all three sides converging to three separate vanishing points.

If our view is expanded to four vanishing points, then we must combine rectilinear with curvilinear perspective. In our example of four-point perspective (Fig. 23.25), the horizontal lines curve, giving us a wide-angle view onto a rectangular shape (like a bench) located below the horizon line. But, the diagram may be given a quarter turn, so the curvilinear lines are now vertical, guiding our view onto a tall rectangular shape (like a skyscraper), converging both above and below the horizon line at the middle.

In continuous perspective (Fig. 23.26), two curvilinear grids overlap, allowing for a continuous panoramic view when we move in a horizontal direction. In painting, the East German artist Werner Tübke (1929 – 2004) created a monumental work, a veritable masterpiece, called *Early Bourgeois Revolution in Germany* (dated 1987 – on permanent display in the Panorama Museum, Bad Frankenhausen) which utilizes just such a continuous perspective.

In five-point curvilinear perspective (Fig. 23.26), straight lines may be seen to converge on a central vanishing point, and on four more points at the top, bottom, left and right of the spherical space. This becomes evident in Dick Termes' depiction of the interior of St. Peter's Basilica (Fig. 23.27), where our vision rises to the domed ceiling or falls to the tiled floor. From Bernini's *baldacchino* at the centre, our vision may enter three of the four main aisles in the cathedral's cruciform plan. Our placement in this architectural space thus gives us five receding views into five vanishing points.

Dick Termes goes on to create six-point perspective, by turning around and drawing the opposite view of St. Peter's Cathedral, so we may now see the fourth main aisle opposite Bernini's *baldacchino* (and hence, the sixth point in perspective). He suggests that the two 5-point perspective pictures be viewed side by side or pasted back to back.

Eventually Termes expanded his perspectival view by painting onto spheres. He explained his theory in a paper 'Six Point Perspective on the Sphere: the Termesphere':

"Six-point perspective comes into being when the other points are pulled around into the three-dimensional space on the surface of the sphere. These six points are arranged like the vertices or points of the octahedron."[18]

When we gaze at his diagram (Fig. 23.28), we must understand that we are looking at one side *only* of the sphere (not *through* the sphere), and another three points lie on the opposite side. In this way, he creates six vanishing points.

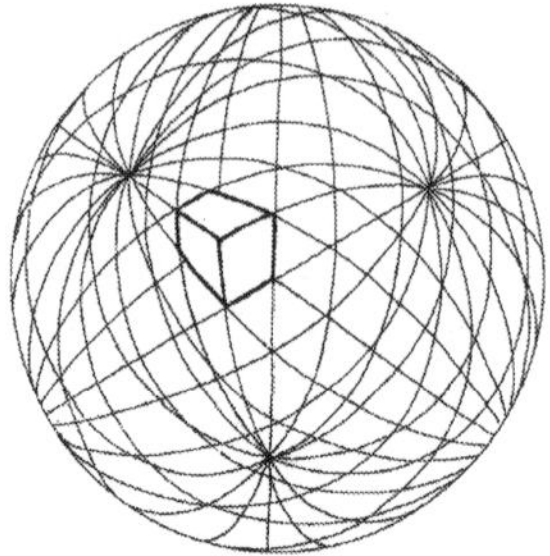
Fig. 23.28 - Six-Point Perspective

In other works, Termes treats the sphere like a perfectly spherical mirror that reflects the room or space around it. As the viewer walks around it, they have the sensation of seeing the entire space reflected yet contained by the painted sphere.

What we learn from Termes' work is that space actually has *an infinite number* of vanishing points. But, our architectural structures, which are essentially six-sided cubes, divide our space into three or six measurable dimensions. A mirrored sphere placed within a cube would, of course, reflect that cube's interior space as six planes. Such a spatial measure reflects our own Human-all-too-Humanist perspective. According to Aristotle, humans perceive space in six directions: up-down, left-right and forward-back (*Physics*, Bk IV, Ch. 1). So, we shape our environment to reflect that, and paint images with a maximum of six perspectives to orient ourselves in that space.

Meanwhile, that same mirrored sphere could be placed within a tetrahedron (reflecting four triangles), an octahedron (reflecting eight triangles), a dodecahedron (reflecting twelve pentagons) or an icosahedron (reflecting twenty triangles). However, we would have to free ourselves of our bodies and, indeed, of our earthly sphere with its gravity and horizon, to ascend to different spheres and experience their different Platonic measures of space. We shall consider this in the final chapters, on the Soul Ascent.

VI. Leonardo's Paradox

One of the most important essays on Perspective in the 20th century was, without a doubt, Erwin Panofsky's *Perspective as Symbolic Form.* The erudite art historian, whose studies in myth, symbol and iconography made him a valued member of the Warburg Institute, called upon a term coined by his friend and colleague Ernst Cassirer to characterize perspective. *Perspektive,* Panofsky decided, *ist eine symbolische Form*:

"The modern vanishing-point construction distorts all widths, depths and heights in constant proportion, and thus defines unequivocally the apparent size of any object, the size corresponding to its actual magnitude and its position with respect to the eye... But if perspective is not a factor of [measurable] *value, it is surely a factor of style. Indeed, it may even be characterized as (to extend Ernst Cassirer's felicitous term to the history of art) one of those 'symbolic forms' in which 'spiritual meaning is attached to a concrete, material sign and intrinsically given to this sign.' This is why it is essential to ask of artistic periods and regions not only whether they have perspective, but also which perspective they have."*[19]

This attitude stands in direct opposition to theorists like Kirsti Andersen, whose *The Geometry of an Art* treats perspective (as its subtitle says) as 'The History of the Mathematical Theory.' Although the geometry of perspective may be nailed down on paper and even proven (Desargues' Theorem of 1648), such constructions side-step vital problems in Optics (distortion of the visual angle) and otherwise ignore the artist's more practical needs of actually drawing objects in perspective.

Panofsky shows that a variety of perspectival constructions have emerged over time, which James Elkins (in *The Poetics of Perspective*) expands into dozens more: workshop methods, curios and arcana. None of these, which are used by artists at a certain time and place in history, can make claims to absolute certainty or accuracy. For this reason, Panofsky sees perspective as a *symbolische Form* – as a means of constructing pictorial space which has a significant (i.e. symbolic) meaning for the culture in question. Indeed, such a symbolic form has a higher *spiritual* meaning.

At the end of his essay, Panofsky seems to be acutely aware of the transition from Hieratic to Humanist art that came about with linear perspective. He describes the shift in perspective that emerged, when the Humanist viewer, and not the Hieratic figure, became the centre of our focus:

"Perspective seals off religious art from the realm of the magical, where the work of art itself works the miracle, and from the realm of the dogmatic and symbolic, where the work bears witness to, or foretells, the miraculous. But then it opens it to something entirely new: the realm of the visionary, where the miraculous becomes a direct experience of the beholder, in that the supernatural events in a sense erupt into his own, apparently natural, visual space and so permit him really to 'internalize' their supernaturalness. Perspective, finally, opens art to the realm of the psychological, in the highest sense, where the miraculous finds its last refuge in the soul of the human being represented in the work of art... Perspective... seems to reduce the divine to a mere subject matter for human consciousness; but for that very reason, conversely, it expands human consciousness into a vessel for the divine."[20]

In the earlier quotation, Panofsky also characterized perspective as a certain 'style' of painting. By our own definition, Style is concerned with the play of the curving line around the invisible straight line (Fuchs), or the emergence of certain forms, once a principle is followed methodically (Viollet-le-Duc). Certainly, this characterizes Renaissance art, which uses the *invisible lines of perspective* to shape space for the curving human figures and straight architectural forms. Perspective is followed *as a principle*, allowing certain distinct stylistic forms to emerge. What makes the Renaissance 'style' is, not just the return to the Classical Greek figure, but *the perspectival shape* of its pictorial space.

What all of this means is – there is no right or wrong perspective. Once the artist gains a thorough grasp of its constructions, they may 'play with the perspective' by adjusting parameters like the horizon line, vanishing point and distance point to arrive at their own unique approach and style. This occurs most clearly with the play of visual angle and the distance point. Although C. D. Brownson, in his article *'Euclid's Optics and its Compatibility with Linear*

Perspective', was able to prove mathematically that Euclid's angle axiom and Alberti's distance axiom *"are compatible,"*[21] this does not negate Panofsky's observation that artists have struggled with that opposition throughout history. From the standpoint of Optics, and of painting in general, the opposition of the Distance and Angle axioms is quite real.

Although Alberti himself was aware of the limitations of his *costruzione legittima,* Piero della Francesca and Leonardo da Vinci struggled against those limitation with unrelenting passion. To characterize the opposition, Leonardo used the terms natural and artificial perspective, where *prospettiva naturale*, like Optics, *"shows all these objects just as the eye sees them diminished,"* while *prospettiva accidentale*, like Geometry, *"is that which is devised by art."*[22] Alberti's construction, which uses only straight lines, was recognized as artificial because it used those lines to gain geometric legitimacy (*legittima*) at the expense of optical veracity.

Since the time of Alhazen, Bacon, Witelo and Peckham, Optical theorists had known that the angle of vision is to be measured by an arc, not a straight line. When the picture plane cuts the angle of vision with its straight, flat surface, perceptual distortions occur. At the centre, where the centric ray is perpendicular to the picture plane, distortion is avoided. But towards the periphery of vision, when extrinsic rays hit the plane at oblique angles, the distortions become more apparent.

Piero della Francesca illustrated this problem in Book I of *De Prospectiva Pingendi,* a book which Leonardo (through Pacioli) read with much interest. Throughout his Notebooks, Leonardo struggles with the problem, which has become known as Leonardo's Paradox (Fig. 23.29). The classical example occurs when one stands before an arcade of round columns.

From the standpoint of Optics, the column in the middle will be the widest, while those to the left and right will *decrease* in width the further out they appear in our angle of vision. But, if that visual angle is cut by the straight line of our picture plane, then distortions arise in our *costruzione legittima.* As the outer columns are projected onto the plane, their width *increases* rather than decreases.

A possible solution, suggested by Leonardo's diagram, is to curve the picture plane so it accords with the arc in our angle of vision. It has been debated for centuries whether Leonardo was proposing curvilinear perspective as a cure to the malady of straight-lined grids. (We shall return to curvilinear perspective momentarily).

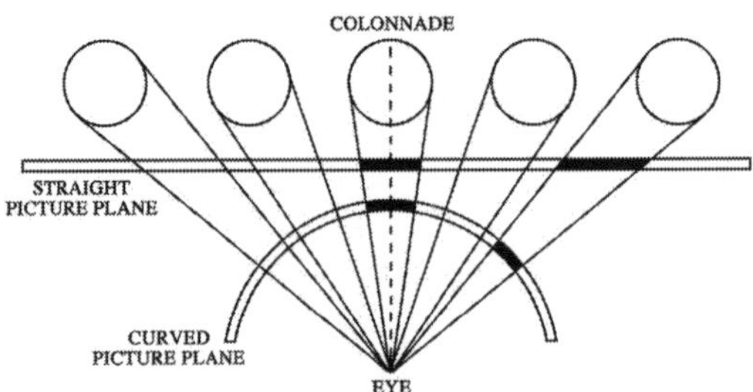

Fig. 23.29 - Leonardo's Paradox

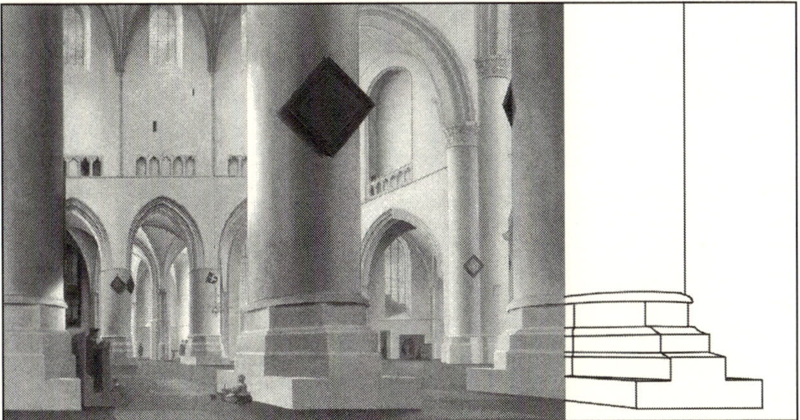

Fig. 23.30 - Pieter Saenredam: *Interior of the Grote Kerk at Haarlem* with Extension of Pillar

Instead, both Piero and Leonardo suggested a more practical solution: painters should *limit the angle of vision*. Piero recommended the rather conservative angle of 60° (according to Frangenberg[23]) while Leonardo held to the traditional angle of 90° already established by the field of Optics.

But this paradox brings to light the basic opposition of the Angle and Distance axioms. As a rule, the closer the Distance Point appears to the Vanishing Point, the greater will be the angle of vision (since, as we saw in Fig. 22.2, when the Distance Point is swung around and becomes the Viewing Point, the viewer stands closer to the painting, increasing the angle of vision through the frame or 'window'). This feature is welcomed by painters who wish to create a wide angle of vision in their works, such as a panoramic view onto a vast landscape. But, the moment that artist adds straight-edged architectural structures to their landscape, they risk peripheral distortion.

Dubery and Willas offer an excellent example[24] through the works of Pieter Saenredam (1595 – 1665), a famous Dutch painter of church interiors. In his *Interior of the Grote Kerk at Haarlem* (Fig. 23.30), Saenredam offers a wide angled view (in one-point perspective) of Haarlem's old cathedral of St. Bavo. On the right, the artist cuts the column with the edge of the picture frame. Had he allowed the wide-angled view to continue, the edge-distortions of his perspective construction would soon have become obvious, since the column would appear massively wide.

VII. Playing with the Vanishing Point

Over time, painters have revealed their talent and ingenuity in getting around Leonardo's Paradox. This is particularly the case with Venetian painters like Veronese and Canaletto, who sought out greater angles of vision in their works without sacrificing the constraints of linear perspective. Instead, they resorted to solutions that date back to Roman Wall painting.

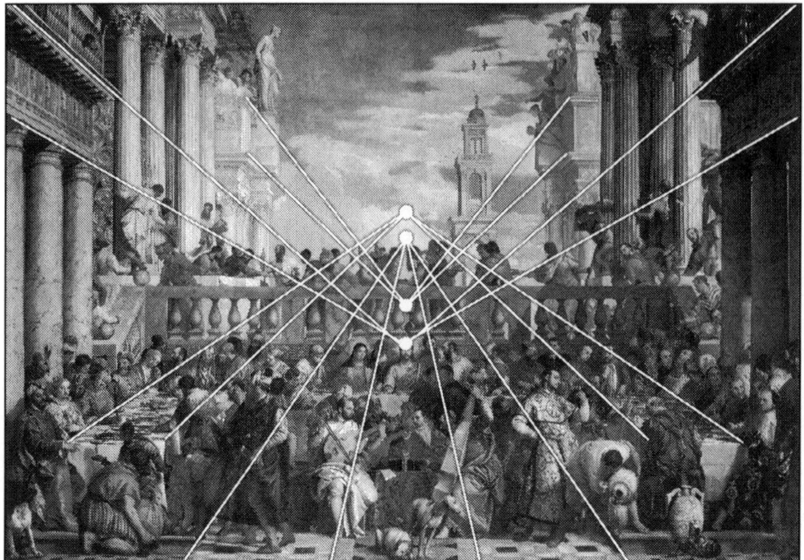

Fig. 23.31 - Paolo Veronese: *The Wedding at Cana* - Vertical Axial Perspective

In 1562, Paolo Veronese (1528 – 1588) created his life's masterpiece, *The Wedding at Cana* (Fig. 23.31), an epic canvas six metres high and ten metres wide (indeed, the largest in the Louvre), where Christ miraculously transmutes water into wine. To increase the viewer's angle of vision, Veronese has created *a hierarchy of parallel horizon lines* with their vanishing points arranged along the main vertical. When the viewer gazes at the table and floor, the convergence of their orthogonals offers him a bird's eye view onto the scene (note the birds hovering in the sky above these points). When he gazes upward at the architecture, he is offered instead a worm's eye view, as the orthogonals converge lower down, on the balustrade and on Christ himself. The saviour occupies a central position, both in the 2D composition and in the 3D perspectival space.

The musicians sitting before Christ are none other than Jacopo Bassano (on flute), Tintoretto (on violin), Titian (on violoncello) and Veronese himself (on viola da gamba) – the four greatest artists of the Golden Age of Venetian painting. In front of them, an hourglass on the table reminds them of the vanities of this world. In this period, Mannerists loved 'to play' with the strict rules of Renaissance Classicism, and Veronese has done this through his ingenious use of Axial Perspective, a technique first used in Roman times.

Sixty years later, in 1730, Canaletto (Giovanni Antonio Canal, 1697 – 1768) painted one of his many views of the Venetian capital. His *Piazza San Marco with Basilica* (Fig. 23.32) offers a panoramic view of the famed square, with its Byzantine basilica dwarfed by the Campanile di San Marco. On the pavement, Andrea Tirali's interlocking floor pattern of squares, rectangles and ovals (laid just seven years before Canaletto's painting) leads the eye to the main entrance of the Basilica San Marco.[25]

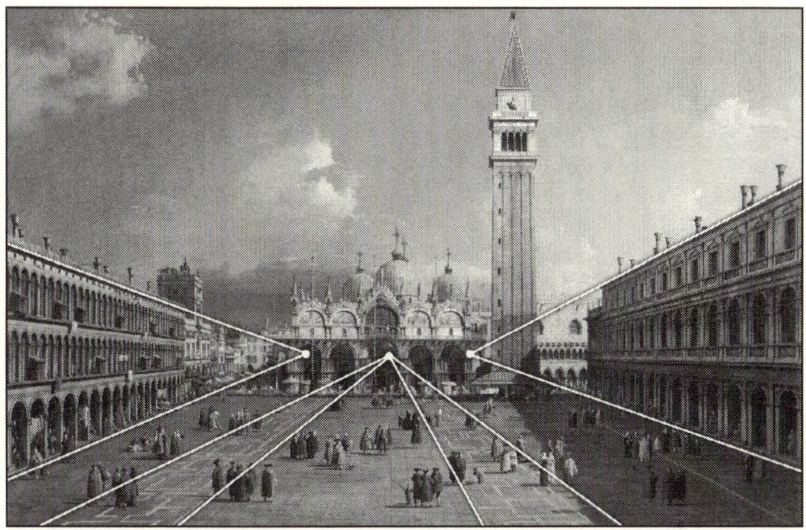

Fig. 23.32 Canaletto: *Piazza San Marco with Basilica* - Horizontal Axial Perspective

Yet, when we measure the perspectival lines of the *procurati vecchie* on the left and the *prourati nuove* on the right, we discover that they converge on vanishing points *to the left and right* of the main vanishing point. The artist has cunningly introduced three vanishing points on the horizontal axis, to broaden our view and avoid the edge-distortions of a single viewing point. Once again, the Venetian has called upon the methods of his ancient Roman counterparts, who introduced Axial Perspective into their frescoes.

The other way in which Mannerist artists played with perspective was by shifting the vanishing point into unlikely places. If we return to Tintoretto's *Venus, Mars and Vulcan* (Fig. 23.33), we notice that the artist has placed the vanishing point high up and to the right, beyond the upper corner of the painting. As a result, the viewer is hovering above, like a fly on the wall, to witness this scene of love and betrayal.

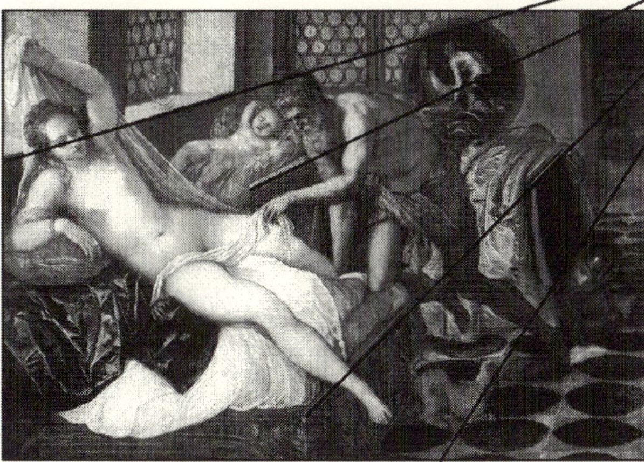

Fig. 23.33 - Tintoretto: *Venus, Mars and Vulcan*

In *The Poetics of Perspective*, Elkins has noted that Mannerist artists still respect the proscenium stage or perspective box of the Renaissance, but they offer views from different seats in the theatre – too low, too high, too far to the side or too far back: *"These displacements, whether back, forward, down, or to one side, have a common result: they create a sense of strain or tension...The painters did not tend to question perspective as a science, nor did they bypass or destroy it. Instead, they 'transformed' perspective in the geometric sense of the word: they skewed, magnified, and displaced the symmetrical perspective box in order to bring out things that were distant, peripheral or hidden... they worked within the bounds of perspectival rules to reshape perspective."*[26]

This 'breach of decorum' gave painting new dynamism and life, as the eye was now free to roam and explore new spaces from new angles. It is this quality which gives Renaissance art its unique quality. Rather than directing the eye onto one fixed point, as happens often with Hieratic art, the eye is encouraged to roam and explore in Renaissance painting. In Humanist art, we must remember, the perspectival view belongs to the human viewer, who is free to turn his gaze along rushing diagonals or pause to admire dynamic figures:

"Perspective requires a rigid, motionless eye fixed on the vanishing point," Elkins writes. *"But this imagined paralysis is only the most extreme form of the kind of seeing peculiar to perspective. The eye never wanders as freely and inquisitively through a perspective picture as it can, for example, through a crowd painted by Brueghel or a trecento townscape. Perspective lines... direct the gaze along orthogonals, up façades, through archways. There are several ways to give the eye the rest it needs to enjoy a painting for more than a few minutes. Organic forms in general slow our roving vision. When figures occlude lines, or parallax disrupts orderly diminution, perspective is softened enough to turn the eye loose. Perspective can also blend with pattern so the eye moves left and right 'along the surface' as well as into depth."*[27]

VIII. Curvilinear Perspective

In 1434, Jan Van Eyck painted the *Arnolfini Wedding Portrait* with its famous convex mirror on the back wall (Fig. 23.34). Within the mirror we have a curvilinear view of the entire scene, including a minute self-portrait of the artist himself, as a witness to the ceremony. (*"Johannes de eyck fuit hic 1434"* he inscribed above the mirror – *Jan Van Eyck was here*).

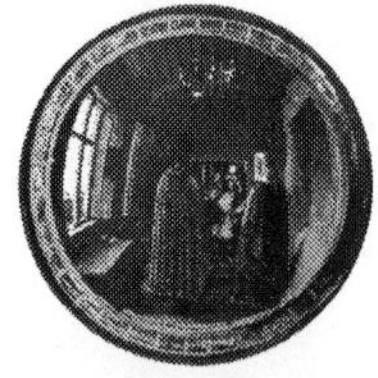

Fig. 23.34

Van Eyck was certainly not the first or the last to use curvilinear perspective. Jean Fouquet's *Arrival of Emperor Charles IV at the Basilica St. Denis in 1378* gives a curvilinear grid for the pavings on the ground, while Carel Fabritus' curvilinear *View of Delft* extends our view in all directions, from a stringed instrument in the foreground to the cathedral in the background. From Parmigianino's *Self-portrait in a Convex Mirror* of 1504 (Fig. 23.35) to M. C. Escher's *Hand with Reflecting*

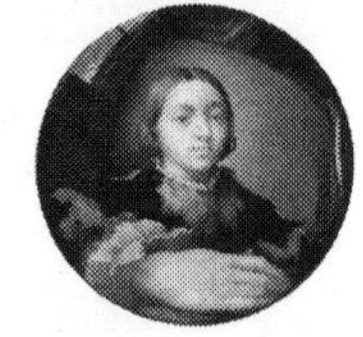

Fig. 23.35

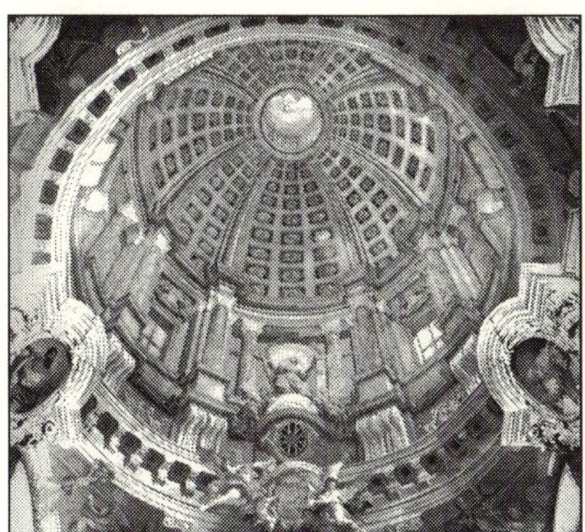
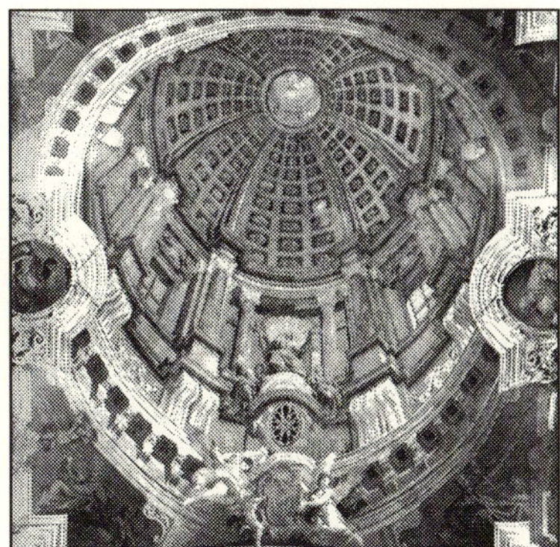

Fig. 23.36 - Andrea Pozzo: *Trompe l'œil Dome on Flat Ceiling of the Jesuit Church Vienna*
Left: View from Marked Tile *Right: View from Directly Below*

Sphere of 1935, artists have always been fascinated by curvilinear views onto space.

The most common application of curvilinear perspective was in illusionistic ceiling painting. This began with Andrea Mantegna's *oculus* (1474) for the *Camera degli Sposi* in Mantua's Ducal Palace, which offers a view *Di sotto in sù* ('from below upward') of a round balustrade with foreshortened *putti* gazing downward.

Mannerist artists like Correggio delighted in creating huge curvilinear compositions for church ceilings – Correggio's acknowledged masterpiece being the *Assumption of the Virgin* (1524) on the main cupola of Parma Cathedral. From its octagonal foundation, a vortex of clouds spirals upward to a blinding golden light, where Christ (who is not visible except from the angle at the altar) awaits the Virgin below, as she rises upward in the company of angels and saints.

Di sotto in sù painting experienced an explosion in the Baroque period, when artists like Giovanni Lanfranco (*Assumption of the Virgin* – 1627) and Pietro de Cortona (*Palazzo Barberini* ceilings – 1639) created complex masterpieces that we can only marvel at today. The Italian tradition continued in Austria with Andrea Pozzo and Paul Troger (*Abbey of Melk* ceiling – 1731) where it reached new heights in the Rococo period.

Andrea Pozzo expanded curvilinear perspective to *trompe l'œil* effects ('fooling the eye'), after he painted the flat ceiling of the Church of St. Ignazio in Rome (1685) to appear like a vaulted dome. Born in the Austrian Südtirol, Pozzo was a Jesuit brother who spent most of his life in Rome, but was called to Austria in 1702, where he painted another *trompe l'œil* cupola in the Jesuit Church of Vienna, six years before his death in 1709.

I have had the pleasure of experiencing the artist's ingenious invention in Vienna (Fig. 23.36). When viewed from a specifically marked tile several metres down the main aisle, the effect of the perspective is remarkable: one has the impression of gazing into a hemispheric dome. When viewed exactly from below, we are able to appreciate even more how the painting is actually constructed: the curvilinear perspective is re-adjusted to take into account the distortions of the viewing angle.

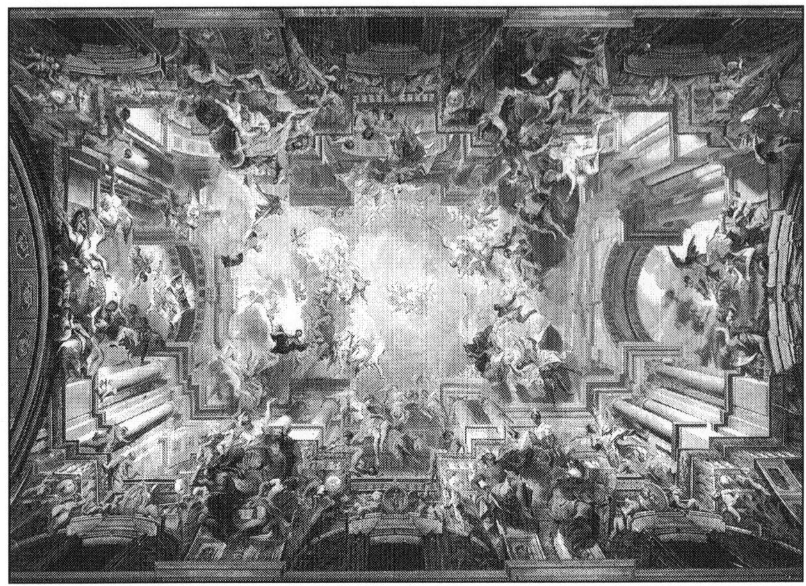

Fig. 23.37 - Andrea Pozzo: *Apotheosis of St. Ignatius* 1694

If we take a moment to examine Pozzo's *Apotheosis of St. Ignatius* (Fig. 23.37), we will note that it is not, strictly speaking, curvilinear in perspective. Instead, the artist has used *di sotto in sù* one-point perspective to unify *four separate triangular compositions*, each one mounting the architectural plane that extends the walls of the church (a technique called *quadratura* in the Baroque period). Near the apex of the composition, four rays of light stream outward from the heart of St. Ignatius – four rays that divide yet unify the four perspectival planes, each one composed with its own allegory, *istoria* and perspectival space. It is, as if, Pozzo has painted Raphael's *Disputation of the Host* four separate times and unified them all into one grand composition.

Andrea Pozzo was not only a master artist but also a master geometer, as evidenced by his two volume work *Perspectiva pictorum et architectorum* (1693, 1698), which was illustrated with 118 engravings and eventually published in six languages. The text gives clear instructions on how to geometrically construct a view in curvilinear perspective.

Piero della Francesca's *De Prospectiva Pingendi* of 1475 was, in fact, the first treatise to demonstrate how to draw the curves of a cupola, followed by Hans Vredeman de Vries' richly illustrated *Book of Perspective - 1604*, which even offered an 'Orbital Diagram of the Visual Field'. In the 19th century, Guido Hauck's *Die subjektive Perspektive und die horizontalen Curvaturen des dorischen Styls* (Subjective Perspective and Horizontal Curvature in the Dorian Style - 1879) attempted a more scientific approach ('Haucksche Perspektive' was championed by Panofsky), followed by Erwin Keller's *Kurvierte Perspektiven* (Curved Perspectives - 1926), which was essentially a mathematical approach of little use to artists. More recently, André Barre and Albert Flocon have investigated the subject in their book *La Perspective curviligne: De l'espace visuel à l'image construite* (Curvilinear Perspective: From Visual Space to the Constructed Image - 1968).

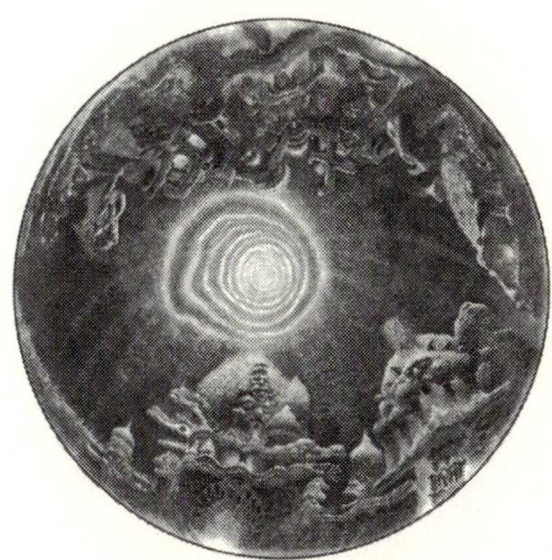

Fig. 23.38 - Maura Holden:
Traveler's Moon 2003

In her circular panels, the contemporary Visionary artist Maura Holden has demonstrated a mastery of curvilinear perspective. For example, in *Traveler's Moon* (Fig. 23.38), she offers a skyward view of the moon experienced while in an elevated state. The moon-lit sky becomes an image of the One exfoliating into the many – first as a burst of light refracting into so many possible geometric shapes, then as rings of spectral colour. Its rays finally plunge into sublunar existence as transparent ethereal shapes and organic architectural forms.

IX. M. C. Escher & the Play of Perspective

When I first entered the living room of Johfra's home in Dordogne, I was drawn to the sight of a mirrored sphere hanging from the ceiling. At that moment, I knew, he too had felt the mystical experience of 'the oneness of all space' – when we suddenly feel ourselves to be *at the absolute Centre* of all creation. The mirrored sphere, which reflects everything around it, is the clearest image we have for this ineffable experience of unity.

For this reason, artists as diverse as Van Eyck, Johfra, M.C. Escher and Alex Grey have shared the same fascination for spherical mirrors. Their work attests to a profound grasp of perspective in all its complexities. The best way to conceptualize perspective, these artists have learned, is to visualize a mirrored sphere within a cube (...and eventually, within more complex polyhedra). That cube becomes the architectural space in which perspective may be visualized. Each plane reflected in the sphere may then have its own vanishing point – up to five, if we see reflected the back wall, two side walls, the ceiling, and the floor.

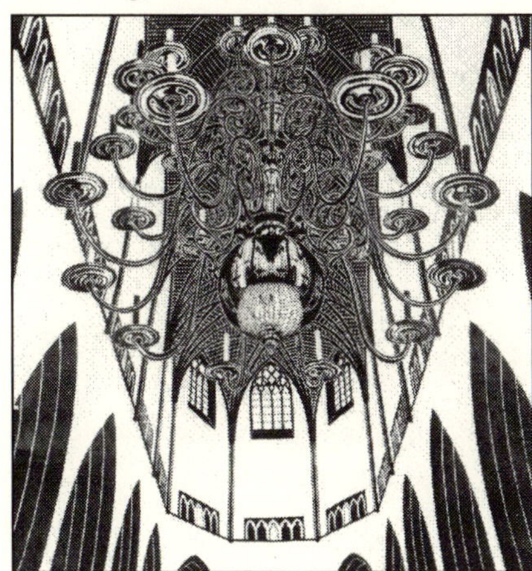

Fig. 23.39 - M. C. Escher
Interior of St. Bavo's Cathedral

An early pen and ink drawing by Escher[28] (Fig. 23.39) shows the interior of St Bavo's cathedral (the same cathedral painted by Pieter Saenredam), where an immense candelabrum reflects the church interior and, indeed, the young artist himself as a minute spectator on the floor. Through his three-point perspective, Escher has managed to render a composition based on a square (the frame), a triangle (the perspective) and a circle (the candelabrum) where the spherical mirror at the centre reflects and unifies the entire sacred space.

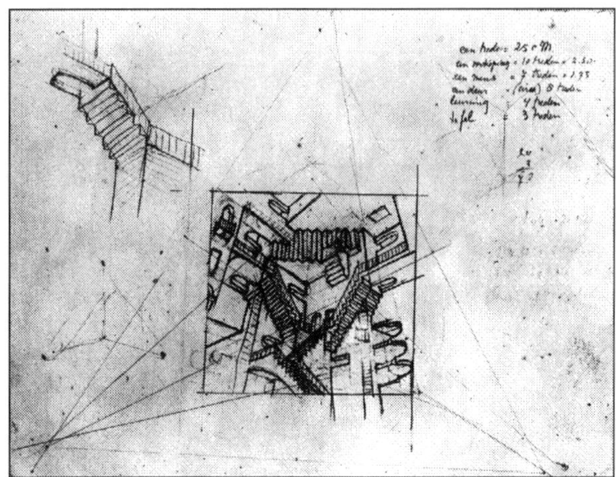

Fig. 23.40 - M. C. Escher: *Relativity - Pencil Study* 1953

Having visualized a mirrored sphere within a cube, Escher was able to consider more complex applications of the same idea. In his *Pencil Study for Relativity* (Fig. 23.40), we can clearly make out the three-point perspective, and the architecture taking shape within the square frame in the middle. That architecture, as the woodcut attests, consists mainly of those arched staircases which Leonardo so loved in his perspective drawing for *The Adoration of the Magi* (Fig. 22.29).

A close examination of the pencil study reveals that those stairs lead us from one plane to another, in an interior space consisting of *three planes.* The steps on each staircase recede sideways to their respective vanishing points. Meanwhile, at the centre of the drawing, we can see the point where the three planes meet, like a view into the interior corner of a cube.

Where Pozzo's *Apotheosis of St. Ignatius* (Fig. 23.37) used one-point perspective *di sotto in sù* to unify the four sides of his architectural space onto a common centre, Escher has done the same with three planes.

To obtain his three-point perspective, Escher drew an equilateral triangle, and from the vanishing point on each corner he drew a centric line (bisecting the angle of perspective) to meet the other lines at the centre, which then continue visibly as the separations between the walls. Because the small square frame of his drawing has its base roughly parallel to the base of the triangle, we are able to orient ourselves within this interior space: the vanishing point at the top tells us we have a worm's eye view onto the scene.

In the *Early Print* (Fig. 23.41), Escher attempted to disorient the viewer by turning his piece of paper round, so the upper vanishing point (worm's eye view) now appears at the bottom (bird's eye view). He has also obscured the central meeting place of the three planes and skewed the main vertical. Most interesting, he has added a figure on the right side who is stepping *into* the picture.

In the *Final Print* (Fig. 23.42), he has returned to his original schema (worm's eye view) by taking the Early Print and turning it 90° clockwise, then flipping it horizontally, so the figure stepping into the picture now appears at the bottom. Although this figure meets our expectations of gravity and

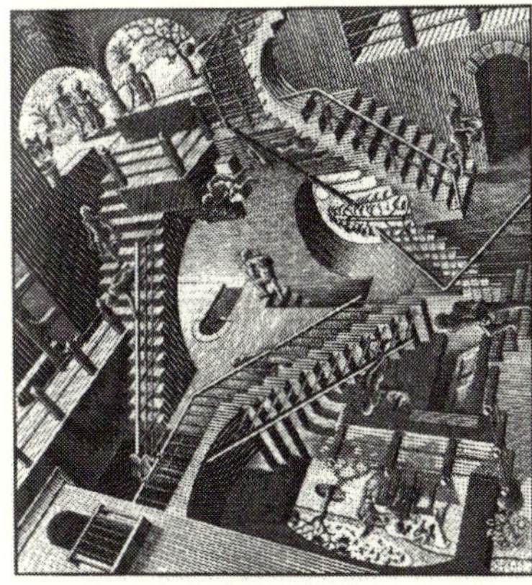

Fig. 23.41 - M. C. Escher: *Relativity - Early Print* 1953

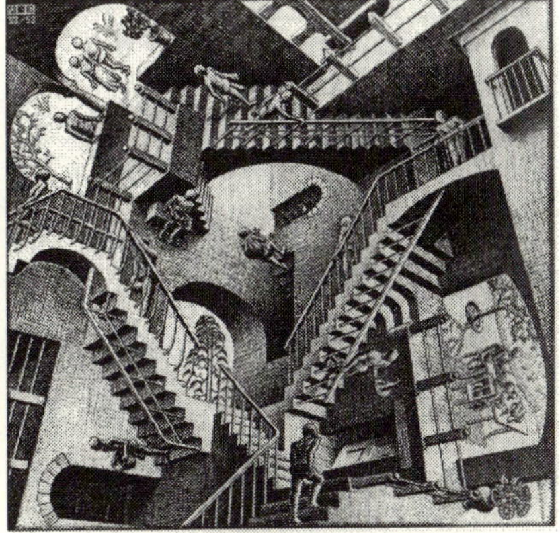

Fig. 23.42 - M. C. Escher: *Relativity - Final Print* 1953

orientation, the remaining scene plays with these expectations, re-orienting the other figures to the other vanishing points and gravitational directions.

In his first pencil sketch for *High and Low* (Fig. 23.43), Escher began with another *di sotto in sù* one-point perspective, this time dividing a square into *four* architectural towers where the top two are seen 'from above' and the bottom two are seen 'from below'. Once again, Escher is repeating Pozzo's schema, and this time the one-point perspective unifies *four* separate towers joined by arches and bridges.

In his second pencil sketch (Fig. 23.44), he has abandoned the orthogonals of his *ad quadratum* grid and oriented the architecture instead to the diagonals. This created a more dynamic rendering of what is, essentially, the same view of four architectural compositions united by a single vanishing point.

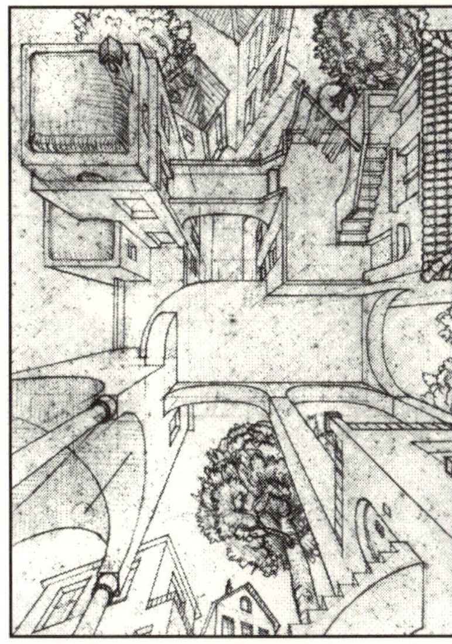

Fig. 23.43 - M. C. Escher: *High and Low - First Pencil Sketch* 1947

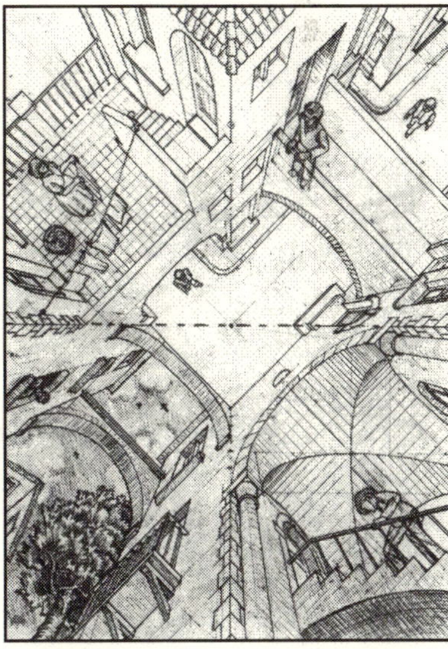

Fig. 23.44 - M. C. Escher: *High and Low - Second Pencil Sketch* 1947

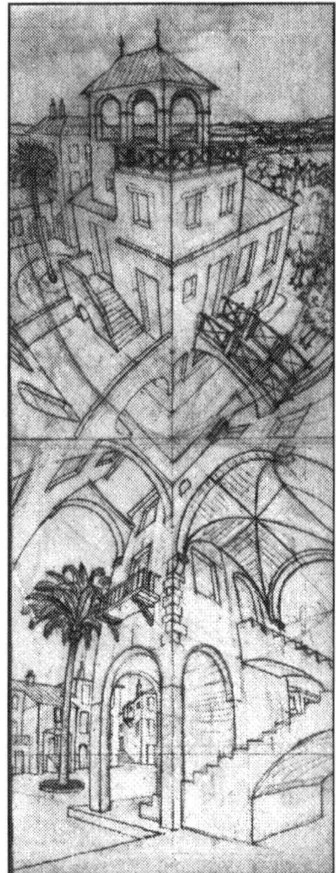

Fig. 23.45

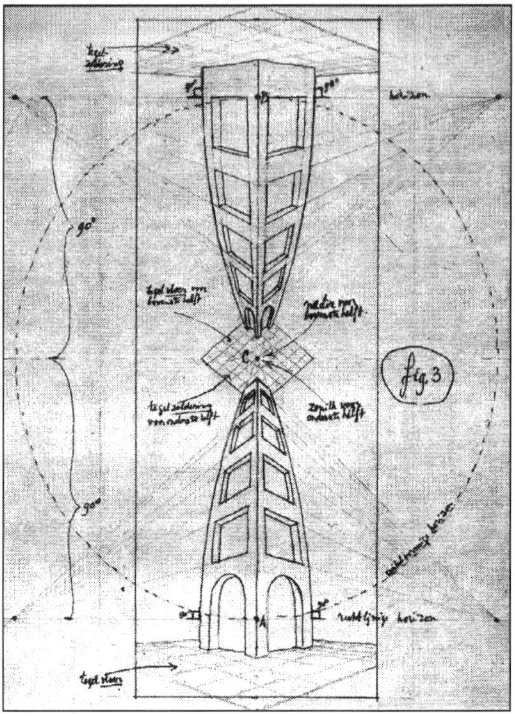

Fig. 23.46 - Escher: *High and Low Explanatory Sketch*

In his third pencil sketch (Fig. 23.45), Escher decided to use a form of curvilinear perspective that unifies two three-point perspectives onto a common vanishing point. A close look at his explanatory sketch (Fig. 23.46) reveals that the tower at the bottom is viewed in three-point perspective, with two vanishing points on either end of the horizon, and a third vanishing point at the apex, which uses curvilinear space from the central circle to bend the straight edges of the tower to the central vanishing point. The tower at the top does the exact same thing, but upside down.

As a result, the third version (Fig. 23.47) now has three horizon lines: near the top (bird's eye view), bottom (worm's eye view) and middle (looking straight up or down – *di sotto in sù*). If we used a mirrored sphere to make sense of this space, we would have to, in fact, use three interpenetrating spheres: one at the top, one below and one in the middle. The top and bottom spheres would reflect their cubes' three outer sides in three-point perspective, while the middle sphere would reflect five interior sides: the back,

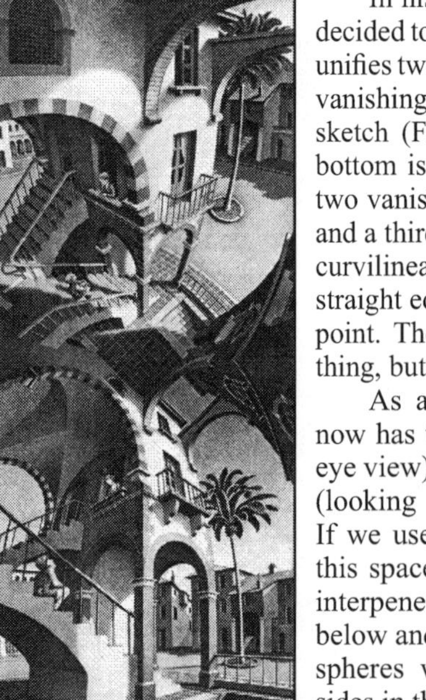

Fig. 23.47 - Escher: *High and Low*

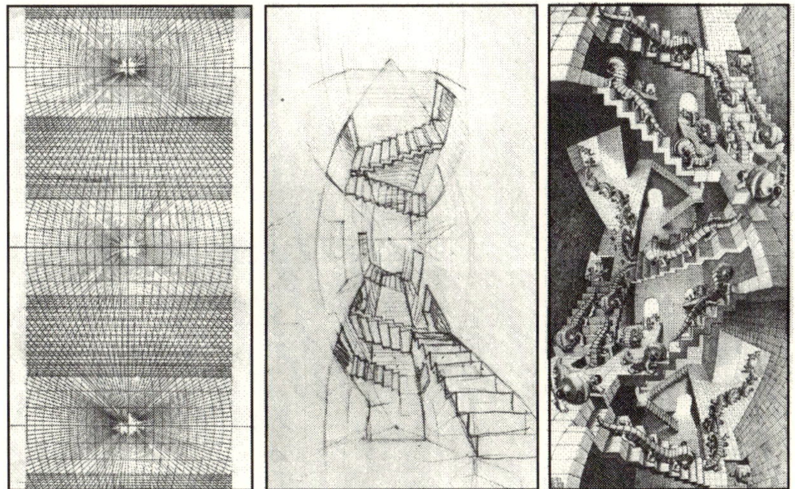

Fig. 23.48 - M. C. Escher: *House of Stairs - Grid - Pencil Study - Final Print* 1951

two sides, top and bottom. The middle sphere shows a view in curvilinear five-point perspective.

For his *House of Stairs* (Fig. 23.48), Escher did in fact create a grid of overlapping spheres (which Termes called Four Point Continuous Perspective). In Escher's grid, we can clearly see how three curvilinear perspectives may overlap. Each of these spheres could, in theory, reflect a cubic space in five point perspective. From here, the possibilities are seemingly infinite...

I will end my examination of Escher here, though I have only scratched the surface. During the fifty odd years that Maurits Cornelis Escher (1898 - 1972) practiced his art, his ever-curious mind explored multiple perspectives (including axonometric), complex polyhedra (Platonic and Archimedean Solids) and elaborate tilings (which he first encountered in the Alhambra in 1922). As a Dutchman, he was deeply inspired by his country's long tradition in perspectival exploration (Van Eyck, Vredeman de Vries, Saenredam, Vermeer etc). And during his stay in Rome (for more than a decade, from 1923 – 1935), he became intimately acquainted with *di sotto in sù* ceiling paintings. Escher's work combines all these influences while remaining individual and stylistically unique.

For those who wish to look more deeply into his constructions, I would recommend Bruno Ernst's *The Magic Mirror of M. C. Escher* (2007).

X. Alex Grey: Spiritual Perspectives

My last meeting with Alex and Allyson Grey, I must admit, was overwhelmingly intense. As our guests at the Vienna Academy of Visionary Art, they stayed with us for five days, while giving a two-day workshop called *Art Spirit Vienna* (February 2nd and 3rd, 2016). The remainder of their free time was spent with my wife Florence Ménard and myself, conversing in cafés or at our apartment in the Josefstadt. During this time I had a dizzying gaze into the endless creativity flowing from these two extra-ordinary individuals.

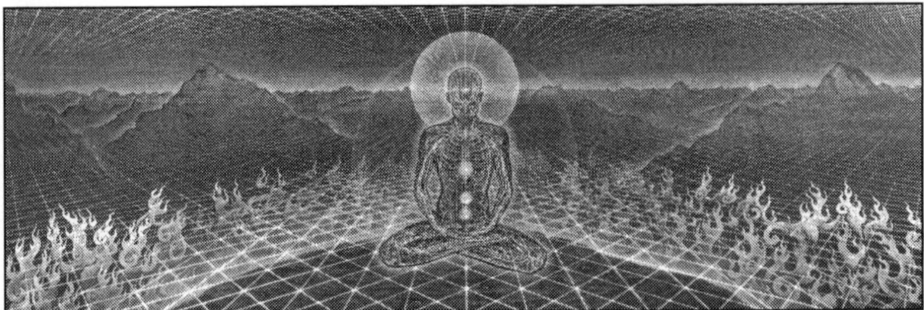

Fig. 23.49 - Alex Grey: *Theologue* 1986

They sketched as they spoke (even on stage during our evening talk on *Sacramental Culture and Visionary Art*), and in their free time their attention was focussed solely on us – the challenges we faced in expanding our Academy and manifesting the Apocryphon Chapel. They shared without hesitation, gave without asking, and freely offered so much wisdom born of experience.

"Life," Alex Grey wrote in one of his Art Psalms, *"is infinite creative play."*[29] Our conversations roamed over many topics, but inevitably returned to Visionary Art, touching on many of the themes I have laboured hard to explain here: of our true Oneness with divinity, of the One manifesting itself through art in the shape of the Divine Eye, of the meditation on art that can lead to divine seeing in the Visionary realms, and of the artist's mission today to revive sacred art, as a transformational source of healing for individuals and the planet. From that place of loving devotion through creativity, we were able to focus on the actual details of making art happen...

A reproduction called *Theologue* (Fig. 23.49) was left to us as a gift, and an evening meditation ('entering through the image') became the starting point for my exploration into his work, from the standpoint of perspective. In a vast landscape of mountainous peaks, the theologue sits in the lotus *asana*, his eyes shut and head bowed in deep meditation. He is meditating upon *"...the sky-like nature of mind. The rootedness of Being is in emptiness, clarity and awareness."*[30]

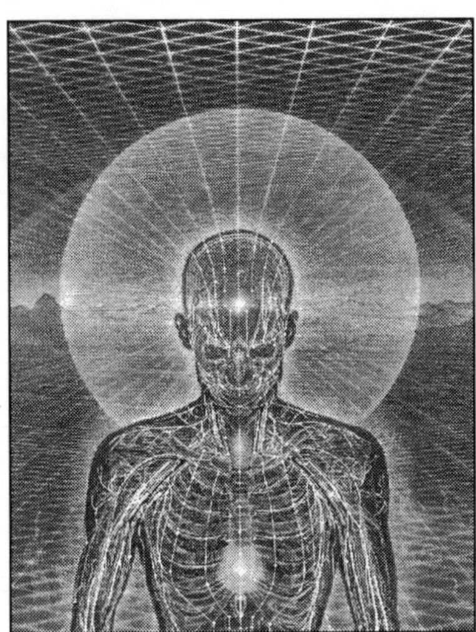

Fig. 23.50 - Alex Grey: *Theologue* (Detail)

From the place of the Third Eye (Fig. 23.50), lines of perspective spread in all directions, creating the first measure of space from a central vanishing point. At opposite ends of the canvas, two more vanishing points provide the transversals of what is, essentially, two planes in three-point perspective – the plane of the ground and the sky – meeting at their shared horizon. That horizon line, we note, traverses the Third Eye.

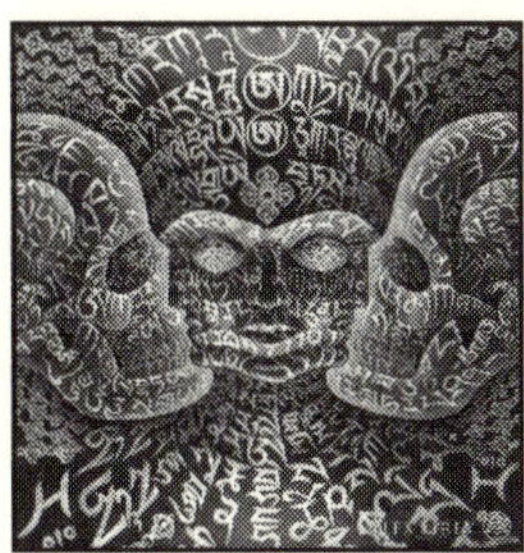

Fig. 23.51 - *Song of Vajra Being*

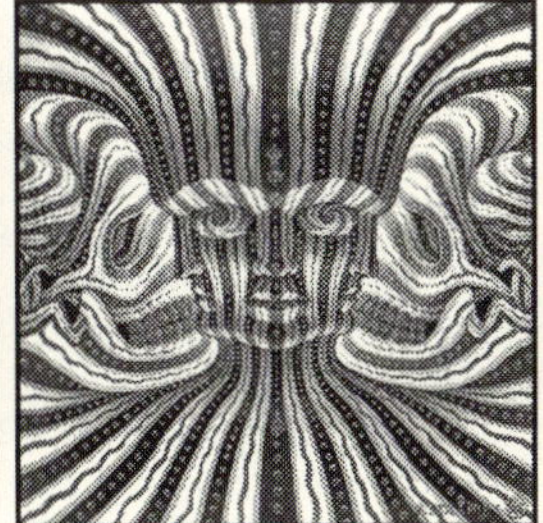

Fig. 23.52 - *Bardo Being*

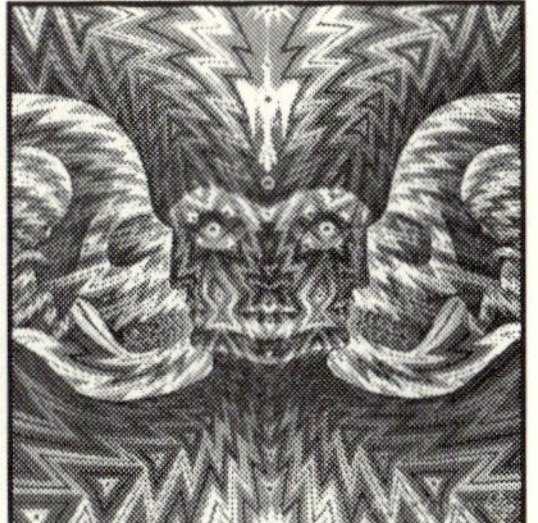

Fig. 23.53 - *Peyote Being*

My meditation on this image revealed that the theologue is, in fact, *creating the spatial measures in which he exists.* The shape of space surrounding us is nothing more than a construct which we, consciously or unconsciously, elaborate and project. From our node in the net, we see and experience those lines as converging onto our point of view. But, there could just as well be two more theologues to the right and left of the one depicted here. *"We are all extensions of the Oneness,"* Alex Grey wrote in another psalm, *"Imagine XYZ axis Extending infinitely in each direction. Thou art that."*[31]

In a series of paintings from 2002 to 2005 (Figs. 23.51 - 53), Alex Grey depicted the bowed head of the theologue as so many Beings (Bardo Being, Vajra Being, Peyote Being, Jewel Being, Diamond Being), where the foreshortened view of his bowed head has now expanded into an elaborate crown that connects its expanded consciousness to other (as yet undepicted) beings. These beings, which have faces on three (and one assumes, four) sides, are surrounded by images of death and new life. In one image after another, their surface is created through sacred patterns, some traditional (peyote stitch and bead patterns, Tibetan prayer glyphs), others entirely original.

Then, in his book *Net of Being*, Alex Grey recounted:

"In 2003, deep in the jungles of Brazil, while on an ayahuasca journey, I entered a great net of being, a fiery jewel-like web of Godselves weaving an endless anthropocosmic tapestry. It was the realm of universal beings with an omnidirectional topology of interconnected heads and hearts, fusing boundless wisdom and love. A luminous ball inside the basketlike head of each four-faced God was the heartglow shining an eerie under-light for the level of Godheads above and beyond sight. The flaming lattice of eyes and galaxies revealed a new order of the x-y-z axis, an endless soul-field of infinite consciousness."[32]

As a result of this experience, Alex Grey began the two large-scale paintings *Godself* (2012) and *Net of Being* (2007) which formed part of a (as-yet unrealized) triptych. In *Godself,* it is the being itself which engages our attention, causing us to focus our vision onto the centrally placed Third Eye. From there, our vision may expand outward to encompass the vast array of beings that make up its network.

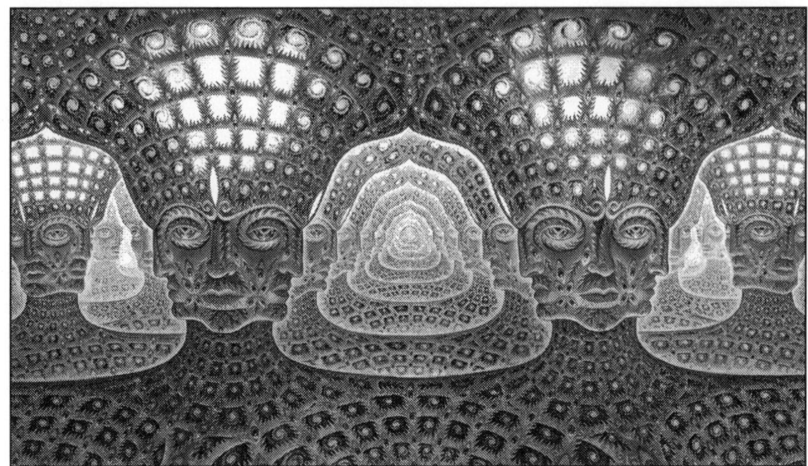

Fig. 23.54 - Alex Grey: *Net of Being* 2007

In *Net of Being* (Fig. 23.54) meanwhile, the wide horizontal composition (4.57 m. x 2.29 m.) draws our gaze down the central passage between two Godselves, creating a more 'transpersonal perspective'. Each of these beings has four faces, with one eye shared by each adjacent face, making four gazing eyes on each pillared being. Although they are arranged like pillars in an *ad quadratum* space, their gazes meet diagonally, criss-crossing throughout the network. The moment we engage one of them with our gaze, we become a part of their network, realizing that we too are divine beings, sharing in their omni-directional grid of unified consciousness.

This brings us back to the theologue, whose Third Eye vision was actively creating the spatial grid while orienting it onto a single point of perspective. While *Godself* also has this capacity, in *Net of Being* the focus is shifted *onto the grid itself,* onto the greater network of Beings, their gazes interlocked, whose vision actively creates and holds together this omni-dimensional space. In a conversation late one night at their CoSM studio, Alex Grey described to me in detail how he could see upward to higher and ever-higher beings in that cubic space.

That Alex Grey was able to depict this vast network of beings in a cohesive perspectival space is no small accomplishment. What divine vision revealed to him in a matter of seconds, he had to spend months figuring out... Such as, how to depict the heads in receding size, and harmonically arranged, in a 2:1 rectangular composition with three-point perspective.

Although there are many works by Alex Grey which inspire my thoughts on perspective, the last to be elucidated is *Monochord* (Fig. 23.55), now on display at the Temple of Music in England. In a geometric space inspired by the Xenolinguistic works of Allyson Grey, the artist has depicted an allegory of cosmic harmony and evolution. The space around the main figure is like a jewelled network of green emeralds, connected by luminous threads that weave an infinite pattern of squares, octagons and turned squares (the *quadrature*).

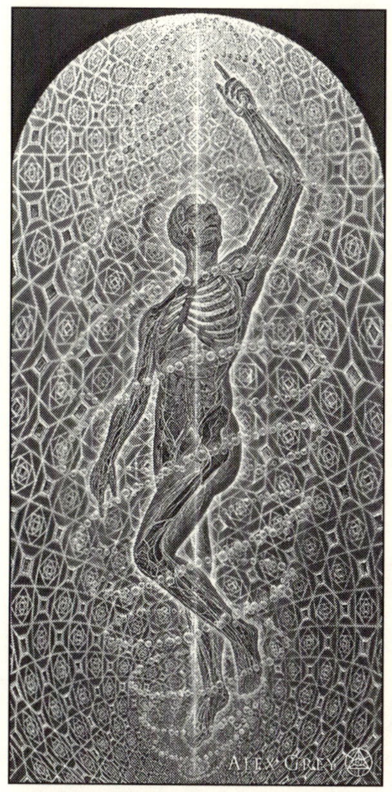

Fig. 23.55 - Alex Grey: *Monochord* 2013

Through the use of curvilinear perspective, Alex Grey has taken that pattern and centered it on two vanishing points, one above, one below. Meanwhile, at the mid-point of the composition, the pattern crosses, to create a vast figure 8 (symbol of infinity). As our gaze rises and falls from the mid-point, we are offered a view into the opposing vortexes of that pattern, from alpha to omega, and beginning to end.

As our conversation at his CoSM studio delved deeper into questions of technique, I asked if he had used digital rendering to map out the spatial grid. He shook his head and muttered with embarrassment, *"It's all done by hand."* Despite the advantages of our present technology, the artist's last resort is always a profound working knowledge of perspective's underlying principles.

In the *Monochord* painting, this extends to many of the 'forgotten principles' which Visionary Art has attempted to revive. The main figure follows the principles of proportion (specifically, Desiderius Lenz, which Alex Grey has cited in many of his works), of the pose (here, a *serpentinata* twist) and anatomy (which he has spent a lifetime studying and teaching). The figure clearly wraps itself around a plumb line which, in this case, *is* the glowing monochord. But, from the raised right heel to the glance of the eye, all the energy and movement of the figure spirals around the plumb line, ultimately transcending the upward-pointing gesture and glance to become focussed on the spiralling vortex above.

More than that, this painting speaks of harmony, unity and transcendence. Twelve times, the rosary of cosmic spheres spirals round the main figure, like the Pythagorean dodecad that brings the *diapason* (6:12), *diapente* (8:12) and *diatessaron* (9:12) into one accord; and also like the cosmic dodecad of the five elements and seven planets that surround us, emanating those harmonies from a higher unity.

"The Monochord is a strand strung from Heaven to Earth," Alex Grey writes, *"We all are that string, and God tunes us."*

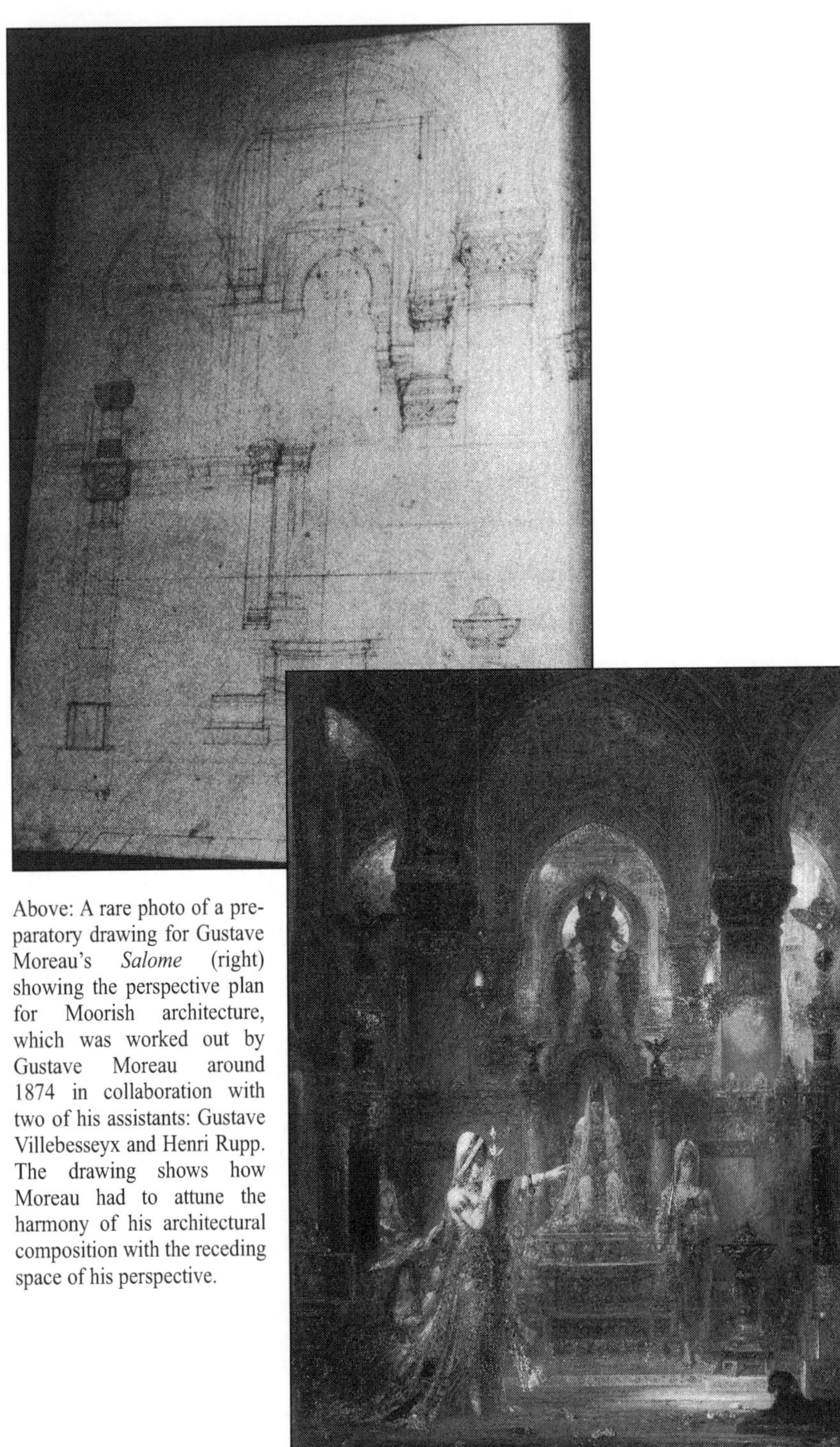

Above: A rare photo of a preparatory drawing for Gustave Moreau's *Salome* (right) showing the perspective plan for Moorish architecture, which was worked out by Gustave Moreau around 1874 in collaboration with two of his assistants: Gustave Villebesseyx and Henri Rupp. The drawing shows how Moreau had to attune the harmony of his architectural composition with the receding space of his perspective.

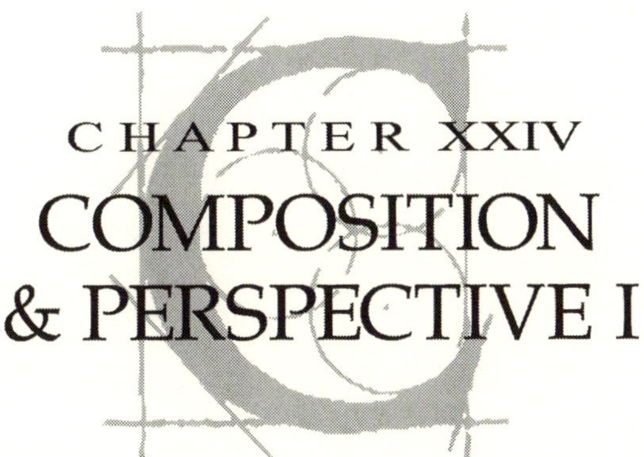

CHAPTER XXIV
COMPOSITION & PERSPECTIVE I

I. The Reconciliation of Armature & Perspective

Late one snowy afternoon in Vienna, I came across a painting which had been stowed away in the apartment reserved for our Academy teachers. I found it in a closet, wedged between a series of other unfinished works. Pulling it out and gazing at it in the wintry twilight, I was immediately struck by the unusual mood and atmosphere of the piece.

At once, I recognized the unique style and handiwork by Daniel Mirante: his fluid brushstrokes, soft scumbles and delicate glazes, all executed in earth tones and semi-neutrals, awaiting a hint of colour. In the midst of an Umbrian landscape, a maiden stood before a reflecting pool, flanked by two figures allegorical in nature. The woman before the pool had paused in mid-action, as if, awaiting a moment that would never actually come to pass. The poetic nature of the piece reminded me at once of Mantegna or Moreau – two inspirations which Mirante and I shared.

The painting transported me in my revery to another afternoon, now in Paris, when he and I along with Timea Tallian had visited the *Musée Gustave Moreau*. Wordlessly we watched and absorbed how the French master had artfully executed each stage of his paintings in their continuous evolution. Though left unfinished, Moreau's work – like Mirante's – had the poet's touch. *Une oeuvre inachevée* by one of these masters said more to me than the most polished and refined pieces by scores of lesser artists.

The pool in Mirante's painting reflected rocky crags and cliffs, like an ancient mausoleum bordered on all sides by tall cypresses. Though receding into the distance, the landscape was met by a huge precipice, making it rise vertically rather than expand horizontally. This, along with the atmospheric haze, gave the painting a unique quality: it spoke of the hidden and often unspoken accord between composition and perspective...

The discovery of perspective immediately added another dimension – and with it, a new and very puzzling dilemma – for the harmonious construction of pictorial space. Because artists, over the course of history, had already worked out a variety of methods (*ad quadratum* grids, root rectangles, etc) for the harmonious arrangement of figures in 2D pictorial space – a pursuit which we have investigated here as armature. But all these invisible lines – particularly the dynamic diagonals – now come into conflict with the receding diagonals of perspectival space. The question thus arises: how can the invisible lines of armature and perspective be harmoniously reconciled?

In the works of Piero della Francesco, Leonardo da Vinci and especially Raphael, we can see how these great minds struggled with the problem – each proposing their own unique solution. The question was first posed, indirectly, by Alberti when he wrote about perspective: "*However, this rule for dividing the pavement belongs to what we shall later call composition.*"[1] This is indeed strange. For most Renaissance artists, 'the rule for dividing the pavement' would belong to the study of, not composition, but *perspective...*

But, as an architect, Alberti was interested in the way the elevation could be developed from the ground plan. The facade was constructed by reproducing the same geometric shapes and harmonic proportions as established in the floor plan. And, as was a long-standing tradition among Gothic and Renaissance architects, traces of that foundational geometry appeared in the *pavimento* – in the tiled floor.

In fact, a closer look at the *pavimentazione* in many Renaissance works reveals a profound concern with geometry and proportion, as the turned triangles (hexagrams) and turned squares (octagrams) form tilings which rival even the finest works of Islamic culture. This is why 'the rule for dividing the pavement' ultimately relates to composition and perspective: the harmonic division of space is first established in the composition (its underlying armature and geometry, as revealed by the floor tiles), and is *then* translated into the perspective. This is especially true of Piero della Francesca's *Flagellation of Christ,* but Raphael's *School of Athens* and Leonardo's *Last Supper* also play with these notions.

II. Piero della Francesca's Flagellation of Christ

The first *quattrocento* artist to grapple with the question of the harmonious reconciliation of composition and perspective was Piero della Francesca. As a pioneer in the field of perspective, his curious, ever-searching intellect sought out possible solutions, which then appeared in his carefully executed paintings. *The Flagellation of Christ* (Fig. 24.1) is perhaps one of his most mysterious creations, a masterpiece in oil and tempera which Kenneth Clarke called, *"a mystique of measurement."*[2]

At first glance, the painting confuses the eye: *why* is Christ relegated to the background, and *who* are the three foreground figures? Why does the young man in the foreground assume a pose similar to Christ, and why is he bare-footed, when the other two are so richly attired? Scholars have debated these questions for centuries.

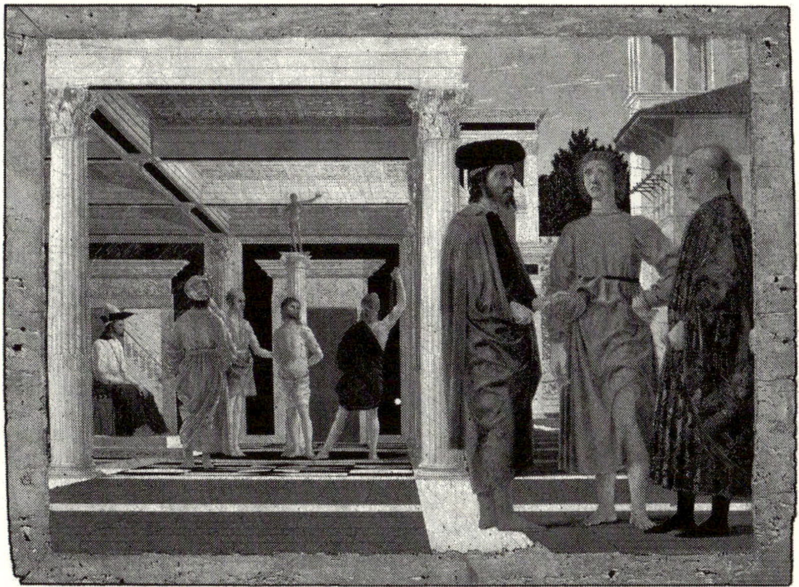

Fig. 24.1 - Piero della Francesca: *The Flagellation of Christ* c. 1460

The young man in the middle is usually identified as Oddantanio da Montefeltro, the first Duke of Urbino, who came to power in 1443 at the tender age of sixteen. Young, brash and extravagant, he exhausted the court coffers until his own advisors conspired against him. These two, Manfredo dei Pio da Carpi and Tommaso di Guido dell'Agnello, appear to his left and right. All three were assassinated on the night of July 21st, 1444, and Oddantonio was succeeded by his half-brother Federico da Montefeltro, who commissioned the painting to commemorate his less-fortunate sibling. The artist has depicted the young duke as an innocent victim, his betrayal and suffering comparable to that of Christ on the whipping column. On the frame, long since lost, were the words *Convenerunt in Unum*, suggesting that Oddantonio's advisors, like the San Hedrin that delivered Christ unto Pilate, had indeed 'conspired as one'.

In the Gospel of John, it is written that the members of the San Hedrin *"...led Jesus from Caiaphas unto the hall of judgment... and they themselves went not into the judgment hall, lest they should be defiled."* (Jn 18:28) This passage explains, in part, *why* the threesome are standing *outside* the praetorium, which the Renaissance artist has lovingly depicted in the Antique style: Corinthian columns, a coffered ceiling, and Christ bound to an Ionic column topped with a golden effigy. Indeed, after meeting with Leon Battista Alberti, Piero modelled his praetorium on Alberti's Rucellai Sepulchre in Florence, since it assiduously reproduced the Holy Sepulchre of Jerusalem.[3]

This explains the squarish proportions, black and white marble, and ornate geometric designs – all of which adorn the Rucellai Sepulchre. But for Piero, the challenge was not *to build* the Holy Sepulchre, as Alberti had done, but *to depict it in perspective.* In one cohesive work, he sought to marry composition with perspective, by combining their respective codes of construction.

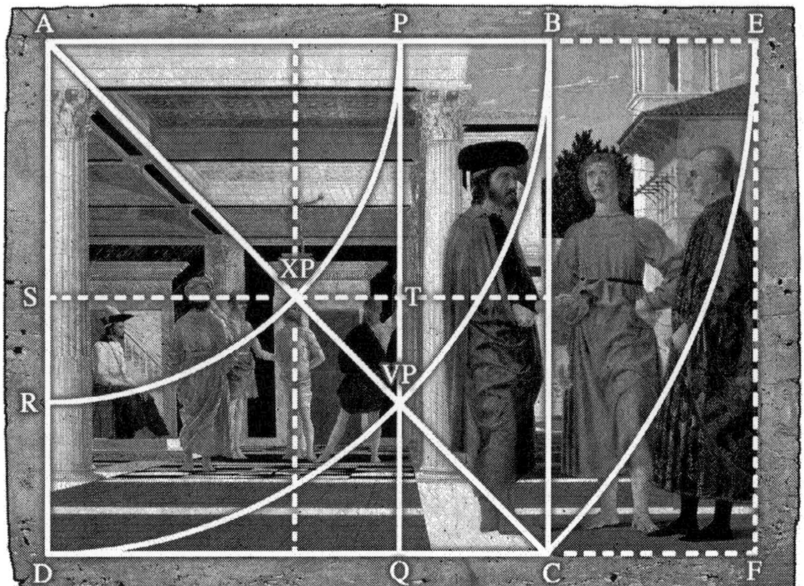

Fig. 24.2 - Piero della Francesca: *The Flagellation of Christ* Establishing the Vanishing Point

The key lay in the placement of the vanishing point. If he could create an armature that integrated the vanishing point, then the perspective would converge onto a harmonious point within the pictorial space. As we can see in Fig. 24.2, Piero began with the square ABCD, through which he drew diagonal AC. From centre A, he arced the AC diagonal up to E, in order to create the root 2 rectangle AEFD, the outer limits of his painting. The right side of the main square, on the vertical BC, determined the end-point of the white strip on the pavement, with its row of Corinthian columns receding, *precipitoso,* in steep perspective. This same vertical also set the limit to the back wall of the praetorium.

To establish the vanishing point, Piero drew another arc *within* the square, based on centre A, and extending B to D. Where this arc cut the diagonal AC, Piero established his vanishing point VP.[4] We have met with this construction before (in Fig. 17.12) where it was used to inscribe a root rectangle *within* a square. Hence, APQD is a root 2 rectangle. In this way, Piero was able to converge the diagonals of the architecture onto an integral point in the armature, harmoniously marrying perspective and composition. We can see this especially with the black divisions of the coffered ceiling (upper left), which precisely follow the diagonal AC towards the vanishing point.

By drawing a vertical through the vanishing point VP, and drawing yet another arc with centre A, this time from P to R, Piero established point XP. The dotted lines crossing through XP established both the height and the plumb line for Christ, whose head lies just below the exact centre-point of the main square ABCD.

The dotted horizontal through XP also reminds us that root 2 rectangles are *recursive*, meaning that the division of a root 2 rectangle into two equal parts leads to two smaller root 2 rectangles. In this case, the dotted horizontal through XP, labelled ST, divides the root 2 rectangle APQD into two smaller root 2 rectangles, APTS and STQD. Meanwhile, the root 2 rectangle APQD is itself one half of the painting's entire root 2 rectangle AEFD (with PEFQ being the other half). The figures round the whipping column and the painting's vanishing point appear within the small root 2 rectangle STQD, which occupies exactly *one quarter* of the pictorial space. By that same token, the three figures in the foreground occupy *one half* of the pictorial space.

III. The Star Octagram Floor Tiles: From Quadrature to Root Two

That Piero was conscious of this √2 division of pictorial space is evidenced by the *pavimentazione* (Fig. 24.5, over). In fact, there are two types of floor tile: the area *outside* the praetorium, which is evenly divided by large squares containing 8 x 8 tiles; and the area *inside*, which is divided by large squares containing star octagram motifs – except for Christ's pillar, which is surrounded by a solid black circle. Hence, the outside space is divided *arithmetically*, with regular whole numbers, while the inside space is divided *geometrically*, resulting in irrational numbers like √2.

In Fig. 24.4 (over), I have recreated Piero's geometric construction of the star octagram *pavimentazione*, which uses the *quadrature* to create the octagram, and root 2 rectangles for the outer square.

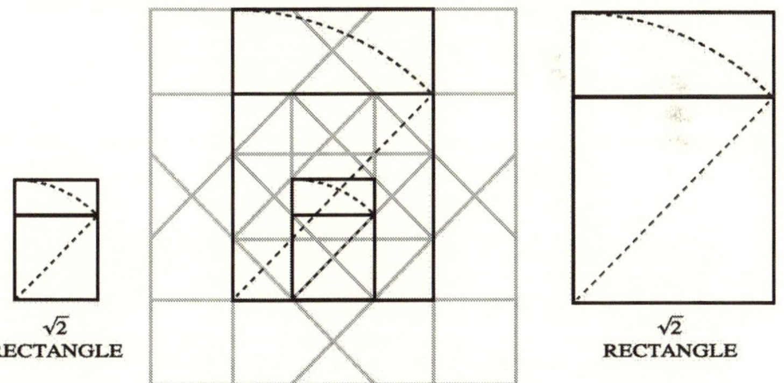

Fig. 24.3 - Piero della Francesca: Root 2 Rectangles in the Floor Tiles

In diagram 24.3 (above), we can see the relationship of root 2 rectangles to the star octagram. In fact, *within* the star octagram itself, the root 2 rectangle appears *four times*. And in the outer frame, it appears *four more times*, making *eight* root 2 rectangles in all. This means that the pictorial space of Piero's composition is governed by the same proportion as the floor tiles. This is the ratio of the square (1) to the root 2 rectangle, or 1:√2.

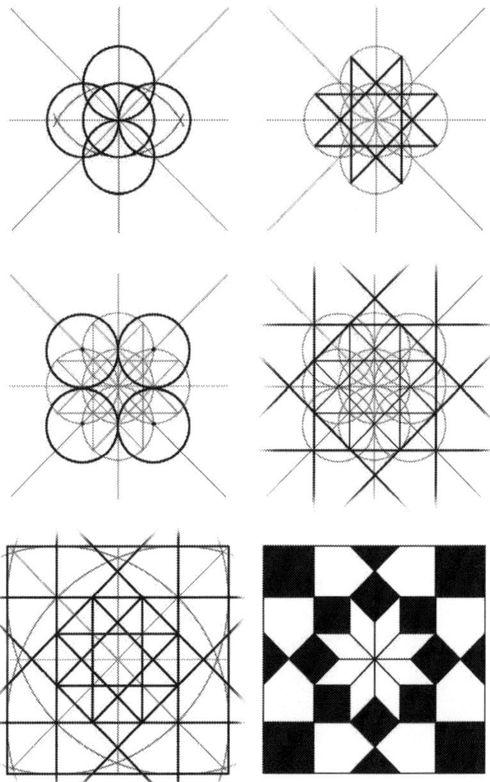

Fig. 24.4 - Piero della Francesca: Star Octagram *Pavimentazione* Construction

Step 1. Beginning *ad circulum*, he drew a vertical line with three interpenetrating circles (the double vesica), then drew the large arcs (*oculus* or 'Eye of God' motif) to create the horizontal line for the centres of two more lateral circles (another double vesica), creating the four-petalled flower. With this, he drew the diagonals.

Step 2. Through the *quadrature*, he drew a square and turned square within the first circle, creating an octagram. By extending the lines of the octagram to the limits of the four circles, he created the star octagram.

Step 3. Setting his compass on the intersection of the first four circles, he drew four more circles of the same size, creating a kind of quatrefoil.

Step 4. Using the points of intersection of the first four circles with the four new circles, he drew the large turned square. Using the intersection of the diagonals with the four new circles, he drew the regular square, thus creating a large octagram. Again, its sides were extended to create a large star octagram.

Step 5. To determine the outer square, he used the diagonals of the inner square, which were arced around, and where they crossed the extensions of that square, he drew his orthogonals to create the outer square. In other words, he drew four root 2 rectangles and then joined them up in the outer square.

Step 6. To create the black and white pattern, he eliminated the lines of the small octagram in the centre, drawing orthogonals and diagonals instead. Then, the smaller squares and turned squares alternated in black and white.

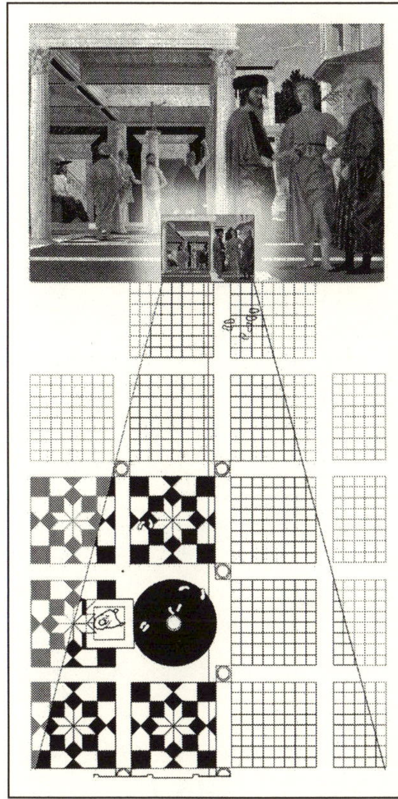

Fig. 24.5 - Diagonal Translation of Orthogonal Floor Plan to Linear Perspective

In *De Prospectiva Pingendi* (On Perspective for Painting), Piero della Francesca developed his own method for constructing perspective, which we referred to as the Diagonal Construction, since it (like the root 2 rectangle) uses *the diagonal* to translate even the most complex shapes from orthogonal to linear perspective.

Obviously, Piero began the complex design of the floor tiles in orthogonal perspective. To apply the Diagonal Construction, he had to work out *the entire floor plan* in orthogonal perspective, and then project it, step by step, to the linear perspective of the painting. Modifying a diagram from Wittkower and Carter's 'The Perspective of Piero della Francesca's Flagellation', I have shown (Fig. 24.5) what the procedure would have entailed.[5] The floor plan was drawn at roughly 17.5 times the size of the original painting (which is 81.5 cm x 58.4 cm large, meaning the floor plan was 1.42 m x 1.02 m). Although the steps for transferring the perspective are exceedingly complex, the resulting painting attests to Piero's diligence and ingenuity.

In another modified diagram from Wittkower and Carter (Fig. 24.6, over), I have shown the visual angle from both the elevation and side view, to show the proportions at work in Piero's perspectival space. The depth of the floor plan is divided by (almost exactly) five large squares, while the back wall is three-and-a-half squares wide. None of this is obvious in the painting itself, but the ground plan shows a conscious division of the *pavimento* into fairly even squares.

Each set of figures occupies the middle of a square. Moving toward the back wall from the front picture plane, we notice that the three foreground figures occupy the first square, the turbaned man observing the flagellation occupies the third square, and the flagellation scene itself takes place in the fourth square. This creates a definite proportion, on the order of 1:3:4.

If we calculate the distance of the viewer to the picture plane, and compare it to that of Christ from the picture plane, we discover that they stand in a relationship of 1:2. Obviously, the viewer is not present in the painting, but the man with the turban occupies a curious position, standing before the flagellation scene as an observer, as if he were indeed the viewer of the painting.

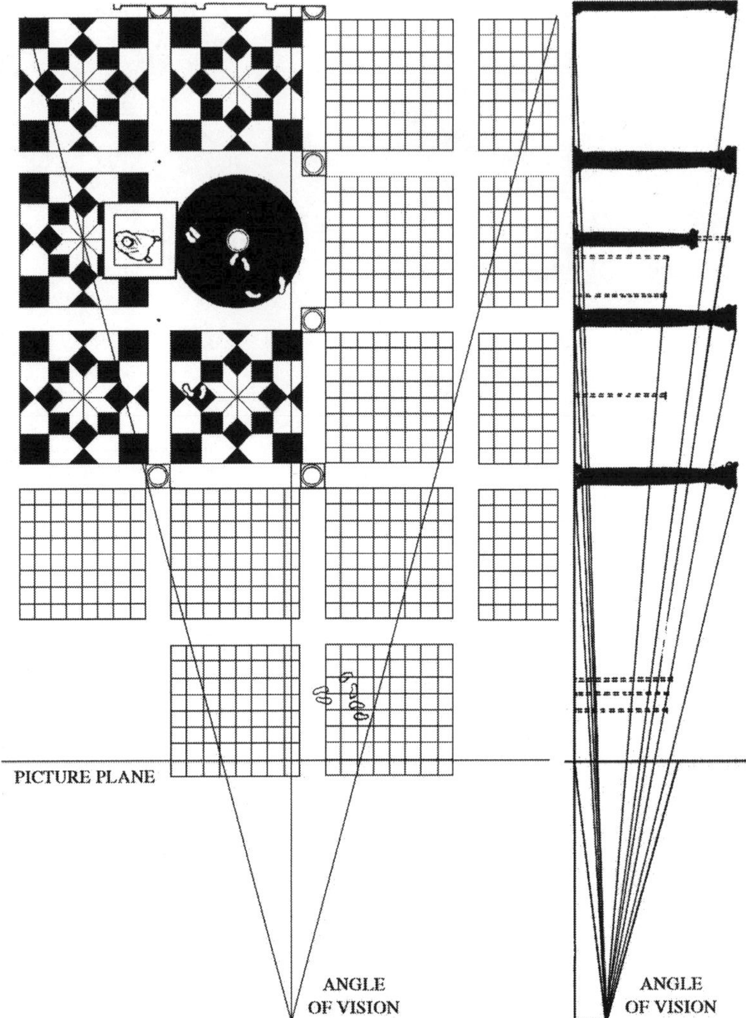

Fig. 24.6 - Visual Angle in Elevation and Side View Showing Proportions in Perspective

The centric ray of perspective, which runs from the eye of the viewer to the vanishing point (cutting the viewing angle in half), runs almost parallel to the Corinthian columns, which appear in very steep perspective. In the floor plan, those four columns are evenly spaced between the large squares. In the painting, they indicate the diminution in perspective through their decreasing heights, as they rapidly recede into the background.

Corinthian columns, when measured from their height to the width of their base, are traditionally 10:1 in proportion. If we treat the foremost column as 10 units high, then measurement tells us that the columns diminish in a proportion of 10 : 8 : 6.5 : 5.5. The difference in height is thus 2 : 1.5 : 1, which is an arithmetic series.[6]

IV. Piero della Francesca: Proportion in Perspective

Piero della Francesca became aware of proportion in perspective and, some fifteen years after painting *The Flagellation*, wrote about it in *De Prospectiva Pingendi*. In an important article called 'Brunelleschi and Proportion in Perspective,'* Rudolf Wittkower traces the development of perspectival proportion from its early beginnings in Brunelleschi and Alberti to its high development in Piero della Francesca and Leonardo da Vinci.[8]

Piero begins the relevant section of *De Prospectiva Pingendi* with a re-statement of Euclid's theorem of similar triangles (Fig. 24.7), which appears in Book VI of *The Elements*.

Euclid's Proposition 4 states, *"In equiangular triangles the sides about the equal angles are proportional."*[9] This means that, if we have two similar triangles, and know the ratio of the side to the base for one, then the ratio of the side to the base for the other must be proportionate. In the example given here, the larger triangle has a ratio of 2:4 (side to base), so the similar smaller triangle has a ratio of x:2 (side to base), where x must equal 1.

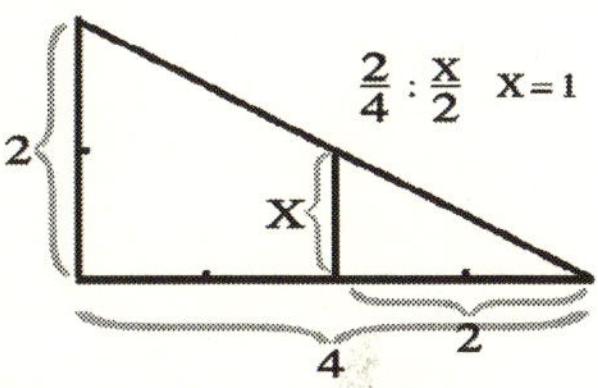

Fig. 24.7 - Euclid's Theorem of Similar Triangles

In terms of perspective, this means that similar triangles are formed when the angle of vision, from the eye to a series of objects, is cut by the picture plane (Fig. 24.8) If we know the height of the object (side) and its distance from the eye (base), then the ratio of that larger triangle (side to base) will be proportionate to the ratio of the smaller triangle. The smaller triangle has, on its side, the height of the apparent image on the picture plane and, as its base, the distance from the picture plane to the eye of the viewer. Through Euclid's theorem of similar triangles, the height of the apparent image on the picture plane can be calculated. In the example given here, four separate objects create *four separate triangles*, each with *two similar triangles*, one with its side on the object and one with its side on the picture plane.

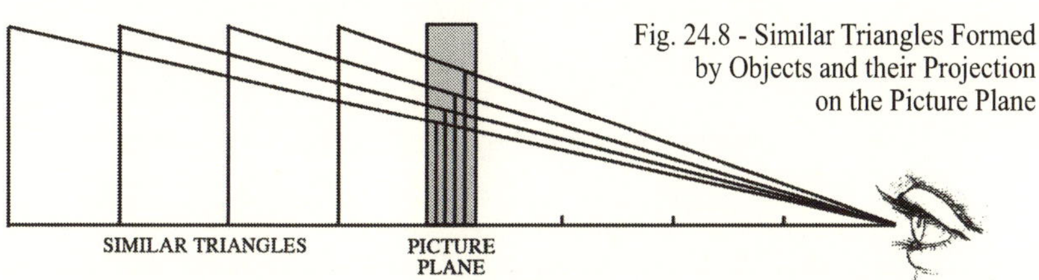

Fig. 24.8 - Similar Triangles Formed by Objects and their Projection on the Picture Plane

*In 'Piero della Francesca and the Renaissance Proof of Linear Perspective', James Elkins questions whether it was actually Piero della Francesca or a later commentator who wrote the important passage for Wittkower's interpretation of *De Prospectiva Pingendi*. Elkins writes: *"His* [Wittkower's] *conclusions are not supported by Piero's text: 'proportion in perspective' is not the subject of Piero's Proposition Lxi, but rather of a scholium or commentary appended to it; and Piero, who is otherwise so thorough about illustrating his propositions, does not even include a diagram."*[7] However, we have no clear evidence as to *who* wrote this proposition, which still demonstrates, nevertheless, proportion in perspective.

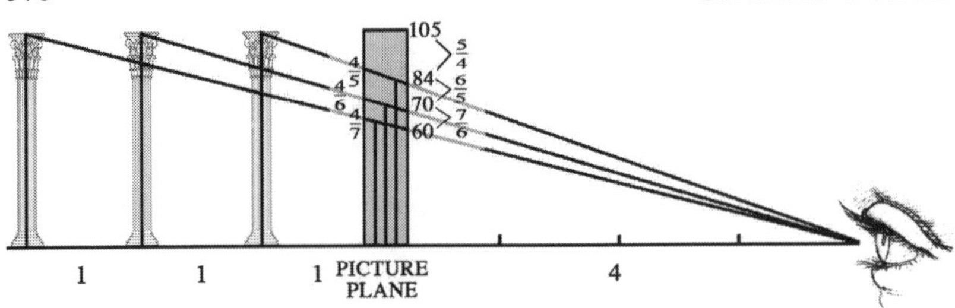

Fig. 24.9 - The Rate at which Objects Diminish on the Picture Plane

In his investigation into proportion in perspective, which he calls *commensuratio*, Piero begins by asking why proportions in perspective do not follow any of the well-known progressions, such as 4, 6, 9 or 9, 12, 16. To work out the proportion of diminution on the picture plane, he gives a series of examples which measure out parallel objects, such as columns.

In the example given above (Fig. 24.9), each column is 1 unit from each other and from the picture plane, while the picture plane is 4 units from the eye. On a picture plane 105 units tall, Piero calculates the apparent size of the columns, from closest to farthest, as 84, 70 and 60.

Given this progression, he then compares each two numbers and reduces their ratio, beginning with 105:84 which, divided by 21, equals 5:4. Then 84:70, divided by 14, equals 6:5. And finally, 70:60, divided by 10, equals 7:6. These ratios express the *relative size* of each object *to the other*. If he expressed each in comparison to the total height of the picture plane (105), he would have arrived at a more regular series: 84/105 = 4/5; 70/105 = 4/6 and 60/105 = 4/7. This creates the new series 4/5, 4/6, 4/7.

Due to the theorem of similar triangles, a distinct pattern emerges. As the distance of the objects increases, their size on the picture plane decreases, creating a diminishing series. If the picture plane were 1 unit from the eye, then the diminishing series would be 1/2, 1/3, 1/4...

For some unknown reason, Piero did not arrive at the 1/2, 1/3, 1/4 series, which is crucial for harmonic proportion in perspective. But, *De Prospectiva Pingendi* worked out the *commensuratio* for the first time: the rate at which objects diminish in size on the picture plane, expressed as a series of ratios. He discovered proportion in perspective.[10]

V. Leonardo da Vinci: Harmonious Proportion in Perspective

It was left up to Leonardo da Vinci to work out *harmonic* proportion in perspective, especially the Pythagorean-Platonic proportions found in music, architecture and the armature of painting. He did this both in his writings and in a painting which, in this case, was his famous *Last Supper* (1498). Through the intermediary of Luca Pacioli, Leonardo had studied *De Prospectiva Pingendi*, and was able to build upon Piero's important groundwork.

Scattered throughout his Notebooks are a series of diagrams and remarks on proportion in perspective. In one remark, from Notebook SKM II (now in the Victoria & Albert Museum), Leonardo asks a crucial question:

"The differences in the diminution of objects of equal size in consequence of their various remoteness from the eye will bear among themselves the same proportions as those of the spaces between the eye and the different objects.

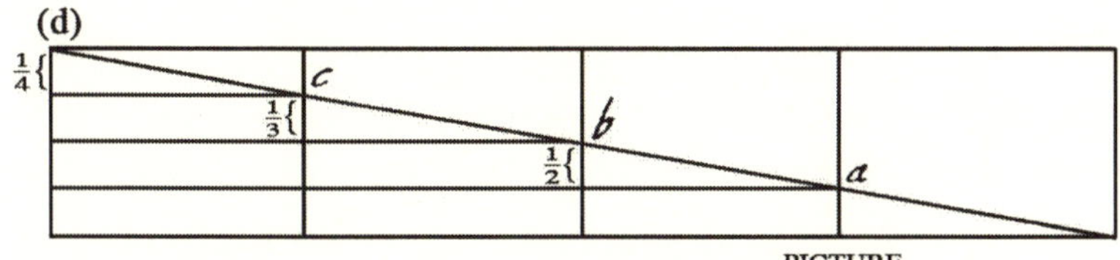

Fig. 24.10 - Leonardo's Diagram on Proportion in Perspective

"Find out how much a man diminishes at a certain distance and what its length is; and then at twice that distance and at three times, and so make your general rule."[11]

The remark is accompanied by a diagram (Fig. 24.10), but Leonardo does not elaborate upon its meaning. And yet, the four distinct lines marked *a*, *b*, *c* (and presumably *d*) are all equally distant, suggesting that *a* is the picture plane, between the eye on the bottom right and the first object, marked *b*, on the left. The diagram shows how object *b* is 2 units from the eye, and will appear on the picture plane at 1/2 its height. Object *c* is 3 units from the eye, and will appear at 1/3 of its height. And object *d*, being 4 units from the eye, will appear at 1/4 of its height. This creates the diminishing series 1/2, 1/3, 1/4.

In another passage, this time from the *Codex Atlanticus*, Leonardo arrives at a general rule:

"If you place the vertical plane at one braccio from the eye, the first object, being at a distance of 4 braccie from your eye, will diminish by 3/4 [and so appear as 1/4] *of its height on the plane; and if it is 8 braccie from the eye, by 7/8* [and so appear as 1/8 of its height]*; and if it is 16 braccie off, it will diminish by 15/16* [and so appear as 1/16] *of its height, and so on by degrees, as the space doubles the diminution will double."*[12]

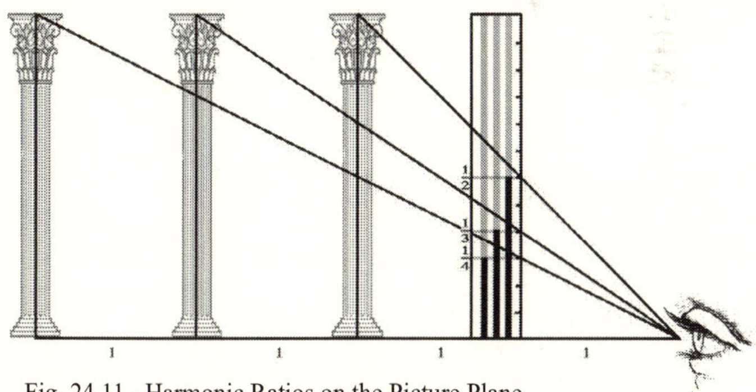

Fig. 24.11 - Harmonic Ratios on the Picture Plane

In this passage, the distance of the objects doubles from 4 to 8 to 16 as the height diminishes proportionally. But the general rule does not concern *the amount* by which the proportion decreases (doubling, tripling etc), but the constant ratio. That ratio is shown in Fig. 24.11, which simply expands upon the first diagram by Leonardo.

Here, we can see how the *diapason* halves, *diapente* thirds and *diatessaron* quarters naturally result on the picture plane, if the columns are spaced 1 unit apart, and the picture plane is 1 unit from the eye. It is a natural outcome of the theorem of similar triangles that this harmonic series will result. This gives us the following general rule.

In the diminishing series 1/2, 1/3, 1/4, the top numerator of the fraction expresses *the distance of the picture plane from the eye*. This is a fixed amount, 1 unit, and so remains constant in all the fractions. The bottom denominator expresses *the distance of the objects from the eye*. This is a variable amount, beginning at 2 and increasing arithmetically. In *Proportion: Science, Philosophy, Architecture,* Richard Padovan expresses this progression in variables, which takes the general form of: A/B, A/(A+B), A/(A+2B), A/(A+3B)..., where A is the distance of the eye from the picture plane and B is the distance of the object from the eye.

With this general rule, we can imagine a variety of proportions in perspective. As Padovan explains, *"the value of B can be anything we like: for instance √2, √3, √4, √5 or ϕ,"*[13] resulting in a variety of series that are not only arithmetic, but also geometric or harmonic.

VI. The Last Supper: the Armature

In Leonardo's masterpiece in Milan (Fig. 24.12), the artist worked out a series of harmonic proportions in both the armature and the perspective. We shall begin with the proportions that appear *in the armature*, granting harmony to the composition. After, we may then approach *the perspective*, to see if a similar harmony rules the depths.

In his writing, the artist explains how the purpose of harmony is to *expand our vision*, so the painting can be viewed in both its parts and as a unified whole:

"The painter in his harmonious proportions makes the component parts react simultaneously so that they can be seen at one and the same time both together and separately; together, by viewing the design of the composition as a whole; and separately by viewing the design of its component parts."[14]

In another remark, this time on the *paragone* that compares painting with its sister arts, Leonardo recognizes that painting and music share in common a sense of harmonic proportion:

"From painting which serves the eye, the noblest sense, arises harmony of proportions; just as many different voices joined together and singing simultaneously produce a harmonious proportion which gives satisfaction to the sense of hearing."[15]

Reports from *The Last Supper*'s chief restorer, Pinin Brambilla Barcilon, allow us to reconstruct part of Leonardo's working method. He began with a smooth surface, called the *intonaco*, which mixed chalk with stone fragments. On top of this, he executed his *sinopia* underdrawing in concise, fluid brushstrokes, using a brick-red earth colour for the figures and black outlines for the architecture. These were fixed with a tonal layer of light-yellow (calcium carbonate, magnesium, and traces of quartz).

Instead of using the usual *fresco* technique (painting into the wet plaster), Leonardo painted in oils, beginning with an *imprimatura* ground of lead white.

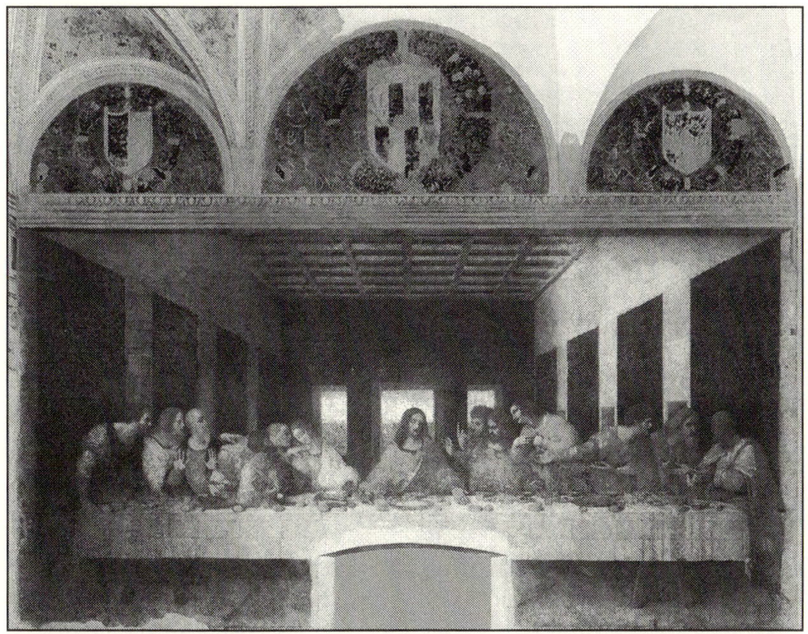

Fig. 24.12 - Leonardo da Vinci: *The Last Supper* with Lunettes and Ornamental Architrave

On top of this, he rendered his forms in a dry *tempera forte* technique, mixing his colours in a protein-based binder, adding small amounts of walnut oil.

During the restoration, a large number of incised lines were found, etched with a sharp instrument (Fig. 24.15). Most likely, these incisions were used to transfer his designs, since none of the usual *spolvero* traces were found, of black charcoal dots pounced through a pricked *cartone*. All of the architectural elements were etched in straight lines, and the main figures were outlined. Leonardo proceeded quite loosely and made many changes while painting, often improvising within the incised lines.[16]

After three years of labour, Leonardo completed his work in 1498. Alas, by 1517, Vasari said the painting was so damaged that the figures were no longer recognizable. Lamazzo recorded in 1582 that it was 'in a state of total ruin.' Around 1652, a door was cut into the refectory wall, and the building narrowly missed total destruction several times. Over the centuries, the image was variously restored and repainted, until Pinin Brambilla Barcilon began a twenty-year conservation project in 1978, removing the excess layers. One interesting find from the fresco's conservation was the discovery of a tiny pinhole that marked Leonardo's vanishing point.

When we gaze at the *Last Supper* today and try to make some sense of its underlying armature, we must naturally begin with its bounding shape (Fig. 24.12). Although Leonardo had the entire upper wall of the refectory to work from, he first created three large decorative lunettes at the very top, and just below them, an ornamental architrave.

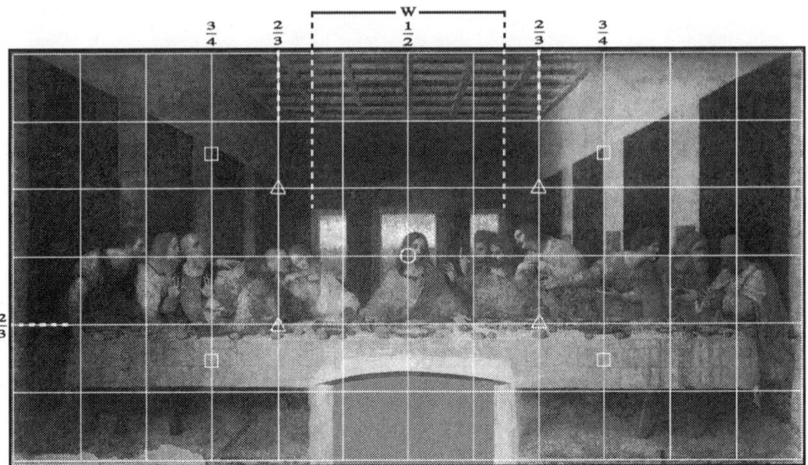

Fig. 24.13 - Armature for Compositional Harmonies

This allowed him to concentrate his design into a wide rectangular space which, when measured, reveals itself to be of *diapason* proportion: a 1:2 rectangle measuring 4.4 m x 8.8 m (with an extra 10 cm on the top and bottom - Fig. 24.13). Scholars have long-since recognized that the coffers lining the top edge of the painting evenly divide the ceiling into six equal parts. Leonardo used this length as his module, since his 1:2 rectangle was evenly divided into 12 squares in width and 6 squares in height.

By dividing his space into a duodecimal system of twelfths, he was able to work out the halves, thirds and quarters with ease, since these fit into 12 (as we saw in Pythagoras' tablet in *The School of Athens*) as 6, 8 and 9 respectively. Indeed, in a sketch for the *Last Supper* (Windsor No. 12542), Leonardo jots down the numerical series *3.4.6.-6.3-6-4=32*. This has been interpreted as the ratios of the *diatessaron* quarters and *diapente* thirds within the *diapason* half (3:4:6), followed by another *diapason* half (6:3), and a *diapente* third (6:4).[17]

To get a better sense of the harmonic proportions in *The Last Supper*, I have marked the exact centre of the painting (the halves) with a small circle, then the thirds with small triangles, and the quarters with small squares. Clearly, Christ has been situated *at the very centre* of pictorial space, on the *diapason* halves. Meanwhile, the back wall of the chamber ends at the *diapente* thirds, and the coffered ceiling meets the top of the painting at the *diatessaron* quarters. On the horizontal grid, the top of the refectory table lies exactly on the two-thirds *diapente*.

The three windows behind Christ (symbolic of the trinity) are marked with a W in the diagram. Their width is exactly three squares, being three-twelfths, and hence, one-quarter of the entire width.

The figures in Leonardo's painting are responding to Christ's profound revelation, *"One of you will betray me – one who is eating with me."* (Mk 14:18) In the wave of reactions breaking left and right across the table of

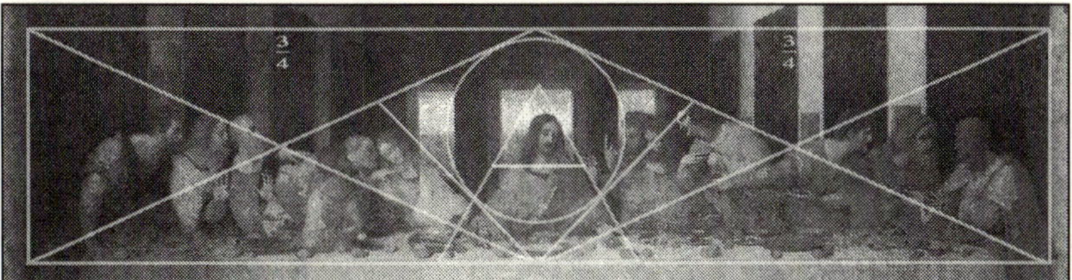

Fig. 24.14 - Armature for the Figures

their repast, we can see each characteristic response as *"...they began to be sorrowful and to say to him one after another, 'Is it I?'"* (Mk 14:19) Only Judas betrays himself by not reacting. Instead, he reaches for a piece of bread just as Christ, also reaching for a morsel, announces, *"It is the one dipping bread into the bowl with me."* (Mk 14:20)

Leonardo has grouped the twelve disciples into four sets of three, which are contained in overlapping scalene triangles (Fig. 24.14). The main pyramid has its apex above the window's circular pediment, and extends to the edge of the foremost tapestry, forming its base along the front edge of the table. When this wide triangle is inverted, it creates two XX shapes that form the overlapping scalene triangles of the figures. The centre of each X, dividing the disciples into their respective groups, falls exactly at the *diatessaron* three-quarters proportion of the painting's horizontal axis.

Christ himself forms a hieratic triangle, inset in the circle that continues the curved arc of the window's pediment. Through this armature, Christ appears to be enclosed within the Eye of God. The painting is a perfect fusion of Humanist and Hieratic codes. The static symmetry of the composition is relieved by harmonic quarters and thirds, which allow us 'to view the design in its component parts' while also expanding our vision 'to the composition as a whole'.

As our vision expands, we take in the architectural space, where the flat frieze of foreground figures contrasts with the chamber's deeply receding perspectival space. To the left and right, the disciples protest, question, confront and deny, each expressing a different Humanist feeling. While at their centre, sorrowful and resigned, a Hieratic Christ surrenders himself with divine love and compassion.

VI. The Last Supper: the Perspective

To appreciate the harmonious proportions of Leonardo's perspective, we must begin with its *costruzione legittima.* However, a diagram of the incisions (Fig. 24.15, over) reveals that the artist changed the perspective of the coffered ceiling more than once. This is particularly evident on the upper left, where several measures are worked out.[18]

Due to these changes, Leonardo often hid key reference points in his painting, and came to write about the importance of 'natural perspective' which treats the objects *"just as the eye sees them diminished, without*

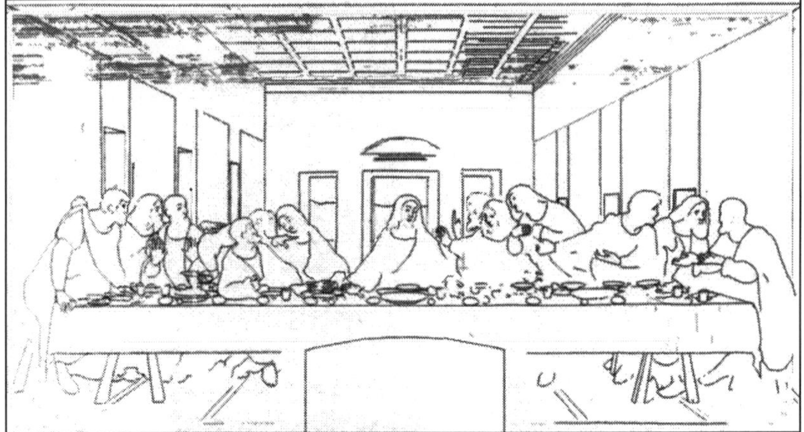

Fig. 24.15 - Incisions for the Perspective Construction

obliging a man to stand in one place," in preference to 'artificial perspective' which is *"the work done by rules* [and] *is devised by art."*[19]

Leonardo called upon natural perspective (*prospettiva naturale*) because his painting appeared high up on the wall, making it impossible to view it properly from the correct Viewing Point (i.e. 'a man standing in one place'). He also took the liberty of altering the artificial perspective (*prospettiva accidentale*), particularly in the tapestries on the side walls, which become larger than they should as they diminish towards the back. The reason for this, as we shall see, was to incorporate Pythagorean-Platonic proportions.

In Fig. 24.16 we have a simplified view of Leonardo's *costruzione legittima*. The main vanishing point (VP) lies directly on Christ. Although Leonardo was not the first Renaissance artist to combine the centre of compositional space with the centre of perspectival space (recall the Annunciation panels with their enclosed garden and bolted door), this device has allowed him to converge all the perspectival diagonals *directly onto Christ*, as if he were at the centre of a crystalline quartz. The Saviour appears, not only at the centre of the 1:2 rectangle, but in a direct line with the viewer, just before the vanishing point.

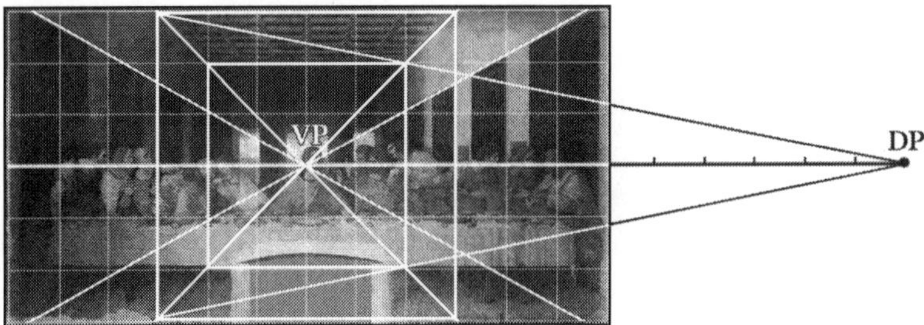

Fig. 24.16 - *The Last Supper - Costruzione Legittima*

The Distance Point has been determined by drawing a diagonal through the coffered ceiling, to the point where it crosses with the horizon line. It falls exactly on a point measured out by the painting's 12-part duodecimal system, standing 6 modules from the painting's edge. Since the Distance Point at the side may be swung around to become the Viewing Point in front of the painting, this means that the perspectival space would be viewed properly by someone standing 6 modules (i.e. 4.4 m) directly before the painting.

The supping chamber is twice as deep as it is wide (i.e. 12 modules deep and 6 modules wide), with Christ and his disciples in a flat frieze quite close to the invisible sixth side of the perspectival box. This means that, if the viewer stands 6 modules from the picture plane, Christ appears 12 modules from the back wall, which is to say, two-thirds of the way (the *diapente*) between the viewer and the back wall.

In Thomas Brachert's 1971 study, *'A Musical Canon of Proportion in Leonardo da Vinci's Last Supper'*, the author reveals the Pythagorean-Platonic proportions at work in the perspective. From Brachert's article, I have re-created and revised two important diagrams.

In the first,[20] we see how Leonardo may have worked out the proportion of the room and the tapestries *along the side* of the painting, in its vertical space (Fig. 24.17). The schema assumes that the room is 12 modules deep, and that the viewer (i.e. the Viewing Point) is 6 modules before of the picture plane.

Leonardo has spaced out the tapestries along the side wall in such a way that their top corners cut the picture plane at harmonious points: from back to front, the back corner of the first tapestry (T1) cuts the picture plane at the two-thirds *diapente*, and the front corner of the fourth tapestry (T4) cuts it close to the six-sixths mark, which is to say, the perfect *unison*. In between, the front corner of the second tapestry (T2) cuts the picture plane at the three-quarters *diatessaron*, and the front corner of the third tapestry (T3) cuts it at the four-fifths mark, which is the *ditone* or major third in Pythagorean Tuning. Last of all we note that the horizon line traverses the picture plane at the one-half *diapason*. In this way, Leonardo has adapted Piero della Francesca's *perspectival* proportion to arrive at *harmonic* proportions in the painting's depths.

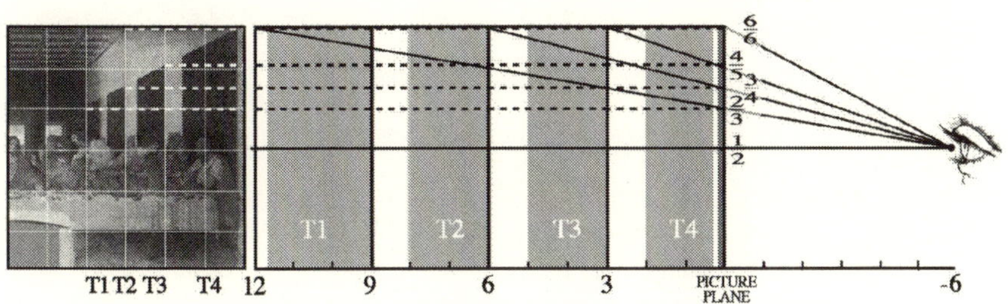

Fig. 24.17 - Harmonic Proportions in the Vertical Space

In the second diagram,[21] we see how Leonardo may have worked out similar proportions *along the base* of the painting, in its horizontal space (Fig. 24.18). Now we can see that the back corner of the chamber falls one-third from the centre along the baseline, and the front corner falls six-sixths or the perfect *unison*. Continuing from back to front, the front edges of the first, second and third tapestries fall respectively on the two-fifths, one-half *diapason* and two-thirds *diapente*, while the back edge of the fourth tapestry falls on the three-quarter *diatessaron*.

In *The Last Supper*, Leonardo respected the Pythagorean-Platonic proportions in both his armature *and* his perspective. On the level of armature, he began with a 1:2 rectangle, which he divided duodecimally into a space 12 modules wide and 6 modules high. On the level of perspective, he began with a 1:2 chamber which, likewise, he divided duodecimally into a space 6 modules wide and 12 modules deep.

By setting his Distance Point, and hence, his Vanishing Point at 6 modules from the picture plane, he was able to create a series of correspondences between armature and perspective. He concentrated on the halves, thirds and quarters of his armature to establish key points for the corners of his tapestries. Then, he translated those points into the perspective by placing the corners of the tapestries at regular intervals behind the picture plane in his perspectival construction. The result was the total integration of armature and perspective, which worked together as one.

In Leonardo's masterpiece, the figure of Christ appears at the very centre, radiating harmony in all directions. By establishing the ritual of the Eucharist, he transforms the architecture around him into a perfect House of God. Each part resonates harmonically with the other, and the whole falls into one perfect geometrico-cosmological arrangement of sacred space.

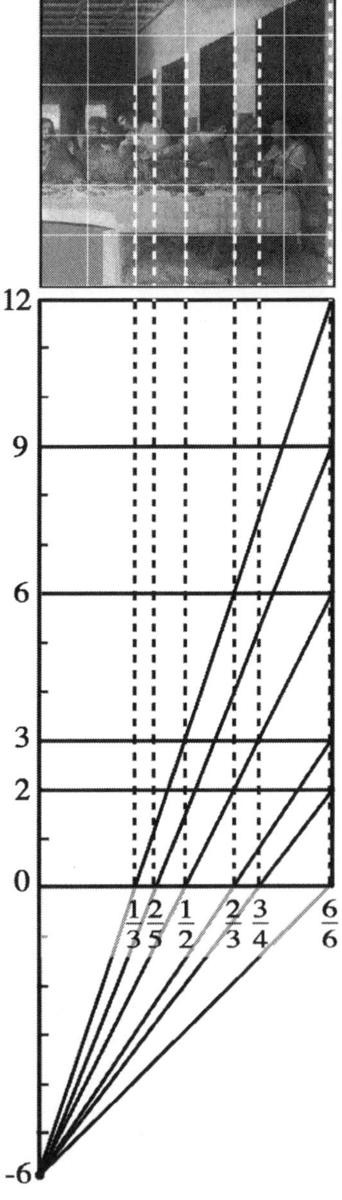

Fig. 24.18
Harmonic Proportions
in the Horizontal Space

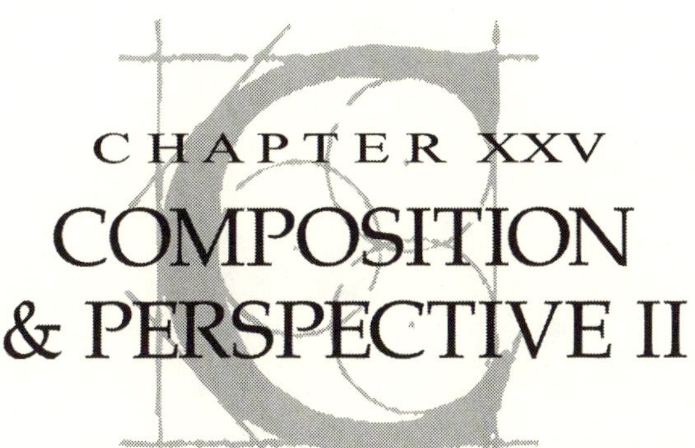

CHAPTER XXV
COMPOSITION & PERSPECTIVE II

I. The School of Athens: Bramante Contemplating a Rhombicuboctahedron

When Pope Julias II saw *The Disputation* that Raphael had painted on the main wall of his library, he was entranced. Immediately, the pontiff ordered the destruction of all previous paintings on the remaining walls (much to the chagrin of masters throughout Italy), so the 25-year old Raphael could design and paint the entire *Stanza della Segnatura*. In 1509 the artist began the designs for *The School of Athens*, which was to appear on the wall directly opposite *The Disputation*.

A number of preparatory sketches still survive, as well as the large *cartone* (Figs. 25.1-2) now housed in the Biblioteca Ambrosiana in Milan. Measuring 2.74 m x 7.95 m, this neglected masterpiece was made on roughly 210 fragments of used drawing paper, glued together into eight squarish sheets. Traces of previous drawings remain on the sheets, making it an immense puzzle for scholars.[1]

The *cartone* carefully works out all the figures on the steps, though the architecture above them is lacking (lines indicate its key features). Using his studio assistants as models, Raphael made preparatory sketches in silverpoint of the main groups ('Diogenes' now in the Städelsches Kunstinstitut Frankfurt; 'the group around Pythagoras' now in the Albertina, Vienna) which he re-drew in silverpoint onto the *cartone*, then went over with charcoal and lead white to deepen the shadows and emphasize the outlines. These outlines were later pin-pricked by assistants for the *spolvero* transfer to another set of drawings for the fresco.

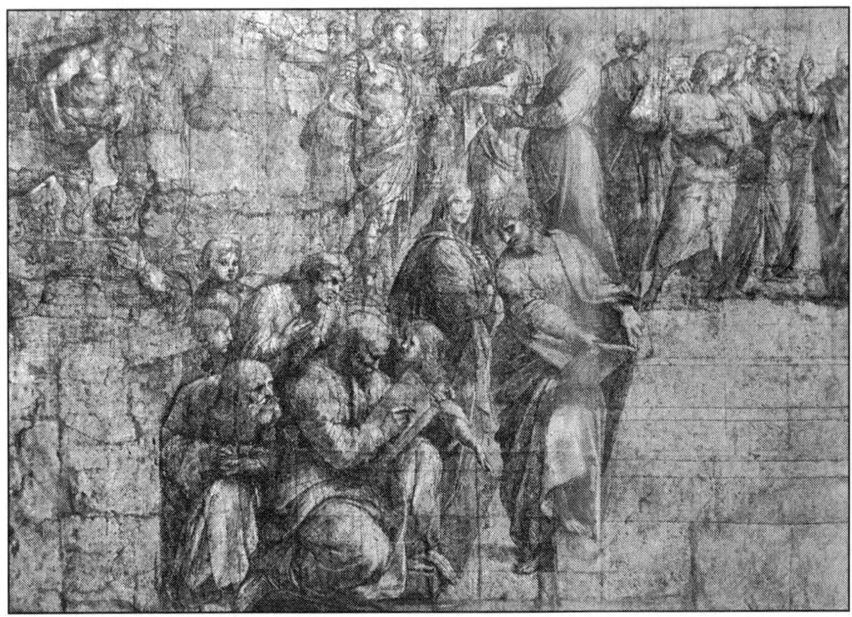

Fig. 25.1 - Raphael: *The School of Athens - Cartone* Left Side

An interesting woodcut by Ugo Panico da Carpi, now in the Albertina, reproduces the preparatory sketch for a figure which, according to Caroline Karpinksi, is not included in the final fresco (Fig. 25.3). In her article, 'Archimedes Salutes Bramante in a Draft for the School of Athens', Karpinski writes that, *"from a visual standpoint, we may suppose that Raphael projected Archimedes to sit in the position that Diogenes now occupies."*[2] The figure of Diogenes, we recall, is sprawled upon the steps, and we may imagine this majestic figure of Archimedes in his place. The 3rd century BCE mathematician and astronomer is contemplating a rhombicuboctahedron – that same 26-sided Archimedean Solid rediscovered by Luca Pacioli and appearing in his portrait as a glass polygon filled with water (Fig. 23.14).

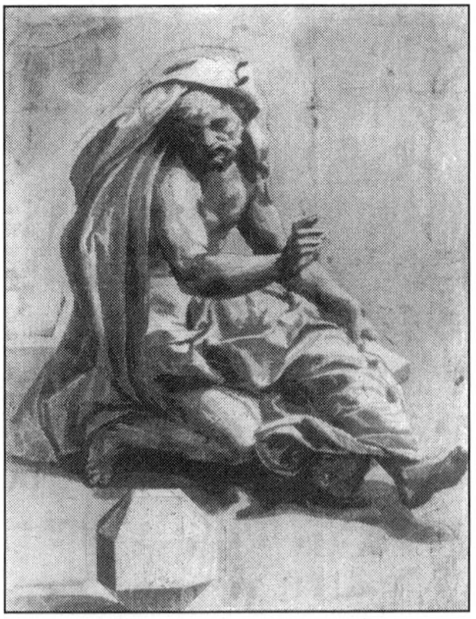

Fig. 25.3 - Ugo Panico da Carpi: Archimedes Contemplating a Rhombicuboctahedron

...Except for the fact that the rhombicuboctahedron in the Pacioli portrait combines 8 triangles with 18 *perfect squares*. Such is the case, as well, with Leonardo's illustration (Fig. 23.15) in Pacioli's *De divina proportione* (On the Divine Proportion – written in 1498, published in 1509).

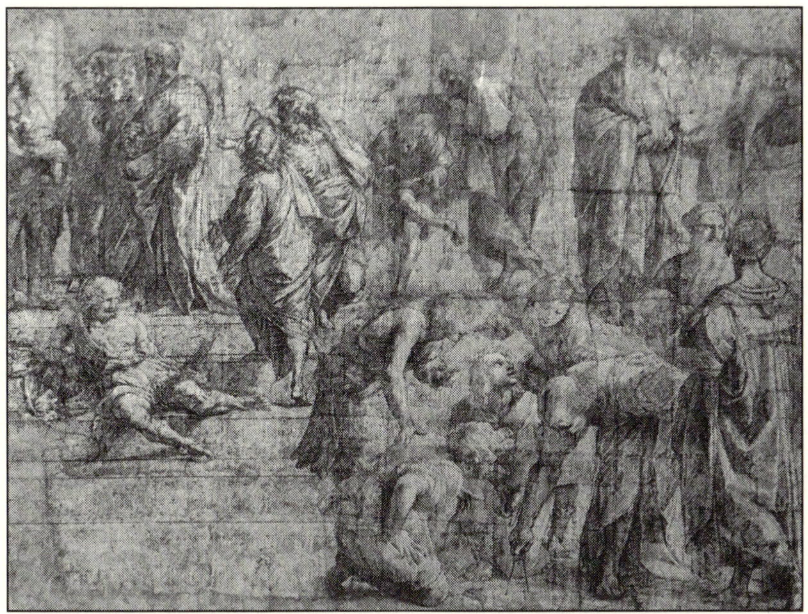

Fig. 25.2 - Raphael: *The School of Athens - Cartone* Right Side

In Raphael's version, however, the sides are *rectangular* rather than square. In his text, Pacioli advises the reader to follow a two-step procedure, first truncating a cube at each side's mid-point to create a truncated cube (or cuboctahedron), and then to truncate this shape to create the rhombicuboctahedron. Leaving aside Leonardo's design, Raphael has followed Pacioli's procedure to the letter, creating a new version of the rhombicuboctahedron, hitherto unseen, with *rectangular* rather than square sides.[3]

As Samuel Y. Edgerton has written: *"It is worth noting that, during the very months Raphael was painting in the Stanza dell Segnetura, Luca Pacioli's Divina Proportione was published, with all its idealized implications concerning the geometry of regular solids."*[4]

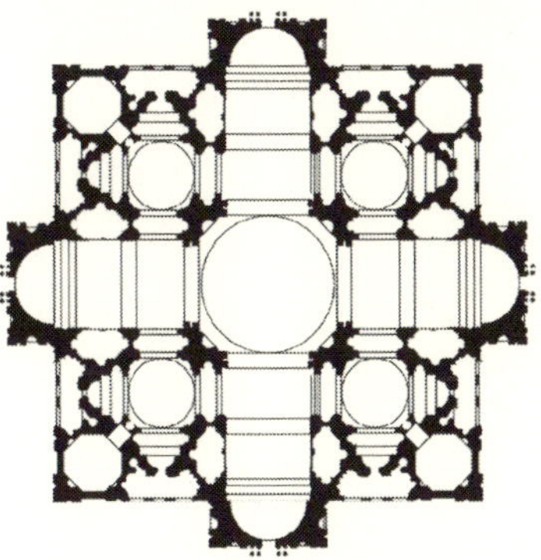

Fig. 25.4 - Bramante: Plan for Basilica of St. Peter

Raphael's drawing was a tribute, it seems, to his friend and mentor Donato Bramante (1444 – 1514), whose features adorn Archimedes. It was the architect Bramante who, just three years previously, had received the commission from Pope Julius II to design *the new* Basilica of St. Peter. Combining a Byzantine floor plan with an Antique elevation, Bramante envisioned a large square structure divided by a Greek cross, so its four long barrel vaults would extend in each direction from a huge central dome. In the corners, four lesser chapels would be topped by their own smaller domes.

Following Brunelleschi's great achievement in Florence, Bramante conceived the supports of St. Peter's dome in Rome as essentially *octagonal*. This explains why Archimedes/Bramante is contemplating a rhombicuboctahedron, since this particular polygon, when cut along its axis of symmetry, *yields a perfect octagon*. Bramante the architect and Raphael the artist were exploring the geometrical and structural possibilities of this unique Archimedean Solid.

In the final version of *The School of Athens*, this rendering of Archimedes does not appear, and Bramante's features come to adorn Euclid instead.

However, Bramante's plans for the as-yet unrealized basilica came to influence Raphael profoundly, since the architecture of *The School of Athens* is based on a large square (or octagonal) structure divided by a Greek Cross. The painting's central perspective provides us with a breath-taking view down the length of the two barrel vaults, and a brief glimpse into the huge dome spanning their breadth. In the foreground of his fresco, the floor before the steps uses inlaid squares. But in the background, the *pavimento* beneath the barrel vaults uses squares *surrounded by octagons* (Fig. 25.5).

That same pattern, of squares surrounded by octagons, appears previously in the *pavimente* of two of Raphael's masters: Perugino's *Annunciation Ranieri* (1497) and Pinturicchio's *Annunciation* (1501) in the church of Santa Maria Maggiore. Perhaps, while working in Rome, Raphael wanted to render homage to his Perugian masters. But the octagon in the *pavimentazione* suggests that the *quadrature* or turned square played a key role in Raphael's geometry, particularly the architecture.

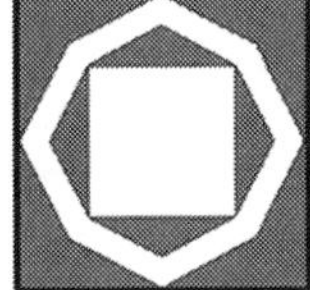

Fig. 25.5 Square-Octagon *Pavimento*

Meanwhile, the actual floor of the Stanza della Segnatura (Fig. 25.6) plays with more patterns, since its *cosmatesque* design reproduces the Byzantine *quincunx* – four semi-circular *eyelets* surrounding a main circle or *guilloche*. As with the Byzantine *quincunx,* the Renaissance *cosmatesque* creates a mosaic of five circles on the floor which reflect the five domes on the ceiling above it, as a result of the Greek Cross floor plan.

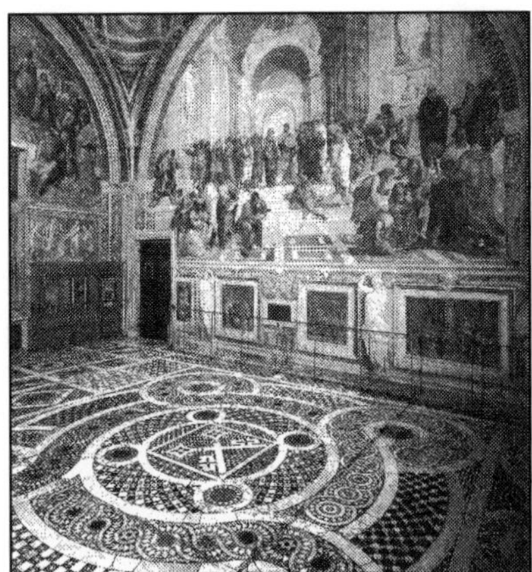

Fig. 25.6 - Cosmatesque Floor Design

II. The Harmonic Division of Pictorial Space

When Raphael conceived the basic design for his fresco (Fig. 25.7), he began with the existing space on the east wall of the Segnatura: a large circle cut along its lower sixth, forming a grand arch decorated with a frieze of meanders. By drawing the horizontal diameter (the dotted line D) through the centre of this bounding circle, and bisecting it to obtain the main vertical (½), he established the lowest of the three points on our diagram. From this point, the horizontal line D establishes the baseline for the architectural facade. It also divides the friezes of figures into two distinct planes.

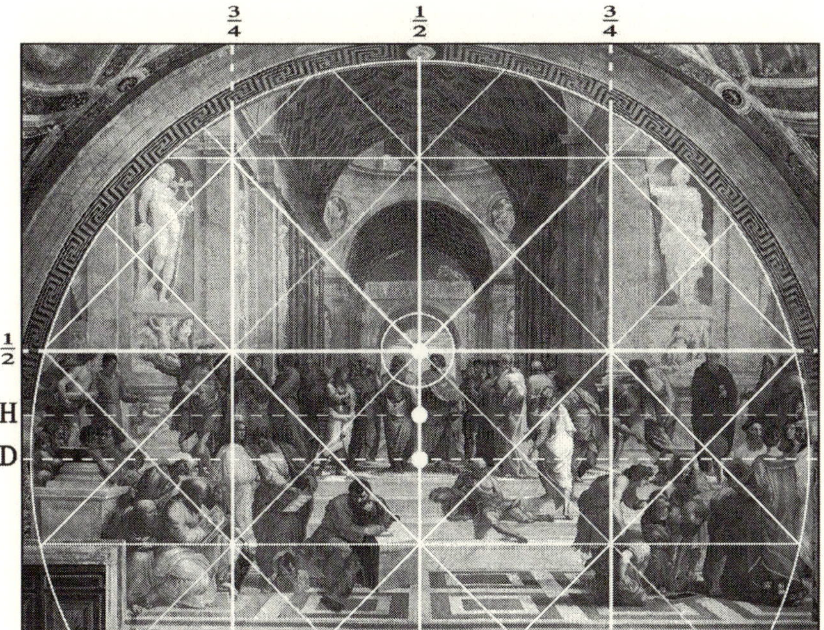

Fig. 25.7 - The Harmonic Division of the Pictorial Space

Moving up along the main vertical, he drew another horizontal (½) at the point which cut the vertical space of the painting directly in half. A small circle drawn around this point marked the round arch of the gate in the background. Indeed, this point became the centre of his flat pictorial space, cutting it in half in both directions.

But, it was not the centre of his perspectival space. By creating a third point, roughly halfway between the first two, Raphael established his vanishing point, cutting it with the dotted horizon line (H). We note that, unlike Leonardo in *The Last Supper*, here the vanishing point does *not* coincide with the centre point of the flat pictorial space.

Returning to that centre point, we note that it divides the flat pictorial space, in both directions, into the *diapason* halves. By cutting the ½ horizontal into four equal parts, he also established the quarters (¾). We note that the vertical edges of the facade, where they turn to recede into the transepts, run exactly along the *diatessaron* quarters. Through the architecture, Raphael has divided his pictorial space horizontally so half of it (the two outer quarters of the facade) are flush with the picture plane, and half of it (the inner two quarters of the receding transepts) run perspectively into the distance. Likewise, the bottom half of the painting is taken up by the flat frieze of figures, while the top half is given over to the Temple of Philosophy with its perspectival depths.

By expanding the squares created by the halves and quarters, a large *ad quadratum* grid results. Following the Antique method for dividing up a frieze of figures, Raphael may have drawn 45° diagonals within the square grid to group his figures. The left foreground group around Pythagoras accords well with this armature, since the youth in white stands at the apex of the resulting triangle, while the books held by the kneeling Pythagoras and turning Parmenides align perfectly with the 45° diagonals (as does the receding top surface of Heraclitus' writing block, while its side straddles the main vertical).

In the right half of the fresco, the line of movement between Diogenes sprawled on the steps and the two dynamic figures above him also follows a 45° diagonal. But the grouping around Euclid seems to follow a different angle, like a scalene triangle.

The addition of the diagonals invites us to investigate the use of the *quadrature* in the development of the composition – that same *quadrature* suggested by the octagons in the *pavimentazione* (Fig. 25.8). When we begin from the outermost edges and converge to the centre point, inscribing squares within turned squares, we discover that certain key lines in the architecture fall upon those measures. The most important is the foremost corners of the first transept which, as we have already noted, run exactly along the *diatessaron* quarters. But now we can see that the first transept *ends* at the next smaller square (inscribed in the turned square) that measures out the *eighths* of the pictorial space.

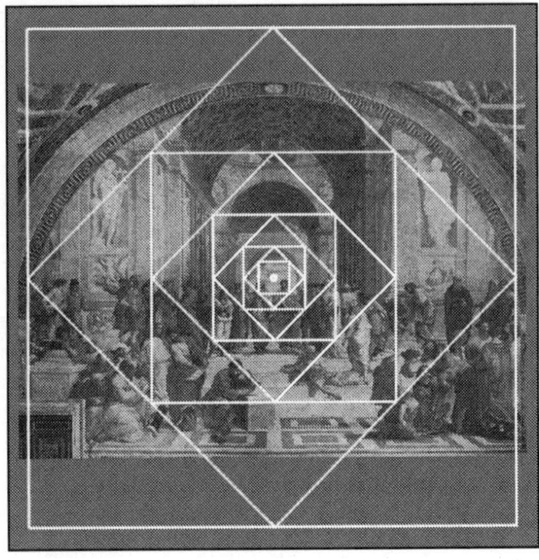

Fig. 25.8 - Quadrature Division of Pictorial Space

Certainly, the division of the flat pictorial space into *diapason* halves and *diatessaron* quarters shows that Raphael was indeed conscious of the classical harmonies inscribed on Pythagoras' tablet.

But the question remains – did he also search out those harmonic proportions in the perspective?

III. Reconstructing the Floor Plan

Our quest for understanding Raphael's floor plan and perspective begins with the *cartone,* and the penetrating analysis by Konrad Oberhuber (former Director of the Albertina) in his *Polarität und Synthese in Raphaels 'Schule von Athen'* (Polarity and Synthesis in Raphael's School of Athens – 1983). In the bottom left section of the *cartone*, where the kneeling Pythagoras appears, Oberhuber was able to re-construct the traces of an architectural design (Fig. 25.9), showing the ground plan of one side of the transept leading to the round space for the dome. Three niches and their accompanying columns are carefully measured out to form one wall of the transept.[5]

A close inspection of the niches and their columns reveals that they are constructed according to a module. Taking this as my starting point, I have used Raphael's niche and columns as a basic building block to reconstruct the entire

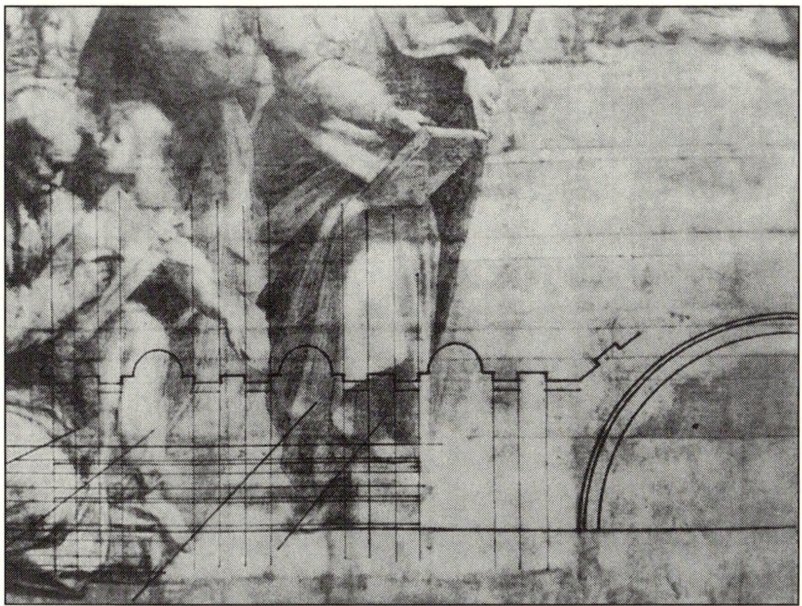

Fig. 25.9 - Oberhuber's Reconstruction of the Architectural Design

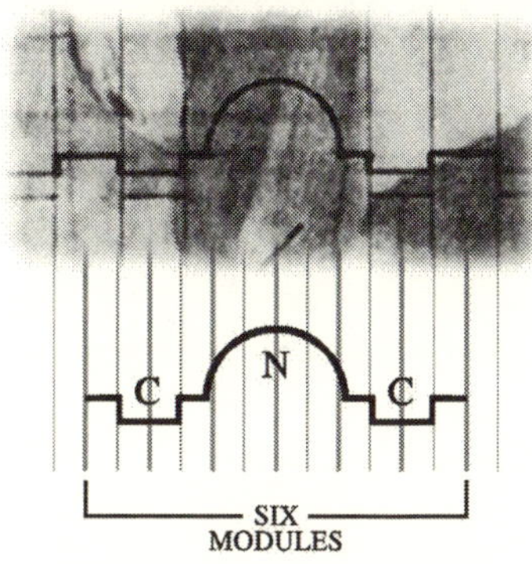

Fig. 25.10 - Module Division of Niche

temple. A close look at Raphael's diagram shows (Fig. 25.10) that each column (C) is 1 module wide, each niche (N) is 2 modules wide (not marked in Raphael's diagram), and each of these is separated by a space of half a module. To construct my building block, I have begun with the half space, to arrive at a total of six modules: 2 modules for the niche (N), 2 modules for the two columns (C), and 2 modules for the four half-spaces between them. This measure is exactly equivalent to Raphael's, but simplifies the procedure for laying one building block next to the other.

Following the lay out in Raphael's fresco, the entire temple has been reconstructed (Fig. 25.11, over). Each transept, when measured from the front column to the back column, is 18 modules long and 12 modules wide. The area under the dome forms a square 18 modules across. The foreground space from the transept's first pillar to the front edge of the floor tiles (i.e. to the picture plane) makes another 18 modules, divided as follows:

- From the transept's first pillar to the facade (i.e. to the forward niches with Apollo and Athena, called *avant-corps*): 6 modules
- The upper row of octagonal floor tiles: 4 modules
- The steps: 4 modules
- The lower row of square floor tiles: 4 modules

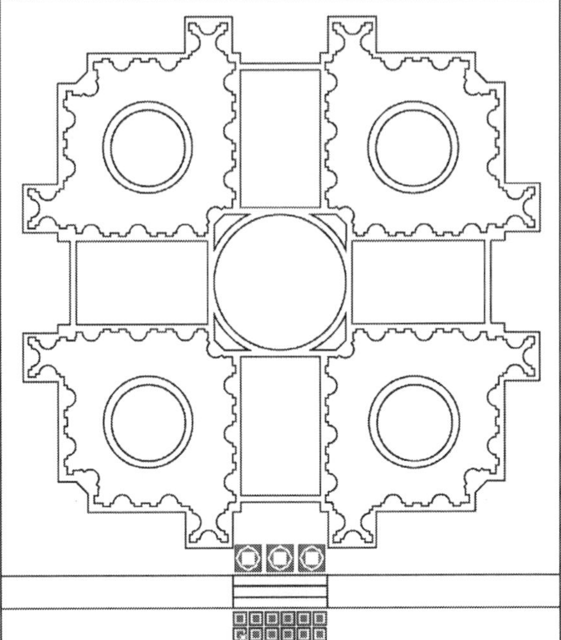

Fig. 25.11 - Reconstruction of the Temple
Floor Plan Based on the Niche Modules

IV. Multiple Perspectives

Using a floor plan similar to this, Raphael's studio would have worked out the entire perspective of the fresco (Vasari suggests that Bramante was, in fact, responsible for the perspective construction). But, *which* method was used?

In *The Science of Art*, Martin Kemp reviews the important contributions made to perspective by Brunelleschi, Alberti, Piero della Francesca and Leonardo da Vinci. When he arrives at Raphael, he admits to being somewhat perplexed:

"Virtually all the new methods were either taken up or invented in the studio of one artist, Raphael Santi... Raphael does not seem to have contributed to the optical and geometrical bases of painters' perspective, whereas he undoubtedly showed how its potential could be developed in an almost bewildering variety of ways... By the age of twenty-one, Raphael had achieved an impressive mastery of the orthodox description of architectural forms in space."[6]

It is known that Raphael's father, the painter Giovanni Santi, was commissioned by the Confraternity of Corpus Domini in c. 1440 to aid Piero della Francesca with the design of an altarpiece.[7] It is probable that Giovanni learned Piero's perspective construction at this time and passed it on to

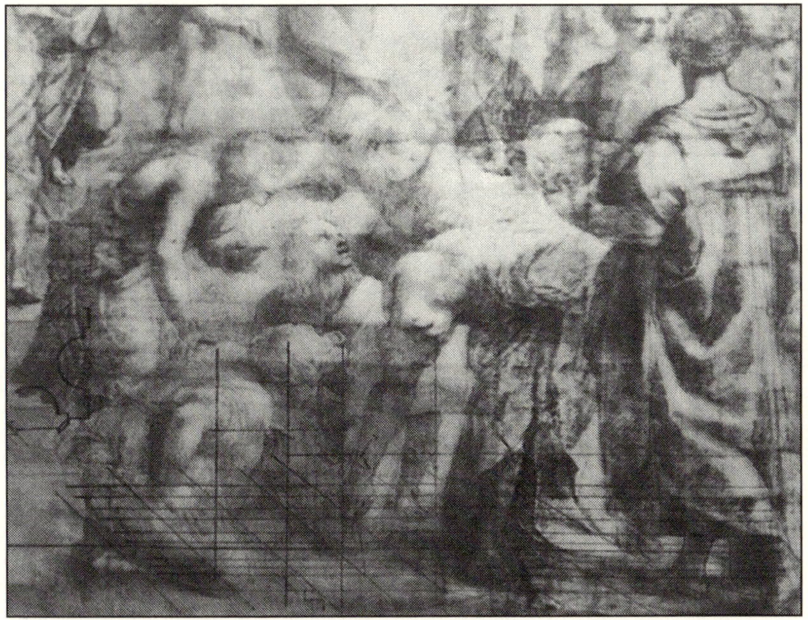

Fig. 25.12 - Oberhuber's Reconstruction of the Perspective Construction

Raphael or to his chief studio assistant, Evangelista, before Giovanni died in 1494. In order to draw Heraclitus' block, *only* Piero's method could have been used, since none of its sides are flush with the picture plane (Fig. 25.13).

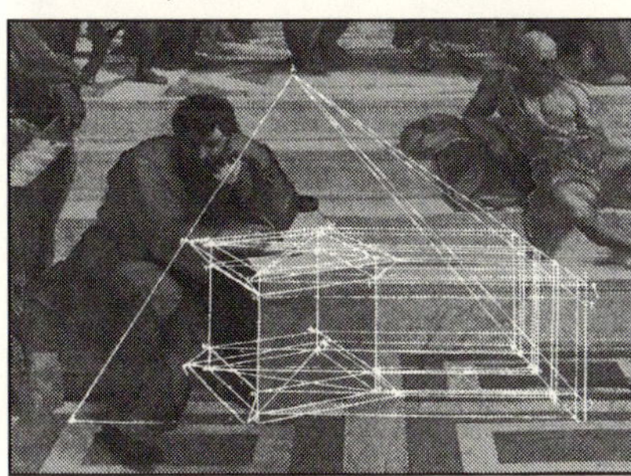

Fig. 25.13 - The Turned Block of Heraclitus

Indeed, when we superimpose Piero's own perspective construction for a turned block on Raphael's block of Heraclitus, we find an almost perfect match. Only the top surface has been re-oriented.

But, Oberhuber found faint traces of a drawing on the bottom right of the *cartone*, this time related to the perspective construction of the steps[8] (Fig. 25.12). Although the construction is not complete, it clearly follows Alberti's *costruzione legittima*. Most likely, the perspective for the foreground floor and the background ceiling of the transepts was worked out with the distance point method.

However, Raphael also had knowledge of the geometrical construction (Fig. 22.23) used in his early *Annunciation Predella*, and he *could have* applied this method for the receding transepts. My own attempts to reconstruct the transept ceiling using this geometrical method, however, had only limited success.

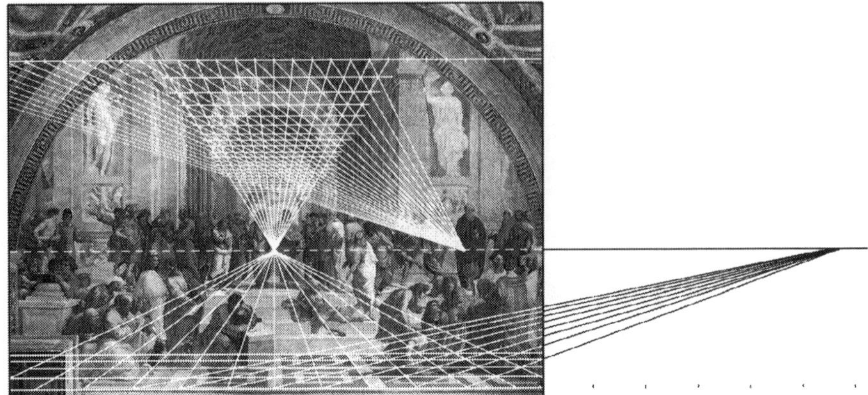

Fig. 25.14 - The Two Distance Points Used in the *Construzione Legittima*

When we apply Alberti's *costruzione legittima* to the architecture, following the transversals to their respective distance points, we make a most startling discovery: *two different distance points were used*, one for the floor tiles in the foreground, and one for the receding transepts in the background (Fig. 25.14).

The foreground floor tiles create transversals that converge to a distance point far outside the painting. Using the module as our measure, we arrive at a distance point of 11.8 modules from the central vanishing point. Given that the fresco is 5 m high and 7.7 m wide, this means that the proper viewing distance from the picture plane is roughly 9 m away – a distance made impossible by the stanza's small size. The proper viewing point is also 4 m off the ground – meaning that the fresco was never intended to be viewed by 'a man standing in one place'.

Meanwhile, the background transepts create transversals that converge to a distance point *within* the painting itself. Indeed, the philosopher in a long magenta cloak, standing apart from the others (usually identified as Plotinus) is mysteriously *pointing* to this distance point. Using the module as our measure, this point stands 3.5 modules from the central vanishing point. If we imagine the picture plane as flush with the first columns of the transept, then the proper viewing point would be 2.7 m.

We have already noted how Raphael divided his pictorial space horizontally into four quarters, with the flat facade taking up the two outer quarters, and the receding transepts occupying the two quarters in the middle. We can now see that the inner two quarters possess *their own* perspective, different from the perspective of the outer two quarters.

This affects our experience of space. The foreground area appears flat and massive because we are, in fact, standing *too close* to view it properly. But when we turn our gaze to the receding transepts, our vision flies through that narrow space, since the closer viewing point *draws us in*. The two perspectives share the same vanishing point and horizon line; it is only the difference in *distance points* which alters our experience of space.

To create the perspective, the floor plan would have been divided at the first columns of the transept. Then, as we can see in Fig. 25.15, the plan of

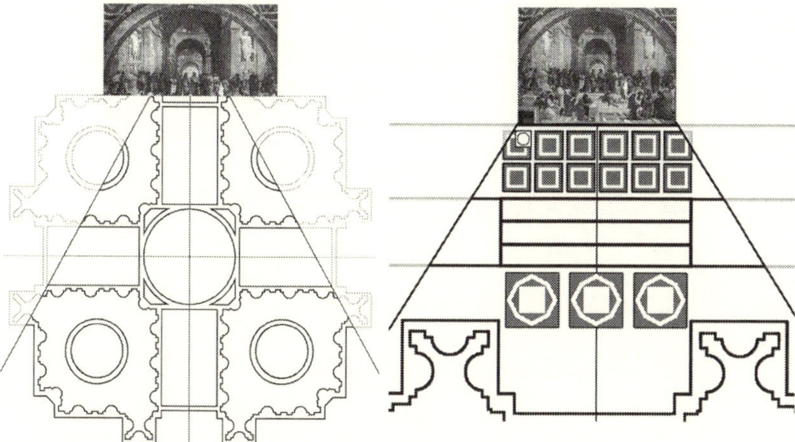

Fig. 25.15 - The Two Floor Plans Necessary for the Perspective Constructions

the foreground space (18 modules - right) would have been placed flush to the bottom of the picture plane, to work out the perspective of the square *pavimentazione*, the steps, the large octagonal *pavimentazione*, and the two forward niches (*avant-corps*). Meanwhile, the plan of the background space (54 modules - left) would have been placed flush to the bottom of the first transept, to work out the perspective of the barrel vaults and receding columns. The plans are of different size, but based on the same module and proportion.

V. The Harmony of Perspective

How did Raphael arrive at the placement of his vanishing point? In Richard Fichtner's *Die verborgene Geometrie in Raffaels 'Schule von Athen'* (The Hidden Geometry in Raphael's School of Athens – 1984), one plausible solution is offered.[9] According to Fichtner, Raphael used the width of the transept (marked as the *diatessaron* quarters in our first diagram) to create a square on his pictorial surface. By arcing the sides of the square to the point where they crossed, Raphael established his vanishing point. This procedure forms an inverted equilateral triangle (like my Trimorphic Matrix Subocularis, but upside down), and its sides follow exactly the perspectival diagonal of the receding architraves. According to Fichtner, a smaller square (with dotted lines in our diagram) may be drawn using the horizon line as its base. This smaller square establishes the width and height of the first transept. Furthermore, a horizontal line drawn through the centre of these squares establishes the height of the second transept.

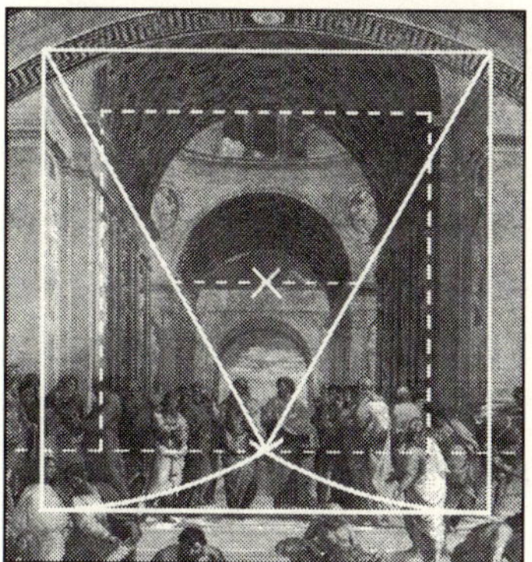

Fig. 25.16 - Fichtner's Placement of the Vanishing Point

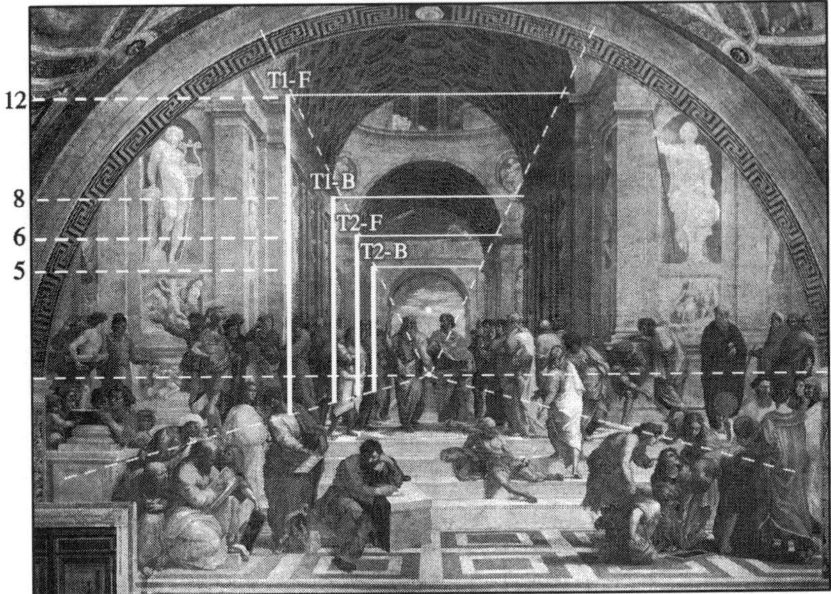

Fig. 25.17 - The Harmonic Proportions of Perspective in the Transepts

More interesting still, Fichtner was able to uncover the harmonic proportions of Raphael's perspective[10] (Fig. 25.17). On either side of the central dome are two transepts, the first one (T1) being closer to us and the second one (T2) being farther away. Each is covered by a barrel vault with a coffered ceiling (the ceiling's hexagon-and-lozenge design is inspired by the Basilica Maxentius, a Roman ruin). Beginning with the first transept (T1), we may designate its front column (F) as T1-F and its back column (B) as T1-B. Likewise with the second transept, we may designate its front column (F) as T2-F and its back column (B) as T2-B. Measuring their respective heights, we discover that T1-F is 12 units high, T1-B is 8 units, T2-F is 6 and T2-B is 5 (actually 4.8).

By using the same method as Leonardo, Raphael was able to create harmonic proportions in his perspective. As we can see in Fig. 25.18, the series 12, 8, 6 and 5 (4.8) can be divided by 24, to create the series 1/2, 1/3, 1/4, 1/5. The top numerator expresses the distance of the picture plane from the eye, which is a constant of 1. The bottom denominator expresses the distance of the respective columns from the eye, which increases arithmetically as 2, 3, 4 and 5.

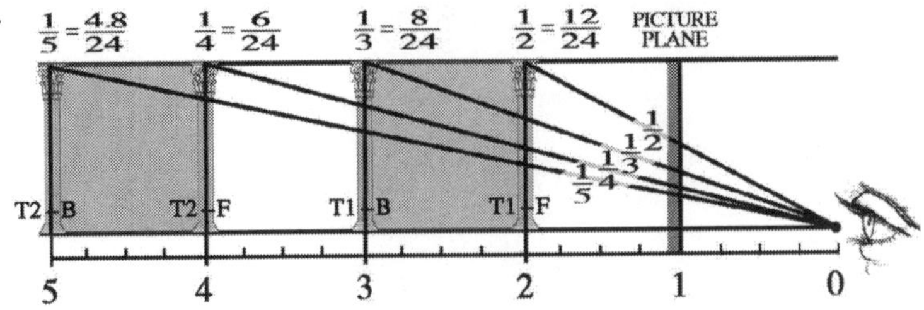

Fig. 25.18 - The Construction of Harmonic Proportion

As a result, T1-F expresses the half *diapason*, T1-B the thirds *diapente,* and T2-F the quarters *diatessaron* in relation to the picture plane. But, more than that, these columns also have harmonic relationships to each other, since T1-B stands in a relation of 8:12 to T1-F, which is the 3:4 *diatessaron.* Likewise, T2-F stands in a relation of 6:12 to T1-F, which is the 1:2 *diapason*, and in a relation of 6:8 to T1-B, which is the 3:4 *diatessaron.*

Because of the constant proportions in his architecture, Raphael was able to achieve Pythagorean-Platonic harmonies in his perspective.

Another interesting feature of Raphael's architecture occurs in the arches, which bear a remarkable geometrical relationship to each other. As we can see in Fig. 25.19, the three receding arches form three circles, which we may designate as large, medium and small. The centre of the small circle, as we already remarked in Fig. 25.7, lies exactly at the centre of pictorial space, divided at the *diapason* halves. However, this point also lies on the circumference of the medium circle, describing the arch of T2-F. But, the centre of the medium circle lies on the circumference of the large circle, which describes the arch of T1-F. The centre of the medium circle also sets the limit to the height of the triumphal arch in the background. Finally, the centre of the large circle describes the upper limit of the round barrel vault ending the first transept.

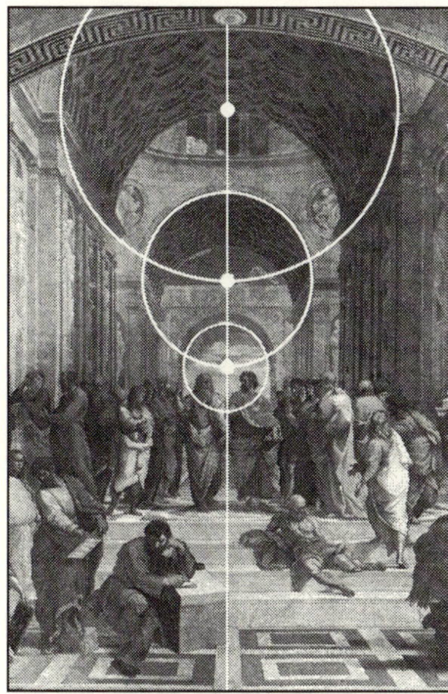

Fig. 25.19 - Harmonic Proportion of the Circle Measures

When we measure the diameter of each circle, we discover that they stand, from largest to smallest, in a harmonic relationship of 1:2:4. This proportion expresses the Geometric Mean, where $B = \sqrt{(AC)}$. Since $A = 1$ and $C = 4$, then $B = \sqrt{(1x4)} = \sqrt{4} = 2$. The medium circle, with a diameter of 2, creates a harmonic relationship between the larger and smaller.

In this case, the small circle is the half *diapason* of the middle, and the middle is the half *diapason* of the larger, meaning that the small circle is also the quarter *diatessaron* of the larger. How Raphael arrived at this harmonic relationship of circles remains a mystery, but it is another clear case of Pythagorean-Platonic proportion *in perspective.*

VI. The Enigma of Euclid's Tablet

A mere glance at Raphael's fresco reveals that Euclid's tablet (Fig. 25.20, over), on the bottom right of the composition, demands as much attention and consideration as that of Pythagoras. As early as 1879, Herman Hettner had recognized in his *Italienische Studien* that the 6-8-9-12 ciphers on Pythagoras' tablet relate to Pythagorean-Platonic harmonies.[11] As we have seen, these harmonies pervade Raphael's fresco in both its composition and perspective.

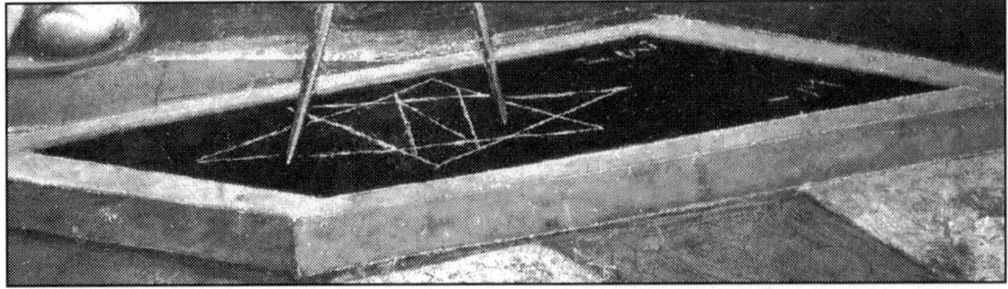

Fig. 25.20 - Euclid's Tablet

What, then, of the message encoded in Euclid's tablet? Despite the fact that art historians have endeavoured for decades to decipher its shapes, no one has yet cracked the enigma.

Indeed, scholars cannot even agree on how to correct the angled perspective to arrive at the original shapes on the tablet. As Fig. 25.21 shows, it remains unclear as to whether the two triangles form a perfectly symmetrical hexagram or some variation on that theme.

Oberhuber (A) decides that the shape must be a perfectly equilateral hexagram, and reads the ciphers as one-half and one-third.[12] Fichtner (D) accepts the equilateral hexagram, but notes that the parallel lines must extend further, to the sides of the triangles.[13] Other scholars, such as Mazzola[14] and Keim[15] (B,E) arrive at two triangles with sides paralleling each other, while Valtieri[16] and Lauenstein[17] (C,F) elongate the hexagram. Only Haas[18] (G) sees the triangles as totally irregular.

In *'La Scuola d'Atene. "Bramante" suggerisce un nuovo metodo per costruire in prospettiva un'architettura armonica'* (The School of Athens: "Bramante" Suggests a New Method of Constructing a Harmonic Architecture in Perspective – 1972), Simonetta Valtieri interprets the shape on Euclid's tablet as an elongated hexagram (C), which she then applies to the architectural perspective (Fig. 25.22). Since the intersecting triangles cut the main vertical at 8, 5, and 4, these measures express, she says, the *diapason* (8), the *diapente* (5) and the *diatessaron* (4).

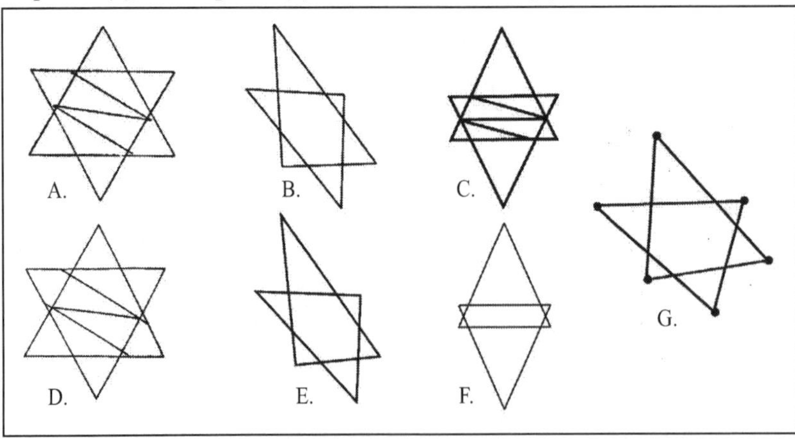

Fig. 25.21 - The Star Hexagram on Euclid's Tablet Interpreted by:

A. Oberhuber B. Mazzola C. Valtieri G. Haas
D. Fichtner E. Keim F. Lauenstein

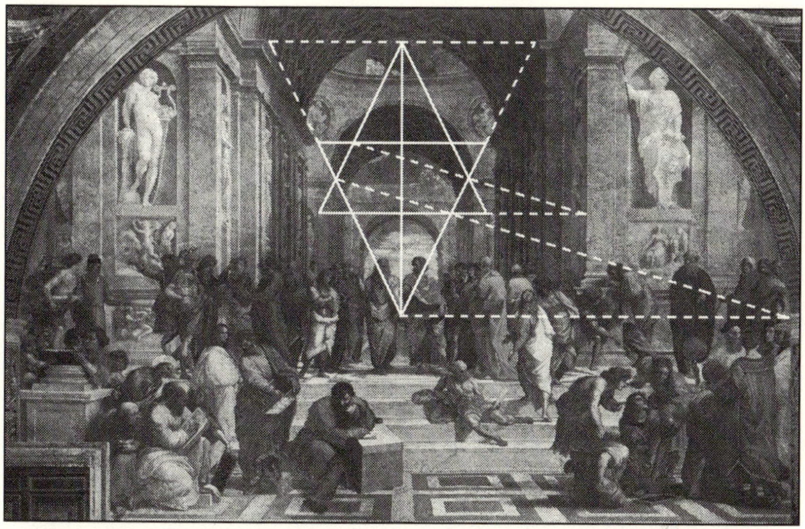

Fig. 25.22 - Valtieri's Application of the Star Hexagram to Raphael's Perspective

After super-imposing her hexagram on the transepts, she is able to show that the arches stand in a harmonious relationship to each other. In further, more complex diagrams, she also demonstrates how the perspective of the entire hall was constructed.[19]

While Oberhuber saw it fit to reproduce parts of Valtieri's research in his authoritative work on Raphael's *cartone,* other authors like Fichtner and Lauenstein roundly criticize her conclusions.[20] Valtieri's results are intriguing, but her starting premise – of an elongated symmetrical hexagram – is questionable. As Fichtner points out, she connects the parallel lines and their diagonal to the intersection points of the triangles, when they clearly extend beyond them (Example D in Fig. 25.21)

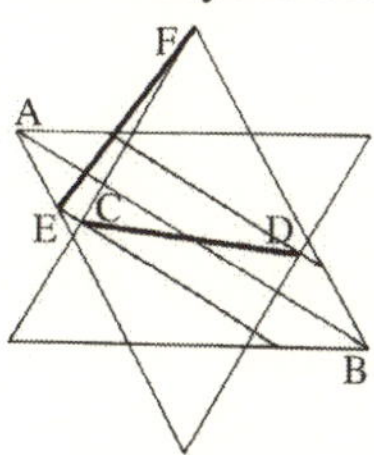

Fig. 25.23

Fichtner becomes the foremost of many scholars who see a geometrical proof in the tablet. Using the Pythagorean theorem, he claims that the shape offers a proof (Fig. 25.23) that EF and CD are the same length.[21] Why he adds EF to the diagram, and thinks it is important to compare its length to CD, remains baffling and inexplicable.

In *Disclosing Horizons: Architecture, Perspective and Redemptive Space*, Nicholas Temple explains the shapes as a demonstration of theorem 47 in Euclid's *Elements*[22] (where, in fact, no star hexagram appears). Temple's explanation, though interesting, requires a six-sided *hexagon*, not the star hexagram drawn on Euclid's tablet.

Finally, in a paper called *Raphael's School of Athens: A Theorem in a Painting?*, Robert Haas reviews for the Journal of Humanist Mathematics most of the known geometrical explanations (Valtieri, Fichtner, Mazzola) and decides that *none* seem plausible. Examining the hexagram, he remarks that *"the figure... is neither a Euclidean nor an Archimedean problem."*[23] Haas concludes with the 'Null Hypothesis' – that there *is no* geometrical problem, and *"...it might simply be misplaced ingenuity to seek an actual theorem on Euclid's slate."*[24]

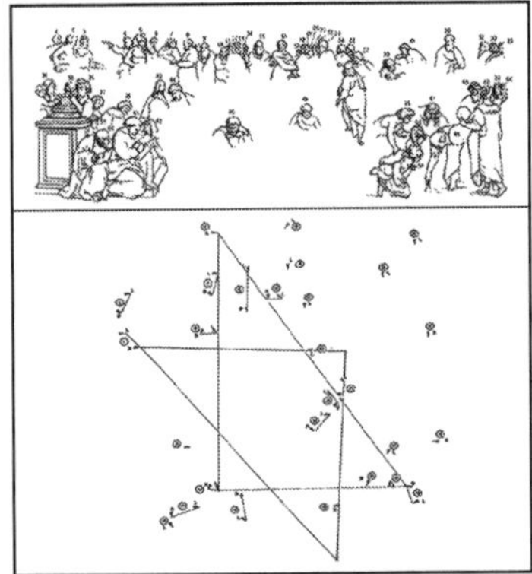

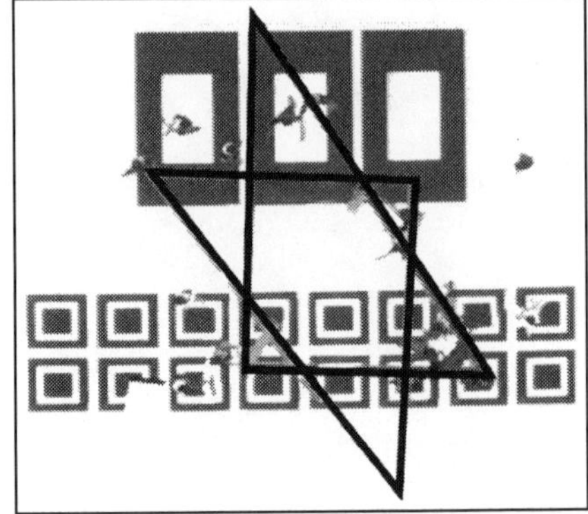

Fig. 25.24 - Mazzola Projection of the Star Hexagram onto the Figures' Foot Placement

I tend to agree with Haas. Had Raphael intended to show a geometrical demonstration, he would have *at least* used regular shapes and straight lines – but the shapes are clearly irregular, and the lines waver unsteadily, making an accurate geometric demonstration impossible.

Another curious interpretation of Euclid's tablet was offered by Guerino Mazzola in *Rasterbild - Bildraster: Anwendung der Graphischen Datenverarbeitung zur geometrischen Analyse eines Meisterwerks der Renaissance; Raffaels 'Schule von Athen'* (Rasterized Image – Image Rasterized: An Application of Graphic Data Processing to the Geometric Analysis of a Renaissance Masterpiece; Raphael's 'School of Athens' – 1987). Using the latest developments in CAD (a Computer Aided Design which, by today's standards, seems primitive), Mazzola and his team of I.T. specialists map out the figures and architecture, creating a computer model which can be viewed from any angle. They also correct the perspectival view of the hexagram, so that it appears as two intersecting, right-angle triangles with all sides parallel each other (Example B in Fig. 25.21).

After numbering all fifty-two figures in the fresco, Mazzola maps out their foot placement (*Fußpunkte*), and compares their various alignments to the hexagram (Fig. 25.24). He claims that specific figures, especially those in white or yellow clothing, appear at significant points.[25] Surprisingly, these key figures do *not* include Plato, Aristotle, Pythagoras or Euclid. It seems rather unlikely that Raphael would have hidden the hexagonal schema in a view of the figures that can only be seen from above, and is otherwise undetectable from the painting's perspectival view.

The final interpretation to be considered here comes from Frank Keim in his *Raffaels Astronomische Tafel entschlüsselt: Kopernikanisches Weltsystem und Jupitermonde in Raffaels Schule von Athen* (Raphael's Astronomical Tablet Deciphered: The Copernican Cosmos and Jupiter's Moon in Raphael's School of Athens' – 2013). For Keim, the tablet is actually a map of the heavens (Fig. 25.25), based on the *Commentariolus* (Little Commentary) that Copernicus distributed to friends (presumably around the time of Raphael's fresco), before publishing *De revolutionibus orbium coelestium* (On the Revolutions of the Heavenly Spheres) in 1543 – the book which announced his revolutionary *heliocentric* view of the cosmos.

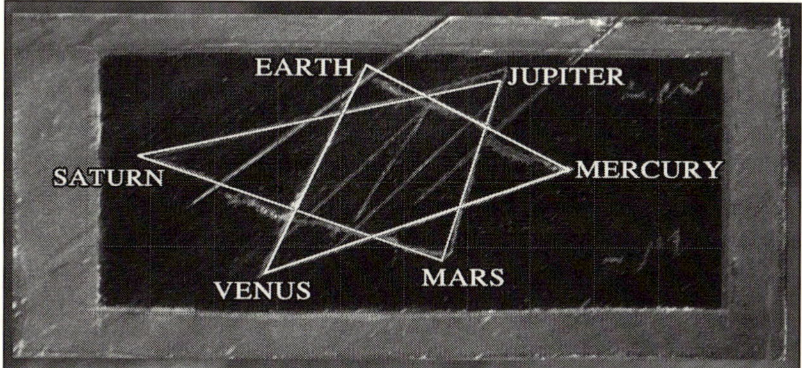

Fig. 25.25 - Keim's Astronomical Interpretation of the Star Hexagram

For Keim, the man with the compass is Copernicus, not Euclid, and he is drawing a circle to show the circular orbits of the planets *around the sun*. The six visible planets in the heavens (the Moon is not included) are correlated to six points on the hexagram. Through a series of measurements and calculations, Keim attempts to show how the lengths of the sides of the triangles correspond to the distances of the planets in the heavens. Thus Venus, for example, is 7 units from the Earth, and 9 units from Mercury – a measure also stated by Copernicus.

What is more, these distances correspond to the 3:4 *diatessaron* ratio, while the distances of Mars to Jupiter, and Mars to Saturn, (100:200) form the 1:2 *diapason*. Thus, the planets are arranged harmonically, and there is a direct correlation between the planetary distances in Euclid's tablet and the harmonies recorded in Pythagoras' tablet.[26]

To support his thesis, Keim calls upon the work of Conrad Doose and Hajo Lauenstein, who were the first to interpret the ciphers at the top of Euclid's tablet (or bottom – depending on how you view it) as harmonic ratios. For all intents and purposes, these ciphers appear as 3 over 1 on the left, and a mirror version of the same on the right (Fig. 25.26).

But, according to Doose and Lauenstein, the 1 and 3 are to be read as the letters I (Iota) and M (Mu), which are the 9th and 12th letters of the Greek alphabet, thus forming the 9:12 ratio which is the 3:4 *diatessaron*. Furthermore, the ciphers on the top right appear as I (Iota) and S (Sigma), which are the 9th and 18th letters of the Greek alphabet, thus forming the 9:18 ratio which is the 1:2 *diapason*.[27]

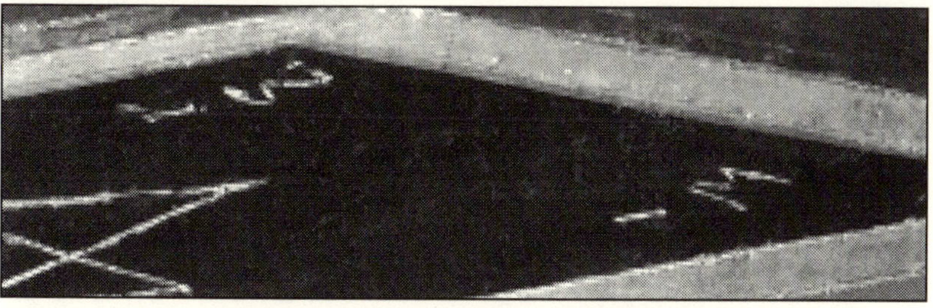

Fig. 25.26 - Ciphers at the Top of Euclid's Tablet

From the foregoing, it seems clear that scholars have gone to great lengths to make some sense of Euclid's tablet – without ever really hitting the mark. Despite their publication in respectable journals, these explanations fly high into the realm of speculation, and seem rather implausible. Such far-reaching hypotheses have nevertheless inspired me to include in this volume an account of my own journey through Raphael's *School of Athens*. Having already provided a more scholarly interpretation (in Ch. 10), I do not hesitate to recount here a more personal and, I dare say, poetic reading of Raphael's timeless masterpiece.

VII. Contemplating the Mysteries of Life & Death

Having meditated upon this image a number of times, I always come away marvelling at its unfathomable layers of mystery. Raphael wanted his fresco to yield up, I believe, a number of possible readings, with different narratives emerging at each level. The scholarly interpretation becomes an allegory of the quest for divine knowledge – of the *Causarum Cognitio* or Knowledge of First Causes. But what if the artist also wove a more personal narrative into the composition?

Although much of Raphael's life remains a mystery, we know that his early years were marked by death and mourning. His mother and sister died in 1491, when Raphael was merely eight year's old, and his father followed soon after, leaving Raphael an orphan at age eleven. With the help of courtiers and patrons, the child prodigy quickly rose to fame and fortune. But, it seems possible that, while painting this fresco, he had some deep presentiment, some dark foreboding that an early death awaited him – a tragedy which did in fact occur in his thirty-seventh year.

Adding this extra dimension to the work, the 'tunnel of light' in the architecture takes on a much more personal meaning: it is not only the source of First Causes, but the great mystery, the heavenly heights into which the artist would one day be drawn against his will.

That artist has depicted himself on the far right of the fresco, gazing at us directly. He has given a prominent place in the composition to his contemporaries, Leonardo (as Plato), Michelangelo (as Heraclitus) and Bramante (as Euclid), while relegating himself, rather humbly, to the outer edges. Yet, a closer inspection reveals that, among the plethora of figures interwoven in the fresco, *only four* stand alone and *gaze outward* at the viewer (Fig. 25.27).

The first is the baby on the far left, at the absolute commencement of the composition. A bit further to the right, almost hiding behind Epicurus (the one with an open book on a pedestal) is the second: a child with fair hair. Further right again is the third: a mysterious youth in white (often identified as Hypatia) standing just above Pythagoras. The fourth, as we have already noted, is Raphael himself at the age of twenty-five. Since we have already established a temporal movement in the composition from left to right, could not these four figures be read as four stages of Raphael's life – from new-born to child to youth to the master artist?

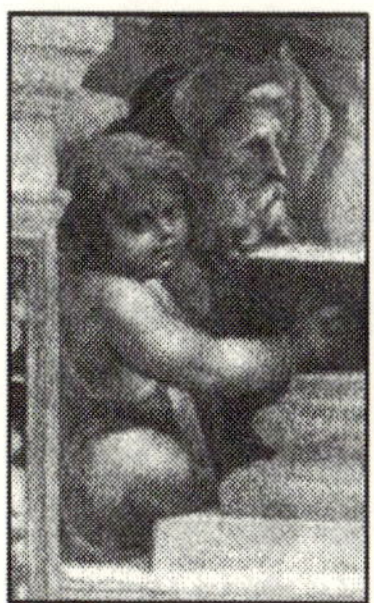
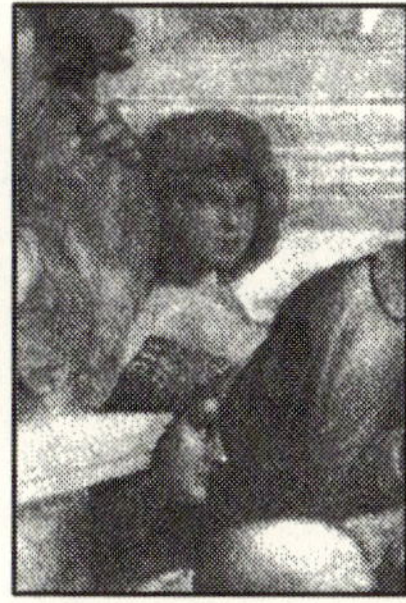
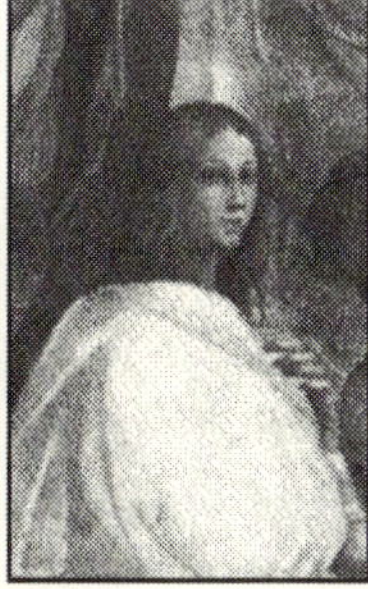
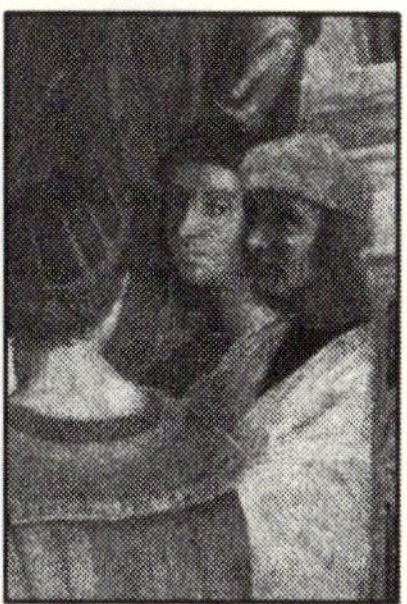

Fig. 25.27 - The Four Figures Gazing at the Viewer

In this way, the personal narrative becomes a contemplation on life itself, and the stages of life we pass through to an inevitable death. As a young man, Raphael has reached for the same high laurels as the elderly Leonardo (thirty-one years his senior) and the mature Michelangelo (his elder by twelve years). Would he reach their honour and wisdom of old age, or perish before attaining such great heights?

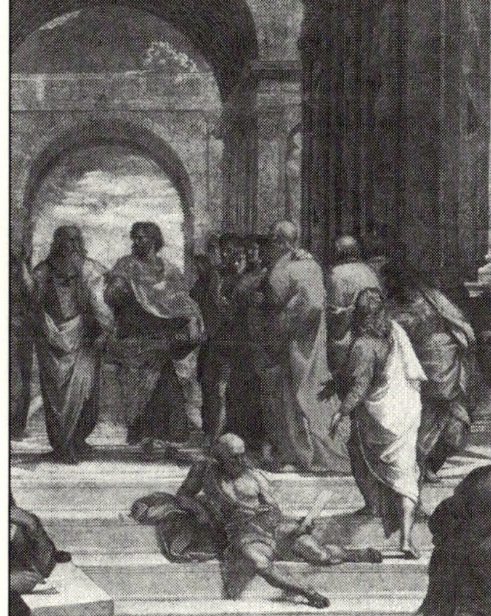

Fig. 25.28 - Diogenes in the Shadow of Two Figures

This invites the question: is there a figure of great age in the fresco, who possibly mirrors Raphael in the later stages of life? A *coup d'oeil* will reveal a great variety of elderly philosophers before the Great Hall. But our eye is inevitably drawn towards the curious old man sprawled upon the steps, while two young men above him gesture dramatically: one turning with open hands, as if to ask the question, *"Why?"* and the other pointing forcefully to the open archway that stands like a gateway to the sacred beyond.

The interpretation of this figural ensemble has puzzled scholars for centuries. The most plausible solution is that the old man is Diogenes, and the action illustrates a famous anecdote by Plutarch, where Alexander the Great came upon the Cynic sprawled in the sun, and offered to grant him whatever his heart most-desired. Diogenes replied, "...That you move away from the sunlight!"

Without a doubt, Raphael has gone to much pains to create a cohesive arrangement of light and shadow in the painting. The left foreground group around Pythagoras stand 'light against dark', while the right foreground group around Euclid stand 'dark against light'. Every figure is carefully sculpted so the light falls from the upper right. But the most conspicuous example occurs with Diogenes, where the gesturing man has clearly *cast a shadow* across the sprawled philosopher.

Scholarly interpretations aside, the ensemble presents an intriguing enigma. In the personal narrative, it may be read as a passionate plea by the young artist striving for the highest laurels: *"What awaits us in this life? Only old age and death? Or is there something more?"* The figure above the old man is clearly pleading with open arms, to beg some important question. The response is given by the second figure, who points to Plato and Aristotle before the divine doorway. Wordlessly, he implies, *"Death is a great mystery, but these two have shown us the way."*

Thus, the whole painting becomes an extended contemplation on the mysteries of life, and what awaits us after death. That Raphael chose Diogenes for the old man becomes singularly important: he is the spiritual ascetic, striving for the light. Alexander, as ruler of the material world, casts a shadow over him: the shadow of materialism and its illusory longings. Only by remaining clearly focussed on the light, may the soul pass unhindered through death's doorway, unrestrained by the body and its passionate attachments to this world.

VIII. The Passage to the Other Side

In this sense, the realms ruled over by Apollo and Athena become spheres of knowledge necessary for the soul's ascent. First, the soul must acquire rational knowledge of the earthly sphere, indicated by Aristotle's outheld hand, which is evenly balanced, echoing the horizon. All the philosophers under his sway sought out a knowledge of Nature, the world of Becoming, the animate region of growth and generation made visible through movement, alteration and transmutation. After that, the soul must navigate the heavenly realm, indicated by Plato's upward-pointing hand. The philosophers swayed by his dialectics sought out knowledge of the higher spheres, the realm of Ideas, an eternal state of Being invisible to the eyes, but circular in motion, geometric in shape, and harmonic in measure.

Beginning at the lower right, we behold Euclid with his compass. Like the divine geometer, indeed, like the great Demiurge, he seeks to establish one fixed point in the cosmos. From this point of reference, all shapes may find their centre, all measures may find their point of origin. Though bound by the horizon, the soul seeks to orient itself within the earthly sphere. For this reason, Euclid's tablet has been interpreted as a plan of earthly perspective, as a schema for the heavenly architecture, or as a map of the entire cosmos. It holds the key for the soul's orientation in the world.

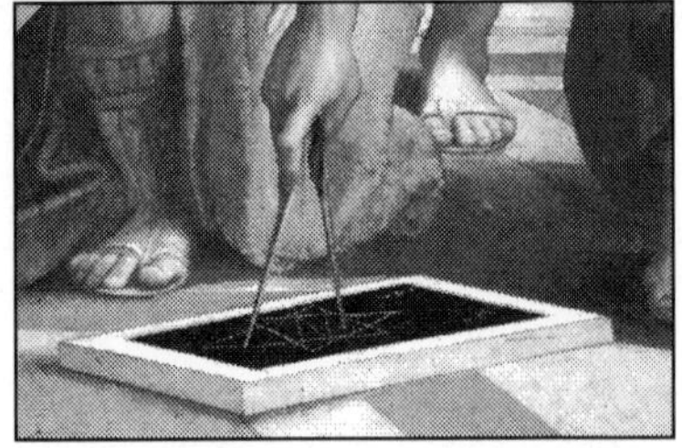

Fig. 25.29 - The Divine Geometer

Moving upward from here, we encounter the geometer and astronomer, each holding their respective spheres. Perhaps the geometer is Strabo and the astronomer is Ptolemy. More importantly, each has sought out a knowledge of the earth and heavens, a map for orienting the soul in its ascent through, first of all, the world with its continents, equatorial zones and axis of rotation; and secondly, the planetary spheres with their order, orbits and epicycles. The goddess Athena gazes down at these two, her line of sight directed upon their terrestrial and celestial spheres that, *in nuce*, orient our awareness in all Space and Time. The soul finds its ladder of vision, a virtual map through the outer and after worlds.

Rising ever higher, it reaches the realm of Ideas, Plato's domain of the *eidé*. No longer guided by sight, having left the body behind, the soul now orients itself with an extra-sensory perception: the mental shapes and conceptual harmonies known only through number and measure. Like a beacon, the divine Creator sends out its signals, at a constant pulse or harmonic frequency, repeating the ciphers 6-8-9-12. Having attuned itself to these harmonies (repeatedly seen and heard in the earthly sphere), the soul now seeks them out intuitively.

We can see this, not only in the kneeling figure of Pythagoras, guided by the sibylline child to record those holy ciphers in his book, but also in the brooding Heraclitus. Though his head is bowed and his eyes are closed, he records, like an amanuensis, the hidden higher harmonies. We know this because Raphael has purposefully altered the perspective of his writing block. Though its front is oriented towards the earthly horizon, its side and upper surface are tilted *higher up*, so their lines converge upon *Apollo Citharoedus* – the patron of art and poetry, the god who holds the eight-stringed harp that eternally emits the 6-8-9-12 harmonies of the higher spheres.

It is also no mere co-incidence that the writing block straddles the painting's main vertical with startling precision. This line, on the flat 2D plane, signifies the *diapason* measure, the division of the whole from one to two. In both the composition and the perspective, the writing block orients the *pensieroso* to the divine source of harmony.

IX. Euclid's Tablet

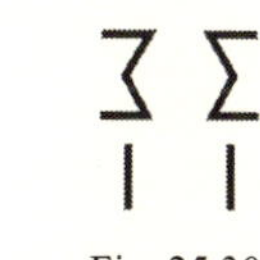
Fig. 25.30

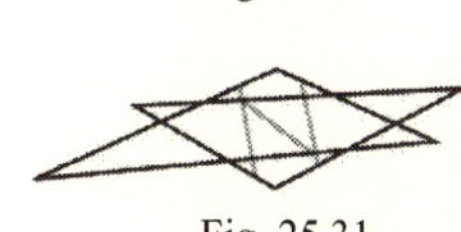
Fig. 25.31

If the Pythagorean harmonies are meant to orient the soul through the invisible afterworld, then what of the designs on Euclid's tablet? Could they not serve a similar purpose? At the top of the slate are the ciphers 3:1, 3:1, appearing twice, but mirroring each other (Fig. 25.30). Below them, two triangles appear, interlocked, also mirroring each other (Fig. 25.31). Could not the 3:1, 3:1 simply be re-iterating, in numerical form, the unique property of triangles? But they also attempt to emphasize their mystery: the divine shape that is three-in-one.

Immediately we think of the Trinity, but that Christian doctrine was developed quite late, primarily by Gregory of Nyssa in the 4th century CE. As early as the 3rd century BCE, Plato thought of the soul as *tri-partite* in nature, and of Divinity *as well*. In Book IV of the *Republic,* Plato says the soul (*psyché*) is composed of three parts, the highest part being like the rational mind (*nous*) centered in the head, the middle part connected to the high-spirited blood rushing through the heart, and the lowest part connected to the appetites and desires located in the belly and loins.

Plato's tri-partite Deity was elucidated most clearly by Plotinus, who described its three levels of being as the One, the Intellect, and the World Soul. As for Aristotle, he basically re-iterated in his *De Anima* Plato's tripartite division of the soul into its rational, sensitive and vegetative parts,

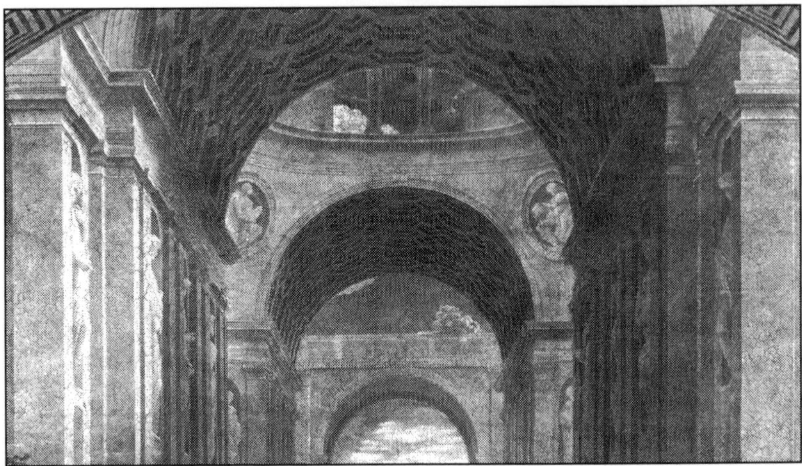

Fig. 25.37 - The Halls of Eternity

while defining Deity in his *Metaphysics* as a tri-partite Being, the *noesis noeseos noesis* or Mind whose first Thought was the Thinking of itself (also called 'Thought thinking itself').

Whether we consult Plato, Aristotle or Plotinus, the ancient world saw both the soul and God as tri-partite in nature. The aim, after death, was to merge the three-part soul with the triune God, leaving the lower parts behind until the higher parts came into one true accord. Or, to use Plotinus' metaphor: until both came to rest *in the same centre*.

In other words, the shapes on Euclid's tablet may simply be read as a kind of *sigil*, as a mnemonic device for the soul to remember in its afterworld ascent. The Deity is tripartite in nature, as is the soul. From above to below, these interlock and fuse, like two triangles in a hexagram, sharing a common centre. This shape mirrors the joining of the macrocosm and the microcosm: 'As Above, So Below'.

Thus it is drawn as a sigil for the polysemous meanings it contains. The triangles need not be accurate, nor the lines perfectly straight. What matters is the magical act *of drawing it*, the initiation into ancient knowledge. Through *anamnesis* – the Platonic path of recollection – the soul wends its way back to the divine Creator. Guided by simple ciphers (6-8-9-12) and the most basic of shapes (two interlocking triangles), it re-unites with the sacred Source of the All.

Entering the heavenly kingdom, the architecture in Raphael's fresco transforms into the Halls of Eternity. From their sculpted niches, the gods gaze out in different directions, each diffusing its own distinct sympathy or sentiment, from Martial strife and division to Venusian love and union. The ceiling's hexagon-and-lozenge shapes echo outward through the vault's *ad triangulum* sacred space.

Of the great dome crowning the Hall of Eternity, we can only see a triple window, like a small eyelet of the three-in-one Deity. The vaults of the Great Hall converge onto a single circular arch that opens to the heavens. Centered on this invisible point, the contemplative soul finds its last point of focus: the heavenly heights, and the clear blissful light of divine awareness.

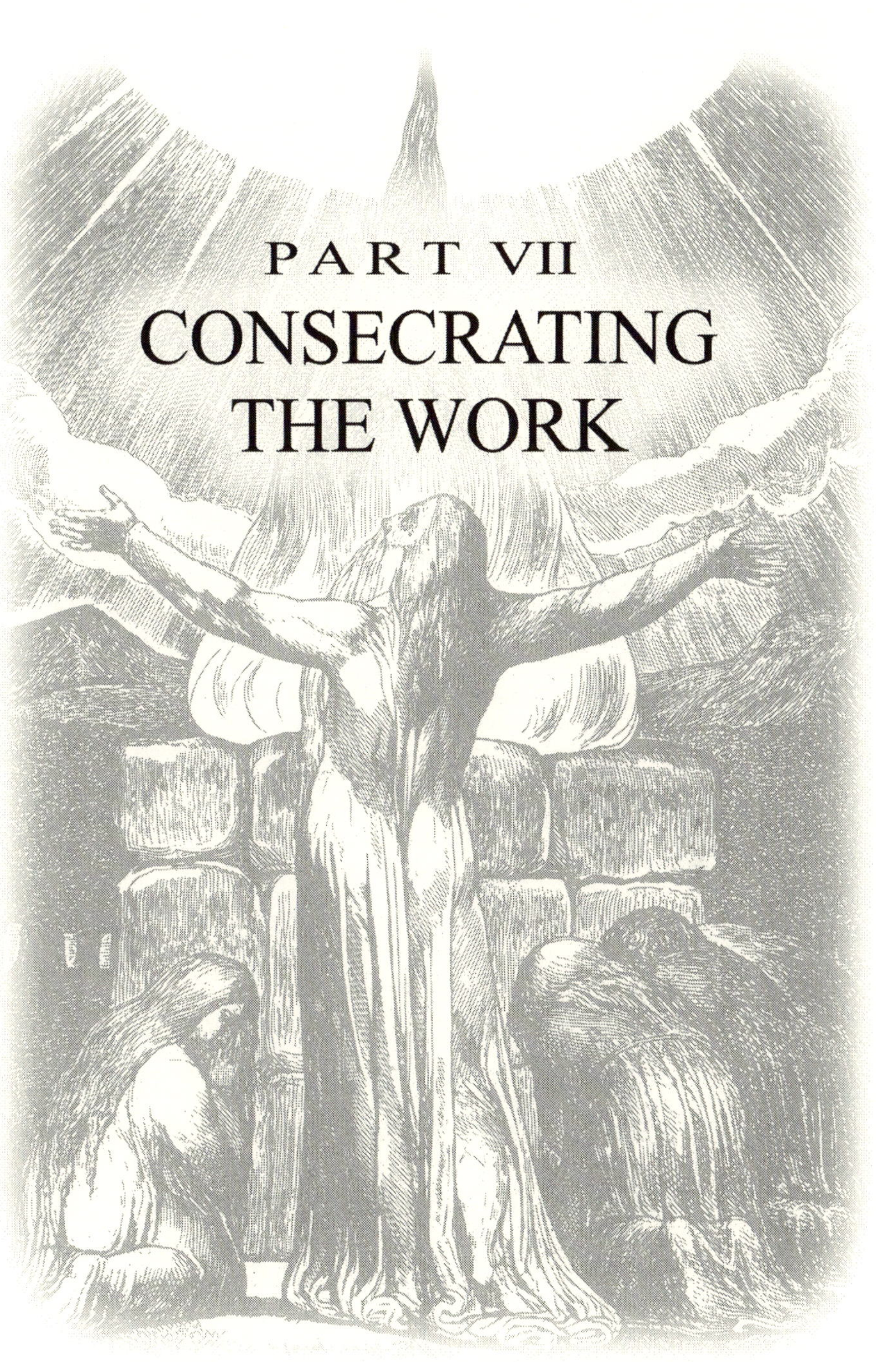

PART VII
CONSECRATING THE WORK

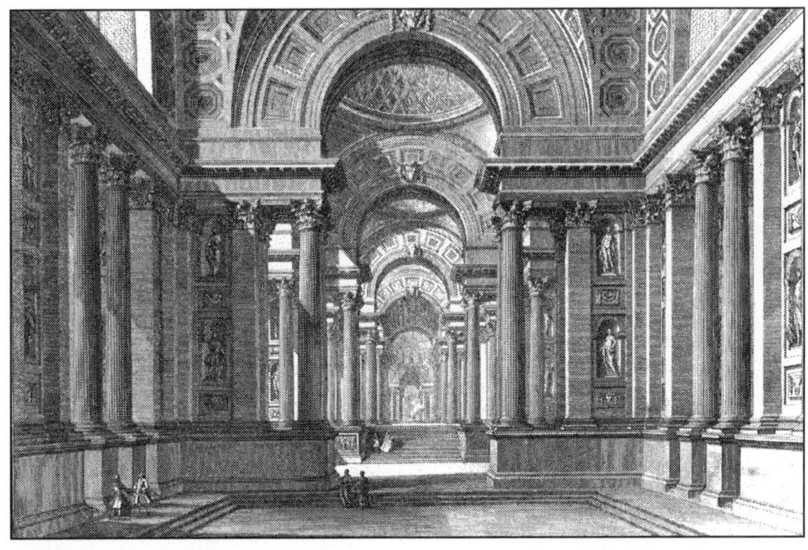

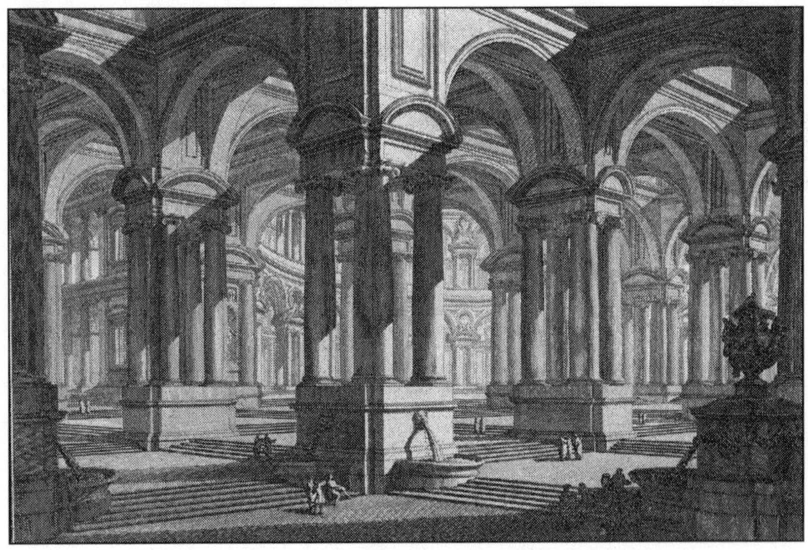

Giovanni Battista Piranesi: *Ancient Temples* c. 1750

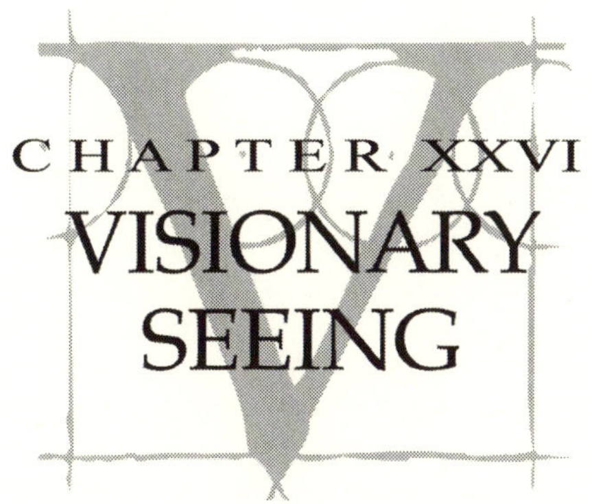

CHAPTER XXVI
VISIONARY SEEING

I. To Share in Divine Sight

In my visions and dreams, I have often entered a vast architectural space which may best be described (using a phrase from Ernst Fuchs) as 'the Hall of the Simultaneousness of All Images'. Like the Hall of Eternity in Raphael's fresco, it has long corridors, well-lit by natural sunlight, and is crowned by a vast dome – its coffered ceiling converging to a circular *oculus* at the summit. Like the interiors of Piranesi, Giger or Escher, it has halls of stairs leading infinitely in all directions, and archways opening like portals to other vast halls with distant passages and corridors. The *Rotunda* of the Pantheon, the *Grande Galerie* of the Louvre, and the *Vestibül* of the Kunsthistorisches Museum – all these places seem to somehow recall this place in my memory, where countless images line the walls, inviting our contemplation.

In this sacred space, the art of all epochs and locales are displayed, almost at random, with little regard for author or chronology. Indeed, our Western obsession for historicity and the cult of the artist seems sorely out of place here, as does our entire manner of *looking at* pictures – admired as *objets d'art* or priceless masterpieces. In this place, the images invite a different kind of seeing, which I can only describe as Visionary.

In Visionary Seeing, the painting becomes a transformational experience for artist and viewer alike. As we enter 'the Hall of the Simultaneousness of All Images', a more timeless experience awaits, an eye-opening transfiguration, as we openly engage the Sacred with our gaze. At first, certain peculiarities in the painting may draw our eye towards it. Regardless of the intended meaning, what matters is the potential for holding our regard and 'entrancing' us with its magic. That enchantment fixes our eye until the painting becomes a doorway or portal: our 'en-trance' into another world.

To fall into a painting... to immerse ourselves in its vision until we become wholly engaged by its life-changing power – this is regarded in our own culture as sheer madness. Yet, Ancient and Eastern cultures have practised a similar form of engagement for centuries, if not millennia. We are thrown, once more, against the age-old division between the Humanist and Hieratic traditions – a division which Visionary art may eventually unite and transcend.

In the Hieratic tradition, a painted image or sculpture may possess beauty and grace, and its artist be regarded with high esteem. But, the image is directed towards a much different end. It is not regarded as 'a work of Art' but *a vehicle* of the Sacred. At times, the artist may innovate and invent a different style, but *the proto-type*, the perfectly proportioned pattern of the original, the authentic and 'first' Divine Image, is always to be venerated and respected. Like the scribe or copyist, who must always respect the original transmission of the Divine Word, the case of the artist is no different: Sacred Codes have been transmitted for generations to ensure the holy purpose of the work.

As this volume reaches its conclusion, I must admit that it has reached greater proportions than originally intended. So many, it seems, are the Sacred Codes forgotten by our culture, that I have gone on at great length in my attempt to revive them. And yet, there remains one more task which neither author nor reader may neglect: the transmission of Sacred Codes for the Consecration of the work.

By investigating ancient methods of meditation and image-creation, I hope to show how our present works of art may be engaged once more in a more holy manner. From ancient Egypt, onward to Greece, India and Tibet, the work was so constructed as to invite a *higher* way of seeing, where the in-dwelling deity opens our eye to Divine Vision. The deity within not only *appears* before our steadfast gaze, but alters our perception inexorably. The greatest benediction, for the seer, is *to be seen* by the deity, and acknowledged as the one who has entered into its holy Presence.

To share in Divine Sight becomes *an act of consecration*. With our tears, we baptize the work, cleansing our vision to behold the true source of vision. The cultures of old possessed this archaic knowledge, and we may revive it, the moment we are prepared to engage the work with a heart open and true, a soul ready for sacrifice, and a mind focussed on the Sacred.

II. The Egyptian Mysteries

A hieroglyphic text inscribed on a doorjamb at the Temple of Edfu warns the Egyptian priests: "*Do not reveal what you see in any secret matter in the sanctuaries.*"[1] And indeed, the Egyptian Mysteries were always guarded in great secrecy, never to be written down. Even pilgrims were warned not to reveal what they saw 'upon pain of death.'

The most explicit account we have of the Egyptian Mystery rites comes to us rather late in that culture's history, from the Roman author Apuleius who describes his initiation into the cult of Isis during the Ptolemaic period. The High Priest warned him that, *"The rites of initiation approximate to a voluntary death from which there is only a precarious hope of resurrection."* Still, through the grace of the goddess Isis, the initiate is *"...in a sense, born again."*[2]

After ten days of fasting, Apuleius was purified in the public baths, sprinkled with holy water and invested with white linen before being brought to the inner recesses of the sanctuary. There, he received the final revelation, which he describes with the words: *"I approached the very gates of death and set one foot on Proserpine's threshold,* [i.e. the Netherworld] *yet was permitted to return, rapt through all the elements. At midnight, I saw the sun shining as if it were noon; I entered the presence of the gods of the underworld and the gods of the upper world, stood near and worshipped them."*[3]

From this fascinating account we may gather that Apuleius was ritually conducted on journey – via the sacraments, the music and sacred imagery – into the afterlife realms (*"I approached the very gates of death"*) which included a 'visionary ascent' through the planetary spheres (*"I... was permitted to return, rapt through all the elements"*) encountering both demonic and angelic beings (*"I entered the presence of the gods of the underworld and the gods of the upper world"*) until he finally gazed upon a sacred statue – a profound experience that constituted, for him, a divine revelation (*"I entered the presence of the gods... stood near and worshipped them."*)

For those who practice Visionary Art today, the art and texts of ancient Egypt are as relevant now as they were three thousand years ago. But – what knowledge remains of their initiatory rites? By what means did the ancient priests access visions of the afterworld? And – even more important for the Visionary artist – by what means did they access the Hieratic style for their art?

The closing strophes of *The Am Duat* describe that sacred text as *"...the excellent guide, the secret writing of the Netherworld, which is not known by any person, save a few."*[4] Whoever they were, and by what means they accessed these visions, their knowledge granted them 'initiation into the Mysteries of the Netherworld.'

This latter expression comes from the *Litany of Re*, where the king is greeted by the gods as one *"...who knows the initiation into the mysteries of the Netherworld, for you are one who has penetrated into their sacredness."*[5] In order to guide their king, the ancient priesthood had also learned 'to enter and leave the Netherworld.' *During their lifetimes*, they had gained a rare glimpse into the Beyond.

Another fascinating text, discovered in 1919, concerns Petosiris, the 4th century BCE High Priest of Thoth at Hermopolis. On his tomb inscription, Petosiris is described as *"The High Priest... who enters into the holy of holies* [i.e., the innermost *naos*, and...] *sees the god in his shrine."*[6] Clearly, Petosiris had achieved a visionary state that gave him a direct experience of the Sacred.

III. Shamanic Wisdom in the Pyramid Texts

One of the more interesting studies written in the last ten years is Jeremy Naydler's *Shamanic Wisdom in the Pyramid Texts*. As a scholar, Naydler notes that traditional Egyptologists feel *"ill at ease"*[7] with mystical interpretations of Egyptian lore. Nevertheless, modern Egyptologists can no longer ignore the abundance of ancient testimony regarding visionary experience. Recent scholars like Erik Hornung and Jan Assmann have also broken that long-standing taboo and written at length about the visionary and mystical nature of Egyptian religion.

In his book on their 'shamanic wisdom,' Naydler performs a detailed analysis of the Egyptian Pyramid Texts – the 228 Spells inscribed on the walls of the Pyramid of Unas (or Wenis) some 4,500 years ago. The Pyramid Texts, it should be noted, are the earliest sacred texts (from *any* culture) that have come down to us intact. Hieroglyphically inscribed on the walls of the Pharaoh's tomb, they describe his Vision Journey through the *Duat* (or Netherworld) where the pharaoh must overcome many demonic foes before ascending to the gods.

The Pyramid Texts date back to the Old Kingdom (c. 2705 – 2180 BCE). During the millennium that followed, fragments of the so-called Coffin Texts emerged during the Middle Kingdom (c. 1987 – 1640 BCE). Inscribed on the sarcophagi of kings, these contain more spells (much like the Pyramid Texts) for the protection of the king as he ascends skyward (like a bird) and is transformed (like a scarab) to become one with the gods. The most important text to emerge during this period, *The Book of the Two Ways*, is the first 'map' of the Netherworld, with a lake of fire dividing the water route from the land route.

More fascinating still are the numerous 'Books of the Dead' from the New Kingdom (c. 1640 – 1530 BCE). Now we enter the Valley of the Kings and find inscribed on the Pharaoh's tombs many essential sacred texts: *The Am Duat, The Book of Gates, The Book of Caverns* and more – all richly illustrated with enigmatic images as yet undeciphered. Typically in these visionary journeys, the initiate joins Re's solar barque on its nocturnal passage through the twelve gates of the Netherworld, overcoming foes at each threshold, before its judgement at Osiris' throne and final deification at sunrise.

Wending our way back to the Pyramid Texts, Naydler's entire thesis is that these books have been interpreted exclusively as 'funerary texts' describing the king's *afterlife* journey. Instead, they should also be viewed as *mystical visions* of the other world, experienced by the king and priesthood *during this life,* to prepare the initiate for the afterworld journey: *"Beyond the funerary rites and cult of the dead, there also existed the possibility of certain individuals entering into a more conscious relationship with the spirit realm, bridging the gap between worlds in an altered state of consciousness."*[8]

Naydler calls the spiritual experience in the Pyramid Texts a state of *"Visionary Mysticism"* which *"...entailed direct experience of the spirit world through states of consciousness in which the soul left the body in an ecstatic flight, to encounter ancestors, gods, and spirits, to experience an inner rebirth."*[9]

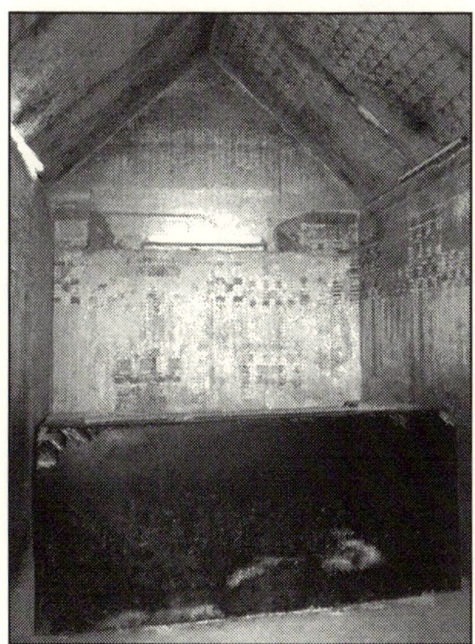

Fig. 26.1 - King Unus' Tomb with the Pyramid Texts Inscribed on the Walls

Although there is no narrative structure *per se* to the Pyramid Texts, the spells are so integrated into the architecture of King Unas' tomb (Fig. 26.1) that they may be read – moving outward from the sarcophagus chamber and antechamber to the entrance corridor – as a visionary sequence describing the king's symbolic death and eventual rebirth involving his ascension and ultimate union with the divine.

To prepare him for this visionary journey, the king is first bathed, anointed, clothed in linen and offered bread and water (compare this to Apuleius' initiation above) – each time accompanied by the sacramental invocation, *"O Osiris, the King, take the Eye of Horus."* (Utt 82 – 171)

In a visionary passage from Spell 93, Horus himself presents his eye to the king with the words, *"I have come and I bring to you Horus' own Eyes; seize them and join them to yourself... Horus has offered them... so that they may guide this king to the firmament, to Horus, to the sky, to the great god."* (Utt 93) And Spell 167 exhorts him, *"O Osiris, the King, open your eyes that you may see with them."* (Utt 167)[10]

Throughout the Pyramid Texts, the king is identified with Osiris, the god of death and resurrection. As Osiris, he acquires the well-known "Wedjat Eye" which Horus lost in his battle with Seth (death) and, once regained, was offered to the dead Osiris to restore him to life. Numerous stunning examples of the Wedjat Eye (Fig. 26.2) have been found adorning the dead: cast in gold, inset with precious gems, and forged in their beautiful Hieratic Style. The Eye of Horus is clearly an image of that eye which gazes *into the Beyond*, the visionary eye which looks *beyond death and rebirth*, to see *as the gods see*. It is the Divine Eye.

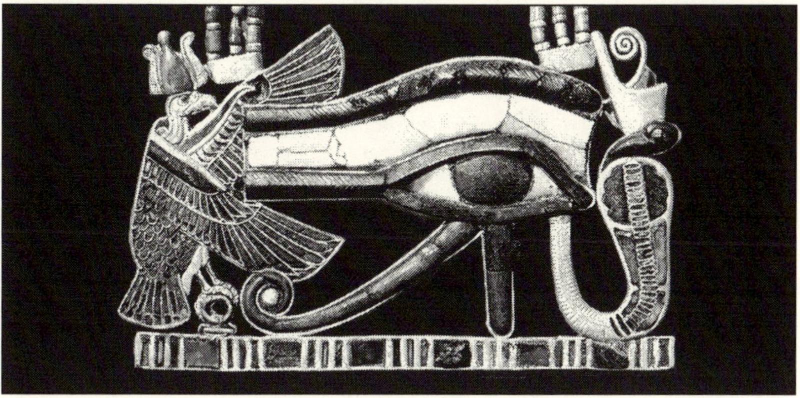

Fig. 26.2 - Jewelled Pectoral of the Wedjat Eye

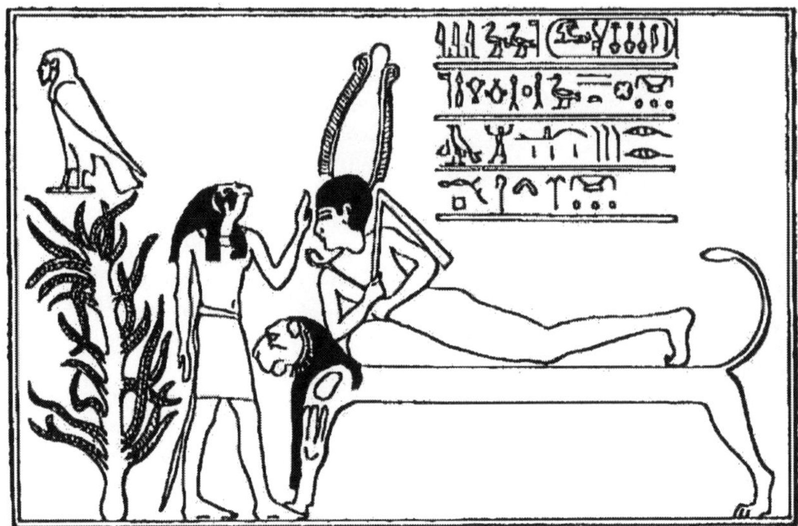

Fig. 26.3 - Relief from the Temple of Dendera:
A Horus-headed Priest Awakens the Initiate King

Having acquired the Divine Eye, the Pyramid Texts then relate the king's visionary journey: he undergoes a 'solar rebirth,' being identified and united with both Horus the falcon and Re the sun. As Horus, he 'ascends' like a falcon; as Re, he is 'reborn' like the rising sun. This is revealed explicitly in a visionary passage from Spell 368: *"O Osiris, this is Horus in your embrace, and he protects you. He has become akh through you, in your identity of the akhet from which the sun emerges."*[11]

As Naydler explains, *"Through the embrace, he* [the king as Osiris] *becomes a shining spirit (akh)... The Egyptian word akhet is usually translated as 'horizon' because this is where the sun first shines each morning, but it is also, in a religious sense, the place of spiritual transfiguration."*[12] And he elaborates, *"From the akhet, the king rises as an akh, an inwardly illumined, 'solarized' being (utt 216-217)."*[13]

It is through his union with the divine triad (Osiris-Horus-Re) that the king's spirit (*akh*) is illuminated and transfigured; he joins with the immortals. And yet, we must not forget that all of this *is a vision*. His union with the divine and entrance into immortality transpires during a brief moment of illumination. Once the transfiguring moment expires, the king returns to his more mundane existence.

This is made explicit in yet another spell, where the king is reminded: *"Awake! Turn yourself about! ... O King raise yourself up to me, betake yourself to me, do not be far from me... I give you the Eye of Horus, I have allotted it to you, may it belong to you."* (Spell 223) As Naydler notes, Spell 223 is *"...concerned with awakening the king from what would appear to be a trancelike state, and ensuring the return of his spirit into his body."*[14] On a nearby page, the author reproduces a relief from the Temple of Dendera (Fig. 26.3) where we behold a Horus-headed priest awakening the initiate king.[15]

Most importantly, the king is reminded of the Eye of Horus, which has been allotted to him during his visionary experience, and which he will retain afterward, as an eye-opening portal into the afterworld dimension. Through his initiatory death and rebirth, accompanied by an illuminating transfiguration, the king has acquired the Divine Eye.

IV. The Egyptian Priesthood

Certain statues of the priests, carved in black alabaster, have come down to us – their eyes opened wide with mysterious knowledge and insight. Contemplating one such statue, the French Egyptologist Serge Sauneron wondered about *"...the vexing riddle of their faces. What thoughts were once concealed behind these serene features, what spectacles were beheld by these large, open eyes that will never flash again with life?"*[16]

In his study *The Priests of Ancient Egypt*, Sauneron notes the strict regimen maintained by these hierophants. To maintain ritual purity they were shorn of all hair, circumcised, bathed twice a day, wore only fine linen and (while in office) abstained from sex and ate no meat. Their induction into the priesthood required nothing less than an 'initiation into the Mysteries of the Netherworld.'

One rare account of a priestly initiation has come down to us, mentioning the neophyte's baptismal cleansing, his anointing with oil and his investment with a linen garment: *"I was presented before the god... I was introduced into the horizon of heaven* [the akhet]... *I emerged from Nun (the primordial waters) and I was purified of what ill had been in me; I removed my clothing and ointments... I advanced before the god in the holy of holies* [the innermost *naos*], *filled with fear before his power."*[17]

Aside from the ritual preparation (compare with Unas and Apuleius), the young priest experienced a transformation and 'solarization' of his *akh* (shining spirit). Like the sun which, at the beginning of time, emerged from Nun's primordial waters, he too 'emerges from Nun' as one illuminated and newly-born. What is more, he was 'introduced into the horizon of heaven' – that is, *into the akhet*, the place of spiritual transformation and illumination. In this visionary state, he 'advanced before the god in the holy of holies' and gazed upon the sacred image 'filled with fear before his power.'

In his study *Death and Salvation in Ancient Egypt*, Jan Assmann suggests that *"Initiation into the temples and cults of Egypt anticipated and prefigured the ultimate initiation into the mysteries of the realm of the dead."*[18] In other words, during his priestly initiation, the novice underwent a visionary death and rebirth, so as to prepare him for his priestly function as psychopomp and guide of the deceased through the Duat: *"During his lifetime, a priest experienced his introduction into the mysterious cultic presence of the divine as a sort of foretaste of his postmortem introduction to Osiris."*[19]

Assmann finds evidence of this in an Egyptian text called The Hymn to the Nocturnal Sun: *"...The mysteries of the Netherworld, an initiation in the mysteries of the realm of the dead ...mysteries that absolutely no one knows for the treatment of the transfigured dead ...You* [the god] *do this, without letting any man see, aside from the one who is truly your intimate and a lector priest."*[20] As such, only the lector priest (i.e. the *kheri heb* [*xry hbt*] who reads the Books of the Afterlife during the entombment) is initiated into the Mysteries of the Netherworld.

It is for this reason that certain priests were called those who *"open the doors of heaven."*[21] One such priest was Chaeremon of Alexandria, a learnèd *hierogrammateis* (Greek for *kheri heb* or Lector priest) from the Temple of Serapis, with its famed Library of Alexandria. All of his writings – *On Hieroglyphs, On Egyptian Astrology,* and *A History of Egypt* – were lost (...no doubt, when early Christians razed the library to the ground). But, fragments of his works describing the Egyptian priests were preserved by Porphyry (the famed disciple of Plotinus). Through Porphyry, Chaeremon offers us a fascinating glimpse into the daily life of Egyptian priests from the late Ptolemaic period.

Like monks in later Buddhist and Christian monasteries, the lives of Egyptian priests were regulated into periods of worship, study and meditation. The priests *"...divided the night into the observation of the celestial bodies, and sometimes devoted a part of it to offices of purification; and they distributed the day into the worship of the Gods, according to which they celebrated them with hymns thrice or four times... The rest of their time they devoted to arithmetical and geometrical speculations, always labouring to effect something, and to make some new discovery."*[22]

The sacred geometry underlying the construction of temples, pyramids and statuary attests to the precision of their 'arithmetical and geometrical speculations,' as do the astronomical orientation of these places to 'the observation of the celestial bodies.' But Egyptian science was not pursued for its own sake; this learning kept the Pharaoh's land in accord with *Maat* – the divine order. Their eyes were ever-turned towards the contemplation of 'the higher': *"These* [priests], *having relinquished every other employment and human labours, gave up the whole of their life to the contemplation and worship of divine natures and to divine inspiration."*[23]

When we wander through Egyptian temples today, admiring the many niches with sculpted images and *bas reliefs*, we should not be surprised to discover that the statues were the main focus of the priesthood's contemplation: *"They chose temples, as the places in which they might philosophize. For to dwell with the statues of the Gods is a thing allied to the whole desire, by which the soul tends to the contemplation of their divinities."*[24]

However, we are misled if we think that the word 'contemplation' means a 'thoughtful observation' or 'philosophical reflection' on lofty and abstract ideas. As we shall see later in this chapter, the philosophical interpretation of the word *theoria* (contemplation) was introduced by Plato. In its primary meaning, *theoria* meant 'to see' and 'gaze deeply' upon a sacred image – especially a statue of a god.

That the priests 'contemplated the sacred images' with a prolonged gaze is brought out more explicitly in another passage: *"They devoted their whole life to contemplation and vision of things divine. By vision, they achieve honour... They practised controlling their gaze, so that if they chose they did not blink."*[25]

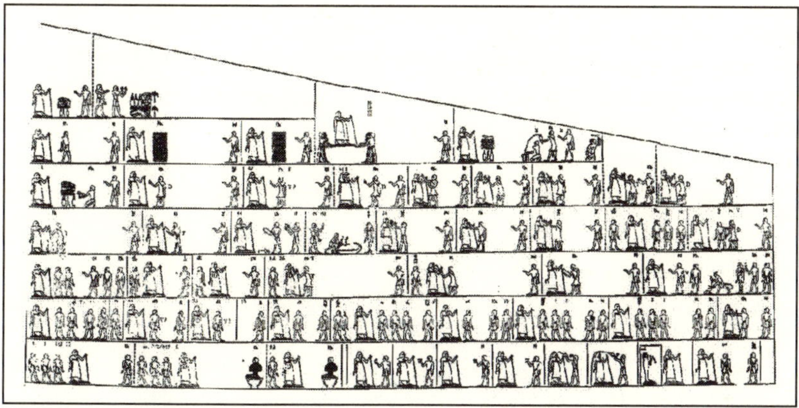

Fig. 26.4 - The Opening of the Eye and Mouth Ritual from Rekhmire's Chapel

Here, we have direct evidence of a kind of Visionary Seeing practiced by the Egyptian priests. As they contemplated the statues – oft times in a visionary state – they 'practised controlling their gaze' into a prolonged, open-eye meditation upon the sacred image. Through this *fixed regard*, the deity within the statue emerged.

V. The Hieratic Style of Egyptian Statuary

In Thebes, the mortuary chapel of Rekhmire offers us a rare glimpse into the visionary inspiration behind Egypt's unique sculptural style. The vizier Rekhmire was both the High Priest of Heliopolis and a high ranking official under Tuthmosis III. On one wall of his richly-decorated chapel (he was buried elsewhere), we have the most complete portrayal of the Opening of the Eyes and Mouth ceremony. This ritual extends from the Old Kingdom right through to the final Ptolemaic period. In it, Egyptian priests consecrate a sacred statue or sarcophagus through a complex theurgic rite involving amulets, an adze and a serpent-headed blade.

The rear chamber of Rekhmire's chapel portrays fifty-one of the seventy-five known steps of the Opening of the Eyes and Mouth, thus being one of the oldest and most complete representations extant (Fig. 26.4). As the ceremony begins, a number of specialized priests (lector priest, imy-khent priest) enter the ceremonial space around the statue and utter the words, *"I enter to see him."*[26] The face of the statue, at this stage, is generic in form, lacking specific traits. The priests must first 'see' these traits and render them onto the statue.

With water and 'smoking incense' (interpret that as you will...) they purify the space (called 'the gold mansion') while invoking the Eye of Horus. E.g.: *"Take the water that is in the red eyes of Horus."*[27]

The next scene (episode 9 at Rekhmire – Fig. 26.5, over) depicts 'The Conception of the Statue.' A new priest enters, called 'the Sem priest.' This

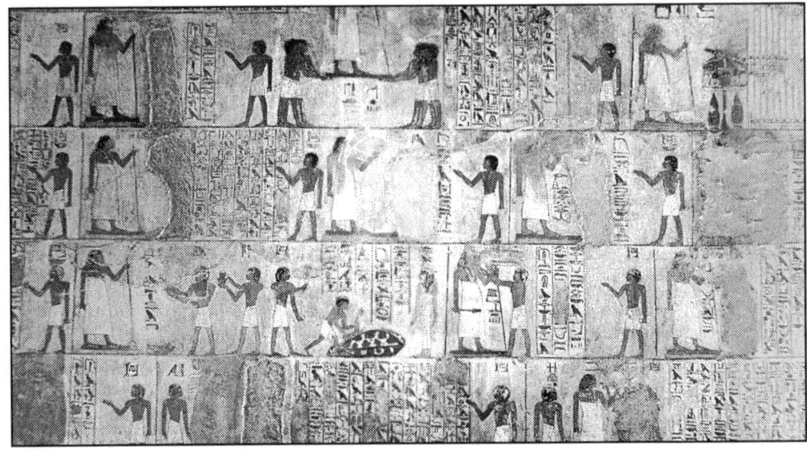

Fig. 26.5 - Rekhmire's Chapel: Episodes 9 and 10 of the Opening of the Eye and Mouth Ritual

rather unique seer, as we shall soon discover, is already in a trance state. The hieroglyphic script accompanying the scene describes the rite as follows: (I have italicized key phrases):

Seclusion in the Gold Mansion: *resting by the Sem priest*
Speech of the Sem priest seated facing it
Words spoken: 'he has struck me'
The Imy-is to stand behind it
Words spoken *'he has outlined me'*
The Imy-is – speech four times
Words spoken by the Imy-is 'My father my father' four times
Waking the sleep of the Sem priest.[28]

We shall elucidate this scene momentarily. In the next part (episode 10), the Sem priest says to the Imy-khent priest: *"I have seen my father in his every outline."* And the Imy-khent priest says in turn to the Sem priest: *"I have seen my father in his every outline."* Next (episode 11) the Sem priest says to the sculptors: *"Mark my father for me... Create, for my father, for me – the divine form, make a likeness of him for me."* As the sculptors render the features of the statue, they say together with the Sem and Lector priests: *"Who are those who approach my father? Who is it striking my father? Who is it forcing his head? ... Who protects those who are to strike your father?"*[29]

The act of rendering the sacred image puts the sculptors in grave danger. The Sem and Lector priests intervene, saying, *"I am Horus and Seth. I do not allow you to make the head shine for my father."* So, the carvers finish their work, but the image is not yet complete; the priests must still 'make the head shine' by performing the theurgic rite of the Opening of the Eye and Mouth.

The Sem priest removes his 'qeni-matting robe' and dons a leopard skin, saying to the statue: *"I have marked your eye for you, your ba-spirit (to be) in it."* All the priests then go outside and oversee the sacrifice of a bull. Its

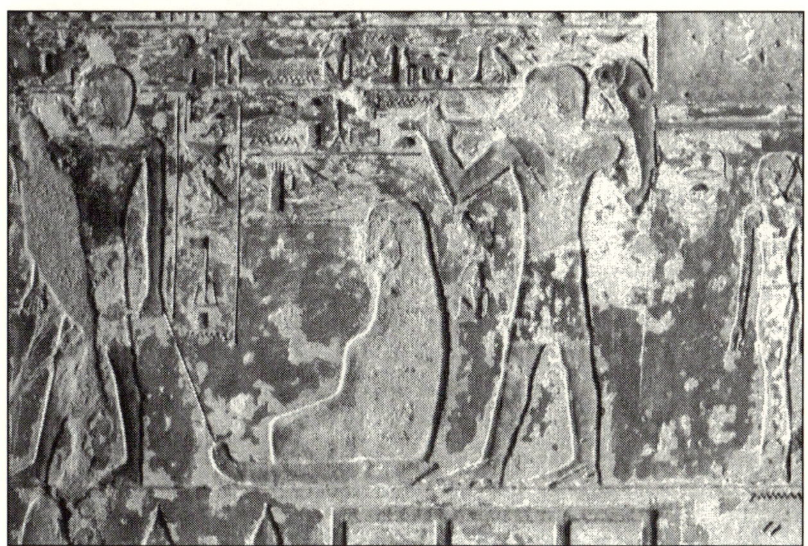

Fig. 26.6 - Tomb of Renni at El Kab 18th Dynasty
Showing the Tekenu (Sem Priest) as a Bundled Man Sitting Upright on a Sled

foreleg is offered to the statue with the words: *"Receive the foreleg, the eye of Horus."* Thus begins the long section for the Opening of the Eye and Mouth. The priests touch the statue's mouth and eyes with a variety of different knives, saying: *"Horus has opened your mouth for you, he opens your eyes for you."* The priests do this, *"so that he may walk and speak with his body before the great Nine Gods in the great mansion."* The ritual concludes with more purifications. Then, the statue is carried to a shrine within the chapel, garlanded and incensed.[30]

As this ancient account makes clear, the unique seer called the Sem priest first *had a vision* of the divine features ('I enter to see him') and then communicated *its distinct style and shape* to the others ('I have seen my father in his every outline'). Only then does he call upon the sculptors *to render the sacred shapes* ('Mark my father for me... – the divine form, make a likeness of him for me'). But the sacred image is not yet *activated* ('make the head shine') until the Eye and Mouth are opened.

How does the Sem priest receive the vision? In a fascinating paper called 'A Rite of Passage: The Enigmatic Tekenu in Ancient Egyptian Funerary Ritual,' Greg Reeder analyzes a number of tomb engravings involving the mysterious *tekenu* figure. This shadowy figure appears as a bundled man on a sled, pulled along by priests during the funerary procession. Sometimes he lies in a foetal position (the pre-dynastic burial position - Fig. 26.7, over), and sometimes he sits upright (Fig. 26.6) with the sack cowled round his head. Some Egyptologists thought that the *tekenu* was a slave sacrificed during the ceremony.[31]

But, this same *tekenu* figure appears in Rekhmire's Chapel, and Reeder is now able to identify *the tekenu as the Sem priest*. In Episode 9 (quoted above), he first appears head down, bundled in his sack (*'resting by the Sem*

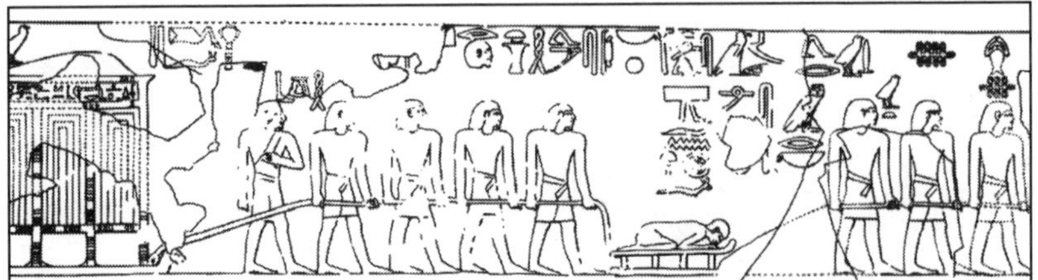

Fig. 26.7 - Theban Tomb of the Fan-bearer Montuhirkhepeshef
Showing the Tekenu (Sem Priest) as a Bundled Man Lying on a Sled

priest') and next appears sitting upward on a lion-footed couch, still bundled and wrapped in the manner of Osiris (*'waking the sleep of the Sem priest'*). Between his sleeping and waking, he receives 'the outline' of the sacred image.[32]

In Reeder's words: *"Here is revealed the metamorphosis of the tekenu... It is the Sem priest who is awakened from his trance... The Sem states that he was 'asleep' but had visited the deceased in the otherworld... As the tekenu he is transported to the tomb wrapped in a shroud to help facilitate his 'death' so that he can be transported to the other world. Thus having visited the spirit world, the Sem was imbued with powers which enabled him to perform the succeeding 'Opening of the Mouth' ceremony for the deceased."*[33]

Not only did the trance give him power to perform the succeeding ceremony, it also allowed him 'to see' and 'to outline' the 'divine form' which 'makes the head shine.' Through his Netherworld journey, the Sem priest was able *to see the hieratically-stylized features* that, once they were carved on the statue and consecrated, thus activated it as a vehicle for the divine.

The statue's eyes were open.

From the preceding, it becomes clear that certain Egyptian priests were adept at entering into visionary states. This began during their initiation into the priesthood, and extended to the ceremonies performed for seeing, sculpting and activating their sacred statues and sarcophagi. Typically, such a trance state involved a visionary journey through the Netherworld, instigated through a death-and-rebirth experience. The statues, ritually rendered in this fashion, bore the marks and signs of the Hieratic Style. Other priests, dwelling in the temples, practiced a form of open-eye meditation ('controlling their gaze') upon these statues. All these activities aided the priests in *seeing,* like the Pharaoh, with the Wedjat – the Divine Eye.

VI. Ancient Greece

One of the most popular feasts of Classical Greece were the Eleusinian Mysteries celebrating Demeter and her daughter Persephone (also called *Koré* – 'the maiden'). Pilgrims throughout the land were invited to Athens to celebrate these initiatory rites, which dramatized Persephone's abduction by Hades, her descent to the underworld while her mother Demeter mourned, and her eventual return to the land of the living. Those who participated in the Mysteries were granted immortality in the afterlife, due to the initiatory vision.

Sophocles extolled the Mysteries with the words, *"Thrice blessed are those mortals who have seen these rites and thus enter Hades: for them alone there is life, but for the others all is misery."*[34] And Pindar added, *"Blessed is he who, seeing these things, goes beneath the earth; he knows the end of life, and he knows the god-given beginning."*[35]

Although the actual events of the rites are shrouded in mystery, we know that the ten day ceremony began with a procession, as the sacred images (*hiera*) were brought to the temple (the *Eleusinion* at the base of the Acropolis) by priests (*hierophantes*) and initiates (*mustés*, *epoptés*) waving myrtle branches. Those called the 'initiates' (*mustés*) were undergoing their first initiation, while those called 'the watchers' (*epoptés)* had already been initiated once, and would now witness 'the higher mysteries.'[36]

After a day of fasting, all the celebrants drank a special brew (the *kykeon* – interpret that as you will) and the next day they entered the great hall (the *telesterion*) which was plunged into darkness. The greatest moment of initiation (*teleté*) began when the hierophants opened the door to an inner central chamber (the *anaktoron*) and the initiates, chanting sacred hymns, entered it to 'see' (*theorein*) and experience a moment of revelation (*epoptika*).

Alas, what was actually seen and witnessed remains unknown. The revelation (*epoptika*) was so powerful, it seems, that no one dared break the vow of silence and actually reveal it in writing. Whatever vision may have befallen the initiates – it granted them knowledge of eternal life.

For us, the key to this entire mystery lies in the verb *theorein* ('to see') from whence the word *theoria* ('to contemplate') is derived. The initiates 'saw' and literally 'contemplated' the mysteries. The Greek word *theorein* combines both the word for god (*theos*) and the word for sight (*thea*). As Andrea Wilson Nightingale notes, *"Ever since antiquity, people have debated whether the word* 'theoria' *derives from* theos *(god) or* thea *(sight, spectacle).... 'sacred spectating' captures this dual signification."*[37]

In her book, *Spectacles of Truth in Classical Greek Philosophy: Theoria in its Cultural Context*, Nightingale performs an extended exegesis on the word *theoria* and what it meant to the ancient Greeks. We today use the word 'contemplation' (*theoria*) to refer to a 'thoughtful observation' or 'philosophical reflection' on lofty and abstract ideas. This is the legacy of Plato and Aristotle, eventually inherited by Christianity. But, in its primordial sense, *theoria* meant 'the sacred vision' witnessed by an initiate at the climax of their pilgrimage to a religious festival, such as the Mysteries of Eleusis.

"In the classical period," Nightingale writes, *"theoria took the form of pilgrimages to oracles and religious festivals... At its centre was the act of seeing, generally focused on a sacred object or spectacle. Indeed, the theoros* [the beholder or contemplator] *at a religious festival or sanctuary witnessed objects and events that were sacralized by way of rituals: the viewer entered into a 'ritualized visuality' in which secular modes of viewing were screened out by religious rites and practices. This sacralized mode of spectating was a central element in traditional theoria, and offered a powerful model for the philosophic notion of 'seeing' divine truths."*[38]

In short, the initiates at Eleusis were 'theorizing' the Mystery: they were 'contemplating' it in the sense of *envisioning the sacred*. This was no ordinary sight, but a very special form of seeing which included a direct gaze upon the

Sacred. Nightingale calls this Visionary Seeing a *'ritualized visuality'* and a *'sacralized mode of spectating.'*

By that same token, the *theoros* is the contemplator, the one who beholds the divine vision. In Nightingale's words, *"the theoros 'sees' a divine revelation that transforms his soul."*[39] And she goes on to say that, *"The theoros witnessed objects and events that were sacralized by way of ritual structures and ceremonies, and was thus invited to engage in a distinct kind of seeing. First of all, the theoros enters a sacred space – a 'liminal site in which the viewer enters the god's world and likewise the deity intrudes directly into the viewer's world in a highly ritualized context.' In this space, the theoroi participates in ritual activities that bring about a certain mode of seeing."*[40]

The practice of *theoria*, of contemplating sacred images, was not unique to Classical Greece. As we have already seen, the ancient Egyptian priesthood also '*chose temples as a place to contemplate their divinities.'* (Chaeremon's words, as conveyed by Porphyry). This contemplation was also a ritualized form of visionary seeing which accessed the Divine directly.

For the ancient Greeks, the object of *theoria* – the object 'seen' at the climax of a pilgrimage to a sacred festival – was an *agalma*. *"In the classical period,"* Nightingale explains, *"the word agalma referred exclusively to the statues and images of the gods."*[41] The Greeks had many words for 'image,' such as *eikon* or *eidolon*. But an *agalma* (plural: *agalmata*) was specifically a *sacred* image. By definition, it evoked the Sacred: *"As Vernant observes in his discussion of agalmata and divine images, the purpose of such an image 'is to establish real contact with the world beyond, to actualize it, to make it present, and thereby to participate intimately in the divine.'"*[42]

As such, to *theorize* an *agalma* – to contemplate a sacred image – was to enter fully into the presence of the gods. This unique experience was granted to all *mustés* (initiates) who participated in the theurgic rites of the Mystery religions.

However, by the time we get to Plato, we find that this status is only reserved for philosophers – and that they are contemplating those higher invisibles which Plato called the *eidé* or archetypes. Through a penetrating analysis, Nightingale demonstrates how *"the model of theoria at religious festivals offered Plato a way to structure and describe the new discipline of theoretical philosophy."*[43]

The result was to replace the *agalmata* – the sacred images contemplated by all initiates of the Mysteries – with the *eidé*, the higher and unseen forms contemplated only by philosophers: *"Plato... takes pains to explicate this new kind of 'seeing.' First of all, he claims, the objects of true knowledge are metaphysical entities called eidé, a term which is generally translated as 'Forms.' "*[44] *"A philosopher who gazes upon the Forms contemplates divinity, an act replete with wonder and reverence."*[45]

During the Italian Renaissance, artists recognized that the Platonic forms were 'invisible' to, what Michelangelo called, *"...weak and wavering eyes... not fixed on things above."*[46] But in his poems, the great sculptor reminded us that the artist, in his quest for 'the Idea of Beauty' could ascend in his visions to the higher spheres: *"This Idea alone lifts my eyes to those high visions / Which I set myself to carve and paint here below."*[47]

In this sense, the artist's pursuit is informed by the *eidé*, particularly by Beauty, Harmony and Unity, as invisible shapes and forms that permeate his work. Through extended contemplation (*theoria*), these invisible forms may momentarily become visible. Any stylized shape, made harmonious through geometrically perfect measures, may reveal the hidden *eidé* or archetype, which the Renaissance writer Giovanni Pietro Bellori referred to as 'the Ideal'.

In 1664, Bellori made a speech at the Accademia di San Luca in Rome – a speech so highly valued that it was published in 1672 as *L'idea del pittore, dello scultore, e dell'architetto* (The Idea of the Painter, Sculptor and Architect). Noting that Renaissance art had fallen into decline after the death of Michelangelo, Bellori criticized the brutal naturalism of Caravaggio while upholding the idealistic art of Carracci and his school.

Bellori went to great lengths to cite the Hermetic and Neo-Platonic texts which revolutionized Florentine art in the late 1400's, when Ficino translated the Hermetica and the works of Plato, Plotinus, Iamblichus and Proclus at the behest of Lorenzo the Magnificent. The divine unity, Bellori wrote, reflected upon itself to create all the forms of Nature. Those above the lunar sphere, as Ideas (the Platonic *eidé*) possess unchanging eternal beauty, while those below are subject to change; their beauty lacks harmony and proportion.

For this reason, *"the noble painters and sculptors imitating that first maker, also form in their minds an example of superior beauty, and in beholding it they emend nature with faultless color or line. This Idea... is revealed to us and enters the marble and the canvases."*[48]

For Bellori, the artist must rise above the sublunar sphere and 'emend nature' to capture the true form, the Idea and 'ideal' of beauty. In a state of theoric vision, the artist beholds the higher form, and renders it in the stylistically altered shape that truly ennobles and transfigures it.

VII. *Darśan* & the Conception of the Hindu Image

A pilgrimage, in Sanskrit, is a *tirtha-yatra* – literally a journey (*tirtha*) to a ford or crossing place (*yatra*), where one *crosses over* into another realm of experience. Just as the pilgrimage requires many steps and unexpected mishaps, so does the creation of the sacred image for *darśan* require many complex steps for the craftsman, which involve at least three phases: Conception, Consecration and Meditation.

In her book *Darśan: Seeing the Divine Image in India*, Diana L. Eck notes that *"Darśan means 'seeing.' In the Hindu ritual tradition, it refers especially to religious seeing, or the visual perception of the sacred."*[49] And she adds, *"One might say that this 'sacred perception', which is the ability to truly see the divine image, is given to the devotee, just as Arjuna is given the eyes with which to see Krishna in the theophany described in the Bhagavad Gita"*[50] – a theophany which we have already quoted in our first chapter.

In the first step of 'Conception', the artisan must first formulate a clear image of the deity in his mind before commencing the work. The process requires both intense concentration *and* visualization.

As Diane Eck observes: *"The śilpin* [sculptor], *before beginning a new work, undergoes a ritual purification and prays that he may successfully bring to form the divine image."*[51] She describes this process in precise terms: *"Entering into a state of concentration by means of yoga, the śilpin* [sculptor] *is to visualize the completed image in the mind's eye."*[52]

Since sculptors created sacred works, the act of creation was, itself, consecrated. If he felled a tree for his materials, the artisan should first, the *Bṛhat Saṃhitā* (57.10-11) says, ask pardon to the spirits residing in the tree, and propitiate them with offerings. Indeed, before the work commenced, the artisan should bless his tools with incense, flowers and unhusked rice.[53]

In his massive two-volume work, *The Art of Indian Asia*, Heinrich Zimmer also describes the Hindu sculptor's visualization methods: *"The night before commencing a new work, the image maker is to pray: 'O thou Lord of all gods, teach me in dreams how to carry out the whole of the work that I have in mind.'"*[54]

He prays like this, Zimmer explains, because *"an Indian image is, properly, an outward vessel corresponding precisely to the inner vision of the divinity."*[55] Indeed, *"the sacred image grows out of the inner vision,"*[56] Zimmer writes in *Artistic Form and Yoga in the Sacred Images of India.* Describing the unique stylization of Hindu figures, he remarks, *"In the fundamental aspects of its style, the sacred image is subject to the laws of the inner vision."*[57]

As such, the unique stylization of the Hindu sculpture is not so much a *cultural* style as it is a *vision-inspired* style – which we have described here by the word 'Hieratic'.

Hence, the Aesthetics of the *Śukranītisāra* conclude: *"Let the imager establish images in temples, by meditation on the deities who are the objects of his devotion. And for the successful achievement of this yoga, the lineaments of the images are described in books, which are to be dwelt upon in detail. By no other means* [...] *is it possible to be absorbed in contemplation, as by this meditation on the making of images."*[58]

VIII. The Hindu Image: Consecration & Meditation

According to an instructional text On Building a Vishnu Temple, the *Hayaśirṣa-pañcarātra*: *"The divinity draws near willingly – if images are beautiful."*[59] Just as the ancient Greeks and Egyptians developed complex theurgic rites for the consecration (*telestikē*) of their statues, so did the priests and craftsmen of India.

"When an image is completed," Diane Eck remembers, *"there are special rites of consecration which take place, for the most part, in a specially consecrated booth outside the temple itself. First, the image is purified with a variety of ritually pure substances, such as darbha grass, honey, and ghee. Then by a ritual called nyāsa, literally the 'touching', various deities are established in different parts of the image: Brahma in the chest, Indra in the hand, Surya in the eyes,"*[60] etc.

As in ancient Egypt, the final act of consecration includes the 'instillation of breath' and 'the opening of the eyes': *"Finally, prāṇa the 'breathlife' is infused into the image in the central rite called prāṇapratiṣṭā, 'establishing the breathlife'. The infusion of the prāṇa ordinarily takes the form of a mantra: 'O Vishnu, approach this image and wake it up with thy embodiment of knowledge and divine energies, which are concentrated in this image.' The eyes of the image, which to this point have been sealed with a thick coat of honey and ghee, are now 'opened' by the brahmin priest, who removes the coating with a golden needle."*[61] Elsewhere, Eck writes, *"the eyes were ritually opened with a golden needle or with the final stroke of a paintbrush."*[62]

In 'The Secret Life of Statues' Angela Voss writes:

"In both Egyptian and Greek traditions, the most significant moment of the statue's creation, the moment of animation, was that of the painting in or inserting the eyes – and again it is Hinduism that preserves this in the ritual of darsan. 'Not only must the gods keep their eyes open', writes Diana Eck, 'but so must we, in order to make contact with them, to reap their blessings, and to know their secrets.' This was the moment of consecration, the 'making sacred', the point at which the god entered the image and it became operative in the world, able to meet the gaze of the onlookers."[63]

Once it is consecrated, the statue henceforth becomes an *arcāvatāra* – an *image-incarnation* of the deity. What this means is that the infinite form of the deity has now acquired *mūrti* or *definite form*, with well-defined contours and limits. What is more, the emblems and hand gestures (*mudra*) give the statue a definite resemblance to the deity, making it a *pratima* or *likeness*. It is the divine proportions and stylistic likeness that make the image 'beautiful' and a wonder to behold.[64]

The subsequent act of Contemplation and worship (*pūjā*) involves many ritual gestures, but at its heart is the act of seeing – *darśan*. At first, the devotee may approach the sacred image with the *upacāras* or 'honourary offerings' in hand, such as fresh leaves, sandalwood paste, incense or betel nuts, and place them on the altar – though the most auspicious offering is the five-wicked oil lamp (*āratī*), which is circled before the deity while hymns are sung and handbells rung.[65]

To show her devotion (*bhakti*), the worshipper may 'touch' (*sparśa*) the statue in various places with her hands, then touch herself to instill the deity's presence within (*nyāsa*).[66]

But, *"the central act of Hindu worship,"* Eck reminds us, *"is to stand in the presence of the deity and to behold the image with one's own eyes, to see and be seen by the deity. Darśan is sometimes translated as the 'auspicious sight' of the divine* [...] *Beholding the image is an act of worship, and through the eyes one gains the blessings of the divine."*[67]

The act of *darśan* or 'sacred seeing', though it is still practiced today, has a more ancient meaning. *"In Vedic India,"* Eck writes, *"the 'seers' were called ṛṣis. In their hymns, collected in the Rg Veda, 'to see' often means 'a mystical, supernatural beholding' or 'visionary experiencing.'"*[68]

IX. *Ekāgratā* – Concentration on a Fixed Point

Some sacred texts describe this unique form of Contemplation as *ekāgratā – the 'one-pointed' meditation on an image*. In an extended passage, Diane L. Eck describes the *ekāgratā* meditation:

"The image is primarily a focus for concentration [...It] *is a kind of yantra, literally a 'device' for harnessing the eye and mind so that the one-pointedness of thought (ekāgratā), which is fundamental to meditation, can be attained. The image is a support for meditation."*[69]

She then goes on to cite the *Vishnu Sāṁhitā*, a ritual text for worshipping statues of Vishnu (Fig. 26.8): *"Without form, how can God be meditated upon? If (He is) without any form, where will the mind fix itself? When there is nothing for the mind to attach itself to, it will slip away from meditation or will glide into a state of slumber. Therefore the wise will meditate on some form, remembering, however, that the form is a superimposition and not a reality."*[70]

In *Artistic Form and Yoga in the Sacred Images of India,* Heinrich Zimmer also describes the *ekāgratā* meditation, which is a vital part of the *prāṇapratiṣṭā* (instillation of breath) into the statue, achieved through the flower offering (*puśpānjali*):

"Upon entering, the worshiper casts aside any possible disruptive influences from the heavenly sphere by staring straight ahead, unblinking, so that his gaze is like that of the gods [...]. *Any distractions lurking in the earthly sphere he drives away by striking the ground three times with his heel.* [...] *Then follows an act of concentrated meditation (ekāgrada-dhyāna) that, guided in the inner visions by a series of spoken formulas and syllables (dhyāna-mantras), constructs the image of the god's essential nature from the feet to the head and back again. This act of inner worship is to precede every external one."*[71]

Zimmer then cites a passage from the Sāktānanda-taranginī: *"After seeing the Ista-devata* [tutelary deity] *in one's heart, one should establish Her in the image, picture, vessel or yantra and then worship her."*[72]

As such, one must concentrate, first, on the *inner image* of the deity, and then project it or instill this into the sculpture. One concentrates on the inner image and sees it through 'inward vision', which is manifestly different from 'outward vision'.

The difference is that one can 'see unity' with the aid of inward vision, while outward vision has great difficulties with this task. *"If our* [physical] *eye actually expects to deal with the multitude of things in its field of vision,"* Zimmer writes, *"it has to roam about, to rove back and forth."*[73]

But, *"How different is our inward vision!"*[74] Zimmer exclaims. *"With equal intensity and without showing favour, our inner eye must illuminate everything gathered before it."*[75] And he adds, *"This particular type of visualization fills up the entire field of view,"* so that *"the mind's focus is directed at the whole as the sum of its parts* [...] *with a clear focus on a single point."*[76] Our focus expands until all the parts are seen *"with equal sharpness"*[77] and the figure stands *"totally motionless"*[78] while being *"sealed in tranquility."*[79]

Having achieved this stupendous inner vision, the contemplative then projects it onto the statue through the flower offering. And so, meditating upon the stone image with the flower offering in his hands, the contemplative performs the ritual 'act of installation'.

According to the Gandharva Tantra: *"Let him think of the identity between the image manifested within and the image without. Next, the energy of consciousness within should be taken* [...] *with the breath along the nostrils and infused into the handful of flowers. Thus, issuing with the breath, the Devata* [the inner image of the deity] *enters into the flowers. The Sādhaka* [devotee] *should then establish the Devata in the* [stone] *image by touching it with those flowers."*[80]

Through this theurgic act of touching the sculpture with the flowers, the stilled statue transforms into a beatific vision of the deity. No longer does the god appear in his limited form of lifeless stone, but expands into an unbounded apparition of divine proportions.

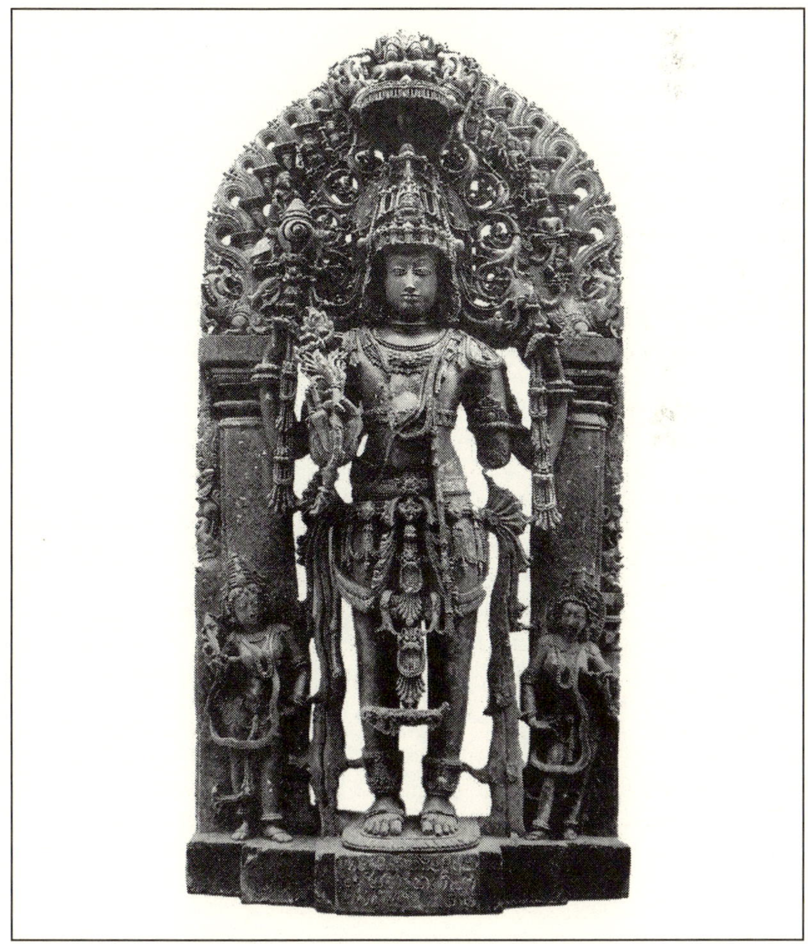

Fig. 26.8 - Standing Statue of Vishnu

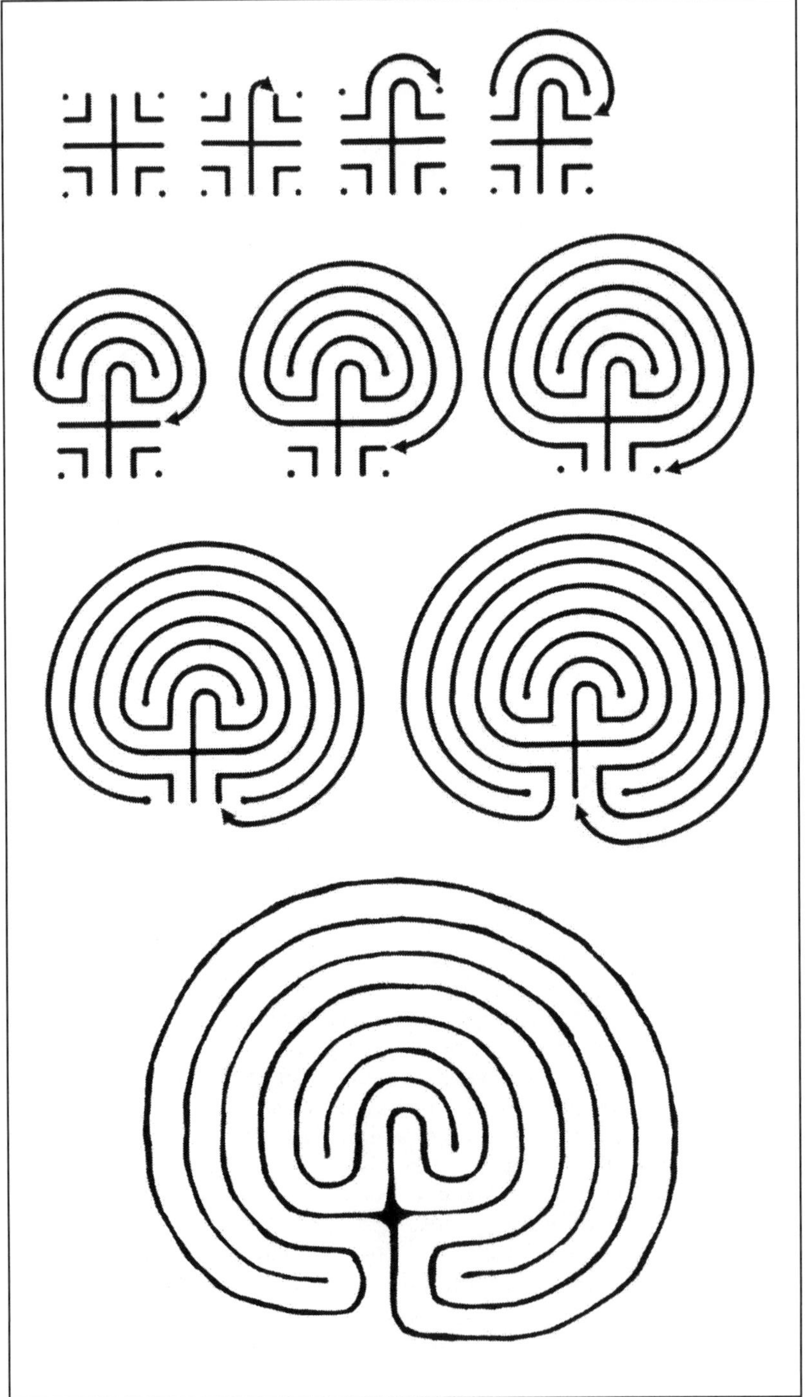

Fig. 27.2 - Expansion of a Minoan Pottery Glyph into the Labyrinth

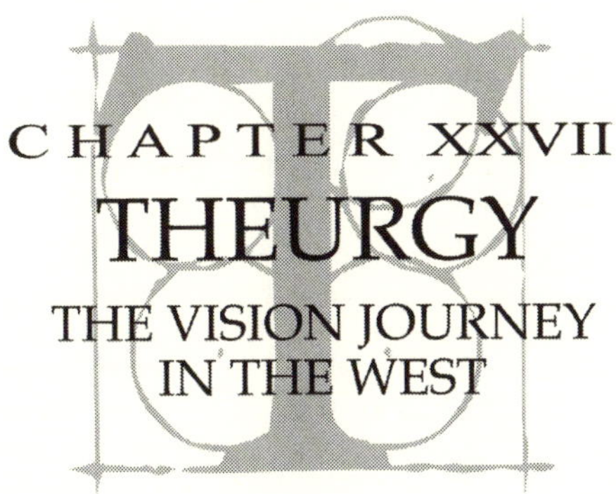

CHAPTER XXVII THEURGY

THE VISION JOURNEY IN THE WEST

I. Theurgic Rites

The Minoan civilization has left us with many mysteries. Because we have no sacred texts to rely upon, the images alone must speak to us of their ancient worldview. Perhaps the best-known image from that Aegean civilization is the labyrinth. But Minoan pottery is also over-run with mysterious glyphs that, at first glance, seem indecipherable (Fig. 27.1). Nevertheless, with time we have learned to read some of these glyphs as mnemonic devices for reconstructing the fabled labyrinth. As the example opposite shows (Fig. 27.2), the second and third glyphs below may be expanded to create the Minoan labyrinth.

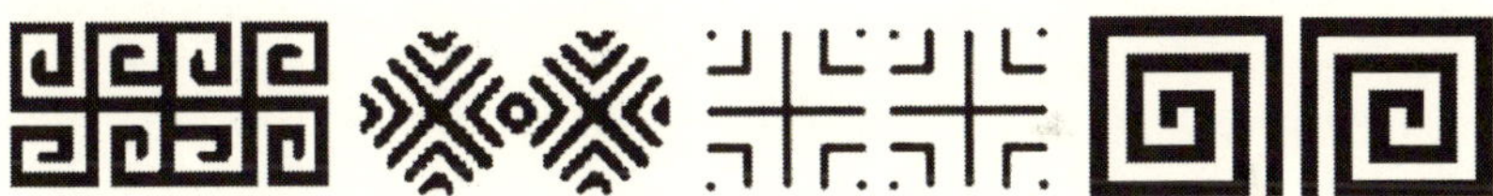

Fig. 27.1 - Minoan Pottery Glyphs

Their ritual purpose becomes clearer when we remember that spirals and other labyrinthine designs often appeared at the entrance to underground mortuary temples. If we interpret the Minoan labyrinth as an image of the afterworld, then we may be surprised to discover that the seven turnings in the labyrinth correspond to the seven visible planets in the heavens. More than that, the labyrinth may have served as a kind of *map* for the ascending soul to navigate its passage through the seven planetary realms – to ultimately arrive at the stilled eternal realm, symbolized by the centre of the labyrinth.

In this sense, the labyrinth and its associated glyphs served as an *aide-mémoire* for the dis-embodied soul to reconstruct and remember its afterlife passage through the planetary spheres. Although we have no proof of this, the sacred art of later civilizations – in both the East and West – attest to the fact that many such mnemonic devices existed, and they all served as carefully-constructed maps for the soul's passage through the post-mortem realms. This is particularly true of mandalas in the East, which we shall examine in the next chapter, and theurgic rites in the West, practiced around Alexandria in the first century of our own era.

The Greek word *theurgy* (from *theos,* 'divine' and *ergeia*, 'workings', hence 'divine workings') describes the ancient practice of invoking the gods through their earthly vehicles or statues – such as occurred during the Mysteries and other religious festivals. Beyond the rituals involved in consecrating a statue, a more contemplative practice evolved, wherein the theurgist ascended through the heavenly spheres to experience a momentary *henosis* or 'oneness' with the Divine source.

Several great theurgists have come down to us through time, such as Julian the Chaldaean and his son, Julian the Theurgist, who are credited with the creation of *The Chaldaean Oracles* (2nd century CE); the Neo-Platonist philosophers Numenius, Iamblichus and Proclus; as well as the 4th century Roman Emperor Julian, whose attempts to elevate Neo-Platonic Theurgy into the state religion earned him the title of Julian the Philosopher from his supporters, and Julian the Apostate from the church.

But the greatest theurgist to come down to us through time is, without a doubt, Hermes Trismegistus. In the Latin *Asclepius*, the thrice-great Hermes conducts a dialogue with Asclepius on the spiritual life of statues:

> *"Humanity persists in imitating divinity, representing gods in semblance of its own features..."*
>
> *"Are you talking about statues, Trismegistus?"*
>
> *"Statues, Asclepius, yes... I mean statues ensouled and conscious, filled with spirit."*[1]

During the consecration of a sacred image, the theurgist performed certain rites which 'activated' the statue – 'ensouling it' (*empsychsis*) and 'filling it with spirit' (*enpneumatosis*). From that time forward, the statue was regarded as a sacred mirror of the Divine. This ancient view onto statues inspired endless debate among Neo-Platonic philosophers – some of whom refused to accept this more ancient, mythopoeic outlook within their rationalist worldview.

Plato (427 – 327 BCE) himself was, in part, responsible for this debate. Although the Athenian philosopher acknowledged the importance of the Mysteries, he upheld reason over rite. While accrediting Pythagoras, the Orphics and even the ancient Egyptians as the true source of wisdom, he introduced *dialectic* and *logos* as superior to *theurgy* and *agalmata.*

To put the Platonic legacy in proper perspective, we must remember that Plato himself wrote in the 3rd century BCE. Over the next six hundred years, his writings were copied, commented upon and re-interpreted – chiefly by Plotinus (204 – 270 CE), a brilliant 3rd century philosopher now called 'the father of Neo-Platonism.' Plotinus framed Plato's philosophy within the 'Emanationist' worldview, where all of creation descends from the One in ever-lower hypostases or levels of being, while remaining fundamentally unified at its core.

Plotinus' chief disciple was Porphyry (c. 234 – c. 305 CE), a prolific writer on many subjects. He wrote his master's biography (*On the Life of Plotinus*) and organized his writings into nine treatises (*The Enneads*). Like his teacher, Porphyry was a rationalist, and they both questioned the efficacy of theurgic rites. Plotinus wrote the treatise *'Against the Gnostics'* and Porphyry penned *'The Letter to Anebo'* which called into question numerous theurgic practices.

Porphyry's greatest student was Iamblichus (c. 245 – c. 345 CE), a brilliant exponent of the Neo-Platonic philosophy who – contrary to his master – defended the value of statuary, ritual and myth. In one of his most well-known texts, he contends with his master Porphyry, refuting the *'Letter to Anebo'* line by line. This book, *On the Mysteries* (*De mysteriis*), becomes one of the best-known defences of theurgy, and offers some rare and valuable insights into those Mystery rites which were otherwise guarded in great silence.

Perhaps the last and greatest of the Neo-Platonic philosophers was Proclus (412 – 485 CE), a fifth century theologian, geometer and mathematician who eventually headed Plato's Academy in Athens. Like Iamblichus, he wrote a staunch defence of theurgy (*On the Sacred Art*), since he himself had been initiated into the Chaldaean, Orphic and Eleusinian Mysteries. Through these experiences, he reported visions of Hecate, Athena and the Great Goddess in her triple-form of Rhea, Demeter and Persephone.

The Hermetica, *The Chaldean Oracles,* and *The Gnostic Codices* also constitute important sources for theurgic practice. All of these emerged from Alexandria in the first century – that rich melting pot of Greek, Egyptian, Jewish and early Christian beliefs during Egypt's Ptolemaic period. *The Hermetica* (which combines the Greek *Corpus Hermeticum* and the Latin *Asclepius*) are like a last desperate attempt to preserve in Greek and Latin the lost Egyptian wisdom which could no longer be read in the hieroglyphs. *The Chaldean Oracles* perform a similar service for Babylonia ("Chaldea" in Greek), in the form of an ancient Mystery poem in Greek hexameters. Both of these late Hellenic works look back upon the demise of Egyptian and Babylonian culture with great regret, trying to at least *preserve* or even *revive* their lost philosophies.

The Gnostic Codices, which were discovered in Nag Hammadi Egypt in 1945, also combine Greek, Egyptian, Jewish and early Christian motifs to give us a rare glimpse into 'the Visionary Ascent' – a contemplative rite which (as we shall see by the end of this chapter) constitutes the highest form of theurgic practice.

The word *theurgia* is a Neo-Platonic invention, borrowed from the *Chaldean Oracles*. The word *theurgist* came to denote anyone who participated in the conception, creation and consecration of sacred images. In the past, this occurred through the combined efforts of hierophants (priests) and craftsmen. Today, the Visionary Artist is called upon to revive these ancient practices – to not only conceive and create a work of art, *but to consecrate it as sacred...*

II. Word against Image: the *Logos* & the *Agalmata*

In one passage from his *Letter to Anebo,* Porphyry wonders aloud how an all-powerful deity may be commanded to descend from above and enter its statue: *"It very much indeed perplexes me to understand how superior beings, when invoked* [through the rite of a statue's consecration], *are commanded by those that invoke them."*[2]

In his rebuttal, Iamblichus elaborates a defence of theurgy that is founded upon the Neo-Platonic worldview: all things come from the One and, as such, are vehicles or reflections of its greatness:

"...The light of the gods shines while entirely separate from the objects illuminated, and, being firmly established in itself, makes its way through all existing things."[3]

Iamblichus then applies this unified worldview onto the animation of divine statues: *"Whether* [in the case of] *holy cities and regions, whether to certain temple-precincts or sacred images, the divine irradiation shines upon them all... This light is one and the same everywhere, and is not only present, undivided, with all things* [but...] *fills all things, as a cause, joins them together in itself, unites them everywhere with itself, and combines the ends with the beginnings. Who, then, that contemplates the visible image of the gods, thus united as one, will never have too much reverence."*[4]

As such, the act of consecration does not 'command' the divine spirit to enter the statue (this is the common misconception of 'magic' directed at theurgists). Rather, through the act of consecration (*telestikē*), the statue becomes a clear reflection or earthly vehicle to the pre-existing divine power that is everywhere. Such a divine reflection, as Iamblichus notes at the end, can only be seen and experienced during the subsequent step of *contemplation – theoria – 'Who, then, that contemplates the visible image of the gods, thus united as one, will never have too much reverence.'*

The debate between Iamblichus and his master Porphyry is the result of differing practices leading to the same experience of divine unity (*henosis*): Porphyry, as a rationalist philosopher, has ascended the heavenly spheres and experienced divinity through the thoughtful contemplation (*theoria*) of Plato's invisible concepts and forms (the *eidé*), while Iamblichus has done the same thing through the *more ancient mode* of contemplation (*theoria* as sacred spectating), based on theurgic rites and statuary (the *agalmata*).

"For it is not," Iamblichus writes, *"the concept that unites the theurgic priests to the gods: else what is there to hinder those who pursue philosophic speculation contemplatively, from having the theurgic union to the gods? ...On the other hand, it is the complete fulfilling of the arcane performances, the carrying of them through in a manner worthy of the gods and surpassing all conception, and likewise the power of the voiceless symbols which are perceived by the gods alone, that establish the Theurgic Union. Hence we do not effect these things by thinking."*[5]

Porphyry, while writing about the life of his master, says that Plotinus experienced *henosis* four times while in his presence, and that he himself experienced it once in his lifetime: *"To this God, I also declare, I Porphyry, that in my sixty-eighth year I too was once admitted and I entered into Union."*[6]

Contrast this to Iamblichus' description of the ways the different beings appear in a vision:

"In the Epoptic vision, the figures of the gods shine brilliantly; those of the archangels are awe-inspiring and yet gentle... those of the dæmons are alarming [and] *those of the archons are terrifying to the beholders."*[7]

Iamblichus goes on to say that, while *"demons present the appearance of smouldering fire,"*[8] the angels, by contrast, *"...are resplendent with light."*[9] Greater still is the appearance of the gods: *"The images of the gods glow with abundance of light,"*[10] he says. Indeed, so beautiful is the vision of the gods that *"...there flashes out from the gods Beauty which seems inconceivable, holding the beholders fixed with wonder, imparting to them an unutterable gladness, displaying itself to view with ineffable symmetry."*[11]

This same acuity of vision was experienced by Proclus, as his biographer Marinus recounts: *"The philosopher was cleansed by the Chaldean purification; then he* [Proclus] *held converse, as he himself mentions in one of his* [lost] *works, with the luminous apparitions of Hecate, which he saw with his own eyes."*[12]

While reading the debates between the Neo-Platonic philosophers, I have always had the clear impression that both achieved a mystical state of oneness (*henosis*). But, the new, more philosophical conception of *theoria* lead to a rare and, indeed, rarified encounter with the One as the source of all conceptual forms (*eidé*), while the more ancient practice of *theoria,* coupled with theurgy, led to overwhelming visions of the One, now as the source of a whole hierarchy of heavenly angels and less-than-heavenly demons.

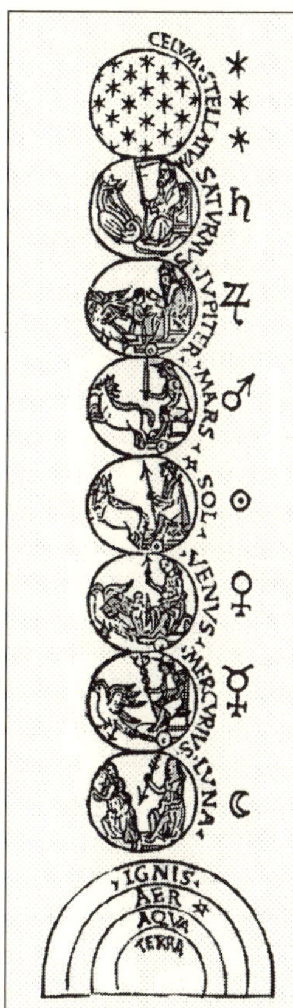

Fig. 27.3 - The Emanations

III. *Sunthêmata:* Proclus on the Sacred Art

In his defence of theurgy, Iamblichus calls upon the more ancient worldview of 'the emanations', where the divine One shines its light into all things – from the luminous planets on high to the darkest and grossest matter below:

"But energy of the divine Fire itself shines forth spontaneously in all directions, and being both self-called and self-operating, is active in like manner through all things, those alike that impart [the divine fire – the planets] *and those that can receive it* [the elements]*."*[13] Indeed: *"Not only does it shine from without, and fill all things, but it likewise permeates all the elements, occupies the earth, and air and fire and water, and leaves nothing destitute of itself."*[14]

While the Divine Light shines through all things, the wise theurgist learned to distinguish its varying degrees of power and the assorted correspondences that result. More specifically, the One 'imparted' its divine fire to the seven luminaries in the heavens – Saturn, Jupiter, Mars, the Sun, Venus, Mercury and the Moon. And each of these, in turn, exerted its influence on 'those that can receive it' – all the images in the sublunary realm, composed of the four elements in the aether – Fire, Air, Water and Earth.

Theurgists brought together the higher and lower powers and, through contemplation, ritually united them – to create symbols of the Sacred:

"The theurgic art in many cases links together stones, plants, animals, aromatic substances, and other such things that are sacred, perfect and godlike, and then from all of these composes an integrated and pure receptacle [for the gods.] *One must select material that is akin to the gods, capable of harmonizing with the construction of the divine dwellings, the consecration of statues, and indeed for the performance of the sacrificial rites in general."*[15]

Proclus, the Neo-Platonic heir to Iamblichus, elaborated upon this worldview. In his text *'On the Sacred Art'*, he showed how all of creation moves, like by like, in accord with the higher powers. Alas, only fragmentary remains of his text have come down to us through time. *'On the Sacred Art'* begins by noting how, individually, each existing thing 'prays in accordance with the rank it occupies':

"How else could it be that the sunflower (hêliotropia) moves in accordance with the sun and the moonflower (selênotropia) with the moon, each, according to its ability, turning around with the luminaries of the world?"[16]

Observing the lotus flower, he remarks: *"Its petals are closed before the appearance of the sun's rays, but it gradually opens them as the sun begins to rise, unfolding them as it reaches its zenith and curling them up again as it descends. What then is the difference between the human manner of hymning the sun, by opening and closing the mouth and lips, and that of the lotus by opening and closing its petals?"*[17]

But even lowly things like stones may become vehicles for the divine emanations: *"For stones as well can be seen to be infused with the emanations of the luminaries, thus we see the rays of the sun reproduced in the golden rays of the sunstone (hêlitên)* [...while] *the moonstone (selênitên) changes both its markings and its patterns along with the moon."*[18]

Thus, a series of correspondences arises between all that is above and all that is below: *"There are seen to be on the earth,"* Proclus remarks, *"suns and moons in a terrestrial form; and in the heavens, all the plants, stones and animals, after a celestial manner."*[19] The philosopher ends with the stirring declaration, *"Thus, all things are full of gods."*[20]

In another text, the *Commentary on the Timaeus of Plato*, Proclus describes how each planet leaves its 'seal' or impression on objects from the lower world: *"For Nature... inserts in bodies the impressions of their alliance to the divinities. In some, indeed, inserting solar, but in others, lunar impressions; and in others again, the symbol of some other god."*[21]

Hence, although the divine One is present throughout the Chain of Being – linking all things into an orderly whole – a series of correspondences evolve between the various levels. These divine signs or tokens are called *sunthêmata* by the theurgists – a word sometimes translated as 'symbols' but usually more distinctly as 'signs' or 'sigils'.

The Greeks already had a word for 'symbol' – *sumbolon*. But a *sunthema* was different; it was a divine token that, like hieroglyphs, immediately manifest the Sacred through its very shape and form; it bore upon its surface the marks or 'impressions' of its heavenly counterpart, and moved in accord with the higher powers. The art of the theurgists, like that of the later alchemists, was to understand 'the divine workings' (*theurgia*) and to perform a series of operations that combined the divine signs (*sunthêmata*) so as to effect a complete transformation, and indeed, 'a perfection' of the material at hand.

During the statue's creation, the appropriate materials were brought together – alabaster, sandstone, gold, precious jewels, meteoric iron – and fused. During its consecration (- *telestikē* means both *'to consecrate'* and *'to make perfect'*), the work was ritually bathed, anointed, incensed and carried into the light of day, thus transforming it into a *sacred* image (*agalma*).

In one passage from 'On the Sacred Art' – the only passage where Proclus describes *theurgy* directly – he says:

"From these facts, the masters of the Sacred Art found the way to pay divine honours to the Higher Powers, by following what lay in front of their eyes... By mixing together many different things, they unified the emanations [to make] *a likeness of that Whole which exists before every thing else comes into being. And so they often constructed images* (agalmata) *and incenses from these mixtures, mingling the divided divine sigils* (sunthêmata) *into one."*[22]

In many Egyptian *bas reliefs,* we behold the Pharaoh offering incense to a divine statue, or leading it out of the temple in a sacred procession, to become irradiated by Ra's light. The Opening of the Eyes and Mouth ceremony (described last chapter), as well as the Eleusinian Mysteries, involve similar such offerings and purifications. While 'incense' was the principal means of consecrating a statue, Algis Uždavinys notes that other theurgic operations were possible: *"The statue (agalma) is regarded as a vessel and container for the divine powers that take up residence inside it. The awakening of these powers is sometimes achieved by the practice of putting* pharmaka *(remedies, drugs, herbs...) into hollow statues and thereby animating them."*[23]

Before his untimely death in 2010, the Lithuanian scholar Algis Uždavinys returned to many ancient texts neglected by time and re-discovered much of value in their pages. This is especially true of the Orphic, Pythagorean, Gnostic, Hermetic and Neo-Platonic writings which he grouped together under the heading of 'Emanationist' cosmologies, since they all share a common core: that the divine Unity unfolded into multiple levels of being (the 'emanations'); and that the fundamental aim of our existence is the return to our original state of oneness with the Divine (*henosis*). Hence, through *theoria* and theurgic rites, we may accomplish *"...the return of our souls to god* [as] *either a fusion with the divine (theokrasia), or a perfect union (henosis panteles)"*[24]

The consecration of a sacred statue, Uždavinys says, ultimately creates a portal for transcendence:

"Telestikē (the term is derived from the verb telein, to consecrate, to initiate, to make perfect) is not a kind of rustic sorcery (goēteia). Rather it is a means to share or participate in the creative energies of the gods by constructing and consecrating their material receptacles, their cultic vehicles, which then function as the anagogic tokens, as sumbola and sunthēmata (symbol and sign)."[25]

Regarding *'sumbola and sunthēmata'* he writes, *"The symbol (sumbolon, synthema) is viewed as the central link between the divine realm and the human world."*[26] And: *"These images... function as 'windows of transcendence' irradiating divine power and grace."*[27]

IV. *Psychanodia* – The Soul Ascent

Theurgy was also called *Hieratike* – 'the Sacred Art.' Like alchemy, it was not only an attempt to re-enact 'the divine workings' (*theurgia*) through a series of ritual operations that 'combined the divine signs' (*sunthēmata*). Rather, a form of meditation was added to these ritual stages, making it a graduated ascent (*anagôgé*) in the mind of the contemplator. Such a 'soul ascent' was known as *psychanodia* in the ancient world.

At the foundation of the Emanationist philosophy, the soul recognizes its true nature: it has *proceeded* from the One (*proôdos*) and it will *return* to the One (*epistrophe*). This fundamental knowledge and remembrance (the *gnôsis*) constitutes our beginning, middle and end. Iamblichus described it as *"The issuing forth of all from the One, the returning again into the One, and the absolute rule of the One in everything."*[28]

Within this lifetime, we may gain knowledge of *the way* of return, through mystical experience. This was the purpose of the ancient Mystery rites, to ritually enact those steps (*theurgia*) and to witness (*theoria*) the self-unfolding of the One, in a moment of revelation (*epoptika*). By engraving those steps in our memory, *the way* of 'the soul's ascent' (*psychanodia*) could be remembered after death.

In some of the more amazing passages from *On the Mysteries* (*De mysteriis*), Iamblichus describes how the ancient Mystery rites, such as those at Eleusis, led to the soul's visionary ascent and union with the Divine:

"From these Performances it is plain, that what we are now discoursing about is the Safe Return of the Soul, for while contemplating the Blessed Spectacles, the soul exchanges one life for another, becomes linked to another energy, and rightly viewing the matter, it seems to be not even human, but is filled with the most blessed energy of the gods... Indeed, the upward way through the invocations effects for the priests a purifying of the passions, a release from the condition of generated life, and likewise a total union to the Divine First Cause."[29]

In another startling passage, he writes:

"By such a purpose, therefore, the gods being gracious and propitious, give forth light abundantly to the theurgists, both calling their souls upward into themselves, providing for them union to themselves in the Chorus, and accustoming them, while they are still in the body, to hold themselves aloof from corporeal things, and likewise to be led up to their own eternal and noetic First Cause."[30]

However, Iamblichus admits that the Visionary Ascent is not easily accomplished. Such a revelation *"...only arises rarely..."*[31] and is only *"...activated by the performance of the perfect sacrifice..."*[32] The priest or theurgist must time the ritual properly, enact the steps perfectly, and be in a sufficient state of purity both physically and mentally.

During the rite, the theurgist's mind must be fully focussed, and his hands faultlessly concentrated on the symbolic manipulations, so as to lead him toward a perfect attunement and oneness with the higher, divine Mind: *"It is the communion of a friendship based on like-mindedness and an indissoluble bond of unity that gives coherence to the performance of hieratic rites,"*[33] Iamblichus writes. But in the end, *"Ascent to the intelligible fire is granted to theurgists – a process which indeed must be proposed as the goal... of every theurgic operation."*[34]

V. The Soul Vehicle

The lower world, for the Neo-Platonists, is a 'place of generation' where our bodies, as material receptacles, constitute a kind of prison and corruption for the divinely-inspired soul:

"The human soul," Iamblichus writes, *"is held fast by a single form, and is obscured by the body on every side; and this condition* [is] *called the river of Forgetfulness or the water of Lethe, or 'ignorance' or 'madness' or 'bondage through excessive emotions'* [or being] *detained in a prison."*[35]

To rise up, through visions, to the higher spheres, the soul must free itself of the body. This 'out of body experience' however, is only temporary; and the soul soon finds itself back in the clasp of matter once more:

"For when we become entirely soul and are outside of the body, and soaring on high with all the gods of the non-material realm, we occupy ourselves with sublime visions. Then again, we are bound in the oyster-like body and held fast under the dominion of matter, and are corporeal in feeling and aspiration."[36]

For the soul to journey upward and away from the body, a vehicle (*ochêma*) was required. This is, perhaps, one of the most amazing ideas to arise within Neo-Platonism – the concept of the Soul Vehicle:

"All this kind of divination..." Iamblichus writes, *"is encompassed by one power which someone might call 'evoking the light.' This somehow illuminates the aether-like and luminous vehicle* [*aitherodes kai augoeides ochêma*] *surrounding the soul with divine light, from which vehicle the divine appearances, set in motion by the gods' will, take possession of the imaginative power in us."*[37]

In *Iamblichus and the Theory of the Vehicle of the Soul*, John F. Finamore explains that one of the chief purposes of the Soul Vehicle, during the visionary ascent, is to *"...act as the organ of sense-perception and imagination,"*[38] so that, once it is fully immersed in the divine light, the vehicle becomes *"...filled with divine images."*[39]

Proclus also wrote about this vehicle, which he described variously as a luminous vehicle (*augoeides ochêma*) or spiritual vehicle (*pneumatic ochêma*). More interesting still, he viewed the Soul Vehicle as spherical in form, though other geometric shapes were possible: *"Our vehicle is rendered spherical, and is moved circularly, when the soul is in a remarkable degree assimilated to the divine mind (nous)."*[40]

The Soul Vehicle is the instrument of higher perception in us. Being 'aether-like and luminous', it temporarily replaces the soul's material receptacle with an ethereal one (*aitherodes ochêma*) to rise up through the sub-lunar realms, and even with a luminous one (*augoeides ochêma*) to journey through the heavenly spheres. Indeed, the rays of divine light become the shafts through which the Soul Vehicle ascends and descends.

VI. The Gnostic Garment of Light

The Neo-Platonic Soul Vehicle resembles, to a remarkable degree, the Garment of Light described by the Gnostics. Like the luminous vehicle, the Garment of Light was needed to ascend through the planetary spheres. However, since the Gnostics perceived the lower guardians of heaven's gates (the *Archons*) to be essentially malevolent, the Garment of Light also protected the soul during its other-worldly passage:

"The powers [Archons] *do not see those who are clothed in the perfect light, and consequently are not able to detain them. One will clothe himself in this light sacramentally in the union."*[41]

It was during the Gnostic rite of baptism that one underwent a visionary ascent and was granted the Garment of Light:

"And I delivered him to those who give robes – Yammon, Elasso, Amenai – and they covered him with a robe from the robes of the Light; and I delivered him to the baptizers, and they baptized him – Micheus, Michar, Mnesinous – and they immersed him in the spring of the Water of Life."[42]

The origin of the concept of the Garment of Light remains laden with mystery. According to one Gnostic text, it was Christ, during his first descent into the world, who put on the Garment of Light, which is composed of all the emanations, from the highest to the lowest: *"Afterwards the mother established her first-born son (...) And she gave to him a garment in which to accomplish all things. And in it were all bodies: the body of fire, and the body of water, and the body, of air and the body of earth, and the body of wind, and the body of angels, and the body of archangels, and the body of powers, and the body of mighty ones, and the body of gods, and the body of lords. In a word, within it were all bodies so that none could hinder him from going to the height or from going down to the abyss."*[43]

When we put on the Garment of Light, during the Gnostic baptism, we were, in essence, putting on an image of Christ, who is referred to in *The Gospel of Philip* as 'the living man': *"The living water is a body* [i.e. the baptismal water becomes a garment]. *It is necessary that we put on the living man.* [i.e. Christ as a garment]. *Therefore, when he is about to go down into the water, he unclothes himself, in order that he may put on the living man."*[44]

To protect himself from evil influences, the Gnostic wore the Garment of Light, both during the Visionary Ascent and during their afterlife voyage through the heavenly spheres. But, once it was acquired, the Gnostic was called upon to wear the garment all the time, so as to become a living image or manifestation of Christ in this world. Once more, in the words of the *Gospel of Philip*: *"You saw Christ, you became Christ."*[45]

But, important as it was, the luminous Soul Vehicle or Garment of Light was only one of the many *sunthêmata* required for the Soul Ascent.

VII. Maps of the Afterworld: Reconstructing the Soul's Route to Salvation

The divine signs (*sunthêmata*) manipulated by the theurgist were not only images, but also sounds, gestures and scents – anything that would stimulate the memory of our true hidden state, as a particle of divine oneness. The *sunthêmata* included chants, mantras, mudras, vocalizations and hierarchies of names. Different kinds of incense stimulated different memory-cues in the mind. The visualized images were not only figurative, but geometric and numerical. All had the 'anagogic' function of lifting the initiate higher, through a series of graduated steps, to union with the Divine (*anagogia* means *'to elevate'*).

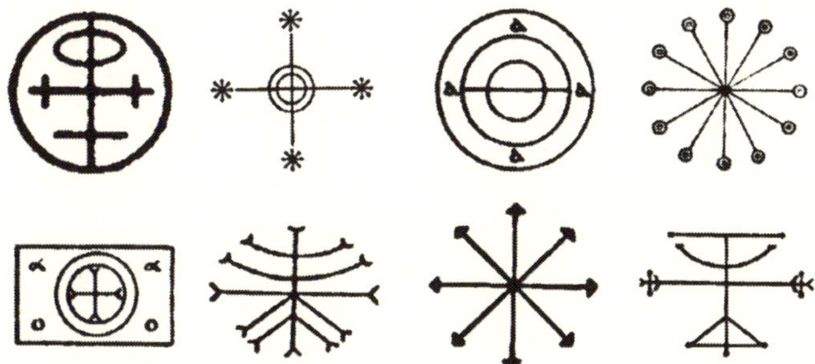

Fig. 27.4 - Gnostic Sigils from *The First and Second Books of IEOU (Jeu)*

Once again, we return to the researches of Algis Uždavinys. The theurgy of the Soul Ascent, he notes, occurred in stages. On the one hand, the theurgist ascended through the use of *"...chains of mantric names, the anagogic sounds of the sacred chants accompanied by inner visualizations and resulting in divine epiphanies,"* to which he adds, *"various divine numbers and geometric shapes, secret names (arrheta onomata) and material objects, all of them serving as theurgic tokens and means of elevation."*[46]

On the other hand, the theurgist also had to remember the deeper meaning of all these symbols. Describing the One as the 'noetic principle' – meaning the higher Mind (*Nous*) which 'thinks' (*noésis*) upon itself and thus 'thinks' *us* into being – he writes: *"Because of its noetic origins, the soul has an inborn (albeit temporarily forgotten) knowledge of these world-creating, world-ruling and, simultaneously, elevating names... When the essential hidden sunthema* [divine sign] *is remembered, re-awakened, and re-sounded, the soul, mythically speaking, returns... to its noetic and supra-noetic principle."*[47]

Thus, through the full enactment of the theurgic Soul Ascent, accompanied by meditation and contemplation, the soul experiences, in Uždavinys' words, *"...the One in its perennial contemplation of itself."*[48]

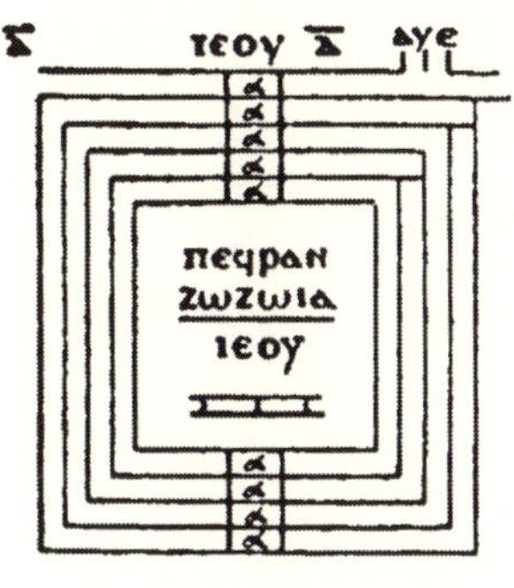

Fig. 27.5 - Diagram from *The First Book of IEOU (Jeu)*

Many of the Gnostic *sunthêmata* have come down to us, and these include geometric sigils (also called 'seals' – Fig. 27.4) and elaborate names with long vowel sequences. Some of the Gnostic diagrams (Fig. 27.5) resemble Buddhist mandalas, and reveal thereby their deeper purpose – *as mnemonic devices.* Once the soul is freed from the body (whether in a visionary state or during the afterlife journey), it must *navigate* its passage through the post-mortem realm, which the Gnostics called the *aeons* and the Buddhists, the *bardos*. Gnostic sigils and Buddhist mandalas served the same purpose: as mental maps or road marks for reconstructing the soul's route to salvation.

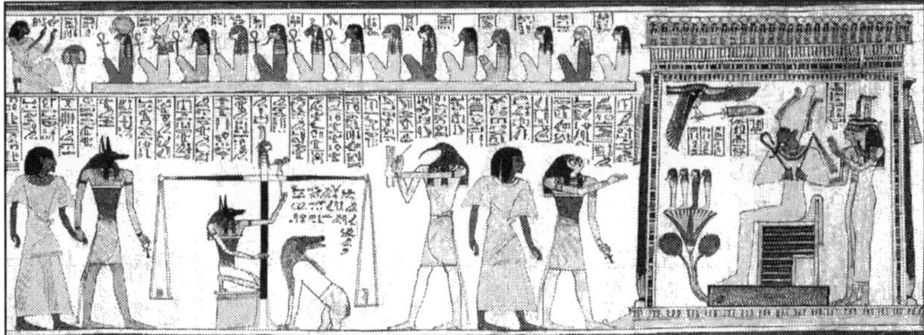

Fig. 27.6 - The Judgement Hall of Osiris

This idea is perennial and pervasive, found in the oldest texts of the Egyptians and Babylonians. Where the Egyptian *Books of the Afterlife* envisioned the soul journey as a *horizontal* boat-trip through the twelve gates of the Netherworld, the Sumerian myth of Inanna portrayed it, instead, as a *vertical* journey through the seven heavenly spheres.

The Egyptian *Book of Gates*, for example, depicts the afterlife journey as a passage through twelve distinct 'gates', one for each hour of the night. Accompanying Re on his solar barque, the soul encounters demons at each doorway, repelling them through a series of protective 'spells'. At the fifth hour (i.e. at the mid-point of the journey, in the very nadir of the Netherworld) the barque reaches the Judgement Hall of Osiris (Fig. 27.6). Here, each passenger's heart is weighed against Maat's 'feather of truth'. Only those *'who have magnified the forms of the god'*[49] pass beyond the fifth gate. On the morning horizon (*akhet*), they fuse with the sun, and are granted eternal life. As 'solarized' beings or stars, they join the eternal cycle of the cosmos.

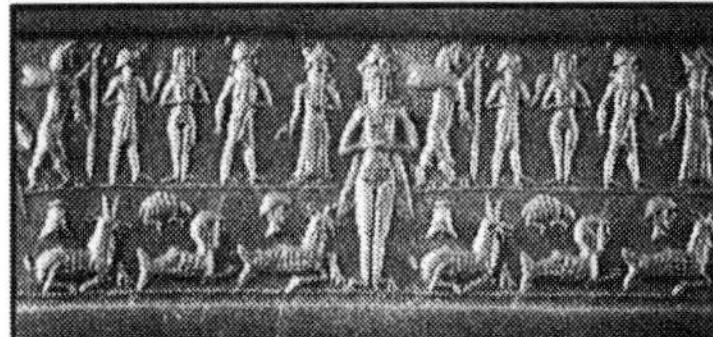

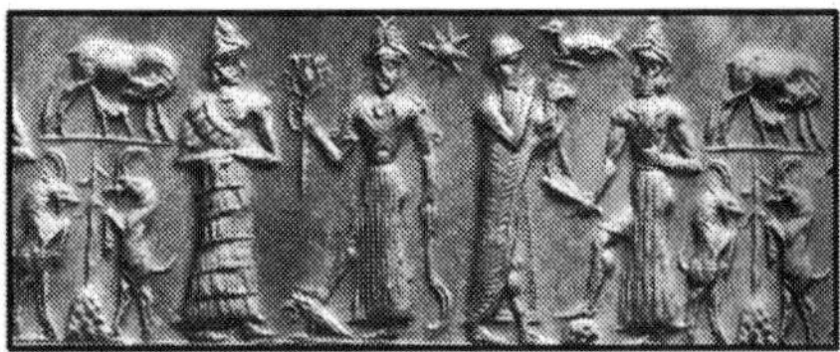

Fig. 27.7 - Roll-out of Sumerian Cylinder Seals: *Inanna's Descent to the Underworld*

In the Sumerian myth of Inanna's *Descent to the Underworld* (Fig. 27.7), the Goddess 'from the Great Above' passes downward through seven gates – corresponding to the seven planetary doorways – and surrenders one of her garments or talismans at each gate until, naked, she enters 'the Great Below'. This ancient mythologem lies at the root of Salome's famous Dance of the Seven Veils.

The recurrence of the numbers seven and twelve are due to the cosmological model of the Egyptians and Babylonians, which persisted from Ptolemy all the way through to the Middle Ages (Fig. 27.8). Seven was the number of visible planets in the heavens, which were envisioned as a series of blackened spheres-within-spheres, so that only the planetary spark was visible – like a doorway to the effulgence of light beyond it. Below the planets lay the 'sublunary' realm ('under the moon's sway'), which consisted of five more spheres-within-spheres – with the aetheric sphere outermost; fire and

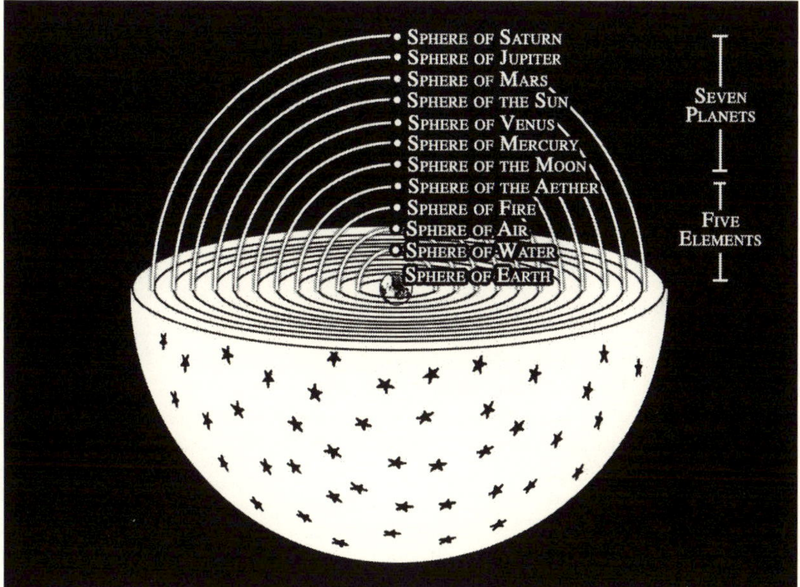

Fig. 27.8 - The Cosmos as Seven plus Five equals Twelve Spheres Within Spheres

air rising naturally to the next two spheres, and water and earth descending to the innermost spheres. Hence, the seven planets and five elements created a twelve-fold cosmos – a hierarchy of twelve realms varying in degrees of light and darkness, of spirit and matter, of order and chaos.

In the Gnostic and Hermetic texts, the soul's release from the five elements of the body and its ascent through the heavenly spheres is described in detail. Take, for example, this passage from the first book of *The Corpus Hermeticum*:

"First, in releasing the material body you give the body over to alteration, and the form that you used to have vanishes... Thence the human being [or soul] *rushes up through the cosmic framework, at the first zone* [the lunar sphere] *surrendering the energy of increase and decrease; at the second* [Mercury] *evil machination, a device now inactive; at the third* [Venus] *the illusion of longing, now inactive; at the fourth* [the Sun] *the ruler's arrogance, now feed of excess; at the fifth* [Mars] *unholy presumption and daring recklessness; at the sixth* [Jupiter] *the evil impulses that come from wealth, now inactive; and at the seventh zone* [Saturn] *the deceit that lies in ambush. And then, stripped of the effects of the cosmic framework, the human enters the region of the ogdoad* [the eighth heaven of the fixed stars]*; he has his own proper power, and along with the blessed, he hymns the father."*[50]

As this passage makes clear, certain qualities were associated with each planet. During her descent, Inanna surrendered a garment or talisman at each planetary doorway. In the Hermetic text, the ascending soul is '*stripped of the effects of the cosmic framework*' and surrenders a certain soul-quality as it rises. The Gnostics, meanwhile, emphasized the *negative* qualities associated with each planet, since they regarded it as an evil threshold-guardian or *Archon*.

According to the Gnostic view, when our soul first separated from the One and descended into dark matter, it 'put on' seven soul-garments – one 'passion of the soul' was granted by each threshold-guardian, leaving a distinct mark or seal on the soul. Descending further into matter, the soul also 'put on' the body – which was a dark material receptacle composed of the four elements in the aether. During its post-mortem ascent (and during a vision), the soul shed the earthly receptacle and attempted to surrender each of its soul garments – like a seal or talisman paid to the planetary Archon or guardian (whom they also called 'toll collectors').

What were the 'passions of the soul' associated with each planet? None of the Gnostic texts quite agreed on this point. In the above Hermetic text, the planetary character of each Greek god is evoked, giving us a clue. In general, the seven negative qualities associated with each Soul Garment may be listed as:

- Delusion – Saturn
- Envy – Jupiter
- Wrath – Mars
- Pride – the Sun
- Lust – Venus
- Greed – Mercury
- Inconstancy – the Moon

By associating further negative qualities with the elements (and their humours in the body), we may add five more:

- Fear – the Aether
- Strife – choleric Fire
- Dishonesty – sanguine Air
- Apathy – phlegmatic Water
- Depression – melancholy Earth

Following Plato, the theurgists saw the body as 'a prison' which holds us *'in bondage through excessive emotions'* (as Iamblichus says above). The Hermeticists had a more mitigated view onto the body (Nature, they said, was divine), while the Gnostics went to extremes (the only escape from this dark material world was to become ascetic or libertine). But all agreed that excess of emotion, or the surrendering of the soul to bodily passions, had a huge and negative impact on the visionary ascent.

For this reason, much preparation was needed, to cleanse the mind of negative thoughts and purge the body of negative feelings. In Gnosticism, a series of sacraments were developed, called the Mystery of the Five Seals. Like the other ancient Mysteries, the experiences at the heart of these initiatory rites were never revealed. But, their purpose was to prepare and cleanse the initiate before receiving the final revelation.

The Gnostic baptism was an ornate ritual that used visualizations and the Visionary Ascent to reveal the full extent of the afterlife journey. Through sacred names, vocalizations and sigils, it ritually engraved in the memory the soul's way of salvation. We may basically reconstruct the Gnostic baptism* as follows:

After a three-fold immersion in water (*baptism*) and a single unction with oil (*chrism*) as well as ingesting a sacrament (*eucharist*), the initiate began the Visionary Ascent (*resurrection*) by 'renouncing' the Archons of the lower aeons (*renunciation*) and 'invoking' the Angels of the upper aeons (*invocation*) through a series of names, vocalizations and sigils. To pass beyond the Archons' planetary gateways, the initiate also had to visualize the 'stripping off' of its five bodily garments and seven soul garments.

Passing into the Upper Aeons, the initiate was then 'called' by their spiritual name (*naming*) and their image was 'sealed' in the watery light of the upper aeons (*sealing*). Thus, eternally clothed in their 'Garment of Light', they experienced a momentary revelation, through union with the Divine (*the Bridal Chamber*).

While many Gnostic gospels attest to the power and beauty of this Mystery, others warn that the soul's passage to salvation is not easily attained. In the *Apocalypse of Paul,* for example, the Archon of the fourth heaven detains a soul, and brings forth witnesses to attest to its worldly corruption. *"When the soul heard these things, it gazed downward in sorrow. And then it gazed upward. It was cast down. The soul that was cast down went to a body which had been prepared for it."*[51] Like the Neo-Platonists and Hermeticists (who were much inspired by Plato's myth of Er), the Gnostics held the view of *metempsychosis*, of the soul's cyclic rebirth in another body.

In *The Dialogue of the Saviour*, Christ describes the afterworld passage, saying to his disciples:

"When the time of dissolution arrives, the first power of darkness will come upon you. Do not be afraid! ...If you are afraid of what is about to come upon you, it will engulf you. For there is not one among them who will spare you or show you mercy. But, look upon the [Archon], *since you have mastered every word on earth. ...The crossing place is fearful, but you, with a single mind, will pass it by!"*[52]

Throughout the ancient world, sacred texts and rituals were designed to help lead the initiate through their visionary experience. Incense and sacraments; visualizations and vocalizations; mantras and mudras – all these *sunthêmata* were ritually deployed to instill in the initiate a deep remembering of *the way* through the visionary afterlife. Leaving the body and ascending the heavenly spheres, the soul received the *gnôsis* of its true nature, witnessing its origin in the One.

But we must not forget that – it was the ancient hieratic works of art, like statues and icons, which momentarily transformed the theurgic experience into a divine revelation. The sacred images were not only 'aesthetically-pleasing' to the eye, but active channels of divine energy which had been ritually consecrated and activated. Through theurgy and *theoria*, the Visionary art of old had that tremendous power.

---

* For a literary reconstruction of the Gnostic Baptism ritual, see Chapter 11 of my novel *The Hidden Passion: A Novel of the Gnostic Christ Based on the Nag Hammadi Texts* (2007)

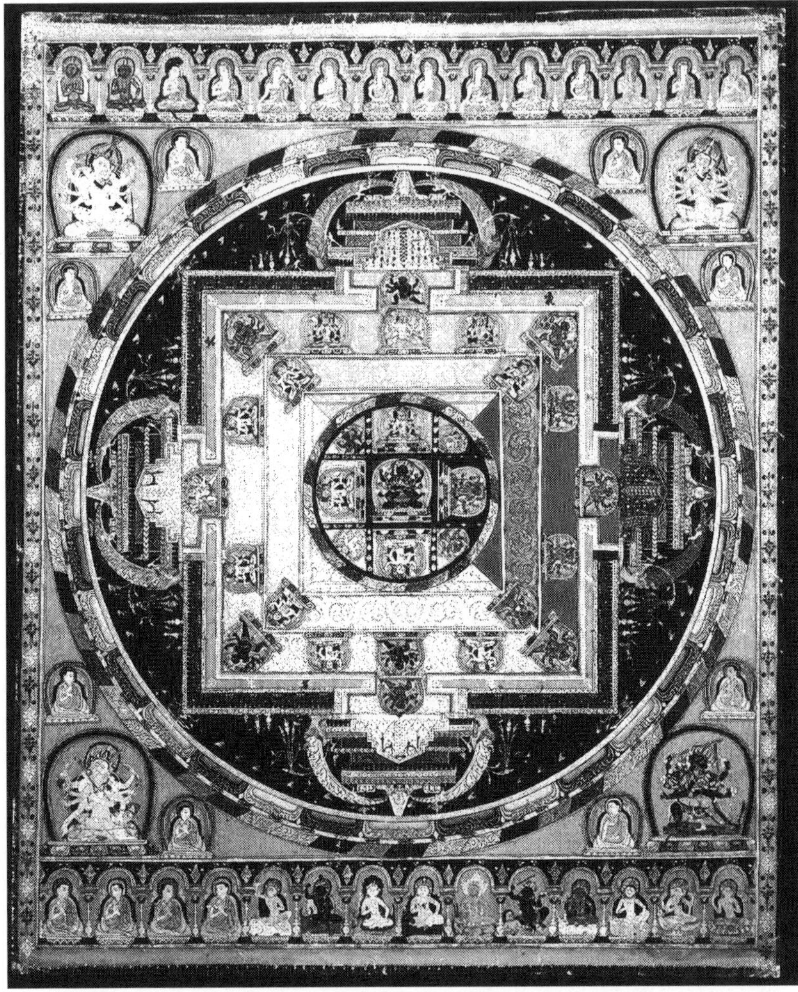

Fig. 28.1 - Thangka of the Guhyasamānja Mandala

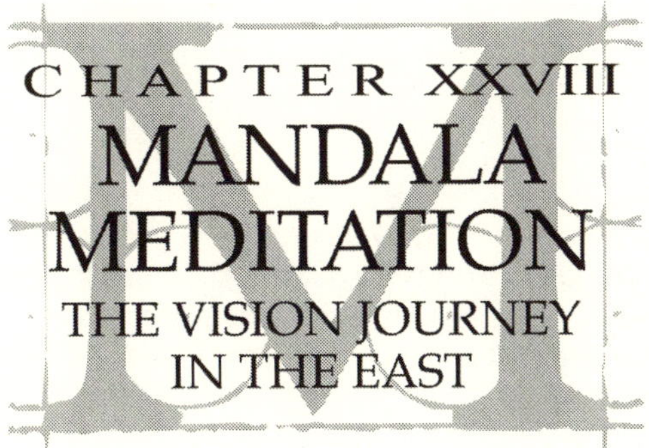

CHAPTER XXVIII MANDALA MEDITATION THE VISION JOURNEY IN THE EAST

I. Mandala Meditation: The Generation & Completion Stages

In February of 2014, during the Winter Trimester at The Vienna Academy of Visionary Art, Vera Atlantia and Kuba Ambrose initiated the students and teachers into a collective project: the creation of a Padmasambhava Mandala. Over the course of the next twelve weeks, we chanted, prayed and meditated while mixing paints and rendering figures on the four-sided design. Thanks to Timea Tallian, who had studied Thangka painting under Master Lopon Sangay Rinchen of the Trongsa monastery in Bhutan, we gained a deeper respect for their sacred traditions, learning how to pray while mixing the paints, and consecrating the final work with a mantra inscribed on the back.

All of this encouraged me to finally fulfill a life-long dream – of better understanding Thangka painting, and immersing myself into its contemplative practice. It was particularly Mandala meditation that absorbed my interest, with its *sādhana* visualizations upon a chosen *yidam* or meditation deity. As I immersed myself deeper in the subject, Andrew Stewart crossed my path. Our long discussions confirmed to me that Mandala Meditation is essentially linked to the Afterlife journey. I am forever grateful to Vera, Kuba, Timea and Andrew for introducing and initiating me to this revered art form.

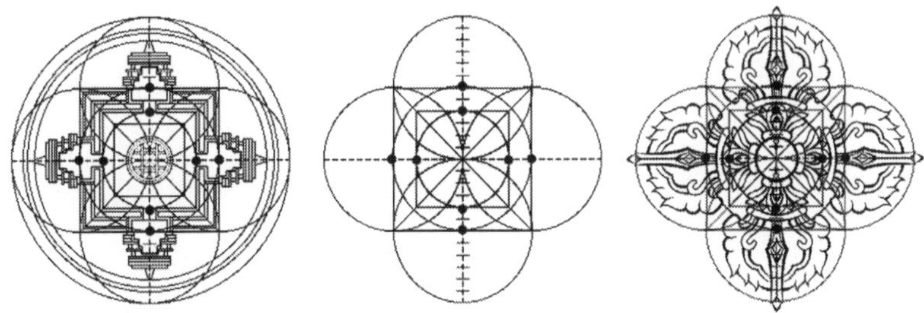

Fig. 28.2 - Geometric Construction of the Mandala and Vajra Diamond-Thunderbolt

In its deepest sense, the *mandala* is a cosmogram of the inner and outer worlds. At one and the same time, this design offers us a map of the mind's inner workings and a reconstruction of the entire cosmos. More than that, it is a clear manifestation of the enlightened mind, and an image of the world made perfect and true – transformed into the heavenly kingdom.

At the very centre of the mandala is the Tantric deity – an image of the yogini, bodhisattva or Buddha who is nothing less than the one true source of all these appearances. Made of clear transparent light, the mandala is an emanation of the enlightening mind at the centre, and all the figures at different levels are varying aspects of its own multiform appearance, whose essence and origin are one.

The Tibetan word for mandala – *dykil-'khor* – means, literally, 'that which encircles a centre.' As we can see in Fig. 28.2, a mandala is constructed through the intersection of six circles around a centre – one inner 8 x 8 squared circle and five more 12 x 12 circles: one inner squared and four outer ones on its circumference. The inner walls of the palace follow the 8 x 8 measures of the inner squared circle, while the outer walls follow the 12 x 12 measures of the main squared circle. Finally, the mandala's three protective rings follow the outer limits of the four outer circles (24 measures).

The principle form of Buddhism practiced in Tibet is Vajrayana Buddhism, which uses the four-pronged *vajra* or *dorje* (meaning 'diamond-thunderbolt') as its main emblem. The vajra is constructed through *the same basic geometry* as the mandala, and becomes in this way a symbolic reminder or microcosmic reflection of the whole. As a kind of sigil or *aide-mémoire*, its basic shape aids the contemplator in mentally reconstructing the mandala's four-fold architecture.

Traditionally, a Tantric practitioner must be initiated by a master through the rite of 'empowerment' (*wongkur* in Tibetan, from the Sanskrit *abhiṣeka* meaning consecration, sprinkling or baptism). This two stage process begins with the *Generation* stage (*utpattikrama* or *bskyed rim*, also called the creation or causal stage), where the mandala's Wrathful and Peaceful Deities are successively visualized, separate from each other and separate from one's self. After this comes the *Completion* stage (*nispanna-krama, sampanna-krama* or *rdzogs rim*, also called the realization or fruition stage), where the adept transcends the illusory separation and fuses (*samadhi*) with all the deities, particularly the Meditation Deity (*yidam*) at the centre of the mandala.

In some rites of empowerment, a painted mandala (or *thangka*) is used as a meditative support; in others, a more temporary sand mandala is ritually created and destroyed. Then again, the entire mandala may become an elaborate mental construct that is memorized by the practitioner and projected – onto their own body or that of their consort. Different texts (*sutras*) from different traditions offer different visualizations (*sādhanas*) – each with its own cosmology, deities and mandalas.

We are interested in the form of Tantra called *Anuttarayoga* ('unsurpassable union'). The *Anuttarayoga Tantra* uses the mandala initiation (or 'rite of empowerment') to recognize one's true Buddha-nature, as reflected by the image of the enlightened deity at the centre. Many steps (called 'purifications') are required to cleanse awareness of the concepts and feelings hindering this realization. The images of Wrathful and Peaceful Deities gradually transform the subtle energies at their root, so the experience of enlightenment may be attained.

There are three main types of mandala initiation. The 'Father Tantras', which include the *Guhyasamānja* and *Yamātaka* mandalas, emphasize 'method' (*upaya*) and 'compassion' (*karuna*) as an active and compelling way to transform one's wrath and anger. Meanwhile the 'Mother Tantras', which include the *Hevajra* and *Caṇḍamahāroṣaṇa* mandalas, emphasize 'wisdom' (*prajna*) as a more peaceful and passive way to transform one's longing and desire. Finally, the non-dual approach, as exemplified by the *Kālachakra* mandala, pursues both these paths equally. The central Meditation Deity often depicts a male and female figure as sexually united in *yab-yum* to symbolize this union.

One of the greatest Western expounders of Tibetan Buddhism is the American scholar Alexander Berzin. After graduating from Harvard with a doctorate in Sanskrit and Chinese, he lived in Dharamsala for twenty-nine years, studying under masters like Tsenzhab Serkong Rinpoche. In his *Introduction the Kalachakra Initiation*, Berzin describes the intensity and transformative power of *sadhana* – the visualization practice:

"From beginning to end, attending a Kalachakra initiation involves visualization. ...Visualization practice, however, involves sights, sounds, fragrances, tastes, physical sensations, mental feelings such as joy, and senses of who and where we are, what is around us and what is happening. ...It is a process of complete transformation, involving equally the mind, heart, feelings, sense of identity and spatial orientation.

During the visualizations, we try to feel that our spiritual master and ourselves are actually Buddha-figures, where we are is actually a mandala, and what we picture occurring is actually happening."[1]

The *Kalachakra Sutra* ('Teachings on the Wheels or Cycles of Time') constructs an elaborate mandala to ritually initiate monks into a deeper awareness of mind, body and the cosmos. From the outside, the mandala's four-sided, five-storey palace may be viewed as a physical map of the cosmos, with the planets revolving around the central axis of Mount Meru. But, from the inside, it is a diagram of the body's subtle energy system, where the red and white 'seeds' or 'drops' (*bindu*) from different psychic 'winds' (*prana*) flow through the three main channels of the subtle body, gathering at the five main focal points (*chakras*). The adept must master an understanding of the mandala on all these levels.

But, most of all, the mandala is a visual support for the Vision Journey. Its basic geometrical shape and many-armed deities all serve as *mnemonic devices* – as elaborate memory cues for remembering and navigating the soul's passage through the visionary realms, particularly the after-death passage through the *bardo* realms.

II. The Three Bodies, Worlds and Bardos

In Tantric practice, the Buddha reflects differing aspects of our true nature. One key to understanding mandala meditation is the *trikaya* doctrine, meaning literally the 'three bodies'. The *Nirmāṇakāya* (*Emanation Body*) describes our earthly, physical nature, which the Buddha manifest to us in Body. We experience this through our own body, and our perception of other bodily incarnations of the Buddha, such as bodhisattvas and gurus. The *Sambhokāya* (*Bliss body*) describes our true spiritual nature, as fully-enlightened beings, which the Buddha manifest to us through Speech. All appearances of the Buddha, in the form of spoken *mantras*, performed *mudras* or painted *thangkas*, fall into this category. The *Dharmakāya* (*Truth body*) describes our absolute nature, as a limitless ocean of 'no-self', which the Buddha manifest to us through Mind. This is the 'clear light mind' of enlightened bliss.

Following the *trikaya* doctrine, there are three principal levels of existence: the *Kamadhatu* or Desire World, where all beings are trapped in the 'gross' realm of the senses, due to desire (*kama*); the *Rupadhatu* or Form World where, freed of desire (*kama*), all the deities have 'subtle' energy bodies (*rupa*) and sense organs of light; and the *Arupadhatu* or Formless World where beings have no form whatsoever (*arupa*) and exist in pure, clear consciousness.

These three aspects of ourselves are reflected back to us during the vision journey or afterlife journey, which also has a three-fold structure. In the *Bardo Thodol* or *Tibetan Book of the Dead*, the visionary journey through three of the afterlife realms (*bardos*) is described in detail. Immediately after death, during the first to third day, one may journey directly into the *Chikhai bardo* which, like the *Dharmakāya*, is a limitless ocean of 'no-self' – the Buddha's clear light mind.

Unprepared for this overwhelming experience, the vision journey shifts during the third to seventh day to the *Chonyid bardo*, where one reaps all the benefits of good deeds (*karma*) sewn over many life times. Now, Peaceful Deities appear, as a reflection of our true spiritual nature – the *Sambhokāya* (*Bliss body*) manifestation of ourselves as fully-enlightened beings.

From the eighth day onward, the journey darkens into the *Sidpa bardo*, where the karmic reflections of our own evil inclinations appear as Wrathful Deities. Fearful and confused, the mind seeks re-birth in another body, and so the *Nirmāṇakāya* (*Emanation Body*) appears as our next earthly, physical refuge.

While the text of the *Bardo Thodol* is read aloud to the deceased, in the hopes of orienting the disembodied consciousness through the post-mortem *bardo* realms; other Tantric texts, such as the *Guhyasamānja Sutra,* offer visualizations and Vision Journeys to adepts *during this life*, in the hopes of orienting consciousness through the *bardos* of their own subtle energies, as personified by the various Peaceful and Wrathful Deities.

III. The Guhyasamānja Visualization

Guhyasamānja means literally *'the Secret Assembly'.* Anyone who has read a Gnostic or Alchemical text will not be surprised by the language of the *Guhyasamānja Sadhana,* which fascinates and confuses at the same time. Images of sex and death intermingle with sacred invocations, veiling literal instructions in metaphor and, at times, leading the initiate into labyrinthine passages of visionary wonder, terror and fear.

First, we must orient ourselves spatially within the mandala, before reading the sadhana to visualize the meditative journey. With the aid of the *Guhyasamānja Akṣobbyavajra* mandala, we may contemplate the *Guhyasamānja* initiation, as an examples of the Vision Journey in the East.

After a series of opening prayers, including one to *"the single eye that has directly seen,"*[2] the *Guhyasamānja Sadhana* evokes the mandala's creation in the form of a myth: *"Within a state of Voidness comes a PAM..."*[3] – this divine seed-syllable erupts like the sun from a lotus, while a wheel appears spinning at its centre. The mandala spreads its petals in all directions, and at the centre, the main Meditation Deity says, *"I arise as Vajradhara... with three faces – white, black and red – and six arms... My consort is white* [Sparsavajra, also called] *Vajradhatu Ishvari, with three faces – white, black and red – and six arms... We embrace each other* [as] *father and mother."*[4] (Fig. 28.7)

The first thing we notice about the *Akṣobbyavajra* (Tibetan: *Mi bskyod pa*) version of the *Guhyasamānja* mandala (Fig. 28.3) is its unique shape and the geometric disposition of its figures.[5] Thirty-two principle deities are arranged onto its flat orthographic projection of a five-storey palace with four gates, surrounded by a protective circle. The inner central circle is divided into nine parts (resembling a 'magic square'). At its centre appears Vajradhara, in the form of Akshobhya, embracing his consort Sparsavajra in the *yab-yum* position. (Hence, Vajradhara embracing Sparsavajra count as two of the 'thirty-two deities' even though there are only 'thirty-one' places or 'seats' in the mandala).

Through their joining (*yab-yum*), the divine pair expands outward in eight directions. First orthogonally, in the four cardinal directions (east, south, west and north – the eastern gate is always at the bottom of mandalas) and then diagonally, in the four inter-cardinal directions (south-east, south-west, north-west and north-east). Ultimately, the divine pair expands outward into all thirty-two deities, the surrounding palace and its protective circle.

Occupying the four cardinal seats are Vairochana, Ratnasambhava, Amitabha and Amoghasiddhi who, together with Akshobhya in the centre, make up the *Five Meditation Buddhas* (or *Dhyani Buddhas* - Fig. 28.6).

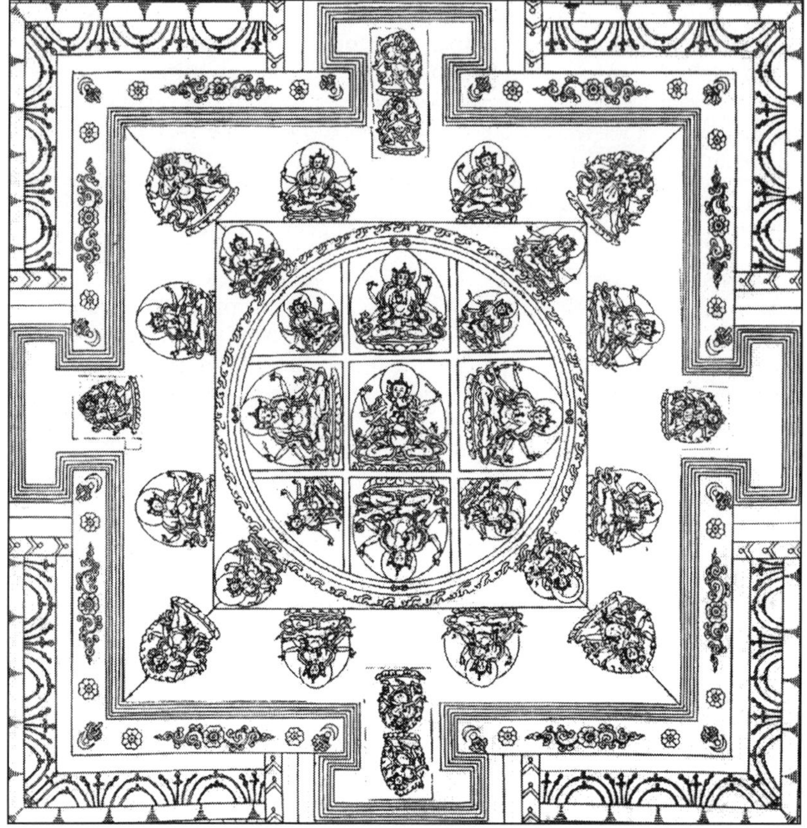

Fig. 28.3 - Central Section of the Guhyasamānja Akṣobbyavajra Mandala
Showing the Palace Interior Without Gateways and Protective Rings

The four inter-cardinal seats, together with their diagonal extensions into the corners of the square one level below, constitute the seats of *"...the eight goddesses* [who] *have their hair half tied up in a knot... They are extremely voluptuous, smiling and slender, beautified with such charming features as slanting eyes glancing to the side. In the prime of their youth, they enjoy the pleasures of the five desirable sensory objects."*[6]

So, sitting in the circle's four inter-cardinal seats are the goddesses Lochana, Mamaki, Pandaravasin and Tara. And moving outward to the corners of the small square, we find Rupavajra, Sabdavajra, Gandhavajra and Rasavajra. These eight are traditionally called the Eight Offering Goddesses (*Astapujadevi*), of which five are the consorts (*prajna*) of the *Five Meditation Buddhas*. Lochana is the consort of Vairochana; Mamaki goes with Akshobhya; Pandaravasin with Amitabha; and Tara with Amoghasiddhi. Sparsavajra, who appears in the centre, takes the form Vajradhatvishvari when she becomes the consort of Ratnasambhava.

On exterior sides of the inner square, flanking the entrance gates, are eight Bodhisattvas, called the *Ashtamahabodhisattva* or Eight Great Bodhisattvas. They are Maitreya and Kshitigarbha (east door), Vajrapani and Khagarbha (also called Akasagarbha) (south door), Lokeshvara (also called Avalokitesvara) and Manjushri (west door), Sarvanivarana-viskambhini and Samantabhadra (north door).

Finally, on the outer edges of the mandala, the Ten Wrathful Deities appear: four stand at the centre of each doorway, four appear in the corners of the palace, and two more occupy the zenith and nadir, just outside the top and bottom doorways.

The four cardinal doorways are guarded by Yamantakrit in the east; Prajnantakrit in the south; Hayagriva in the west; and Vighnantakrit in the north. Meanwhile, in the south-east corner stands Achala; in the south-west is Takkiraja; in the north-west is Niladanda and in the north-east is Mahabala. At the zenith above stands Ushnisha-chakravartin, and in the nadir below appears Sumbharaja.

In all, then, Vajradhara appears as thirty-two deities:

• The Meditation Deity Vajradhara with his consort Sparsavajra – at the centre
• The Five Meditation Buddhas – at the centre and four cardinal points
• The Eight Offering Goddesses – at the eight inter-cardinal points
• The Eight Great Bodhisattvas – two on each side of the inner square
• The Ten Wrathful Deities – four at the doors; four in the corners, one above and one below

IV. Wrathful Deities: The Protective Outer Circle

When we read the text of the *Guhyasamānja Sadhana,* Vajradhara appears first at the centre, in the embrace of his consort Sparsavajra. But, from there, the mandala is visualized *from the outside in.* The first deities to emerge from their tantric union (*yab-yum*) are the Ten Wrathful Deities on the periphery, with Aksobhya at the centre (as a form of Vajradhara). Vajradhara proclaims:

"Rays of light from the concentration being at my heart – with us in union as mother and father – bring forth Akshobhya surrounded by the ten wrathful ones."[7]

Their purpose is protective, to guard the space from any disruptive element:

"...From the wrathful ones and the daggers, blazing vajra fire and light is emitted in the ten directions, burning and disintegrating all interferers and evil ones of samsara.

TAKKI HUM JAH – beyond the wrathful one is an iron vajra fence.
TAKKI HUM JAH – beyond this is a fence of water.
TAKKI HUM JAH – beyond this is a fence of wind."[8]

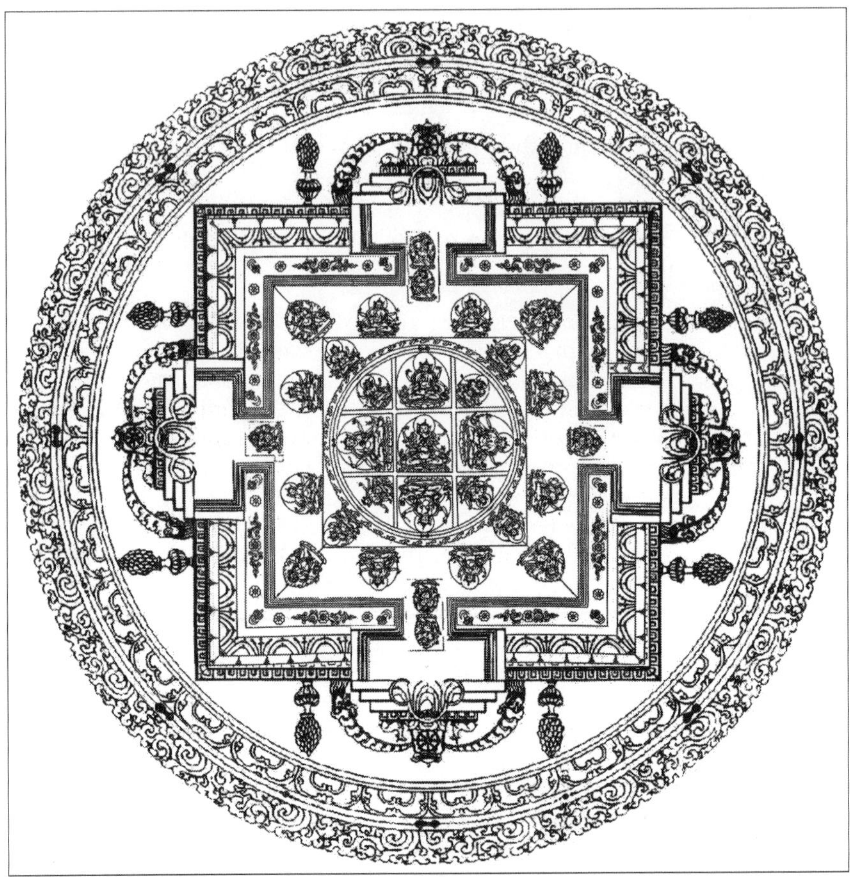

Fig. 28.4 - The Entire Guhyasamānja Akṣobbyavajra Mandala (as handed down by Mar-pa of Lhobrag) including the Gateways and Protective Rings

With the utterance of these three seed-syllables, three rings on the periphery of the mandala emerge (Fig. 28.4). The outermost one, which moves thirty-two times through the colours of white (space), yellow (earth), red (fire), green (wind) and blue (water), is the 'fence of water and wind', as can be seen in its dynamic swirling shapes. Within this is the narrow ring of sixteen vajra thunderbolts, the 'iron vajra fence'. The innermost ring consists of a lotus with thirty-two petals – the original lotus that appeared from the sound PAM at the beginning.

Since we are to visualize the mandala as a whole, we must keep our eye focused *on the centre*. But, the first thing that happens, during the *sadhana* visualization, is that our vision expands *to the outermost periphery.* At first, this 'vision of the whole' may frighten and distract us. And so, through calm meditation on a fixed point, we learn to see and visualize the outermost boundary as a stable, fixed shape, free of 'all interferers'. According to the

Guhyasamānja Sadhana, the vajra thunderbolts in the hands of the Ten Wrathful Deities transform into vajra-hooks and daggers, which seize and transfix any 'interferer' until *"...they become unwavering and unmoving in their body, speech and mind."*[9]

Once the outermost shape has become fixed, it also becomes a kind of vehicle for our vision journey. As with Proclus and the Neo-Platonists, the Soul Vehicle here *is circular or spherical* in shape, and *fills the imagination* with heavenly images. If we wish, we could imagine this shape, from centre to periphery, as a device that mirrors the Divine Eye.

V. Dissolutions & the Different Types of Experience

But there is more going on during this visualization. The Vision Journey, we should not forget, is actually a journey through the afterlife *bardo* realms. As the *Guhyasamānja Sadhana* unfolds, we find that we are journeying ever further, *during this life,* through the visionary experience *of death* which, in Tantric Buddhism, is experienced as *a series of dissolutions*.

As consciousness separates from the body, it experiences that dissolution through a series of visions. These may take the form of specific memory-images (*vāsanās*) of past events, which are memory-imprints from one's karmic past. But, at their root, these memory-images are fundamentally illusory, since different 'types of experience' have led to their creation. In order to recognize these memory-images as 'fabrications' (*saṅkhāras*), the initiate must go down to their core, and become fully aware of the different 'types of experience' that gave rise to them in the first place.[10] These different categories or 'types of experience' include:

• The five elements, that consciousness experiences as the physical body
• The five bodily senses through which consciousness senses the world
• The five 'sense-objects' or faculties that create the mental categories of sensation
• The five *skandhas* or 'aggregates' that create the mental categories for conceptualizing the world
• The five *kleshas* or 'passions' that drive consciousness to experience the world
• The five *jñānas* or wisdoms that liberate us from these experiences.

We shall examine these in detail later on. As the visualization of the mandala progresses, we visualize each of the deities *as personifying one 'type of experience'* (i.e. as symbolic of one element, sense, sense-object, aggregate or passion). But that only 'generates' awareness of the categories. It is typical of the *Generation* stage to successively visualize the Wrathful and Peaceful Deities, one after the other, in the attempt to recognize *each* type of experience and dissolve it *individually*.

But during the *Completion* stage, all these categories or types of experience must be recognized as illusory and transcended completely. In a single moment, *all* the deities are dissolved *simultaneously*, once we fuse (*samadhi*) with their source – with the Meditation Deity (*yidam*) at the centre of the mandala.

This deity, who is a mirror of ourselves, has generated the entire mandala from the sacred seed syllable PAM. But as the first lines of the *Guhyasamānja Sadhana* remind us:

"In the sense that the nature, causes and results of all phenomena are all three void of existing inherently by their own definition, everything becomes void. Within a state of Voidness comes a PAM..."[11] From the outset, the mandala and all its deities are said to be illusory constructs arising from the formless world (or 'state of Voidness') of the clear light mind.

In this sense, each of the Peaceful and Wrathful Deities is visualized, in order for us to become aware of the different categories generating those illusions. Each deity 'removes an obstacle' that is blocking our awareness from its true state of being, which is the Buddha-state of infinite bliss. One by one, they free consciousness of an element, sense, sense-object, aggregate or passion – each of which forms a part of our illusion-creating faculties. As veil after veil is removed, we become increasingly aware of, what Alexander Berzin calls, *"our not-yet-happening enlightenment, our individual enlightenment which has not yet happened."*[12] In truth, we *are* enlightened – we *are* the Enlightened Buddha at the centre of the mandala – but we have not realized this *yet*.

VI. Visualizing the Celestial Palace & Peaceful Deities

And so, the Vision Journey into the mandala takes on a deeper level of meaning. Thus far we have visualized Vajradhara at the centre of the circle, the Ten Wrathful Deities, and the outermost rings – as a 'safe' space for our consciousness to witness its own inner workings.

The *Sadhana* then creates the celestial palace through a series of mantras-within-mantras, each producing geometric shapes-within-shapes, accompanied by specific elements and colours. In all, four mandalas are created: a blue bow-shaped wind mandala, a red triangular fire mandala, a white circular water mandala and a yellow square earth mandala (recall Fig. 28.2). *"These four mandalas merge into one and transform... into a square celestial mansion with four doorways. Its jeweled walls going all around have five layers."*[13]

Through this visualization, the inner space of the mind has now taken on a recognizable shape. Although a variety of shapes were considered, the square ultimately emerged as the simplest delineation of space within 'the circle in the void'. Viewed from above, the square is actually a four-sided pyramid, with five levels ascending to the central shrine on top.

It is not merely by chance that four-sided pyramids have been used in the sacred architecture of all cultures. The circle describes the dome of the heavens, while the square defines the four cardinal directions of earthly space. These rise up, in the shape of four triangles, which co-align and unite at their summit. The pyramid is so archetypal in shape that it becomes the *'templum'* or template for all sacred space. It is the shape, *par excellence*, for our memory palace.

When considered as a Soul Vehicle, the pyramidal shape takes on a new meaning, since the human figure in a lotus position will naturally assume just such a three-dimensional shape. The *Guhyasamānja Sadhana* hints at this realization when it says, mysteriously: *"This excellent pure mansion... has its inside clearly visible when looking from the outside, and its outside clearly visible when looking from the inside."*[14]

In the next stage of the visualization, the original joining (*yab-yum*) of Vajradhara with Sparsavajra is repeated (Fig. 28.7). From their union emerges the Five Meditation Buddhas, the Eight Offering Goddesses and the Eight Great Bodhisattvas – all disposed in their appropriate places on the cardinal and inter-cardinal points of the celestial mansion.

But, no sooner do they appear in the celestial mansion than Vajradhara visualizes them again, this time as appearing on different points of his body (*kaya*). The Five Meditation Buddhas and their consorts appear on his five chakra points, while the five Offering Goddesses appear at his sense faculties. This section ends with a passage entitled *"Meditation on taking Death into the Path of Dharmakāya."*[15] In a single recitation, all thirty-two deities are named, then visualized as *"deities on my body"*[16] and, one by one, they *"...dissolve into clear light."*[17]

The *Dharmakāya,* it is to be recalled, is our '*Truth body*', our absolute nature as a limitless ocean of 'no-self'. In this section, the initiate is invited to realize their true nature, as an 'already-enlightened being'. We are called upon to experience this vision as a *death and transformation*, entering directly into the *Chikhai bardo* – a limitless ocean of enlightened bliss, the Buddha's true state of clear light mind.

To do this, we must visualize the thirty-two deities as successively removing all the obstacles to enlightenment – the elements, senses, sense-objects, aggregates and passions that generate illusory existence – each dissolved one by one.

But, rather than ending here, the *Guhyasamānja Sadhana* continues with two more sections entitled *"Meditation on taking the Intermediate State* [i.e. Bardo] *into the Path of Sambhokāya* [the bliss body]" and *"Meditation on taking Rebirth into the Path of Nirmanakāya* [the emanation body]."[18]

Now, Vajradhara visualizes his body as transforming, part by part and piece by piece, into the architecture of the celestial palace: *"The front, back, right and left sides of my body are the four corners of the mandala."*[19] Having achieved this total identification of the body with the celestial mansion, a much more detailed process of identification begins. Step by step, with the enunciation of a seed-syllable, one 'type of experience' is associated with a Peaceful Deity located in the body-palace.

The Generation stage of the *Guhyasamānja Sadhana*, in its three stages, comes to resemble the three-stage *Bardo Thodol*, which portrays the after-death journey as, first of all, the immediate entry into the clear light mind (experiencing the limitless *Dharmakāya* 'truth body' in the *Chikhai bardo*), followed by an intermediate stage of spiritual existence (experiencing the

Sambhokāya 'bliss body' in the *Chonyid bardo*), and concluding with our rebirth due to fear and longing (putting on the *Nirmanakāya* 'emanation body' in the *Sidpa bardo*).

Alexander Berzin has noted that, after we go into the clear light mind in the first section of the *Guhyasamānja Sadhana*, a sudden 'reversal' occurs in the second and third sections: *"First of all, the dissolution process is going into the clear light. But then, you have the reversal process of coming out of the clear light, with the attainment of a bardo body* [the *Sambhokāya* 'bliss body'] *...and with attaining a rebirth body* [the *Nirmanakāya* 'emanation body']."[20] Hence, the remaining sections of the *Guhyasamānja Sadhana* describe how we pass from potential enlightenment to earthly rebirth.

The text, as we have elucidated it so far, only describes the Generation stage of the visualization (indeed, only the first of three main parts). The subsequent Completion stage does not (normally) exist in print form, since one should be initiated into this stage through a master. However, we do know that the Completion stage involves a more complex visualization of the mandala as a diagram of the subtle energy system, where the red and white 'seeds' or 'drops' (*bindu*) from different psychic 'winds' (*prana*) flow through the subtle body's three main channels (the left *rasana* and right *lalana* entwined around the central *avadhuti* channel), to activate the five energy centres (the *base, gut, heart, throat and crown chakras*). The intonations of seed-syllables, the breathings, postures, mudras and resulting visualizations all play an important part of this process – and so one must be initiated by a master.

It is worthwhile, at this point, to go back to the Generation stage, with its dissolution of the thirty-two deities, and examine in detail how they remove all the obstacles to enlightenment.

VII. The After-death Journey

By meditating on the deities' dissolutions, we begin to gain a much clearer view onto the mandala as 'a map of the mind's inner workings' and, indeed, as a Vision Journey through the afterlife realms. During the dissolution process, and hence, *during death*, our consciousness experiences visions of the various elements, senses, sense-objects, aggregates and passions passing away one by one. This is because it is progressively being severed from each.

This begins with the body. During the agonies of death, element after element dissolves, causing consciousness to experience visions. In the Eight Stage Dissolution Process[21], this is described as follows:

1. Earth dissolves into water – hallucinations begin, like a mirage
2. Water dissolves into fire – vision grows hazy, like smoke
3. Fire dissolves into air – sparks erupt, small and intense, like fireflies
4. Air dissolves into space – the flickering of a flame grows still
5. Space dissolves into consciousness – a transparent bluish light emerges

At this point, the heart and brain have ceased all function, and the body is clinically dead. Consciousness survives the death of the body, and experiences the last three stages on a more 'subtle' level, as the appearance of white, red and black lights.

When consciousness first entered the body, during conception, the white *bodhichitta* drop from the father's sperm rose upward from the heart to the crown chakra, while the red *bodhichitta* drop from the mother's menstrual blood descended downward from the heart to the navel chakra. During death, the white and red drops return to the heart in a three stage process.

6. White drop returns to the heart – a radiant white light appears, 'like moonlight'
7. Red drop returns to the heart – a glowing red light appears, 'like sunlight'
8. The red and white drop re-unite – a radiant blackness emerges

The *Guhyasamānja Sadhana* allows the initiate to visualize the dissolution of the body's elements by associating each one with a different deity. But, more than that, a specific sense, sense-object, aggregate and passion is also associated with a particular deity. By generating the image of that deity and 'dissolving' it, we consciously move through the death process as, not only the dissolution of the body's five elements and three *bodhichitta* drops, but also *the dissolution of the mind's mental categories* – the senses, sense-objects, aggregates and passions that have generated all types of experience in the first place. The after-death journey is a visionary passage through the dis-embodied mind, and the mandala offers a map of its innermost workings.

During death, we witness this as the appearance of so many Peaceful and Wrathful Deities. As the *Bardo Thodol* expresses it: *"Thou wilt beget fear and be startled at the dazzling white light and wilt wish to flee from it."*[22] And so, one is taught the prayer:

"With every thought of fear or terror... may I recognize whatever visions appear, as the reflections of mine own consciousness... May I not fear the bands of Peaceful and Wrathful deities, mine own thought-forms."[23]

During the *Guhyasamānja* visualization, we prepare ourselves for the death journey. With full awareness, we attempt to *consciously* journey into the after-death world (the *bardos*) – and return with a clear knowledge of how to 'navigate' those post-mortem realms. With this new awareness, we may consciously enter the *Chikhai bardo* – and *remain there*, as a *Dharmakāya* or limitless ocean of enlightened bliss. Or, we may consciously enter the *Chonyid bardo*, to 'put on' our *Sambhokāya* – our 'bliss body' or 'vajra body', which is nothing less than an appearance of the Buddha, in the form of a bodhisattva or yogini seeking the compassionate enlightenment of all beings.

With a clear knowledge of our illusion-creating faculties, we can accomplish this. This occurs when each and every Peaceful or Wrathful Deity removes its 'obstacle' blocking our consciousness from its true state of enlightenment, the Buddha's clear light mind.

VIII. Dissolving the Mind's Mental Categories

In the *Guhyasamānja Sadhana* the initiate pronounces a seed-syllable (such as OM, AH, HUM) which 'names' or evokes a specific type of experience (a sense, sense-object, aggregate or passion), which then 'transforms' into a deity generated on a specific point on the body. A typical line from the text runs: *"At my navel is a LAM, the nature of my body's entire element of earth, which transforms into a white Lochana with an Akshobhya crowning his head."*[24]

Or: *"Between the crown of my head and my hairline is a white OM, the nature of my aggregate of form, which transforms into a white Vairochana with an Akshobhya crowning his head."*[25]

In the case of the elements, four of the Eight Offering Goddesses (located on the four inner inter-cardinal points) personifies one of them: earth as Lochana, water as Mamaki, fire as Pandaravasin, and wind as Tara. (Space, as Vajradhatvishvari, is not mentioned in the text).

In the case of the sense faculties, five of the Eight Great Bodhisattvas (located on the four sides of the small square) personifies one of them: the eyes as Kshitigarbhas, the ears as Vajrapanis, the nose as Khagarbha, the tongue as Lokeshvara and the body as Sarvanivarana-viskambhini.

With sense objects, five of the Eight Offering Goddesses (located at the centre and the four outer inter-cardinal points) personifies one of them: sight as Rupavajras, sound as Shabdavajras, smell as Gandhavajra, taste as Rasavajra and touch as Sparshavajra.

Last of all, the five aggregates (*skandhas*) have the Five Meditation Buddhas (in the centre and four cardinal points) to personify one of them: 'form' as Vairochana, 'recognition' as Amitabha, 'consciousness' as Akshobhya, 'feeling' as Ratnasambhava, and 'mental constructs' as Amoghasiddhi.[26]

Once the five aggregates are transformed into images of the Five Meditation Buddhas, they may be dissolved. One way of dissolving an aggregate is to transform its negative quality into a positive one. The Five Meditation Buddhas have this capacity because each one is associated with an element, sense faculty, sense object, aggregate and passion – *as well as a form of wisdom to liberate it.*

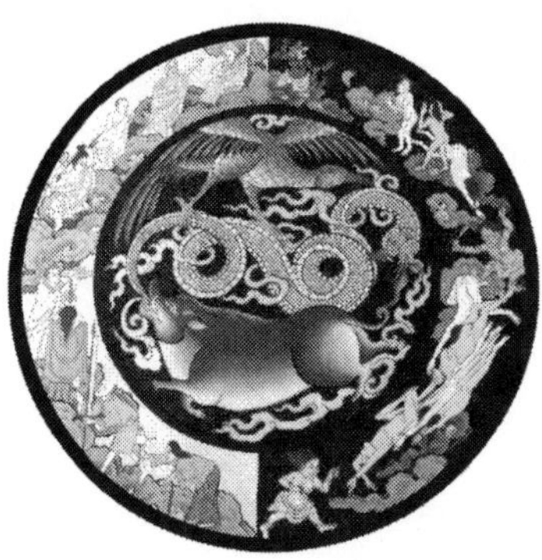

Fig. 28.5 - The Three Poisons

This brings us to a more detailed examination of the passions (*kleshas*), aggregates (*skandhas*) and wisdoms (*jñānas*) of the Five Meditation Buddhas.

The Five Passions (*kleshas*) lie at the root of all suffering. Initially they were considered to be three – the Three Poisons (*triviṣa*) of ignorance, attachment and aversion. These appear at the centre of the Wheel of Life mandala as the pig (ignorance), cock (attachment) and snake (aversion) (Fig. 28.5).

When expanded into five, through the addition of pride and envy, they became the Five Passions[27] (*kleśaviṣa*):

- Ignorance (delusion, deceit)
- Attachment (desire, passion, lust)
- Aversion (wrath, anger)
- Pride (arrogance, ego-centricity)
- Envy (jealousy, injustice)

It is both fascinating and disturbing how the Five Passions of Tantric Buddhism tally with the Seven Soul Garments of the Gnostics. If we translate ignorance, attachment and aversion into their more emotional forms of delusion, lust and wrath, then all five of the Buddhist Passions fall within the seven Soul Garments of the Gnostics: Inconstancy, Greed, Lust, Pride, Wrath, Envy and Delusion. Only the first two, Inconstancy and Greed, are missing.

The Five Passions (*kleshas*) lie at the root of our desire to experience the world. But, our experience is further interpreted through the Five Aggregates (*skandhas*), which are our mental constructs – the categories or ideas we use to conceptualize the world. A *skandha* is literally a 'bundle', and we use these conceptual categories to 'bundle together' our experiences into distinct notions, prejudices and ideas which, fundamentally, are illusory. In truth, the mental categories are nothing less than our 'illusion-creating faculties'. The Five Aggregates (*skandhas*) are:

- Form – the sensorial shape and impression left by an object
- Feeling – the pleasant or unpleasant sensation left by an object
- Recognition – the awareness of an object as separate and distinct
- Mental constructs – the words and categories associated with an object
- Consciousness – the simple awareness of the object

The only way we may free ourselves of the aggregates and their underlying passions is *to dissolve them in deeper forms of awareness*. Each of the Five Meditation Buddhas (Fig. 28.6) manifests a distinct *form* of wisdom, a different *way* of being aware. The Five Wisdoms are:

- Vairochana – Pure clear awareness (*Tathatā-jñāna*) of the unmanifest, beyond all forms and concepts
- Ratnasambhava – Equalizing awareness (*Samatā-jñāna*) of the sameness or commonality of all existence
- Amitabha – Discerning awareness (*Pratyavekṣaṇa-jñāna*) of the distinct uniqueness of all existence
- Amoghasiddhi – Active awareness (*Kṛty-anuṣṭhāna-jñāna*) of perfecting all beings through compassion
- Akshobhya – Mirror-like awareness (*Ādarśa-jñāna*) of reflecting all things without attachment

By meditating on each of these Buddhas, one passion and aggregate may be transformed into a deeper form of awareness. More than that, since an element, sense faculty and sense-object are also related to them – all of these may also be liberated in this way.

It is for this reason that the Five Meditation Buddhas appear in the middle of the mandala, as liberating sources of energy. Their five consorts, who are located on the four inter-cardinal points, bring them the five elements to be liberated. The same is true of the remaining Goddesses and Bodhisattvas, who bring them the five senses and sense-objects to be liberated.

As we visualize the *Guhyasamānja Sadhana,* the Five Meditation Buddhas[28] exercise their liberating power over each element, sense, sense-object, aggregate and passion:

• Through Vairochana's pure clear awareness (*Tathatā-jñāna*), water, eyes, sight, form, and ignorance (delusion) are dissolved.
• Through Ratnasambhava's equalizing awareness (*Samatā-jñāna*), earth, ear, sound, feeling, and pride are dissolved.
• Through Amitabha's discerning awareness (*Pratyavekṣaṇa-jñāna*), fire, nose, smell, recognition, and attachment (lust) are dissolved.
• Through Amoghasiddhi's active awareness (*Kṛty-anuṣṭhāna-jñāna*), wind, tongue, taste, mental constructs, and envy (jealousy) are dissolved.
• Through Akshobhya's mirror-like awareness (*Ādarśa-jñāna*), space, body, touch, consciousness, and aversion (wrath) are dissolved.

Although the initiate should visualize the deity as part of the mandala, they should also zoom in and visualize its figure in the finest detail. All the deities are given headdresses crowned with one of the Five Meditation Buddhas, to identify them as belonging to that Buddha's 'family' (*kula*). So, in the case of the Buddha Vairochana: his consort Locana, the offering goddess Rupavajra and the bodhisattva Khagarbha all wear crowns with his emblem, to show they belong to his family.

More than that, the mudras, emblems and ornaments of the many-armed deities also form complex mnemonic devices. During the visualization, the *Guhyasamānja Sadhana* announces:

"All the deities, from Vairochana through Samantabhadra, have jewel ornaments and garments... They sport a crown, jeweled earrings with an utpala flower above their ears and beautified with a hanging ribbon, a jewelled choker necklace, a pearl long hanging necklace, strands of jewels, bracelets, anklets, and a jewelled girdle-belt."[29]

Each ornament symbolizes a specific wisdom:

• Crown ornament – Mirror-like awareness
• Earrings – Discerning awareness
• Necklace – Equalizing awareness
• Bracelets and anklets – Pure clear awareness
• Girdle-belt – Active awareness

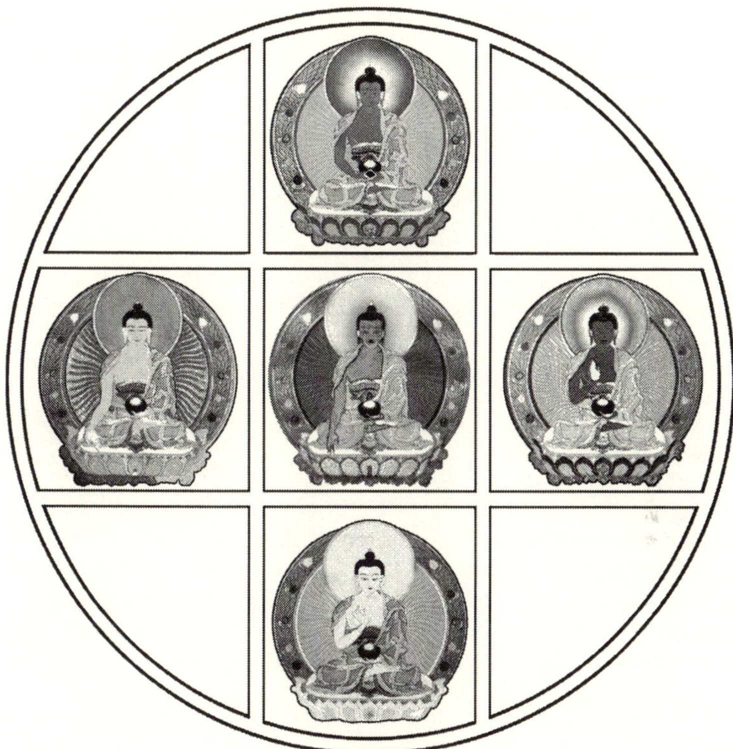

Fig. 28.6 - The Five Meditation (*Dhyani*) Buddhas - Top: Amitabha
Left: Ratnasambhava Middle: Akshobhya Right: Amoghasiddhi
Bottom: Vairochana

The same is true of the mudras, emblems and bone ornaments of the many-armed Wrathful Deities. This complex iconography creates intricate levels of association between the various gods and goddesses. Up to the very edges, the fractalline parts of the mandala reflect the whole, while the Meditation Deity at the centre brings them all into one accord.

Sitting on a white lotus in the splendour of the sun, Vajradhara embraces Sparsavajra, whose many attributes are a symbolic and symmetrical reflection of his own: the blue-toned skin, three faces and six hands which hold a variety of theurgic instruments. Each implement offers its own method or way for achieving enlightenment, because it is associated with one of the five Meditation Buddhas,[30] as follows:

- Wheel – Vairochana
- Jewel – Ratnasambhava
- Lotus – Amitabha
- Sword – Amoghasiddhi
- Thunderbolt and bell – Akshobhya

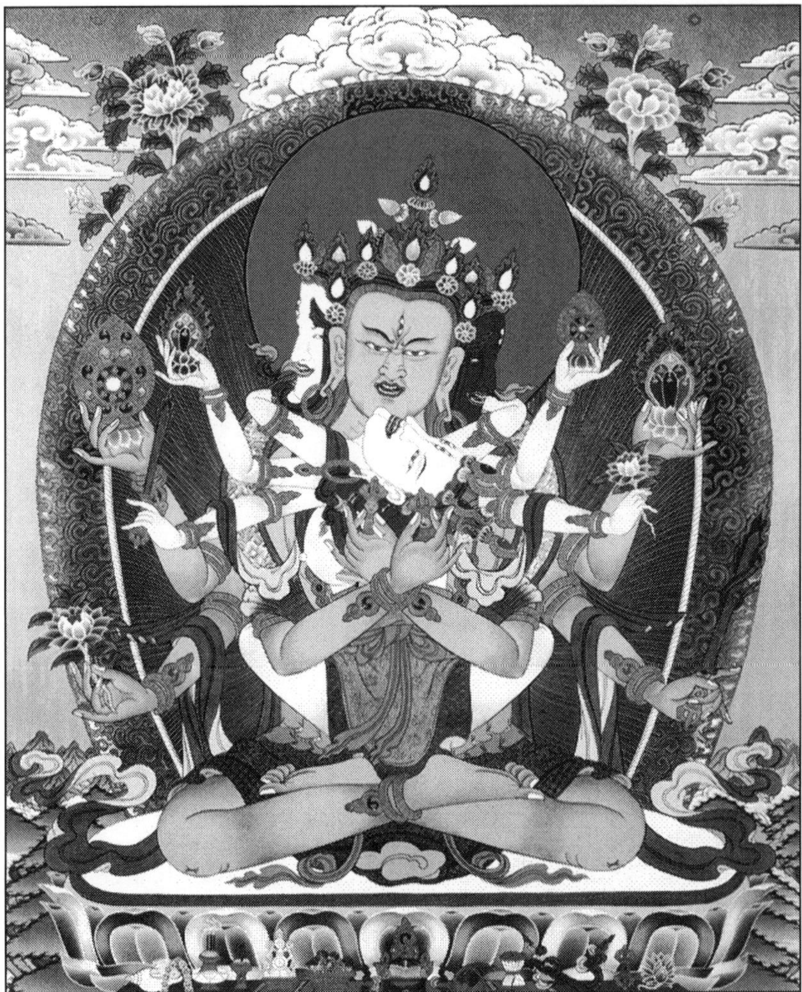

Fig. 28.7 - Vajradhara Embracing Sparsavajra

With a semi-peaceful, semi-wrathful expression on his face, Vajradhara wraps his arms around his consort, his crossed hands holding the thunderbolt and bell, as symbols of the union of *upaya* and *prajna* – of method and wisdom – the Father and Mother of the tantras. All in all, the mandala is a multi-leveled diagram of the mind, body and cosmos integrated as a whole – all to be recognized in their complex inter-relationships and ultimately transcended as illusion. The not-yet-happening enlightenment, once actual, plunges us into a limitless ocean of compassion and clear light.

Despite its complexity, the mandala's main purpose remains clear: it uses basic geometrical shapes and emblematic figures as mnemonic devices for memorizing the dynamic inter-relationship of the mind, body and cosmos. When we journey through the afterlife *bardos*, we are journeying, in essence, through our own karmic imprints and remaining thought-forms. The mandala and all its figures becomes an integrated structure or map for navigating that experience.

Indeed, during the second stage, when we enter the *Chonyid bardo* and attempt to 'put on' our *Sambhokāya* – our 'bliss body' or 'vajra body' – we are attempting to *mentally reconstruct a perfect body* – what is also called a 'diamond body'. With a profound knowledge of its inner workings, we are able to navigate, not just the *bardo* realms, but our every-day existence, as an active appearance or manifestation of the Buddha's five-fold wisdom.

In this sense, the 'diamond body' resembles the Gnostic 'Garment of Light'. Despite its initial resemblance to the theurgists' Soul Vehicle (which is spherical or geometrically-shaped), the Gnostic Garment of Light was more likely a human-shaped envelope with a twofold purpose: to 'protect' us by repelling negative influences, and to actively 'manifest' the light and wisdom of the enlightened saviour. Whether we 'put on' the Light Garment of Christ or the Diamond Body of the Buddha, we become an active source of love and wisdom, light and compassion.

Each image of a spiritual saviour, be that Christ, Quetzlcoatl, Vishnu or the Buddha, is intended as a mirror-image of our higher self. To see ourselves in that mirror, and become one with the reflection, is the eternal task of Visionary art. We consecrate the work, the moment that reflection becomes true.

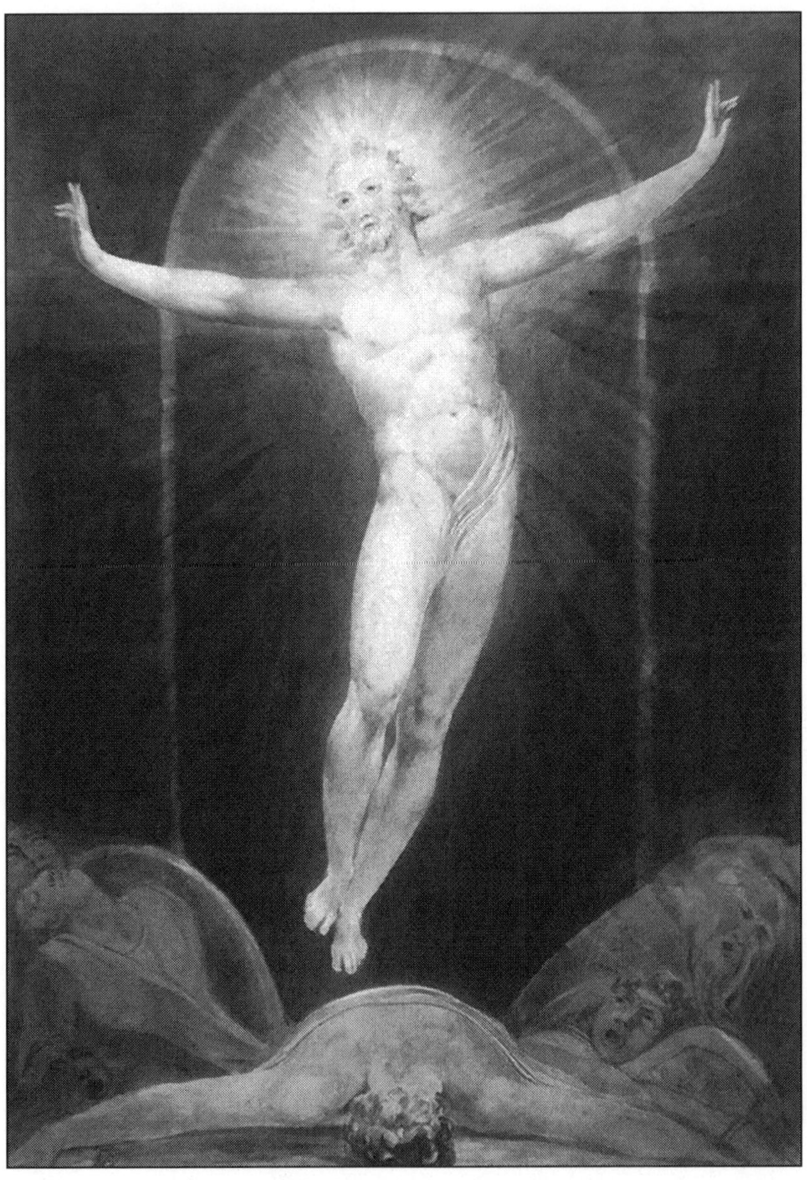

Fig. 29.1 - William Blake: *The Resurrection* c.1805

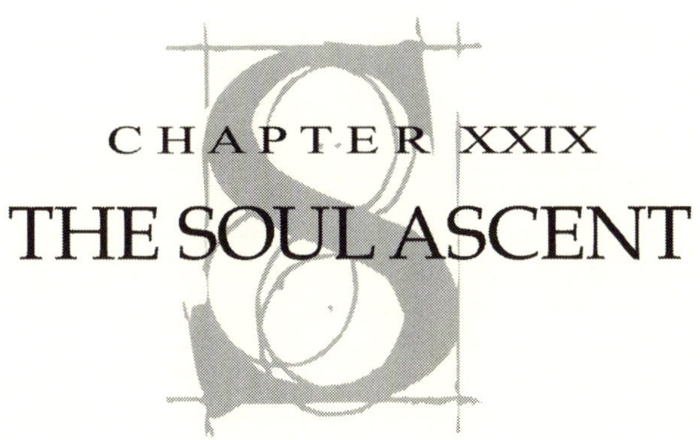

CHAPTER XXIX

THE SOUL ASCENT

I. Late Thoughts & Concluding Considerations

In a variety of cultures, visionary practices have emerged through the ritual use of sacred plants. This extends from the ceremonial smoking of cannabis by rastafarians and saddhus to the shamanic use of mushrooms, peyote and ayahuasca, *et al* by Tribal cultures. Although many cultures in the past may have practised similar rites (the Mystery traditions of Egypt, Babylon and Greece), certainly our present Western culture has experienced a resurgence in sacred plant knowledge, from the Psychedelic Sixties to the Trance Festivals of today.

I have experienced visionary states with a variety of sacred plants. As an artist and writer, I have also participated in a variety of conferences or colloquia dedicated to Psychedelics: i.e. to integrating and understanding sacred plants in our contemporary culture. At each event, I was struck by the inability of our present philosophy and science to adequately describe and integrate these experiences. The language and conceptual outlook are still lacking, though researchers are labouring hard to forge a new paradigm or cohesive worldview. Still, all I write here will appear, at best, esoteric and speculative.

Having experienced full-on visions for periods of up to six hours, (where it did not really matter if my eyes were opened or closed), I can best describe or liken the experience to *being immersed in a mirrored sphere*, where each thought, feeling or intention is immediately materialized and reflected, in the form of a fully-immersive environment. Since we are not always in control of the thoughts or feelings which cross our consciousness, random and unexpected images may appear. Our response to these images constitutes one of the rare opportunities we have to navigate the experience.

At the same time, our awareness is plunged into an altered reality where the usual structures of space, time and causality are no longer apparent. Time may lose its regular, linear measure and assume a bewildering variety of forms, from frighteningly slow to fractured milliseconds of disjointed attention-spans. Then again, time may endlessly cycle round, as in Hindu-Buddhism, or assume arcane calendrical measures familiar only to the Mayans and Aztecs. In certain blissful moments, time loses its usual measured pace and stands eternally still.

Our customary three-dimensional space also seems skewed, as our mind is suddenly freed of that gravity and horizon which keeps our body balanced and oriented in the earthly architectural space of cubic shapes. Freed of those physical and mental constraints, futuristic and alien architectures may abound, oriented to different gravities and dimensions (see, for example, Jonathan Solter's works). Ancient cosmologies and models of the cosmos suddenly make sense, assuming new importance and relevance. If we are fortunate, all these spatial constructs may finally fall away, and we discover ourselves to be situated in the absolute centre and still-point of creation.

More disorienting still, a rational outlook based on causality or cause-and-effect thinking becomes sorely out of place. 'If I do this, then that will happen' becomes a mental trap or paradox best-avoided, since moments of retro-causality cause us to experience the effect before the cause, or the cause after the effect (for retro-causality, see Romuald Leterrier's contribution to *Ovnis et Conscience*). Synchronicities appear obvious, co-incidences abound, and numbers take on a magical or oracular significance. Freed of causality, the past and future acquire different meanings, and the present moment comes to possess both infinite possibility and complete surrender to the experience.

Although our mind may experience itself as freed of the body, it may also immerse itself into its materiality with frightening autonomy, exploring cellular patterns or DNA strands, neural networks or somatic rhythms, all organized with bewildering complexity. New forms of healing seem possible, but the mind may equally lose itself in this interior labyrinth of faeces, phlegm, blood and bile.

Long-forgotten memories from the past may resurface, with all their childhood wonder and enchantment. Traumas are relived, whether real or imaginary, and the boundary between true vision and hallucination is always flimsy, malleable and diaphanous. In this place, even the absolutes of true and false, good and evil, or real and unreal are momentarily suspended and rescinded. Indeed, a whispered prayer of intention, made at the beginning of the journey, may become too difficult to re-construct and remember. Even one's own name or identity may be forgotten.

The boundaries between self and others are transcended, in both positive and negative ways. Freed of the ego, we may plunge into a blissful ocean of no-self, at one with the all; but we may also be torn apart and devoured by hordes of hungry ghosts or demonic forces. All this time, the visionary experience is encountered in waves, as we periodically plunge and resurface from these alternate realities.

Given all of that – how can we possibly navigate the visionary experience?

II. The Correspondences: As Above; So Below

On the fringes of our culture, in the underground and alternative scene, a variety of practices have emerged to help us navigate these currents. However, I have likened the visionary experience to a mirrored sphere, a fully-immersive environment where each thought, feeling or intention is immediately materialized and reflected. *That core experience* teaches us to navigate day-to-day experience as we would the visionary sphere. Indeed, *there is no difference:* in a heightened state of awareness, our thoughts, feelings and intentions influence our physical reality as much as they do our imagined one.

The only difference, perhaps, is that in the visionary sphere there is *less physical reality* to prevent our wishes and desires from immediately becoming manifest. What we experience immediately in the visionary sphere, materializes slowly in the earthen sphere. During that process, we often lose sight of our original intentions, as our thoughts and feelings are continually blinded or distracted by time, space, causality, material wants and bodily needs.

To hold an intention, to stay focussed on our higher aims, to respond to each situation with readiness, courage, intuition, a sharp mind and an open heart – these are the qualities necessary for navigating the soul through visions and through life itself.

In order to remain focussed, some form of spiritual practice is recommended. Today, these practices include various forms of breathing, posture, chanting, vocalizations, seed-syllables, mantras, visualizations, sigils, mudras – many of which we have already encountered in Theurgy and Mandala Meditation.

As our scientific paradigm shifts toward a multi-dimensional view of reality, composed of energy states in differing frequencies of vibration, so do we begin to understand how these theurgic and *sadhana* practices have the capacity *to shift* our internal energies, from one state to another; from distraction and confusion, for example, to one-pointed focus and attention.

While deeply immersed in visions, the internal vibrations produced by chanting, vocalizations and other techniques may profoundly influence our mental and emotional states, to the extent of *altering the images* that immediately appear in the mirrored sphere.

In this sense, the chaos of full-on visions may gain some order, and become a full-on vision journey, the moment we guide ourselves with the appropriate shapes and sounds. It may also become a full-on Soul Ascent, if we immerse ourselves into a cosmology that 'holds together', both in space and in time, for a decent portion of the visionary experience.

Our aim is to identify specific vibrational frequencies, in shape or in sound, for each level of the Visionary Ascent. These correspond to a graded series of emotional and mental states in the individual, and a hierarchy of divine powers in the greater cosmological structure. In the East, these are encountered in mandala meditation as the various 'types of experience' (sense-objects, passions, mental aggregates) symbolized by peaceful and wrathful deities which, in the subtle energy system, relate to the five or seven centres of chakra energy. In the West, this hierarchy is encountered in theurgy as the lower passions of the soul and higher states of mind, which the Gnostics symbolized through planetary Archons in the lower aeons and angelic beings in the upper aeons.

This brings us to the Emanationist philosophies, which we have already encountered in Theurgy, Neo-Platonism, Gnosticism, Hermeticism, Astrology and Alchemy. Their basic tenet states: As Above; So Below. Particularly Hermeticism seeks out *the correspondences* between the cosmos above (as the macrocosm) and the human being below (as the microcosm). So, certain vowel sounds, musical tones or visible shapes link us as individuals to the heavenly spheres.

In the Visionary Ascent, the theurgist attempts to attune his or her internal state to one of the planetary influences, gradually ascending the heavenly ladder, step by step (the alchemist, engaged in the *opus alchemicum*, performs a similar such ritual with metals and their planetary influences). Through the laws of sympathy and 'like attracts like', the theurgist rises up by harmonizing himself with each deity, mirroring its energy and reproducing their vibrational frequency within himself. The aim is to acknowledge and transcend these influences, one by one, to finally center ourselves within the Divine Source.

When the tripartite mind, body and soul are fixed on the action, then the movement and transformation can occur. It is not enough for the theurgist to perform the action in body – the mind and soul must also be ritually focussed and engaged. For the mind, this includes a complete mental picture of the cosmos, to guide the soul through a labyrinth of emotional states. For the soul, this is to fully engage the images and re-experience the emotional states they evoke. In all their aspects, the cosmic spheres must be experienced and transcended.

In the Platonic tradition, we live in a mirrored cosmos, where the lower world of Becoming reflects the upper world of Being. The Gnostics divided these two realms into the lower aeons (the five elements and seven planets ruled over by Archons) and the upper aeons (ruled over by Angelic beings that *are* the Platonic archetypes or *eidé*). The Demiurge modelled the lower world on the upper, except the lower world is a dark, divided, material, visible and temporal sphere of Becoming that dimly reflects the higher world of light, unity, spirit, invisibility and timelessness in pure Being.

In this cosmology, the earth lies at the centre and absolute bottom of the armillary spheres-within-spheres of the lower aeons (Fig. 27.6). But, when the soul *"rushes up through the cosmic framework,"* (*Corpus Hermeticum* I.24) it meets with the boundary of the outermost sphere, called *horos* or the limit. Through merit and divine grace, it may pass beyond the limit, through the cosmic mirror, and finally enter the upper aeons. Then, *the ascent continues*, but the soul now moves inward through the spheres-within-spheres of the upper aeons, to finally unite with the One at its centre.

III. The *Mysterium Cosmographicum*

I return to the idea of full-on visionary experience *as total immersion in a mirrored sphere*, where each thought, feeling or intention is immediately materialized and reflected, in the form of a fully-immersive environment. Given this paradigm or worldview, then the Visionary Ascent may, in fact, be the passage from one visualization to the next in that mirrored sphere. Through breathing, chanting, etc we attempt to navigate the journey through these different vision-spheres, mentally situating ourselves in each new space.

Personally, I do not believe that a complete movement, step by step, through *all* twelve or twenty-four spheres is necessary. But we are trying to construct a model or map – an ideal picture of the complete journey. With this greater cosmology in mind, we can then navigate the individual parts, moving from one sphere to another.

For the theurgists, the Soul Vehicle was the traditional means of transport through the visionary realms. Iamblichus and Proclus described it variously as spherical or geometrical in shape. I would like to suggest that the Soul Vehicle, and the visionary state in general, is indeed like being immersed in a mirrored sphere. But, we may mentally construct and visualize a geometrical shape around us, as our main means of transport through the all-inclusive visions.

In this visualization, each new shape harmonizes and resonates with the particular design and spatial dimension of that visionary sphere. It is like a key that unlocks our passage through multi-dimensional realms, allowing us to navigate their different measures of space. Each new shape opens our mind conceptually to a differently-shaped dimension. All of us can mentally navigate a cubic space, since it is reflected to us daily in our natural and architectural environment. But, in the ascent through the higher spheres, the soul must be prepared for other dimensional constructs. It is not by mere chance that a new literature is emerging on, for example, the correspondence of sacred geometry to 'merkabah vehicles'.

Kepler's *Mysterium Cosmographicum* (*The Cosmographic Mystery* - 1596) was the astronomer's attempt to measure the distances between the planets with the Platonic Solids. From the standpoint of modern astronomy, it is flawed. But, in the visionary sphere, it 'suddenly make sense' as an ancient cosmology or model for navigating the planetary hierarchy.

In a manner similar to Eastern Mandala Meditation, we may mentally construct and visualize each Platonic Solid as a differently-shaped Soul Vehicle, for a graded visualization of the Soul Ascent. Each planetary dimension measures out its space with different geometrical shapes, constructing an elaborate mental picture of the cosmos.

To construct his model, Kepler envisioned each planetary orbit as a circle inscribed on a sphere. In Fig. 29.2, the spheres are cut in half, resembling cups, and the planetary orbit forms its rim. Following Copernicus' heliocentric model, Kepler placed the sun at the centre of our cosmos. He then inscribed

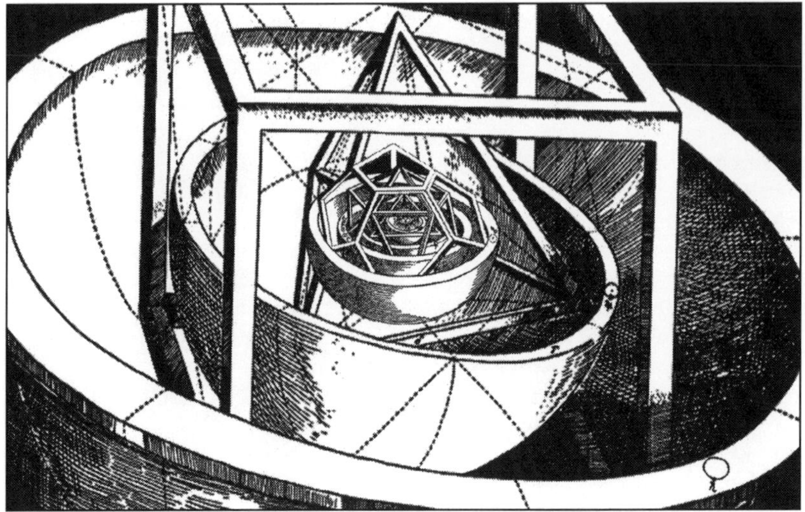

Fig. 29.2 - Kepler's *Mysterium Cosmographicum*

a sphere around it to show Mercury's orbit. Around Mercury's sphere, Kepler inscribed an 8-sided octahedron to show its distance to Venus, whose orbit appeared on the next sphere. Continuing in this fashion, Kepler created the following model of the cosmos (with the Sun at the bottom as the centre):

• Saturn's orbital sphere
- 6-sided cube
• Jupiter's orbital sphere
- 4-sided tetrahedron
• Mars' orbital sphere
- 12-sided dodecahedron
• Earth's orbital sphere
- 20-sided icosahedron
• Venus' orbital sphere
- 8-sided octahedron
• Mercury's orbital sphere
• The Sun

The only problem with Kepler's *Cosmographicum* is that it places the sun at the centre of a heliocentric cosmos. To align our sacred geometry with the cosmos of the Emanationist philosophies, we must return to an even-more ancient model or cosmology. From ancient Babylon and Egypt through to Greece and the Middle Ages, the Ptolemaic model showed us the seven planets that are actually reflected back to us when we, on the earth, turn our eyes to the heavens.

Basically, the Ptolemaic and Copernican models exchange the placement of the Earth and Sun. In the Ptolemaic cosmos, the Earth appears at the centre, with the Moon just above it, while the Sun occupies the place between Venus and Mars. Thus, in the Ptolemaic variation on Kepler's *Cosmographicum*, we arrive at the following configuration:

• Saturn's orbital sphere
- 6-sided cube
• Jupiter's orbital sphere
- 4-sided tetrahedron
• Mars' orbital sphere
- 12-sided dodecahedron
• Sun's orbital sphere
- 20-sided icosahedron
• Venus' orbital sphere
- 8-sided octahedron
• Mercury's orbital sphere
• The Moon's orbital sphere
• The Earth

In this model, the Lunar sphere has no corresponding shape, which is perhaps appropriate, since the Lunar realm is one of inconstancy, variability and shape-shifting fluidity. In the initial step of the vision journey, we are often met with dis-orienting, maze-like, kaleidoscopic imagery, which is appropriate to the lunar sphere.

The seven-fold model of the cosmos can be expanded to twelve, once the five elements are included. In the *Timaeus*, Plato had already established the geometric shapes of the four elements (with Xenocrates adding the fifth element, the aether, shortly thereafter). Following Kepler's model, we may envision each geometric solid as surrounding and enclosing an elemental sphere, with the earth at the bottom:

- 12-sided dodecahedron
• Aether's sphere
- 4-sided tetrahedron
• Fire's sphere
- 8-sided octahedron
• Air's sphere
- 20-sided icosahedron
• Water's sphere
- 6-sided cube
• Earth's sphere

IV. The *Voce Magicae* & *Musica Universalis*

In the Classical period of Western thought, philosophers and theurgists worked out a whole array of correspondences, such as that of the planets with specific vowel sounds or harmonic notes. From the *Papryi Graecae Magicae*, (a Greek papyrus collection of small magic scrolls) to the so-called Gnostic Gems (collections of Roman magic amulets – see the Campbell Bonner Magical Gems Database[1]), we find a mixture of Greek, Egyptian,

Jewish and early Christian practices where mantric words with long vowel sequences were ritually intoned. The Church Fathers called them, in Latin, *voce magicae* (magical voices) and *nomina barbara* (strange names).

The Gnostic texts in particular give us some stunning examples,[2] where IAΩ ('IAO') becomes the hidden name of the Demiurge, while the silent name of Jesus is expressed through the five vowels of IHOY ('IEOU') or all seven vowels of the Greek tongue: IHOYEAΩ ('IEOUEAO'). The correspondence of the seven Greek vowels with the seven planetary spheres occurs in Porphyry's *Commentary on Dionysius of Thrace* (not the Neo-Platonic philosopher Porphyry) and Nichomachus of Gersa's *Manual of Harmonics*, among other sources.[3] Although the order is sometimes inversed, so the alpha (A) corresponds to Saturn and the omega (Ω) to the Moon, the usual order of vowel intonations is (from bottom to top):

Saturn	- Ω, ω	- omega
Jupiter	- Y, υ	- upsilon
Mars	- O, o	- omicron
Sun	- I, ι	- iota
Venus	- H, η	- eta
Mercury	- E, ε	- epsilon
Moon	- A, α	- alpha

The *Musica Universalis* or 'harmony of the spheres' is slightly more complicated, depending on which musical scale we use. Nichomachus of Gersa[4] used the oldest system, called the Lesser Perfect System, where two conjunct tetrachords are tuned to the Dorian Diatonic scale, giving us the basic Pythagorean Tuning of seven tones (heptatonic scale with five whole and two half steps) as follows:

- Saturn - E - hypate
- Jupiter - F - parypate
- Mars - G - hypermese or lichanos
- Sun - A - mese
- Venus - B♭ - paramese
- Mercury - C - paranete
- Moon - D - nete

We are only now beginning to rediscover and experience for ourselves how these visualizations (with Platonic Solids), vocalizations (with Greek vowels) and intonations (with Greek tones) can alter internal energy states. Particularly during vision journeys with sacred plants, when our internal energy states are immediately reflected back to us, we can experience their transformative power directly.

Already in the 2nd century, the Gnostics had begun to explore the ritual use of sigils and vowel sounds to elevate the soul in a Visionary Ascent through the cosmic framework. Those vowel sounds are our Western equivalent of Tantric seed-syllables. The anagogic *sunthêmata* of the Gnostics may indeed have been specifically designed, like the Tantric Buddhist seed-syllables, mudras and ritual implements, to 'remove obstacles' during the Visionary Ascent – to dispel the illusory power of the Archons, who continually generate images of fear, anger and lust to keep us 'imprisoned' in a perpetual state of distraction, confusion and delusion.

Particularly during strong entheogenic experiences, this labyrinth of emotional states can entrap the unwary soul, binding it with anxiety or paralyzing it with fear. It risks becoming trapped in vicious circles, where fears produce more images of fear; or madness, ongoing images of madness. During these moments, techniques like posture and breathing can help release the flow of blocked energy.

While the mind seeks ways to continually navigate the experience, the soul will become emotionally engaged with the imagery that emerges. During those moments, feelings should not be suppressed. Rather, the soul may engage the visions to integrate, acknowledge and transform them. It does this by acknowledging them within the greater framework of the cosmic journey, where Archons attempt to entrap us in their realms, just as angels attempt to lead us higher upward to the heavenly spheres.

Through this transformative process, a full range of emotions may be expressed, experienced and recognized. In both their negative and positive aspects, they constitute a hierarchy of energy centres that are continually activated, both in visionary experience and our day-to-day encounters. By remaining focussed on the Sacred, we call to mind our inner core of divinity, a spark of light illumined by self-awareness. We center ourselves in that knowledge (or *gnosis*) of the fundamental oneness that pervades all things.

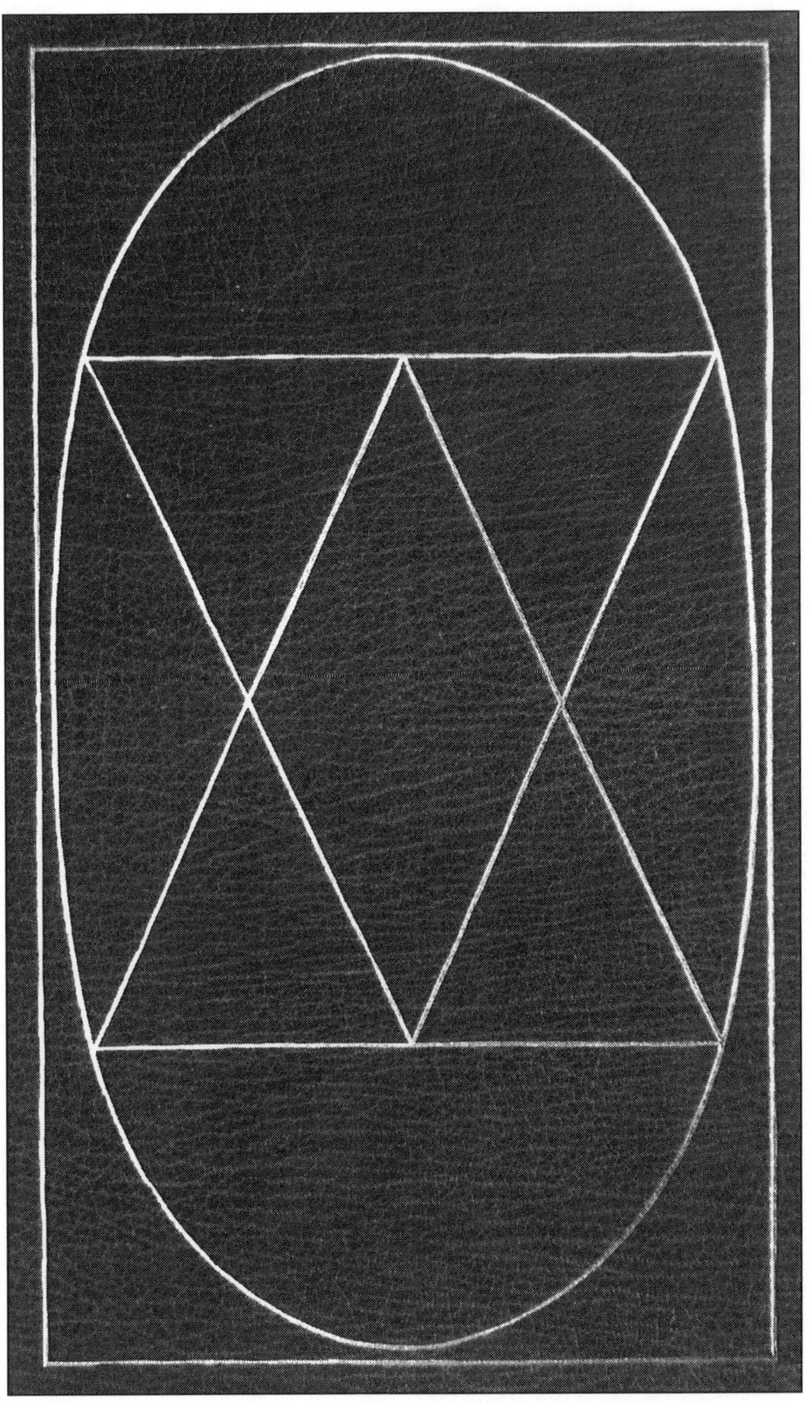

Ernst Fuchs: Ornamental Cover Design from *Symbolik des Traumes* 1968

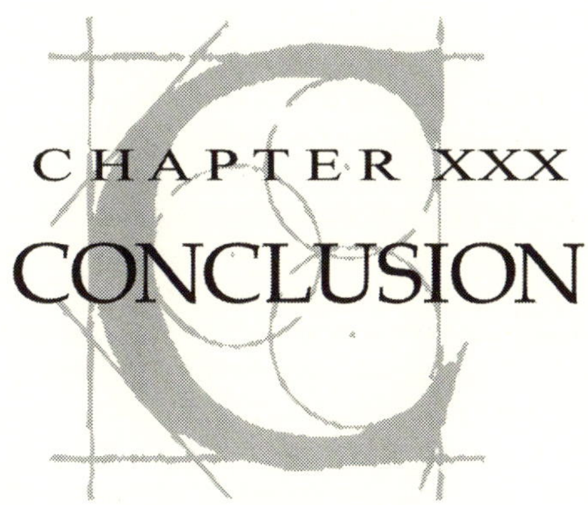

CHAPTER XXX
CONCLUSION

I. *"A large sculpted book, massive and made of stone..."*

I feel called upon to conclude this long study with some personal remarks. I have been fortunate, through the founding of The Vienna Academy of Visionary Art, to encounter individuals who, as a result of their deep passion for certain practices, have increased my awareness of the Vision Journey. Whether as students or colleagues, they have become my guides and teachers.

I have integrated their teachings in my own way, by pursuing image-meditation on a regular basis. Each Saturday evening, while the studio stands empty, I close the door and meditate upon a variety of images. In these last pages, I would like to share the results of this personal practice.

But, I am fortunate to live in a city that is resplendent with masterpieces from the entire history of civilization. Other times, I enter museums, fully equipped with sketchbook, drawing materials (and headphones...) to immerse myself in the majestic works of art.

It is particularly the Kunsthistorisches Museum which has called me back, time and again, to contemplate the works of old. Each time I enter that palace dedicated to painting, I am immediately transported into a dream. I recollect, with unusual clarity and wonder, the ambiance and feelings of a specific dream, which I dreamt (so my notes tell me) on Easter Monday, April 13th, 1998 – a full two years before ever meeting Ernst Fuchs.

In the dream I am together with Ernst Fuchs, and we are admiring the architecture of a building that he has constructed. There is the sense that he and I know each other, but not very well.

His building is mostly made of some bizarre concrete (like the alchemical *prima materia*) poured into molds, resulting in a dark, Romanesque style of a basilica. But, the more I turn my head to explore this dark interior, the more the architecture transforms into an ever-changing panoply of styles from all epochs of history: Gothic, Islamic, Mannerist and Baroque.

From where we are standing, on the floor of the huge basilica, there is also a fantastic, Escher-like effect. Numerous portals, passages, and long Gothic vaults are gracefully ascending in all directions. I notice that, no matter where I turn my gaze, my view plunges into a steep perspective, as if peering up into high Gothic spires, down long Romanesque colonnades, or deep into ancient Celtic wells. So many simultaneous points of perspective seem impossible, but in my dream they create a marvellous sense of harmony, filling me with a strong feeling of elation.

I comment to Fuchs that this place reminds me of a line from Helter Skelter. Fragments of the song return to my memory: *"When you get to the bottom, you go back to the top of the slide, then you turn and you stop and you go for a ride, then you get to the bottom, then you see me again..."*.

"What's that?" Fuchs asks.

"From the Beatles," I reply,

He nods, seemingly unfamiliar with the Beatles. But on a piece of paper, he makes a note of it.

Then I go off on my own, to further explore this amazing space, which fills me with such strong euphoria and enchantment. Soon, I find myself on the upper mezzanine of the museum (which, upon waking, I recognize as the Kunsthistorisches Museum). On the upper floor there are various displays of alchemical retorts and astronomical instruments, like athanors and alembics, astrolabes and armillary spheres. There is also a large sculpted book, massive and made of stone, which draws my attention. But, before I can read the words inscribed on its huge granite pages, a loud voice announces that the museum will be closing. And so the dream ends.

This is only one of a whole series of dreams that I had about Ernst Fuchs, *before* meeting him in person. When we did actually meet in the flesh, and he brought me to his studio in Castel Caramel, I was thunderstruck: we were now standing on same mezzanine which I had encountered numerous times in my dreams: gazing out over his large studio space.

He and I worked together in that studio, and his other *atelier* on the *Quai des Artistes* in Monaco, for the better part of a year. Then we went our separate ways, meeting up only occasionally over the next ten years, until the Academy called me back to Vienna in September of 2013. As fate would have it, he and I formed a much different relationship – during what turned out to be – the last two years of his life.

At times, he sent me on bizarre missions to retrieve objects that existed only in paintings, such as a chalice from a painting by the 19th century Biedermeier artist Ferdinand Georg Waldmüller. Indeed, at times, it seemed that delirium had gripped his mind forever, but towards the end he returned to startling moments of clarity, during which he would recite to me long poems from memory. Or, while composing a poem, he would read it aloud with such fervour and prophecy that he would close his eyes and continue to read the words that were now taking form behind his closed lids. Always, these poems returned to the same theme, of the everlasting and eternal state of being, evinced by that unique German word, *Ewigkeit*.

As he reclined on his sick bed, I upheld various monographs and we gazed fixedly at plate after plate by Michelangelo, Moreau, Delville, Dalì, or Fuchs himself. Silently, we entered into the Hall of the Simultaneousness of All Images.

Professor Ernst Fuchs passed away on the night of November 8th, 2015, at the age of eighty-five. I received the news while staying at my apartment in Paris. Sitting in the Jardin Luxembourg, I wrote a poem of remembrance beginning with the words, "My father in art, eternal..."

Since his passing, I have felt the call, stronger than ever, to pursue the path of painting – *to revive*, as the subtitle of this book says, 'The Forgotten Principles of Painting', through the practice of Visionary Art. All the students and teachers drawn to the Academy in Vienna feel this same sense of purpose, this strong dedication and duty. In the poverty of our present era, we must rediscover the lost Art of Painting. Over the last year, those words have echoed in my mind continuously – always uttered with tremendous power by the voice of Ernst Fuchs: the sacred Art of Painting.

He continues to visit me in my dreams, as every Master should. But his presence is most palpable when I visit the Kunsthistorisches Museum. Immediately upon entering, I stand in the middle of the marbled floor and gaze up into the circular aperture in the ceiling, which offers a steep perspectival view into the copula and its crowning octagonal dome. At that moment, the immense *oculus* becomes the Eye of God, and I am transported into a dream-like state, filled with joy and euphoria.

Strangely, the architecture from Raphael's *School of Athens* also returns to me – the same Great Hall, with rows of sculptures set in niches, going on for infinity. I have re-entered that dream-space where images, like endless corridors, invite immersion into timeless vision. As I penetrate the first galleries and behold the paintings arranged in row upon row, I know that this place is more real, more familiar, than any earthly place of sojourn. It is a timeless space, abundant and infinite – the hall of eternal images. Within moments, the spirit of my master joins me, and guides me on a timeless journey through the history of art.

Often, I should add, I cannot even manage to get past the Egyptian collection. I thought that this peculiar habit was entirely my own, until Mark Lee (Somnio8) and Justina Azrienne invited me, during the 2013 Winter Trimester, to accompany them there on their weekly visits for museum sketching. Not once did we manage to move beyond the Egyptian section, since the three of us were always so entranced by the sacred beauty of those ancient statues. Like Mark and Justina, I felt that this place was a spiritual home, long-forgotten, but slowly being recollected and truly remembered – image by image, piece by piece. In this section near the entrance (carved out to resemble a huge Egyptian Temple), a Spiritual Art still resonates through

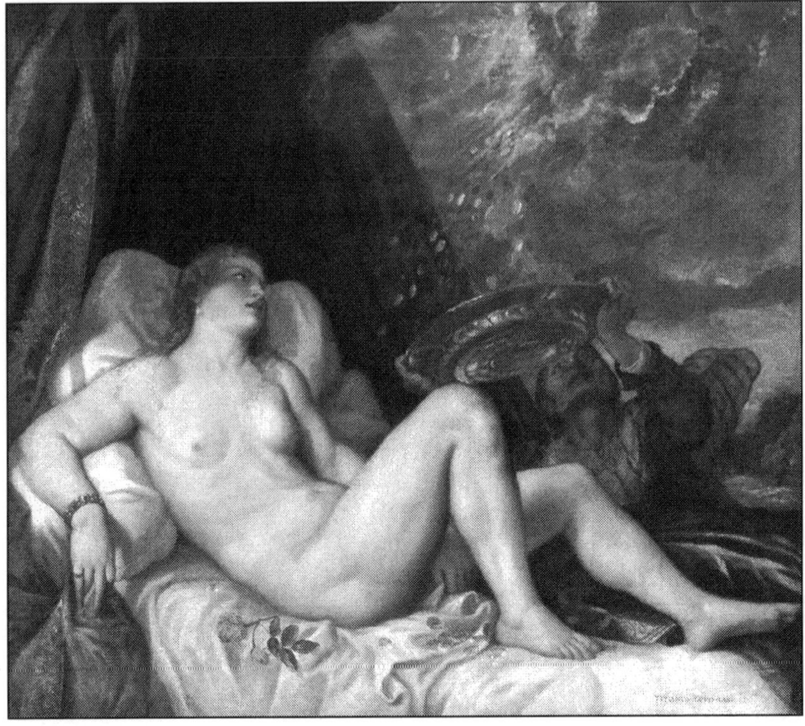

Fig. 30.1 - Titian: *Danaë* 1554

the aeons with a higher, holy purpose. Each work is consecrated, each stone becomes a vessel for the Sacred, and each image opens up as a portal to another time and dimension.

With this Hieratic purpose in mind, I am often guided by my master, beyond the Egyptian section, into the halls of Humanist art. And suddenly, I see it all through new eyes, with a renewed sense of purpose. I awaken to the Holy Presence that is shining through these works, and experience their allegories as timeless myths, enacted by the gods, to inform and enlighten us. In Fuchs' words, I witness *"the eternal prefiguration of a human life"* in each mythic allegory.

II. Tantric Approaches to Renaissance Art

Having practiced image meditation as a *sādhana* – as a form of visualization upon a chosen deity or *yidam* – I then ponder the question as to whether Eastern spiritual practice can be translated into our Western works of art. As I have tried to explain in the preceding chapters, all the pre-requisite knowledge has been given to us. In the West, especially through theurgy and alchemy, the rudiments of image meditation have survived. And the wisdom of the East, with its meditations on Buddhist mandalas and consecrations of Hindu deities, may help us to revive it. Even Tribal cultures, as experienced at Transformational Festivals, invite us to enter into altered states, dance before the images, and interact with the forms elucidated by each brush-stroke.

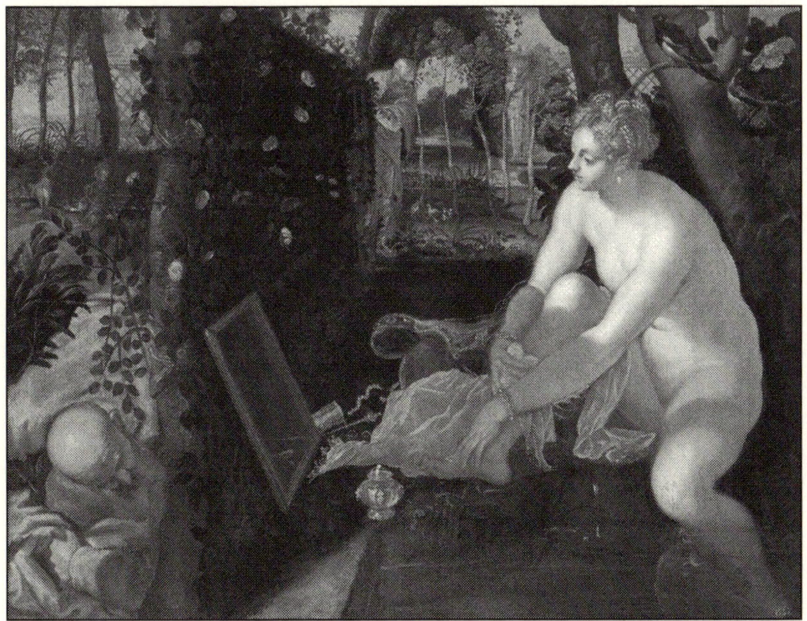

Fig. 30.2 - Tintoretto: *Susanna and the Elders* c.1555

What we have forgotten is the purpose of gazing upon a work of art. If we are there for an aesthetic experience, we will surely find it. For Beauty is always there, in harmony and balance, enlivening the figures in their composition and perspective. But, on a much deeper level, these works are capable of transforming our human experience into a soul-shattering experience of true wonder and awe. We are not just there *to see* the deity, but *to be seen*, to enter into the divine presence. Like Semele, we surrender to Divine Sight – an eye-opening experience that ultimately annihilates our more human way of seeing.

Such an overwhelming vision may only be granted by Divine dispensation. But, in my experience, it may also be earned through constant practice. There is no shortcut or way around daily discipline. And, as a spiritual practice, these methods have enriched my soul immensely. When I stand before a work of art, I begin by asking that the Deity grant me eyes to see, a mind to understand, and a heart to be opened by the image's transformative power.

Then begins the *sādhana*, which takes the form of a soul quest. I ask myself what feeling is being evoked by the image before me. In the hall of works by Venetian painters, this may be Titian's *Danaë* in a shower gold (Fig. 30.1) or Tintoretto's *Susanna and the Elders* (Fig. 30.2). When I first studied painting in Vienna, in the Fall of 1989, I was not moved in the least by these images. At the age of twenty-seven, I did not even know how to read them, and could not imagine why anyone would engage them seriously. Renaissance art seemed much too mannered and theatrical. How was I supposed to identify with this antiquated scene transpiring before my eyes?

With age I have learned that a knowledge of myth helps guide the viewer through the painting. But, even if the specific myth is not known, I can still resonate with the image if I recall the classical meaning of myth in Occidental culture. In the Humanist tradition, the Greek and Roman gods eternally enact human situations, so we may reflect upon our given response. Along with their Hebrew and Christian counterparts, they portray feelings, and allow us to visualize the various passions of the soul, so we may feel empathy and undergo a transformation.

Aristotle described this as fear (*phobos*) and compassion (*eleos*) before the hero's tragic suffering, leading to a deep *catharsis*. In a well-constructed plot (*mythos*), the main figure falls victim to a situation (*catastrophe*) that brings on an excess of feeling (*pathos*) but also a reversal and transformation (*peripeteia*), when they recognize and acknowledge *(anagnorisis*) their genuine human flaw (*hamartia*).

That is the power of Humanist art: to evoke our feelings, so as to acknowledge and transform them. The scene is set, the figures are posed, and the story unfolds as foretold. When we refuse to participate in the drama, because the gestures seem too overdone or theatrical, we are in fact failing to see the Hieratic dimension of the piece. These are not human actors from an earlier era, but sacred beings eternally portraying the seven passions of the soul for our benefit. Their graceful poses and stylized gestures reminds us that this play has a higher, allegorical purpose: to help us navigate the soul's passage through this lifetime and the next.

What passions? The Wisdom Traditions of the East and West have reduced them to specific number, so we may remember and recollect each one. There are basically seven and sometimes twelve. It does not matter that Charles Le Brun, in his *Expressions des Passions de l'Ame,* enumerated the simple passions as six; or Bharata, in his *Nātyaśāstra* set the iconography of the primary *rasas* as eight. What matters is that the feelings can be clearly recognized and recalled.

As we have seen, in Classical times each negative emotion was associated with a planetary deity: Saturn's delusion, Jupiter's envy, Mars' wrath, the Sun's pride, Venus' lust, Mercury's greed and the Moon's mind-bending madness. To these we may add the five negative influences arising from the elements and our own bodily humours: the Aether's quintessential fear, the strife of choleric Fire, the dishonesty of sanguine Air, the apathy of phlegmatic Water, and the depression of melancholic Earth. (In the East, we recall that envy, pride, aversion, attachment and ignorance form the Five Buddhist Passions or *kleśaviṣa* that echo our Western sentiments, as do the seven *chakra* centres in the Hindu Kundalini tradition).

In the heavens, the planets are constantly orbiting through the band of constellations. That is to say, certain eternal dramas are being constantly re-enacted, for all of eternity. The gods cast their feelings outward into the cosmos, like sympathetic waves or vibrations, and we receive them – knowingly or not. The ones most sensitive to these harmonic frequencies are the eternal poets, the painters and sculptors, who give contemporary shape to these ever-repeating forms, guarding the age-old adage: As Above, So Below. This perennial philosophy permeates their works, like the upward-pointing, downward pointing triangles of a hexagram, as a hidden sign or sigil: As Above △; So Below ▽.

Painting after painting has been designed for a meditation on specific feeling-situations – the fall of the hero or heroine because of too much pride (*hubris*) and their ignorance of some hidden human flaw (*hamartia*). Some suffer from a deep fascination with Venus' desire; others, with Mars' compulsion for violence and rage. Jupiter goads us on with envy, while Mercury entraps us with greed for this world's material illusion. Touched by the Moon, some suffer madness and mental disorder; while others, under the sign of Saturn, fall into deep melancholy and delusion. The astrological linkage of the planetary movements with the passions of the soul gives us a means of navigating these currents.

Returning to Titian's Danäe or Tintoretto's Susanna, it does not matter, necessarily, what myth is being portrayed. Beyond that, a specific feeling emanates from the image. Perhaps Susanna, gazing at herself in the mirror, is manifesting vanity and pride. And Danaë, with her eyes fixed on the shower of god, is expressing greed and desire. There is no right or wrong answer here – only our true feeling response to the image. What passion of the soul does this painting evoke?

III. In the Solitude of My Studio

The next step in the meditation, which I always find to be terribly difficult, is to experience *pathos* and *peripeteia*, which is to say, feeling and transformation. Since this involves a genuine *catharsis*, I prefer the safe confines of my studio. (I have indeed been moved to tears by a painting in a museum – an experience which some museum-goers find disturbing, incomprehensible, or just plain mad...).

Therefore, in the solitude of my studio, I am more free to explore my soul's feelings to the full. This involves a number of techniques, which I have learned thanks to my students and colleagues.

Kevin Campeau, for example, has taught me how to go on an 'inner journey'. Having mastered this technique for himself, as the result of complete bodily paralysis in his youth, he taught it to me, guiding me verbally through the realms of vision. Since then, he has facilitated many people on their inner journeys – each of whom reaped such benefits that they learned this technique for themselves.

First, upon entering the visionary sphere, we express gratitude for this moment and the journey that awaits. With mindful appreciation, we set an intention for the journey. Then, each detail of the landscape and architecture are named and noted down. Spaces from dreams or distant travels re-awaken in our memory, as we willingly immerse ourselves in their evocative environment.

At a certain point, we call upon a guide, be that human, animal or some bizarre combination of these two, in all their various manners and movements. Like the landscape, the guide is envisioned to the full: each detail of their gestures and dress is carefully noted, named and remembered. Allowing our hand to move freely, in automatic drawings inspired by our guide, we may record these moments in images or words. Willingly, we enter the spaces conjured by our inner spirit, who may lead us to unexpected places and introduce us to other forms of guides.

Over time, Kevin Campeau has constructed an immense 'Memory Palace', with chambers and doorways leading in multiple directions on many levels. Like the five-storey palace of mandala meditation, surrounded by four gates and three protective circles, so does this Memory Palace correspond to places in the body, to energy chakras and their associated feelings. The mind enters this imaginative realm and encounters autonomous powers, be they angelic or demonic, which await us at each turning of the mind's labyrinth.

From remaining perfectly balanced with slow even breathing, I have also learned (thanks to Kathleen Schmieder) that one may gradually begin to rock back and forth, moving with the breathing, alternating from one side of perfect balance to the other. These movements bring awareness down through body's central channel, re-activating heart-centered actions that express the passions of the soul, both positively and negatively.

I must also mention another student, who has unknowingly become my guide and teacher. Paul Hughes taught me a method called Vivation which serves to activate or 'vivate' certain feelings through four distinct types of breathing. By identifying the breathing pattern associated with a certain feeling, *and breathing deeper into it*, we can increase its power (not just joy, but anger, fear or pain) to more fully activate its informative power.

Among my colleagues, some have practiced chanting, vipassana or Holotropic breathwork. These methods open up new pathways for the spirit: exploring how different passions of the soul may be activated by different types of breathing. In deep visionary states, posture and breathing are our greatest aids and allies, combined with meditative techniques.

For me, all these approaches – and there are many more – serve the same essential purpose: to guide us on a visionary journey that evokes certain passions of the soul. Through such a meditation, we can not only re-activate and re-experience the strong emotions from our distant or recent past, but view them with our mind and spirit, from a higher point of view. And, for each negative emotion there is a positive one that mirrors it. In a full meditation or visionary journey, we pass through symbolic scenarios that allegorize our present-day soul struggles. To be brought to tears when faced with a painted allegory of this – is to reach the momentary feeling of revelation and redemption.

IV. Shedding Tears of Laughter

When artists like Michelangelo, Blake, Moreau or Fuchs composed their paintings, they did so as poets. Each of these artists wrote poetry, and knew how to compose allegories through verse. They were acquainted with the transformative power of symbols, to guide our soul in a narrative ascent or descent.

And so, they proved themselves to be poets of painting as well, drawing vast allegories that portray the soul's struggles, step by step, image by image. Their masterpieces are equivalent to Dante's Divine Comedy, which displays the power of allegory to guide us through various levels of heaven and hell.

In our imagination, the painting becomes an epic poem or play, a theatre of the mind, where sculptures pass through a series of movements to direct our gaze through the narrative unfolding.

This eye-movement may be errant, or begin as so, until the sudden focus and fixation on a distinct configuration of images allows us to recognize and reflect upon a situation in our soul's present journey. This situation, and the feeling at its core, is recalled through the image configuration so the feeling may be re-activated and considered from the higher point of view.

Certain types of negative feeling appear again and again in different situations. These negative feelings arise because we are acting from one of the seven ego-needs rather than our higher Self. These seven ego-needs are what we have described as the Seven Passions of the Soul.

Yet, for each of these, if it is re-experienced to the full, there is a form of redemption. If, in the first entry into the visionary realm, I experience massive confusion, overwhelming complexity, evoking terrible fear – especially the fear of insanity – then I have encountered and mastered 'fear in the face of inconstancy' – the lunar powers that provoke so-called 'lunacy'. I have traversed the lowest of the seven negative feelings, the lowest 'Passion of the Soul'.

After Inconstancy, comes Greed, Desire, Pride, Anger, Envy (or Injustice) and Delusion. Painting after painting has been designed for us to meditate on allegories of these feeling-situations. Not just Tintoretto's Susanna or Titian's Danäe, but myriads of figures from the Hall of Simultaneousness of All Images.

Those who go on vision journeys are able to investigate these feelings as they manifest in their own life-dramas, and re-experience them to such a degree of profound transformation, that the cleansing power of tears allows them to see it in a different light. The *pathos* and *peripeteia* of the well-constructed *mythos* evoke our feelings and transform them; the *anagnorisis* and *catharsis* allow us to acknowledge our inner flaws and cleanse them.

Indeed, through the act of crying, specific tensions in the body are powerfully released – blocked energies are liberated, and we free ourselves of those bodily forces that were drawing upon negative emotions, as if the body feeds on them just as surely as demonic spirits feed upon our fears and desires. Each organ, each chakra centre, cycles through its need for a certain energy-type, provoking negative feelings that we come to manifest in day-to-day situations. But now, through meditation, we recognize it and view it all from a higher point of view – as a soul centered in the Sacred.

The negative feeling transforms into a positive one – not just any positive one, but the one that mirrors it in the higher sphere. If we feared the overwhelming confusion of the lunar power, then suddenly we experience clarity, stillness and order. The sacred world appears as a place of silence, light and distinct form. We are able to focus upon it for timeless moments, feeling absolutely safe and eternal, a particle of divinity, above the seven lower passions of the soul, now experienced in their true and undistorted form, as spiritual joys.

Pride finds its higher reflection in Humility; Anger becomes Love; Desire transfigures into the soul's Beauty; Injustice is matched by a Balance for justice, truth, and equality; Greed is met by Generosity and Sharing.

In Aristotle's vision of Tragedy, our feelings of fear (*phobos*) and compassion (*eleos*) undergo a transformation and purification (*catharsis*) when we shed tears of sadness. But, the second book of his *Poetics* – which was *on Comedy* – failed to survive the vagaries of time. Nevertheless, we can reconstruct parts of it to show how Comedy mirrors Tragedy. Instead of fear and compassion, it is now our feelings of envy (*phthronos*) and angry indignation (*nemesan*) which undergo a purification and transformation (*catharsis*), but this time through laughter. We may purge and purify ourselves of negative emotions, *by shedding tears of laughter*.

In each re-enactment of an allegorical situation, whether portrayed in a painting or remembered in our vision-journey, we hear the calling for us to respond from the higher feelings in us. We learn to act upon those elevated feelings, while navigating this earthly existence. When called upon, time and again, to respond with either pride or humility, we choose humility. Our anger, after much self-reflection and practice, comes out to others as love. We gaze at an object of desire and see only its higher beauty.

V. *"The external world falls away, like a veil..."*

In so many of Dalì's paintings, there emerges the small detail of an older man taking the hand of a child and gesturing to the horizon. Now, when I walk through the halls of Painting, my master is beside me. I hear his voice and see things, as he guides me through the eternal halls of art. Yes he, the eternal artist, takes my hand and guides me down corridors of time into distant cultures, where new forms of seeing await.

I have attempted to faithfully record those different inner forms of sight, but no words can adequately express the full glory of their epiphany. When immersed in the sacred art of painting, the external world falls away, like a veil, revealing the true, beautiful and timeless nature of the world. In such a stilled and dream-like world of enchantment, we think we must surely be hallucinating. But hallucination is the name which fear gives to the full effulgence of the Sacred.

The visionary state is a state of madness, of the continuous disconnect between the paradise you know that exists in your heart, and the external world which is mediated to you. Functioning in the visionary state requires an extraordinary degree of detachment (sustained by hidden personal sacrifice), while maintaining a complete and thorough engagement in inter-personal and worldly affairs.

For the true visionary artist, painting becomes not only a technical skill, or a form of soul expression, but a spiritual practice – a means of perfecting ourselves, so we may bear the jewelled crown (knowing it is a crown of thorns) and put on the robe of glory (knowing that it is a torn and bloodied garment). We suffer, so that Divinity may penetrate our art, like the arrows in St. Sebastian's flesh. That same Divinity may move through our art with all the Beauty and grace of a Goddess.

Every allegory of the soul has two meanings, and how we read the symbols depends upon how we view them – from which side of the spiritual divide; do we see with the Divine Eye or its distorting twin? Do we passively drink in the darkness, believing that the worlds conjured by fear and hate are the only possible worlds? Or do we actively envision the light, seeing the opportunity for redemption in each conflict?

The lower world mirrors the upper: As Above; So Below. As Visionary artists, our task is to manifest that hidden world, made visible to the tearfully cleansed and awakened soul. How can any of us describe that experience? Words, scrawled randomly in a sketchbook while deeply immersed in the visionary state, come rushing back to my memory:

And I wept with joy to gaze upon it.

END NOTES

A.T. = Author's Translation

PREFACE

1. Aristotle, Metaphysics, quoted in Padovan, Richard, *Proportion: Science, Philosophy, Architecture,* (1999), p. 123.
2. Vasari, Giorgio, *The Lives of the Artists* (1965), p. 316.
3. My principle writings on Visionary Art may be found in:
   - *The First Manifesto of Visionary Art* (2000)
   - Chapter 12: 'Symbols in Modern Visionary Art' in *Enter Through the Image* (2009)
   - A series of articles for *The Visionary Revue* - Summer 2001 - Fall 2007. Two articles from the fourth issue, called 'A Mirror Delirious' and 'Myrette', contain earlier versions of research and results published here.

PART I - ENVISIONING THE WORK

CH. 1 – SEEING UNITY

1. Moreau, Gustave, *Écrits sur l'art, Volume I,* (2002), p. 143-144, A.T.
2. 'Book of Exodus', *The Holy Bible*, New International Version.
3. Ovid, *Metamorphoses*, (1955), p. 81.
4. Moreau, Gustave, *Écrits sur l'art, Volume I,* (2002), p. 142, A.T.
5. *Bhagavad Gita* (1962), *passim.*
6. 'Apocryphon of John' in *The Nag Hammadi Library in English*, (1990), pp. 104 - 123.
7. Fuchs, Ernst, *Architectura Caelestis: Images of the Hidden Prime of Styles*, (1970), p. 170.
8. *Ibid.,* p. 170.
9. Plotinus, *Enneads*, (1975), *passim.*
10. Plato, 'Symposium' 210a-211e *passim*, (trans. by Michael Joyce and Benjamin Jowett) in *The Collected Dialogues of Plato*, (1961).
11. Fuchs, Ernst, 'About My Pictures' in *Catalogue for the Ernst Fuchs exhibitions in the National Tretjakow Gallery Moscow*, (2001), p. 23.

CH. 2 – ENTER THROUGH THE IMAGE

1. Vasari, Giorgio, *Vasari on Technique*, (1907), p. 211.
2. Fuchs, Ernst, 'The Hidden Prime of Styles' in *Architectura Caelestis: Images of the Hidden Prime of Styles*, (1970).
3. Caruana, L., 'A Mirror Delirious' in *The Visionary Revue*, Issue 4, Paris, (2007).

CH. 3 – THE PRINCIPLES OF VISION

1. Lindberg, David C., *Theories of Vision From Al-Kindi to Kepler*, (1976), p. 161.
2. Vinci, Leonardo da, Notebook G37a in *The Notebooks of Leonardo da Vinci,* Volume I, (1970), p. 30.
3. Empedocles, 'Fragment 86' from Burnet, John, *Early Greek Philosophy*, (1892) p. 217.
4. Empedocles, 'Fragment 84', *Ibid.*, p. 217. Translation amended.
5. Lindberg, David C., *Theories of Vision From Al-Kindi to Kepler*, (1976), p. 5.
6. *Ibid.*, p. 5. 7. *Ibid.*, p. 5. 8. *Ibid.*, p. 12.
9. Blake, William, 'The Everlasting Gospel' (c. 1810) section 5, line 101 from *The Rossetti Manuscript* (*aka* MS. Book; c. 1793 – 1811).
10. *pūjā* is a form of 'worship' involving *sparśa*, touching the statue with one's hand, and *nyāsa*, touching the limbs of one's own body, to establish the presence of the deity there. See: Eck, Diana L., *Darsan – Seeing the Divine Image in India*, (1981), p. 11.

11. Rilke, Rainer Maria, 'The Panther' in *Selected poems / Ausgewählte gedichte*, trans. by Stanley Appelbaum, (2011).
12. Fuchs, Ernst, *Architectura Caelestis: Images of the Hidden Prime of Styles*,(1970), p. 184.
13. Blake, William, 'The Tyger' in *Songs of Innocence and Experience: Shewing the Two Contrary States of the Human Soul, 1789-1794*, (1977).
14. Viollet-le-Duc, Eugène, Entry on 'Style' in Volume 8 of *Dictionnaire raisonée de l'architecture française du XIe au XVIe siècle*, (1875), A.T.

PART II - THE FIGURE: PROPORTION & POSE

CH. 4 - HIERATIC PROPORTION: ANCIENT & MODERN

1. Barbillon, Claire, *Les Canons du Corps Humain Au XIXe Siègle – L'Art et la Règle*, (2004), p. 254, A.T.
2. Lenz, Desiderius, *The Aesthetic of Beuron and other writings*, (2002), p. 7.
3. *Ibid.*, p. 56. 4. *Ibid.*, p. 17. 5. *Ibid.*, p. 16.
6. *Ibid.*, p. 19. 7. *Ibid.*, p. 27. 8. *Ibid.*, p. 20.
9. *Ibid.*, p. 20. 10. *Ibid.*, p. 34. 11. *Ibid.*, p. 70.
12. *Ibid.*, p. 72. 13. *Ibid.*, p. 70. 14. *Ibid.*, p. 64.
15. *Ibid.*, p. 72. 16. *Ibid.*, p. 41. 17. *Ibid.*, p. 61. 18. *Ibid.*, p. 31.
19. Tomoum, Nadja, *The Sculptor's Models of the Late and Ptolemaic Periods*, (2006) p. 149
20. *Ibid.*, p. 170.
21. Edgar, C. C., 'Remarks on Egyptian Sculpture Models', (1905), p. 137.
22. *Ibid.*, p. 141.
23. Viollet-le-Duc, Eugène, Entry on 'Style' in Volume 8 of *Dictionnaire raisonée de l'architecture française du XIe au XVIe siècle*, (1875), A.T.
24. Diodorus Siculus, Book I, chapter 98, *Library of History*, (1933).
25. Robins, Gay, *Proportion and Style in Ancient Egyptian Art*, (1994), p. 26.
26. Barbillon, Claire, *Les Canons du Corps Humain Au XIXe Siègle – L'Art et la Règle*, (2004), p. 166.
27. Robins, Gay, *Proportion and Style in Ancient Egyptian Art*, (1994), p. 169.
28. Guralnick, Eleanor, 'The Proportions of Kouroi', (1978), p. 461 - 472.
29. Clark, Kenneth, *The Nude*, (1960), p. 86.
30. Panofsky, Erwin,'The History of the Theory of Human Proportions as a Reflection of the History of Styles' in *Meaning in the Visual Arts*, (1955).

CH. 5 - HIERATIC PROPORTION: EAST & WEST

1. Kramrisch, Stella, 'Traditions of the Indian Craftsman', (1958), p. 224.
2. Zimmer, Heinrich, *The Art of Indian Asia*, (2001), p. 322.
3. Kramrisch, Stella, 'Traditions of the Indian Craftsman', (1958), p. 225 - 227.
4. *Ibid.*, p. 228.
5. Mosteller, John F., 'The Problem of Proportion and Style in Indian Art History' (1990), Footnote 9, p. 394.
6. Kramrisch, Stella, 'Traditions of the Indian Craftsman', (1958), p. 227.
7. *Vishnudharmattara* Part III, Ch. 38, Verses 1-28 in *Vishnudharmottara (Part III): A Treatise on Indian Painting and Image-Making*, (1928) p. 42.
8. Mosteller, John F., 'The Problem of Proportion and Style in Indian Art History'(1990), p. 389
9. Kramrisch, Stella, *The Hindu Temple*, Vol. II, (1976) p. 309.
10. *Ibid.*, p. 309.
11. *Vishnudharmattara* Part III, Ch. 36 in *Vishnudharmottara (Part III): A Treatise on Indian Painting and Image-Making*, (1928) p. 36.
12. Haja, Nilofar Shamim, 'Celebration of Life: A study of sculptural and mural depictions of dance and music in Buddhist art of India, (2007), p. 22.
13. Mostellar, John, F., 'The Study of Indian Iconometry in Historical Perspective' (1988), p. 105.
14. Mostellar, John F., 'A New Approach for the Study of Indian Art' (1987), p. 58.

15. Mosteller, John F., 'The Problem of Proportion and Style in Indian Art History'(1990), p. 393.
16. Gega Lama, *Principles of Tibetan Art,* Vol I, (1983), p. 75.
17. *Ibid.*, p. 11. 18. *Ibid.*, p. 57 - 58.
19. Jackson, David P., Jackson, Janice, *Tibetan Thangka Painting,* (1988), p. 71.
20. *Ibid.*, p. 69.
21. Gega Lama, *Principles of Tibetan Art,* Vol I, (1983), p. 57 - 58.
22. *Ibid.*, p. 57.
23. Jackson, David P., Jackson, Janice, *Tibetan Thangka Painting,* (1988), p. 13.
24. Dionysius of Fourna, p. 7, ¶ 39 of *The Painter's Manual*, (1989).
25. *Ibid.*, p. 5, ¶ 36. 26. *Ibid.*, p. 38, ¶ 112 (70). 27. *Ibid.*, p. 34, ¶ 103 (61).
28. Sendler, Egon, *L'icône – image de l'invisible*, (1981), p. 108 - 109, A.T.
29. *Ibid.*, p. 112, A.T.
30. *Ibid.*, p. 110, A.T.
31.Mako, Vladimir, *The Art of Harmony,* (2007), pp. 56 - 57.
32. Dionysius of Fourna, p. 15, ¶ 60 (16) of *The Painter's Manual*, (1989).
33. Mako, Vladimir, *The Art of Harmony,* (2007), p. 26.
34. Villard de Honnecourt, *The Medieval Sketchbook of Villard de Honnecourt*, (2006). All citations refer to the Plates in this edition.
35. Viollet-le-Duc, Eugène, Entry on 'Sculpture' in Volume 8 of *Dictionnaire raisonée de l'architecture française du XIe au XVIe siècle*, (1875), A.T.
36. *Ibid.* 37. *Ibid.*

CH. 6 – HUMANIST PROPORTION: CLASSICAL & RENAISSANCE

1. Galen, *De placitis Hippocratis et Platonis*, v, 448 in Stewart, Andrew, *'The Canon of Polykleitos: A Question of Evidence'* (1978), p. 122.
2. Leftwich, Gregory V., 'Polykleitos and Hippokratic Medicine' in Moon, Warren G., editor, *Polykleitos, The Doryphoros and Tradition*, (1995), p. 38.
3. Tobin, Richard, 'The Canon of Polykleitos' in *American Journal of Archaeology*, Vol. 79, No. 4, (1975), pp. 307 - 321.
4. Zeising quoted in Padovan, Richard, *Proportion: Science, Philosophy, Architecture,* (1999), p. 308.
5. Cook, Theodore Andrea, *The Curves of Life,* (1914), p. 420.
6. *Ibid.*, p. 464. 7. *Ibid.*, p. 463.
8. Pliny, *The Natural History*, Bk. 39, Ch. 61, (1893).
9. Politt, J. J., *Art and Experience in Classical Greece*, (1972), p. 176.
10. Carpenter, Rhys, *Greek Sculpture*, (1960), p. 107.
11. Politt, J. J., *Art and Experience in Classical Greece*, (1972), p. 176.
12. Vitruvius,, *The Ten Books of Architecture,* Bk III, Ch. I ¶1 in Lester, Toby, *Da Vinci's Ghost*, (2012), p. 38.
13. Vitruvius, *The Ten Books of Architecture,* Bk III, Ch. I ¶3, (1960), p. 72.
14, Cennini, Cennino d'Andrea, *The Craftsman's Handbook: "Il Libro dell' Arte"* (1954), Ch. LXX.
15. Da Vinci, Leonardo, *Codex Arundel* in in Lester, Toby, *Da Vinci's Ghost*, (2012), p. 184.
16. Vitruvius, *The Ten Books of Architecture,* Bk III, Ch. I ¶2, (1960), p. 72.
17. Lester, Toby, *Da Vinci's Ghost*, (2012), p. 212.
18. *Ibid.*, p. 212.
19. Cousins, Jean, *Livre de perspective*,(1560).
20. Cousins, Jean, *L'art de dessiner*, (1778).
21. Paul Richer in Barbillon, Claire, *Les Canons du Corps Humain Au XIXe Siègle – L'Art et la Règle*, (2004), p. 186, A.T.
22. Michelangelo, *Zeichnungen und Zuschreibungen*, (2009), p. 47.
23. *Ibid.*, p. 51.

CH. 7 - THE HUMANIST POSE: CLASSICAL

1. Spike, John T., *Young Michelangelo: The Path to the Sistine*, (2010), p. 193.
2. *Ibid.*, p. 193.
3. Volume III, Book 9, line 774 of *The Greek Anthology: The Declamatory Epigrams*, (1917).
4. Herodas, *Mime 4*, lines 32-34 in *Theophrastas, Herodas, Saphron*, (2003).
5. Aeschylus, 'Papyrus Oxyrhynchus 2162' in *Fragments*, (2009).
6. Plato, *Cratylus* 399d (Jowett trans) in *The Collected Dialogues of Plato*, (1961).
7. Plato, *Phaedro* 245e (R. Hackfourth trans) in *The Collected Dialogues of Plato*, (1961).
8. Plato, *Phaedo* 109d in *The Collected Dialogues of Plato*, (1961).
9. Plato, *Phaedo* 79d in *Ibid.*
10. Plato, *Phaedo* 79c in *Ibid.*
11. Plato, Timaeus, 28a in *Ibid.*
12. Neer, Richard, *The Emergence of the Classical Style in Greek Sculpture*, (2010), p. 41.
13. Pliny, *The Natural History*, Bk. 34, Ch. 19, (1893).
14. Pausanias, *Description of ancient Greece*, Book I, ¶ 24, line 5, (1918).
15. Neer, Richard, *The Emergence of the Classical Style in Greek Sculpture*, (2010), p. 150.
16. *Ibid.*, p. 148.
17. Politt, J. J., *Art and Experience in Classical Greece*, (1972), p. 24.
18. *Ibid.*, p. 43.
19. Aristotle, *Poetics*, I. 4-9, (1895).
20. Aristotle, *Poetics*, 1452a (1965).
21. Xenophon, *The Memorabilia, Recollections of Socrates*, Bk II, section 10, (1897).
22. Politt, J. J., *Art and Experience in Classical Greece*, (1972), p. 56.
23. Clark, Kenneth, *The Nude*, (1960) p. 31.
24. *Ibid.*, p. 32.
25. *Dictionnaire de L'Académie française*, 8th Edition (1932-5).
26. Neer, Richard, *The Emergence of the Classical Style in Greek Sculpture*, (2010), pp. 72 - 73 (89).
27. *Ibid.*, p. 91 (108).

CH. 8 - THE HUMANIST POSE: RENAISSANCE

1. Spike, John T., *Young Michelangelo: The Path to the Sistine*, (2010), p. 64.
2. Alberti, Leon Battista, *On Painting*, (1970), Bk II, ¶45, p. 73.
3. Michelangelo, *The Poetry of Michelangelo*, (1993), p. 106.
4. Blunt, Anthony, *Artistic Theory in Italy: 1450 - 1600*, (1962), (Poem trans. by K. T. Butler), p. 69.
5. Panofsky, Erwin, 'The First Two Projects of Michelangelo's Tomb of Julius II' in *The Art Bulletin*, (1937), p. 561.
6. Blunt, Anthony, *Artistic Theory in Italy: 1450 - 1600*, (1962), Poem trans. by K. T. Butler, p. 68.
7. Vasari, Giorgio, *The Lives of the Artists* (1965), p. 382.
8. Lomazzo, Giovan Paolo, *Tracte Containing the Artes of curious Paintinge, Caruinge, Buildinge*, (1598) Bk. 1, Ch. 1, p. 22.
9. *Ibid.*, Bk. 1, Ch. 1, p. 23.
10. *Ibid.*, Bk. 6, Ch. 4, p. 296.
11. Clark, Kenneth, *Leonardo da Vinci*, (1939), p. 152.
12. Alberti, Leon Battista, *On Painting*, (1970), Bk I, ¶11, p. 44.
13. *Ibid.*, Bk. I, ¶13, p. 45
14. *Ibid.*, Bk. II, ¶22, p. 68.
15. Dolce, Lodovico, *Aretin: A Dialogue on Painting*, (1770), p. 71.
16. Alberti, Leon Battista, *On Painting*, (1970), Bk. II, ¶ 22, p. 68.
17. *Ibid.*, Bk. III, ¶ 13, p. 95.
18. *Ibid.*, Bk. II, ¶ 42 , p. 73.
19. *Ibid.*, Bk. III, ¶ 5, p. 92.
20. *Ibid.*, Bk. I, ¶ 28, p. 51.
21. *Ibid.*, Bk. II, ¶ 31, p. 70.
22. *Ibid.*, Bk. II , ¶ 52, p. 74.
23. *Ibid.*, Bk. II , ¶ 54, p. 76.
24. *Ibid.*, Bk. II , ¶ 52, p. 74.
25. *Ibid.*, Bk. II, ¶ 53, p. 76.
26. *Ibid.*, Bk. III, ¶ 1, p. 90.

27. Dolce, Lodovico, *Aretin: A Dialogue on Painting*, (1770) p. 71.
28. Alberti, Leon Battista, *On Painting*, (1970), Bk. III, ¶ 17, p. 96.
29. For the former, see Frances A. Yates, *The Art of Memory*, (1966); for the latter, see: Carruthers, Mary J., 'Ars oblivionis, ars inveniendi: 'The Cherub Figure and the Arts of Memory', in *Gesta*, vol. 48, (2009).
30. Vasari quoted in Stowell, Steven F.H., *The Spiritual Language of Art: Medieval Christian Themes in Writings on Art,* (2014), p. 279.
31. Vasari, Giorgio, *Vasari on Technique: Being the Introduction to the Three Arts of Design, Architecture, Sculpture and Painting*, (1907), p. 210.
32. Vasari, quoted in Blunt, Anthony, *Artistic Theory in Italy: 1450 - 1600*, (1962), p. 89.
33. Vinci, Leonardo da, from 'Small codex on the flight of birds in the Royal Library at Turin' 20v, quoted in *The Notebooks of Leonardo da Vinci,* (1980), p. 4.
34. Vinci, Leonardo da, from MSS. A and B, called B.N. 2038, 19r in the Bibliothèque Nationale, quoted in *The Notebooks of Leonardo da Vinci*, (1980), p. 4.
35. Vinci, Leonardo da, from *Trattato della Pittura* (Codex Urbinas 1270), p. 28 quoted in *The Notebooks of Leonardo da Vinci*, (1980), p. 110.
36. Blunt, Anthony, *Artistic Theory in Italy: 1450 - 1600*, (1962) Poem trans. by K. T. Butler, p. 69.
37. *Ibid.*, p. 63.
38. Vasari, Giorgio, *Vasari on Technique: Being the Introduction to the Three Arts of Design, Architecture, Sculpture and Painting*, (1907), p. 205.
39. Alberti, Leon Battista, *On Painting*, (1970), Bk. III, ¶ 6, p. 93.
40. Maximus of Tyre, *Philosophical Oration* 17, iii in Söran, Görbum, 'The Classical Concept of Mimesis' in *A Companion to Art Theory,* (2008), p. 25.
41. Aristotle, *Poetics*, 1460b, (1895).
42. Pliny, *The Natural History*, Bk. 35, Ch. 64, (1893).
43. Cicero, *De inventione* II.1.1-3 in Söran, Görbum, 'The Classical Concept of Mimesis' in *A Companion to Art Theory,* (2008), p. 25.
44. Blunt, Anthony, *Artistic Theory in Italy: 1450 - 1600*, (1962) Poem trans. by K. T. Butler, p. 72.
45. *Ibid.*, p. 64.
46. Clark, Kenneth, *The Nude*, (1960), p. 54.

PART III - NARRATIVE & STYLE

CH. 9 - THE ACADEMY & THE GUILD

1. Ames-Lewis, Francis, *The Intellectual Life of the Early Renaissance Artist,* (2000), p. 18.
2. *Ibid.*, p. 19. 3. *Ibid.*, pp. 20 - 21. 4. *Ibid.*, p. 19.
5. Cennini, Cennino d'Andrea, *The Craftsman's Handbook: "Il Libro dell'Arte"* (1954), Ch. II, p. 2.
6. *Ibid.*, Ch. III, p. 3. 7. *Ibid.*, Ch. CIIII pp. 64 - 65.
8. Ames-Lewis, Francis, *Drawings in Early Renaissance Italy* (1981), p. 36.
9. *Ibid.*, p. 36. 10. *Ibid.*, p. 55. 11. *Ibid.*, p. 56. 12. *Ibid.*, p. 47.
13. Ames-Lewis, Francis, *The Intellectual Life of the Early Renaissance Artist,* (2000), p. 36.
14. *Ibid.*, p. 57. 15. *Ibid.*, p. 31.
16. Bouleau, Charles, *Charpentes – La Géométrie Secrète des Peintres*, (1963), p. 101.
17. Ames-Lewis, Francis, *The Intellectual Life of the Early Renaissance Artist,* (2000), p. 32.
18. Goldstein, Carl, *Teaching Art – Academies and Schools from Vasri to Albers*, (1996), p. 27.
19. *Ibid.*, p. 28. 20. *Ibid.*, p. 137. 21. *Ibid.*, p. 21.
22. *Ibid.*, p. 45. 23. *Ibid.*, p. 150. 24. *Ibid.*, p. 150. 25. *Ibid.*, p. 42.
26. Schaller, Catherine, *L'expression des passions au XIXe siècle* (2003), p. 10.
27. *Ibid.*, p. 9, A.T. 28. *Ibid.*, p. 10, A.T. 29. *Ibid.*, pp. 11 - 12.
30. Goldstein, Carl, *Teaching Art – Academies and Schools from Vasri to Albers*, (1996), p. 42.
31. *Ibid.*, p. 41. 32. *Ibid.*, pp. 162 - 163. 33. *Ibid.*, p. 61.
34. Bonnet, Alain; Goarin, Véronique; Jargot, Hélène; Schwartz, Emmanuel; *Devinir Peintre Au XIX Siècle* (2007), p. 49.

35. Schaller, Catherine, *L'expression des passions au XIXe siècle* (2003), p. 52, A.T.
36. Bonnet, Alain; Goarin, Véronique; Jargot, Hélène; Schwartz, Emmanuel; *Devinir Peintre Au XIX Siècle* (2007), p. 69.
37. *Ibid.*, p. 49. 38. *Ibid.*, p. 91.
39. Goldstein, Carl, *Teaching Art – Academies and Schools from Vasri to Albers*, (1996), p. 79.
40. Barbillon, Claire, *Les Canons du Corps Humain Au XIXe Siègle – L'Art et la Règle,* (2004) p. 133.
41. Goldstein, Carl, *Teaching Art – Academies and Schools from Vasri to Albers*, (1996), p. 137.
42. Barbillon, Claire, *Les Canons du Corps Humain Au XIXe Siègle – L'Art et la Règle,* (2004) p. 48, p. 132.
43. *Ibid.*, pp. 71 - 72, A.T. 44. *Ibid.*, p. 151, A.T.
45. Lifchez, Raymond, 'Jean-Galbert Salvage and His Anatomie du gladiateur combattant: Art and Patronage in Post-Revolutionary France', (2009) p. 164, A.T.
46. *Ibid.*, p. 171, A.T. 47. *Ibid.*, p. 171, A.T.
48. Goldstein, Carl, *Teaching Art – Academies and Schools from Vasri to Albers*, (1996), p. 58.

CH. 10 - THE NARRATIVE MOVEMENT IN PAINTING

1. See the Preface of Rubens, Pierre-Paul, *Théorie de la Figure Humaine*, (2003).
2. Rubens, Pierre-Paul, *Théorie de la Figure Humaine, Considerée dans ses principes, soit en repos ou en mouvement* (1773), Ch. II, p. 9, A.T.
3. *Ibid.*, Ch. II p. 9, A.T. 4. *Ibid.*, Ch. III p. 11, A.T. 5. *Ibid.*, Ch. III p. 16, A.T.
6. *Ibid.*, Ch. III p. 12, A.T. 7. *Ibid.*, Ch. III p. 12, A.T. 8. *Ibid.*, Ch. III p. 12, A.T.
9. *Ibid.*, Ch. III p. 14 10. *Ibid.*, Ch. III p. 16, A.T.
11. *Ibid.*, Ch. III pp. 14 - 15 *passim*, A.T.
12. Vasari, Giorgio, *The Lives of the Artists* (1965), p. 249
13. Bober, Phyllis Pray, 'Polykles and Polykleitos in the Renaissance: The "Letto de Policreto"' in *Polykleitos, the Doryphoros, and Tradition* (1995), *passim.*
14. Vasari, Giorgio, *The Lives of the Artists* (1965), p. 356.
15. Le Brun's lecture was recorded by three different auditors and published after his death in three different versions: Henry Testelin: *Sentiments des plus habiles peintres sur la pratique de la peinture et de la sculpture mis en tables de préceptes*, Paris, (1680, 1696); Gaëtan Picard: *Conférence de M. Le Brun sur l'expression générale et particulière*, Paris, (1698), and Jean Audran: *Expressions des passions de l'âme, représentées en plusieurs testes* Paris, (1727). Picard's version appears in English in Jennifer Montagu: *The Expression of the Passions: The Origins and Influence of Charles Le Brun's Conférence sur l'expression générale et particulière*, Yale University Press (1994).
16. Le Brun, Charles, trans. by Jennifer Montagu in *The Expression of the Passions: The Origin and Influence of Charles Le Brun's "Conference sur l'expression generale et particuliere"* (1994).
17. *Ibid.* 18. *Ibid.* 19. *Ibid.*
20. *Ibid.* 21. *Ibid.* 22. *Ibid.* 23. *Ibid.*
24. Schaller, Catherine, *L'expression des passions au XIXe siècle* (2003), p. 27.
25. *Ibid.*, p. 52, A.T. 26. *Ibid.*, p. 52, A.T.
27. *Ibid.*, p. 50, A.T. 28. *Ibid.*, p. 106, A.T.
29. Félibien, André, *Principes de l'Architecture, de la Sculpture, de la Peinture* (1699), p. 288, A.T.
30. *Ibid.*, p. 288, A.T. 31. *Ibid.*, p. 288, A.T.
32. *Ibid.*, p. 288, A.T. 33. *Ibid.*, p. 288, A.T.
34. *Ibid.*, p. 288, A.T. 35. *Ibid.*, p. 289, A.T.
36. Letter of 28th April, 1639 in Poussin, Nicolas, *Collection de lettres de Nicolas Poussin*, (1824) p. 18, A.T.
37. *Ibid.*, p. 91, A.T. 38. *Ibid.*, p. 91, A.T.
39. Fuseli, Henry, *Lectures on Painting* (1801), p. 251.

40. Palmer, Richard E., *Hermeneutics: Interpretation Theory in Schleiermacher, Dilthey, Heidegger and Gadamer*, (1969) p. 84.
41. Le Brun, Charles, *Conferences* (1669), Sixth Conference, p. 83, A.T.
42. *Ibid.*, p. 103, A.T. 43. *Ibid.*, p. 105, A.T.
44. Aristotle, *Poetics*, V. 4 (1965).
45. Hénin, Emmanuelle, *Ut pictura theatrum: Théâtre et peinture de la Renaissance italienne au classicisme français*, Librairie Droz (2003).
46. Fuseli, Henry, *Lectures on Painting* (1801), p. 246.
47. Le Brun, Charles, *Conferences* (1669), Sixth Conference, p. 134.
48. Blunt, Anthony, *Nicholas Poussin*, (1995) *passim.*
49. Alberti, Leon Battista, *On Painting*, (1970), Bk. II , ¶ 52, p. 74.
50. Le Brun, Charles, *Conferences* (1669), Sixth Conference, p. 98, A.T.
51. *Ibid.*, p. 94, A.T. 52. *Ibid.*, p. 90, A.T.
53. Poussin, Nicolas, *Collection de lettres de Nicolas Poussin*, (1824) p. 353, A.T.
54. Letter of 28th April, 1639 in Poussin, Nicolas, *Collection de lettres de Nicolas Poussin*, (1824) p. 18, A.T.
55. *Ibid.*, p 18, A.T.
56. Le Brun, Charles, *Conferences* (1669), Sixth Conference, p. 91, A.T.
57. *Ibid.*, p. 86, A.T. 58. *Ibid.*, p. 94, A.T. 59. *Ibid.*, p. 106, A.T.
60. Aristotle, *Poetics*, 1452a (1965)
61. Fuseli, Henry, *Lectures on Painting* (1801), p. 246

CH. 11 - THE HIERATIC POSE: EAST & WEST

1. Trop, Hjalmar, *The Integrating System of Proportion in Byzantine Art,* pp. 120.
2. Ouspensky, Leonid, *Theology of the Icon*, Vol I (1992) p. 51n.
3. *Ibid.*, Vo. I, p. 170. 4. *Ibid.*, Vo. I, p. 180.
5. Ouspensky, Leonid; Lossky, Vladimir, *The Meaning of Icons* (1982), p. 26.
6. Ouspensky, Leonid, *Theology of the Icon*, Vol I (1992) p. 161.
7. *Ibid.*, Vo. I, p. 162. 8. *Ibid.*, Vo. I, p. 158.
9. *Ibid.*, Vo. I, p. 156. 10. *Ibid.*, Vol. I, p. 157. 11. *Ibid.*, Vol. I, p. 181.
12. Ouspensky, Leonid; Lossky, Vladimir, *The Meaning of Icons* (1982), p. 41.
13. *Ibid.*, Vol. I, p. 42.
14. Joseph of Volokolamsk (1439 - 1515) excerpted from Lazarev, V. N., *Andrei Rublev i ego shkola*, Iskusstvo, (1966), pp. 75 - 78, trans. by Robert Bird.
15. Pseudo-Dionysius, *Ecclesiastical History* IV. 3, p. 3 cited in Torp, Hjalmar, *The Integrating System of Proportion in Byzantine Art* (1984) p. 121.
16. Cennini, Cennino d'Andrea, *The Craftsman's Handbook: "Il Libro dell' Arte"* (1954), Ch. LXVII.
17. Jackson, David P., Jackson, Janice, *Tibetan Thangka Painting,* (1988), pp. 45 - 47.
18. Mezzalira, Giovanni; Ambrosi, Annarosa; Borgato, Daniela; Pegoraro, Wilma, 'La ricostruzione dell'icona costantinopolitana' *Contributo scuola di iconografia san Luca al Convegno Internazionale su San Luca del 2000*, (2001).
19. Jackson, David P., Jackson, Janice, *Tibetan Thangka Painting,* (1988), p. 91.
20. Ouspensky, Leonid, *Theology of the Icon*, Vol I (1992), p. 171.
21. Ouspensky, Leonid; Lossky, Vladimir, *The Meaning of Icons* (1982), p. 40.
22. Beer, Robert, *The Encyclopedia of Tibetan Symbols and Motifs*, (1999) p. 4.
23. Ouspensky, Leonid; Lossky, Vladimir, *The Meaning of Icons* (1982), p. 41.
24. *Ibid.*, p. 40.
25. Beer, Robert, *The Encyclopedia of Tibetan Symbols and Motifs*, (1999), p. 4.
26. Ouspensky, Leonid, *Theology of the Icon*, Vol I (1992), p. 185.
27. Beer, Robert, *The Encyclopedia of Tibetan Symbols and Motifs*, (1999), p. 4.
28. Schönborn, Christopher, *God's Human Face: the Christ-Icon*, (1994), p. 227.
29. *Vishnudharmottara* (1928) Part III, Ch. 43, Verses 1 - 39, p. 59.
30. Haja, Nilofar Shamim, 'Celebration of Life: A study of sculptural and mural depictions of dance and music in Buddhist art of India' (2007), p. 25.

31. *Ibid.*, p. 30.
32. Politt, J. J., *Art and Experience in Classical Greece*, (1972), p. 56.
33. Tagore, Abanindranath, *Some Notes on Indian Artistic Anatomy*, (1914), p. 13.
34. Haja, Nilofar Shamim, 'Celebration of Life: A study of sculptural and mural depictions of dance and music in Buddhist art of India' (2007), p. 25.
35. Vatsyayan, Kapila, *The Square and the Circle of Indian Arts*, (1997), p. 122.

CH. 12 - THE FUSION OF HUMANIST & HIERATIC STYLES

1. Moreau, Gustave, *L'assembleur des rêves*, (1984), p. 197, A.T.
2. Ackroyd, Peter, *Blake*, (1996), p. 40.
3. *Ibid.*, p. 37. 4. *Ibid.*, p. 43. 5. *Ibid.*, p. 47.
6. William Blake, 'Marginal Note' in Raine, Kathleen, *William Blake* (1970) p. 18.
7. Ackroyd, Peter, *Blake*, (1996), p. 273.
8. William Blake, 'Letter to George Cumberland' in Raine, Kathleen, *William Blake* (1970), p. 27.
9. *Ibid.* p. 115. 10. *Ibid.*, p. 195. 11. *Ibid.*, p. 263.
12. *Ibid.*, p. 315. 13. *Ibid.*, p. 318.
14. Blake, William, 'A Vision of the Last Judgment' in *The Portable Blake*, (1948), p. 653.
15. Blake, William, 'Marriage of Heaven and Hell' in *The Portable Blake*, (1948), p. 249.
16. Blake, William, 'A Vision of the Last Judgment' in *The Portable Blake*, (1948), p. 653.
17. *Ibid.* 18. *Ibid.*
19. Ackroyd, Peter, *Blake*, (1996), p. 227.
20. *Ibid.*, p. 299. 21. *Ibid.*, p. 214.
22. *Ibid.*, p. 299. 23. *Ibid.*, p. 217.
24. Cooke, Peter, *Gustave Moreau: History Painting, Spirituality and Symbolism*, (2014) pp. 16 - 18.
25. *Ibid.*, p. 131.
26. Moreau, Gustave, *Gustave Moreau: l'homme aux figures de cire*, (2010), p. 81.
27. *Ibid.*, p. 75.
28. Forest, Marie-Cécile, 'Gustave Moreau et la sculpture: l'homme aux figures de cire' in *Gustave Moreau: l'homme aux figures de cire*, (2010), p. 16.
29. Moreau, Gustave, *L'assembleur des rêves*, (1984), p. 80.
30. See the chapter 'La genèse du tableau et les techniques du peintre' in *Gustave Moreau: Monographie et nouveau catalogue de l'œvre achevé*, Pierre-Louis Mathieu, (1998), pp. 229 - 252.
31. Moreau, Gustave, *Gustave Moreau: l'homme aux figures de cire*, (2010), p. 40.
32. Moreau, Gustave: *Gustave Moreau: Monographie et nouveau catalogue de l'œvre achevé*, Pierre-Louis Mathieu, (1998), p. 257.
33. Cooke, Peter, *Gustave Moreau: History Painting, Spirituality and Symbolism*, (2014), p. 47.
34. Ibid., p. 47.
35. Lessing, Gotthold Ephraim, *Laocoon*, (1987), Ch. XVI, p. 92.
36. Moreau, Gustave, *Écrits sur l'art*, Volume II, (2002), p. 349, A.T.
37. Moreau, Gustave: *Gustave Moreau: Monographie et nouveau catalogue de l'œvre achevé*, Pierre-Louis Mathieu, (1998), p. 230.
38. Fuchs, Ernst, *Architectura Caelestis: Images of the Hidden Prime of Styles*, (1970), p. 182.
39. *Ibid.*, p. 180. 40. *Ibid.*, p. 186.
41. *Ibid.*, p. 183. 42. *Ibid.*, p. 161. 43. *Ibid.*, p. 145.
44. Caruana, L., *The First Manifesto of Visionary Art*, (2000), p. 27.
45. Fuchs, Ernst, Preface to *Robert Venosa: Illuminatus*, (1999), p. 13.
46. Caruana, L., *The First Manifesto of Visionary Art*, (2000), p. 7.
47. Fuchs, Ernst, *Architectura Caelestis: Images of the Hidden Prime of Styles*, (1970), p. 177.
48. *Ibid.*, p. 181. 49. *Ibid.*, p. 171. 50. *Ibid.*, p. 188.
51. *Ibid.*, p. 184. 52. *Ibid.*, p. 157. 53. *Ibid.*, p. 177.
54. *Ibid.*, p. 165. 55. *Ibid.*, p. 182. 56. *Ibid.*, p. 182.

PART IV - GEOMETRY & ORNAMENT

CH.13 - SACRED GEOMETRY: THE FOUNDATION OF HIERATIC COMPOSITION

1. Plutarch: *"Plato said God geometrizes continually" Convivialium disputationum*, liber 8,2.
2. Pythagoreans described in Aetius of Antioch, *Opinions of the Philosophers*, 1.3.8 (Text reconstruction by H. Diels from pseudo-Plutarch, *Opinions of the Philosophers* and Stobaeus, *Selections*).

CH. 14 - HIERATIC PATTERN & DESIGN IN ISLAMIC & GOTHIC ART

1. Abas, Syed Jan and Salman, Amer Shaker, *Symmetries of Islamic Geometrical Patterns,* (1994).
2. Burckhardt, Titus, 'The Void in Islamic Art' in *Studies in Comparative Religion,* Vol. 4, No. 2. (1970).
3. *Ibid.*
4. Necipoglu, Gülru, "Early Modern Floral: The Agency of Ornament in Ottoman and Safavid Visual Cultures' in *Histories of Ornament: From Global to Local*, edited by Gülru Necipoglu and Alina Payne (2016), p. 136.
5. Porter, Yves, 'From the "Theory of the Two Qalams" to the "Seven Principles of Painting": Theory, Terminology, and Practice in Persian Classical Painting' in *Muqarnas* Vol. 17 (2000), p. 110.
6. *Ibid.*, p. 117.
7. Necipoglu, Gülru, "Early Modern Floral: The Agency of Ornament in Ottoman and Safavid Visual Cultures' in *Histories of Ornament: From Global to Local*, edited by Gülru Necipoglu and Alina Payne (2016), p. 139.
8. Porter, Yves, 'From the "Theory of the Two Qalams" to the "Seven Principles of Painting": Theory, Terminology, and Practice in Persian Classical Painting' in *Muqarnas* Vol. 17 (2000), p. 113.
9. Necipoglu, Gülru, "Early Modern Floral: The Agency of Ornament in Ottoman and Safavid Visual Cultures' in *Histories of Ornament: From Global to Local*, edited by Gülru Necipoglu and Alina Payne (2016), p. 137
10. Necipoglu, Gülru, 'Geometric Design in Timurid/Turkmen Architectural Practise: Thoughts on a Recently Discovered Scroll and its Late Gothic Parallels' in Lisa Golombek and Maria Subtelny, editors, *Timurid Art and Culture: Iran and Central Asia in the Fifteenth Century,* (1992), *passim.*
11. *Ibid.* 12. *Ibid.*
13. Nasr, Seyyed Hossein, *Religion and the Order of Nature*, (1996), p. 62.
14. The diagram of *girih* construction is reproduced from El-Said, Issam; Parman, Ayşe, *Geometric Concepts in Islamic Art*, World of Islam Festival Publishing Co. Ltd., (1976), p. 13.
15. The diagram of proportions in the square is attributed to Tons Brunés in Kappraff, Jay, "The Arithmetic of Nicomachus of Gerasaand its Applications to Systems of Proportion", *Nexus Network Journal*, vol. 2, no. 4 (October 2000). My research on proportion in Islamic Geometry was aided by El-Said, Issam, *Islamic Art and Architecture: The Systems of Geometric Design,* (1998), p. 132.
16. The diagram of three *girih* patterns and their circular matrices (top two rows) is derived from Broug, Eric, *Islamic Geometric Patterns*, (2008), p. 3. The remainder of the diagram is my own.
17. Abas and Salman give the five basic shapes in their *Symmetries of Islamic Geometrical Patterns,* (1994).
18. The diagram of the 17 pattern cells originally appears in Schattschneider, Doris, 'The Plane Symmetry Groups: Their Recognition and Notation', *American Mathematical Monthly*, Volume 85, Issue 6, (1978), p. 442.
19. The diagram of the 17 wallpaper patterns is created from materials furnished by Owen Jones' *The Grammar of Ornament* (1910) and organized into wallpaper groups by Martin von Gagern in *Computergestütztes Zeichnen in den Symmetriegruppen der euklidischen Ebene*, (2008).

20. For information on radial grids, I am indebted to: El ouaazizi, Aziza; Nasri, Abdelbar; Benslimane, Rachid, 'A rotation symmetry group detection technique for the characterization of Islamic Rosette Patterns' in *Pattern Recognition Letters,* Volume 68, Part 1, December (2015), pp. 111 - 117.
21. See for example: Ulu, Ebru and Şener, Sinan Mert, 'A Shape Grammar Model To Generate Islamic Geometric Pattern', paper presented at The 12th Generative Art Conference (2009).
22. Abas, S. Jan, 'Islamic Geometrical Patterns for the Teaching of Mathematics of Symmetry' in *Symmetry: Culture and Science* vol 12, Nos 1-2, p. 61.
23. Shelby, Lon R., 'The Geometrical Knowledge of Mediaeval Master Masons' in *Speculum* Vol 47, No. 3, (July 1972), p. 398.
24. Popper, K. R., *The Open Society and its Enemies*, (1962), vol. I, p. 249 quoted in Padovan (1999), p. 66.
25. Padovan, Richard, *Proportion: Science, Philosophy, Architecture,* (1999), p. 68.
26. Bork, Robert, *The Geometry of Creation: Architectural Drawing and the Dynamics of Gothic Design*, (2011), p. 9.
27. Vitruvius, *The Ten Books of Architecture,* Bk III, Ch. I ¶1, (1960), p. 72.
28. Wittkower, Rudolf, 'The Changing Concept of Proportion' in *Daedelus* Vol. 89, No. 1, The Visual Arts Today (Winter, 1960), p. 202.
29. Wittkower, Rudolf, *Architectural Principles in the Age of Humanism*, (1971), p. 159
30. Wittkower, Rudolf, 'The Changing Concept of Proportion' in *Daedelus* Vol. 89, No. 1, *The Visual Arts Today* (Winter, 1960), p. 201
31. Schuttermayer, Hanns, 'Preface' to *Fialenbuchlein* (c. 1487), trans. by Lon R. Shelby and quoted in: Dudley, Colin Joseph, *Canterbury Cathedral: Aspects of its Sacramental Geometry*, (2010), p. 12.
32. *Ibid.* p. 12.
33. Villard de Honnecourt, *The Medieval Sketchbook of Villard de Honnecourt*, (2006), plate 29.
34. Bucher, François, 'Medieval Architectural Design Methods 800 - 1560' in *Gesta*, Vol. 11, No. 2 (1972), p. 38.
35. Villard de Honnecourt, *The Medieval Sketchbook of Villard de Honnecourt*, (2006), plate 27.
36. *Ibid.* p. 43. 37. *Ibid.* p. 43. 38. *Ibid.* p. 44.
39. *Ibid.* p. 43. 40. *Ibid.* p. 44. 41. *Ibid.* p. 41.
42. Bork, Robert, *The Geometry of Creation: Architectural Drawing and the Dynamics of Gothic Design*, (2011), p. 1.
43. *Ibid.* p. 5. 44. *Ibid.*, p. 34.
45. *Ibid.*, p. 437. 46. *Ibid.*, p. 437.
47. Schneider, Michael S., *A Voyage From 1 To 5* (2006), pp. 16 - 17.
48. Diagrams reproduced from Viollet-le-Duc, Eugène, Entry on 'Meneaux' in Volume 6 of *Dictionnaire raisonée de l'architecture française du XIe au XVIe siècle*, (1875).
49. Viollet-le-Duc, Eugène, Entry on 'Style' in Volume 8 of *Dictionnaire raisonée de l'architecture française du XIe au XVIe siècle*, (1875), A.T.
50. Fuchs, Ernst, *Architectura Caelestis: Images of the Hidden Prime of Styles*, (1970), p.184.
51. Bucher, François, 'Medieval Architectural Design Methods 800 - 1560' in *Gesta*, Vol. 11, No. 2 (1972), p. 48.

CH. 15 - ORNAMENT & FORM

1. Jones, Owen, *The Grammar of Ornament*, Bernard Quaritch, (1910). p. 1.
2. *Ibid.*, p. 5. 3. *Ibid.*, p. 6. 4. *Ibid.*, p. 154. 5. *Ibid.*, p. 156.
6. Trilling, James, *The Language of Ornament*, (2001), p. 31.
7. *Ibid.*, p. 104. 8. *Ibid.*, p. 111. 9. *Ibid.*, p. 6.
10. Necipoglu, Gülru, "Early Modern Floral: The Agency of Ornament in Ottoman and Safavid Visual Cultures' in *Histories of Ornament: From Global to Local*, edited by Gülru Necipoglu and Alina Payne (2016), p. 137.
11. *Ibid.*, p. 141.

12. Baltrušaitis, Jurgis, *Le Moyen-Âge fantastique : Antiquités et exotismes dans l'art gothique*, Flammarion (1992), p. 80.
13. *Ibid.*, p. 96. 14. *Ibid.*, pp. 100 - 111.
15. Villard de Honnecourt, *The Medieval Sketchbook of Villard de Honnecourt*, (2006), plate 35.
16. I am indebted to Stuart Whatling and his website 'The Corpus of Medieval Narrative Art' (http://www.medievalart.org.uk) for documenting the glyptic art of Gothic Cathedrals. All photos are by Stuart Whatling; the armatures are my own.
17. Coomaraswamy, Ananda K., *Yaksas* (1993), p. 48.
18. *Ibid.*, p. 47.
19. Schele, Linda; Miller, Mary Ellen, *The Blood of Kings: Dynasty and Ritual in Maya Art*, (1992), p. 282.
20. Miller, Mary Ellen; Taube, Karl, *An Illustrated Dictionary of the Gods and Symbols of Ancient Mexico and the Maya*, (1997), p. 180.
21. Schele, Linda; Miller, Mary Ellen, *The Blood of Kings: Dynasty and Ritual in Maya Art*, (1992), p. 45.
22. *Ibid.*, p. 285.
23. Powell, Christopher, 'The Shapes of Sacred Space: A Proposed System of Geometry used to Lay Out and Design Maya Art and Architecture' (2010), p. 24.
24. *Ibid.*, p. 24. 25. *Ibid.*, p. 24.
26. Schele, Linda; Miller, Mary Ellen, *The Blood of Kings: Dynasty and Ritual in Maya Art*, (1992), p. 284.
27. The 'Long Paragraph' of Dionysius' *Hermeneia*, from Papadopoulos-Kerameus' Source A in Torp, Hjalmar, *The Integrating System of Proportion in Byzantine Art,* (1984), p. 39.
28. Fuchs, Ernst, *Architectura Caelestis: Images of the Hidden Prime of Styles*, (1970), p. 162.
29. *Ibid.*, p. 162. 30. *Ibid.*, p. 188.
31. Trilling, James, *The Language of Ornament*, (2001), p. 186
32. *Ibid.*, p. 206. 33. *Ibid.*, p. 206.
34. Fuchs, Ernst, 'Ernst Fuchs Speaks' Interview with L. Caruana, *The Visionary Revue*, Paris, Spring (2004).
35. Fuchs, Ernst, *Architectura Caelestis: Images of the Hidden Prime of Styles*, (1970), p. 182.
36. For more information on the Golden Chain of Being, see E. M. W. Tillyard, *The Elizabethan World Picture,* Vintage Randam House, Ch. IV, passim and C.S. Lewis, *The Discarded Image: An Introduction to Medieval and Renaissance Literature,* Cambridge University Press, 1964, which are summarized in Caruana, L., *Enter Through the Image*, (2009), Ch. 9 'Symbols of the Sacred'.

PART V - COMPOSITION

CH. 16 - RECTANGULAR COMPOSITION

1. Bouleau, Charles, *Charpentes – La Géométrie Secrète des Peintres*, (1963), p. 56, A.T.
2. *Ibid.,* p. 59. 3. *Ibid.,* p. 65.
4. *Lenz, Desiderius, The Aesthetic of Beuron and other writings,* (2002), p. 41.
5. Callen, Anthea, *The Art of Impressionism: Painting Technique and the Making of Modernity,* (2000), p. 18.
6. *Ibid.,* p. 19.
7. Béguin, André, articles 'châssis' and 'organisation des surfaces' in *Dictionnaire technique de la Peinture, pour les arts, le bâtiment et l'Industrie*, tome 1, ed A.Béguin, (2001), p. 263.
8. Sendler, Egon, *L'icône – image de l'invisible*, (1981), p. 86, Fig. 16.9, in a slightly modified version, also appears in Sendler.
9. Bouleau, Charles, *Charpentes – La Géométrie Secrète des Peintres*, (1963), p. 45.
10. Sendler, Egon, *L'icône – image de l'invisible*, (1981), p. 88, A.T.
11. Bouleau, Charles, *Charpentes – La Géométrie Secrète des Peintres*, (1963), p. 45.
12. *Ibid.*, p. 126, A.T.

13. Iamblichus 'On the Pythagorean Way of Life' in Uždavinys, Algis, *The Golden Chain: An Anthology of Pythagorean and Platonic Philosophy*, (2004), pp. 28-29.
14. Iamblichus, *Ibid.*, p. 15.
15. Iamblichus, *Ibid.*, p. 20.
16. Iamblichus, *Ibid.*, p. 21.
17. Iamblichus, *Ibid.*, p. 14.
18. Stobaeus, *Anthology* I. 22. 1d in *Ibid.*, p. 48.
19. Iamblichus, *Ibid.*, p. 21.
20. Aristotle, *Metaphysics*, cited in Padovan, Richard, *Proportion: Science, Philosophy, Architecture,* (1999), p. 63.
21. Alberti, Leon Battista, *On the Art of Building*, (1991), p. 305.
22. *Ibid.*, Bk. IX, Ch. 6, section 167, p. 305.
23. *Ibid.*, Bk. IX, Ch. 6, section 167, p. 306.
24. Bouleau, Charles, *Charpentes – La Géométrie Secrète des Peintres*, (1963), p. 197.
25. Alberti, Leon Battista, *On Painting*, (1970),, Bk II, ¶29.
26. Bouleau, Charles, *Charpentes – La Géométrie Secrète des Peintres*, (1963), p. 106, A.T.
27. *Orphicum Fragmenta* 165 in Guthrie, W. K. C., *Orpheus and the Greek Religion* (1952), p. 139.
28. Plato, *Timaeus* 31c (Hamilton Cairns trans) in *The Collected Dialogues of Plato*, (1961), p. 1163.
29. Plato, Timaeus 35c, *Ibid.*, p. 1165.
30. The elucidation of Nichomachus of Gerasa's Tables comes from: Kappraff, Jay, "The Arithmetic of Nicomachus of Gerasa and its Applications to Systems of Proportion", *Nexus Network Journal*, vol. 2, no. 4 (October 2000).
31. Plato, Timaeus 50c, *Ibid.*, p. 1177.
32. Plato, Republic 461d (Hamilton Cairns trans) in *The Collected Dialogues of Plato*, (1961), p. 700.
33. Fontaine, *Conférences inédites de l'Académie royale de la peinture et de sculpture*, Paris, p. 117 cited in Bouleau, Charles, *The Painter's Secret Geometry* (2014), p. 111.
34. *Ibid.*, p. 111.
35. Gerbino, Anthony, *François Blondel: Architecture, Erudition, and the Scientific Revolution*, (2010), p. 151.
36. Wittkower, Rudolf, 'The Changing Concept of Proportion' in *Daedelus* Vol. 89, No. 1, *The Visual Arts Today* (Winter, 1960), p. 202.
37. *Ibid.*, p. 204.

CH. 17 - DYNAMIC COMPOSITION

1. Chai, Jean Julia, 'Introduction' to *Gian Paolo Lamazzo's The Idea of the Temple of Painting*, (2013), p. 3.
2. Bouleau, Charles, *Charpentes – La Géométrie Secrète des Peintres*, (1963), p. 87
3. *Ibid.*, p. 155.
4. This armature is my own invention, applying Bouleau's principles.
5. Lomazzo, Giovan Paolo, *Tracte Containing the Artes of curious Paintinge, Caruinge, Buildinge,* (1598), Bk. 1, Ch. 1, p. 23.
6. The derivation of root rectangles from harmonic triangles in the circle is mentioned briefly in: Hambridge, Jay, *Dynamic Symmetry: The Greek Vase*, (2007), p. 42.
7. Powell, Christopher, 'The Shapes of Sacred Space: A Proposed System of Geometry used to Lay Out and Design Maya Art and Architecture' (2010), p. 266.
8. Schneider, Michael S., *Dynamic Rectangles* (2006), p. 122.
9. Schneider, Michael S., *Fibonacci Numbers and the Golden Mean*, (2006), p. 103.
10. Nagy, Dénes, 'Golden Section(ism): From Mathematics to the Theory of Art and Musicology - Part 2', *Symmetry: Culture and Science*, Vol. 8, No. 1, 74-112, (1997), *passim.*
11. Schneider, Michael S., *Fibonacci Numbers and the Golden Mean*, (2006), p. 110.
12. Bouleau, Charles, *Charpentes – La Géométrie Secrète des Peintres*, (1963), p. 136.
13. *Ibid.*, p. 248.

CH. 18 - COMPOSITION & FIGURATION

1. Mâle, Emile, *The Gothic Image: Religious Art in France of the Thirteenth Century*, (1958), p. 369.
2. *Ibid.*, p.369.
3. Blake, William, 'A Vision of the Last Judgment' in *The Portable Blake*, (1948), p. 653.
4. Ackroyd, Peter, *Blake*, (1996), p. 315.
5. See *Gustave Moreau: 1826 - 1898*, Catalogue de Galeries nationales du Grand Palais, 29 Septembre 1998 - 4 janvier 1999 (1998), pp. 210 - 225.
6. Petrie, W. M. Flinders. *The Pyramids and Temples of Gizeh*, (1883), Ch. 7.
7. Fuchs, Ernst, *Architectura Caelestis: Images of the Hidden Prime of Styles*, (1970), p. 157.
8. *Ibid.*, p. 184. 9. *Ibid.*, p. 181. 10. *Ibid.*, p. 159.

CH. 19 - THE NARRATIVE MOVEMENT THROUGH COMPOSITION

1. Moreau's cartone of Lust (cat. 807) is reproduced as fig. 88 in: Cook, Peter, *Gustave Moreau: History Painting, Spirituality and Symbolism*, (2014).
2. This Moreau drawing is reproduced as plate 66 in: Kaplan, Julius, *The Art of Gustave Moreau: Theory, Style, and Content*, (1982).
3. de Plancy, J. Collin, *Dictionnaire Infernal*, Paris, (1863), p. 55.
4. Moreau, Gustave, *Écrits sur l'art, Volume I*, (2002), pp. 146 - 147, A.T.

PART VI - PERSPECTIVE

CH.20 - HIERATIC PERSPECTIVE I

1. Naydler, Jeremy, *Temple of the Cosmos: The Ancient Egyptian Experience of the Sacred*, (1996), pp. 21 - 23.
2. Vasiljevi, Slobodan, 'Les grands traceurs de plans: d'un ingénieur à l'autre, de Micheli du Crest à Dufour: les tracés effacés de la structure urbaine entre 1720 et 1860' in *Ingénieurs et architectes suisses* Band (Jahr): 114 (1988) Heft 4.
3. Tyler, Christopher W. and Chen, Chien-Chung,'Chinese Perspective as a Rational System: Relationship to Panofsky's Symbolic Form' in *Chinese Journal of Psychology*, Volume 53, Issue 4 (2010), p. 5.
4. *Ibid.*, p. 7. 5. *Ibid.*, p. 7.

CH. 21 - HIERATIC PERSPECTIVE II

1. Thackston, Wheeler M., *Album Prefaces and Other Documents on the History of Calligraphers and Painters*, (2001), p. 43.
2. *Ibid.*, p. 43.
3. Guest , Grace Dunham, 'Shiraz Painting in the Sixteenth Century', *Smithsonian Institution Freer Gallery of Art Oriental Studies*, No. 4, (1949), p. 25.
4. *Ibid.*, p. 25. 5. *Ibid.*, p. 25. 6. *Ibid.*, p. 28.
7. Kleiss, Wolfram, 'Safavid Palaces' in *Ars Orientalis*, Vol. 23, (1993).
8. Thackston, Wheeler M., *Album Prefaces and Other Documents on the History of Calligraphers and Painters*, (2001), p. 42.
9. Grignon, Iffet Orbay, 'Remarks on the Concept of Pictorial Space in Islamic Painting' (1996), p. 47.
10 *Ibid.*, p. 49.
11. Nasr, Seyyed Hossein, 'The World of the Imagination and the Concept of Space in the Persian Miniature' in *Islamic Art and Spirituality*, (1987), p. 178.
12. *Ibid.*, p. 179. 13. *Ibid.*, p. 179. 14. *Ibid.*, pp. 180 - 181 *passim.*
15. Buchwald, Hans, *Form, Style and Meaning in Byzantine Church Architecture*, (1999), p. 299.
16. *Ibid.*, pp. 297 - 298.
17. Florensky, Pavel *'Obratnaia perspektiva' – 'Reverse Perspective'* in *Trudy po znakovym sistemam* (1967), pp. 381-416.
18. Zehgin, Lev, *Iazik zhivopisnogo proizvedeniia: uslovnost' drevnego iskusstva - The Language of the Work of Art: Conventionality of Ancient Art*, Moscow, (1970).

19. Uspensky, Boris, *The Semiotics of the Russian Icon*, ed by S. Rudy, Lisse (1976), p. 33.
20. Antonova, Clemena, *Space, Time, and Presence in the Icon: Seeing the World with the Eyes of God*, (2010), p. 103.
21. *Ibid.*, p. 2. 22. *Ibid.*, p. 2.

CH. 22 - HUMANIST PERSPECTIVE I

1. Lucretius, *De Rerum Natura*, Bk IV, line 430 in *On the Nature of Things* trans. by Cyril Bailey, (1910).
2. Vitruvius, *Ten Books of Architecture*, Bk. I. Ch. I. ¶2, trans. by Morris Hickey Morgan, (1914)
3. *Ibid.*, Preface Bk. VII, ¶11.
4. Stinson, Philip, 'Perspective Systems in Roman Second Style Wall Painting', *American Journal of Archaeology* 115 (2011), p. 415.
5. *Ibid.*, p. 418. 6. *Ibid.*, p. 418. 7. *Ibid.*, p. 419.
8. *Ibid.*, p. 419. 9. *Ibid.*, p. 403. 10. *Ibid.*, p. 424.
11. Andersen, Kirsti, *The Geometry of an Art: The History of the Mathematical Theory of Perspective from Alberti to Monge*, (2007), Preface p. XX.
12. Glick, Thomas F.; Livesey, Steven; and Wallis, Faith, *Medieval Science, Technology, and Medicine: An Encyclopedia* (2005), p. 165.
13. Manetti, *Life of Brunelleschi*, (originally published c. 1501), Trans. by Howard Saalman, (1968), *passim.*
14.Vasari, Giorgio, *The Lives of the Artists* (1965), *passim.*
15. Alberti, Leon Battista, *On Painting*, (1970), Bk I, ¶6, p. 42.
16. *Ibid.*, Bk. I, ¶ 18, p. 46. 17. *Ibid.*, Bk.I, ¶16, p. 45.
18. *Ibid.*, Bk. I, ¶19, p. 46. 19. *Ibid.*, Bk. I, ¶40, p. 55 *passim.*
20. Brown, J. H., 'Unscrambling Giotto's Perspective', (2004), *passim*
21. Mitrović, Branko and Massalin, Paola, 'Leon Battista Alberti and Euclid' in *Albertiana*, 9 (2008), p. 4.
22. *Ibid.*, p. 1.
23. Euclid, *The Optics of Euclid*, Burton translation (1945), p. 357.
24. *Ibid.*, p. 358.
25. Euclid, *The Optics* Postulate 1, Lindberg tranlsation in: Lindberg, David C., *Theories of Vision From Al-Kindi to Kepler*, (1976), p. 161.
26. Euclid, *The Optics* Postulate 2, Lindberg translation, *Ibid.*
27. Euclid, *The Optics of Euclid*, Postulate 3, Burton translation (1945), p. 357.
28. Euclid, *The Optics of Euclid*, Postulates 4, 5, 6, Burton translation (1945), p. 357.
29. Panofsky, Erwin, *Perspective as Symbolic Form*, (1996), p. 35.
30. Brownson, C. D.,' Euclid's Optics and its Compatibility with Linear Perspective' in *Archive for History of Exact Sciences* Vol. 24, No. 3 (1981), pp. 165-194.
31. *Ibid.*, p. 184.
32. Alberti, Leon Battista, *On Painting*, (1970), Bk I, ¶46, p. 56.
33. *Ibid.*, Bk I, ¶46, p. 56 34. *Ibid.*, Bk I, ¶45, p. 55 - 56.
35. Kang, Eun-Sung, 'Raphael's Annunciation Predella panel and a perspective drawing', in *Burlington Magazine*, 148, (2006), pp. 545-548.
36. Edgerton Jr., Samuel Y., 'Alberti's Perspective: A New Discovery and a New Evaluation' in *The Art Bulletin* Vol. 48, No. 3/4 (1966), pp. 367-378.
37. *Ibid.*, p. 374 As scholars, Edgerton cites Miriam Schild Bunim, *Space in Medieval Painting and the Forerunner of Perspective,* et al.
38. *Ibid.*, p. 373.
39. Euclid, *The Optics of Euclid*, Proposition 13, Burton translation (1945), p. 359.
40. Euclid cited in Edgerton Jr., Samuel Y., 'Alberti's Perspective: A New Discovery and a New Evaluation' in *The Art Bulletin* Vol. 48, No. 3/4 (1966), p. 373.
41. Alberti, Leon Battista, *On Painting*, (1970), Bk I, ¶46, p. 56.
42. Moffitt, John F., 'Domenico Veneziano's "Saint Lucy" Altarpiece: The Case for "Uterine Perspective"' *Notes in the History of Art*, Vol. 16, No. 4 (1997), p. 19.

CH. 23 - HUMANIST PERSPECTIVE II

1. Field, J.V., *Piero della Francesca: A Mathematician's Art*, United States of America: Yale University Press, (2005), p. 15.
2. For a clarification of this construction, I am indebted to: Hammack, Richard, 'Piero della Francesca's Diagonal Construction' - http://www.people.vcu.edu/~rhammack/Math121/Handouts/Francesca.pdf.
3. Francesca, Piero della, De Prospectiva Pingendi edizione critica di G. Nicco Fasola con XLIX tavole fuori testo, G. C. Sansoni editore Firenze, (1952), p. 88.
4. David, Margaret Daly, *Piero della Francesca's Mathematical Treatises: The Trattato d'abaco and Libellus de quinque corporibus regularibus*, Longo Editore, Ravenna p. 57.
5. *Ibid.*, p. 20.
6. MS Urb. Lat. 1270, datable .ca 1540 in the Biblioteca Apostolica Vaticana, Vatican City.
7. Ash. I. 17b in Vinci, Leonardo da, *The Notebooks of Leonardo da Vinci,* Edited by Jean Paul Richter, Vol I, (1970), p. 16.
8. *Ibid.*, p. 16.
9. G37a in *Ibid.*, p. 30.
10. Euclid, *The Optics* Postulate 1, Lindberg tranlsation in Lindberg, David C., *Theories of Vision From Al-Kindi to Kepler*, (1976), p. 161.
11. Leonardo quoted in: Kemp, Martin, *The Science of Art: Optical Themes in Western Art from Brunelleschi to Seurat*, (1990), p. 47.
12. 7. Ash. I. 17b in Vinci, Leonardo da, *The Notebooks of Leonardo da Vinci,* Vol I, (1970), p. 158.
13. *Ibid.*, p. 160. 14. *Ibid.*, p. 129. 15. *Ibid.*, p. 159
16. Viator (Jean Pèlerin), *De Artificiali Perspectiva*, (1509).
17. Termes, Dick, 'New Perspective Systems: Seeing the Total Picture - One through Six Point Perspective', (1998).
18. Termes, Dick A., 'Six-Point Perspective on the Sphere: The Termesphere', *Leonardo*, Vol. 24, No. 3 (1991), p. 290/
19. Panofsky, Erwin, *Perspective as Symbolic Form*, (1996), p. 41.
20. *Ibid.*, p. 72.
21. Brownson, C. D.,' Euclid's Optics and its Compatibility with Linear Perspective' in *Archive for History of Exact Sciences* Vol. 24, No. 3 (1981), p. 84.
22. Codex E, 16b in Vinci, Leonardo da, *The Notebooks of Leonardo da Vinci,* Edited by Jean Paul Richter, Vol I, (1970), p. 62.
23. Frangenberg, Thomas, 'The Angle of Vision: Problems of Perspectival Representation in the Fifteenth and Sixteenth Centuries' in *Renaissance Studies*, Vol. 6, No. 1, (1991), p. 6.
24. Dubery, Fred and Willats, John, *Perspective and Other Drawing Systems*, Van Nostrand Reinhold, Revised Edition (1983).
25. Lien, Barbara, 'The Role of Pavement in the Perceived Integration of Plazas: An Analysis of the Paving Designs of Four Italian Piazzas', M. Sc. thesis in Landscape Architecture, Washington State University, (2005), p. 85.
26. Elkins, James, *The Poetics of Perspective,* (1996), p. 158.
27. *Ibid.*, p. 177.
28. Escher's plans and drawings may be found in: Ernst, Bruno, *The Magic Mirror of M. C. Escher*, Taschen, (2007).
29. 'The Vast Expanse' in Grey, Alex, *Art Psalms*, North Atlantic Books, (2008).
30. *Ibid.*
31. 'Calling the Soul Home to Source Reality' in Grey, Alex, *Net of Being*, (2012), p. 125.
32. *Ibid.*, p. 151.

CH. 24 - COMPOSITION AND PERSPECTIVE I

1. Alberti, Leon Battista, *On Painting*, (1970), Bk I, ¶49, p. 57.
2. Clark, Kenneth, *Piero della Francesca*, (1951), p. 20.
3. Lavin, Marilyn Aronberg, 'Piero della Francesca's Flagellation: The Triumph of Christian Glory' in *The Art Bulletin*, Vol. 50, No. 4 (Dec., 1968), p. 324.

4. See: Kemp, Martin, *The Science of Art: Optical Themes in Western Art from Brunelleschi to Seurat*, (1990), p. 32.
5. Wittkower, R and Carter, B. A. R., The Perspective of Piero della Francesca's 'Flagellation', *Journal of the Warburg and Courtauld Institutes*, Vol. 16, No. 3/4 (1953), pp. 294-295.
6. Cf, *Ibid.*, p. 295.
7. Elkins, James, 'Piero della Francesca and the Renaissance Proof of Linear Perspective', *The Art Bulletin*, Vol. 69, No. 2 (Jun., 1987), pp. 226.
8. Wittkower, R, 'Brunelleschi and Proportion in Perspective', *Journal of the Warburg and Courtauld Institutes* Vol. 16. No. 3/4 (1953), pp. 275-291.
9. Euclid, Bk VI, Prop. 4, *The Elements of Geometry*, trans. by Richard Fitzpatrick (2007).
10. Wittkower, R, 'Brunelleschi and Proportion in Perspective' (1953), p. 284.
11. Note 104 from Notebook SKM II in Vinci, Leonardo da, *The Notebooks of Leonardo da Vinci,* Edited by Jean Paul Richter, Vol I, (1970), p. 61.
12. *Ibid.*, Note 100, p. 60 - amended.
13. Padovan, Richard, *Proportion: Science, Philosophy, Architecture,* (1999), p. 219.
14. Trat 21 in Vinci, Leonardo da, *The Notebooks of Leonardo da Vinci,* Richter, Vol I, (1970), p. 146.
15. *Ibid.*
16. Brambilla Barcilon, Pinin, *Leonardo: The Last Supper*, (1999), *passim.*
17. Brachert, Thomas, 'A Musical Canon of Proportion in Leonardo da Vinci's Last Supper', in *The Art Bulletin*, Vol. 53, No. 4 (1971), p. 464.
18. Landrus, Matthew, 'The Proportions of Leonardo's Last Supper' in *Raccolta Vinciana* 32 (2007), p. 64.
19. Codex E 16b in Vinci, Leonardo da, *The Notebooks of Leonardo da Vinci,* Richter, Vol I, (1970), p. 62.
20. Brachert, Thomas, 'A Musical Canon of Proportion in Leonardo da Vinci's Last Supper', in *The Art Bulletin*, Vol. 53, No. 4 (1971), p. 463.
21. *Ibid.*, p. 463.

CH. 25 - COMPOSITION & PERSPECTIVE II

1. Oberhuber, Konrad, *Polarität und Synthese in Raphaels 'Schule von Athen'*, (1983), p. 12.
2. Karpinski, Caroline, 'Archimedes Salutes Bramante in a Draft for the "School of Athens"' in *Artibus et Historiae*, Vol. 31, No. 61, (2010), pp. 117.
3. *Ibid.*, p. 120.
4. Edgerton Jr., Samuel Y., *The Heritage of Giotto's Geometry: Art and Science on the Eve of the Scientific Revolution*, (1991), p. 222.
5. Oberhuber, Konrad, *Polarität und Synthese in Raphaels 'Schule von Athen'*, (1983), fig. 5, p. 72.
6. Kemp, Martin, *The Science of Art: Optical Themes in Western Art from Brunelleschi to Seurat*, (1990), p. 69.
7. Forcellino, Antonio, *Raphael: A Passionate Life*, Polity Press, (2012), p. 21.
8. Oberhuber, Konrad, *Polarität und Synthese in Raphaels 'Schule von Athen'*, (1983), fig. 5, p. 73.
9. Fichtner, Richard, *Die verborgene Geometrie in Raffaels "Schule von Athen"*, (1984), fig. 16, p. 28.
10. *Ibid.*, fig. 86, p. 81.
11. Valtieri, Simonetta, 'La Scuola d'Atene. "Bramante" suggerisce un nuovo metodo per costruire in prospettiva un'architettura armonica' in *Mittelungen des Kunsthistorischen Institutes in Florenz* 16, Bd., H, 1 (1972), p. 63.
12. Oberhuber, Konrad, *Polarität und Synthese in Raphaels 'Schule von Athen'*, (1983), fig. 3/4, p. 59.
13. Fichtner, Richard, *Die verborgene Geometrie in Raffaels "Schule von Athen"*, (1984), fig. 6, p. 14.

14. Mazzola, G., Kromker, D., Hofmann, G.R., *Rasterbild - Bildraster: Anwendung der Graphischen Datenverarbeitung zur geometrischen Analyse eines Meisterwerks der Renaissance; Raffaels 'Schule von Athen'*, (1987), fig. 11 p. 72.
15. Keim, Frank, 'Raffaels Astronomische Tafel entschlüsselt: Kopernikanisches Weltsystem und Jupitermonde in Raffaels Schule von Athen (1509-14)', Universität Ulm. Kommunikations- und Informationszentrum, (2013), fig. 12.
16. Valtieri, Simonetta, 'La Scuola d'Atene. "Bramante" suggerisce un nuovo metodo per costruire in prospettiva un'architettura armonica' in *Mittelungen des Kunsthistorischen Institutes in Florenz* 16, Bd., H, 1 (1972), p. 66.
17. Lauenstein, Hajo, *Arithmetik und Geometrie in Raffaels Schule von Athen. Die geheimnisvolle Schlüsselrolle der Tafeln im Fresko für das Konzept harmonischer Komposition und der ungeahnte Bezug zum Athena-Tempel von Paestu,* (1998).
18. Haas, Robert, 'Raphael's School of Athens: A Theorem in a Painting?', *Journal of Humanist Mathematics*, Volume 2, Issue 2, July (2012), p. 12.
19. Valtieri, Simonetta, 'La Scuola d'Atene. "Bramante" suggerisce un nuovo metodo per costruire in prospettiva un'architettura armonica' in *Mittelungen des Kunsthistorischen Institutes in Florenz* 16, Bd., H, 1 (1972), *passim.*
20. Fichtner, Richard, *Die verborgene Geometrie in Raffaels "Schule von Athen"*, (1984), p. 15; Lauenstein, Hajo, *Arithmetik und Geometrie in Raffaels Schule von Athen* (1998), p. 270
21. Fichtner, Richard, *Die verborgene Geometrie in Raffaels "Schule von Athen"* (1984), fig. 97, p. 102.
22. Temple, Nicholas, *Disclosing Horizons: Architecture, Perspective and Redemptive Space,* (2007), p. 64.
23. Haas, Robert, 'Raphael's School of Athens: A Theorem in a Painting?', *Journal of Humanist Mathematics*, Volume 2, Issue 2, July (2012), p. 12.
24. *Ibid.*, p. 22.
25. Mazzola, G., Kromker, D., Hofmann, G.R., *Rasterbild - Bildraster: Anwendung der Graphischen Datenverarbeitung zur geometrischen Analyse eines Meisterwerks der Renaissance; Raffaels 'Schule von Athen'*, (1987), *passim.*
26. Keim, Frank, 'Raffaels Astronomische Tafel entschlüsselt: Kopernikanisches Weltsystem und Jupitermonde in Raffaels Schule von Athen (1509-14)', Universität Ulm. Kommunikations- und Informationszentrum, (2013), *passim.*
27. Doose, Conrad; Lauenstein, Hajo, Raffaels Fresko „Die Schule von Athen" : Die Tafeln des Pythagoras und Euklid vor und nach der Restaurierung, Förderverein Festung Zitadelle Jülich e.V. 2RWTH Aachen, Fakultät für Architektur pp. 12 - 13.

PART 7 - CONSECRATING THE WORK

CH. 26 - VISIONARY SEEING

1. Sauneron, Serge, *The Priests of Ancient Egypt*, (2000), p. 23.
2. *Ibid.* p. 239. 3. *Ibid.* p. 241.
4. Hornung, Erik, *The Ancient Egyptian Books of the Afterlife*, trans. by David Lorton, (1999), p. 423.
5. Piankoff, A., *Litany of Re: Egyptian Texts and Representations,* (1964), p. 36.
6. Lichtheim, Miriam, *Ancient Egyptian Literature, Volume III: The Late Period*, (2006), p. 45
7. Naydler, Jeremy, *Shamanic Wisdom in the Pyramid Texts: The Mystical Tradition of Ancient Egypt,* (2004), p. 12.
8. *Ibid.*, p. 8. 9. *Ibid.*, p. 8.
10. All Utterances from: Faulkner, R. O. *The Ancient Egyptian Pyramid Texts: Supplement of Heiroglyphic Texts*, Clarendon Press, (1970).
11. Naydler, Jeremy, *Shamanic Wisdom in the Pyramid Texts: The Mystical Tradition of Ancient Egypt,* (2004), p. 69.
12. *Ibid.*, p. 69. 13. *Ibid.*, p. 318. 14. *Ibid.*, p. 216. 15. *Ibid.*, p. 217.
16. Sauneron, Serge, *The Priests of Ancient Egypt*, (2000), p. 5.
17. *Ibid.*, p. 48.

18. Assmann, Jan, *Death and Salvation in Ancient Egypt*, (2005), p. 204.
19. *Ibid.*, p. 201 20. *Ibid.*, p. 201.
21. Sauneron, Serge, *The Priests of Ancient Egypt*, (2000), p. 59.
22. *Ibid.* 23.*Ibid.* 24. *Ibid.* 25. *Ibid.*, p. 8.
26. 'Opening of Mouth Ceremony' Selection of 51 episodes in the tomb-chapel of Rekhmira, *Digital Egypt for Universities.*
27. *Ibid.* 28. *Ibid.* Episode 9. 29. *Ibid.* Episodes 10 - 11. 30. *Ibid.*
31. Reeder, Greg, 'A Rite of Passage: The Enigmatic Tekenu in Ancient Egyptian Funerary Ritual' in *KMT: A Modern Journal of Ancient Egypt,* vol. 5 no. 3, (Fall 1994), p. 55.
32. *Ibid.*, p. 55.
33.Reeder, Greg, http://www.egyptology.com/reeder/enigma/tekenu.html.
34. Nightingale, Andrea Wilson, *Spectacles of Truth in Classical Greek Philosophy,* (2004), p. 85.
35. *Ibid.*, p. 85.
36. Nightingale, Andrea Wilson, 'The Philosopher at the Festival: Plato's Transformation of Traditional Theoria' in Elsner, Jaś, and Rutherford, Ian, *Pilgrimage in Graeco-Roman and Early Christian Antiquity: Seeing the Gods,* (2005), p. 174.
37. Nightingale, Andrea Wilson, *Spectacles of Truth in Classical Greek Philosophy,* (2004), p. 45.
38. *Ibid.*, pp. 3-4.39. *Ibid.*, p. 86.
40. *Ibid.*, p. 46 citing Elsner's Introdution to: Elsner, Jaś, and Rutherford, Ian, *Pilgrimage in Graeco-Roman and Early Christian Antiquity: Seeing the Gods*, (2005).
41. *Ibid.*, p. 163. 42. *Ibid.*, p.164. 43. *Ibid.*, p. 73.
44. *Ibid.*, p. 79. 45. *Ibid.*, p. 81.
46. Blunt, Anthony, *Artistic Theory in Italy: 1450 - 1600*, (1962), Poem trans. by K. T. Butler, p. 69.
47. *Ibid.* p. 69.
48. Bellori, Giovanni Pietro, *The Idea of the Painter, Sculptor and Architect,* (1672).
49. Eck, Diana L., *Darsan: Seeing the Divine Image in India,* (1981), p. 3.
50. *Ibid.* p. 6. 51. *Ibid.* p. 52. 52. *Ibid.* p. 52.
53. Kramrisch, Stella, 'Traditions of the Indian Craftsman' in *The Journal of American Folklore*, Vol. 71, No. 281, (1958),, p. 226.
54. Zimmer, Heinrich, *The Art of Indian Asia: Its Mythologies and Transformations,* Vol I, (2001), p. 320.
55. *Ibid.* p. 318.
56. Zimmer, Heinrich, *Artistic Form and Yoga in the Sacred Images of India*, (1984), p. 53.
57. *Ibid.* p. 53.
58. Zimmer, Heinrich, *The Art of Indian Asia: Its Mythologies and Transformations,* Vol I, (2001) p. 321.
59. *Ibid.* p. 318.
60. Eck, Diana L., *Darsan: Seeing the Divine Image in India,* (1981).
61. *Ibid.*, p. 53. 62. *Ibid.*, p. 7.
63. Voss, Angela, 'The Secret Life of Statues' in: Campion, Nicholas and Curry, Patrick M., eds. *Sky and Psyche: The Relationship Between Cosmos and Consciousness,* (2006), pp. 201-234.
64. Eck, Diana L., *Darsan: Seeing the Divine Image in India,* (1981), p. 38.
65. *Ibid.*, p. 47. 66. *Ibid.*, p. 11. 67. *Ibid.*, p. 3.
68. *Ibid.*, p. 9. 69. *Ibid.*, p. 45. 70. *Ibid.*, p. 45.
71. Zimmer, Heinrich, *Artistic Form and Yoga in the Sacred Images of India*, (1984), p. 43.
72. *Ibid.*, p. 44. 73. *Ibid.*, p. 54. 74. *Ibid.*, p. 55.
75. *Ibid.*, p. 60. 76. *Ibid.*, p. 51. 77. *Ibid.*, p. 59.
78. *Ibid.*, p. 61. 79. *Ibid.*, p. 63. 80. *Ibid.*, p. 45.

CH. 27 - THEURGY: THE VISION JOURNEY IN THE WEST

1. *Asclepius* 24 in Copenhaver, Brian P. (editor and translator) *Hermetica: The Greek Corpus Hermeticum and the Latin Asclepius* in a New English Translation, (1995), p. 81.
2. Porphyry, *The Letter to Anebo*, Section 9 in *Iamblichus, On the Mysteries of the Egyptians, Chaldeans, and Assyirans*, trans. by Thomas Taylor, (1821), p. 9.
3. Iamblichus I.9 in *Theurgia or The Egyptian Mysteries,* Trans. by Alexander Wilder (1911).
4. *Ibid.* Iamblichus I.9. 5. *Ibid.* Iamblichus II.11.
6. Porphyry, 'The Life of Plotinus' Ch. 22 in Plotinus, *The Six Enneads*, trans. by Stephen Mackenna and B. S. Page, (1952).
7. Iamblichus II.3 in *Theurgia or The Egyptian Mysteries,* Trans. by Alexander Wilder (1911).
8. *Ibid.* Iamblichus II.4. 9. *Ibid.* Iamblichus II.4.
10. *Ibid.* Iamblichus II.4. 11. *Ibid.* Iamblichus II.3.
12. Proclus, *Proclus' Hymns: Essays, Translation and Commentary*, R. M. Van den Berg, (2001), pg 75.
13. Iamblichus IV.1 in *Theurgia or The Egyptian Mysteries,* Trans. by Alexander Wilder (1911).
14. *Ibid.* Iamblichus III.12.
15. Iamblichus V.23 in *On the Mysteries*, trans. by Emma C. Clarke, John M. Dillon, Jackson P. Hershbell, (2003).
16. Proclus, 'On the Sacred Art' trans. by Stephen Ronan, (1988).
17. *Ibid.* 18. *Ibid.* 19. *Ibid.* 20. *Ibid.*
21. Proclus, Bk. II, 65A in *The Commentaries of Proclus on the Timaeus of Plato, in Five Books*, Trans. by Thomas Taylor, Vol. I., (1820).
22. Proclus, 'On the Sacred Art' trans. by Stephen Ronan, (1988).
23. Uždavinys, Algis, *Philosophy & Theurgy in Late Antiquity*, (2010), p. 151.
24. *Ibid.*, p. 81. 25. *Ibid.*, p. 80. 26. *Ibid.*, p. 143. 27. *Ibid.*, p. 155.
28. Iamblichus I.19 in *Theurgia or The Egyptian Mysteries,* Trans. by Alexander Wilder (1911).
29. *Ibid.* Iamblichus I.12, Amended. 30. *Ibid.* Iamblichus I.12.
31. Iamblichus V. 15 in *On the Mysteries*, trans. by Emma C. Clarke, John M. Dillon, Jackson P. Hershbell, (2003).
32. *Ibid.* Iamblichus V. 9. 33. *Ibid.* Iamblichus III.31.
34. *Ibid.* Iamblichus III.31. 35. *Ibid.* Iamblichus III.20.
36. *Ibid.* Iamblichus V.15. 37. *Ibid.* Iamblichus III.14.
38. Finamore, John F., *Iamblichus and the Theory of the Vehicle of the Soul*, The American Philological Association, (1985), p. 1.
39. *Ibid.*, p. 146.
40. Proclus, Bk. III, 161B in *The Commentaries of Proclus on the Timaeus of Plato, in Five Books*, Trans. by Thomas Taylor, Vol. I., (1820), p. 445.
41. Gospel of Philip 70:5 in *The Nag Hammadi Library in English*, (1988), p. 151.
42. Trimorphic Protennoia 48:15 in *The Nag Hammadi Library in English*, (1988), p. 520.
43. 'The Untitled Text in the Bruce Codex' in *The Books of Jeu and the Untitled Text in the Bruce Codex*, Carl Schmidt and Violet MacDermot, (1978).
44. Gospel of Philip 75:44 in *The Nag Hammadi Library in English*, (1988), p. 154.
45. Gospel of Philip 61:30, *Ibid.* p. 147.
46. Uždavinys, Algis, *Philosophy & Theurgy in Late Antiquity*, (2010), p. 118.
47. *Ibid.*, p. 219. 48. *Ibid.*, p. 256.
49. Fifth Hour, The Book of Gates in *The Short Form of The Book of Am-Tuat and The Book of Gates*, trans. by E. A. Wallis Budge (1905).
50. Corpus Hermeticum I.24 in Copenhaver, Brian P. (editor and translator) *Hermetica: The Greek Corpus Hermeticum and the Latin Asclepius* in a New English Translation, (1995), p. 5.
51. Apocalypse of Paul 21:15 in *The Nag Hammadi Library in English*, (1988), p. 258.
52. Dialogue of the Savior 122:3, *Ibid.* p. 246.

CH. 28 - MANDALA MEDITATION: THE VISION JOURNEY IN THE EAST

1. Berzin, Alexander, *Introduction to the Kalachakra Initiation*, (2011), p. 124.
2. Berzin, Alexander (trans), *Medium-Length Guhyasamaja Sadhana*, (2001), p. 2.
3. *Ibid.*, p. 4. 4. *Ibid.*, p. 5.
5. Wayman, Alex, *Yoga of the Guhysamajatantra: The Arcane Lore of Forty Verses - A Buddhist Tantra Commentary,* (1977), pp. 122 - 123. cf. Wright, Roger, *The Guhyasamāja Piṇḍikṛta-sādhana and its Context*, (2010), p. 57.
6. Berzin, Alexander (trans), *Medium-Length Guhyasamaja Sadhana*, (2001), p. 8.
7. *Ibid.*, p. 5. 8. *Ibid.*, p. 5. 9. *Ibid.*, p. 6.
10. Berzin, Alexander, *What Is Guhyasamaja Practice?* (undated) The Eight-stage Dissolution Process.
11. Berzin, Alexander (trans), *Medium-Length Guhyasamaja Sadhana*, (2001), p. 4.
12. Berzin, Alexander, *Introduction to the Guhyasamaja System of Anuttarayoga Tantra* - Transcript, (2012).
13. Berzin, Alexander (trans), *Medium-Length Guhyasamaja Sadhana*, (2001), p. 6.
14. *Ibid.*, p. 7. 15. *Ibid.*, p. 9. 16. *Ibid.*, p. 9.
17. *Ibid.*, p. 9. 18. *Ibid.*, p. 9. 19. *Ibid.*, p. 10.
20. Berzin, Alexander, *Introduction to the Guhyasamaja System of Anuttarayoga Tantra* - Transcript, (2012).
21. Berzin, Alexander, *What Is Guhyasamaja Practice?* (undated) The Eight-stage Dissolution Process.
22. Evans-Wentz, W. Y., Editor, *The Tibetan Book of the Dead*, (1960), p. 109.
23. *Ibid.*, p. 103.
24. Berzin, Alexander (trans), *Medium-Length Guhyasamaja Sadhana*, (2001), p. 10.
25. *Ibid.*, p. 10.
26. Wayman, Alex, *Yoga of the Guhysamajatantra: The Arcane Lore of Forty Verses - A Buddhist Tantra Commentary,* (1977), pp. 122 - 123 cf. Wright, Roger, *The Guhyasamāja Piṇḍikṛta-sādhana and its Context*, (2010), p. 57.
27. Wayman, Alex, *Yoga of the Guhysamajatantra: The Arcane Lore of Forty Verses - A Buddhist Tantra Commentary,* (1977), p. 212.
28. Fremantle, Francesca, *A Critical Study of the Guhyasamaja Tantra*, London, (1971), p. 24.
29. Berzin, Alexander (trans), *Medium-Length Guhyasamaja Sadhana*, (2001), p. 8.
30. Laundau, Jonathan; Weber, Andy, *Images of Enlightenment: Tibetan Art in Practice*, (1993), pp. 120 - 123.

CH. 29 - THE SOUL ASCENT

1. For The Campbell Donner Magical Gems Database, see:.http://classics.mfab.hu/talismans.
2. See for example 'The Gospel of the Egyptians' in *The Nag Hammadi Library in English*, James M. Robinson, General Editor, (1988).
3. See: Godwin, Joscelyn, *The Mystery of the Seven Vowels: In Theory and Practice*, (1991), pp. 20 - 23.
4. See: Godwin, Joscelyn, *The Harmony of the Spheres: The Pythagorean Tradition in Music*, (1992), p. 408, Note on Nichomachus.

BIBLIOGRAPHY
OF CITED WORKS

Abas, S. Jan, 'Islamic Geometrical Patterns for the Teaching of Mathematics of Symmetry' in *Symmetry: Culture and Science* vol 12, Nos 1-2 p. 61.

Abas, Syed Jan and Salman, Amer Shaker, *Symmetries of Islamic Geometrical Patterns*, World Scientific Publishing Company, (1994)

Aeschylus. *Fragments,* edited and translated by Alan H. Sommerstein. Loeb Classical Library, Harvard University Press, (2009)

Ackroyd, Peter, *Blake*, Vintage Books (1996)

Alberti, Leon Battista, *On Painting*, trans. by John R. Spencer, Yale University Press, (1970)

Alberti, Leon Battista, *On the Art of Building, In Ten Books,* trans. by Joseph Rykwert, Neil Leach and Robert Taverner, M. I. T. Press, (1991)

Ames-Lewis, Francis, *The Intellectual Life of the Early Renaissance Artist,* Yale University Press, New Haven and London, (2000)

Ames-Lewis, Francis, *Drawings in Early Renaissance Italy,* Yale University Press, (1981)

Andersen, Kirsti, *The Geometry of an Art*: *The History of the Mathematical Theory of Perspective from Alberti to Monge,* Springer, (2007)

Antonova, Clemena, *Space, Time, and Presence in the Icon: Seeing the World with the Eyes of God,* Ashgate, (2010)

'Apocryphon of John', trans. by Frederik Wisse, *The Nag Hammadi Library in English*, edited by James M. Robinson, HarperSanFrancisco, (1990)

Aristotle, *Poetics*, translated with a critical text by S. H. Butcher, MacMillan and Co. (1895)

Aristotle, *Poetics* in Aristotle; Horace; Longinus, *Classical Literary Criticism: Poetics; Ars Poetica; On the Sublime,* translated by T. S. Dorsch, Penguin Classics, (1965)

Assmann, Jan, *Death and Salvation in Ancient Egypt*, trans. by David Lorton, Cornell University Press, (2005)

Baltrušaitis, Jurgis, *Le Moyen-Âge fantastique : Antiquités et exotismes dans l'art gothique*, Flammarion (1992)

Barbillon, Claire, *Les Canons du Corps Humain Au XIXe Siègle – L'Art et la Règle*, Odile Jacob, (2004)

Beer, Robert, *The Encyclopedia of Tibetan Symbols and Motifs*, Shambhala, (1999)

Béguin, André, articles 'châssis' and 'organisation des surfaces' in *Dictionnaire technique de la Peinture, pour les arts, le bâtiment et l'Industrie*, tome 1, ed A.Béguin, (2001)

Bellori, Giovanni Pietro *The Idea of the Painter, Sculptor and Architect*, (1672), English passages in Dr William Sieger: http://homepages.neiu.edu/~wbsieger/Art316/316Read/Bellori.pdf

Berzin, Alexander, *Taking the Kalachakra Initiation*, Ithaca, Snow Lion, (1997)

Berzin, Alexander, *Introduction to the Kalachakra Initiation,* Snow Lion; 2nd ed. (2011)

Berzin, Alexander, What Is Guhyasamaja Practice? (undated) http://studybuddhism.com/en/advanced-studies/vajrayana/tantra-advanced/what-is-guhyasamaja-practice

Berzin, Alexander, *Introduction to the Guhyasamaja System of Anuttarayoga Tantra*, (Transcript of a talk given inMoscow, Russia, October 2012) http://www.berzinarchives.com/web/x/ nav/group.html_1104057603.html

Berzin, Alexander (trans), *Medium-Length Guhyasamaja Sadhana*, based on discourse by His Holiness the Fourteeth Dalai Lama and Tsanzhab Serkong Rinpoche, Tushita Retreat Centre, Dharamsala (2001) http://www.chakrasamvara.com/articles/practice/8-gelug-practice-texts. html

Bhagavad Gita, trans. by Juan Mascaró, Penguin Books, (1962)

Blake, William, 'The Everlasting Gospel' (c. 1810) from *The Rossetti Manuscript* (*aka* MS. Book; c. 1793 – 1811)

Blake, William, 'The Tyger' in *Songs of Innocence and Experience: Shewing the Two Contrary States of the Human Soul, 1789-1794,* Oxford Paperbacks, (1977)

Blake, William, 'A Vision of the Last Judgment' in *The Portable Blake*, Selected and Arranged by Alfred Kazin, Penguin Book, (1948)

Blunt, Anthony, *Nicholas Poussin*, Pallas Athene, (1995)

Blunt, Anthony, *Artistic Theory in Italy: 1450 - 1600*, Oxford University Press (1962)

Bober, Phyllis Pray, 'Polykles and Polykleitos in the Renaissance: The "Letto de Policreto"' in *Polykleitos, the Doryphoros, and Tradition,* edited by Warren G. Moon, University of Wisconsin Press, (1995)

Bonnet, Alain; Goarin, Véronique; Jargot, Hélène; Schwartz, Emmanuel; *Devinir Peintre Au XIX Siècle: Baudry, Bouguereau, Lenepveu*, Fage éditions, (2007)

(The) Book of Gates in *The Short Form of The Book of Am-Tuat and The Book of Gates*, trans. by E. A. Wallis Budge. http://ancientegyptonline.co.uk/bookgates5.html (1905)

Bork, Robert, *The Geometry of Creation: Architectural Drawing and the Dynamics of Gothic Design*, Routledge, (2011)

Bouleau, Charles, *Charpentes: La Géométrie Secrète des Peintres,* Éditions du Seuil, (1963)

Bouleau, Charles, *The Painter's Secret Geometry: A Study of Composition in Art*, Dover Publications, (2014)

Brachert, Thomas, 'A Musical Canon of Proportion in Leonardo da Vinci's Last Supper', in *The Art Bulletin*, Vol. 53, No. 4 (1971), pp. 461-466

Brambilla Barcilon, Pinin, *Leonardo: The Last Supper,* University of Chicago Press, (1999)

Brown, J. H., 'Unscrambling Giotto's Perspective', paper presented at the *(Re)Discovering Aesthetics Conference* at University College, Cork, July 10, 2004 - http://faculty.philosophy.umd.edu/jhbrown/Giotto/index.htm - (2004)

Brownson, C. D.,' Euclid's Optics and its Compatibility with Linear Perspective' in *Archive for History of Exact Sciences* Vol. 24, No. 3 (1981), pp. 165-194

Broug, Eric, *Islamic Geometric Patterns*, Thames & Hudson (2008)

Bucher, François, 'Medieval Architectural Design Methods 800 - 1560' in *Gesta*, Vol. 11, No. 2 (1972), pp. 37 - 51

Buchwald, Hans, *Form, Style and Meaning in Byzantine Church Architecture*, Ashgate, (1999)

Bunim, Miriam Schild, *Space in Medieval Painting and the Forerunners of Perspective*, Columbia University Press, (1940)

Burckhardt, Titus, 'The Void in Islamic Art' in *Studies in Comparative Religion*, Vol. 4, No. 2, (1970)

Burnet, John, *Early Greek Philosophy*, A. & C. Black, London, (1892)

Callen, Anthea, *The Art of Impressionism: Painting Technique and the Making of Modernity*, Yale University Press, (2000)

Carpenter, Rhys, *Greek Sculpture: A Critical Review*, University of Chicago Press, (1960)

Carruthers, Mary J., 'Ars oblivionis, ars inveniendi: The Cherub Figure and the Arts of Memory' in *Gesta*, vol. 48, University of Chicago Press, (2009)

Caruana, L., *The First Manifesto of Visionary Art*, Recluse Pub., (2000)

Caruana, L., 'A Mirror Delirious' and 'Myrette' in *The Visionary Revue*, Issue 4, Paris, (2007)

Caruana, L., *Enter Through the Image*, Recluse Pub., (2009)

Cennini, Cennino d'Andrea, *The Craftsman's Handbook: "Il Libro dell'Arte"* translated by Daniel V. Thompson, Dover Publications; 2nd Edition (1954)

Chai, Jean Julia, 'Introduction' to Gian Paolo Lamazzo's *The Idea of the Temple of Painting*, Penn State University Press, (2013)

Clark, Kenneth, *Leonardo da Vinci*, Penguin Books, (1939)

Clark, Kenneth, *Piero della Francesca*, London, Phaidon Press, (1951)

Clark, Kenneth, *The Nude,* Pelican Books, (1960)

Cook, Theodore Andrea, *The Curves of Life: Being an Account of Sprial Formations and their Application of Growth in Nature, to Science and to Art*, Constable and Company Ltd, London, (1914)

Cooke, Peter, *Gustave Moreau: History Painting, Spirituality and Symbolism*, Yale University Press, (2014)

Coomaraswamy, Ananda K., *Yaksa*s, Oxford University Press, (1993)

Copenhaver, Brian P. (editor and translator) *Hermetica: The Greek Corpus Hermeticum and the Latin Asclepius* in a New English Translation, Cambridge U. Press, (1995)

Cousin, Jean, *Livre de perspective*, l'imprimerie de Jean le Royer, Paris (1560)

Cousin, Jean, *L'art de dessiner*, Jacques-François Chereau, Paris, (1778)

Cüppers, Christoph; Van Der Kuijp, Leonard; Pagel, Ulrich; *Handbook of Tibetan Iconometry - A guide to the Arts of the 17th Century*, Brill, (2012)

David, Margaret Daly, *Piero della Francesca's Mathematical Treatises: The Trattato d'abaco and Libellus de quinque corporibus regularibus*, Longo Editore (1977)

Dictionnaire de L'Académie française, 8th Edition (1932-5)

Diodorus Siculus, *Library of History*, Bk I, Ch. 98, Loeb Classical Library Vol. I, (1933)

Dionysius of Fourna, *The Painter's Manual of Dionysius of Fourna*, translated by Paul Hetherington, First edition Sagittarius Press, London, (1974, Reprinted by Ωakwood Πuplications, (1989)

Doczi, György, *The Power of Limits – Proportional Harmonies in Nature, Art & Architecture*, Shambhala Publications, (1981)

Dolce, Lodovico, *Aretin: A Dialogue on Painting*, Printed for P. Elmsley, (1770)

Doose, Conrad; Lauenstein, Hajo, *Raffaels Fresko „Die Schule von Athen" : Die Tafeln des Pythagoras und Euklid vor und nach der Restaurierung*, Förderverein Festung Zitadelle Jülich e.V. 2RWTH Aachen, Fakultät für Architektur

Dubery, Fred and Willats, John, *Perspective and Other Drawing Systems*, Van Nostrand Reinhold, Revised Edition (1983)

Dudley, Colin Joseph, *Canterbury Cathedral: Aspects of its Sacramental Geometry*, Xlibris, (2010)

Eck, Diana L., *Darsan: Seeing the Divine Image in India,* Columbia U. Press (1981)

Edgar, C. C., 'Remarks on Egyptian Sculpture Models' in the *Recueil de Travaux relatifs à la Philologie et à l'Archéologie égyptiennes et assyriennes*, (1905), vol. XXVII, Librairie Émile Brouillon, p. 137-150

Edgerton Jr., Samuel Y., 'Alberti's Perspective: A New Discovery and a New Evaluation' in *The Art Bulletin* Vol. 48, No. 3/4 (1966), pp. 367-378

Edgerton Jr., Samuel Y., *The Heritage of Giotto's Geometry: Art and Science on the Eve of the Scientific Revolution*, Cornell U. Press, (1991)

Elkins, James, 'Piero della Francesca and the Renaissance Proof of Linear Perspective', The Art Bulletin, Vol. 69, No. 2 (Jun., 1987), pp. 220-230

Elkins, James, *The Poetics of Perspective*, Cornell University Press, (1996)

El-Said, Issam; Parman, Ayşe, *Geometric Concepts in Islamic Art*, World of Islam Festival Publishing Company Ltd., (1976)

El-Said, Issam, *Islamic Art and Architecture: The Systems of Geometric Design*, Garnet Publishing Ltd, (1998)

El ouaazizi, Aziza; Nasri, Abdelbar; Benslimane, Rachid, 'A rotation symmetry group detection technique for the characterization of Islamic Rosette Patterns' in *Pattern Recognition Letters*, Volume 68, Part 1, December (2015) pp. 111 - 117

Ernst , Bruno, *The Magic Mirror of M. C. Escher*, Taschen, (2007)

Euclid, *The Elements of Geometry*, Greek text of J.L. Heiberg (1883–1885) from *Euclidis Elementa*, edidit et Latine interpretatus est I.L. Heiberg, in aedibus B.G. Teubneri, (1883–1885), edited, and provided with a modern English translation by Richard Fitzpatrick (2007), http://farside.ph.utexas.edu/Books/Euclid/Euclid.html

Euclid, *The Optics of Euclid,* Trans. by Harry Edwin Burton, Journal of the Optical Society of America, Vol 35, No. 5, (1945) pp. 357 - 372

Evans-Wentz, W. Y., Editor, *The Tibetan Book of the Dead*, Oxford University Press, (1960)

Faulkner, R. O. *The Ancient Egyptian Pyramid Texts: Supplement of Heiroglyphic Texts*, Clarendon Press, (1970)

Félibien, André, *Principes de l'Architecture, de la Sculpture, de la Peinture* Troisième edition, Chez la Veuve & Jean Baptiste Coignard, fils (1699)

Fichtner, Richard, *Die verborgene Geometrie in Raffaels "Schule von Athen"*, R. Oldenbourg Verlag München, Deutches Museum, (1984)

Field, J.V., *Piero della Francesca: A Mathematician's Art*, Yale University Press, (2005)

Finamore, John F., *Iamblichus and the Theory of the Vehicle of the Soul*, The American Philological Association, (1985)

Fischer, Helmut, *Die Ikone,* Verlag Herder Freiburg im Breisgau (1989)

Forcellino, Antonio, *Raphael: A Passionate Life*, Polity Press, (2012)

Forest, Marie-Cécile, 'Gustave Moreau et la sculpture: l'homme aux figures de cire' in *Gustave Moreau: l'homme aux figures de cire*, Somogy éditions d'art, (2010)

Francesca, Piero della, *De Prospectiva Pingendi edizione critica di G. Nicco Fasola con XLIX tavole fuori testo, G. C. Sansoni editore Firenze,* (1952)

Frangenberg, Thomas, 'The Angle of Vision: Problems of Perspectival Representation in the Fifteenth and Sixteenth Centuries' in *Renaissance Studies*, Vol. 6, No. 1, Oxford University Press, (1991)

Fremantle, Francesca, *A Critical Study of the Guhyasamaja Tantra*, London, (1971)

Fuchs, Ernst, *Architectura Caelestis: Images of the Hidden Prime of Styles*, Residenz Verlag, (1970)

Fuchs, Ernst, Preface to *Robert Venosa: Illuminatus*, Robert John Ltd., (1999)

Fuchs, Ernst, *Phantastiches Leben: Erinnerungen*, Kindler verlag (2001)

Fuchs, Ernst, 'About My Pictures' in *Catalogue for the Ernst Fuchs exhibitions in the National Tretjakow Gallery Moscow*, (2001)

Fuchs, Ernst, 'Ernst Fuchs Speaks' Interview with L. Caruana, *The Visionary Revue*, Paris, Spring (2004)

Fuseli, Henry (Füssli, Johann Heinrich), *Lectures on Painting Delivered at the Royal Academy, March 1801*, Printed for J. Johnson, St. Paul's Chruch-yard, (1801)

Gega Lama, *Principles of Tibetan Art: Illustrations and explanations of Buddhist iconography and iconometry according to the Karma Gardri School, Vols I and II*, Darjeeling India, (1983)

Gerbino, Anthony, *François Blondel: Architecture, Erudition, and the Scientific Revolution*, Routledge, (2010)

Glick, Thomas F.; Livesey, Steven; and Wallis, Faith, *Medieval Science, Technology, and Medicine: An Encyclopedia* Routledge, (2005)

Godwin, Joscelyn, *The Mystery of the Seven Vowels: In Theory and Practice*, Phanes Press, (1991)

Godwin, Joscelyn, *The Harmony of the Spheres: The Pythagorean Tradition in Music*, Inner Traditions, (1992)

Goldstein, Carl, *Teaching Art – Academies and Schools from Vasri to Albers*, Cambridge University Press, (1996)

(The) Greek Anthology, Volume III: Book 9: The Declamatory Epigrams, trans. by W. R. Paton, Loeb Classical Library, (1917)

Grey, Alex, *Art Psalms*, North Atlantic Books, (2008)

Grey, Alex, *Net of Being*, Inner Traditions (2012)

Grignon, Iffet Orbay, 'Remarks on the Concept of Pictorial Space in Islamic Painting' in *O.D.T.Ü. M.E.T.U. Mimarlik Fakültesi Degisi, Journal of the Faculty of Architecture*, 16 i-ii (1996) pp. 45 - 57

Grimm, G. D., *Proportsionalnost' v arkhitekture,* Leningrad, (1935)

Guest , Grace Dunham, 'Shiraz Painting in the Sixteenth Century', *Smithsonian Institution Freer Gallery of Art Oriental Studies*, No. 4, (1949)

Guralnick, Eleanor, 'The Proportions of Kouroi', *American Journal of Archaeology*, Vol. 82, No. 4, (1978), p. 461 - 472

Guthrie, W. K. C., *Orpheus and the Greek Religion: A Study of the Orphic Movement*, Princeton University Press, (1952)

Haas, Robert, *'Raphael's School of Athens: A Theorem in a Painting?'*, Journal of Humanist Mathematics, Volume 2, Issue 2, July (2012)

Haja, Nilofar Shamim, 'Celebration of Life: A study of sculptural and mural depictions of dance and music in Buddhist art of India' Madras Craft Foundation & Dakshina Chitra, (2007)

Hambidge, Jay, *The Elements of Dynamic Symmetry*, Dover, (1967)

Hambridge, Jay, *Dynamic Symmetry: The Greek Vase*, Merchant Books, (2007)

Hammack, Richard, 'Piero della Francesca's Diagonal Construction' - http://www.people.vcu.edu/~rhammack/Math121/Handouts/Francesca.pdf

Handbook of Tibetan Iconography: A guide to the Arts of the 17th Century, edited by Christoph Küppers, Leonard Van Der Kuijp, Ulrich Pagel, Brill (2012) – facsimile edition of an iconometric handbook, preserved in a late 17th century manuscript, of the 'Illustrations of Measurements: A Refresher for the Cognoscenti' (Cha tshad kyi dpe ris Dpyod Idan yid gsos) produced by Sangs rgyas rgya mtsho (1653 – 1705), regent of the 5th Dalai Lama.

Hauck, Guido, 'Die subjektive Perspektive und die horizontalen Curvaturen des dorischen Styls: eine perspektivisch-ästhetische Studie' *Eine Festschrift zur fünfzigjährigen Jubelfeier der Technischen Hochschule zu Stuttgart*, (1879)

Hénin, Emmanuelle, *Ut pictura theatrum: Théâtre et peinture de la Renaissance italienne au classicisme français*, Librairie Droz (2003)

Herodas, *Mimes* in *Theophrastus, Herodas, Sophron. Characters. Herodas: Mimes. Sophron and Other Mime Fragments,* edited and translated by Jeffrey Rusten, I. C. Cunningham. Loeb Classical Library, Harvard University Press, (2003)

Honnecourt, Villard de, *The Medieval Sketchbook of Villard de Honnecourt,* edited by Theodore Bowie, Dover Publications, (2006)

Hornung, Erik, *The Ancient Egyptian Books of the Afterlife,* trans. by David Lorton, Cornell University Press, (1999)

Iamblichus, *On the Mysteries of the Egyptians, Chaldeans, and Assyirans*, translated from the Greek by Thomas Taylor, London: Bertrum Doebell, (1821)

Iamblichus, *Theurgia or The Egyptian Mysteries – Reply of Abammon the Teacher to The Letter of Porphyry to Anebo* – Translated from the Greek by Alexander Wilder, M.D. F.A.S., London: William Rider & Son Ltd; New York: The Metaphysical Publishing Co. (1911)

Iamblichus, *On the Mysteries,* translated by Emma C. Clarke, John M. Dillon, Jackson P. Hershbell, Society of Biblical Literature, Bilingual Edition, (2003)

Jackson, David P., Jackson, Janice, *Tibetan Thangka Painting: Methods & Materials,* Illustrated by Robert Beer, Snow Lion, Shambhala Publications, (1988)

Jones, Owen, *The Grammar of Ornament*, Bernard Quaritch, (1910)

Kang, Eun-Sung, 'Raphael's Annunciation Predella panel and a perspective drawing', in *Burlington Magazine*, 148, (2006) pp. 545-548

Kaplan, Julius, *The Art of Gustave Moreau: Theory, Style, and Content*, UMI Research Press (1982)

Karpinski, Caroline, 'Archimedes Salutes Bramante in a Draft for the "School of Athens"' in *Artibus et Historiae*, Vol. 31, No. 61, Konrad Oberhuber in memoriam: part I, (2010), pp. 115-132

Keim, Frank, 'Raffaels Astronomische Tafel entschlüsselt: Kopernikanisches Weltsystem und Jupitermonde in Raffaels *Schule von Athen* (1509-14)', Universität Ulm. Kommunikations- und Informationszentrum, (2013)

Keller, Erwin, '*Kurvierte Perspektiven*' Sitzungsberichte der Akademie der Wissenschaft in Wien, mathematische-naturwissenschaftliche, Klasse 135_2a: 547-561, (1926)

Kemp Martin, *Geometrical Perspective from Brunelleschi to Desargues: A Pictorial Means or an Intellectual End?* Aspects of Art Lecture Series, British Academy, Oxford University Press (1985)

Kemp, Martin, *The Science of Art: Optical Themes in Western Art from Brunelleschi to Seurat*, Yale University Press, (1990)

Kleiss, Wolfram, 'Safavid Palaces' in *Ars Orientalis*, Vol. 23. Gülru Necipoglu, ed. Ann Arbour: Department of History, University of Michigan, (1993)

Knee, Karyl M., *The Dynamic Symmetry Proportional System is Found in Some Byzantine and Russian Icons of the Fourteenth to Sixteenth Centuries*, Oakwood (1988)

Kramrisch, Stella, *The Hindu Temple, Vols I and II*, Motilal Banarsidass, (1976)

Kramrisch, Stella, 'Traditions of the Indian Craftsman' in *The Journal of American Folklore*, Vol. 71, No. 281, American Folklore Society, (1958), pp. 224 - 230

Kappraff, Jay, "The Arithmetic of Nicomachus of Gerasaand its Applications to Systems of Proportion", *Nexus Network Journal,* vol. 2, no. 4 (October 2000), https://www.emis.de/journals/NNJ/Kappraff.html

Laundau, Jonathan; Weber, *Andy, Images of Enlightenment: Tibetan Art in Practice*, Snow Lion Publications, (1993)

Landrus, Matthew, 'The Proportions of Leonardo's *Last Supper*' *Raccolta Vinciana* 32 (December 2007), pp. 43-100.

Lauenstein, Hajo, *Arithmetik und Geometrie in Raffaels Schule von Athen. Die geheimnisvolle Schlüsselrolle der Tafeln im Fresko für das Konzept harmonischer Komposition und der ungeahnte Bezug zum Athena-Tempel von Paestum*; Frankfurt a. M. (1998)

Lavin, Marilyn Aronberg, 'Piero della Francesca's Flagellation: The Triumph of Christian Glory', *The Art Bulletin*, Vol. 50, No. 4 (Dec., 1968), pp. 321-342

Lawlor, Robert, *Sacred Geometry Philosophy & Practice,* Thames & Hudson, (1982)

Le Brun, Charles, *Expressions des Passions de l'Ame, Representées en plusieurs testes*, Jean Audran, (1727)

Le Brun, Charles, *Conferences de l'academie royale de peinture et de sculpture pendant l'année 1667* (edité par André Félibien) Chez Frederic Leonard, (1669)

Lee, Rensselaer W., *Ut Pictura Poesis: The Humanistic Theory of Painting,* W. W. Norton & Company, (1967)

Leftwich, Gregory V., 'Polykleitos and Hippokratic Medicine' in Moon, Warren G., ed., *Polykleitos, The Doryphoros and Tradition,* U. of Wisconsin Press, (1995)

Lenz, Desiderius, *The Aesthetic of Beuron and other writings*, translated by John Minihane and John Connolly, Francis Boutle Publishers, (2002)

Lessing, Gotthold Ephraim, *Laocoon*, trans. by Ellen Frothingham, Roberts Brothers, (1987)

Lester, Toby, *Da Vinci's Ghost: Genius, Obsession, and How Leonardo Created the World in His Own Image,* Free Press, (2012)

Leterrier, Romuald, in *Ovnis et Conscience: L'Inexpliqué au coeur du nouveau paradigme de la physique*, par Collectif, Le Temps Présent (2015)

Lichtheim, Miriam, *Ancient Egyptian Literature, Volume III: The Late Period*, University of California Press, 2nd Revised Edition, (2006)

Lien, Barbara, *'The Role of Pavement in the Perceived Integration of Plazas: An Analysis of the Paving Designs of Four Italian Piazzas'*, M. Sc. thesis in Landscape Architecture, Washington State University, (2005). http://citeseerx.ist.psu.edu/viewdoc/download?doi=10.1.1.513.8302&rep=rep1&type=pdf

Lifchez, Raymond, 'Jean-Galbert Salvage and His Anatomie du gladiateur combattant: Art and Patronage in Post-Revolutionary France', *Metropolitan Museum Journal* 44, The Metropolitan Museum of Art, New York (2009)

Lindberg, David C., *Theories of Vision From Al-Kindi to Kepler*, U. Chicago Press, (1976)

Lomazzo, Giovan Paolo, *Idea of the Temple of Painting*, Edited and translated by Jean Julia Chai, Penn State University Press, (2013)

Lomazzo, Giovan Paolo, *Tracte Containing the Artes of curious Paintinge, Caruinge, Buildinge*, written first in Italian by Paul Lomatius painter of Milan and Englished by R. H. (Richard Haydock), Printed at Oxford by Joseph Barnes, 1598

Lucretius, *On the Nature of Things* (*De Rerum Natura*) trans. by Cyril Bailey, Oxford The Clarendon Press, (1910)

Macrobius, *Commentary on the Dream of Scipio,* translated by William Harris Stahl, Columbia University Press, (1990)

Mako, Vladimir, *The Art of Harmony: Principles of Measuring and Proportioning in Byzantine Wall Painting*, The Orion Art, (2007)

Mâle, Emile, *The Gothic Image: Religious Art in France of the Thirteenth Century*, translated by Dora Nussey, Harper Torchbooks, (1958)

Manetti, *Life of Brunelleschi,* (originally published c. 1501), Trans. by Howard Saalman, Pennsylvania State University Press (1968)

Mazzola, G., Kromker, D., Hofmann, G.R., *Rasterbild - Bildraster: Anwendung der Graphischen Datenverarbeitung zur geometrischen Analyse eines Meisterwerks der Renaissance; Raffaels 'Schule von Athen'*, Springer, (1987)

McClain, Ernest G., *Pythagorean Plato: Prelude to the Song Itself,* Nicolas-Hays (1984)

Meurer, Moritz, *Vergleichende Formenlehre des Ornamentes und der Pflanze*, Dresden, Kühtmann, (1909)

Meurer, Moritz, *Die Ursprungsformen des griechischen Akanthusornamentes und ihre naturlichen Vorbilder*, Berlin, G. Reimer, (1896)

Mezzalira, Giovanni; Ambrosi, Annarosa; Borgato, Daniela; Pegoraro, Wilma, 'La ricostruzione dell'icona costantinopolitana' *Contributo scuola di iconografia san Luca al Convegno Internazionale su San Luca del 2000*, (Posted on January 7, 2001) at http://www.iconografi.it/?p=304

Michelangelo, *The Poetry of Michelangelo*, trans by J. M. Saslow, Yale U. Press, (1993)

Michelangelo, *Zeichnungen und Zuschreibungen*, Michael Imhof Verlag, (2009)

Miller, Mary Ellen; Taube, Karl, *An Illustrated Dictionary of the Gods and Symbols of Ancient Mexico and the Maya*, Thames & Hudson, (1997)

Mitrović, Branko and Massalin, Paola, 'Leon Battista Alberti and Euclid' in *Albertiana*, 9 (2008), pp. 165-249 at https://www.academia.edu/4540841/Leon_Battista_Alberti_and_Euclid

Moffitt, John F., 'Domenico Veneziano's "Saint Lucy" Altarpiece: The Case for "Uterine Perspective"'. *Notes in the History of Art,* Vol. 16, No. 4 (Summer 1997)

Montagu, Jennifer, *The Expression of the Passions: The Origin and Influence of Charles Le Brun's "Conference sur l'expression generale et particuliere"* Yale University Press (1994)

Moon, Warren G., ed., *Polykleitos, The Doryphoros and Tradition,* U. of Wisconsin Press (1995)

Moreau, Gustave, *L'assembleur des rêves, Écrits complets de Gustave Moreau*, A Fontfroide, Bibliothèque Artistique & Littéraire, (1984)

Moreau, Gustave, *l'Inde de Gustave Moreau*, Paris Musées, (1997)

Moreau, Gustave: *Gustave Moreau: Monographie et nouveau catalogue de l'œvre achevé*, Pierre-Louis Mathieu, ACR Édition, (1998)

Moreau, Gustave, *Gustave Moreau: 1826 - 1898*, Catalogue de Galeries nationales du Grand Palais, 29 Septembre 1998 - 4 janvier 1999, Réunion des musées nationaux, Paris, (1998)

Moreau, Gustave, *Écrits sur l'art, Volume I, Sur ses oeuvres et sur lui-même*, présentés et annotés par Peter Cooke, A Fontfroide, Bibliothèque Artistique & Littéraire, (2002)

Moreau, Gustave, *Écrits sur l'art, Volume II, Théorie et critique d'art*, présentés et annotés par Peter Cooke, A Fontfroide, Bibliothèque Artistique & Littéraire, (2002)

Moreau, Gustave, *Gustave Moreau: l'homme aux figures de cire*, Somogy (2010)
Moreaux, Arnold, *Anatomie Artistique de l'Homme*, Éditions Maloine, (1959)
Mostellar, John F., 'A New Approach for the Study of Indian Art' in *Journal of the American Oriental Society*, Vol. 107, No. 1, (1987), pp. 55 - 69
Mostellar, John F., 'The Study of Indian Iconometry in Historical Perspective' in *Journal of the American Oriental Society*, Vol. 108, No. 1, (1988), pp. 99 - 110
Mosteller, John F., 'The Problem of Proportion and Style in Indian Art History: Or Why All Buddhas in Fact Do Not Look Alike', *Art Journal*, Vol. 49, No. 4, (1990), pp. 388 - 394
The Nag Hammadi Library in English, James M. Robinson, General Editor, 3rd Edition, Harper and Row, (1988)
Nagy, Dénes, 'Golden Section(ism): From Mathematics to the Theory of Art and Musicology - Part 2' in *Symmetry: Culture and Science*, Vol. 8, No. 1, 74-112, (1997)
Nasr, Seyyed Hossein, 'The World of the Imagination and the Concept of Space in the Persian Miniature' in *Islamic Art and Spirituality*, SUNY Press (1987)
Nasr, Seyyed Hossein, *Religion and the Order of Nature*, Oxford University Press, (1996)
Naydler, Jeremy, *Temple of the Cosmos: The Ancient Egyptian Experience of the Sacred*, Inner Traditions, (1996)
Naydler, Jeremy, *Shamanic Wisdom in the Pyramid Texts: The Mystical Tradition of Ancient Egypt*, Inner Traditions, (2004)
Necipoglu, Gülru, 'Geometric Design in Timurid/Turkmen Architectural Practise: Thoughts on a Recently Discovered Scroll and its Late Gothic Parallels' in Lisa Golombek and Maria Subtelny, editors, *Timurid Art and Culture: Iran and Central Asia in the Fifteenth Century*, E.J. Brill (1992)
Necipoglu, Gülru, "Early Modern Floral: The Agency of Ornament in Ottoman and Safavid Visual Cultures' in *Histories of Ornament: From Global to Local*, edited by Gülru Necipoglu and Alina Payne, Princeton University Press, (2016)
Neer, Richard, *The Emergence of the Classical Style in Greek Sculpture*, University of Chicago Press, (2010)
Nicomachus the Pythagorean (Nichomachus of Gersa), *The Manual of Harmonics*, Phanes Press; Revised edition, (1993)
Nightingale, Andrea Wilson, *Spectacles of Truth in Classical Greek Philosophy,* Cambridge University Press, (2004)
Nightingale, Andrea Wilson, 'The Philosopher at the Festival: Plato's Transformation of Traditional Theoria' in Elsner, Jaś, and Rutherford, Ian, *Pilgrimage in Graeco-Roman and Early Christian Antiquity: Seeing the Gods*, Oxford University Press, (2005)
Oberhuber, Konrad, *Polarität und Synthese in Raphaels 'Schule von Athen'*, Urachhaus, (1983)
'Opening of Mouth Ceremony' Selection of 51 episodes in the tomb-chapel of Rekhmira, *Digital Egypt for Universities*: http://www.ucl.ac.uk/museums-static/digitalegypt// religion/wpr2.html
Ouspensky, Leonid, *Theology of the Icon, Vols I & II,* St Vladimirs Seminary Press (1992)
Ouspensky, Leonid; Lossky, Vladimir, *The Meaning of Icons,* translated by G. E. H. Palmer and E. Kadloubovsky, St Vladimir's Seminary Press, (1982)
Ovid, *Metamorphoses*, trans. by Mary M. Innes, Penguin Books, (1955)
Padovan, Richard, Proportion: Science, Philosophy, Architecture, Taylor & Francis, (1999)
Palmer, Richard E., *Hermeneutics: Interpretation Theory in Schleiermacher, Dilthey, Heidegger and Gadamer,* Northwestern University Press, (1969)
Panofsky, Erwin, 'The First Two Projects of Michelangelo's Tomb of Julius II' *The Art Bulletin,* Vol. 19, No. 4 (Dec., 1937), pp. 561-579
Panofsky, Erwin, editor: *The Codex Huygens and Leonardo da Vinci's Art Theory*, Pierpont Morgan Library, Codex M. A. 1139, London, Warbrurg Institute (1940)
Panofsky, Erwin,'The History of the Theory of Human Proportions as a Reflection of the History of Styles' in *Meaning in the Visual Arts*, U. of Chicago Press (1955)

Panofsky, Erwin, *Perspective as Symbolic Form*, Zone Books; Revised edition (1996)

Pausanias, *Description of ancient Greece*, Book I, translated by W. H. S. Jones, Loeb Classical Library, Harvard University Press, (1918)

Petrie, W. M. Flinders. *The Pyramids and Temples of Gizeh.* 1st ed. London: Field and Tuer; New York: Scribner & Welford, (1883)

Piankoff, A., *Litany of Re: Egyptian Texts and Representations*, Bollingen, (1964)

Plato, *The Collected Dialogues of Plato*, edited by Edith Hamilton and Huntington Cairns, Bollingen LXXI, Princeton University Press, (1961)

Plato, *Great Dialogues of Plato*, trans. by W. H. D. Rouse, New American Library, (1956)

Pliny, *The Natural History*, trans. by John Bostock and H. T. Riley, George Bell and Sons, London, (1893)

Plotinus, 'Enneads' in *The Essential Plotinus*, trans. by Elmer O'Brien, Hacket (1975)

Politt, J. J., *Art and Experience in Classical Greece*, Cambridge University Press, (1972)

Popper, K. R., *The Open Society and its Enemies*, Rutledge and Kegan Paul, (1962), vol. I.

Porphyry, 'The Life of Plotinus' in Plotinus, *The Six Enneads*, Translated by Stephen Mackenna and B. S. Page, Encyclopedia Britannica, (1952)

Porphyry, 'The Letter to Anebo' in Iamblichus, *On the Mysteries of the Egyptians, Chaldeans, and Assyirans*, translated from the Greek by Thomas Taylor, London: Bertrum Doebell, (1821)

Porter, Yves, 'From the "Theory of the Two Qalams" to the "Seven Principles of Painting": Theory, Terminology, and Practice in Persian Classical Painting' in *Muqarnas* Vol. 17 (2000), pp. 109-118

Poussin, Nicolas, *Collection de lettres de Nicolas Poussin*, Imprimerie de Firmin Didot, (1824)

Powell, Christopher, *The Shapes of Sacred Space: A Proposed System of Geometry used to Lay Out and Design Maya Art and Architecture* Ph. D. Dissertation, U. of Texas at Austin, (2010)

Proclus, *The Commentaries of Proclus on the Timaeus of Plato*, in Five Books, Translated from the Greek by Thomas Taylor, Two Volumes, (1820)

Proclus, 'On the Sacred Art' translated by Stephen Ronan, http://www.esotericism.co.uk/proclus-sacred.htm (1988)

Proclus, *Proclus' Hymns: Essays, Translation and Commentary*, R. M. Van den Berg, Brill publishers, (2001)

Raine, Kathleen, *William Blake*, Oxford University Press, (1970)

Recht, Roland, 'Torsion et hanchement dans la sculpture gothique' in *Gesta* Vol 15, No. 1/2, (1976), pp. 179 – 184

Reeder, Greg, 'A Rite of Passage: The Enigmatic Tekenu in Ancient Egyptian Funerary Ritual' in *KMT: A Modern Journal of Ancient Egypt*, vol. 5 no. 3, (Fall 1994)

Ridgway, Brunilde Sismondo, *Fifth Century Styles in Greek Sculpture*, Princeton University Press, (1981)

Rilke, Rainer Maria, *Selected poems / Ausgewählte gedichte*, edited and translated by Stanley Appelbaum, Dover Publications, (2011)

Robins, Gay, *Proportion and Style in Ancient Egyptian Art,* University of Texas Press, (1994)

Robinson, James M. (editor), *The Nag Hammadi Library*, Harper & Row, (1978)

Rubens, Pierre-Paul, *Théorie de la Figure Humaine, Considerée dans ses principes, soit en repos ou en mouvement*, Charles-Antoine Jombert, Pere, Librairie de l'Artillerie & du Génie, (1773)

Rubens, Pierre-Paul, *Théorie de la Figure Humaine*, Édition de Nadeije Laneyrie-Dagen, Æsthetica, Éditions Rue d'Ulm, (2003)

Salvage, Jean-Galbert, *Anatomie Du Gladiateur Combattant,* A Paris, Chez l'Auteur, Cul-de-Sac Saint-Dominique D'Enfer, N. 6, De l'Imprimerie de Mame, (1812)

Sangpo, Phuntsog, *The Clear Mirror Depicting the Pearl Roseries of Thanka Painting of the Tsangpa Tradition of Tibet,* (1996)

Sauneron, Serge, *The Priests of Ancient Egypt*, New Edition, trans. by David Lorton, Cornell University Press, (2000)
Saxl, Fritz, *The Codex Huygens and Leonardo Da Vinci's Art Theory*, The Warburg Institute, (1940)
Schaller, Catherine, *L'expression des passions au XIXe siècle: Le concours de la Tête d'expression à l'Ecole des Beaux-Arts de Paris. Théories de l'expression des passions et analyse des toiles du concours.* Thèse de Doctorat présentée devant la Faculté des Lettres de l'Université de Fribourg, en Suisse (2003).
Schele, Linda; Miller, Mary Ellen, *The Blood of Kings: Dynasty and Ritual in Maya Art*, George Braziller Inc., (1992)
Schattschneider, Doris, 'The Plane Symmetry Groups: Their Recognition and Notation', *American Mathematical Monthly*, Volume 85, Issue 6, pp. 439 - 450 (1978)
Schneider, Michael S., *A Voyage From 1 To 5 - Create and Explore Geometric Patterns of Nature and Art,* Volume 1 of *Constructing the Universe Activity Books,* Michael S. Schneider (2006)
Schneider, Michael S., *A Voyage From 6 To 12 - Create and Explore Geometric Patterns of Nature and Art,* Volume 2 of *Constructing the Universe Activity Books,* Michael S. Schneider (2006)
Schneider, Michael S., *Fibonacci Numbers and the Golden Mean,* Volume 3 of *Constructing the Universe Activity Books,* Michael S. Schneider (2006)
Schneider, Michael S., *Dynamic Rectangles – Explore Harmony in Mathematics and Art,* Volume 4 of *Constructing the Universe Activity Books,* Michael S. Schneider (2006)
Schönborn, Christopher, *God's Human Face: the Christ-Icon*, Ignatius Press, (1994)
Sendler, Egon, *L'icône – image de l'invisible – eléments de théologie, esthétique et technique*, Desclée De Brouwer, (1981)
Shelby, Lon R., 'The Geometrical Knowledge of Mediaeval Master Masons' in *Speculum* Vol 47, No. 3, (July 1972), pp. 395 - 421
Söran, Görbum, 'The Classical Concept of Mimesis' in *A Companion to Art Theory*, edited by Paul Smith, Carolyn Wilde, Wiley Online Library, (2008)
Spike, John T., *Young Michelangelo: The Path to the Sistine*, Vendome Press, (2010)
Stewart, Andrew, 'The Canon of Polykleitos: A Question of Evidence' in *Journal of Hellenic Studies* Vol. 98, (1978), pp. 122 - 31
Stinson, Philip, 'Perspective Systems in Roman Second Style Wall Painting', *American Journal of Archaeology* 115 (2011) pp. 403-26
Stowell, Steven F.H., *The Spiritual Language of Art: Medieval Christian Themes in Writings on Art*, Brill, (2014)
Tagore, Abanindranath, *Some Notes on Indian Artistic Anatomy*, translated by Sukumar Ray, Indian Society of Oriental Art, Calcutta (1914)
Temple, Nicholas, *Disclosing Horizons: Architecture, Perspective and Redemptive Space*, Routledge, (2007)
Termes, Dick, *'New Perspective Systems: Seeing the Total Picture - One through Six Point Perspective'*, pdf (1998) - http://termespheres.com/6-point-perspective
Termes, Dick A., 'Six-Point Perspective on the Sphere: The Termesphere', *Leonardo*, Vol. 24, No. 3 (1991), MIT Press, pp. 289-292
Thackston, Wheeler M., *Album Prefaces and Other Documents on the History of Calligraphers and Painters*, Brill (2001)
Tobin, Richard, 'The Canon of Polykleitos' in *American Journal of Archaeology*, Vol. 79, No. 4, (1975), pp. 307 - 321
Tomoum, Nadja, *The Sculptor's Models of the Late and Ptolemaic Periods – A Study of the Type and Function of a Group of Ancient Egyptian Artefacts,* translated by Brenda Siller, National Center for Documentation of Cultural and Natural Heritage and the Supreme Council of Antiquities, Egypt, (2006)

Torp, Hjalmar, *The Integrating System of Proportion in Byzantine Art,* Giogrio Bretschneider Editore, Norwegian Institute in Rome, (1984)

Trilling, James, *The Language of Ornament*, Thames & Hudson, (2001)

Tyler, Christopher W. and Chen, Chien-Chung,'Chinese Perspective as a Rational System: Relationship to Panofsky's Symbolic Form' in *Chinese Journal of Psychology*, Volume 53, Issue 4 (2010)

Ulu, Ebru and Şener, Sinan Mert, 'A Shape Grammar Model To Generate Islamic Geometric Pattern', paper presented at *The 12th Generative Art Conference* (2009)

('The) Untitled Text in the Bruce Codex' in *The Books of Jeu and the Untitled Text in the Bruce Codex*, Text Edited by Carl Schmidt, Translation and Notes by Violet MacDermot, Nag Hammadi Studies (Book 13), E. J. Brill (1978)

Uždavinys, Algis, *The Golden Chain: An Anthology of Pythagorean and Platonic Philosophy*, World Wisdom Books, (2004)

Uždavinys, Algis, *Philosophy & Theurgy in Late Antiquity,* Sophia Perennis, (2010)

Valtieri, Simonetta, 'La Scuola d'Atene. "Bramante" suggerisce un nuovo metodo per costruire in prospettiva un'architettura armonica' in *Mittelungen des Kunsthistorischen Institutes* in Florenz 16, Bd., H, 1 (1972), pp, 63 - 72

Vasari, Giorgio, *The Lives of the Artists*, a selection translated by George Bull, Penguin Classics, (1965)

Vasari, Giorgio, *Vasari on Technique: Being the Introduction to the Three Arts of Design, Architecture, Sculpture and Painting, Prefixed by The Lives of the Most Excellent Painters, Sculptors and Architects*, trans. by Louisa S. Maclehose, J. M. Dent & Co., (1907)

Vasiljevi, Slobodan, 'Les grands traceurs de plans: d'un ingénieur à l'autre, de Micheli du Crest à Dufour: les tracés effacés de la structure urbaine entre 1720 et 1860' in *Ingénieurs et architectes suisses* Band (Jahr): 114 (1988) Heft 4

Vatsyayan, Kapila *The Square and the Circle of Indian Arts,* Abhinav Publications, (1997)

Viator (Jean Pèlerin), *De Artificiali Perspectiva, Summe faber rerum qui perspicis omnia solus ad te directo calle Viator eat.*, Impressum Tulli, (1509)

Villard de Honnecourt, *The Medieval Sketchbook of Villard de Honnecourt*, Introduction and Captions by Theodore Bowie, Dover Publications, (2006)

Viollet-le-Duc, Eugène, *Dictionnaire raisonée de l'architecture française du XIe au XVIe siècle*, Vols I - VIII, V. A Morel & Cie, (1875)

Vinci, Leonardo da, *The Notebooks of Leonardo da Vinci*, Complied and Edited from the Original Manuscripts, by Jean Paul Richter, in Two Volumes, Dover, (1970)

Vinci, Leonardo da, *The Notebooks of Leonardo da Vinci*, Selected and Edited by Irma A. Richter, Oxford University Press (1980)

Vishnudharmottara (Part III): A Treatise on Indian Painting and Image-Making, translated by Stella Kramrisch, Ph. D., Second Revised and Enlarged Edition, Calcutta University Press, (1928)

Vitruvius, *Ten Books of Architecture*, trans. by Morris Hickey Morgan, Dover, (1960). Reprint of Harvard University Press (1914)

von Gagern, Martin, *Computergestütztes Zeichnen in den Symmetriegruppen der euklidischen Ebene*, Diplomarbeit in Informatik, Fakultät für Informatik der Technischen Universität München (2008) - http://martin.von-gagern.net/publications/2008-diploma/Diplomarbeit.pdf

Voss, Angela, 'The Secret Life of Statues' in: Campion, Nicholas and Curry, Patrick M., eds. *Sky and Psyche: The Relationship Between Cosmos and Consciousness*, Floris Books, Edinburgh, pp. 201-234 (2006)

Wayman, Alex, *Yoga of the Guhysamajatantra: The Arcane Lore of Forty Verses - A Buddhist Tantra Commentary*, Motilal Banarsidass, (1977)

Wellesz, Emmy and Blauensteiner, Kurt, 'Ilustrationen zu einer Geschichte Timurs' in *Wiener Beiträge zur Kunst- und Kulturgeschichte Asiens* X (1936)

Whatling, Stuart, 'The Corpus of Medieval Narrative Art' - http://www.medievalart.org.uk

Wittkower, Rudolf, 'Eagle and Serpent. A Study in the Migration of Symbols' Journal of the Warburg Institute Vol. 2, No. 4 (Apr., 1939), pp. 293-325

Wittkower, R and Carter, B. A. R., The Perspective of Piero della Francesca's 'Flagellation', Journal of the Warburg and Courtauld Institutes, Vol. 16, No. 3/4 (1953), pp. 292- 302

Wittkower, R, 'Brunelleschi and Proportion in Perspective', *Journal of the Warburg and Courtauld Institutes* Vol. 16. No. 3/4 (1953), pp. 275-291

Wittkower, Rudolf, 'The Changing Concept of Proportion' in *Daedelus* Vol. 89, No.1, The Visual Arts Today (Winter, 1960), pp. 199 - 215

Wittkower, Rudolf, *Architectural Principles in the Age of Humanism*, W. W. Norton & Company, (1971)

Wright, Roger, *The Guhyasamāja Piṇḍikṛta-sādhana and its Context,* Prepared as part of the MA Study of Religions (Buddhist Studies Pathway) MA (Religions), School of Oriental and African Studies, University of London, (2010)

Xenophon, *The Memorabilia, Recollections of Socrates*, Translated by H. G. Dakyns, Macmillan and Co., (1897)

Yates, Frances A., *The Art of Memory*, Routledge and Kegan Paul, (1966)

Zeising, Dr. A., *Neue Lehre von den Proportionen des menschichen Körpers*, Rudolph Wiegel, Leipzig, (1854)

Zimmer, Heinrich, *The Art of Indian Asia: Its Mythologies and Transformations*, Vols I & II, Motilal Banarsidass, (2001)

Zimmer, Heinrich, *Artistic Form and Yoga in the Sacred Images of India,* translated by Gerald Chapple and James B. Lawson, Princeton University Press (1984)

Zimmer, Heinrich, *Myths and Symbols in Indian Art and Civilisation*, Princeton University Press, (1972)

Made in the USA
Monee, IL
02 July 2020

35481393R00420